More praise for
THE SOVIET CENTURY

"[Schlögel] and his wonderful noticing of things and how
they sit in space is on full display."
—SHEILA FITZPATRICK, *Foreign Policy*

"Formidable. . . . The emergence of this book in our intellectual
landscape is timely, as we seek to better understand Russia in an era
when systematic political, economic, social, and even cultural
approaches have failed to explain or predict the current resurrection
of the 'Soviet Leviathan.' Indeed, perhaps 'the devil is hidden in the details,'
and by diving yet again into these minute but culturally rich details of
Soviet banal routine, spiritual life, and rituals, we can make a step
forward in our comprehension of why the dark side of
'Soviet civilization' keeps reemerging."
—OKSANA ERMOLAEVA, *EuropeNow* (editor's pick)

"[A] magnum opus. . . . Invaluable."
—*Publishers Weekly* (starred review)

"Who knew that, apart from his experiments with dogs, Ivan Pavlov
wrote a preface concerning nutrition for a bestselling Soviet cookbook?
That's one of just many oddments Schlögel assembles in this utterly
absorbing tour through the material goods that defined the Soviet era,
from pulpy wrapping paper to the medals veterans wore,
from canned goods to perfume and tchotchkes and everything
in between. . . . A superb blend of social history and material culture."
—*Kirkus Reviews* (starred review)

"A pinnacle in Soviet studies. . . . A splendid book."
—*Library Journal* (starred review)

"If the past is a foreign country, *The Soviet Century* is a unique
travelogue from one of the world's most innovative observers
of urban space and material culture. Karl Schlögel's scholarly
Baedeker is the culmination of a lifetime of study, travel, and thought.
It guides us across nothing less than a continental empire and a
century of upheaval. But Schlögel's greatest accomplishment
is to connect stunningly eclectic new detail to the big picture,
allowing us to see and feel a lost civilization anew."
—MICHAEL DAVID-FOX, Georgetown University

THE SOVIET CENTURY

THE SOVIET CENTURY

Archaeology of a Lost World

KARL SCHLÖGEL

TRANSLATED BY RODNEY LIVINGSTONE

PRINCETON UNIVERSITY PRESS
PRINCETON AND OXFORD

First published in Germany under the title *Das sowjetische Jahrhundert*, by Karl Schlögel, copyright © Verlag C.H.Beck oHG, München, 2018

English translation copyright © 2023 by Princeton University Press

Published by Princeton University Press
41 William Street, Princeton, New Jersey 08540
99 Banbury Road, Oxford OX2 6JX

press.princeton.edu

First Princeton paperback printing, 2024
Paper ISBN 978-0-691-23729-9
Cloth ISBN 978-0-691-18374-9
ISBN (e-book) 978-0-691-23238-6

British Library Cataloging-in-Publication Data is available

Editorial: Priya Nelson, Thalia Leaf, Barbara Shi, and Emma Wagh
Production Editorial: Jill Harris
Jacket/Cover Design: Lauren Michelle Smith
Production: Danielle Amatucci
Publicity: James Schneider and Kate Farquhar-Thomson

Jacket/Cover photo: Film still from Dennis Adams's *Malraux's Shoes*, 2012, courtesy of Kent Fine Art, New York

This book has been composed in Kazimir Text and Industry

Printed in the United States of America

For my wife, Sonja Margolina,
who has always both inspired me and challenged me

CONTENTS

Translator's Acknowledgements   xi
Abbreviations   xiii
Preface   xvii

Introduction: Archaeology of a Vanished World   1

I. Shards of Empire   7
  1. *Barakholka* in Izmailovsky Park, Bazaar in Petrograd   9
  2. The Soviet World as Museum   19
  3. Return to the Scene: Petrograd 1917   40
  4. The Philosophy Steamer and the Splitting
        of Russian Culture   58

II. Highway of Enthusiasts   75
  5. *USSR in Construction*: The Power of Images   77
  6. DniproHES: America on the Dnieper   83
  7. Magnitogorsk: The Pyramids of the Twentieth Century 98
  8. Black and White: The Photographer's Eye   115
  9. Excursion to the White Sea Canal   122
 10. Landscape after the Battle   141

III. Soviet Sign-Worlds   157
 11. The Writing on the Wall   161
 12. Decorations and Medals: Chest Badges   170
 13. Body Language: Tattoos   178
 14. Moscow Graffiti: In the Beginning Was Futurism   184
 15. Names Are Not Just Hot Air   189

IV. The Life of Things   195
 16. Wrapping Paper, Packaging   197
 17. The Fate of the Great Soviet Encyclopedia: The
        Organisation of Knowledge amid the Tumult of History   200

18. Galleries of Private Possessions: The China Elephant
      on the Shelf   213
19. The Piano in the Palace of Culture   219
20. Rubbish: A Phenomenology of Cleanliness   227
21. Krasnaya Moskva: Chanel in Soviet-Speak   231
22. Stalin's Cookbook: Images of the Good Life
      in the Soviet Age   245

V. Oases of Freedom   261
23. Geologists' Field Work and Other Breathing Spaces   263
24. Dacha: Chekhov's *Cherry Orchard* in the
      Twentieth Century   272
25. Health Resorts for Workers: The Sanatorium as a
      Historical Locus   283

VI. Interiors   301
26. Doorbells: Nameplates and Signals   303
27. *Kommunalka*, or Where the Soviet People Were Tempered   305
28. The Interior as a Battlefield   326
29. Hostel/*Obshchezhitie*: Soviet Melting Pot   338
30. Tent Cities, World of Barracks: Finding One's Way in
      'Russia in Flux'   343
31. Palm Trees in the Civil War   348
32. The Soviet Staircase: Towards an Analysis of
      Anonymous and Anomic Spaces   361
33. Ilya Kabakov's Installation: The Toilet as a Civilising Space 366
34. The 'Moscow Kitchen', or the Rebirth of Civil Society   376

VII. Landscapes, Public Spaces   397
35. Gorky Park: A Garden for the New Human Being   399
36. Diorama: View of a Landscape with Heroes   413
37. 'Zhilmassiv', or the Sublime Vistas of the Prefab Mountains 420
38. Russkaya Glubinka—the Country beyond the Big Cities   438

VIII. Big Data   453
39. *Spetskhran*: Catalogue of Forbidden Books   455
40. Diagrams of Progress, Diagrams of Catastrophes   466

IX. Rituals   481
41. The Border at Brest—Rites of Passage   483
42. Choreographies of Power: Parades on Red Square
    and Elsewhere   496
43. A 'Temple of Modernity': The Crematorium   513
44. ZAGS, or the Rituals of Everyday Life   523
45. Queues as a Soviet Chronotope   531
46. 'Think of the Parties We Had . . .'   552

X. Bodies   567
47. *Fizkultura*: Soviets as Athletes   569
48. Clothes for the New Human Being, or Christian Dior's
    Return to Red Square   585
49. Manly Grace: Nureyev's Gesture   608

XI. Kolyma: The Pole of Cold   619

XII. The Solovetsky Special Camp—Laboratory of Extremes:
Monastery Island as Concentration Camp   649

XIII. Corridors of Power   665
50. K. in the Labyrinth of Everyday Soviet Reality   667
51. The 'House on the Moskva': Machine for Living,
    Trap for People, Gated Community   678
52. The Aura of the Telephone and the Absence of the
    Phone Book   691

XIV. The Noise of Time   699
53. The Bells Fall Silent   702
54. Levitan's Voice   713
55. Back in the USSR: Sound Traces   726

XV. Alien Territory, Contact Zones, In-Between Worlds   731
56. 'The Little Oasis of the Diplomatic Colony'   735
57. The Journalists' Ghetto: The View from Outside,
    Fixation with the Centre   741
58. Beryozka Shops: 'Oases of Affluence'   745

59. Genius of the Collector: George Costakis and the
        Rediscovery of Soviet Avant-Garde Art   752

**XVI. The Railroads of Empire: Time Travel Back into
the Russian Twentieth Century**   769

XVII. Red Cube: The Lenin Mausoleum as Keystone   791

**XVIII. The Lubyanka Project: Design for a *Musée Imaginaire*
of Soviet Civilisation**   807

Acknowledgements   821
Notes   823
Selected Reading   879
Index   881

TRANSLATOR'S ACKNOWLEDGEMENTS

I wish to express my gratitude to Angela Livingstone for help with Russian transliteration and her part-translation of Yuly Kim's poem in the chapter on Moscow kitchens. I am grateful to Professor Ralph Cleminson for a brief but illuminating conversation. Help and encouragement from Benjamin Livingstone and Professor Sonia Livingstone were immensely supportive. I owe thanks also to Karl Schlögel for his prompt and kind replies to my queries. I am deeply indebted to the Princeton editing team led by Jill Harris, who oversaw the process with tact and consideration. In a volume containing references in multiple languages, Irina du Quenoy successfully devised a system for harmonising the transliterations of Russian names and words. My greatest debt is to Kim Hastings, who meticulously scrutinised my translation, correcting stylistic and grammatical slips, removing Germanicisms and making imaginative suggestions.

Translator notes appear in square brackets throughout. When available, English translations have been cited in notes. The transliteration of Russian words and names in the text has been designed to be as user-friendly as possible. Endings have been simplified. Names familiar in English have retained their customary spellings (Khrushchev, Gorbachev). Texts cited in German or English and, more rarely, French retain their original spellings.

ABBREVIATIONS

ARA American Relief Administration
BAM Baikal-Amur Mainline
BSE (Bolshaya sovetskaya entsiklopediya), Great Soviet Encyclopedia
CEC Central Executive Committee
Cheka (VChK) Russian Extraordinary Commission for Combating Counter-Revolution, Profiteering and Corruption (1917–1922), the first in a series of Soviet secret-police organisations
CIAM International Congress of Modern Architecture
CPSU Communist Party of the Soviet Union
CSKA Central Sports Club of the Army
Dalstroy (Glavnoe Upravlenie stroitelstva Dalnego Vostoka/Severa), Construction Trust of the Far East, or alternatively, of the Far East and North (1931–1957)
DniproHES (Dniprovskaya Hidroelektrostantsiya), also known as Dniprostroy (1929–1932), Dnieper Hydroelectric Station
DOSAAF (Dobrovolnoe obshchtestvo sodeistviia armii, aviatsii i flotu), Volunteer Society for Cooperation with the Advancement of Army, Airforce and Navy—a paramilitary sport organisation
FSB Federal Security Service, the chief Russian security agency since 1995
GDR German Democratic Republic (1949–1990)
GOELRO State Commission for the Electrification of Russia
Gosplan State Planning Commission
GPU See OGPU
GTO (*Gotov k trudu i oborone SSSR*), Ready for Labour and Defence
GUM Department store
KEPS Commission for the Study of Natural Productive Forces
KGB (Komitet Gosudarstvennoy Bezopasnosti), Committee for State Security (1947–1991)
LFZ Leningrad Porcelain Factory trademark
MVD Ministry of Internal Affairs
Narkomfin People's Commissariat for Finance

Narkompros People's Commissariat for Enlightenment, i.e., education

Narkomtrud People's Commissariat for Labour

Narkomvneshtorg People's Commissariat for Foreign Trade

NEP New Economic Policy (1921–1928)

NKGB People's Commissariat for State Security. It became the MGB in 1946. Both it and the MVD were headed by Lavrenty Beria until 1953.

NKTB (Narkomtyazhprom), People's Commissariat for Heavy Industry

NKVD (Narkomvnudel), People's Commissariat for Internal Affairs. Originally established in 1917 and tasked with conducting regular police work and overseeing the country's prisons and labour camps. It took over the OGPU (the secret police) in 1934 and thus acquired a monopoly over law enforcement activities until the end of the Second World War. It became the MVD in 1946.

NOT Scientific Organisation of Labour

NPO VILAR All-Russian Scientific Research Institute of Medicinal and Spice Plants

NTS (Narodno-trudovoy soyuz rossiyskikh solidaristov), National Alliance of Russian Solidarists, a Russian anticommunist organisation founded in 1930 by a group of young Russian anticommunist White émigrés in Belgrade, Serbia. Its centre for underground revolutionary activity was dissolved in 1991 after the fall of the Soviet Union.

OGPU (GPU 1922–1923), an organisation for investigating and combating counterrevolutionary activities in the former Soviet Union, replacing the Cheka. It became the NKVD from 1934.

OKB (Osoboe konstruktorskoe byuro), Special Construction Office

OSOAVIAKhIM (Obshchtestvo sodeistviia oborone aviatsionnomu i himicheskomu stroitelstvu), Association for the Advancement of Defence, Aviation and Chemistry (precursor of DOSAAF)

OVIR Office of Visas and Registration

Pomgol Hunger Relief Committee

ROSTA Russian Telegraph Agency

RSFSR Russian Soviet Federated Socialist Republic

Sevvostlag (Severo-Vostochny ispravitelno-trudovoy lager), the North-Eastern Corrective Labour Camps

Shirkost (Soyuzny trest vysshey parfiumernoy, shirovoy, mylovarennoy i sinteticheskoy produktsii), Union Trust of Distinguished Perfumery, Fat-processing, Soap-making and Synthetics Production

SLON Solovki special camp

Spetskhran Special Storage Section, i.e., for books with limited access

SR Socialist Revolutionaries

STO Council for Work and Defence

STON Solovetsky prison

TASS Russian News Agency

TseKUBU Central Commission for the Improvement of the Everyday Lives of Scientists

TsSU (Tsentralnoe statisticheskoe upravlenie), Central Administration of Statistics

TsUNKhU (Tsentralnoe upravlenie narodno-khozyaystvennogo uchota), Central Administration of Economic Record-Keeping

UFA (Universum Film-Aktien Gesellschaft), German motion-picture company (1917–1945)

VChK All-Russian Extraordinary Commission, i.e., the secret police, commonly known as the Cheka

VDNKh Site of the Exhibition of the Achievements of the National Economy

VOKS All-Union Society for Cultural Relations with Foreign Countries

Vsevobuch (Vseobshchee voennoe obuchenie), Universal Military Training Organisation

VTsIK All-Russian Central Executive Committee

ZAGS (Zapis aktov grazhdanskogo sostoyaniya), Office for the Registration of Personal Information

ZhAKT (Zhilishchno-arendnye kooperativnye tovarishchestva), Housing cooperative

Zhilmassiv (Zhilishchny massiv), Housing massif

ZIL (Zavod imeni Likhachova), a former car and truck factory in Moscow

PREFACE

Historians are sometimes contemporaries who discover they are witnesses of what specialists refer to as a 'caesura', a 'historical juncture' or 'the end of an era'. This was the case with the Soviet Union. What had come to an end was not history itself, but an empire, whose time had run out. Suddenly almost everything appeared in a different light: the past, the setting and the people caught up in the historical process. And nowhere, perhaps, was this harder to endure than in a country that had been subjected to a series of wars, civil wars and revolutions, a country with a vast territory and individual destinies of a kind seen only amid an utterly cataclysmic historical tumult. However, the end was also a beginning. There was now a plurality of voices, where hitherto there had been a strictly controlled public sphere. People could now step out into the world, where previously the borders had been closed. They could fix an uninhibited gaze on their history with its many open questions. The archives could be opened and stories could at last be told. From outside it was difficult to grasp the radical nature of this rupture with the past. Longstanding habits were cast aside, life plans consigned to the rubbish heap; borders sprang up where previously none had existed. Millions had to reorganise their entire lives. This meant social disaster for some, improvement for others. The quarter of a century that has elapsed since that time has shown how painful this process of transforming the former Soviet Union has been and how the political leadership has exploited postimperial phantom pains, nostalgic yearnings and fears of the loss of social status to pursue an aggressive policy, not excluding war against neighbouring states, so as to maintain its own power.

Both these experiences—that of the historical turning point and that of the longer timespan since then, which has brought the impact of 'deeper' structures to the surface—identify the historical locus for the origins of the present book.

Its appearance to coincide with the centenary of the Russian Revolution was unintentional but has its advantages however much we may object to the recycling of such events. History does not move according to the whims of anniversaries. At best, they are opportunities to express ideas that have finally matured. Our gaze has become more focused and feels challenged to make a new assessment of the 'Ten Days That Shook the World' and of the civilisation sui generis that emerged from it and contrived to assert itself down to the end of the twentieth century. This is what it is to see the twentieth century as Soviet: as a breakaway from the Europe of the First World War, as the reestablishment of the Russian Empire in a new form, as the outpost of the revolution against colonialism, as the antipode of the capitalist world market and as the experimental site of an unprecedented surge of modernisation, as a war to assert itself against Hitler Germany's barbaric wars of annihilation, as the growth into the world's second most powerful nation extending from the Elbe to the Pacific and as the last great multinational empire at the end of the twentieth century in Europe. There are good reasons to accept the idea of a Soviet century alongside the American one. When it finally came to end, many people asked how the Soviet Union was able to survive for so long, while others had already accepted that it would last forever. Everyone was blindsided by the course of events that led to perestroika and ultimately the demise of the USSR.

I have personally experienced a major portion of Soviet history, of its late period. Ever since my first visit in 1966, I have travelled all over the Soviet Union, explored and studied in it. Like many people who come from the smaller spaces of Central Europe, I was endlessly fascinated by its landscapes, rivers, history and people. I was touched and moved by the generosity of members of the war generation, who had undergone such horrific sufferings, towards a young German whose father fought as a soldier of the Wehrmacht on the 'Eastern Front'. I listened to their life stories, the likes of which were not to be found even in great literary accounts, but again and again I found myself confronted by people's depressing experiences, the images of stolen lifetimes and the expectation that after all the terrors and monstrosities, Russia might finally become a 'normal country'.

Working on the Soviet Union has been a lifelong preoccupation—and for me, as a historian socialised through the study of the Russian language and history, this has meant Russia above all. In my book *Jenseits des Großen Oktober, Petersburg 1909–1921: Das Laboratorium der Moderne* (1988) (Beyond October 1918, St. Petersburg 1909–1921: Laboratory of modernity), I worked on the period in which Russia became more or less the centre of the world. My book *Berlin: Ostbahnhof Europas* (1998) (Berlin: Europe's eastern station) was devoted to Russo-German relations, highlighting the fate of the Russian diaspora. With *Terror und Traum: Moskau 1937* (2008) (*Moscow, 1937*), I attempted to clarify what happened during the 'Great Purges' of the Stalin era. Portraits of Eastern European cities written from the 1980s on enabled me to gain access to the Soviet lifeworld and the cultural landscape of Eastern Europe. If there was one topic I avoided, it was the war of annihilation that Hitler inflicted on the nations of the Soviet Union. I shrank from this, afraid that I would not be able to do it justice.

It was not my intention to provide a balance sheet, a sort of final account of my studies of Russia or the Soviet Union; I had other plans and priorities. But then came the final drop that made my cup run over. What decided and urged me on was Putin's annexation of the Crimea and the undeclared war on Ukraine. It was this—so I found—that forced me to take one more look at the empire that had disappeared. This was the context in which I formed the plan for the present book. In June 2014 I gave a talk to the Carl Friedrich von Siemens Foundation in Munich when I presented an outline of my thinking under the title 'An Archaeology of Communism: Forming an Image of Twentieth-Century Russia'. The fact that I was able to concentrate on this book and bring it to completion under such privileged conditions was made possible by the generosity of the Carl Friedrich von Siemens Foundation and its director, Professor Heinrich Meier. I would like to express my warmest gratitude to them. And I am delighted that C. H. Beck has agreed to include the book in its programme.

Karl Schlögel
Berlin, May 2017

Postscript to the English Edition

The appearance of the English edition gives me particular pleasure. I would like to thank Rodney Livingstone for his wonderful translation. I am grateful to Brigitta van Rheinberg and everyone at Princeton University Press for the friendly and efficient cooperation that has made its publication possible.

July 2022

Archaeology of a Vanished World

What will be presented here as the 'archaeology of a vanished world' does not set out to be a new history of the Soviet Union but attempts to imagine the history of this country in a novel way, certainly one that differs from many of the impressive histories currently available. The Soviet Union was not only a political system with a datable beginning and an end, but a form of life with its own history, maturity, decline and fall. With its practices, values and routines, it shaped the citizens of the nation for many generations to come.[1] I term this longstanding lifeworld 'Soviet civilisation', disregarding the validity or otherwise of its claims to be superior to the old world, capitalism or the West. Lifeworlds may be older and more stable than political systems and they may live on even after the end of a system has been proclaimed and established.[2] They leave their traces well beyond that end, as everyone who has lived in any of the states that have emerged from great empires knows: languages, the style of schools and administrative buildings, infrastructure and railway lines, manners, educational institutions and biographies, the hatred of or sentimental attachment to the masters of former years—these phenomena can be seen everywhere, whether in the former territories of the British Empire, the Ottoman Empire, the Danube Monarchy or even the German Reich. The situation with the Soviet Union is not very different. Its vestiges will persist—as physical traces and on the mental maps of inhabitants of what is now a postimperial, postcolonial world—long after the USSR as a political entity has passed away.

This is where archaeology comes in. It takes the territory of a former empire as its field of operations. It then inspects and secures the various traces; it sets up probes and carries out excavations— literally and metaphorically. Archaeologists do not dig in a haphazard fashion; they follow up clues that can lead to further findings. They have their navigation tools and maps and, above all, entire libraries in their heads. What they are looking for are the remains of earlier generations. They lay bare one stratum after another, secure their findings, catalogue the fragments and take all steps necessary for subsequent conservation and analysis. Their findings are destined to inform them about a world that has ceased to exist. The fragments they have learned to decipher enable them to create a picture, the text of a past era. Each of these fragments has its own past and the trick is to make them speak. Together these fragments form a mosaic and the stories these lifeless objects yield up all come together to create what we think of as 'history'. On occasion, archaeologists unexpectedly encounter strata and objects that force them to reject interpretations, periodisations and contexts that have been handed down to them. These are their moments of epiphany.

Uncovering objects, rescuing them, making them speak—that is the archaeological path proposed here. It implies also a rather broader definition of a 'document', a 'source'. To imagine the world of a past epoch calls for more than merely written documents, reports, testimony, a collection of files, all of which are basically the objective products of human existence (if we ignore for the moment the accretions of nature). The world can be read via the history of things, the analysis of signs and modes of interaction, places and routines. The totality grows out of the details so that, if everything counts, the principal question in a project relating the history of Soviet civilisation is where to begin and where to stop. Do you start with the great buildings of communism or the little porcelain figurines of the 1930s, with the voice of the speaker on Radio Moscow or the parade of athletes, with Gorky Park or the camps on the Kolyma River, the building of a mausoleum or the beaches on the Red Riviera? This list is not uttered in the spirit of anything goes, nor is it a game involving a quest for the unusual and the exotic. It points to the infinite complexity of a society, particularly if that society is drawn into a sequence of war, civil war and revolution and if over great expanses of time life is no more than a struggle for survival. The history of civilisation aims at totality; it is not the history of politics or daily life, of the reign of terror or enthusiastic approval, of culture or barbarism, but both together and much, much more—often at the same time and in the same place.[3] If we assert the idea of *histoire totale* as a desirable, albeit unachievable ideal, and if we are prepared to accept the risks implied, then for all our 'panoramic openness', we have to face up to the criteria for selection, the question of 'relevance'—in other words, the decision about what is envisaged in such a study and exactly what is to be analysed.

The present book is not a collection of essays assembled over the years, although some were written at different times. Instead the chapters listed in the table of contents represent a journey whose stages have been deliberately chosen by the author. This selection can of course never achieve encyclopedic completeness and whether it is plausible and convincing or artificial and even forced must be left to the reader to decide. I would like to have added a few more sections, had I not feared outstaying my welcome and overburdening the reader. For example, I would have liked to add chapters on the Artek camps, the summer camps for children, and examined their effects on childhood; also a chapter on the 1957 World Festival of Youth and Students in Moscow. Then there is Yury Gagarin, the glorious hero. No advance commentary can take from the individual chapters what only they can do, namely provide evidence. We are reminded of the awesome statement that Walter Benjamin concealed in the gigantic corpus of his *Arcades Project*: 'Method of this project: literary montage. I needn't say anything. Merely show.'[4] A statement he was himself barely able to satisfy, having developed from the flaneur of the nineteenth century into the refugee of the twentieth.

As can be seen from the structure of the contents, this book consists of around sixty individual studies of varying length, arranged in eighteen sections. They constitute the stages of a journey undertaken between the first chapter—a stroll through one of Moscow's flea markets at the end of the Soviet Union—and the final section, that amounts to a *musée imaginaire*, a museum of Soviet civilisation situated in a memorably central location, the Lubyanka, the heart of darkness of Soviet history. One line of inquiry could take its cue from Heinrich Mann's title 'An Age under the Microscope'. Another accepts the invitation to 'read time by looking at space',[5] with the two approaches coming together in what Mikhail Bakhtin calls the chronotope.[6] The different chapters address the major creations of communism, what we might call the pyramids of the twentieth century. They range from the scent of the Empire, a brand of Soviet perfume, through the meaning of –49°C for the prisoners in Kolyma and the 'Ten Days That Shook the World', to other themes in which all the senses with which we perceive the world come into play. Even if there is no point in attempting to explain the relevance of each of these themes here or justify their inclusion, it is important to explain why these particular topics were chosen. The selection is based on the author's own first-hand experience. It is not the product of current academic controversies or of any change of direction in Russian or Soviet studies.

For someone such as me, who has spent a lifetime thinking about the world of the Soviets and has had almost three decades of direct experience of the Soviet system, it has long been clear which areas should be explored and which key points probed. Hence the problem was that of the book's 'architecture', the structure to be adopted, once I had abandoned any simplistic encyclopedic or chronological organisation of the key topics. These topics included my first impressions of the period of East-West confrontation, an alien world obscured by the smokescreen of the Cold War. Then there was the world of the 1960s, when it became possible to explore the USSR by moving from one campsite to the next. This was the time of the student movements, when I was able to study the world through the seminars held at the Free University's Institute of Eastern Europe in West Berlin, where the theory of totalitarianism had been superseded by a neo-Marxist approach. It was the world of the Soviet Union and its allies, whose tanks could be seen in Prague. And lastly, it was the world of the Soviet Union in the age of glasnost and perestroika, when things that had been inconceivable until then happened. In particular there was the return of free speech and living thought to the public sphere, an almost silent historical miracle just when the world had been prepared for the very worst—Stephen Kotkin caught the spirit of the moment with the title of his book, *Armageddon Averted.*[7] All these events amounted to a stock of experiences acquired by travelling through the country, by bus, train, boat and even hitchhiking. The subjects addressed in this book are based on that foundation, on my first-hand experience and the system of coordinates developed from that, so what decided whether something was significant and worthy of analysis was not any preexisting discourse, nor any secondary material from books or the media, but my own direct perception—what I saw with my own eyes and what could serve as a basis for analysis. This book, then, deals only with places and things that I have seen for myself, whether dams, monasteries or the Costakis collection in Thessaloniki. Of particular interest were the 'common places' that Svetlana Boym first brought to the attention of academic researchers: the queues, the communal apartments, the public toilets, the parades, the large-panel prefabricated mass-housing estates and the Moscow kitchens. In each case the object concerned had a visible exterior that had been overlooked by academic researchers for decades, because they believed the search for the 'essence' or the 'system' to be more important than the description and analysis of the actual realities of life.[8]

However, it would fall short of the mark to think of the present project as no more than a personal story, a 'merely subjective' view, an account with some such title as 'My Soviet Union: Memories of a Vanished World'.

A generation that has passed through every conceivable academic controversy in 'Soviet studies' is well able to resist the fetish of 'subjective impressions' and a concept of 'direct intuition' that is as portentous as it is naïve. It was schooled in the debates around totalitarianism, 'bureaucratic degeneration' and the subtle distinctions and ramifications that have developed since the 'paradigm shift of social history'. Its members were after all the direct witnesses of the transformation of the Soviet Union itself, when the country found its own voice once more and began to get to grips with the 'blind spots' in its past.[9] If the figure of the flaneur—that is, the idea of excursion as a method—plays such a crucial role, then it is because direct experience and reflection coincide here in a way that is both unforced and compelling.

Mention must be made of a further factor that supports the methodology adopted here. The present book has profited from the revival of interest in a type of cultural history that aspires to foster an interdisciplinary approach. In Germany this approach is associated with such divergent names as Karl Lamprecht, Georg Simmel and Aby Warburg. It is built on the insight that all human socialisation expresses itself and becomes concentrated in cultural forms. This being the case, the analysis of cultural and symbolic forms—in whatever genre—must move into the focus of attention. Analysis of this kind is very different from the analysis of 'culture' conceived as a separate subsystem, comparable to the economy or politics. Instead, it aims at the concrete exploration of cultural forms involving all the disciplines that have ever succeeded in contributing to them.[10] Who could deny that eclecticism and dilettantism are a danger here, all the more so since many of the essays in this book are just opening moves which still await a systematic analysis and cultural research?

Now, having identified the experiential space and the (intersubjective and transgenerational) frame of reference for the present studies, I would like to make two important reservations.

First, the end of an empire has epistemological consequences—and the USSR is no exception. We experience a shift in our viewpoint. The academic socialisation that has put its stamp on historians of Russia and the Soviet Union—and not just on me—was, as a rule, Russocentric and focused on Moscow or Leningrad. It operated in Russian, the lingua franca of the Empire. This points to a limitation of our competence that cannot be easily rectified. Here we can only take note and bear it in mind as we proceed. That a museum tour on the postimperial periphery of the former Soviet Union would in many respects look completely different is self-evident.[11]

Second, what began with the bazaar ends—unexpectedly for me and yet with something approaching inevitability—with the collection of objects in the museum where people, natives and foreigners alike, come together because they wish to imagine the Soviet world and enter into a dialogue—mediated by the exhibits—with generations who are no longer present and can no longer speak. The idea of providing Soviet civilisation with what André Malraux called a *musée imaginaire* or Matteo Ricci a 'memory palace' turns out to be the logical form into which the present research has flowed.[12] The book is an invitation; people can follow their curiosity, inclinations, their own interests. Visitors roam around autonomously, more as if through a labyrinth than in a linear fashion. No single lesson is provided, apart from any conclusions they may reach as they review the age, the places and the objects together with their history and destinies.

PART I

Shards of Empire

CHAPTER 1

Barakholka in Izmailovsky Park, Bazaar in Petrograd

It's only a few stations on the metro from the centre of Moscow to Izmailovo. You get out at Partizanskaya and follow the signs or even just the crowds of people moving towards where everyone wants to be: the bazaar, or the *barakholka*, as the flea market used to be called in Russia even before the Revolution, the market where second-hand articles are bought and sold.[1] Following the collapse of the socialist centralised distribution system, the entire country—indeed the entire former Eastern bloc—found itself covered by a network of thousands and thousands of such bazaars and flea markets in parks, at the last stations of the underground lines, with thousands and thousands of visitors and customers. Examples are the 'Seventh Kilometre' near Odesa and the market that spread itself out in the Luzhniki Stadium in Moscow. When the centralised distribution system collapsed, the value of the currency fell and a barter economy reemerged temporarily; these markets became the chief arenas for the struggle for survival, with millions of people travelling to and fro to do their shopping, shuttling back and forth like a weaver's loom, even across frontiers.[2] The bazaar in Izmailovsky Park was something special. This was because of its proximity to the city centre; in the 1930s it had been called Stalinsky Park and was Moscow's second largest park after Gorky Park, with a statue of Stalin at its entrance. It was where the Stalinsky Stadium was to be built. If it still attracts Muscovites and foreigners today, that has less to do with the magnificence of the parkland and gardens than with the attractions of this vast bazaar.

Svetlana Alexievich visited another street market and has described her walk through the Arbat in Moscow. She gives a sensitive account of how an entire world-historical era was being sold off on the cheap.

On the Old Arbat, my beloved Arbat, I found rows of pedlars, selling *matryoshka* dolls, samovars, icons, and portraits of the last tsars and the royal family. Portraits of White Guard generals—Kolchak and Denikin, next to busts of Lenin. . . . There were all sorts of *matryoshkas*: Gorbachov *matryoshkas*, Yeltsin *matryoshkas*. I didn't recognize my Moscow. What city was this? Right there on the asphalt, on top of some bricks, an old man sat playing the accordion. He was wearing his medals, singing war songs, with a hat full of change at his feet. Our favourite songs . . . I wanted to go up to him . . . but he was already surrounded by foreigners . . . snapping pictures. . . . They were . . . having a lot of fun. Why wouldn't they be? People used to be so scared of us . . . and now . . . here you go! Nothing but piles of junk, an empire gone up in smoke! Next to all the *matryoshkas* and samovars there was a mountain of red flags and pennants, Party and Komsomol membership cards. And Soviet war medals! Orders of Lenin and the Red Banner. Medals![3]

There are and always have been bazaars, flea markets and street markets like this one in every town and city of the Soviet Union and what you can see there are the shards, the debris and the fragments of the world of objects belonging to the empire that has ceased to exist. There is nothing you cannot find there. Objects belonging to the world of generations long past change ownership and become the property of people living now. We witness the circulation of objectified forms and their reappropriation by others. You can find cast-iron irons that used to be heated up by charcoal and that may have come from a peasant house in the north of Russia destined to be torn down. But you can also see modern, electric irons that were perhaps handed out to the factory workers in lieu of the wages they had long since ceased to receive or which had become worthless during the 1990s. You can find individual sheets, still in good condition, of a Party newspaper, which was formerly printed in millions of copies. They have now become historical documents, thanks to the portrait of Stalin and the text of an important decree. You can find photograph albums documenting the stages of an entire life—the grandparents, the family, the pioneer years, school, the start of a working life, and perhaps even time spent in the army—in which the transition from one phase to the next is in-

FIGURE 1.1. As with marketplaces everywhere in the world, the entire inventory of past ages is spread out on display. And so it was in a bazaar in Moscow's Izmailovsky Park in the 1990s. © moscowwalks.ru.

dicated by the transition from sepia to black and white and, in the case of a long life, to colour prints. You can find postcards from holidays on the Black Sea. Happy days! You can see them all lying there, spread out in the dust, in plastic folders, just like other kinds of documents that register the toils of a life of work, such as the 'Arbeitsbuch' containing a person's employment record, with entries in elegant handwriting recording the stages of a working life.

Sometimes, when someone has died or a household has been broken up, you find a whole bundle of documents reflecting an entire life. There are photographs enabling us to get the measure of someone's appearance and their entire trajectory—their school reports, their sporting successes, their party membership and so on right down to the end of their life. In the bazaar you can find the sort of furniture the grandchildren don't know what to do with because it is too old-fashioned, insufficiently 'modern'. Entire libraries are to be found there testifying to the taste of past generations of readers. Many of the books contain underlinings and notes in the margins. The objects up for sale are absolute compendiums of past trends and fashions. Here you can see how a young generation that wanted nothing to do with the old turned its back on the world of yesterday with its leather jackets and sailor tops. Things that had previously been carefully stored and preserved until the end of people's lives—distinctions, work records, diplomas and even medals—all find themselves up for sale in the flea market once material needs have become sufficiently pressing and the sense of reverence has evaporated. Among the post-imperial junk you can find the wall rugs that have been brought from Central Asia and the radios people could not bring themselves to discard, since they might, after all, come in handy again one day. The expert connoisseur of graphic art can barely suppress his excitement when a clueless dealer offers him a valuable print. Plunder, junk, second-hand goods, unique items—it is all testimony of one sort or another. These markets all have something of interest to bored tourists, but also to highly specialised experts. In the battered biscuit tin they discover the design of the prerevolutionary confectioners founded by Theodor Ferdinand von Einem or the Mosselprom cigarette trust of the 1920s. On the bookstall they recognise the exquisite binding of the editions of the classics published by the Academy of

Sciences in the 1930s. In the chest full of hundreds of artfully designed bottles of scent, they search out the ones called 'Red Moscow' or 'Lilac Eau de Parfum'. No one can match the expertise and aesthetic judgement of the dealers offering china figurines for sale. They know the designers, the factories and the signatures on the base of each piece. In such markets you can find specialists who know all about Dresden China, about the various incarnations of the Pathé gramophone and the endless sets of matchboxes and cigarette packets. Certain notorious relics of the Stalin period, such as the book about building the White Sea Canal, edited by Maxim Gorky and illustrated by Alexander Rodchenko, are particularly costly. There are still large numbers of collectors of memorabilia from the Soviet-German War—belt buckles, pay books and service records, helmets with bullet holes, the labour records of former 'eastern workers' as well as of German soldiers who never managed to return home—all these things are readily available. Entire collections are sold en bloc, ranging from those that have been sorted out systematically to those where everything is lumped together—tea mats, stamps and coin collections (especially those of the Civil War period with their dozens of competing local currencies). In the midst of all this, you suddenly come across class photographs from 1937, the year of the Great Terror.

Today's barakholka has its predecessors.[4] We might even say that every great crisis, every revolution, the end of every era finds expression in bazaars where the shards of the vanished world are offered for sale on the cheap. 'Fragment of an Empire' is the title of a 1929 film by director Fridrikh Ermler, a masterpiece of the Soviet silent cinema.[5] A soldier in the Civil War who has lost his memory as the result of a wound regains consciousness in Leningrad, where he is unable to find his bearings. Everything has changed—the tempo, the faces, fashion and women. There are even skyscrapers to be seen (evidently the House of Industry in Kharkiv, only recently finished). The soldier wanders through the metropolis in his fur cap and peasant's coat, trying to return to the city, but finding only shards, ruins and fragments. He finally succeeds in gaining access to the factory committee, the new masters of the city, and everything ends well. Ermler has staged the great transformations wrought by the war, Revolution and Civil War by presenting them as an age of splintering and fragmentation.

The age of turmoil was also the age of the barakholka. Class distinctions disappeared from the marketplace; deprivation and the
struggle for survival made everyone equal, regardless of whether they
were workers, former civil servants, members of the intelligentsia or
just peasants. 'Grain was the absolute standard, the hard currency
throughout all the years of the Civil War.'[6] The hierarchy of values was
turned upside down. Mikhail Ossorgin describes this from the standpoint of a bibliophile: 'I found a complete first edition of Lavoisier's
works. Extremely rare for Moscow. And I saw a curious little book on
mathematics, with ecclesiastical print, dated 1682, the first I should
think, ever published in Russia. The title was curious too: *A Convenient
Method of Calculation whereby any Man may conveniently discover the
Number of Any Kind of Things when Buying or Selling*. There are also
logarithmic tables there that go back to the time of Peter the Great.'
Editions from the time of Peter and Catherine can be more cheaply
obtained than the latest editions of the Imaginists.[7]

In those days too, everything ended up in the marketplace if it
helped to alleviate hunger and cold. The wealth of the entire capital, doomed to disappear, was up for sale often at throwaway prices.
The postrevolutionary situation was one of unlimited squandering of
riches accumulated over generations: one pair of boots in exchange
for ten kilos of books or one uniform in exchange for one kerosene
stove. A Rubens painting that had disappeared from a palace in exchange for a loaf of bread. For connoisseurs who had not emigrated,
a moment of glory had arrived. During the Civil War, St. Petersburg/
Petrograd must have been the greatest street market of European
art. Furniture by Abraham Roentgen, paintings by Poussin, the most
venerable examples of the goldsmith's art were all to be had by anyone
who could offer a bag of flour.[8] This was the place for the poorest of
the poor. During the Civil War everyone went there to barter. Money
had ceased to have any value. Every social class was represented
and you could buy whatever you wanted: porcelain figurines, chandeliers, telescopes, cameras with Zeiss lenses, chamber pots, Underwood sewing machines, ostrich feathers, volumes of *Niva* magazine,
French perfume. Barakholka Petrograd—that would be the history of
a place where a city devastated by the collapse of all social relations
maintains its unity, a place for trade where everything merges: buying and selling, swindling, the activities of professional thieves, the

worldly expertise of art dealers, the meeting ground for everyone expelled from their habitual social roles and compelled to present themselves anew.[9]

There is plenty of testimony to the world of the open city of Petrograd with its palaces, libraries, art and painting collections, the everyday wealth that piled up in the dwellings of an affluent class. Literary reflections of the dispersal of this great wealth in the bazaars, secondhand bookshops and trading on commission can be found, for example, in Boris Pilnyak's *The Volga Flows to the Caspian Sea*.[10] There we find two Moscow antique dealers who buy up old furniture in Kolomna, a town flooded during the building of a new dam. The antique furniture stands for the Russia that has disappeared. About the church, where the goods are all stored, we learn:

> The church looked like a pile of objects rescued from a fire. Round the walls were heaped cupboards, wardrobes, sofas and a vast number of sewing machines. . . . On a level equal to the height of three men a dinner table had been placed on two wardrobes; on it there was a chair together with a small table and a hammer for the auctioneer. Only a few people had collected in the auction room, where they were inspecting the goods, looking very business-like and loudly discussing the prices at which the bidding was to start; these, with the numbers of the lots, were posted up on the various wardrobes, beds, armchairs, sofas and sewing-machines. A dim light forced its way through the iron bars and the dust of the church windows. The professor, following the example of the others, aimlessly wandered from object to object. They were holding sales of goods that had not been redeemed from the pawnshops, sales brought on by misfortunes of every kind. Cotton cushions alongside brass bedsteads and lime wood dining-tables narrate the chronicle of Russian impoverishment.[11]

The room of the curator of the Museum of Antiquities in Kolomna is described as follows:

> In his house, somewhat like a storehouse, there lay scattered about rare bibles, stoles, albs, cassocks, chasubles, patens, veils and altar cloths of the thirteenth, fifteenth and seventeenth centuries, and

amidst this dust there reigned a naked statue of Christ in a crown of thorns, a work of the seventeenth century taken from the monastery at Bobrenev. His study was furnished with antiques which had once belonged to the landowner Karazin. On the writing-table there stood a nobleman's cap in porcelain with red trimming and white crown, which served as an ashtray.[12]

Furniture items tell their own story.

The art of Russian mahogany furniture, started in Russia by Peter the Great, has its own legends. This art of the serfs has no written records, and time has not deemed it necessary to preserve the names of its masters. It has always been the work of individual and known men, in cellars in the towns, in small backrooms in the country, a work of bitter vodka and cruel solitude. Georges Jacob and André Charles Boulle, the French master cabinet makers, were their inspiration.

Young serfs were sent to Moscow, St. Petersburg, Paris and Vienna; there they were taught the craft. Then they were brought back from Paris to the cellars of St. Petersburg and Moscow, from St. Petersburg to small serfs' quarters on the estates, and there they created. For decades one of them would be employed in making a couch, a dressing-table, some small bureau or book-case; he worked, drank and died, leaving his art to his nephews, for a master was not supposed to have children, and the nephews either carried on their uncle's art or copied it. The master died, but what he created lived on in landowners' estates and private houses. People made love and died in their beds . . . in the secret drawers of the secretaries clandestine correspondence was kept; in the mirrors on the dressing tables brides gazed on their youth, old women on their age. Elizabeth, Catherine—rococo, baroque, bronze scrolls, fleurons, mahogany, ebony, rosewood, satinwood, Persian nut. . . . Under Paul it is a soldier's life with a soldier's Freemasonry, a calm severity. The mahogany is overlaid with a dark lacquer, there is green leather and griffons and black lions. Under Alexander I it is all Empire style, Classical and Greek. . . . This was how the spirit of the times was mirrored in the joiner's craft.[13]

Later on, too, the barakholka remained a fixture in everyday Soviet life. From time to time, it would be banned and it was always subject to controls and bureaucratic interference, but remained irreplaceable as a counter to the failings of the planned economy. The economist V. V. Sher thought of the Moscow bazaar as the rebirth of capitalism. 'The Sukharevka is conquering Red Square in the name of transforming the whole of Moscow into a New York or Chicago.'[14] In 1936 Moscow also had the Yaroslavsky and Dubininsky bazaars where you could buy rubber galoshes, shoes, off-the-peg clothes, gramophone records, and more. The bazaars of the 1930s and 1940s existed side by side with the state shops.[15] In the 1940s, Aleksander Wat, the Polish writer banished to Alma-Ata [now Almaty] after the occupation of eastern Poland, wrote about the Tolkuchka bazaar:

I had to walk across the flea market, which played a certain role in my life, and so maybe I should describe it a little. An enormous square, perhaps as large as Red Square. By day it was Sodom and Gomorrah, a whirlwind of rags and people. Colorful. You could buy anything there. Nails, one rubber boot at a time, but there were also very substantial items—gold. They all held onto their goods for dear life. They slung them over their arms or held them in their hands, or the entire family would barricade them because *urks* cruised the market. And policemen too. It should be said that while in Russia the NKVD was a menace, the police were mostly undernourished and very anaemic, like sleepy flies in the late autumn. They hung around the market. Incredible shouting in twenty languages, dialects. That was by day.[16]

The flea markets and black markets were places that enabled people to survive, especially in the towns ravaged by war in the west of the Soviet Union before state supplies had been properly restored. According to Yury Nagibin, what you could find in the barakholka in postwar Moscow were old shoes, used clothing, soldiers' overcoats, splendid furs, gold rings and antiques—from balalaikas without strings to accordions, pistols, medals, forged documents, padded jackets, priests' robes, Brussels lace and American summer suits—in fact everything under the sun.[17] These markets acquired a rather different meaning during the Thaw and the late Soviet phase. The Thaw generation did away with the furniture of the 1930s and 1940s— it had put behind it the fears and basic privations of the Revolution and the industrialisation phase. It discarded the cumbersome furniture that looked out of place in the new, modern homes; it threw out the complete works of Marxism-Leninism, while retaining the children's books by Korney Chukovsky and Arkady Gaidar, the Academy editions of the Russian classics and the great cookery book from the Stalin era. In the 1960s the 'organs of the state' took a harsher view of the flea markets because they saw in them a biotope for speculators, currency dealers and *fartsovshchiki* [illegal traffickers].[18]

However, the most serious clearing-out campaign took place at the end of the Soviet Union. The clear-out of the past became a paroxysm of hysteria, for a brief period at least. People could not rid themselves fast enough of the furniture, clothes and books of the Soviet era. But this phase is over and done with. Today the barakholka is fast disappearing from the post-Soviet consumer landscape with its super-malls, shopping centres with carparks and logistics complexes. What survives in the barakholka is what is unobtainable in the expensive modern consumer world focused on the latest fashions, namely the shards of empire.

CHAPTER 2

The Soviet World as Museum

Museum visits were not normally the top priority of visitors to the Soviet Union or Russia. Of course, there were always highlights and still are, places that were required viewing and could not be omitted: the art collections, first and foremost the Hermitage and the Russian Museum in St. Petersburg or the Tretyakov Gallery and the Armoury Palace in the Kremlin in Moscow. But how many people find themselves in the Railway Museum in St. Petersburg or the Bakhrushin Theatre Museum in Moscow, not to mention the many museums with impressively large collections that might be inspected outside the two Russian metropolises?[1] These collections are sought out by experts who know that important works of art belonging to Soviet Modernism can also be found outside the capital and in the so-called provinces: in Samara on the Volga or in Novosibirsk. They had been sent there once upon a time by a People's Commissariat for Enlightenment that believed in the idea of education and the principle of just redistribution and decentralisation of cultural goods. This is how masterpieces by Boris Kustodiev or Kazimir Malevich can still be found in remote locations where no one would ever expect to find them.[2]

But the world of museums is not confined to art. Museums are far more than that, as can be seen from what has become a vast literature on the subject.[3] They are storehouses of cultural memory, for both major events and minor details; memories of families, tribes, nations, empires and enterprises. Their exhibits and the way they are presented enable us to imagine time—both time past and the time in which we live. This is how a nation or a city wishes to be seen. This is the self-image that one wants sent out into the world or at least anchored in visitors' minds. Museums resemble time capsules or time machines. They may take the form of cabinets of curiosities, glassed-in galleries complete with dust and spiders' webs or else modern high-tech museums with moving images, audio guides and the production of sound worlds that catapult visitors to other places or other times in an 'interactive' relation to generations long since extinct. Museums can be structured strictly chronologically so that visitors follow what might be termed an arrow of time. Such exhibitions have an order of their own, much like that of old-time school textbooks, so that whoever follows the narrative line cannot really go astray. They follow the red thread and at the end of the trail, having successfully negotiated all the vicissitudes and dangers, arrive at an end point, which is indispensable in any historical narrative. Such a narrative needs an end, a goal, a telos, which admittedly varies. It may be an end with a clear message, a 'lesson', or else one full of contradictory information or interpretations, leaving visitors confused—as after a rollercoaster ride.

At the heart of the museum, we find the collector and the collection. Prolonged periods of peace are beneficial for the labour of accumulation, while disruptions, with their uncertainties and iconoclastic outbursts, can lead to irreversible losses. Museums put objects on display—the heritage of humankind—but they never do so without the desire and the intention to display something of themselves. The exhibition of the material legacy of the past in its thousand different forms has its own history, as we well know. For that reason, however 'dry and dusty', however 'permanent' they seem, museums are true likenesses and barometers of time.[4] Every exhibition and every change in the course of events is significant—one way or another. They proclaim that an alteration has taken place, a revision, a revaluation or a change of perspective. This can be seen very dramatically following the end of the Soviet Empire and the construction of national museums in the 'post-Soviet space'. The history of museums in the 'Time of Troubles' of the 1990s and the process of de-Sovietisation has still to be written. There is much to be said here about the partial collapse of the security systems, the boom in smuggling antiquities and works of art, and the fact that the life's work of an entire generation of museum professionals, curators and restorers was threatened and in many instances ruined. But we should also raise a monument to the dedication, bravery and indeed heroism displayed by these 'servants of culture'—not for the first time in history—in the defence of 'their' museums. Think of the courage and persistence with which the staff of the National Art Museum doggedly defended the museum round the clock for weeks on end amid the battles on the Maidan. Think of the numerous movements that sprang up to prevent secularised churches that had been converted into museums from being returned to the Russian Orthodox Church, one case in point being St. Isaac's Cathedral in St. Petersburg.[5]

Museum Empire: Lifeworlds of the Empire

Those who have familiarised themselves with the world of museums during decades of travel here, there and everywhere in the Soviet Union and taken the trouble to reflect on the importance of 'seeing with one's own eyes' to understand history will have become something of experts on museums, whether by design or not.[6] There is a simple but cogent explanation for this. During the Soviet era, when these central institutions of knowledge and information were on hand and accessible, visiting museums was a simple necessity. The local and regional museums were the most important places to discover information about a particular location. This was particularly so for foreign visitors, but also more generally in a country where literature on local history was in short supply or totally absent. Bookshops had little to offer—in many you could not even find a local town plan. Even when publications on aspects of local history existed, they quickly went out of print since they became instant rarities that had appeared in minieditions of between one hundred and five hundred copies as part of an under-the-counter literature, unavailable for the most part in the large municipal or university libraries. Another indispensable method of familiarising oneself with what Italo Calvino called 'the invisible cities' was to visit the cemeteries, insofar as they still existed and had not been levelled in favour of new roads, stadiums or culture parks.

The museums repeatedly visited did not just serve to provide local information but stood for a kind of museum culture, which has almost died out in Western countries and, notwithstanding all the Soviet rhetoric about progress, has a lot to do with the traditional idea of museums as places of education and culture that prevailed in the nineteenth century. This becomes very clear in the museums of local

FIGURE 2.1. The conquest of the North Pole by Soviet pilots can be seen in the Museum of the Arctic and Antarctic that was installed in the former St. Nicholas Church in St. Petersburg in 1937. © Martin Jeske, Basel.

and regional history outside the large towns (*istoricheskie i kraeved-cheskie muzei*), that is, in the ancient Russian towns lying outside the more recent metropolises, such as Dmitrov, Tver and Yaroslavl. Opening up the cultural landscape defined by a river, the Volga region, for example, was (and is) unthinkable without visits to the well-stocked museums of Nizhny Novgorod, Saratov, Samara or Astrakhan. Simply reading the inscriptions in museums of the non-Russian metropolises such as Tbilisi, Tashkent, Yerevan, Kyiv and Riga taught you very quickly that the Soviet Union was a state with many languages and alphabets. How could you begin to understand something of the force of the modernisation process in the Russian Empire or the Soviet Union without a visit to the museums of such industrial towns as Ivanovo-Voznesensk, Donetsk, Yekaterinburg? In the period of perestroika, the regional museums were frequently the first port of call for information about the local impact of the Great Terror, the opening-up of mass graves and the camps. In short, museum visits played a preeminent, indeed irreplaceable role in a country that for a long period had fallen out of the 'Age of Gutenberg' with its production of publications that were always universally accessible. Up to now, there has been to my knowledge no analysis of the uncommonly rich and multifaceted museum landscape of the former USSR.[7]

One is overwhelmed not simply by the number of large, medium and small museums, but also by their range, which covers the infinite variety and wealth of the Soviet or Russian world. The regional collections introduce you in a classical interdisciplinary—one is tempted to use the old-fashioned term 'holistic'—manner to the development of a region, starting with a description of its natural space and the classical questions about its geology, geography, botany, flora and fauna, right down to the events of the present day. But alongside these museums with a local focus to be found in most larger places, you can also find magnificent permanent exhibitions, dedicated to such topics as the conquest of the Arctic and Antarctic (in Leningrad/ St. Petersburg), the history of the railways in the Russian Empire (St. Petersburg, Novosibirsk, among others), the history of the theatre (the Bakhrushin Museum in Moscow); numerous museums of architecture and town planning; museums of river boats and barge traffic (Nizhny Novgorod, Rybinsk); and memorials and museums of Soviet despotism (Solovki, Medvezhyegorsk on the White Sea Canal). More recently, we have seen the emergence of museums that following independence in 1991 were set up to break radically with their predecessors (the Museum of the Occupation of Latvia in Riga, the Genocide Museum in Vilnius). An important role is played by all the museums, memorials and dioramas relating to the Great Patriotic War (dioramas in Sevastopol, Volgograd, Rzhev, as well as in Independent Ukraine in Dnipro and Kyiv). War—including recent wars such as those in Afghanistan or Chechnya—is a fixture of all museums, with monuments and memorials often shown as a background to important events of personal life, such as photos of the first day at school or at weddings.[8] A further unusual feature is the number of museums dedicated to enlightenment or atheism, both associated with the aggressively anticlerical policy of the Bolsheviks and the Godless movement of the 1930s. This was given visual expression in the exhibition of relics and Foucault's pendulum, which was suspended above the paving in the centre of Kazan Cathedral in Leningrad. A type of museum that in my experience is far less common in other cultures are the so-called apartment museums (*muzei-kvartiry*), museums located in the former dwellings of famous people such as Pushkin, Dostoevsky, Alexander Blok, Rimsky-Korsakov, Dmitry Mendeleev, Ivan Pavlov and others—places they lived in either permanently or for a limited period. In the Soviet era there were many museums devoted to the 'life and works' of representatives of the state and Party leadership— Lenin, Kirov, Lunacharsky, and so forth. A similar genre features the 'lifeworlds' of the nobility, the country mansions—the homes of the nobility that managed to survive the waves of plundering, arson or else systematic destruction and demolition after 1917 and as a result of the Soviet-German War.

Looked at from the bird's-eye view of the historian, the Soviet space still seems to be infinitely homogenised and uniform. But to do justice to the 'Soviet Union' you really need an 'on-site' inspection. Once there, you see that despite all the unifying and the censorship, you have the vast variety of a great country that simply cannot be fitted into a 'short course'.

A Linear History of Progress and the Magic of Shop Windows

Museums of the Soviet type—but not only them—followed a simple, plausible narrative, if we may be allowed such generalisations. It is the (Marxist) history of progress, advancing step by step from the origins of the world and on to flora and fauna, the Stone Age, primitive society, slave-owning society, feudalism, capitalism, the workers' movement and socialism. This is a simple chronological system; it is as informative as a school lesson and quite comprehensive. Visitors learn a lot—or find themselves reminded of what they once knew when in high school. The arrangement of the exhibits provides a firm framework. This linear approach is of course intentional, carefully constructed and linked to an ideological interpretation and a specific educational thrust.

Just what a narrative about the Soviet museum might look like was not apparent initially. Its genesis was a highly conflicted process which reflected the Soviet power's struggles to establish its relation to history. It took a while for a kind of standard narrative to crystallise. 'Vladimir Ilyich was no great lover of museums,' his wife Nadezhda Krupskaya tells us.[9] The issue was not Lenin's personal opinion but the question of the role of museums in the new society and how they could become places that would guarantee a continuity of knowledge and tradition that transcended the rupture created by the Revolution. There was no more than a decade between the radical critique of museums as an outmoded and obsolete institution, as asserted by Kazimir Malevich, for example, and the emergence of a new pedagogical institution based on dialectical materialism, but this decade was marked by a debate still topical and relevant today. This can be seen from the list of people who expressed their views on the subject of revolution and the museum: Kazimir Malevich, Alexander Rodchenko, Osip Brik, Andrey Platonov and Pavel Florensky spoke up on behalf of the avant-garde, while philosophers and art critics of the Stalin period included Ivan Luppol and Alexey Fyodorov-Davidov; as an invisible third party and theoretical reference point, there was the philosopher Nikolay Fyodorov, whose chief work *The Common Cause* was concerned with establishing a relation between the generations, between the living and the dead and ultimately with resurrection.[10] Michael Hagemeister summarises Fyodorov's position as follows: 'The museum is no shop full of dead objects, but the place where the dead are remembered through artefacts of all kinds (including books)—where they are recalled to life, if only in the mind initially. Thus the museum serves the purpose of overcoming death and making mortals immortal.' In Fyodorov's own words, 'the museum is no collection of things but an assemblage of persons; its activity is not to pile up dead things but to return to life the remains of those who have passed away; its purpose is to enable the active living to deploy the products of those who have died so as to restore them to life once again.'[11] For anyone who has had anything to do with the 'mature' museums of the late phase of the Soviet Union, it is difficult to recall to mind the radical interrogations, at once inspirational and irritating, of the early period of Soviet museum discourse.

From the 1930s, with the ascendancy of Stalin's 'Short Course', the narrative was fixed for decades to come. Whatever did not fit in with the history of progress was simply omitted or else 'transcended' in the course of dialectical movement. Specific phases or events of history are entirely absent: the cruel behaviour of the Bolsheviks in the Civil War, the Holodomor famine in Ukraine during the period of collectivisation and industrialisation, the repression of the nationalities, the nonheroic side of the Great Patriotic War with its horrendous sacrifices.

The difficulties experienced by museums in producing a new, non-ideological and myth-free narrative since the end of the Soviet history of progress can be seen in many of the museums of the republics that have (once again) regained their independence. In the National Museum of Tbilisi, for example, the period 1920–1991 is represented without exception as the 'Period of Occupation', just as if the Soviet Republic of Georgia were simply and solely an occupied territory—without its own Soviet modernisation drive and without any pride in 'Stalin, the greatest son of the Georgian people'.

It is not easy to explain why Soviet museum culture should also be seen as an achievement sui generis, when we consider the prescribed images of history, the modelling of the past on political events and the shameless falsifications. Nevertheless, the museums are more than just mere indoctrination and propaganda institutions. They are also the meeting point of traditions that have more in common with the nineteenth century, with the belief in the 'spirit of Enlightenment' and the 'betterment of humanity through education and culture' than with the utopian project of communism.

The Soviet-Russian museum merits a phenomenological study, a 'thick' description that would bring many things together—the location: often splendid old urban villas, palaces of the nobility or else churches; the rituals involved in the cumbersome production of the entry ticket; the cloakroom procedures; the stern looks of the museum attendants, frequently older women; and the feeling of loneliness unless a class of children happens to be on a school visit.

Among the stand-out characteristics of the Soviet museum, we note its insistence on the concrete nature of material objects—whether stuffed bears, clay pots or an issue of a prerevolutionary underground newspaper. Museums the world over have objects on display. But Soviet museums did not yet have sequences of rapidly changing images, interactive screens, play stations and machines with which to distract onlookers. Given their educational function with its doctrinaire narrowness and imposed limitations, they remained places of learning. To a greater degree than elsewhere, they remained pedagogical and moral institutions. Visitors were not left to their own devices but taken by the hand and gently guided. It was not the individual who moved through the exhibition rooms but the escorted group that wanted and was supposed to learn something. The outing was packed full of information that no one could retain, even though some people took notes. It was an intensive study experience that called for great self-discipline.

A further feature of Soviet museums was the wish to make visible the 'spirit of the age' or of a particular milieu.[12] The effort to re-create the appropriate atmosphere, dismissed by postmodernists as naïve, is still impressive today, where it has survived. It cannot be achieved without an emphasis on style, stereotypes and clichés. We can even speak of a regular stylistic canon of 'the spirit of the ages'. Whatever museum you visited between Brest and Vladivostok, there was always a particular interior with wallpaper, a piano and Art Nouveau lamps that stood for the world of the Russian intelligentsia. Another setting—glassed-in veranda, chandelier, Empire furnishings with antimacassars—stood for the nesting place of the Russian nobility, while yet another stood for the world of the merchant—frequently the alcove with an icon or private chapel. We could almost draw up a list of the objects belonging to the programme: Thonet bentwood chairs, Mercedes or Underwood typewriter, Singer sewing machine, the metal-framed bed standing for the asceticism of revolutionary youth. The typology and image worlds of sociocultural milieus took many decades to become established and be passed from one generation to the next. There was no sensational original to form the centrepiece but instead you had to create as close an image as possible to an atmospherically accurate, convincingly colourful staging of the kind of world familiar from Russian novels, the photo albums of past generations or posters that have become iconic. These stagings revealed an astoundingly secure sense of style and, significantly, were

more compelling in their reconstruction of bourgeois milieus than of
the world of the proletariat.[13]

Reading History Anew

The dissolution of empires is always something of a happy catastrophe. With all their uncertainties and instabilities, they are a threat
to such sensitive institutions as museums with their dependence on
order and their need to grow over many generations. On the other
hand, the ends of eras are a great opportunity because we can make
a fresh start, the museum cosmos can be rearranged, stories can be
told that were never told before, new narratives can be formulated,
new objects retrieved from the warehouse and new pathways developed. A 'change of decor' in a literal sense.[14]

Rethinking and reinterpreting a nation's entire history can be one
of the most exciting events in its intellectual life. Such processes of
seeing things anew and reevaluating them are risky, full of potential
conflicts that may result in the formation of new mythologies and
ideologies. At stake is the discovery and visualisation of topics that
were hitherto taboo even though they embodied life experiences of
central importance. They inevitably lead to a greater animation of
the museum scene and the museums themselves move out of the
quiet realm of educational institutions into the centre of public debate. They become the contested sites of new orientations, the battleground to determine who has the right to lay down the law. As a
rule, provincial museums followed the lead taken in the capital—on
historical matters too—but with a certain time lag. This doesn't always happen. Their very distance from the public life of the capital
enables curators and museum directors to put their own projects and
ideas into effect—usually emphasising the 'special nature' of local
and regional conditions and drawing on treasures that have long
lain around in warehouses. This means that there is no exhibition
on 'collectivisation' or 'the' Great Terror, but there will be something
on the collectivisation of the peasantry or the Terror aimed at particular regional elites, based on local sources, testimony and archives.
This is the concrete nature of materials on the spot that then trickle

into the wider discourse, transforming it in the medium and longer term. The ability of the supercentralised state to force everything into line with its 'vertical lines of power' is immense, but it is childish to imagine that in a country as vast as Russia historical knowledge and concrete memories can be totally controlled and coerced into a particular philosophical direction. Furthermore, the internet has now joined up the remotest Russian 'province' with the centres of global culture. (Think of the young curators in the year 2000, who sat with their laptops discussing a joint exhibition with colleagues in Rotterdam and New York from a 1930s seaplane hangar on the Solovetsky Islands in the White Sea.)

Exhibitions can play a key role in changing people's historical consciousness of themselves. They can act as veritable turning points just as much as new openings can. This is how it was with the exhibition *Ten Years Khrushchev* on Komsomolsky Prospekt in Moscow during the perestroika period in the mid-1980s, when the public was visibly shaken to find itself confronted with the experiences of its own generation for the first time: with life in the *kommunalka*, that is, communal apartments; with the return of the inmates from the Gulag after Stalin's death; with the USA Exhibition, the World Youth Festival of 1957 and Christian Dior's fashion show put on display by models on Red Square. Visitors discovered their own world here; for the first time, the 'banality of everyday life' had become the subject of an exhibition, in contrast to earlier presentations which consisted exclusively of peak performances, records in fulfilling the plan and heroic deeds. Visitors were moved to tears, recognising themselves and their own age and finding themselves recognised: it was a moment of self-perception and self-enlightenment. Another example was the exhibition coorganised by the photographer Yury Brodsky on the grounds of the Solovetsky Monastery. For the first time, the history of the camp-archipelago was represented there, with constant references to the traces of the camp that were still visible at the beginning of the 1990s—the quay where the boats arrived with their prisoners, the church rooms that had been converted for use as prison cells, the canals and workshops built by the prisoners, and the decaying churches on the islands in which the political prisoners were locked up.[15] One new initiative was the exhibition of Soviet underwear in

the Russian Museum in St. Petersburg. This exhibition was concerned with fashion, but above all with the relation of Soviet men and
women to their bodies, the relation of private to public—a subject for
which there had been no room in a history of prudish, official Soviet
high culture.[16] It is almost always the stupendous materiality of such
exhibits that creates their powerful effect—the Primus stoves in the
Soviet kitchen, the transistor radio from the Riga factory, the pattern
on the Azerbaijani wall rugs and the encounter with a now vanished
lifeworld.

Historical events are played out in space as well as in time. History
happens in a place; history takes place. Not for nothing do we speak
of the genius loci, the magic (or curse) of a place to which a historical
event becomes attached and which becomes a point of mediation
between the living and the dead, between different generations, in
their virtual conversation: so this is where it all happened!

Cities are marked by historical events, either because those events
have left physical traces—bullet holes or ruins, for example—or else
by being imagined as authentic historical backdrops. These physical
or symbolic topographies can be revealed, made visible or decoded.
The historical events of different epochs overlay one another like a
palimpsest in which layers of meaning are superimposed. The Soviet
practice of *memorialnaya doska*, the commemorative plaque that reminds us of important contemporaries, was, like the museum, a way
of making 'history' visible: 'Here lived and worked the outstanding
artist of the people . . .' However, the uniform nature of these plaques,
which are ubiquitous throughout the Soviet Union, points to the fact
that an elaborate system lay behind them, from the commission that
awarded the distinction down to the design that is supposed to attract
attention and survive for all eternity in defiance of wind and weather.
Plaques for poets, scholars, Party leaders, war heroes, tank and aircraft manufacturers, 'outstanding male and female artists of the
people', theatre people, composers, engineers and top workers—the
list includes both geniuses and officials no one remembers anymore;
executioners and their victims. Cities such as Moscow and Leningrad
were (and still are) punctuated by these plaques, by the symbolic
presence and celebration of people who were significant or honoured
as such. No less illuminating is the identity of those who were not

thought worthy or whose names were expunged at a particular point in time. Putting the two groups together would provide a landscape both fascinating and shocking. In many cases, it would be the starting point for dramatic accounts of people's lives and deaths in exceptional times. We need only consider the plaques on the façade of the Hotel Metropol, that Art Nouveau luxury liner on Theatre Square in the centre of Moscow. We see there (by no means all) the names of the members of the first Soviet government, prominent visitors from everywhere in the world on their passage through Moscow, fellow travellers from every country. Or the plaques on the legendary House on the Embankment, the almost American-looking compound built in the 1930s for the Party and government elite. Just as victims and perpetrators had often lived together on the same floor, so now they appear side by side in plaques on the wall of the building. An analysis of these commemorative plaques would probably amount to a history of the selective appreciation of some residents together with a silence that speaks volumes about the deviationists, renegades and nonconformists, and especially of the many who remain nameless. To restore names and dates to those intentionally forgotten, to make visible their fate and the theatre of their lives, is one of the great tasks of the activists of 'Memorial'. They have begun—motivated possibly by the 'stumbling stone' movement in Germany—to put plaques with the inscription 'The Last Address' on the dwellings of the people who disappeared in the Terror. By doing so, they have opened a new chapter in the memory culture of the post-Soviet era.

The territory of the former Soviet Union bears the scars of mass suffering from the storms of violence that have passed over it. We might speak of a commemorative landscape of death and survival to which every age and every generation has contributed its share.[17] It is possible to take a virtual journey through the world of the Soviet camps, but also an actual journey.[18] These include places of mass execution by the NKVD [the secret police] and the Gulag: the forest of the Levashovo Memorial Cemetery or the Kresty Prison in Leningrad, the clearing near Sandarmokh in the zone along the White Sea Canal, the firing-squad sites and mass graves in Butovo and Kommunarka in southwest Moscow, Bykivnia near Kyiv and many others. Alongside these, a number of other commemorative sites could only obtain

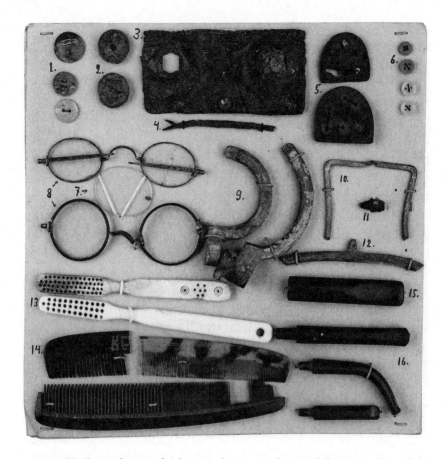

FIGURE 2.2. Vestiges and traces of violence. In the perestroika period, there were almost daily announcements about discoveries and excavations in places where spectacle frames, boots, buckles, cartridge cases and smashed skulls were found. This picture shows finds from a mass grave from the 1930s in Dubovka near Voronezh. © GULAG Archives/Tomasz Kizny.

public recognition in the course of perestroika and after the demise of the Soviet Union. Examples are the memory of victims on both sides in the Civil War, the victims of collectivisation, the deportation of ethnic groups or the mass murder of Polish officers in the Forest of Katyn, in Mednoye near Tver and in Kharkiv. Many of these memorial sites from the period following the end of the Soviet Union are most impressive; visitors fall silent at the sight of them. Family members of the victims often travel great distances to visit and nail a letter or a photo to a tree because the exact location of their grave is unknown.

With the addition of a brief inscription, a bare stone, one just lying around, seems to be the main form of commemoration—as is the case with the boulders from Solovki on Lubyanka Square in Moscow and in Troitskaya Square in St. Petersburg.[19] Travellers, especially if from Germany, also find themselves discovering another quite different topography of violence, namely the ubiquitous traces of the German war of annihilation on the soil of the former Soviet Union; the sites of the massacres of the Jews—Babi Yar in Kyiv, Botanichesky Sad in Dnipro, Drobytsky Yar and the tractor factory in Kharkiv, Odesa and Kamianets-Podilskyi, the obelisk on the site of the former ghetto in the centre of Minsk, the memorials to the massacres of Rumbula and Bikernieki near Riga, the Klooga concentration camp in Estonia—the sites of prison camps and the execution of partisans, of the mass deaths in besieged Leningrad. There is scarcely a village without an obelisk or a grave.[20]

It was not just because of the Soviet Union's ideological claim to be the 'Workers' Fatherland' that political attention was concentrated on the world of work and the world of the working class. This claim flowed naturally from the fact that it was an agrarian country developing into an industrial one. Factories and businesses were focal points around which life was organised—not unlike the situation in Western Europe during the phase of industrialisation. The factory environment included the workplace, provision for the works canteen (*stolovaya, fabrika-kukhnya*), the allocation of living rooms, school and further education, the system of evening schools and company schools, as well as the palaces of culture belonging to the company and financed by it, the system of health resorts and sanatoriums vital to the structure of holidays. The life of the population revolved around the factories—not unlike the company towns in North America, in which the life even of larger towns was organised around the enterprise, as was the case with US Steel in Gary, Indiana, and General Motors in Detroit. All of this helps to explain the particular importance of the factory and works museums that were set up from the early days of the Revolution and subsequently expanded and maintained at considerable cost. They are to be found in almost all larger factories and sometimes also in smaller ones, including the legendary Putilov Works and the Baltic Shipyard in Leningrad, AMO or ZIL in

Moscow, the car plant in Gorky, and the tractor factories in Chelyabinsk, Stalingrad and elsewhere. They opened access to the history of
industrialisation beyond knowledge of a particular factory and paid
heed to the world of every day, the lifeworld. In these museums you
can read almost the entire history from the exhibits: the origins of
the great factories, stretching back into the nineteenth century and
frequently financed by foreign investors; the emergence of the Russian workers' movement; the growth of technology and production
methods that become increasingly independent of foreign influences;
the disruptions to industry arising from the Great Terror, the effects
of the war, and finally, the postwar reconstruction. The cars in the
works museum in Gorky/Nizhny Novgorod illustrate the history of
the Soviet motor industry. The history of construction gives us an
insight into the development of industrial architecture, engineering
and technology; the account of living conditions clarifies the transition from communism to the consumerism of the post-Stalin era.
The histories of factories and industrial plants have never been so
professionally reconstructed and put on museum display as in the
former Soviet Union (presumably, the industrial museums in Manchester, Sheffield and Leeds offer the closest comparison).[21]

Museums of this type are accompanied by a specific scientific and
literary genre: the works history, biographies of outstanding builders,
engineers, top workers or sportsmen who have made their way from
the workbench to a gold medal in boxing or weightlifting. It was no
less a figure than Maxim Gorky, the most prominent Soviet writer,
who promoted this genre with the assistance of a publishing house
he helped to launch: Zemlya i Fabrika (Country and Factory). Together
with the works' archives, the works museums await the day when they
shall all be opened for a microhistory of Soviet industrialisation.

Nikolay Pavlovich Antsiferov:
Material Culture, Excursion as Method

Works histories and works museums did not emerge spontaneously
but developed on an elaborate theoretical foundation under the heading of *Muzeologiya*, *Kraevedenie* (regional studies) and *Gradovedenie*

(urban studies). Nikolay Antsiferov (1889–1958) seems to me to be a key figure in this context. He wrote a book legendary in its day—*The Soul of St. Petersburg* (1922)—that has appeared in a large number of reprints and new editions since the end of the Soviet Union.[22] Antsiferov, himself a pupil of Ivan Mikhailovich Greaves, a specialist in ancient history and Italian urban culture, played a leading role in developing a method known as excursionism (*ekskursionistika, ekskursologiya*), which entered Soviet museum science and historiography and became a dominant influence in the genre of the Soviet excursion. The idea was that once the palaces of the aristocracy had been opened to the public and once private libraries and galleries had become generally available, the population as a whole should be granted access to the world of the ruling class. 'Museums of material culture' sprang up everywhere, showcasing the domestic interiors and lifestyle of class society. Visitors were supposed to gain a vivid insight into social and cultural living conditions from inspecting the places where people actually lived.[23] Antsiferov and his school were convinced that you needed a concrete view, that you must 'experience' a city by touring around in it. Regional and national studies were rigorously planned with this in mind. We are dealing with a 'history from below' avant la lettre, with a trend that anticipates the Western 'history workshops' and the 'museums of everyday culture'. Antsiferov shows himself to be a contemporary of a Franz Hessel, who developed the art of taking a walk in Berlin, or of a Walter Benjamin, who made the flaneur a central figure of his historical hermeneutics.[24] Like the entire trend of national and regional history, Antsiferov's school fell under the wheels of Stalinist repression and was caught up in the increasingly dogmatic approach to historiography of the later 1920s/ early 1930s. More than a few representatives of Kraevedenie and Gradovedenie were murdered.[25] The Antsiferov tradition lived on in the underground and in the circles of nonacademic historians, who collected materials, traces, pictures, eyewitness accounts and maps, but could find no salaried posts among officially approved historians. The history of marginalised historians, who made a crucial contribution to the survival of a critical tradition, is rich in stories of persecution and victimhood, but has yet to be written. The fact that they were compelled on occasion to defend themselves from accusations of dilettantism and lack of professionalism tells us something not only about the self-assurance of academic historiography, but also about the failure to understand even today the enormous contribution of so-called hobby historians to the development of a vital way of thinking on the margins of Soviet society.

Search for Identity: Between the Urge to Throw Things Out and the Creation of New Myths

A quarter of a century after the demise of the Soviet Union, museums have become contested spaces. The freedom that had opened for museums brought movement into the museum landscape, which had seemed ossified hitherto. A plethora of exhibitions appeared everywhere, with an emphasis on 'small-scale history'. Things that had lain mouldering in depots were now put on show.[26] There was no sense of direction or a unified script for a post-Soviet narrative. What some regarded as unprecedented freedom, others experienced as a dangerous vacuum. It seemed easier to fill this vacuum in the non-Russian republics, since the newly recovered history of the nation offered itself as a substitute for history imposed by 'the Russians'. All the mistakes and tragedies could now be laid at their door, while the Russians themselves were left alone with their Soviet heritage.[27] In the 1990s the project of a post-Soviet Russian identity was everywhere proclaimed. Since then, even the 1990s have become history and are themselves the object of historicising and moralising, initially on paper and then, at some point, in reality. 'The museum of the 1990s is the terrain of liberty.'[28]

But the phase of seeking, of self-discovery, of the plurality of historical interpretations inaugurated by perestroika ended a decade later in a new historical turn, imposed in a clampdown by the new leadership and introduced step by step. Its results can be followed in school textbooks, TV series, popular literature and the erection of monuments. They also impinge on museums that received enormous subsidies for modernisation during the oil and gas boom of the affluent 2000s. Everything now was high tech instead of old-fashioned glass display cases, and video installations instead of staged live scenes. More concerning was the ideological and political turn which privileged the celebration of the Russian state, the greatness of the Empire, and the spiritual superiority of the Russian world, above all the Russian Orthodox world, in contrast to other cultures. The familiar early nineteenth-century formula rooted in the trinity of autocracy, orthodoxy and populism was now tailored to the needs of the twenty-first century.

This soon showed itself in the way museum display rooms and exhibitions were reconfigured or newly conceived. Whole thematic complexes or historical periods were simply phased out, eliminated from the permanent displays and banished to the cellars. Nowadays, the Tsarist Empire basks in a nostalgic halo, while the histories of the Revolution and the Civil War are consigned to the rubbish heap. In the local museum in Rybinsk, for example, they have been stored in the building of the old Corn Exchange, directly on the Volga where an entire era—'Building Socialism' in the 1920s and 1930s—has disappeared for the time being and been replaced by portraits of the Tsars and an exhibition on the relations between the Romanovs and the city's merchants. This process of reorganisation frequently involves not just a new exhibition concept, but also the existence and definition of the very museum buildings themselves. Holdings that form part of the core stock of a museum—such as the icon collections—are to be returned to the churches from which they were removed during the period of 'nationalisation'. Churches deconsecrated by the Bolsheviks and the Godless movement and transformed into 'museums of scientific atheism' have to be 'remuseumised' and reconsecrated—as has been the case with the Kazan and St. Isaac Cathedrals in St. Petersburg— although synagogues and mosques could also be mentioned in this context. In short, museums have become places that are doubly contested. This applies also to a number of wonderful apartment museums whose former inhabitants have ceased to be judged museum-worthy and whose buildings often rouse the appetite of estate agents because they occupy the best locations.

Before all else, however, we hear the question: what should be put into a museum and how should it be displayed? In other words, what historical narrative should the exhibitions follow? Needless to say, these disagreements are settled, or primarily settled, not by museum

FIGURE 2.3. 'Metaphysical sphinx' is the name given to this monument to the victims of political repression in Leningrad/St. Petersburg by the Russian/American sculptor Mikhail Shemyakin. It was erected in 1995 on the Voskresensky Embankment of the Neva facing the Kresty Prison. © shutterstock.

experts, but by the great 'ideological apparatuses', to take up the term coined by Louis Althusser—in short, by the powers-that-be that preside over interpretation. These range from the academies to the popular writers, from advertisers to the tourist industry, and from sponsors to religious organisations. Above all, however, they include those who believe it is their prerogative to determine the historical consciousness of the nation as they wish: the political elites and their ideological advisers.

We have long since found ourselves engaged in a struggle to find a new 'grand narrative' for Russian history, especially twentieth-century Russian history. This can be seen in the monument war that has been fought throughout the land: the war about the monument for Felix Dzerzhinsky on Lubyanka Square that was demolished in 1991; or about the building of a monument in the Kremlin for St. Vladimir, Grand Duke of Kyiv, which was originally supposed to be posted on the façade of Lomonosov University in the Sparrow Hills, towering high above the Moskva River. In the controversies about the development and acceptance of a new grand historical narrative, the interpretation of the Russian Revolution and the Great Terror will play a crucial role. No one knows what that history will look like in the future. A well-known joke from Soviet times claimed that 'nothing is so unpredictable as the past'.

CHAPTER 3

Return to the Scene: Petrograd 1917

Entire libraries have been written about the Russian Revolution and thousands of studies of the events of 1917 have immeasurably increased our knowledge, as have the memoirs of participants or those affected by it. From almost every vantage point light falls on the scene; from the heights of world history; from the viewpoint of the victors and of those who barely escaped with their skin; from the viewpoint of officers who mislaid their army; and from that of the proletarians who were supposed to become the ruling class, at least in name. We have the testimony of people who popped up from underground movements, and of others in Bolshevik Russia who were compelled to flee underground or else across the frontier. Diplomats who stayed at their posts through the turbulence and became the involuntary witnesses of world-historical events also made their own small contributions to the mosaic that makes up the vast panorama. The memory of the Revolution has been 'preserved for all eternity' and locked up in Soviet archives or published abroad in the form of memoirs in the 'Archive of the Russian Revolution', listed in the reference catalogues of the Hoover Institution at Stanford, and last but not least, stored in the minds of millions whom no one has asked and who have left behind no written 'testimony'. Taken together, these resources have delivered the material for the reconstruction of the events from which the main lines and turning points of developments could be distilled. They attempt to explain why it all happened and how it came about that the Soviets were able to seize power. They are the starting point from where, further along in time and from a higher vantage point, accounts emerge that in one respect at least surpass all contemporary witnesses: they know how the story continued.[1]

And yet, it was a privilege to have been around at the time, a privilege nothing can replace. It makes up for the limitations experienced by the participants and which those born later were spared. Some eyewitnesses of those 'Ten Days That Shook the World' were still alive when the Soviet power that was created then came to an end.

Eyewitnesses lead us back into the tumult in which everything was still open and no end, let alone 'a logical end', was in sight. They depended on their own eyes to form a judgement that frequently could be no more than a first impression. They could not yet base their opinion on the knowledge available to those born later. They were compelled to 'come to their own view' without outside assistance. But their imperfect knowledge can redound to their advantage. However limited their knowledge of the larger context, they had the entire scene, fresh and undivided, before their very eyes; they lacked the specialisation that carves up into different objects and spheres things that belong together.

Ten Days That Shook the World

It is an unearned piece of good fortune to be in the right place at the right time. Of those who have made something of it, the American journalist John Reed and the Russian socialist Nikolay Sukhanov belong in the first rank. It is only right that all subsequent commentators on the Russian Revolution should have appealed to them as crown witnesses. Thanks to them, everyone could be caught up in the whirl of events and become an involved spectator, a reporter of things as they happened and the creator of an authoritative narrative.

When John Reed arrived in Petrograd in September 1917, he already had considerable experience. Born in 1887 as the son of a businessman in Portland, Oregon, he attended private school and then Harvard, where he edited a student magazine, became an enthusiastic sportsman and formed a friendship with Walter Lippmann, a contemporary. He had been on a Grand Tour through Belle Epoque Europe and formed friendships with left-wing intellectuals of Greenwich Village—Lincoln Steffens, Max Eastman—and his own later wife, Louise Bryant. As a journalist, he had reported on factory disputes in the USA but above all on the Mexican Revolution. The art scene in prewar Paris was not the best place for a pacifist activist and so after the outbreak of the First World War, he went as a war reporter to Southern and Eastern Europe: to Salonika, Bulgaria, Serbia, Romania and Constantinople, as well as to the Jewish settlements of the Russian Empire, which had become a war zone. In September 1917 Reed arrived at the place where, as a reporter who made no secret of his political convictions and eagerness for a scoop, he could deploy all his talents.[2]

Nikolay Nikolaevich Sukhanov came from a very different world, even though he belonged to the same generation. Born in Moscow in 1882 to a rather more middle-class family—his father, who came from a family of Russified Germans, was a railway employee—he went through the stages typical of an alert young man of his generation. After high school, he undertook a journey to Paris, where he made contact with the political emigration. Following his return to Moscow, he took up the study of philology and philosophy. He was incarcerated in Taganka Prison, from which he was freed by demonstrators during the 1905 revolution. This was followed by further travel abroad, this time to Switzerland. On his return he was sentenced to exile in Arkhangelsk; from 1913 he was active in St. Petersburg, writing for various journals. As an adherent of the Zimmerwald antiwar movement among the Mensheviks and the representative of the 'socialist writers' group', he found himself right at the start of the February revolution a member of the Executive Committee of the Petrograd Soviet, which was the rival of the other main pole of power in Petrograd, the Provisional Government. Throughout 1917 he remained in positions—often in charge—from which he was in frequent contact with the leading figures in every party and through all the changes of government. After Maxim Gorky's *Novaya zhizn* was shut down by the Bolsheviks, he started work on his *Notes on the Revolution*, published by Grshebin Verlag 1919–1923.[3]

The paths of the two reporters frequently crossed with those of the actors in the events (Lenin, Trotsky, Antonov-Ovseenko and many others). Reed described their own appearance on the revolutionary stage; Sukhanov cited them as reliable eyewitnesses. At one point Lenin came even closer to Sukhanov than may have been to the latter's taste: the 10–23 September 1917 session of the Bolshevist leadership, at which the armed insurrection was decided upon and at which Lenin appeared disguised with a wig, took place in Sukhanov's apartment on the Karpovka Naberezhnaya, No. 32, Flat 31—without Sukhanov's knowledge.[4] Trotsky repeatedly quoted from Sukhanov as a reliable chronicler and even described John Reed as the 'observer and participant, chronicler and poet of the insurrection.'[5]

John Reed and Nikolay Sukhanov describe periods of widely differing length, but for both men the dissolution of the Constituent Assembly which had long been proclaimed and upheld as the chief concern of almost all participants remained outside the framework of their accounts. Both aimed to follow the dynamic of events and the coalition changes that signalled shifts in power. This process began with the abdication of the Tsar, and that led to the establishment of a Provisional Government, which was forced in turn to share power with its adversary, the Soviets. This lasted through a number of attempted coups from both right and left, when power finally slipped from its hands in a brilliantly conducted campaign by the Bolsheviks. In less than a year, a series of blows led to the end of a three-hundred-year-old dynasty, the collapse of an empire, and the disintegration of its most powerful supports—above all, the army. Russia was transformed into what was at the time the freest country in the world, thanks to the collapse of power and subsequent anarchy. The imperial capital became a law-free space in which power lay in the hands of whoever controlled the armoured cars. The details of this tectonic shift, the disintegration and establishment of a new power, are familiar:

On 23 February/8 March [see chapter 46 on the introduction of the Red calendar], strikes, food shortages and demonstrations of women for International Women's Day metamorphosed into revolution; regiments stationed in the capital went over to the insurgents. On 27 February/12 March, the Provisional Executive Committee of the Petrograd Soviet of worker delegates and the Provisional Committee of the Imperial Duma took over political leadership. On 2/15 March, the Tsar abdicated and on 3/16 March the Provisional Government was formed under the chairmanship of Prince Lvov—all of this accompanied and supported by violent clashes in the streets of Petrograd with large numbers of victims. In early April, after years of exile, Lenin arrived at the Finland Station in Petrograd. On 3/16 June, the First All-Russian Congress of Soviets, consisting of workers' and soldiers' deputies, convened. The demands for bread, land and peace intensified but the Bolsheviks' attempt early in June to use the increasingly radical movement for an uprising failed initially. The continuation of the war and the refusal to confirm the spontaneous occupation of land by peasant soldiers returning from the front increasingly undermined the authority of the Provisional Government. General Kornilov's attempt to restore 'peace and order' by means of a coup (27/29 August–9/11 September) failed abysmally. Other attempts in the form of a 'Democratic Conference' that would stabilise the situation by means of a so-called Preparliament until elections could be held and a constitutive assembly convoked went awry. On 10/23 September, the Bolshevist leadership settled on an armed uprising. This was prepared in minute detail, thanks to the authority of the Military Revolutionary Committee of the Petrograd Soviet. This ensured that the Second All-Russian Congress of Soviets, convened on 25 October/7 November, was confronted with the collapse of the Provisional Government and actual takeover of power by the Bolsheviks. In the days that followed, the Congress of Soviets adopted all the proclamations issued by the Bolsheviks including the ending of the war, the transfer of land to the peasants and the self-determination of the peoples of Russia. Following a protest and subsequent walkout by the Mensheviks and right-wing Socialist Revolutionaries, the Congress approved the formation of a government of people's commissars. The election for the Constituent Assembly took place, as previously arranged, on 12/25 November, but when it convened on 5/18 January 1918, it was violently dispersed by the Bolsheviks. These, then, were the chief events, turning points and forks in the road.

Topography of the Revolution

Chroniclers who wish to keep track of events inevitably become topographers. Whoever follows the actors must seek out the locations where the decisions are taken.[6] It is essential to describe the stage on which opponents confront each other; a glance into the auditorium tells you who garners the most applause and who is shouted down. Speeches and proclamations can usually be read *post festum* but whether a speaker holds an audience or the mood in the auditorium changes depends on a situation in which the spoken word is decisive. And in general, hardly anything about mass movements can be explained without knowledge of the relevant public space. It is there that arguments (whether considered or demagogic) are put forward, the willingness to act is aroused or reinforced, resignation overcome or strengthened. The 'Cirque Moderne' on the Petrograd side, Nicholas II's People's Palace in the park near the Peter and Paul Fortress, the Alexandrinsky Theatre—these are not empty place names but generate attitudes and convictions. Places and spaces have their own specific public, one that alters with time. The moment comes when the public mood changes and speakers who were once applauded are no longer allowed to open their mouths. The festively illuminated halls of the Mariinsky Palace, the Municipal Duma, the Tauride Palace or the Smolny theatre auditorium are worlds away from the regimental barracks and the factory buildings on the periphery of the city. 'In the softly glittering halls of the Marian Palace there was no revolution at all. It was all in Smolny, in the working-class sections of the capital and in the provincial towns and districts. And that revolution was racing down an inclined plane to a *dénouement*.'[7] Another scene is set in the Tauride Palace: 'The limitless spaces of the Palace swallowed up effortlessly and unnoticeably many hundreds of people, scurrying about with a busy look or obviously bored with inactivity. These were the deputies who "belonged" here, and looked like masters of the house rather shocked by the roistering of their uninvited guests. . . . But they were in the minority. The Palace was obviously filling up with an alien population, in fur coats, working-class caps, or army greatcoats. Among these, well-known figures from the intellectual political circles of Petersburg were seen at every step. All the Petersburgers active in political and public life were already gravitating there.' We have here 'a melting pot of events'. 'I was in the very crucible of great events, the laboratory of the revolution.'[8] Different again was the atmosphere in Smolny: 'In the rows of seats, under the white chandeliers, packed immovably in the aisles and on the sides, perched on every window-sill, and even the edge of the platform, the representatives of the workers and soldiers of all Russia waited in anxious silence or wild exultation the ringing of the chairman's bell.

There was no heat in the hall but the stifling heat of unwashed human bodies. A foul blue cloud of cigarette smoke rose from the mass and hung in the thick air.'[9]

A city of two million people like Petrograd was an organism built on routines that functioned; a demonstration, a skirmish was not enough to disrupt the normal flow of activities—the trams, the armies of droshkies, the arrival and departure times of the trains. On Nevsky Prospekt, Reed notes, 'Few people passed and there were no lights; but a few blocks away we could see the trams, the crowds, the lighted shop-windows, and the electric signs of the moving-picture shows—life going on as usual. We had tickets to the ballet at the Mariinsky Theatre—all the theatres were open—but it was too exciting out of doors.'[10] Even in parlous times, the town markets where domestic servants and messengers did their shopping still functioned. But if the servants preferred to join demonstrations, and if waiters in restaurants thought it beneath their dignity to accept a tip, then an era was drawing to its end. It could take quite a long time before a city started to grind to a halt. Even on 8 November, following the Bolshevik coup, Reed noted: 'Superficially all was quiet; hundreds of thousands of people retired at a prudent hour, got up early, and went to work. In Petrograd the street-cars were running, the stores and restaurants open, theatres going, an exhibition of paintings ad-vertised. . . . All the complex routine of common life—humdrum even in wartime, proceeded as usual. Nothing is so astounding as the vi-tality of the social organism—how it persists, feeding itself, clothing itself, amusing itself, in the face of the worst calamities.'[11] Nor did theatre or opera performances get cancelled just because there were clashes with demonstrators at a crossroads in the city centre. The city turned into a huge marshalling yard: 'The soldiers flowed through the countryside from the rear and the front, recalling a great migra-tion of people. In the cities they blighted the trams and boulevards, and filled all the public places. There were reports here and there of drunkenness, rowdiness and disorder.'[12]

John Reed and Nikolay Sukhanov went on undeterred, each on his own chosen route. They also ventured into no-go areas. If they wanted to keep up with events, they had to adjust to the rhythm of the committee meetings and St. Petersburg was the focal point of an

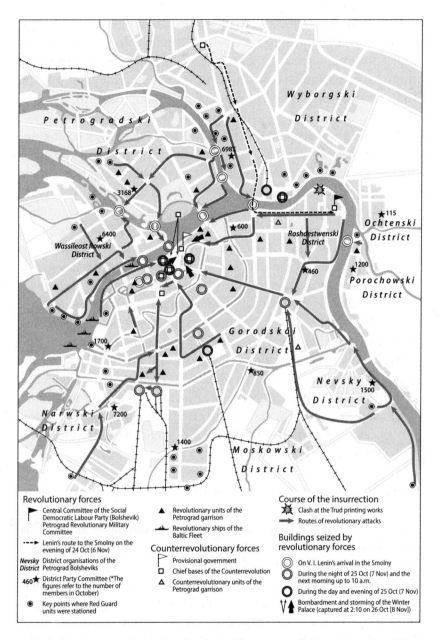

Revolutionary forces

▶ Central Committee of the Social Democratic Labour Party (Bolshevik) Petrograd Revolutionary Military Committee

--▶ Lenin's route to the Smolny on the evening of 24 Oct (6 Nov)

Nevsky District organisations of the *District* Petrograd Bolsheviks

460★ District Party Committee (*The figures refer to the number of members in October)

◉ Key points where Red Guard units were stationed

▲ Revolutionary units of the Petrograd garrison

⚓ Revolutionary ships of the Baltic Fleet

Counterrevolutionary forces

▷ Provisional government

☐ Chief bases of the Counterrevolution

△ Counterrevolutionary units of the Petrograd garrison

Course of the insurrection

✳ Clash at the Trud printing works

➡ Routes of revolutionary attacks

Buildings seized by revolutionary forces

◎ On V. I. Lenin's arrival in the Smolny

◉ During the night of 25 Oct (7 Nov) and the next morning up to 10 a.m.

○ During the day and evening of 25 Oct (7 Nov)

▼▲ Bombardment and storming of the Winter Palace (captured at 2:10 on 26 Oct [8 Nov])

FIGURE 3.1. An attempt to capture and represent the scene and the dynamic of events in October 1917 on a map: town plan of Petrograd. From *Illustrierte Geschichte der Großen Sozialistischen Oktoberrevolution*, Dietz Verlag, Berlin 1973, 131.

endless series of congresses, committees, conferences and meetings. The talks and debates in the brightly lit palace frequently did not begin before midnight and they resembled magnificent waiting rooms where exhausted passengers hoped to catch up on their sleep. The whole city was caught up in a permanent talking session:

> All Russia was learning to read and *reading*—politics, econom-ics, history—because the people wanted to know. . . . In every city, in most towns, along the front, each political faction had its newspaper—sometimes several. Hundreds of thousands of pam-phlets were distributed by thousands of organizations. . . . Then the Talk . . . lectures, debates, speeches—in theatres, circuses, school-houses, clubs, Soviet meeting-rooms, union headquarters, barracks. . . . What a marvellous sight to see Putilovsky Zavod (the Putilov Factory) pour out its forty thousand [workers]. . . . In railway trains, street-cars, always the spurting up of impromptu debate, everywhere. . . . And the All-Russian Conferences and Congresses, drawing together the men of two continents—conventions of Sovi-ets, *Zemstvos*, nationalities, priests, peasants, political parties, the Democratic Conference, the Moscow Conference, the Council of the Russian Republic. There were always three or four conventions going on in Petrograd. At every meeting, attempts to limit the time of speakers [were] voted down and every man [was] free to express the thought that was in him.[13]

To Sukhanov we are indebted for a cinematically precise depiction of the reception Lenin received at the Finland Station; Eisenstein sub-sequently adapted it for film. 'There was a throbbing of many motor cars. In two or three places the awe-inspiring outlines of armoured cars thrust up out of the crowd. And from one of the side-streets there moved out on to the square, startling the mob and cutting through it, a strange monster—a mounted searchlight, which abruptly projected along the bottomless void of the darkness tremendous strips of the living city, the roofs, many-storeyed houses, columns, wires, tram-ways, and human figures.'[14] Nor did the interior of the Kshesinskaya Palace escape his attention: 'The apartments of the famous ballerina had a rather strange and inappropriate look. The exquisite ceilings and walls out of all harmony with the unpretentious furnishings, the primitive table, chairs, and benches set casually about as required by business. There was very little furniture. Kshesinskaya's movable property had been put away somewhere, and it was only here and there that the remains of former grandeur were visible.'[15] And he registered the shock, the frenzy that overcame those present when Lenin appeared. 'I shall never forget that thunder-like speech, which startled and amazed not only me, a heretic who had accidentally dropped in, but all the true believers. I am certain that no one had expected anything of the sort. It seemed as though all the elements had risen from their abodes, and the spirit of universal destruction, knowing neither barriers nor doubts, neither human difficulties nor human calculations, was hovering around Kshesinskaya's reception-room above the heads of the bewitched disciples. . . . In those days this alone . . . was enough to make his listeners' heads spin.'[16]

The city moved fast, at least as long as taxis still ran and the telephone connections were intact. Cars and armoured vehicles succeeded droshkies and coaches; they gradually became mobile power centres. Again and again, the 'monstrous, dark armoured cars' recurred: 'whoever controlled the Bronneviki controlled the city'.[17] The leather-clad chauffeur now prescribed the tempo, not the Cossack on his horse or the flaneur along the Nevsky. The acceleration of events had something to do with the new means of communication—the telephone above all. In Reed's and Sukhanov's Petrograd, people were constantly on the phone. You can even find the emergency number— 104-6[18]—and in the last analysis, the fate of the besieged Provisional Government in the Winter Palace, the General Staff and the garrisons was decided by the fact that the telephone lines were cut, breaking off contact to the city. We are indebted to John Reed for his report on entering the Winter Palace, where the Provisional Government had barricaded itself in the hope of eventual rescue.

At the end of the corridor was a large ornate room with gilded cornices and enormous crystal lustres, and beyond it several smaller ones, wainscoted with dark wood. On both sides of the parqueted floor lay rows of dirty mattresses and blankets upon which occasional soldiers were stretched out; everywhere was a litter of

cigarette butts, bits of bread, cloth and empty bottles with expensive French labels. More and more soldiers, with the red shoulder-
straps of the *yunker* schools, moved about in a stale atmosphere of
tobacco smoke and unwashed humanity. One had a bottle of white
burgundy, evidently filched from the cellars of the palace. . . . The
walls were covered with huge canvases in massive gilt frames—
historical battle scenes . . . '12 October 1812' and '6 November 1812',
'16–18 August 1815'. . . . One had a gash across the upper right hand
corner.[19]

'The Crucible of Events'

Whoever follows in the footsteps of Reed or Sukhanov during those
weeks will learn something about the interaction between the political nerve centres and the locations where the decisive action
took place. The two men roamed tirelessly between the magnificent
buildings of the capital that had become 'laboratories of the revolution', the newspaper offices and print works, the crossroads where
critical situations developed, and in between they frequented the
Café Vienna, which kept on going despite all the unrest. Armoured
cars crossed the path of Easter Night processions. The routes taken
by the chroniclers create a map of the capital's terrain with all its
'hot spot' frontiers, front line networks and junctions. It is not by
chance that map readers keep popping up. Reed, for example, saw
them in Smolny: 'A blast of stale air and cigarette smoke rushed out,
we caught a glimpse of dishevelled men bending over a map under
the glare of a shaded electric light.'[20] 'At the centre table, the huge
Dybenko bent over a map, marking out positions for the troops with
red and blue pencils. In his free hand he carried, as always, the enormous blue-steel revolver. Anon he sat himself down at a typewriter
and pounded away with one finger; every little while he would pause,
pick up the revolver, and lovingly spin the chamber.'[21] With this Reed
had an insight key to the course of the Revolution, the crucial link
between cartographical knowledge (knowledge of the territory) and
armed power (the ability to occupy it). Thus Reed's and Sukhanov's
contributions are more than just a chronology of events and their

temporal dynamics; they provide a history of a transformation of the power arena.

Their depiction of the course of the Revolution allows us to read off the topography of revolutionary Petrograd without difficulty, a city guide sui generis. Whoever reads their reports from this angle will find it easy to identify the key intersections, the principal inter-connections, the neuralgic points.

These include, first, the crucial locations. They were important not just symbolically but because they were technically and spa-tially in a position to secure what Habermas termed the 'structural transformation of the public sphere'. Chief among these locations was the Tauride Palace, a vast estate built by Ivan Starov for Count Potemkin, the favourite of Catherine the Great and the founder of Novorossiya or New Russia. Between 1906 and 1917 the palace was the seat of the Imperial State Duma and now it became the seat of both the Provisional Committee of the State Duma and the Executive Committee of the Soviets. With its huge adjacent park, the palace became the setting for numerous demonstrations and assemblies. This was where Lenin proclaimed his April Theses and with the vi-olent dissolution of the Constituent Assembly, this was where the lights of parliamentarianism went out in Russia.[22] The Smolny com-plex with its magical cathedral, built by Francesco Rastrelli, and a gigantic convent, which functioned as a boarding school for young, aristocratic ladies, served as the engine room of the opposing forces, which, situated somewhat away from the centre, was well protected and able to act as the venue for the Second All-Russian Congress of Soviets and the seat of the Council of People's Commissars.[23] In a prominent position, opposite St. Isaac's Cathedral, stood the Mariin-sky Palace, designed by the court architect Andrey Stackenschneider at the beginning of the nineteenth century. It had been extended before the Revolution to house the State Council of Imperial Rus-sia and subsequently became the temporary seat of the Provisional Government until the latter moved to the Winter Palace, the Tsar's residence, which had become 'free' following his abdication.[24] Here and in the General Staff Building, which was located on the opposite side of the Palace Square, the Provisional Government was arrested and imprisoned on 7 November.

The Municipal Duma enjoys a special status here, if only because architecturally (it was designed by Giacomo Ferrari) it resembles Western European town halls and remained the focal point of resistance to the dictatorship of the Bolsheviks to the end.[25]

Second, standing at the opposite pole to the city that was the centre of power, we find the factories referred to again and again, by both Reed and Sukhanov. The attitude of the workers who kept the war machine going determined the course of events generally. The experience of the first Russian Revolution, which had taken place barely more than a decade previously, was still almost physically present: the strikes, the demonstrations and the massacres initiated by the Cossacks, the police and the army. Nor had the chauvinistic mobilisation for the Great War succeeded in undermining the St. Petersburg proletariat's experience of class struggle. With the coming of the Revolution, the social topography of the industrial landscape of St. Petersburg started to shift once more. The workers moved from the periphery to the centre. At its heart, initially, were the factories on the Vyborg and Petrograd side—many belonged to international firms, such as Lessner, Erikson, Promet, Langsiepen, Vulkan, Siemens & Halske, Nobel Brothers, the Tube Mill, the Baltic Shipyard, the Cable Works, the San Galli workshops, the Putilov engineering works, the Skorokhod shoe factory, the cotton spinning plant, Siemens-Schuckert and Russky Renault.

The third complex that can be identified is that of the barracks, the guards regiments and the military and officer schools. With their parade grounds, schools, accommodation, riding schools, garages and workshops, they almost constituted a city within a city, with the prevailing powers depending on their stability, loyalty and reliability. With its 200,000-strong garrison, the capital was a city of barracks and soldiers, and the 'peasants in grey military overcoats' were soon to become the chief agents in the dissolution of the old order. The history of revolution in Petrograd can be traced, therefore, by the decisions taken in the barracks, by the change in attitude that took place there, among the Lithuanian, Volhynian, Izmailovsky, Finnish, Semyonovsky, Pavlovsky, Preobrazhensky and other regiments.[26]

The fourth complex relates to the infrastructure that held the city together and kept it going. Whoever controlled it, controlled the city.

That began with basic geographical factors. St. Petersburg is divided by numerous river arms and canals and is held together only by its bridges. Whoever controls the bridges, controls life in the metropolis— only in winter, when the Neva is frozen and rail tracks and streets are laid down over the ice, does the role of the bridges become less dominant; without the bridges there could be no history of revolution in Petrograd. In Reed and Sukhanov, the bridges turn up again and again in the struggle for control of the city—the Dvortsovy Bridge, the Nikolaevsky Bridge, the Troitsky Bridge, the Liteyny Bridge and the very important Sampsonievsky Bridge linking the Vyborg and Petrograd sides of the river.[27] The same may be said of the railway stations, the city gates and the junctions linking the capital with its hinterland, with the Empire. These links enabled Petrograd to be supplied with food and raw materials: through them the peasant soldiers entered the city in the hundreds of thousands; they were the transit stations for the great migration of nations, for people, weapons, ideas and slogans. And what is true of the St. Petersburg railway stations—the Finland, the Nikolaevsky, the Baltic, the Warsaw and the station on the line to Tsarskoe Selo—holds for the control of the telephone and telegraph communication networks, for the energy supply—the electricity works—and for the circulation of money, that is, the control of the state bank and banking network.[28]

There is even a map to represent the battle for minds. It displays the offices of such papers as the *Russkaya volya*, *Pravda*, *Robochy i soldat* and *Novaya zhizn*, which contained texts, appeals and posters as well as the printers which in the emerging age of mass movements could make the difference between victory and defeat.

Many organisations remained active and merely changed their personnel. Prisons, places of repression and incarceration, were kept up despite the ruptures of history and remained intact. This held for the Petrograd prisons—the Peter and Paul Fortress, the Kresty and Shpalernaya Prisons, from which inmates of the old regime were released, replaced by inmates of the new regime.

The most volatile were the public spaces and squares where the confrontation of power and populace unfolded. The Petrograd of 1917 had its zones of contact and conflict, its squares for parades and locations for barricades—often a repeat of the revolutionary clashes of 1905. Above all, it was Nevsky Prospekt that repeatedly became the arena, the mighty parade ground, together with the Znamenskaya Square in front of the Nikolaevsky Station, the square in front of Kazan Cathedral and the Palace Square between the Winter Palace and the General Staff Building.

There has been no lack of attempts at a cartographic representation of the landscape of power, its dissolution and regrouping. The available methods are well known: map symbols, lines, hatched surfaces, arrows, the use of colours and points together with dates. The colour red signifies 'on the march', blue 'in retreat'. Little red flags mark Bolshevist underground bases, the seat of Party committees and the large factories in the grip of strikes. Universities and institutes that have joined the revolutionary movement are highlighted. Dotted lines trace the routes taken by demonstrators and red circles mark the most important meeting points. Crosses are used to indicate clashes. Arrows show where troop units have gone over to the Revolution while yellow circles indicate the buildings occupied by the insurgents on 24 October. The bridges are especially highlighted. The centres—Smolny, Tauride Palace, Mariinsky Palace—are shown on the map as outline façades. The regiments are indicated by name. Lenin's route from the underground to Smolny on 24 October is shown by one broken line, while another is supposed to show the shot fired by the *Aurora* on 25 October at 21:40 and the bombardment of the Winter Palace from the Peter and Paul Fortress. The surrounding and capture of the Winter Palace is dated 26 October at 2:10.[29]

The crispest account is the view of the military situation in the city as described by the chief organiser of the conquest—Leon Trotsky:

The city was divided into military divisions, each subordinate to the nearest headquarters. At the most important points, companies of the Red Guard were concentrated in coordination with the neighboring military units, where companies on duty were awake and ready. The goal of each separate operation, and the forces for it, were indicated in advance. All those taking part in the insurrection from top to bottom—in this lay its power, in this also at times its Achilles' heel—were imbued with absolute confidence that the victory was going to be won without casualties. The main operation began at two o'clock in the morning. Small military parties, usually with a nucleus of armed workers or sailors under the leadership of commissars, occupied simultaneously, or in regular order, the railroad stations, the lighting plant, the munition and food stores, the waterworks, Dvortsovy Bridge, the telephone exchange, the state bank, the big printing plants. The telegraph station and the post office were completely taken over. Reliable guards were placed everywhere. Meager and colorless is the record of the episodes of that October night. It is like a police report.[30]

Soviet cartography has taken the very greatest care to indicate 'Lenin's places', in other words, all the locations—apartments, meeting places, spots where he gave speeches, offices—that had any connection with Lenin's life. There is also an intensive mapping of proletarian Petrograd. These maps may well create the impression that victory was predestined and that there never was a moment when the future was in doubt. Until a method has been devised to capture the revolutionary movement entirely by cartographical means, the eyewitness accounts of yore—those of Reed and Sukhanov—will continue to be the best-informed guides to the historical setting.

'On s'engage et puis . . . on voit'

Eyewitnesses at the time could not know what events would play out on this stage. John Reed, who in 1918 had temporarily returned to the United States in order to enlist support for Soviet Russia in the country of the 'Red Scare', returned to Moscow for the Second World Congress of the Comintern and died there of typhus on 19 October 1920. Nikolay Sukhanov returned to the second rank, occupied various positions abroad in the 1920s and worked on economic and cooperative issues. In 1931 he was sentenced to ten years in gaol in the show trial against the Mensheviks, which he spent in the notorious Verkhneuralsk politisolator political prison. Scarcely had he been freed—he had been working as a German teacher in Tobolsk—when he was rearrested in 1937, the year of the Great Terror—this time as a German agent. Subjected to torture, he confessed and was sentenced

FIGURE 3.2. Kliment Redko (1897–1956) painted *Insurrection* in 1925 with Lenin as its centre of energy, but one under threat since those close to him would later fall victim to the Terror. Acquired by George Costakis. © State Tretyakov Gallery, Moscow. Photo: culture-images/fai.

to death on 29 June 1940. He was executed on the same day in the prison in Omsk. Trotsky, himself a brilliant journalist and historian who always spoke highly of both Reed and Sukhanov, was murdered on 21 August 1940 in Coyoacán in Mexican exile, almost at the same time as Sukhanov in Omsk and in the same country where John Reed's career as reporter had begun.

Even Lenin could not know what would become of the scene in which he had acted as the 'demon of world destruction', to cite Sukhanov's words. In the last year of his life, Lenin read Sukhanov's personal record of the Revolution. In his response there is no dearth of disparaging comments or derogatory remarks about a political opponent—'pedantry', 'incomprehension of the dialectic', 'irrepressible phrase-mongering', 'clichéd thinking'. But Lenin's cursory reading of Sukhanov's very substantial book ends in a not exactly typical reflection about the prospects for the Russian Revolution and his own part in it. In a kind of dialogue with Sukhanov, he wrote:

> You say that civilization is necessary for the building of socialism. Very good. But why could we not first create such prerequisites of civilization in our country by expelling the landowners and the Russian capitalists, and then start moving toward socialism? Where, in what books, have you read that such variations of the customary historical sequence of events are impermissible or impossible? Napoleon, I think, wrote: 'On s'engage et puis . . . on voit.' Rendered freely this means: 'First engage in a serious battle and then see what happens.' Well, we did first engage in a serious battle in October 1917, and then saw such details of development (from the standpoint of world history they were certainly details) as the Brest peace, the New Economic Policy, and so forth. And now there can be no doubt that in the main we have been victorious. It never occurs to our Sukhanovs, to say nothing of Social-Democrats still further to the right, that revolutions cannot be made any other way. It never even occurs to our European philistines that subsequent revolutions in Oriental countries, which possess much vaster populations in a much vaster diversity of social conditions, will undoubtedly display even greater peculiarities than those dished up by the Russian Revolution.[31]

People who think that the course of world history could be foreseen in a textbook are simply fools in Lenin's opinion. He himself preferred to leave his readers perplexed—this text appeared in *Pravda* on 30 May 1923—by the confession of his own perplexity.

CHAPTER 4

The Philosophy Steamer and the Splitting of Russian Culture

In autumn 1922 two steamers—the *Oberbürgermeister Haken* and the *Preußen*—set sail from the harbour of the city that was to be renamed Leningrad two years later. They had a curious cargo on board: philosophers, writers, university teachers and agronomists, members of learned societies, journalists, cooperative representatives and public intellectuals. They were all handpicked, selected in a procedure that had been personally instigated and worked out by Lenin. Included were people renowned in Russia as well as individuals known only to initiates. They had all been forced to leave Soviet Russia against their will. 'Banishment instead of shooting' had been Lenin's motto. When the passengers docked in Stettin a few days later, Russia was the poorer by the loss of some of its ablest minds and the world richer by a novel experience—the expulsion of independent thinkers from the territories of the first socialist country on Earth.[1] This was the beginning of a practice that was to endure for decades, in fact right up to the end of the Soviet Union, except that fifty years later, in 1974, Solzhenitsyn—who also left against his will—was expedited not in a steamer to Stettin but on board an Aeroflot Tupolev 154 bound for Frankfurt am Main. That many of those who implemented the expulsion of representatives of the Russian intelligentsia would find themselves similarly driven into exile has an irony of its own. Such was the case with Leon Trotsky, who was put on a boat for Constantinople in 1929 only to be murdered later in Mexico by Stalin's agents. Having earlier supplied the arguments which helped to establish the practice, he fell victim to it himself. The deportation of leading representatives of the Russian intelligentsia harks back not just to a macabre version of repression known ever since Ovid but also to a history that even now is far too little known: the history of the Russian diaspora, the Russia beyond its frontiers, the exodus of between one and two million people after the Revolution and Civil War, who spread out through the entire world with wave after wave of refugees, émigrés and nonreturnees—especially after the Second World War and during the latter years of the Soviet Union—and have settled in the world's metropolises right down to the present day.[2] Unlike the movements of refugees and émigrés away from Hitler-dominated Europe, the general public is not aware that the Russian emigration is the other great exodus of the twentieth century, even though there are great names representing the achievements of the Russian diaspora: writers such as Vladimir Nabokov and Ivan Bunin, economists and sociologists such as Pitirim Sorokin and the Nobel Prize laureate for economics Simon Kuznets, musicians such as Igor Stravinsky and Serge Koussevitzky, philosophers such as Nikolay Berdyaev and Alexandre Kojève. Traces of Russian learning and culture are to be found to this day around the globe. The philosophers' steamer is emblematic of the ruthlessness of Bolshevist power, of the delusions of its efforts to bring everybody into line, of the divisions within Russian culture that persisted for a century and could come together again only after the demise of the Soviet regime. It is one of the tragic paradoxes that the first exiles outlived many of those who drove them away in the first place and that deportation proved to be their salvation.

Lenin's Surgical Intervention

Now that the archives have been opened up, the process of expulsion can be reconstructed in detail. It advances from Lenin's first thoughts on the subject as early as 1921, about the candidates to be selected for deportation, the committee meetings of both the Party and the state, the arrests and interrogations, the obtaining of visas and so on down to the ship's crossing and the landing in Stettin as well as the journey onward to Berlin.[3]

We are no longer solely dependent on the detailed accounts of people directly affected; we can now also read the transcripts produced by the officials of the GPU (the then current name for secret police). Not all the deportees were sent into exile on the philosophy steamer; some emigrated with their families to Warsaw or Riga at

their own expense, while others were sent via Odesa to Constantinople. For many, the only option was exile within Soviet Russia itself.[4] What becomes very clear, however, is that Lenin himself was
the driving force behind the expulsions even though he was already
marked by the after-effects of the strokes he had suffered. As early
as January 1922, he initiated the departure of prominent Mensheviks
who had resorted to hunger strikes to protest about being sent into
internal exile. He then began to make a mental list of people whom
he regarded as the protagonists and spokespeople of an opposition
to the Bolshevik regime. He took note of authors, had texts sent to
him, wrote polemical pieces and required his team to painstakingly
study periodicals such as the *Ekonomist* or a collection of essays on
Spengler's *Decline of the West*, whose authors he lumped together as
members of the 'White Guard', even though they had not the slightest connection with the White movement. To make these men—in
actuality, they included one prominent woman: Yekaterina Kuskova—
leave the country became something of an idée fixe for Lenin. In an
urgent letter of 15 May 1922 to the People's Commissar for Justice,
Dmitry Kursky, he called for an extra paragraph to be inserted into
the Penal Code that would provide for 'the right to commute the death
sentence to deportation'. In a letter listing numerous candidates for
expulsion, Lenin wrote, 'arrest a few hundred and *without giving the
reasons*—they will all emigrate, ladies and gentlemen! All the writers
from the "House of Writers", the periodical "Der Gedanke" in Piter [i.e.,
St. Petersburg]; Kharkiv should get what it deserves too, *we do not
know anything about it*, it is "a foreign country" in our eyes. We need
to purge *quickly*, not *later* than the trial against the SR. Don't let the
literati in Piter out of our sight (their address: Novaya russkaya kniga,
No. 4, 1922, p. 7) nor those on the list of private publishers (p. 29). With
communist greetings, Lenin.'[5]

In a further letter, he called for the systematic survey and compilation of the candidates and even supplied the first batch of names
which in his view were the most important. He insisted that the process should be speeded up; the relevant people's whereabouts had to
be discovered so that they could all be arrested in a planned raid on
16/17 August 1922 and then interrogated. At the end of August, Trotsky
swung into action. In an interview with an American journalist, John

Reed's widow Louise Bryant, printed in *Pravda* on 30 August 1922, he summed up the meaning and purpose of the deportations with characteristic precision:

> You ask me [said Trotsky] what the explanation is of the decree to expel abroad elements hostile to the Soviet regime. And does it not mean that we are more afraid of them within the country than on the other side of the frontier?
>
> My answer will be very simple. Recently, you witnessed the trial of the SRs, who, during the Civil War were the agents of foreign governments fighting against us. The court judged them as warranting the death penalty. Your press, for the most part conducted a despairing campaign against our cruelty. Had we got the idea straight after October [i.e., the Revolution] to send the SR gentlemen abroad we could have saved ourselves from being called cruel. Those elements whom we are sending or will send [abroad] are politically worthless in themselves. But they are potential weapons in the hands of our possible enemies. In the event of new military complications—and these, despite all our love of peace, are not ruled out—all these unreconciled and incorrigible elements will turn into military-political agents of the enemy. And we will be forced to shoot them according to the regulations of war. This is why we prefer to send them away in good time. And I hope that you won't refuse to accept our far-sighted humanity and will take it upon yourself to defend it in the face of public opinion.[6]

In an article 'A First Warning' in *Pravda* on 22 August 1922, signed by 'O' and attributed to Trotsky, we read, 'The Soviet government has shown far too much patience. Now it has sounded a first warning. The most active counter-revolutionary elements are being exiled partly abroad and partly to the Northern provinces. For the workers and peasants all this will serve as a reminder they will soon need their own worker-peasant intelligentsia.'[7]

The lists were assembled, commented on and adopted; then the visas had to be organised and the costs of the journey secured. Those affected had to settle their family affairs and, liquidating their entire lives up to that point, sell everything they owned and set out to discover how they would keep their heads above water once they were out of the country. The very basis of their existences was ruined by their being debarred from their professions, censorship and the closing-down of their professional organisations. In the German consulate, Stepun came across an old acquaintance from his university days in Heidelberg who helped him obtain a visa; Sorokin took the train to Berlin via Riga.[8]

Internal correspondence and the interrogation transcripts make clear why the Bolshevist leadership of those years was obsessed by the idea of forced exile. With the resolutions of the Tenth Party Congress, the Bolshevik Party had responded to the explosive situation that had developed following the end of war communism with the peasant uprisings, famine and mutiny of sailors in Kronstadt. The Bolshevik government was concerned about the high standing of the Hunger Relief Committee (Pomgol) managed by Russian politicians and of the American Relief Administration (ARA), which had taken up the fight against the famine that had claimed millions of victims in 1921–1922. It was nervous about the international protests and the solidarity campaigns on behalf of the left-wing Socialist Revolutionaries who had been accused in a show trial in June 1922, and they feared the erosion of the success they had achieved with the conclusion of the Treaty of Rapallo. Anyone who relaxed the laws against the market, trade and business, as had happened with the decision to approve the New Economic Policy (NEP), was compelled at the same time to tighten controls and eliminate any forces whose mere existence cast doubt on the ruling powers. Lenin was well aware of the nature of 'ideological hegemony'. At a time of economic liberalisation, it was essential to maintain and indeed tighten control over the public sphere. For this reason, in the efforts to achieve social conformity, the figures to be targeted first were the spokesmen of the intelligentsia, the leaders of recently formed organisations—the congresses of doctors, engineers, cooperatives and student organisations, university rectors and institute directors. This all took place long after the spokesmen of political parties had been arrested or murdered or fled the country. In its efforts to rebuild the country, Soviet power was dependent upon the collaboration of the intelligentsia, without whose professional expertise it would have been lost. All the more reason for it on the one hand to enlist the support of the noncommunist, bourgeois intelligentsia, the 'former people'—without a doubt the overwhelming majority—and on the other to isolate everyone who offered intellectual resistance to Soviet power. It was idle for those affected to protest their loyalty to the state and their obedience to the law under the new regime. The campaign to proceed with the exile programme testified to Lenin's sensitivity to ideological currents within the opposition, his consciousness of the feeble legitimacy underpinning Soviet rule, but equally to his ruthless determination to assert his power.

The list that was gradually compiled in the spring and summer and the subsequent arrests were in line with these goals. The interrogations all followed a particular pattern, as is evident from transcripts; the transcripts themselves were read and commented on by the higher GPU command—Unshlikht, Agranov, Yagoda and Dzerzhinsky. The most important questions, the ones always put to the prisoners, were as follows:

1. What are your political views?
2. What is your view of the structure of Soviet power and of the proletarian republic?
3. What is your view of the role of the intelligentsia?
4. What is your attitude to the Savinkovites, the 'Change of Landmarks' people and the trial of the Socialist Revolutionaries?
5. What is your attitude to the professors' strike, to sabotage and other similar ways of fighting against the Soviet regime?
6. What is your view of the Soviet regime's policy towards higher education and to the reforms taking place at the university?
7. How do you see the prospects of the Russian emigration abroad?[9]

All those arrested consistently emphasised their loyalty to the Soviet state, while simultaneously rejecting the worldview and practices of Bolshevism. There were a number of curious discussions in the offices of the GPU. In one example, Lev Karsavin, the philosopher-brother of Tamara Karsavina, the prima ballerina, discussed ballet with his interrogator; in another, Nikolay Berdyaev debated philosophical questions in the Lubyanka with Felix Dzerzhinsky.[10]

At first glance, the people destined for deportation do not have much in common. We are talking about 225 individuals in all, the largest group among them from Moscow (37), Petrograd (22), and a few other cities (Kazan, Kharkiv and Perm).[11]

Names on the Moscow list included those of Vladimir Abrikosov, a Uniate priest and Tolstoyan; the prominent literary critic Yuly I. Aykhenvald, even though his sons were convinced Marxists; the journalist and Socialist Revolutionary Ilya Yurievich Bakkal; well-known philosophers Nikolay Berdyaev, Ivan Alexandrovich Ilyin, Boris Vysheslavtsev; writer Mikhail Ossorgin; historians Alexander Alexandrovich Kizevetter, Prince Sergey Yevgenievich Trubetskoy and Venedikt Alexandrovich Myakotin; Archaeological Institute members Vasily Bardygin and Sergey Nikolaevich Tsvetkov; cooperative movement representative Nikolay Ivanovich Lyubimov; Moscow University rector Mikhail Mikhailovich Novikov; and Dean of the Faculty of Mathematics Vsevolod Viktorovich Stratonov. The most politically prominent was probably Alexey Vasilievich Peshekhonov, an economist, journalist and former minister in the Provisional Government.

The Petrograd list contained the names of respected philosophers such as Sergey N. Bulgakov, who was also a priest, Lev Platonovich Karsavin, Ivan Ivanovich Lapshin and Nikolay Onufrievich Lossky. Then there were Alexander Solomonovich Izgoev-Lande, the liberal journalist who was a pet hate of Lenin's, the sociologist Pitirim Sorokin, the economist and demographer Boris Davidovich Brutskus, as well as the publisher Abram Saulovich Kogan.

Among those who made their own way into exile were the writer and philosopher Fyodor Stepun, the historian Sergey M. Melgunov, the leaders in the famine aid programme Yekaterina D. Kuskova and Sergey Prokopovich, the writer Vladislav Khodasevich and his life partner, Nina Berberova. Among those subsequently reprieved from exile abroad were the publisher of the Spengler volume Yakov Markovich Bukshpan and the economist and cooperative member Nikolay Dmitrievich Kondratiev. Likewise reprieved were Pyotr Ioakimovich Palchinsky, one of Russia's leading engineers who had already spent much time in exile abroad, the writer Yevgeny I. Zamyatin and the philosopher Gustav Shpet. Many of this latter group would later lose their lives in Soviet camps.

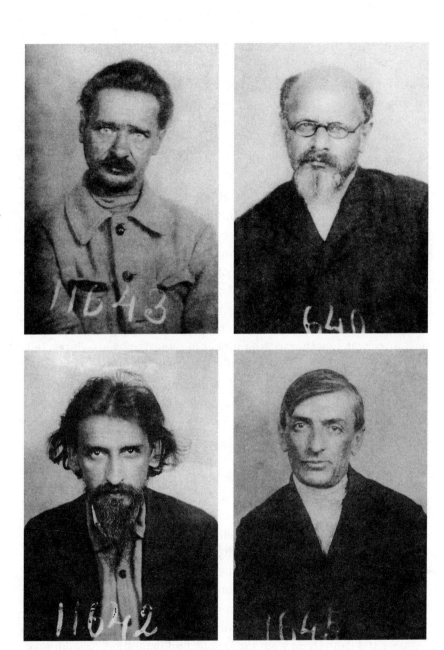

FIGURE 4.1. Photo portraits of some of those exiled in 1922, taken during the preceding interrogations. Clockwise from top left: A. B. Petrishchev, A. S. Izgoev-Lande, B. I. Khariton, L. P. Karsavin. From V. G. Makarov and V. S. Hristoforov (eds.), *Vysylka vmesto rasstrela: Deportatsiia intelligentsii v dokumentah VChK-GPU 1921–1923*, Russkii put', Moscow 2005.

For all the differences between them, the political and cultural profile of the targeted group can be readily distilled. The main blow is aimed at the so-called third element of Russian society, as the intelligentsia was frequently known. If we dissect the list of names according to their professions, we find 45 doctors, 41 professors, 12 engineers, 126 lawyers, 22 writers and journalists, 30 economists and agronomists, 34 students, 9 politicians, 2 ministers of religion and 6 others.

Of the total, 67 were exiled abroad, 49 sent into internal Soviet exile, while the sentence of exile was withdrawn in 33 cases. As to political allegiance, 26 were regarded as Mensheviks, 3 as Social Democrats, 13 as left and right Socialist Revolutionaries, 8 as Popular Socialists, 23 as Kadets, 2 as monarchists and 4 as of no party. The biggest cohort was of those born between 1871 and 1880—that is to say, the generation to which Lenin, Trotsky, Dzerzhinsky and Stalin all belonged.[12]

For most of the deportees, not only the interrogation records have survived, together with a number of remarkable anecdotes, but also the police photos that the GPU took just before the expulsion. This resulted in the production of a portrait gallery of the Russian intelligentsia and, for its part, the archive of the secret police became a repository of cultural memory.

Berlin, Prague, Paris and New York—The Russian Diaspora

When the deportees arrived in Western Europe, they were met by a Russia beyond Russian frontiers, which with 1.5 to 2 million people was already the largest exile community of modern times. Its centres lay along the escape routes leading away from a Russian Empire torn apart by civil war and foreign intervention and towards the metropolises of Europe. Starting out from Odesa and Novorossiysk, these great evacuation campaigns followed the roads to Constantinople, Gallipoli and Lemnos and from there went on to Sofia and Belgrade. Thousands of people went by ship to Athens and Marseilles. Key staging posts in the north were Helsinki (Helsingfors in Tsarist Russia), Tallinn (Reval in Tsarist Russia), and Riga as well as Warsaw and Stockholm. The largest communities formed in Berlin, the capital city of the erstwhile enemy;

Prague, capital of the newly founded Republic of Czechoslovakia; and later in Paris, above all. When Hitler overran Europe, the centre of the Russian diaspora shifted to North America. In the Far East, Harbin and Shanghai were the first anchorages for a large and productive albeit somewhat out-of-the-way Russian community, which left traces in the cityscape that are still visible there to this day.[13] In practice, scarcely anywhere in Europe and overseas remained untouched in one way or another by the flood of refugees. Wherever there were family links, visas were issued. Language skills or pure chance proved helpful, as Russians settled for shorter or longer periods in Varna, Beirut, Cairo, Madrid, Copenhagen, London, Bizerte (where a part of the Russian fleet had found refuge), Paraguay and South Africa. A new class of human beings had emerged from the breakup of the Tsarist Empire— the stateless people Hannah Arendt would later identify as the new 'outlaws' of the twentieth century, barely keeping their heads above water and furnished with a document issued by the League of Nations, the so-called Nansen passport.[14]

What was the diaspora? It was the wretched plight of hundreds of thousands who, having been expelled from their normal lives and deflected into unfamiliar surroundings, were forced to make a new start in refugee camps, mainly former makeshift housing for POWs or military barracks—a society condemned to stay in the waiting room of history in the hope that they would be able to return to their homes once the Soviet republic had collapsed, but also what R. C. Williams has called 'a community of despair'.[15] The diaspora was a copy of the old society, especially of its elite and with a high proportion from the military, of officials from the old governmental apparatus, but with even more representatives from the middle classes—industrialists and businessmen, the professions and the intelligentsia, that is, writers, journalists and lawyers—what Vladimir Nabokov once described as an inverted pyramid of prerevolutionary Russian society. The Russia that persisted beyond its borders had its own infrastructure—its associations, cafés and restaurants, its own higher world but also its underworld. It contained a whole spectrum of political parties, from monarchists to anarchists, from constitutional democrats to extreme right-wing terrorists and anti-Semites. The émigrés were visible in the cities but even so they lived in a parallel universe in which the host nations for the most part showed little interest. They continued fighting for their own political interests on foreign soil even though these were of steadily diminishing importance for the course of events, that is, for the permanent establishment of the Soviet order of things.

Each centre of the Russian diaspora had its own profile, a tone of its own, something quite unmistakable. In the years 1922–1924, with over three hundred thousand émigrés, Berlin was for the moment the capital of exile, with dozens of publishers, numerous daily papers, endless journals and a Russian Scientific Institute with some outstanding members. The leading party politicians driven into exile, the Mensheviks, for example, had brought their expertise with them. Berlin was, after Rapallo, the 'third location' where people in exile with Soviet passports could meet and renew conversations that had become impossible in Soviet Russia itself. Examples were representatives of the Silver Age, such as Yuly Aykhenvald and the Futurist poet Vladimir Mayakovsky. Berlin was not only a centre of emigration; it was also an advance post of the Communist International and an extraterritorial battleground between White Russia and Red Russia.[16] The situation was completely different in Russian Prague, which thanks to the 'Russian campaign' of President T. G. Masaryk, a man with an intimate knowledge of Russian culture, was to become the 'Russian Oxford' with its own institutes, newspapers and, above all, the Archive of Russia Abroad, which until it was removed from Prague by the Red Army in 1945 had been the central meeting point for Russia beyond its frontiers. The Olšany Cemetery in Prague is a veritable necropolis of Russian learning.[17] The Czechoslovak Republic, like other 'new' states, such as Yugoslavia, profited from the brain drain out of the former Russian Empire, and used it to help modernise their country, in particular their roads, railway and the construction of technical high schools.

The close relations between Russia and Paris dated back to before the war. Even before the First World War and the Revolution, Paris had been a kind of Mecca for Russians. Artists (Larionov, Goncharova and Chagall) lived there; Serge Diaghilev's Ballets Russes was enjoying huge success with Stravinsky, Nijinsky and Bakst. France was an ally in the First World War and so Paris was a haven for many generations of revolutionaries who had been forced to leave the Tsarist Empire. It is no wonder that even after the Revolution it became the strongest and most enduring focal point of the diaspora. It had the most important congresses, at which the 'strategy and tactics' of the emigration could be debated; it had a rich intellectual and literary scene (Lev Shestov, Nikolay Berdyaev, Pyotr Struve, Ivan Bunin, Mikhail Ossorgin); but it was also the seat of the old aristocratic and industrial Russia (with such families as the Shakhovskoys and the Ryabushinskys). A notable element of Russian Paris was provided by the legendary taxi drivers, who had been landowners in their former lives, as well as the Renault car workers in Billancourt, who had been officers in the Tsarist army. The importance of Russian Paris can be gauged today by the graves in the cemetery of Sainte-Geneviève-des-Bois.[18] The German occupation of Paris was to become a lethal threat to Russian Paris and after the Second World War, many people had no choice but to move on to America, which became the most important destination for refugees and émigrés fleeing from the Soviet Empire. This was when Vladimir Nabokov's 'American years' began; this was where the archival legacy of the diaspora was rescued and looked after—in the Hoover Institution on War, Revolution and Peace, the Houghton Library in the case of Trotsky's papers and the Bakhmeteff Archive of Russian and East European Culture at Columbia University. It was here, in these new institutes and think tanks, that Russian scholars found the opportunity to refine their knowledge and to train a new generation of experts on Russia and the Soviet Union, whose expertise went far beyond the period of the Cold War. (I have in mind here Harvard's Russian and Ukrainian Research Center, Pitirim Sorokin at Harvard and Merle Fainsod's research projects.) American universities became the leaders in all things Soviet and Russian. In a certain sense, the history of the diaspora also comes to an end in America. Anyone who becomes an immigrant in the USA ceases to be an émigré. Little Odessa in Brighton Beach in the last decade of the twentieth century does not represent the continuation of the history of Russians in exile, but the beginning of a different history—a worldwide migration that has become normal and whose end result is that you become an American.

Glory and Tragedy in 'The Age of Extremes'

For the exiles of the revolutionary period, hopes of an early return were doomed. The debates about what strategy to adopt in the struggle against Bolshevism ran into the sand the longer the Soviet regime managed to survive. But many who had been forced to give up their homes for life abroad found that they had made the better choice; they had escaped with their lives while many of their age group, friends, colleagues and relatives had lost their freedom or even perished in the maelstrom of persecution or extermination. Even many of those who had been responsible for the expulsions of 1922—Unshlikht, Yagoda, Agranov and Yenukidze—died later in the execution cellars of Stalin's purges. What kept the Russian diaspora together—the longer it lasted, the stronger it became—wasn't a political programme but the consciousness of a cultural mission. This found its clearest expression in the annual festivals and jubilee celebrations all over the world for Pushkin, Tolstoy and Dostoevsky. The Russian emigration succeeded in helping Russian culture survive the Revolution. In so doing, it made a visible contribution to world literature, as in the cases of Ivan Bunin, Vladimir Nabokov and Marina Tsvetaeva; it ensured growth of knowledge and understanding in the scholarly institutes of the West, as in the work of major scholars such as Michael Rostovtzeff, George Katkov at Oxford, Georges Florovsky and George Vernadsky at Harvard. But it also existed in 'small doses', in the simple presence of Russian culture and intellectuality in the micromilieus of the Bloomsbury Group or the Tanglewood Music Festival with the participation of Serge Koussevitzky. Both Europe and America profited from the transfer of refinement and stylishness that accompanied the expulsion of the aristocracy and the luxury industries from St. Petersburg/Petrograd to the fashion houses of Berlin, Paris and New York. We saw the aristocrat of yore transformed into the fashion designer and milliner who taught the Paris and Berlin publics the meaning of form and elegance.[19]

It is infinitely harder to monitor precisely the intellectual leakage that spread to 'the West' via the diaspora. But there is no doubt that the structuralism of Roman Jakobson, who had originally gone to

Prague as a member of the Soviet diplomatic corps, had a powerful influence on American literary studies at Yale. Mention must also be made here of the sociological and demographic gaze, schooled in the experience of crises and catastrophes, that Pitirim Sorokin brought with him to Harvard via Prague. And we should not forget Ayn Rand, who was born in St. Petersburg in 1905 and had immense success in America with 'Objectivism' and *Atlas Shrugged*. Her fundamentalist liberalism is barely comprehensible without her experience of Leningrad, from which she fled in 1926. And can it be of no importance that philosophers—existentialists such as Berdyaev and Shestov, the phenomenologist Lossky, and Hegelians such as Koyré and Kojève, all of whom had a Russian and Soviet background—should have made their appearance at a particular time and place, namely the Paris of the interwar period? Of course, there were other currents of thought that had come together at that time: alongside the Russian exiles, the 'Protocols of the Elders of Zion' had also arrived in Germany and made a crucial contribution to the spread of an anti-Semitic International in Munich and Berlin, with the struggle against 'Jewish Bolshevism' as its core theme.[20] All this would find its appropriate place in a global history of culture and ideas that also included the experience of the Russian emigration and refugee movement.

It would then become evident that the links between Soviet and pre-Soviet Russia were never entirely broken, despite all attempts to erect barriers between them or to criminalise elements of the past. The Cheka/GPU/OGPU/NKVD/KGB and today's FSB never failed to keep an eye on whatever was thought, written, printed and conveyed across the frontiers by post. We need only read Nabokov's novel *The Gift* to see how the two worlds remained connected, and we need only call to mind the kidnapping of 'White generals' such as Alexander Kutepov in 1930 and Yevgeny Miller in 1937 by agents of the Soviet secret services to understand that the Soviet side never freed itself from the objects of its hatred, the 'White émigrés'.

Europe, which was first divided by the Hitler-Stalin Pact, then overrun by Hitler's troops and finally liberated and occupied by Stalin's armies, remained a life-threatening place for Russian émigrés.

In the eyes of the Nazis, the exiles were always suspect and inferior, despite Alfred Rosenberg's Baltic connection and the right-wing views of Russian extremists. This applied even to later collaborators associated with Pyotr Krasnov, author of the popular trilogy *From Double Eagle to the Red Flag* who was executed in Moscow in 1947. Whenever they were tracked down, Russian Jews were always executed by the Germans. This was the fate of the great Jewish historian Simon Dubnow. Dubnow had escaped from Petrograd to Berlin in 1922, moved to Riga in 1934 and was captured there and murdered by the advancing German killing squads. It was also the fate of the demographer and journalist Alexander Kulischer, who like many others in exile in Paris was arrested and sent to his death in a German camp. Stalin's henchmen also took a keen interest in their former fellow countrymen. There was Grigory Landau, a philosopher and journalist who had lived first in Berlin and then in exile in Riga—even before Spengler he had published a spectacular book, *The Twilight of Europe*. He was arrested by the NKVD in 1940 and perished in a camp, as did the philosopher Lev Karsavin, who had taught in Kaunas, was sentenced to forced labour in 1949 and died of its effects in 1952.[21] The guardians of the Archive of Russia Abroad were deported to the Soviet Union together with the archive in 1945, when the Red Army occupied the city on the Vltava. After lengthy exile and imprisonment, they were finally able to spend the evening of their lives in their old homeland. Some of those 'repatriated' were able to make their peace with the Soviets in their later years—one of them, Vasily Shulgin, born in 1878, a prominent monarchist and rabid anti-Semite in prerevolutionary Russia, was even invited as a guest to the Twenty-Second Congress of the CPSU.[22]

Unlike the situation with the Russian revolutionaries of the nineteenth century, who had found refuge in Zurich, Lausanne, Paris and London, there was no safe bolthole for the Russian émigrés of the twentieth century. Caught between the hammer and anvil of Hitler's and Stalin's henchmen, denigrated and under suspicion, constantly coopted and instrumentalised for propaganda purposes during the Cold War, the Russian diaspora has probably never been given its proper place among the expatriates and outlaws of the twentieth century.

Return to an Altered Homeland

The exiles have now returned home. Most of them did not live to see the end of the regime that had banished them or their forebears. But they have at least returned in their books, in mass reprints of their works: Nabokov, Berdyaev, Stepun and Teffi. Many others belonging to the 'third wave', that is, the émigrés of the 1970s, were able to return home for a visit or even to settle. For Alexander Solzhenitsyn, the most prominent of the late exiles, return became a triumphal progress to Moscow on the Trans-Siberian Railway. World congresses of fellow Russians were officially organised; members of the Romanov dynasty flew in, bringing with them the mortal remains of the Tsar's family to lay to rest in the city that once again bore the name St. Petersburg. Some shifted the focus of their lives once again to Russia—the writer and logician Alexander Zinoviev (from Munich) was one such person. Others, like the writer and satirist Vladimir Nikolaevich Voynovich, acquired a second home there. The opening of exile libraries and exile archives revealed a whole continent that up until then had been accessible only to the privileged and those in the know.

But while some people returned home, former Soviet citizens now swarmed out into the world for the very first time. Among the sights they wished to visit was the grave of Vladimir Nabokov, member of the Provisional Government and father of the writer, in the cemetery in Berlin Tegel. Then there were the graves of Joseph Brodsky, Serge Diaghilev and Igor Stravinsky in the San Michele cemetery in Venice. The end of exile and what amounted to a state of emergency went together with the opening of what had become a global universe without limits. In the decade following the fall of the Iron Curtain, Russian communities sprang up everywhere: in Paris, Berlin, Helsinki, New York, Bangkok and London. These new communities had nothing in common with the exiles of yesterday, but a lot to do with tourism, business and great streams of money and capital flows. The new Russia beyond the old borders took on the characteristics of a brain drain reminiscent of the loss of human talent in the first wave of emigration. Admittedly, Russia beyond its borders was now represented less by members of the intelligentsia, artists, writers, theatre people and journalists than by the enormous numbers of tourists, who were bent on discovering the world that had been closed to them for so long. And then there were the 'new Russians', who had made something of themselves or transferred their wealth abroad—whether thanks to their own business acumen, their connections or perhaps even through Mafia-like organisations. But in an age of global capitalism this normalisation trend cannot blind us to the fact that, in a divided and indeed hostile culture, returning home, reappropriation and re-union are complex and painful processes and cannot be successfully accomplished simply by taking advantage of a newly acquired cross-border freedom of movement. Two decades on from the end of the Soviet Empire, the question of what we are to understand by the re-united 'Russian world' remains quite unresolved. For some, it means the reacquisition of an ability to conduct internal conversations, a self-renewal, regenerating the inner tension of a culture that had been paralysed and even destroyed by violence and exile; for others, the state-controlled TV channels and culture apparatuses in Putin's Russia define the new 'Russian world', which is the name for claims as old as they are new to the right to exercise power, especially in the so-called 'near abroad'. As with the annexation of the Crimea and the continuing aggression in Ukraine, these claims are being asserted in part at least through the use of force.

PART II

Highway of Enthusiasts

CHAPTER 5

USSR in Construction: The Power of Images

The idea the world has formed of socialist construction consists of images created by photographers. They all belong to a long-vanished era when colour pictures did not yet exist, or if they did exist, were purely experimental or the private hobby of enthusiasts. To this day our notions of authenticity, objectivity and ultimately of truth, the unvarnished truth, are almost inseparable from black and white images. 'Black-and-white photographs function ... like scientific procedures that operate with the contrast between True and False, just as society operates with the contrast between trust and distrust or theology with the distinction between good and evil. Black and white remains relevant because it answers the need for a symbolically informed economy of perception and orientation, for an indispensable reduction of complexity in a world of colour.'[1]

The modern observer has difficulty in coping with the force of these images even today. The dam of the DniproHES power station, the blast furnaces of Magnitogorsk, the lock chambers of the White Sea Canal, originally named after Stalin, the rhythm of the workshops of the tractor factory in Kharkiv—all shape our image of socialist construction to this day; they became the international symbols of modernity and the leap of a backward agrarian country into the twentieth century. Printed in newspapers with a mass circulation, they migrated into the picture memory of generations; they were displayed in international exhibitions and shown again and again in newsreels. Since then, whole libraries have been devoted to the Soviet photography of the 1920s–1940s. Its masterpieces circulate in the international exhibition business. In the world's leading auction houses, the prices they command increase the more remote the era which found its definitive shape in them becomes. The disciplines of art and photography have traced the genealogy—and decline—of this brand of photography in all its nuances. Nevertheless, its impact on later generations shows little sign of fading. These images enable us to connect with an age that developed a common pictorial language that extends far beyond the USSR. It is represented by such names as Alexander Rodchenko, Margaret Bourke-White and John Heartfield, as well as by the emergence of a new type of magazine—the *Arbeiter-Illustrierte Zeitung, USSR in Construction, Fortune, Life*—magazines that created the media history of the twentieth century.

No magazine presents us with such a concentrated image of the age as *SSSR na stroike*, which appeared as a monthly in four foreign languages between 1930 and 1941: *USSR in Construction, USSR im Bau, URSS en construction, URSS en construcción*.[2] Each of these large-format, lavishly illustrated magazines was dedicated to a particular aspect of the social revolution in the Soviet Union and behind each issue stood a group of photographers, designers, writers and graphic artists, each of whom made a name in the history of photography and design.[3] The list of contributors over the decade reads like a Who's Who of Soviet photography and Soviet literature: El Lissitzky, Alexander Rodchenko, Varvara Stepanova, Roman Karmen, Georgy Petrusov, Boris Ignatovich, Arkady Shaikhet, Yevgeny Khaldey, Mark Markov-Grinberg, Max Alpert, Dmitry Debabov and John Heartfield. Texts were supplied by Maxim Gorky, Isaac Babel, Mikhail Koltsov, Valentin Kataev, Yakov Belsky, Eduard Tisse and Sergey Tretyakov. Leading officials of the Party and the state were members of the editorial office: Georgy Pyatakov, head of the People's Commissariat for Trade; Valery Meshlauk, chairman of the State Planning Commission; Alexander Kosarev, chairman of the Komsomol. The muse of the editorial board was Yevgeniya Khayutina, the wife of Nikolay Yezhov, who later became the head of the People's Commissariat for Internal Affairs (NKVD). In her salon, representatives of the literary intelligentsia came together with the secret police.[4] The inner core of the editorial board did not outlive *USSR in Construction*; Pyatakov, Meshlauk and Kosarev were arrested and executed in 1937/38, the year of the Great Terror. Yevgeniya Khayutina died by her own hand in 1938; her husband was arrested in 1939 and executed in 1940. The editorial archive vanished along with the victims of the Stalinist purges and has never reappeared.[5]

FIGURE 5.1. John Heartfield stayed in Moscow from April 1931 to January 1932 and designed several issues of *USSR in Construction*. This is a photomontage of oil rigs in Azerbaijan. © The Heartfield Community of Heirs/VG Bild-Kunst, Bonn 2018. Photo: culture-images/fai.

The fact that qualitatively pictures would play a new role was something of a platitude among the Soviet leadership who had come to power in a country in which large parts of the population were not yet able to read and write. Agitation and propaganda campaigns, the meaning of revolutionary posters that could trace their heritage to the Russian tradition of the *lubok*, and the advances of Russian cinematography all made clear the new significance of visual media in the social revolution. Magazines that worked with pictures already existed: *Ogonyok* (The little flame), which had a circulation of five hundred thousand copies in 1929 alone, *Soviet Photo* and Maxim Gorky's *Nashi dostizheniya* (Our achievements). The acceptance of the Five-Year Plan and the ideological mobilisation on all 'fronts' enabled the emergence of a new magazine in which the advances of industrialisation and life as a whole could be not only documented but above all propagated. This led to the swift development of a new genre which combined the advanced picture language of Soviet photography with succinct, memorable texts. It was primarily the collaboration of journalist Alexander Smolyan, photographer Max Alpert and painter Nikolay Troshin that created the foundations for the new type of photo essay, which amalgamated the experience of cinema narrative, photomontage and reportage.[6] The January issue of 1932 with the title 'Gigant i stroitel' (Juggernaut and construction worker) was devoted to the construction of Magnitogorsk and employed a 'type of photomontage that came very close to the technique of cinematic narrative. . . . The montage of contrasting images made it possible to display the direction of change, their gigantic proportions and the contradictions on the vast construction site.'[7] In the process, the photo narrative went beyond mere juxtaposition in the form of a photomontage; it became the form in which narratives of upheaval and development could be conveyed—such as the transitions from old to new, reactionary to revolutionary, capitalism to socialism.

A survey of the issues devoted to particular themes allows us to elaborate a certain recurrent typology. There is the contrast between the wooden plough on the one hand and the array of tractors on the other, the contrast between 'yesterday and today' in the horse cart on the one hand and the Moscow bus garage designed by Konstantin Melnikov on the other, or even the cabriolet on a Moscow boulevard. The sack carriers of olden times are contrasted with the automated conveyor belt of the present. *USSR in Construction* shows the Soviet Union as the country of technical innovation: the car factory; the wind tunnel in which aircraft engineers work; the *Maxim Gorky*, the largest passenger plane in the world; the Moscow Metro, which opened in 1935; the new Turksib railway line in a region where up to then there had been nothing but a trackless waste. The transformation of the geographical space of the Union comes into view thanks to the combination of maps and pictures: automobile races as far as Central Asia, canal building and the opening-up of mineral deposits in the Kuznetsk Basin. We are presented with the entire spectrum of nationalities living in the Union. Expeditions lead into the wide open spaces of the Empire. The picture of space and the map depicting the Northeast Passage opens up the prospect of routes only then entering into the realm of the possible and the accounts of the journeys undertaken by Soviet tourists open our eyes to the world of the Volga basin. All compass points and all regions of the Empire come into view: the tropical south of the Black Sea coast with its palms and lemon trees, the austere landscape of Karelia and the mountains of the Caucasus. The issue focusing on frontier troops takes us to the Soviet border with Manchuria. The view of Moscow presents a highly modern city—with escalators, café automats and elegant limousines; the view of the hinterland—Turkestan, the Russian village—reveals what the future holds for the periphery. In this way we begin to see a picture gallery of the contrasts and diversity of the multiethnic Soviet Empire and the persistence of the old amid the new as it has been captured and preserved in *USSR in Construction*: horses and carriages vs rows of automobiles, bazaars vs modern department stores, wooden huts vs apartment blocks. Every issue is designed not just—or not primarily—to present contradictions, the clash of cultures, but to show how they are overcome, thanks to the energetic and wise leadership of the state and of Stalin personally. This holds good for many of the reports: on the health service, the care of children and young people, the school system, the army and the fleet, sport and theatre. All the reports contain pictures of great, suggestive power: the sportsmen's bodies, the beauty inherent in the idea of the series—whether of machines or parades—the visualisation of the transformation from a 'wild', natural landscape into a manmade one.

And yet, there was one, almost insoluble problem. How could the transformation of the world by Bolshevism be shown to be superior given that at the same time, Russia was visibly, irrefutably backward?[8] But it is precisely the revelation of this chasm between the 'old' world and the 'new' that supplies the visualisation process with its vitality, its enormous impact. It is the unbridgeable contrast between the current state of affairs and the transformation brought about by an enormous concentration of human energy that makes these pictures so seductive. The observer of these illustrations has the same experience as Valentin Kataev, who travelled to the Magnitogorsk construction site and was flabbergasted by what he saw. This arose not simply from the sheer magnitude of the blast furnaces that had just been completed but from the fact that this had been achieved in the vastness of the steppes, where there was simply nothing to prepare for and facilitate the building of an iron and steel works of this kind. It was a situation in which the only option was to start believing in the kind of miracle that can move mountains. It is pointless to confront *USSR in Construction* with a reality that has been set aside and ignored. A photographer such as Alexander Rodchenko did not even bother to ignore the existence of forced labour; he aestheticised it. He even identified with the idea that forced labour was good for the character, transforming the old person into the new one, the criminal or the prostitute into the best worker or the shock worker who earned the right to retire prematurely or be awarded a medal.

The large-format title pages of *USSR in Construction*, lined up year by year, would produce not merely a chronicle and panorama of the Soviet upheaval, but also a sequence of images, of suggestion, of complicity, of joining in and even submitting. The fascination exerted by *USSR in Construction* must be understood and succumbed to in order to break its spell and arrive at a fair appraisal of the Soviet Union in the course of its construction. *USSR in Construction* is not just for art historians and iconographers, nor even for the analysis of aesthetic forms. It is a case of seeing how the power of images enters into history, of realising that images play a part in the creation of reality—both for contemporaries and for those born later.

CHAPTER 6

DniproHES:
America on the Dnieper

The four-lane carriageway that sweeps up out of the Ukrainian industrial town of Zaporizhzhia to the top of the Dnieper Hydroelectric Station dam follows the line of the gently curving dam wall that was erected here over eighty years ago. DniproHES, the abbreviation for Dniprovskaya Hidroelektrostantsiya, also known as Dniprostroy, was at the time Europe's largest hydroelectric power station and even today is still one of the most important dams in the world. Visitors who want to get a feel for its dimensions should walk the two kilometres between the banks of the Dnieper, even if, in doing so, they have to put up with the ear-splitting noise of the trucks thundering past, clouds of exhaust fumes and a vibrating asphalt road surface. The reward is a panoramic view that would elude travellers in a car or bus. Pedestrians will work their way along the top of the dam metre by metre, advancing along the sixty-metre-high dam wall, its piers plunging down into the depths and passing beneath the great cranes required for the operation and maintenance of the dam and the weir. Upriver is the Dnieper, which is dammed up to a distance of fifty kilometres, creating the reservoir in which the former Dnieper rapids lie submerged. Downriver, the island of Khortytsia can be seen in the distance, the former headquarters of the Zaporizhzhia Cossacks—that is to say, 'the Cossacks beyond the rapids'. In 1926 Vladimir Mayakovsky wrote:

> Our Debt to the Ukraine
> Where, with burning vodka,
> with daring,
> even with blood,
> The Zaporozhskaia Sech'
> seethed,

Taming the Dnepr
with a bundle of wires.
They'll force
the Dnepr
to flow across turbines
And the Dnepr
through wire whiskers
will flow through the blocks
As electricity . . . [1]

Far below, the surface of the Dnieper ripples in circles as if it had used up its energy in the turbines of the twin power stations at the ends of the dam wall. Pedestrians can also glance down at the two lock gates that enable even larger sea-going ships to pass. On the left bank, the grandiose backdrop of the industrial plants and the smoking factory chimneys of Zaporizhzhia can be seen; on the right bank, the tower blocks of Greater Zaporizhzhia.[2]

The Curved Clasp

The entire ensemble consisting of the dam, the locks and the power stations is overwhelming in its cyclopean dimensions and with its patina of grey reinforced concrete. But the most powerful impression springs not from the vantage point of the passing observer but from a bird's-eye view, which was in fact the viewpoint of the builders who designed and executed the project. From a distance and from above, you find the image of DniproHES that has left an indelible impression in the minds and memories of generations. It is the image of the curved dam with the supporting piers at regular intervals that Georgy Petrusov captured, indeed created.[3] Among those who have grasped this best we must also count Margaret Bourke-White's film, in which the dam is staged like an artificial waterfall. It was Petrusov's picture that went round the world and became fixed in people's memory over generations down to this day. It is the image of a curving dam wall which although of gigantic dimensions is like an elegant clasp, a hinge that has been inserted at the only point where it belonged, namely at the point in the relief where the energy of the entire river can be

FIGURE 6.1. The photographer Georgy Petrusov (1903–1971) was one of the most important contributors to *USSR in Construction*. The photo shows the top of the dam looking east. The foreground shows the turbine hall designed by the brothers Viktor, Alexander and Leonid Vesnin. © House of Photography, Moscow. Photo: culture-images/fai.

trapped, forced into the turbines and transformed into electricity. 'The dam that is being erected in Dneprostroi will raise the water for some ninety miles above the upstream and will one day rise through 120 km of its course concealing all the variations of the Dnieper gradient. The rocks making up its six rapids, regarded with anger or wonder by many generations of Russians, will sink into the trough and so the rapids themselves will be cheated of a privilege they have enjoyed for ages, ruining this noble stream for purposes of navigation. . . . The sight of the rapids is starting to acquire a certain rarity value.'[4] What Paul Scheffer called the 'Eichendorff idyll' [after the German Romantic poet] would give way to the roar of turbines.

This elegant structure is the expression of human genius in its taming and utilisation of the natural world. Humankind has done more here than simply build a plant; it has demonstrated its superiority. With its technical expertise, it has dammed the river and flooded the rapids, thus eliminating them as an obstacle to traffic; it has forced the river to drive the turbines and generators, which in turn facilitated the growth of an entire cluster of new industries. It makes ingenious use of the best place to achieve the maximum effect. Once we know that DniproHES has become the centre of a great industrial region and that it supplies the entire Donbass region with electricity, we can readily see what a powerful centre has been created here. DniproHES is not merely the sum of the labour of prospectors, geologists, hydrologists, engineers and the mass workforce, including forced labour; it is notable for the precision of its architectural design and its construction, in which beauty and function have achieved perfect harmony.[5] The cameras of Bourke-White and Petrusov made iconic what the builders had already succeeded in creating.

The Genius of the Builders:
Alexandrov, Vinter, Vedeneev, Rottert and Vesnin

DniproHES is a 'classic' of Soviet Constructivism. It is the definitive exemplar of the work of the engineers who conceived the project and thought it through—Ivan Gavrilovich Alexandrov (1875–1936), Alexander Vasilievich Vinter (1878–1958), Boris Yevgenievich Vedeneev (1885–1946) and Pavel Pavlovich Rottert (1880–1954). DniproHES might well have been the place that led someone to coin the new construction formula 'form follows function'. The entire DniproHES complex comprised the dam, the hydroelectric power station together with the turbine hall, the generators, the locks and the two bridges over the 'old' and the 'new' Dnieper. It also included the 'socialist city' (Sotsgorod) with such notable buildings as the canteen, the hospital, the summer theatre and the sports facilities on the site of present-day Zaporizhzhia, which had originally been named Alexandrovsk in honour of Alexander Golitsyn, one of Catherine the Great's favourites.

Viktor Alexandrovich Vesnin (1882–1950) was responsible for the design and construction of the power station and the turbine hall on the western side of the dam, but what he said about the shape of the turbine hall holds for the entire project. He summed it up in 1932: 'In DniproHES we achieved the maximum synthesis of functionality and beauty. We found the most powerful architectural expression for the technical idea embodied in Dniprostroy by erecting a building whose beauty did not consist of stucco ornaments or rows of columns. We used materials such as glass, glass tiles, etc., to a hitherto unknown degree. Because of that, we could draw the walls apart and achieve an unprecedented spaciousness in the building, whose width did not exceed 20 metres and length 250 metres.'[6]

Vesnin's colleagues were Nikolay Kolli, a partner of Le Corbusier, and his assistant Georgy Orlov. Together with the design for a theatre to stage musical mass actions in Kharkiv in 1930 (project abandoned) and the Proletarsky District Palace of Culture in Moscow (1931), DniproHES (1929) was the high point in the work of Viktor Vesnin, who together with his brothers Leonid and Alexander were the leaders of the Soviet architectural avant-garde. His training and first buildings date from before the Revolution. After 1917 he took part in important architecture competitions and was part of the Soviet architecture establishment until his death.

The decision in favour of this union of form and function was not a foregone conclusion, as can be seen from the public controversies that raged around the projects. In the course of a discussion with Anatoly Lunacharsky, the 'intellectual' among leading government ministers, Viktor Vesnin explained, 'I belong to the school of thought that does not believe it is possible to make a sharp distinction between the architect's and the engineer's contribution to a building. In any given case, the form of the building is only a consequence, and if we work on the form, it is only in the sense of providing a greater precision and a greater perfection in our treatment of the data laid down for us by the fundamental functional decision."[7] He adopted a similar position in connection with the planned Dnieper bridges: they were to be functional but not ponderous. The decision in favour of Vesnin's solution was not a given; it was rather the product of a struggle between two different approaches. The closed competition had also attracted prominent representatives of the neoclassical school, in particular Ivan Zholtovsky and Vladimir Shchuko, who were both members of the St. Petersburg Academy of Arts. Zholtovsky came up with a neoclassical project, Shchuko with a somewhat more modern design. They were the complete antithesis of the plans put forward by Colonel Hugh Lincoln Cooper (1865–1937), the American consultant working on Dniprostroy, who insisted on a straightforward technical design, dismissed all talk of aesthetic form as unimportant and was categorically opposed to Vesnin's proposal. In the debate about the project, the leading figures of the Soviet architecture scene took opposite sides. Academician Alexey Shchusev defended Zholtovsky, while Moisey Ginzburg and Ivan Leonidov spoke out in support of Vesnin's Constructivist and functionalist design. All the submissions were put to a session of the Central Executive Committee in the Kremlin in December 1929 for the final decision.[8] The power-station building in reddish tuff with huge windows at regular intervals that enabled light to enter the turbine hall was in harmony with the dam's flowing arches. The concrete piers provided the dam with a rhythmic articulation and ensured a smooth transition to the lock complex.

DniproHES was not only a triumph of human beings over nature technically and aesthetically, however. It was also the symbolic victory of a new age over the past, of the Soviet Union over the Old Russia, the age of electricity over the age of steam. The former Cossack heartland now stood in the shadow of the gigantic dam wall. No less a figure than Mayakovsky thought that the Empire's guilt towards Ukraine had been expiated by the construction of DniproHES. The rapids that had spelled the ruin of shipping in the past were now flooded and disappeared into the reservoir, where they ceased to be an obstacle. The sound of their rushing waters had fallen silent, transformed into the hum of the turbine paddle wheels. Three point five million cubic metres of earth and rock had been excavated and over one million cubic metres of concrete had been poured into the dam, the powerhouse and lock structures; forty-seven sluice gates were mounted between the piers; and nine turbines and generators installed.[9] On 1 October 1932, everything was ready. Thousands of people marched with banners over what had been the building site; the scaffolding had been removed; prominent politicians turned up from Moscow and Kharkiv; speeches were given from the tribune that had been erected on the steep bank. Someone pulled the lever that set the turbines and generators in motion. The first electricity passed through the transformer station and from there to the high-voltage cables and out into the factories. The electric bulbs illuminating the mighty dam wall came on and with them the enlightenment that had triumphed over darkness. The steady rhythm of the piers was further emphasised by the thousand-fold illumination and when the letters LENIN appeared on the dam wall, it seemed as if a new age had dawned, not in words but in reinforced concrete. It has been said, and may well be true, that Alexander Vinter, the chief engineer of DniproHES, had tears in his eyes. From this day on and far into the future, the image of the illuminated dam and those letters was fixed in the memory of Soviet citizens. In scarcely more than a decade, what in 1920 had seemed no more than the far-fetched fantasy of the 'dreamer in the Kremlin'—as H. G. Wells had described Lenin after a visit—had become a reality. GOELRO, the State Commission for the Electrification of Russia, had been described by Lenin as the 'second Party plan'. It was Lenin who coined the saying 'Communism is Soviet power plus electrification of the whole country'. This was the formula for the ambitious modernisation programme for his backward nation. 'Dneprostroi is a profoundly Russian enterprise, not just in its methods but also in its entire trajectory. It mirrors the fact that Russia has been little changed by human labour of a technical kind and that "colonial" Russia still survives in its readiness to take to any new initiative and its willingness to change everything from the bottom up.'[10]

The Century of Engineers

Lenin did not invent the electrification plan but he made a reality of something that had been in the air for decades and prepared for by specialists eager to create a modern Russia—geologists, hydrologists, soil scientists, power engineers and artists. GOELRO, which was set up on 21 February 1920, brought together everything they had long been waiting for. Ever since Catherine II's conquest of the Cossack Hetmanate and the shores of the Black Sea, the minds of generations had been focused on making the Dnieper navigable, in other words, overcoming the rapids that made navigation impossible. Even before 1914, plans to dam the river had been produced by the dozen. Later on, the idea of navigability was gradually superseded by that of the river as a source of energy. Creating a source of energy would make it possible to open up the entire southern region of the Tsarist Empire, with the ore and coal deposits of the Donbass and industry in Yekaterinoslav, Kherson and Mykolayiv. The steps needed to realise this project were obvious: geological and hydrological surveying of the terrain; economic analysis; construction of the dam, power station, high-voltage power lines and a new city around the power station. Decisions were taken: for DniproHES and against the Volga-Don Canal. Satisfying the claims of the newly established and hugely self-confident Ukrainian Soviet Socialist Republic was not the least important consideration. Vlas Chubar, a leading Ukrainian communist, had even threatened to take Ukraine out of the USSR. Furthermore, a positive decision was made to seek foreign advice and foreign financial support.

The Soviet government was able to call on the services of outstanding specialists from the ranks of the old engineering elite, who for their part saw in GOELRO the opportunity to realise their life's dreams as engineers and technicians. The management team at Dniprostroy included Ivan Gavrilovich Alexandrov, who for many years had been a leading intellectual force and the builder of the first great peat-fired power station in Shatura near Moscow. He was now put in charge of the entire project. Then there were Alexander Vasilievich Vinter, the chief engineer of DniproHES; Boris Yevgenievich Vedeneev, Vinter's deputy; and Pavel Pavlovich Rottert, senior engineer and another of Vinter's deputies.

Among the architects, Viktor Vesnin was in charge of building the power station and the Sotsgorod housing estate. The chief consultant from the United States was Colonel Hugh Lincoln Cooper, a civil engineer from Minnesota with great experience of dam construction. These men could call on the advice of other leading engineers with experience building power stations. One such was Genrikh Osipovich Graftio (1869–1949), the builder of the Volkhov Hydroelectric Station, the first to be built after the Revolution.[11] They were all from the cohort that had learned from the technical revolution at the end of the nineteenth century. At the same time, they grew up in an age of profound social and political change. They had all benefited from a first-class training and gained practical experience working on projects throughout the expanses of the Russian Empire. Some of them had sympathised with oppositional and revolutionary trends—as was the case with Vinter. Others were regarded with some suspicion as being of dubious loyalty either as 'former people', because of their background and membership of the old elite, or as capitalist foreigners like Cooper. And the start of the first Five-Year Plan together with its mobilisation of revolutionary youth coincided with a campaign against 'bourgeois experts' which could easily slip into lethal repression—as was the case with the 1929 Shakhty trial of leading engineers in the Donbass. Ivan Alexandrov received his training in Moscow and had been to the USA on a study visit in the 1920s. Alexander Vinter, who came from Bialystok, had gone through the St. Petersburg elite education of the Polytechnic Institute of Civil Engineers. Boris Vedeneev had been born in Tbilisi. Pavel Rottert came from a German family also from Bialystok. He had graduated from the Institute of Civil Engineers and directed the construction of new government buildings in Kharkiv. Like many of the technical specialists and intellectuals who had not gone into exile, they sought a modus vivendi with the new regime that systematically doubted their loyalty and was in a position to marginalise or even eliminate them at any time. Their entire life's work was dedicated to the modernisation of Russia, and when the Tsarist regime was no longer able to achieve this, it was the power of the Soviets that would enable them to pursue the same goal. They seized their opportunity with passion, sustained by their professional ethic as engineers but also as patriots for whom the modernisation of the country took priority over party-political affiliation. Soviet power offered them scope for planning and action roughly comparable to what was available following the founding of the Commission for the Study of Natural Productive Forces (KEPS) in the emergency brought about by the First World War. The establishment of this commission is generally regarded as the actual birthdate of the GOELRO plan.[12] Something similar can be said of the builders and architects. The first decade following the Revolution was concerned with the renovation and maintenance of the preexisting building stock. Not until the first Five-Year Plan did independent building activity start up again on a large scale. After a decade of 'architecture on paper', it was time for actual construction, primarily in industry and infrastructure. The energy sector, the construction of power stations, was one of the principal links in this chain, since the building of industrial complexes or the planning of new towns depended on a form of energy that could be transported overland and was independent of any particular location. The impact of the building boom of the first Five-Year Plan can still be seen down to the present day; indeed the Soviet industrial landscape is the product of that period.

In the final analysis, the construction of DniproHES was possible only because of what must have seemed like an inexhaustible supply of labour. With its aid, the construction site came to resemble a giant quarry with its colossal rock-crushing and milling machinery, cement works, towering wooden constructions, makeshift housing, as well as canteens, cinemas and a stage for summer theatricals. The workforce was basically cost-free as a consequence of the collectivisation of agriculture that also began with the Five-Year Plan. This drove hundreds of thousands of peasants out of the villages into the towns and what were termed the 'building-sites of socialism'. The problem was not the lack of workmen but their qualifications, which were minimal or altogether absent. 'It would seem that the instinct for using complicated machinery is not as highly developed in Russia as in countries of long-standing industrial traditions.'[13] Skills had to be acquired in the shortest possible time through on-the-job training by workers who themselves had only recently qualified. Forms of organisation that guaranteed the cohesion of the workforce had to be developed; the rhythm of seasonal work—in which peasants returned to the fields in summer—had to be superseded by the continuity of work in industry, including the acquisition of reading and writing as basic skills. All this was forced through by means of a quasi-colonial, hierarchical system in which punishment and reward played a prominent part. Because of the use of imported machinery and tools—Caterpillars, cranes, concrete mixers, sawmills, turbines and generators—Dniprostroy was regarded as a relatively privileged building site. And these special conditions were purchased at the price of impoverishing the village. The peasants were the 'social pariahs' on the building site—or so Paul Scheffer claimed.[14] The village handed workers over 'at zero cost'. It handed over its own surplus value which was then exported abroad, converted into foreign currency and used to buy technologically more advanced products because it was forced to do so; in other words, it was expropriated. As can be seen from the statistics, labour came from every region of the Soviet Empire, but especially from the disaster areas of the collectivisation in Ukraine, where later on the Holodomor, the manmade famine, raged with millions dead. To this extent, the elegant arc of the Dnieper dam is inconceivable without the violence that controlled and subjugated the workforce. Elegance and barbarism were intertwined. Paul Scheffer, the journalist attached to the *Berliner Tagblatt* and a fascinated visitor to Dniprostroy in October 1928, summed it up succinctly: 'We shall see! All in all this will become the largest power plant in Europe. Soviet industry is in its infancy, yet it plunges into an enterprise of this colossal magnitude! Where will its enormous energies take it once it has succeeded in dealing with its origins? Yet the consumers for it have still to be invented! . . . The Soviet regime feels itself master of all such possibilities!'[15]

America on the Dnieper

The most surprising members of the corps of DniproHES builders were the Americans, who contributed engineers, technicians, companies and know-how. And all this, even though there were as yet no diplomatic relations between the USA and the USSR (these were not established until 1934). But America had more to offer than the Germans, who were also competitors, despite the fact that the Russians had close, longstanding ties with Germany in science and technology—many Russian and Soviet engineers had studied in German technical universities. Moreover, German firms such as Krupp and Siemens-Bau-Union had in fact obtained contracts. But North

America had an early lead in constructing dams as well as the most efficient turbines and generators. Most important of all, it was the United States, the country of the future, which set the standards, not 'Old Europe'. The Soviet leadership looked to the most advanced capitalist country, which was the USA, especially at the time of the first Five-Year Plan. According to Hans Rogger, there was such a thing as 'Soviet Americanism' (*sovetsky amerikanizm*), whose impact went far beyond the economy. Charlie Chaplin, Mary Pickford and Douglas Fairbanks were stars in the eyes of Soviet cinemagoers and American musicals enjoyed great popularity. In many respects people felt closer to America; America had left behind the class barriers and snobbery of Old Europe. America was less hierarchical; you could rise socially, something otherwise possible only in postrevolutionary Russia, where class barriers had broken down and equality had been universally imposed by brute force. There had never been a war with America, if we set aside the US intervention force in the Civil War. American aid had been generous in the famine of 1920-1922. More than a few Russian revolutionaries had spent time in American exile—including Bukharin and Trotsky—and many who had fled there from Tsarism returned after the Revolution in order to put their anarchist or libertarian projects into practice. A number with more advanced skills found work on the construction sites. A further factor was that after the onset of the Great Depression of 1929, thousands of mostly young Americans, workers but also students, travelled to the Soviet Union in search of jobs. It is to them—the engineers, skilled workers and translators—that we owe some of the most acute observations on the lives of Soviet citizens.[16]

The Great Depression had triggered the policies of the New Deal, a policy which propagated a regulated form of capitalism that imposed rules on workers and bosses alike in a kind of concerted action. In particular, it set out to combat unemployment and the misery it caused by instituting large state-funded job programmes. Public buildings, community centres, roads and dams—these were all new even to America. The outstanding project of the New Deal, the construction of the Boulder Dam on the Colorado River in 1931-1935, subsequently renamed the Hoover Dam, can almost be described as a parallel project to DniproHES—from both an engineering and an aesthetic point of view. It is little wonder, therefore, that Soviet visitors to America, with many engineers among them, should have felt at home in the USA and experienced a great resonance with the country of the New Deal. And conversely, many Americans, once they had recovered from the shock of the backwardness of revolutionary Russia, got on well with the talent for improvisation and the can-do approach of Soviet managers who had themselves come from very modest circumstances. The Americans were present in force in Dniprostroy. The chief consultant at Dniprostroy was Colonel Hugh Lincoln Cooper. Under his supervision, the Wilson Dam had been built (1918–1924) on the Tennessee River, a major project with many similarities to the Dnieper Dam and one which later formed part of the Tennessee Valley Authority programme. US companies Newport News Shipbuilding and later on General Electric supplied the majority of the high-powered turbines and generators. An American colony lived in privileged conditions in Dniprostroy—in specially built houses with tennis courts and a car pool. Special food supplies were even said to have been shipped in via Odesa.[17] Together with other US engineers and technicians, Colonel Cooper was awarded the Order of the Red Banner of Labour after the completion of the project on 17 September 1932. So there were not just the 'Yankees from the Arbat', as a text from the 1920s by Ilya Ehrenburg was titled, but also Yankees on the Dnieper. Stalin himself spoke enthusiastically of the synthesis of 'American pragmatism and Bolshevik passion'. In 1927, when Dniprostroy began, it could not have been foreseen that 'Soviet Americanism' was no more than a passing phase.

It is not difficult to grasp the essence of the Soviet passion for America. It consists primarily in the belief that basically all problems are capable of a technical solution and that technology is a tool that can also help resolve social conflicts. In Soviet Russia quasi-utopian expectations latched on to technology and technical progress. Electricity, the light bulb, known as 'Ilyich's little lamp', was supposed not simply to provide illumination, but also to lead the country out of the 'gloom of the Middle Ages' and catapult it onto the sunlit uplands of what would surely become a classless society in a not too distant future. The century of electricity would supersede the century of steam, according to Gleb Krzhizhanovsky, the moving spirit behind GOELRO.

Technical advances were credited with problem-solving capacities
that they couldn't live up to. This applies with equal force to the idea
of an 'overall state plan' or the Soviet Fordism of an Alexey Gastev.[18]
The fascination of the machine, of technical apparatus and the images
created by them can also be seen in Margaret Bourke-White, but in
her case without the redemptive pathos implicit in the photographs
of DniproHES and other construction sites of the future. She wrote,
'Machine worship was everywhere; it permeated even the classic Russian ballet. Little girls with gear wheels in gold or silver painted on
their chests danced Machine Dances. The people were worshiping at
new shrines with the fervor of religious zealots. It was as though they
needed to replace their religion—which was being taken away from
them step by step. They looked on the coming of the machine as their
Saviour; it was the instrument of their deliverance.'[19]

Dynamiting a Building of the Century

A few weeks after Hitler Germany's assault on the Soviet Union, the
German army stood on the Dnieper. The Red Army could not afford
to let the energy capital of the entire south fall into the hands of the
conquerors. They attempted to remove important technical equipment and finally dynamited the dam on 18 August 1941. The photo,
with the gaping hole torn in the top of the dam by the explosion,
shows that the colossal efforts of an entire country can be destroyed
in a second. No one knows how many people lost their lives through
the destruction of the dam and the tidal wave that was unleashed in
the Dnieper valley; estimates ranged from 20,000 to 100,000.[20] The
Germans tried to plug the hole and put the power station into operation again in 1942, but as the Red Army advanced to the Dnieper, the
dam was blown up for a second time in autumn 1943.

Whoever stands before the vast installation today needs to be
aware that what one sees is the new dam wall that was built at top
speed between 1944 and 1947. After the war the power station became
the centre of a major industrial region once again. But the town has
grown—today it has a population of around 760,000; the electric power
has nurtured the car factory that produced the Zaporozhets and also

the aluminium plant. Since 1980, there is also the Zaporizhzhia nuclear power station, consisting of six reactor units, the largest on Ukrainian soil after Chernobyl. DniproHES has set a precedent, as can be seen from the dams, power stations and reservoirs since erected on the territory of the former USSR. Many of them are run-down, having deteriorated and become obsolete. The time for hydrological megalomania, the flooded fields, the salinisation of the earth through irrigation, the irretrievable loss of ancient towns and cultural monuments to flooding—all are in the past. It's now the turn of a new cost-benefit calculation. In general, the century of 'electric rivers'—to use the term coined by Richard White in his study of the Columbia River—is over. Tourists still come to marvel at this grandiose engineering monument of the twentieth century, but many of the visitors, especially the children, are drawn more to Khortytsia Island downriver from the dam. There they can see the old Cossack settlement—the *stanitsa*—in the open-air museum and gaze in wonder at the equestrian skills of the Cossacks. Quite recently, the Lenin Monument towering above the dam in the riverside park—the monument to the man whose name, LENIN, lit up by a thousand bulbs, had once proclaimed the arrival of a new world—was removed.

CHAPTER 7

Magnitogorsk: The Pyramids of the Twentieth Century

Whoever wishes to see what we might call Soviet civilisation in its pure form must go to a land where everything was poised for an unprecedented new beginning, a place whose wealth of natural resources promised development without limits. Unconfined by any historical tradition, it would be a space where the ruthless exercise of power could work wonders. Nothing would be allowed to stand in the way of the self-creation of the new human being. Only a tabula rasa could be considered as a construction site fit for the new world.

A 'Marxist theory' yields very little for an understanding of the processes of change in postrevolutionary Russia. We get somewhat nearer the mark if we explore the scene of a modernisation without modernity and of a grandiose civilising process powered by forces that were anything but civil, let alone forces that followed the 'American star' that Alexander Blok had seen rising at long last over Russia. On its flight path lie the 'great buildings of socialism' of the 1930s, which in a mere decade transformed an agrarian nation into an industrialised one. On this road we can see the Stalingrad of the tractor factories or the car plants of Nizhny Novgorod that had been erected with the assistance of Henry Ford, the camp cities of Karaganda and Norilsk, the DniproHES Dam, Novokuznetsk or the canals that link the Volga with the Moscow River and the Don. But the starting point of this journey is called Magnitogorsk—a name that itself seems to be made of ore.

Machines in the Steppes

Magnitogorsk lies twelve hundred kilometres from Moscow. In summer 1993, foreigners were permitted for the first time simply to get on a plane and fly to what had been a closed city beyond the Urals.

The flight lasted around two hours. The pilot of the Yak-42 was nice to the passengers. He flew low over the steppe, which unfolded in gentle waves while the Ural River carved its way through the landscape. He then circled round his goal, as if aware that battlefields and ruined landscapes could be surveyed only from a great height and at a great distance. Far away on the horizon, the line of the Ural mountain range shimmered blue. Beneath us, a large town with almost half a million people stretched out some fifty kilometres along the river—a white agglomeration consisting of many housing cubes, endless highways and right angles. We looked in vain for a city centre, a concentration of buildings. But there was no such thing, for the centre of this city consisted of the largest steelworks in the world, the Magnitogorsk Iron and Steel Plant.

Who would be able to describe the sight of it? There is no vantage point and no camera lens that would encompass the panorama that we know otherwise only from the sight of the forces of nature at work. Viewed from the air, it seems to be a pink, artfully created gigantic plaything, hurled down by titans or left lying around by them. Looked at closer, from, say, the surrounding hilltops, it is a grandiose silhouette of chimneys and blast furnaces, blackened by fire and rust. And from the ground, it is a landscape of iron and steel, smoke and gas so vast that it seems pointless to try to ride around it by tram, let alone explore it on foot. Unlike when I first made this journey, there is now a pioneering study of the founding and development of the city—Stephen Kotkin's *Magnetic Mountain*.[1]

The conglomerate has an area of around twenty by ten kilometres. The Magnitogorsk combine is roughly the size of a region from Manchester to Sheffield, compressed into a single point, a Pittsburgh beyond the Urals. As Stephen Kotkin observed at the end of the 1980s, the Magnitogorsk engineering complex was far more than just a 'steel factory'. It consisted of dozens of plants, ten mighty blast furnaces, thirty-four open hearth furnaces, rolling mills and finishing mills that produced more steel annually than Canada or Czechoslovakia and almost as much as the whole of Great Britain. In the old Union, more than ten thousand businesses depended on Magnitogorsk—from tank factories to the automobile industry. If the Urals were the 'industrial heart of the Union', Magnitogorsk was the capital of the steel empire. The original ore mountain has long since been exhausted and has left behind an excavation the size of a crater. What we now see resembles nothing so much as a pile-up of cathedrals made of iron and steel. One hundred and thirty factories form part of the complex, a craggy immensity with its vast heap of blast furnaces, cooling towers, coking plant, foundries, power stations and heating plant, rolling mills and workshops; at the same time, it is one huge enterprise secretly governed by the logic of the work process. Obsolete though its technology may be today, this does not detract from the strict regularity and powerful precision with which the pipes and tubes have all been joined, tracks laid and chimneys erected. We often realise what human labour and engineering genius are capable of only when we gaze on the ruins of their work. Even the orgy of smoke and rust that filters down over the city day by day and night by night obeys a mysterious rhythm. The sixty thousand people whose labour and life's blood have been consumed by this Moloch, day by day, year by year and generation by generation, must surely be somewhere.

The onset of the Industrial Age in North America, as depicted by Leo Marx in *The Machine in the Garden*, seems quite innocuous when set beside this megamachine in the steppes—as innocuous as the nineteenth century in comparison with the twentieth, which understood the potential of total mobilisation only too well. It is this process that was launched in Magnitogorsk in 1929, the year of the 'great breakthrough' and of Stalin's 'revolution from above'.

The Magnitka Myth

The pictures and posters of the first Five-Year Plan always show the first two blast furnaces to have been built. We can see from this that there was more at stake than the construction of a modern steelworks in an inhospitable location. They were the symbols of radical novelty, of complete otherness. There could be no Constructivist image montage without DniproHES and Magnitka. The magazine *USSR in Construction* used modern design and the example of Magnitogorsk to illustrate what Stalin meant when he spoke of the union of 'Bolshevist spirit and American technology'.[2] Leading architects such as Ivan Leonidov, and Ernst May of Frankfurt, worked on the designs for Sotsgorod, the city of the future.[3] Magnitostroy or Magnitka, as the giant construction site that was set to become a city was called, became the symbol of modern Soviet Russia and its foundation contains all the elements of a modern myth. 'Working as if on Magnitostroy' meant total commitment, dedication and discipline. Magnitka became the byword for the idea that nothing was impossible if only the workers could master machines and technology. The Moscow Metro—another megaproject of the 1930s—was known as 'Magnitka underground'. In Magnitka, a backward Russia prevailed over itself. Tractors prevailed over the wooden plough and modern industry prevailed over peasant land, the town prevailed over the village and the twentieth century prevailed over the 'dark Middle Ages'. Magnitka was the incarnation of *per aspera ad astra*, a motto that can still be read today on the entrance to the works laboratory. In Magnitka, communist youth showed that they could refute the pessimistic calculations of the old 'bourgeois specialists' any day, while the Party proved that it could literally move mountains. The year of the birth of Magnitogorsk, 1929, was also the year of the Great Depression. Beyond the Urals, skilled workers were in demand, whereas in the capitalist world workers and engineers had been thrown into the streets. In New Deal America, films and books about projects like Magnitogorsk were all the rage. Without Magnitka it would not have been possible to produce the literature of the 'heroic age' with its population of 'new human beings with their unprecedented readiness to make sacrifices'. This was where the 'steel was tempered', from which the forthcoming generations would be forged. Other time scales and standards operated here. At a time when the USSR was shaken by crises and civil-war-like conditions—though it was not alone in this respect—Magnitka was a cornerstone of the future. The building site was a magnet for thousands of volunteers from the entire Union and even abroad. One such volunteer was John Scott from Wisconsin, to whom we owe the best report about the foundation period of Magnitogorsk.[4] Magnitogorsk was inconceivable without the supply of human beings from the Gulag empire. The imagination of an entire generation circled round Magnitogorsk, which preoccupied such different minds as Vladimir Mayakovsky and Ernst Jünger, who discerned there the emergence of the 'figure of the Worker', a new humanity and extraordinary developments.[5]

One who took all this seriously and went to Magnitogorsk in 1931 was Erich Honecker, a young German communist who later became the leader of the German Democratic Republic. That was also when the Dutch filmmaker Joris Ivens went to make his film about the young Komsomol members on the building sites.

Magnitogorsk remained a model long after its foundation. Miniature copies sprang up everywhere in occupied Eastern Europe: in Eisenhüttenstadt (originally Stalinstadt), Sztálinváros and Nowa Huta—with similar consequences for the present day.[6] The iconic figure of the worker, that herculean embodiment of a proletarian Siegfried, started out from Magnitogorsk on his journey round the world, although it was of course by mere chance that a worker from Magnitogorsk became the model for the figure of the soldier in the Soviet war memorial in Treptower Park in Berlin.

Not everything in this myth is a straight-out lie or revolutionary kitsch nor is it true that sweat, blood and tears are absent from the images of the youthful heroes. Stalin's party never concealed the nature of those condemned to forced labour in Magnitka—the kulaks, prostitutes and priests—but instead displayed them in film chronicles that were shown to the entire nation—as examples of 'turning people into new human beings through reeducation'. The enigma consists in what emerges to the public gaze—that indissoluble amalgam of enthusiasm and terror, of construction and destruction at the very heart of Magnitka.

Work as the Front, Magnitka as Battlefield

When the first settlers arrived in the Urals in 1929, they found basically nothing there. Up to the decision of the Council of People's Commissars on 17 January 1929, there is little more than a prehistory: the legends of the Mongol Batu Khan, whose horses' hooves are supposed to have stuck to the magnet mountain; and then information from the memoirs of the thirteenth-century Franciscan monk Giovanni da Pian del Carpine about the unusual behaviour of the compass needle in this vicinity. The peasant rebel Yemelian Pugachev set up his camp in the Cossack station on Mount Magnitnaya, something even referred to by Pushkin. Ever since the eighteenth century, scientists from everywhere in Europe have swarmed around the mountain on the Ural meridian. Alexander von Humboldt discovered unknown minerals there on his journey in 1829. Even so, during the nineteenth century, only one Belgian-German firm, Bogau and Co., arrived in nearby Beloretsk to exploit the fabled resources, while at the start of the twentieth century there was talk of selling the mountain to a Japanese consortium.[7]

It was the Soviet government that first suggested opening up the supposed mineral resources of the remote Magnitnaya mountain and that decided to make this a central plank of the GOELRO national development programme. If coal could be brought from the Kuznetsk Basin or Karaganda, 270 million tonnes of high-grade iron ore could be extracted. Even so, it was still a decade before action was taken. The risks, uncertainties and challenges were too great. The decision was finally taken at a time of crisis: the regime hoped to free itself by agreeing to the Five-Year Plan, which aimed at collectivisation and industrialisation at any price, even at the risk of restarting the Civil War. The construction site at the magnet mountain was one of the battlefields on which peasant Russia would be destroyed and forged anew. In this battle, there were commanders and field marshals on the 'labour front'; the general staff of the 'battle for steel' was located in the people's commissariat of Sergo Ordzhonikidze, shock brigades and the war against 'spies and parasites'. Even the steppes had to be 'beaten down'. The whole country became the backdrop to this 'front' on which 'heroes were born' and 'enemies were smashed'. News bulletins from the 'economic front' were like those of war reporters.

After 17 January 1929, developments came thick and fast. There was no rail link, but as early as 30 June 1929 the first locomotive passed over the 150-kilometre single track section from Kartaly to Magnitogorsk. The technology for 'the most modern steelworks in the world' that was not to be found in its own country was supplied under contract by the US company McKee of Cleveland for 2.5 million gold rubles. And for the US and German engineers who were unable to dispense with central heating, running water and the *Saturday Evening Post*, a little America was created in Beryozka consisting of 150 cottages that can still be marvelled at to this day. On 10 March 1929, the

FIGURE 7.1. Magnitogorsk, built in 1929, at the time Europe's largest iron and steel works, an icon of the first Five-Year Plan and of Soviet industrialisation. In the background, the pre-fabricated concrete blocks of flats of the 1970s–1990s. © akg-images/Sputnik.

first 256 people arrived; by summer 1931 there were already 40,000. In 1939, the last year before war broke out, the town had almost 150,000 inhabitants.

Even before people began to think about housing, excavations for the first blast furnaces started up. With winter outdoor temperatures of –30°, the combined male and female workforce lived in tents, caves and, later, huts—often with up to eight hundred people squeezed into confined spaces. There was no water for the works buildings to be erected, so a weir was built in six months to dam up the Ural River. There were no brickworks, no workshops—they had to be built from scratch. Labour was often begun before the plans were ready. What that all looked like could be seen by summer 1992 in the Museum of the Metallurgical Complex on Victory Square. There, in addition to a diorama of the first excavation pit, the relics of the heroic era are preserved: shovels, buckets, wheelbarrows, measuring instruments and the engineers' fountain pens, everyday objects such as wooden cupboards, earthenware crockery, loudspeakers, gramophones with the record of a foxtrot on the turntable, as well as decorations and documents honouring the top workers. Vyacheslav Polonsky's book *Magnitostroy* of 1932 is on display. Pieces of the first cast iron to be produced are on view, as well as the plaque commemorating the first production of molten steel on 3 July 1933: 'Yesterday, at 7hrs 45, the first Magnitogorsk molten steel'. There was initially no workforce, so one had to be procured. This was done by advertising in the factories in Leningrad, Sverdlovsk and Mariupol. Magnitostroy was a project for the young: half of those working there in 1931 were under twenty-four. Others were conscripted by force from the ranks of 'de-kulakised' peasants and Gulag prisoners. A good third of the workforce was under the supervision of the GPU.

In the shortest possible time, millions of cubic metres of earth were moved, cement was poured, bricks and steel were put in place. The necessary know-how was supplied by contracts with the US company McKee and the German Demag. The original plan envisaged the production of 650,000 tonnes but this was subsequently quadrupled. There were delays in fulfilling the plan but even so, the first coking plant was commissioned by the end of 1931, the first cast iron was produced in February 1932 and the first steel in 1933. A little later, the production cycle was complete; in 1935 Magnitogorsk supplied one-quarter of total Soviet steel production—as much as Czechoslovakia, Italy and Poland combined. The empire of the People's Commissariat for Heavy Industry did not grow over generations, like those of Carnegie or Krupp, but grew within the bounds of the first Five-Year Plan. There were no specialists, so people had to be trained. The construction site became a school and the decade became the decade of engineers. In 1932 the State Technical University was opened, followed by the Pedagogical Institute and night schools. There were no bricklayers so beginners learned from workers who became 'instructors'. The advice of 'experienced specialists' was ignored and so a high price was paid in the shape of accidents and a high reject rate—but workers did learn from their mistakes. There was no forum for the forty or so nationalities working on the site, so a cinema was built in the style of a Doric temple and a newspaper was established, which exists to this day. There were no traditions in a place like this, which had started from scratch, but in 1937, the year of the Great Terror, this city of the future celebrated the centenary of Pushkin's death and erected Merkulov's Pushkin statue. There was no culture, but a culture and recreation park was created, with plaster-cast statues, a chess club and parachute towers. The first settlers had lived in mud huts and tents but shortly before the outbreak of war the tent city became a fortified town. And two years later, Magnitogorsk—which, unlike Krivoy Rog, Mariupol and the whole of the Donbass, was beyond the reach of German forces—produced the steel for every second tank made in the Soviet Union.

The construction site is a place from which we can see a major turning point: teams of horses and shovels alongside American Caterpillars, concrete being mixed by hand alongside automated steelworks and rolling mills, the most modern equipment rotting away because people didn't know how to use it. No one has counted how many fell from the scaffolding, froze to death during excavations, or were killed by collapsing buildings or in explosions. Whatever damage the Party and management wreaked with the murderous work rate, incompetence or sheer stupidity was blamed on 'wreckers'. In the purges of the 1930s, Magnitostroy devoured its 'heroes of labour' and its officers, while peasants' sons were promoted to the rank of 'Red directors' and catapulted into positions of authority. Magnitogorsk became a place of death for many but a place of survival for even more, a place where you could escape your origins through hard work and have an unprecedented career.[8]

The 'New Human Being'

The new human being was the product not of any faith in a utopia, but of a tumult in which existing lifeworlds were destroyed and new ones born. The 'Homo Sovieticus' was no fiction to be casually mocked but a reality with whom we usually only start to engage in earnest when we realise that analysing the decisions of the Central Committee is less crucial than commonly assumed. What happened in Magnitogorsk during the 1930s was replicated throughout the Soviet Union. Between 1936 and 1939 the urban population of the USSR grew from

26.3 million to 55.9 million people. Never before in modern history had there been social development on this scale. The urbanisation of a nation that was simultaneously a ruralisation of the town centres took place not over two centuries but in one or two decades. And there can be no history of the Stalinist era as long as the scenery of this secular tumult is inspired solely by the records of the Party, the secret police and the documents fabricated by them.[9]

Peasant Russia came to its end at a time when urban Russia had not yet been born. In reality we are talking about towns that were no more than factory settlements and about town dwellers who had been village dwellers the previous day. The new town was born out of the factory of which it was no more than an appendage. It was the product of a targeted population policy and internal colonisation. Its basic form of housing was the barracks, a provisional type of building built for the duration. The town combined features of a lifeworld that had not been fully eliminated with features that had not properly developed; it was neither peasant-like nor proletarian, while something resembling a 'style' could be found only in the atrium of the powerful in Stalinist high society.

Peasants who escaped from the rhythm of the seasons and acclimatised to the regular pulse beat of the megamachine ceased to be the countrypeople they once were. Time dissolved; it divided into worktime and free time, calendar time. They began to submit to the discipline of the clock. The young woman who made a career as a shock worker was no longer the bride who could be married off to the man who made the best offer. Galiullin Khabibulla, the illiterate Tatar woman who learned how to build a blast furnace, was just as much a 'new human being' as Viktor Kalmykov, the peasant's son who rose to the post of 'Red director' at the age of thirty.[10] Magnitogorsk was a human workshop with forty different nationalities and what developed there was in fact a new Soviet human being who regarded assimilation into the new social fabric as more important than preserving national characteristics. Young people did indeed lose their old faith, but were more than happy to exchange their beliefs for the experience of a visit to the cinema once a month—especially if they could see Charlie Chaplin in *City Lights*. Work continued into the night by floodlight and even so the evening trams were filled with students of both sexes studying at the workers' faculty or the technical college where they learned something about Hegel and took the engineering exams. There were few newspapers and none beyond the control of the Party but people who learned to read and write were capable of having their say, even if they were condemned to keeping their mouths shut for the time being. Margaret Bourke-White, who greatly admired Russia as the country of the 'Day after Tomorrow', noted during her visit to Magnitogorsk, 'Great prestige was attached to literacy. In the Ural Mountains, where the Magneto-Gorsk steel mills were under construction, I saw night classes in reading and writing held in the nearby villages. The pupils were middle-aged peasants; the teachers, high-school girls.'[11] We can smile at the harmless pleasures and the attempts at 'cultured behaviour' organised by clubs or palaces of culture, but that does not detract from the basic desire of these young people to absorb everything that smoothed their path into the world. The peasants who had been driven from the land had to give up their own skills and ways of speaking, but they were also fascinated by the luxury goods of this new world—the bicycles, sewing machines and gramophones. All of these are on display in the Local History Museum. The new human being was the skilled worker who became the Red director in the steel empire or the working-class woman who wore lace dresses and danced the foxtrot, things previously reserved to the old elites.

In Magnitogorsk, that workshop for manufacturing human beings, the ways of living in which more than one generation would grow up, kept expanding. There was a private sphere, which found itself constantly under surveillance by fellow inhabitants of barracks and apartment blocks. The simplest purchases turned into a chain of endless complications consisting of ration cards, queues and wangling, and you were only safe if you could look after yourself. This explains why workers planted their own potatoes on the edge of the construction site and if they were especially well-off, they grazed their cow there too. It also explains why even at the high point of the Stalinist Terror, the city could not survive without the bazaar or the slummiest of settlements that were to be found on every large construction site from Magnitogorsk to Vorkuta and inevitably nicknamed Shanghai. You gave the state everything, but not so much that you found yourself at its mercy—that was the beginning of a lifesaving hypocrisy.

Life circled round the factory, which had overall responsibility for every amenity in a growing town—supplies, clubs, sports facilities, polyclinics, schools—but in the first instance you counted on yourself and people like you.

In Magnitogorsk, which was more of a chaotic town than a transparent, planned one, fresh and even brutal energies collided with one another. They were set free when the bonds and values of a traditional culture were destroyed by the mobilising force of a ruthless modernity. It is scarcely possible to conceive of greater tensions than here, where the struggle for survival was everything. And it was this desperate struggle that fed the dream of a utopian world.[12] Precisely because there was no experienced, independent labour organisation, military discipline and collective fear stepped in to fill the gap. The redemptive power of technology can get a grip only where the handcart and the shovel constitute the basic available equipment. 'Never did a country fall beneath the spell of another country technically or materially as much as Russia has fallen under the spell of the United States today', observed Theodore Dreiser in 1927. People admire America the more, the less they possess its qualities—the skills of its immigrants, its pragmatism, its pleasure in taking responsibility. This explains why the Futurist myth of the machine flourished to excess in backward, agricultural Russia. And nowhere was the dictatorship of the clock the subject of such rhapsodic poetry as in the country of the universal *nichego* [nothing]. The impotence of the masses was the inevitable concomitant of the omnipotence of the Party, and the fetishisation of the Plan only confirms that the forces of chaos were far stronger than those of spontaneous coordinated action. Considered from this angle, the socialist doctrine of the period is not the handy key with which to explain an endlessly chaotic reality, but merely an aspect of that reality, which itself stands in need of explanation.

'Gorod Budet'—'A City Arises'

Once a start had been made, everything generated its own dynamic. What started out as a construction site soon turned into a factory settlement. And when the time was ripe, the factory settlement developed into a town, one that had ceased to be a mere appendage of

the megamachine. 'Gorod budet'—'A city arises', Mayakovsky wrote
in a poem. In the process, generations came and went. The city did
indeed arise from a plan, but it went its own way, following the path
of its own growth.

No one who travelled through the city of Magnitogorsk in the early
1990s found anything very exciting—only what was already known
from other new towns in the socialist world: a monotony intensified
to the point of infinity; running parallel to the Ural River, a series of
avenues seemingly without vanishing point; the absence of any kind
of individual façade or intimate square. Measured against towns
that have had two thousand years to develop features of their own,
Magnitogorsk is monotony itself. But measured against the fact that
as late as the end of the 1920s there was nothing here but a collection
of shacks in the shadow of a blast furnace, the result is staggering.
What appears to the outsider's gaze as the embodiment of a nontown
is in truth the birthplace of late Soviet urban culture. The privacy
that could not exist in the barracks world grew between four walls,
even if those walls were shaped by 'monotonous', prefabricated concrete panels.

The different historical strata of the town are easily identified.
Each has its centre and specific physiognomy. What we can see is that
Magnitogorsk quickly departed from the original plan and moved its
centre from close to the combine on the left bank of the river to the
right bank. It could be said to have fled from the heap of rust and
smoke and pushed the reservoir between itself and the combine to
make a barrier. The history of Magnitogorsk found expression in the
buildings of the Constructivists and the Bauhaus people on Ulitsa
Kirova and Ulitsa Mayakovskogo, where around ten three-storey
houses painted green, yellow and red and with large windows can
be seen. The 1930s are represented by the municipal theatre and the
monumental front of the Institute of Mining and Metallurgy, the Mag-
nit Cinema, the State Bank and the spacious squares, especially the
view of the iron and steel works and the monumental frontage of the
Institute. The most impressive features, however, are the districts
shaped initially by Khrushchev's mass-housing programme and after
that by the new quarters built in the large-panel, prefabricated style
and stretching out to the horizon. In numerous places, the barracks

and individual houses surrounded by little gardens have survived and become the starting point for private dwellings. With the combine's administration, the central laboratories, the fire service, Hotel 'Asia', the State Bank, the old NKVD headquarters, the cinema, as well as the culture and recreation park, Komsomol Square was the main entrance to the works. It was also the central assembly point and the parade square facing the blast furnaces and chimneys. The earlier statue of Stalin has been replaced by one of Lenin. The second centre, the actual 'socialist city'—with its palace of culture, polyclinic, schools, municipal theatre and housing estates—was designed by Ernst May of Frankfurt. Although sometimes mocked as 'matchboxes', parts of the estates built by him in 1932 on Mayakovsky Street bring a breath of the garden city, as well as echoes of Bruno Taut's Uncle Tom's Cabin in Berlin-Zehlendorf, into faraway Magnitogorsk.[13] The district of Beryozka is similar. There one can see the cottages built for American engineers that had long since been transformed into communal apartments. After the war, building moved to the other riverbank, where a tent-shaped monument reminds us of the first arrivals in the steppes. The signature of the Leningrad architects is easily recognised: they built the impressive view of the iron and steel works with the monumental Institute of Mining and Metallurgy: they added squares and avenues à la St. Petersburg and built chessboard-like quarters, each grouped around a park, a school, a hospital or a department store. The façades are ornamented, the apartments fitted with parquet flooring and glass doors: big-city luxuries for the worker aristocracy. You can even find a piece of German Romantic architecture here: German POWs added a street in the style of their native land. In the distance you can see the domes of a church—in a town that envisaged no church in its original plan.

Now that the the city is all built, it has entered a new phase. If you had happened to gaze on it in the summer of 1993, at a moment when the wind was favourable, it might have seemed as though all was well with both the city and the combine. Hardly anything would have pointed to the momentous developments once again confronting Magnitogorsk. However, the dissolution of the Soviet Empire posed an imminent threat to the capital of the steel empire, which is what Magnitogorsk was. The city, entirely dependent upon the iron and steel works, was forced to set out on a new path, as was the combine itself. To put it even more forcefully, the city can only survive if it sets its face against the industrial megamachine that has now become an existential threat. There have been many days when the city has been shrouded in clouds of red and sulphurous yellow soot. In winter, black snowflakes have fallen. Year after year, 870 million tonnes of rust fell on the surrounding area because the filtration unit was too unsophisticated, faulty or switched off at night to cut costs. Every hectare of the city area received seven tonnes of poisonous fall-out annually. Coal dust, phenol and sulphur poisoned the air, the water and the earth itself.[14] The old questions—Who can do what to whom? What comes first: metals or people?—gained a new urgency in the cities of the Ural region, one that even the most radical thinkers of the early Soviet period couldn't have imagined. Closing down these operations may be the only solution, if the finances to modernise them are not available. It may very well be the case that the residents will simply have to make a new start elsewhere because life there has become impossible. Magnitogorsk may well become the 'mausoleum of Soviet industrial civilization', to quote Stephen Kotkin.

Liberation from the megamachine and the power apparatus that kept it going has become a question of survival. Magnitogorsk's response has been that of a city whose energies have been shaped and simultaneously wrecked by the rhythms of 'shock work'. The civilising mills of labour grind slowly. Hardly any of the generation of 'heroes of labour' are still alive today. The heroic age is now the stuff of legend—whether of an idealising nostalgia or of bitter memories. But no one there today has to be taught how to read and write. Even so, the soldiers at the labour front have turned into the civilians of an everyday existence that calls for just as much courage and risk tolerance as their predecessors showed. In 1991 over one hundred thousand citizens of the town gathered to celebrate Russia's independence. Magnitogorsk has left the period of Sturm und Drang behind and reached adulthood. It has outgrown the utopia it needed for its survival and can now be allowed to rest in peace.

This must be why the city, which voted for Yeltsin in the referendum, failed utterly to confirm the horrific visions of the Moscow intelligentsia with its profound ignorance of life in the provinces. Admittedly, drunks could be seen staggering around on the streets in the evenings. There was a stabbing incident in a hotel room near my own and on occasion shots could be heard. But the true sensations in summer 1993 were very different. In the city all was peaceful—perhaps because the real crisis in the once-powerful and wealthy iron and steel works had not yet begun. The streets and avenues were immaculate. Young people went for an evening stroll in the parks as they had always done. The goods in the shops were plentiful and bazaars opened up at many points in the city. Magnitogorsk was reconnected to international trade once again and the corner kiosks gave customers the choice between Berlin Schultheiss beer and fruit juices from the Weser region. More than a few Western cars drove down the avenues, having travelled in convoy down the long roads from the used-car markets in Tallinn or locations around Berlin. At the airport you might bump into American guitar players or a manager from the Ruhr. Encountering foreigners had ceased to be anything special. Magnitogorsk had renewed contact with America and took part in a symposium on the experience of reviving the fortunes of a steel town such as Pittsburgh. In the Museum of the Metallurgical Complex you could now see, in addition to the photographs of the heroes of labour, the pictures of the victims of the Great Terror. The neoclassical Gorky cinema was showing *Blondes Like It Hot*. At the station, the Russian edition of *Penthouse* was a greater attraction than the first steam engine ever to have entered Magnitogorsk. The shops on the ostentatious Avenue of the Metallurgists still had the old signboards—Fishmonger, Grocer and Hairdresser. But in reality they too had already passed into new hands. The shop windows were full of the rivalries between Reebok and Adidas or Sony and Grundig. Opposite the Municipal Soviet, the firm A. V. Gorenko Enterprise had rented space and another company sold furniture imported from Slovakia. In front of the factory gates, you could see the Saab limousines of the works' directors who had been promoted to chairmen of the supervisory boards of the thirty joint-stock companies that succeeded the old industrial complex.

At long last, Magnitogorsk has started to work for itself and not just for iron and steel. Whether the numerous activities that have mushroomed will suffice to lead the city out of the Iron Age is as yet unknown. The calmness of the citizenry at a time when everything has changed suggests a positive outcome. At the same time, people are preparing for a worst-case scenario by harvesting tomatoes and potatoes on their allotments outside the city and are already tilling the fields for the following year.

CHAPTER 8

Black and White:
The Photographer's Eye

The central concern of Alexander Rodchenko, the pioneer and master of Soviet photography and photomontage, was to learn how to see the world anew. The way he went about this brought him considerable acclaim. To track down the effect of his pictures we need only follow the gaze of the photographer, who gave his own account of his working methods. Looking back, he provided this description: 'In his hands, the black Leica of nickel and glass began to work with a lover's passion. He would show this world—the familiar and ordinary world—from new points of view. He would show the building of Socialism and its people more intensively and exaltedly. He would propagandize with photography. For everything new, young and original.'[1] It is evident that his aim was not simply photographing and documenting the external world but acquiring a new mode of perception, a new way of seeing.

'In order to teach man to see from new viewpoints, it is necessary to photograph ordinary, well-known objects from completely unexpected viewpoints and in unexpected positions; and photograph new objects from various viewpoints, thereby giving a full impression of the object.'[2] The photographer must as it were 'estrange' the object to which we have become accustomed and ceased to 'notice', so we can perceive it as something new and fresh. 'It's possible that we often look at things like this, but don't see them. We don't see what we're looking at. We don't see marvellous perspectives—foreshortening and the positioning of objects. We, who have been taught to see what we have grown up with, must discover the world of the visible. We must revolutionize our visual thinking.'[3]

Thus the issue for Rodchenko was not the creation of photographic paintings, constructed scenes, panel-painting photography. It was not just a matter of different subjects—the worker instead of the bourgeois.

In other words, it was a matter not of a different 'what' but a different 'how'. 'The destruction of the old photography. The struggle for a photographic language to illustrate Soviet themes, the search for camera angles, agitation for discovery of the world by means of photography, for facts, for reportage.' That was the programme. 'The revolution in photography was that the photographed fact—thanks to its quality, i.e., "how it's shot"—acted so strongly and unexpectedly with all the value specific to photography; that it was possible not only to compete with paintings but to show everyone a new, perfected way of discovering the world in science, technology, and the everyday life of contemporary humanity. LEF as the avant-garde of Communist culture is obliged to show how and what needs to be photographed. What to shoot—is something every photo group knows, but how to shoot—only a few know.'[4] To achieve this, we must set out on new paths. 'We must experiment. To simply photograph facts, just as simply to describe them, is nothing new'. We need a new aesthetic 'for the photographic expression of our new social facts'.[5] For camera work, for the production of a new pictorial language appropriate to the matter in hand, you need point of view, perspective and lighting. An essential part of this, according to Rodchenko, is a change of perspective: 'The artist rises up above the crowd. . . . His field of vision always lies above that of the crowd. So as to give a good view of their spatial positioning.'[6] The photographer must adopt a specific stance on this if he wishes to see: 'We must tear down the veil that is called "navel level" from our eyes' means . . . photograph from all viewpoints, except the "navel" until all viewpoints are recognized.'[7] He didn't lay down rules for his colleagues and comrades, but he did make suggestions. 'And the most interesting modern shots are those "from the top down," the "bottom up" and their diagonals.'[8] The camera should not simply document an object. 'For us, a photo of a reconstructed factory is not just the photo of a building. The new factory in the photo is not a simple fact but a fact that is the pride and joy of the industrialization of the Land of Soviets, and we have to figure out "how to photograph" this.'[9]

Rodchenko's instructions together with his illustrations show how he himself learned to 'see things anew'. To be specific, he did this in the context of a new megaproject of the first Five-Year Plan, the construction of the White Sea–Baltic Canal, also known as the White Sea

Canal or the Belomor Canal, which was built between 1929 and 1932 by more than two hundred thousand prisoners of the OGPU, the later NKVD. Rodchenko visited the Canal Zone three times between 1930 and 1933 and took around two thousand photos, a selection of which was used to illustrate the collective work on the canal by a group of prominent Soviet writers.[10] This volume, subsequently withdrawn from circulation because important participants and representatives of the project had fallen out of favour and into the hands of the executioners, tells the story of the canal from projects going back to the time of Peter the Great up to the opening in 1932, but concentrates above all on the so-called process of 'reforging' (*perekovka*) the inmates, which meant transforming them into 'honourable and deserving Soviet citizens' through forced labour. The principle of not taking photographs 'at navel height' but from above or below is carried through in exemplary fashion. There are views from above of landscapes of rocks and water, logging, lock chambers and lock gates. We see the clearings stripped of timber, the path already surfaced, the tracks for a railway trolley, and the filigree constructions for the lock chambers built of tree trunks and the smooth concrete walls— in short, the visual transformation of what had originally been wild nature into geometrical and linear forms. Observers find themselves gazing at the image of nature changed into a humanmade landscape, the marvel of human labour in a hostile environment. Humans do not exist there as simple creatures, but as objects in the process of being 'reforged'. They count only to the extent that they undergo a dynamic development. Rodchenko had no interest in the simple reproduction of a wooden crane with which to remove blocks of stone; he was not interested in the 'crane in itself' but only in the crane as a tool for transforming the landscape. Humans do not appear in a state of being, something that 'is', but as the representatives of a self-shaping, a self-creation. The rocky Karelian landscape forms the backdrop to the concreted-over canal bed; where previously there had been only a modest railway station, an imposing administrative building was now built in Medvezhyegorsk, the capital of the Canal Zone.

Natural landscape is replaced by perspectival formations, diagonals, the contrast of light and shade, of black and white; everything is straightened out and made geometrical. The monumental rocky

FIGURE 8.1. The photographer Alexander Rodchenko at work at the White Sea Canal 1933. Photo by Anatoly Skurikhin. © Rodchenko & Stepanova. Photo: culture-images/fai.

Karelian landscape is contrasted with the monumental construction of the lock chambers; the waterfall with the artificial embankment; the deported peasants, clad only in rags, with visitors to the camp theatre who owed their presence there to the literacy and education programmes. The bearded peasant has been transformed into a clean-shaven young workman in a white shirt. Taken together, these images teach a lesson and show the way forward.

The mere copying of a fact—of primitive wheelbarrows, the throng of thousands of prisoners on the building site, the visits of the *nachalniks*, bosses, casually posing for a group photograph—none of that satisfied an art photographer like Rodchenko. Those things were 'only' documents, 'only' reportage. He preferred to take a picture of a brass band, viewed diagonally from above, while below men were hard at work on the floor of the lock chamber. 'This picture was intentionally taken like this in order to show that the members of the band are also workers, that this is not a solemn performance but an ordinary work environment.'[11] This fit entirely with his longstanding credo: 'The artist rises up above the crowd. . . . His field of vision always lies above that of the crowd. So as to give a good view of their spatial positioning.'[12] The Rodchenko of a minimalist, laconic, matter-of-fact photography of the late 1920s turned into a storyteller in the camp situation of the White Sea Canal; not content to rely just on pictures, he instead constructed, in Leah Dickerman's words, 'a sense of over-arching narrative [that] replaced his earlier aggregate structures, which had allowed the reader to negotiate between component parts and potentially multiple meanings.' The upshot was a kind of coercive narrative created by an artist who was doing violence to himself in order to 'reforge' his own nature. He thought of the building of the White Sea Canal as a 'passage to a new life', a way of taking leave of the past and redeeming himself through his work as a photographer. His work for the White Sea Canal project represents a break in Rodchenko's oeuvre. 'In celebrating the canal, Rodchenko lent his artistic authority to one of the most coercive and irrational projects in the Stalinist period, one that, for those willing to see, exposed the Communist dream of unalienated labor as myth.'[13]

Other picture sources can be found today in the photo archive established on the orders of the NKVD—for the information of the Moscow centre—and now located in the Karelian National Museum in Petrozavodsk. These sources come from Viktor Karlovich Bulla (1883–1938), son of Karl Bulla (1855–1929), the owner of an important photographic studio in St. Petersburg and himself a professional photographer. Viktor Bulla, who was shot in 1938 during the Great Terror, had been charged by the NKVD with documenting the progress of work on the canal. His photos were not 'art' but served to inform project managers in Moscow and Leningrad. From Rodchenko's point of view, they achieved 'only what any group of amateurs can achieve, namely, they can copy something.' The truth is that they are even better suited to producing a picture of the Canal Zone that is not subject to the imperatives of ideological mobilisation.[14]

Despite initial scruples which had less to do with the White Sea Canal than with his own state of mind, Rodchenko wholeheartedly identified with the Gulag project as a great project of reeducation and modernisation. In his critical and self-critical memoir 'Reconstructing the Artist' of May/June 1936, he noted: 'I went to the White Sea Canal in a very bad mood. In *Sovetskoe foto* it had become fashionable to abuse me in every Issue . . . this abuse stuck to me. It became creatively unbearable for me to work in Moscow.'[15]

The invitation to the construction project, which he could in fact have turned down, proved to be his 'salvation', 'a ticket for life. From that point on the goal became clear. I wasn't afraid of the criticism, all the persecution dimmed.' What he saw on the construction site filled him with new courage:

> A gigantic will gathered here, on the canal, the dregs of the past. And this will was able to raise such enthusiasm in people, the likes of which I hadn't seen in Moscow. People were on fire, they sacrificed themselves, heroically overcoming all the difficulties. People whose life, it seemed, was over, showed that it began anew, full of extraordinary interest and struggle. They took gigantic cliffs and quicksand by storm. This was a war of man with untamed nature. Man came and conquered, conquered and reconstructed himself. He arrived downcast, penalized, and angry, and left with his head held proudly high, a medal on his chest, and a ticket to life. And life opened to him in all the beauty of genuinely heroic creative labour.
>
> I was bewildered, amazed. I was caught up in this enthusiasm. It was all familiar to me, everything fell into place. I forgot all about my creative disappointments. I took photographs simply, not thinking about formalism. I was staggered by the sensitivity and wisdom with which the re-education of people was conducted. There they knew how to find an individual approach to each person. At that time we didn't have this sort of sensitive attitude to the creative worker. Things went this way with us; reject formalism and go work as best you can. There, on the canal, that's not the way they worked. They didn't sit a bandit down to work at an accountant's desk or put a thief to work on payroll, they didn't make a prostitute into a laundress. The bandit worked in demolition or as a driver, a member of a shock team or emergency brigade. The thief or embezzler was made director of a club or cafeteria, or a purchasing agent. And the prisoners worked miracles.

After spending a month on the canal I left for Moscow, developed the material I had shot, and . . . began to miss the construction group. I couldn't help thinking about it. How was life going on there? I felt that it was too calm here and that everyone was too self-involved. I left for the White Sea Canal again. I went a third time, as well, before the construction was finished.[16]

Rodchenko's material appeared in all the great Soviet newspapers and magazines—*Pravda, Izvestia, Komsomolskaya pravda, Prozhektor, Ogonyok, Smena.* He edited an entire issue of *SSSR na stroike/USSR in Construction* (12/1933) and *Nashi dostizheniya* (Our achievements). He delivered the greater part of the illustrations for the writers' collective work. He was represented and as it were rehabilitated vis-à-vis his former critics from *October* in the *Masters of Soviet Photo Art* exhibition in 1935. In a letter to his wife, Varvara Stepanova, he wrote, 'I'm photographing, even though it's freezing. The sun is wonderful. It's interesting here, more than in the Caucasus. The air is wonderful. One should come in the spring.' And 'This is where we should go on vacation—in winter. What snow, light and mountains!'[17] This was written from the Canal Zone, a place of terrible privations for thousands upon thousands of slave workers. As Leah Dickerman summed it up: 'For Rodchenko, the canal photo-story seems to stand as an allegory for his own punishment and transformation. The terrible irony is that the coercive nature of the White Sea Canal project did not hinder Rodchenko's work—it became his main inspiration.'[18] Read in this way, his photos speak also of the violence he did to himself and for which he paid a high price: it became a process of what Walter Benjamin termed 'the aestheticizing of violence'.

CHAPTER 9

Excursion to the White Sea Canal

Every Soviet citizen knew about the Belomor Canal, even if they knew little or nothing of its origins. A stylised picture of the canal, which connects the Baltic with the White Sea, featured on the packet of one of the Soviet Union's strongest and most popular cigarette brands. With its blue and red lines on a white background, the picture circulated by the millions every day in the Soviet space—and still does today in post-Soviet Russia. 'The Stalin Canal between the White Sea and the Baltic Sea' was also the title of a book of 1934, which Soviet dissidents condemned as betrayal and corruption of the intelligentsia.

Even today, three-quarters of a century after its completion, anyone who has time and luck can go in search of traces of the canal. You have to board a ship in St. Petersburg at one of the landing stages on the Neva and it will take you via Lake Ladoga and Lake Onega to the Belomor Canal; from there you travel on to the Solovetsky Islands in the White Sea. If you wish to be spared the journey on this notorious canal, you can also go by train. The old Murmansk line travels within sight of the canal route for long stretches so that during the White Nights you gain a vivid impression of the Karelian landscape with its forests, waterways and far-flung settlements. At the time of the first Five-Year Plan (1928–1932), this was the setting for the largest slave-labour Soviet project under the direction of the OGPU. This was where two hundred thousand human beings lived and worked during the construction, which was completed early, in twenty months. Thousands succumbed to 'death by labour', dying of hunger, disease and accidents. With Belomorstroy, as the building site was known in Soviet jargon, a new chapter was opened; it was the transition from a mere concentration camp, such as had existed since the Civil War, to the Gulag system, which consisted of labour and reeducation camps and spread from here as an archipelago covering the entire Soviet Union. What that all meant has been vividly described by Alexander Solzhenitsyn.[1] Visitors who travel along that route today need some imagination to be able to picture the scene during those years. In Leningrad, as St. Petersburg was known at that time, construction offices were hard at work. Machines and tools for building the canal came from Leningrad factories; there was a lively commuter exchange of engineers, technicians, managers and Chekists between the City on the Neva and the administration centre of the Canal Zone in Medvezhyegorsk. On Nevsky Prospekt posters spread propaganda about transforming 'the dregs of society' into model workers. Nowadays not much happens along this stretch. Freight traffic and tourism have collapsed. You need a specific reason for a journey here. Visitors might include Finns on a nostalgic return to Karelia, the ancestral land from which they had fled or been expelled; pilgrims on their way to the monasteries on Lake Onega or the White Sea; even holidaymakers returning to Murmansk from vacations in the south. Perhaps also the children and grandchildren of prisoners in search of the places where their forebears toiled and died.

A museum was established in the former Stalin Hotel in Medvezhyegorsk on the seventieth anniversary of the completion of the canal. At Povenets, at the entrance to the canal from Lake Onega, a chapel commemorates the inmates of the Belbaltlag camp that supplied the labour force. And in Sandarmokh, not far from the canal, family members and delegates from every corner of the former Soviet Union come together every August to commemorate the 1,111 inmates of the Solovki camp who were executed in the forests in a 'mass operation' in 1937. These victims were Russians, Ukrainians, Uzbeks, Poles, Jews and adherents of various religious confessions. When the archives were opened during the 1990s, historians from all over the world came to Petrozavodsk, the capital of Karelia, in order to reconstruct the true history of the building of the canal.[2] Since that time, the topography of the camp has been investigated and documented with photographs.[3] If you fly over the former camp zone in a helicopter, you can still make out the remains of the inmates' shacks, the watchtowers, a cart wheel, a rusty steam-driven sawmill that has sunk into the swampy ground and iron gratings from the prisoners' huts.[4] Despite evidence that products of the modern age have appeared in such remote places as Kem and Povenets—a Mercedes in front of a brick building, mobile ringtones everywhere—you soon realise that the buildings were originally built by deportees and the victims of forced resettlements.

An Old Guide to the New Age

The best guide to the Canal Zone is still *The Stalin Canal between the White Sea and the Baltic Sea: A History of Its Construction*,[5] a deluxe commemorative volume in Russian edited by Maxim Gorky, L. L. Averbakh and S. G. Firin in the series History of Factories and Companies and published in 1934 by the state publishing house Gosizdat. This joint production by thirty-six writers appeared in an edition of thirty thousand copies to coincide with the Seventeenth Party Congress, but fell out of favour because it contained the names and photographs of people who had subsequently been condemned. It was withdrawn from circulation, and from then on, with photographs blacked out for fear of the secret police, it became a bibliographical rarity. As a sumptuous, large-format, prestige edition, with pull-out maps, graphics and photographs by important photographers, it made the perfect gift for special occasions. My own copy, bought second-hand, had been presented to Moisey Lvovich Kogan in 1962, together with a certificate for being the 'Best Worker of the Central House Committee', by Apartment Block Administration 12 of the Lenin District of the City of Moscow. The reprint of 1998 was regarded in intellectual and dissident circles as one of the key reference works to be consulted when wishing to document the moral collapse of the communist elite and left-wing intelligentsia. This is no accident since the book contains the clearest imaginable statement of the task facing the impressive roster of leading Soviet writers who conceived, wrote and published the volume as a collective work within six months. On 15 August 1933, the publishers' editorial board took the decision to commission the volume; on 12 December the manuscript was delivered; on 20 January 1934 the book appeared in print.

As a modest 'Annotation' proclaimed, the volume aimed to show the following:

The history of the construction of the Stalin White Sea Baltic Sea Canal, which was accomplished on the initiative of Comrade Stalin with the energies of former enemies of the proletariat under the leadership of the OGPU.

Shining examples of the labour and reeducation policies of Soviet power, which has reforged thousands of socially dangerous people into the conscious builders of socialism.

The heroic victory of the collectively organised energy of human beings over the elemental forces of the savage nature of the north, the realisation of a grandiose hydro construction.

The type of construction leaders—Chekists, engineers, workers— but also former counterrevolutionists, parasites, kulaks, thieves, prostitutes and speculators who have been reeducated by labour and who have obtained a work qualification and returned to a decent working life.[6]

The list of contributors included writers who were prominent at the time and Soviet authors still widely respected today. Among them were Maxim Gorky, G. Gausner, B. Lapin, S. Budantsev, M. Kosakov, G. Korabelnikov, D. Mirsky, P. Pertsov, V. Shklovsky, Vera Inber, S. Alymov, A. Berzin, Vs. Ivanov, V. Kataev, L. Nikulin, S. Khasrevin, B. Agapov, K. Selinsky, A. Erlikh, Mikhail Zoshchenko, S. Gekht, L. Averbakh, Alexey Tolstoy and Bruno Jasieński. Some of them were liquidated in the course of the purges. One example is the 'Eurasian' prince Dmitry Mirsky, who had returned to Soviet Russia from exile in England. Another was the Polish writer Bruno Jasieński. Mikhail Zoshchenko became the butt of a smear campaign. Most of the illustrations came from Alexander Rodchenko and Alexander Lemberg; the cover was designed by I. Ilyina. Master artist Alexander Deineka was involved in the design of the maps. Some of the writers had had a look at the canal route; others—like Rodchenko—had paid several visits. Most had been present at the inaugural voyage on the canal on 17 August 1933. The only member of the collective who actually came from the camp was Sergey Alymov.

Panama Canal on the Arctic Circle

The volume is a visitor's guide, but above all it is a guide to a new era. It contains maps and graphics, showing the extent to which the entire country had been on the move at the beginning of the Five-Year Plan. It describes the harsh and inaccessible Karelian landscape as well as how rock formations and mountains were moved and waterways diverted. It introduces us to the technical personnel—ageing experts trained in the Tsarist Empire but with international experience—and reveals how they changed under the pressure of the superhuman tasks they faced. The inmates are characterised by their origins, but what counts is what they became in the course of their work on the canal. What was at stake here was not first and foremost the complex history of a building project but the building project as part of a mighty debate, a debate of almost planetary dimensions. Questions of work style became questions of attitude and ideology. Discipline and self-sacrifice were always combined with questions of loyalty or betrayal. Every activity in the zone, however modest in nature, was part of a global mission. The only group that was complete in itself—perfect and no longer in need of change—was the group of Chekists. They were the axis on which everything turned; models of self-confidence and resoluteness, ruthless and dedicated to a single task. The Chekists and their social reeducation were at the very centre of the enterprise and it is an irony that it was precisely the heads of the OGPU/NKVD who had been showered with honours for their achievements—Yagoda and Firin above all—who would be dismissed and destroyed shortly after their promotion (1936, 1937)—expunged, struck out and eradicated from all copies of the book.

It is no coincidence that the volume opens with the chapter titled 'Socialist Truth'. It aims at a mental operation that sticks not to things as they are, but rather to what they should become in obedience to the command of the leader: Joseph Stalin. The authors not only show us what they have seen; they explain how they have understood and interpreted it. They are concerned not with the facts but with their encounter with the facts, the angle of their gaze, the contours of a way of speaking in which experience becomes significant and capable of communication. Only people who have themselves engaged in such mental gymnastics and adopted that particular angle can see what the authors saw.

Together with the Moscow-Volga Canal and the Volga-Don Canal, the Belomor Canal was the first project in the framework of an integrated system of waterways as envisaged in the first Five-Year Plan.[7] The 227-kilometre canal between Lake Onega and the White Sea would radically shorten the 4,000-kilometre sea journey around Scandinavia and create a link between the Northeast Passage to Vladivostok and Central Russia. It would also open up the hitherto rather isolated province of Karelia with its natural resources—timber, fish, iron ore and other minerals. To accomplish this, a difference in altitude had to be overcome between Lake Onega, which was 33 metres above sea level, and the watershed, 102 metres above sea level. The natural course of the rivers could be exploited over great stretches, but even so a 37.1-kilometre passage had to be excavated through a rocky landscape. To overcome the difference in water levels and the impoundment of water, a comprehensive hydraulic engineering system needed to be created. Altogether 19 locks—13 double and 6 single—15 dams, 12 spillways and 45 dykes had to be built. This made it possible to overcome a difference in height from 69 metres to the south to 102 metres to the north. The period during which the canal was navigable lasted only 165 days on average. The climate and logistical problems made the construction process extraordinarily taxing. The builders were forced almost exclusively to use materials available on the spot; above all, wood, rock and peat. Soil was moved on a vast scale. Up to 21 million cubic metres were shifted, of which around 10 million cubic metres were sheer rock. Despite the demanding logistic and climatic conditions—temperatures fell as low as−30°C at times— the canal was completed ahead of schedule. Its costs worked out at 95 million rubles, the major portion of which was actual construction of the canal and the locks. In a number of places, the 'Murmanka' rail track built during the First World War had to be moved to make way for construction.

Even when compared to other major canal projects, such as the Suez and Panama Canals, the scale of the Belomor Canal remains huge. Large boats, sea-going vessels, couldn't pass through the canal because it was too shallow and the lock chambers too narrow.

FIGURE 9.1. The Head Office in Moscow was kept informed about the progress of works with the aid of thousands of photos that can be found today in the Karelian National Museum. Photograph around 1932. © akg-images.

Submarines dispatched to the White Sea from Leningrad had to be transported on barges. Altogether 126,000 people worked in the Canal Zone—almost all of them prisoners. Given the constant influx of new prisoners and the departure of others, this added up to over 250,000 'Canal Army soldiers', as the quasi-military expression had it. According to incomplete records, around 12,800 people lost their lives in the process.[8]

Figures of this order are also to be found for other major hydrological projects of the colonial era. Thus the building of the 80-kilometre Panama Canal between 1906 and 1914 resulted officially in the deaths of 5,609 people from accidents and disease, but the total for the entire project totalled around 28,000. It is thought that around 1.5 million workers were involved during the ten-year construction period of the 193.3-kilometre Suez Canal. Tens of thousands are believed to have paid with their lives.[9] After the completion of the construction works in August 1933, 12,484 inmates were released, 59,516 had their sentences commuted and a large number received certificates and testimonials. Many former prisoners and the special settlers who had acclimatised to the zone remained in the region.[10]

The opening of the canal seemed to spell the success of something long in the making. Ever since Peter the Great, projects to construct a waterway had repeatedly been proposed, planned and worked on. It was thought that boats could be hauled along certain stretches. But the railway proved to be an increasingly powerful competitor, so the Tsarist Empire and 'the anarchy of capitalism' could never rise to the challenge of a project of these dimensions.[11]

The building of the canal and the colonisation and industrialisation of a region by means of forced settlement appeared to be the final implementation of a centuries-old project: Soviet power as the consummation of an inexorable development. The new empire took over completion of a mission that the old empire had been too feeble to carry out. The repeated comparisons with Panama and Suez show only that the imperial and colonial mission still survived—only now it sailed under a new flag.

In the Soviet-German War the canal became a front. German and Finnish planes bombed the canal route; on 5 December 1941, a German and Finnish force conquered Medvezhyegorsk. The Soviet defenders dynamited the locks and the hydraulic structures, especially in the southern sector, so that after the cessation of hostilities they had to be completely rebuilt or newly built, with further widenings and deepenings of the canal over the following decades.

Miracles in a Rocky Landscape

All the prerequisites for the beginning of the construction works had to be obtained from elsewhere. The first was to create the enforcement organs of the OGPU, to assemble the work brigades from the prisoners deported to the site by force. Yakov Berman was in charge during the initial stages. 'It seemed as though the entire abcess that had been cut out of the country had turned up here—7,000 priests in lilac robes, officers in blue-grey coats.'[12] Everything needed for preparing the construction site had to be built by prisoners who had been dumped in the wilds of Karelia: caves, huts and tents, without which basic organisation and planning couldn't have begun. The key planning committees were grouped under the OKB (Osoboe konstruktorskoe byuro; Special Construction Office) and were located in Moscow, in Furkasovsky Pereulok close to the Lubyanka, in Leningrad and locally in Medvezhyegorsk. Communication between these organisations took place via telegraph and included the photo documentation that was regularly sent on to Moscow. The latter took the form of glass plates and its survival today makes it the most important resource for a visual reconstruction of the progress of the building project. These photos help us form an idea of the difficulties to be overcome. The planners had opted for the 'easier' variant of the canal, the one lying farther to the east. This route had a lower flow capacity but its advantage was that it followed the natural lay of the land so that building was less costly. Even though the builders took care to incorporate the existing lakes and rivers of Karelia where possible, it still meant constructing an artificial waterway through the hardest rock, marshland and the clearing of enormous boulders. The planners had opted for a drywall construction method, which meant temporarily diverting rivers. The adverse geological and climatic conditions—extremely hot in summer, extremely cold in winter—and the absence of basic infrastructure for the building works were countered by technical equipment that at first sight can be described only as hopelessly inadequate. There was no means of transport and only gradually were narrow-gauge rail lines introduced—and their tracks were actually made of wood; even the wheels were of wood held together by an iron ring. The earthworks were carried out by hand, with shovels, spades and wheelbarrows. Dynamiting took place in the most inaccessible places. Only the most primitive lifting tackle or self-made wheelbarrows—known as the 'Belomor Ford'—were available to move the many cyclopean boulders.[13] Access to the marshy sections was provided by building wooden footpaths. In contrast to the construction at DniproHES, no Cat machines were available. A great sensation was caused by the arrival of a floating excavator that could be used to increase the depth of the shipping channel. Whatever industries were needed had to be built on the spot: sawmills, workshops for the few machines they had, the carpark for the use of OGPU management or technical specialists. Concrete was in short supply and concrete mixing was a huge problem in the winter temperatures. It could only be used at certain especially sensitive places in the hydrological system; elsewhere alternative solutions had to be found. The canal builders had to rely entirely on building materials that were available on site: timber and rock. The excavations simultaneously supplied the rock material required for making up and stabilising the dams and embankments. Since concrete was mainly unavailable, boxes the size of the storey of a house were made with logs and then filled with stone and debris—at first by way of experiment but afterwards on a large scale. This produced huge blocks of material that were then joined to one another and used to make the canal banks and the walls of the lock chambers.

The pinnacle of an elementary technology born of necessity can be seen in the lock chambers. These are constructed of wood, as are the lock gates, only a few of which were made of metal imported from Leningrad. What we see is the supreme craftsmanship of these workers in wood—wood as 'Karelia's gold'. We see just how conversant the peasants and craftsmen in the Canal Zone were with this basic material. Wood in every conceivable variation—from the construction of an administration building or clubhouse for the OGPU bosses, from workshops and garages to a public swimming pool, whose mere outlines reveal the skills of a prerevolutionary builder, on through the lock chambers several storeys high, whose walls are made from precisely sawn-off logs and timber-cladding, as was the 'paving' of the lock floors. How twenty-metre-high lock gates could be made from tree trunks is a mystery that perhaps only the inventor and builder V. N. Maslov and his craftsmen could explain. It is the beauty of these constructions, of their geometric lines, and the precision of the workmanship involved, their consummate craftsmanship, in short, that has made the engineering system of the Belomor Canal into a technical masterpiece—whatever we think about its other purposes or indeed its often-alleged senselessness.[14] This beauty is not the least significant reason the Belomor Canal became the starting point for the aestheticising of power and violence despite its cost in terrible suffering and thousands of human lives. This process of transforming a landscape of rocks and skerries into a technogenic landscape can be followed step by step in the photo documentation reproduced in Medvezhyegorsk. We can see how an 'ant-heap' of thousands and thousands of slave labourers, a vast tangle of columns of wheelbarrows, horse-drawn carts and wooden cranes, gradually give birth to a canal bed, in which we cannot detect the slightest sign that it was made entirely of slave labour and intelligence, blood and sweat and thousands of industrial accidents. Under Rodchenko's editorship, the Belomor special issue of *USSR in Construction* lives entirely from aestheticising this forced-labour project.

'Canal Soldiers': Soviet Society as a Mobilised Society

Only an army, or a quasi-military organisation, was adequate to the challenge of building the White Sea Canal from scratch in twenty months. What was needed was a body with boundless authority over life and death—the OGPU; a staff of outstandingly trained and experienced engineers and experts; 'human material' that did not in fact possess the necessary qualifications but was present in absolutely unlimited numbers, that is, the work slaves drawn from the entire nation; and lastly, an ideological propaganda agency that would equip the 'Canal Army' politically and hold it together morally and politically. The style adopted by all those involved in the project— thousands and thousands of people who had had no prior contact with one another—was that of a wartime operation in which nature had to be vanquished and every sacrifice was justified in the cause of victory. The commanders on the spot, all of whom received the highest honours that Soviet power could confer after the victorious struggle, were recruited from the leadership of the OGPU: Genrikh Yagoda, Lazar Kogan, Matvey Berman, Semyon Firin, Yakov Rappoport, Sergey Zhuk, Naftaly Frenkel, Konstantin Vershbitsky. Most of them had the sort of biography that could arise only in the conditions that obtain following revolutions, wars or civil wars. Their task was to create a power structure and a hierarchy that did not shrink from extremes of brutality and cruelty to achieve their goals. It is difficult to explain how such a small group of violent men was able to hold down and control a hundred thousand people and force them to work. In the Belomor volume, the commanders are all depicted as individuals, complete with portraits and biographies. They had all had experience of foreign countries before the First World War or in the postwar emigration—in Sofia, Constantinople or Berlin—and as managers of power had proved themselves as talented as they were cruel. In a state which lacked trained administrators, there was an above average number of social climbers with a Jewish background, who wanted nothing more than to burn all the bridges to the milieu from which they came—the Shtetls of the Pale of Settlement. Equipped with the typical insignia of Bolshevik power—the commissar's leather coat, Nagant revolver, leather cap and rhombus badge—they appear in a variety of poses in the photos of the time, as the very epitome of the anti-Semitic stereotypes rife throughout Russia as in Europe as a whole.[15]

Mere power would not have achieved anything had the specialists lacked skills and competence. N. I. Khrustalyov, who was present at the opening of the Berlin-Stettin navigation route in 1913, was the chief engineer in Belomorstroy in 1932 and was awarded the Order of the Red Banner. Other engineers included Orest V. Vyazemsky and Georgy K. Riesenkampf, both of whom received their training at the best technical high schools of the Russian Empire or Western Europe, as well as having international experience. For them the project was a technical challenge. Professor V. N. Maslov developed new timber frames for the lock gates. For his contribution to 'socialist hydrotechnology', he was prematurely dismissed in 1932 and honoured with the Order of the Red Banner. Sergey Zhuk, unlike most of the engineers, was an 'independent engineer' whose career went from Belomor to the Moscow-Volga Canal and from there to most of the dams and hydroelectric works on the Volga. Behind almost all of these careers was a history of radical loss of status because of the Revolution, followed by stigmatisation and criminalisation when these men were condemned and treated as 'wreckers' and 'former people'. The path to the technical commanding heights of the Gulag was for them the road to survival, to rehabilitation and regaining their status in the technocratic elite without which the Stalinist dictatorship could not have hoped to implement its ambitious modernisation plans. Within the state propaganda system they acted as perfect examples of the reeducation of the old intelligentsia to become the loyal servants of the new state.[16]

The hardest thing is to picture the vast mass of forced labourers. In the official photographs of the Gulag, they generally appear as a faceless, barely distinguishable mass on the floor of the canal bed or felling trees in the forest. Again and again we see them in the group photos of various brigades competing in socialist rivalry—the Afanasiev Brigade, Falanga No. 7, Krasny Kavkaz Brigade and others—where they have been picked out as record-breaking workers (*rekordisty*), or else standing by characteristic work tools that identify them as belonging to a specific trade: chauffeur or mechanic. There are also women with jackhammers. The thousands of slides that document all of this systematically allow us to separate faces from the masses and pinpoint social and cultural profiles. This holds for the relatives of almost every nationality—known as *natsmeny*—working on the canal and making the collectives look like miniature editions of the great melting pot of Soviet society. The overwhelming mass of forced labourers were recruited from the peasants deported to the north under the label of 'kulaks'. They brought with them the physical constitution and experience to enable them to survive and work on such building sites. They provided the large numbers of lumberjacks; workmen armed with picks and shovels for digging; workers who built the barracks and paths, bred and tended the cattle and grew vegetables in cold frames to feed the camp management. They also supplied the mass of labourers who were trained on the spot, principally by workers who had come from the Leningrad factories, to become mechanics, tractor drivers, metalworkers and fitters. And in general, the Canal Zone was a camp for learning and training that specialised in learning by doing. Furthermore, a large proportion of the forced labourers came from the ranks of people who had suffered dislocation from the social upheavals, the war and the Revolution, been pushed to the margins of society and robbed of their political rights. Many were casual thieves or professional criminals, genuinely or labelled as such. Their ranks included members of professional groups who had been déclassé, discriminated against and persecuted—clergy, monks, adherents of the numerous sects, former members of the defeated White Army and the non-Bolshevik parties, representatives of the nobility, the merchant class, former house-owners, drug dealers and prostitutes. Such people—'former people' and representatives of the 'anarchic petty bourgeoisie'—were treated with utter disdain. They were made to feel the full destructive fury of Bolshevik delusions about the transformative powers of education. Even on this model construction site of the OGPU, the true enemy of communist power was not the external foe, but the inner enemy, the 'anarchic petty bourgeois' or the mass of people who refused to fall into line.

Perekovka. Reforging. Slave Labour as Rebirth

'Belomor ne karaet, no ispravlyaet'—'Belomor does not punish, it rectifies'. This is just one of the slogans in which the peremptory tones of the OGPU guards blend with the laconic matter-of-factness of the avant-garde.[17] Another adage of the same kind is 'The Belomor Canal is our second home; on the Belomor Canal we were reborn'.[18] Unmasking the propagandistic content of this rhetoric does not take us very far, nor does worrying about the inquisitive, travel-loving writers who strove to make sense of what they saw or cynically endorsed it. There is something qualitatively new in the idea that here were slave labourers who not only acquiesced in their fate but even thought of it as an opportunity for self-development and self-improvement. 'They didn't just blow up rocks; they blew up their old world.'[19] The rhetoric of 'reforging', 'rebirth' and 'a second life' in the canal book can only be subverted by reading the memoirs of people who survived but were unable to speak about their experiences in the Belbaltlag until decades afterwards.[20] To have been deported by night from one's hometown, as was the fate of hundreds of thousands of people at the end of the 1920s/early 1930s—all the suspect candidates for resettlement, banishment, arrest and execution are listed in the catalogue of outcasts—to have been torn away from the modest comfort of a peasant holding, from family and a village community, really does amount to the loss of one's 'first home' and to uprooting and displacement. It is the end of one's 'first life'. In this perverted sense we can regard arrival in the rocky Karelian landscape and submission to the new coercive life imposed by force as the beginning of a 'second life'. One might even describe one's survival there as a 'rebirth'. More generally, a way of life had been destroyed; those who had been deported became 'former people', members of a vanished world. Nothing was more plausible or even inevitable than for everyone who wanted to go on living to adapt to their new circumstances, to start afresh, to make the best of the new situation. And this happened a hundred thousand times over in the rocky landscape of Karelia and after that in building sites all over the new Soviet world. It may well be true that peasants who were used to difficult conditions were the most likely to find their feet in their new situation. But what about all the ladies in high-heeled shoes and summer clothes, who had never had previous contact with swamps and marshes, swarms of mosquitoes and the stony ground the prominent writers found so entertaining? Or the scholars who knew their way around libraries or laboratories, but had no experience labouring with pickaxes or primitive wheelbarrows? Their only option was to go under, or learn to cut corners—a practice known as *tufta*—in short, to practise passive resistance or somehow join in—in the brigade, in the literacy campaign or in 'perfecting one's own personality'.[21] A certain self-hatred may also have been involved, a rejection of one's own bourgeois origin and guilt about being an intellectual who previously enjoyed a privileged status. And the prospect of an early release from hellish conditions may well have played a role in the attraction of the idea of reforging with its slogan 'Work can make you free'. And wasn't the situation in the canal camp, where norms could be met and even surpassed, always better than conditions in the villages in Ukraine and on the Volga, which were being overwhelmed by collectivisation, famine and vast numbers of deaths? At first, 'reforging' was not a concept but simply the name for the wish to survive at whatever cost. This held true even for the writers who travelled through the canal on 17 August 1933 aboard the *Karl Marx* and followed this up with an enthusiastic report on the successes of reforging, of self-improvement, as a motive force in producing all the miracles that they could see. In writing this, they were in effect also writing about themselves: about their flight from their precarious existence, which was always on the brink of failure—even if we are talking here only of the loss of a contract or restrictions on opportunities to publish—and their escape to the protection of a power, to whose whims they like everyone else were subject. The description of 'reforging' 'alien social elements' and 'criminal' and 'counterrevolutionary individuals' was also a description of them, of their own careers, plagued by doubts, weighed down by hankerings after their 'first life', their struggle with their own suspicions about themselves and their search for an identity that conformed to the new order.[22] Now that the old Russia had been destroyed, the entire nation was in search of a new identity and in the process of finding and reinventing itself. Belomorstroy was a great crime scene and the setting for such self-reinvention. This drama was enacted in the ominous shadow of the unconstrained violence of the OGPU and its master, who finally visited the canal on board the steamship *Anokhin*. He handed out medals to the bosses of this special task force, patted the engineers on the back, but was ready to take any of them to court at any time, accuse them of being spies and wreckers, and then have them killed. All this would soon happen in fact, as could be seen from the arrest and execution of Yagoda and Firin and thousands of others for whom the Belomor Canal was supposed to signify the dawn of a new era.

Even though we know so much about cruelty, violence and betrayal in the twentieth century, it continues to be one of the great puzzles that operas could be produced in places where human beings were dying of cold and exhaustion, that a wind orchestra could play above the brigades building the lock chambers, that on the canal bank where the overseers of the slave workers glided by aboard a ship called *Chekist*, canal poets could declaim poems by Baudelaire, and that talks about the religion of Ancient Egypt could be given in the culture houses of the camp zone. There was a restaurant where even the inmates could order food and meet the stars of the Moscow theatre and opera scene. The holiday calendar of the Revolution was maintained even in the camp, where decorations were awarded for the best workers and for those who had passed the literacy test on stages festooned with flags and propaganda posters. On the occasion of the solemn opening of the canal, the Canal Army soldiers had to remain in their barracks, but a little later many of them departed on boats to the next battle: the construction of the Moscow-Volga Canal, the greatest forced-labour project of the second Five-Year Plan, which would turn Moscow into the 'Port of Five Seas'.

'We Are Travelling Now to the Capital City of the Russian Intelligentsia'

Among the people deported to Belomor Canal was Nikolay Antsiferov, author of the legendary book *The Soul of Petersburg* of 1922, a melancholy memoir of leave-taking from the ancient capital. He described his journey from Leningrad to Medvezhyegorsk as a journey 'from the Palazzo to the tents [*palatki*]' and 'from the baroque to the barrack'.[23] He was badly shaken but obtained a commission which not only enabled him to get around but was one he learned from. Having been made responsible for the distribution of newspapers, he came to know the Canal Zone, including its bosses Kogan and Frenkel, whom he described as committed and competent. The inventor of the scientific historical excursion, he created a programme of excursions along the canal. As a historian, he developed into an expert on petrography; he was able to select his coworkers from among the prisoners: the Arabist V. Ebermann and the German teacher Libikh-Lipold. He conducted seminars on petrography, topography and mineralogy. He came across an old friend of Andrey Bely, a translator of Jakob Böhme, an anthroposophist who had helped build Rudolf Steiner's Temple, the Goetheanum, in Dornach. He met a great-grandson of the Decembrist Kondraty Ryleev and listened to Igor Weis, a professional organist and Bach specialist. He met acquaintances from his Leningrad days—whether as prisoners or visitors. In a circle of 'book friends', the philosopher Alexander A. Meyer, who was working in the planning department but also preparing a major study of Goethe's *Faust*, gave a talk. Inmates performed the opera 'Dam No. 6' by Igor Weis and a satire with the title 'Mister Stupid', about an English correspondent who, having found himself in a Soviet camp, wrote home about the incredible things he saw. There was theatre in drag and a genuine ballerina who, having danced the dying swan, returned to her work in the camp laundry. There was scarcely a topic that was not debated—the poetry of the age of Tsar Nicholas [I], Mikhail Bakhtin's

studies of Dostoevsky's novels. Antsiferov, an urban historian who
became a mineralogist, was charged with setting up the Museum of
Canal Construction in Medvezhyegorsk, which was housed in the so-
called Stalin Hotel, architecturally a mixture of Bauhaus simplicity
and Stalinist Empire style. This was where the brains trust was located and where the telephone and telegraph lines were housed. At
the end of the 1990s, shops and a market moved to the building, a
bazaar, but also the local museum. The exhibits here consist of objects salvaged from the past or viewed as characteristic of the past.
We find a china elephant—the symbol for SLON, the 'Solovki special
camp'—a china concertina, the writing instruments of the *nachalnik*
(boss), together with his telephone, radio and loudspeakers of the
sort that were ubiquitous in the zone at the time, an 'ABC of Communism', the obligatory Thonet chair and sewing machine, a clock—the
instrument with which to enforce the discipline needed for the new
age—a gramophone and a prison-cell door from *lagpunkt* 22 of the
Belbaltlag. It goes without saying that the maps, graphics and statistics that tell the story of the superlative achievements of the Belomor
construction project are also present: the 21 million cubic metres of
soil, the 2.5 million cubic metres of rock, the 380,000 cubic metres of concrete poured and the million cubic metres of timber. On
show are the tools: pickaxes, saws, shovels, wheelbarrows—and the
everyday implements: cast-iron stoves, wooden tables, spoons and
tumblers. On the wall we see the gallery of commandants: Vyazemsky,
Maslov, Khrustalyev, Frenkel, Zhuk, Firin, Zubrik, Kogan and Berman.
The newspapers that lie open on display bear the titles 'Perekovka',
'Stalinskaya trassa' and 'Medvezhyegorsky bolshevik'. Musicians from
the Moscow conservatoire played in the Canal Zone; they performed
Carmen and *Belugin's Wedding*.

Nikolay Antsiferov, who had become the founder of his own form
of excursion in his years in Petersburg and Leningrad, had also
worked out a project for the Canal Zone to introduce readers to the
geology and landscape of Karelia, to teach them to see nature in a
new way and gain an understanding of the unrelenting harshness
of the battle with the rocky landscape. Anyone who returns today to
the site of the museum he established will find his ideas highly topical. Medvezhyegorsk could well be the starting point for exploring

a unique topography along the canal route. The excursion would include a boat trip on the canal, with a view such as was possible from the deck, a further view from the bridge, a view such as the one available to the writers who had journeyed from Moscow and one from the height Alexander Rodchenko deemed appropriate to get a good overview. It would lead along the embankment from where it might be possible to obtain a view from below and take in the swampy ground reclaimed from the Karelian forest where it is still possible to make out the outlines of the barracks which have long since lain derelict. In Sandarmokh the excursion would pause in a clearing in front of a granite boulder from the Solovetsky Islands with the inscription 'On this spot 1,111 inmates of the Solovki prison camp were shot between 27 October and 4 November 1937'. Every year the children and grandchildren of the murder victims gather here from every republic of the former Soviet Union.[24] No one can say where exactly any particular person is buried. Karelia's skies spread their stars over Stalin's mass graves.

CHAPTER 10

Landscape after the Battle

The twentieth century has ended and the landscapes that it gave birth to in its Sturm und Drang phase have dissolved. We gaze transfixed at the miracles it brought forth but also contemplate the lunar landscapes it left behind. We do not know what will survive or what must be dismantled or modifed. In the case of the Soviet Union, we only now have an inkling of the extent and radical nature of the destruction wrought by human beings. The system has given up its spirit; the megamachine that ploughed up the entire country in three generations has lost its rhythm. The generators have been switched off but it is too soon for the all clear. The decay rates of the elements liberated in this process surpass the limits of the memories even of generations. Nature's reconquest of the earth, which has been scorched and laid waste by human beings, would be a blessing. The jungle may have overgrown the ruins of Angkor Wat and the Mayan cities, but the jungles, tundras and ice-covered regions of the entire world are not enough to wipe Chernobyl from the map. So we must continue to live with the legacies of the century. They are our environment.

We can complain about the delusions of earlier generations but they did what they could with the means available to them at the time, and with the expectations and hopes that fulfilled their lives. Whether we have truly surpassed them is unclear. As is well known, the human race only sets itself tasks that are within its capabilities. As always, everything is done with the best intentions. The goals aspired to with a good conscience by earlier generations often enough lead to headaches and a guilty conscience for us, their successors. We roam the terrain on which others have perished, and we feel drained, distanced, as we contemplate the scene with the serene gaze of people who know better than those who were actually present. Russia is in many respects merely a radicalised version of Nietzsche's 'all future things', which occur elsewhere too but emerge more clearly here because the inhibitions, mediations and counterpressures to be found everywhere civil institutions exist are absent. In Russia radical changes and cat-astrophic experiences occur in their pure form.

When I first saw Magnitogorsk, I was speechless. I was aware of the statistics about the quantities of rust and poison gas raining down daily, weekly and annually on the inhabitants of the mining town in the southern Urals. I knew that thousands upon thousands of poison-ous particles were released into the air over the town when plumes of smoke of every conceivable colour poured out of the chimneys over the industrial complex. I knew that Magnitogorsk ranked highest in every publication about air and water pollution, that the incidence of cancer was higher than elsewhere and that this was not a good place for babies to come into the world. And of course I knew of the circum-stances in which the town had come into existence and the victims this had created. It had been built with thousands of 'kulaks' who had been deported to the site, 'criminals' from the towns and priests side by side with volunteers from the communist youth movement. At temperatures of–40° and under the watchful eyes of the NKVD, they churned up the soil, pushed ore cars, fell from scaffolding and died anonymously. I knew all of this, but that did not prevent me from feeling an amalgam of horror and fascination when I glanced out the plane's window and saw the megamachine of the industrial complex that was built in the steppes in 1929.

Sturm und Drang

I attempted to reconstruct in my mind what must have attracted the young American John Scott to come to this place along with thou-sands of his generation—of his own free will; no one forced him to do so. And he had remained despite that being an extraordinary time, full of privations. I tried to grasp the thinking of the McKee Company engineers who found things of interest beyond their salaries and the bonus payments they received for having agreed to come to Soviet Russia. I knew something of the ideas of the great Nikolay Milyutin on the subject of Sotsgorod and of Ernst May's plans for Magnitogorsk, which he was able to realise in part. The tent city of the Komsomol pioneers of 1929 was transformed in a decade into a large town and, even more importantly, had become the capital of the Soviet steel empire. John Scott, Ernst May and Nikolay Milyutin, the engineer Arthur McKee from Cleveland and the thousands of workmen who had come of their own free will—this was the other, very different, far more enigmatic aspect of Magnitogorsk.

I had only ever seen anything comparable in the United States, in the Ohio cities of Akron and Cleveland and also in Detroit. In the 1970s I had travelled through iron country—past mile after mile of factories, through areas with blast furnaces that had been shut down, rusting away for years, yet still gave me a sense of what human labour can achieve.

I learned that Pittsburgh was twinned with Magnitogorsk and that a Magnitogorsk had existed before Magnitogorsk, namely in Gary, Indiana. Gary had been founded on the banks of Lake Michigan in 1906 and, following its own cult of personality, one that was even older than the well-known Soviet version, had been named after the president and chairman of the board of US Steel, Judge Elbert H. Gary. The town of Gary too had been conjured out of thin air in a place where previously 'there had been nothing at all'. In its day, Gary was the biggest steelworks in the world. In Gary, a stream of immigrant workers from all over the world came together to create the American working class. Gary was not a town in the usual sense, since everything depended on the company, and what in other places would be a town centre or a Main Street was just the factory complex in Gary.

I visited Gary and Pittsburgh after I had been in Magnitogorsk. From Chicago, Gary, Indiana, can be reached in under three-quarters of an hour. You drive along the southern shore of Lake Michigan, that you hardly get to see because the highway passes through a landscape that is neither town nor factory but an intermediate zone, half suburbia, half factory. The highway soon swings up and then down again, giving a view from the car like one from a mountain pass over the monumental landscape of US Steel. You see rail tracks, abandoned living areas, warehouses, water towers and, above all, industrial plants and workshops of a size that would enable each of them to shelter a medium-sized town. Everything is rust-coloured. Between these industries from another age, you see illuminated sites belonging to refineries and power stations. At the time, the early 1990s, Gary was said to have the highest murder rate in the USA. Nobody goes there without a special reason.

But there is a special reason and a good one too. Gary itself, a town that had 175,000 inhabitants around 1970, compared with 80,000 today, has little to offer by way of tourist attractions. There are a few manufacturers' villas that show the visitor that large sums of money could be earned here at one time. Today, the town is in decline because steel is no longer in demand. Gary, the centre of the American steel empire, has not been spared by the wave of deindustrialisation.

No less impressive is the backdrop to the coal and steel town of Pittsburgh, on the western slopes of the Appalachians, at the confluence of the Allegheny and Monongahela Rivers. Pittsburgh has a history that goes back long before it became the 'forge of the universe' in the nineteenth century. Every period of American history has left its traces in Pittsburgh. But here, too, the most impressive phase is the era of modern industry, which is now on its way to becoming history. It has given shape to the grandiose silhouette of the town with the Hazelwood coke works and the Cathedral of Learning towering behind it and has made the town a museum of modernity with impressive works by Henry Hornbostel, Albert Kahn, Frank Lloyd Wright, Walter Gropius and Ludwig Mies van der Rohe. Pittsburgh was—and this is much clearer than in Gary—not merely one of the smithies of America but one of the centres of American wealth. Andrew Carnegie, Henry Clay Frick, and the Mellons, the epitome of American wealth and patronage, all put their stamp on Pittsburgh. With the Gothic skyscraper of the Cathedral of Learning in the centre—and in sight of the steelworks—a city of the sciences and the arts has come into being, with laboratories, clinics, museums and art galleries. The Cathedral of Learning, built between 1925 and 1929, is taller than the blast furnaces and has become an icon of the age, just like the Hoover Dam on the Colorado River and the DniproHES hydroelectric plant in the Soviet Union. The Age of Steel had its genius loci too. Gary, Pittsburgh and Magnitogorsk were among them. Whatever they achieved and however they may have been misused, they tell us something about the genius and power of human labour. We understand little of the twentieth century as long as we fail to take cognizance of the peculiar beauty of industrialised and planned landscapes. That is why we find ourselves drawn to such places. We do not go to Magnitogorsk, Gary and Pittsburgh to see derelict rolling mills and chimney stacks but because we want to see something of the vigour of the age with our own eyes. These are the places in which the USA and the USSR became what they were in the twentieth century—superpowers. Everything that America has become is connected to Gary or Pittsburgh. Everything the Soviet Union was is connected to the half-mythical, half-real town of Magnitogorsk. We might say that the United States consists of the American Constitution plus Carnegie. There could have been no Wonder of the World like New York, no Brooklyn Bridge, no John Roebling, no Golden Gate Bridge, no transcontinental railways, no American tanks and Flying Fortresses over European battlefields, and no victory over Hitler without the machinery and chimney stacks of Gary and Pittsburgh. The same holds good for Magnitogorsk: no industrialisation and no victory over Hitler without Magnitogorsk.

The Age of the 'Plan': The New Deal

This sounds almost like an apologia, even though our concern is simply to observe that these are the places where the work that has underpinned the world as a whole ever since was done. It was in this sense that Ernst Jünger entitled his 1932 essay 'The Worker' and with it identified the central 'figure' of the age. The physiognomy of the Worker, his pathos and his style confront us in both hemispheres. He bears various names and has a variety of prophets: Henry Ford and Alexey Gastev among them. The tone of his speech is determined by his confident belief that there is nothing that cannot be achieved by total commitment and heroic effort. The heroic era had a tone and a language of its own. There were no translation problems. M. Ilyin's 'Story of the Great Plan' was a bestseller in New Deal America. The bronze statues that used to be built in honour of engineers and workers on the dam crests of Boulder and DniproHES are of the same style, one more Art Deco, the other more classical naturalism, without the sculptors knowing anything of one another. Because of the Great Depression, the need for a new approach to work and living was a commonplace notion. And the new way was that of the Plan.[1]

Everyone made plans: two-year plans, four-year plans, five- and even ten-year plans. This expressed not just the self-confidence of the age but also a good measure of despair, hatred of the old world and a certain perplexity. Thinking in terms of plans, of planned landscapes, was a response to the social chaos of the postwar situation and the world economic crisis. It provided something to go on when everything had become uncertain.

Great projects are, as we know, not without preconditions; they are not the ideas of madmen but halfway rational solutions to the problems of the age. Those we have described were the desperate actions of communities that had been deeply shaken. The Roosevelt Dam, the Hoover Dam, the entire gigantic project of the Tennessee Valley Authority, perhaps the greatest technical work of art in history—these are not the unanchored dreams of fantasists, but the inspired actions of intelligent politicians and efficient bureaucracies. We might think of the New Deal and the first Five-Year Plan as the American and Russian responses to the crisis of the 1920s were it not for the fact that the Russian response—'the harvest of sorrow', to use Robert Conquest's phrase, with millions dead in the wake of the process of collectivisation—precludes any meaningful comparison.

Nowhere, perhaps, was the dream greater than in the tormented, desperate country of Russia. No sacrifice seemed too great. Dreams are born of despair. And this truth holds good for the dreams which gave rise to the Moloch of Magnitogorsk.

The transition from the 'workshop' landscape to the 'planned' one about which Jünger had written so eloquently took place almost instantaneously, as if there had been a worldwide understanding that we must all work differently in future. The plan became the cipher of an entire era—and not just in the homeland of the Five-Year Plans. A 'plan' means doing something on a large scale, one that surpasses the financial and organisational resources of individual enterprises, however impressive. 'Plan' means the interaction of heterogeneous branches and sectors—from agriculture to the development of turbines, from research departments to sales. The plan is interdisciplinary. It presupposes authorities who can not only plan but also put things into practice. With 'planning' landscapes, we see the growth of bureaucracies that will risk everything to maintain their hold on power: their lifespan, their health and the wealth of the nation.

What the plan represented in the minds of contemporaries can be seen from photographs of the time. On 22 December 1920, when the plan of the State Commission for the Electrification of Russia was presented and approved at the Eighth All-Russian Congress of Soviets, this was done with the necessary graphic illustrations. A map of Soviet Russia was spread out over the stage of the Bolshoi Theatre, where the Congress met. The motto 'Russia must be electrified' was not so much utopian as timely, long overdue and vividly present to all enlightened minds. The GOELRO Plan, as the electrification plan was named, merely confirmed this. The map of an electrified Russia with an entire network of routes, canals and pipelines became the emblem of the new, Soviet Russia. This map was unfurled on town squares on public holidays and lit up with hundreds of coloured lights. 'A sixth of the Earth', as the Soviet Union was called, became bathed in light at the push of a button; it was rescued from 'the darkness of backwardness' and 'guided towards the light of enlightenment'! These metaphors soon obscured the actual effects of the modernisation process that had been set in train. The huge map with its diagrams and lights, rising production curves, balance sheets, ever-accelerating record numbers of kilowatts, tonnes and increasing outputs was designed to register the arrival of a new world. It was no longer necessary to comfort oneself with the thought of the world to come.

At the end of the road, in the late 1940s, we find the plan of plans, the ultimate total work of art, elaborated by the Academy of Sciences, the Komsomol, environmentalists, the Gulag administration and the secret police: Stalin's Great Plan for the Transformation of Nature.[2] In this plan, Earth—or at least the sixth of it that belonged to the Soviet world—was transformed into the Garden of Eden. The Planning Authority represented social rationality, if not indeed the World-Spirit. The dictator was playing God. The Book of Genesis was reproduced in the form of a ukase. Everything ought to be possible. Where there had been a steppe, there was now an ocean of grain; instead of caravans, there would now be motorways, and the yurts of the nomadic peoples would be replaced by modern cities. The rivers of the north would be reversed and flow southwards. Waterways from the Black

Sea to the Pacific were included in the maps and plans were afoot to
use atomic bombs to blow up entire mountain chains that were in
the way. These were no mere fantasies; they were projects on which
hundreds and thousands of scientists and organisers laboured for decades. Moreover, they were projects with consequences, since in the
1950s a whole generation of young people journeyed to the steppes of
Kazakhstan in order to plough up the virgin soil. But nothing came of
the plan as a whole. Even more seriously, the struggle to reverse the
north-flowing rivers and the rivers of Siberia, as had been envisaged
in the projects of the 1940s, became one of the factors leading to the
downfall of the Soviet Union.

What all these terrestrial projects had in common was a militant
resolve, a hubristic mentality, a heroic attitude of either-or, of now or
never. Nature was not simply stuff, matter with which one had to come
to terms and whose 'laws' had to be painstakingly discovered. It was
an adversary, an enemy to be fought, defeated and eliminated. The
construction sites of Magnitogorsk, Novokuznetsk and DniproHES
were the battlefields on which peasant Russia was annihilated and
'reforged'. In this battle there were commanders and field marshals on
the 'labour front', a general staff in the 'battle for steel', shock brigades
and the battle against 'spies and wreckers', that is, fatal casualties,
the wounded, tortured and traumatised. Even the steppes had to be
defeated. The entire country became the hinterland of this front on
which 'heroes were born' and 'enemies' destroyed. Bulletins from the
'economic front' were bulletins from the 'reporters from the front'. At
stake was always something more than a mere building site or blast
furnace. The language of war and military command prevailed on the
building sites of the new world. Management teams were modelled on
military hierarchies. Engineers became strategists and construction
teams became battalions. A lack of discipline at work was treated
as a betrayal of the great cause and correspondingly punished—as
desertion. Everything was dragged into the vortex of great conflicts
with an omnipresent foe. Accidents at work were sabotage, the work
of wreckers. The construction sites simply teemed with evil spirits,
unrecognised enemies and deviationists. The new world was emerging from a pandemonium of betrayals, suspicions and purges. Nature and the human beings living in it were things whose resistance

had to be broken. The novels of the time all turned on the battle with nature, the overcoming of resistance on the part of matter and the mastery of technology. They bore titles like *Cement, Driving Axle, Hydroelectric Power Station, Time, Forward!, The Assembly Line* [=*Das große Fließband*—the title of the German translation of *The Flivver King*, Upton Sinclair's novel about Henry Ford], *The Russian Forest* and *The Volga Flows to the Caspian Sea*. Their heroes or heroines came from *How the Steel Was Tempered*. They were hard on themselves and others; they remained impassive when the battlefront passed over them as it advanced, if only victory was certain. Individuals were only of importance as long as they strengthened the whole. If they were left behind, the collective had every right to abandon them, to rid itself of such individuals. Heroic self-sacrifice was as indispensable to the new society as iron ore and cement. Discipline replaced machines, subordination the absence of organisation. Pathos compensated for the lack of know-how. The more limited the technology, the greater the belief in its omnipotence. Soviet Americanism and the fetishising of technology in the 1920s and 1930s was, as Hans Rogger has shown, the ideology with which to compensate for backwardness.[3]

The militarisation of work and work as military service—the distinctions became blurred at the high point of the mobilisation of society during the Stalin era. Such construction sites were actually battlefields, and there were dozens of them in the Soviet Union during the period of socialist construction in the 1930s. On these battlefields the Soviet Union grew, along with the type of human being that held it together, for over a generation. Apart from Magnitogorsk, they included the Stalingrad tractor works, the automobile factories of Nizhny Novgorod, the Moscow Metro, the Moscow-Volga Canal, the tractor factory of Chelyabinsk and the Novokuznetsk combine. These battlefields are now forgotten, thrust aside by others, the battlefields of the Second World War: Stalingrad, Kursk and the defence of Moscow. In brief, the modern Soviet Union was the product of those battles.[4]

The system that emerged from the movement of millions, from the 'total mobilisation', to use Ernst Jünger's phrase, could only survive if it remained in motion and kept on growing. Its end had to come the moment the factors propelling it forward were shut down and the heroic human being vanished. At some point the heroic men and women of the mobilised society were transformed into the peacetime consumers who had settled down. They regarded the refrigerator in an apartment of their own as more important than the products of the iron and steel works, and preferred a car to a truck. In a society where people had become sedentary, civil war types of human being seemed quite incongruous. The hectic stress of a war that has long been running down simply gets on the nerves of people who have moved into their two-room apartments. This was how consumers were born at the very heart of communist society. Modest though their expectations may have been initially, they already belonged to the species of nonheroic, civilised human beings. Beyond war and civil war and beyond the battles surrounding steel, a new type of human being began to emerge from the prefabricated mass-housing estates of the Khrushchev and Brezhnev era. We can think of the entire post-Stalin Soviet Union as the calming and consolidation of a society exhausted by hypermobilisation and war. It represented the transformation of many millions of uprooted migrants into settlers and town dwellers, and the demobilisation of an entire society following decades of excessive turbulence and mobility.

Figuratively speaking, the stuff of the new age is not steel, the basic material for the manufacture of the means of production, but plastic as the basic material of goods produced for mass consumption. Khrushchev's de-Stalinisation, which created space for the birth of consumerism at the heart of communism, will always be associated in the minds of that generation with plastic and chemicals, with the smell, feel and colour of plastic objects introduced to ease the harsh realities of daily life. The role of the iron and steel factories in Stalin's time was replaced by the chemical combines under Khrushchev. In the judgement of contemporaries, Khrushchev's age was humdrum and marked by a loss of form and style that was not outweighed by a feeble remake of pre-Stalinist modernity. But the true achievement of the Khrushchev era lay in the fact that it left 'society' in peace. That was decisive for a nation utterly exhausted after the cruel blood-letting, the Sturm und Drang, the Great Terror and the Great Patriotic War.

The megamachine that grew out of social mobility, enthusiasm, terror and the yearning for progress is breaking apart, and indeed has broken apart. Chernobyl in 1986 spelled the end of Soviet civilisation even before the formal dissolution of the USSR, which only confirmed what had long been fact.[5] The megamachine had run out of control. The world then became intoxicated by the images of the events of 1989 and was delighted to have found in those events the historical caesura that we can all hold onto. But radionuclides have a different rate of decay from the pictures that helped generations form their image of the world. Nineteen eighty-six, or more precisely, 26 April 1986 at 1:23:58 p.m., is the moment that will remain when the era-making events of 1989 have long since been forgotten. Whole societies do not collapse because of differences of opinion or true or false guidelines or even the decisions of party bosses. They perish when they are utterly exhausted and human beings can go on living only if they cast off or destroy the conditions that are killing them.

Out of Control

Even before Chernobyl there were numerous signs showing what happens when the megamachine liberates itself from all constraints and spins out of control. Human beings paid for its continued existence with rapidly falling life expectancy, extremely high infant mortality and greater vulnerability to life-threatening toxins of all kinds. They paid with their lives for a doomed system that survived only through inertia. They had fallen hostage to the megamachine. Such dependency is not confined to the Soviet case; but nowhere else, perhaps, has it manifested itself with such clarity and ruthlessness. It is not inappropriate that this major nuclear meltdown should have occurred first in a country where technical megalomania knew no limits. The Soviet Union lacked the institutional brakes that might have helped to moderate the large-scale operations of an all-powerful state. It also lacked the property rights whose mere existence represents a sort of veto. State egotism—dominant both as an apparatus and in terms of personnel—was able to unleash a lethal force because it was never challenged by other egos or by the egos of as many others as possible. The peculiar absence of 'individuals' to act as leaders in the Soviet planned economy brought anonymity and negligence in its wake. It was, as Rudolf Bahro once observed perceptively, 'an economy of irresponsibility'.[6] Since everything belonged to everybody, it belonged to nobody, and since no one was responsible, no one could be held responsible. Nowhere were the riches of nature and society squandered so casually and senselessly as in the Soviet Union. Nowhere were the costs as high as in a social system that was based on state and collective property. In comparison, the criticism of 'senseless capitalist wastefulness'—for which advertising was the classical example—appears like a harmless relic of the old days. There was no power of veto—whether economic or institutional—to limit the ruthless, unconstrained expenditure of human and material capital. There was no authority that might have been in a position to resist the structural waste of effort and prevent the overexploitation of the forests, the eternally flowing water taps, the leaking oil and gas pipelines, the gratuitous disposal of nuclear waste in the Barents Sea, and so forth. The history of progress in Russia in the twentieth century is marked by its ravages. The ancient Russian belief in the inexhaustible riches of nature joined forces with the indifference of the new Soviet masters. Soviet civilisation brought forth engineers and managers but no Rockefellers, Carnegies or Duponts.

What was lacking was the rivalry, the competitiveness that creates the space to move in a society stuck fast in the very first stages of development. The only things that could jolt the megamachine out of its rhythm or slow its movements were internal friction and competition between rival bureaucracies or the paralysis that results from dysfunction, the sweet poison of corruption and the go-slow inefficiency of bureaucratic procedure. In short, the less well the system functioned, the greater the scope for exploitation.

This makes it clear that the difference between the American and Soviet variants was fundamental, even during the phase of heroic industrialisation and the planned landscape, which was the moment of their greatest similarity. And no less fundamental are the routes that lead out of the world of industrialism. Pittsburgh is not Magnitogorsk.

Who knows what will become of the iron landscapes in post-Soviet Russia? There are places which—unlike the Maya temples of Yucatán—no human being will ever be able to set foot in again. But there are

FIGURE 10.1. The city of Berezniki in the Urals, one of the greatest centres of phosphate mining worldwide. It became a 'Russian Atlantis'. © Alexander Gronsky, Moscow.

also new developments. Signs of the postindustrial world, of the service society, are already starting to spring up in the Soviet landscape created by iron and steel—especially in such metropolises as Moscow and St. Petersburg.

One possible consolation in the light of these depredations is that Russia is huge and evasive action can be taken even if some of the contaminated areas are as large as Germany. To this day barely explored and almost inaccessible natural regions large enough to contain several middle-sized European states still exist. Even so, the tundra is full of oil lakes and the mountains of rubble lurking in the forests give the impression that an entire civilisation has been emptied out there. Notwithstanding all that, snowy landscapes, forest clearings and rivers as pristine as on the First Day of Creation can be found, and not far away.

Ever since the megamachine stalled, the sky has become visible once again, often for the first time in decades. There has been no ecological reform; the mere shutdown of industry, bankruptcy, has sufficed. The mining towns that were built beyond the Arctic Circle by forced labour decades ago may well be dying. New towns may yet be built outside the polluted zones. The advanced posts of industrial civilisation that are too costly and require too much effort to maintain are being abandoned. And it will be up to individuals, such as are to be found everywhere, to undertake something new. For the time being, the excessive efforts of the past are over and done with; the overreach is being corrected. After decades of overexploitation, Russia is learning to husband its resources in a new way. There is a move towards greater reflection, greater concentration, and towards retrieving the most important aspects of every culture, a sense of form and a more measured approach.

The ruins of the megamachine lie scattered all over the country. As Alexander Solzhenitsyn observed years ago, they are a source of great danger. But the arts of political compromise are of no avail against the physical and moral decline of the megamachine. Steel rusts, pipes break, containers fall apart. Dismantling and deactivating weapons after a battle long-since ended continues and has even become a priority.

But what has come to an end in the post-Soviet world is not just the metallurgical world and the metallurgical worldview. Time is up also for the human beings who inhabited that world and appropriated that worldview for themselves. The heroic worker and the engineer who served as models for an entire era have long since disappeared from the stage. Their last great moment was on 26 April 1986 and the days that followed. The 'liquidators', that is, the 410,000 men who dug the tunnel under the Chernobyl reactor, who collected up the graphite blocks with their bare hands and extinguished the burning reactor, saved Europe. In so doing, they sacrificed their lives, their health and their happiness. Next time, Europe will have to do without them.

PART III

Soviet Sign-Worlds

The Soviet sign-world went into meltdown during the 1990s. We shall see what remains of it or has been revived. The script that once put its stamp on the Russian city has become indistinct, utterly extinguished or exchanged for something else. Our observations are, as always, centred on Moscow, because our experience is mainly in the capital. The vast country beyond gets by with fewer signs and symbols. It almost seems as if they were swallowed up or vanished on the distant horizon. One would like to recall them. They have disappeared, although once upon a time they marked out and defined the living space of cities. The course of world history does not always proclaim its arrival with flashes of lightning; it also makes use of advertisements in small print or in neon lights. While heated debates were still raging in the Central Committee about nuances of meaning in the communiqué announcing the new age—perestroika—the battle of the signs had already been proceeding at full tilt. Signs simply bide their time. When the moment is ripe, they burst forth from the surrounding gloom. Lights go on where beforehand all was darkness. The entire stage is plunged into a new brightness hitherto unseen. The system changes colour literally, visibly. New names and new inscriptions appear everywhere. The metro station that previously went by the name of the founder of the Cheka—Dzerzhinskaya—is now called Lubyanka, which had been the name of the square a century earlier. The former Karl-Marx Prospekt station has once again become the old Okhotny Ryad, Hunters' Row, Gilyarovsky's 'belly of Moscow'. And on it goes. Even Moscow's Broadway, Gorky Street, which is so firmly anchored in the collective memory, has now been renamed Tverskaya after the town to which the street led. Such are the changes in the capital and these have been gradually followed in other town centres, not to mention the capitals of the various republics which want to do away not just with the Soviet legacy but also with the Russian past. The recoding of the Soviet world has proceeded in a series of waves, not to say shock waves. First its streets and then its squares, monuments and institutions: that is the simplest way to effect a transformation. You change the names; there is a great universal onomastic revision, the unavoidable accompaniment of every genuine revolution. On the other hand, we can say that when the renaming process has reached the level of everyday life, a revolution has become irreversible. Party-congress resolutions can be reversed but not the transformation of an urban landscape. Names are not hollow words, as Faust believed; they are the manifestations of a status quo, a marking-out of terrain. But the contrary is also true: names can be changed, whereas institutions, structures and biographies are relatively inert and of long duration. Everything else can stay the same even when names and titles have changed.

In times of transition these markers are merely expressions of a chaotic course of events. Everything is caught up in the struggle; the granite façades of 1930s buildings now bear the logos of Yves Rocher, Reebok and Cartier. That means more than a change of a company name; it is a declaration of war, a friendly takeover, the downgrading of the somewhat outdated, dusty Soviet design by pristine, radiant glory. On the streets, above the heads of the passersby, the war of signs has broken out between the new investor and the building that is in the process of becoming a piece of real estate, a capital investment. The signs define a front that runs straight through the city. Logos that hitherto stood for the alien, distant and hostile world effect their entry, make inroads, take possession or are repulsed once again: Ernst & Young, McDonald's, Siemens, Apple, Radisson, Kempinski, Auchan, Mercedes, Apple, BMW and Samsung. They break up the line formed previously by the slogans of the Soviet universe: Gastronom, Ryba, Knigi, Produkty, Aviakassa and Aeroflot. A new vocabulary makes its entry onto the streets. The hieroglyphs of the Soviet Empire make way for the lingua franca of globalisation: *rieltory*, *brokery* and *developery*. Latin script has thrown down the gauntlet to Cyrillic. Russian appears infinitely receptive in its breadth and adaptability; it can absorb all the idioms in the world as if nothing were more natural. At some point in the 1990s Yury Luzhkov, then mayor of Moscow, demanded that the inscriptions in advertisements on Tverskaya be in Cyrillic script. Fantasy names were constructed, as was fitting for transitional phases and hybrid situations. They had an olde Soviet flavour about them and also seemed ripe for globalisation. There were labels from a hybrid world, coined in the excitement of creating something new. All this happened at a breathless pace, as if every day that passed were a day wasted—at least in the capitals and cities of over a million people. They wanted to leave the old world and its names behind. So Nestlé was preferred to Produkty (food store), McDonald's instead of Stolovaya (canteen), Hyatt instead of the Hotel Minsk. Nowadays there is not just one bank, the state Sberbank, but a whole host of other banks, including Raiffeisen, Deutsche Bank and Banque Nationale de Paris. Nowadays people do not just read either *Pravda* or *Izvestia*; they have infinite choices—or else abandon the world of newsprint in favour of the internet. Glossy magazines specialising in furniture, fashion or building your own dacha have arrived at the newspaper kiosks. Thanks to these turbulent changes in setting, Muscovites no longer recognise their surroundings and, overwhelmed by the breakneck pace of change, feel like outsiders in their own city. A backdrop that had been fixed and unambiguous for an entire lifetime seems to have dissolved. People have to reorientate themselves. The signs of Soviet Russia stood for a social order; they marked out an entire living space in which generations grew up and on which they could rely. The neon signs on the wall represent the end of an era, the loss of a sense of direction that accompanied it and which human beings have to come to terms with. We do not need to be experts in semiotics or to have read Roland Barthes's *Empire of Signs* or Umberto Eco's studies to understand the meaning of the erosion of this sign-world. It means the dissolution of the Soviet lifeworld.[1]

CHAPTER 11

The Writing on the Wall

When you look at old photos of Russian cities, you are struck by the chaotic variety of shop signs, advertising posters and their polyglot scripts. The façades seem to be completely covered by them and by looking at them you can almost read off the general structure of trade, the dominant fashions and stages of the business cycle, and identify *le dernier cri*. No doubt, this was no less true of Europe in general, at least in the multilingual nations. Everything was handcrafted and revealed something of the nature and quality of particular trades; the scripts used the old orthography and had something of the elegance of Art Nouveau. There were branches or offshoots of firms that operated nationwide and internationally—in Łódź, Riga, Vladivostok, Tbilisi, Kyiv, Kharkiv, Warsaw and Helsinki. There were addresses of firms from the late Tsarist Empire and the first globalisation, a display of luxury and fashion.

The Revolution did away with all that—from sheer necessity. The owners had fled or the firms had collapsed. The inscriptions faded and became memories of past times. There were new users and the firms ceased to bear the names of their former owners or founders. They bore the names of the organisation, the institution, the collective, the cooperative, the Soviet trust. This did not happen all at once and in the 1920s the shopping streets of the towns even witnessed a Babel-like revival. Trade and the market returned for a few years and with them firms with familiar names. But that spelled the end of the initial phase of the planned economy. The public arena began to find new occupants. It is possible, though hardly straightforward, to follow and systematise the process of recoding as it was dictated from above. While the sign-world of the past faded and became illegible, the new one was installed in powerful colours.

The slogans and mottoes, when arranged chronologically, provide something like a chronicle of public life as produced by the Party. They provide a sketch of political developments with all their ups and

downs. The lettering of each new set of slogans and mottoes tells us
about the projects, plans and opposing fronts central to the mobilisation of the masses at any given time. From them we can discover
whether we find ourselves in the NEP phase or the first Five-Year
Plan. We can gauge the international situation and the lettering tells
us whether people still understood the old orthography or whether
they had adapted to the clear, uncluttered letters inspired by avant-
garde graphic artists. Every age has its own adages, phrases and
watchwords—warnings about enemy agents and the proclamation of
relentless repression in the time of the Great Terror look very different from the guidelines that were posted at the time of peaceful coexistence and the World Festival of Youth and Students of 1957. Every era
has its slogans, but also its physiognomies, authoritative quotations
and profiles of its leaders. The heads of Marx, Engels, Lenin and Stalin
in profile, one behind the other, stood for the heyday of Stalinism,
while the disappearance of Stalin's profile made it clear that Soviet
citizens could or had to dispense with him. The leave-taking from
the sign-world of the Congresses of the CPSU was duly celebrated on
a grand scale, in Erik Bulatov's paintings, masterpieces of Moscow
conceptualism, for example. With these paintings, the signs of the
Soviet world migrated into the art galleries of the world.[1]

The Soviet order, which aimed to bring the old world into line
behind it, developed a new sign language. It was supposed to be terse
and pregnant with meaning. Abbreviations were to be a characteristic feature of the new age. Foreign visitors were puzzled by the
staccato tone of the abbreviations: Gosplan, GOELRO, ZI, Zik, NOT,
Komsomol, OSOAVIAKhIM, VOKS, VChK, OGPU, NKVD, Narkom, STO,
Narkomtyazhprom, CPSU, CC—the entire vast, multilevel organisation
of the administrative and controlling apparatus became concentrated in these cascades of unpronounceable but visually comprehensible sign-monstrosities. They can all be decoded: State Planning
Commission (Gosplan), State Commission for the Electrification of
Russia (GOELRO), Council for Work and Defence (STO), Central Executive Committee (CEC), Scientific Organisation of Labour (NOT),
and so on. They could well be subjected to analysis to show how
they formed an integral part of the hierarchical structures of the
state, the Party, the unions or the people's commissariats. Behind

such abbreviations stood institutions, organisations and ultimately collectives consisting of individuals. The abbreviations stood for the 'pillars' supporting the social order. They were the power structure made visible, radical reductions of complex structures, short forms of organisation charts or symbolic architectures of power. In Soviet times you could inspect this architecture by reviewing the signs on the brass plates on the portals of ministries and other institutions.[2] Found predominantly in the centre and on the monumental buildings erected in the 1930s and 1940s, they were the visual aids for what the German historian Dietrich Geyer has described as 'society as a state production'.

Even people unfamiliar with the country and the language learned to cope with this language of abbreviations. The acronyms entered the political jargon of the news reports and leading articles of Western newspapers, in such snippets as 'The Soviet news agency TASS has announced'; they became part of the linguistic household of an internationally networked world. Other examples included Aeroflot and Intourist as the flagship enterprises of the USSR. Another term to gain acceptance in international jargon was *troika*, which covers an extremely broad semantic field ranging from the horse team of a sleigh ride in winter to the three-man team that pronounced death sentences every few minutes at the time of the Great Terror.

The signs on the nameplates leave no doubt that we find ourselves in an imperial or even cosmic space. Hotels in Moscow were called Minsk and Ukraina (now a Four Seasons luxury hotel in one of the Stalin skyscrapers). In Kyiv the leading hotel was called Moskva (it has since become the Ukraina). Distinguished old hotels for wealthy tourists from the West were allowed to retain their prerevolutionary names: L'Europe and Astoria in Leningrad, Metropol, National and Grand Hotel in Moscow, the London in Odesa. In the capitals of the republics, the leading hotel—built mainly by the Japanese or Scandinavians—bore the name of the country: the Latvija in Riga, the Lietuva in Vilnius. Friendly relations with socialist countries were also expressed in hotel names: Warszawa, Berlin (the old Savoy), the Pekin (a perfect exemplar of the late Stalin period). In the Empire there was of course ethnic cuisine; it was easily recognised—*Aragvi* for Georgian cuisine, *Yerevan* for Armenian.

But most important of all was that the network marking out the lifeworld pointed to the places that had the greatest difficulty coping with everyday life. Here too we see the fundamental difference from the sign-world of the West. The writing didn't represent individual firms and individuals, a make or a brand; it stood for things, objects of daily use. It didn't celebrate consumer goods but use-values. The names were the names of the objects they referred to. Of course, that didn't mean that the object described actually existed. The queues might well indicate that the object concerned was in short supply. Every inscription was also associated with a specific aroma, a specific ambience or a specific light. You had to be familiar with the circumstances to know which of the many shops labelled *Khleb*/Bread were really selling tasty bread. In Soviet times, you might have to go far to find that out. Among the various points of orientation, we could list the following:

Аптека/Apteka/Pharmacy. These places to go for medicines were of the greatest importance. Even better, however, was having connections in the German Democratic Republic or Czechoslovakia, where the preferred producers of pharmaceuticals were located.

Булочная/Bulochnaya/Bakery. Muscovites always knew where the best bread was to be found. But it was always a great event when the many different kinds of bread for which Russia had once been so famous ('Filipovs') reappeared.

Хлеб/Khleb/Bread. This lovely sign always evoked a variety of contrasting memories. It could remind you of the impersonal doling-out of a box-like loaf of bread whose cost—a few kopeks— remained stable over decades. It could also remind you of extreme poverty and even hunger, but also of the warmth and light to be found in old bakehouses.

Мясо/Myaso/Meat, **Мясные продукты/Myasnye produkty/ Meat products**. It is hard to describe this range of goods when you come from a world where there are always dozens of different sorts of meat and sausage, an experience that always came as a shock to Soviet dissidents encountering Western affluence for the first time.

Мебель/Mebel/Furniture. Here too you had to be in the know. It was important to discover whether the furniture came from 'home' production or from foreign socialist countries. Analysing the furniture probably gave some insight into changes in Soviet interiors.

Продукты/Produkty/Food. This is the most neutral name imaginable and made it easy to forget that it frequently cost a lot of time to find the 'product' you were looking for.

Овощи/Ovoshchi/Vegetables. Western visitors accustomed to buying fresh produce year round were reminded that the availability of fruit and vegetables is tied to the rhythm of the seasons and the life cycle of nature.

Вино/Vino, **Винный магазин/Vinny magazin/Wine**. Here queues were common, especially before holidays; choice was limited. You saw the lucky customers hurrying off. If you knew your wines and had connections, you could obtain rarer wines from Georgia or Moldova. A comparative account of the differences in drinking cultures is a specialist topic which has already filled entire libraries.

Фарфор/Farfor/China. This sign pointed to household goods but specialised in china. On occasion, you might even have been able to buy the wonderful cobalt-blue dinner services from the Lomonosov Factory in Leningrad.

Бижутерия/Bizhuteriya/Jewellery. Crystal was greatly sought after and often adorned people's display cabinets at home. This was where the Czechoslovak glass industry probably found its most faithful customers.

Канцтовары/Kantstovary/Stationery. Here you could find paper, school exercise books and notepads—all at a time before laptops and iPads became available. These establishments smelled of paper and worries about children at school. Before the start of the new school year on 1 September was always a busy time.

Ткани/Tkani/Textiles. This simple sign led to clothes and clothing materials. There was a time when sewing and making your own clothes, often using patterns from *Burda* fashions, was a matter of course.

Кулинария/Kulinariya/Ready-Meals and Delicatessen. This sign pointed to a time when Soviet people had already emerged from the worst deprivations of the postwar and reconstruction period. 'Delicatessen' is perhaps putting it too strongly, but once inside the shop customers were on the lookout for something special with which to bring pleasure to others and also please themselves.

Торты/Torty/Gâteaux. Yes, there were in fact shops that specialised in gâteaux, such as the Prager Torte in the Praga shop. Bonbons and confectionary in colourful wrapping paper—manufactured in the Bolshevik sweet factory or the Red front—were also to be had. The legendary brands included Ptitchie Moloko and Krasnaya shapochka. The boxes for the cakes—famous in their own right—needed careful folding and tying up so that you could cautiously walk home with them in the dark.

Союзпечать/Soyuzpechat/The Soviet press. The kiosks set up by Soyuzpechat in the towns sold newspapers, magazines, city maps, illustrated magazines, TV programmes, and theatre and concert tickets. They were focal points for the distribution of official and unofficial information and opinion.

Рыба/Ryba/Fish. The simple, unadorned word told you nothing about the source or type of fish being sold. Further information had to be sought elsewhere. It was more like the abstract concept of a concrete fish variety.

Гастроном/Gastronom/Delicatessen. The sign with a beautiful 'Г' pointed to a largeish supermarket with long shelves on which the packs and packages were heaped.

Елисеевский/Yeliseevsky. These iconic food halls were easily recognisable as luxury businesses—with lots of stucco, glass, mirrors, palm trees and chandeliers. There was one on Gorky Street in Moscow and another on Nevsky Prospekt in Leningrad. The staff knew that they were working in a special place and that they were not so much servants of the public but persons of authority supplying the needs of the hordes of customers.

Таксофон/Taksofon/Telephone. There were entire batteries of these with from two to six phones for conducting conversations within the city at the cost of two kopeks. They could be found in popular locations: entrances to metro stations, underpasses, cinema foyers. The telephone was an uncommonly important means of communication in such a large city where every misunderstanding about how to meet up was a minor catastrophe, a waste of precious hours. The telephones were also a drastic illustration of people's indifference towards their fellow human beings, who may well have already been standing in line. And it goes without saying that these phones were the primary, highly vulnerable objects of hatred and vandalism. The mobile phone has caused these 'taxi phones' to retreat to a past that now seems infinitely remote.

Парикмахерская/Parikmakherskaya/Hairdresser. This is an excellent example of the elegant import of a foreign term into the Russian vocabulary. [The Russian word for hairdresser/hairstylist comes from the German 'Perückenmacher', literally, wigmaker.]

Бутербродная/Buterbrodnaya/Sandwich bar. Here too the German origin of this bistro-like establishment is easily detected. [Cf. German 'Butterbrot'.]

Книги/Knigi/Books, **Книжный магазин/Knizhny magazin/Bookshop**. This sign, enlarged sometimes by 'Books' or 'Bücher', pointed to central institutions of Soviet life. There was no house without books or where books were not read. Their stock revealed the stability of the reading culture as well as the shifts in the intellectual climate of the day. Here too, of course, there were specialisations: *Akademkniga* had academic books for serious students; *Dom knigi* were major bookstores, although these were often places of permanent disappointment and frustration since interesting and banned books were absent.

Букинсит/Bukinist/Second-hand books. This was where the hunting instinct of readers, collectors and bibliophiles was aroused. It was a world of its own, where the most improbable discoveries could be made. Examples were editions of Nietzsche or Freud dating from 1910, editions otherwise unavailable in the USSR at the time.

Квас/Kvas/Kvass. This sign was printed on the sides of brown or ochre-coloured tankers for the most part, while olive green

tankers bore the inscription *огнеопасно/ogneopasno*/inflamma-
ble. It was hard for a foreigner to believe that the kvass, a liquid
drawn from a tap, was a kind of weak beer that could be drunk.
Here too the locals knew exactly which tankers were carrying
the good brews and which the inferior.

Газированная вода/Gazirovannaya voda/Sparkling water.
Automats with this inscription were an achievement of the postwar period, an index of the arrival of automation in the realms
of consumption and the service industry. You pushed down the
glass that was there in order to rinse it out, put a kopek in the
slot and fizzy water poured into the glass. If you put in three kopeks, the water would be mixed with red syrup. The refrigerator
mechanism made the automat vibrate. Astonishingly, no one
took the glass but always put it back.

Авиакасса/Aviakassa/Plane tickets. You could find these all
over the city, as well as in the branch offices of the railway. This
was a reminder that the land was infinitely vast and that both
flying around and railway journeys that lasted for days on end
were nothing unusual but an everyday experience that determined the rhythms of life.

Универмаг/Univermag/Department store. Department store
architecture had been developed even before the Revolution; a
Moscow example was the Art Nouveau–style Voentorg Building
that was demolished on the orders of Mayor Yury Luzhkov. Its
floors were mainly built around a large light well. You could buy
almost anything there except foodstuffs. City planning from the
1930s on was concerned with the construction of such department stores.

This list is neither exhaustive nor representative. It shows only that
the cycle of everyday Soviet life was defined in specific ways. People
grow up with signs and logos that mark out their ambient world and
enable them to orientate themselves. These signs were part of the
immediate, physical organisation of daily life. Distances played a role,
as did the adverse features of the climate. By listing these elements,
we are not concerned to provide what Natalia Lebina calls an 'encyclopedia of banalities', but an encyclopedia of fundamentals. And if we

were to draw a map of the daily movements of Soviet citizens, above all in the towns, these, together with a few others, would be among the chief points of orientation. Each of these keywords possesses an entire semantic penumbra made up of experiences, aromas, rumour and knowledge. Most of them surface in literature in the form of background and milieu. People's lives ran their course surrounded by them. If you know about the seeming permanence, the sheer stability of this horizon, you begin to understand the violent impact felt when it dissolved. The USSR has made way for ROSSIYA. TASS has ceased to exist; instead we have ITAR-TASS. The logos of GAZPROM adorn the tower of the state enterprise in the south of Moscow, and the illuminated signs of LUKOIL shine out above the country's petrol stations. Bookshops now bear names such as BIBLIOGLOBUS or FALANSTER or RESPUBLIKA. Travel bureaus have fantasy names that somehow evoke the beaches of the Red Sea or Thailand. In the midst of all this, we see such names as APPLE and SAMSUNG.

CHAPTER 12

Decorations and Medals: Chest Badges

The most interesting but also most puzzling corners in the bazaars and flea markets found in all Russian towns and cities are those with stalls devoted to *znachki*, medals. They are all neatly laid out there, creating the effect of a densely wrought colourful mosaic. When it rains, they are covered over with a plastic sheet. These stalls are always surrounded by people who speak with expert knowledge of the medals on view. Together with the workbooks that log the life and career development of Soviet citizens year by year and workplace by workplace; alongside the diplomas for special achievements, certificates of merit and photograph albums, it is the medals that lure customers, enthusiasts, collectors and the sellers of personal effects and heirlooms to come here every weekend. The spectrum of these insignia ranges from ordinary sports badges, from distinctions such as 'New Marksman' or 'Young Tourist' for both girls and boys, to Young Pioneers or Communist Youth (Komsomol) badges. There were endless reasons for creating badges: in honour of the foundation of towns, sporting events, Spartakiads, the Olympic Games; in honour of famous sons and daughters of particular towns; for long service in a factory or institute; for early years' service spent reclaiming land or building a pipeline; in honour of the first space flight. They are made of shiny metal or tin-plate and have a logo or else a red flag, hammer and sickle, or the logo of the combine making the award. The entire universe of Soviet symbols is represented in all its diversity and beauty: cogwheels, hammer and sickle, axe, anvil, plough, spade, head frames, chimneys, tractors and industrial plants. There were additional symbols for agriculture: sheaves of corn, cotton flowers, horses, riders and cattle.[1] The weightier and hence more expensive pieces are decorations or even medals on which an entire life depended, not simply a working life, but survival in a life-and-death struggle for the defence of the realm or the destruction of the enemy, that is, of German fascism. Such medals have found their way into the flea markets and, even more commonly, to the electronic bazaars and auction houses. If there is an element of humiliation here, it lies in the fact that these emblems of self-sacrifice to the point of death are being sold off like this. We might well prefer not to imagine what goes on in the minds of veterans when they see these military decorations, the more distinguished of them in velvet cases, being offered for sale as if they were just any old goods.

Medals and decorations in their sheer quantity and profusion are not just on view in bazaars and flea markets. Soviet society had a medal culture and cult all its own. Decorations for both preschool- and schoolchildren were only the beginning in a life full of decorations for merit of one kind or another. On approaching a town that resisted the German invasion—Moscow, Leningrad, Kyiv and Odesa among others—monumental signs remind you of the achievements of the 'heroic city'. Plaques listing awards can be found in stations, factories and institutes. Works entrances are often flanked by granite or marble colonnades on which the top workers' names have been engraved, or there are display cabinets containing their portraits. The most obvious evidence of this culture was the medals proudly worn on the appropriate occasions—1 May, 9 May, 7 November—by veterans, members of the Red Army, wartime industry and the partisan movement. The further the war receded into the past, the more their wearers appeared bowed down beneath the weight of their honours, though they evidently still had the strength to wear them, as is the way with those who have been through a baptism of fire. A strange mixture of sadness and pride prevailed when the fighters of yore turned up on the dance floors of the culture and recreation parks for a waltz on those days of remembrance. Veterans of both sexes were ubiquitous but not always popular when they made their appearance and, protected by the imposing decorations on their chest, exercised their privilege of bypassing the queues in the delicatessens, in being served with drinks or at theatre ticket offices. But a medal also created an aura of respect and generated a kind of positive discrimination for its bearer, who claimed its benefits as a matter of course.

FIGURE 12.1. Those familiar with the significance of medals, decorations and insignia can use them to gain an understanding of military organizations, social hierarchies and the experiences of different generations. © culture-images/fai.

The military in general lived off the nimbus of heroic sacrifice. The military were easily recognisable, just as if they were a specially constituted class of human beings. They always seemed exceptional, thanks to their stature, peaked caps visible above other people's heads in the metro, military overcoats with fur collars and insignia that revealed their rank, as long as you knew enough to identify it, which of course was far from a given in a generation that grew up in peacetime.

The greatest experts when it comes to the world of medals and distinctions, apart from the civil servants and museum staff concerned with such matters, are of course the collectors, since they have usually studied the specialist literature, which they sometimes carry around with them in plastic folders and files. They know all about the finer details of a five-pointed star or a medallion, can tell you all about production locations and award numbers, how to attach the insignia to clothing—with a grub screw and nut—and on which occasions it was to be worn. Conversation with the collectors is redolent of a stroll through the Soviet-Russian past narrated through the history of medals and honours. Where the layman can obtain no more than a general overview, such connoisseurs enable the mosaic to speak and you learn about the design, material, origins and hierarchy inscribed as well as about the rise and fall of the Soviet-Russian state.

Statistics confirm the impression created by the Soviet honours system that it has developed in connection primarily with military achievements, while civil awards—for scholarship, the economy and culture—are very much in second place. The statistics of the Soviet honours system in general provide a key to the sociological analysis of elite formation. It shows a status structure and a meritocracy sui generis.

What is an honours system and what is it supposed to achieve? The Constitution of the Honours System of 1936 states: 'Honours are the highest distinctions in the country. They can be awarded both to individuals and to military units and sections, businesses, institutions and organisations. . . . Those who are honoured are required constantly to give a good example in the fulfilment of their duties as citizens. Those who are honoured are entitled to particular rights—a monthly sum of money, rent and travel reductions, exemption from income tax, lowering of the pensionable age.'[2] The Soviet honours system did not emerge all at once with a decree, but rather, emerged spontaneously, starting with the Civil War. On 20 August 1918, a unit of the Red Army was awarded the Honorary Revolutionary Red Banner— an award made to a collective, not an individual. The honours chapter of the Tsarist court was abolished but the Mint, which produced the medals, remained the same. Awards were now made not to dignitaries but to deserving fighters of the Revolution—the honours system underwent a social revolution. The crosses and eagles disappeared from the medals and were replaced by the Red flag, which had become the state flag of the Russian Soviet Republic after 8 April 1918, as well as the hammer, sickle, ploughshare, red star, torch, rifle and bayonet—all symbols of the new honours system. Over time other honours were created, both centrally by the Soviet Union, which was established in 1922, and by the national republics. Important additions included the establishment of the Order of Lenin and the Order of the Red Star on 6 April 1930, which were intended above all for politicians, people involved in the economy, scientists, technologists, doctors, as well as artists and writers. The decoration with the bust of Lenin encircled by a wreath of wheat and with a Red flag was awarded to such diverse figures as top worker Alexey Stakhanov, director Konstantin Stanislavsky, botanist Ivan Michurin, writer Maxim Gorky and military officer Kliment Voroshilov. On 16 April 1934 the most important honour, that of Hero of the Soviet Union, was established to reward those who participated in the rescue of the crew of the *Chelyuskin,* which had been imprisoned in Arctic ice. On 27 December 1938 the order of Hero of Socialist Labour was established with a gold star, hammer and sickle and red ribbon.

The Soviets broke with the forms and practices of the Tsarist honours system. Peter the Great had been the pioneer in this sphere, as in so many others, and established honours and medals. Military awards predominated in the magnificent honours system of the Tsars, the most outstanding of which can be seen today in museums. They included the Order of St. Andrew of 1698, which was the highest, very sparingly awarded decoration, originally a military honour; the Order of St. Catherine, founded in 1714, a high distinction for women; the Order of St. Alexander Nevsky, established in 1725 for serving officers of the rank of general; the Order of the White Eagle, founded in 1723 for military and civil achievements; the Order of St. George the Martyr, a military honour dating from 1769; the Order of St. Vladimir of 1782; the Order of St. Anna, established in 1735; the Order of St. Stanislaus, created in 1765 by Stanisław August Poniatowski, king of Poland, and adopted by the Tsarist Empire.[3] Apart from these honours, there were memorial crosses, decorations for merit during the overthrow of oppressed and rebellious peoples—the conquest of Warsaw in 1861, the crushing of Hungary and Transylvania in 1849 and the conquest of the Western Caucasus in 1864—decorations for the regiments and military colleges, for the Page Corps and the Cadet School. The honours system bore the marks of the caste system. Decorations were tied to a particular ranking. There were five categories of eligible persons: all clerical, military, civil and court ranks, then merchants and members of other estates. Petty bourgeois and members of the peasantry were excluded. In the Patriotic War against Napoleon, peasant soldiers were denied medals. Not until the crisis of the Tsarist Empire in the

First World War did the ordinary rank and file qualify for honours as a reward for fighting. The Cross of St. George, which went back to the year 1807 but was initially intended exclusively for officers, was awarded over one million times in the First World War up to 1917—as a mass decoration for patriotic soldiers.

It was during the Great Patriotic War of 1941–1945 that the honours system was revamped and brought to its full flowering—with visible traces that persisted far into the postwar period. In January 1943 military ranks and shoulder boards were reintroduced. Prerevolutionary military traditions and the names of the great generals were explicitly invoked. Orange ribbon with vertical black stripes was chosen for the Order of Glory. This was consciously modelled on the prerevolutionary Cross of St. George. The actual conditions of war made it necessary to simplify procedures for rewarding mass heroism. Hence commanding officers were given the power to award medals to members of their units. Soldiers, NCOs and officers were presented with decorations on the battlefield and in the presence of their comrades. New medals were created using the names of famous Russian generals: Alexander Suvorov, Mikhail Kutuzov, Fyodor Ushakov, Bogdan Khmelnitsky and Alexander Nevsky. These were followed somewhat later by the highest military decorations of the country, the one-class Order of Victory and the three-class Order of Glory with a five-pointed star and the Spassky Tower of the Moscow Kremlin. The rules governing the award of the medals were strict: a fixed number of planes had to be shot down or tanks destroyed. Most recipients were the sons of workers and peasants.[4]

After 1944 decorations were also introduced for persons active behind the lines: workers, collective farmers, scientists, technicians, teachers and medical staff. The medal 'For Valiant Labour in the Great Patriotic War 1941–1945' was bestowed over sixteen million times, making it the most frequently awarded decoration. Even after the war was over, thousands of additional medals and decorations were conferred since many heroic deeds came to light only later on.[5]

The honours system after the end of the war reflects the nation's return to civilian life and the labour of rebuilding in the 'Fourth Five-Year Plan for the Reconstruction and Further Development of the Economy of the USSR for the Years 1946–1950'. As medals for war service inevitably receded into the background, the number of awards for civil achievements grew. Between 1941 and 1945 there were 5,122 awards of the Order of Lenin; these increased to 212,880 for the period 1946–1964.[6] Decorations and medals now had such designations as 'For the Restoration of the Donbass Coal Mines', 'For the Restoration of the Black Metallurgy Enterprises of the South' and 'For the Development of Virgin Lands'. It was also the age of jubilees, with medals 'In Commemoration of the 800th Anniversary of Moscow', 'In Commemoration of the 250th Anniversary of Leningrad' and 'In Commemoration of the 1500th Anniversary of Kyiv'. Because of the extreme economic constraints of the postwar years, decorations were not linked to any financial privileges. At their core was service for the common good—saving lives in the fire service, for example—and achievements in science and culture. On 4 October 1957, the first satellite, Sputnik, was sent into space; on 12 April 1961, Yury Gagarin became the first man in space. During this phase, titles such as National Artist of the Russian Federation; Creative Worker in Theatre, Film or Music; Honoured Test Pilot or Honoured Pilot of the USSR; Architect of the Nation; Doctor of the Nation; Teacher of the Nation; Honoured Inventor of the USSR; as well as Honoured Agronomist of the USSR predominate. Long after the war was over, decorations were created for twelve heroic cities and the Fortress of Brest. On the fiftieth anniversary of the October Revolution, the order named after it was created, the second most important after the Order of Lenin. The honours system established in the USSR was also extended to foreigners and internationalists, including Germans such as Konrad and Friedrich Wolf, the so-called enlightener Ruth Werner (a notorious spy) and cosmonaut Sigmund Jähn.

A chest covered in medals sometimes resembles a bas-relief whose subtle shadings can be read and interpreted. The men and women wearing decorations resemble living monuments; they represent the history that extends into our present world. As a statistic, one thing stands out: the rapid growth of military decorations in the war, a sign of a society caught up in a struggle for self-assertion and survival. The statistics of the medals and decorations awarded between 1918 and 1964 reveal a dramatic surge in the war years. Between 1924 and 1927 there were only 60 Heroes of the Soviet Union, between 1938 and 1940 there were only 561, while between 1941 and 1945 there were as many as 11,025. If all honours and medals are taken together, there were 18,145 between 1924 and 1937, 119,911 in 1938–1941 and as many as 13,144,303 in 1941–1945.[7] A population scarred by war. A sociological breakdown would reveal a hierarchical society that produced an aristocracy of its own while at the same time reverting to prerevolutionary traditions.

The holdings of the Central Museum of the Revolution show that up to 1982 1,038 decorations of different kinds were collected. This turns out to be a catalogue of an elite divided into three groups— the USSR in general, the Soviet republics on a regional level and, lastly, individuals.[8] When broken down according to the sectors of the economy—iron and steel, coal, oil, chemicals, shipbuilding, timber, etc.—the statistics of decorations conferred between 1918 and 1964 reveal a more or less exact mirroring of the principal emphases of the development of Soviet industry. They show, furthermore, that workers in agriculture were honoured far less frequently.[9] All of this would constitute material for study of a class that has never existed in this form. It would consist of physicists, physiologists, polar explorers, directors of trusts, chemists, aircraft engineers, hydroelectrical engineers, geologists, directors of truck factories, partisans, participants in the Spanish Civil War, former revolutionaries, microbiologists, pilots, Party and state officials. For the sake of completeness, we should include the honours systems of enemies of the Soviet Union, such as the White movement, the volunteer army. They too had their decorations and medal rituals, such as the Order of St. Nicholas the Wonderworker.[10] Taken together, these awards amount to something like a relief of Russo-Soviet excellence in the twentieth century, especially in the military sphere.

CHAPTER 13

Body Language: Tattoos

It is a far cry from tattoos as the stigmata of the Middle Ages to the bodily accessory of modern fashion. Well into the twentieth century they were a sign by which seamen, itinerant adventurers, members of the foreign legion and other exotic characters could be recognised. Now tattoos have become an omnipresent ornament, a drawing on what are mainly beautiful, bronzed bodies—a memento of a holiday in the south, an encounter that presages or ought to presage major developments in one's future life. The 'normal' world long resisted tattooing. It was something for outsiders, for people who did not quite fit in. In the Soviet Union, too, it was associated with sailors, that privileged group who had been able to explore the great wide world, or with soldiers recalling their time spent in garrison towns. Overall, however, it was a practice that had drifted into everyday normality from the criminal world, long before it became fashionable during perestroika or the postperestroika period. A tattoo would catch the eye of strangers; it might be a cross on the back of a hand, a date or a pierced heart on an arm in a sauna or the figure of Stalin with a halo on a truck driver's chest—almost as striking as the picture of Stalin on a taxi windscreen. We are not speaking here of the burn marks on the shoulder blades or forearm inflicted by the prison system on convicted prisoners—army deserters, major or minor criminals, convicts sentenced to banishment or forced labour. Those were the slave marks of doomed people. Setting aside the seamen, tattoos in the Soviet Union up to the Second World War were for criminals, recognition signs of a subculture which had in many ways become the dominant culture, at least in the prisons and camps. They were part of a secret language of a population running into the millions, the distinguishing feature of a hierarchy which, under the control of clans and bosses, could decide a person's life or death.

No one can describe this world or contribute to the deciphering of its peculiar body language better than a person who has spent a life studying and experiencing it, a person who has analysed it as a kind of linguist of the body. The multiple volumes of the *Russian Criminal Tattoo Encyclopaedia* were published by two such experts: Danzig Baldaev and Alexey Plutser-Sarno [and photographer Sergey Vasiliev].

Danzig Baldaev comes from the family of a famous ethnologist and a specialist in Buryat national customs. At least fifty-eight members of his family lost their lives in the repressions of the GPU and NKVD. They were all educated people—doctors, technologists, teachers, engineers, surveyors and mining experts. Baldaev's baptised Buryat-Mongol family had achieved prosperity and recognition under the Tsars, but, as often happened, was divided and joined opposing factions in the Civil War. Following the Great Purges, his father was arrested in 1938, while Danzig, as the 'son of an enemy of the people', was placed in a special camp for children. Starting out from this experience, he spent decades collecting material about the language and folklore of the criminal world and visiting penal colonies and reformatory camps in Central Asia, the Caucasus, Ukraine, Northern Russia and the Baltic. For a long time, he worked in the Criminal Investigation Department of the Ministry of the Interior in St. Petersburg.[1]

The coauthor of the *Encyclopaedia* hails from language studies, more particularly, the Tartu-Moscow Semiotic School of Yury Lotman, which produced pioneering studies on the development of semiotics in the Soviet Union. Plutser-Sarno writes in his contribution to the illustrative material provided by Baldaev,

> Strange as it may seem, the tattoo-covered body of a *vor v zakone* (legitimate thief) is primarily a linguistic object. Tattoos are a unique language of symbols and the rules for 'reading' them are transmitted via oral tradition. . . . Esoteric in nature, this language resembles thieves' argot and it performs a similar function to protect itself against uninitiated outsiders. In exactly the same way as argot is a masked language, neutral words with coded meanings, tattoos convey 'secret' symbolic information through the use of allegorical images which at first glance may seem familiar to everyone (a naked woman, a devil, a burning candle, a dungeon, a snake, a bat, etc.). This is a language that is both highly socialized and politicized. A thief's tattooed body is like a 'depiction' of a full-dress

uniform covered with regalia, decorations and badges of rank and distinction. In thieves' jargon the traditional set of tattoos is called *frak s ordenami* (a tail-coat of decorations), an expression that is included in Danzig Baldaev's dictionary of thieves' slang.[2]

And in fact the signs resemble the epaulettes, rings, chains and crosses found on uniforms. These tattoos do indeed contain the complete 'professional actions' of a criminal, his entire career. All his successes and failures are listed, his promotions and demotions, 'disciplinary transfers' to gaol and 'moves' for various 'purposes'. A thief's tattoos are his 'passport', his 'case file', 'awards record', 'diplomas' and 'epitaphs'. In other words, they represent his full set of official bureaucratic 'documents'. A man who is tattooed is one of the old lags and initiates; for those in the know, a man with no tattoos stands right at the bottom of the ladder. This is how prison inmates are identified and distinguished from one another.

Once you understand the secret meanings, what looks at first like a chaotic jumble of symbols turns out to be a system of communication and information. The body conveys a message; it becomes a kind of living letter. Thus 'tattoos', according to Plutser-Sarno, are a sort of 'mass medium of the underworld', symbols of an identity put on public display, a demonstration of social self-awareness and collective memory. They set out the rituals and rules necessary for maintaining order in the world of thieves. The Russian word *bog* (God) stands for 'I shall rob again'; *zhuk* (beetle) stands for 'I wish you successful robbing'; *mir* (peace) for 'Shooting will reform me better'; *NKVD* (People's Commissariat for Internal Affairs) for 'Nothing is stronger than friendship among crooks'. These tattoos express an entire legal code. The tattoos 'brand' a man and transform him into a 'character'. Each tattoo tells a story, narrates a history. 'The corpus of modern thieves' tattoos devoted to historical events is immense. Practically the whole of Russian history has been drawn on the bodies of Russian convicts.'[3] Anyone who wears a tattoo to which he is not entitled is 'wiped out'—and that goes from the amputation of a finger with a false ring right down to stigmatising a fellow inmate as a despised 'cockerel' who can be 'used' by anyone at any time. Tattoos acquired for no good reason have to be removed by whatever means

FIGURE 13.1. '"Legitimate" thieves in the Gulag were as privileged as modern-day bureaucrats.... Criminal prisoners in the Gulag ranked three times higher than the "enemies of the people." Authoritative or "legitimate" thieves with numerous previous convictions usually did not work.' From Danzig Baldaev, *Drawings from the Gulag*, translated by Polly Gannon and Ast A. Moore, Murray & Sorrell FUEL, London 2010, 83.

available—knives, razor blades or a lump of brick. The very terms that the tattoo artist/*kolshchik* uses have a deterrent effect. The needle is called an 'ice-pick'/*peshnya*; the machine for applying tattoos is called a 'typewriter'/*mashinka*, 'sewing machine'/*shveynaya mashina* or 'drill'/*bormashina*; the ink, 'fuel oil'/*mazut* or 'dirt'/*gryaz*. The tattoo itself is called 'advert'/*reklama*, 'regalia'/*regalka*, 'painting'/*raspiska*, or alternatively 'brand'/*kleymo*.

Tattoos determine people's conduct and their place in a hierarchy; they structure the social space. The body, which is covered over and over with hieroglyphs, with magic signs becomes a stage 'on which ritual scenes are produced'. They are also a kind of talisman—like pictures of guardian angels or of churches. There are symbols of death, such as crosses, axes, snakes and scythes. The skull stands for death, which the crook does not fear. Tattoos are also the mark of initiation when the young criminal is branded with the sign of death that signifies his death as a bourgeois subject. 'The language of tattoos reveals to us that thieves regard themselves as characters from the world beyond. Prison itself is symbolically regarded as a grave, and visiting it is a major part of the life of a thief.'[4]

Whether signs can be interpreted as messages of political resistance has often been debated. But, as Alexander Solzhenitsyn has shown in detail, the principal dividing line in both prisons and camps runs between criminals and the prison or camp personnel on the one hand, and the political inmates on the other. The life of a 'politico', however lengthy his sentence, counted for nothing in the eyes of the criminals. There are indeed political, anti-Soviet tattoos: 'Lenin as the Chief Boss of the CPSU', 'Stalin as Head of the Camp of Socialism', 'Brezhnev as the chief arse of the Kremlin', 'Gorbachev as the Slave of Marxist-Leninist lies and deceptions'.[5] Hammers and sickles often have barbed wire wrapped round them. The common image of Lenin is a concealed acronym for VOR, roughly, a 'thief', but also an abbreviation of 'Leader of the October Revolution'. Police are represented as devils with horns and tails or as vampires and bats. According to the *Encyclopaedia*, it would be a misunderstanding to interpret all this as the work of 'dissidents'; it is rather the categorical rejection of a 'system' to collaborate with which would be judged the very worst form of treachery and punished as such. The tattoos of criminals speak the language of hoodlum law; they are declarations of war on the 'cops'.

The principal symbol of a VOR is the playing-card colour black of clubs or spades. Among the basic hoodlum signs, we find pictures of skulls, the suit of clubs (as in playing cards) and animals such as cats, panthers, leopards, tigers, snakes and eagles. Cats symbolise smartness and thieves' luck; knives stand for power, strength and ruthlessness. There are erotic tattoos—a heart, two hearts pierced by arrows, the name of a wife or girlfriend—but these symbols may have nothing to do with sex; they can also refer to gambling debts. *Blyad*/'tart' is the word for the greatest possible humiliation—for men stigmatised as prostitutes. The diamond is the sign for 'stool pigeon'/*stukach*, engraved by force. Nor do pictures of the sex act have anything to do with sex; they are a matter of humiliation/*opuskanie*, a licence for rape, in other words, for the exercise of power or domination. Erotic tattoos on the bodies of prostitutes, in contrast, point to their profession inside the camp and so amount to a form of protection and privilege that exempts them from work.[6]

The body is treated as a sculpture and furnished with artificial scars. Armed penises as instruments of torture or rape, or ears cut off, and strips of skin peeled off from the head—these are practices that evidently occur in prisons the world over.

Here, however, there is another significant factor: the mass of people who were swept through the camps, especially after the Second World War. Having been released after Stalin's death by Khrushchev's great amnesty, they invaded the 'normal world', where they spread fear and terror far and wide. With their arrival, underworld slang entered the standard language, infiltrated and merged with it so that tattoos ended up going far beyond the criminal world. In consequence, 'millions of absolutely honest, upright citizens bear these tattoos. And this has happened simply because every fifth inhabitant of our country has passed through the camps and one in every two has been in the army zone.'[7]

CHAPTER 14

Moscow Graffiti: In the Beginning Was Futurism

Probably the world's most significant graffiti are the ones made by the troops of the Red Army after they forced their way into the monster's cave and introduced them on the blackened walls of the Reichstag in Berlin. This was an occupation first by force of arms, then by chalk marks. There was a huge scramble at the conclusion of the campaign that had ended in Berlin with the defeat of Nazi Germany. The troops had arrived with their last reserves of strength. Finally, victory had come. But there were no triumphant orgies; it was all laconic—a name, the town and the date. Here we were: Major Bondarev, Colonel Yakovlev. In bold, legible letters, the inscriptions of those who had come through.

Those aside, inscriptions and writing on the walls were meagre in the Soviet world. Public spaces were the property of the Party; graffiti, to say nothing of proclamations, amounted to sabotage and treason. Whether there were subversive messages in any quantity can be ascertained only in the archives of the secret service. The graffiti I saw were all on station entrances in the larger towns, on firewalls and in courtyards backing onto railway tracks, on the sides of garages and the concrete walls surrounding factories. You could travel through corridors and, on the Trans-Siberian Railway, pass through thousands of kilometres with rear views of towns. There wasn't much to see. There were signs put up by the fans of football clubs or ice-hockey teams—the D of Dynamo fans, the abbreviation CSKA of the Army Sports Club, the capital S of Spartak Moscow or Zenit in Leningrad. The battle between rival teams was continued on fences and house walls, as everywhere else the world over—D became *Dura*/idiot, Spartak became *myaso*/ meat. People mocked, ridiculed and threatened on walls. These were the pronouncements of passionate fans. Over time, other voices made themselves heard. You could see the words PEACE or MAKE LOVE NOT

WAR when Soviet troops were being sent to Afghanistan. It was risky to put up such messages and they were certainly noted by state security. Moreover, the fact that symbols and words started to appear in English was new and amounted to a breakout from linguistic provinciality— FUCK OFF. Alongside the football fans, you could now also see the supporters of rock bands who made their own marks: PUNK, ROCK, Beatles, Led Zeppelin, ABBA, AC/DC.

Further developments in graffiti and the leap into the public, political sphere came in the 1980s, following perestroika. Since then, a subculture that has established contact with the global scene of street art in its has developed language, materials and aesthetic, especially in the large towns. There is a lot of pleasure in imitation at work. It is all greatly inspired by the New York or Berlin scene that could have been viewed on visits abroad, but it also has its own, autonomous language. Displayed in galleries, it had long since reached the level of high culture; its masters had emerged from anonymity and competition for the most original tag was fierce. Graffiti had been prohibited and so were all the more tempting, just as conduct that was actually an expression of opposition was frequently punished as hooliganism. The graffiti showed how society ticked—whether passionate idealists or suburban youth who wished to show they were the equals of the intelligentsia of the capital. Hence alongside such slogans as THE WIND OF CHANGE you find BEAT THE JEWS, BEAT THE BLACKS (by which was meant people from the Caucasus) and RUSSIA FOR THE RUSSIANS! Swastikas and SS runes were not uncommon, and it is not easy to decide whether these were intended as dirty words with which to provoke the official antifascist line or to be taken at face value.

In his study of Moscow graffiti, John Bushnell has provided a 'thick description' of the stairwell in the building at Bolshaya Sadovaya 10 that leads to Apartment 50. He sees it as an arena where opposing sides fight for control of the graffiti on the walls.[1] Again and again, young people gathered around the spot; these were the fans of Mikhail Bulgakov, who had lived in this building and this apartment for a long time, immortalising it in his novel *The Master and Margarita*. The stairwell has become a cult location, a site of the Moscow underground in the process of striving to leave that world and the subculture behind it. The walls of the stairwell are covered in painting and

FIGURE 14.1. The chalk inscriptions of the Red Army troops on the walls of the Reichstag in Berlin are among the most famous graffiti of the twentieth century. © Getty Images/The LIFE Picture Collection/William Vandivert.

writing but the concierge regularly whitewashed and painted them over. The novel was not published in the Soviet Union until later on and the quotations from it that migrated into the graffiti make clear why they were not tolerated. They read, 'Manuscripts don't burn', 'The greatest sin is cowardice' and 'Never talk to strangers'. But the graffiti artists finally triumphed and, after pressure by a civic group, the apartment in Bolshaya Sadovaya became the first graffiti location to be turned into a museum, the Bulgakov Museum. What began as a meeting point of the Moscow scene has grown into a stopping place on the Moscow visitor tour.

While public spaces in Soviet times provided little scope for spontaneous, uncensored speech—which was treated as 'vandalism'—the risk of monotony and a feeling of emptiness were met with more than official posters and slogans. In public places, in Kunst am Bau [that is, the so-called 'percent for art' principle in building projects], art even enjoyed a special flowering in the late Soviet period. Murals, frescoes and mosaics adorned underpasses, bridges and foyers, which had previously been ideal spaces for the handwritten products of anonymous graphic artists. What might be called the artistic public space became immunised against spontaneous incursions.

The works of the graffiti and spray-paint pioneers have meanwhile begun to populate the great art collections but what their creators have forgotten is that they are simply taking up practices long since introduced into the world—by the Russian Futurists in the years directly after the Revolution. At that time too—the end of the Tsarist Empire—artists wished to break into the space reserved for a controlled, quasi-official public realm. What was at stake was taking possession of the streets and squares and turning them into great stages and graphic surfaces. The abstract installations of the Suprematists covered several storeys of the façades of neoclassical palaces, proclaiming the victory of the world proletariat. These graffiti have entered the history of twentieth-century art. Their authors were not anonymous but went by such names as Kazimir Malevich, Ivan Puni, David Burlyuk, David Shterenberg and Natan Altman.[2] Such spectacular redecorations of squares and streets was not something organised from above but could base itself on what amounted to a takeover of the streets by the 'revolutionary masses'. It took a while before the powers-that-be were able to regain control of language in public spaces and give it a fixed, standardised or, as many people might say, congealed and fossilised form, namely as the banners and slogans that were brought out annually on 1 May, 9 May and 7 November.

In contrast, the takeover of public space by the graphic artists could be seen typically in the Futurist document of February 1918, with its title 'Decree #1: On the Democratisation of Art':

Comrades and citizens, we, the leaders of Russian futurism—the revolutionary art of youth—declare:

1. From this day forward, with the abolition of tsardom, the domicile of art in the closets and sheds of human genius—palaces, galleries, salons, libraries, theaters—is abrogated.
2. In the name of the great march of equality for all, as far as culture is concerned, let the Free Word of creative personality be written on the corners of walls, fences, roofs, the streets of our cities and villages, on the backs of automobiles, carriages, streetcars, and on the clothes of all citizens.
3. Let pictures (colors) be thrown, like colored rainbows, across streets and squares, from house to house, delighting, ennobling the eye (taste) of the passer-by. Artists and writers have the immediate duty to get hold of their pots of paint and, with their masterly brushes, to illuminate, to paint all the sides, foreheads, and chests of cities, railway stations, and the ever-galloping herds of railway carriages.

    From now on, let the citizen walking down the street enjoy at every moment the depths of thought of his great contemporaries, let him absorb the flowery gaudiness of this day's beautiful joy, let him listen to music—the melody, the roar, the buzz—of excellent composers everywhere.
    Let the streets be a feast of art for all.[3]

Much can be said in support of the idea that the painters of post-Soviet graffiti have taken up where their predecessors left off. At any rate, we can certainly think of the campaign of the St. Petersburg group Voyna in this way. They succeeded in spray-painting a giant 'Penis under Arrest by the KGB' on the Liteyny Bridge in St. Petersburg. The bridge, which had been raised for a few hours at night, aimed this monumental graffiti penis at the St. Petersburg night sky with its message to the Great House that is (and always has been) universally known in St. Petersburg as the seat of the NKVD/KGB/FSB.

CHAPTER 15

Names Are Not Just Hot Air

Name changes coincide with changes of era. This can be seen in toponyms—the renaming of towns, squares and streets—but also in people's names. The latter are bestowed by parents and as a rule accompany a person for life. They become part of his or her persona. Changing them can signify a change of social or marital status, apostasy or departure from one's original family. Names can be stigmas, but also protective masks.

How abrupt the breach may have been can be seen from a survey of first names that became current after the Revolution. This selection is quite arbitrary and is listed in Russian alphabetical order:

Avangard for avant-garde; *Aida* after Verdi's heroine; *Almaz* the diamond; *Arlen* formed from Armiya Lenina [Lenin's army, i.e., the workers]; *Vilen*, a composite of Vladimir Ilyich Lenin; *Vladlen*, also from Vladimir Lenin; *Volt* from the electrical term; *Gely* for the chemical element helium; *Dzhonrid* for John Reed, the American journalist and witness of the Revolution; *Zhores* to commemorate Jean Jaurès; *Istmat* from *istorichesky materialism*, i.e., historical materialism; *Karlen*, a combination of Karl Marx and Vladimir Lenin; *Kim*, the official abbreviation of Kommunistichesky internatsional molodyozhi (Young Communist International); *Lyublen* from *lyubov Lenina*, 'love of Lenin'; *Magnita*, a reminder of the founding of Magnitogorsk; *Marat*, a tribute to the French revolutionary Jean-Paul Marat; *Marlen* in honour of Marx and Lenin; *Mauzer* from the notorious pistol in widespread use in the Civil War; *Mels* for four of the fathers of communism: Marx, Engels, Lenin, Stalin; *Ninel*, Lenin backwards; *Oktyabrina* from *Oktyabrskaya revolyutsiya*; *Pravlen*, an indissoluble union of the truth and Lenin (*Pravda Lenina*); *Rady* for the element radium; *Remark*, an abbreviation of *Revolyutsionny Marksizm (Revolutionary Marxism)*; *Revolt* identical with the English 'revolt'; *Roi* from *Revolyutsiya, Oktyabr, Internat-sional* (Revolution, October, International); *Rem* from *Revolyut-siya, Elektrifikatsiya, Mir* (Revolution, Electrification and Peace/ World and the Russian village community *mir*); children are also named after revolutionaries: *Spartak* from Spartacus; *Stalen* from Stalin and Lenin; *Torez* from Maurice Thorez; *Trolen* from Trotsky and Lenin; *Fed* from Felix Edmundovich Dzerzhinsky, the founder of the Cheka; *Evir* from *Epokha, Voyna, Revolyutsiya* (Epoch, War, Revolution); *Elem* from Engels, Lenin, Marx; *Erlen* from the era of Lenin. Additional names include *Traktor/Traktorina, Turbina* and *Elektrina*.

Richard Stites has attempted to bring some sort of order and logic into this plethora of new names. He has divided them as follows.

- Revolutionary heroes and heroines: Spartak, Marks, Engelina, Libknekht, Lyuksemburg, Roza, Razin, Mara, Robesper, Danton, Bebel; Vladlen, Ninel, Ilyich, Ilyina (all variants of Lenin); Bukharina, Stalina, Budena, Melor (Marx, Engels, Lenin, October Revolution)
- Revolutionary concepts: Pravda, Revmir (revolution and peace), Barrikada, Giotin (guillotine), Bastil, Tribuna, Revolyutsiya, Krasny (red), Kommuna, Parizhkommuna (Paris commune), Proletary, Buntar (rebel), Fevral, Mai, Oktyabrina, Serpina (from sickle), Molot (hammer), Smychka (alliance of workers and peasants), Volya (will or freedom)
- Living the Revolution: Svoboda (freedom), Dinamit, Ateist, Avangarda, Iskra (spark), Marseleza (Marseillaise)
- Concepts of modernisation and progress; industrial, scientific, and technical imagery: Tekstil, Industriya, Traktorina, Dynamo, Donbass, Smena (shift), Radium, Geny (genius), Ideya, Elektrifikatsiya
- Concepts taken from the world of culture, myth, nature and place names: Traviata, Aida, Les (forest), Luch (light), Okean, Orel (eagle), Solntse (sun), Zvezda (star), Razsvet (dawn), Atlantida, Minevra (*sic*), Monblan (Mont Blanc), Kazbek, Singapur.

In stories by Mikhail Bulgakov, we find names such as Bebelina [referring to the German Social Democrat August Bebel] and Pestelina (no doubt alluding to the Dekabrist Pavel Pestel).

In times of general innovation, misunderstandings can easily arise, for example, when a girl is baptised Markiza or Vinegret, while otherwise customary names, such as Tatiana, Andrey, Sofiya, Pyotr or Nikolay, are casually discarded.[1]

Looking back on these developments from a linguistic point of view, Lev Uspensky comments in *Ty i tvoye imya* (You and your first name, 1960):

> Today hardly anyone remembers that a number of bold attempts were made in the Twenties and Thirties to create a kind of 'Soviet Saints calendar' for the inhabitants of our nation. Over a number of years various publishers issued more than a few calendars containing lists of recommended names. These lists contained a large number of suggestions, not all of them bad. And yet, if you go through the list of your acquaintances or else an arbitrarily chosen list of citizens born after the October Revolution, you will see that the overwhelming majority have quite ordinary, traditional names, i.e., names introduced by the Church. What is going on here? Why is this happening? Why did our nomophiles' experiments fail to catch on for the most part? There was no reason, after all, for our people to cling so firmly to the old times. Why should they not have adopted a number of novel names that sounded good and were meaningful, alongside the familiar ones?
>
> In order to determine why that has not happened up to now, let us have a look at these 'Red Saints' calendars that I have just referred to. Just try to imagine these naïve people proposing all sorts of curious names! They probably imagined that you could use any old word, as long as it had a meaning and referred to something new in the life of our nation. In this way they recommended girls' names such as Electrification, Chemification and boys' names such as DniproHES, Magnitostroy or Donbass and the like. In so doing, they completely forgot that no one likes having an elongated name of seven or eight syllables that won't 'fit into an elegy' and is quite

useless in ordinary life. As an ingenious young boy once put it, 'My mouth finds it hard to utter such words'. And he was only being asked to pronounce the simple name Lyudmila. Of course, everyone wants a name that is easy to pronounce, short and sounds well. A name like Chemification lacks brevity and El-ek-tri-fi-ka-tsi-ya is neither short nor easy to pronounce. Our language tends to shorten all long words where possible; we say 'metro' rather than 'metropolitan', we have 'kino' instead of the lengthier 'cinematograph'. . . . Language is lazy. It dislikes superfluous labour where one can succeed without great effort. Why should anyone put up with a name that consists of separate details joined together by an ingenious wordsmith? 'What is your name?' 'Me? I am called Elektrifikatsiya Magnitostroevna. . . .' Would you like to introduce yourself to your acquaintances like that? Of course not. Everyone wants to like their own name and even feel a little proud of it.

'My parents gave me the name Anna when I was baptized / The sweetest name for a person to hear and to say.' Anna Akhmatova wrote this about herself, not without pride. This pride is understandable. But just try once more to acclimatise yourself to such names as Detsentralisatsiya or Mingetshaurstroy! Needless to say, you won't succeed. Life simply casts them aside in fury.[2]

Needless to say, this entire phenomenon did not escape the notice of astonished contemporaries and was roundly satirised. In an article titled 'The Mother', Ilf and Petrov mocked the procedure of an 'atheist' baptism:

The new-born baby was brought before the Local Committee. Here the ceremony of handing over the present took place. The present was always the same—a satin coverlet. But the chairman of the Local Committee was quick to take revenge for this coverlet. Over the baby's cradle he gave a two-hour talk on the international situation. The new-born baby naturally did not stay still, but the experienced orator had no difficulty shouting him down. The grown-ups stood around sadly, smoking. The orchestra repeatedly played a fanfare. Once the talk was over, the baby, who had now gone a bit blue, was given a name. They called him Dobrokhim [an insecticide] while a baby girl was called Kuvalda [sledge-hammer] in the hope that they would keep these names their entire lives. . . . Back at home everything proceeded as normal. Dobrokhim was called Dima and Kuvalda was known as Klavdiya. But the feeling of disappointment lasted a long time.[3]

Korney Chukovsky explores the question of name-giving in the period following the Revolution in his volume of stories *Alive as Life Itself*.

Today the universal passion for abbreviating words has died out. There are children who were punished at birth by being given such exotic names as Avantchel (*Avangard Chelovechestva*/Avant-garde of humanity), Slachela (*Slava Chelyuskintsam*/Fame to the Chelyuskin heroes), Novera (*Novaya Era*/New era), Dolkap (*Doloy Kapitalizm*/Down with capitalism), etc. Now they are already forty years old, no less, and have reverted to more human names for their children: Tanya, Olya, Volodya and Vanya. And here is one more who has suffered: Sivren—the abbreviation of four noteworthy words: *Sila*/strength, *Volya*/will, *Razum*/reason and *Energiya*/energy. We can be quite certain that not a single one of his sons will be called Sivren Sivrenovich.[4]

Samuil Marshak feels regret that children given such 'monster names' as Proton or Atom may well suffer from it for the rest of their lives, while in a song about the *oktyabriny*, that is, the 'atheist baptism', Yevgeny Dolmatovsky believes he can foresee the demise of this practice. 'People are now trying to call children Sergey, Andrey, Ivan, Irina, Marina and Tatiana. But there was a time when fathers and mothers gave them some very curious names. . . . They grew up and even grew old with their old names—Energiya, Vanzetti, Volodar and Voenmor—in homage to the Red Army—and Trudomir, in honour of peace and work.'[5]

PART IV

The Life of Things

CHAPTER 16

Wrapping Paper, Packaging

Eras have their surfaces. They can be smooth or rough. They can vanish or dissolve. They can be felt. What wrapping paper was and what it meant is something one only begins to understand now that it has disappeared. It has vanished in the flood of plastic bags. To know what it felt like can no longer be experienced in a world in which everything is wrapped in wafer-thin, milk-coloured and sometimes blank film that hints at what is inside: the shrink-wrapped book that calls for a certain cunning to release it from its packaging; the packet of salt or sugar that can be opened only at one corner; the milk carton from which the milk often squirts out once the tab has been removed. Packaging has become a complicated business. Packaging materials have been refined, created by designers, and people who carry purchases around with them have perforce become advertisers whether they want to or not. We can no longer imagine the ubiquitous competition between brands and logos, the manifestations of taste and trends, without these plastic bags. In contrast, how basic, how simple, the world of Soviet wrapping was. It was the very apotheosis of materiality. You could grasp it in your hands; it wasn't smooth but rough; you could almost feel the fibres of the cellulose pulp it had come from. Wrapping was secondary: you did not have to think about it; the important thing was what was inside. There was no choice of wrapping. The same greyish-brown paper could be used for a loaf of bread or for a newly bought ring intended as a gift. In its plain materiality, this paper would go soggy in the rain and melt away or a sudden movement would cause it to tear. It might rot and then fall apart and disappear.

All the more astonishing, even enchanting, were the many things you could do with this simple material. Buying books—always a happy moment in Soviet times—reached its end point when the books you had bought were wrapped in that strong, brown, resistant paper and then tied up with an equally sturdy piece of string. Book buying had something celebratory about it and unpacking the books at home meant more than ripping off the cellotape and taking them out of a plastic bag. You had to untie the string and the knots, and smooth the wrapping paper for reuse. You gradually built up heaps of brown paper that would be saved, not thrown away. Paper was costly, as were newspapers and magazines. They would be collected as wastepaper and neatly piled up and tied with string. They could then be disposed of in return for a voucher which went towards the purchase of the keenly desired volumes of the Akademie Verlag's editions of the classics. Yes, paper really was precious. If you had no better-quality paper on hand, you could use newspaper to roll your *makhorka* tobacco and then smoke your *papirosa*. In times of extreme cold and hunger, you could feed the round iron stoves known as *burzhuyki* in individual rooms with the stocks of paper that could still be found in the towns. Their brief flaring-up enabled many people to survive the cold and prevented whole towns from freezing to death. War and revolution had meant a lengthy setback for the paper and cellulose industry and the rough surface of papers such as *Pravda* and *Izvestia* with their five to six pages was familiar to all Soviet people: a quality that seemed to repel colour and meant that frequently you could barely recognise the outlines of the subjects in the illustrations—whether state visits, heroes of labour or the harvest in the sovkhozy in the Kuban. It took a long time before the standards of paper-making and printing—standards that St. Petersburg typographers had long since achieved and even set for the rest of the world—could be retrieved once again, and when they were, this probably began in the workshops of the Akademie Verlag.

People's full attention was focused not on the objects they had purchased but on political posters.[1] There was never any shortage of good-quality paper, and the graphic art and design of the early Soviet period left their stamp on the language of twentieth-century signs worldwide. The stiff, not easily foldable wrapping paper that was used for every conceivable purpose stands for the era of shortages, when not the slightest thought was given to exchange value. To take hold of a piece of it today is to step back into a bygone age and a world in which use value triumphed over exchange value and scarcity over surplus production. On the other hand, the most prominent graphic artists, designers and poets—from El Lissitzky to Mayakovsky—devoted themselves to producing advertising slogans and posters on behalf of state trusts. There was no such thing as consumer research but people did research the impact of aesthetic forms on human productivity.

The radical transition to plastic containers, plastic bags and plastic rubbish in the post-Soviet era reminds us that the coarse grey-brown wrapping paper really had been representative of an entire period. Plastic foil is transparent; it reveals the object it is covering—every fibre of the marbled piece of meat, for example. It hides nothing. It is always part of the display of the object concerned. It is almost like a shop window, whereas the sheet of coarse wrapping paper hid the object it covered. And yet, just as the wrapping-paper world was based on the timber and the pulping and paper industries—an entire infrastructure—so now the production of plastic foil and plastic bags can be seen to have concealed the issue of recycling waste, which had not been a problem previously. At present, vast quantities of plastic form hills, mountains and even mountain ranges; these do not return to the earth, they do not become ash or compost, nor do they melt away. The film does not simply vanish; it survives and becomes a mighty wall driven by the wind—almost like a sand dune. Wherever you go in post-Soviet Russia, you encounter these heaps of detritus, the mountains of the new plastic civilisation—on both sides of the Trans-Siberian tracks. Water bottles, beer bottles, tins, piles of rubbish, which society is not equipped to dispose of. Rubbish that gleams in the sun and disappears only briefly when the snow covers the plastic-coated plain.

CHAPTER 17

The Fate of the Great Soviet Encyclopedia: The Organisation of Knowledge amid the Tumult of History

The concept of an encyclopedia comes from the Greek 'all-round education' and signifies reference works in which the knowledge of the age is stored in the most concise form imaginable. Such books usually owe their existence to large long-term projects; whole generations work on them. They recruit if not the very best minds, then at least some of the leading, representative scholars of the age. From reading them you can discover what a particular age deemed worthy of an entry and on what it chose to remain silent. Encyclopedias deploy the power of definition and establish the nation's *façon de parler* and its stock of canonic knowledge. No self-respecting national culture can dispense with them. The row of gilt-backed volumes forms part of the interior furniture of the educated European citizen; they are still the plinth on which our libraries stand. The rhythm of the series of volumes, the inexorable sequence of the alphabet, the unity of the book binding and embossed gold lettering—all that stands for stability, solidity and objectivity. Encyclopedias ignore the fluctuations in day-to-day knowledge, but keep their gaze fixed on what has lasting value. They are treasure troves of knowledge and even future generations should still be able to profit from them. They are the ancient dream of Alexandria in a handy format.

All this holds good for Russia with the Great Soviet Encyclopedia (in Russian, the *Bolshaya sovetskaya entsiklopediya, BSE*), which appeared in three editions between 1927 and 1978. But the Great Soviet Encyclopedia is not like others of its kind. It is no Brockhaus, no new version of the Grand Larousse, and aspires to be more than the

Encyclopedia Britannica. At best, the publishers might have accepted the comparison with Denis Diderot's *Encyclopédie.* The Great Soviet Encyclopedia is the work of a century; from it one might study the rise and fall of the Enlightenment, the progressive nationalisation of knowledge and memory, a new order of knowledge and a different 'dialectics of Enlightenment'. Its world of books collapsed in ruins along with the Soviet Empire. The reassessment of values has not left the corpus of the Great Soviet Encyclopedia unscathed. It now lies on the shelves of the second-hand bookshops devalued and almost worthless. Even so, it remains a precious document sui generis, a compilation in miniature of the Soviet history of knowledge. We could spend the rest of our lives analysing it volume by volume. It is like samples of moon rock; by examining them, we can learn something about the origin of the planetary system just as we can from analysing in our laboratories meteorites that have fallen to Earth. It is like lava from the origins of our century that has gone cold.

'A Monument of Our Great Revolutionary Epoch'

Of the three editions of the *BSE*, the first, which appeared between 1927 and 1948, is undoubtedly the most enigmatic and fascinating. Its origin coincided with a sequence of unprecedented violent acts: the cultural revolution of 1928–1930, during which the positions of the old intelligentsia were demolished; the collectivisation of 1929–1933, which was nothing but a war against the peasants; the industrialisation of the first two Five-Year Plans, which were implemented in a quasi-military campaign; the unleashing of the Great Terror, which reached its climax in 1937 and cost hundreds of thousands of people their lives; and lastly, the Great War with its many millions of dead. War, famine, mass deportations, a terror that could strike down anyone at any moment—that is the stuff of which the two decades during which this first edition was supposed to appear were made.[1]

None of this failed to leave its mark in the *BSE*. What was once intended as a bold new venture in enlightenment ended in obscurantism and sycophancy. What began as a fragmentary work ended in the totalitarian obsession that everything had to be cast 'from a single mould'. Where once equality before the alphabet took precedence, this degenerated in its final stages into the arbitrary despotism of a 'Stalin cult' that could do just as it pleased. The editors and authors of the *BSE* were in great danger from the very outset. Every swerve of the 'general line' and every resolution of the Central Committee dragged someone else down into the abyss. People often paid with their lives for 'errors' in individual contributions to the encyclopedia. The term 'purge' acquired an elemental, deadly meaning. The further the edition progressed, the longer the list of the purged became. It may well be the case that never before was a literary work subjected to such systematic revision with the aid of the censor's pen and razor to strike out, scratch out or erase offending faces. People who were once known to every Soviet citizen became unpersons and to have known them was an offence. In this way a Who's Who became a reference work of omission and suppression.

The Great Soviet Encyclopedia was no private enterprise but a great state project decided on by the Central Executive Committee of the USSR on 13 February 1925. It was concerned not with the updating of knowledge but with the radical revaluation of all previous human knowledge. It is a work of revolution, not evolution; of the Great Leap Forward, not of gradual progress. It went all out and aimed to create something utterly different. Its goal was not profit but the enlightenment and adult interest of the masses—and it would settle for nothing less. It had a different public and a different circle of readers. 'The Revolution has created new readers with new needs and the profound desire to orientate themselves in the present in all its variety, to systematise its knowledge, to consolidate the revolutionary and materialist world view and to familiarise themselves with the latest scientific discoveries.' The *BSE* did not wish to remain a reference work for the intelligentsia but offered its services to the 'fundamental cadre of Soviet construction', namely 'progressive workers', trade-union activists, agronomists, cooperative workers, judges, teachers and journalists. In former times, encyclopedias were written for intellectuals with literary and historical interests, whereas the *BSE* placed emphasis on economics, politics and political and technical practice. The *BSE* aimed to be entirely up to date and so was concerned primarily with technical discoveries, radio, flight and electrification. It aspired to leave the ivory tower of abstract knowledge and satisfy the requirements of practice. It was the encyclopedia not of philosophers or theologians but of mathematicians, engineers, botanists, aeroplane makers, geographers, geologists and physicists. We learn further in the preface to volume 1 in 1927: 'Our age is the transitional age from capitalism to socialism in which both material and social relations, as well as ideology are all fundamentally transformed.'[2] It follows that the editors were drawn not just from the realms of science and learning but also from the world of practical activity. Among them we find people's commissars for heavy industry, experienced diplomats, polar explorers, former professional revolutionaries and underground fighters alongside members of the former Imperial Russian Academy of Sciences. All the disciplines are represented. It almost reads like a summons for the new creation of the world when the editors begin by proclaiming: 'Our encyclopedia shall become a monument of our great revolutionary epoch and a pillar for the future construction of socialism borne aloft by the masses and founded on the latest state of knowledge.'

Exuberant Enlightenment:
Surpassing the First Phase of Modernity

The Russian revolutionaries who created the Great Soviet Encyclopedia had a great, indeed monumental model to build on. That was the legendary Encyclopedic Dictionary of Brockhaus-Efron, which had appeared between 1890 and 1907 in eighty-two volumes and four supplements. This work constitutes a testimony to Russia's entry into modernity that remains impressive to the present day—as impressive in its way as the Trans-Siberian Railroad or the technical masterpiece of the bridge over the Volga in Syzran.[3] The joint venture of F. A. Brockhaus in Leipzig and I. A. Efron in St. Petersburg involved not merely the publication of the encyclopedia, whose first edition amounted to a hardly inconsiderable 75,000 copies. It also included the Small Encyclopedic Dictionary, the Jewish Encyclopedia, a library of industrial knowledge and even a history of European culture. Brockhaus-Efron was a bastion of positivism and European

FIGURE 17.1. 'The gold spines of the Brockhaus and Efron encyclopedias gleamed on the bookshelf' (Ludmila Ulitskaya, *The Big Green Tent*, translated by Polly Gannon, Farrar, Straus and Giroux, New York 2015, 479). Two eras of knowledge—the Great Soviet Encyclopedia and Brockhaus-Efron. Private collection.

classicism. This enabled the publisher to continue with its work for a while even after the Revolution, until it went into exile in Berlin in 1920, where it perished in 1933.[4]

The people behind the *BSE* shared the Enlightenment passion of the publishers of Brockhaus-Efron and perhaps even the belief in the omnipotence of books and words. 'Knowledge is power' did not start out as a Bolshevist slogan. The creators of the *BSE* did not just measure themselves against the culture of book production in the late Tsarist Empire or the standards of printing techniques in Leipzig; they aimed at surpassing these legendary forebears. That was no easy matter since the Brockhaus-Efron venture employed more or less all the prestigious scholars of the Russian learned world: philosophers such as Ernest Radlov and Vladimir Solovyov, the historian Vasily Klyuchevsky and world-class scientists such as the chemist Dmitry Mendeleev. But for all the pathos that united the Russian Enlighteners both before and after the Revolution, the difference was fundamental. Whereas the editors of Brockhaus-Efron still spoke of 'objective facts', the editors of the *BSE* mocked such ideas as naïve. In tune with this, in the relevant 1934 entry an alphabetical sequence is described as a 'mask' behind which 'class attitudes of the world were propagated'. Encyclopedias, it was said, represented the 'concentrated reflection of class attitudes and their popularisation', an 'instrument of class struggle' and the 'in-house education of the cadres of the ruling class'. Correspondingly, the *BSE* discerned in Brockhaus-Efron an 'excess of data' and the 'use of facts' to obscure the class character of knowledge. Authors such as Solovyov or Lenin's rival Pyotr Struve were dismissed as 'idealists'; and a further criticism took aim at their allegedly defective communication of the realities of life and politics. The merits of the Great Soviet Encyclopedia, on the other hand, were said to be self-evident. It was supposedly built on a unified foundation— Marxism; it claimed to consist exclusively of original contributions, unlike Brockhaus-Efron, which was based on the German Brockhaus. It was all of a piece, whereas in bourgeois encyclopedias different or even conflicting attitudes could stand side by side. The plurality of positions was viewed as a deficient form of knowledge when compared with the 'totalising view of dialectical materialism'. The fact that Lenin was once able to have articles on 'capitalism in Russia' incorporated in one of the volumes of the prestigious prerevolutionary Encyclopedic Lexicon of the Granat brothers was ridiculed by the Bolsheviks, once they were in power, as a bourgeois prejudice and liberal lapse.[5]

An Encyclopedia Devours Its Authors

What the editors praised as the principle of a superior organisation turned out to be their own undoing. Denouncing the alphabetical order as a mere mask opened the floodgates to whim and caprice. By defending the cause of partisanship, they cut the ground from under their own feet since henceforth the Communist Party or the ruling group of the moment would decide the situation, and revalue and reinterpret history. The politicisation of reference works strikes back and hits those who have come out in favour of one side on a topical political or party issue. It follows that the sponsors and editors helped to build the very machine that would crush them.

The list of editors and contributors of dictionary articles contains notable names from the academic world and the political elite of Soviet Russia. They include Abram Yoffe, the Göttingen-trained physicist; the chemist Vladimir Ipatiev, who subsequently emigrated to the USA and made a career there; and Karl Krug, an engineer trained in Darmstadt who played a pioneering role in the electrification of Russia. Anatoly Lunacharsky, the cultivated Old Bolshevik, wrote about theatre and art; Mikhail Pokrovsky, a pupil of Vasily Klyuchevsky, was responsible for history; music was in the hands of Yevgeny Braudo, the doyen of St. Petersburg music criticism; and military questions were entrusted to Mikhail Tukhachevsky, a former officer of the Tsarist army and subsequently the commander in chief of the Red Army. Responsibility for the entire work lay initially with a group of prominent Old Bolsheviks including such men as Nikolay Bukharin, Yury Larin and Valerian Osinsky, a Bolshevik of aristocratic lineage. Political questions were dealt with by such well-known representatives of Bolshevism as Grigory Zinoviev, Karl Radek and Leon Trotsky. Legal questions were the province of the Marxist legal scholar Yevgeny Pashukanis; economic issues were assigned to Lev Kritsman and Georgy Pyatakov. Heat transfer was the responsibility of a famous engineer condemned to death as a 'parasite' in 1930 but awarded the Stalin prize in 1943: Professor Leonid Ramzin. In the earlier published volumes of the *BSE* we still find informative and partially objective essays about liberal émigrés such as Yosif Gessen or writers such as Hermann Hesse. The thirty-page essay on Goethe came, as is well known, from a group of authors, one of whom was Walter Benjamin.

All this would be no more than a form of senseless name-dropping but for the fact that these names in the *BSE*'s index also appeared in other contexts. Some of them reappeared as the accused in the approaching show trials—examples are Nikolay Bukharin, Georgy Pyatakov, Karl Radek and Valerian Osinsky. A number would have to let their names stand in for the abhorrent conspiracies allegedly unleashed by them against the socialist fatherland. Mikhail Pokrovsky would enter the Soviet history of the world as the head of a 'left-deviationist denial of the progressive role of Tsarism in the formation of the Russian Empire'; Lev Kritsman and Yevgeny Preobrazhensky confessed themselves guilty of the capital offence of Trotskyism. Some would be presented as the leaders of groups of wreckers and saboteurs who had been commissioned by Japanese fascists to derail trains, while others, such as the philosopher Abram Deborin, were supposed to have 'been guilty of the abhorrent crime of Menshevik-like idealism'. None of the 'Encyclopedists' was immune from such absurd accusations; neither the Marxist legal scholar Yevgeny Pashukanis, who was accused of 'right-wing nihilism', nor Marshal Tukhachevsky, shot as a 'traitor' and 'agent of German fascism', nor even the mathematicians and philosophers doomed at the end of the 1940s by their 'cosmopolitan thinking'. Few of the prominent editors—among them the indestructible mathematician and polar explorer Otto Yulievich Schmidt—died a natural death or even lived to see the completion of the edition. The obverse of this list of martyrs is the rise of the profiteers of the Great Terror. Among these are such figures as Andrey Vyshinsky, the former Menshevik and future prosecutor in the Moscow show trials, who oversaw the department dealing with 'law and the state' on behalf of the *BSE*. We might also mention Mark Mitin, who owed his rise to the elimination of 'idealising and Hegelianising' colleagues from the institute. The completion of such a scholarly venture presumably never before involved the destruction of so many victims. Outstanding figures of Russian science, such as the world-famous botanist Nikolay Vavilov, would perish in prison—while his brother Sergey led the *BSE* to its completion.

Changes in the membership of the collective running the edition during the 1930s point to a process of the survival of the fittest—or perhaps only of the power of fate. Following Tukhachevsky's execution in 1937, Kliment Voroshilov was put in charge of military matters. On legal matters, Vyshinsky of all people became the lead figure, while for foreign affairs it was Vyacheslav Molotov. An altered practice of quotation tells us something about the new attitude towards sources. Judgements and evaluations from a 'class standpoint' became more important than original quotations. We can even discern a trend towards the 'Russification' of texts at the end of the 1940s. In the 1920s, citing Western European and American sources was still normal practice. Volume 5 (1927) contains a detailed appreciation of an anti-Bolshevist thinker such as Nikolay Berdyaev. Volume 8 (1927) features a portrait of Nikolay Bukharin wearing a leather jacket. The portrait was protected by fine *washi* paper and had a detailed bibliography. Alphabetical order, with its inherent 'democratic' disdain for hierarchies and maintenance of proportionality between the entries, survived in volume 17 (1930). This contains a brief entry on Adolf Hitler (Gitler) by E. Mayer adjacent to Sasha Guitry (Gitri), the French actor, whereas later on, the alphabetical order was increasingly undermined by the proliferation of ideological and judgemental contributions. Volume 55 (1947) contains an entry on Trotskyism but there is nothing on the individual known as Leon Trotsky, beyond the fact that he was murdered in 1940 by one of his supporters. The encyclopedia editors had evidently been overwhelmed by history—this can be seen clearly in the dogmatic account of fascism by Georgy Dimitrov in volume 56 (1936). The Second World War disrupted publication, as we can see from the delay between volumes 49 (1941) and 50 (September 1944). The heroes of yesterday could easily disappear between the publication of individual volumes. Thus volume 12 (1936) still has an entry on Nikolay Bukharin, Lev Kritsman and Valerian Osinsky, none of whom would remain among the living for very long. And in volume 33 (1938), we find that only Voroshilov was still responsible for military matters since Tukhachevsky had been executed in the interim.

Volume 31 (1937) no longer contains any reference to Lev Kamenev but only to a Russian Romantic of the same name. On occasion, the repression struck faster than the censorship so that a person might already have been annihilated before printing or distribution of the volume could be halted. We may suppose that the publisher's reader E. M. Krasovskaya who is named on the masthead was one of those at greatest risk since, living in an age when no one was safe, her decisions about who should be included in the encyclopedia and who should be left out were quite often 'wrong'.[6] At some point, named articles disappeared and made way for the anonymous contributions that were such an important feature of the emerging Soviet culture of books and knowledge, a process that can barely be comprehended wherever the fear of taking individual responsibility is absent. The entrance of lies into the *BSE* was accompanied by that of kitsch. Photos show collective farmers on bicycle outings, orphan children in sanatoriums and palaces of culture in the villages at a time when the country was being laid waste by famine and deportations. Nonsimultaneity, the disjuncture between historical reality and the production cycle of the *BSE*, fostered the *damnatio memoriae,* the process of excluding people from official accounts. A person who had been a hero of socialist construction in volume 1 might well be denounced as a 'saboteur' or even omitted entirely from a subsequent volume. And someone not even mentioned in the first volume had a good chance of being included in the last volume because of the blood-letting caused by the purges. For many people, the appearance of two volumes might be separated by a life-and-death decision.

The editors of the *BSE* were very aware of the turmoil of events and vertiginous tempo of change and with their decision as early as 1931 to hasten the publication of the final volume, they helped only to intensify the general confusion. They decided to accelerate the editorial work and continue the edition simultaneously from the beginning and the end of the alphabet. With the publication of volume 65, they began a reorganisation of the various segments on the grounds that the previous volumes contained a number of essays full of 'incorrect statements that were false from the standpoint of Marxism-Leninism'. This created a situation in which a gigantic encyclopedia devoured an ever-larger number of authors and editors; the further it progressed and the more it advanced towards completion, the less anyone wished to take responsibility for it.

By 1948, when the two special volumes devoted to the USSR appeared, the work was enormous. In reality, however, what was left was an impressive ruin that could not be salvaged by the contributions of mathematics geniuses nor by those of a Nobel Prize winner such as Ivan Pavlov. A new theory of knowledge in which a quotation from Stalin's 'Short Course' rendered all empirical evidence superfluous was established in it. Over huge tracts, it spoke not of the world in which Soviet citizens actually lived but of a phantasmagorical world of ghosts. It spoke of 'historical movements' that were fictions, and of processes that never took place. Conversely, it contained murders without murderers and achievements whose originators remained anonymous. It contained articles that were far worse than simply the products of a sick mind that had lost all contact with reality. We are looking at a 'Phenomenology of Mind' in a society traumatised by terror, fear and violence.

Return to the Alphabetical Order

It took a long time before there was any return to reality, and by then the Empire had begun to dissolve.[7] The second edition of the BSE, which appeared in fifty volumes between 1950 and 1958—the 'Blue edition'—was produced by members of the generation that had made their careers during the Great Purges. It was still filled with the euphoria that came from Hitler's defeat and from socialism's victory parade through Central Europe and East Asia. The Soviet Union featured as the 'centre of world civilisation'. But the Thaw had already begun to make its influence felt in the second edition, the period of de-Stalinisation and 'peaceful coexistence'. That left its traces, not indeed immediately, but with the hesitations and delays characteristic of long-term projects. There was a change of tone. We suddenly heard about 'Stalin's errors', 'which had put a brake on societal development'. There was a new enthusiasm in talk of 'the scientific and technical revolution'. Where the 'Red edition' described the Sturm und Drang years of the founding of the Soviet Union, the 'Blue edition' was an encyclopedia of peaceful times, of modestly improving living standards, the fridge that had become affordable, the mass-housing projects and the trade-union holiday on the Black Sea, but equally, the acknowledgement of a society that was gradually regaining its vigour.[8]

The arrival of the third edition, which appeared between 1969 and 1978, coincided with the Soviet Union's late phase.[9] The tanks had rolled into Prague in 1968, while in Moscow the first dissident circles around Solzhenitsyn and Sakharov had begun to stir. However, production of the encyclopedia continued as though nothing had changed. It produced no new ideas but expanded into an 'encyclopedic system'. Today there are specialised encyclopedias of every kind and the republics of the former Union are all acquiring their own reference works. The *BSE* now appears in Ukrainian, Latvian, Lithuanian, Kazakh, and even English and Greek.

Perestroika and glasnost have devalued the Great Soviet Encyclopedia almost to the point of worthlessness. People attempted at first to make do with the Great Russian Encyclopedic Dictionary that had quickly been brought onto the market by a private company. This and other reference works signalled Russia's return to the normal ways of accumulating and transmitting knowledge.[10] It circles around the 'problems of a new, sovereign Russia'; it reveals for the first time the 'people who have suffered under the repression of the totalitarian system'. Where a date of death is uncertain, it gives 'unkn.' Trotsky has finally been given a murderer and the murderer has a name: NKVD agent Ramón Mercader. Alphabetic order has been reinstated while Stalin has been given a ten-line entry and disrespectfully placed next to Sylvester Stallone; Marx is adjacent to the Marx brothers, and the Russian philosopher Nikolay Berdyaev has been placed next to the mass murderer Lavrenty Beria. There is a Berlin Wall with a length of 162 kilometres and a town called Nizhny Novgorod, which was once known as Gorky. There is an entry for Gulag. A flood of specialist encyclopedias has gradually made its way onto the market. Where this does not suffice, Russia has settled for provisional solutions—such as the *Encyclopedia Britannica*, which is to be found in every flea market as a CD-ROM, on the internet or in reprint. The post-Soviet era is an age of reprints. At the end of the twentieth century, there was a return to the nineteenth century—albeit in digital form—and editors took up the narratives where Russia had previously broken off contact, namely with the Brockhaus-Efron in which the twentieth century with all its horrors and achievements did not yet figure.

In the days of the Revolution, books had simply been the symbol of the bourgeoisie. In her diary of 16 September 1918, Zinaida Gippius noted: 'Since the Bolsheviks have no money a tax has been levied on behalf of the Soviets; this will be followed by the "immediate housing of workers in middle-class homes". This means that I shall shortly cease to be the owner of my own desk and my own books. Books are the first hallmark of the "middle class". We own so many that our apartment is of course the most "middle class" in the entire building.'[11]

Right down to the present day, the Brockhaus-Efron Encyclopedia occupies a place of honour in many intellectual households, however small the apartment may be and even though the rooms may be filled to bursting point with books. It may well be the most precious legacy, passed down from one generation to the next, and perhaps regarded as a rarity to be acquired under the counter from an antiquarian bookshop or else discovered during a trip to a provincial town. Whatever the case may be, it stands there in all the glory of which Russian book craft was once capable, just as if it knew that it was in many respects in advance of the time that presumed to supersede it.

CHAPTER 18

Galleries of Private Possessions: The China Elephant on the Shelf

Soviet porcelain of the 1920s obtains top prices at international auctions, while in the design sections of arts-and-crafts museums unique exemplars of Soviet agitprop art stand out as being among the most precious objects, luminous in the display cases. There are plates of the finest porcelain, rimmed in red and gilt, with stylised hammer-and-sickle emblems and ears of corn, also of gold, in the middle of the well. Another plate shows a commissar in a yellow jacket, with belt and boots, standing in front of the gleaming red headquarters of the General Staff in Petrograd. And on yet another, with a fine gilt rim, a Red Army soldier in a gleaming red uniform and holding a bayonet comes towards us. But there are also other, highly colourful motifs from the world of Russian sagas, fairy tales and folklore in general, always done with consummate artistry, and framed by cobalt-blue rims and flowers or ears of corn applied in gold. It is not difficult to understand why lovers of this material and this art form were beguiled from the start. The interaction of the swirling colour and the delicacy of the material is altogether enchanting. Soviet porcelain design inaugurates a new chapter in the history of art.

By way of contrast, interest is rather muted in the later development of 'small forms of applied decorative art' or the Soviet 'small sculptures', as this genre is generally called in specialist literature. Following Vera Dunham's pioneering work on middle-class values in Stalin's time, this theme is generally viewed as a stage in the development of petty-bourgeois taste in the 1930s.[1] To find artefacts of this kind, you have only to venture into the flea markets and antique shops or look about the apartments of friends and acquaintances. You can be certain that the bookcases and cabinets will contain specimens of what has been rather condescendingly described as 'socialist trinkets'. At the same time, the world of trinkets and knick-knacks says a lot about the development of a Soviet lifestyle, undoubtedly more than the highly spectacular porcelain bowls and dinnerware decorated with Suprematist designs from the first decade after the Revolution.

Incredible what there was to be found: bears playing or fighting; a flask of 'Odaliska' perfume from the 1920s, made in the Comintern factory; a Red Army man in a leather jacket; a group of figures from Valentin Serov's celebrated painting *The Rape of Europa*; figurines from the series 'The Harvest' showing a Georgian woman with a jug of wine on her shoulder; a figure of a frontier guard; figures from Pushkin's poem 'The Fountain of Bakhchisaray'; a statuette of a girl with a cat and a dog; polar bears, penguins, an arctic fox; a figure of a Cossack in baggy Turkish trousers; characters from Gogol's *Inspector General*; fairy-tale figures and busts of Lenin, boys flying balloons, hockey goalkeepers, a young man playing an accordion, sportsmen and sportswomen of every kind, swimmers, skiers, and dancing sailors.

The spectrum of this world of figurines seems unlimited. Looking more closely, however, you can see that here too the historical process has left its traces and has even been steering the course of events. Overtly political messages can be found even in later years, but with the passage of time there are fewer cups, plates and sauce boats decorated with mottoes and slogans such as 'Long live Soviet power!', 'Struggle gives birth to heroes!' and 'He who does not work, neither shall he eat'. Slogans such as these had been all the fashion in the agitprop china of the 1920s. The Red Army soldier with the bayonet in the well of a plate and the inscription in German 'We shall set the world ablaze with the fire of the Third International' belong to the Civil War phase, which was entirely dominated by the idea of a new revolutionary beginning. Running in parallel to that is a conception of form radically reduced to function, as could otherwise be found in the European Functionalism and Constructivism of the 1920s. This line is continued further in the 1930s, where we find tea and coffee services decorated with industrial buildings, crane arms, scaffolding and dams. Themes such as 'From the Taiga to the Construction Site', the building of the Moscow Metro or projects that were part of the General Plan were taken up in the design of tableware or groups of figurines. Similarly, the Great Patriotic War introduced yet again all the great historical events into the world of small-scale art. Patriotic motifs were developed, such as the wounded tank driver, the commemoration of the fallen woman partisan and the storming of Berlin. Again and again we can see how the postwar period too prompted the inclusion of designers' motifs and commissions from the great political events of the day. However, as we can see from Yelena Yakhnenko's survey, the overall development went in a different direction.[2] Following the period of turmoil, chaos and destruction, yearning for the restoration of order and form appears to have been overwhelming—if this was not possible in society as a whole, then at least on a small scale, in private life and beyond the reach of the overtly political. No doubt, busts of Lenin and Dzerzhinsky still stood on the bookcase or the piano, but the bust of Pushkin, the icon of both Russian and Russo-Soviet culture, was even more important. No doubt, there was the frontier guard with guard dog—the embodiment of vigilance towards the external enemy. But there were even more examples of all sorts of comic animals—colourful wood grouse, black and white elephants, circus monkeys, penguins and, again and again, 'Russian' bears depicted not as dangerous but as familiar and almost friendly creatures. The many different shapes and colours of the peoples and cultures of the Soviet Union are reflected in the porcelain microworld: the Ukrainian bandura players, the woman who no longer wears a veil, the Orient and the world of the Caucasus. The microcosm of figurines and bric-à-brac reflects that of the multiethnic empire; it has a purely ethnographic dimension. The porcelain commissar is replaced by the fairy-tale figure of the humpbacked horse or the little golden fish. The figurines made of blue-white *gzhel* porcelain do not send out any political message but want to be of use to their owners. The master craftsmen of Palekh have learned to paint representatives of the new man on their black caskets—polar pilots and engineers, for example—but their most important message is quite different. It is that the ancient art of Palekh handicraft is still alive or has been revived and that the robust forms and explosive colours that have been practised for generations will come into their own once more. The age of aesthetic asceticism was over.[3] The new class had clung to it only half-heartedly anyway—it was well known that

Felix E. Dzerzhinsky was himself the most important embodiment of revolutionary asceticism. The nomenklatura class that emerged from the revolutionary upheavals began by helping itself generously to the stocks of table silver belonging to the expropriated classes of the court and the plundered estates. There are numerous reports by diplomats and foreign visitors of having received hospitality in the shape of precious dinner services from the silver collections of the court. Vases, tableware, groups of figurines turn up again and again in households which could have obtained them, as was perfectly plain, only through plundering, expropriation or the black market. From the 1930s on, the new class began to create a style of its own appropriate to this new wealth. But their ambitions went further. Objects in daily use had themselves to satisfy their aesthetic needs and harmonise with the culture of a cultivated and matured taste. In a society in which all significant modes of production lay in the hands of the state and artists and designers no longer lived private lives but were dependent upon state educational facilities and commissions, unsuspected opportunities had opened up to undertake the 'cultural' reshaping of everyday objects on a mass scale.

The postrevolutionary elite knew all about the qualities of Tsarist culture and the potential of handicrafts, as well as the uncommonly high standard of craftsmanship, especially in the luxury sector, which had always been frank about its debts to the French, Swiss and English industry. The Soviets took over the great porcelain factories of the Tsarist Empire and turned them into the fundamental pillars of a renewed, modernised arts-and-crafts branch of industry. Proof of this is to be found in the Imperial Porcelain Factory in St. Petersburg, which was transformed after the Revolution into the Leningrad Porcelain Factory; its trademark LFZ lasted until the end of the Soviet Union itself. The private Dmitrovsky Porcelain Factory belonging to Francis Gardner in the village of Verbilki likewise became a state company, as was the case with the Dulevo Porcelain Factory close to Moscow. As Yelena Yakhnenko has shown, these factories stand for incisive examples of the renewal of traditional craftsmanship and for the establishment of special and even regional manifestations of schools of porcelain design. They are connected by such names as Sergey Vasilievich Chekhonin and Natan I. Altman.

Artists such as Alexandra V. Shchekochikhin-Pototskaya and Nata-lia Y. Danko produced classics of modern design. Nikolay Suetin, who worked in Vitebsk with Kazimir Malevich, kept on with his Suprema-tist compositions even in the 1930s and struck out on new paths in porcelain design together with his Leningrad associates. The fact that Soviet porcelain designers of the 1920s and 1930s achieved the highest prices and awards at the 1937 World Exhibition in Paris was no mere coincidence. The combination of experience in production and the aesthetic lines of the prerevolutionary luxury-goods industry with the imaginative ideas of the Soviet avant-garde, the association of the folklore tradition with modern methods of mass production—as in the Palekh workshops—as well as a growing 'market' of interested buyers with money to spend created the foundation that enabled this aspect of Soviet craftwork to flourish as a mass-produced artefact of the highest quality.[4]

The Great Patriotic War represented no more than an interruption and postponement for this development of a new trend towards con-sumerism and private prosperity, which resumed with an increased impetus once the war was over. In the late 1940s and 1950s the models of a form-conscious, mass consumer-goods culture began to have an impact when the troops returning home from Germany and occupied Europe found their way into the Soviet Union. The objects discovered in German homes, including decorative figurines, were frequently the only things that soldiers who had lost everything in the war were able to bring back with them. This explains why it is not unusual to come across terracotta putti, woodpeckers and kingfishers, and groups of figurines in the Dresden style in even the remotest flea markets. They could only have come from conquered enemy territory.

China figures of the socialist type probably reached their peak in the period after reconstruction, when the Soviet world began to develop a consumer culture of its own, in other words, in the 1950s and 1960s. At the same time, that was also the end point since the 1960s brought a 'second modernism', with its goal of functionality, its dislike of ostentation and the practised pomp of the 'grand style' of the Stalin period. Whereas the imposing neo-Renaissance sideboard still had a place in Stalin-era homes, the more constricted space of postwar living conditions ruled out owning large, bombastic pieces of furniture. The neomodernity of the 1960s regarded the grand style as outmoded and ceased to admire groups of figurines, where it did not dismiss them as petty-bourgeois kitsch. Other objects that were deemed worthy of preserving and remembering now emerged in the family galleries: souvenirs of trips to the Soviet west—Tallinn or Lvov; presents brought from Soviet citizens' dreamlands, such as Georgia and Armenia; embossed copper pots, glazed bowls and tiles; even mementos of business trips that took an engineer to Peking, Havana or Aswan. There might also be mementos from trips to countries in the socialist camp—a mug from the spa promenade in Karlsbad, a model of the Goethe and Schiller memorial in Weimar. At some point—as early as the dying phase of the Soviet Union—even icons of Western consumer culture made it onto the bookshelves, where they formed curious galleries of intimate and private museum-making. They might include an empty Marlboro cigarette packet or an empty Coca-Cola bottle. We can undoubtedly speak of the corruption of the Soviet conception and vocabulary of form. If Soviet porcelain figurines find renewed interest and even customers today, this tells us two things. One is that this world of forms has become historical; they are contemplated and respected as past objects. Something found its own proper expression and became a distinct form of its own. The other is that changes of the small objects to be found on shelves mirror precisely the changes in taste and the yearning for beautiful things in times when large-scale beauty was withheld from contemporary Russians. People were able to create their own private galleries which changed throughout the course of their lives.

CHAPTER 19

The Piano in the Palace of Culture

Not only do books have their destiny; pianos have one too. 'In my room we got to talking about the "piano" as a piece of furniture that functions in the petit-bourgeois interior as the true dynamic center of all the dominant miseries and catastrophes of the household', Walter Benjamin remarked during his visit to Moscow in the winter of 1926. His girlfriend Asja Lacis had been 'electrified' by the idea that his friend Bernhard Reich was planning to write a dramatic sketch and he himself wanted to write an article of his own on 'furniture'.[1] Benjamin not only was fully aware of the central importance of pianos in the middle-class and lower-middle-class world but also understood the threat posed to this symbol of bourgeois privacy in the conditions obtaining in the postrevolutionary Soviet world. At this point in time—1926–1927—following the confusions of the war, the bourgeois and petty-bourgeois worlds were just starting to find their feet again, but in the very next moment, in 1927–1928, they would find themselves utterly destroyed by the hammer blows of the culture revolution that accompanied the industrialisation and collectivisation plans. The piano perceived as the embodiment of bourgeois private life became the symbol of a way of life whose time had run out.

The circles where piano-playing and listening to music are a normal part of life are not left unscathed by revolutions. The routines of practising, the peace and quiet that musicians need for their get-togethers are disrupted. Even the external conditions of care and upkeep may deteriorate, if houses stop being heated and life has to retreat within the constraints of one's own four walls. This was what it was like during the Civil War in towns deprived of heating fuel and beset by crises of household supplies. In his novel *Quiet Street*, Mikhail Ossorgin described the gradual extinguishing of city life in a residential district in Moscow, in a street and a house during the Civil War. In the dining room of the Professor's household, icicles hang down from the ceiling, the samovar has already disappeared and parts of his library have been used as firewood to withstand the cold. But something like an ultimate place of refuge remained. 'He had his grand piano, and that was the main thing after all; some people had had theirs taken away.'[2] However, at some point his piano too is confiscated, requisitioned for the Workingmen's Club and all that is left behind are white spots where the legs had stood. The piano stool, which no longer has any purpose, just stands around and becomes an object of meditation. 'Without an instrument, it's impossible not only to work out a symphony, but even to sketch in the simplest little song. And, well—how can one live without it? If that goes, what is left?'[3] Dmitry Likhachyov remembers his schooldays: 'In those days every classroom had a piano that had been confiscated from the *Burzhui* [bourgeois].'[4] Pianos were among the objects confiscated in the general furore of expropriation and nationalisation so that the forces of revolution might distribute them among workingmen's clubs, schools or factory theatres, even though they frequently could not be used as intended and so ended up in depots. 'At the depot, the warehouse of a large business premises that had been closed down, were quantities of furniture, carpets, pictures with broken frames, writing-desks, pianos, mirrors—everything scratched and chipped during the hasty removals. There were two grand pianos, and Tanyusha had no difficulty in recognising the one she knew so well, the one that belonged to Eduard Lvovitch. But, heavens, what a state it was in! Dusty, grimy, its lid all scratched.'[5] In the anomic world of the Civil War, pianos stood around without a master and vulnerable. In the best case, they ended up in the household of a member of the newly arrived elite who might have known what to do with it, or in one of the educational institutes, where it would at least have been used. Yury Orlov gives an account of what the revolutionary peasants did with the furniture, including pianos, that they had seized from the landed estates:

In one of the villages . . . There was an estate there—the manor house was completely preserved, two floors, luxurious, all boarded up. The estate owner, they told me, had already been killed at the German front, and where his family was no one knew. I hung up a sign on it: 'Do not touch! The people's property.' The peasants read it. One, two days passed, and an orderly raced in: 'They're looting!'

We rushed there on a machine-gun cart. What a picture! The peasant men, women and children were hauling off everything they could get their hands on. Whatever couldn't get through the door they didn't dismantle but sawed or chopped and threw the parts out of the window. They dragged off halves of chests of drawers, divans—it was a mob scene, just like at a fire. . . . They very carefully carted away a grand piano and a huge cheval glass—you see, they could be careful when they wanted to, the sons of bitches—and set them down at the village well. . . . And they found a use for the piano. The strings went for a wire. They also carried off the houses brick by brick. That's how it was. And you talk of 'democracy'. Those people need the kind of 'democracy' which wasn't even dreamed of at hard labour under the Tsar. Don't you tell me.[6]

Thousands of pianos must have found new owners and users one way or the other in this lawless period, if indeed they were not simply lost or destroyed.

Until the outbreak of the First World War and the Revolution, Russia was a country with a highly developed tradition of manufacturing pianos, whose roots go back to the eighteenth century. Piano builders, for the most part immigrants from Western Europe, had worked their way up to among the best in the world over the course of the nineteenth century. They had become purveyors to the court and been awarded Grand Prix medals in the World Exhibitions in Paris. A solid craft tradition, technical know-how, numerous innovations and patents, as well as the sheer inexhaustible market of the Russian Empire led to Russia's joining the world's leading piano manufacturers. In 1913 there were dozens of piano factories, especially in St. Petersburg, the centre of luxury-goods production. In the first rank were the piano makers who had emigrated from Germany and established market brands: Jakob Becker, Schröder, Diederichs, Lichtenthal, Blüthner and Rönisch. This chapter came to an end in 1924 when German piano makers were declared foreign enemies and were forced to give up their firms and leave the country. Then, following the chaos of the Revolution and the general deprivation of the Civil War years, the workshops and factories were shut down—this was said to have affected sixteen piano factories and forty-one workshops in

St. Petersburg alone. Company archives were plundered or destroyed. Finally, production in general came to a halt and the craft tradition fell by the wayside. Other Russian piano makers left the country as part of the great emigration and started up new companies elsewhere— 'Estonia' in Tallinn, for example.[7]

The new beginning, the creation of a new Soviet-Russian production, initiated by the People's Commissariat for Enlightenment, took the form of consolidating the nationalised piano makers. What previously had been Becker Bros., Schröder, Rönisch, Mühlbach and Diederichs now became the state trust Red October, which began to operate in 1927 on the tenth anniversary of the October Revolution. In 1934, the first Soviet-made concert piano was produced in the works set up in the former premises of the Jakob Becker factory. Red October would become the leading brand among Soviet pianos and in the following decades factories opened in a good three dozen Soviet towns that would supply the country with countless thousands of instruments. These pianos came from factories with names like Belarus, Ukraine, Riga-1, Lira and Sarya and could not compete in quality, as every pianist in the Soviet Union was fully aware, with the top models made by Red October. They bore names like Belarus-3, Oktava, Akkord, Sonata, Chaiyka, Noktyurn, Elegy and Jubilee.[8] The German war against the Soviet Union was another profound historical rupture that not only left its traces in music and musical life but literally scarred the instruments themselves. Anatoly Kuznetsov described a situation that occurred in Kyiv under German occupation:

> In the hall which had been used for amateur theatricals there was a wrecked piano. It looked as if someone had gone to work on it with a heavy instrument, a sledge-hammer or an axe, because the lids were smashed, and the keys were pulled out and lying all over the floor, like teeth that had been knocked out. What harm had it done them, to make them treat it like that?
>
> I tried to lift away the casing and the splinters of wood and discovered that the sounding board and the strings were unharmed, and that the keys and the strikers had only jumped out of their slots, so that it was possible to put some of them back again. I set about restoring two octaves and when I succeeded I sat there

for a while strumming on the keys, watching the little hammers jump about and listening to the sound ringing down the empty corridors.[9]

In the same way, pictures of the end of the war frequently feature pianos, fragments of a world in ruins, vestiges of an unknown prosperity that became booty, trophy, as we see from the accounts from Breslau once it had been taken by the Red Army.

Oh yes, pianos were a real Soviet specialty. They are expensive, beautiful and elegant. In any case, the Russians are a musical nation. In our tenement, there were five pianos, one for every family. . . . Then one day, a Soviet truck drew up. *Davai!* [Hand them over!] We beg them: 'Leave us just one.' But it's *Niet, Niet, Niet*. Then my father hit a keyboard to show it wasn't working. So they left us that one. And that's how I remember it: a forlorn piano lying on the street amid the ruins.[10]

Many people believe that after its terrible losses in the Revolution and the Civil War, as well as two world wars, Russia had been forced back to where it had started. On this view, not until it won the Grand Prix at the World Exhibition in Brussels in 1958 with its Red October models did the Soviet Union recover the status that Russia had achieved once before—in 1913.

However, this evaluation of musical life in Soviet Russia does not withstand scrutiny. After all, the Soviet education system produced a never-ending cluster of virtuoso pianists, each surpassing his or her predecessor, confirming the world-class status of Soviet pianists down to the present day: Vladimir Sofronitsky, Heinrich Neuhaus, Svyatoslav Richter, Maria Yudina and Yevgeny Kissin, not to mention exiles Vladimir Ashkenazy and Vladimir Horowitz. Such musicians had access to the best of the pianos requisitioned by the state when they were studying. The fact that a time of great deprivation and danger could coincide with a breath-taking flowering of musical talent can only be explained by the coming together of two trends: the interaction of a traditional musical high culture that kept producing virtuoso players and inspired interpretations with a highly developed system of music education that was able to attract huge reserves of talent regardless of their location and social background.

The universal importance and routinisation of the piano as a specific cultural symbol and mark of social status, as well as a career option, are made doubly visible: by virtue of its omnipresence in public spaces and its status in the intellectual middle classes of the later Soviet Union. Joseph Brodsky described how following Stalin's death his family wanted to sell their piano 'which nobody in our family could play anyhow (notwithstanding the distant relative my mother invited to tutor me: I had no talent whatsoever and even less in the way of patience)'.[11] Pianos were everywhere. Dmitry Likhachyov witnessed how the pianos that had been confiscated turned up again in the classrooms.[12] Later on, pianos could even be found in the Solovetsky Islands, the birthplace of the Gulag, to assist in the 'reeducation', resocialisation and cultivation of the prisoners. Somehow or other Lenin managed to bring in music and the piano when he formulated the sentence familiar to all Soviet schoolchildren that even when listening to Beethoven's *Appassionata* you have to remain hard and beat people over the head—in other words, you should not become soft and sentimental in the course of 'improving humankind'. Sometimes the whole of life appears to turn on playing music.

For would-be musicians there were affordable music scores and parents did everything in their power to send their children to special music schools.[13] Pianos stood in the music rooms of the pioneer palaces, in the auditorium of the university theatre and on the stage of the workingmen's clubs. The piano migrated from the interior of the petty-bourgeois home, where Benjamin had located it, into society at large, and once there it attracted that potential and built up a broad range of talents from which the crème de la crème finally emerged.

At some point, the old, never-to-be-forgotten desire for a piano returned. It was during the late 1950s and 1960s, when life became calmer after the exigencies of war and returned to something like a more normal routine. People at long last left the communal apartment and moved into their own homes. It was the quintessence of a life that could be lived in peace and quiet. On the list of consumer products in the 1970s and 1980s, the piano stood in fourth or fifth place—far behind the most desirable object, namely the car, of course—and it

FIGURE 19.1. Pianino. No palace of culture without a piano. Kaluga 1995. © Silvia Voser, Zurich.

varied slightly in line with educational attainment. Even so, the piano was a symbol at the very centre of a life that yearned for 'normality'.

But the late Soviet period was followed by a new, dramatic chapter. What future could there be for a music culture that was being steamrollered by MTV and overtaken by global sound? How could committed piano teachers in the palaces of culture compete with the disc jockeys in the clubs? If pioneer palaces and workingmen's clubs wanted to survive once state or municipal subsidies dried up, they would have to seek out new funding streams. In many places, cafeterias were converted into discotheques or else rented out to restaurants; grand foyers were turned into exhibition spaces for all sorts of trade fairs and funfairs. Palaces of culture from the 1930s managed to survive by renting out entire floors. Self-help courses—where can I learn how to knit or use a camera?—had become obsolete. Financial support had faded away, essential repairs were neglected, and the former monuments of new cultural beginnings fell into decay. The corridors with pianos were abandoned; instead the music rooms filled up with IT nerds who brought new life into them. The *kulturnost* propaganda of yesteryear had grown stale. Supply and demand had changed radically. The former Soviet people now converted their longing for cars, travel, computers and new furniture into deeds. Whoever could afford to do so replaced old furniture with new in the EuroRemont, that is, Western style. And the first thing many people disposed of was their piano, to the point where the second-hand market for pianos collapsed. A commentator familiar with the situation reported that pianos were piled high in abandoned factories or storage hangars, waiting for buyers.[14] Whoever could afford it switched from the domestic brand Red October to Yamaha or Blüthner—with the inevitable consequence: the company Red October, which had just reverted to the old, world-famous name J. Becker, went bankrupt in 1996. The red-brick factory building where the firm had had its headquarters—in Vasilievsky Island, Line 8, No. 63, with a depot in Morskaya 35—became a business hotel. That spelled the end of a tradition of manufacturing pianos that had lasted almost a century.[15] It may be that what was happening in Russia was no different from what had been seen much earlier elsewhere, namely the incorporation of a once elitist musical world that was always orientated towards high culture into a world based on mass culture.

If only one had enough time and good fortune, it would be possible to write the biographies of pianos. Eginald Schlattner, the Transylvanian German writer, attempted this with his *Piano in the Mist*. In that novel, the piano is the only thing left on the platform after the entire village was deported from Transylvania to Soviet labour camps at the end of the Second World War.[16] Historians need no fiction; they have to stick to the facts. In the case of pianos, the identification number is engraved in the cast-iron frame. It is something like an identity card that makes it possible to trace the ownership changes the piano undergoes. The history of the piano belonging to Sergey Rachmaninov that was discovered in the attic of School No. 19 in Moscow would be a case in point: Julius Blüthner L. E., Leipzig, Purveyor to the Royal Court of Saxony, with a coat-of-arms of two crowned lions, the owner of numerous patents and distinctions—Paris 1867, Vienna 1873, Philadelphia 1876 and many others. Even the production number has survived: 36419.[17] But there are many other examples of the same sort. We need only seek them out and tell their stories.

CHAPTER 20

Rubbish: A Phenomenology of Cleanliness

Societies can be identified by the way they dispose of their waste. All societies generate rubbish; all dispose of unwanted, obsolete objects at some point or another. Wherever there is order, there is also waste and every kind of order produces its own specific form of waste. The discovery of rubbish pits of past centuries can be a magic moment for archaeologists. Entire eras can be reconstructed from their debris.[1]

In Russia people are accustomed to dealing with metaphors. After all, they knew the statement attributed to Trotsky to the effect that political systems could be consigned to 'the dustbin of history' when the time was ripe. To foreigners gazing at an unfamiliar world from a distance, Soviet society had always appeared to be without rubbish, almost as if there were nothing that could simply be thrown out. When paired with the rational consideration that the materials of discarded or worn-out objects could still be put to some use, the scarcity of almost everything appeared to provide the basis for an adequate disposal system. In the West, from a certain point in time, people started to talk about the 'limits of growth', and recycling began to catch on in both theory and practice. In Russia, by contrast, these had always existed. Glass was never thrown away but collected up. There used to be collection points in every district or along the street at points where queues would form at certain times when you could obtain money in exchange for glass of all kinds—milk bottles, jam jars, bulbous preserving jars. In the same way, there were collection points for wastepaper—heaps of newspapers, school exercise books and even books, in return for which you would be given a new copy of a book. There were bazaars where you could find the most out-of-the-way car parts for a 1952 model on a stall that was organised as efficiently as a Chinese pharmacy under the watchful eye of connoisseurs and specialists. I have no memory of having seen in Soviet towns what we think of as bulky waste that can be left out on the street once a year to be rummaged through and stripped by students or experts in old furniture or removed by the council. That fact too was presumably a reflection of the general scarcity and the care taken with available resources.

But where did you in fact come across rubbish as a physical, sensory and even olfactory reality? Rubbish could normally be found in the vicinity of dacha colonies, in the woods, beyond the fences that enclosed the colonies. There was no rubbish-disposal service, or if there was one, it was inadequate to the task, and so it was customary simply to dump waste materials in the surrounding forests. Nature—in this instance, the forest—appeared sufficiently vast and impenetrable to absorb even larger quantities of waste. That in its turn reflected a view of nature as something eternal, invulnerable and indestructible. The environment would surely cope with the legacy of the negligible society of human beings. This view of nature had graver consequences in actions of a completely different magnitude, such as disposing of nuclear waste in rivers and lakes, in the 'pristine expanses' of the Urals, or else dumping it in the Barents Sea; actions that could only be uncovered and documented after the demise of the Soviet Union. Nuclear deposits have even been found in locations inside the towns. The rubbish problem could also be encountered in the widely used waste-disposal units that were based on the model found in Swedish buildings and widely praised as great achievements. These were located in stairwells and sometimes even in the apartments themselves. They became known for the special smell they emitted as well as the permanent presence of all sorts of living creatures, which gradually migrated throughout every floor of the building, calling for the sustained vigilance of the inhabitants. The ravens and crows crowding around the iron rubbish bins pointed to the fact that these contained mostly organic waste, remnants from kitchens and not the mass of plastic packaging to be found in rubbish bins in the West.

Rubbish in Western cities, like vandalism, is a good indicator of the processes of social deprivation, the withdrawal of state or municipal services and the emergence of zones of anonymity and anomie. Social and state control in Soviet times meant that waste and litter were simply not allowed in public spaces, even though there is truth in Ilya Utekhin's assertion that citizens feel responsible solely for their own strictly circumscribed private realm, while no one other than the communal authorities is willing to accept responsibility for the general, public space.[2] The rubbish bins were shaped like classical 'vases'—the name by which they were known. These silver-painted 'urns' stood in readiness on the promenades along the boulevards and in the culture and recreation parks. The tiles in the concourses of the metro stations shone even on days when the frozen slush stuck to people's shoes. Undeterred, the army of concierges, the *dvorniki*, were on the march, determined to make sure everything was in order, to keep an eye on everything going on in the courtyard and to put a stop to any misbehaviour. They were undeviating in their attention to sweeping and mopping up—in front of house entrances, on pavements, in foyers, station concourses, public squares and exhibition spaces, and in the corridors of the long-distance train stations or the local train service. Soviet citizens have not forgotten the *subbotniki*—the worker collectives who came freely or under duress to work on weekends and who restored order and cleared away the dirt and rubbish that emerged after the remnants of snow and ice melted in the spring. This custom has even been revived in a number of places. Nor have people forgotten the scent that spread out through the dacha colonies in autumn when the leaves and remains of summer activities were all swept up and burned. Sweeping and mopping up are part of the public or semipublic sphere no less than the personnel who used to enjoy a certain authority in matters of 'cleanliness in public places' and were indeed themselves a part of the civic order.

Just how important the rubbish-free, well-ordered public space was for the Soviet lifeworld can be seen even more clearly when we look more closely at the upsurge of rubbish in the post-Soviet world. For that is what happened when the hustle and bustle of the 'black markets' and bazaars overwhelmed the towns, when kiosks shot up everywhere like mushrooms after rain and the wave of Western goods and the entire packaging industry broke over Soviet towns and cities both large and small. The municipal services responsible for maintaining 'cleanliness and order' seemed to have capitulated momentarily to the massive influx of goods and packaging. Previously, the housing administrator had been responsible for the convoluted timetable for disposing of the waste from the *kommunalka*. When the shared apartment system began to break down, individuals were forced to carry their own rubbish in plastic bags down to the containers in the courtyard.[3] For a time the sweeping and clearing-up duties could no longer keep pace with the activities of small-time traders and kiosk owners. Visitors to the markets had to clamber over mountains of waste packaging materials. In a society where consumer goods had always been in short supply, the entire universe of things to buy had flooded into everyday life like the bursting of a dam. And with it came all the other features of a throwaway society without that society's having the tools to deal with it.

This anarchic turmoil that swept away the orderly world of the Soviets also had a fascinating, inspirational aspect. It demonstrated the superiority of spontaneous, uncontrolled, hitherto suspect and suppressed elements over an order established by state power. Every cigarette packet casually thrown away became a demonstrative gesture: No one is going to tell me what to do. Litter was not simply the result of people letting themselves go; it was the tamest way of breaking the rules, the messy, perhaps even ugly side of a society that had begun to enjoy the taste of freedom. When people think back to the wild 1980s and 1990s and talk about chaotic, anarchic years, they are speaking the truth, albeit a truth with a variety of interpretations.

It took a while before the civic and municipal administrations found a proper response to the new chaotic circumstances. This could be seen in Yury Luzhkov's Moscow, which gradually reestablished control over the anarchy of spontaneous activity. But the strategies for rubbish disposal and the introduction of more orderly conditions by the mayor of Moscow went along with the growth of an increasingly authoritarian regime. The strong arm showed itself in its control of a modernised armada of waste-disposal groups and its popularity increased in part at least from the struggle against 'filth and chaos' that the new regime retrospectively equated with democracy and anarchy.

CHAPTER 21

Krasnaya Moskva: Chanel in Soviet-Speak

Krasnaya Moskva or 'Red Moscow' was the most sought-after and popular perfume of the Soviet Union. We might even describe it as the scent of the Soviet era. 'Every year the parfumiers offer women new scents', wrote Maria Bykova, soon after the end of the Soviet Union. 'But by no means all fashionable perfumes have had the good fortune to become a classic and to remain one over many years, as was the fate of this, the best-known perfume of the Soviet era. It is likely that everyone knows of the legendary Krasnaya Moskva; the name has long since referred to a leading brand.'[1] Everywhere that people were celebrating and women dolled themselves up, the scent of this perfume hung in the air. It might be in theatres or concert halls when the scent drifted through the foyer, or else on the first day of school or on graduation day, at family parties or on 8 March, International Women's Day, when society gave official public expression to its appreciation of women. As we have known since the days of Baron von Haxthausen [1792–1866], Russia has been ruled by men but dominated by women. Women have always held up more than half the sky, as Mao Zedong observed. The scent of Krasnaya Moskva even wafted beyond the frontiers of the Empire and made its presence felt everywhere Soviet forces were stationed and officers' wives in garrison towns together with their husbands acted as the representatives of the Soviet Union's friendship with its allies. The scent is associated with particular scenes that stand for the more attractive, beautiful and joyous sides of Soviet life—an evening at the theatre beneath bright chandeliers, women teetering on high heels, tables lavishly overflowing with food. Even the perfume's packaging was special. The bright red with the zig-zag white markings had something electrifying about it, the curved design with the shiny white lining, the clasp with the pom-pom reminiscent of a jewellery box; the polished crystal flask stood for something exotic and precious. In short, ever since its invention in the 1920s, Krasnaya Moskva was the epitome of beauty and refinement in an oppressive, uniformly grey everyday world.

Perfumes and scents have their own history. Taste and smell are generally undervalued in comparison to sight and hearing. They are not mentioned by great sociologists such as Comte, Durkheim and Weber, although they can be found in Georg Simmel and Norbert Elias. And an understanding of its scent world should undoubtedly form a part of a history of Soviet civilisation. Alain Corbin's history of odours in *The Foul and the Fragrant* should be expanded to include the Soviet sphere of fragrances. Once they read Patrick Süskind's *Perfume*, even historians realised that the 'social semantics of smell' might be relevant to history.[2] Numerous aspects of the subject would come into play. No doubt the negative ones that are experienced as repellent, disgusting and unpleasant would have priority: the odours that arise when human beings are forced to live together in a highly confined space—as in the *kommunalka* or a hostel; the stench in a third-class sleeping carriage during a railway journey lasting several days; the acrid and hence stimulating smell of petrol being poured into canisters at a petrol station; the smell in supermarkets which reminds us that sell-by dates have been ignored; the odour of passengers crowded together in buses and tube trains. But there would also be the smell of the icy, clear air once you have left the city behind and settled into your dacha in a forest clearing or indeed the light aroma of a perfume such as Krasnaya Moskva that makes you forget all of that for the moment at least, since it both envelops and sets you apart.

The Composed Fragrance

Perfumes are literally compositions and people who wish to discover the secret of a particular fragrance would have to analyse its components, ingredients and blends. They would need to understand something of the top notes, the infinite nuances and facets of the oils and essences that make up its basic tone. They would need to know something of heart notes and base notes, rounding effects, spicy accents, violet notes, iris themes and, above all, something of the chemical compounds, such as the aldehydes—one can learn this vocabulary by consulting the home pages of the individual perfumes of Chanel, Gucci or Guerlain. An olfactory expert would be able to identify the basic formula, the DNA, of a fragrance that laypeople would be able to describe only approximately, mostly in metaphorical or literary terms and by appealing to the emotions and sensory impressions. Laypeople simply follow their own sense of smell and, instead of deciding on the basis of the chemical formulas that the perfumers understand, will go by the smell of a sample in the cosmetics department of one of the world's major department stores or in the perfume studios or boutiques with their well-informed, fairy-like personnel. We might conceive of a museum for scents and fragrances in which the scents of the age are displayed in showcases and shelves and made available to the public with the aid of sprays: the Soviet Union as a perfumery, a country of aromas or 'scentscapes', as people might say today.[3]

Perfume specialists offer the following descriptions of Krasnaya Moskva. With its more than sixty components, the brand has 'a delicate, warm, subtle aroma with an accent of *fleur d'orange*'. In Rudolf Fridman's book *Parfyumeriya* of 1955, Krasnaya Moskva is 'associated with elegant warmth, playful and flirtatious languor, melodious, plastic harmony. The basic tone is that of a 'violet complex', whose aroma is 'essentially sentimental, but thanks to the change of timbre and the introduction of a number of harmonising substances, it has acquired a special beauty and richness of smell'. 'The perfume Krasnaya Moskva, consisting of a mixture of the bases of iris, violet, carnation for perfection (rounding) of all these primary materials and for enhancing their delicate smell, requires a significant proportion of jasmine essence.' Renata Litvinova describes the perfume as 'sugary, concentrated . . . giving rise to a feeling of normal healthy nostalgia'. She points out that in 1958, it was awarded a prize at the World Exhibition in Brussels. Maria Bykova offers this description: 'Only natural ingredients are used in the production of this scent. Its dominant notes are bergamot and neroli, complemented by grapefruit and coriander; they quickly attract attention. The sharpness of these aromatic compounds is softened by the velvet notes of jasmine, roses and ylang ylang, with a slight admixture of nutmeg. And lastly, as a trail, a magnificent compound of iris, vanilla, amber and patchouli. The subtle aromas blend wonderfully and the classical aroma of Krasnaya Moskva stuns the imagination with its astounding combination of rigour and sexuality, tenderness and firmness. It is probably this blend of things that cannot be combined that has ensured such a long life for this perfume.'[4]

The scent that bewitched many generations of Soviet women and men is, however, older than the Soviet state and we see here that the world of fragrances can survive even revolutions.

How the Scent 'Red Moscow' Emerged from the 'Bouquet de Catherine II'

Krasnaya Moskva was invented in 1925 and put on sale in 1927. The age of Soviet perfumes had begun a little earlier, in 1921, when the TeZhe essential oils trust was established, a French-sounding abbreviation. Behind that name, however, the Shirkost, one of those abbreviations typical of the Soviet Union, lay concealed. It stands for the Union Trust of Distinguished Perfumery, Fat-processing, Soap-making and Synthetics Production (Soyuzny trest vysshey parfiumernoy, shirovoy, mylovarennoy i sinteticheskoy produktsii). The trust brought together almost all the companies of the perfume sector that had been expropriated and nationalised after the Revolution. After years of closure and plundering in the Civil War, of flight and emigration by their owners, perfumers and lab experts, this industry was to be revived—after all, a firm such as Brocard & Co. had employed as many as one thousand workers before the Revolution. Most of the French-managed firms of the perfume industry were brought back under new names. The Alphonse Rallet works became Factory No. 4 Svoboda (Freedom); the Genrikh Brokar (Henri Brocard) company was transformed into Company No. 5 Novaya Zarya (New Dawn). This spelled the end of a long and impressive chapter in the history of Russian perfume-making and the share foreign companies had in it.

Even before the involvement of foreign enterprises, Russia had a perfume culture of its own, one based on the specific features of the climate and the local traditions of medicinal herbs and spas. Perfumery in the modern sense began in the eighteenth century when

FIGURE 21.1. Bottle of the Bouquet de Catherine II, empress Catherine the Great's favourite scent, produced by the St. Petersburg fragrance manufacturer Brocard & Co. and presented in 1913 on the three hundredth anniversary of the Romanov dynasty. © culture-images/fai.

FIGURE 21.2. Bottle of Chanel No. 5, presented on 5 May 1921 at the end of the Russian Civil War in Coco Chanel's boutique in the Rue Cambon 31 in Paris. Wikimedia Commons.

FIGURE 21.3. Bottle of Krasnaya Moskva, 'Red Moscow', created in 1927 for the tenth anniversary of the October Revolution. A post-Soviet remake in 2016.

what was an essentially French court culture gained a foothold in the Russian Empire. From then on, the production of fragrances became an index of the inroads made by European cultural standards in Russia. At home, in France, the perfume industry and the production of luxury goods in general were threatened existentially by the Great Revolution of 1789. Aristocrats fled abroad and settled there; in their wake came the producers of French cultural life—craftsmen, merchants, industrialists, scholars and artists. They arrived in Russia in the hope that they would achieve success and make large profits in that vast country. Russia owed the development of its perfumes and cosmetic industries, as well as the production of other luxury goods, to the impact of the French Revolution. Marina Koleva has documented this process in detail.

In 1843 the Frenchman Alphonse Rallet set up the first soap factory in Sushchevo close to Moscow where 'extracts' as well as glycerine and strawberry soap were produced. Rallet was followed to Moscow by Henri Afanasievich Brocard (1836–1900), who not only became a purveyor to the court over the coming decades but also managed a business that showed great ingenuity and originality in opening up a new mass market for what had hitherto been luxury goods. Vladimir Karlovich Ferrein was another person to become involved in soap-making. He owned the country's largest pharmacy, which was situated in Nikolskaya Street in Moscow. Likewise in Moscow, the Frenchman Adolphe Siou opened a business producing olfactory oils, soaps and perfumes, which soon developed into a label for expensive and prestigious cosmetics and articles of hygiene. With its splendid boutiques in the vicinity of Kuznetsky Most and Tverskaya Street, Moscow soon became the centre of the perfume industry.

The businesses of Brocard, Siou and Rallet not only had expertise in making perfumes; they also had the very best connections in the modern fashion and luxury-goods industries in which France was, of course, the leader. They manufactured perfumes and organised the large-scale shipment of plants and materials from plantations in the colonies. They built up workshops for making glass and other artistic goods; they worked with graphic artists and designers who produced prospectuses and advertising copy, bottles, and right on down to the interiors of cosmetics and fashion shops. They also created a worldwide distribution and advertising network. As early as 1900 François Coty had built up a regular fragrance empire whose branches circled the globe. Firms such as Brocard could depend on a sophisticated infrastructure when setting out to open the as yet unexplored market offered by the seemingly boundless Russian Empire. The cosmetics ranges, advertising posters and interiors in the style of the times— Art Nouveau, *Jugendstil* or what Russians called *stil modern*—could soon be found from one end of the Empire to the other. With them the scents of the entire wide world, exotic fragrances, penetrated beyond the capital cities into the provinces where they became symbols of progress and culture. If you come across representations of the Russian middle classes in provincial museums nowadays, there is inevitably a piece of glycerine soap with a picture of Egyptian pyramids on show or a powder compact from the House of Brocard.

But the true secret of the tradition and its long history lay in its ability to hand down not the crystal flasks or graceful soap containers but the 'formula' of a definite, successful fragrance, which might not exactly be a state secret but certainly was a company secret, a particular form of *arcanum imperii*. The formula for Krasnaya Moskva had been developed before the Revolution and was the foundation of the 'Bouquet de Catherine II', familiar in Russian as the *Lyubimy buket Imperatritsy*, 'the Empress's favourite bouquet'. It was presented to Maria Fyodorovna, Tsar Nicholas II's mother, in 1913 on the three hundredth anniversary of the foundation of the Romanov dynasty. It was a gift developed at considerable expense by the court purveyor Brocard & Co. According to one version, it was the creation of Ernest Beaux (1881–1961), the 'Napoleon of perfume', who had previously worked as perfumer in the business of Alphonse Rallet. After the Revolution and the expropriation of the Rallet company, Beaux had emigrated to France, where he continued to work in the Rallet factory of La Bocca in Cannes. It was from there that he passed the formula for the 'Empress's favourite bouquet' on to Coco Chanel, and from there it became the perfume industry's greatest success of the twentieth century under the name Chanel No. 5.[5]

According to another version, the man who created this perfume, or was at least involved in the research on it, was Auguste Ippolitovich Michel (dates unknown), another perfumer originally from

France, the son of a soap maker from the Cannes area and employed at Brocard. Following the expropriation and breakup of the company, Michel too was on the point of leaving the country. It seems, however, that his passport had gone astray among the Soviet bureaucrats who were dealing with it so that he was unable to depart but received a residence permit instead. This meant that even when France had resumed a diplomatic relationship with the Soviet Union, he was not given any help for a long time. Having found himself stuck in Russia partly against his will, he resolved to make the best of it. So, having made contact with survivors of the old workforce, including a number of specialists, he helped to set up the first perfume business of the Soviet Union. This was called 'New Dawn' (Novaya Zarya), a name that he is claimed to have proposed. Remnants of stocks of extracts and basic materials were discovered in the old studios.

Thus the names of the old companies were changed—Brocard, Siou and Rallet were all merged to produce 'New Dawn'. In the same way, the perfumes too acquired new names: '1 May', 'Red October', '8 March', 'Red Poppy' and indeed 'Red Moscow'. In the coming decades this became the most desirable scent of all to millions of Soviet women. The perfume that had been dedicated to the Tsar's mother and bore the name of Catherine the Great now became the fragrance of choice for modern Soviet womanhood—albeit with slight modifications such as the addition of musk. The fact that the perfume was altered was associated with the shortage of some of the ingredients, but partly also with a more scientifically driven perfume production that was less dependent on exotic natural products and more inclined to use synthetic materials from the new chemical laboratories.

Class Struggle in the World of Fragrances

From the standpoint of the new state, perfume belonged to the world of luxury goods, and even decadence—how could it be otherwise? Of course, this did not prevent its emancipated representatives of both sexes from helping themselves to the remaining inventory of the prestigious but now expropriated companies or by stocking up on supplies from their subsidiaries when they found themselves abroad.

How wonderful it was to receive a present of English soap in those days! Even so, powder and perfume were widely regarded as unworthy of a class-conscious working woman. In 1924 you could even read in the magazine *Rabotnitsa* that 'cosmetics will be liquidated by raising the cultural level of women'.[6] But the claims of real life could not be suppressed in the long run. No sooner had something like normality returned at the end of the Civil War than the newspapers were full of advertisements for creams and perfumes—mostly the old, prerevolutionary brands—and powders and lipsticks reappeared in shop windows.

At the same time, during the transitional phase of the 1920s, the world of scents and fragrances became the highly contested arena of class struggle. The scents and fragrances of the old world collided with those of the new world. We may even speak of a sociology of fragrances, as does Marina Koleva, of overlaps, blendings and confrontations. Perfumes stood for the 'individual note', the need to stand out from the 'grey mass' and indeed from the grey reality more generally. The personal fragrance provided a counter to the general levelling; in times of shortages and deprivation, the crystal flask was felt to be a provocation, a manifestation of excess. It stood for the profound gulf between the old settled urban milieu and the new social strata who had drifted in from the countryside. There is an olfactory equivalent of the clash of cultures in a confined space, for what is known in the social sciences as the contemporaneity of the noncontemporaneous:

> The constant mixing of great fragrances with the smell of cabbage soup or roast onions does not simply degrade a scent and turn it into something disagreeable and intrusive, it falsifies the very meaning of perfume as a concept. Thus in the everyday world of the Soviets, certain fragrances came to be seen as almost ordinary and even colourless. The external surroundings and inner state of a human being ceased to be in harmony and might even clash. The secret pleasure a woman takes in her perfume became fragile and was swiftly terminated once she found herself criticised as petty bourgeois or oppressed by the grinding hardships of daily life. We can only marvel that despite everything the Soviet era not only

produced a string of exceptional fragrances that were a match for anything in Western Europe but that it actively promoted its own perfume and cosmetics industry at all.[7]

The time for discrediting the perfume industry drew to a close following the Sturm und Drang phase of the late 1920s and early 1930s. Auguste Michel invented a wonderful new perfume in 1932 with a 'hint of the summery aroma of cloves and lily of the valley' and the name Manon, surprisingly elegant for the period.[8] The perfume industry was rebuilt and even expanded. In 1934 the Leningrad factory produced as many as seventy thousand flasks a day of Severnoe Siyanie (Northern Lights); by 1936 there were as many as thirty-six retail outlets of TeZhe, the cosmetics trust, throughout the country,[9] and when in 1937 the newly built Hotel Moskva opened in the centre of Moscow, a prestigious TeZhe specialty shop was of course included. TeZhe's fragrances became associated with the faces and style of film stars and other public favourites, such as Lyubov Orlova and Valentina Serova. The cosmetics industry was energetically promoted by Polina Zhemchuzhina, the elegant and cultivated wife of Vyacheslav Molotov, the Politburo member and, later, Soviet foreign minister. TeZhe's product range was displayed in full in the newspaper advertisements and shop windows of Stalinist socialism. The new elite needed not just evening dress and jewellery for its celebrations but also creams and fragrances whose production became increasingly mechanised and scientific—a process resumed and expanded in the late 1940s and 1950s after the interruptions caused by the war with Germany. It is very much to Auguste Michel's credit that he passed on his expertise to his two pupils, A. V. Pogudkin and P. V. Ivanov—who spoke disparagingly of him as a foreigner and a man whose time had passed, however.

Nevertheless, a lengthy article by Mikhail Lokutov in a 1937 issue of *Nashi dostizheniya*, a magazine published by Maxim Gorky, did provide a sympathetic portrait of Michel—'the old Frenchman'—the 'citizen of the French Republic'. It contained reminiscences of the bourgeois world he had come from, the perfume business on the Côte d'Azur, the everyday luxury of the days before the Revolution as well as the continuation of the industry after the Revolution together with Michel's contribution. The cosmetics industry of the 1930s is depicted as an exemplary branch of industry, equipped with modern chemical laboratories. It went beyond all romantic ideas of the empire of fragrances and served a highly cultured mass market. According to Lokutov, Michel's last efforts were devoted to the creation of a perfume that would capture the scent of the new age, one marked by the input of technology and engineers. Cement, concrete, iron and steel were to contribute the olfactory notes for the brand, which was to be called 'Palace of the Soviets' and sold in a bottle inspired by the greatest building in the world, the 420-metre-tall Palace of the Soviets. In the event, no more came of this than of the proposed palace itself.[10]

It is not known what became of Michel, who had been arrested once in 1934. Various accounts of his fate are in circulation. Some claim that his French citizenship was restored and that he returned to his native country; others report that he was evacuated to Sverdlovsk during the war; while yet others assume that he was caught up in the turmoil of the Stalinist purges at the end of the 1930s and died in a Gulag. Could the designer of the Soviet perfume have been a parasite, a saboteur and an agent of a hostile power? If so, he would not have been the only person to suffer such a fate in Stalin's empire.[11]

Mikhail Bulgakov and the Chanel Connection

In Mikhail Bulgakov's novel *The Master and Margarita*, the magician, Woland, and the ghostly cat appear in a variety show, and the audience, enraptured by the cat's magic tricks, is ready to believe in the most extravagant promises and take the tricks as real. One of the high points of the performance is the cat's entrance, when he calls out to the audience, the women above all, and with a grand gesture—as if it were nothing special—hurls a number of perfume bottles into the hall: 'Guerlain, Chanel, Mitsouko, Narcisse Noir, Chanel Number Five, evening dresses, cocktail dresses', casting the audience into a frenzy of delight.[12] All the names are of actual perfumes and reveal that, apart from the thrill of their exotic names in a literary text, the author takes it for granted that people are familiar with the names of luxury goods from the West. In fact, there is a link between the world of perfumes in Moscow and the Paris of Chanel No. 5, that now legendary fragrance of the already famous Coco Chanel, a link that does not seem so extraordinary when we consider the relations along the Moscow-Paris axis that persisted into the 1930s. We need think here only of the to-ing and fro-ing of the literary and artistic elite: Ilya Ehrenburg in Moscow and Paris, Romain Rolland's Moscow visit and the journeys undertaken by Pasternak and Bukharin to the Culture Congresses in Paris, or the close relations between Liliya Brik, Elsa Triolet and Louis Aragon.[13] But the interconnections are in fact far closer; they are not simply atmospheric but are tied concretely to places, times and people.

Krasnaya Moskva and Chanel No. 5 arose from the same scent code, namely the 'Bouquet de Catherine II' or *Lyubimy buket Imperatritsy* creation. They were brought into circulation even before the Revolution and then split into two lines: the world of fragrances that had gone into emigration and the one that had been continued in the Soviet Union. Both scents were represented by perfumers of French origins, men of genius who had spent part of their lives on Russian soil: Ernest Beaux and Auguste Michel.[14] Both names have been linked to the mystery of the 'Bouquet' that made millions of women happy following the war and the Revolution. Coco Chanel, who, it seems, did not initially like women's fragrances—'Women only wear perfume when they need to hide bad smells'—subsequently changed her mind. She came into contact with exiled Russians early on and had an affair with Grand Prince Dmitry Pavlovich Romanov, a close relative of the Tsar. Via her links with exile-Russian circles she met Ernest Beaux, which represented the starting point for the series of fragrances from which Coco Chanel then selected the fifth variant, which under the name Chanel No. 5 became the trademark and guarantor of her financial success.

At the end of the Second World War, after the years of privation, the blockade and widespread destruction, the need for a more orderly normality and the yearning for beauty were intense. Production of the Krasnaya Moskva brand resumed as early as the victory in Stalingrad and the cosmetics industry as a whole expanded after the war ended. Plantations for olfactory oils were set up in Central Asia, in the

North Caucasus and especially in the Crimea. There was progress in expanding the scientific basis of production and this included setting up an institute for researching natural and synthetic materials and establishing chairs in the subject. Auguste Michel's pupils had by now been succeeded by the next generation, people such as V. L. Gutsait and I. G. Volfson. Perfumes with wonderful names appeared in the shops—'Pique Dame', 'Carmen Powder', 'Persian Syringa', 'White Syringa' and 'Silver Lily of the Valley'. Fragrances with enchanting designs—bottles in the shape of Stalinist high-rise towers—appeared in the shops. And the larger world of the Eastern bloc brought new brands into play. The queues for fragrances no longer formed in front of the shops selling the 'Red Moscow' brand, but for the creations from Riga, the People's Republic of Poland and the GDR. Quite often, young people regarded the Soviet brands as fit only for grandmas and ancient aunts, identifying them with the stagnation and the past of the Soviet Union. At a later date, in the mid-1980s, with the opening of the Russian market, Soviet cosmetics firms were forced to face competition from international companies. New labels appeared in the towns: Givenchy, Guerlain, Yves Rocher, Lancôme, Gucci—and Chanel. The Soviet perfume industry launched its own brand on the market with the name Tolko ty (You alone) and confirmed its faith in the point of perfume manufacture, which was to enable people to experience themselves as individuals. But at the very same moment, this chapter in the history of Soviet perfume came to a close. Soviet perfumeries with traditions going back over 140 years, traditions in which the Russian and French schools had been merged, were now privatised and even the largest Russian factory—Svoboda—struggled to compete. It survived only by importing ingredients and recipes that aimed at the world market. For many people who disliked the scent of 'Red Moscow' or even found it repellent, the arrival of new fragrances from abroad seemed like a message announcing the arrival of new, more liberated times. For many others, it meant the dissolution of a world that had traumatised them. The scent of the Soviet era now appeared in the perfume stores and duty-free shops of international airports open to all. The cosmetics sets with their velvet inlays and ornamental ropes and names evoking lily of the valley or Scythian gold were cleared out or vanished into drawers. But the faster the era disappeared into the past, the higher the vintage bottles rose in price—whether empty of the precious perfume or not. They have now become museum exhibits or vessels full of nostalgic memories. Chanel No. 5 and 'Red Moscow' have a common origin in 1913, and their history symbolises the division of the world in the twentieth century.

CHAPTER 22

Stalin's Cookbook: Images of the Good Life in the Soviet Age

Mass editions for cookery books are nothing special. After all, the genre treats the most ordinary matters imaginable, namely the preparation of the food people eat day by day, month by month and year by year. Such books deal with enduring continuities that are maintained despite all other historical ruptures. The genre has developed from guides for small, mainly courtly circles down to the households of modern consumer societies. Every generation, or rather every decade, adds to our knowledge of food and drink. Guides that have been thrown together more or less adventitiously turn into regular encyclopedias in which this knowledge is stored and systematised. They are constantly kept up to date by further editions.

For many reasons, the *Book of Tasty and Healthy Food*, which first appeared in the Soviet Union in 1939, may justly claim a special place in the genre of cookery books.[1] From its first publication down to the end of the Soviet Union, the book appeared in eight editions with a presumed total circulation of around 3.5 million copies. The various publication dates mirrored breaks in the life of the country and were also linked with editorial interventions and alterations. The dates for the new editions were 1945 (in an abbreviated version at the end of the war); 1952 (for the Nineteenth Party Congress and at the high point of the anti-West, anticosmopolitan campaign: punch, ketchup and sandwich were deleted from the book's repertoire); 1965, 1971, 1974, 1981 and 1985 (the years of tentative reforms and a prolonged stagnation, which ended with the onset of perestroika). The volume was published in an oversize format usually reserved for reference works and encyclopedias. With these it shares superior quality, in particular that of the illustrative photos and large colour plates. It bears all the features of a systematic and even scientific publication, initiated at the highest level and with contributions from the stars of the discipline. The cookbook was commissioned by the USSR Ministry of the Food Industry, presumably at the instigation of People's Commissar Anastas Mikoyan no less. The content was authorised by the Institute for Nutrition at the Academy of Medical Sciences of the USSR and the book was published by Pishchepromizdat, in other words, the ministry itself.

A Political Economy of Eating and Drinking

What distinguishes the book most clearly from ordinary cookbooks is the fact that it aims to be, and is, an explicitly political book, particularly in the preface and table of contents, where it opens with a quotation from Stalin: 'The special nature of our revolution consists in the fact that it has not just given the people its freedom back, but also the material goods and the possibility of a life in prosperity and culture.' A lengthier introduction with the title 'Towards Abundance!' follows. This provides the four-hundred-page framework for instructions, recipes and illustrations. Readers are told that nutrition is a fundamental precondition for human existence and that malnutrition is one of the fundamental problems of human culture. They should reflect on the ways in which the range, quality and choice of foods, their quantity and regularity, determine human beings' health, longevity and ability to work. Readers learn that, with the Nineteenth Party Congress in 1952, seven years after the war's end, it is finally time, following the decades-long priority given to heavy industry, to develop the consumer-goods industry. Everything that has been lacking should now be produced in abundance: fish, meat, butter, sugar, confectionery, textiles, shoes, furniture, etc. These detailed explanations are integrated into illustrations designed to enable readers to visualise the new abundance: tins of food heaped into pyramids, displays of fish and sausage, fishing vessels at sea, mountains of melons and citrus fruits, and combine harvesters on infinitely vast fields of grain. The development of consumption in the Soviet nation would differ both from capitalism and from prerevolutionary Russia. Whereas capitalism was said to favour reduced consumption, socialism was allegedly concerned with its continuous growth; where capitalism lowered wages, socialism raised them. The fundamental difference was allegedly visible in every aspect of the provision of consumer goods. The Soviet system was claimed to be superior to that of prerevolutionary Russia in every respect. Equipment in the food industry represented the latest developments in hygiene; the workforce was a self-contained collective of technologists, doctors, chemists, connoisseurs, engineers and workers. Quality was guaranteed by regular state inspections. The liberation of women from domestic drudgery is emphasised with the aid of a quotation from Lenin and a reference to the production of tinned and processed foods. New, scientifically approved products were envisaged—for example, tomato juice, with its vitamins and mineral salts, as a healthy mass drink. But all this progress in providing expanded consumption did not mean 'we should eliminate individually cooked dishes or abandon feeding the family at home'. In short, with every day that passed, life in the Soviet Union was growing better. The aim of economic development was abundance, emancipation from capitalism's law of the jungle and from hunger, poverty, chronic malnutrition. They would be replaced by developing and using the boundless riches of the homeland.

Rational Nutrition, Systematic Training in Manners

Most of the book consists of recipes, arranged systematically. However, this section is preceded by a kind of scientific introduction to the rationality of provision and the nature of nutrition. It was provided by none other than the Russian physiologist and Nobel Prize winner Ivan P. Pavlov. His task was to demonstrate the connection between the development of an organism and its natural and social surroundings. He produced a treatise on nutrition, proteins, fats and carbohydrates, and the differences between animal fat and plant fat, showing the importance of vitamins and minerals and their relevance to the cooking of potatoes.

The editors challenge readers to engage in a more conscious relationship with their own eating habits, arguing that this begins with the rational subdivision of the day into breakfast, lunch and dinner and the rational sequence of buying, preparing and serving food. They do not fail to mention that the dishes should be washed up after a meal. Indeed, they go so far as to say that it is 'absolutely impermissible' to leave the washing-up until the following day, emphasising that this would attract flies and create unpleasant smells.

In the same way, how to lay the table is explained systematically and in detail. The tablecloth should be white and properly ironed. It should have a flannel underlay to keep it in place and prevent the crockery from clattering. This chapter tells us how many parts a service has, how the tableware and bread should be put out on the table, when the champagne should be uncorked and how to place spoons, knives and forks, as well as to note that napkins should be folded into triangles. Children should have to learn not to swing on their chairs, not to pull at the tablecloth and not to put knives into their mouths, in part because of the risk of hurting themselves. Readers learn what can and cannot be cut with a knife, that meat should not be cut up all at once but one bite at a time, and that children must learn to chew their food carefully right to the end and not to eat noisily.

There is a special section on kitchens. The illustrations show a model kitchen, furnished with hanging cupboards, a gas oven, sink and kitchen stool. The most important things to bear in mind in the kitchen are cleanliness and hygiene. However good the foodstuffs may be, all is in vain unless they are put away properly, in compliance with the rules of hygiene. Kitchen appliances must always be clean; the oven and floor should be scoured regularly and at frequent intervals; the waste bin should be emptied at least once a day. The kitchen should be bright and well aired, the refrigerator large enough to hold supplies for two to three days. The cooking appliances are introduced—coal-burning oven and kerosene or Primus stove. The editors have added tables with weights and measures, a list of kitchen implements and a summary of the vitamin values of different foodstuffs.

As is only fitting for a cookbook, recipes stand at its heart. It really is an encyclopedia of foods, a lexicon that enables the kitchens of the multinational Soviet Empire to show what they can do. This book can only have been put together and written by genuine food experts, specialists in assembling components and connoisseurs of the infinite nuances of the rarest spices, theoreticians who know their way around laboratories and practical people who have spent their lives in kitchens and pantries. Around two thousand dishes of every kind are represented here, systematically arranged and described. The everyday knowledge of housewives joins forces with the specialised knowledge of culinary high culture, which makes amateurs feel their entire naïvety—not least when it comes to the vocabulary of the menus, which belong, as is well known, to the most difficult and complex fields of language acquisition. Thus we learn something about cold delicacies and hors d'oeuvres, endless varieties of salads, the divisions and subdivisions of fish species and seafood, as well as the different types of caviar. We are inducted into the spectrum of preserves that had just come into fashion in the 1930s. Some forty pages are used to describe hundreds of soups, of which Russian soups such as borscht, *rassolnik* and *solyanka* are only the best known.[2] The realm of fish fills twenty-five pages,[3] including sections on catching fish and caviar production. We also find out about meat in all its most important varieties, as well as about the drinks that complement particular meats.[4] Simple dishes—*bliny* [pancakes] and noodles—are given in alphabetical order alongside exquisitely sophisticated dishes such as lemon mousse. Other sections are devoted to vegetables and mushrooms, with a survey of edible mushrooms. Noodles and other dough-based dishes, a rich assortment of desserts, sweets, jellies, creams and ices are unveiled. Further chapters emphasise that nutrition and eating are closely linked with health and convalescence, particularly the sections on preparing food for children, the sick, people with diabetes or heart disease, as well as on the correct diet for pregnant women and babies. Those who wish to find their way around in this encyclopedia of tasty and healthy cuisine will find assistance in the index at the end of the volume. One noteworthy fact is the brevity of the section on drinking and drinks, although Anastas Mikoyan himself takes up the cudgels against the legends about Russian drinking habits then in circulation. On a mere two pages (79–80 in the Russian version), we find Stalin calling for a greater variety of alcoholic drinks. Mikoyan quotes Stalin: 'Comrade Stalin is preoccupied with the greatest questions of the construction of socialism in our country. He concentrates on the economy as a whole, but he does not overlook the details, since every detail has its importance. Comrade Stalin says that Stakhanovite workers now earn well, as do engineers and other workers. And if they want to buy champagne, are they able to obtain it? Champagne is a sign of material prosperity, a sign of affluence.' The vastness of the Empire includes a great variety of wine-growing districts and even such an exclusive brand as Abrau-Dyurso. The cookbook recommends in the main the consumption of wine and beer. Vodka, by contrast, should be consumed only in small quantities.[5]

A Socialist-Realist Still Life: Images of a Better Life

The rich and complex culinary lexicon we have described was probably more of an obstacle to its broad practical use than otherwise and so it was presumably the book's illustrations that contributed to its fame, indeed its legendary status. There is so much of interest to see alongside the numerous somewhat technical photographs of kitchen utensils and kitchen furniture! There are pictures of lavishly laid tables with white tablecloths, gold-rimmed plates and linen napkins, while champagne stands ready and waiting in coolers. Readers can even make out some of the labels on the bottles: Abrau-Dyurso, red wine from Georgia, muscatel, Borjomi water. Bowls filled with caviar can be seen, as well as fish in aspic and a suckling pig. A glass bowl glows with little clusters of red caviar. Blue grapes, juicy pears, peaches and apples spill over the sides of a fruit bowl. Another photo shows a table laid for dessert; on it stands a flower-patterned tea service as well as a fruit bowl with grapes, peaches and plums. Here too the wines on display include champagne, Georgian wine Nos. 20 and 19, the Yerevan brand of Armenian cognac, and muscatel, among other drinks. We can also recognise Slava chocolate, a box of chocolate creams, chocolate-coated pastries, doughnuts dusted with sugar, an eclair and a meringue, two Asian-looking jugs and more floral bouquets. The entire volume contains glorious illustrations of sumptuously laid tables, representing affluence and good taste. Even people not all that familiar with the role that still lifes, *nature morte*, have played in European history will see at once the connection between these lavish scenes in Stalin's cookbook and the stylish Dutch still lifes of the late sixteenth and seventeenth centuries. Everything in the photos is beautifully arranged; there are clever camera angles and the colour quality is amazing. The book has done away with the black and white photography of the prewar era even though it cannot be said to have kept pace with modern image reproduction. Nevertheless, the comparison with still-life painting of the Dutch Golden Age is compelling. In the latter, too, the magnificent, incomparably precise depiction of fish with their scales, dead eyes and gills are clearly identifiable. Here also we see flowers and fruit, slaughtered animals, gleaming goblets, exotic fruits and roast fowl. Silverware has been placed on an expensive-looking tablecloth and everything is reflected in a silver tray or perhaps in a mirror hanging on the wall in the semidark. The sparkling gleam of goblets reveals the nature of an entire era and the way the game has been carved gives us insight into the level of civilised manners reached at table. Since in Dutch painting we also see the world of ordinary people—peasant weddings, holidays and funeral feasts—we further gain the impression of a universally rich and successful life. The wealth of some people does not mean covering up the poverty and misery of others less fortunate. The profusion of flowers on show, the slaughtered game, the exotic fruits, the parrot's feather in the background are not there to compensate for anything, for war or poverty or hardship.

But how is it with the pictures in Stalin's cookbook? These images were created not by painters but by photographers, albeit by outstanding masters of their trade, such as Dmitry Baltermants. Could the memory of the horrific famine—which claimed the lives of millions in the villages but was on such a vast scale that it seeped into the towns as well—have evaporated? How are we to think of extravagance like this in a country where rationing and the ration-card system of the 1930s had only just been abolished? And how could anyone enthuse about all these delicacies when hundreds of thousands of people had only just put behind them the privations of the war, the hunger in the lands devastated by the Germans, and the sufferings of the many millions of people uprooted by the war who had now flooded back into the liberated territories? How could recipes be printed and recommended when the basic foodstuffs and ingredients were simply not available, when they could not be found in either the shops or the bazaars? Are they in denial about something? Compensating for something? Are they images of a world designed to dispense confidence and hope now that the war and violence and famine had been overcome? Isn't the situation comparable to the one we find in the film *Cossacks of the Kuban* (1949) by Ivan Pyriev, in which the luxury of a marketplace in a Cossack village assumes altogether fantastic features, not to say surreal ones? It is said that Stalin, who saw the film several times but was himself long since removed from reality, thought the film gave a true picture of the real world.[6] At a time of total exhaustion perhaps the country needed a dream image of a land of milk and honey, strong and succulent, in order to overcome its own inertia? What is the meaning, the function, of these still lifes, which might well, following Pushkin, bear the title 'A Feast in Time of Plague'?

The recipes for a better life and the pictures of superabundance stem from a particular period when the sorely tried population appeared to have left the worst of its privations and sacrifices behind it. The Civil War lay in the past; it had produced its own icons of distress, of sombre reflection and extreme austerity in Kuzma Petrov-Vodkin's highly individual still lifes with fish and bread. Gone too were the 1920s, with their feverish revival of the prerevolutionary economy and prerevolutionary culture, which had seemed like harbingers of a return to the prewar normality of 1913. That was when you could find the tables of the NEP restaurants groaning with food and cheek by jowl with the asceticism of the avant-garde until both perished in the turmoil of the late 1920s—the culture-revolutionary furore and the horrifying devastation of the countryside wrought by collectivisation.

These were the years of food rationing and the ration-card system, with the nomenklatura in the lead, followed by the manual workers and after them the rest of society. Once the village had been subdued, the collective system was imposed and the state obtained a monopoly of all resources, including food and other consumer goods. This meant the ration-card system for bread could be abolished in 1934, followed a year later by that of other foodstuffs. That enabled a second kind of free market to be introduced in the kolkhoz system. Two new people's commissariats were created—one for the food industry, the other for domestic trade. The consumer-goods industry was started up, notably under the direction of Anastas Mikoyan. Mikoyan had toured America

FIGURE 22.1. Frontispiece of the 1953 Russian edition of the *Book of Tasty and Healthy Food*. 'The special nature of our revolution consists in the fact that it has not just given the people its freedom back, but also the material goods and the possibility of a life in prosperity and culture' (Joseph Stalin, preface to the cookbook). From *Kniga o vkusnoi i zdorovoi pishche*, Pishchepromizdat, Moscow 1953.

in 1936 and visited the slaughterhouses in Chicago and the car industry in Detroit, where he had met the vegetarian Henry Ford. He had been powerfully impressed by the degree of automation and technical innovation in the canning industry and by restaurants with automated food and drink dispensers.[7] Moscow now built its own abattoirs—the meat processing plant was named after Mikoyan—and started up the manufacture of refrigerators. Chains of specialist shops were set up—Gastronom, Bakaleya, Ryba, Moloko—and a food-supply system that lasted until the end of the Soviet Union. New products were successfully launched with the aid of an aesthetically pleasing advertising campaign—ice (in every season), *gazirovannaya voda* (sparkling water obtainable from automats) and caramel sweets.[8] By this time, doing without and austerity had ceased to be the principal themes. The policy now was that achievement should be honoured and differences of achievement should be reflected in different levels of consumption. This led to the emergence of special shops for the privileged and special channels for grocery supplies. Gastronom No. 1, formerly the delicatessen on Tverskaya in Moscow, became the primary delicatessen once again, just as it had been before the Revolution. Now, however, people could shop there without a guilty conscience and the stigma of being bourgeois. It became the place to reward hard-working and well-earned privilege.[9]

Gastronom No. 1 on Tverskaya and the Gastronom in the GUM department store became the places where the old, cultivated luxury was maintained but exclusively for the new elite and its special dietary requirements. The old Yeliseev Food Hall, a survivor of the old world, emerged as the home of abundance in the new society. Stucco, mirrors, display cabinets, the splendour of its cakes, the bonnets and white aprons of the staff—all provided a breath of luxury. The business has been recorded as *kommerchesky*, signalling its inclusion in the world of capitalism. We must picture to ourselves all the things it had on display beneath gigantic chandeliers and surrounded by Chinese vases: salmon, seafood, various sorts of caviar, the fish specialty *bychki v tomate*, exotic varieties of cheese, sausages of every conceivable kind, and a select range of chocolates. To judge by the impression all this created, Stalin's slogan must have come true: 'Life has got better, Comrades, life has become more joyful'. As a prominent instance of the further development of the ancient culinary tradition, we mention a salad introduced to Russia in the 1860s by the French chef Lucien Olivier and named after him. In the 1930s, the Olivier salad returned to menus under the name *stolichny* (Russian salad) and later on *myasnoy* (meat salad); it contained boiled potatoes, carrots, eggs and sausage together with a hefty dose of mayonnaise.

The Second World War was a hard time of hunger and privation. After the war it was difficult to depart from the course set by the first Five-Year Plans—which put heavy industry as the top priority, followed by light industry and the service industries. But change was unavoidable if the new demands made by a society whose needs had continued to grow were to be satisfied. Despite efforts to apply the brakes, the age of consumerism prevailed even in the Soviet Union, albeit belatedly in the 1950s.

The *Book of Tasty and Healthy Food* satisfied the heightened expectations of the 'new class', the nomenklatura, but it is also an educational work concerned with manners and the development of good taste, with the education and self-improvement of the 'rising class' (*vydvizhentsy*) that had emerged from the upheavals in society. *Kulturnost* (cultured behaviour) was a key term during the time of the culture revolution of the first Five-Year Plans, when many millions of people were torn from their villages and—whether by force or freely following a general movement—found they had landed in urban settlements. The basic cultural techniques included not only reading and writing, and not only the internalisation of the rules governing behaviour in the towns—a process that had occurred in large Western cities generations previously—but also 'culture' in the domestic sense: the culture of eating and drinking, and conduct at the dinner table.[10] The entire scientific and pedagogic impulse fits in with the typical gestures of an educational dictatorship on the threshold separating a traditional agrarian society from the new urban and industrial setting. If we look more closely, we can see that the *Book of Tasty and Healthy Food* represents not so much a breach with the old, prerevolutionary eating culture as a continuation of it in different conditions. The pictures and recipes for a better life had already existed for the middle class in the Tsarist Empire before 1917.

Yelena Molokhovets's Prerevolutionary Cookbook

The publication of Stalin's cookbook in 1939 was overshadowed by another cookery book and manual that pursued more or less the same objectives. It had disappeared from the shelves and the public sphere around twenty years previously, but had by no means vanished from the everyday consciousness of (urban) society. It must have continued to thrive on the horizons of the generation that reached adulthood before 1917. The cookbook referred to here, *A Gift to Young Housewives or a Help to Reducing Housekeeping Charges*, or simply *A Gift to Young Housewives*, was written by Yelena Ivanovna Molokhovets.[11] The book first appeared on 21 May 1861, but was then published in twenty-nine reprints with a total of around three hundred thousand copies. It was a genuine bestseller that made the author and publisher rich. As the newspaper *Birzhevye novosti* wrote on the fiftieth anniversary of its first appearance, on 20 May 1911, 'There is no corner of Russia, no family, in which this book is not present. And the name of Y. M. Molokhovets enjoys tremendous respect.' Molokhovets's book long remained a classic of Russian gastronomic and culinary literature; the fourteenth edition of 1904 contained 4,163 recipes. And it is strange that one of the few writers to interest himself in her and her work should have written: 'The woman who taught Russia how to cook was a person without a biography. And rightly so. The book by Yelena Molokhovets has long since become part of a national myth, and myths do not call for precise dates.'[12]

Nevertheless, the design and genesis of the *Gift to Young Housewives*, its ambitions as well as the personality of the author, are of great significance. We are indebted to the Dutch journalist Egbert Hartman for a biographical sketch of the author.[13] She was born Yelena Ivanovna Burman on 28 April 1831 in Arkhangelsk to the family of a customs official. Thanks to a series of chance circumstances, she was educated at the Smolny Institute for Well-Born Girls in St. Petersburg, where she received a solid but strict upbringing and from which she graduated with distinction. She married the urban architect Franz Molokhovets and moved to Kursk, where she published *Gift to Young Housewives* in 1861. Her intention, she wrote in the introduction, was to help young housewives manage the household, that is, to keep house thriftily, avoid unnecessary outgoings and yet produce a great variety of dishes. She evidently believed it was her mission to help young married couples find their own way. 'She did not just teach people how to cook; she designed and created a way of living and gave very detailed instructions about how to achieve it. Here you can see a menu calendar with recipes for each day, paying heed to the dates of religious fasts as well as the cost of ingredients, depending on season. The more affluent reader can choose the dearer variants, poorer people find less expensive recipes recommended. Vegetarian recipes, which had just started to become fashionable, are also given. In this way, the collection of recipes became a detailed list for everyday use throughout an entire year.'[14]

It is easy to see that the layout for the *Gift to Young Housewives* provided the blueprint for Stalin's own cookbook, but the differences are equally clear. It is divided up in a similar way—hors d'oeuvres, soups, meat, fish, salads and desserts, etc. But where the Stalin cookbook

provides a scientific preface for the preparation of the food, Molokhovets is more concerned with practical cooking. Large sections of
her book follow the calendar of the Russian Orthodox Church, especially during Lent and at Easter. She also provides more detailed and
authoritative instructions on such matters as how to lay the table
and how to serve up the food. She goes even further and includes the
entire household, explaining how apartments and individual rooms
should best be furnished—and how the serving personnel is to be
integrated in the family household, while at the same time keeping
a proper distance. For example, there should be a space where common prayers could be said—together with the servants. In addition,
she offers advice about the layout of the children's rooms, the relationship between the kitchen and the pantry, the optimal height of
the rooms and how to install the piano. Molokhovets's book has no
illustrations, let alone coloured ones, but she leaves us in no doubt
about the sumptuousness and rich variety of Russian cuisine. Her
accounts of soups, sauces, *pirogi*, *blinchiki*—Russian pancakes—*kasha*,
oatmeal, preserves, juices and cakes bring to life all those pictures in
which the painter Boris Kustodiev depicted the energetic and colourful abundance of the world of Russian merchants and farmers of the
end of the nineteenth century. It is not hard to understand how later
on, Soviet citizens would have contemplated the infinitely sumptuous
range of foods described in Molokhovets, the associations such food
would have brought to mind, and the astonishment and sarcasm
that would have been provoked by the sight of ingredients that had
long since disappeared from the shops.

The cookbook is aimed primarily at young housewives. It was an
ideal wedding present, with much detailed information that was far
from trivial. River carp are tastier than pond carp. The tastiest of all
are the carp caught between May and August. To improve the taste
of pond carp, you have to strike the fish so that it doesn't die on the
spot. The *Gift to Young Housewives* is a universal reference work for
food prices. You can get help here if you want to distinguish fresh and
unfresh meat or learn how best to lay in stocks of food. Molokhovets
does not teach; she tells you how to save on the shopping bill and
how to lay the table properly. No one who has read her is left feeling
inadequate. 'Advice for young housewives' describes how a family
belonging to the Russian middle class might lead a proper life.

But evidently Yelena Molokhovets was not satisfied with her success as author of a cookery book. She aspired to something higher. Because cooking had something to do with health or convalescence, she felt it had a connection to healing or saving one's soul. She was not simply a cook measuring out her ingredients but a woman eager to save the world. Hence, following her move to the capital, she fell in with starry-eyed idealists, occult and even nationalist circles. They exploited the fame of the bestseller writer and her propensity for apocalyptic scenarios. In her missionary activities she sought out the great figures of the cultural and political establishment, such as Konstantin Pobedonostsev, Chief Procurator of the Most Holy Synod, a man as enlightened as he was reactionary, and Vasily Rozanov, one of the leading intellectual writers in St. Petersburg. It was he who in hindsight referred to her as *baba-povarikha*, a Russian lady cook, which presumably was intended as a compliment to the original mother of Russian cuisine. The mother of Russian cuisine died, unnoticed by the public, in a starving Petrograd in 1918.[15] There was neither an obituary nor a funeral ceremony appropriate to a woman who had once been so prominent. The cookery books from the pen of a declared monarchist were used to feed the iron stoves in Petrograd apartments in which the temperature had sunk below freezing point. During the Civil War, the ingredients needed for the recipes she recommended were no longer available. Cooks ought to be able to govern the country, as had been claimed in a statement ascribed to Lenin, but the communal apartments no longer contained the kitchens that a cook might have ruled over; dining rooms of one's own were now out of the question and the mistress had become the household maid of all work. Restaurants had given way to the large canteens known as *fabrika-kukhnya* and eating had become a rational process aimed at reproducing labour power instead of an activity as pleasurable as it was useful.

Towards a History of the Education of the Soviet-Russian Middle Class

Fewer than twenty years passed before work on the history of education of the Soviet middle class resumed—even if it was not thought of in those terms. The guide to a better life surfaced in an altered form even if no one referred to its author by name. This new kitchen was poorer in many respects, but it had a novel addition that lasted until the end of the Soviet Union—and probably beyond. We need only recollect the salads and hors d'oeuvres that were transferred from the Molokhovets recipes to Stalin's cookbook and have survived to the present day. Think also of the lavishly laid tables preserved in the still lifes, a sight that could be seen replicated in the Moscow kitchens of the 1970s and 1980s: the batteries of bottles, the crystal ware, the little saucers of jam, the fruit bowls, the platters for sliced fish and the bowl of caviar. All the tableware and culinary utensils of an era had come together: the robust, fluted glass, the tea service, the crystal bowls, the *chaynik*—the bulbous teapot in which hot water stood ready until it was poured onto the tea extract—instead of the samovar, which had long since lost its dominant position in tea-drinking society. Indeed, the *chaepitie* itself, the agreeable ritual of drinking tea, the slowing down of one's movements, had withstood all the storms of the age. It was Vasily Rozanov who at the start of the twentieth century had succinctly answered the eternal question 'What then shall we do?', that had always preoccupied the Russian intelligentsia: 'Pick berries in the summer and drink tea with jam in the winter.'

The Rediscovery of Russian Cuisine in the Age of Globalisation

The *Book of Tasty and Healthy Food* must have seemed to the generation that looked at it after the end of the Soviet Union to be a picture book from an age long since passed. (My copy acquired in Rostov-on-Don showed none of the signs of having been used that one would expect from a cookery book, which suggests that it was intended for a bookshelf rather than as a kitchen aid.) That, at any rate, is how Alyona Dvinina saw it after perestroika. 'To turn the pages of this book, and I have the 1985 edition in my hands, is a fantastic pleasure; it's just like looking through an old family album. The decades-old photos that show the proper way to lay a table are full of products of the past. There they are—the unforgettable kefir in the glass with a green top, the milk in the triangle-shaped carton, the cheese spread. Yes, it was all like that. But some of the 1985 recipes, the start of *perestroika* and the mass deficit—have got something sarcastic about them. Especially, chapter headings like "Seafood", "Roast Squid", "Stuffed Cabbage—*golubtsy*—with shell-fish".[16] Despite the *longue durée* of the tea-drinking ritual, Soviet cuisine gradually loosened up under the pressure of new experiences and temptations. The Soviet table was cleared and the globalised world has left its mark even on Russia. In January 1990, when McDonald's opened its first restaurant in Russia—in Pushkin Square in Moscow—this amounted to a revolution. For the first time in decades, restaurant-goers could experience fast, clean and above all friendly service—even in a fast-food restaurant. The world of gastronomy has been internationalised. And McDonald's was soon followed by Russian restaurants under their own names such as Mu-Mu or Tri Tolstyaka, which restored Russian cuisine to its place of honour. The paying public now has a choice. The *Book of Tasty and Healthy Food* can still be found in the second-hand bookshops (though prices are rising) and Yelena Molok-hovets's *Gift to Young Housewives* has become available again. There are museums such as the Museum of Social Nutrition in Moscow,[17] which was founded in 1977, then closed and finally reopened in 2006. By visiting it, later generations can work their way through the history of the Russian twentieth century, but on this occasion by strolling past menus, models of gâteaux and lavishly laid tables.

PART V

Oases of Freedom

CHAPTER 23

Geologists' Field Work and Other Breathing Spaces

It was not all that long ago that the vastness of the world appeared to Soviet citizens to be identical with the sheer infinity of Soviet territory and people could even move from one continent to the next, from Europe to Asia, without crossing a single border or producing their passports. People could pass from one time zone and one linguistic and cultural realm to many others. And people moved around every year with the seasons; when summer came, they simply set out for the seaside, into nature and to the towns and provinces they wanted at long last to see for themselves. All this has changed radically in the quarter of a century since the disappearance of the Soviet Union. Russian tourists as well as tourists from the other former Soviet republics can now be encountered all over the world—in metropolises as well as in remote locales. Until the fall of the Iron Curtain, Soviet citizens were rarely seen abroad; they were often recognisable by their clothes or by the fact that they were in a tour group under the leadership of a knowledgeable guide. Russian tourism was confined largely to the territories of the USSR itself or else to the Soviet bloc—from the Elbe to the Pacific, from Cuba to North Korea. The destinations that now appear on the departure boards in Russian airports were largely unknown to many people in the Soviet Union: Antalya, Sharm El-Sheikh, Malaga. By contrast, the names on the train carriages pointing to the destinations within the Empire longed for during the summer were familiar to everyone. There were various rail links: Kuzbass-Adler (the terminus on the Black Sea); Vorkuta-Adler; Novosibirsk-Simferopol (terminus and hub on the Crimea); Leningrad-Sevastopol (terminus on the Crimea); Komsomolsk-Amur-Novorossiysk (port on the coast of the Black Sea) and even Sverdlovsk-Riga (on the Baltic). These train links connected the towns at the other end of the Soviet Union with the mining and industrial basins, the zones of labour with the coasts of light, day by day, week by week and year by year—for almost a century, the length of a human life, outlasting generations.[1]

Recreation, leisure time and tourism were yet other activities reorganised in Soviet Russia. When the Bolsheviks came to power, holidays and leisure time were not among their top priorities. But it was not long before the old tourism, travelling and holidays that had existed in Tsarist times came to be opposed by a new 'revolutionary', 'proletarian' form of tourism. A representative explained: 'While admiring the beauty of Caucasus landscape the [proletarian] tourist should at the same time investigate class struggle in the Chechen *aul* [village].'[2] This programme, formulated in the mid-1920s, emphasised the organisation of leisure time and recreation, the importance of familiarising oneself with the history and cultural centres of the now socialist homeland, and keeping fit and healthy so as to survive in working life and the struggle on the labour front. And it was important to form a picture in an international spirit of the multinational empire that no longer wished to be a 'prison of the nations'. Prerevolutionary tourism, the Grand Tour of the educated classes—Berlin–Vienna–Bad Ems–Munich–Lake Lucerne–Lake Geneva–San Remo–Florence or Paris and Biarritz—in fashionable hotels and spa visits for a cure had all now come to an end.[3] At issue was not foreign travel and recreation for a small, affluent and educated elite—but holidays for workers or people hungry for education. 'What is tourism? It is travel. . . . You see what you have never seen before and this opens your eyes, you learn, you grow. . . . And then you go back to the city, to work, to struggle— but the time has not passed in vain: you have become stronger and richer. This is tourism.'[4] The old lodging houses and villas on the sea were handed over to the trade unions for this new proletarian tourism. Informative and cultural routes were set up for proletarian tourists—in the former Tsarist residences or on the sites of revolutionary struggles, but also on the building sites of communism that had only just come into being, the sites for power stations, new settlements and other prestige projects of the new society. Proletarian tourism was a 'conscious activity', not just for pleasure. In the 1930s this 'Red' tourism became organised; what had been the Riviera of the Russian aristocracy in the Crimea now became the Red Riviera. The palaces, dachas and hotels became the holiday homes for the bureaucrats of

the people's commissariats. They now all had proletarian names—
The Metalworker, The Fisherman, The Coalminer, and so forth—and
welcomed top workers for their holidays. Not until the 1960s did tourism develop into a mass phenomenon with a corresponding infrastructure: new hotels, promenades, restaurants, lodging houses and
an expanded travel capacity from building new railway stations and
airports. Thousands of tourist routes were developed both centrally
and locally.[5]

Going to One's Limits

It was impossible not to notice the exodus from the towns at the onset
of the holiday season. People assembled in front of the stations, ready
for the off, easily recognisable by their kit: jackets of grey canvas,
hoods and strings. At one time you saw a lot of training outfits; they
were superseded by camouflage gear. You could see broad-brimmed
hats, which had something adventurous about them, something of the
Wild West. The crucial thing, however, was the piled-high rucksack,
which contained everything needed for a great expedition: canned
food, water filters, saucepans, oars for paddleboats and, above all,
a guitar. These were the features of a well-worn routine. Everyone
had already travelled to regions far from the capital, to places where
there were no roads, where you had to wait days for the next boat or
for a bus that ran only once a week, and where you might have the
good luck to be picked up and given a ride by a passing helicopter.
That could be on a promontory in the middle stretch of the Yenisei
River, in the Altai Mountains or in Karelia. The equipment of these
groups standing in front of railway stations or on the platforms had
something professional about it and yet they were masters of improvisation who knew how to deal with any emergency situation, no
matter how complicated. They evidently had a model to follow: the
expeditions of geologists, soil scientists, cartographers—the core
troop of those opening up the expanses of the Empire, people who
were forced to make their own way for weeks on end without anyone to rely on but themselves. These expeditions before and after
1917—ethnographic, geological or linguistic—with their preparations,

FIGURE 23.1. Time-out for a rest somewhere in the infinitely vast land of the Soviets. From *Fotoal'bom Sovetskii Soiuz*, Planeta, Moscow 1972.

logistic adventures and evaluation phases—not only wrote important chapters in the history of Russian and Soviet science; they also
represented the love of adventure and the excitement of making new
discoveries. The image of these adventure-seeking groups includes
their preparations—assembling maps and rail tickets and having
experienced people check the equipment so as to be ready for all
eventualities. A novel of the early 1950s gives us the picture: 'Geological explorers march over the bare rocky shores; the sun rises more
gloriously by the day; the boat sails swiftly along the steep banks; the
campfire flickers in the dark. . . . How lovely to spread your sleeping
bag on a bed of twigs in the Taiga, to spend the night beneath the
stars, listening to the rustling of the trees and the muted calls of the
night birds! As dawn breaks, the piece of sky framed by dense pine
trees assumes a different colour at every moment, while the clouds
seem to be formed of coloured wax.'[6] This is vaguely reminiscent of
the romanticism of the young Germans of the Youth Movement at the
turn of the twentieth century with their songs and guitars round
the campfire and the celebration of community far from the society
whose stresses they had escaped for a few weeks.[7] We probably cannot
understand how Soviet society held together without being aware of
these enthusiastic communities and friendship circles which found

one another in remote locations and then returned fortified to their confined lives in the towns. Hiking over the isolated Karelian wastes or sailing down the Yenisei surely ranked among the great experiences of a generation for whom it provided compensation for the uniformity and tedium of ordinary life. Such sentimental journeys produced memories that lasted a lifetime; they yielded knowledge of a country that people living in a large town would otherwise have known about only from hearsay. In such regions you come into contact with a breath-taking natural world, but also with a godforsaken land into which the orderly time of revolution, Five-Year Plans or TV has never succeeded in making inroads.[8]

The Vorkuta to Adler (Sochi) Train and Sex on the Beach

The north is the landscape for putting yourself to the test, for survival training and extreme sports; it is the country for expeditions. The south is everywhere something very different: no one needs to dig in here or protect against the rigours of nature. People who go to the coast absorb enough sun and natural fragrances to last them for the rest of the year. The coast has plenty of culture to offer: Greek ruins, vestiges of the Kingdom of the Cimmerian Bosporus, the citadels of Genoa and Venice, the palace of the Khans of the Crimean Tatars, the Livadiya summer palace of the Tsars, Anton Chekhov's white dacha and the neo-Gothic toy fortress on a rocky crag—the Swallow's Nest near Foros. But the journey to the south has other attractions too: the beaches, even though those on the Black Sea are mainly of coarse shingle; and the sun, which rises early out of the mist and goes down as a magnificent fiery-red ball far away in the west over the Bulgarian and Romanian coast. The promenades are relatively restrained, or at any rate, they do not have much hustle and bustle. Every Soviet citizen knew the local place names long before arriving there: Yevpatoriya, Yalta, Gelendzhik, Hurzuf. The train carriages from the north reflected the blistering summer heat, the windows down or opened out; the passengers, already exhausted by two, three or several days' travel, longed for nothing more than for the train to come to a halt in the stations by the sea or at least for the sea to come into view. The passengers from the north, their food supplies running out, had long since made themselves comfortable in training suits and feverishly anticipated arrival in the definitive dream landscape. Dreams and expectations accompanied every train from the coal-mining districts of Vorkuta or Kotlas. Miners, mining officials, families who had finally managed to get approval for a holiday in the trade-union health resorts, singletons who came here year after year to experience the adventure, perhaps even the romance of their lives: every train arriving disgorged thousands of people hungry for light and life onto the platforms and from there onto the beaches and into the grand hotels built since the 1960s or else into the arms of privately rented accommodation. Finding a place to stay during the season was hard. Between 50 and 83 percent of all annual holidaymakers in the Soviet Union were said to have made their own arrangements and even in Sochi these so-called 'wild' tourists outnumbered group travellers by a factor of two or three. There was no space that wasn't exploited: cellars, sheds, attics, barns.[9] Towns abandoned in winter turned into metropolises a hundred thousand strong in the summer months without there being an infrastructure adequate to cater for their needs. Hence even the happy days at the seaside in the south were marred by queuing, improvising, overcrowded living quarters and people on top of one another; beaches for hundreds of thousands, bodies next to bodies, close contact between the sexes, relaxation zones, multinational beaches of every conceivable type. 'The journey to the south' became code for the search for happiness or an erotic adventure.[10] In this respect, too, routines and rituals gradually developed in which every year thousands of people set out for a 'reunion'. Vacationing among the Caucasian Black Sea lovers was not entirely without risk for women travelling on their own: the southern beach as the site of sin. Viktor Erofeev called Yalta the 'health resort with the most sex in the whole of Europe', created not for recreation but for never-ending orgies, madly developing love stories, sleepless nights and dangerous relationships. The air was redolent of perfume, sin and boxwood.[11] In the southern holiday resorts, dreams took wings; it was not possible to make them a reality in such cramped living quarters—that could be done only on the beach and to the accompaniment of the rhythmic beat of the waves.

The Baltic as a Substitute for Europe: Itinerary of the Intelligentsia

Travellers of the 1960s outdid each other in discovering parts of the country barely opened up until then: monasteries on the Upper Volga that had fallen into ruins; Repin's summer house and atelier in Kuokkala, which has now been renamed Repino. The intelligentsia felt drawn to Europe, to the Europeanised city par excellence, namely Leningrad/St. Petersburg. Anyone who wanted to go farther aspired to visit the Soviet republics on the Baltic, but not just because of the tourist attractions such as the Gothic St. Olaf's Church or the Town Hall in Tallinn, St. Peter's Church in Riga or the Art Nouveau buildings in the Alberta Iela designed by Eisenstein's father around 1910. The Baltic region became something of a cult, a landscape for people in the know, who spent their vacations in seaside resorts such as Loksa and Haapsalu on the Estonian coast or in Jūrmala near Riga. People ventured into extraterritorial regions without ever leaving the Soviet Union, and into Europe within the frontiers of the USSR. There you could not only see something special; there were also differences of manners and a different tone.

Thus the tourist routes and trajectories reflected the mental maps of Soviet citizens, but in very different ways. There were overlaps between the vast spaces of the Empire from the Polar Circle to the subtropical zones, between the winding towers and slag heaps of the north and the palm-studded terraces leading down to the sea. Once a year you went through all the time zones that held the Empire together and so with each year that passed, the routine and the experience of a way of life that was ubiquitous and omnipresent were consolidated, even at the vanishing points of everyday Soviet life. An image became fixed in people's minds and became something familiar and a goal by which to orientate oneself, one that never left you wherever it might be. Even on the beach at Pitsunda [Abkhazia], the local food store was called Gastronom and standing in a queue was the normal reality, despite the exotic nature of the surroundings.

This knowledge and the memories of journeys to the four ends of the Empire formed a dense layer in people's minds. Family photograph albums are filled with happy moments. You see pictures of the white villa with the palm tree or the balcony of the hotel built of concrete and glass, depending on whether they depict the 1930s generation or that of the '60s.[12] You would see mountains of dream landscapes piling up, if it were worth the labour of collecting them. One could effortlessly create the archive of the century with the postcards displaying the topography of the landscapes of desire and the sites of bliss—from White Nights on the Solovetsky Islands to the valleys of Georgia. Group photos against the backdrop of nature in the wild would bring back memories to anyone who had ever been there and evoke that sense of community that lives on in people's minds even when the state in which they grew up had imploded. Community meant something you could rely on in a society where normally you trusted no one, and certainly not any institutions. This was an age at home in holiday photos. Anyone who wanted to find out about it or to reconstruct people's trajectories in greater detail would have endless material to work with: guidebooks, brochures, town plans and maps with which to reconstruct their journeys; logbooks and navigation charts of past explorations—by the thousand, indeed the hundred thousand.

But then the Empire that provided the framework for these souvenir images disappeared. The goal of people's yearnings has now moved to different, more distant horizons. Beyond the beaches of the Black Sea is the Côte d'Azur, and beyond the beaches of Jūrmala in Latvia are the beaches of Miami. For a long time, the only art you could see was in the Hermitage, whereas now the Prado, the Louvre and the British Museum have joined the list. People have long since transferred from the train to the plane and where there used to be a crush in the concourse and on the platforms of railway stations, you now have the queues to the security check in the terminals for foreign flights. Ever since you could book hotel rooms on the internet, people have almost forgotten that at one time you could not be sure of finding accommodation at all. And at the time the most powerful desire to pave the way to the outside world was itself the product of necessity: it was to smash a hole in the Iron Curtain. The collapse of the Empire, and with it of all the institutions responsible for the supply and distribution of goods, forced the opening of the borders overnight. Millions of tourists in the 1990s set out to go shopping between Moscow and Dubai, Sverdlovsk and Ürümqi, Odesa and Istanbul, Vladivostok and Tianjin. This was the prelude for the 'normal' tourism that developed, in which the 'Turkish Riviera' around Antalya came to take the place of the old 'Red Riviera'.

CHAPTER 24

Dacha: Chekhov's *Cherry Orchard* in the Twentieth Century

Every flight from one of Moscow's airports in the 2000s enables you to see that the tapestry of dacha settlements surrounding the capital is starting to break up. Earlier, in the days of the Soviet Union, the patchwork of small gardens had been uniformly interwoven. The lands on which the dacha colonies were built and which mostly belonged to a cooperative, a business or an institute were all roughly the same size. The network of roads in the colonies was clearly marked as if cut out from the surrounding forests. The dachas now seem to be losing their importance. From a bird's-eye view (or from Google Earth) we can see new, wide access roads that make it easier for dacha owners to make a quick exit from the capital. The motorway ring and the new roads have assumed greater importance than the bridle paths that lead from the nearest suburban rail station—usually the so-called elektrichka trains—through the forest to the dacha colony. In earlier times, hardly any house stood out from the finely textured and patterned tapestry whose colour changed with every season. Medium tones predominated—the weather-bleached timber from which both buildings and fences were constructed, the dull grey of the tin roofs, the green and blue of the freshly painted carvings on the façades. In winter, when everything was covered in snow, you could easily make out the clear geometric structure of the housing plots. This disappeared in the summer amidst the greens of the apple and cherry trees that covered the dacha world like down. Nowadays, the uniform appearance of the dacha colony has been broken up by the large number of two- and even three-storey brick buildings with their freshly painted and newly installed metal roofs. The colony has changed colour. Some buildings rise up like great steamships and stand out from their surroundings. The plots of land now have high walls or solid metal fences that block the view, and entry gates that often feature surveillance cameras and can be opened automatically. There are 'dacha skyscrapers' in what is for the most part forested terrain dotted here and there with natural or artificial ponds. Every year sees the completion of further massive buildings that have long ceased to be mere summer houses but are more like second homes that can be occupied even in winter. Every summer witnesses a growth in the commuter traffic between the city and the surrounding region, with the difference that it does not proceed via the elektrichka but on the road network, which itself has been expanded. There are endless tailbacks leaving the city on Friday afternoons and even longer ones returning to the city on Sunday evenings. Dotted among the old-style dachas you suddenly find *cottages* and *town-houses*—with their fairy-tale overtones; the terms too are new, exotic, chiefly Anglo-Saxon imports for buildings, whose whereabouts are advertised in advance on motorway *billboards*, announcing the birth of the new *gated communities*. Walls are springing up separating the 'newcomers' from the 'longtimers' in a world where everyone knew everyone and where, if you had business to attend to in town, you could call on a babushka from next door who would look after a child or grandchild at a moment's notice. Instead of a community, you now have a retreat to a world of one's own cut off from the outside.

There is much to be said on this score. There are the cars for which there was no parking space in the old-style dacha colonies; the satellite dishes that produce immediate contact to the world in settlements that once upon a time had no phone, could be reached only on foot and were cut off from the normal sense of time. The dacha has long since ceased to function as the irreplaceable source of provisions, the place where flowers, tomatoes and potatoes were planted and harvested and where this produce helped people survive the winter in an emergency. The dacha plot of land has scarcely anything to do with self-sufficiency anymore, as it had done for past generations, especially in times of crisis. Whatever you need for living over the weekend or indeed the entire summer, you bring with you in your car from town or fetch from one of the supermarkets or malls that have sprung up on the city outskirts. The decibel levels make it clear that there is no need to stick to rules about keeping the noise down. The garbage and waste on the margins of the colony have become a significant problem since the development of infrastructure and communal services lag hopelessly behind the expansion of consumption. The out-of-town building boom probably tells us even more about the growth of a new middle class than the building activity in the town centres. It would not be difficult to compare the pictures produced by Google Maps over the last two decades to gauge the changes that have taken place. These may well pass unnoticed at first sight as well as in the long view, but when looked at on fast-forward the speed of change is staggering. The history of the dacha as a central site of Russian-Soviet culture is far from over, but has now entered a new phase. This sharpens our sense of what the dacha used to be.[1]

'Summer Guests'

The dacha is no Soviet invention but rather the continuation of a Russian 'institution' under novel conditions.[2] Famous dacha suburbs still visible today have existed since the second half of the nineteenth century, especially in the environs of St. Petersburg and Moscow. They are themselves the heirs of the country estates built by the nobility or 'given' by the Tsars to deserving dignitaries to be used as summer houses ('dacha' comes from *dat = to give*).

But the heyday of the dacha as temporary accommodation close to town and either purpose-built or else rented for the summer belongs historically in the second half of the nineteenth and the early years of the twentieth century. This was the boom time of the industrialisation and urbanisation of the late Tsarist Empire, which had been accompanied by the formation of a fast-growing middle class of state officials, white-collar workers, entrepreneurs, businessmen and freelance professionals. The building of the railways provided the infrastructure needed for commuting between work and leisure, between the urban centre and the surrounding region. A boom in dacha building followed—not unlike the current one—developing along the newly laid rail track. In St. Petersburg this followed the route along the coast of the Gulf of Finland to Lisy Nos and Kuokkala, Novaya Derevnya, Ozerki and Shuvalovo on the route to Vyborg in the north, and along the route to the 'Petersburg paradises' of Tsarskoe Selo,

Pavlovsk, Gatchina and Oranienbaum in the south and southwest. The situation in Moscow was similar. There are important dacha settlements on the Nikolaevsky line to St. Petersburg, on the route to Smolensk, and on the Kazan, Nizhny Novgorod and Yaroslavl line important dacha settlements have grown up which define the space around Moscow to this day. The dacha settlements for the nomenklatura on or close to the Moscow River acquired particular importance in the Soviet period.[3]

The characteristic nature of a dacha existence was succinctly summarised by Fyodor Dostoevsky when he observed following his arrival in Staraya Russa in 1872: 'It's cheap, it's quick and easy to move here and finally, the house comes with furniture, even with crockery, the station has newspapers and journals, and so on.'[4] The railway track created a corridor of intensive building activity and speculation. Gradually, the dacha emerged as a special kind of house—you can see this from the catalogues and architects' plans of the day. The basic features of the dacha were defined by its function. It had to be located 'in nature', that is, on a plot looking out onto the natural environment, the forest. It had to have a spacious staircase and a glassed-in veranda or balcony leading outdoors. All the amenities needed for a family or sometimes even several generations to live together had to be present, albeit in a simplified or reduced form. The house was inhabited only in the summer months and had to be weatherproofed against the winter cold. The fin-de-siècle dacha architecture has survived as a model of the versatility of a wood architecture that passed through the entire gamut of stylistic trends—from neo-Russian to neo-Gothic, from the Swiss chalet to the English country house. Russian Art Nouveau achieved its most fantastic flowering in its timbered buildings.

The dacha was not just a place but a form of life, a biotope, the setting for an intelligentsia that sought constantly to distance itself from the stresses of public life in the capital. It was a place for meditation and reflection that was tied to the idiosyncrasies of what Dietrich Geyer has called a self-referential community of like-minded people. The dacha and its inhabitants became topoi, if not stereotypes, of Russian literature. In his drama *Dachniki* (*Summerfolk*), Maxim Gorky erected a monument to the summer visitors in the shadow of the

failed 1905 Revolution—a play spectacularly directed by Peter Stein at
the Berlin Schaubühne and premiered in London in 1974 by the Royal
Shakespeare Company under the direction of David Jones. It is no
mere coincidence that in *The Cherry Orchard* Anton Chekhov chose a
summer house as the backdrop to the social drama of the decline of
the old land-owning nobility and the rise of the new, capitalist class of
entrepreneurs and businessmen. The dacha as a social biotope meant
the periodic retreat from the urban hustle and bustle, entry into a
different daily rhythm and submission to nature's changing seasons
from early summer to autumn. The veranda with its basket-weave
furniture, the preservation of a more formal dress code even in the
summer resort, and the presence of servants from the local village—all
of this has been captured in countless memoirs and literary works as
the *lieux de mémoire* in the topography of Russian culture. The summer
house as both the starting point for projects to reform one's life and
a Gesamtkunstwerk has rewritten the history of art in the artist colonies of Abramtsevo and Talashkino. The dacha functioned as a zone
of contact between town and village for a social stratum that had lost
its relationship to the countryside. 'The intelligentsia—that's not us!
We're something else . . . we are dachniki in our own country . . . some
kind of foreign visitors. We rush about, try to make ourselves comfortable niches in life . . . we do nothing and talk a disgusting amount.'[5] In
short the dacha was a way of life of the newly emerging middle class
beyond the 'nests of gentlefolks' and beyond the workers' accommodation in the growing industrial towns.[6]

Even in the turbulent times of the Revolution, commuting between
the dacha and the city continued, or so we can read in the diaries of
Zinaida Gippius, when she writes, on Thursday, 17 August 1917: 'It is
warm, still summer. We ought rather to drive out to the dacha for the
last days. But everything is still seething here and leaving is difficult.
The dacha is on Prince Wittgenstein's land, not far from the Siverskaya
estate where the war has been raging. The newspapers will come the
same day, there is a telephone and a beautiful house. The connection
to St. Petersburg would not be disrupted—how I love the old park in the
autumn!—but I can't bring myself to leave here. The Siverskaya estate
reminds me of the "sufferings of war" but the dacha prophetically and
appropriately is now called "Red Dacha" . . . (it is actually painted red

all over).'[7] Or in the entry for 21 September 1917: 'It's dark outside. Day and night are almost indistinguishable. Damp and slippery. We should drive out to the dacha. The birches out there gleam like gold and there is the illusion of peace and quiet.'[8] On the change of ownership of dachas, Gippius notes on 5 July 1918: 'The estate has been "taken away" from the Prince, of course. A "commissar", a young monkey, is now installed. He has already got rid of about half the furnishings, spends his time shooting the thrushes and takes his new patent-leather shoes out for walks. Acts like a genuine boor.'[9]

Biotope of Social Climbers and the New Middle Class

An autonomous, specifically Soviet dacha culture arose from the mid-1930s when it was believed that simply redistributing and redeploying properties taken over from prerevolutionary times—an example was the Arkhangelskoe estate near Moscow—was no longer sufficient. The state intervened and made plots of land available for establishing dacha colonies and resources were provided for building dachas for the new elite, Party and state personnel, star achievers from among Red directors, top workers and members of the Academy of Sciences. An entire archipelago of generously appointed and even luxurious dacha colonies came into being. The relevant professional organisation or the people's commissariat had the responsibility of finding worthy tenants. The right to live in a dacha was time-limited and lapsed with the death of the privileged occupant or his widow. The nomenklatura dachas—such as those in Barvikha, Serebryany Bor, Nikolina Gora among others—look architecturally like a continuation of the old, prerevolutionary dacha world. Nikita Mikhalkov, who himself comes from a Soviet-Russian artist dynasty, attempted to depict this milieu in his feature film *Utomlyonnye solntsem* (*Burnt by the Sun*), a version of *The Cherry Orchard* transposed to Stalin's Russia, with its mixture of relaxed serenity in luxurious surroundings and the entry of brutal violence at the time of the Stalinist purges. Alexander Rodchenko is just one of many to remind us of the 'relaxed tension' on weekends when Mayakovsky, the Briks, Shterenberg and Pudovkin were guests in his dacha. Some of them sat around and conversed while others played mahjong, gorodki or cards. 'Everyone was fed from Saturday to Monday. There was a dinner with masses of wild berries, all kinds of piroggi were baked. Anichka, who came specially for the summer, was really good at this.'[10]

As the biotope of this new elite, the dacha makes an appearance in many of the memoirs of the Great Terror as a place of retreat, fictive conspiracies but also fantastic orgies, and as the setting for a privileged existence that could end in catastrophe at any moment.[11] For most of the population, the dacha plots of land which became increasingly available from the mid-1930s on were largely a resource to ensure self-sufficiency and a refuge for hundreds of thousands of city dwellers fleeing to the countryside to escape overcrowded accommodations. By the mid-1930s around half a million Muscovites fled to the dacha suburbs on summer weekends.[12]

Self-Sufficiency and Resistance to Crises

The struggle for survival during the war and the postwar period gave the dacha a purpose that it retained until the demise of the Soviet world: it served not just as a place of recreation but as the basic source of provisions that one could rely on even when public supply had utterly failed. The economies of the large towns were based in great measure on the exchange between 'the country and the city', as this was mediated by the commuters in the suburban trains, the rhythm of the seasons and the alternation of weekend and working week. The indissoluble links between the city and the dacha were revealed by the hectic, pulsating movements of hundreds of thousands heavily weighed-down passengers moving between stations as they travelled every week on the elektrichka with their rucksacks, bags and trolleys. Surveys in 2010 revealed that 48 percent of the inhabitants of the large cities had access to a dacha, while in Russia as a whole the figure rose to around 60 percent.[13]

During the summer the dacha became the focal point of life. Even the railway stations were a world of their own—at the end of the 1980s they might have had a single telephone, a newspaper kiosk and stalls selling vegetables and fruit seeds from the gardens of the local kolkhoz farmers. Once you reached the dacha colony after an extended march, you were 'outside', 'unreachable' and subject to a different time scale. For children the long summer began at the end of May with the start of the school holidays, which would not draw to a close until the new term on 1 September. For them this was nothing less than an entry into a world of adventures and a carefree existence. For adults, however, country life also meant work. Professors devoted themselves to 'urban gardening', planting potatoes and tomatoes in the summer. White-collar workers were kept busy repairing the water pump or making sure that the cesspit at the end of the plot was in good working order. But more importantly and aside from the economic self-sufficiency, the dacha was compensation for the overcrowded conditions in the towns. Here was a place where the generations could meet up but at a distance, whereas normally they were forced to live more or less on top of one another. And similarly, the couples who otherwise had nowhere to be on their own could get together undisturbed. This was a place where people brought the old furniture that was no longer wanted in town. There would be a stool from the '40s, crockery that had survived the war—the dacha acted as a depot for the discarded furniture of past times. Here children and adolescents could form their teams and gangs. The inexorable annual cycle called for skills that town dwellers had forgotten: how to prune trees or change gas cylinders. Dachas were where people brought books they had finished or that were out-of-date and where, conversely, you read papers that were already days old because current papers were unavailable. The books that had not been recycled because people couldn't bear to part with them formed the basis of a second library in the country. So the modern visitor did not actually end up living 'in nature', but in a second urban world in the countryside. It was not until later, when the Soviet order of things was coming to an end, that new anxieties manifested themselves. What shall we do in winter when the dacha is empty and uninhabited? Who will keep an eye out? Who will intervene if homeless people or *narkomany*, that is, drug addicts, come in search of a roof to put over their heads or if thieves are in the vicinity? The post-Soviet dacha world has solved this problem with metre-high walls, modern surveillance cameras and the alarm systems of a booming security industry.

Peredelkino—Lieu de Mémoire

The end of the dacha culture can best be observed in one of the most prominent settlements in Russia—in Peredelkino, beyond the motorway ring, southwest of Moscow, on the railway line to Kyiv. At Gorky's suggestion and in response to Stalin's decree, Peredelkino was established in 1933 for the benefit of the Union of Soviet Writers. Its aim was to provide elite authors and artists with privileged working and living conditions.[14] Originally a piece of woodland, twenty-five hectares in size and containing around thirty summer houses, it gradually attracted the crème de la crème of Soviet writers. The catalogue of its inhabitants is a Who's Who of Soviet literature. Peredelkino even became known to a Western public when reporters visited Boris Pasternak, the author of *Doctor Zhivago* and winner of the Nobel Prize in 1958, in his summer house (today the Pasternak Museum is located in his house in Ulitsa Pavlenko 3).[15] The inhabitants of Peredelkino include some of the classics of Soviet literature—Korney Chukovsky; Marietta Shaginian; Margarita Aliger; Vera Inber; Nikolay Pogodin; Fyodor Panfyorov; Alexander Fadeev, the chairman of the Writers Union who took his own life in 1956; Ilya Ehrenburg; Valentin Kataev; Lev Kassil; Konstantin Paustovsky; as well as the leading figures of the then younger generation of Soviet literature such as Yevgeny Yevtushenko, Andrey Voznesensky, Bulat Okudzhava, Bella Akhmadulina and Chingiz Aitmatov. The children of Friedrich Wolf, the German political émigré, enjoyed happy days in Peredelkino. This was where Lev Kamenev spent his summers before he was condemned to death in a show trial in 1936 and executed. And so did Isaac Babel, whom Beria's men murdered as an 'agent' and 'parasite' in 1940. It is no exaggeration to say that this dacha colony has become a *lieu de mémoire* of Russian and Soviet culture—as well as a memorial to the end of an era.[16]

The end of the Soviet era produced a flare-up in the conflict around land, the dacha colonies and the preservation of traditional privileges and new claims. The oasis of recreation and seclusion has become a battlefield between the old inhabitants, the anything but disinterested defenders of the status quo, and the new settlers, the social climbers resolved to make their way. Peredelkino, too, 'Stalin's Cherry Orchard', has become a stage on which the 'new Russians' can perform. Even the Russian Orthodox Church has plunged into the battle for the inheritance of Peredelkino. The church has built a prestigious and even ostentatious summer residence there for the Patriarch of Moscow and all Rus. Peredelkino makes a statement about social status; Peredelkino is also expensive. The new wealth encapsulated in the 'dacha boom' is as divisive socially as it is visibly. No stylistic extravagance is too gross to be put on show. Anyone who lacks the opportunity to stroll in the well-sheltered precincts of the newly affluent Rublyovka can gain an impression of the taste of the new Russians in the glossy magazines that delight in displaying interiors created by Italian or French designers. There is no style that has not been tried out, no eclecticism that is too fantastic. The great dachas of the old elite—the heroes of the Soviet Union, the aircraft and atomic bomb builders, the distinguished composers, Academy members and writers—look almost Spartan, modest and even puny in comparison. For the new Russians, in contrast, there seem to be no rules at all. Their taste is derived from Western glamour—or what they imagine glamour to be. They build however and wherever suits them because the people who might wish to defend Peredelkino against ruthless development are too old and feeble. So they have set their sights on transforming the dacha colony into a museum. A Peredelkino Museum already exists; tours are available for the friends of literature and culture; the cemetery is being promoted as a pantheon of Russian literature. The houses of writers and artists who used to live and work there are already being turned into museums: Pasternak, Chukovsky, Okudzhava, Yevtushenko and even Zurab Tsereteli. But to turn everything into a museum means that an era has reached its end point.

In his wonderful book about the dacha, Stephen Lovell writes, 'If the tag "middle-class" refers to anyone in Russia, it is to the dachnik. Not that this observation can bring us much moral or intellectual succour. One could have no stronger confirmation of the enduring social weakness and political marginalization of this putative middle than the fact that so many of its members are called, every Friday night or Saturday morning, to don rubber boots and depart for their plot of land. In the modern dacha, if we care to look closely enough, we find much of what has made Russia in the last century so incredibly resilient and so disastrously dysfunctional. What it does not do,

FIGURE 24.1. Dacha built in Peredelkino in 1935 and belonging to the writer Leonid Leonov (1899–1994); it is now falling into disrepair. From *Itogi*, 29 May 2001, 28.

unfortunately, is suggest how the symbiotic relationship between these two characteristics can ever be broken.'[17]

That is to say, if ever there was a place where something that might be called a Russian middle class was formed and consolidated, then it must have been the summer house, that temporary social space which was indispensable for coping with the needs of ordinary life and for survival in hard times. The dacha, the summer house that succeeded the old manor house, the 'nest of gentlefolks', in the late nineteenth and early twentieth centuries, is itself on its way to being superseded. This development takes different forms. The most important is doubtless the transformation of the dacha landscape into something familiar to us from other parts of the world where urbanisation and urban sprawl have proliferated. But the fact that the dacha cooperative Ozero in the north of St. Petersburg, an all-male society composed of old sports comrades, secret servicemen, Mafiosi and kleptocratic oligarchs, would become the birthplace of the Putin regime was probably not foreseen in any history of the Soviet dacha world.[18]

CHAPTER 25

Health Resorts for Workers: The Sanatorium as a Historical Locus

Thomas Mann's novel *The Magic Mountain* inscribed the sanatorium as a topos in the literary map of Europe for all time. In it Europe's last days before the continent plunges into the abyss of the First World War play out. Under a strict regime, medical interventions alternate with solid lunches and festive dinners in contravention of every recommended diet. Everything moves in tune with a routine of interludes that bridge the passage of time and with amusing conversations where tensions find expression and give rise to the intimacy in which people beset by illnesses or already doomed all come together as patients. This exceptional situation high up in the Swiss Alps where you feel close to the heavens and nature but have no need to renounce the comforts of civilisation creates the sense of freedom that enables people to talk about matters of ultimate importance. It is a place where people have barely had time to come close to one another before having to face up to their own death. Thus the sanatorium becomes a place in which Europe takes leave of itself: Hans Castorp, Madame Chauchat, Joachim Ziemßen, Hofrat Behrens and all the others.

Two contemporaries of Thomas Mann—who was born in Lübeck in 1875 and died in Zurich in 1955—found themselves in a sanatorium at the other end of the world and in utterly different circumstances. There they wrote *Correspondence across a Room*, which subsequently became famous. The authors were Mikhail Gershenzon, perhaps the most important literary historian and Pushkin specialist of the Russian Silver Age—he was born in Kishinev in 1869 and died in Moscow in 1925—and Vyacheslav Ivanov, a philosopher of religion and a poet, who was born in Moscow in 1866 and died in Rome in 1949. In 1920 the two men spent some months together in a sanatorium—*dom otdykha* in Russian—established by the Soviet government for older scientists, scholars, writers and artists who, lost in the confusion, cold and hunger of the Civil War, might otherwise not have survived. Through TseKUBU (an abbreviation for Central Commission for the Improvement of the Everyday Lives of Scientists)—an institution set up largely under the influence of Maxim Gorky—a number of sanatoriums were established in requisitioned villas and aristocratic country houses in Petrograd and Moscow. In one such place, these two scholars lived together and began to send questions and answers back and forth across the room. This led to a correspondence that Ernst Robert Curtius published in German as early as the 1920s, believing it was one of the most important testimonies to an intellectual understanding after the war, the Revolution and the Civil War, and the demise of the Old Europe.[1] Nothing could make the distinction between the two books clearer than their settings: the Schatzalp Sanatorium in the mountain world of Davos in one case; a confiscated tenement block in 2nd Neopalimovsky Pereulok 5 in central Moscow (according to Boris Zaytsev) in the other. The first was a sanatorium with all the comfort of a luxury hotel; the second, a shabby tenement block cheaply converted into communal apartments, with no army of servants, but maintained with nothing more than the rations approved by the people's commissariat for deserving elderly scholars. In the first instance, we have Thomas Mann's reconstruction of the premonitions of a prewar era that already lay in the past; in the second, a real-time exchange of opinions during the Civil War that had not yet concluded, after which the two occupants of the room on 2nd Neopalimovsky Pereulok would go their separate ways. Gershenzon would remain in Moscow, though with periodic stays in Badenweiler, while Ivanov went via Baku into exile in Rome. The sanatorium: the health resort viewed as an end point, a place of survival, a place for meditation in catastrophic times. With 'Stalin's dacha' in Sochi, in contrast, we learn about a very different meaning.[2]

Health Resorts, the Clinic as Topos

When compared to the exclusive and sophisticated world of Davos or the shabbiness of the Moscow scholars' residence hall, places that go by such names as rest home (*dom otdykha*), boarding house (*pensionat*),

sanatorium (*sanatory*) or even hotel (*gostinitsa*) seem quite unspectacular and very ordinary. And yet health resorts or sanatoriums have
a specific place in the experience of Soviet citizens. Just consider the
numbers: in the 1970s there was a network of around six thousand
sanatoriums, health centres and boarding houses in which some 13
million people were looked after annually. The health resorts run by
the trade unions accommodated more than 9 million people annually,
around 90 percent of whom were looked after in privileged conditions
paid for by the state.[3]

Many things came together here. Obtaining a place was anything
but straightforward. You had to belong to a trade union or a similar
professional organisation—of writers or composers—to gain a spot
in one of the homes managed by these organisations. Health resorts
were 'places in the sun'; compared to tourist camps (*turbaza*), themselves relatively comfortable, they were in great demand and short
supply. Here too there were queues, waiting lists on which you inched
forward, often for years on end. Gaining approval, the so-called *putyovka*, was itself something of a triumph. You could get lucky and
be allocated a place at the seaside in the Caucasus, on the Crimean
coast or else in one of the spas on the Baltic; or perhaps even in one
of the older spa towns around the capital, such as Staraya Russa or
Zvenigorod, or in one of the recreation and leisure complexes gradually built up by the large combines in the forested regions of the
Urals, the Altai or the Tian Shan mountains.

The network covered the entire Union. There was a spa town for
every ailment—climatic spas, thermal baths and peat baths. The system, which was essentially under the control of the trade unions,
aimed 'to act as healing and prophylactic institutions designed to
restore the health of the workforce and their ability to work, to educate them to look after their own health, improve their hygiene and
to carry out a comprehensive and varied programme of culture and
enlightenment.'[4] The sanatoriums included a large number of departments with medical specialists, laboratories and units for diagnosis
and therapy. Not least were the culture programmes and leisure activities. Particular emphasis was placed on the scientific nature of the
entire operation. 'The Soviet system of health care and spa treatments
is based on strict scientific principles.'[5] In their endeavours they were

supported by numerous 'institutes of spa science' (*kurortologiya*). This complex approach to health probably helped to explain the sheer magnitude of the Soviet health resort system, which saw a massive building boom in the 1970s. By way of illustration, the United Health Resorts in Adler provided 7,000 beds, Pitsunda 3,000, the Leninskie Skaly in Pyatigorsk more than 1,300, the Piket Sanatorium in Kislovodsk more than 1,200, and Kuyalnik in Odesa over 4,000.[6] Every spa town was a self-contained world which called for total commitment from the moment of arrival. And even if you were there just for relaxation, you could not escape the education, the scientific plan and the thoroughgoing balneological counselling. The daily routine provided for entertainment and cultural activity: visits to natural wonders or ancient ruins in the vicinity, a regional museum or the performance of a folklore ensemble. The moments captured on countless photos and postcards allow us to read off the evolution of the rest and recreation landscape—from its beginnings down to the present. All the historical styles can be found there: the neoclassical pump rooms of Pyatigorsk, the hotel and sanatorium façades in Yessentuki and Mineralnye Vody in the Caucasus, the neoclassical porticos in the Sochi of the 1930s through to the skyline of the hotel towers that create the silhouette of Sochi today.

A Glorious Heritage: The Spas of the Russian Empire

It is easy to see how Soviet power could latch on to the development of the prerevolutionary spa and leisure industry and build on it right down to the present day. The buildings inherited from the Tsarist Empire—where not destroyed by the Germans during the war—form the kernel or historical centre of almost all today's prominent spa towns. The most accurate information about the rich and diverse spa landscape in Russia can be gleaned from the guides and Baedekers that lured the new, affluent public to the places that were on the rise during the years 1880–1913.[7]

You can learn from them just when the building boom began and what was essential to the creation of the spa and leisure infrastructure. This meant chiefly the military conquest and 'pacification' of the

Caucasus and building the railways that brought the Black Sea coast closer. Everything needed by spa towns is to be found there right down to the present day: the grand train station with waiting rooms for different classes, the hotels with expensive boutiques and arcades, the water towers and electricity generators, the pumping stations, the mountain and cable cars, the bars and reading rooms, the promenade, the casino and the local telegraph office. And we mustn't forget the arrangements for the different centres of worship—churches, mosques and synagogues.[8] The spa culture began in Russia as early as 1717 with the discovery of sources of medicinal mud near Petrozavodsk in Karelia; somewhat later came the mineral springs on the middle and lower Volga near Samara and Lipetsk. The first spas based on the rich mineral springs of the Caucasus were opened as early as 1803. After the Russian Empire had conquered the Black Sea coast and the Caucasus, the Russian elite took possession of them culturally in the period leading up to the First World War. They no longer catered just to the nobility, the aristocracy, but increasingly also to the entrepreneurs and the middle classes who discovered and indeed invented 'the Russian south'. The affluent and educated Russian classes had always travelled to Western Europe for its spas and culture. Now they set about creating their own spas together with everything associated with them. The elite of the Russian Empire—and increasingly of a Russian middle class—no longer felt compelled to go as far as Antibes, Biarritz, Deauville, Ostend or Baden-Baden. The 'Caucasian Riviera', a hotel complex built around 1900 in the centre of Sochi, provided not only central heating, a library, a lift and a theatre for six hundred spectators but also five international newspapers and a maître d'hôtel who spoke English, French and German. All the major architects who had made their name in the capital cities built in the spa towns of the south: Nikolay P. Krasnov, Karl I. Eshliman, I. A. Monighetti, Auguste de Montferrand and Andrey Stackenschneider. Well-known doctors from the capital such as Sergey P. Botkin opened their practices in the blossoming spa towns.

All the wealth of the Russian Empire seems to have been concentrated in a zone of luxury and comfort. The infrastructure and level of culture created in the decades before 1914 or 1917 set standards that remained valid even for the succeeding Soviet regime.

FIGURE 25.1. Postcard of the Caucasian Riviera Hotel in Sochi at the beginning of the twentieth century. From E. I. Kirichenko, E. G. Shcheboleva and M. V. Nashchokina (eds.), *Gradostroitel'stvo Rossii serediny XIX–nachala XX veka: Goroda i novye tipy poselenii*, vol. 2, Progress-Traditsiia, Moscow 2003, 15.

Every conceivable style would be tried out here: Renaissance, English country house, neo-Russian, neo-Gothic, Louis Seize and Art Nouveau. The names of the sanatoriums and hotels are similar to those in Biarritz, Opatija/Abbazia and San Remo: Metropol, Hotel Central, Hôtel de France, Europe, etc. From the standpoint of the subsequent Soviet welfare state, the 36 spa towns with their 60 sanatoriums and 3,000 beds which were said to have existed on the coast on the eve of the Revolution were relatively few in number and relatively backward. From this vantage point, the beneficiaries of this 'pleasure ground' were exclusively the exploiting classes. The social composition of the spa guests as recorded in the spa lists is unambiguous: in Mineralnye Vody in 1907 41.9 percent were landowners and nobility, 23.8 percent bourgeoisie, 10.5 percent officers and 23.8 percent officials. The spas were not accessible to the wider public, to the 'masses'.[9] What is also true, however, is that this was when the foundations were laid for the Soviet leisure landscape: the broad beaches with the promenades, the sloping terraces, the parks, the villas and guesthouses surrounded by palm trees and flowering bushes. Every subsequent era added its own piece of the mosaic: the neoclassical pavilion of 'Spring No. 4' and the temple-like peat bath in Yessentuki, the Pushkin pump room in Zheleznovodsk, the white dacha that Anton Chekhov had built and the white palaces dotting the southern coast of the Crimea.[10]

The Crimea: How the Pearl of the Empire Turned into the Soviet Sanatorium

The first health resorts were established by the Soviets in 1920 as a kind of emergency measure for the benefit of select groups—scientists and writers. In May of that year, one was opened in Kamenny Ostrov in Petrograd; this was followed in August by one of the palaces in Serebryany Bor and then in Tarasovka and Zvenigorod close to Moscow. On 21 December 1920 Lenin signed a decree of the Council of People's Commissars 'On utilizing the Crimea for the medical treatment of working people'. In the decree we read: 'Sanatoriums and spa towns of the Crimea, which previously were the privileged resorts of the big bourgeoisie, the wonderful dachas and villas used by large landowners and capitalists, and the palaces of former Tsars and Grand Dukes, shall be used now as the sanatoriums and treatment centres of workers and peasants.'[11] By the end of 1921, twenty-three sanatoriums had already been opened. The Crimea was destined to become the collective sanatorium of the Soviet nation. A central spa administration (KurUpr) was set up for the whole of the peninsula. Sanatoriums were established in the available villas and hotels and taken over by state or trade-union organisations, which following the style of the day were given names such as Glavdortrans, Ukrastrakhkass, Narkomzdrav, Narkomsem and so on. By 1924 there were already 37,137 spa guests. Initially the Soviets did not build sanatoriums and health resorts themselves but took over existing buildings. The transformation of the Crimea from a playground of the Russian Empire's elite into a 'workers' paradise' was essentially a matter of renaming and appropriation. You can see that from various guidebooks in which the old and new names are listed next to each other.

Yalta alone is home to the Red Cross health resort, the former Hotel Petrogradskaya, and the All-Russian Central Executive Committee (VTsIK) health resort in the Erlanger Park; the Bezobrazov summer house has become a health resort of the Council of People's Commissars of the Russian Soviet Federated Socialist Republic (RSFSR). To this, add the health resorts of the Central Committee of the Federated Trade Unions of Communal Workers (Ulitsa Chainaya 5), of the Central Committee of the Federated Trade Unions of Water Transport Workers (Ulitsa Proletarskaya 8–10), of the People's Commissariat for Labour (Narkomtrud) (Ulitsa Khalturina), of the People's Commissariat for Workers' and Peasants' Inspection (RKI) (Ulitsa Botkinskaya 18), of the Central Committee of the Federated Trade Unions of Transport Workers (Ulitsa Kommunarov 36), of the People's Commissariat for Posts and Telegraphs (Ulitsa Kommunarov 5) and of the Revolutionary War Council of the Republic (the former Dacha Vasiliev on Issarskoe Chaussee). The Palace of the Emir of Bukhara, built in Moorish style at the beginning of the twentieth century, has been transformed into a Museum of the East and subsequently a sanatorium (Ulitsa Kommunarov).

Livadiya, built in 1911 after Nikolay Krasnov's designs in the Italian Renaissance style, used to be the site of the summer residence of Tsar Nicholas II. A guidebook describes the museum that opened in the palace after the Revolution: 'The museum shows the last Tsar's way of life in all its petty-bourgeois manifestations. . . . The upper storeys contain the Tsar's seven tastelessly decorated private chambers. The walls, adorned with exotic varieties of wood, display vast numbers of cheap drawings, religious images and icons. The rooms are filled with period furniture.' In the German-language guide to the USSR of 1928 we learn that in 1923 a sanatorium with three hundred beds was opened exclusively for peasants in the castles of Livadiya. The former surgical unit in the castle now contained the Livadiya Sanatorium No. 6 which was managed by the central health insurance fund. The building of the former entourage of the court was turned into a guesthouse with seventy rooms. The land formerly belonging to the Palace of Oreanda became the health resort of the print-workers' union, under the name Proletarian Health. The former Palace Kichkine in Gaspra, once property of the grand duke Dmitry

Konstantinovich, was transformed into the sanatorium of the Council of People's Commissars of the Crimea; Dyulber, the palace of Grand Duke Pyotr Nikolaevich, housed a sanatorium for political workers. Dyulber was built at the end of the nineteenth century in Moorish revivalist style to a design by Nikolay Krasnov. Even the spectacular neo-Gothic 'Swallow's Nest', perched on a rocky outcrop, now contained a sanatorium. Numerous properties along the coast were transformed into agricultural collectives. In Miskhor, what was the estate of Prince Dolgorukov in the first half of the nineteenth century has become the 'Red Dawn' (Krasnye Zori) along with several other sanatoriums with up to eighty-five rooms. One of them, 'Mountain Sun' (Gornoe Solntse), was nationalised and used by the GPU as a tuberculosis sanatorium. In Gaspra, another former estate from the nineteenth century belonging to Count Panin became a health resort of the TseKUBU, while the estate of Prince Yusupov in Koreiz, with its precious interiors, furniture and paintings, was converted into a health resort for the GPU and used by Felix Dzerzhinsky.

Alupka is famous for its Vorontsov Palace with rare plants, gigantic cedars, Wellington trees, pines, oleander and magnolias. The two-hundred-room castle, built in a half-Tudor, half-Moorish style, once served as a sanatorium of the People's Commissariat for Enlightenment and can be visited nowadays as a museum. The vineyards of Massandra and the Nikitsky Botanical Gardens, established in 1811 on the initiative of the Duc de Richelieu, are a veritable Garden of Eden. The Nikitsky Gardens, constructed from plans by Peter Simon Pallas, have hundreds of species of trees, around 2,000 roses and 260 different vine varieties, as well as older plants: date palms, Persian silk trees and thousand-year-old amorphophallus trees. Gurzuf has the house of the Raevsky family, with whom Pushkin stayed in 1820, as well as parks and gardens. Alushta, renowned for its vineyards and tobacco cultivation, has a district known as the 'Workers' corner' (Rabochy ugolok), a large beach and the rest and recreation homes of the Council of Trade Unions and the Red Cross. The monastery of Kozmodemiansk was transformed into a labour colony of the Commissariat for Social Welfare. In Feodosiya, a town on the sea shaped like an amphitheatre, a city was established for eight hundred children. In the spa season many private guesthouses offer accommodation.

Between 1921 and 1940 around 3.5 million people spent their vacations on the south coast of the Crimea. But not until the 1930s, when the Moscow architect Moisey Y. Ginzburg developed a plan for 'socialist reconstruction', were truly new sanatorium buildings erected in the Crimea, and especially in Yalta. Later, together with Andrey Burov, Ginzburg led the reconstruction after the liberation of the German-occupied areas. Construction in the Crimea was disrupted by the German occupation, which lasted from November 1941 to May 1944. It left behind not only great physical destruction but also a peninsula depopulated by war, deportations and mass murder.

Matsesta: A New Health Resort for the New Human Being

The principal site for the conversion of the prerevolutionary spa towns lies elsewhere, however; namely on the Caucasian Riviera, the strip of coast stretching from Sochi to Batumi. There the Soviets developed a new spa region in accordance with their own ideas. From the beginning of the twentieth century, this area counted a number of resorts and a preexisting railway line with all the essential amenities. With the Caucasian Riviera hotel complex, Sochi even had the largest and the most luxurious resort of the entire Black Sea coastline. Sukhumi on the Abkhazian section of the coast was famous for its fantastic subtropical gardens, parks and white villas.

But the Soviet government had even more ambitious plans here, beginning as early as the 1920s with studies and projects, which did not become reality until large investments poured in during the 1930s. During the second Five-Year Plan (1933–1937) more than 600 million rubles were invested in this sector.[12] It became the meeting place of all the period's important architects and town planners.

Representatives of the avant-garde like the Vesnin brothers and Alexey Shchusev were just as involved here as the leading minds of the neoclassical school, Ivan Zholtovsky, Vladimir Shchuko, Vladimir Gelfreikh and Stalin's personal favourite, Miron Merzhanov.[13]

Matsesta had an important architectural heritage from before the Revolution: Voronov's summer house, the harbour hospital, the villa later used to house the malaria isolation station, the Pushkin Library in an enchanting Moorish-style building surrounded by parkland. But the most significant complex, one that represented the standard for Soviet architects, was the truly impressive Caucasian Riviera, built after 1906 to architect V. A. Yon's plans, with two four-storey hotels, a theatre for six hundred spectators, cafés and restaurants, its own water supply and sewerage system and an independent electricity supply. In subsequent years it was expanded and provided with all the marks of comfort, swimming pool, reading room, casino, car park, landing stage and even darkrooms for camera buffs. This hotel complex, nationalised in 1918, was surpassed and gave way to something new.[14] 'The architects of our spa town seek successful paths towards the creation of a new Soviet style in spa architecture, in rest and recreation homes aimed at the broad mass of workers and not restricted to a handful of exploiters, as was the case before the Revolution.'[15] Sanatoriums were also planned and erected elsewhere—for example, in Mineralnye Vody and Barvikha near Moscow where in 1929–1934 Boris Yofan, architect of the Palace of the Soviets and the House on the Embankment, built the most ambitious sanatorium complex, which now serves as a department of the Kremlin Hospital.[16] But Matsesta near Sochi was the showpiece, the architecture exhibition for the new, Soviet 'spa and pool architecture'. 'What architecture should there be in our spa town, what new buildings best satisfy the requirements of Soviet architecture?', asked M. K. in the *Sochinskaya pravda* on the occasion of a conference in 1936.[17] The answer was that everything should be different from the old architecture. The spa town was now viewed as a totality rather than a series of single buildings; from the railway station to the pool house, from the design of the parks to the building of the restaurants. The communal arrangements were key. The planning was not limited to individual ideas, but followed a 'scientific' rationale, affecting such matters as the positioning of balconies, the changes in lighting according to the seasons, the building of the sports facilities, the professional services and the laboratories. Recreation was not simply leisure time but the 'conscious, cultural' activity fostering the development of 'the human being to the fullest possible extent' and embracing further education, theatre, area studies and gymnastics. Technically everything was to be as up-to-date as possible, including hydroplanes that would link up the different resorts along the coast. The daily routine focused on the processing and management of collectives, not on providing for individual guests.[18] The individual sanatoriums were overseen by a trade union or a professional organisation, a people's commissariat or a ministry. To be put in charge of sanatoriums or health resorts was henceforth one of the most important symbols of power; it also resulted in a certain communality or sociability since control was always exercised by the relevant sector. Writers and their relatives and clans always stayed together, just like the members of the fishing union.

The Matsesta 'Building Exhibition' can best be divided into two different stylistic tendencies. The first is represented by the architects of 'classical Soviet modernity', the Constructivist architect Leonid A. Vesnin, who designed Sanatorium No. 7, and Alexey V. Shchusev, from whom we have the plans for Sanatorium No. 8. Both buildings are large, on a hill high above the sea, with central staircases and verandas, long balconies and large windows, generous foyers, dining rooms, a library, restaurants and a billiard room. The façades are smooth and austere.[19] Other sanatoriums in the same vein are the Sanatorium of Narkomvod, with its unbroken balconies, the Sanatorium of the People's Commissariat for Light Industry and the Sanatorium of the People's Commissariat for Agriculture.

On the other hand, there is the neoclassical trend with its massive, indeed ostentatious buildings which continue the Caucasian Riviera's line of 'white palaces'. They include a number of noteworthy public buildings—a pump station of 1935, a viaduct of 1936 (both the work of Ivan Zholtovsky), the Ordzhonikidze Sanatorium of 1934–1937 (by architect I. S. Kuznetsov) and the Burevestnik Hostel of the 1930s.

The most impressive examples, however, are the Palladian-style sanatorium designed by Ivan Zholtovsky for the People's Commissariat for Heavy Industry (Narkomtyazhprom) that might be described as a grandiose 'palace of healing'; the building for the directorate of the Plenipotentiaries of the Central Executive Committee of the USSR, the four-pillared portico of which evokes a classical temple; and the Winter Theatre, surrounded by ninety-two white columns and built in 1937, codesigned by Shchuko and Gelfreikh, architects of the Palace of the Soviets in Moscow.

FIGURE 25.2. The Voroshilov Sanatorium of the Red Army in Sochi, 1932–1934. Architect: Miron I. Merzhanov (1895–1975). © Shchusev State Museum of Architecture, Moscow. Photo: culture-images/fai.

Without a doubt, the outstanding building in the entire Union, universally praised as exemplary, was the Voroshilov Sanatorium of the Red Army, which was built between 1931 and 1934 from a design by Miron Ivanovich Merzhanov. With five storeys, it stands on the crest of a hill, facing the sea, with flights of steps and lift-shafts that give shape to the frontage, balconies that flow round the building and large windows. The complex is divided by a rack-and-pinion railway that brings guests up from the valley. The combination of glass and the funicular creates the effect of a high-tech building. This is underlined by the glassed-in and hence bright and airy dining room extending over two storeys. Similarly, the station in Sochi with its two cubic corner towers can be regarded as part of the trend towards a subtle Late Constructivism. Newly rebuilt after the ravages of the war, the station and its long arcaded hall as well as a campanile and passenger port reveal the signature of the transitional phase of the 1920s–1930s.[20]

'Stalin's Dacha': The Capital by the Sea

Measured against the aforementioned prototypes of Matsesta, the building that actually incorporated the real political power is a modest affair. 'Stalin's dacha' is one of several summer houses that the dictator had built on the Abkhazian coast. It is located in Matsesta, Kurortny Prospekt 113, lit. A; others, far better known for their location and beauty, can be found in Gagra and on Lake Ritsa. What the prominent building of the Voroshilov Sanatorium and Stalin's dacha have in common is that both were designed or converted by the same architect, Miron Ivanovich Merzhanov (1895–1975). Originally, Stalin's dacha had been a nineteenth-century villa belonging to a certain M. A. Sensinov. In 1937 Merzhanov had it converted for Stalin in a way that showed great sensitivity both to the place and to Stalin's needs. Today it is accessible as a museum so that the visitor can gain an impression of its inner workings with its blend of asceticism and modest comfort. This atmosphere is even more pronounced in the dacha complex of Kuntsevo outside Moscow, also built by Merzhanov.[21] For reasons of both health and sentiment—the spa waters, but equally the proximity to his Georgian homeland—Stalin spent much time in the summer houses of the south, especially the dacha in Matsesta. Distant from the capital for weeks and often months on end, he kept his eye fixed on political events at the centre from his Caucasian periphery. From there he orchestrated the unprecedented wave of violence that drove the process of collectivisation, unleashing the famine and above all the mass operations of 1937, the Great Purges that ravaged the nation. The trains, the couriers, the protocols and queries all came to Matsesta. From Matsesta poured out all the instructions, the lists and a day-by-day correspondence concerning every last detail of the machinery of state. We could read the correspondence between Stalin and Molotov or Stalin and Kaganovich as one between the capital in the Kremlin and the capital by the sea.[22] Stalin's comrades-in-arms were summoned here when necessary. Photographs of these places reproduce precisely the milieu of this capital with its blend of family, politics, bureaucracy and clannishness, this mixture of formality, the father-daughter relationship between Stalin and Svetlana and the informal chumminess of what Sheila Fitzpatrick calls 'Stalin's team'. Residency

FIGURE 25.3. A dacha for Stalin by his favourite architect, Miron I. Merzhanov. The likeness to Frank Lloyd Wright's villa Fallingwater is no coincidence. Drawing by Merzhanov from memory since photography was not permitted. From Peter Noever (ed.), *Tyrannei des Schönen: Architektur der Stalin-Zeit*, Prestel, Munich and New York 1994, 56.

beneath the palms must have included visits by leading personnel of the Comintern, whose luxurious stays there might have been interrupted, however—like lightning from a clear sky—by nocturnal arrests and shootings. The relaxed atmosphere in the parks and on the verandas alternated with mutual suspicions, denunciations and betrayals, as has been reported by one who knew: Margarete Buber-Neumann.[23] In this way the sanatorium of the privileged turned into the point of departure from a privileged life and what had been a sanctuary became a dangerous and even life-threatening place. When we look at the seemingly innocuous and beautiful properties today with their parks and gardens, we fail to notice that in reality they were state apparatuses and high-security zones in disguise, designed to defend the paranoid dictator from the spectre of enemy terrorists. And more generally, government personnel had developed a taste for exclusive, specially secured spaces that were mostly referred to as 'dachas', 'government dachas', 'rest and recreation areas'. These were the venues for lavish hunting parties with hundreds of specimens of game slaughtered and put on show at the end.[24] Stalin died on a carpet in the Kuntsevo dacha and his era died with him. Failed leaders of Party and state were consigned to sanatoriums and rest and recreation homes. This was Khrushchev's fate. In August 1991 Mikhail Gorbachev was arrested by putschists in the government residence in Foros on the south coast of the Crimea. If the seaside residences were power centres of state terror at a distance in Stalin's time, in this instance they served as the locus of an attempted coup d'état which was soon followed by the end of the entire USSR.

Leisure Resorts as Battlegrounds

During the final decades of the Soviet Union, there was an impressive expansion of the spa and health resort sector. There was a boom in organised travel and, more especially, spontaneous, individual tourism. The summer months witnessed an exodus from the city centres to the world of the main tourist destinations, holiday homes, guesthouses and sanatoriums. These centres reproduced the growth of mass tourism that had long since gained momentum elsewhere— albeit with the financial assistance of the welfare state that had long since ceased to be affordable. New horizons had opened up with the elimination of borders, the new opportunities for travel, the convertibility of the ruble and the overwhelming yearning to see the world with one's own eyes. People no longer had to rely on the trade-union voucher (*putyovka*) or membership in an organisation; the longed-for comfort was less expensive, less stressful and more readily available in places that were far away but now accessible. At the same time, the world of guesthouses and health resorts began to break up. With the acquisition of plots of land, the privatisation of hotels and holiday homes, speculation with the best locations, corruption and increasing dilapidation, the previously well-ordered and tranquil world of holidays and vacations dissolved into chaos and visitor numbers plunged. In many places the infrastructure collapsed into disrepair; elsewhere high-rise hotels sprang up without building permits, while ancient villas that had stood in their way were torn down without further ado. This process can be followed in any number of places—in the skyline of Sochi or Yalta, in the brutal privatisation of public spaces, in the proliferation of gated communities or in the architectural monstrosities created by private investors and developers.[25] Globalisation spread to regions that had previously lagged behind. The spa towns once known for peace and quiet have become louder. People arrive in their own cars, for which there is inadequate parking space. Early-morning group sport has been supplanted by fitness trainers. All this too points to the disappearance of a way of life. Where once there was a tranquil promenade, you now hear the roar of Formula 1 racing cars. In the palaces that President Putin has had constructed in Sochi, there are audiences appropriate to summer residences, but the pomp on show goes far beyond the measure and proportionality of the ancient buildings of the new Matsesta. The most shocking development of all in recent years is in Sukhumi on the Abkhazian coast: guests have ceased to come to the white palaces now surrounded by burnt-out palm tree gardens and native inhabitants too have fled the ruins of the city. In the Crimea, which was occupied by Putin's special troops in a coup in the spring of 2014, warlords and their armies fight for ownership of the villas with the loveliest views. The landscape of rest and recreation has once again become a parade ground and war zone.

PART VI

Interiors

CHAPTER 26

Doorbells:
Nameplates and Signals

Visitors made their first acquaintance with communal apartments even before entering one, namely at the front door itself. There they would find a bell to one side of the door and next to the bell a notice, saying how many times to push the button to get a response: ring once for Occupant A, twice for Occupant B and so forth. This bell system resembled Morse code. The apartment occupants internalised the signals and everyone knew who had just received a visitor. Given the large number of people in the apartments, the bell ringing was no minor nuisance. To reduce the stress the occupants devised an alternative system whereby each person had his or her own bell and a cable going directly into his or her own room. The visible evidence of this communication system was the battery of bells with nameplates at the side of the door. In both cases the entire block was kept informed of fellow tenants' contacts and frequency of visits. All were involuntarily drawn into their neighbours' circle of acquaintances. This not infrequently led to complications and conflicts when a visitor rang the wrong bell and woke up the 'wrong' occupant or someone returning home late at night inebriated pressed all the buttons at once.

Klaus Mehnert, who lived in a six-room communal apartment in Moscow with eight other families in 1937, recalled: 'There were disturbances from the very first night. The bell was rung loudly and persistently several times. Everybody woke up, except for the intended person. At one point I was woken up by the bell being rung three times. That was our signal. . . . I thought that something serious must have happened as it was 3 a.m. And so I rushed out. A complete stranger had rung the bell on the left, while ours was the one on the right. Later on, our ears became better attuned and we learned to distinguish the two bells, which were an octave apart.'[1] Here too a routine developed over time; one became accustomed to this acoustic communal space and learned to live with it. And there were times when the knock at the door or the ring of the bell could decide a person's fate. They became deeply ingrained in the memory of all who experienced nightly visitations or were actually arrested at the time of the Great Terror. Conversely, the disappearance, the literal elimination of the battery of bells—that symbol of having to live with other people against one's will—stood for the departure from the world of communal apartments as such.

CHAPTER 27

Kommunalka, or Where the Soviet People Were Tempered

People who didn't grow up in the Soviet Union have no conception of the *kommunalka*, the communal apartment. Nadezhda Mandelstam, who grew up in an upper-middle-class environment in Kyiv, was well aware of this, having been forced to spend her life moving from one communal apartment [ZhAKT] to another. She recorded in her memoirs: 'Future generations will never understand what "living-space" means to us. Innumerable crimes have been committed for its sake, and people are so tied to it that to leave it would never occur to them. Who could ever leave his wonderful, precious twelve and a half square meters of living-space? ... Husbands and wives who loathe the sight of each other, mothers-in-law and sons-in-law, grown sons and daughters, former domestic servants who have managed to hang on to a cubby-hole next to the kitchen—all are wedded to their living-space and would never part with it.'[1]

Even less could they imagine what is obvious to every Soviet person who hears the word *kommunalka*, the colloquial term for *kommunal-naya kvartira*, in other words, for the communal dwelling inhabited by people who had nothing in common apart from the fact that they were fellow occupants, 'neighbours', because they had been forced into sharing an apartment. It was an artificially created community of strangers living together, not for the short term but for the long run and perhaps even a lifetime—an emergency situation that became an everyday experience. This peculiar and specifically Soviet biotope was generally located in an older building, constructed before the Revolution for well-to-do bourgeois families, their dependants and staff. In the best city districts, especially of St. Petersburg and Moscow, the generously sized and luxuriously appointed six-to-twelve room apartments provided a comfortable home even for larger families. Following the Revolution and expropriation, however, 'members of the

revolutionary class'—workers, soldiers and peasants—were accommodated there and divided the rooms up among themselves. Whole families shared a single room so that former upper-middle-class apartments became the residence for between forty and sixty people, who
had to arrange their entire lives within these cramped spaces.[2]

To gain a rough idea of the scale of these 'social localities': by
the end of the 1950s around 25 million families in the USSR lived in
kommunalkas, huts or hostels. Until 1958 the communal apartment
was the basic type of urban dwelling. In Moscow, in 1960, around
60 percent of the population lived in kommunalkas or similar communal accommodations; in the 1970s, it was still 40 percent even after
an accelerated building programme. And as late as 1989, 23.8 percent
of the Leningrad population still lived in kommunalkas.[3] The end of
the Soviet Union spelled the end of the kommunalka too. The last
inhabitants were moved out of the old buildings—often by force—and
relocated to apartments that the *developery* and *rieltory* (as speculators and estate agents are known in post-Soviet Russia) procured for
them far out in newly developed districts. There they sit dreaming of
days which may not always have been happy but were their lifetime.
The disappearance of the kommunalka meant the disappearance of
a social space that was at the innermost core of the Soviet way of life
and that now, with its decay, can be seen as one of the sites, perhaps
even the very laboratory, from which the Soviet people were born. It
represented the permanent state of emergency that was everyday
reality for those affected or surrounded by it.

The Lifeworld in the Blind Spot of Soviet Studies

It took quite a while before the kommunalka attracted the attention
that it merits, given its place at the heart of the Soviet lifeworld.
This is remarkable and deserves explanation. Research into communism, the Soviet Union and totalitarianism has published entire
libraries of documentations designed to inform us about the functioning of the 'Soviet system'. And there are countless analyses of
Marxist-Leninist doctrine and the pronouncements of the CPSU. Cutting a path through all the obfuscation, we have found our way into

the heart of the Politburo's decision-making processes as well as its barely comprehensible factionalism; we have analysed the literature both serious and popular to uncover what it might reveal to us about the spiritual life of Soviet society. Entire institutes have spent years dissecting every utterance of the Kremlin—but before the end of the Soviet Union not one study about the kommunalka, the primary living space of millions of Soviet citizens, had appeared. This could perhaps be explained by a lack of source material, which is the case in several instances. For example, the administrative records of the ZhAKTy (housing cooperatives) were destroyed during the siege of Leningrad. Furthermore, this topic was unpopular with Soviet officialdom since it might have exposed the darker sides of the Soviet way of life and so was blocked by censors. These arguments miss the point, however. Very detailed information did exist in reports by foreign correspondents who for a long time were the only people to concern themselves with the 'banality of everyday life'. Examples included Hedrick Smith, Klaus Mehnert and Christian Schmidt-Häuer.[4] Nor is there any truth in the claim that there were no accounts of the ordinary life of Soviet citizens. There are many films whose plots and conflicts play out against the background of a communal apartment—comic, conciliatory or cheap and sentimental—and a cinema that simply ignored the experience shared by every spectator would have lost not only some of its credibility but also any impact it might have had.[5] Many Soviet novels were set in communal apartments.[6] If the kommunalka failed to become an object of scrutiny by Soviet social scientists, this was primarily because it was seen simply as part of ordinary life and hence as so 'natural' that it did not warrant looking into. Evidently time had to elapse before it could be seen as worthy of analysis. With her work on the 'common places' of Soviet life, Svetlana Boym opened the door to exploring hitherto overlooked questions.[7] Since the dissolution of the Soviet Union, the kommunalka has become an object of study by sociologists, ethnologists and, finally, by historians, so that today we may say that many disciplines have looked at it, and even appropriated it from their own point of view. It is certainly no coincidence that the heavy lifting has been done by social scientists who have closely examined the available sources 'in the street', nor is it a coincidence that the most important studies have focused on the 'capital of communal housing', namely Leningrad/St. Petersburg.[8] In their wake have come major studies from outside the post-Soviet space.[9]

Thus we can now speak of an interdisciplinary and multiperspectival approach to a core topic of the Soviet lifeworld. The initial contributions were made not by social scientists and historians, however, but by writers and artists, especially outsiders looking at the lifeworld that had become narrow and alien to them. They were able to make visible things that had become too familiar to be articulated.

The Poet's Eye: Joseph Brodsky's Essay 'In a Room and a Half'

Born in Leningrad in 1940, the poet Joseph Brodsky was forced by the Soviet authorities to emigrate from the Soviet Union in 1972. He was awarded the Nobel Prize for Literature in 1987. His essay 'In a Room and a Half' is about his immediate experience of a world he grew up in but he wrote about it from the great distance of a completely different way of life.

His gaze fixes on the parquet flooring, a feature of all the communal apartments in Leningrad. He thinks of the kommunalka in olfactory terms—as a space of perspiration, sweaty feet, kitchen odours—and the meticulous way in which the one and a half rooms that had been carved out of the large apartment had to be arranged and furnished so as to house a family of three. He describes the heterogeneous society that coexisted in this building without having come together voluntarily, as well as the precarious nature of a cohabitation that persisted for years and simply had to be endured and overcome. 'There were three of us in that room and a half of ours: my father, my mother and I. A family, a typical Russian family of the time. The time was after the war, and very few people could afford more than one child. Some of them couldn't even afford to have the father alive or present: great terror and war took their toll in big cities, in my hometown especially. So we should have considered ourselves lucky, especially since we were Jews. All three of us survived the war (and I say "all three" because I, too, was born before it, in 1940); my parents, however, survived the thirties also.'[10] They strove to make the best of their situation despite their poverty and powerlessness. 'What dishes, utensils, clothes, linen we had were always clean, polished, ironed, patched, starched. The tablecloth was always spotless and crisp, the lampshade above it dusted, the parquet shining and swept.' His parents were constantly on their feet. 'Cooking, washing, circulating between the communal kitchen of our apartment and our room and a half, fiddling with this or that item of the household.'[11]

The home he grew up in, on the corner of Liteyny Prospekt and Ulitsa Panteleymonovskaya, is a grand apartment block, famous in St. Petersburg and architecturally significant. Built by a wealthy merchant at the end of the nineteenth century, the Muruzi House embodies the history of St. Petersburg like no other, from the Silver Age through the Revolution and the Civil War, Stalinist terror, the German siege and the long postwar period down to the present. Its exact address was Liteyny Prospekt 24, Apartment 28.

Our room and a half was part of a large enfilade, one-third of a block in length, on the northern side of a six-story building that faced three streets and a square at the same time. The building was one of those tremendous cakes in so-called Moorish style that in Europe marked the turn of the century, erected in 1903, the year of my father's birth, it was the architectural sensation of the St. Petersburg of that period and Akhmatova once told me that her parents took her in a carriage to see this wonder. On its western side, facing one of the most famous avenues of Russian literature, Liteiny Prospekt, Alexander Blok had an apartment at one time. As for our enfilade, it was occupied by the couple that dominated the pre-revolutionary Russian literary scene as well as the intellectual climate of Russian emigration in Paris later on, in the twenties and thirties; by Dmitry Merezhkovsky and Zinaida Gippius. And it was from our room and a half's balcony that the larva-like Zinka shouted abuse to the revolutionary sailors.[12]

Brodsky is well aware of the transformation of this luxurious dwelling in the course of the 'redistribution of apartments' during the Revolution and the Civil War. 'Walls were erected between the rooms—at first of plywood. Subsequently, over the years, boards, brick and stucco would promote these partitions to the status of architectural norm', which led to infinite transformations of the original space. The Brodskys were fortunate in that only eleven people were accommodated in their communal apartment, not twenty-five or even fifty, as was sometimes the case. And he sketches an account of the social world that developed through maximum 'densening-up' in a single space. 'Of course, we all shared one toilet, one bathroom and one kitchen. . . . [The "basic laundry"] hung in the two corridors that connected the rooms to the kitchen and one knew the underwear of one's neighbours by heart.'[13] Living together like this 'bares life to its basics: it strips off any illusions about human nature. By the volume of the fart, you can tell who occupies the toilet, you know what he/she had for supper as well as for breakfast. You know the sounds they make in bed and when the women have their periods. It's often you in whom your neighbour confides his or her grief, and it is he or she who calls for an ambulance should you have an angina attack or something worse. It is he or she who one day may find you dead in a chair, if you live alone, or vice versa.'[14] And in fact Brodsky's father was found dead in his chair in the empty room and a half by a neighbour. For Brodsky, the communal apartment became a school of the senses and a school of life. 'This is where one learns life's essentials: by the rim of one's ear, with the corner of one's eye. What silent dramas unfurl there when somebody is all of a sudden not on speaking terms with someone else! What a school of mimics it is! . . . What smells, aromas and odors float in the air around a hundred-watt yellow tear hanging on a plait-like tangled electric cord.' In the communal kitchen he discovers an archaic anthropological primordial scene: 'There is something tribal about this dimly lit cave, something primordial—evolutionary, if you will; and the pots and pans hang over the gas stoves like would-be tom-toms.'[15] In his own way Brodsky has given a description of themes that have been taken up and elaborated by others in a different language: the 'exposure' of people who can no longer retreat into a private sphere, what Richard Sennett has called the 'tyranny of intimacy'.

The Kommunalka as a Contested Space

Ilya Kabakov also had recourse to a primary experience filtered by
distance. He too experienced the communal apartment as a living
space before he could reimagine and bring it to the stage as an objective reality. The installation put on display in Leipzig in 1996 was
strictly historical in 'building upon the submissions, complaints and
petitions of the tenants of communal apartments in Moscow to the
police or the arbitration tribunals'.[16] He wished to present the kommunalka not as something exotic but as a way of life coming to terms
with everyday reality. 'We see here utterly normal, average citizens
of the "Soviet nation", who in other circumstances would be completely ordinary but who have now been forced to live their entire
lives in an enclosed space with only one bathroom, only one toilet
and only one kitchen and so have been condemned . . . to a permanent war against one another from which no one can escape and in
which they all without exception are doomed to become the victims
of a never-ending battle.'[17] All the quarrels, running battles, settling
of accounts and animosities brought to the tenants' meetings are
described in meticulous detail by the tribunal which is supposed to
resolve them. All the trivial disagreements that make life a hell are
brought up for discussion; the pot that was put in the wrong place,
the light that wasn't turned out or the ski that wasn't put away. 'But
in the communal apartment all these little things turn the life of the
individual and all the individuals together into a daily domestic penal
colony, entirely comparable to a genuine punishment camp and all
the more terrible for not being seen as such by the outside world.'
Kabakov starts by talking about the origins of the kommunalka: 'In
our big cities, especially in Moscow and Leningrad immediately after
the 1917 Revolution, "consolidation" and "settling" were started. In the
big luxury apartments they began to house the basement dwellers,
people of another class who had come from other cities. There were
not enough homes, and the new waves of people and the existing
residents moved into the homes of the departing "bourgeoisie" and
the "royal protégés" by special "order", handed out by the new organ
of proletarian power. But even without such "orders" they simply

occupied the apartments, and almost instantly a completely new society of people appeared in these 12 and 16 room apartments, people
who often did not know who their neighbour was, what he did, where
he worked.' Each family was entitled to one room, but since the families tended to grow, there were often several generations living in
one room. 'Often three or four generations were there for practically
all their lives—great grandmother, grandmother, father and mother,
children, relatives.'[18]

Kabakov gives a precise description of the ground plan of such a
former stately home:

> The layout of a tenement block is generally familiar. There are
> three or four apartments on every floor of a building that is usu-
> ally between five and seven storeys high, with a 'white' spiral stair-
> case leading up from the 'entrance halls' where the hall porter is
> located. ... After the Revolution the entrance halls were blocked
> off and the new apartments were built which had their own hall
> and passageway.
>
> Right beside the door of these apartments was a large hall which
> led into a corridor. On one side of the corridor there was frequently
> a suite of rooms, but each with their own entrance off the corri-
> dor: (i) the sitting room, (ii), the dining room, (iii) the small sitting
> room, (iv) the library, (v) the master's study. On the other side the
> rooms were generally smaller: (vi) the guestroom, (vii) a nursery,
> (viii) a room for the older children, (ix) the grandparents' room,
> (x) the owners' bedroom, (xi) the mistress's study. The end of the
> corridor was the domestic area: the kitchen, the servant's bedroom,
> a second room, a bathroom and toilet. The door from the kitchen
> led onto the 'back' staircase so that neither the cook nor the porter,
> nor the laundress nor their children and friends would appear in
> the 'apartment'.[19]

After 1917 the entire floor plan changed. Each room was occupied
by one or more families; they were forced to rearrange themselves.
They divided up rooms that were too large for single people, blocked
up windows or broke through walls to insert new doors, blocked off
enfilades and connecting rooms and then sectioned off spaces with

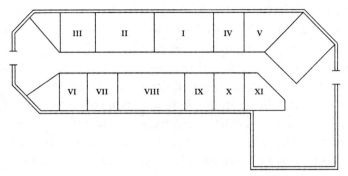

Layout of a bourgeois apartment before the Revolution of 1917

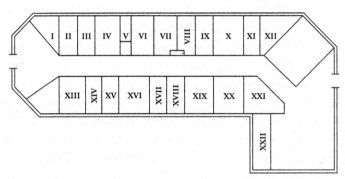

Layout of a communal apartment

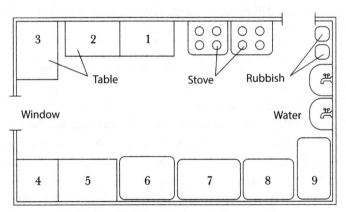

Layout of the kitchen of a communal apartment

FIGURE 27.1. Ground plan of a communal apartment. From Ilya Kabakov, *1964–1983: Stimmen hinter der Tür*, Galerie für Zeitgenössische Kunst, Leipzig 1998, 35. © 1998 Ilya Kabakov and Galerie für Zeitgenössische Kunst.

the aid of cupboards, shelves and partitions so as to create their own 'homes'. Living together called for a minimum of internal organisation and agreement about cleaning, putting out the rubbish bins and cleaning the corridors, the kitchen and the toilet. Most of the occupants called for votes on use of the toilet, the bathroom and the kitchen. 'And if in the morning there is a queue of people outside the bathroom with towels over their shoulders, then there is obviously no queue for the toilet. The tenants simply lurk behind their own doors in order to work out from the sounds and the footsteps when the toilet is free so that they can make a dash for it.'[20]

The secret centre was the communal kitchen. 'There you find the most varied aspects of life shimmering and twinkling as if in all the facets of a magic crystal; there people reveal their illnesses, their problems and their hopes. Everything has its place here—the meanest and the best, the everyday and the romantic, love and bitter quarrels about a broken glass, boundless generosity and petty squabbles about the electricity bill, sharing the freshly cooked *pirogi* and disagreements about taking out the rubbish. It is the marketplace of a medieval town and also a theatre where spectators and actors exchange roles, where the scenes drag out for hours and follow one another like avalanches.'[21]

But with its roughly forty square metres, the communal kitchen itself stood in need of further differentiation given the large numbers of people using it.

Tables stand along the walls, as many tables as there are families in the apartment—five, six or seven, etc. Every family or every housewife has its or her own little table. This table can be of any kind: new, repainted or old. The only thing it may not be is larger than the others. Each table abuts its neighbour and over each table there is an individual shelf with pots and jugs, etc. When fridges began to appear in the Soviet Union, the tenants kept them in their own rooms because there was no space in the kitchen and it was also safer: no neighbour could go to someone else's fridge at night and help themselves to food. The dishes were the only things to stay in the kitchen and everyone took good care to keep the floor swept and mopped around the tables . . . next to the row of tables came the cookers, one, two or even three, depending on the number of tenants.

It wasn't just food that was cooked in the kitchen; there was also the washing, which was boiled on the stove and afterwards hung out to dry on lines in the hall. 'Almost every problem can lead to a scandal involving the entire community. Demagogues, troublemakers, informers, loudmouths are always to be found. Then where to keep all the junk? The whole corridor is blocked up with piles of suitcases, boxes, bundles and bags. Metal bowls, bicycles are hanging up on hooks, chairs hang from the ceiling. There is constant shrieking; children are rampaging around, you can hear other people's conversation through the thin partition walls. People dole out advice, do each other favours and entertain each other from time to time. But little acts of this kind can also lead to quarrels—dishes not returned, sitting too long on the toilet, the dirt that your guests have "brought in with their feet".' Such quarrels could be conducted at the top of people's voices in the kitchen or corridor and if needed, before the residents' administrative committee, then the police or even the district criminal court.[22] The kommunalka then turned into a battlefield between hostile parties or even a war of all against all—and given the general housing shortage, this was not a war you could escape just by moving out.

The Kommunalka Community:
Everyday Reality as a State of Emergency

The Soviet-type communal apartment did not just turn up overnight, nor was it the final version of an idea that had haunted the minds of revolutionary youth in the late nineteenth century. Representative examples are to be found in the idea of the phalanstery taken over from the French socialists by Robert Owen and formulated in *What Is to Be Done?*, the utopian novel of 1863 by Nikolay Chernyshevsky, the demi-god of the student generation of the day. This utopia was a space beyond heteronomous control by the family, the church or the state, a paradise of self-determination and self-realisation for both men and women. The development of the kommunalka into an actual, already institutionalised form of life was also largely independent of the debates among the architects and designers of the Soviet avant-garde who racked their brains trying to devise buildings and dwellings appropriate for the revolutionary class. Their ideas formed part of the background noise of a high culture that had more to do with international networking between the Bauhaus, Vkhutemas, Weissenhof Estate, Ville Radieuse and CIAM Congresses than with the disagreements about how to deal with the housing shortage as a practical reality.[23]

Even before the Revolution the big cities had their housing dilemmas and the Revolution had promised to solve these en passant. Hundreds of thousands of peasant workers who had poured into the industrial towns with their exploding populations lived in conditions that now form part of a familiar story about the periphery of capitalism and colonialism: slums, mud huts, now and then a workers' estate. At the beginning of the 1890s, of the 1.4 million people living in St. Petersburg, around half a million lived in small rooms, cellars and attics, while 150,000 could at best rent by the night or the hour a shelter bunk or corner to sleep in. It was a kingdom of darkness in the shadow of the booming cities and gave Russian literature a wealth of material about poverty, violence and disease. The First World War with its streams of refugees, columns of evacuees and deportations had already, even before any shock of revolution, accustomed the population to the destabilisation of traditional living conditions.[24] People were probably not too surprised to discover that the nationalisation of housing was to be one of the first steps taken by the Soviet government and that in 1918 and 1919 around 65,000 families in Petrograd were moved out of the industrial suburbs into the former middle-class and aristocratic centre. Even without the renovation projects that Lenin proposed in 'The Immediate Tasks of the Soviet Government', it was not absurd to surrender the city of the old ruling classes and allow it to be taken over by 'the new class'. It may well be that the chief effect of this takeover was not so much the 'solution of the housing question in favour of the proletariat' as the humiliation and demoralisation of the old ruling classes. There were even complaints that the workers did not really feel at home in their new luxurious surroundings. The huge rooms were difficult to heat and the journeys to the factories were now made longer so that the workers would have preferred to remain in the environment they were accustomed to.

However that might be, an emergency measure in the Civil War times had led to a lasting innovation and the communal dwelling became a cross-generational institution that endured until the downfall of the Soviet Union. The reason it did endure was that the influx of people looking for housing in the towns never dried up. The expropriation of home ownership and property was permanent. In the process of 'housing redistribution'—a term alluding to the dividing up of manorial estates by the peasantry—the entire housing stock went into the hands of the state, the communal economy, the soviets of the towns and regions. This was the origin of the term 'communal apartment'. On 30 August 1918 the Soviet government legalised the more or less violent confiscation of dwellings with the decree 'On the abolition of the right to private ownership of real estate' and inaugurated the process of a thoroughgoing 'municipalisation'. The introduction of the New Economic Policy brought a temporary relaxation of the legislation. Thus in December 1921 the decree 'On the conditions governing the demunicipalisation of dwellings' was introduced and a regulation of May 1922 permitted the private ownership of housing. By the mid-1920s around 5 percent of the Leningrad housing stock was in private hands and 75 percent was placed under the authority of the housing cooperatives (ZhAKTy), which reintroduced rents so as to be able to renovate houses. In this way the arbitrary appropriation of dwellings and forms of privatisation and individual responsibility were built up again. The owners and housing managers (kvartirokhozyaeva) would acquire the right to make decisions about the tenants and to take the process of 'self-densification' into their own hands instead of relying on arbitrary allocations or appropriations from outside, a process that led to a consolidation and greater social homogeneity.[25] By the spring of 1925 there were as many as eight thousand housing cooperatives in Moscow.

This situation did not last long, however. Given the forced pace of industrialisation and the mass migration from the villages resulting from collectivisation, the pressure on the 'housing market' grew and houses were transferred completely to the authority of the local soviets in 1929 and communalised, while even the housing cooperatives were abolished by 1937. This in fact concluded the process of nationalising the housing problem; state control of housing remained in place until the end of the 1950s when the housing cooperatives were reintroduced in the wake of Khrushchev's de-Stalinisation and the new course in housing policy.

Every alteration in the general political line resulted in changes in the 'specific organic composition' of the kommunalka community. While the bourgeois world thinned out, the 'proletarianisation' of the centre increased. Where the former owners remained, they had to content themselves with one room and move closer together, while the staff, servants, nursemaids and chauffeurs had to share the accommodation with incoming families. This meant the coming-together of worlds and social milieus that normally had little or no contact. The clearest differences were between the 'former people' and the 'new people'. The 'former people'—businessmen, officials, representatives of the Third Estate, lawyers, university professors and intellectuals—had already lost their legal standing. They had been deprived of the franchise by the constitution, were excluded from political activity in general and discriminated against in ordinary life.[26] In the kommunalka they were assigned a marginal, despised and spatially reduced position, while the 'insulted and injured' of yore occupied the privileged spaces. Seamen and their girlfriends who had never lived in decent quarters were now able to enjoy the pleasures of panelled rooms decorated with fresco paintings—formerly music rooms. The former cook could choose to move into the former maid's room next to the kitchen. The professor at the technological institute who had become indispensable to the new regime could even lay claim to a second room to house his library. The former house-owner could stay where she was since she was able to deploy her cultural capital and give French lessons. Another won the favour of the children through her ability to play the piano, which had been left behind. Almost all who turned up had years of wandering through the Empire behind them, along the fronts and lines of evacuation. They came from diametrically opposed worlds. What was seen here was a clash of cultures in miniature! Lifestyles, worlds of experience, the contemporaneity of the noncontemporaneous in which the old relations of domination and subordination were turned upside down, in which the old official versions lost their authority and terrible things could occur to anyone at any time: Red Guards might enter a house in search of 'counterrevolutionaries' or 'speculators' and simply take whatever they wanted—a ball gown for a girlfriend, an Art Nouveau vase, or even the former house-owner, handy as a hostage. Such company normally came together only in exceptional circumstances. The kommunalka community was like passengers in a train compartment, brought together by chance, for better or worse, only in this case, the encounter might last a very long time.

The New Economic Policy brought about a certain relaxation in which living conditions 'sorted themselves out'; the remnants of urban society got their second wind, began to succeed and in a certain sense regained lost ground. They found some protection in the ruined landscapes of their 'world of yesterday'. But this brief recovery was followed by even graver consequences, scarcely foreseeable in their implications. Industrialisation drew a stream of millions of peasant migrants into the towns and these filled to brimming the last nooks and crannies of the already 'overcrowded' living spaces. At the same time, the survivors of the 'world of yesterday', otherwise known as *lishentsy*—that is, those deprived of their civic rights in concerted campaigns in 1925 and 1935—were driven out of the towns and banished to the provinces. These included the middle classes, the homeless, vagrants, the believers, the prostitutes and intellectuals who were expelled from Leningrad and other towns in the thousands after Kirov's assassination in 1934. This was a blood-letting of the old society that simultaneously created space for their successors, who took over the places that had been freed up in the overfilled communal apartments.

The struggle for accommodation took a far more sinister twist during the purges of 1937 and 1938, when denouncing one's housemates became the easiest way to acquire a place in an apartment. When thousands of people were denounced and arrested as spies, counterrevolutionary elements and wreckers, thousands of highly desirable and almost unobtainable rooms became vacant. At the same time, the chaotic and opaque conditions prevailing in overcrowded apartments made them ideal places for people who wished to disappear, become invisible. The kommunalka was both an extremely dangerous place in times of total mistrust and denunciation and a refuge for people who wanted to go into hiding to escape the wave of repression.[27]

The destruction of hundreds of thousands of dwellings in the towns directly affected by the war dramatically exacerbated the housing problem, as did the ensuing increase in waves of migration. Along with Stalin's death, these were the chief driving forces behind the radical U-turn in housing policy after 1953. The change meant abandoning prestigious public buildings and planning in favour of simpler, more functional forms made possible by the industrialisation of construction. Khrushchev completed the process of abandoning the old construction policy and this paved the way for the end of the communal apartment. The late 1950s and early 1960s witnessed the creation of gigantic construction firms which ensured that between 1966 and 1970 942,000 people were able to obtain accommodation in Leningrad alone, the overwhelming majority of them—809,000—in new-build homes.[28]

Thus the expansion of the kommunalka meant far more than a policy of redistributing living space that had sprung from a crisis. It was rather a key indicator of the success or failure in dealing with the processes of industrialisation and modernisation unleashed by the war and the Revolution.

The Dictatorial Control of Intimacy, the Destruction of Privacy, Lessons in Indifference

The organisation of space in the kommunalka gives us a good idea of the existential plight of their occupants as well as of negotiating processes that are as basic as they are complicated. The kommunalka's cramped nature led to a never-ending struggle between private and public spaces. The question is whether the separation of the two could be sustained in such circumstances and whether we should not rather speak of a collapse of privacy. The public areas in the kommunalka were the entrance hall, the corridor, the kitchen, the toilet and the bathroom. The private ones were the rooms of the individual families. But such clear distinctions could not be maintained in practice.

The entrance hall contained the telephone together with a stool and perhaps a shelf or a blackboard for notices, perhaps from the house management, and those concerned everyone. The telephone was used by everyone; the conversations were generally audible. Everyone could hear them whether they wished to or not. To make more space in their own rooms, people put things in the hall that were not needed for immediate use. The space that belonged to everyone belonged to no one; whoever was there first simply claimed the right to occupy it. The corridor was the ideal place to put up a washing line. The occupants all put their clothes on show *coram publico* and this included underwear, however intimate. Similarly in the kitchen; however vigilantly you guarded your 'own turf'—your own small table, your own gas hob or fridge—as long as you had not imported these things into your own four walls, the confined nature of the space brought these 'territories' closer together and made it easier for others to encroach on your space. As the space for food preparation and hospitality, the kitchen was the communal area par excellence. It could therefore easily become a battlefield for competing users (right down to the kerosene that someone threw into a neighbour's soup). The bathroom too was used by everyone, but given the varying ideas and practices of hygiene, length of occupancy and different notions of cleanliness, the bathroom, that most intimate space, inevitably became a focal point of bitter disagreements and practices. The same may be said of the toilet, a secluded place visited by everyone living in the kommunalka. The individual rooms can also be described formally as belonging to the private sphere, but this did not stop you from hearing—against your will—whatever went on behind the thin, retrofitted walls: snoring, loud conversations between the occupants and so on down to the sounds of sexual intercourse. From Ilya Utekhin, the author of the most thoroughgoing ethnographic study of the kommunalka, we have the formula of a 'transparent space'.[29] A kommunalka was a space of noises, smells and movements shared by all, and however considerate people might be, they were inevitably drawn into each other's world. The house rules regulated all sorts of things—sharing electricity and gas bills, putting out the rubbish and routine cleaning of the kitchen and corridor. A community interested in at least minimal cooperation will create consummate rituals that make living together possible. Hence the queues for the toilet or the bathroom first thing in the morning when the need is greatest because everyone has to go to work or school, and hence too the unwritten rule not to permit noise after a certain hour. But such agreements are not always honoured by everyone; where many people live together there are many exceptions and where everyone wants to have his or her way, precedents are created by the dozen. Cramped conditions produce a proximity that makes it almost impossible to keep any sort of distance. You take a peek into your neighbour's pot on the stove even though it is none of your business. You keep bumping into your neighbours, who are in the habit of spending the entire day in gym trousers or pyjamas, making their way topless, if not entirely naked, from their room to the communal bathroom. Yury Orlov recalled the childhood he spent in a communal apartment in a cellar: 'In the closet without a window lived a janitor with her schoolboy son, who had something wrong with his legs and went about on crutches. The mother moonlighted as a prostitute on the bed. At such times, the son slept on the floor on a narrow mattress wedged into the space between the bed and the wooden-plank wall. And all this was in the heart of the capital of a nation that wished to teach the rest of the world how to live!'[30]

All energy went into the demarcation and defence of one's own realm, which itself had to be artfully subdivided: a child would sleep on a bed that had to be separated by curtains, umbrellas or shelves from the divan on which his parents spent the night. The greatest economy was needed to make it possible to live in that room. We haven't even begun to discuss what it was like when emergencies arose in such cramped conditions—when, for example, a binge drinker went on a bender and terrorised the community; or when the school-boy in the next room tried his first joint, to say nothing of prostitutes going about their business. Everything that took place in seclusion 'in normal circumstances' took place in public in the kommunalka community. And the question is not just how did this 'microcosm' cope but what consequences did this communal life have for the larger society as a whole?[31]

This form of cohabitation in fact produced the sorts of behaviour appropriate to it. In this respect robustness was as important as the cultivation of a certain indifference towards behaviour that would

FIGURE 27.2. The kommunalka kitchen: 'Tables stand along the walls, as many tables as there are families in the apartment . . .' (Ilya Kabakov). Photo © George Kiesewalter.

normally be deemed coarse and insulting. Coarseness and indifference were needed to steel one's psyche. Since space for relaxation
was not available indoors, people went elsewhere in search of peace
and quiet: the conservatoire, the museum, the theatrical performance
in the palace of culture. People felt more at home out of the house
than in it. This led to a different—and indeed enhanced—evaluation of
cultural institutions. One had to develop a register of actions and reactions in order to put up with 'neighbours' who could not be avoided.
Unavoidable encounters with fellow tenants who were in fact also
'neighbours' and who could be met with any day or indeed any hour
of the day might well be one of the reasons for the breakdown of
polite forms of speech and gestures which appeared superfluous or
to require too much effort. The fact that so many things demanded
one's attention—footsteps in the hall which signalled who was on the
way to the bathroom, for example—made it clear that living together
in a cramped space against one's will called for strategies to spare
one's own energies in the daily struggle for survival. The elaboration of household rituals was one way of husbanding one's strength;
abandoning extravagant expressions of pleasant surprise or of demonstrative self-distancing was another. This gave rise to a 'median'
type of behaviour—an attitude resembling indifference and distance
since it revealed little or nothing about what one really felt—not too
far removed from the 'indifference' that Georg Simmel identified as
the outstanding 'virtue' of the modern city dweller. Of course, this
'indifference' does not seem to be the appropriate response in the
confined, intimate space of the kommunalka. It's a stance that had
a lot to do with the need to maintain a preestablished harmony and
not feel threatened by scandals under any circumstances. Looked at
from outside, the kommunalka appeared to be a group of people who,
although interdependent, held one another in check. It is difficult to
overstate the effect on society as a whole of a situation in which the
physical, psychological and mental energies of its countless communities were absorbed in maintaining this precarious equilibrium,
even when allowances are made for the various forms of relief that a
hierarchical and dictatorial system can offer. A private space, which
normally facilitates relaxation, had become a focus of relentless
strain, expenditure of effort and exhaustion. This background gives

us some idea of the significance of abandoning the kommunalka in the 1960s to the 1980s in favour of the birth of the private sphere in prefabricated tower blocks.

Considered in this way, the history of the kommunalka can be seen as a history of the decline and fall of bourgeois subjectivity in the twentieth century. However, this does not apply to the millions of new city dwellers determined to rise in society, people who had poured in from the countryside or been expelled from it and for whom the kommunalka represented entry into a new, modern way of life. The kommunalka— which on the one hand appears to represent the dissolution of a stage of urbanism, a deurbanisation—is, when seen from this perspective, the first step towards an urbanism in statu nascendi.

Yuri Slezkine once compared the Soviet Union to a communal apartment. The end of communal apartments coincided with the end of the Soviet Union.[32] Whoever has been able to move out of the old, long-neglected apartments in the centre of Moscow or St. Petersburg has moved to the edge of the city where people can be together on their own in moderate comfort. In the last Soviet phase, it was having four walls of one's own that saw the birthplace of the 'Moscow kitchen', a public place all of its own. In post-Soviet times a violent struggle has erupted over the apartments in the larger, older buildings which were transformed into communal apartments after 1917. 'New Russians' are making every effort to return to the best locations in the town centres.[33] A housing war has broken out, a second 'housing redistribution' after the first one a century ago. If other methods fail, violence is employed: water pipes are blocked or fires started in order to drive out the survivors of the kommunalka period. Dilapidated buildings are renovated, though more often people prefer to demolish whatever the kommunalka period has left behind in a run-down state for lack of funds. There is now a second expropriation; the process of communalisation has been succeeded by decommunalisation. It almost looks as though places like the Muruzi House in Leningrad, in which Joseph Brodsky was born in 1940, have returned to what they were. At least Liteyny Prospekt 24, Apartment 28, now has a museum that tells the story of how it all happened.

CHAPTER 28

The Interior as a Battlefield

Interiors reveal as much about their own times as public spaces. Walter Benjamin, who was in Moscow in December 1926, took lodgings in 'an example of petit-bourgeois domesticity, it would be hard to imagine a more horrid specimen. The sight of hundreds of slipcovers, consoles, upholstered furniture, drapes is nearly enough to suffocate you; the air must be thick with dust. . . . These petit-bourgeois interiors are the battlefields over which the devastating assault of commodity capitalism has victoriously swept, and nothing human can thrive here.' Thanks to his 'penchant for cave-dwelling,'[1] however, he remained there while a new battle was getting underway—for the revolutionary, modern interior appropriate to the proletariat.

The history of this struggle can easily be imagined from viewing the original locations or visits to museums and exhibitions. These might include the great bourgeois houses on Kamenoostrovsky and Kronverksky Prospekt in St. Petersburg/Leningrad where the Leningrad elite had set up house (today's Kirov Museum). In addition, there are the communal dwellings or the interior design of the reading room of the Workers' Club that Alexander Rodchenko produced for the Paris Exhibition in 1925, the furnishing of the Milyutin penthouse in the legendary Narkomfin Building by Moisey Ginzburg—both are icons of Soviet interior design and indeed of the European avant-garde. Another building that might be mentioned would be the Mayakovsky Museum in Moscow; it conveys an idea of the restrained if not Spartan style of the late 1920s. The avant-garde was succeeded by the search for a style of one's own that would be distinct both from the ascetic rigour of modernism and from petty-bourgeois cosiness. To inspect these interiors, one need only go to places where the rise of the new elite of the Stalin period, the *vydvizhentsy*, is documented, namely in the houses and offices of the managers, the bureaucrats whose increased power and prestige can be seen not least in the houses assigned to them or conferred on them. The people behind the 'Government House' in Moscow have preserved some of this as has Kirov's house in Leningrad—with its wireless set, polar bear bedside rug, arms collection and bookcase that was specially made for him.[2] New forms were developed in the dwellings built after the war, with their bombastic display shelves, enriched by the trophy furniture brought back from Germany, in particular heavy dressers and cupboards from *Gründerzeit* buildings, whereas dwellings from the 1960s are distinguished by their simplicity, colour and light.

Making Oneself at Home in the Ambience of the Old World: Revolutionaries and Plush

The postrevolutionary world was able to take possession of the public space and newly encode it in one fell swoop—with the demolition of traditional monuments and hasty construction of new ones in materials such as plaster, whose temporary nature was foreseeable, and with the redecoration of streets and squares, as was the case with the abstract panels introduced by Ivan Puni and Kazimir Malevich in Petrograd. The situation was different with the houses that had been taken over: it was vital for the revolutionaries to preserve those that were at least somewhat intact and bring them back into operation, ideally to settle into them. The new powers-that-be entered the palaces of the authorities they had superseded, the grand hotels of European stature—the Yevropeyskaya and Astoria in Petrograd, the National and Metropol in Moscow—where the new masters were served by concierges in old-fashioned uniforms. The Revolution and the Civil War had temporarily brought furniture manufacture to a standstill. People lived in surroundings created and inhabited by others and even after years had passed it was possible to guess who had previously owned a particular house or apartment. Ground plans and furnishings were permanent and telling. A woman who lived in a Petrograd kommunalka years after the Revolution recalled:

> The etagere and the little table both date from before 1917; they belonged to an engineer who had lived here before 1917 and who had this entire apartment to himself. I have been here since 1932

and have never once caught sight of him. The first room, the one
with the glass doors, that was where his cleaning lady lived; it was
15 square metres in size. The second room—that had 40 square
metres . . . 38–40 square metres, it was big. That was their ballroom.
The room next to that has now become two rooms, with plywood
walls; previously there hadn't been any rooms there at all but
only a small hallway. They had made it into two rooms before the
war. The next room, just opposite, was 24 square metres in size. . . .
Now the room after that, this small one, was a smoking room. Then
there is one further room that was his study . . . the kitchen had
a floor made of pinkish tuff. Now it has got a clay-coloured vinyl
floor covering and when you mop the floor you can see the trouble
the mop has absorbing the water. Our room was the nursery. The
door dates back to before the war; previously there hadn't been a
door there at all. . . . There had been a stove here before the war, a
white stove like a low chest of drawers. I don't know where it has
disappeared to.[3]

The revolutionaries—as you can see from photos—found themselves surrounded by the trappings of the old world with its plush
sofas. Egon Erwin Kisch wrote in the 1920s that every street urchin
could make his home in an ancient palace. If you want to know what
these expropriated dwellings looked like, you need to look up architecture magazines of the period 1880–1914: pictures from the
Gründerzeit, lampshades, soft carpets, 'boudoir' furniture, velvet,
plush, lots of embroidery, Thonet chairs and kitchens that assumed
you had servants. This world, used, eviscerated and laboriously held
in check, was dusted off and brought back to life at the end of the Civil
War. When Benjamin arrived in Moscow, he could still see 'the last
monuments of an ancient culture of dwelling'. The old routine, the old
way of life had lost its footing, but a new one had not yet established
itself. Disorder ruled with the decay of the old interior that seemed
to have become completely outdated, antiquated, coated with dust,
even unhygienic and threatening. Modern people familiar with the
writings and theories of Giedion, Mendelsohn and Le Corbusier are
even more impressed with the radicalism of the Russian modernisers
who not only made traditional spaces transparent but intended to
abolish Sundays and so intervene in the rhythm of time itself.[4]

Revolutionary Living: A New World for the New Human Being

The innovative designs of Constructivism have become icons of architectural history and especially of architectural theory, but they have remained isolated experiments. And yet we are speaking largely about the interiors of public buildings: libraries, and theatre auditoriums, sports facilities and cafeterias, as can be seen to this day in the Zuev Workers' Club built by Ilya Golosov in Moscow in 1927–1929 or the reading room of the Gorbunov Palace of Culture by J. Kornfeld in Moscow 1929–1938. These examples illustrate the programme very clearly: bright rooms thanks to windows that often take up a whole wall, lofty ceilings, simple milky-white glass lampshades, shelves and greenery. In the centre, there are simple, unadorned wooden tables and rows of chairs—the perfect place to read and study. Truly unique achievements were Rodchenko's reading room for a Workers' Club that was in fact never built but constructed simply for the 1925 Paris Exhibition, where it won a Grand Prix, and Nikolay Milyutin's penthouse in the Narkomfin Building, which, after decades of neglect, has survived only in photographs. These were icons of the international style; they had the character of an 'aesthetic proclamation'[5] and were received as such on the international circuit between Rotterdam, the Weissenhof Estate in Stuttgart and the Bauhaus in Weimar. At their core were spaciousness, functionality, light and cleanliness. Curtains were permissible, but no longer the heavy blinds that darkened the room. Where possible, curtains were to be made of cloth created by modern designers—in bright colours with red communist stars. The preferred material for furniture was not wood veneer but simple lacquered wood that was easy to clean. A simple wooden table, or even better, a space-saving folding table, was ideal. Prerevolutionary furniture with its carvings and ornamentation was generally thought to be unhygienic: beetles and other parasites could be nesting in it, a hazard for small children. Dressers, sideboards and chests were undesirable, whereas built-in furniture promised to be the solution to many problems. Beds absolutely had to have metal frames to keep bedbugs and other vermin as far away as possible. Wood was generally regarded as the building material of the village and outmoded. Decorative cushions and wall tapestries were to be avoided because they were dust traps, nesting places for microbes of all sorts, and made for extra work. There had to be room for a small desk under the window as well as a bookcase. In the dining room there was to be space for a children's corner with the obligatory portrait of Lenin and a map of the USSR or images of the Soviet Union's flora or fauna. Pretty, ornamental objects needed not be avoided entirely, but it was vital to ensure that the apartment was not packed full of superfluous pieces that would only attract dust and vermin. 'Let the proletarian house be light, spacious, decorated with flowers and only with those objects which preserve the health of the body and the health of the revolutionary spirit.'[6] The kitchen range or its more modern version, the Primus stove, was regarded as the symbol of the enslavement of the housewife. However, the building of communal kitchens or cafeterias for an entire apartment block was possible only in a few select and privileged places, such as the communal house in Ulitsa Rubinshteyna in Leningrad or the student residence hall in Ordzhonikidze Street in Moscow.[7]

Icons were a particular thorn for designers of the new interior projects. These were manufactured and sold by the millions in Orthodox Russia and continued to circulate after the Revolution. It took a long time before the icon corner could be superseded by the 'Lenin corner', with pictures of Party leaders, Marxist literature, gramophones and radios. The icon was 'the fiercest foe in the arena of the domestic front', at the place of honour of every Russian house. Kissing an icon was believed to transmit contagious diseases such as syphilis, tuberculosis, diphtheria and scarlet fever. Mayakovsky wrote against unhygienic icons. 'These new krasnye ugolki served as the new communal hearths of socialism. They supplanted the old individual petit-bourgeois "hearth" and served as the new communal focus for agitational speeches, lessons and other group activities.'[8]

In the transformation of the old world, one element stood out above all others: light. Electrification had become the practical yardstick of modernisation. 'Lenin's lamp', as the electrical light bulb was called, became the preeminent symbol for Russia's leaving the dark and entering into enlightenment. 'The dirt of the old world, the characteristics of the "traditional psychology" not only appear in relations of production, in the inability to labour, the lack of labouring culture, but also in private life, in byt, where the vestiges and traditions of the past burst forth in particularly splendid colours, revealing the great tenacity of the spirit of petit-bourgeois individualism.'[9]

The Desperate Struggle against the 'Petty Bourgeoisie'

Whenever innovations were proposed or experimented with, they largely remained at the level of assertion and declaration of faith rather than practical changes on a mass scale. The avant-garde experimented with new materials, including plastic and sound-absorbent floor coverings; they experimented with theoretical questions about new colours and acoustics, but the craft skills and industrial preconditions for adopting these ideas in practice were largely absent.[10] Building the new Soviet world included creating a new milieu of things—in both housing and the social interior. However, artistic aspirations in this sphere remained basically on paper.[11]

Interior design too remained largely a paper exercise. Moreover, the incompatibility between avant-garde projects and users' needs could not be denied. 'The inhabitants arrive in the new hearth of the new *byt*, with Primuses, icons, washboards, and sundry trash, which has no place in socialist homes. People bring into new homes not only icons and Primuses, but old, bulky uncomfortable furniture. Can one blame them for this, when no one is concerned with the furnishing of new buildings appropriate to contemporary conditions, which is comfortable and occupies little space?'[12] People brought their old world with them into the new one and the comments of this observer express his sense of his own powerlessness, but also his deep-seated hostility to the 'petty bourgeois'. The new inhabitants could not be induced to give up their own likes and dislikes and so they continued to go to the markets to buy knick-knacks—plaster casts of roses, figurines depicting Mephistopheles and girls bathing. 'These articles, born of the most reactionary petit-bourgeois taste, come to the market, enter into use, thanks to the fact that our industry and cultural organisations don't give any attention to these matters.'[13] Left-wing Bohemians and the avant-garde made fun of the triumph of bad taste and the kitsch that resonated in the yearning for 'socialist cosiness' and were unrelenting in their

mockery of the corny decorations in bedrooms and living rooms, the
samovars, the portraits of Marx framed in red, the singing canaries
and the clothing materials decorated with hammers and sickles or
geraniums and rubber trees. The left-wing avant-garde once again
entered the fray on behalf of its principles during the industrialisation campaign at the end of the 1920s. These included rigour, simplicity and functionality and with their huts and dormitories seemed to
meet the needs of the accelerated industrialisation process. But the
unprecedented harshness of life together with the fact that a proportion of the workers were better off materially unleashed a yearning
for withdrawal and safe places. Thus the triumph of the aesthetics of
the Stalin period over both 'left' and 'right' deviations was inevitable
even in matters concerning domestic interiors. Critiques of the 'left'
focused on its excessive rigour and the authoritarian attitudes with
which it sought to impose its notions of modern life—the elimination
of private spaces, the abolition of individual kitchens, the outsourcing
of children's upbringing, among other things, while ignoring the prevailing social and economic conditions. 'The concept of the "interior"
was actually dead; it had vanished from the dictionary.'[14]

Yearning for 'Cosiness' in Chaotic Times

The construction of the first large housing complexes in the first
half of the 1930s witnessed the return of efforts to create a totality,
to conceive of dwellings as a complete work of art. Nothing was to
be left to chance—not the ground plan, which had to be rational and
comfortable, nor the wallpaper or the seating. The interior came back
into fashion with this totalising approach, only the circumstances
had changed: the traditional rights of the family were restored; the
housewife was to return to her kitchen and devote herself to her
'primary' task—child-rearing. The dwelling no longer had to be 'transparent' but rather comfortable and cosy because its chief purpose
was to help regenerate labour power as effectively as possible. The
previous emphasis on equality and levelling was replaced by the dif-
ferential rewarding of achievement. Special efforts had to be appre-

ciated and whoever showed the greater efficiency at work should be able to spend more than the average person and acquire different things. 'Prestige' became the new word of the moment. The recently emerged middle class was branded by some as the 'new bourgeoisie' or the 'new class'. It could afford many fine things, choice furniture, a private tailor, silk shawls and antiques, which had been frowned upon in revolutionary circles as symbols of decadence. Apartments were decorated and even filled with costly objects that had been scorned as kitsch in the 1920s. In a sense this implied the rehabilitation of the prerevolutionary interior, albeit with significant differences. The upwardly mobile who wished to leave their 'uncultured' selves behind now lived cultured, hygienic lives and concentrated on their work. The insignia of social advancement now included the gramophone, and the obligatory newspapers and portraits. The metal-framed bed stood against the wall and was properly made with pillows and blankets. Wall tapestries were permissible once more. The patterns on rugs and sofas were familiar: swans on a lake, camels with pyramids in the background and other symbols of desire. The dresser ceased to be the emblem of the petty bourgeoisie. It now held a mirror, perfume bottles, family photos, porcelain figurines and vases. Embroidered cloths attested to the skill of the mistress of the house.[15] The wife of the writer Mikhail Prishvin described her husband's study: 'The study in Moscow is finished; it has dark-blue matt walls and old furniture from the nineteenth century. Now and again an antique makes its appearance. These things begin to live here, each with its own mood, history and meaning, and at the same time they express the soul of the master of the house. In this peaceful room nothing is simply what it is. In the centre of the room hangs the old chandelier made of the purest Venetian glass. The lightness and clarity of the material makes it splendid. In its form it resembles a complicated transparent flower.'[16] Not all apartments were as refined as this, as can be seen from the description of the modest circumstances of the writer N. Lashko. 'The dining room had a simple wooden table, covered with an oilcloth. Viennese chairs of different heights stood around the table. In a corner against the wall stood an oak sideboard with simple crockery behind glass. Similarly, the study had nothing but an unprepossessing desk covered by an oilcloth that had been patched up in two places. There was nothing on the table except for an inkstand, schoolboy fountain pens and heaps of cut paper. Nothing on the walls apart from a winter landscape by Byalynitsky-Birulya and a little portrait of Gogol.'[17]

Boris Yofan's Armchair and the Labour
of Producing a Soviet Style

The furniture in 'Government House' in Moscow was supposed to be all in the same style and at the forefront of modern technology. Everything aimed at maximum comfort: glass doors, American locks, security chains, lift keys, lampshade holders, telephones, gramophones, built-in freezer compartments beneath the windows, built-in cupboards. Of course, the new occupants of these apartments had to familiarise themselves with the requirements of modern civilisation; they had to learn, for example, that the switches could only be activated by turning them clockwise, that cigarette packets and cigarette butts must not be thrown down the sink or into the toilet. They had to learn to treat the furnishings responsibly since these were state property, specially made in the workshops that had been set up in the nearby church of Nicholas the Wonderworker (Nikolay Chudotvorets).[18] The interior, then, was not just the expression of modernity, but a teaching aid to help educate tenants. In the designs for the Government House furniture—the wooden armchairs, for example—we detect the cultivated taste of the architect Boris Yofan, who had received his training in Rome. He succeeded in blending the upwardly mobile class's old-new need for luxury and comfort with the style of his own Constructivist buildings of the 1920s. The sterling craftsmanship and sense of form schooled in the Constructivist years created a Soviet version of Art Deco, whose heyday and expansion, however, were even briefer in Russia than in the capitalist West. The exhibition for the Eighth All-Union Congress of Soviet Architects in 1940 that was dedicated to 'Soviet style' was overshadowed by the onset of the Second World War—and so belongs in a very different chapter.[19]

FIGURE 28.1. Furniture designed by Boris Yofan for Government House, on view in the museum there. Private collection.

After Victory: The Grand Style,
Neo-Empire—and Its Dissolution

It had been clear since the 1930s that the hyperurbanisation unleashed by the accelerated process of industrialisation could only be compensated for by a great plan for housebuilding on a massive scale. The destruction wrought by the war accentuated the problem, but Stalin had other priorities. What he wanted after 1945 was to build or rebuild the ruined towns and cities in a monumental style. Moscow would be the city of skyscrapers and of the great Palace of the Soviets which should at long last be completed. That would be one development, in the direction of monumentalism, neo-Empire and the grand style. In contrast, there was the shortage of basic housing, the need to create emergency accommodation for troops returning from the front, demobilised soldiers—housebuilding on a massive scale. Two distinct trends thus developed. On the one hand, there were bombastic furnishings enriched by the trophy furniture brought back by soldiers returning from Germany; we might describe this trend as neo-Empire, echoing the Empire style imported into Russia following the Patriotic War against Napoleon. On the other hand, there was a house design that aimed at standardisation and was to benefit everyday people. The grand style—to use the term introduced by Natalia Lebina—was to be found above all in the newly built Moscow high-rise buildings. The Moscow Furniture Factory No. 1, Glavmosmebelprom SSSR, manufactured furniture in the neo-Empire style for a large customer base: the nomenklatura. High-quality woods were used—red woods or Karelian birch. Walnut became popular in Moscow apartments and even rivalled Yofan's designs. Antique furniture was in great demand. 'The furniture and interior designs of the 1950s are easily recognisable. Inspired by the era of the other Patriotic War with its upsurge of nationalism following the victory over Napoleon, this style sometimes provoked curious propagandistic effects.'[20] Conscious efforts were made to promote the grand style, for example, via pictures of an apartment with a magnificent chandelier, a sideboard with glass doors and beautifully grained veneer, fine porcelain on the table and heavy blinds [shtory].[21] But it soon became obvious that the postwar period could no longer concern itself with the search for out-of-the-ordinary or luxury apartment designs. What was wanted were furnishings that were as simple as possible, robust mass furniture that could be easily produced on an industrial scale. Chairs of this type—the so-called kontorskie made of wood and with rigidly upright backs—remained popular for decades thanks to their robustness and simplicity.

The mass housebuilding programme under Khrushchev produced radical changes. This was not without consequences for interior design. New trends could be seen as early as 1956 at the All-Union Furniture Exhibition in the Manege in Moscow: furniture now became bulky and bombastic, fitted into the new room height of 2.5 metres and could be moved around in tune with variations in the new apartment design. The early modernity of the 1920s was rediscovered; new magazines were founded—*Dekorativnoe iskusstvo* was one. Soviet design became a talking point. People wanted everything to be lighter and to get rid of heavy furniture (which had often been used in the kommunalka to create private spaces). Synthetic materials were the coming thing—artificial veneers and sometimes steel or aluminium furniture. There was a growing market for adjustable cupboard walls and bookshelves imported from Czechoslovak, Polish and GDR manufacturers. People no longer just sat around the dining table in the middle of the room, but on the sofa which could be transformed into a bed overnight. Even the lighting arrangements had changed since members of the household no longer had to sit under the 'cosy' central lampshade above the table in the middle of the room. 'The housing boom created spaces that were inimical to the use of old furniture' and this helped to bring about 'the dissolution of the old material order in favour of a new one [that] helped heal the wounds of the past such as the privations of wartime, the Terror and any number of related personal tragedies.'[22]

This may be regarded as the end of a period of accumulation and normalisation. Soviet citizens had arrived at their own private sphere and created their own interior space. The fate of Soviet interiors reflects fairly accurately this journey from the dissolution of society and loss of a sense of form during the Revolution and the Civil War. It had advanced from projecting an entirely different, new world in the 1920s, continued through the labour expended on the grand style demanded and fostered from above, until it arrived at the dissolution of that style when the housing question was finally about to be resolved, from the late 1950s on.

The end of the Soviet Union represents once again a further radical break in the design of interiors and furnishings. The privatisation of housing initiated a wave of modernisation known as EuroRemont, which was accompanied by an unprecedented campaign to dispose of unwanted items. Residents of the Empire who could afford it—and many could—bid farewell to their accustomed surroundings so as to acquire new furnishings. Some did this with the assistance of Italian and other interior designers; others relied on the branches of a Swedish furniture company. It is not possible to predict when prices for antique furniture 'Sdelano v SSSR'/'Made in the USSR' will rise again.

CHAPTER 29

Hostel/*Obshchezhitie*: Soviet Melting Pot

The road out of the village and into the town, to the construction sites, the factories and the universities led hundreds of thousands and even millions to spend time in a hostel: simple workmen, would-be scholars and scientists, the political personnel of the future.[1] In a country that wished to put former times and the old world of the village behind it, that wanted to achieve the great leap forward into modern industry and the town in the shortest possible time, hostels were inevitable; for generations of peasants, workers and students they were the point of transition that they all aspired to and lived through. The struggle to obtain a place in a hostel was harsh and embittered. One of the worst imaginable punishments was to lose a place previously secured, to be thrown out for some dereliction—be it excessive alcohol use, a violation of house rules or attracting attention for one's political views. For this reason, the hostel turns up as a particular phase of one's life in countless Soviet biographies. The young Andrey Sakharov, for example, who, at the start of his life as a specialist, went to work in an ammunition factory in Ulyanovsk on the Volga, reported on the extreme conditions that the exhausted workers had to contend with. Exposed to acid fumes at work, they had to stand in queues for bread early in the mornings before going on shift in the afternoons.

Single workers coming from outside Ulyanovsk were assigned to a hostel. I lived in one from September 1942 until July 1943. Each room in the one-story barracks could accommodate six to twelve people sleeping in three-tiered plank bunks. People were too exhausted to make any noise, so it was usually pretty quiet, but occasionally one of my comrades would be a talkative type, and the conversations could be quite informative. The toilet was in the courtyard, about seventy-five feet away. Since many people didn't feel like walking that distance at night, there were always frozen puddles of urine outside the door. Lice were common. But there was always cold water for washing, and hot boiled water for tea from a 'titan' [a wood- or coal-heated water tank]. Every morning women from the surrounding villages brought oven-heated milk (I always bought a half pint for breakfast), carrots, and cucumbers.

I still recall with horror the day a roommate of mine came back from his shift after drinking a cupful of the methyl alcohol used in the plant. He became delirious and went berserk. Half an hour later, he was taken away in an ambulance and we never saw him again. He was a giant of a man, exceptionally strong, with fair hair and the light blue eyes of a child.

As I learned later, conditions were better in some places and worse in others: life at plants in the Urals was harder and hungrier. And Leningrad—under siege—was unspeakably worse. Everywhere, life was hardest for 'outsiders'—among them young evacuees from western parts of Russia, and especially for young apprentices (students from trade schools) working alongside adults.

This is just one of the many thousands of voices recalling conditions in a workers' hostel, albeit the voice of one of the privileged.[2]

The biography of the young Mikhail Gorbachev also includes an important period of residence in a hostel. This was the legendary Moscow University dormitory in Ulitsa Stromynka in the northeast of the city during the postwar years, when the university was still in the centre of town and the new buildings in the Lenin Hills not yet finished. The dormitory lay in a three-storey barracks building dating back to the time of Peter the Great and in its inner courtyard was a chapel that had been transformed after the Revolution into a reading room and luggage store. Following the end of the war, the complex was turned into a student hostel of Moscow University. Gorbachev, who had come to know his future wife, Raisa, among other students there, stood out as a bright student of law eager to learn. He had come to the capital from the southern provinces and soon acquired a certain authority as someone who was outgoing and sociable, ready to share food sent from his south Russian homeland—a common practice since it meant he could in exchange borrow shoes or a better suit for important occasions.

Since the Ulitsa Stromynka dormitory figures in so many of the biographies of students who were later to make important careers, we know a lot about what went on there. One former occupant wrote:

> The colourful, polyphonic community of post-war youth became a melting pot for the non-Muscovites for whom it took the place of the parental home and whom it welded together into a unified organism. This was a Soviet nucleus in a former barracks, built in the age of Peter, from which the barracks mentality that permeated the building and its entire structure had not yet faded. Down to the point in time when the students moved into the 'Great House', the high-rise block of the MGU on the Lenin Hills, they lived with several students to the room which contained no furniture but the beds under which they kept their trunks and personal possessions. A long corridor stretched all the way through the ochre-coloured building and everyone who was fed up with being confined in his own smoke-filled room walked up and down there as if on the principal avenue of this student city, which was constantly abuzz and hardly ever slept.
>
> A further location of the shared time as a student was . . . the toilet. Because of the disruptions of the post-war period, the cubicles and the doors had gone missing and so the toilets consisted simply of a row of lavatory basins. However, the toilets were not just used for their basic purpose. It was not uncommon for them to become the arena for political and theoretical debates and you could often see a student reading a philosophical tractate with a pencil in his hand or simply lost in thought, like Rodin's 'Thinker', albeit in a less aesthetic pose.

The harshness of everyday life in these conditions brought the characters of the students living there to the surface and into conflict with each other, almost as in an experiment. It is easy to understand how alongside the amiable Mikhail Gorbachev there were residents of a very different temperament. One could escape from them into the nearby parks, the library or the sports facilities.[3]

Hostels had to be built for single men or small families (many students married early because it increased their chances of obtaining a room in a kommunalka or even an apartment of their own). This was essential because otherwise workers could not have been found for the new large building sites or to fill the student courses. As a rule, hostels were thought of as temporary accommodation, but even in the 1950s and 1960s, long after the housing programme had got underway on a large scale, the hostels continued to be indispensable, especially for single men and women. If such individuals found no partner, the hostel could even become a lifelong home. The major projects of the first Five-Year Plan and the opening-up of Siberia and Kazakhstan after the Second World War saw a boom in hostel building. In the 1950s, thousands of young people, Komsomol members from the European part of Russia, journeyed to such places as Omsk, where an oil-worker town was being built, or to Novosibirsk, where a scientific research complex was being established. The first stage of housing in Omsk consisted of a tent city for seven hundred people, as well as hostels, and later, university buildings, where rooms with large windows and high ceilings housed between twelve and twenty women. During the day both men and women worked on the construction sites; in the evenings they attended classes. The standard furnishings included double or triple metal bunkbeds and a table in the middle of the room for both eating and studying. Lunch was to be had in the canteen (*stolovaya*); in the evenings people cooked for themselves. In higher-end hostels there were beds for four people, bedside tables, a wardrobe, a mirror, perhaps a bookshelf and a radio connection. Hostels usually had a communal room for games or for reading, a washroom and, later, a TV.[4]

As with the kommunalka, all this meant living with other people, in other words, sharing a toilet and a kitchen and being subjected to house rules, which did not always go smoothly. Until new hostels were developed—a special type of building as early as the 1920s—prerevolutionary models were used and adapted, if possible: military barracks, homes for clerical academies, monastery grounds, and the like. The different nationalities of the Soviet Union encountered one another in this school of enforced togetherness: Kazakhs, Uzbeks, Russians and Armenians. There was also the possibility of contact with students from outside the Soviet Union, with the children of émigrés from the Spanish Civil War and later with students from the socialist nations and the Third World. Whether the years spent in the hostel were remembered retrospectively as a time of filth, neglect and psychological terror or whether it was possible to make interesting friendships and concentrate on one's studies depended on the composition of the student population. Hostels were a sort of melting pot in several respects: utterly different lives came together often for the first time (from the villages or towns). The numerous nationalities of the Soviet Union all converged here. For many, this living arrangement provided a kind of substitute family, of great importance for the formation of personality in adolescence; for others, it was a dead end and more than a few took refuge in alcohol. It is difficult to speak of the 'dorm' as a place to withdraw. The opposite is more like the truth when one considers the extraordinary importance of all the institutions that provided an escape beyond the hostel: the parks, sports facilities, cinemas, canteens and palaces of culture with all their amenities. It may be that the 'self-seeding', provisional nature of these encounters contributed to a specially active social life, to a sociability that crossed the boundaries of the subjects and disciplines one was studying, and that made Akademgorodok, the small university town close to Novosibirsk, one of the most innovative and liberated places in the Soviet Union in the 1960s. The ballads of Okudzhava could be heard coming from its hostel windows, where students practised the twist on the club terraces, and where poets who were banned from appearing on stage in Moscow and Leningrad could publicly recite their verses to an exceptionally youthful and self-confident audience. What was once a part of the 'shanty-town' subculture became the place where the samizdat literature of dissidents began to circulate.

CHAPTER 30

Tent Cities, World of Barracks: Finding One's Way in 'Russia in Flux'

Nothing survives today, or practically nothing, of the shanty towns of the workers who built the great buildings of communism. What has come down to us from the early days of Soviet industrialisation, the age of the first Five-Year Plan of the late 1920s and 1930s, or indeed the postwar period, are the objectivised results of that labour, in other words, the great buildings themselves: the iron and steel factories of Magnitogorsk, in the Kuzbass, in Chelyabinsk; the car plants in Gorky, now called Nizhny Novgorod once again, in Rostselmash in Rostov-on-Don; the tractor plant in Stalingrad or Uralmash in Sverdlovsk, now renamed Yekaterinburg. There is a landscape of iron, factory workshops that are kilometres long, foundries, blast furnaces and warehouses. What has survived are the industrial buildings originally constructed in stone, the administration, guesthouse and other buildings that represented the life of the new society: the palace of culture, the workingmen's club, the stadium, the school or the mining institute, the technical university for mechanical engineering, and public amenities such as the baths, the library and the park for cultural activities and recreation. Some of these projects have even gone into architectural history under the heading of 'Sotsgorod'—the estates of the car workers in Gorky, the Stalin tractor works, the Chekist township in Sverdlovsk or—quite remarkably—the district around Kharkiv's Government House.

But these cities were the exceptions, like the owner-occupied homes and villas that were built for managers, technical personnel or foreign experts. It is not by chance that in Magnitogorsk these were known as 'Amerikanka'. The plant, Sotsgorod and the estates for specialists formed the core of the newly founded or enlarged towns, whereas the workers' accommodations consisted of wood huts, that is, of nonlasting material. What remained was what Marx called 'objectified' labour, while the living space from which the living labour power had emerged dissolved into nothing. Like a sea, these huts surrounded the high-rise buildings constructed for the future of the nation, for eternity. To gain a proper picture of industrialisation means leaving the core of steel and stone before our very eyes and entering the zone that was once defined by the endless agglomeration of hostels in which workers and their families resided. If we are to gain some idea of subsequent developments, we must think ourselves back to the very beginnings, to a time before the large-panel, prefab estates that were later built on a massive scale came into existence.[1]

The shanty town of the early 1930s was the locus of 'accelerated industrialisation', where the labour power of an entire large nation was sucked up and pulled together at a single point, a hyperurbanisation which succeeded the initial hyperindustrialisation. It was visible in a town such as Magnitogorsk, which was founded in 1929 in what had been an eighteenth-century Cossack *stanitsa*. A decade later it had 150,000 inhabitants; it then received a further, unprecedented boost following the evacuation of more than thirty large engineering works from the western regions of the Soviet Union at the onset of the German invasion. The foundation of the town could not have been more symbolic—on 30 June 1929 the first train arrived on a new stretch of line. It provides the picture of an instant city in which hundreds and, not much later, thousands of mainly young workers literally put up their tents on the banks of the Ural River. A tent city at the birth of a new town, one which would soon advance to the next stage: the shanty town. It too was essentially provisional, due to last perhaps five to ten years. In the event, it endured for one, two or even three generations, unintentionally but long term. Today in Magnitogorsk, at the entrance to the Veterans' Park, stands an expressive monument to the 'First Tent' that is supposed to memorialise the enthusiastic pioneers of 1929 about whom Boris Ruchyov wrote: 'We lived in a tent with a green window / Washed by the rain, dried by the sun / Yes, we lit golden campfires at the doors / On the reddening stones of the Magnetic Mountain.'[2] It would be no less instructive to imagine oneself back into a barracks city of the kind from which Magnitogorsk and many other towns of the Soviet Union grew.

Barracks

Barracks appear wherever large groups of people are required to stay a specific length of time and need accommodation. Hence the term 'hut' (barak), not house. Barracks had to be erected for refugees who had lost their shelter overnight; for the sick from whom society sought to protect itself by isolating them; for people in transit and migrants on their way out of the country. With its many convulsions and mass movements, the twentieth century had great need of emergency shelters. In the modern military, barracks became an imposing institution. In the world of modern autocracies, the camp with its large-scale complexes and streets became a permanent fixture. In the world of industrial megaprojects, the barracks town was omnipresent—whether in the construction of the Hoover Dam or in the labour and reform camps such as those linked to the Volga Dam projects where forced labourers languished. The period of accelerated industrialisation was synonymous with the establishment of the barracks towns which grew up around the heavy-industry projects to which they were subordinated in every respect, above all financially. The blast furnace was more important than the creation of a halfway bearable infrastructure or decent accommodation for the workforce.

If we set aside their historical core, the cities of the 1930s to 1950s consisted largely of workers' settlements situated in the immediate vicinity of the combines, not unlike the company towns of the USA. Only a fraction of the housing consisted of buildings with several storeys, running water, and connection to the sewerage system. In a town like Krasnoyarsk near Perm before the war, two-storey wooden buildings made up most of the housing stock. Paths and roads were in poor condition; many roads had paths made of wood blocks (which were needed for the transitional seasons of spring and autumn when the roads turned into mud).

The design and planning of the barracks were largely the same everywhere. In the settlement of the A. I. Mikoyan Meat Processing

Plant in Moscow, the most important and modern slaughterhouse of the Soviet Union, each barrack had a central entrance with a porch and a kitchen opposite the entrance with hotplates on the longer sides, heated by logs or oil. There were also washbasins. A corridor led in both directions with twenty doors per side, for a total of forty rooms, each around 12 square metres in size. Every room or section—the rooms were often separated only by a curtain or screen—had a stove that could be heated from the corridor. The barracks were scattered around the settlement in clusters and had a common room in which hot water was available.[3]

Conditions were similar in the Krasnoyarsk settlement near Perm. There, in barracks without tap water or sewerage systems, were twenty-two rooms, each with an area of 18.4 square metres; two kitchens with a larder; two heated toilets; a washroom, entrance hall and two corridors. Furthermore, the barracks had a room for firewood, two waste pits, a room for delousing clothes and washing, an oven with iron plates, a jet nozzle and grate for disinfecting clothing, as well as a laundry with seven tubs. Often, of course, sanitary standards were not maintained and the buildings themselves were frequently of the worst quality since the work had to be carried out by the occupants themselves: insulation was poor, stoves frequently didn't work so that repairs were soon needed, walls and ceilings weren't plastered; there was only a single electric bulb in the corridors, and there were no separate washrooms for men and women. Yury Orlov, evacuated to Nizhny Tagil with his mother during the Second World War, described their accommodation as follows:

She and I were quartered in a just-excavated barracks together with a pair of newly wed workers and an unmarried adjuster of automatic milling machines. The barracks had an earthen floor three steps below the street, tiny windows, nails in the wall instead of hangers, stools (there was no room for a table), and four wooden bunk beds. All our belongings went into suitcases under the beds. There was a small iron stove in the centre and firewood outside near the door. The walls got covered with frost in winter, and with large drops of dew in spring and fall. To make up for it, the barracks was not flooded in spring. Our neighbors' did flood once, and their suitcases and stools were left floating.[4]

Costs had to be kept down compared to the magnitude of the investments for the production units. Conditions were so hard, not to say unbearable, that even the Komsomol felt constrained to take up the cudgels for improvements with the slogan 'The struggle for a warm barracks—that is the struggle against the class enemy who exploits our weak points to the detriment of socialist construction.'[5]

The barracks gradually disappeared as the dominant feature of the Soviet city, which increasingly was rebuilt around the historical centres or else designed from scratch. Once again it was Khrushchev's policy of mass-housing construction that brought about the end of the barracks world and transported its former occupants into confined habitations of a different kind.[6] The microdistrict with prefab apartment blocks spelled the end of the barracks life as an institution and led to an urbanisation that was something other than village life forced into a workers' settlement. The ruralisation of the town may only recently have come to an end. But this does not mean that all traces of what sociologist Natalia Lebina has defined as the 'subculture of the barracks' have been eliminated. There are forms of conditioning that persist even when their origins have long since vanished.[7]

CHAPTER 31

Palm Trees in the Civil War

The palm is a product of the south and the subtropical world, while in the north it is a symbol of luxury—like pineapple or strawberries in winter. The fact that the palm tree keeps recurring throughout Russian and Soviet history must have its own significance, even though it does not appear as a chief protagonist but only ever on the margins, as part of the background. The palm was seen in the Kremlin during the First Congress of the Communist International in 1919. There were palms in the festively lit Hall of Columns in the House of the Unions, where Lenin's body lay in state in 1924. Sergey Kirov, the Party leader assassinated in Leningrad in 1934, appears laid out beneath a palm forest in a large-format oil painting by Alexander Samokhvalov. The hundreds of thousands of people who filed past Stalin's body did so against a background of palm fronds. The palm is present in photos that show families on vacation on a sanatorium veranda in the Crimea or in Sochi. Visitors to the later Soviet Union encountered palms chiefly in official and public spaces: in the foyers of ministries and organisations, in the entrance halls of student residences or institutes, in delicatessens with reputations dating from prerevolutionary times, in the lobbies of grand hotels such as the National in Moscow and the Astoria in Leningrad. In the palace of culture at the car plant in Gorky the lamps were shaped like palm trees. Palms stood beneath the dome of the Hotel Metropol dining room and on the stage where jazz bands performed. The restaurant in Yaroslavsky Station was 'crowded with palms', making Walter Benjamin 'feel as if [he] were at the zoo in the antelope pavilion.'[1] Palms recur in countless feature films as aspects of the interior, as symbols. But as symbols of what? The greatest surprise for me was a 1931 poster by Sergey Yakovlevich Senkin with the caption 'We're making our factories and workshops green'. This poster from the time of the Soviet avant-garde shows a woman with a red headscarf and protective goggles at a long workbench; above her head a palm extends its branches. Palm fronds in an otherwise incomparably stark world! The green of the tropical plant contrasts with the white of the workshop and the red of the worker's headscarf. A palm stands by each workbench—serial palm trees, a palm forest in a modern factory. I had never seen such a thing before. I felt the need to follow it up. The palm tree, the symbol of an exclusive and elitist world in the midst of a world that had appeared on stage to do away with all that.

The Other Palm-Tree World: Siegfried Kracauer's 'Under the Palms' of 1930

What, then, does the palm tree stand for? In his feuilleton 'Under the Palms' in the Travel section of the *Frankfurter Zeitung* of 19 October 1930, Siegfried Kracauer wrote: 'The palm tree is the chief constituent of that Fata Morgana that rises nowadays again and again on the horizon of Berlin's wasteland normality.' With palms everywhere, the southern tree had become fashionable, the symbol for escape from the wicked world. Walter Benjamin no longer identified the palm tree with 'the dark soil' but with 'the drawing room'.[2] For Kracauer, it became a sign of crisis. 'The growth of palm trees is in exact proportion to the growth of poverty.' Palm trees in a café in western Berlin, painted palm groves, palm clusters and palm fronds as a fixture of the interior, palm restaurants everywhere. In the centre of Berlin, between the Stadtbahn stations and the world-class traffic, there was a 'lively growth of vegetation' in which employees, businesspeople, students and lovers sought refuge. 'They are not escaping from ordinary life into the cosy comfort of the "parlour"; at most they discover what they already possess and develop abilities they didn't know they had. The palm tree is a signpost to happiness. They dance with flushed cheeks, tenderly embracing in the booths. The muted lighting obliterates the shabbiness of their jackets and blouses. It switches from red to green, mirroring the feelings of the dancing couples. And as in the Paradis Bleu in Paris, the air is suffused with the sense of sorrow that surrounds those who are happy.'[3] The palms here are 'not merely an echo of a distant world, a mirage which consoles the observer for

FIGURE 31.1. Isaak Brodsky (1883–1939), *Around the Leader's Coffin*, 1925. The colours—the green of the palm trees and the bright yellow of the chandeliers—hardly seem to suggest a funeral scene. © State Historical Museum, Moscow. Photo: akg-images.

FIGURE 31.2. Dmitry Baltermants (1912–1980), *Stalin's Funeral*, 1953. A palm forest in the Hall of Columns in the House of the Unions, originally the Club of the Russian Nobility. © Courtesy of Dmitry Baltermants. Photo: culture-images/fai.

the ills of his home, but real domestic plants that adorn a home that continues to exist despite all the misery."[4]

There really are palm-tree restaurants in Berlin; they form part of the decor of big-city society. The palm tree of the Soviet world has a different background and we would be remiss if we were to transfer Kracauer's remarks to Soviet-Russian conditions. In the Soviet world, the palm tree is not the exotic accessory of metropolitan mass culture, but instead points to a culture with a very different genealogy. It leads us into the world of the nobility, the court, the Enlightenment and the representation of power.

In the northern climate, the palm tree is imaginable, viable, only in conditions that have been created and maintained artificially. Without a shelter manufactured by human hands, the palm would not survive the winter. It is a plant entirely dependent a priori upon the power that can produce and guarantee the conditions needed for its survival. The collapse of that power spells the end of the culture to which it owes its existence.

Palm Trees, Absolutism and Enlightenment

Exotic plants and animals made their entry into the Muscovite Empire relatively early, chiefly as gifts from diplomatic embassies at the Tsarist court. The systematic cultivation of plants began with Peter the Great. As early as 1706 he started an apothecary's garden for medicinal herbs in Moscow, which subsequently developed into the Botanical Garden with its avenues, ponds, paths and greenhouses and which exists to this day.[5] After transferring the capital to the Neva, in 1714 he also moved the *aptekarsky-prikaz*, the apothecary office, from Moscow to St. Petersburg and established a herb garden on Aptekarsky Ostrov, Apothecary Island, which became the foundation for the future botanical garden. Over an area of 300 × 200 *sazhen* [one *sazhen* = around seven feet] medicinal herbs were cultivated, chiefly for the army and navy—camomile, sage, mint, wall germander, juniper, lavender—but also roses and peonies for the court's floral decoration needs. In the 1730s the garden already had more than three hundred species. We can tell just how important the garden was to Peter when we see that its direction was entrusted to one of his leading reformers—Archbishop Feofan Prokopovich. The St. Petersburg herb garden developed largely under the leadership of foreign botanists, above all Germans, Swedes and Swiss. The catalogue of 1736 already contained 1,275 species and the first greenhouses were built of wood. Foreign visitors marvelled at the numerous plants from Asia, Persia and China. 'Pineapples grow here to maturity. They are harvested and brought to the table.' The orangeries contained aloe, myrtle, boxwood, citrus fruit, figs, geraniums and canna lilies. But alongside medicinal and scientific concerns, the greenhouse and especially the orangery served as expressions of courtly and aristocratic power. Following the conquest of the Crimea in 1784, when Catherine II had the Tauride Palace built in St. Petersburg for her commander and favourite Prince Grigory Potemkin, it was taken for granted that it would contain a huge park in the English style along with an orangery with palm trees, laurels and oleanders—the orangery was in fact subsequently built on a different site.

The Patriotic War against Napoleon was not without its consequences. The Botanical Garden suffered from shortages. In winter 1818, around 180 plants died of the cold. It took a while for the Botanical Garden to recover, but under Count Viktor Kochubey and the German botanist Friedrich Ernst Ludwig von Fischer, the St. Petersburg garden became one of the most important in Europe. In 1824 there was a square with twenty-five greenhouses; 15,000 living species were counted in 1823. The Botanical Garden was placed directly under the management of the imperial court. It now had better funding and could even finance costly expeditions to Brazil, Chile, Turkestan, the Caucasus, Mongolia and northwest China. Following the fashion of the times, this resulted in the growth of greenhouses, palm gardens and orangeries. In 1847 a palm-tree house was built in St. Petersburg; in 1855 this was supplemented by a library and a herbarium. Further orangery buildings were added in 1896–1899 as part of projects by leading St. Petersburg architects. By now they had become an indispensable part of the new St. Petersburg cityscape. Thus by the beginning of the twentieth century, behind the figure of the palm tree stood an almost two-hundred-year-old history, leading from the Tsarist herb garden to the modern botanical garden. This history represents an amalgam of economic utility, scientific interest and the pleasure taken in nature's exotic splendours. The palm house owes its existence to the Tsar, who had by then become an Imperator, as well as to the impetus of science, which has to collect natural objects and organise and classify them so as to increase the national wealth. The palm stands for imperial power and enlightenment as well as luxury and beauty.

Vsevolod Garshin's 'Attalea Princeps': Revolution as the Demolition of the Greenhouse

Vsevolod Mikhailovich Garshin (1855–1888) is known to Russian schoolchildren as the author of children's tales, but what he wrote in simple children's language was a story anticipating the Revolution. The highly gifted and precocious Garshin, who had been wounded in the Russo-Turkish War of 1877, must have been badly traumatised when he learned of the execution of a young revolutionary of his own generation: he hurled himself out of a window and died when he was barely thirty-three years old. One of his children's stories tells of a palm tree—*Attalea princeps*—that breaks through the glass roof of the greenhouse in which it is imprisoned and pays for its love of liberty by dying in the freezing cold of northern St. Petersburg.

> In a certain large town there was a botanical garden, and in this garden an enormous greenhouse of glass and iron. It was a very handsome building. Graceful spiral columns supported the whole structure, and on them rested ornamented arches interwoven by a whole web of iron frames, in which panes of glass were set. This greenhouse was especially beautiful when the setting sun was reflected redly against it. Then the whole building seemed alight. Crimson rays played and transfused just as in some gigantic, delicately-cut, precious stone.
>
> Through the thick, but transparent, panes could be discerned the captive plants. Notwithstanding the size of the greenhouse its inmates felt cramped for space. Roots interlaced and robbed each other of moisture and sustenance. The branches of the trees interfered with the enormous leaves of palms, rotted and broke

them, and pressing against the iron framework themselves rotted and snapped. The gardeners were constantly lopping off boughs and binding the palm-leaves with wires, so that they should not grow where they wished. But these efforts were of little avail. They needed space, their homeland and freedom. They were natives of hot climes, tender, luxurious creations. They remembered with longing the lands of their birth. However transparent the glass roof it was not the clear heavens. Occasionally in wintertime the panes became frosted, and then the greenhouse became quite dark. The wind would howl and beat against the iron framework, causing it to vibrate. The roof would be covered with drift-snow. The plants standing within would listen to the beating of the wind, and recall another wind, warm and moisture-laden, which used to give them life and health. And then they would long to feel its breath once more so that it might sway their boughs and play with their leaves. But in the greenhouse the air was motionless, excepting when winter storms shattered some of the glass panes; then a cutting cold current, a veritable icicle, would burst in on them, leaving faded, shrivelled leaves in its wake.[6]

The Director of the Botanical Garden was an outstanding scholar who tolerated no disorder and was proud of his science, which had given the most splendid of palm trees the name *Attalea princeps*, although at home in Brazil it had a completely different name, as a Brazilian visitor had assured the orangery. Whereas the visitor was able to travel back to his homeland, the palm tree had to remain where she was. Life was now harder for her. She was quite alone. She had outgrown all the other plants and they envied her for that. All her companions in the orangery—the sago palm, the cactus, the cinnamon tree and the fern—quarrelled and pleaded with her, but the proud palm tree urged them to end their quarrel and act in concert. "'Listen to me! Grow taller and wider, throw out branches, press against the iron framework and glass panes, and then our greenhouse will break up into bits, and we shall gain freedom. If only one branch presses against the glass they will, of course, cut it off, but what will they do with a hundred strong and daring trunks? It is only necessary to be more friendly and to work together, and victory is ours!'"[7] The palm tree was rebuked and mocked; she now knew where she stood: "'I alone will find a way for myself. I want to see the sky and sun direct, not through this glass and grating . . . and I will." And the palm proudly glanced with her green top at the forest of comrades displayed below.' She found encouragement only from a small plant, a frail, insignificant species of grass which felt too feeble to take up the struggle for liberty. The palm tree now made preparations for escaping from the greenhouse that had become her prison. To the astonishment of all the other plants, she grew even taller. She braced herself against the iron beams and the glazing; she wanted freedom at any price. "'I shall free myself or die or live in freedom."' At a stroke, she smashed her way through the orangery dome, whose debris and splinters fell down on the Director while 'the green crown of the palm had straightened itself, and was proudly protruding above the glass dome'. The cold descended all around the palm tree, but she could not now find her way back. 'She would have to stand in the cold wind, feel its gusts and the biting touch of snowflakes. She would have to gaze at the drab sky, at beggarly Nature, at the unsavoury backyard of the botanical garden, at the huge wearisome town looming through the fog, and wait until people below in the greenhouse decided what to do with her. The Director gave instructions to saw the palm down.' Other solutions, such as enlarging the orangery, did not occur to him. 'They fastened ropes round the palm so that when it fell it should not destroy the walls of the greenhouse, and low down at its very roots they sawed it through. The little herb which had grown around the trunk did not wish to part from its friend, and also fell under the saw. When they dragged the palm out of the greenhouse, the torn stalks and leaves spoilt by the saw fell on to the stump that remained.'[8] The palm tree ended up on the waste tip. The Director would doubtless think of something new to plant in its place.

The Palm Tree in the Civil War

In his legendary book *The Soul of St. Petersburg* of 1922, dedicated to the demise of the capital, Nikolay Antsiferov cast a glance at the Botanical Garden. 'On the edge of the city, behind the little Karpovka River, there are other prisoners from hot countries in the tropical corner of the Botanical Garden, namely the palm trees familiar to the sphinxes, among them the romantic *Attalea princeps,* the heroine of a story by Vsevolod Garshin. And there was also the "distant palm" that filled the dreams of the lonely pine tree covered with a white blanket of ice and snow and had migrated "from the East" into the "bare north".[9] The city, where there was no exhibition opening or hotel reception without the accessory of a palm tree, was scarcely in a position to guarantee the living conditions of its inhabitants, let alone the existence of orangeries (or of zoos for that matter!). Looking back at the Silver Age, Alexander Benois recalled the opening of a Serge Diaghilev exhibition in the Stieglitz Museum: 'This time the hall seemed particularly festive, thanks to an extravagant abundance of hothouse plants and flowers which Serioja had placed everywhere regardless of cost. A certain section of the advanced intelligentsia of the capital was displeased at the pomp—unprecedented at any exhibition—with which the opening took place.'[10] The palm tree was something of a commonplace, as we see from a scene in Nabokov's *Speak, Memory,* in which, standing beside his father and Korney Chukovsky, he quotes Alexey Tolstoy's couplet 'Vizhu palmu i Kafrika / Eto—Afrika' (I see a palm and a little Kaffir. That's Africa.).[11]

During the weeks and months of the Revolution, it was difficult to maintain normal conditions in the greenhouses. Even in the Kremlin the difficulties could not be ignored: 'The hard-pressed city government, with few roubles to spare for building-maintenance (and none for more utopian schemes), devoted part of the summer of 1917 to selling off exotic plants from the palace hot-houses.'[12] In the spring of 1917 over half of the dried-out plants and some large and rare tropical ferns perished in the Petrograd orangery. The Museum Park grounds and collections could no longer be looked after. Trees perished; bushes could no longer be pruned and cared for. Weeds spread unchecked. Nature began to reclaim the terrain wrested from it. The Tauride Palace Palm House ran wild and was dismantled towards the end of the 1920s and transferred to the Botanical Garden. But gradually the grounds were restored and the orangeries reinstated. In 1925 a large number of tropical and subtropical plants were collected from the orangeries of the imperial residences and private palaces and handed over to the Botanical Garden. Whatever had survived until then in the Tauride Palace, in Tsarskoe Selo, in the greenhouses of the Durnovo Villa and Brusnitsyn Mansion was concentrated in the Botanical Garden, which was itself put under the control of the Academy of Sciences in 1930. In the years 1930–1935 a modern 'Orangery No. 2' was built and once it was completed the surviving stocks of the Tauride Palace orangery were transferred to it so that before the outbreak of war the orangery in the Botanical Garden contained as many as 6,367 species in twenty-five greenhouses.

But scarcely had the Botanical Garden facilities recovered from their losses in the war and the Revolution than the Second World War broke out and struck the greenhouses once again, especially during the siege of Leningrad. The collections in the orangeries were particularly affected. Unique specimens of palm trees and ferns were lost. An important part of the cactus collection, some rhododendrons, some specimens of sago palm ferns and some seedlings could be saved. The restoration of the orangery collection began as early as spring 1943. This was assisted by donations of subtropical cultures from the Botanical Garden of Sukhumi, as well as fern spores from plants that had perished in the winter of 1941/42. In spring 1944 a packet of seeds arrived from Lisbon. Some of the palms and agaves donated by the Botanical Garden of Sukhumi can still be seen today in the orangery of the Botanical Garden in St. Petersburg.

Palms versus Rubber Plants

In the debates about the type of housing appropriate to the new society, the question of indoor plants also played a role. Even though in general people were inclined to reject plants because they posed a hygiene risk, there was nonetheless a dispute about room plants quite apart from the fact that palm trees, because of their sheer size, required large spaces normally available only in public buildings and organisations—such as hotels, people's commissariats, institutes, clubs and hospitals. The literature shows a clear dividing line: the essence of a petty-bourgeois lifestyle could be found in certain plants, including the rubber plant, geraniums and African hemp. The rubber plant featured in many poems of the Futurists, Constructivists and supporters of a modern style of living as the epitome of the petty bourgeoisie. You can read about it in Mayakovsky, Zoshchenko, and Ilf and Petrov. The palm was not affected by this polemic; it appeared in festive, official, prestigious and opulent contexts—in congresses (photos of sessions of the people's commissars or the Comintern in the Kremlin); at funerals, as in the crowd scenes filing past the coffin at the funerals of Lenin, Kirov, Ordzhonikidze and Stalin. A palm tree can even be seen in the mausoleum for Lenin that had been provisionally built of wood in 1924.[13] Or again, in receptions in the best hotels for prominent foreign visitors such as Feuchtwanger, Shaw and Romain Rolland, or when an especially luxurious setting was called for, as in the first-class dining room of the Volga steamer *Josef Stalin*, sailing between Nizhny Novgorod and Astrakhan.[14] In pictures of hotels and spas on the Black Sea coast and the Caucasus, the palm, as a subtropical plant, hinted at the broader expanse of empire; it stood for a sphere of comfort and luxury to which even ordinary Soviet citizens could aspire if they worked to earn it and had the requisite political consciousness. This was the palm tree as the background to upward mobility. It was so symbolic of officialdom and social mobility that it confirmed the veracity of a statement uttered in Poland that held for the Soviet Union. In 1982, at the time of martial law in Poland, a state radio and television official said: 'Some comrades say that this Solidarność was a kind of paper tiger that was destroyed overnight on December 13th and that it is no longer dangerous. . . . Such certainty has led some of us to declare that in principle we had won and that it is time to celebrate our victory— time to curtail or abolish the State of War, that everything is back to normal. That is the attitude of those Comrades who have installed themselves in their official armchairs under large potted palms . . . and under the protection of the Military. Such a view of the situation is quite wrong . . . and very damaging.'[15] The 'large potted palm' had become the symbol of a complacent political class that made itself at home in its 'official armchair', the status quo.

FIGURE 31.3. The revered palm in the prototype building of Constructivism, an apartment of the Narkomfin Building in Moscow, Novinsky Bulvar 25. Architects: Moisey Ginzburg, Ignaty Milinis, Sergey Prokhorov, 1928–1932. From E. Ovsiannikova and E. Miliutina, *Zhiloi kompleks 'Dom Narkomfina'*, Tatlin, Yekaterinburg 2015.

FIGURE 31.4. Sanatorium in the Crimea, Yalta 1938. Photographer unknown. From Leah Bendavid-Val, *Propaganda and Dreams: Photographing the 1930s in the USSR and USA*, Edition Stemmle, Zurich and New York 1999.

Hydroculture and Empire

Since the end of the Soviet Union, Russia has ceased to be a country of the north, as far as the supply of flowers and exotic plants is concerned. It has been incorporated into global supply chains that can deliver roses from Peru, palm trees from the Netherlands and lilies from Thailand to anywhere on Earth at any point in time. Brightly lit florists with opulent displays in metro entrances and passages form part of the new image of post-Soviet cities and towns. The Botanical Gardens were affected by the temporary setback to public organisations. Real-estate speculators and investors cast an eye over the desirable locations, the beauty and the aura of gardens and parks that had grown over generations.[16] Why shouldn't the orangery in the Tauride Palace be turned into an internet café? A vigilant public and sometimes new pathways to a public-private partnership have prevented the worst and ensured that such trees as the Siberian larch planted by Peter the Great or the three-hundred-year-old willow that Catherine II had seen, were saved. The palm trees that can be seen in great numbers in Moscow at present are only rarely the distinguished-looking exemplars that bear the marks of the years and all they have experienced in that time. That too indicates a historical end point when the revered fossils of empire are replaced by the neat and highly polished palm trees produced by Dutch hydroculture. During the years of the latter-day Soviet Union, they stood around in hallways and foyers like forgotten or abandoned monuments of a past era. Needing little and accustomed to neglect, the palms were tended exclusively by women at least as old as them. Palm trees were barely tolerated out of the kind of token reverence felt towards contemporaries who had grown old with honour. Now, however, the era of the Soviet palm tree appears to have run its course.

CHAPTER 32

The Soviet Staircase: Towards an Analysis of Anonymous and Anomic Spaces

Staircases are problematic zones the world over and we ought not to make things easier for ourselves by generalising about 'the' Soviet staircase in the singular. There were neglected and well-maintained staircases there as everywhere, staircases where it was evident that the building occupants cared about their condition and others that exhibited all the signs of indifference. And everyone knows that the appearance of staircases is influenced by many factors: the social composition of the area, the cultural habits of the occupants and the economic status of the people.

Nevertheless, it would be overhasty to simply ignore the irritating impression Soviet staircases left on foreign visitors. We should rather look into the signs of neglect, indifference, filth and vandalism. What is called for is something like a 'thick description', a specific analysis that would do justice to the phenomenon. What is of interest are not the extreme cases of neglect to be found all over the world in run-down buildings or districts, but the fact that neglect can be found where it is least expected: in areas inhabited by average middle-class people so that visitors from outside are immediately struck by the sharp contrast between the apartment and the staircase, between the private and the semipublic.

Once you found the right entrance (*podyezd*)—and in large apartment blocks there could be many entryways—you looked for the door number you had been given. The door might be open or ajar or it might have had the kind of lock requiring a numbered code. Doors were mainly of wood or metal, rarely of glass; they couldn't easily be opened and once you entered, they banged shut behind you. The hall you entered was dark. The walls were painted in floor coatings—blue, grey or turquoise, rarely white. This made them more durable. The obligatory list of house rules was nailed to the wall. This was where you would find the letter boxes—*pochta*—which were often broken into and hence are no longer used. A bulb or neon light produced a feeble light, if indeed it hadn't fallen out or been unscrewed. The weather outside left its marks in the hallway and the staircase, especially in the autumn and spring when the ground was slushy in front of the door. Lifts, supplied mainly by the Soviet monopoly company Moslift, were part of the basic furnishings. Their mechanism was reliable even if they were scuffed, stained and smelled bad. There were no nameplates on the doors, only the number and the bell, which did not always work. A 'thick description' would add that tiles were often missing, the stairs had not been washed for ages and the walls were disfigured with graffiti. Moreover, the light was too faint to illuminate the entire space and the waste bins did not close so they spread a stench that was especially strong in winter because heating was indispensable. Nor would such an account fail to mention the debris in the staircase and the lifts, the broken windowpanes that had not been replaced, and the banisters that should have been repaired and freshly painted.

Even if the apartment occupants had nothing to do with one another, the staircase and the lift were where, like it or not, they ran across each other. These were unavoidable contact zones. People did not know the other tenants and if you happened to be wandering through the building in search of an apartment and asked for help, you would be looked at warily or even with outright suspicion. Greeting other people was not only unusual but might have provoked puzzled and even hostile glances. Personal demeanour made clear that everyone wanted to be left in peace. Even in a crowded lift you needed to keep your distance. A friendly word or a well-intentioned greeting was likely to produce not a friendly reaction but an evasive or dejected look. No one spoke, let alone laughed. Such innocent utterances were regarded as breaches of the peace. The contact zone was bereft of communications. But the converse was also true. The anonymous space everyone tried to leave as quickly as possible also provided the opportunity to do things that you would not do in your own apartment or in the presence of others.

FIGURE 32.1. Staircase: 'These are the stairs leading up to my studio in the attic and to which I climbed six floors every morning. On every floor the doors from the communal kitchens on each side opened onto the landing and every time I climbed up I could hear scolding and shouting behind the doors. Sometimes a door opened and I could glimpse a woman in a dressing gown scraping food remnants from a plate or from a saucepan into the waste bin' (Ilya Kabakov, *Auf dem Dach/On the Roof: Installation Palais des Beaux-Arts de Bruxelles*, Richter Verlag, Düsseldorf 1997, 114). Photo © George Kiesewalter.

There are very many reasons why 'people'—that is, quite ordinary fellow residents—tolerated such living conditions.

The magnificent staircases of the old apartment houses in the centre of St. Petersburg, solidly built as they were, nevertheless bore the marks of the passage of time: the broken downpipes in the cold winters during the Civil War and the Revolution, the improvised tinkering with the electrical wiring and telephone cables at times when light bulbs were in short supply and removed on the sly, the shortage of craftsmen who might have repaired the Art Nouveau windows and banisters that had survived until then. The fact that the most basic essentials were unobtainable undoubtedly helps to explain this situation. The decades-long wear and tear took its toll. These staircases saw generations going up and down without their ever having been properly maintained. There was hardly ever enough money to undertake repairs because the rents were so low. Also lacking was the robust interest that would normally be shown by a house or apartment owner.

But indifference and neglect in these semipublic spaces could be seen not just in older buildings but even in the buildings erected in the 1960s. Barring an explanation rooted in a supposed national psyche, there remains nothing but to look to social and sociopsychological causes. People care about their own, private space, but wish to have nothing to do with the public space. The staircase which forms the intermediate zone of every building is secondary, peripheral when viewed from one's own dwelling. The space that belongs to everyone belongs to no one. In a society as socially heterogeneous as the Soviet one, where the traditional segregation into 'classes', professional groups and milieus simply did not exist, the contact zone was rather a non-meeting place of people who had nothing to say to one another and preferred to avoid each other. Everyone looked after their own. People avoided the semipublic space; to effect any change cost energy and commitment. Hence the semipublic space was used furtively to get rid of anything you had no room for in your, for the most part, highly constricted private space. People accepted responsibility for their own possessions but felt exempt from any wider obligation. They retreated within their own four walls and abandoned to the outside world the semipublic space over which they had no influence. The emergence of the anonymous and anomic space followed from the retreat of the inhabitants on whom the battle over the semipublic space made excessive demands. This battle ended with their surrender.

Once this space was vacated, everything became possible—from harmless graffiti to mugging and murder. On 20 November 1998 Galina Starovoytova, a member of the St. Petersburg Duma and a prominent defender of human rights, was murdered by a contract killer on her way back to her apartment on Griboedov Canal 91. She was shot down on the stairs by two bullets. Anna Politkovskaya, the fearless journalist of *Novaya gazeta*, was murdered in the lift by a contract killer on 7 October 2006 when she was on her way to her home at Ulitsa Lesnaya 8 in Moscow. And the explosions in Ulitsa Gurianova 19 in Moscow on 8 September 1999, which brought down the houses there, were facilitated, if not made possible, by the atmosphere of anonymity in which the locals had long since ceased to show any interest in what was happening all around them.

A new trend started with the privatisation of the housing stock. One of its effects has been segregation and social divergence. A new struggle has broken out for the control of semipublic space. Whether appropriation, *reconquista* or flight—however the battle for the borders between public and private on the staircase ends up—will tell us something about the battle between power and impotence in Russia as a whole.

CHAPTER 33

Ilya Kabakov's Installation: The Toilet as a Civilising Space

No special explanation is needed to include the 'restroom' in an attempt to comprehend the Soviet lifeworld. It was indispensable, as in every society. It was not like the car which could be done without, if necessary; you could get from A to B in a number of ways. The toilet will be treated here not simply from a wish to provide a comprehensive picture, which is unattainable anyway. Rather, as historians have long known, the toilet is an extraordinarily compelling subject. Archaeologists are always delighted to encounter toilet remains since they can reconstruct whole eras of human development from the vestiges of human faeces: from the state of food production, eating habits and food culture right down to the course of sieges and epidemics. Interest in the Soviet toilet has primarily a different source: the perplexity—shock even—felt by foreigners when confronted by the general state of the toilets, especially public toilets, whose use they depended on in town or on their travels and not just as an object of aesthetic or historical reflection. As an outsider, a foreigner, I would prefer not to treat this topic if only because discussing it at all implies a patronising attitude, however subtly disguised, and perhaps even an assumption of superiority that we are all too familiar with from the history of colonialism. That this is a delicate matter is evident from my tentative approach to the subject lest we be thought offensive or insulting, especially if we appear to be looking at a 'scandal of civilisation' from the viewpoint of the outsider, the foreigner or the 'Westerner'.

Now that the Soviet lavatory has ceased to be a taboo subject and Russian society has begun to concern itself with the condition and importance of toilets, self-justifications from a foreigner's perspective are no longer needed. We can simply leave reconstruction of the history and culture of the Soviet loo to the self-analysis of post-Soviet

Russian society. The toilet in its various gradations both private and public—*sortir, ubornaya* and *tualet*—has become the object of essays, exhibitions and films. In 1991 Timur Kibirov devoted a poem to the toilet with the title 'Sortiry' (Loos); the Czech dramatist Pavel Kohout wrote a play titled *Nuly* (Zeros). [In Germany, Eastern Europe and Russia, public toilets are commonly identified by two zeros on the door.] In 1999, Vladimir Putin, who had just been appointed President, adopted the vocabulary of the toilet in his response to terrorist attacks in Buynaksk, Volgodonsk and Moscow in a press conference at which he announced he would have 'terrorists drowned in the latrines'. In 2004 the Water Museum in St. Petersburg curated an exhibition with the title 'The Evolution of the Toilet'.[1] Probably the most sustained treatment of this theme, however, is Ilya Kabakov's installation 'Tualet' in the Moscow art space Vinzavod. There could be no further doubts about the seriousness and relevance of a topic that was normally passed over in embarrassed silence.

In the introduction to his monograph on the 'commode', Igor Bogdanov identified the changing tone: 'There is a topic that it is not agreeable to discuss in public even though it becomes increasingly explicit in the press, in the works of writers and poets and in film. Yes, I am speaking of lavatories, of the need to answer the call of nature. In our society, people have tried to ignore the subject out of embarrassment right down to the era that has become known by the name "perestroika".[2] Bogdanov is not alone. Andrey Konchalovsky, the Russian film director who worked in Hollywood for many years, has spoken of his plan to make a film about the history of the Russian lavatory, since the lavatory enables us to judge 'the standard of a nation, its civilisation and its political consciousness'.[3]

What I referred to above as a 'scandal of civilisation' was the experience that no sooner did you leave the world of high culture—the public rooms of the Bolshoi Theatre, the Leningrad Philharmonic, the galleries and museums and the better or even the best hotels—than, you, as a user of public toilets, were confronted with conditions that for simplicity's sake we may call revolting, disgusting and intolerable, quite apart from the fact that in all towns fewer and fewer conveniences were to be found or were recognisable as such. Similarly, as a rail passenger compelled perhaps to spend more than a day and night on a journey, you might well have found toilets that with the best will in the world were barely usable, or alternatively, at a stop along the way, you would see passengers relieving themselves in standing-only toilets that did not even have swing doors to separate them off. Even in the Lenin Library, the largest library in the country, the toilet was a place to avoid if at all possible. It was located underground close to the refectory (*stolovaya*); you entered it through a lobby dimly lit by a single ceiling bulb. Smokers stood around its walls, filling the semidark room with clouds of smoke that merged with the acrid smell of the adjacent toilets. Even if you employed a certain artistry in the use of these conveniences, it wasn't just a matter of the congestion and the hard-to-describe and even harder-to-put-up-with concentration of filth, stench and semidarkness. The question was rather why these conditions were tolerated in a place where library patrons came day after day to do their work—until more civilised conditions were introduced with the end of the Soviet Union.

It goes without saying that these public toilets were an exception and very different from the toilets in people's own homes. However, a large portion of the urban population lived in communal apartments for over a generation, and the problem of the general, public use of toilets existed in the kommunalka as well. The lavatory was in fact a semipublic place, since the occupants of the kommunalka knew who was in the toilet for how long and perhaps what his or her habits were. A queue would form in front of the toilet door—especially first thing in the morning—with all you might expect: impatience, irritation and gossip. One became the involuntary witness of what was going on in the closed space—which was not really closed. This was where differing ideas of what constituted discretion and cleanliness for people of different backgrounds and upbringing met up. A toilet for over thirty people, which according to Ivan Bogdanov was not untypical, is hard to keep clean and various strategies were used to cope. Individuals or families in the shared apartment often had their own toilet seats, which hung on the lavatory wall, where there was a regular gallery of toilet seats.

In his study of life in the kommunalka, Ilya Utekhin writes: 'Nowadays toilet seats for the family and individuals are less common than they used to be. We more frequently encounter the situation where all the occupants of the kommunalka use the toilet seat fixed to the toilet bowl and take care of hygiene by covering the seat with the sheets of paper or old newspapers found in a bag on the toilet door (sometimes together with a roll of toilet paper, although this is not typical). The paper used as a cover prevents physical contact with the toilet seat. The used paper is thrown away—sometimes in a special bucket or basket nearby. It is forbidden to throw the paper down the toilet bowl since that leads to blockages (a frequent occurrence that leads to trouble for the person on duty [*dezhurny*], who has to clean the toilets if the person responsible for the blockage cannot be identified).'[4]

In memoirs of life in the kommunalka we learn too about the individualising of light since each apartment resident had their own light switch; we are told also that paper and matches were on hand to produce smoke to blot out unpleasant smells—as substitutes for nonavailable deodorants. Like the corridor, the bathroom and the kitchen, the toilet was a space for everyone but also a place of utmost privacy. As a room used by all, it suffered the most acutely from community indifference. At the same time, it was the space most urgently in need of individual discretion and hygiene, of mutual consideration. This is where conflicting modes of behaviour meet in the most confined space imaginable. Research into this 'social space' would be worthy of the attention with which a Norbert Elias and others scrutinised the genesis of everyday culture in Western Europe. The great exception here is the subtle and 'thick' description given by Vasile Ernu in his 'Ode to the Soviet Toilet' after his return from the Soviet Union.[5]

We make it too easy for ourselves if we explain such fundamental customs of ordinary life in terms of an ideological programme. It is true that in a speech on the New Economic Policy that Lenin gave on 5 November 1921, on the fourth anniversary of the October Revolution, he referred to public conveniences, which would all be built of gold in the streets of some of the largest cities after the worldwide victory of the proletariat. Toilets of gold—and this at a moment of total economic collapse with millions of people starving. Why must

FIGURE 33.1. Ilya Kabakov, 'Life in the Toilet'. Installation at the Documenta in Kassel, 1992. © VG Bild-Kunst, Bonn 2018. Photo: Emilia and Ilya Kabakov.

'gold toilets', of all things, have to stand as proof of the superiority of socialism?[6] No less noteworthy is the scene in Sergey Eisenstein's film *October*, which was produced for the tenth anniversary of the October Revolution. After the storming of the Winter Palace, a Red Army soldier smashes the porcelain lavatory pan in the imperial apartments. Here the toilet—as an institution and a material object—figures as the symbol of the old world doomed to vanish, as the achievement of the world of 'former people'. St. Petersburg was on its way to becoming a modern metropolis.

To achieve this called for adopting the most modern sanitary facilities, including water closets. British firms were in the lead here, in particular companies such as Tornado, Lawrence and Unitas, all of which supplied the city, and above all the hotels and districts of the middle class, with the latest models and fittings. The 'class hatred' of the insulted and the injured would be aimed at these symbols of bourgeois culture. Maxim Gorky captured scenes from the days of this civil war.

I recollect with revulsion the following event: In 1919 the Congress of Village Poverty took place in St. Petersburg. Several thousand peasants had come from the northern regions and hundreds of people had found accommodation in the Winter Palace of the Romanovs. When the Congress was finished and the delegates had departed it turned out that they had left not only the bathrooms of the Palace in a filthy state, but also a vast number of the most valuable porcelain vases from Sèvres, Dresden and the Orient, which they had used as chamber pots. This was not because there was no alternative—the lavatories of the Palace were in working order and the water supply was adequate. No, this barbarity was the expression of their desire to damage and defile beautiful things. In the two revolutions as well as the war, I have observed hundreds of times the same wish to smash and destroy, to ridicule and befoul objects from the same obscure longing for vengeance.

Viktor Shklovsky had seen Red Army soldiers in Moscow drilling holes in the floor that went right down through to the floor beneath and then using them as lavatories for an entire year.[7]

It is very clear that the antibourgeois feeling of the political elite played a certain role here, even though its members belonged to the bourgeois intelligentsia and obviously enjoyed taking advantage of the facilities and the comfort of the so-called Soviet houses, that is, the old luxury hotels such as the Astoria and L'Europe in Petrograd and the National and Metropol in Moscow. The rhetoric that extended the class struggle to interiors, bathrooms and toilets fuelled the vandalism of the peasant and soldier masses that ran amok in the prevailing absence of punitive measures. 'The toilets, clean and shiny, heated and regularly serviced, together with the various urinals that had become prevalent, had become a symbol of "yesterday's society" for which they could feel only class hatred and proletarian contempt. They had to be destroyed—like churches, public baths and country houses—and history had to be started over again.'[8] Following the Civil War, things calmed down somewhat and certain customs were rehabilitated, as witnessed by the reintroduction of public conveniences. There were even architecture competitions for the construction of underground conveniences in which prominent architects such as

Alexander Gegello took part. As new vocabulary acquired currency, the prerevolutionary *klozet* (WC) or *retiradnik* (restroom) was replaced by the simpler and earthier lavatory (*ubornaya*).

The fact that the toilet crisis—both the public and the private one—was never-ending was less the consequence of any ideological programme than of its inexorable link to the shared apartment and to permanently overcrowded conditions. The light in the kommunalka was always on. This led to disputes at the tenants' meetings in Ilya Ilf and Yevgeny Petrov's *The Little Golden Calf*,[9] in Mikhail Zoshchenko's story 'Guests' of 1927[10] and even in Mikhail Bulgakov's early novel *The Heart of a Dog* of 1925 (not published until 1987) in which Professor Preobrazhensky sums up his view of the matter: 'If, when I go to the lavatory, I, if you'll forgive the expression, begin to piss and miss the bowl, and Zina and Darya Petrovna do the same, then we get Disruption in the lavatory. So it follows that Disruption is in the head.'[11]

The overpopulation of the towns as a consequence of the rapid influx of immigrants from the countryside, as well as the overcrowding in the kommunalkas converted the state of emergency in the lavatories into a permanent crisis. An additional factor was the need for people who had never known of lavatories in their lives to acquire the rituals of basic sanitation and be initiated into the forms of urban life together. An example of the acquisition of basic cultural techniques of the kind that we are familiar with from other large European towns a century earlier is found in rules for the use of toilets in shared apartments:

1. Absolute cleanliness and hygiene are to be observed in the toilet.
2. It is forbidden to throw paper into the toilet basin; it must instead be put into the special bucket or basket placed there for that purpose.
3. The toilet may only be used for a definite length of time. Consideration must be shown to other people in the apartment.
4. The toilet may be used only by fellow occupants (not by guests and relatives) and the hygiene rules must be observed.

5. The toilet must not be filled with extraneous objects (except for those approved by the house committee). Order must be maintained; it is forbidden to burn paper.
6. Standing with one's feet in the toilet basin is forbidden so as to avoid accidents and possible damage.[12]

The introduction of public toilets failed utterly to keep pace with an urban population that grew by leaps and bounds, while the expansion of public services lagged far behind. The denunciation of the toilet as a symbol of a bourgeois lifestyle, combined with mass immigration to the towns, created almost insuperable problems. These problems were merely exacerbated by war and reveal an aspect of the Great Patriotic War that normally goes unmentioned or at best is only ever hinted at. With its bombardments, German armed forces focused heavily on destroying the infrastructure of towns and cities—water supply, sewerage systems, heating and waste disposal—so as to render them unlivable. Ivan Bogdanov is right to point out that 'The fact that there were no epidemics in Leningrad must be regarded as one of the heroic achievements of its citizens. Disease is more terrible than hunger and enemy fire.'[13] Urban destruction meant that there could be no more heating, so water and sewage pipes froze and cracked; people were too weakened to be able to keep lavatories and public conveniences in good order and dispose of waste. Excrement had to be removed manually in buckets and was heaped up in courtyards until it thawed in the spring, turning courtyards and streets into cesspools in the process.[14] The plan of the German besiegers was not just to starve the city's population but to demoralise them as well. Their goal was to ensure that 'the Palmyra of the North', this centre of culture, should die amid its own filth and stench. The speed and discipline with which the inhabitants set about cleaning up and restoring order following the lifting of the siege is all the more astonishing.

The start of the mass-housing programme in the 1960s and the consequent gradual dissolution of the kommunalka played a crucial role in the 'Evolution of the Toilet' (to quote the title of the exhibition in St. Petersburg in 2004). The lavatory became a genuinely private place. The situation of public conveniences was still pretty bad; in comparison with, say, Berlin or Beijing, there were still too few in all Soviet towns and cities. The opening of new public conveniences was always a great event, as was the case when the Kremlin was opened to tourists and had to be equipped with the corresponding facilities.[15] The same can be said of the public toilets opened at the new Kremlin Palace in 1974. As contemporaries recall, this was a sensation. In their splendour and with modern air-conditioning systems, these conveniences were reminiscent of the dressing rooms for dancers: 'Unlike the lavatories outside the Kremlin gates, the underground facilities here were faced with marble, the doors had locks, and the paper came in real rolls, not from the grudging hands of an attendant by the door. Even the soap was free, and it was smooth, just like the stuff that delegates used to receive in Stalin's time.'[16]

The problem of public conveniences had still not been resolved by the very end of the Soviet Union. Real change came only when they were transferred from state and municipal authority into private hands. Then it suddenly became possible to find clean, brightly lit and regularly cleaned toilets. They had become the source of a lucrative business—as had been the case in prerevolutionary times with the 'Assenisatoren', that is, the waste-disposal crews who emptied town cesspits and were also called *zolotari* (goldmakers), because they had turned waste disposal into a business and were able to convert human leftovers into gold. *Pecunia non olet*—money does not stink. As in Roman times, this proverb became current once again. Admittedly, it took a while before people overcame their inner reluctance to pay for the elimination of human excrement. The introduction of pay toilets may have been the most important sign in many people's minds that the communist era in which everyone was equal but treated equally badly really had come to an end. A new era was dawning—the 'capitalist grimace' at the *tualetnaya revolyutsiya*.[17] And in fact, the expansion of the relevant amenities was a far-from-despicable aspect of the improvement in the quality of life in contemporary large towns and cities in Russia, thanks not least to the contribution of cheap labour from the Central Asian republics. It formed part of the emerging service-industry culture, which revolutionary authorities had stigmatised as the culture of menials, of subalterns, as something humiliating and debasing. To their way of thinking, the needs of ordinary citizens were disturbing and the customer an enemy. Stigmatising services as degrading activities had gone alongside the practice of demonstratively changing the use of culturally significant locations—both profane and religious—by transforming them into public toilets. Many churches and chapels were transformed and desecrated in this way. In 1936, for example, the Church of the Kazan Icon of the Mother of God by the north entrance of Red Square was torn down and replaced by a summer café and a public convenience—an iconoclastic action that was supposedly reversed with the rebuilding of the church in 1993.

It was left to the great artist Ilya Kabakov to create an installation that presented the Soviet toilet as a cultural and social topos and to display it in a way that sought neither to unmask nor to denounce, but to inform. His achievement was to anticipate the end of an institution, to provide a historical context for a place that hitherto had not featured in historical accounts but which had never ceased to be vitally important in the everyday life of Soviet citizens.

CHAPTER 34

The 'Moscow Kitchen', or the Rebirth of Civil Society

Nothing ends without some forewarning. In 1969 Andrey Amalrik wrote his essay *Will the Soviet Union Survive until 1984?* in which he analysed the crisis of the late Soviet Empire with what was for the 1960s striking diagnostic accuracy. His prediction of its demise in 1984 was rather more than a playful allusion to George Orwell. At the time, Amalrik had completed his history studies and had already experienced a period of banishment in Siberia. At the end of his text, he invited readers to send feedback to his address at USSR, Moscow G2, Ulitsa Vakhtangova 5, Apartment 5.[1]

The space in which he imagined the end happening, where freedom of speech would be regained, was the Moscow kitchen, a memorable place for those who knew it of old, a legend and distant myth for those born later.

But when the turning point arrived and the Soviet Union dissolved, the community of kitchen inhabitants was taken by surprise and even overwhelmed. The end of the Soviet Union was accompanied by that of its opponents and challengers. With the perestroika years, when everyone could venture at least tentatively to speak their mind, the underground catacombs became superfluous; when the passionate debates about 'What is to be done?', 'Whither Russia?' and 'Who is to blame?' emerged from intimate circles and entered the Palace of Congresses in the Kremlin, reaching millions of people over the TV channels, the need for such subterranean refuges ceased. The samizdat books that had been copied by small groups of people and passed from hand to hand were now available in mass editions and could be bought in bookstalls and newspaper kiosks. In a country where a public sphere had been created, escape underground had become meaningless. People who still engaged in conspiracies had simply failed to keep up with the times.

What the Moscow kitchen was must now be reconstructed from the tales of people who were there, many of whom are still alive. It must be gleaned from the memoirs of people who have now been scattered to the four corners of the globe—the émigrés and exiles who have left the country or were forced to leave it and who have now settled in Tel Aviv, New York, Bloomington or Paris; from the literary remains now archived in Stanford, Leeds or Bremen; in the abandoned bookstalls whose contents are now sold off cheaply by clueless and indifferent descendants in book bazaars in Moscow or the provinces; in the photograph albums containing group portraits of the farewell evening before departure; in the world's art galleries where the works of artists long derided and demonised as decadent nonconformists are now on display.[2] What the Moscow kitchen was can now be gleaned from the chansons and songs of the bards who were born there, who discovered their first audience there and who were helped to discover their own sound by the time of exciting new change in the 1960s and the period when dissidents were persecuted. I have in mind here Bulat Okudzhava, with his guitar and his melancholy voice; Vladimir Vysotsky, his voice hoarse with anger; and the satirical protest songs of Alexander Ginzburg.[3]

Yuly Kim's Memorial for the Moscow Kitchens

It was the bard Yuly Kim who created a memorial for the Moscow kitchens as early as 1991 at 'The End of a Beautiful Era', to quote the title of a poem by Joseph Brodsky. In the initial stanzas of Kim's lengthy poem 'Moscow Kitchens', we find

> Exotic tea-room (pancakes, pies),
> A study, an impassioned den,
> Reception room cum sitting-room
> Or in old-fashioned speech—a salon;
> Pub, for a wild youth dropping in,
> Night's lodging for a homeless bard—
> In a word, it's a Moscow kitchen:
> Ten metres for a hundred folk!

Cut glassware, a confusion of glasses,
Green bottles
With the beloved . . . you know what,
And oh how much of the beloved
Was already tried out with sprats and mint
And offloaded onto the grubby tablecloth
For whole centuries!

The polished glasses
Sometimes with cognac!
And the jokes, the salty ones
About all sorts of things.
Ah pipe-cigarettes, asp-like gloom.
O "Sem Sorok" and "Gypsy maid"
Hey! In chorus and down to the ground!
Hey! Once and once more
L'chaim, you Boyars!
That's how it was, we drank and drank.
We dropped in, sat, smoked
The whole evening until sunrise.
Countless poems were recited and heard.
Tea, the guitars of Vysotsky and Galich,
They too were born here.
Tea with sugar and intellectual bread—nowhere else,
And from time immemorial
The most important thing of all—is the Russian conversation
     by night,
In which everything comes back to the one theme, regardless of
     where You start out, just as everything homes in on a candle
     in the night:
Russia, wondrous Mother!
Where to? Where from? How?
Endless yearning,
Forays out of the darkness into the dark . . .
Where can we find even harder and more convoluted paths?
How to experience so much and to pick up the burden once
     again!

O "Black Marusyas"! [i.e., Black Marias]
O Potma and Dalstroy!
O Lord Jesus!
O Alexander II!
The sleepless cooking in the kitchen
Has gone on forever . . .
And I was there,
Have drunk mead and beer,
And the food all went down well.[4]

Yuly Kim, the son of a Korean who was deported to Central Asia and shot during the Great Terror of 1937, has been one of the legendary bards of the Moscow scene since the 1960s. In this introduction, he conveys a foretaste of the numerous voices, the many genres that could find expression in these nocturnal conversations. The kitchen speaks the language of the multinational state as a whole. Here we find the Central Asian tearoom—the Chaikhana—and the Jewish dance "Sem Sorok", as well as the Hebrew greeting to the Boyars. Here too are the inmates released from the camps in the Far North and the Far East—Potma, Dalstroy—as well as the young people preparing to go into exile. Further on in the poem, the dishes are washed up; the news from the BBC, Voice of America and Radio Liberty blare out from the Spinola radio on the subject of dissident protests. A *nachalnik* (boss) and his assistant make their appearance in the trial against the five people who demonstrated in Red Square against the entry of Warsaw Pact troops into Czechoslovakia on 25 August 1968. Ilya Gabay, condemned and exiled to a camp for anti-Stalinist activities, speaks but so do 'ordinary' Soviet people who embody the vox populi condemnation of people who think differently. Alyona reads out the statement of protest and support on behalf of the accused and condemned dissidents. Alyona knows that this letter will be auctioned for millions one day—'in 200 years'. It becomes absolutely clear by the end of the poem that we are not dealing with the evocation of an idyll. Many of the heroes of that time have gone abroad; many died prematurely, exhausted and marked by their persecution. Ilya Gabay took his own life. Vadim Delaunay, one of the five who helped prepare for the protest on Red Square against the occupation of Czechoslovakia, died in exile in France in 1983 at the age of thirty-five. Yury Galanskov, a veteran of the 1960s, had been given seven years in a camp and died a year before the completion of his sentence in 1972, following the failure to provide him with adequate medical treatment. Anatoly Marchenko died in 1986 after nineteen years' incarceration in the prison in Chistopol. Yuly Kim mentions by name others who died or were driven into exile: Tosha Yakobson, Grisha Podiapolsky, Ira Kaplun, Sasha Galich and Vika Nekrasov.

Kim's poem concludes with a chorus:

> Eternal memory.
> Eternal memory.
> Memory to the end of time.
> O how cruel, how dark and meaningless
> Is our path to the light of day.
> But patiently and undeterred
> the dawn comes nearer with every loss.
> Eternal memory.
> Memory to the end of time.

Yuly Kim's poem is no sentimental reminiscence of a past time but an epitaph for an era and those who created it—without whose voice Russia would never have found its way out of the blind alley of stagnation and onto the road to freedom.

The Moscow Kitchen: A Topography

The Moscow kitchen is not simply a metaphor but also a concrete place, a challenge to a sociology of the late Soviet era which hitherto adopted this phenomenon under the heading of 'dissident movement' insofar as the Academy deigned to notice it at all.[5] Yet the dissident movement itself did not live in a vacuum but had its own place. The 'ten metres' in Kim's poem are to be taken literally. Kitchens of that size had been fitted in the five-storey Khrushchyovki ever since the late 1950s and the subsequent high-rise, large-panel concrete prefabs that were ubiquitous. With the departure from the shared apartment and the move to the two- or three-room apartment, one could for the first time speak of one's own four walls and a private life. One could even put up visitors.[6] Occasional meetings had taken place in the kommunalkas, where the kitchen was the only sizeable room that could be used for private celebrations on a set day after prior agreement with the other parties in the kommunalka. We learn this, for example, from the widow of Alexander Ginzburg, who tells us about the 'Ginzburg kitchen' in a two-storey nineteenth-century timber frame house near the Moscow Polyanka metro station where seventeen families were housed: the Ginzburgs' room was used as a meeting place and subsequently became legendary.[7] The actor Dmitry Nikolaevich Zhuravlyov and his wife, Natalia, conducted discussions in their tiny two-room apartment on the ground floor of the Vakhtangov Theatre cooperative in Ulitsa Vakhtangova. These took place after concerts or theatre performances in the kitchen, between hotplates, washbasins and a constantly dripping water pipe. They featured a sometimes illustrious cast of doctors, actors, writers and musicians, including Anna Akhmatova, Svyatoslav Richter, Boris Pasternak and Alexander Vertinsky. There were readings from new works; new recordings of the Matthew Passion or *Lohengrin* with Dietrich Fischer-Dieskau were played. For over twenty-six years the painfully cramped apartment of the poet Mikhail Aisenberg in Bolshoi Kazyonny Pereulok provided a regular meeting place for a changing set of guests which included poets, critics and authors. Studios too, such as that of the painter Dmitry Bisti on Povarskaya or of the sculptor Vadim Sidur, acted as meeting points. The historian Vadim Borisov conducted his Moscow kitchen in a five-room kommunalka in an old building where as many as forty to fifty people might turn up on special occasions, often unannounced.[8] No great effort would be needed to produce a map of the Moscow-kitchen landscape and describe the various patterns and calibre of this form of sociability more precisely, much as the literary historians of Russian Formalism did for the nineteenth century. In addition, seminar-like sessions in which talks were given and discussed, or meetings involving formal invitations—the opening of a research institute or an evening of lieder in a palace of culture—can be included in the same category as the 'Moscow kitchen'.

Even a casual glance will reveal some of the phenomenological features of this form of social interaction. Many different functions, motives and individual groups came together. They included circles of friends, albeit open circles—guests could be brought along. There was an inner circle but no conspiratorial grouping. Few such groups had any kind of agenda; instead they discussed issues of the day: the current situation, the latest broadcasts from foreign stations, solidarity actions for fellow campaigners or dissidents who had been threatened or arrested, such practical matters as collecting medicines, food parcels, the addresses of interested parties or the names of sympathetic lawyers. The kitchen was a substitute for such nonavailable public institutions as cafés,[9] where successful and prominent figures of Moscow society met one another. But the prototype was the Moscow kitchen, where members of the intelligentsia—mostly writers, academics from diverse disciplines, friends and acquaintances—met up to debate the 'eternal questions' about Russia: 'Whose fault is it?' and 'What is to be done?' In this improvised realm of hospitality, which had become something of a routine, there was always something to eat—rice salad, fried bread/*grenki*, Olivier salad—and always something to drink as well—vodka, Bulgarian or Moldavian wine, Armenian cognac, presents from the Beryozka shops (where purchases had to be made with Western currency).

These were meetings of like-minded people who made fun of dogmatism, censorship, officialese and disciplinary action, people who supplied one another with forbidden literature or who even copied such writings over days and weeks so as to maintain the circulation of self-published writings. They were a paradise for people who regaled their friends with jokes and anecdotes, for people who enjoyed listening to the stories brought back from visits abroad or from the Siberian 'province'. Sometimes there were quarrels with the neighbours if things got too loud or too many guests had come. There was a great deal of smoking. The boundaries of academic disciplines were not respected: physicists expressed their opinion about versification; poets discussed plans for diverting Siberian rivers. Foreigners were welcome—journalists for the most part, the correspondents of foreign newspapers who could make themselves understood in Russian. This was where the Western left, who for the most part had no idea about 'actually existing socialism', met Russian dissidents who were able to explain to them just what the Soviet realities were.[10] Long before the proclamation of the 'new opacity' (by Habermas), the distinction between 'left' and 'right' became increasingly confused. For foreign visitors—academics on short stays in Moscow, directors and artists in transit—there was much to learn if they were concerned to make contact with the Moscow scene. Thus the German filmmaker Hark Bohm and Jane Fonda turned up at the soirées of Alexander Mitta, the film director; the US beatnik poet Allen Ginsberg could be seen chez Alexander Ginzburg.[11] The Moscow kitchen became the meeting point for the home-grown intelligentsia and foreigners of every kind: Wolf Biermann at the home of Yevgeniya Ginzburg, Heinrich Böll at the home of Lev Kopelev and Raisa Orlova, Hans Magnus Enzensberger chez Margarita Aliger at the House of Writers in Lavrushinsky Pereulok.[12]

Moscow kitchens were also to be found in dachas, the nests of networks, of literary and intellectual clans. The Moscow kitchens built bridges not only between disciplines and professions but also between generations. There people who had experienced the Stalin era and the war came together: there were the offspring of parents who had been oppressed, condemned and shot; there were returnees from the camps as well as the young intelligentsia experiencing censorship and repression for themselves. They included Yevgeny Gnedin, Walter Benjamin's contact; the captivatingly elegant Liliya Brik and her salon; Yevgeniya Ginzburg; Nadezhda Mandelstam, the widow of the poet Osip Mandelstam, who had died in the camps. The Moscow kitchens became the centres of networks where ideas, manuscripts and books smuggled in from abroad circulated. Here you could find the insider tips of the day, such as Abdurakhman Avtorkhanov's classic *The Technology of Power*, which had appeared in samizdat. You could hear gramophone records of works by Mahler, Berg and Schoenberg. Kitchen communities crystallised around political trials and gained their strength from mutual help and support. The wave of repression that began in 1965 with the trials of Andrey Sinyavsky and Yuly Daniel, the publication of the trial proceedings in the 'White Book', the records of the trial of Joseph Brodsky, the trial of Andrey Amalrik, the press conferences, the battle to prevent sentencing members of the

FIGURE 34.1. 'Moscow kitchen' in the house of Yuly Aykhenvald and Valeriya Gerlina-Aykhenvald, Moscow 1978–1979. Gathered here are—from left to right—Joels, Tamara Margolina, unknown (with a beard); Vladimir Rudov and Alexandra Aykhenvald, standing in the doorway; in front of them: Sonja Margolina, the back view of an unknown man, the bard Yuly Kim, Kolya Miletich, the Swedish journalist Disa Håstad, Valeriya Gerlina-Aykhenvald; in front of them Lena Zhumilova and Alyosha Chantsev. © Memorial Society Archive, Aykhenvald Foundation.

opposition to enforced stays in psychiatric units, the defence of the group that protested against the occupation of Czechoslovakia, the solidarity with the dissidents fighting to be allowed to emigrate to Israel—these were the moments when the Moscow kitchens came into their own.

The guest book in the salon of the translator Yelena Golyzheva and the screen writer Nikolay Otten was representative of an important aspect of Russian literature, according to one of her regular guests. More generally, we can say that the guest books that were or could have been maintained would provide a Who's Who of an intelligentsia that had been awakened to a new life. Group photos showing the departure of friends to travel abroad or into exile depict what amounts to the elite of civil resistance. One of the photographs from the Ginzburg kitchen shows such veteran dissidents as Boris

Shragin, Natalia Gorbanevskaya, Sasha Anonov, Grigory Pomerants, Alexander Yesenin-Volpin and Yuly Kim; we can also recognise Andrey and Gyuzel Amalrik, Pavel Litvinov, Arina Ginzburg and Alexander Ginzburg.

The fact that the concept of Moscow kitchens has become established shows that we are dealing essentially with a phenomenon based in capital cities. There were also Kyiv, Tallinn, Tashkent and Riga kitchens that have become known as 'provincial kitchens' and often functioned as 'boosters' for the formation of regional and local elites during the perestroika phase.

In summary we can say that the Moscow kitchens served as a substitute for the missing public sphere and such semipublic institutions as cafés. They were a rebirth of the salon and the circle (*kruzhok*) of the nineteenth and twentieth centuries, which were still to be found in the 1920s, only now of course they subsisted in conditions of unlimited control at the hands of an omnipotent state and the emergence of an international press.[13] They were cosmopolitan in a nation shut off from the outside world; they ignored the boundaries of discipline and status and were interdisciplinary in an eclectic and dilettantish way. Conversation was in many respects a substitute for political action, which was closed to nonconformist intellectuals and liable to penalties. A place of nighttime conversations, 'conversations about God and the world', a place of self-exploration and reflection, a congregation of the marginalised, a bolthole for the oppressed—the Moscow kitchens were all that and much more; a space in which something new was born or expressed.

The 1960s Generation and the Formation of the Dissident Movement

The place we are speaking about here belongs to an era that has been given different names by contemporaries and historians: de-Stalinisation, the Thaw, era of 'détente and peaceful coexistence', Renaissance.[14] Each of these names puts the emphasis on a particular aspect of the period. There was Khrushchev's settling of accounts with the 'personality cult' of Stalin's era. 'The Thaw' was the title of

a 1954 novel by Ilya Ehrenburg which used the meteorological metaphor to speak of the new liberal spirit. 'Peaceful coexistence' signalled
that the Cold War, the potential Third World War, was at an end and
a new age of collaboration between different systems should begin,
coexistence between East and West based on mutual recognition.
'Renaissance' referred mainly to linking up once again with a culture
that had been cut off and destroyed by the Revolution and, above all,
by the Stalinist regime.

The age may be best characterised by Alexander Solzhenitsyn's assertion, in the collection of essays *From Under the Rubble* (reprinted in
1974), that the intelligentsia was now 'able to breathe again'.[15] He was
referring to an intellectual climate in which political reforms, a generation change, an opening to the outer world, a greater acceptance of
domestic conflict, a new self-confidence on the part of Soviet society
and a general willingness to look to the future had all come together.
The Moscow kitchen, which was no institution but an informal means
of communication, of networking, was a creation of the 1960s; it had
been incubating in the decade since Stalin's death and was broken off
when Khrushchev was forced to resign in 1961, an event followed by a
renewed phase of repression—a re-Stalinisation—and a long decade of
stagnation under Brezhnev, which lasted until it was finally superseded
by Gorbachev's policy of glasnost and perestroika. The turning point
was marked by the trial of Yuly Daniel and Andrey Sinyavsky in 1965
and the government backlash against the growing feeling of solidarity
with the victims of persecution for whom the new term 'dissidents' soon
gained acceptance, although the latter preferred the Russian term for
nonconformists: 'people who think differently'.

The trial of Daniel and Sinyavsky was a turning point ideologically
as well. The new beginning in the late 1950s and early 1960s had aimed
at returning to a true Marxism, a true Leninism and a socialism with
a human face—the key slogan of the Prague Spring. With Brezhnev's
persecution of the domestic Soviet opposition and the overthrow of
the Prague Spring, the call for a 'true socialism' was finally exposed
as an illusion. The opposition began to coalesce around the idea of
the defence of basic human and civil rights, independently of the
political or ideological orientation of the groups or individuals affected by state repression. The key difference was the adherence in

practice to the rights of free speech, free travel and freedom of assembly, rights guaranteed even in the Soviet Constitution. The Thaw and de-Stalinisation of the 1950s were implemented with the idea of renewing Marxism and it is not just coincidence that the major Twenty-Second Party Congress of 1961, where the decision was taken to remove Stalin's body from Lenin's Mausoleum and to engage in an even more thorough settling of accounts with Stalinism, should also have been the Congress that resolved on the new Party Programme, which proclaimed that the current generation would be the one to experience the advent of communism.[16]

Whatever ideological emphases were prominent at the time, something fundamental had shifted—however unintentionally and gradually—namely the mood, the life feeling, people's behaviour and modes of interacting with one another. Political rivals were no longer executed but sent to the provinces or into retirement (as was the case with Kaganovich and Molotov). Hundreds of thousands of inmates returned from the camps and, emblematically, a single ordinary prisoner became the literary sensation of the 'Thaw': Alexander Solzhenitsyn's *One Day in the Life of Ivan Denisovich* appeared in 1962 in a mass edition of *Novy mir*, the literary magazine. After decades of retreat, isolation and quarantine, the Soviet Union, Russia, resumed contact with the outside world. Tens of thousands of young people came from all over the globe to the World Festival of Youth and Students in Moscow in 1957. Hundreds of thousands poured into the American National Exhibition in Moscow in 1959. Tens of thousands gathered at the Mayakovsky statue for the readings on the 'Day of Poetry' with such eloquent stars of the young generation as Yevgeny Yevtushenko and Andrey Voznesensky. Soviet engineers built the Aswan Dam and were active in many countries of the Third World; in the same way, Moscow received state visits from nonaligned nations (the Bandung Conference of 1955). Soviet athletes triumphed in Melbourne in 1956, in Rome in 1960 and in Tokyo in 1964. A new cult of heroes that went beyond the military became popular; young people wanted to become champion high jumpers like Valery Brumel or the goalkeeper Lev Yashin and even among intellectuals there were some who had a foible for the intellectual weightlifter Yury Vlasov. Something of the fascination of the Cuban Revolution, of Fidel Castro and Che Guevara even extended to the Soviet Union, which was grey and bureaucratic in comparison. The 1960s were years of discovery and rediscovery. Soviet artists fed up with socialist realism discovered the Soviet avant-garde of the 1920s; architects proclaimed a 'second modernism' and started to reappear at the world exhibitions. Christian Dior got his models to parade and be marvelled at in Red Square and GUM. Scholarship separated itself from the Procrustean bed of dialectical materialism. Thousands of the victims of the Stalinist purges were rehabilitated; topics taboo hitherto—the crimes of the Stalin era, Stalin's role in the run-up to the Soviet-German War—began to be studied by historians even if they did not reach the point of a general settling of accounts, let alone legal proceedings.[17] Entire disciplines that had suffered gravely were reinstated—from genetics to sociology. A new passion for truth spread rapidly, concentrated initially among the natural scientists, mathematicians and physicists. The launching of Sputnik into orbit round the Earth on 4 October 1957 was something of a triumph, as was Yury Gagarin's journey into outer space in 1961. These were dramatic times in which everything seemed possible. Harvey 'Van' Cliburn's participation and triumph in the First International Tchaikovsky Competition in 1958 and Khrushchev's 1959 tour of the United States are instances of this. This was a Khrushchev who was not plagued by an inferiority complex, was more self-assured and appreciative of the country so that he was able to express his admiration for the American way of life, while his wife Nina enchanted both press and public with her charm and sagacity. But this was the same Khrushchev who produced his famous outbursts against abstract art and 'decadent bohemians' during the Manege Exhibition of 1962, the Cuba crisis, the capricious swings of economic policy and administrative reform, the massacre of the protesting workers of Novocherkassk which was carried out with his knowledge and the malicious and disastrous atheist campaigns against the Orthodox Church.[18] And yet, notwithstanding all this, the Khrushchev years succeeded in bringing about a 'climate change' in Russia. The Twenty-Second Congress of the CPSU in 1961 did in fact approve a programme for communism but the true revolution that transformed the lives of millions in a very short time was really more concerned with consumption, with cars that one could actually buy, albeit only after a lengthy wait, and above all, with the ability to move out of the shared apartment and into one's own four walls.

Alexander Genis and Pyotr Vail may have painted the most subtle portrait of the 1960s and the generation that profited from the Thaw but which was driven into confrontation with the newly emerging state power at the end of the Khrushchev years.[19] A number of factors contributed to this fundamental change in mentality: the impact of Hemingway, Faulkner and Salinger on the Soviet-Russian literary scene; the perception that many Soviet citizens had experienced the assassination of US President Kennedy in 1963 as a tragedy; the opening-up of their world, with Heinrich Böll and Hans Magnus Enzensberger in Moscow, the reunion of Russian jazz and American jazz: Duke Ellington's tour in the Soviet Union in 1971. There had been two or three decades in which the political system and its institutions had remained unchanged, while the atmosphere, the lifeworld and the 'soft structures' had altered irreversibly. A new tone had become possible, sustained by irony and distance. Now there were everyday heroes, little truths before which the great truth of class, the classics and the Party all capitulated. The current situation was that scientists like Sergey Korolyov or Andrey Sakharov and bards like Vladimir Vysotsky could unobtrusively become the key figures of their era. This was the age of an inner détente, a period when people could catch their breath and gather their strength—and it had a sharp dénouement in 1968.

Since all non-Bolshevik groups, parties and organisations had been suppressed and destroyed from the beginnings of Bolshevik rule (and in the Stalin years, Khrushchev had been one of the most steadfast executors of the reign of terror), the independent creation of autonomous associations, however discreet, was a radical innovation. Every form of independence questioned the legitimacy of the enforced conformity and the all-powerful state felt justified in reacting as brutally as if its very existence were threatened—it was in fact under threat, given the fragility of its own achievements and legitimacy. As early as the 1940s and early 1950s there had been illegal and conspiratorial underground organisations—the Communist Party of Youth, the Fighting League for the Revolutionary Cause, the All-Russian Social and Christian League for the Liberation of the People; most of these had a 'truly revolutionary' programme that was directed against 'Stalinist deformation'.

And yet there was no continuity with the currents of the period before the Revolution or the 1920s. The brutal hunting down, internment and exiling of all non-Bolshevik groupings, the systematic physical destruction of every conceivable anti-Soviet opposition in the 1930s—the members of conservative organisations, officers of the White Armies, Socialist Revolutionaries, Mensheviks, returning émigrés, representatives of nationalist communist trends, supporters of Trotskyites or other factions—had done away with continuity and tradition of every kind. This meant that after the war the core of all resistance groups was recruited from among the rebellious young and activists from national underground movements, above all in Western Ukraine and the Baltic states. The texts of the 'Old Guard' had disappeared into the poison cupboards; to be found in possession of them or even just reading them had grave repercussions.[20]

The rise of the dissident movement and the founding of associations to defend civil rights can therefore be regarded as something new following the creation of a tabula rasa. Of course this does not exclude the possibility that historical precedents were in the air. The circles/*kruzhki* of the democratic intelligentsia may well have had the—often terrorist—groups of Narodniks and Socialist Revolutionaries, the conspiratorial tradition of the professional Russian revolutionaries, in mind.[21] All groups and movements were affected by the enforced conformity and suppression. That includes the humanist and scientific intelligentsia, the western-liberal and the Orthodox-Pan Slavist intellectuals, the Great Russian nationalists and the various national oppositions—Lithuanian, Estonian, Ukrainian and Georgian, etc. The antitotalitarian consensus arose less from any coherent theory of totalitarianism than from direct experience and the need to defend oneself. It grew, in other words, from the solidarity with people likewise under threat. That is what generated the explosive power of the dissident movement and exposed the impotence of Soviet power.

A further factor was that the conditions for disagreements between individuals and the state were radically altered by the new methods of communication and obtaining information. Every event in Moscow or some other distant point could now be relayed back to the nation by foreign broadcasters. An event in one place could become a news item for discussion throughout the nation. The introduction of press conferences, the dissemination of statements and open letters meant that whereas formerly one had to reckon only with on-the-spot protests, there were now worldwide reactions that required a response, even once the self-interest of the Western powers engaged in the Cold War had been discounted. The radio station became a powerful platform, the mouthpiece of a small but influential minority. The different groupings did the obvious thing. They were less interested in elaborating ideological programmes than in organising ways of defending themselves, in communicating and in sticking together in the face of persecution, isolation and fragmentation, and in strengthening aids to self-help and self-publication. In the process they constantly appealed to the rights embedded in the constitution. By insisting on basic human and civil rights, what was in quantitative terms a minority and even a peripheral movement was able to develop an explosive force, albeit assisted by the state's evident inability to produce a modus vivendi with its detractors.

A number of key moments can be identified in the emergence and growth of the civil rights movement.[22]

- The demonstration in Pushkin Square on 5 December 1965, the 'Day of the Soviet Constitution', to achieve permission for the public to attend the trial of Daniel and Sinyavsky. It was the first unofficial demonstration in Moscow for many decades.
- The trial of Daniel and Sinyavsky and their sentencing to a labour camp in 1966 unleashed a broad movement of solidarity between prominent artists and intellectuals.
- The demonstration on 22 January 1967 against the arrest of Yury Galanskov, Alexey Dobrovolsky and Vera Lashkova.
- On 30 April 1968, the 'Chronicle of Current Events' appeared in Moscow for the first time. For fifteen years this constituted the intellectual 'backbone' of the civil rights movement. The impetus behind the founding of this samizdat bulletin came from Natalia Gorbanevskaya and provided information about human rights violations in the Soviet Union and the struggle to establish

human rights there. Up to 1983 sixty-four editions of the 'Chronicle' appeared. For publishing the 'Chronicle', the following were arrested and sentenced to various periods in the camps: Yury Shikhanovich, Gabriel Superfin, Ivan Sergeevich Kovalyov, Alexander Lavut, Tatiana Velikanova and Anatoly Yakobson.

— The demonstration in Moscow on 17 May 1968 by the Crimean Tatars. Several hundred Tatars demonstrating to be allowed to return to the Crimea were sent back to Uzbekistan.

— The protest in Red Square in Moscow on 25 August 1968 against the occupation of the CSSR by troops of the Warsaw Pact. Beneath the slogan 'For our freedom and yours', Natalia Gorbanevskaya, Larisa Bogoraz, Viktor Faynberg, Konstantin Babitsky, Vadim Delaunay, Vladimir Dremlyuga and Pavel Litvinov met at the place of execution.

— The 9–11 October 1968 trial of five of the Red Square demonstrators: Konstantin Babitsky, Larisa Bogoraz, Vadim Delaunay, Vladimir Dremlyuga and Pavel Litvinov.

— The arrest of Petro Grigorenko in 1969 followed by committal to psychiatric institutions, emigration and loss of citizenship in 1977.[23]

— The expulsion of Joseph Brodsky in 1972 after several trials and periods in prison, as well as the loss of citizenship.

— The expulsion of Alexander Solzhenitsyn in 1974.[24]

— The bulldozing of the exhibition of the Moscow Conceptualists in December 1974.[25]

— The foundation of the Moscow Helsinki Group in 1976, followed by its successors in Kyiv, Vilnius and Tbilisi.[26]

— The foundation of working groups to investigate psychiatric abuse.

— The deportation of Vladimir Bukovsky in 1976 (exchanged for Luis Corvalán, general secretary of the Communist Party of Chile).

— The condemnation of the Jewish human rights activist Anatoly Shcharansky (now known as Natan Sharansky) in 1976 and deportation in 1986 (exchanged for a Soviet spy on the Glienicke Bridge in Berlin).

— The arrest and forced committal to a psychiatric hospital of Vladimir Klebanov, the founder of the Association of the Free Trade Unions, in 1977.[27]

— The internal exile of Andrey Sakharov to Gorky in 1980, accompanied by his wife Yelena Bonner.[28]

When Andrey Sakharov and Yelena Bonner returned to Moscow in 1986 from exile in Gorky, the entire system holding power together at the time was in the process of dissolution. Until then the common opponent—the CPSU, the Soviet authorities, the secret service—had held the various oppositional groups together. This alliance constituted the strength of the movement, in other words, the democratic movement tended to be defined by their common enemy. This led them to defer their disagreements among themselves, scarcely leaving them enough energy to develop their own 'positive' programmes for the future.

The dissident movement formulated and concentrated all the ideas and forces already taking shape in the thinking population of the late Soviet Union. This was also the basis of the ideas with which the Party leadership operated. It was well aware—once the grey-haired leadership was out of the way, following the deaths within a very brief timespan of Brezhnev, Chernenko and Andropov—that things could not go on as they were. It had therefore introduced perestroika to rescue the prevailing system by revamping the old idea of 'socialism with a human face'. Everything pointed to the fact that at long last the hour of the 1960s generation had struck, the moment for which that generation had waited a lifetime.

'The Great Don't Stay Great, the Order Is Turning'

The 1960s generation helped pave the way for change but they didn't expect it to come from above, let alone from the general secretary of the CPSU. The dissident milieu provided the key ideas, the spokespeople, the slogans and the authors; it defined the new language regime, the *sound* of perestroika. But the more their demands were met, the less their opinion was wanted. The cohorts of 1968 worked to make sure they were no longer needed. They supplied the editors-in-chief of magazines such as *Ogonyok, Druzhba narodov* and *Novy mir* which now published subject matter that previously circulated only in samizdat. They could now devise programmes to publish everything previously

banned and in this way they changed the image that Soviet people
had of themselves. What used to be the viewpoint of the marginalised,
the outsiders, went mainstream—or so it seemed for a moment. The
discussions about Russia, about 'Who is guilty?' and 'What is to be
done?', vanished from the Moscow kitchens and entered the public
sphere. They could be heard in the Kremlin Palace of Congresses, in
live transmissions of parliamentary debates whose conclusions no
one could predict in advance, in the headlines of the popular press,
and in the newspaper kiosks where everything from the *Wall Street
Journal* to *Libération* to *Der Spiegel* was freely available.

What had kept the opposition together—the common enemy, the
censorship and the KGB—had disappeared.[29] What once had called
for a struggle full of sacrifices—emigration to Germany, to Israel or
to the United States—now depended more on the procedures of the
target countries and their readiness to accept immigrants and to
grant visas. Soviet Germans who had counted in the millions now
left the country in hordes to return to their 'first homeland'. The
number of Jews dwindled once the post-1968 Aliyah got underway,
while new Jewish communities came into being elsewhere in the
world. Nationalists, Pan-Slavists and monarchists could at long last
spread their wings and rewrite history in their search for the Holy
Russia that had vanished. Eurasians who had hitherto been confined
to tiny intellectual circles around such figures as Lev Gumilyov were
now appointed to university chairs and built up think tanks close to
the Kremlin. The ideas of the liberal intelligentsia, which understood
little enough about the market economy—where, indeed, could they
have learned about it?—turned out to be far removed from reality and
in many ways little short of disaster. There was a collapse of the central economy and its supply chains; the liberal intelligentsia started
on reforms which resembled chaos more than a planned transformation of the nation into a society with a functioning rule of law. And in
general, the Moscow kitchens bore the stamp of humanist and literary ideas; participants understood a lot about values and traditions
but hardly anything of the economy, the market or investments. They
boasted brilliant essayists and journalists, scholars who had long
waited for their opportunity to return to the international scientific
community, and museum experts who at once joined in the world

of exhibitions and festivals. But the successful organisers of the post-Soviet world tended to come not from the Moscow kitchens but rather from the upper echelons of the Komsomol organisations; from the new blood on the Party career ladders, the dacha cooperatives of the ministries, including the KGB; from the families of diplomats and the elite schools, the faculties of economics, computer sciences, mathematics, finance and the international business schools. These individuals had learned early on to navigate in the black markets and when the crisis point arrived, they knew just where to be in order to acquire their first million. Quite soon the brain drain to the richer pickings abroad started up—the more so, the more sluggishly their own country responded to the great opportunity that had finally arrived. Never in history had a kleptocratic class been swept into power at such speed.

The intelligentsia from the contemplative spaces of the capital had no chance at all compared to such greed and will to power. Their loss of significance and status was dramatic, as was the realisation that they had ceased to be the conscience and voice of the nation, now that the people had spoken—in elections, parliament and demonstrations. The intelligentsia had thought of themselves as a community of the spirit with claims to be a moral authority; now, they were abandoning this position in order to proclaim their rebirth or transformation into intellectuals of a European type. But it was too soon to speak of the end of the intelligentsia in the 1990s. A quarter of a century after the demise of the Soviet Union and living as they are under the aegis of Vladimir Putin, the mission of the intelligentsia has not yet been exhausted. Free speech is again under attack, the media have been forced into line, and independent groupings that aspire to organise into political parties are being silenced and criminalised. Vigorous independent thought is expressed on the internet and in social media. Just as the dissolution of the Moscow kitchen was once an index of normalisation, so now the renewed withdrawal from the public sphere is the best proof that the return to normality has been thwarted. The heirs of the 1960s generation have come under pressure once again, only this time they need not retreat to the Moscow kitchens. Instead, they have an incomparably larger and more effective space at their disposition, namely the internet, social media, as well as the return to the streets and squares—something we can see from the demonstrations against electoral fraud and corruption.

The birthplace of civil society can be reconstructed today from the literary estates of people who went into exile, where they died. It can be seen from the memoirs and autobiographies of the protagonists that were greatly in demand during the Cold War but have been largely forgotten. These intellectuals are recalled in a few places, such as the exhibitions of the Sakharov Centre or the civil rights society Memorial. The members of the 'second liberation movement' will be as significant as those of the first, which led to the downfall of the Tsarist Empire. The names of the liberators of the 1960s—from Amalrik to Solzhenitsyn, from Larisa Bogoraz to Sakharov, from Gorbanevskaya to Alexander Zinoviev—stand for the ancient insight that Bertolt Brecht gave expression to in his 'Song of the Moldau':

> On the bed of the Moldau, the stones are churning,
> The days of our rulers are ending fast.
> The great don't stay great, the order is turning,
> The night has twelve hours, but day comes at last.
> The times are now changing, the darkness receding
> The plans of the mighty must finally fail.
> They're strutting like cocks with severed necks bleeding
> The times are now changing. Force cannot prevail.
> On the bed of the Moldau, the stones are churning,
> The days of our rulers are ending fast.
> The great don't stay great, the order is turning,
> The night has twelve hours, but day comes at last.[30]

PART VII

Landscapes, Public Spaces

CHAPTER 35

Gorky Park: A Garden for the New Human Being

Parks have always been more than just slivers of nature. They were designs for a happy life and every age, even the Soviet age, has had its own dream landscapes. 'Parks of culture and recreation', as they were known, were to be found everywhere in the USSR—in Leningrad, Baku, Tashkent, Magadan. Their entrances were imposing gateways and broad avenues with extraordinarily comfortable benches of an identical design throughout the entire Union. There were central squares for 'social activities' but also secluded corners to which to withdraw. The basic elements of these culture and recreation parks included the giant wheel you could see from afar and the artificial lake you could ride around in pedal or rowing boats. The open-air theatres featured stars of the Soviet stage or folklore ensembles. On holidays, military brass bands played patriotic marches in music pavilions—'The Farewell of Slavyanka' and 'On the Hills of Manchuria'. Elsewhere in the park there were children's playgrounds with swings, carousels and sports fields. The gravel paths usually led to a central fountain. Urns, plaster statues of athletes and sometimes sculptures of frogs and bears stood beneath the trees. In the winter, skaters and ice-hockey players circled on the artificially frozen asphalt surface until late at night. The parks filled up on major Soviet public holidays. The loudspeakers blared; there was dancing. Silence did not fall again until the fireworks were over.

The culture and recreation parks were an institution of Soviet life—like the parade on Red Square, the kommunalka, the queue, the club and the performance of *Swan Lake* in the Bolshoi Theatre. This 'new type of park' was created in the heroic phase of the Soviet Union during the 1930s. The 'new human beings' were supposed not just to recuperate there but also to enjoy themselves; not just entertain themselves but also seek further education and physical fitness. The divide between work and leisure time was to be eliminated, as was the distinction between individual and society, between 'conscious organisation from above' and 'spontaneous agency' from below.[1] As we learn from a document from the early 1930s, the Soviet park ought to be a 'recreation, amusement and culture complex'. Nothing about it was accidental, neither the lines of vision nor the style of the sculptures, neither the organisation of the programme nor the signposts governing the movements of the streams of visitors. As a total artwork of organised happiness, it combined elements of education—and Luna Park, stadium and children's playground, 'strength through joy' and Disneyland. And yet it was something quite unique, containing as it did the history of Soviet civilisation, its early power of mobilisation and its drawn-out agony later. The rise of the park to the status of a topos of Soviet culture began where it ended: in Moscow's Gorky Park.[2]

The Staging of a Gesamtkunstwerk

In the General Plan for the Transformation of Moscow of 1935, a space was set aside for the Central Gorky Park of Culture and Recreation, one of the principal projects alongside the building of the metro; the construction of the Moscow-Volga Canal, which would turn Moscow into the 'Port of Five Seas'; and the building of the monstrous 420-metre-high Palace of the Soviets.[3] With a fivefold increase in green spaces, Moscow would become 'the richest in parks of any capital city in the world'. Gorky Park would be a civic garden at the very heart of the city, in addition to the large, already existing park areas such as Sokolniki and Izmailovo and the parks of the nobility's town houses. Before the Revolution the space had been occupied by a municipal rubbish dump. In 1923 the first All-Russian Agricultural and Handicraft Industrial Exhibition was opened there to display the achievements of this agrarian country and the extent of its recovery under the New Economic Policy. Over three million people visited what was an exhibition, a fair, a market and a trading centre all in one. The Soviet Union's top architects had designed the pavilions, built of wood. They included Konstantin Melnikov's Constructivist Makhorka

Pavilion, an icon of Soviet avant-garde art.[4] In 1928 the exhibition site was vacated in favour of establishing a provisional park, which was then renamed in Maxim Gorky's honour. In the Sturm und Drang years of the first Five-Year Plan, it was primarily the stage for meetings and for mass processions to celebrate the cultural-revolutionary aspirations of communist youth—not, in other words, a place for people out for a stroll or general relaxation. Only after numerous competitions and inclusion in the General Plan for the Transformation of Moscow did the park acquire the shape that turned it into the prototype of the Soviet culture and recreation park.[5]

Moscow's planners took up the idea, originally floated before the Revolution, of a city park close to the centre; in this respect they were merely following other large metropolises. This location was all the more essential as Moscow had experienced an unprecedented population explosion. Between 1929 and 1939 the population had doubled to over four million, chiefly because of the flight of peasants from the land following the imposed collectivisation. The planners and architects of the new Moscow looked around for precedents in Berlin, London, Paris and New York. The Soviet architecture and town-planning journals of the day are full of articles about Renaissance gardens, the grounds of Versailles and Frederick Olmsted's Central Park.[6] The architects studied the native Russian tradition as found in the great parks of Pavlovsk, Peterhof and Tsarskoe Selo. Overall planning was put in the hands of Konstantin Melnikov.[7] Alexander Vlasov was an admirer of classical and Renaissance architecture, as emerges from his notes on a study trip that took him to Athens, Rome, Nîmes and Paris. He knew his way around the problems of the modern big city and was also familiar with the semantics of the English landscaped garden. He was critical of the radical designs of the Soviet Constructivists of the 1920s, accusing them of thinking of gardens purely as parade grounds for political demonstrations with no room for individual recreation or culture.[8]

Gorky Park could be easily reached from the new Park Kultury metro station. It stretches along the Moskva, whose water level had been raised and whose embankments had been enclosed in granite right up to the natural 'Sparrow Hills Amphitheatre' where the towers of the Lomonosov Moscow State University would later be built. The

aim was to create a coherent complex with the Luzhniki sports facilities. The park incorporated parts of the old Neskuchny Garden that
had belonged to an aristocratic estate which subsequently housed the
Academy of Sciences. From Gorky Park a view had been created that
went via the monumental Krymsky Bridge built in 1928 to the historical city centre, to the point where the Cathedral of Christ the Saviour used to stand and where, after its demolition in December 1931,
the Palace of the Soviets was supposed to reach up to the heavens.
No matter where park visitors chose to stand, they would never be
surrounded purely by 'nature' but would always move in sight of the
Lenin statue on the Palace of the Soviets and the axes leading up to
or away from that.[9]

A Complex for a Happy Life

Visitors reached the central fountain square via the principal avenue
and then spread out over the park paths into the different sections—
the squares of 'collective enthusiasm' with agitprop, dance and song;
the secluded reading rooms and pavilions where you could play
chess; and the 'picnic zones'. The herbaceous borders changed according to the seasons and the general political line and depicted the
profiles of Party leaders, the blast furnaces of Magnitogorsk, rising
production graphs or the 'Sixth of the Earth', as the Soviet Union was
known. Urns, sculptures and pavilions in neoclassical style punctuated the landscape. At key points, statues could be seen, which
soon, reproduced a thousand times in plaster or bronze, became the
aesthetic core and cultural code of the park throughout the Soviet
Union: Samuil Makhtin's *Boy with Fish*, Abram Telyatnikov's *Woman
Pioneer with Gas Mask*, Ivan Shadr's *Girl with an Oar*, criticised by an
overzealous critic as a 'boudoir figure'.[10] In the depths of the park
there was an open-air theatre that would seat twenty thousand, a
central summer circus, restaurants and the various facilities essential to bringing thousands of visitors through the park every day
without a hitch: a police station and first-aid centre, the park administration and even a kindergarten, known as 'a living cloakroom',
to use the nomenclature of the day, where parents could deposit

their children. In addition, there were numerous sports facilities, including a parachute jump, a swimming stadium on the Moskva and a jetty for river excursions and regattas.[11]

The key feature of the culture and recreation parks of the Stalinist era, however, was not the creation of a park landscape but the movement of 'mass visitors'. The park became the stage of an awe-inspiring drama. It was this drama that attracted the many prominent visitors to the Soviet capital to Gorky Park—from Lion Feuchtwanger and George Bernard Shaw to Oskar Maria Graf and Romain Rolland. Even such an experienced and critical observer as Klaus Mehnert confessed: 'Like all foreign visitors I too spent a day in the Park of Culture and Recreation, as it is so nicely named. I am always happy to go to Gorky Park, a gigantic park that can accommodate tens of thousands of people and reflects the life of the nation.' He too looked 'for something new, signs that leisure too was something that should be transformed collectively.'[12]

Foreign visitors made discoveries, especially at the opening of the summer season. That was when some forty orchestras, including the State Symphony Orchestra of the USSR, could be heard performing at different locations in the park. The repertoire was as varied as the public and went from Beethoven's Coriolan Overture to Russian folk tunes, Georgian sabre dances and Viennese waltzes. Leonid Utyosov's jazz band brought a whiff of Odesa to the park. Thousands of people whirled around to the waltz and practised the tango or foxtrot. Songs from the musical comedy *Rio Rita* enjoyed particular success. The summer season was filled with the best of what the national republics had to offer the capital by way of dance, music and ballet. Renowned operatic tenors competed with the hit tunes of Vasily Lebedev-Kumach and professional folklore ensembles with accordion players who couldn't read a note yet kept their audiences transfixed for hours on end. Scarcely anyone needed coaxing since everyone wished to learn and was endlessly inquisitive. Sports teachers explained the sequence of steps in the new dances. Elsewhere, a girl recited the text of a new song that was then rehearsed by the choir. On the parachute tower Red Army trainers instructed boys and girls how to jump. In the regattas on the Moskva there were boats with forty oarsmen—to train 'the collective spirit'. There were talks in the House of Culture for people

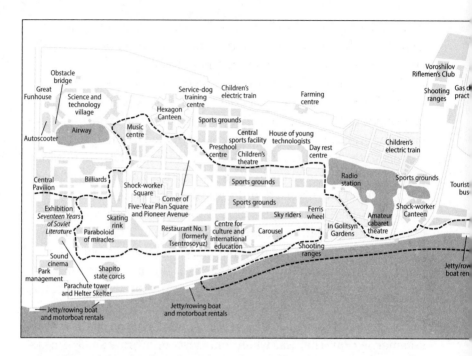

FIGURE 35.1. Ground plan of Gorky Park in Moscow, the model for culture and recreation parks throughout the Soviet Union. From Betti Glan and P. A. Portugalov (eds.), 'Parki kul'tury i otdyha Moskvy. Putevoditel' po TsPKiO im. M. Gor'kogo, PKiO . . . , Proletarskmu PkiO Parku TsDKA', Moscow 1935, in Katharina Kucher, *Der Gorki-Park: Freizeitkultur im Stalinismus 1928–1941*, Böhlau Verlag, Cologne, Weimar and Vienna 2007.

starved of intellectual fodder and the reading rooms had illustrated magazines from all the republics. The physicist and later dissident Yury Orlov spent the summer of 1936 in Moscow and was able to visit Gorky Park without having to pay, thanks to his grandmother, who worked there as a toilet attendant: 'I no longer had to slither through holes in the fence. I would draw Red Squares in the graphic arts group, then visit Grandmother, and then look after rabbits and all kinds of peas in the tiny garden of the "House of the Young Naturalist". Experiments were being done with the peas there. Had Grandmother worked a little longer in her public toilet, I might have turned out to be a geneticist. (And been sent to a camp for that.)'[13]

But Gorky Park also witnessed the end phase of the political carnivals and masquerades that had become fashionable since the Revo-

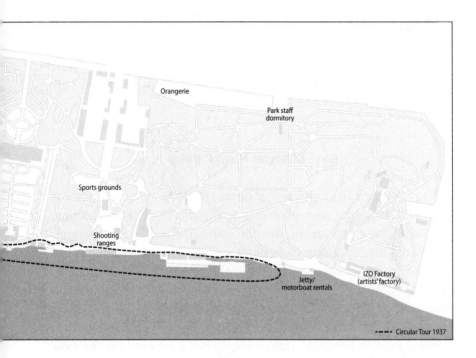

Orangerie

Park staff
dormitory

Sports grounds

Shooting
ranges

Jetty/
motorboat rentals

IZO Factory
(artists' factory)

╺╾╸ Circular Tour 1937

lution. At various times the park was transformed into a sequence of
'theatricalised meetings' with several hundred thousand performers.
On these occasions dozens of heavy trucks with papier-mâché figures
depicting world events would parade past: Trotsky on a lead held by
fascists, Churchill playing golf with a worker's head, Mussolini at a
wedding with the Pope, the struggle of an enslaved India represented
by an elephant bursting its chains, the new Constitution of the USSR,
Valery Chkalov's pioneering flight to the USA, the rescue of the North
Pole pilots from a drifting ice floe. There was action on land, at sea and
in the air, amounting to what we would nowadays call a multimedia
spectacle: military units and mobile propaganda, speedboats on the
Moskva, airships, projectors whose rays pierced the heavens, and
orchestral music playing over the loudspeakers.[14]

In reality, however, we are not speaking of a mere spectacle. The
directors of these performances—including once again pioneers of
the Soviet avant-garde such as Sergey Radlov—belonged to a generation who had studied Wagner's dream of the fusion of art and life,
theatre and reality, in its youth and now wished to abolish an aloof

art by turning life into theatre. The audience was to cease being the mere consumers of a show and become the fellow actors of a political demonstration that would transform life itself. Even in the most innocuous performances there was to be more at stake than simply distraction and entertainment.[15]

Birth of Soviet Mass Culture

The city in which all this was going on was Moscow in 1937—the city of the Great Purge, the wave of arrests by the NKVD; of denunciations, show trials and spy mania. Anyone—whether poet, army general, member of an Esperanto club, outstanding fighter in Spain—could turn at any moment into an 'enemy of the people', a 'British' or 'Japanese' spy. But this very same Moscow was also the city in which the pilots of the flight to America were rapturously greeted with confetti parades, where Soviet violinists returned home with medals from competitions in Brussels, where cornflakes were sold for the first time, where Pushkin was crowned as the greatest poet on his centenary and where 'Circus', a Hollywood type of musical comedy, celebrated its premiere. Gorky Park stood for happy days in the life of the young Wolfgang Leonhard or the youths of the 'Troika' depicted by Markus Wolf.[16]

Gorky Park had its place in the landscape of terror and normality. It was the totalitarian fairyland *and* the place of small moments of happiness in times of cholera. It was the idyll staged by a dictator *and* the scene in which the indomitable will of hundreds of thousands strove to escape from poverty and backwardness. In the Gorky Park of the 1930s there was much that could more easily be explained by the despair and enthusiasm of a youthful nation on the move than by the seductive powers of the dictator. Something surfaced here that was not invented by Stalin and could at best be controlled by him. It is not difficult to discern the old Russian tradition of a happy-go-lucky people (*narodnoe gulyanie*). The scenes containing comedians and clowns, Marusya and Petrushka, hark back to the heroes of the Russian carnival. Alexander Blok's *balagan*—fairground booths—returned in a modernised form. The rollercoasters (*amerikanskie gorki*) that used to be put up in the large squares before the Revolution to mark the beginning of spring now operated all year long. Even political carnivals and parades seemed to be contemporary forms of the old pleasure in play and fancy dress. People at play could at least pretend to enjoy the freedom that was denied them in reality. This explains why General Köstring, who grew up in Moscow before the Revolution and worked as a military attaché in the German embassy in the 1930s, was a regular visitor to Gorky Park. He was there to study 'popular opinion'. 'For this purpose, these parks were a mine of—authentic—information.'[17]

After the destruction of peasant Russia and the Great Leap Forward into the Industrial Age, the old forms in which all these things took place could no longer survive. Tractors, heavy trucks, speedboats, airships, projectors—all came from the arsenal of the Machine Age. The new heroes had ceased to wear beards and peasants' smocks; they were young clean-shaven pilots or engineers, in white shirts. The prerevolutionary park had baroque aviaries and Turkish-style bathing huts; the new park had a planetarium, parachute-jump tower and Ferris wheel. The new park was a place for young people, whose image has been preserved in Alexander Rodchenko's snapshots, and it was to them Osip Mandelstam had called from afar and in a spirit of resignation: 'I'll never walk in step with the lads / into the regimented sports arenas. / I won't jump from my bed at dawn, / woken by the dispatch rider with my call-up papers.'[18] For many workers who could still remember how they used to have to hold their May celebrations illegally in the clearings of Sokolniki Park, always on the lookout for the spies and truncheons of the Tsarist police, it must have been satisfying to have become 'masters of the loveliest park in the world'.

And this must have brought satisfaction to the immigrant peasants who had poured into Moscow in the hundreds of thousands during the 1930s, turning the city into a 'peasant metropolis', to use David Hoffmann's expression. The city needed workers and it was large and sufficiently impersonal for those who wished to shed their 'kulak' identity. These immigrants now lived in Moscow-Shanghai, the name given to those suburbs consisting of bunkhouses and mud huts where there was no water, no light and no tramway. There they

FIGURE 35.2. Couple dancing. Picture taken by Henri Cartier-Bresson, the most sensitive ob-server of Moscow life in the early 1950s. © Henri Cartier-Bresson/Magnum Photos/Agentur Focus.

sat, torn from their lifeworld and deracinated—no longer peasants, but not yet workers. What they brought with them into their new environment were their songs, customs and constrained desire to escape their backwardness and wretched situation. The park of cul-ture and recreation meant experiencing things they had never seen or known about. It was their point of contact with a new world. They went there with their accordions, their curiosity and their dreams of a place in the sun. This was where they learned the difference between *kulturno* and *nekulturno*, civilised and uncivilised. No one has recorded the sincerity of these aspirations and the grace of this learning process more charmingly than Henri Cartier-Bresson in his photo collection *People of Moscow*.[19] There the people practised the new Soviet etiquette that had become a matter of urgent necessity for those living in the 'quicksand society' (Moshe Lewin) of the 1930s, which had run out of control. This was where the younger generation committed to memory what should be thought beautiful and what ugly. In short, this was where the cultural code was formalised. Further, people were ashamed of being illiterate and convinced that one became a better person simply by being able to read and write. Linked to this was the transition from card games and dominos, which stood for village backwardness, to chess, a sign of higher education. The people learned here that drinking was not simply 'an obstacle to productivity' but part of a world that was 'doomed historically'. People respected high culture and the classical in all its forms: the Greek statues in the park, Beethoven and the singers of the Bolshoi Theatre. They started by learning the crude distinctions and then went on to the subtler ones. They learned that spitting on the ground was wrong and gradually overcame the prejudice acquired in the Sturm und Drang years of the 1920s that fashion shows were not places for workers and peasants. They came to believe that leisure time was time wasted if not put to 'creative' use and so they acquired knowledge at every opportunity, whether of technical drawing, in the balalaika orchestra or in the football club. They firmly believed that culture was sublime and extraordinary and that it called for great teachers. Vasily Svarog's monumental painting *Stalin and the Politburo among Children in Gorky Park* of 1939 shows the Great Teacher in the middle of his entourage, surrounded by a throng of boys and girls in their Sunday best and gazing up at Stalin and Kalinin with reverence and gratitude. It took only a generation for the new human being to overcome this infantile stage of development.

Paradise Lost: Luna Park in the Post-Soviet Era

In the 1990s little was left to remind us of what Gorky Park used to be. What has survived are the ground plan, the planetarium, the Ferris wheel and a toilet hut in the shape of a grotto with Doric pillars. The kids on roller skates ignore Yury Shchyuko's bombastic colonnade at the park entrance and are interested solely in the condition of the asphalt. Many do not even know who the Lenin whose visit to the park on 19 August 1923 is memorialised on a plaque. Opposite the main entrance, there is a sculpture park called Muzeon, filled with the statues of Soviet heroes that have been taken down over recent decades. The park, an inner-city wasteland in pre-Soviet times, now serves as a museum of relics of the Soviet age.

For over a decade a hint of the fairground hung over Gorky Park. All at once, you had to pay to enter. International showmen discovered Moscow. They came from Holland and Germany, from the Czech Republic and Slovakia, and from Italy. Disappointed and bored, the public ambled past the ghost train installed by the Prague company New Alpina, past the T-Vision tent and the fun slide. Bungee jumpers hurled themselves over the Golitsyn Pond and down into the depths from the Tarzan catapult. Motorboat races were run on an artificial lake. In the middle of the Great Square, a dragon flicked its tongue above the portal of a Russian fairy-tale castle. Dream ships whirled shrieking people through the air. A roller coaster rattled through a silver mine in New Mexico and over Niagara Falls, past dolphins and palm trees. The most impressive installation had been set up on the Moskva embankment—a copy of the Soviet space orbiter *Buran*, from which you could experience how it would feel to peer down at Earth from a height of 250 kilometres, eat cosmonaut food and have your heart and kidneys tested by a doctor. Elsewhere in the park a 'USA Space Ball'—unique in the world—turned on its own axis. An announcer on the park's loudspeaker quoted from Dostoevsky—'Beauty saves the world'—but this referred to a newly opened French beauty salon. Numerous ships lay on the Moskva, including the old poets' ship *Valery Bryusov*, converted into a casino. At the entrance to the park were notices and posters promoting events on such matters as 'Self-Help', 'Music and the Soul' and 'The Technology of Success'.

Preparations for the expulsion from Paradise were well underway before the end of the Soviet Union. After the war, the park twice became the setting for events of Union-wide importance. The first was in 1947, when the festival for the eight hundredth anniversary of Moscow included a parade celebrating the city's history with floats carrying luminaries from Ivan Kalita to Lazar Kaganovich. The second was in 1957, when the World Festival of Youth and Students took place. This marked the decisive turning away from the Age of Stalin since it reestablished contact between Moscow and the world after years of isolation. Anyone who wished to experience the surreal nature of 'actually existing socialism' had to seek out the 'Exhibition of the Achievements of the Economy' in the northeast, with its gilt fountains and bundles of grain.

The society for which Gorky Park had been designed in the 1930s began to dissolve in the late 1950s. Consolidation, peace and quiet, concern about one's own private life succeeded the dynamism and heroism of the foundation years. The idyll of the Khrushchev years was elsewhere, namely in the newly acquired four walls of one's own and in the dachas outside the city of which the bunkhouse dwellers of the first Five-Year Plan could only dream. The rendezvous points of the Soviet youth of that time became the preferred meeting spots of pensioners and veterans—or else a children's playground. The park loudspeaker that blared incessantly was replaced by the home radio that could be switched off at will. Propaganda now remained outside. No one had to be taught how to read and write and no one was forced to depend on the agitprop of 'living newspapers'. What TV provided went far beyond anything Gorky Park had to offer, however spectacularly staged. Gorky Park ended up as the setting for a spy thriller of the late phase of the Cold War, followed by a spectacular film version that turned the Soviet park of culture and recreation into something even the Western public could understand.[20] The new consumerism and the introduction of Western mass culture had done their job.

After an interim period of neglect and isolation, the Moscow city government revived Gorky Park with a subtle reconstruction and turned it into a leading attraction for citizens of the capital and for tourists. Now you can choose between restaurants, cafés, the glass building of the 'Garage' museum for modern art (by architect Rem Koolhaas) and an international bookshop. You can listen to lectures by international stars such as Slavoj Žižek, try out the mountain bikes or simply do your laps on the running track.

It has all ended up as a well-maintained municipal park which has replaced its lofty goal of educating the new human being. The final product is as unspectacular as all civilisation processes that take time. The children of yore have overcome their illusions and matured. As adults, they insist on no longer being treated as children. Yesterday's enthusiastic *komsomoltsy* have become pensioners; a heroic generation has become a generation of veterans. The parades of the *fizkulturniki*, that is, the sports brigades organised in the spirit of socialism, have been replaced by fitness centres and the parachute towers by bungee jumping (admittedly, the parachute-jump tower of the 1930s has been painstakingly reconstructed). People have ceased to practise for war but are keen to show their dates how to hit cardboard figures in the shooting range. The collective body of 'mass visitors' of the old days has disappeared. Instead there are people out for a fitness walk, locals having a look, hipsters chatting by phone with friends travelling somewhere in California. But perhaps this is just one aspect of *panem et circenses*, while the mobilisation is going on elsewhere.

CHAPTER 36

Diorama: View of a Landscape with Heroes

The nineteenth century was the great age for panoramas in Europe. Citizens looking at them could satisfy a yearning to see the world and undertake imaginary journeys into the past.[1] Ever since Louis Jacques Daguerre, the inventor of photography, first presented his diorama in 1822, European metropolises competed to build the sensational establishments that proclaimed even from outside, from their architecture, that something new was happening. This was the staging of a deceptively compelling illusion—whether of a landscape or a historical event, most often a battle—which, for a fee, could be surveyed from a raised platform. From an elevated position, viewers gazed through a peephole in the wall of a rotunda in which a stereoscopic image was created on a huge screen. There were dioramas in London and other large British towns, as well as in Paris, 'the capital of the nineteenth century'. Walter Benjamin explored the phenomenon of the panorama theatre in his *Arcades*.[2] Dioramas could also be found in Berlin, which demonstrated its world-ranking status with the building of the Kaiserpanorama, in North America and at the heart of the Russian Empire. In a globalising world the themes and subjects were not very far removed from one another: historical events of relevance to the European public, such as the battles of Waterloo or Murten/Morat; scenes from the Passion of Jesus; the panorama of the Alps, which had become a major tourist destination and could now be experienced close to home and risk-free.

It is not difficult to discern the beginnings of modern mass culture in the panoramas and dioramas. Here was an interested and solvent public in need of entertainment and in search of something to compensate for the stress of a modern working life. With his *Historique et description des procédés du daguerréotype et du diorama*, Daguerre had pushed open the door to a new world. Basically, all the elements that would make dioramas a great attraction developed in the nineteenth century; they summarised an old world: mural painting, realism with its meticulous attention to detail, the stage and its lighting. At the same time, they pointed forward to a new form of spectacle that would undermine both the art of the diorama and its business prospects: the cinema of the Lumière brothers.

In the Soviet Union the dioramas, as they were called, had to wait until the later years of the twentieth century for their great moment.[3] Visitors could not really avoid them, especially in the final years of the Empire. It was almost inevitable that anyone who wished to gain an idea of important episodes of history would end up in these curious historical constructions. They stood out even in a museum landscape that never denied its own roots in the nineteenth century—thanks to belief in their ability to narrate and illustrate significant historical moments, the realism in capturing the fine detail of events, and the importance attached to presenting exhibits, if not forever then at least for the duration. Every museum, no matter how remote, had learned the art of reproducing the world vividly and with realistic precision: moorland landscapes with reeds and stuffed waterfowl, the Scythian grave that had been excavated from the hilly terrain of the steppes, the felt upholstery and the telephone on the desk of the Red director in the office of the 1930s power station.

Simply by virtue of their size, dioramas provided an intensified experience of place. It is easy to imagine them. The Central Museum of the Great Patriotic War in Victory Park (Park Pobedy) contains huge dioramas depicting the defence of Moscow in winter 1941, the Battle of Stalingrad, the Siege of Leningrad and the 'Storming of Berlin' in spring 1945. Anyone interested in Napoleon's Russian campaign will not want to miss the diorama of the Battle of Borodino on 26 August to 7 September 1812. It focuses on the moment when Mikhail Kutuzov called his generals together—in Kutuzov's hut—and we can see how Napoleon's fate, and that of Europe as a whole, was decided. Dioramas that reimagine the great battles of the Soviet-German War are also to be found in many other towns—in Rzhev on the Upper Volga, in Dnipro on the Dnieper and, not least, the giant diorama of the Battle of Stalingrad in today's Volgograd. Sevastopol is perhaps where the role of the diorama in Soviet historical culture is clearest.[4]

Sevastopol provides an extremely compressed memorial landscape. It begins with the panorama of 'The Defence of Sevastopol 1854–1855' during the Crimean War and continues with the diorama of 'The Storming of Sapun-Gora', that is, the reconquering of Sevastopol from the Germans in May 1944; the Vladimir Cathedral, where the heroes of Sevastopol—General von Torleben, Admiral Nakhimov and others—lie buried; and the Museum for the Defence of the Malakhov Heights, the Partisan Museum and the Museum of the Black Sea Fleet. The all-round picture of the defence of Sevastopol in the Crimean War was opened in 1904 to celebrate the fiftieth anniversary of the battle and was restored after the Second World War, during which the building had been severely damaged. The circular panorama was cut in half at the outbreak of the war, evacuated across the Black Sea and brought to Novosibirsk. It can now be seen in the white neo-Renaissance building high above the city. Its subject is the Anglo-French attempt to storm the heights on 6 June 1855 and was created under the direction of Franz Alexeevich Roubaud (Russian: Frants Alekseevich Rubo, 1856–1928), in part in the Munich Academy of Arts. It is 115 metres long and 14 metres high; its overall area of 1,610 square metres fills the horizon of the rotunda with its 36 metres in diameter and height. Roubaud's work—he also painted the mural commemorating the centenary of the Battle of Borodino in 1912—remained the model for circular diorama pictures, which continued to influence Soviet painting collectives like the Mitrofan Grekov workshop, which specialised in panoramas.[5] The memorial complex of the Central Museum of the Great Patriotic War on Poklonnaya Gora in Moscow includes an entire ensemble of dioramas cheek by jowl in the Central Building—the Battle of Stalingrad, the Battle for Moscow, the Siege of Leningrad, etc.[6]

If we are to describe and analyse the diorama effect, we must begin by noting some quite simple operations. Visitors enter a darkened building; they climb stairs to a viewing platform in the middle of the building from where they can see the panorama, from which they are separated by a balustrade. Visitors can turn a full 360°; they find themselves in the centre of a space in which an event is being enacted, which they can view in large and fascinating detail, yet is so far away that they are under the impression that they are looking out onto a large vista. Just think of the things they can see, the details in which they can immerse themselves! Accurately modelled soldiers with all the details absolutely correct—down to the buttons, cockades and facial expressions; the line-up of the troops; the lines of the trenches and earthworks; the figure of the drummer boy; the shattered wheel of a broken-down cart; bastions veiled in smoke; the army doctor with his surgical instruments; the tricolours marking the troops on the attack. The plethora of details and the expanse of a landscape churned up by artillery fire; the actual weapons in the foreground that you can take hold of with your own hands and the painted weapons in the background—all merge and form a compelling illusion, thanks to the precise calculation of the perspective and the astute use of lighting effects. And yet no more than a single moment has been captured, one that is precisely dated—6 June 1855. It has been scrupulously researched to establish the personnel involved, their ranks, the types of weapons deployed, the contours of the terrain and the exact location of the front.

Dioramas are supposed to offer as exact a reconstruction of an event as possible; everything must come together to capture the historical moment. The production of dioramas is an interdisciplinary activity. They bring together knowledge of the material, visual and sculptural elements, familiarity with—in this instance—military events and knowledge of the terrain (at a particular season). In a certain sense they embody the idea or dream of a *histoire totale* in which many perspectives, not just one, stand alongside each other but can be absorbed in an all-embracing glance. It is a vision in which all the registers of perception are activated—fanfares announce the coming battle, smoke rises from the campfires—and generally the second dimension of the surface of a painted picture merges seamlessly with the third dimension containing the real, concrete objects in the foreground. These features of the diorama—vividness, plasticity, information content—are what made it a lasting attraction for millions of visitors. The same effects can be seen in other dioramas—such as the panorama of Racławice brought from Lemberg (Lviv) to Breslau (Wrocław) that depicts the victory of the Polish army under General Kościuszko over the Russian army in 1794 or that of the US landscape transformed by industrialisation to be seen in the Museum of Science and Industry in Chicago. Such panoramas attract millions of visitors down to the present day.

It is easy to see that even more is involved. The diorama doesn't just contain images of dramatic action—a battle in this instance; the images are also part of a 'guided tour', with elements that go beyond mere information and education. There is the choice of place, the close links between panorama and genius loci. *This* is where it all happened! This is how it was in Sevastopol, in Dnipro, in Rzhev, in Stalingrad/Volgograd or Moscow. You seem to gaze beyond the diorama to its surroundings, to the actual terrain. The diorama becomes a magnifying glass which enables visitors to gaze directly at the historical scene. It generates a solemn mood that automatically makes visitors lower their voices or even fall silent—classes of schoolchildren are told to keep their voices down. Dioramas are places where visualisation, education and the solemnity and earnestness of thought are synthesized. They help to create a sense of patriotism; they are like lock chambers through which young visitors especially are brought into contact with the experiential worlds of past generations.

For many visitors, entry to the dioramas is bound up with the feeling that they are being imposed upon. This is because the dioramas' cylindrical shape bears some resemblance to a technical apparatus. Visitors feel as if they have left the light of day and find themselves in an orbit so that when they leave, it is with a sense of relief. It is not by chance that battles—the battlefield, defence against an external enemy—are the preferred subject for dioramas; they can be seen as a pendant to the paintings of battles and heroic actions in the Museum of Military History in Vienna. Here the heroic moment is made permanent; dioramas are true depositories for the hour of the hero. Their time might well draw to a close should the country cease to need heroes or if heroes had to prove their worth in areas other than the battlefields of yesteryear.

The art of the diorama will continue to thrive, then, and perhaps even achieve a second flowering. You can obtain a glimmering of this if you take a look at the large model of Moscow on the top floor of Mosproekt. Visitors move along a gallery that leads all the way round

FIGURE 36.1. The Battle of Stalingrad, one of the seven dioramas in the Central Museum of the Great Patriotic War in Moscow. © akg-images/Elizaveta Becker.

this model and gaze at the detailed, true-to-scale city of Moscow. Or there is the Moscow panorama completed in the 1950s which now, after having been mislaid in depots for decades, can be seen in the lobby of the Hotel Ukraina. It comes as no surprise to find that the dioramas continue to work their magic—as can be seen from Yadegar Asisi's panoramas of the Battle of the Nations in the gasometer in Leipzig and the Pergamon panorama in Berlin. The fact that most of the Soviet dioramas were built in the 1970s shows that they are not the product of an unpolitical desire to entertain a mass public. On the contrary, what they do is to capture the moment of heroism in the Second World War, the heroism of the generations of veterans to which Leonid Brezhnev also belonged. They are the monuments of a late phase that found it hard to compete with *Star Wars*, Disneyland and 3D animation and more especially with a reality that stands behind

the horizon of the circular image and beyond the diorama itself. No one foresaw that the dioramas erected in the late phase of the Soviet Union and dedicated to the memory of the victims and heroes of the Great Patriotic War could be used to justify military actions against former 'fraternal nationalities'.

CHAPTER 37

'Zhilmassiv', or the Sublime Vistas of the Prefab Mountains

Of the numerous abbreviations that became common currency in the Soviet Union, 'zhilmassiv' is one of the most incisive and one of the few to have positive associations. It derives from *zhilishchny massiv*, which means roughly 'housing massif' and so includes overtones of 'mountain range'. And in fact, to this day every journey from an airport serving a Soviet city involves travelling through a vast agglomeration of prefab estates that tower on both sides of the highway. Whether you are approaching the city centre from St. Petersburg Pulkovo airport or Novosibirsk Tolmachevo, Moscow Domodedovo, or Kyiv Borispol, you must cross a ring of residential districts that all look the same and seem to have been constructed to the same design. What you are crossing are not just suburbs but estates, entire towns populated by a hundred thousand people. The buildings have a certain rhythm and are arranged according to a specific geometry; the distances between them are large but from afar the buildings rise up like massive mountainous landscapes. Although the buildings were designed and constructed by human beings, and humans live in them, people tend to use the language of nature when describing them. Even the seasons and lighting conditions play a major role. In midseason, such as late autumn or early spring, the buildings are as grey as the overcast sky and the slush in the streets. In summer, the peaks of these housing mountains gleam white and they are even whiter in the winter snows. You get the most powerful impression, however, at nighttime the whole year through when the housing mountains twinkle and shine with thousands and thousands of lights. Every window is a luminous spot; every block, floor by floor, is a row of lights; every 'council estate' (the so-called *mikrorayon*) is not an agitated sea of lights but a geometric set of gleaming points, each of them standing for a life, a destiny, for the constant passage from life to death. By night, they lose their monotony, their sameness, the boringness peculiar to the layout of streets and blocks that come straight from the drawing board. The way the streets and housing blocks flicker at night evokes the beating pulse of human life in the big city. 'The scarcity of living quarters here creates a strange effect: unlike in other cities, here the streets in the evening are lined with large and small houses with almost every window lit up. If the glow cast by these windows were not so uneven, you might imagine you were looking at an illumination. There is another thing I have noticed these past few days; it is not merely the snow that might possibly make you nostalgic for Moscow, but also the sky. In no other metropolis do you have so much sky overhead. The low buildings largely contribute to this. In this city you always sense the vast horizon of the Russian steppes.'[1]

The prefab mass-housing estates have changed the face of the cities, the face of the Soviet Union and, beyond that, the Eastern Europe dominated by the Soviets.[2] They are not simply a purely municipal or architectural peculiarity; they are the objectification of a specific form of life in which generations have grown up. They stand for the process of urbanisation, indeed for the birth of urbanisation in a traditional world that remained shaped by agriculture well into the twentieth century. Understanding this is especially difficult for Europeans familiar from childhood with the history of the polis, the agora, the forum, the features of the marketplace and the medieval town, the medieval watchword 'town air makes you free', right down to Georg Simmel's 'culture of the large town'. In their eyes a metropolis designed on the drawing board, built on a green-field site and assembled from factory-made components is the very reverse of urbanity; it is the negation of everything that made the town a European achievement. That achievement starts out from private property, individual representation and a developed community life. These, taken together, have defined the face of the European town in its endless variety and—notwithstanding the levelling process of the 'mass age' and the physical destruction of towns in wartime— continue to define it down to this day.

Mass housing began with the industrialisation and urbanisation of the Western world, but its historical 'face' was first defined in the Soviet world.[3] With this development, towns in the USSR changed their appearance; many settlements became towns only when mass housing arrived. In 1991, at the very end of the Soviet Union, large-panel, pre-fabricated housing amounted to 75 percent of the overall housing stock and in some places the share of prefab buildings was even greater, up to 90 percent.[4] The Soviet form of urbanisation had found its own expression. Over 170 million people lived in industrially manufactured—that is, prefabricated—dwellings in the territories of the former Soviet Union. Everywhere you go, you encounter the contrast between the old town and the new town where the majority of the population lives—whether in Czernowitz or Kharkiv, in Tbilisi or Irkutsk—but nowhere is the contrast so crassly expressed as in the Ukrainian capital of Kyiv, where visitors who stand on the Dnieper heights have the thousand-year-old town with the grounds of the Monastery of the Caves, its cupulas and towers, at their backs, while on the plain on the other side of the river, they see the housing mountain of the new district of Darnytsia stretching out to the horizon.

The world of large-panel, prefabricated housing became a com-monplace and a self-ironising platitude of Soviet citizens, something that can also be seen in the art of the day. In 1959 Dmitry Shostakovich wrote an operetta with the title *Cheryomushki*. Its subject, the struggle to take possession of a new apartment, was bound up with all sorts of intrigues, corruption and romantic entanglements.[5] The last creative phase of Yury Pimenov, probably one of the most important Soviet painters, seems to have been inspired entirely by his experience of the new *mikrorayon* or microdistrict. His neo-Impressionistic paintings record the half-finished prefabs, the soil churned up by excavators, the entrance of a young couple into a bright new apartment. They show the exit from the world of the shared apartment and entrance into an apartment of one's own.[6] The housing revolution found its most successful expression in all its ambivalence in the TV film *Irony of Fate* (1975), a masterpiece by the director Eldar Ryazanov. Over decades and until well into post-Soviet Russia, the film was broad-cast annually on TV at New Year. Zhenya, arriving from Banya in a drunken state, boards a plane for Leningrad and finds himself in an apartment identical to his Moscow apartment, from the address, the apartment block, the key with which he opens the door, right down to the floor plan. Only the beautiful woman he finds in the apartment is new and unknown to him. The comedy of mistaken identity runs

FIGURE 37.1. Five-floor Khrushchyovki in the Grazhdanka district in Leningrad. RIA Novosti and V. Nikitin 1977, from Philipp Meuser, *Die Ästhetik der Platte: Wohnungsbau in der Sowjetunion zwischen Stalin und Glasnost*, DOM Publishers, Berlin 2015, 458.

its course and concludes with a happy ending. *Irony of Fate* became a cult film because everyone was familiar with the commonplace idea of standardised apartment types down to the very last detail. 'Only in the Soviet Union could you mistake someone else's home for your own', wrote a viewer. 'But why just say "home"? Entire districts! And you wouldn't actually need to be drunk like Zhenya Lukashin.'[7] The film was actually made in Vernadsky Prospekt in southwest Moscow, the chief location of new dwellings since the 1960s.

Cheryomushki as Prototype

It all began in Cheryomushki, a rural suburb of southwest Moscow until the 1960s. A country estate of the Menshikovs and Golitsyns, it had been rebuilt several times since the eighteenth century and adapted to the fashionable style of the period; in the nineteenth century it had become a dacha suburb outside the railway ring. In 1956 experimental building started up. Quarters 9, 11 and 12 were filled with five-storey prefabricated houses; the building shell was constructed in fifty-two days and the buildings were completed one hundred days after start-up. By the end of the 1950s/early 1960s construction of Novye Cheryomushki had begun from the south.[8]

The Cheryomushki model was soon followed by other council estates and new urban quarters such as Khimki-Khorino, Mosfilm-ovsky and Chertanovo. Somewhat later saw the building of more wide-ranging new council estates on the outskirts of Leningrad—on Thorez Prospekt, in the municipalities of Kupchino and Dachnoe. Soon all the larger towns and especially the capitals of the republics had their new prefab council estates: in the Darnytsia and Rusani-vka districts of Kyiv, in Vilnius-Lazdynai and in Tallinn-Mustamäe. Large parts of Tashkent were rebuilt using prefabricated materials after the great earthquake of 1966. In his large-scale study *Towards a Typology of Soviet Mass Housing: Prefabrication in the USSR 1955–1991*, Philipp Meuser provides a description of the basic type of prefabri-cated building—the five-storey, concrete-panelled Khrushchyovka—and its subsequent development:

In Moscow from 1958 on, the first houses were ready for people to move into the district of Novye Cheryomushki. This was a show-piece project consisting of five-storey residential blocks of prefab-ricated apartments built on former kolkhoz fields. . . . As long as the production of prefabricated large panels could not be rolled out na-tionally, the architects used conventional brick or masonry. Typical for the new building method was to group two to four apartments around a centrally placed double stairwell with an intermediate landing. As a rule, the ground floor was connected above the first flight of stairs so that the cellar spaces had natural light and the lower apartments were slightly raised above the plot. The staircase was standardised and provided the backbone of the design. With two units per floor the apartments had windows in both directions so that the living space was highly adaptable. Windows at the sides of the section unit were not included in the plan since otherwise adding on further apartments would not have been possible. By and large, there was a high degree of similarity in the design and layout of the five-floor blocks between Leningrad in the north and Erevan in the south, between Kaliningrad in the west and Novosibirsk in the east. The hall, WC and bathroom were designed for the smallest apartments possible. In the first generation of this type of building, the kitchen was accessible only through a narrow corridor close to the bathroom and toilet. The regulations stipulated that the largest room, normally the living room, should measure at least 14 square metres. A bedroom of 8 square metres was regarded as sufficient for two people. The smallest rooms—if present—were designed as children's rooms. Each floor was large enough for two apartments of four rooms each. If more rooms were included in the design, this was achieved at the cost of the number of rooms and the size of the apartment. The individual sections had a depth of 12 metres, which followed from the 6-metre-long staircase, and a width of between 14 and 20 metres. The industrial prefabrication process made it possible to reduce the size of the rooms and the bathroom and toilet facilities to a standard module of 1.20×1.20m or else to scale them up by a multiple of the standard module.[9]

The flaws in this building type are obvious: the limited room height of 2.4 metres; the thin walls, which meant you could hear everything that went on in the neighbours' apartment; the bathroom too small for anything larger than a hip bath; and the kitchen that was no more than 6 square metres. The drawbacks of this model known as K-7 and designed by Vitaly Lagutenko were compensated for by decisive advantages: given the extreme shortage of housing, apartment blocks could be built on a massive scale at low cost and in an exceedingly short time.

The annual construction rate of residential buildings doubled in comparison with the Stalin period. The five-storey post-and-beam structure was retained until into the 1980s: 'Between 1956 and 1965 108 million Soviet citizens were able to move into a new apartment. In purely numerical terms this meant that living space had been created for over one-third of the total Soviet population.' The prefabricated buildings that had become synonymous with residential buildings in the USSR as well as the other countries of the Eastern bloc were not especially beautiful, and moreover, because the technology was in its infancy, there were many defects in the quality of the materials, weaknesses in joint construction and in assembly accuracy.[10] In the later design versions with nine and twelve storeys, which were introduced to increase population density in the microdistricts, the room height was increased to 2.7 metres and both external and internal walls were strengthened. 'But over 75% of the new-builds had been industrially prefabricated as standard models. No other country the world over had rationalised its construction industry like the USSR. However, that made the system inflexible and almost incapable of adapting to new conditions. The Khrushchyovka doubtless belongs among the most popular models actually to be built. Just in the RSFSR alone 290 million square metres of living space were constructed using this model. That amounts to some 10% of the entire surface area of Russia.'[11] Monica Rüthers gives this description of the typical apartment in the Khrushchyovka:

> The current model, a two-room apartment circa 44 square metres floor space, provided 27 square metres of pure living space—kitchen, bathroom and hallway were normally not included in the count. Such an apartment was supposed to house three people. Two occupants had to share 18 square metres, while a family of four had a right to 36 square metres of pure living space. The high proportion of small apartments is a mark of the earlier new-build estate. The design is based on the assumption that up to three generations lived together in these apartments which consisted mostly of a large living room and a recess or small bedroom. That meant that the rooms had to be rearranged mornings and evenings and that you sat, worked, lived during the day and slept at night in the same space. This style of living followed on from the kommunalka where everyone had likewise lived in the same room. The advantage of the new apartments was that you had a bathroom and a kitchen of your own and could lead an undisturbed family life.[12]

The expansion of housing in the new microdistricts brought with it improvements and greater sophistication in both planning and construction methods. Microdistricts were designed for up to 150,000 people who could reach all the key social amenities such as schools, kindergartens and cultural centres in five to fifteen minutes on foot. The ground plans followed the natural lie of the land, modern town strategies were adopted and the insights of sociological studies were applied. In designing the different neighbourhoods, visual axes were respected and dominant points established with tower blocks of varying heights; landscape architects were commissioned to create artificial ponds, parking areas and playgrounds—ideas conceived with a view to creating an environment with a profile of its own, one with which the inhabitants could identify. Needless to say, these improvements could not cancel out the systemic defects: because of the policy on ownership, there could be no property market, no competition, and no fundamental occupant interest in maintaining the condition and quality of the communal areas. Planning and implementation remained in the hands of government project offices and state construction companies and variety was strictly limited to the prescribed building types. 'The construction of residential housing in the Soviet Union was exclusively the responsibility of the state whose design institutes produced the series and whose construction units built the houses.'[13] Even so, we could arrive at a proper evaluation of the achievements of the mass-housing projects of the Soviet type only if, in addition to criticising the uniformity and monotony of the estates, we showed our appreciation of the professionalism, inventiveness and practical skill of the planners, builders and building workers.

De-Stalinisation before De-Stalinisation

Nikita Khrushchev's 'secret speech' to the Twentieth Congress of the CPSU had unleashed a shock wave throughout the world of communist parties and his revelations about Stalin's crimes and 'the errors of the cult of personality' sent a signal that the 'Thaw' was irreversible. It has been largely overlooked that the general attack on the Stalinist system had actually begun two years earlier in full view of the public and in connection with a problem that had made life difficult, even intolerable, for Soviet citizens over generations. This was the housing problem. Millions of people lived in barracks, dormitories, mud huts and communal apartments. The war had shrunk the inadequate supply of housing even further; whole cities were uninhabitable and millions of people had been left homeless. With the liquidation of the camps, some of the former inmates—both criminal and political— settled in the vicinity of the camps as 'free people' and stayed there for the rest of their lives, while hundreds of thousands of others poured out and returned to their place of origin, exacerbating the already dramatic housing shortage in the process. The Stalin regime had admittedly already started to experiment with factory-production methods even before the war, but given its fixation on the means of production and on heavy industry as well as on the armaments sector, which had been brought to a high pitch of activity by the war, it proved impossible to reorientate the construction and housing sector in the same way. The imperatives of a centrally planned economy established the absolute priority of industrialisation and this took precedence over the immediate life needs of the population, 'the proletarian masses'. The 'housing problem', then, remained pressing. Engels's writings had put housing at the forefront of his radical critique of a society based on capitalist modes of production and this weighed all the more heavily on a Soviet Union that had only just emerged victorious from the war. Alongside the capricious cruelty of state-organised terror, the appalling and misanthropic overcrowding of the population in the living quarters of the socialist state was the other defining traumatic experience of Soviet citizens. Criticism of the Stalin regime's housing programme and the promise to find answers to this existential problem were at the very heart of the lives of Soviet citizens. In February 1956, articulating them was as urgent as settling accounts with the 'cult of personality' and the crimes of Stalin and his clique against their own people.

As early as the end of 1955, the State Council passed the Resolution of the Central Committee and USSR Council 'Concerning the Elimination of Excess in Design and Construction'. This attacked the building policies of the Stalin period, but in reality its target was the Stalinist system itself. It sounds like an aesthetic critique of architecture and construction when we read in the Resolution: 'There should be less concern with decorating façades and more effort devoted to planning issues leading to an improved quality of living conditions. The money that is invested in towers, pillars, cornices and porticos could be used for the construction of millions of square metres of living space.' There follows what is for a decree an astonishingly detailed critique of key buildings in Moscow and other cities. Objects of criticism are the elaborate and expensive details in shaping the façades while simultaneously sacrificing the efficient design of the ground plans, extravagant opulence in ceiling frescoes and gilding while neglecting the planning and design of the apartments. Archaic decorations, pilasters, complicated cornices, ostentatious ornamentation and overly lavish use of expensive materials combined with 'wasteful costings' are also targeted. Above all, there is scathing criticism of the bombastic style used in constructing public buildings in towns and cities laid waste by the war. We hear about new railway stations, for example: 'Walls were given marble and oak cladding. Outside, the building was decorated with the addition of pilasters and stucco capitals. For the railings around the building 360 tonnes of metal were used up.' The Resolution does not forbear naming architects prominent at the time, including the recipients of Stalin Prizes, and it calls for the systematic development of standardised design models: 'When planning and building, architects and engineers should pay particular attention to economies that could be made, the function and utility of dwellings, schools, hospitals and other buildings as well as the establishment of residential districts. . . . Soviet architects must in future be simple and rigorous with regard to design and cost-effectiveness. The attractive appearance of a building should not be achieved by means of ingenious and costly ornamentation, but by a harmonious combination of the architecture with both the function of the building and its proportions, as well as attention to the need for high-quality workmanship in the treatment of materials, construction and architectural details.'[14] In concrete terms, it calls for housing models for between two- and five-storey apartment blocks, models for schools for 280, 400 and 880 pupils, hospitals of different numbers of beds, kindergartens, sanatoriums, hotels and holiday homes, cinemas and food shops.

Criticism of the Stalin Prize winners is criticism of Stalin-era architecture. Criticism of the pomp, extravagance and façade-like character of public buildings, such as the façade for the 'Palaces of the Working Class' built for the new elite, and of their creators puts the entire hierarchy of planners and the aesthetics of the Stalin era into question. It creates space for a debate that brings the pragmatism, functionalism and simplicity of the Soviet avant-garde of the 1920s back onto the agenda and links up once more with the town-planning projects and principles that underpinned the Karl-Marx-Hof in Vienna, the estates of Bruno Taut in Berlin and Le Corbusier's postwar projects. In the 1960s a 'second modernity' picked up from where the first modernity, before Stalin, had left off. This time, however, it was not a minority current—as Constructivism and the Bauhaus had undoubtedly been—but thanks to advances in manufacturing technology and under the pressure of an unprecedented migration from the countryside to the towns and cities, it developed on a mass scale to the point where the face of Soviet cities was formed and, we must add, deformed by functional mass housing. The task facing the Soviet mass-housing programme of the postwar period was not simply that of clearing away the war damage in the occupied territory (of the European part of the Soviet Union), not just a matter of correcting the 'excesses' of the bombastic, imperial style of the Stalin era, but of overcoming the problems arising from the mass migration that had been spontaneously and violently set in motion by collectivisation and industrialisation in what Moshe Lewin has described as 'the quicksand society'. The builders of the new towns had to confront a 'Russia in flux';[15] they had to get to grips with a society consisting of millions and millions of migrants whose unpredictable movements resembled those of shifting sand dunes. What seems at first glance to be a desert of large-panel, prefabricated apartment blocks is discovered on closer inspection to be those same shifting dunes of forced and spontaneous migrants that had ceased to move. An uprooted population had settled; it had become a staging post in the great social transformation of a nation, and perhaps a final destination and resting place of the great movement that began with the uprooting of the millions by collectivisation and industrialisation.

FIGURE 37.2. Yury Pimenov (1903–1977), *Wedding in Tomorrow Street*, 1962. © VG Bild-Kunst, Bonn 2018. Photo: State Tretyakov Gallery, Moscow/culture-images/fai.

The Large-Panel Prefab Estate as the
End Point of a Great Migration

'The changing ratios between urban and rural populations take us to the heart of the matter,' writes Moshe Lewin in *The Soviet Century*, referring to urbanisation, the transformation from a rural society to an industrial nation, as the 'crucial phase in Russia's history'. The results of the censuses leave no room for doubt about this quantitative shift.

According to the Census of 1926, 26,314,114 people (17.9 percent) lived in towns while the rural population amounted to 120,718,801 (82.1 percent). In January 1939 there were circa 170.5 million inhabitants in the prewar USSR, of whom 114.4 million (67 percent) were rural while 56.1 million (33 percent) lived in the towns. The urban population had doubled in twelve years, which meant an additional 9.4 percent in the towns every year, 'an exceptionally rapid rate of urbanization by any standards'.[16] Elsewhere, Lewin speaks of 'hyper-urbanization'. While the country as a whole was 'de-ruralized' and lost people through deportations, mass deaths through famine, flight and emigration, growth in the towns was explosive. In 1939 62 percent of the new town dwellers came from the countryside. In the course of thirteen years 450 new towns were founded, which meant an increase in the population density of the large towns: in 1939 there were 27 towns with a population of between 100,000 and 500,000. The number of towns with over 500,000 had grown from three to eight. Many towns were simply set down in the wilderness, wherever the new industrial building sites and industrial complexes of communism were to be found.

But even numbers like this fail to convey the magnitude of these developments when we consider that millions of peasants were deported or had settled in the towns in order to escape deportation and persecution, but had also fled from the towns in their thousands to avoid discrimination and persecution. The country was not at all prepared for what Moshe Lewin calls 'a veritable human maelstrom'.[17] In these circumstances—famine in the countryside, a housing shortage in the towns as well as administrative chaos—those who could find accommodation in the already overcrowded communal apartments could think themselves fortunate. What in quantitative terms might have the appearance of urbanisation was initially a 'ruralisation' of the towns whose existing population became a minority and could only complete the laborious task of urban integration with the greatest of difficulty. 'The influx of peasants seeking work or fleeing the countryside made urban expansion a major problem for the regime. Flight to the cities was *ipso facto* a massive rural exodus.' It was a precautionary measure by those who felt threatened—the 'kulaks' above all—by deportation, displacement to remote regions or forced labour.[18] In particular, would-be upwardly mobile peasants interested in training and bettering themselves looked for an escape route by fleeing to the towns. Millions of people circulated throughout the country; they poured into the towns and major construction sites, but then sometimes abandoned them. Their movements could not be controlled; even the new internal passport requirements of 1932 were unable to stem the flow, for all their strict rules governing migration to the towns and no less strict punishments where the rules were flouted. For their part, the towns became the setting for a demographic and sociocultural revolution with all the negative side effects of hooliganism, criminality and a gang culture. When war broke out, the country as a whole and even Russia was far from being a modern industrial state. 'Sociologically, but also culturally, it was in many respects an extension of its agrarian past including in the very mould of its modernizing state.'[19] What this meant culturally and sociologically, but above all mentally, was summed up by Hoffmann in the phrase 'peasant metropolis'.[20]

The Soviet-German War, with its destruction of the towns, of industrial plants, and its forced evacuation and migration, retarded this transition while also accelerating and radicalising it. For this reason we can think of the postwar period as the time of a second urbanisation. In architecture and town planning, neoclassicism in all its variants was moving towards its apogee, as can be seen from the spectacular high-rise buildings in the capital—more particularly, however, in the reconstructed or newly built towns, such as the public buildings in Stalingrad and Minsk, the railway stations in Kharkiv and Odesa, the Khreshchatyk as the central urban space in Kyiv, showpiece buildings such as the Academy of Sciences in Riga, and later, the Palace of Culture in Warsaw and the Stalinallee in East Berlin.

In the 1960s, the Soviet Union in toto became 'semi-urban'; Russia, Ukraine and the Baltic Republics were urban for the most part.[21] The migrant flows from the countryside to the town and from the towns to the country were impressive. In the years 1961–1965 around 29 million people migrated to the towns while 24.2 million left, which makes a total of 53.2 million on the move. The movement was particularly strong from the east, from Siberia, to the European part of the Soviet Union, even though originally these migrants wished or

were supposed to settle east of the Urals. One reason for this was the
drastic housing shortage in the towns of Siberia and the Far East.
The migrants headed for the towns, largely because that was where
the greater opportunities for both jobs and advancement were to be
found, rather than to the smaller and medium-sized towns whose
populations were relatively stagnant or which had even gone into
decline. The large towns sucked in the Russian villages and absorbed
them; the council estates were the points of maximum concentration
in this vast country, while the flip side of the hyperurbanisation process meant that entire stretches of land had been bled white and villages stripped of their working populations. Moscow can be regarded
as a peasant metropolis, as a village consisting of many-storeyed,
high-rise housing blocks and as a school of urbanity.

Post-Soviet Erosion: Search for the New City

Moving into an apartment in the large-panel, concrete block—the
Khrushchyovka—once seemed to be the true solution to the housing
problem, the true release from the oppressive nature of everyday
Soviet housing. But it is showing its age and not just through physical
and moral wear and tear. It has long since ceased to satisfy more progressive ideas about space and comfort, and moreover, in the overall
picture of rapidly expanding towns, it brings far too few people together in too great a space. As early as the 1990s housing blocks of the
Khrushchyovka type were starting to be demolished and replaced by
even taller blocks. A regular building boom changed the landscape of
council estates. But the increased population density of the building
land freed up by the demolitions and the construction of high-rise
blocks with over twenty floors is just one of the forms marking the
transformation of the post-Soviet town. The most serious change is
the privatisation of housing with all the consequences that entails.
As owners, people are entitled to modernise their own four walls.
New windows were installed in the millions; millions of burglar-proof
doors were fitted; bathrooms and toilets were renovated, balconies
repaired and new furniture introduced. Since tenants were replaced
by owners, the main entrances, which used to be open to everyone

at all hours, have been fitted with an access code or perhaps even an intercom. But this means of course that the charges associated with ownership fall directly on the former tenants; it became necessary to concern oneself with obligations that had always been ignored previously: whether the letter boxes are intact and the staircase cleaned, for example. Changes of this kind call for a radical rethink. Slowly but surely, the social composition of the estates altered. The social mix dissolved; like was drawn unto like. Class segregation had been suppressed in the Soviets' desire to level and equalise. The 'new Russians' who could afford the move left the high-rise block in Chertanovo or Kupchino and tried to relocate into one of the now empty kommunalkas, that is, blocks in the town centres that had been sold off or whose occupants had been evicted—buildings dating back to the early twentieth century or the massive buildings of the Stalin period, so-called German housing, (i.e., those built by German POWs). They were spacious and called for new furnishings; frequently they were transformed into a kind of collection of antiques by people who had come into a fortune overnight. The entrances now are guarded, the former *dezhurnaya* has turned into a *concierge*; the courtyard, which once was the adventure playground and focal point of the house community, now provides parking space for limousines mainly of foreign origin. The wealthy, the upper middle class, the new bourgeoisie has moved into the buildings from which the old bourgeoisie was driven out in 1917, while oligarchs and public officials renew the tradition of the landed gentry in the suburbs and commission Russian or French architects to build properties in the Rublyovka or other hip districts, fenced in by metre-high gated walls under the watchful eye of electronic cameras.

The town as a whole has changed its appearance. It has ceased to need buildings for a Central Committee but it does require them for banks and companies. The new wealth has entered the palaces of the old wealth or has constructed towers that have changed the city skyline in short order. Moscow, for instance, has built the Gazprom Tower, Federation Tower and Moscow City. Formerly, the city had hardly any individual traffic; now it is choking in traffic jams; it needs motorways, garages, car parks, and new regulations to control traffic flows. It creates its own entertainment centres—nightclubs, arcades, malls, gyms and shopping centres. After having been a dull grey for decades, it has changed colours and by night is as brightly lit as the Las Vegas Strip. The HQ of the secret service in the Lubyanka is bathed in searchlights at night. In the outer suburbs, tower blocks are clustered in landscaped parks. The Stalinist high-rise buildings are copied in large residential areas. The housing market is booming since anyone who has come into money in Russia invests it in Moscow. It is not just the city that is changing under the pressure of investors and speculators. Not even in the period of the Stalinist General Plan were so many old buildings torn down; entire districts were gutted and flattened during Yury Luzhkov's tenure as mayor of Moscow. No landmark, however remarkable, has been safe from demolition or a deliberate act of arson. This even included the Hotel Moskva designed by Alexey Shchusev in 1937. Everything happened so fast that this renewal by means of a process of destruction took even the most vigilant observers by surprise.

For a long time, it looked as if the metropolis was being reappropriated by its inhabitants once they had overcome the estrangement between citizens and city caused by the state bureaucracy. This view was confirmed by the hundreds of thousands of people who took part in the demonstrations without their having been sent to join them or been given time off from work. These people streamed over the great boulevards, filled the squares and sometimes pulled down the monuments of a hated past—an example being the monument to Felix Dzerzhinsky in front of the Lubyanka—or defended their newly won freedom behind barricades, as in August 1991.[22] While the oligarchs doled out property and power among themselves, ordinary citizens were busy mastering and indeed relishing their everyday lives. The city acquired a new urbanity and new social manners. There seemed to be no limit to the new initiatives. Kiosks, stalls and tents sprang up, improvised at first but eventually in an organised form. Where previously the high-rise blocks stood at intervals and seemingly in no particular pattern, suddenly there were shops that stayed open day and night, snack bars and modest garden pubs, all of which transformed the council estates into zones full of life. There was no denying that the bazaars and kiosks could also act as bases and contact points for Mafia-type organisations. But now, two decades later, when raiding parties have come in with bulldozers to clear away the kiosk landscape systematically and on orders from the top, one can see very clearly how the kiosks had transformed Moscow and other towns into improvised urban spaces with a 'high quality of life'.

In the long run, people living in the council estates, the Soviet version of David Riesman's 'lonely crowd', will not remain content with this withdrawal into their own four walls. Initially, they were fully occupied with the new arrangement of their lives and homes. But the inhabitants of these estates are not simply silent residents of these minidistricts with their shopping centre, kindergarten, school and metro link; they are also the citizens of a major city in search of ways to publicly discuss the country's problems and resolve them. Following decades when the social and the political took precedence over the private and individual, this withdrawal into the private realm has been overwhelming. It looks like the last stop at the end of a long journey. This began with the flight from the countryside and went via barracks and the kommunalka to private housing in the large-panel prefab estate and from there possibly to a house of one's own. The fences and walls around these properties tell us something about the dream, both old and new, that one's home is one's castle, as well as about the proliferation of crime and fear. Decisions about the future and the reconquest of the town will not be reached in the forests and meadows of the surrounding countryside, but in the town itself. No one can predict how this new town will look. It will become a kind of 'third town' (Dieter Hoffmann-Axthelm), one that goes beyond Stalin's General Plan of 1935 and beyond the large-panel prefab estates of late socialism.[23]

CHAPTER 38

Russkaya Glubinka—the Country beyond the Big Cities

No one who travelled in the Soviet Union could fail to notice the gulf between Moscow and the 'Russian provinces', the flat land all around. It was like time travel between the centuries. An observant commentator, the German journalist Christian Schmidt-Häuer, reported his impressions from a journey by land in the Upper Volga region at the end of the 1970s.

> It is an abandoned village. Not a single person is to be seen, not even a dog or a cat. The windowpanes are broken in most of the peasants' huts; the doors hang loose on the hinges; the rain falls through holes in the roofs. . . . Above the river source there is a wooden hut, which is reached by a narrow footbridge leading from the village. The hut is closed up. My guide told me that there was an old woman still living in the village who had a key to the hut and the Volga. We find her in one of the farmsteads. Yes, she says, she has the key; she is the custodian of the source of the Volga. Her wrinkled face is half covered by a dark cloth. Only her toothless mouth and nose are visible. She says she is 69. We had thought she was 80. 'I was born here', she says, 'I grew up here, I was married here, I buried my mother here and gave birth here to my sons.' 'But in recent times the village has become very empty,' we tell her. 'Of course, it has become empty. There used to be 58 farms here. Now there are only a few old people. The young have all gone to the towns. Nobody wants to live in a village anymore.' 'What does the word Volga mean to you?' 'Volga', she says and thinks about it for a while. 'This place here on the Volga used to be very beautiful. When there were still people here.'[1]

There have been some changes since the source of the Volga became an attraction for the new patriotic tourists. The house above the source has been renovated; the church has likewise been repaired; there is a warden; and yet in all the books that correspondents write at the end of their period of service there is an almost obligatory chapter dealing with the Russia outside the capital and other towns with over a million people and almost all of them contain passages like the one quoted here. I might report on similar impressions from my own travels through the countryside: a bus journey from Leningrad through the Novgorod and Pskov territories; walking tours from Torzhok to Lake Seliger, and from Ostashkov to Rzhev; car journeys from Yaroslavl to the area around Kostroma, to Vologda and Lake Beloye; trips by regular bus from Nizhny Novgorod to Arzamas, by ship down the Volga, by car from the Don to the Caucasus through the fields of Stavropol and Krasnodar that reminded me of the Midwest of the USA, but also upriver on the Yenisei in Siberia near Krasnoyarsk. On such journeys you learn to see the many-sidedness of the country (*mnogolikost*). Wherever you go, you encounter regions, towns and villages whose bleakness and desolation would not be worthy of mention but for their size and extent. For in other countries too, in the American Rust Belt, in La France profonde or in Brandenburg, it is possible to find places and entire regions that people have given up on and abandoned. The fact that we are not talking about mere irritations or overreactions on the part of naïve foreigners but about a serious social malfunction can best be discovered by listening to the Soviet and Russian writers who have spent a lifetime worrying about the emptying-out of the countryside, the slow death of small and middle-sized towns and the collapse of a settlement structure and cultural landscape that grew up organically over centuries. Tatiana Nefedova belongs to a circle of sociologists, ethnologists, demographers and cultural geographers who have investigated the dramatic changes that have taken place beyond the large towns.[2] What Nefedova has called the 'proliferation of black holes in space' has been described no less vividly by the East European historian Carsten Goehrke, who draws a historical parallel with the 'Time of Troubles' at the end of the sixteenth century: 'For the first time since the population expulsions of 1560 to 1620, a new "Wasteland" spread through the nation.'[3]

'A New Wasteland'

In a territory as large as the Soviet Union it would be misleading to speak of units such as 'the village' or 'the countryside'. The climatic conditions as well as the nature of the space and the soil are too varied, to say nothing of the diverse cultural traditions and economic activities in a multinational state, differences that could not be extirpated by the homogenising aspirations of the Soviet state. What could settlement and economic policies have in common where climate and soil conditions diverge so sharply? What could the Russian village—whether the rural commune or, later, the Soviet kolkhoz and sovkhoz—have in common with the economies of the nomads in the Far North or the steppes of Central Asia? Who would want to set the same standards for the immensely fertile Black Earth belt and the arid terrain regularly plagued by overpopulation and drought in the non–Black Earth regions?[4] Little connected agriculture in the Russian North, which had never known serfdom, with the territories where servitude, being tied to the soil and village life, put its stamp on the labour and life of generations. You need only examine the property maps to see that there is a world of difference between the endless fields of the virgin territories of Siberia and Kazakhstan and the miniparcels of private land in Central Russia. Even within the Russian part of the Soviet Union, climate, land and settlement conditions varied so greatly that it is scarcely possible to speak of a homogeneous 'Russian village' or a homogeneous 'Russian province'. But since there was something like an overall Soviet conception of the organisation of agriculture, it follows that something like an organisation of space derived from it—an organisation of the economic, social, cultural and mental space, which continued to be influential in the period following the end of the Soviet Union and for a long time afterward.[5]

We can speak of the common fate of the regions that were the first to pay the price for the industrialisation and urbanisation of the nation. The human energies and material resources that were pumped out of them made the Soviet Union into what it was up to the moment of its dissolution.

The depopulation and disempowerment of the vast hinterlands are the flip side of a process marked by violence, social upheaval and destruction in war that mostly remains hidden from those whose gaze is fixed on modernisation and urbanisation. Down to the present day, townspeople who are focused on themselves and who regard the West as the measure of all things still have very little idea about what goes on in the countryside. A gaze obsessed with the city is part of the professional blindness produced by urbanisation itself.[6] If they know anything about the countryside, it is only through their contacts with other town dwellers who themselves came from a rural background and whose friends and relatives were still living there, or else through a renewed acquaintance with the countryside as a consequence of the new dacha boom in the regions adjacent to big cities. A new link was established once the flight from the countryside was completed. The town moved closer to the country again, that is to say, to its own hinterland, bringing new energies that had been sucked out of it over decades by successive generations. But the dacha boom, the acquisition and transformation of the surrounding countryside by town dwellers in their search for a weekend cottage or a summer holiday home, has created a blind spot with regard to the zone that has expanded beyond the metropolises and large towns. This includes the dying village that has been left to its own devices and the township that has been allowed to rot and about which nobody cares a jot— neither the Kremlin nor the world of oligarchs or foreign investors. Here we find a country that seems to have given up on itself and that everyone wishes to abandon as fast as possible, the energetic, the young and the vigorous above all.

The Central European whose gaze is accustomed to smaller spaces is inclined to explain the impression of emptiness and abandonment that one receives in these 'depressing' regions and localities by pointing to the vastness and 'emptiness' of the country itself. This is a country where the population seems vanishingly small, where the distances between larger settlements and towns seem infinite and settlements often appear to be advance posts of human self-assertiveness in a natural world to whose will one must bend because the energies required to shape and create it are all too limited.[7] This undoubtedly holds good for the almost entirely uninhabited regions of Siberia and the Far East. These regions cover over half the total territory of the Soviet Union or Russia and contain no more than a small fraction of the population. The establishment of the few urban centres beyond the Arctic Circle—Norilsk or Vorkuta, for example—would not have been possible without force, forced labour (in the Gulags) and economic incentives (especially high wages). These deserted spaces contained natural resources such as oil and gas whose yield when sold on the world market enabled first the USSR and then the Russian Federation to support itself financially.[8]

The desolation of which we speak here does not refer to a natural environment almost irredeemably hostile to human settlement, but to an exhaustion arising from the overextension of human capacities, a depletion of what is in any case a fragile network created by human effort and activity, a retreat from the superior power of nature at a moment when the labour of civilisation reached its outer limits. Roads that have ceased to be regularly maintained have become impassable in spring and autumn to the point where they can only be cleared with heavy equipment such as Caterpillar tractors and heavy-duty trucks.[9] The lowest point is reached when villagers realise that it is no longer possible to call a doctor, the village shop can no longer be supplied and no one is left to look after the club or the culture centre. The houses in the village street have been nailed up because not even the young people who have moved to the village can or wish to do anything about them; fences have not been mended, wells fall into disuse and houses sink because the foundations have collapsed. You can see from the fruit trees against which the few remaining cows rub themselves that there was once a garden here. Fixed forms dissolve and what used to be a solid house built from massive tree trunks is now losing its shape; the carvings have fallen off and the roof has caved in. Panes of glass are not replaced because there are no workmen close by and anyway there are no materials. Repairs are not carried out. Houses and barns that have burned down are left alone. Why should anyone try to take the building materials to use elsewhere when there is no longer anyone in the neighbourhood? The only people left are those too old to move and they are still able to provide for themselves by planting potatoes, cucumbers, tomatoes and pumpkin and collecting mushrooms and berries to sell. They may even know someone from the town who would like to rent one of the empty houses—holiday homes 'beyond the bounds of civilisa-

FIGURE 38.1. No thoroughfare in spring or autumn. Such is fate. From Nikolai Borisov, *Povsed-nevnaia zhizn' russkogo puteshestvennika v épohu bezdorozh'ia*, Molodaia gvardiia, Moscow 2010.

tion' for stressed-out townsfolk. Nature encroaches on the settlement and regains its hold on the terrain wrested from it. If occasionally a Humvee with black-tinted windows turns up or the babushka who has refused to move while everyone else is leaving makes all her family arrangements at the top of her voice on her mobile phone, this just underscores the desolate state of affairs in places where the twenty-first century meets up with the eighteenth—a newly built church with golden domes amidst a collection of rotting timber houses and collapsing fences.[10] But basically, nothing further can happen to this world, which has been abandoned, left behind, and forced to rely on

itself. It is practised in survival at the most basic level. These settlements produce no surplus for the market; they have not developed
any greater efficiency based on the division of labour; all they have
are the mechanisms of providing for themselves that enable them to
survive the next winter. They know all about crises and do not panic
even when the situation is hopeless.

A different scene is that of rural landscapes shaped by kolkhozy
or sovkhozy. They are dominated by agribusinesses, granaries, garages, stables, silos, grain elevators and water towers. The newly built
houses are made not of wood but of brick or perhaps of large concrete panels. Everything is on a large scale: the built area, the animal
husbandry, the Caterpillar tractors. Working hours and holidays are
dictated by industrial practice. But the size of the cultivated area is
all out of proportion to the yields; milk production per cow cannot
compete with farms in Western Europe or the USA. Agrotechnology is
omnipresent but poorly maintained and frequently defective because
of the lack of spare parts. Many storage areas full of rusting equipment resemble scrap heaps and cemeteries for farm machinery. Compared to the success of the secondary activities pursued by members
of the collective farms, average productivity is worse than poor. It may
sometimes be the case that the collective farm known as 'October'
owns planes for spraying insecticide, that there is an agronomist on
hand to oversee the scientific management of the farm, and that a
gigantic vehicle park is available; none of that guarantees an efficient
and productive farming operation—particularly when compared to
what goes on in the tiny but intensively farmed private plots and
gardens belonging to the collective farmers.

It is obvious that the collective farms are too big to work efficiently.
Familiarity with farming practices, the willingness to work in the particular and ever-changing climate and soil conditions, the ability to
develop a work rhythm that takes account of these conditions and is
aware that industrial standards are unattainable—all of these remain
beyond the capacity of the collective farms. Defective technology and
poor organisation were never the causes of the failure of the giant
agribusinesses of the Soviet Union but a side effect. Those who wish
to pursue something else and have other skills leave the country-

side. Bitter though this sounds, the countryside becomes the field of 'negative selection'. Its most visible consequence is the ubiquitous excessive drinking and accompanying inability to work. Experts who know the phenomenon speak of a process of *lumpenizatsiya* [going downhill, going to the dogs]. But for the women, life would long since have broken down entirely in these godforsaken places. In many of them the only hope are the seasonal workers from the Caucasus or guest workers from Central Asia who come from alcohol-free cultures and just knuckle down to the job.

The poor yields and low productivity of Soviet agriculture were always known facts and served as the starting point for new attempts at reform and reorganisation without ever addressing the real causes: the inadequate motivation of the immediate producers; the direct, long-term consequences of the expropriation of the peasants; and the restoration of a modernised form of serfdom. The living proof has always been the highly intensive and efficient economy in the 'private sector' or the fact that what used to be the 'granary of Europe' ended up having to import foodstuffs. The subjection of the entire vast nation to the demands of 'socialist accumulation' in the early 1930s also meant the subjection of the peasants to the imperatives of industrialisation and the towns, which amounted to upending ex-change relations between the two. For decades, the inhabitants of the countryside or small towns had to travel to the big cities for pro-visions, and right to the very end of the Soviet Empire, Muscovites only travelled to the countryside if they had brought with them the food that was unobtainable there.

Even though the reasons for the Soviet agriculture catastrophe were widely known, there was a general conviction that in a peculiar blend of euphoria and apocalyptic expectation the end of the USSR would spell the end of the collective farms. Once the bureaucratic superstructure of the kolkhozy had been stripped away, wouldn't a new, longed-for Russian farming economy blossom? Was this not the moment for agriculture to combine the advantages of rational large-scale farming with the powerful impetus arising from the lure of private prosperity? Once the new agricultural code was approved in the 1990s, surely there would be a turnaround, a run on land and property and the convalescence and even renewal of the Russian village that had been destroyed by the sequence of disasters in the twentieth century.

It took a while for the intelligentsia concentrated in the urban centres to respond to this challenge and then they did so only gradually. They had first to rediscover the countryside, take a look around and familiarise themselves with it. A time of discovery, which had actually begun in the late Soviet phase but had not yet entered into the culture of the capital, was approaching. The products of village literature and the so-called *derevenshchiki* (village writers) had their readers but their influence remained marginal in the discourse dominated by an urban public. In the 1960s, the years of dramatic changes in the village, Fyodor Abramov, Viktor Astafiev, Vasily Belov and Valentin Rasputin had all made their contributions to literature, but most people considered their works to be nostalgic and provincial, even nationalistic and reactionary. As in many other fields, the elite of the capital showed itself to be largely unprepared and at a loss when called on to offer solutions to the 'rural question'. In consequence, for a long time—throughout the 1990s and even later—a curious indecision held sway. Some preferred the radical division and redistribution of the former collective farms among private owners. Others chose to retain the kolkhozy and sovkhozy and transform them into modern, capitalist agribusinesses, while members of the old nomenklatura wanted to get their hands on former kolkhoz country in league with the new oligarchic elite. As a result, the debate about the rebirth of the peasantry or the emergence of a modern class of farmers tended to remain somewhat peripheral. Both capital and credit were in short supply, as was experience. The infrastructure needed for individual farmers was lacking as well, and not infrequently the envy seen in village life towards those who were better off or who wanted to escape from the general misery led to people's setting fire to the farm buildings built by the more enterprising farmers against the odds. This envy had previously been disguised as egalitarianism but was now aimed by passive individuals at more active ones, by the lazy at the diligent, by the losers at the winners, and by the left-behinds at those who were striving to better themselves—it was probably one of the most onerous mental legacies of the Soviet village following decades of levelling. Amid this general exhaustion, this apathy and resentment towards those with any initiative, the only people who had a chance were self-evidently the ones who could combine the power of the old establishment with the (often criminal) vigour of the new entrepreneurs. Built on the ruins of the old Soviet collective farms, the new rural estates of post-Soviet agro-holdings easily came to equal in size the possessions of the favourites of Catherine II, the Potemkins, the Orlovs and the Razumovskys—especially in the vast wedge-shaped Black Earth region in the Kursk-Belgorod-Krasnodar triangle. Within two decades a post-Soviet landscape of latifundia had been created, reminiscent of Latin America in many respects. The process of creating this new world of large estates was more or less spontaneous; it has been controlled by Mafia-like organisations and accompanied by gang wars. Thus it did not signify a more or less equal division and distribution of the nation's landed wealth, the social basis of an autonomous society founded on ownership. Instead, it represented an extreme polarisation into large enterprises on the one hand and small-scale businesses based on barter and self-sufficiency on the other.

The breakup of the kolkhozy and sovkhozy was especially dramatic in central and northeast Russia outside the Black Earth region. This was alleviated solely by the dacha boom and the emergence of a highly intensive small farm culture to supply the large towns with vegetables, fruit and milk. It is from here—the periphery of the regions around the big towns—Tver, Pskov, Rostov, Veliky Novgorod and Kostroma—that we find the most vivid pictures of depopulation, decline and the dissolution of the traditional cultural landscape. They now look like 'in-between' zones, nonplaces in which time has not stood still but has slipped backwards.

At particular risk were the towns that had been on the periphery of development in Soviet times and slipped down the supply chain. This included old Russian towns and former provincial capitals—Vologda, Serpukhov, Kaluga, Torzhok, Smolensk, Murom, Ivanovo-Voznesensk, Vyatka and many others. Not infrequently they had lost their status as administrative centres and failed to become focal points of industrialisation in the Five-Year Plan. Quite often, they had also lost their ancient function as hubs of trade and local fairs. By the same token, they were frequently so-called monotowns, their economies entirely dependent upon a single industry and hence vulnerable in a crisis. Many were 'closed cities', part of the 'military-industrial complex', and so had fallen off the maps, as well as off citizens' mental maps.[11] Small and medium-sized towns did not enjoy the benefits of support and modernisation; small towns were low on the list of housebuilding and renovation; they fell into decline and were abandoned. Many were only rediscovered much later, when they became the goal of a nostalgic tourism in search of the 'Old Russia' that had disappeared. Such small and medium-sized towns were remote from the great railway lines, through-roads and pipelines. Since the supply situation was still poor, the inhabitants were dependent on working their own gardens and small fields and keeping their own livestock; this added to their semirural appearance, enabling them to survive 'somehow or other'. When in the late Soviet period there was something of a building programme after all, it only hastened the decline of the older buildings in the abandoned town centres. This amounted to a direct blow to the core of the old government capitals, the centre of the Russian province.

The magical, mythic aspect of the Russian province captured in the great literature of the nineteenth century was based on the configuration of governmental buildings: cathedrals, rows of merchant houses, assemblies of the nobility, the higher education college, the priestly seminar, a few representative streets arranged on the pattern of a chessboard, as well as a few factories and breweries; larger places also had an inn and a station along with the associated workshops.[12] The imminent decline of these centres of Russian cultural development has now provoked the beginnings of a preservation movement as with manor houses and monasteries, and has stimulated the rebirth of local pride and new interest in the history of one's own region.[13]

The Soviet Village: Bled White, Scorched Earth

The history of the Soviet provinces is not simply the reverse side of a history of modernisation and urbanisation. The rural space is rather the scene of an unprecedentedly dense sequence of changes in which the brutal impact of external and internal processes, un-predictable acts of violence and a demographic wasting away over generations went hand in hand. The Revolution had given land to the peasant soldiers streaming home from the Great War. This was a moment of fulfilment for the hopes and expectations of millions, with a shadow side of misery, violence and the senseless destruction of a rural economy already showing sporadic signs of modernisation. In the process, mansions, authorities, relationships of trust and cultural achievements perished—all essential features for a peasantry that had come into possession of land. The party of redistribution—the Bolsheviks who had taken over the agrarian programme of the So-cialist Revolutionaries—was kept in power by the peasantry, against the return of the large landowners promised in the programme of the Whites. The struggle for bread also defined the fronts in the Civil War, which were divided between the rural parts of the Empire, which produced the grain, and the urban parts, which consumed it.[14] The gains achieved by the peasantry from the redistribution of land out-weighed—so they hoped—the unprecedented brutality with which the Bolshevik rulers confiscated the grain under 'war communism' in order to maintain their hold on the towns, 'the besieged fortress'. However, in a few years the village communities revived; the fairs and markets and village craftsmanship blossomed in the mid-1920s, as they had in the days of the Tsarist Empire. The village community, which had thrived through all the disruptions, had maintained itself as a social form and thought of its own survival rather than of the exorbitant industrialisation projects of a political leadership resolved to extract surplus value from the peasants to finance the country's industrialisation.[15]

The assault on the village was planned and executed by the military beneath the innocuous-sounding banner of 'collectivisation'. In fact, it was the first great blow designed to destroy the peasant lifeworlds in the territory of the revolutionised Russian Empire.[16] This is why the years 1928–1932 witnessed the deportation of the most productive and resilient core of the rural population, the 'kulaks', as well as the unleashing and acceleration of a famine designed to break forever the resistance of a peasantry in all its national variations and the de-struction of a cultural and spiritual world with the goal of producing an entirely novel form of society: Soviet society. However resilient the forms, mental world and traditional practices of communal village life might be, and however much the old village community strove to preserve itself within the constraints of the collectivised economy, the fact is that its resistance was broken. None of the many thousands of acts of resistance, attempted murders and actual attacks, or 'women's uprisings' against the pillars of the new establishment were able to do anything to change this. Nor was the underground world of churchgoers or even the flight of people to the cities any more successful.[17] The so-called mass operations of 1937/38 following Instruction No. 0047 were directed in the first instance at the kulaks, who were said to be in league with 'anti-Soviet elements' who wanted to organise an uprising behind the backs of Soviet rulers at the bidding of external enemies.[18] Even today, it is not possible to gauge the full impact of the death toll paid by the peasantry in the 1930s. The statistics will yield only an abstract picture as long as we remain unable to trace the victims district by district, village by village, family by family, name by name and properly record them. But for that we should need a community of people able and willing to bear witness and a society willing to assume responsibility for the witnesses of a Soviet Golgotha. The majority of them did not survive long enough to write down their memories, if indeed they were even able to write.

Most of those who had lost their property, their families and their children in the NKVD campaigns to pacify and annihilate them were called upon a few years later to join the war in defence of the country that had deprived them of everything. The Red Army of Workers and Peasants—to use the official title—was really a peasant army, certainly by name and even more in its social composition. This was true of the ordinary soldier right up to prominent and popular generals who not infrequently owed their promotions to the purges of the old officer corps in 1937. The German war against the Soviet Union cost that country around 27 million dead; it destroyed towns and cities, exterminated the mass of Jews living on Soviet soil, destroyed thousands of villages in a 'scorched earth' campaign, and wiped out whole generations of soldiers, most of whom came from the countryside. The consequences of this were huge: the disruption of the generations and balance between the sexes, not to mention the vast material losses, injuries and psychological traumas. The damage inflicted on the countryside by the war can be seen from the thousands of photographs taken by German troops and national socialist propaganda units of villages set ablaze in Belarus, Ukraine and Russia itself. It can also be seen in the reports and documents of Soviet journalists and photographers of the villages subjected to the scorched earth policy. Blackened chimneys rise up in the snowy landscape, marking the scene of arbitrary and total destruction. To this day there is no village in the countryside afflicted by the war with Germany without a modest memorial to the soldiers born there or who lost their lives there. If we can say that the Soviet village has never recovered from the losses of life, the famine and the moral collapse of collectivisation, this applies even more powerfully to the victims of the Great Patriotic War.

Century-Long Exhaustion

Despite exceptional efforts at reconstruction and numerous reforms as well as greater opportunities and incentives for the kolkhoz peasants, the Soviet village has never really recovered—notwithstanding record harvests, medals for women tractor drivers and an armada of threshing machines duly reported on the front pages of *Pravda* and *Izvestia*—and despite Soviet citizens' ability to cope with apparently hopeless situations. The flight from the village continued after the war—as it did the world over—but without the obstacles built in elsewhere in the shape of property relations and inheritance laws, the attachment to the soil and the desire to live as a farmer. There were attempts to overcome the gulf between town and country, efforts to 'modernise' peasants by turning them into 'workers', which ended up reducing them to the subaltern status of agricultural labourers, who until quite late in the Soviet Union, as late as the 1970s, in fact, never even achieved full freedom of movement. There were also attempts to urbanise the villages by building agro-towns and introducing consumption and greater living space by building large-panel prefab estates even in the countryside. But none of these reforms were able to lead the rural economy out of the blind alley it was stuck in. Even the massive subsidies for kolkhozy and sovkhozy often had the opposite effect. They merely prolonged the extensive form of farming instead of helping the peasants make more intensive use of the existing land and resources. The basic problem—the extremely low productivity—could in this way be prolonged and concealed for decades. The strength to open up the country and develop it, to appropriate it in short, was exhausted. When the Soviet world was in meltdown, it was no longer so surprising that the forces needed to bring about a rebirth of a peasant's or farmer's way of life were not to be found. Instead there was a renewed interest in outsize properties that actually surpassed those of the estates in the Tsarist Empire, except that the modern properties were formed under the aegis of companies, joint ventures and agro-holdings. But this need not be the last word on the subject. Some see a 'normal process' in the expansion of the 'black holes in space',[19] in the depopulation and abandonment of the land, and even an overdue tribute to be paid by modern society to the environment. Thus the reconquest by nature of the manmade world is a project enabling post-Soviet Russia to become a leader in the worldwide environmental movement. Others view the increased population density in the large towns while shrinking the population in their hinterland—as expressed in the dacha boom with the accompanying growth in the local economy—as not just a form of recovery but a way forward for the longer term. As the political scientist and economist Yevgeny Gontmakher has put it: 'we must learn to live in a large territory with a shrinking population.'[20]

PART VIII

Big Data

CHAPTER 39

Spetskhran: Catalogue of Forbidden Books

For foreign scholars the 'Leninka', the State Library in the centre of Moscow with more than twenty million volumes, was often the first and most important address. At the intersection of three metro lines, it was easily and speedily reached. You went up from there, past the Dostoevsky memorial, to the plateau with the long, horizontal building with tall windows, a colonnade of dark stone and sculptures on the roof and you were right in the middle. It was not far to the Kremlin Wall and the Alexander Gardens and even in winter you could go from there to the open-air bath with its clouds of steam rising up, a place where there used to be a building site on which the foundations for the Palace of the Soviets had been laid—all of this at the point where the Cathedral of Christ the Saviour was demolished in 1931 and has since been rebuilt. The library, a masterpiece by the architects Vladimir Shchuko and Vladimir Gelfreikh, who had also delivered the blueprint for the Palace of the Soviets, is a modern, functional 1930s building which tells the observer that its designers had once been supporters of the modernist school. The building is as representative as other great, nationally important libraries: the Library of Congress in Washington, DC, the New York Public Library, the British Library in London, Henry van de Velde's Book Tower in Ghent, the Bibliothèque Nationale de France in Paris, the later State Libraries of Ernst von Ihne and Hans Scharoun in Berlin—knowledge silos of overwhelming dimensions, repositories of everything ever printed and published, depots of national memory and incomparable treasure houses. This impression is maintained through the entrance inspection guarded by two militia men and advances over a broad, gently rising staircase to the first floor, where among the columns and in broad daylight stands the general catalogue: the key, the navigation tool with which to find one's way around the realm of universal knowledge.

Most people who went there for the first time knew the story with the catalogue. The library, the nation's largest ever since it moved from Petrograd, with more or less unlimited resources and supplied with obligatory volumes year after year, nevertheless failed to provide the information expected from general catalogues supposedly serving as repositories of the nation's knowledge. Anyone who had occasion to visit in the 1970s or early 1980s needed only to try it out. The wooden index-card boxes—altogether the central catalogue was supposed to contain around 70.5 million index cards—revealed nothing for Trotsky under T nor for Solzhenitsyn under S, nothing for Nietzsche under N and nothing of Berdyaev under B. Such random samples were not simply a matter of people passing the time confirming their anti-Soviet prejudices; they did in fact tacitly prove what everyone knew. The most illustrious library of the nation and one of the greatest in the world provided no access to many a famous name, great book titles or even entire branches of knowledge, scholarship and culture.[1] Many former users of the Lenin Library will readily recognise their own experience in the description by Soviet library authority Peter Bruhn, who gave this account at the end of the 1980s:

Since the end of the Fifties I have frequently worked in Soviet libraries. As a Western foreigner in the Moscow Lenin Library, for example, one received permission to use Reading Room No. 1, which was quite obviously reserved for privileged users, a remarkable fact if one thinks about external conditions at the time. In other accessible parts of the Library, for example, the hall with the cloakrooms and entrance and exit points, which were overseen by armed militiamen, you would find a constant stream of visitors so that even the catalogues and the reading rooms open to the public were so overwhelmed that for sensitive people working there this could become a real problem of concentration. In contrast, when you opened the door to Reading Room No. 1 and then closed it behind you, you were overcome by a soothing peacefulness and tranquillity. Unlike the overcrowded spaces of the Library, the seats in this room at least in my experience were as a rule not even half-full and sometimes less than a third. You sat comfortably on your own at a desk intended for two, with a lovely view of the Kremlin walls and towers through the tall windows. With its antiquated interior and furnishings that might well have been used by many generations the ambience made you feel truly nostalgic. When darkness fell you switched on the ancient table lamp with which every desk was outfitted. Its old-fashioned design made it look as if it dated back to the days of Lenin's electrification programme. The external circumstances in themselves made you feel you were being given exceptional treatment. However, the true privilege consisted in obtaining books here that were not available to everyone. I soon learned that the books you were looking for were not to be found in the catalogues. As a reader in Reading Room No. 1, you ordered books on unsigned forms that you handed to the librarian. The books were then looked up in catalogues that were evidently available only to insiders and which contained references for books that had long since been removed from the public catalogues. One could see how dangerous this banned literature was considered to be from the fact that this procedure was evidently not thought to be sufficient. In addition (and analogously to locking up poisons in special cupboards in pharmacies), this forbidden literature was separated out and kept in secret stacks (in Russian, *spetskhran*).[2]

The number of books and journals deposited in the spetskhran of the Lenin Library is impressive, as emerged when these items began to be returned to the ordinary collection in March 1987. They amounted to 300,000 book titles, 560,000 journals and a million newspapers.[3]

We may recall similar practices of limited access to documents and archives of state importance obtaining in other countries; an obvious example is the Index Librorum Prohibitorum of the Roman Catholic Church, which listed some 6,000 works—including writings by Kant, Diderot and Balzac—well into the 1960s. There were also the poison cabinets containing inflammatory racist writings or pornography.

The *spetskhrany* which survived in the libraries right up to the time of perestroika or the *spetsfondy* in the archives are of a different kind and only the tip of an iceberg. Both in scope and nature they represent something quite different from simple censorship. In reality what we have here is a state-organised and historically unprecedented purging of the library holdings of an entire nation. During the perestroika years, this was given a name whose drastic nature seems appropriate to the facts of the case. The *spetsfond* was dubbed the 'book-gulag', the special collection a 'concentration camp for books'. 'Everyone knows that during the years 1955–1956 hundreds of thousands of oppressed human beings returned from the camps. But far from everyone knows that quite recently, in 1987–1989, hundreds of thousands of books were liberated from the special concentration camps where they had been pining for as long as fifty or even sixty years', S. Dzhimbinov wrote in 1990 in connection with the dismantling of the spetskhran and the return of the books to the ordinary stacks accessible to the public.[4] The elimination of the 'book-gulag' spelled the end of a practice that had been an integral part of the culture of Soviet scholarship over several generations whose internal logic could not be gainsaid, for all its absurd implications.[5]

Where else could we find entire disciplines—theology, for example—expunged from the catalogues? How can important representatives of the intellectual tradition simply be eliminated from the holdings? Where else has there ever been a requirement that books be read but quoting from them forbidden? Where else were important academic editions and anthologies excluded from general circulation simply because they contained a footnote or an obscure reference to someone who had fallen out of favour at some point during the time of repression? Seldom have we seen a greater contrast between the external spaciousness and munificence of library buildings—whether from prerevolutionary times, as in the case of the Publichnaya in Leningrad, or newly built, as in Moscow—and the private offices in which specialist staff were involved in protracted procedures about whether the call number on a reader's order form should be approved or rejected—without giving any reason. 'The reader neither knew nor could know what was being withheld from him. The special stacks for quarantined literature contained simply an alphabetical catalogue. Only the staff in the special stacks could use its special catalogue, ordinary readers had no access to it. And the amount of information that a researcher could obtain, even if he had the relevant credentials, depended entirely on the good will of the librarian.

FIGURE 39.1. Card-index cabinets in the Catalogue Room of the Lenin Library, today the Russian National Library in Moscow. © Ed Annink, Den Haag.

'The first thing to suffer as a result of the Jesuitical rules of the special repository was bibliography. No precise references to foreign publications were allowed. Special-repository literature could be referenced neither in the catalogues nor in bibliographical lists.'[6] Deep inside, hidden behind their special catalogues, the library staff decided, over decades—doubtlessly with a meticulous attention to detail—what could be read, studied, cited and published. Or more precisely, it was not the knowledgeable experts who were privy to the mysteries of the excluded world of books—who made the decisions—but those who had created the system in the first place and who continually modified it down to every last detail, adjusted it to the new political situation and perfected it.

The beginnings of the special stacks coincided with the Bolshevik takeover of power. The newspaper of the party of Constitutional Democrats was banned as early as 26 October 1917; the ban on all other non-Bolshevik newspapers followed in the summer of 1918. The institutional form in which book production was to be selected and censored in the future gradually took shape. Decisive steps towards this goal were undoubtedly the setting-up of the central authorities, such as Glavlit, who were to be responsible for management, control and censorship. From the end of the Civil War in 1920, Glavarkhiv and Knizhnaya Palata were responsible for printing, publication and libraries. The founding of these central authorities went together with a double, contradictory process. On the one hand, large, public and private libraries were confiscated and opened to the public; the closed holdings of the old Tsarist archives were opened and made available in impressive editions designed to expose the incompetence of the ancien régime, the suppression of the revolutionary movement and the imperialist foreign policy. On the other hand, new collections of books and documents were put into depots to which only the privileged had access. From the very first days, the Bolshevik leadership laid down guidelines for the 'cleansing' of public libraries and began to set up the relevant special sections in the libraries and archives.

By 1920, with the creation of Glavlit, Glavarkhiv and Knizhnaya Palata, the institutions needed to centralise libraries and publication were mainly in place. These specified what had to be collected, segregated and locked away. Alongside the book collections, Knizhnaya Palata, the other legal deposit libraries were the Petrograd Publichnaya and the Moscow Rumyantsev Library (Moscow's old public library in Pashkov House from before the Revolution), all of whom were entitled to receive a copy of every new book, including books from the Russian emigration. Narkompros (the People's Commissariat for Enlightenment) and the Cheka (All-Russian Extraordinary Commission, i.e., the secret police) were instructed to draw up guidelines for dealing with the incoming publications. Leading positions in these activities were taken by Lenin's widow, Nadezhda Krupskaya, and Pavel Ivanovich Lebedev-Polyansky.[7] In the early 1920s the spetskhran of Moscow Library preserved not just the secret documents of various people's commissariats, the General Staff of the Army and the GPU, but also the journalism and press of the White movement and Vasily Shulgin; of Sergey Witte; the correspondence of Tsarina Alexandra Fyodorovna with Nicholas II; the history of the Second Russian Revolution by Pavel Milyukov; and Nikolay Sukhanov's memoir *The Russian Revolution*.

Gradually, four large groups were identified for sequestration in the spetskhran up to the time it was dismantled in 1991. There were spetskhrany in two to three dozen large libraries. In the majority of cases, books that were 'purged' in this way were simply pulped—that is, destroyed.

The first group consisted of books, magazines and newspapers published between 1917 and 1921 which had failed to pass the censorship. These were publications by the Whites, the 'Greens', the Ukrainian Makhno movement, and the White generals Denikin, Wrangel and Kolchak.

The second group consisted of publications on Soviet territory during the years 1918–1936 which were banned by the censorship because they contained names or quotations of nonrehabilitated members of the Bolshevik Party. These included Leon Trotsky, Grigory Zinoviev, Lev Kamenev, Nikolay Bukharin, Alexey Rykov and others. This group comprised around 8,000 titles, with many propagandist pieces among them.

The third group was made up of books, magazines and newspapers in Russian emanating from Western Europe, the USA, South America, Asia and Australia—in other words, publications by Russian émigrés. Precise figures are not available, but it has been estimated that 99 percent of Russian émigré literature ended up in the spetskhran. The Lenin Library experienced extraordinary growth with the transfer of the Prague foreign literature archive—the principal émigré archive—to Moscow at the end of the Second World War. The means were lacking for the systematic acquisition of Russian émigré writing after the war, although this deficit was partly rectified by the confiscation of 'illegally' imported émigré writing (often with handwritten dedications).

The fourth group—foreign-language books, magazines and newspapers—constituted the largest collection in the spetskhran because it included the whole of 'bourgeois', non-Marxist, anti-Soviet Western literature—from *Time*, *Le Figaro*, *Stern*, *Newsweek*, right down to *Der Spiegel*. There were also around 260,000 books in which an offensive paragraph or footnote sufficed to withdraw a valuable edition from circulation.[8]

The guidelines for the purification of public libraries and the locking-away of noxious literature were followed by decrees. Thus the 'Guide to the Elimination of All Forms of Literature from Libraries, Reading Rooms and Book Bazaars' of 1924 listed over one thousand titles, including schoolbooks from the Tsarist period, texts in old, prerevolutionary orthography, biographies of non-Bolshevist personalities and a history of the Makhno movement. Trade unionists independently set about purifying their own libraries—which shocked such well-versed people as Krupskaya. There followed the 'Instruction Concerning the Monitoring of Books in Libraries' (1926), which criticised the excessive purification of libraries and destruction of books. In the same fashion, access to the special collections was regulated by further instructions.[9] The Party archives set up at about the same time, as well as those of other institutions, also became de facto special archives to which access was strictly controlled and restricted. All this made it inevitable that documents and printed matter—from before the Revolution or from internal party struggles—were increasingly deployed as *kompromat*, as a weapon in the battles of the group around Stalin with oppositional factions.

The most important phase in the formative period of the spetskhrany was during the 1930s when public libraries at all levels—right down to local and village libraries—were combed for works that could conceivably be connected to suppressed parties and organisations in any way. The purging of libraries became an ongoing practice. With every show trial, every change of political direction, new groups were picked off—after the so-called Academy Affair, it was the works of historians such as Yevgeny Tarle and Sergey Platonov. The condemnation of the Trotskyite-Zinoviev faction was followed by the eradication of all writing associated with this 'group'. These campaigns to destroy books were not just initiated and stimulated from on high but were echoed by similar attacks 'from below' and together they developed into 'bacchanals of purification'. Attempts were made to explain them with reference to the lower levels of education and the iconoclastic, anti-intellectual attitudes 'of the people'. At a local level, responsible librarians competed to enlarge the number of proscribed books on the lists that had come down from Glavlit. This in turn led to chaotic situations in the acquisition and cataloguing departments because no one wanted to take on more responsibility for purging the libraries. Confronted by this chaos, librarians did not trust themselves to assign specific titles to the general collections—for example, books on military subjects were felt to be especially risky. Important journals such as the *Communist International*, the *Bolshevik*, *Unter dem Banner des Marxismus* and even some of Marx's own writings, such as *The Class Struggles in France*, were pulled from circulation. Just between 1935 and 1936, 49,000 domestically published titles migrated into the *spetskhran*.[10] This process culminated in Stalin's version of history in the *History of the Communist Party of the Soviet Union (Bolsheviks)*, the so-called Short Course.

By 1937 Glavlit had become an instrument for the total control of libraries as an institution and the dominance of the spetskhran system. In 1938–1939 a further 199 regulations (*prikazy*) for prohibiting additional book titles were introduced. The works of 1,869 writers and 7,809 more titles were banned, as well as 4,512 individual publications and 2,833 anthologies; 1,299 titles were pulped. Altogether during these years 24,138,799 books were destroyed (*unichtozheno*). In October 1938 the system for the 'special treatment' of newspapers and journals was perfected. In 1940, after war had broken out, seventy-five decrees about segregating books were issued. In them, 362 authors were prohibited, while 3,700 monographs and 757 titles were pulped (i.e., not diverted to the spetskhran). The system of special collections was then extended to include other products. In August 1938 setting up spetsfondy in museums which possessed 'harmful' exhibits, such as six hundred portraits and photos of Trotsky, slides of the Romanov family and other exhibits of no 'historical and artistic value', was proposed. In practice, special collections sprang up everywhere in the large museums and in 1938 the management of archives was transferred to the NKVD.[11]

After the war even books by former friends and sympathisers of the USSR vanished. Authors included Lion Feuchtwanger, Ernest Hemingway, André Malraux, Upton Sinclair and Howard Fast, who broke with communism after the crushing of the Hungarian uprising in 1956 and whose books were then banished. It is not difficult to imagine

the consequences of treating libraries in this way. Libraries ceased
to act as meeting points of universal knowledge and unlimited access to it. They became places where education and the circulation of
ideas turned into filters and defensive barriers, promoting isolation.
Catalogues of forbidden writings and books withdrawn from circulation turned into documentary records of intellectual tutelage and
oppression. They became keys to opening up the world of forbidden
knowledge, instruments for navigating an intellectual topography
beyond the censorship of an all-powerful party.

The control of the spetskhrany resulted in a curious distortion
of discourse and a special pathology of intellectual and academic
work. It led to isolation from the general flow of living and boundary-
crossing thought; it slowed the exchange of ideas, bifurcated the
world of knowledge and produced a general provincialisation. However, it was not able to destroy the flow of thought and knowledge
absolutely, only to impede and severely disrupt it. Where there was no
open access to sources, smugglers' routes for intellectual contraband
were sought and found. Not for nothing were the most sought-after
objects at customs checkpoints reading ranging from Solzhenitsyn's
Gulag Archipelago to the latest edition of *Cosmopolitan*. Literature not
found or listed in local catalogues was somehow procured. People's
inventiveness knew no bounds. Russia had its own newspapers and
journals beyond its borders: *Novy zhurnal* in New York; *Kontinent*,
Sintaksis, the *YMCA Press* and *Russkaya mysl* in Paris; *Overseas Press
International* in London; *Posev* in Frankfurt am Main; *Ardis* in Ann
Arbor. They all printed and delivered *tamizdat* writings that were
simply unavailable in the native land of poets and scholars who had
been expelled and banished: Nikolay Berdyaev, Nikolay Lossky, Lev
Shestov, Pyotr Struve, Ivan Ilyin and Pitirim Sorokin. The culture of
reprints blossomed in the shadow of the prohibition and they found
their way into the Soviet Union. People wrote, copied other people's
writings, created large numbers of carbon copies (*samizdat*), sometimes even using the Xerox photocopiers that were few and far between but could occasionally be found in scientific institutes. In this
way the writings of both old and young members of the intelligentsia
bypassed the libraries and their spetsfondy and found readers or
perhaps listeners—via Western radio stations.[12] It was in vain that

the authorities strove to prohibit or criminalise these writings or call a halt to this wave of publications. Radio Svoboda set up the 'Arkhiv Samizdata' in the latter years of the Cold War and research centres focused on collecting underground literature in the Soviet Union and the Eastern bloc. These were in a sense the necessary complement to the literature available in the official catalogues. Together they represented the reunion of all the knowledge that had accumulated on both sides of a frontier that had now become obsolete.[13]

Ultimately, the guardians of the spetskhrany were doomed to defeat. In 1990 the Lenin Library mounted an exhibition 'Publications from the Special Collections of the Lenin Library That Have Been Restored to the Open-Access Shelves'. It displayed around eight hundred exhibits, which could be seen as a kind of epitaph to this chapter of spetskhrany, especially taken together with the enthusiastic comments in the visitors' books. These conveyed a feeling of arriving at a state of adulthood, a sense of freedom regained and hence an experience of the very first order. The exhibition was a reminder of a period when the powers in the land had taken it on themselves to declare their citizens too immature to have access to these writings; they presumed to pronounce what was true and what was false. Today's generation cannot comprehend such an experience: it can discover for itself everything it wants to know in the vast spaces of the internet; it can discover the catalogues of libraries large and small, the archives of the entire globe. It now has unrestricted access online to hundreds of thousands of documents kept secret until quite recently whose possession could have led to a prison sentence or detention in a camp; it has at its disposal the digitalised version of all Russian literature regardless of whether it was published within the country or beyond. For such a generation, the catalogue boxes with lists of forbidden books are historical documents, at once a memorial and a reminder.[14]

CHAPTER 40

Diagrams of Progress, Diagrams of Catastrophes

The nationalisation of the economy after 1917 produced the new institutions and apparatuses of the centralised command economy but over and above that it created a new language—the language of plans and bureaucratic planners. The plan stood for the common good as against the egoism of private interests, for conscious action as against anarchy and chaos, for the superiority of collective rationality as against the irrationality of an unplanned and anarchic economy. As early as December 1917, the Supreme Soviet of the National Economy was established. This was followed by the Council for Labour and Defence, the State Planning Commission (Gosplan) and others. An early form of the central planning of the economy had been the State Commission for the Electrification of Russia (GOELRO), established in 1920. The coordination and decision-making of these organisations depended on the gathering of information and its onward transmission. The new planning functions and management arms required data about what was going on throughout the gigantic empire; the development of agriculture, the 'cut-off line' between agriculture and industry, the state of technical and mechanised development, the degree of literacy and other professional qualifications, all of which would chart the recovery of an economy badly dislocated by the war, revolution and Civil War.

With the end of the New Economic Policy, during which the economy had recovered and reached prewar levels, and with the passing of the first Five-Year Plan for 1928–1933, something quite new emerged. After prolonged debates about minimal, maximal and optimal variations, medium- and long-term directives were developed for the overall economy and for individual sectors. The principal priorities for capital investments were now fixed and production increases set. The Five-Year Plan became the great project, the 'great change' in which a backward agricultural country was to be transformed into an industrial nation in the shortest possible time, a nation that would be in a position to catch up with and overtake the developed nations of the capitalist West.[1] The violent consolidation of the millions of traditional peasant holdings and the forced industrialisation with reckless production increases stand at the centre of the first Five-Year Plan, which would be followed by many others right down to the end of the Soviet Union.

Metaphors for the New Age

The first Five-Year Plan launched a great flood of data, tables, charts and diagrams. Before the new world became reality, it appeared in the shape of tables and columns of figures. Party congresses defined production targets with dizzying growth rates. No target, however ambitious, seemed unattainable. The production quotas for coal and oil, the quantities of shoes and garments, the areas under cultivation and the size of the harvests, the key figures for the number of freight cars and passengers transported by rail, the numbers of trucks and threshing machines rolling off the production lines—all contributed to an irrefutable panorama of progress encapsulated in figures. The signs of this progress—headframes, blast furnaces, high-tension cables, water towers—were projected onto building walls and façades. Steeply rising curves and production figures became a feature of public spaces. The title pages of newspapers could no longer appear without graphics and tables showing the latest production records. The socialist 'emulation' unleashed between the different collectives was reflected in the competition between production teams and their achievements were illustrated in impressive graphs. Charts illustrated the worldbeating growth rates in the numbers of primary schoolchildren, and the curve symbolising improvements in health care rose dramatically, while the graph for venereal disease showed a decline to almost zero. Maps displayed towns that had sprung up from nothing, new roads and canals. Columns of figures showed the expansion of kindergartens—in a country that was still being destabilised by gangs of homeless orphans. Tables of all kinds depicted growing numbers of members—in trade unions, sports clubs and reading rooms. It is the picture language of a mass mobilisation that embraced all the available human and material resources in the territory of the Soviet Union.

From that time on, the images of progress belonged to what later came to be known as the 'world of the media'. The development of this world involved statisticians who collected and analysed the data, as well as artists and designers who translated the dry figures into images. The Soviet Union even set up an institute at the end of 1931 to cater to this and ensure that it all took place in accordance with the highest possible academic and aesthetic standards. This was Izostat— the All-Union Institute of Pictorial Statistics. It survived formally until 1940. Its publications give us a good idea of the nature of the picture language at work during the first Five-Year Plan.[2] A series of maps with the title 'Catching Up with the Capitalist Countries in Ten Years and Overtaking Them' dating back to 1931[3] contained a set of pictures consisting of pictograms, symbols and photographs illustrating the nature of sugar production—each sugar loaf stood for 200,000 tonnes of sugar produced; the picture of a threshing machine showed the growth in production between 1930 and 1933. The annual increase in university students was illustrated by a growing number of stick figures, each of which stood for 20,000 students. The sixty-sheet folder entitled 'The Struggle for Five Years in Four' of 1932[4] compared steel production levels in capitalist countries with that of the Soviet Union over the past twenty years, or the growth of unemployment, in which the figure of an out-of-work person stood for 500,000 unemployed; the comparison of construction projects in the USA and the USSR in 1929–1932 was designed to illustrate the contrast between the Great Depression and the Soviet take-off. Another publication—'15 Years October' of 1932[5]—was designed to explain tractor production and the worldwide growth of unemployment, in simple symbols, pictograms and the appropriate colours. The English edition of 'The Second Five-Year Plan in Construction' of 1934[6] portrayed the dramatic expansion of collectivisation in graphics reduced to a minimalist design—there was no mention of the hundreds of thousands of deported peasants and their families, no hint of the famine triggered by the collectivisation policy or its millions of dead.

The 'Vienna Circle' and Moscow

The staff at Izostat—around seventy between 1932 and 1934—were not alone in developing simple statistical diagrams based on scientific data that also contrived to produce catchy pictograms to convey information about society.

You need only glance at a selection of charts to see the similarities between international approaches to data visualisation about social conditions. The primary model of innovation in the field was *Gesellschaft und Wirtschaft: Bildstatistisches Elementarwerk*, initiated and published by Otto Neurath. The original project was an exhibition mounted by Neurath in the Vienna Town Hall in 1925 to mark the foundation of the Gesellschafts- und Wirtschaftsmuseum. The exhibition displayed modes of production, social orders, cultural stages and life attitudes. Subsequently, the exhibits were reduced to a portfolio of one hundred coloured plates which could be easily transported and employed as a popular educational tool.[7] 'The aim was to make use of symbols to depict social phenomena, with easily grasped arrangements of lines, shapes and figures to represent social interconnections. Statistically comprehended facts would be brought to life.'[8] In his introduction to the portfolio, Neurath wrote,

> The present elementary work on pictorial statistics *Gesellschaft und Wirtschaft* is the first systematic attempt to build on the careful editing and linking-up of available data and combinations of every conceivable sort so as to present people with *a colourful picture* of contemporary human civilisation and its development. Whoever wishes to understand, for example, the meaning of international trading relations, the colonial economy, migration, the modern trading organisations of America and Europe, the position of the Soviet Union in the overall production and consumption of the world within the framework of the great social drama being presently enacted ... will find an initial enlightenment in these colourful plates. What these plates show in the form of simplified, vivid images will be further developed and supplemented by the text and accompanying tables. But the pictograms remain the key elements. Following Comenius, they aspire to be the beginning of a new *Orbus pictus*.[9]

This use of imagery was the result of a systematic development of symbolic images or what Neurath referred to as the 'Viennese method', whose success had gone far beyond Vienna itself and reached Holland, America and the Soviet Union. Its aim was to make use of signs to render relative quantities visible. 'A new pictorial language is being developed, which is not just coherent and precise but which also shapes signs and creates order in an attractive and pleasing manner.'[10] The new visual language, which would later be codified as the ISOTYPE (International System of Typographic Picture Education), was based on transforming abstract, scientific knowledge into concrete, socially relevant propositions, of translating abstract numbers into easily grasped signs that would be useful for a concept of 'museums for the future'.[11]

Neurath said about these signs: 'As far as possible, the signs must be clear in themselves, without the aid of words, that is to say, they must be "speaking signs". They must differ from one another so that there can be no doubt about their correct name when you see them for the second time. They must be so simple that they can be arranged in sequence like letters. The signs must be shaped so that the viewer does not tire of seeing rows with the same sign.'[12]

Basically, there is nothing that cannot be expressed in such pictorial signs—systematised into a lexicon of pictograms. A pedagogic motif becomes visible too: 'The pedagogic aspect of the social sciences is still undeveloped, more particularly, a systematic account of visual modes of representation. With increasing frequency you come across attempts to borrow graphs and tables from scholarly works and make them cruder and more colourful. This turns out to be too difficult; such abstract figures frighten readers off. So the answer is pictures! But this insight does not go far enough; you have to know how to make proper use of pictures.'[13]

Neurath spoke of the importance and memorability of 'statistical hieroglyphs': 'Hieroglyphs fascinate me chiefly because their colours and shapes attract me and because one can evidently join the little figures together so as to develop a picture language. I regretted the fact that the old picture writing had gradually gone out of usage instead of becoming the foundation for an international picture language that might have brought all the peoples of the earth together.'

Neurath repeatedly emphasised the importance of the visual: 'Anyone who wishes to make a quick and lasting impression will make use of images. . . . Modern people receive a large part of their knowledge and their general education through the impressions created by images, illustrations, photographs and films. The newspapers publish more pictures year on year. This is supplemented by the advertising industry which operates on the one hand with optical signals and on the other with visual representations.'[14] Again, '*Modern* man is primarily a *visual creature*. Advertisements, information posters, cinema, illustrated papers and magazines bring a major portion of all education to the broad masses. Even people who read a lot of books derive an ever-increasing stimulus from pictures and picture series. The tired person can take in quickly something that would be harder to grasp just by reading. Over and above that, visual instruction is a means for educating more disadvantaged adults who tend to be more receptive to optical impressions as well as to provide greater opportunities for more disadvantaged young people who would normally have no access to them. . . . Words separate, images bring together.'[15]

The 'Viennese method' reveals the hand of the brilliant Otto Neurath, a central figure of the Vienna Circle, that unique group of philosophers, scientists, sociologists, mathematicians and town planners who, following on from Ernst Mach's Empirio-criticism, were intent on a critical renewal of philosophy and a cross-disciplinary, synthetic view of the individual sciences. Their intellectual stance was that of a populist enlightenment and a desire to educate ordinary people that had developed around Austro-Marxism.[16] Rarely has there existed such a closely linked, free association of thinkers inspired by high ideals of learning and wishing to apply that learning in practice—in town planning, in the democratisation of education but also in the natural sciences. It is no accident that members of the Vienna Circle such as Rudolf Carnap and Otto Neurath should have followed 'the Soviet experiment' with close attention and established contact with avant-gardist circles in Moscow as early as the late 1920s. Neurath took a lead in setting up an institute in Moscow on the lines of the Vienna Museum; he also instructed its personnel in the Viennese method and visited Moscow frequently for that purpose. Between 1931 and 1934 Neurath and his key collaborators, Marie Neurath, Gerd

Arntz and Friedrich Bauermeister, regularly spent time in Moscow, where Neurath also made the acquaintance of Nikolay Bukharin. They even floated the idea of using Moscow as a base for a 'Museum of the Future', a parallel to the Viennese Museum of the Economy and Society. It was to be built on the present-day Theatre Square opposite the Bolshoi Theatre. The architect Josef Frank—likewise a member of the Vienna Circle—had even begun to produce designs for the museum.[17]

When Neurath and his colleagues came to Moscow, the ground had long been prepared. The most important members of Izostat, the Institute of Pictorial Statistics, founded in 1931, had been experimenting quite independently during the 1920s: Mayakovsky's ROSTA Windows—with text and pictures—the revolutionising of book design, the tradition of posters and wall newspapers and the school of Soviet design. Walter Benjamin was one of the first to become aware of the walls covered with illustrative materials in a club for peasants: 'The material here consisted largely of statistics, some of which had been illustrated with little coloured pictures, posted here by the peasants themselves (village life, agricultural development, production conditions and cultural institutions were all recorded), but the walls are also covered with displays of tools, machine parts, chemical retorts, etc.'[18] Among Neurath's social and professional contacts were El Lissitzky and his wife, Sophie Küppers.[19] The Russians, then, were in no need of tutorials but cooperated with their 'guest workers' from Vienna on equal terms. This can easily be seen from the works of Ivan Ivanitsky, who even wrote a study of the Viennese method.[20]

The 'Viennese' kept out of Soviet politics but did not fail to notice that things were happening in the country that could not be reconciled with their promise to illustrate the world and provide a rational account and explanation of what they witnessed. Gerd Arntz, the designer in chief of the Viennese method, was fully aware of the devastating famine and the arrests of Soviet citizens. En route to Sochi in 1932/33—a stay on the Black Sea coast was part of his fee—he passed through the hunger lands of Ukraine and was able to see how people around him and in the neighbourhood simply disappeared without a trace. He knew about the dark sides of the 'Great Change' that were simply absent from the pictorial statistics of progress, the graphs showing successes and increasing progress, and the growth rates in the visual representations of the first Five-Year Plan.[21] The gap between the charts that depicted the world as it should be and the way it was in reality was too great. The relationship between the Vienna Museum and Izostat came to an end in 1934. But for Neurath, there was no way back to Vienna. The Civil War in Austria and the establishment of the Austro-fascist Dollfuss regime made it impossible for him and his colleagues to return to Vienna. The Vienna Museum closed down. Neurath travelled from Moscow via Prague directly into exile in the Netherlands until the Germans occupied Holland, forcing him to flee still farther, to Britain.

The Missing Millions and the Destruction of Statistics

The destruction of pictorial statistics and their transformation from a tool of enlightenment into an instrument of totalitarian propaganda began with the destruction of the foundations of statistics of every kind: the establishing and processing of the empirical data. Tables, graphs and diagrams are simply the visual rendering of those 'dry figures'. As far as Russia was concerned, the situation seemed to be as it appeared to the perceptive Astolphe de Custine early in the nineteenth century: 'Russia is the country of directories; when you look at the inscriptions, everything seems splendid, but one should beware of going any further. If you open the book, you discover nothing of what has been proclaimed. . . . The more remote regiments are cadres without any men; the towns, the streets are simply projects, the nation itself is nothing but a notice to Europe which has let itself be deceived by an ill-advised diplomatic fiction.'[22]

In the early Soviet Union too, a conflict of this kind arose between political power and decision-making on the one hand and an independent statistical practice on the other. The latter could take its lead from prerevolutionary statistics, which had been based on international standards. The massive Census project of 1897 in the Tsarist Empire had been one of the admirable achievements in that tradition. Statistical machinery was set up at the same time as institutions of central planning and economic management. In June 1918 the first

All-Russian Congress of Statisticians was held and the Central Administration of Statistics (Tsentralnoe statisticheskoe upravlenie, TsSU) established. Important statistical surveys duly followed: at the end of 1918, the first all-Russian census of industry and the professions; August 1920, census of professional groups; 1920, survey of data for the State Electrification Plan. There was a 'period of enthusiasm' especially in the community of experienced *zemstvo* statisticians.[23] In fact, with all its upheavals and conflicts the situation of postrevolutionary society must have been a fascinating field for innovative and experimental statisticians. Important theoretical and methodological developments all owed a debt to the state of affairs that obtained in the 1920s. Typical examples were Vasily Leontiev's 'input-output' matrix, Nikolay Kondratiev's model of long wave cycles, Alexander Chayanov's work on cooperatives and the discourses on the economics of the transitional phase.

With Stalin's 'top-down revolution' and the much touted 'disappearance of the exploiting classes' because of collectivisation, statistics found itself assigned quite new challenges by the Communist Party. While the statisticians based their studies on the complex realities of a backward agrarian economy, the political leadership relied on the 'Five-Year Plan in four years'. Empirical reality had to give way to the goals that had been set. And if the statisticians showed reluctance or failed to comply, they were dismissed or even murdered—as was the case in 1937. As Alain Blum has shown, the precarious nature of independent surveys became visible in the rapid turnover of its leading figures.[24] Between 1918 and 1941, the TsSU directorate had eight different directors; five of them were sentenced to death and shot in the year of the Great Purge. Three-quarters of the personnel in the TsSU were replaced during that period. There had been disagreements as early as the 1920s, whether about the estimated quantities of grain to be delivered by the peasants or the forecasts of the investments needed for the renewal of industrial plants. Experienced statistician Pavel Popov was replaced by Valerian Osinsky, a member of Bolshevik leading circles, only for him to be criticised in turn for his 'opportunistic right-wing attitude' on the collectivisation question and forced to cede his position to another leading Bolshevik, Vladimir Milyutin. Osinsky had once spoken about the 'death of statistics'. In

1932 disagreements reached the point of a frontal attack on the TsSU and its chief Ivan Kraval, who had drawn attention to the famine of 1932 and the consequent decline in population. In 1934 the Central Administration of Economic Record-Keeping (Tsentralnoe uprav-lenie narodno-khozyaystvennogo uchota, TsUNKhU) was accused of sabotage. At the Seventeenth Party Congress, Stalin ignored all the existing data and proclaimed that the population of the Soviet Union had reached 168 million, which was 7.5 million more than the information provided by the TsUNKhU. The statisticians' objections to these figures were dismissed as slanders.

The history of the Census of 1937 is the most tragic event in the history of Soviet statistics and that year the—lethal—culmination of a conflict that ended with the destruction of an independent statistics service and the murder of leading experts—a still largely unknown chapter in the history of European science.

Following Stalin's pronouncement that between 1930 and 1933 the population had grown from 160.5 to 168 million, the statisticians were initially unable to confirm his figures. In interviews and discussions with the leadership, Ivan Kraval made attempts to explain about 'the missing millions'. He pointed to the famine following collectivisation, to the Central Asian nomadic tribes who attempted to elude collec-tivisation by fleeing across the border and to the numbers who had perished in the camps. In the wave of purges in 1937/38, half the direc-tors of the TsSU were shot, including Kraval himself, and many were sent to the camps. In 1938 Ivan D. Vermenichev, who had succeeded Kraval, also fell victim to the wave of repression.[25]

The results of the 1937 Census were not published until after the fall of the Soviet Union. In the Great Soviet Encyclopedia (volume 47, 1940), it does not even merit a mention. The new census planned for 1939 delivered numbers that corresponded to the wishes of the political leadership. As we can see from the records of Kraval's inter-rogations, which have now become available, as well as the memoirs of survivors such as Mikhail Kurman, the professional ethics of the Russian-Soviet statisticians of the old school were upheld despite the threats of torture and death. The victims included Nikolay Kon-dratiev, who was given a prison sentence in 1930, condemned to death by a military tribunal on 17 September 1938 and then shot.

In the Second World War it became clear that statistical surveys were indispensable if the necessary technical and human resources were to be fully mobilised for the front, just as they had been for the period of reconstruction. In 1959 the first all-Union census after the war was carried out; it demonstrated the long-term effects of the human losses during the war as well as the changes in the relative populations of the different ethnic groups in the Soviet Union. Diagrams, tables and other visual representations on the front pages of the newspapers in the 1950s and 1960s documented not just the expansion of cultivated land in the new territories, and not just the increase in steel production, but also the transition to the socialist welfare state, as illustrated in the columns and figures pointing to the growth of consumption: of living space, refrigerators, vacuum cleaners, motorbikes and longer holidays—all in crass distinction to the alleged stagnation or actual decline in the capitalist West.

Otto Neurath's Project, Still Unfulfilled

Otto Neurath died in 1945 in exile in Oxford. Had he had the opportunity to put his plan for a worldwide network of 'museums of the future' into practice, he would undoubtedly have recalled his idea of making Moscow a base. If what he had prescribed for his Vienna Museum and his Mundaneum project was true, namely that all forms of production, social orders, stages of culture and life attitudes can be grasped empirically and represented in pictorial diagrams—both their history and compared with each other—then stating what post-Soviet museum personnel ought to have done is straightforward. They should have made use of pictorial statistics to show what Soviet power was incapable of showing. They should have presented not just the diagrams showing what had been achieved, diagrams with which the country had been flooded for decades, but also the dark side of events. They should have put the diagrams of progress together with the catastrophes and disasters and merged the two. The requisite data are now all available even if not everything about them has been clarified. The Viennese method would still be capable of converting the quantities of information into pictorial statistics, but could be enhanced by data centres, digitalisation and global networks. Only combined would these yield a true picture of the miracles of human capabilities and the horrors of humanity's descent into barbarism, the inextricable tangle of rising and falling curves of violence and mass deaths. Alain Blum's monograph—*Naître, vivre et mourir en URSS*— would be an apt description of the resultant assemblage of rising and falling curves.

The population explosion that could be observed in the late phase of the Tsarist Empire moved in parallel to the numbers of victims of the chronic famines caused largely by periods of drought.[26] This was followed in 1914–1921 by what Peter Holquist calls 'a continuum of crisis' with millions of victims.[27] We can glean an approximate picture of the extent of the human losses from Manfred Hildermeier's *History of the Soviet Union*.[28] The military activities of the First World War brought death to 1.7 million soldiers, created 4.95 million war invalids and left 2.5 million prisoners of war. The Revolution and the Civil War killed 9–10 million people—four times more than the First World War itself; a further 2 million were lost to the nation through flight and emigration.[29] The population of the big cities declined drastically—from 2.1 million to 700,000 in Petrograd by the end of the Civil War. The introduction of the New Economic Policy led to the rapid restoration of agriculture and the recovery of industry, but the termination of that policy in 1928 saw a radical shift in conditions in the countryside. Whereas in 1928 only 1.7 percent of farming businesses had been collectivised, this figure had reached 61.5 percent by 1932. The record figures for the expansion of collectivised farmland contrast with the imminent collapse of crop production and animal husbandry—the peasants resisted the forced collectivisation and confiscations by slaughtering their own animals and consuming the remaining grain themselves.[30] The numbers of victims of collectivisation increased by leaps and bounds in parallel to the rapid rise in the number of collective farming businesses. A million peasants were deported together with their families; between 315,000 and 420,000 died in the process because of the dire conditions in the north of the country. As a consequence of the famine unleashed by collectivisation and drought, around 5 to 6 million lost their lives.[31] Because of the extreme mortality rates and the fall in birth rates, the demographic curve simply came to a stop.

Debates about the numbers of inmates in the camps and prisons, and the numbers of dead or executed, are often unclear about who and what is being referred to: in particular, about whether the totals are over a lengthy period or for any given year. Overall, between 1929 and 1953, when the Gulags existed, around 18 million people were detained, and it should be noted that the high point came not in the 1930s but in the later 1940s.[32] Though the divergences in the estimates of historians and demographers may be great, there can be no doubt that we are talking about 'very large numbers', in other words, a socially significant and excessive quantity. It can be shown that before the war there were 2 million inmates in all the work and correctional camps, which together with prisoners in gaols and deported kulaks added up to 3.5 million people. But among the huge numbers of arrests and camp inmates between 1929 and 1953, 1937/38 stands out as a peak year, what Alec Nove calls 'the excess of excess'. In that year around 2.5 million arrests as well as around 680,000 shootings were documented. These figures alone make it clear that the mass character of the repression, the mass deaths and the planned mass murder are indisputable facts. More than a few researchers, however, believe in much higher numbers of arrests, camp inmates, deaths and executions.[33] 'Excesses of excess' also affected particular social and ethnic groups who were targeted, deported or killed on a grand scale: 'bourgeois nationalists', that is, national Ukrainian or Tatar elites; 'enemy agents', that is, Japanese, Koreans, Poles, Germans and Lithuanians, and others, living close to the frontier; tables and diagrams of 'life and death' could also be constructed for certain professions, such as military high-ups, geologists or historians.

These numbers are surpassed only by the numbers of dead in the Second World War and the consequent decline in the birth rate. After many years in which the numbers of victims of the war had been downplayed or suppressed altogether, the monstrous proportions of the death toll among the peoples of the Soviet Union finally became visible. Technically, the diagram would presumably exceed the limits of a normal graph: 26.2 million dead, of whom 19 million were men and 7.2 million women. Fifteen million dead came from among the civilian population; the Jews, the single largest group, amounted to 2.5 million dead, murdered on USSR territory. Eight hundred thousand

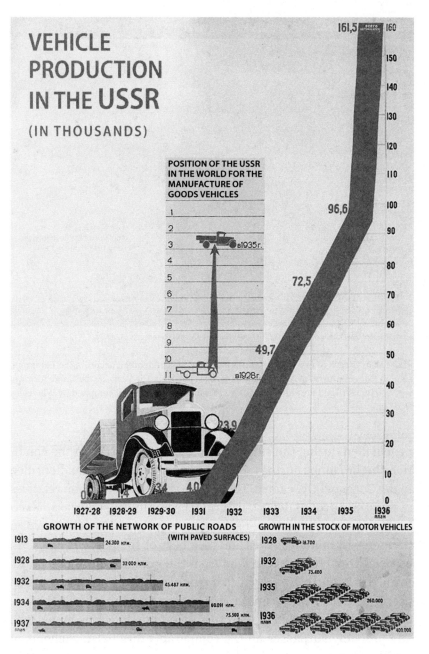

VEHICLE PRODUCTION IN THE USSR

(IN THOUSANDS)

POSITION OF THE USSR IN THE WORLD FOR THE MANUFACTURE OF GOODS VEHICLES

в1935г.

в1928г.

161,5

96,6

72,5

49,7

1927-28 1928-29 1929-30 1931 1932 1933 1934 1935 1936

GROWTH OF THE NETWORK OF PUBLIC ROADS
(WITH PAVED SURFACES)

1913   24.300 км.
1928   32.000 км.
1932   45.487 км.
1934   60.091 км.
1937   75.500 км.

GROWTH IN THE STOCK OF MOTOR VEHICLES

1928   18.700
1932   75.600
1935   260.000
1936   400.000

FIGURE 40.1. Growth of motor vehicle manufacture between 1927 and 1936. Karl Schlögel Archive.

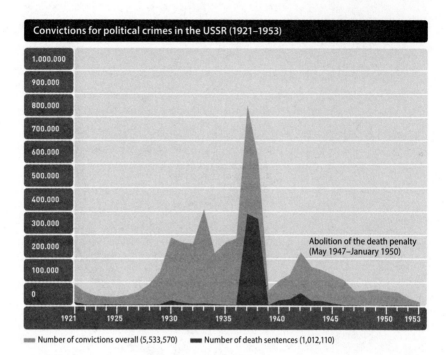

FIGURE 40.2. 'Excess of excess'. The statistics of people condemned according to Paragraph 58, 1–14 (for counterrevolutionary activity) rose sharply in the years of the Great Terror of 1937/38. Buchenwald and Mittelbau Dora Memorials Foundation, compiled by Wladislaw Hedeler.

people died during the siege of Leningrad; 622,000 from the conditions in the camps during the war. Over 3 million Soviet soldiers died in the German POW camps. There were more than 3 million relatives of the ethnic groups deported during the war under suspicion of having collaborated with the enemy—Crimean Tatars, Chechens, Volga Germans, Ukrainians, Poles and members of the Baltic peoples. An especially high proportion died from the horrific conditions in the cattle trucks and places in which they were settled. Roughly 10 million people died from such consequences of war as disease, exhaustion, cold and hunger. 'A blood toll of these proportions was monstrous and probably surpasses all the comparably dire balance sheets of world history.'[34]

In all likelihood, no diagram, however intelligent, could encompass the sheer horror of the events that engulfed the Soviet people.

PART IX

Rituals

CHAPTER 41

The Border at Brest—
Rites of Passage

Border crossings are moments of tense, even intensified awareness. Their details become engraved on our minds. The move from one side to the other is a slowing-down moment in which you become more conscious of everything and store it in your memory. For a long time, the border between the Soviet Union and the West was a border between two worlds. Entire generations of border crossers have recorded their observations, sensing that this was no normal frontier line. One traveller in the 1920s, the writer Joseph Roth, was well aware that he was 'entering a new world': 'It seems clear then that this frontier is not the normal border between one world and another . . . there can be no doubt that this frontier has historical significance.'[1] This feeling was shared by many visitors to the Soviet Union both before and after him.

Crossing borders is one of the most important human experiences of place, especially in times when territories are defined along national lines. Borders are historical structures, created, drawn and altered by men, but contrary to a currently fashionable view they are not virtual, arbitrary constructs. People who have been penned in for decades by good, solid, well guarded state borders and prevented from moving freely in the world would be the first to confirm this. Borders, including the Soviet borders, are like 'peripheral organs', like the skin that covers the body—that was the view of the great geographer and ethnographer Friedrich Ratzel, around 1900. They are permeable or sealed, porous or hermetic; they tell us something about the community of the time, and whether the traveller will be welcomed or turned away. Borders enable us to distinguish between open and closed societies; we can draw conclusions about the state of affairs in a country and its relations to neighbouring states from its domestic mood swings and the modifications it makes to border-crossing procedures. The beginning and end of a historical phase can be decoded not just from the centre but also on the periphery. According to the prediction of the Russian philosopher and publicist Vasily Rozanov on his death-bed in 1918, an 'Iron Curtain' was about to descend on Russia, and between then and its fall or elimination at the end of the twentieth century stretched a long, fascinating and sometimes dramatic history of border crossings.

The Brest Experience: Slowing Down, Stopping

Everyone has experiences of frontier checkpoints, when movement suddenly comes to a halt and you find yourself held up, forced to stand idle and be subjected to an exact registration process. Wherever you crossed the Soviet frontier—at the Polish-Soviet border at Brest, at Mamonovo (formerly Heiligenbeil) on the Polish-Soviet border to the present-day Kaliningrad region (formerly East Prussia), at Chop on the Soviet-Hungarian border or at Zabaykalsk on the border with China—there was always what might be called a 'basic situation'.[2] This was also the case at Moscow Airport—all air travel to the USSR began at the sole airport in Moscow (there are now five as well as direct flights to many other cities).

Up to 1991 the most important gateway for travellers arriving from the West by train was Brest, the old Brest-Litovsk. The transit process for passengers of all kinds has been described thousands of times: by diplomats, journalists, returning soldiers, members of friendly delegations of workers and other nationalities, fellow travellers, cultural tourists, Intourist travel groups, academic exchange visitors, agents retired or still active, reunited families, Soviet Germans and Soviet Jews on their way to their new homes. But there is an obvious asymmetry. What dominates throughout is the Western gaze with all its expectations. Westerners could travel where they wanted; only select categories of Soviet citizens could do the same. In Brest trains arrived from every direction; there were through coaches from every European capital: Paris (Gare du Nord), London (Victoria Station), Vienna, Budapest, Rome, Bucharest and Copenhagen. The tracks all ran to a junction, through a kilometre-wide corridor with endless lines of freight trains, bathed in the glitter of searchlights at night and surrounded by echoing announcements over loudspeakers. There was a river marking the border—the Bug—where the German-Soviet frontier had run from 1939 to 1941. This was a barren strip of land with watchtowers and isolated frontier patrols. All this lay behind you as you entered a different time zone, EET (Eastern European Time) instead of CET (Central European Time), a difference of two hours. Then began the regauging operation: the carriages were raised one after the other and lowered again onto bogies suitable for Soviet broad-gauge track. Everything took its precisely calculated course; border guards entered the carriage and collected people's passports, which would be handed back stamped with a visa at the end of the journey. After that, customs officials arrived with a list of questions and pocket torches. When it was all finished, travellers could visit the station restaurant, buy newspapers (*Pravda*, the *Daily Worker, L'Unita, Neues Deutschland*) or cigarettes (although not Marlboros) and experience the first contacts with the other side. The lifting and lowering of the carriages was like boats passing through a river lock—and in fact Brest is something like a lock chamber between two worlds, full of the tension arising from the entire procedure, closely observing the uniforms, the correct behaviour that oscillates between friendliness and distrust, sometimes bringing to the surface the resentment felt towards people enjoying the privilege of being able to cross this frontier. The inspection of luggage deserves a chapter of its own. There was an intensified interest in publications—Bibles, dissident literature, porn mags. Cameras would be laboriously registered in the customs declaration, so that they could be re-exported.[3] There was always some nervousness on the part of those passing through, the guilty feeling that you might have overlooked something or would be caught in some transgression.

Even so, the actual border crossing had a lengthy prehistory. You needed a visa that had to be applied for well in advance. You also had to fill in a questionnaire, giving precise details of your travel plans, which then could not be altered; you had to present your hotel vouchers from Intourist, without which the journey was impossible. This all amounted to a kind of bureaucratic anticipation of your journey long before it actually began. You really needed to want to travel to overcome the frontier before you even reached it. And once you had this frontier behind you, there were still further obstacles when you arrived, such as registration in the OVIR (Office of Visas and Registration).

Now that train stations have been replaced by airports, this experience has homed in on another location: Sheremetievo, gateway between the outside world and the interior, with a human through-put that hopelessly overtaxes the staff, particularly at peak times and when travellers come laden with unusually large bundles and parcels and when rigorous inspections combine, especially in winter, with overheated halls and the crowds of people pressing up against the security barriers can barely be held in check. And these transit situations can only count as concluded once the final obstacle has been surmounted and you have managed to get the last taxi and it has finally brought you to your destination. As always, first impressions are crucial when crossing a border. Twentieth-century travel writing is full of such first impressions, albeit frequently reduced to stereotypes and clichés.

'This Is a Very Special Frontier'

There have been many transit points like Brest on the thousand-kilometre-long frontier of the USSR, even if they have been less well frequented and less closely observed. Taken together, they confirm the impressions of visitors during the late phase of the Soviet Union. Over decades these border procedures proved to be stable, long-lasting and seemingly fixed for all eternity. The actual border lines may have been redrawn following peace treaties (such as the Treaty of Riga between Poland and the USSR in 1920), occupation (such as after 17 September 1939) or the German invasion of the Soviet Union (on 22 June 1941), and then again at the end of the war. In the guidebooks and travellers' accounts between the wars we read chiefly about two frontier crossings: Eydtkuhnen/Wierzbołów [currently Chernyshevskoe] (between the German Reich and Lithuania, and later Kaliningrad, USSR) and Stolpce/Negoreloe (between Poland and the USSR).[4] Travellers in the 1920s may even have had memories of the older frontier posts between the German Reich and the Tsarist Empire at Thorn/Alexandrov or Eydtkuhnen/Wierzbołów.[5] But with the Revolution and the establishment of Soviet power, the frontier marked out not only a new territory but also a new mental map. The territorial frontier had developed into a hard social and ideological border and this at a moment when a world without frontiers, led by the Soviet Union, was supposed to come into being.

At the time, the border crossings in Sebezh (between Latvia and the USSR) and Stolpce/Negoreloe were distinguished by monumental gateways designed by Constructivist artists and inscribed 'Workers of the world, unite!' The smallest details were loaded with significance, whether positive or negative. The border officials in Negoreloe were dressed in white linen suits, many of them spoke excellent German, English and French, the railway station concourses were clean, and frontier troops with fixed bayonets escorted the incoming trains. All such details, which might otherwise have been insignificant, told you something not only about the country you were about to enter but about the travellers themselves. The frontier became a surface on which every conceivable expectation or fear was projected. Taken together, all the observations made in these 'obligatory chapters' on the frontier experience would probably yield a magnified image of the Soviet Union even before one had set foot in the place.

Here is a very accurate description of an entrance, from an account by Erich Czech-Jochberg in 1937: 'All at once, you see barbed wire fences, a dense thicket of iron all around the station. And where the forest has been cleared, you suddenly catch sight of tall watchtowers, with entire houses on top, with hatches from which machine-guns protrude, slender, corrugated towers, hides for hunting people.... On one of the watchtowers I can see large searchlights'.

How naïve the enthusiasm now seems: 'Suddenly a murmur went through the entire train.... The huge red flag was waving on the roof; tall, slender men in long brown coats arrived with rapid, lively movements, pointed cloth helmets on their heads. A star gleamed on the helmet, the braid on their chest was bright red, there was a red star and a stripe on their left sleeve—these were the soldiers of the Red Army, the border guards of the workers' state.' That was Kurt Kersten

FIGURE 41.1. 'Workers of the world, unite!' At every border crossing, as we see here at Sebezh on the line between Riga and Moscow, thousands of travellers passed through a gate with the Red star. Privately owned, from Karl Schlögel, *Das russische Berlin: Ostbahnhof Europas*, Carl Hanser, Munich 2007, 59.

in 1924. Here is Alfons Goldschmidt in an even more exalted tone: 'As I strolled along the platform in Sebezh, something overwhelming came over me. I felt an almost humble respect, as if I had been overtaken by a great will. A gleaming red wind passed over me from the East. The flags with the sickle and the hammer waved in this luminous red wind that blew from many millions of hearts and had been born from the earth itself. . . . That was my first impression. Who would prevent me from saying something else if I chose to do so!'

The suspicion that this was the self-dramatisation of the Soviet state was fully justified. In the words of F. A. Kramer, in autumn 1932, 'The wish to create a good impression was in fact unmistakable and irritating: tables scrubbed until they were squeaky-clean, laid with carafes of water and glasses for the thirsty, tasteful ashtrays, comfortable, gleaming, freshly varnished benches around the hall, pretty lights and even parquet floors, with everything scrupulously clean. Was the whole of Russia like this?'[6]

Workers sang the 'Internationale', engineers on their way to a job in the country of the Five-Year Plan gazed out the window with a reserved, matter-of-fact expression on their faces, fellow travellers were sympathetic or even ecstatic. The entire spectrum of responses became visible at the frontier.

Astonishingly perhaps, cross-border procedures were at their least complicated during the periods of the nonaggression pact and the subsequent friendship pact between the Germany of national socialism and Stalin's Soviet Union, nations that would soon share a border transporting raw materials from the Donbass that made possible Hitler's war preparations. This frontier would also be crossed by the trains carrying German communists and Jews being held in Soviet camps who were to be transported into Hitler's Reich—many of them moving straight from a Soviet camp to a German one. One such person was Margarete Buber-Neumann, who crossed this border en route from a camp in Karaganda to Ravensbrück. Another was Alexander Cybulski Weissberg, who leapt from the train and joined up with the Polish underground.[7]

On 22 June 1941 the Germans crossed the Bug and turned the border into a battlefront in a war of ideologies and annihilation against the Soviet Union. The station building and the crossing point through which travellers passed after the war were newly constructed on ground that had been scorched and drenched in blood a thousand times over.

The Border Guard as Hero and the Invention of the Enemy

In the calendar of Soviet festivals there was also a Border Guards' Day (Den pogranichnikov). This has been fixed ever since 28 August 1918 and dates back to the early period of the Civil War which was waged against the internal enemy, the White counterrevolution and its allies, the fourteen interventionist powers. The history of the border guards is on show in the FSB Central Border Guard Museum in Moscow (Tsentralny pogranichny muzei FSB, Yauzsky Bulvar 13).

The frontier plays a great role in the intellectual stock-in-trade from which Russian statehood and culture have been constructed. The stages in the history of frontier changes include the bringing together of the Russian territories under Ivan III; the conquest of the Kazan Khanate by Ivan IV in 1552, which led to the incorporation of the first non-Russian peoples into Muscovy; the advance of Yermak, the Cossack ataman, to the Pacific, which resulted in Siberia's becoming a permanently expanding border society; the shift of the border on the southern periphery in a struggle against the khanate of the Crimean Tatars and their allies the Ottoman Empire; the transformation of the borderland in the southwest—Ukraina—into the province of Little Russia within the Russian Empire; the Polish Partitions, which brought the borders of the three empires—of the Romanovs, the Habsburgs and the Hohenzollerns in Central Europe up to the end of the First World War—into contact; the redrawing of borders with the new or resurrected states of East Central Europe after the Revolution and the Civil War, followed by their brutal revision initially by Hitler and Stalin in 1939, then by the German invasion of the Soviet Union in 1941 and once again after the end of the war in 1945. On the continent with what Joseph Roth called 'wandering frontiers', the borders of Russia, the Muscovite Empire, the Russian Empire, the Soviet Union and the post-Soviet Russian Federation have been in constant motion.[8] The border in the Far East seemed to have been reached only when countervailing forces—China and Japan—stood in the path of further expansion. In this way, Russia embraced a territory which, according to Pyotr Chaadaev, the historiographer and founder of a Russian national consciousness, stretched from the Oder River to the Pacific and made geography Russia's destiny: a territory so large that no power would ever be able to encompass it.

And yet the idea of encirclement has always been central to the idea of a Russian empire so that stoking the fear of being threatened and surrounded has always been a constituent part of the imperial idea. Encirclement, threat and foreign bogeymen as essential elements of an ideology of integration have always come to the fore whenever the unity of the Empire appeared fragile. Producing threatening scenarios and hostile stereotypes helped to stabilise an extraordinarily diffuse, fragmented and heterogeneous territory. The creation of enemies became a substitute for the failure to fully enter into the spirit of the gigantic empire and take possession of it. The invasions by Napoleon and Hitler, which threatened the very existence of the Russian or alternatively the Soviet state, led de facto to a rebirth, a strengthening and indeed a new foundation of that state. Invasion was followed on each occasion by a thrust to the very heart of Europe, which was endorsed in the Europe of the Congress of Vienna in 1815 and followed up in subsequent decades by a variety of Russian interventions in its role as the 'gendarme of Europe' (the crushing of the Polish uprisings of 1830 and 1861, and of the 1848 Revolution), or the creation of the Soviet-dominated Eastern bloc after the victory over Hitler's Germany (and with comparable interventions beyond their own borders in Berlin 1953, Budapest 1956 and Prague 1968). A continuous discourse about frontiers runs through the whole of the nineteenth and twentieth centuries highlighting relations between Russia and Europe, from Nikolay Danilevsky's *Russia and Europe,* through the 'Eurasians' around Nikolay Trubetskoy in the 1920s, right down to the Russkiy Mir Foundation at the beginning of the twenty-first century.

The Russian Empire generated its greatest attraction in the shape of the newly born USSR in 1922 as a reaction to the terrors of the First World War, when there was not only a 'Wilsonian moment' of self-determination but also a Leninist version in which an 'affirmative action empire'[9] briefly came into being; its dynamism and short-lived blossoming were violently killed off by Stalin's 'revolution from above'. The Soviet people, Stalin's national community which had come into the world amidst Stalin's violence, could not survive without enemies. The Stalinist universe was peopled by fifth columnists, spies, saboteurs and agents of the Polish, Japanese, British and German secret services. At the end of the Stalinist era the role of enemy was taken over by cosmopolitans, agents of American imperialism and Zionism as part of the mobilisation for the Cold War. This meant that anyone who could be deemed to have a connection with the world beyond Soviet borders was a deadly threat to be extirpated root and branch.

The relatives of peoples close to the frontier or people who had connections to foreign countries fell victim in the hundreds of thousands to the second, 'ethnic' wave of the 'mass operations' of the Great Terror of 1937/38, to the deportations and mass executions: returnees from emigration, Koreans, Poles, Lithuanians, Latvians, Estonians, German and Austrian émigrés and antifascists, as well as ethnic groups who were accused of collaborating with the enemy during the Second World War and deported in the hundreds of thousands to the interior of the Empire—Volga Germans, Crimean Tatars,

Chechens, Kabardin-Balkars and members of the western frontier zones in the Baltic and Ukraine.[10]

During all these decades the border guards were more than one armed formation among others. They stood ready for defence against sabotage and subversion; they embodied the virtue of vigilance; they were a dedicated order in themselves, an elite troop, an icon. They had special uniforms, ribbons and medals, and went around accompanied by German shepherd dogs. They operated in the desert regions on the Iranian frontier, the savage mountainous landscapes of the Caucasus and the Tian Shan, the Pacific coasts and along the Amur, the Karelian forests and the Finnish border; but there were also guards who had to escort the trains in Negoreloe or Brest. Images of *pogranichniki* on posters, in newspapers and films sent a powerful message.[11] Illegal border crossings were crimes against the state and almost impossible in practice although a few succeeded from time to time. The state expected unconditional obedience from its subjects even beyond the border. Failure to respond to a command to return home from abroad, as happened with a number of diplomats and agents in the 1930s, amounted to treason and invited the death sentence. Anyone who was suspected of disloyalty within the Soviet Union, by contrast, if not murdered or arrested, had to reckon not just with ideological excommunication but also with expulsion from the fatherland, a practice that began with the deportation of scholars and writers on the philosophy steamer in 1922 and continued to the late phase of the Soviet Union when dissidents such as Vladimir Bukovsky (1976) and Alexander Solzhenitsyn (1974) were forcibly flown out of the country.[12]

Open Sky and the End of Empire

In 1991 the citizens of the Soviet Union made a shocking discovery. Suddenly there were borders where hitherto there had been nothing but seemingly boundless space. Frontier posts and transit points were no longer to be found on the external lines of the USSR, which had now dissolved, but in places where up to then there had existed only the barely noticeable internal borders between the Soviet republics, which were of no importance in everyday life. Overnight, citizens of the indivisible Soviet Union had become citizens of independent sovereign states. One could now become a stranger or a second-class citizen in the very country where one had grown up. What had been an infinitely accessible space had now been blocked. In time the improvised and indeed provisional checkpoints of the early 1990s turned into regular border-crossing points. Trains no longer just passed through without stopping and passengers no longer just went about their business without let or hindrance. Now they were stopped and had to prove their identity. Since the vast majority of people had never been outside the borders of the Soviet Union, they had never had a passport. They now found that their closest neighbourhood had become a foreign country. This discovery was made hundreds of thousands of times at the new border crossings—between the Russian Federation and Lithuania, on the Memel Bridge at Tilsit/Sovetsk, between Belgorod and Kharkiv and between Russia and Kazakhstan. In this way Russia found itself undergoing the same process as the citizens of the defunct Habsburg Empire almost a century earlier. They had woken up after a war and a revolution to find themselves in a world full of new countries. The single, all-embracing space with a single language, a single sign system and a single system of government had ceased to exist.

Even more significant than this transformation of internal borders into external frontiers was the opening-up of the country as part of the 'globalisation process'. The chief points at which the frontier was now opened, where in fact it disappeared, were the airports. Soviet citizens could now travel not just to friendly Soviet states, but to wherever they wanted, as long as they had an international passport and could afford the journey. It was no longer the case that only privileged state-approved cadres could travel; anyone could go if they had the courage and the means to do so. To travel and move around was a universal human right. This was a revolution that was now exercised every day on a massive scale, a wave of human travellers unprecedented in recent history.

It began with shopping tourism, an activity born out of necessity, but this pushed open the door to the world. Mass tourism developed later, following the stabilisation of the economy in the 2000s—thanks to which Russian citizens became ubiquitous and the most active group of tourists worldwide. This was the beginning of an exploration of the world of which people had had only hearsay knowledge hitherto, from newspapers or films. They could now see the world with their own eyes; they could begin to understand what made the world tick and what it was like to live where there were no queues, no restrictions and far less poverty and destitution than they had always been told about by home-produced propaganda. Travel became an object lesson and the most effective form of enlightenment. People learned from what they saw rather than from books.

Every social group had its own Grand Tour. The shopping destinations were the Grand Bazaar in Istanbul, the ports of Beirut, Alexandria, Athens, Palermo, Marseilles, as well as the malls of Dubai, Abu Dhabi and the bazaar of Ürümqi—not for the tourist attractions but because of the prices for leather goods, jeans, cigarettes and electronics. The intelligentsia travelled to realise the dream of a lifetime: at long last they could visit Paris and London, Florence and Rome. Yet others sought out even more exotic destinations, whether for financial reasons or because no visa was required. A further group caught up on postponed family visits and travelled to see relatives who had long since emigrated to Israel, the USA or Germany. And lastly, there was mass tourism, the grandiose experience of the lightness of being, holidays under the palm trees in the Canaries, Antalya, Sharm El-Sheikh or on a beach in Thailand.

The public we see in the departure and arrival halls is now dressed in the leisure clothing and holiday fashions of international brands. Luggage is lightweight. Everyone has adapted to the security checks that have become ubiquitous in airports the world over and they move through the corridors in the rhythm that has become typical of globalised travel. A country that has allowed millions of its citizens to go out into the world in a few short years is no longer the same once they have returned. As Walter Benjamin noticed after his return to Berlin from Moscow in 1927, you look at the city you left behind with fresh eyes. You have passed through the school of seeing with your own eyes, of comparing, appraising and trying things out. You have brought ideas of 'normal living' with you. It is a school in which you learn a new language and about a new world. Such rites of passage involve essential learning processes that cannot be acquired at school and you gain a power of judgement that enables you to confront authorities and bosses at home. The latter have grasped the fact that the more porous the borders, the more essential it is to have an enemy who can be invoked to intimidate the centrifugal parts of society into staying together and so rescue the 'fatherland when it is in danger'. In future you will have only to look at the border and you will see clearly enough what is going on at the centre.

CHAPTER 42

Choreographies of Power: Parades on Red Square and Elsewhere

Few rituals of power became as potent in the twentieth century as the parades on Red Square. And anyone who was just an ordinary TV viewer and hence unfamiliar with historical dates, anniversaries and jubilees would be regularly reminded—especially during the Cold War—on 1 May, 9 May, 7 November or other particular times of year that there were celebrations in Moscow for International Labour Day, Victory Day and the Day of the Great October Socialist Revolution. Even people not especially familiar with Moscow's topography could recognise at a glance the setting, which was always the same: the slightly sloping, paved, nearly rectangular space of Red Square stretched from the red brickwork of the State Historical Museum in the Russian Revival style on the north side to the exotic-looking St. Basil's Cathedral at the southern end. One long side was occupied by the façade of the GUM department store covered with larger-than-life portraits of Soviet leaders and slogans in Cyrillic script. Opposite this was the Kremlin Wall with the graves of state luminaries, the silver firs and above all Lenin's Mausoleum surmounted by the tribune on which the Soviet presidium stood to receive the march-past of the parading armed forces. Each date had its own season—a radiant May or a November when the first snowfall covered the city. Every broadcast brought with it the analyses and commentaries that drew conclusions about infighting in the Politburo and the current hierarchy of Kremlin leaders from their relative position on the podium. And as always, at least during the Cold War, the military attachés, analysts and Kremlinologists concentrated chiefly on the weapons rolling past on gigantic carriages, especially the missiles on public display for the first time. Even though these events occurred regularly year after year and were broadcast worldwide, they always contained an element of excitement and the expectation that the parades would send out signals about whether rearmament or disarmament, threats or détente were on the agenda. Many other important features came together here: the astonishing discipline and precision with which thousands of soldiers performed on parade; the fact that there were no untoward incidents—which might well have been possible, given the vast numbers involved and the tight organisation of the events; the jolly mood that took over once the military proceedings had concluded—as demonstrated by summer clothes, children on their fathers' shoulders, brightly coloured balloons. Even the bands contributed to the generally cheerful and relaxed atmosphere, notwithstanding their military repertoire—at least this is how it appeared in the age of television and the late phase of the Soviet Union when there was more talk about raising the standard of living than of sacrificing one's life for the fatherland.

And yet, what stayed in the minds of the TV audience—both abroad and at home—was not so much the festive mood of a national holiday as the rhythm of marching columns, the rather darker colour—olive green—of the camouflaged artillery and other military hardware rolling past, and foremost, the extremely precise organisation of a highly trained and disciplined collective body which had the feel of a mighty machine rather than of an informal parade or festive promenade that might be expected in the centre of a capital city. In short, it was a demonstration of power and where there is power there is a certain fascination—the shiver that runs down your spine when tanks roll past to the sound of marching music, but also the sense of dread that you might find yourself caught up in something unpredictable and overwhelming.

Sequence of Events: The Script

The parades were based—necessarily—on scripts that had been worked on to the very last detail. Nothing was left to chance.[1] Taking part in the parades was an enormous privilege—for both the active participants and the observers. For decades on end, obtaining one of the sought-after places was a matter of professional honour and prestige for both members of the diplomatic corps and the press. Access to Red Square was blocked from a particular time beforehand; the streets were cleared to make way for the troops and especially for the military hardware. The city made grand preparations for the festivities. The newspapers published in advance the current slogans, which had all been approved by the highest authorities; banners and posters for the occasion were produced in the factories, institutes and trade unions. Delegations were chosen; they convened at prearranged times and formed columns that moved towards Red Square at a given signal. As a rule, the processions were led by the military contingent, followed by the sportsmen and -women and the workers. The parades did not always feature a military section and not all parades were military.

The parade choreography was fixed from beginning, when the bells rang out from the Kremlin's Spassky Tower, to end, when either the grand salute was fired or the celebrations concluded with a firework display. It started with the succession of military formations, the different uniform colours, and went on with the commanding officer's order of the day, the sequence of orchestras and music ensembles, the addresses and shouts of hooray from the soldiers in the square. The parade was a Union-wide media event, at least since the invention of the radio, but more especially since the arrival of TV.

In the photographs of the parades on Red Square the course of events has become completely identified with the locality. However, it is not the place that has been the defining factor here but rather, the nature of the square has been determined by the events that have taken place in it. Red Square was the key marketplace of an aspiring Moscow, where all trading routes met up: the road to Tver in the north, the roads to the Golden Horde in the south, the square in front of the fortress walls of the Kremlin, a meeting place and place of execution where peasants were drawn, quartered and their bodies consigned to the flames. In the plans for the Fourth Rome of Communism, this square was also envisaged as the site of the Red Forum—with a monumental, terraced People's Commissariat for Heavy Industry, which would have entailed sacrificing the GUM department store, which fills an entire square in itself; even St. Basil's Cathedral would have had to make way for a skyscraper, according to designs from the early 1930s.[2] Its centre, however, is the red-granite Mausoleum, which with the tomb of the founder of the Soviet Union and the Lenin cult turned Red Square into both a quasi-religious space and the focal point of the parades. From the podium, the political leadership looks past the sarcophagus and down onto the marching masses. They review the passing troops as in olden times. The podium above the Mausoleum is like the commanding officer's dais or the Tsar's rostrum. The images of the parades become highly concentrated in meaning—a historical setting, the very centre of Empire, the centre of the capital, the necropolis of the Revolution, the constructed sphere of power, a granite cube that dominates the entire space and holds it together. Is this the triumph of the dead over the living?

Parades: The Offspring of War and Revolution

Parades are as old as war itself. With Peter the Great's toy army and Paul I's admiration of Prussia, some of the Romanovs had proved to be absolute fanatics of parade-ground drill. But the beginnings of the Soviet parade coincide with the Civil War. Red Army regiments that were in the process of formation moved straight from the parade ground to the front. They began not with a ritual that had been worked out down to the last detail but with improvisation and emergency measures. The parade on Red Square is an example of the invention of a tradition and at the same time an index of the ageing process of the Revolution. You can read everything off of it: the rise and fall of a world power, the emergence and disappearance of the protagonists of revolution, the transition from improvised actions to the development of stable structures. Parades are not so much about a display or putting on a show as they are about drill: preparation for a battle that has not yet been decided but which may end up as a victory celebration. The Red Army was the core of the parade culture, but when it celebrated on 1 May 1918, it was only just then being created. Both the concrete posts supporting the overhead cables for the trams whose tracks still ran across Red Square and GUM were festooned with fir branches and red flags; this was to commemorate the fallen revolutionaries buried in the

FIGURE 42.1. 'Long live the great, invincible banner of Marx, Engels and Lenin.' Poster by Nikolay Dolgorukov for the parade on Red Square in 1934. © Russian State Library Moscow/culture-images/fai.

Kremlin Wall. But all of this was a bit rough and ready. The speakers, Lenin and Trotsky among them, stood on the back of a pickup truck; the Maxim guns were drawn across the square by horses; there were no loudspeakers; the cannon still bore the emblem of the Tsarist eagle. A plane made of laminated wood and canvas rose into the air above the square and threw down leaflets. With the parade on Red Square and Khodynka Field in the north of the city, the authorities were eager to prove that, technically speaking, the USSR had arrived in the twentieth century. There were regular opportunities for demonstrations and for elaborating a canon: for the first anniversary of the October Revolution—once again with planes—or for the congresses of the Comintern in the capital whose delegates were impressed by Soviet power. Planes and balloons were regular features as were hot-air balloons that carried slogans and constantly set new records. In 1921 the Red Army displayed the demobilisation of the army which had swollen to over 5.5 million men. All this was followed by illuminations and street theatre. Technical progress was celebrated in the display of tractors and automobiles.

'The Clockwork of the Post-Revolution'

The end of the Civil War and demobilisation were followed by a certain quietening down and demilitarisation of the parades. Paul Scheffer, a discerning observer, gave this account in 1927:

In accord with a custom nine years old, numberless groups of workers 'of hand and brain' filed past Lenin's tomb—over a million in all. They paraded with floats, placards, caricatures, cartoons. Here, too, foreign policy supplied the majority of the subjects: countless the number of unflattering portraits of poor Mr. Chamberlain, and of the men prominent in the League of Nations. The other outstanding feature of the demonstration was the strict discipline of the masses, and therefore, as it seemed to me, the decline in originality, in spontaneity. I noted much less singing, in fact hardly any singing at all. Jests at the expense of the chance bourgeois whom the parade encountered during its progress of several hours through the city were not so insulting or gross as five years ago. The march of the million factory workers followed a review of picked troops, such as might be seen in any country. After the Russian cavalry, riding in impeccable formation, came a brigade of Caucasian horsemen in the black, broad-shouldered hairy jackets traditional in their country; and my thoughts went back to the regiments that paraded here in 1921, badly armed, garbed, partly in khaki uniforms confiscated from the British Relief, and neither brilliantly mounted nor cleverly handled. And yet, this time—nothing electric! Just discipline, organization, routine, perfect routine! In the evening the Caucasians again rode out of the Kremlin and manoeuvred in the Red Square under a play of searchlights. 'Stalin's Pretorians!' remarked one of those unfortunates whose sole surviving, and it would seem inalienable, right is to make a political jest from time to time at the expense of the Red Omnipotents. Yet, for myself, I could detect no trace of the romantic, nor even of the uncertain, in the magnificent clockwork of the Post-Revolution. Stalin does not want, or need, any Pretorians![3]

With the end of the NEP this somewhat carnivalistic version of the parades was transformed into a new, more militant phase.

The Parade of the Five-Year Plans, the Parade of the Soviet People

The parade on Red Square became the propaganda arena for the violent shake-up of the entire country. The Mausoleum began in 1924 as nothing more than a temporary cube made of wood, the predecessor of the permanent granite monument installed in 1929. In the May parade of 1930, which began at 9 a.m., Kliment Voroshilov charged up through Saviour Gate on a horse. Those present for the 7 November procession included relatives of the leadership who would be condemned as traitors, spies and enemy agents only a few years later. Examples were Jānis Rudzutaks and General Avgust Kork. To open access to Red Square for military vehicles and large processions, the Iberian gate and Iberian Chapel were both torn down; in November 1933, units from the Military Academy, schools, sailors, fighters from the divisions of the Moscow proletariat, sniper units, the victors in socialist competitions and shock workers divided up according to their branch of industry and their achievements and, identified by their posters and banners, all poured out onto the square. Outstanding people were always to the fore. Figures, statistics, diagrams and production curves set the tone of the Five-Year Plan parades. Tank drivers, aviators, chauffeurs, artillerymen, machine-gunners, radio operators and pioneers marched past the Kremlin VIPs who noticeably changed from one show trial to the next—as was easily recognisable by the initiated. Vsevolod Vishnevsky, author of *The Optimistic Tragedy*, wrote admiringly of the *virtuozy-tankisty*, the virtuoso tank drivers, who poured out around the Historical Museum in a 'river of steel'. The five hundred tanks and eight hundred 'home-produced' planes were supposed to demonstrate that Russia had become an industrial nation and was capable of the highest technical achievements in the field of military endeavour. The parade then branched out to include airspace. The largest plane in the world, the 'Maxim Gorky', led the parade in the skies, followed by the four-engine TB-3 bombers and the R-5 reconnaissance aircraft and fighters. People discovered the names of aircraft designers who would one day become world-famous: Andrey N. Tupolev and Alexander A. Arkhangelsky. The slogan of the time ran *Krylaty narod—moguch i nepobedim*—'a nation on the wing—powerful and invincible'.

General Köstring, the military attaché to the German embassy, closely observed the parade of November 1935. His interest was focused above all on comments about Germany:

The march of the workers that always follows on from the parade was around 1.75 million this year, slightly fewer perhaps than previously. As I hear it, the pressure to take part this year was somewhat feebler as for the first time 'voluntary' participation had not been declared a duty for everyone. In comparison to earlier occasions the regular theatre props of capitalists, drunken priests and gruesome generals were entirely absent. Stalin, 'our traditional glorious leader and friend', and the 'iron' Voroshilov were what was mostly on view. Similarly, the emphasis was on the now so happy lives of

our well-fed people, the development of Moscow into a garden city
and other props which actually only apply to the decent bourgeois.
I did not see any posters aimed directly against Germany. There
were a number of tactless banners aimed at 'Fascism' in general,
but since they featured the swastika we were the intended target.
The rather sparse and intrusive posters calling for 'Freedom for
Thälmann' appeared somewhat feeble.[4]

In May 1936, when Voroshilov showed off his new field marshal's
uniform, it was clear that ancient traditions and decorations were
back in fashion. The task of the parade now was to present 'the Soviet
people' by calling on the faces and names of the numerous national
groups: the Ukrainian Pyotr Didok, the Belorusian Josef Chabunya,
the Turkmen Sariy Annadov, the Tatar Alexander Abukekirov, the
Chuvash Faddey Stepanov, the Mordvin Alexey Kolasin and the Roma
Mikhail Sukhoy.[5] Köstring remarked in his report of 1 May 1936:

Outwardly, the progress of the parade was familiar. Voroshilov's
speech before the recruits all swore their oath remained moderate in tone. His assurance of Soviet Russia's love of peace and his
warning to the alleged disruptors of peace are old stage props. The
march of the masses—there must have been around two million
people present—produced few direct tasteless attacks on us in
the slogans and the carnival floats. They praised the Empire, the
ostensible prosperity and received the children's thanks to Stalin, the 'leader of all nations'. On my return from the parade I was
caught up in the mass traffic jam for a long time because of the
mismanagement of the police. The Reich flag on my car and my
recognisably German uniform occasioned only friendly humorous
comments, but no jeers or catcalls. The hostile propaganda does
not appear to have penetrated to the ordinary people.[6]

The year 1937 was special: the twentieth anniversary of the October Revolution and the year of the Great Terror. Rehearsing for the 1
May parade went on for months on Khamovniki Field. Alongside the
greying heroes of the Civil War marched the Young Communists, the
parachutists and snipers from the aviation clubs with their symbols;

there were planes, tanks, automobiles, motorbikes and radios. The official opening of the Moscow-Volga Canal was accompanied by a flotilla of boats and steamers that went right up to the Kremlin walls. 'Our capital became a port for five different seas.' The parade was led by Marshal Semyon Budyonny, the commander of the cavalry in the Civil War and one of the very few leaders to survive the massacre of the officer corps of the Red Army. The growing tensions around the world were reflected in the presence of Yan Berzin, a foreign agent and a fighter in the Spanish Civil War. Foreign observers were particularly numerous on the guest tribunes that year on 7 November, trying to figure out the meaning of the *chistka*, Stalin's purges. Was it his intention to forestall a military putsch or some other conspiracy? The legendary ANT-25, the plane in which Mikhail Gromov had flown to the United States via the North Pole, flew over the square. 'Stalin's hawks', who had set many world records, wrote the initials SSSR and XX in the sky over Moscow to celebrate the anniversary. Moscow had lost a major proportion of its military leaders in the bloodbath of the purges but ensured a succession with its dozens of military academies, officer training schools and institutes for political workers and other specialists.

In the parades of 1940—six months after the start of the Second World War and the joint military parade of the Soviet Army and the Wehrmacht in Brest—representatives of countries occupied by Soviet forces now also appeared on the guest tribunes—the Lithuanian, Latvian and Estonian SSR, as well as representatives of the 'liberated' territories: West Ukraine, West White Russia and the northern part of Bukovina. The parade on 7 November 1940 was led by Semyon Timoshenko, a former soldier in the Tsarist army, hero of the Civil War and future Marshal of the Soviet Union. The T-34 tanks that were to become crucial for the outcome of the war rolled over the square.

Survival and Triumph: Perfecting the Ritual

Soviet military parades acquired their final shape in the blazing heat of war. Neither a totalitarian plan nor a strategic coup but rather the life-and-death struggle brought the entire ritual to its apogee. As so often happens, it was the moment of crisis that finally created a unified whole. Place, time and action all converged unpredictably and unplanned, as is frequently the case. On 7 November 1941, the anniversary of the October Revolution, Red Square, which Hitler had already selected for the victory parade of the Wehrmacht following the fall of Moscow, became the chosen venue for a parade whose participants would march straight on from there to the front. On 24 June 1945, the square became the scene of the triumph of the Soviet armed forces together with the nations who had smashed Hitler's armies. The pictures of this event were not provided by UFA, the dominant German film company, which had previously marshalled its film teams for victory parades in Paris, Warsaw and even Moscow, but by Soviet cameramen and photographers.[7]

The distinctive nature and the precision of the images of these parades point us in a certain direction—to the succinct lines and measured gestures familiar from the designs of the Constructivists. This is probably no accident: the brothers Georgy and Vladimir Stenberg had choreographed the Moscow parades from 1932 and it was Vladimir who, following the death of his brother in a car accident, oversaw the artistic direction of the parades until the 1960s. We can perhaps say without exaggeration that the parades represented a synthesis of the aesthetics of the Constructivists and the force and momentum of the victorious Soviet army in a single set of images.

It was far from self-evident that the parade would go ahead on 7 November 1941 when Moscow was facing the imminent threat of being surrounded by the Wehrmacht. The journalist Vadim Sinyavsky had been summoned to the capital from the front the previous evening to prepare the radio report on the parade from the GUM department store. His brief was to report on the parade and make clear to the nation and indeed the whole world that although Moscow was under siege, it was still alive. He led the production team which broadcast interviews, listeners' letters and original sound feeds from the GUM building.

Everything started promptly. Budyonny rode out from the Spassky Gate. Everyone thought that he would take the lead at the parade and give the speech. To their surprise it was Stalin himself who spoke. The fact that the parade took place—even under artillery fire—'is some-

FIGURE 42.2. End of the parade celebrating the victory over Nazi Germany on Red Square on 24 June 1945. © Tass/UIG/Bridgeman Images.

thing that will never be forgotten'.[8] The celebrations in honour of the anniversary of the October Revolution had taken place the previous day, underground in the Mayakovskaya metro station. The rehearsals that would normally have taken up weeks beforehand were not possible on this occasion. The army units that took part in the parade went to Red Square with live ammunition in their weapons and headed straight from there to the front. They took up their positions at 5 a.m. As always, a special permit, a *propusk*, was required to gain entry to the square. Shortly before 8 a.m. Moscow time, Yury Levitan's voice announced the start of the broadcast. In his speech, Stalin set the tone for the fight against the aggression of Hitler's Germany: 'The whole world is looking to you as the force capable of destroying the plundering hordes of German invaders. The enslaved peoples of Europe who have fallen under the yoke of the German invaders look to you as their liberators. A great liberating mission has fallen to your lot. Be worthy of this mission! The war you are waging is a war of liberation, a just war. Let the manly images of our great ancestors—Alexander Nevsky, Dmitry Donskoy, Kuzma Minin, Dmitry Pozharsky, Alexander Suvorov and

Mikhail Kutuzov—inspire you in this war! May the victorious banner of the great Lenin be your lodestar!'[9] The images from this day show a gloomy, overcast sky. Snow had fallen. This was the black and white picture of the Battle for Moscow.

The situation was quite different for the victory parade on 24 June 1945. Stalin had insisted on holding the parade even though the war in the Far East was not yet over, but there was time enough to prepare. There had been parades on a smaller scale as early as 1944, following the liberation of Soviet territory, but now, following the capitulation of Hitler's Germany, Red Square had the eyes of the world upon it. On 23 May 1945 a celebratory reception for the generals had been held in the Georgievsky Hall of the Great Kremlin Palace, a high point in the evolution of Soviet state ceremonial and of the Great Russian chauvinism that was becoming ever more pronounced. Time was needed for all the detailed preparations: for making at least one thousand dress uniforms and for training the military units. Forty thousand troops took part in the parade. Each front was to be attended by a thousand combatants; all the armed services were to be represented. The parade was to be reviewed by Marshal Georgy Zhukov. The whole of Moscow prepared to welcome the troops; barracks were polished to the nth degree, roads were cleaned up, plans for lighting and a firework display were produced. The skies would be emblazoned with balloons bearing the symbols of the Order of Victory and the Order of the Red Star. The evening before the parade, the Supreme Soviet had passed a law ordering the demobilisation of millions of people. The GUM façade displayed the arms of the Union Republics and early in the morning troops representing the fronts from Karelia to the Black Sea took up their positions.

Ten chimes from the Kremlin towers gave the signal to strike up the 'Heroes' March'. Marshal Zhukov rode out from the Spassky Gate on a white horse—having begun as a peasant soldier in the Tsarist army, he had now reached the pinnacle of the Soviet army. He had been the hero of the battle of Khalkhin Gol and then an army commander at the storming of Berlin.

Fanfares sounded. In the centre of the square a 1,400-strong military orchestra played Glinka's 'Slavsya, russky narod' (Glory to the Russian people). Zhukov spoke from the Mausoleum podium. Then the

FIGURE 42.3. Fireworks on 9 May 1945, the day of the capitulation of Hitler's Germany. © Courtesy of Dmitry Baltermants. Photo: culture-images/fai.

anthem of the Soviet Union rang out and a roar of applause echoed around the entire square. This was followed by reading out the list of names of the famous generals. Then the orchestra fell silent. A drum roll sounded and gradually in a precisely orchestrated choreography, the soldiers stepped forward in their dress uniforms and, with a gesture that expressed their disdain for the defeated enemy, cast the trophies seized from the Germans onto the ground at the foot of the Mausoleum. Two hundred flags and banners were hurled below the podium to the crescendo of the drums: a prolonged moment of contempt, pride and dignity all in one. This was followed by the approach of the light and heavy artillery, the motorised units and the T-34 tanks. It took them two hours to pass. The march-past of workers was cancelled because of a heavy downpour, but in the evening all of Moscow poured into Red Square to hear orchestras playing songs and dances, celebrating the soldiers returning from the war. Searchlights probed the night sky; at 11 p.m. the day was concluded with a firework display, a peaceable civil version of the din of battle. The next day, 25 June, a reception was announced for those taking part in the victory parade. Setting aside the subsequent parade of athletes, the twenty-five thousand *fizkulturniki,* on 12 August 1945, this party was the culmination of the ritual celebrating the end of the war and inaugurating the return of an exhausted nation to everyday life.

Military Parades in Peacetime

The annual parades on 1 May and 7 November—Victory Day on 9 May was only introduced in 1965 under Brezhnev—almost became symbols of the uniformity, the immutability of the USSR, which had positioned itself for the duration, if not for eternity. Anniversaries are welcome high points in the otherwise humdrum course of everyday life and its rituals. This was the case, for example, with the fiftieth anniversary of the October Revolution in 1967. The parades were proof of the continuity of a power that had found its place in the world and had in fact become a global power. Delegations arrived from all over the world and relished the public acclaim from the podium. Among them were Fidel Castro (1963) and, increasingly, other leaders from the Third World. The posters proclaimed with tedious repetitiveness the constant economic progress, the successes of the Soviet Union's peace missions, the rise in production and the increase in new-build houses. And if the feeling of triumph was to be repeated, then the latest advance into space supplied the occasion—most recently in 1961 when Yury Gagarin, the youngest and most popular Hero of the Soviet Union, could be seen on the Mausoleum podium.

Even though there was no lack of crises—Suez in 1956, the interventions in Hungary and Poland, Berlin in 1960, Cuba in 1963 and the suppression of the Prague Spring in 1968—the trend was towards a de-dramatisation and a reversion to the everyday that is generally referred to as a 'ritualisation'. The passion and the enthusiasm essential for general mobilisations had faded. The surviving heroes and heroines of former times had become veterans; the war-wounded and the invalids had vanished from the public eye. Historical quotations became the fashion: the flag that had once flown over the Reichstag was unfurled once again in 1965 for the twentieth anniversary; survivors of the 'storming of the Winter Palace' were invited for the anniversary of the Great October in 1967. In 1972 the fiftieth anniversary of the founding of the Soviet Union was celebrated. But these events did nothing to alter the fact that a new generation had grown up, the postwar generation, that knew about the war only from the stories told by their parents and grandparents. Not even the approval of the new Party Programme that was decided on at the Twenty-Second Party Congress in 1961 and that promised the current generation of Soviet people that the arrival of communism was imminent could succeed in rekindling the spark of enthusiasm. The parades tended more and more to assume the features of a reenactment: 1967, the fiftieth anniversary of Red October, became a self-dramatisation; it was not the beginning of a struggle but a great show for the political establishment and delegates from ninety-five countries. As always, white lines were painted on the paving to guide the marching columns and the artillery, and the entire history—the cruiser *Aurora*, Budyonny's cavalry, the storming of Berlin—passed in review. Planes drew the name LENIN and the number 50 in the sky. Even so, this anniversary too was more concerned with increases in production and prosperity than with revolution—and always in contrast to and in competition with the West. What remained in the memories of the millions of onlookers and participants—of the children, above all— were the bright lights, the tunes, the atmosphere, the salute and the great firework show in the night sky over Moscow.

However, beneath the surface of the routine and on the margins of the great parade, something else was beginning. People started to absent themselves, to enjoy the free days in May to work on the allotments attached to their dachas. A very few people began to use Red Square to express their dissent. On 25 August 1968, seven Moscow intellectuals briefly protested against the suppression of the Prague Spring. They unfurled their posters on the Monument to Minin and Pozharsky, the old place of execution—'For your freedom and ours', 'Hands off the CSSR', 'Shame on the occupiers'—before they were arrested by the secret police. In the trials that followed, the seven were condemned as 'anti-Soviet' and sentenced to a number of years in prison or exile:

Natalia Gorbanevskaya
Konstantin Babitsky
Vadim Delaunay

Vladimir Dremlyuga
Pavel Litvinov
Viktor Faynberg
Larisa Bogoraz[10]

It took almost twenty years, until the end of the 1980s, for millions of Soviet citizens to bid farewell to the choreography of the Soviet parades and begin to stroll across Red Square as and when they felt like it. They had their own posters, their own slogans; they didn't march in step but walked like people moving freely in their own city for the first time and, as it were, taking possession of it. The First of May became a special kind of spring festival, a *sacre du printemps*, but without Stravinsky's stamping rhythm which had proclaimed the coming disaster in 1913. Demand for the military parade had largely dried up so it was taken off the programme. The nation now had other concerns. Something had come to its natural end and how the old ritual, which had become firmly established, was to be replaced was as uncertain as the future of Russia itself. This uncertainty persisted— until the tanks reappeared on 9 May 2005, Victory Day, sixty years after the end of the war, almost a quarter of a century after the end of the USSR and on the eve of a new ideological mobilisation against an enemy without which the Putin regime evidently cannot survive. The other holiday—7 November—was abandoned without comment and replaced by 4 November, which was supposed to commemorate the expulsion of the Poles from Moscow in 1612. This was to be celebrated as 'Unity Day', a day whose meaning was a mystery to most Russian citizens.

CHAPTER 43

A 'Temple of Modernity': The Crematorium

Every age, every society develops its own ways of dealing with death. It seeks to contain this existential fact by developing forms, rituals and gestures to enable it to cope with the inevitable. The history of death cults shows that the whole of human history is filled with the quest for interpretations and attempts to make sense of death and invent rituals with which to come to terms with the process of leave-taking. Soviet Russia was no exception.[1] Even so, we detect elements here of a much disputed but obvious continuity, an evolution that can easily let us forget that the new response began with a clash of unprecedented harshness. It centred on the construction of the first state crematorium in 1927, on the eve of the tenth anniversary of the October Revolution. Everything connected with this event appears strangely exotic but in fact it is an exemplary instance of a society's search for a new relationship to death.

Cremation and the New Age

The opening of the Moscow crematorium has been described by an assiduous observer. The first test cremation took place on 11 January 1927 when the body of a dead workman from the Mytishchinsk Water Pumping Station, F. K. Solovyov, was cremated. He was only fifty-three. The process lasted an hour and a half and was filmed. The crematorium officially opened in October 1927—in time for the tenth anniversary of the October Revolution. The crematorium itself had been built on land belonging to the former Moscow Donskoy Monastery in the rebuilt church of St. Seraphim of Sarov and St. Anna of Kashin, which had been consecrated in 1903 at the urging of Tsar Nicholas II.

FIGURE 43.1. The church rebuilt in the Constructivist style in Donskoy Cemetery (architect D. P. Osipov) was opened as a crematorium in 1927. The crematorium furnaces were supplied by the Erfurt company J. A. Topf & Söhne; the Sauer organ came from the Lutheran Church of St. Michael. © culture-images/fai.

After the Revolution, the Donskoy Monastery was nationalised and converted into a Museum of Atheism and a home for the elderly. After an architecture competition in which the legendary Konstantin Melnikov took part, the church was rebuilt according to plans prepared by the Constructivist architect Dmitry Osipov and adapted in accordance with the latest innovations in crematorium design. The church's ground plan was preserved on the whole but the dome and a bell tower were replaced by a square tower reminiscent of a skyscraper. This fit in well with the surrounding space as this was also the location of the Radio Comintern transmission tower erected by Vladimir Shukhov in the early 1920s, a bold, still unsurpassed technical masterpiece. Everything had been well thought out and prepared. The crematorium underwent a year's testing; the furnaces came from the Topf & Söhne company, which subsequently used its expertise in the mass cremation of human bodies in the Auschwitz concentration camp and extermination centre.[2]

As for the furnishing of the rooms envisaged for the memorial services, a Sauer organ was obtained from the Lutheran St. Michael's Church that was due for demolition in 1928. There can be no doubt that Osipov's Constructivist building introduced a new note into the monastic space with its church life and graveyard. But nothing is as revealing as the report of D. Mallori which appeared in *Ogonyok* on 11 December 1927 under the title 'Flaming Burials' ('Ognennye pokhorony'). In it, a catafalque is unloaded from a horse and cart at the entrance to the crematorium. Two old women discuss the new institution and the zinc caskets used to hand out the 1.5 kilos of ash and remnants of bone with a metal plaque on which the name, a number and the date are inscribed. They wonder whether it is true that the bodies of the dead rise up vertically in the flames and whether cremation is compatible with the Bible, as the priest affirms, since it means that ash returns to ash whether in the flames or in the earth. A delegation of three hundred workmen arrives to accompany their dead comrade; there are speeches and music; the relatives take their leave of the departed, who is lying in his open coffin. The reporter is fascinated by the precision of the procedure: the brief sound of the bell, the lowering of the coffin, that only two of the closest mourners may enter the 'work station' where the cremation takes place. Everything is hygienic and clean. There are isolation rooms for people who have died of plague or anthrax, a small space for forensic anatomy, the actual cremation room, the coffin on tracks. The bouquets of flowers are removed and returned to the relatives. A fireproof number is placed on the coffin to avoid any possibility of confusion. The coffin is lowered and goes up in flames. Behind the tiles the temperature rises to 850°–1100°. The body burns slowly, the skull explodes—heavily medicated bodies burn more slowly; men take longer to cremate than women. The technicians control the fire; ventilation ensures optimal conditions. The crematorium charges 50 rubles for an urn in the columbarium; burial in the cemetery is free. Cremation of an adult costs 20 rubles; of a child, 10 rubles. The crematorium can handle ten bodies daily and sometimes goes on working until 10 p.m. Mourners take leave of the dead on the upper floor of the building—with sayings by Rabindranath Tagore, the poet from the land of cremations, who was celebrated in the Soviet Union as a kind of sage.

The reporter from *Ogonyok*:

Fire that turns everything to ashes! It is to you that this modern temple has been erected. This is the blazing cemetery, the crematorium.

Crematorium—the glowing breach in the Chinese Wall of popular ignorance and superstition, with which priests of all religions have played their games.

Crematorium—that spells the end of all relics and other marvels.

Cremation—that means hygiene and a simplified burial, it is the emancipation of the earth from the dead on behalf of the living.

We leave this blazing cemetery. Powerful and light, the radio tower soars into the sky. . . .

Businesses and factories are being built. The nation breathes powerfully beneath the white covering of snow.

Streetcars travel past. Guided tours are organised in the Museum of the Donskoy Monastery. You can hear the howl of the factory sirens. . . .

Live, live from the depths of your soul.

And when we die—they should take us to the crematorium so that instead of a world plagued by cemeteries, life should spread out everywhere full of joy and youthful vitality.[3]

Discourse about the Petrograd Crematorium

The Moscow crematorium in the Donskoy Monastery was the first built by the Soviet state, but it was preceded by lengthy debates about the building of the Petrograd crematorium. As Natalia Lebina has shown, the example of Petrograd makes it clear that what was at stake fundamentally was the new ruling power's attitude towards the experience of death.[4] Consequently, 'crematorium' became part of the common currency even in everyday speech, as the satires of Ilf and Petrov have shown.[5]

The Metropolitan Garden belonging to the Alexander Nevsky Monastery was the site chosen for the construction of the first state crematorium. With the sepulchre of St. Alexander Nevsky, the monastery was not only the most important religious complex of the imperial capital, but also the most important necropolis in the prosperous town on the Neva, a city with many cemeteries rich in traditions. The nationalisation and what amounted to the confiscation of churches and monasteries was one of the first actions of the revolutionary state. In January 1919 the Bolsheviks deployed armed guards against the faithful who wished to defend the churches and prevent the confiscation of gold and silver vessels, icon mountings and diamonds. Metropolitan Benjamin handed them over to avoid bloodshed but even so there was a huge procession to Kazan Cathedral in the city centre. After nationalisation, the monastery buildings were used as a workers' hostel. The state takeover of church property was accompanied by a set of new regulations for cemeteries. As early as 7 December 1918 a decree proclaimed: 'For all citizens there will henceforth be equal burials. Separate categories for funerals or memorial ceremonies are hereby abrogated.'[6] Despite the new egalitarianism, the old cemeteries used for the rich and famous at once became resting places for members of the new elite. Parts of the graveyards were set aside for famous communists—the victims of the Kronstadt uprising, for example. In 1929 Z. I. Lilina, the wife of the former chairman of the Petrograd Soviet, Grigory Zinoviev, who was a notorious militant atheist and opponent of the Orthodox Church, was buried at the entrance to the Svyato-Troitskaya Church. This was a clear provocation to all believers who had to accustom themselves to the fact that in future, graveyards would become museums, if indeed they were not simply abandoned and replaced by parks, cinemas and recreation facilities. The new powers-that-be brought a new order to God's acre. It was they who decided whose grave should be abandoned and done away with and who should be more equal than everyone else in the new age of universal equality.

Something like the gradual extinction of cemeteries began. Funerary monuments were broken up and their precious materials reused. Railings and ornaments were dismantled; graves were raided by robbers. The announcement that there would be a transition to cremation and the call for applications for the design of a crematorium shocked the country with its deep roots in Russian Orthodoxy. Cremation was not actually permitted in the Orthodox ritual, even though there had been debates in the Duma before the First World War about whether crematoriums should be viewed as an integral component of the rapid urbanisation process, just as they were everywhere else. There was an additional ideological factor in revolutionary Russia, which was the need to compensate for Russia's backwardness. Trotsky deemed it advisable to write an article on cremation, calling on the communist leadership to set a good example and have themselves cremated.[7] In the periodical *Church and Revolution*, the crematorium was even praised as the 'professorial chair of godlessness'. Every citizen was to have the 'right to cremation'. Ultimately, however, the rising numbers of dead from cold, hunger and the exodus became the decisive factor in the decimated city.

On 27 March 1919 the city soviet decided to build a crematorium on the site of the Lavra—the monastery—overruling the objections of Metropolitan Benjamin. The invitation to tender listed the requirements for the new building, which was intended to be both a symbol and a prototype for modern urbanism: a vestibule and a large hall for the ceremony, a gallery for singers and an orchestra, and several other smaller rooms with galleries and waiting rooms for family members, priests and coffin bearers. There were many interested applicants, including such prominent architects as Noi A. Trotsky and Sergey S. Serafimov. The winner was Ivan A. Fomin with his project 'The ineluctable path'. Since both materials and manpower were in short supply, the decision was to build a provisional crematorium on Vasilievsky Island, Line 14, at the corner of Ulitsa Kamskaya, the former Rozhkov House, subsequently used as a sugar factory, then a public bath (*banya*). The commission presided over by Boris G. Kaplun, an engineer and 'Bolshevist bon-vivant', called for funds from Moscow and evidently started a test plant in mid-1920. The scene has been described several times as Kaplun invited some of his poet friends to witness the spectacular process, including the poet Nikolay Gumilyov and the artist Yury Annenkov, who left an account of the cremation in the reconstructed *banya* of the first 'test subject', Ivan Sedyakin, a workman, whose body had been brought over from the city morgue. In his diary entry of 1 January 1921, Korney Chukovsky left the following account: 'Everything is bare and exposed. No religion, no poetry, not even the simplest expression of piety obscured the site of the cremation. The

Revolution has abolished all the rituals of yesterday but has not replaced them with anything new. Everyone just stood around with their caps on, smoking and chatting about the dead as if they were dogs.'[8] Such crudeness cannot be explained away primarily by the harsh conditions of the Civil War years. The lack of reverence was also a demonstration against a society in which religion was in some ways still as potent as ever but equally it shows the revolutionary actors demonstrating against one another. Given this kind of rupture, there was no way back to a world from which considerateness towards others had not yet been eliminated. In the same way, the disregard and neglect of cemeteries, which endured for decades—and were not simply the consequence of material deprivation—had their origins here in the onslaught against the mysteries of death.

Red Pantheon and the Ashes of the Victims and Their Executioners

Alongside the attack on traditional funeral and burial rites, the Revolution set about introducing rituals of its own from the very first day. It spontaneously invoked church rites; more especially, however, it drew on the rituals of the workers' movement and the revolutionary traditions of Europe. In Petrograd immediately after the Revolution the central square—the Tsaritsyn Meadow, the Field of Mars—became the burial ground for the first victims of the Revolution. The dead whose names were known were buried here in mass graves—known as *bratskie mogily* in Russian, 'brothers' graves'. Later the entire Field of Mars was transformed. Important representatives of the Petrograd architecture elite entered the open competition for this task, notably Alexandre Benois, but also Peter Behrens, the architect of the German embassy in St. Isaac's Square, and Eliel Saarinen, the master of Nordic Art Nouveau.[9] The parade ground for the guards' regiments, and also the square that turned into the largest fairground of the capital once a year, complete with slides and roller coasters, was transformed into a pantheon for the fallen of the Revolution. In the centre, a square granite block was erected after a design by the young Lev Rudnev, who in the 1950s would create his masterpiece in the shape of the

Moscow State University, complete with an inscription by Anatoly Lunacharsky, the intellectual among the leading Bolsheviks. During the 1920s, well-known members of the Russian working-class movement were buried on the Field of Mars, the last one in 1933. But even at that time another Red Pantheon grew in importance, namely the Mausoleum built in Moscow in honour of Lenin. Increasingly, the urns containing the remains of prominent Soviets were laid to rest in the Kremlin walls or else in Novodevichie Cemetery.

For ordinary people, too, burial rituals were altered by the introduction of cremation. In 1929, two and a half years after the opening of the Moscow crematorium, over 9,600 cremations were registered. Yury Orlov, the physicist and subsequent dissident, describes the cremation process in his childhood memoirs:

> The factory organized a civil funeral: speeches and orchestra. They put me on top of the hearse, next to the coachman. In the back lay my father. To the tune of funeral marches the white horses carried us unhurriedly. It was a warm spring day. Small boys ran around us in circles, eyeing me with envy. I felt embarrassed and wanted to get there faster.
>
> In the crematorium that had just been built alongside the fortress walls of the International Youth Day Leather Goods factory, which before the Revolution had been the Donskoy Monastery, they burned my father. Curious people clustered around, waiting politely for the corpse, enveloped by flame, to raise itself a little, and for the muscles to jerk in spasms. But Father didn't raise himself.
>
> They cut the tendons in his arms and legs, here and here! That's why he didn't get up. You understand? You, his son?.... In those years it was permitted to watch corpses being cremated, so that even the most ignorant citizens should know that there is no mystery in death.

In the 1950s Orlov's mother was also cremated in the crematorium in the Donskoy Cemetery.[10]

The crematorium that had been opened in the Donskoy Monastery in 1927 had much to do in the coming years and decades. While the cemetery grounds became the storage site for sculptures and historically valuable building fragments from the demolished Cathedral of Christ the Saviour, the cremation business was running at full blast. Prominent political and cultural figures were cremated there: Vladimir Mayakovsky; Maxim Gorky; the test pilot Valery Chkalov, who had pioneered the first flight over the North Pole; Sergey Kirov, who had been assassinated in Leningrad; Valerian Kuybyshev; Commissar for Heavy Industry Sergo Ordzhonikidze, following his suicide; 'Lenin's rival' Alexander Bogdanov and many others.[11]

As far as we can reconstruct the history, the victims of the Terror in the 1930s were executed in the Moscow prisons, the Lubyanka, Butyrka Prison, the Lefortovo, and then sent to the crematoriums. The lists of those who were cremated and whose ashes were then buried in pits include such members of the military as V. K. Blyukher, A. I. Yegorov, M. N. Tukhachevsky, I. P. Uborevich, I. E. Yakir, Komsomol official A. V. Kosarev, the Party bosses S. V. Kosyor, P. P. Postyshev and P. A. Alexandrov, M. N. Ryutin, N. A. Uglanov, Vlas Chubar, as well as writers such as Mikhail Koltsov, Vsevolod Meyerhold, Isaac Babel and many others.[12] During the Second World War the dead from the Moscow lazarettes were cremated here. The crematorium was shut down in 1972 following protests by neighbours, although it continued to be used in isolated cases until 1982. The last person cremated here is said to have been Defence Minister and Marshal of the Soviet Union Dmitry Ustinov. In 1992 the monastery was returned to the Russian Orthodox Church, the ovens dismantled and the square tower replaced by a dome once more. The columbarium with the urns of selected personages survived, as did the wall with the names of those who had fallen in the Great Patriotic War. What had previously been a 'combine of progressive interment' has once again become a church where baptisms and weddings are celebrated.

Not far from the monument erected in 1992 to the murdered victims of Stalinism, whose ashes were scattered in anonymous graves, lies the grave of Vasily Blokhin, an executioner whose work rate was that of a Stakhanovite record-holder. He was responsible for thousands of executions, including the murders of thousands of Polish officers in Tver in spring 1940. Blokhin died in his bed on 3 February 1955 and his body rests next to that of his wife and not far from the ashes of his victims.[13] The land belonging to the Donskoy Monastery contains the ashes of the various waves of Stalin's purges, as well as victims and perpetrators who were caught up in the maelstrom of subsequent purges.[14] This is why we must suppose that Grave 1, which has been erected by historians, human rights activists and family members in memory of the victims, contains both sorts of ashes—those of the victims of the show trials, such as Nikolay Bukharin, but also those of the executioner Nikolay Yezhov.

CHAPTER 44

ZAGS, or the Rituals of Everyday Life

Even in a system as prolific in abbreviations as the Soviet linguistic cosmos, ZAGS stands out as especially prominent and popular. Soviet citizens knew at once what was meant by it and had dealings with it on many occasions throughout their lives (in post-Soviet Russia, too, the name and the institution have continued to exist). What is called ZAGS in ordinary speech is officially and rather cumbersomely known as Zapis aktov grazhdanskogo sostoyaniya: the Office for the Registration of Personal Information. Institutions like ZAGS exist in every social system; they stand for the regulation and organisation of life from birth to death. Every change in status, all the important stages of life are recorded here: birth, marriage or divorce, adoption, name changes and death. Given its opening hours and its powers, ZAGS is an unavoidable part of the physical and mental topography of a town, a parish and a municipal district. Frequently it is notable just for its prominent buildings, especially when they are used for weddings. Because these buildings offer clues to the permanence or changing nature of the rituals that hold together and sustain a society, they are useful points from which to observe the consolidation or erosion of community life. What goes on in them has been well described in a standard work on rituals:

> What we mean by ritual in the narrower sense is a human practice characterised by the standardisation of its external forms, repetitiveness, nature of its enactment, performativity and symbolic significance and that has a fundamental, socially constructive impact. In contrast to this, one speaks of ritualisation in the wider sense when a particular form of behaviour repeats itself regularly in its outward forms.[1]

During its existence, the Soviet Union generated specific rites and rituals that influenced and shaped people's lives and have left a permanent mark in the memories of all citizens. We are talking about vitally important documents after all. The birth certificate testified to the arrival of a 'new member of Soviet society'. The issuing of a passport by the militia transformed you into what Vladimir Mayakovsky called 'the proud citizen with a red passport and the object of envy to the citizens of other states'.[2] This was where the 'covenant for life' was established—or else dissolved, whereupon a death certificate would be issued.

The most important ritual connected with ZAGS between birth and death was the wedding, if we go by the typical photographs in family albums. This was when the couple, dressed in their very best clothes, came to the wedding palace, accompanied by no less well-dressed family and friends to take part in a ceremony whose forms developed over decades. The very location and its surroundings were significant. Wedding palaces were often situated in special buildings, former businessmen's villas, bank buildings, the pavilions of the late Tsarist Empire, such as Wedding Palace No. 2 in Ulitsa Furshtatskaya, one of the best districts of St. Petersburg; the wedding palace in the Peterhof close to St. Petersburg; or the Astrakhan wedding palace in a magnificent Art Nouveau building dating back to 1910 that was originally intended to be the Stock Exchange. These prominent buildings almost always had magnificent entrances, impressive staircases and halls, enfilades, wood-panelled drawing rooms, parquet flooring, opulent stucco ceilings and chandeliers. The atmosphere was dignified, solemn, with net curtains and heavy draperies, the portrait of the President and the city's coat of arms. Where prerevolutionary splendour was in short supply, as in newly built towns, a specific interior architecture developed in the wedding palaces. They were places where you could order festive music according to your own taste: Tchaikovsky's Piano Concerto, a Glazunov Polonaise, but most frequently, Felix Mendelssohn's Wedding March, which rang out as the bridal couple, accompanied by witnesses and friends, mounted the stairs to the hall where they listened to the address of the deputies of the town soviet, likewise in their Sunday best and a sash. The substance of the address differed little from the earnest exhortations heard elsewhere.

FIGURE 44.1. Wedding ceremony in the wedding palace: 'My sister is getting married. As witness, I stood on the left; the groom's witness stood on the right. The Registrar read an introductory speech. Then we all stood up. It all went quickly and without undue solemnity. We were all dressed quite informally and wore everyday clothes' (Emiliya Kabakov). From Ilya Kabakov, *Auf dem Dach/On the Roof: Installation Palais des Beaux-Arts de Bruxelles*, Richter Verlag, Düsseldorf 1997, p. 114 (with the kind permission of Emiliya Kabakov).

You were told that a new life was beginning, that marriage entails a special bond of fidelity and that children should be brought up in a Soviet and patriotic spirit. The ceremony was often followed by a buffet and perhaps a glass of champagne in front of the wedding palace, but perhaps also by a ride to one of the places where the lives of individuals met up with the great life of the nation and one's forebears. That might have been to the Memorial to the Unknown Soldier or the Piskaryovskoe Memorial Cemetery in Leningrad, to lay flowers where the victims of the siege are commemorated.

These festive marriage rites did not always exist. The wedding palaces were late innovations probably not introduced until the 1960s. They signalled the stabilisation of rituals that the Russian Revolution initially wished to abolish. The ZAGS have come a long way. From starting off as a place of registration, they have developed into the sites of elaborate celebrations.

In the first weeks of the ZAGS' existence, on 18 December 1917, the Soviets had decreed that church weddings should be abolished and civil marriage introduced. A year later, on 16 September 1918, a new Civil Code was introduced. This did away with the church rituals for weddings that had existed since time immemorial. Or that was the intention. Registration became a matter of signing a piece of paper in an office; this was true for both marriage and divorce. The family, it was claimed, had been replaced by the collective; instead of marriage there would now be camaraderie between men and women, and where previously children had been brought up by their parents, education would now be delivered by social organisations. The designation ZAGS itself stands for the loss of meaning of a ceremonial world that had once borne the stamp of church influence. The ease with which couples could now be joined in wedlock, and more especially, the ease with which they could now divorce became a constant theme of literature and everyday folklore in the 1920s. Under the guise of emancipating women, men could now escape their obligations as breadwinners; women found themselves held responsible for the children the men had abandoned. The reforms, then, took place at the expense of women and children who were often simply deserted. And although these innovations seemed exemplary even to Western observers such as Fannina Halle, they contributed more to fragmentation than to social cohesion.[3] At the same time, the revolutionary marriage legislation of the 1920s was presumably itself no more than the formal acknowledgement of the breakdown of the family as an institution following the collapse of the social order as a whole. Among the catastrophic consequences, we should mention the uprooting of the *besprizorniki* amid the chaos and civil war, the millions of orphaned children who were left to fend for themselves and who represented a huge challenge to the state.[4] This resulted in an abrupt volte face in the mid-1930s by politicians, who called for the rehabilitation of marriage, the old ideas of family and the restoration of women as 'housewives'—a revision that then suffered a further major setback with the Second World War and its catastrophic social and demographic consequences.

The rise of wedding rituals and everything they entailed—the ceremonies, the palace, the hospitality and the lavish private celebrations—was an important index of how postwar society became consolidated.

Yury Pimenov's 1962 painting of a bridal couple in the new Moscow district of Novye Cheryomushki became iconic [see fig. 37.2].

Following the separation of church and state, the 'Decree on Civil Marriage, Children and Civil Registry Bookkeeping', issued on 18 December 1917, as well as the 'Code of Laws Relating to Marital Status: Marriage, Family and Guardianship' agreed on by the Central Executive Committee of the RSFSR on 16 September 1918 put an end to the Orthodox Church's monopoly on marriage. In European terms, this was a normal act of secularisation, admittedly one with major implications. They also affected other religious communities, such as those of Judaism and Islam. At the same time, opportunities opened up for millions of people, above all the young, eager to escape the old repressive customs and develop new modes of living for themselves. The reduction of marriage to the formal act of 'registration', however, unsettled the sense of social responsibility, much as people were shocked by such developments as Alexandra Kollontai's 'glass of water theory of sexuality' and notions that love is merely 'the gratification of a physical need'.[5] The minimum of ceremony that became the norm in the ZAGS of the 1920s was representative of the new casual attitude, the general loss of the importance attached to family bonds and hence of social cohesiveness more generally. These had after all been subjected to the greatest imaginable strain by war, revolution, civil war and migration. People spoke of a state of 'legal nihilism' (Bogdan Kistyakovsky) in the postrevolutionary period, and in the same way, one can speak of a 'nihilism of formality' and a 'hostility to formality', since all formalities per se—rites and rituals—had been discredited as 'bourgeois' and 'reactionary'. Great efforts were needed to develop new rites and rituals, new ceremonies that might help to create a new cohesion or perhaps even enable a new positive formality to develop in a society that had become fragmented in the extreme.

This invention of tradition had perforce to adhere to the stock of formalities that had been handed down, whether in the traditions of the socialist workers' movement, which was feeble in Russia, in the religious communities or in historical models, above all, the French Revolution. This led to the crystallisation of a particular chronology known as the 'Red calendar' that acted as the successor to the calendar of saints and the religious festivals of Russian Orthodoxy, as well as the calendar of Jewish and Muslim festivals. Where desirable, 'usable' elements of these cultures were incorporated into the Red calendar. In this respect, the Soviets were astonishingly productive and innovative. It was as if they had set out to compensate aesthetically and ritually for their lack of legitimacy. The religiously based names of patron saints were replaced by the names of revolutionaries; the archaic course of the religious year was replaced by the rhythm of industrial labour. Where previously lines of succession had been based on wealth and power, new worker dynasties would develop their own initiation rites.

Bolshevism and the Soviets found themselves in a country still imbued with traditional, peasant values, although admittedly in an almost hopeless confrontation with an overpowering cultural rival. The new elite's attempts to develop its own 'modern rituals' and anchor its own system of values was therefore far more than a matter of 'cultural management'. It was a huge effort, a veritable life-and-death struggle.[6] The Party and the state had to do battle with the very core of all community and society, namely the family, even though that institution had been severely damaged by the upheavals. They had to try to replace the rites of membership and initiation of the religion-based communities—such as baptism or circumcision. Hence in the period after the Revolution, the state introduced the *oktyabriny, oktyabrenie* (October rite) as a substitute for the *krestiny*, the traditional baptism ceremony. The aim was to transform the mere entry in a register of births and the giving of a name into something more festive and to combine it with some helpful advice: 'Dear parents! Today is a great and significant event for you—a new member of the family has been born. This is a reason for rejoicing not simply for you but for our whole society. Children are our happiness, our joy, our future. . . . Raise and educate your children (to become) healthy, joyful, bold and unafraid of difficulties. From childhood implant in them a love of work and of our great Motherland.'[7] There were also special locations for the registration of newborn children, although not such magnificent ones as the Malyutka Palace that was later built in a former palace at Ulitsa Furshtatskaya 58 in St. Petersburg. The *oktyabriny* did not succeed in gaining general acceptance except among communist enthusiasts in the 1920s.

Birth registration was followed by the organisation of the Young Pioneers, which was intended for the age group between nine and fourteen and then by the Komsomol for those between fourteen and twenty-eight. Membership of the Young Pioneers was pretty general, whereas Komsomol membership was more a matter of political decision and personal choice. Each of these organisations developed its own rituals. In the case of the Young Pioneers this meant taking an oath, an act of dedication during which two older pioneers tied a red kerchief around the novice's neck, after which the youngsters would all march off carrying banners and accompanied by the sound of fanfares and trumpets. All of this was supposed to take place in a location of historical significance such as the Lenin Museum or the Finland Station.

Komsomol membership was also associated with a vow, weighty speeches and a commitment to the working class, the fatherland and the heroes who had preceded them in the Komsomol. Following speeches by veterans and the handing-out of membership cards, new members swore an oath on the ideals of the Komsomol, vowed to study, work and remain true to their parents' ideals.

Other—outwardly nonpolitical—rituals in the lives of young people may have been even more significant: the start of the school year on 1 September, school open days, final exams and the handing-out of school-leaving certificates as well as enrolment in a university. An event of great importance for young men was the day of the call-up to the armed forces, as in the Tsarist Empire, together with bidding farewell to the family, the work collective or even the entire village. This was a day on which to take leave of 'civic life', a tearful day, full of foreboding, when young men were separated from their usual surroundings. It was a brief interlude before entering into the exceptional circumstances of military service, which was associated with a toughening process, discipline, subordination, humiliation and, as we now know, high suicide rates. The departure was preceded by a day of unrestrained high spirits with vast quantities of alcohol beneath the gaze of a sympathetic public—shortly—before 'things became serious'.

Even in post-Soviet Russia, ZAGS has remained a stable institution, essential for every citizen. But these registry offices are no longer the only or even the primary places people look to when seeking orientation and support in life's rites of passage. Russia is secular but religion, whether superficial or profoundly spiritual, has informed people's ideas and behaviour far more powerfully since the end of the

Soviet Union. Many people claim to be 'religious' without being regular churchgoers. More and more people have their children baptised, church schools are popular and there is a growing interest in the rites and customs of other faiths—Judaism and Islam. Whether we should equate this with a genuine renaissance of religious belief or whether it is a passing fashion is unclear. Weddings nowadays are outstanding events—with rented droshkies or American old-timers, bands, lavish buffets and champagne—in the better-off Russian middle classes at any rate. Church weddings have become the norm again while the ZAGS 'registration' and finger-wagging sermons by presiding officials persist unchanged. But the visits to the tomb of the Unknown Soldier that became obligatory in Soviet times or to the viewing platform on the Sparrow Hills (formerly called the Lenin Hills) show that there neither has been nor can be a straightforward return to the religious rituals of prerevolutionary Russia.

As an example of successfully inventing tradition by taking over and adapting a (religious) festival, we should mention the 'invention' of celebrations for the New Year. The Soviets abolished Christmas as an official holiday and created confusion in the calendar by introducing the five-day week in 1929. By way of compensation, they put all emphasis on New Year as a new, secular holiday. This worked because it involved taking over Christmas trees and everything associated with them from the former Christian holidays: 'Father Frost' (*Ded Moroz*), families united beneath the Christmas tree, presents for the children and a general Christmas atmosphere generated with the assistance of Russian salad. The rehabilitation of the Snow Maiden— *Snegurochka*—was a later addition.[8]

The post-Soviet world has rediscovered and revived pre-Soviet festivals and rituals; it has been unable to detach itself from generation-long Soviet festivities and so celebrates Christmas and New Year according to both the Orthodox and the Soviet calendars. It follows the pattern, therefore, of people who find themselves caught up in times of transition, between disruption and continuity. They celebrate according to both the old calendar and the new; if one does not suffice, they can have recourse to the other and celebrate twice over. Taken together that comes to two weeks, a kind of time-out from world history.

CHAPTER 45

Queues as a Soviet Chronotope

'Together with the Soviet social order and the Soviet way of life, history has also been made by the Soviet line.' The memory of the queue, which determined the daily life of Soviet citizens, will persist for a long time. We owe a debt of gratitude to the Russian historian Yelena Alexandrovna Osokina, for her pioneering study *Our Daily Bread: Socialist Distribution and the Art of Survival in Stalin's Russia, 1927–1941*, where she summarises the topic in a 'Farewell Ode to the Soviet Queue'.[1] Such queues may still be found in a number of offices where issuing references and documents and carrying out complex investigations continue, but the queue as an everlasting ritual, an integral component of everyday life and indeed the epitome of the Soviet way of life itself has been relegated to history. People born later or foreigners who have never had any contact with the Soviet world will have difficulty imagining what it was like.

It is in any case strange how long it took before this centrepiece of ordinary Soviet life became the object of scholarly scrutiny and reflection even though visitors and journalists couldn't help but notice it the very first day of their stay in the Soviet Union. They were astounded and quickly concluded that it was proof of the superiority and greater efficiency of affluent Western societies, but they failed to look at the matter in any greater depth. The same can be said by and large of Soviet citizens themselves, even though they were well aware that without standing in line you could not really obtain anything. As Osokina puts it: 'It can be said without exaggeration that almost the entire nation stood in the Soviet queue. The queues were visible, there were depressed and angry queues, queues in which you stood for hours and queues that went on for days, there were silent ones and noisy ones where being lucky enough to obtain something was combined with the tragedy of time wasted and of a wish that had not been fulfilled. And there were also the invisible queues such as the years'-long wait for a car or an apartment—and in fact many people ended up frustrated because the entire Soviet era turned out to be shorter than the queues it had produced.'[2] An entire complex of experiences and contacts was linked to queues—the memory of a bargain, a piece of furniture that had been acquired, perhaps a bookcase made in Czechoslovakia, or an edition of a classic such as Alexander Dumas in exchange for a few kilos of wastepaper—*makulatura*. There were many recollections of small defeats and small victories and the cunning that occasionally enabled individuals to triumph over the long-term shortages dictated by the system. The queue was a social theme of utmost importance, one that left its mark on the lives and attitudes of entire generations of Soviet citizens.

Soviet Chronotope

'In the sense that we can speak of Soviet time-space as a utopian chronotope,' Andrey Lebedev writes, 'we can describe the USSR not just as a utopia but also as a uchronia. What are its fundamental features? It is well known that utopias either look back to the past or forwards to the future, but never at the present. The Soviet uchronia was resolutely future-orientated. Communism was something that had yet to be built and its creation was defined ideologically as a race against time: "Five-Year Plan in four years! Let's fulfil the Year's Plan by 7 November"—the nation lived under the hail of the columns of numbers coming from the loudspeakers and the aim of this mendacious radio violence with its promises of victory was the transformation of all life into an endless race leading "Forwards to the victory of Communism!"'[3] 'Everything was working. More precisely, everything appeared to be working where the official myth coincided with the nonofficial reality. And the chronotope of this everyday reality was the chronotope of the queue. . . . The queue is the antithesis of the Communist chronotope and the literal expression of stasis, *zastoi*. It was not individual people who stood in the queues but time itself: it stagnated, it solidified, it turned to stone and when it did move on, it was in short tortuous bursts, constantly stopping and starting. The collective Soviet body reminds us of an organism suffering from chronic constipation. You queued for everything: a car, an apartment, a sausage, theatre tickets or an exhibition.' Queuing was the ritual you underwent in order to become a Soviet human being. An essential part of that was spending the night at the entrance to the department store; when it opened the next morning you waited until you were called up by name, until the number inscribed in ink on your hand began to run—'these were the tribal insignia, the marks of the *rod-plemya*, in short, the queue was a mode of socialisation and a form of social sculpture par excellence.'[4]

However, precisely because the queue was so prevalent in Soviet reality, it was accepted as a natural phenomenon which simply could not be altered. It existed, but not as an object of social concern. It was the open secret not worth speaking about. The queue was the locus of squandered living time, an indispensable way of coping with everyday life, day by day, month by month, year on year. It was the barometer that provided an indication of the pressures at work in society—not the expression of poverty or deprivation, but of a socially produced scarcity. It was as ubiquitous as the infinitely vast Empire itself; its topography was that of the Empire. The queue was a familiar reality that had long since ceased to cause surprise, both in the principal cities, which in fact were privileged where the distribution of consumer goods was concerned, and in the remote estates where people were accustomed to fending for themselves. It was the inevitable fact of life to which people had to submit if they wished to get by. To circumvent the queue or to ignore it, to disregard its rules would have led to the collapse of a social order that was based on an established routine. This was not the queue that citizens join to enter a bus in an orderly manner without crowding one another; it was a permanent form of stress that had to be endured with patience but which almost always ended in verbal abuse and sometimes even pushing and shoving. The queue had as many voices and faces as the Empire itself. Since scarcity was systemic it could affect anyone—apart from those who were provided for through other channels. For all other people no article of consumption was always readily available. This was true even of tomatoes and potatoes in a country with no shortage of either. There might be underwear in sizes that were not in demand and had been in stock forever or hats and caps gathering dust on the shelves because they had long since fallen out of fashion, summer clothing in winter and winter clothing in summer—all delivered according to plan but not in tune with the rhythms of life.

The queue was even to be found in the shared apartment, as noted by the ethnologist Ilya Utekhin: 'As we have seen, the queue reflects the spatial arrangement of the rooms in the apartment—in this sense everything does go round in circles.' That begins with the *dezhurstvo*, the arrangements for dealing with the general tasks of looking after the apartment, starting on one side of the hallway and then proceeding to the other.[5] The queue is the place for outfoxing others, for pulling a fast one, for swindling one's way to the front. 'What is characteristic of the Soviet queue with all its ingenious organisation and innumerable exceptions and unwritten rules is the importance of the many mutual "agreements"/*ogovorki* and the private arrangements of the people standing in line. Of equal importance is what might be called the "human" aspect', in other words, a highly subjective set of informal but stable relationships.[6] But even the process in a bus where people handed tickets and money over the heads of other passengers can be regarded as a type of queuing.[7] There were the visible queues that formed outside the department stores or kiosks and there were the invisible queues consisting of waiting lists where names advanced year by year, seven years perhaps in the case of an independent apartment, ten years or even longer for a car.

Standing in a queue was life in the community, a state of affairs you simply had to adjust to, created by forces the individual was powerless to resist—unless you opted for a change of scene and moved to the black market and the shadow economy where everything could be obtained.

The Queue—An Attempt at a Literary Treatment

It took almost to the end of the Soviet Union for one of the most typical manifestations of everyday Soviet life to find artistic expression. Not surprisingly, literature was the medium. Literature is sufficiently alert and flexible to mould language, objects and human beings and depict their interaction. Vladimir Sorokin's novel *The Queue* is a significant literary and sociological testimony of one of

the first-rank experiences of ordinary Soviet life. His book inaugurates the study of a topic that other disciplines—sociology, history,
ethnology—began to explore only much later from a historical distance.[8] The very first sentence captures the essence of the primal
scene familiar to every Soviet citizen in which the new arrival joins
the queue:

— Comrade, who's last in the queue?
— I am, I think, but there was a woman in a blue coat after me.
— So I'm after her?
— Yes, she'll be back in a moment. You stand behind me in the
  meantime.
— You're staying here then are you?
— Yes.
— I just wanted to nip off for a moment—I'll literally be a minute.
— I think you better wait for her, 'cos what can I say if somebody
  else comes along? If you hold on a moment, she said she wouldn't
  be long.
— Okay then, I'll wait. You been queuing long?
— Not really . . .
— How many are they giving per person, d'you know?
— God knows . . . haven't even asked. Do you know how many each
  they're giving out?
— Don't know about today. I heard yesterday it was two each.
— Two?
— Uh-huh. First it was four each, then two.
— Not a lot, huh! Hardly worth waiting, really . . .
— You should get into two queues at once. Those guys from out of
  town have got places in three different queues.
— Three each?
— Uh-huh.
— Then we're going to be here all day!
— Nah, don't worry. Service is very quick here.
— I'm not so sure. We haven't budged an inch . . .
— That's 'cos those people have just come back again. Whole bunch
  of them—they'd all gone off for a while.
— They all go off and then all pile in at once.[9]

That is how Sorokin's novel begins. And that is how it goes on for almost 250 pages. The novel consists of a multivoiced conversation, whose heroes are ordinary citizens who have come together simply because they have joined a queue. They have no idea what they are waiting for, although they have learned from experience that where people are queuing there must be something that makes standing there worthwhile. The queue moves forward and becomes a communication space made up of suppositions, rumours, recommendations and insults. It is the social space of chance acquaintances and uncensored speech because its universality offers anonymity and protection. The text also contains long pauses and blank spaces—literally, empty, unprinted pages—and then again, entire pages filled with the roll call of the names of people with a right to be in the queue. The queue is plagued by permanent doubts about whether it might be better to leave and switch to another queue. It is the information marketplace where people exchange news about where things are to be found and where one might get on faster—assuming the rumours are true. The entire range of judgements and prejudices about the peoples who inhabit the Soviet Union are rehearsed and foreign enemies are denigrated. People waiting encourage one another to keep their spirits up, offering the reassurance that despite the lengthy wait things will move on in due course. They get to know one another—even by name: Lena is one person, Vadim is another. They all comment on the increasing nervousness. They push into the people in front of them but sometimes they push too hard and find themselves being pushed back. The queue continues through the midday heat, which they all have to endure, or they find themselves soaked in a sudden shower of rain. People are loud in their condemnation of anyone who tries to jump the queue of people waiting patiently. They talk about films they have seen. At some point a megaphone announces the arrival of whole busloads of people who want to be served out of turn. The level of excitement, envy and anger moves up a few notches. The orderliness of the queue is under threat. People get worked up about Georgians and Jews or about the privileged representatives of top workers who are whisked to the front of the queue. They express their views on the passing limousines belonging to diplomats and talk about accidents they have read about or even witnessed.

They argue about Soviet writers, opera productions, geography. Some people swear—every kind of accent can be heard, ranging from the uneducated to the highly cultured. Recommendations fly to and fro—about radios, materials, the superiority of imported goods from other socialist countries, the quality of BASF cassettes, the achievements of the Americans and the music of Scriabin and Rachmaninov. Views are aired on every conceivable aspect of ordinary life: the state of the apartment blocks, the price of meat, the exhibition in the Pushkin Museum. At some point, crush barriers are set up. The roll call is taken again—fifty pages of names. People display their expert knowledge about LPs, albums, Tarkovsky's films, the merits of the poetry of David Samoylov and Pushkin. People get to know one another and escape from the rain into an apartment where they enjoy passionate sex. The queue is the home of chance encounters, a place where energies that demand to be released build up. The enforced standstill is a place of pent-up energies, of wasted, squandered life. The entire scene is a chaotic bubble, a cacophony, a corridor of voices and sounds, swearing, suppressed aggression, conversations about God and the world that has stopped caring about the passage of time because time has become meaningless.

Agents of the Secret Police and Queues:
Listening in on Society

No one has grasped the importance of the queue as a source of public opinion more fully than the state and its organs. Yelena Osokina produced her history of the Soviet system of distribution from her research in the archives of the NKVD. 'Queues have vanished from our lives but the historical documents and the memories of them have survived. . . . The queue can tell us something about the age, the people and about power. As a historian of Stalinism, I have chosen the Stalinist pre-war years. My sources are the reports of the People's Commissariat for Internal Affairs (NKVD) for the years 1938–1941.'[10]

Since the queues were a sensitive barometer of the changing moods in Soviet society, a place of noncommittal, informal conversations and discussions, without naming names and addresses, there

FIGURE 45.1. Queuing at a bread shop in Chelyabinsk. © culture-images/fai.

were always agents present—*lyudi v shtatskom*—collecting information for their ministry. These agents, dressed in civilian clothes, provided a service not only to the government but also to the historian
because they have passed useful material down to us. 'The people's
voice' has been recorded in the reports and memorandums of NKVD
informers.

We can think of the queue as a mass phenomenon, a movement created by the system of organised scarcity that could skid out of control
at any moment. After a brief period in 1935–1936 during which a 'free
market' held sway and ration cards were abolished, the supply crises
again increased in frequency and then became permanent. Queues
tens of thousands strong waited for days on end, engaging in a kind
of cat-and-mouse game with the militia, scattering and reforming. Not
even bans, arrests or expulsions were powerful enough to force them
out of the city. We learn from the NKVD reports of 1938–1939: 'On the
night of 13–14 April, 33,000 customers waited outside the stores. On
the night of 16–17 April, 43,800 people lined up outside stores.'[11] Queues
of people in their thousands stood outside every large department

store. 'At six o'clock in the morning a line formed at a department store in the Dzerzhinskii district, taking over the nearest streets, tram, and bus stations. By nine o'clock there were 8,000 people in line.' Or, 'lately the narrow side street of Stoleshnikov has been transformed into something like the Yaroslavskii market.'[12]

One person in the queue commented: 'So many working days are wasted in line! For these working days it would have been possible to build two textile factories in Moscow.' The NKVD informers emphasised the ability of those waiting in the queues to organise themselves: 'The line starts to form several hours before the store closes, in the yards of the nearest houses. Someone makes a line list, and, after getting on the list, some people leave to find a place on the street or in a yard to rest. Some citizens bring big winter coats and blankets to keep warm. Some also bring kitchen chairs to sit on.'[13]

The people in the line seethed, especially the younger ones. They complained about having money but nothing to buy with it because the shelves were empty. 'I don't know where to put my money. . . . In the villages there is nothing and here you have to be tormented in the lines—there's no time to sleep at night. Many people don't have places to stay, but it's forbidden to sleep in the train station. It's all very bad.' Someone else remarked, 'I have money, but I can't buy anything. It's already the fourth day I've camped here, and it seems that I have to go home with nothing.' Or, 'I'm walking in torn pants. I got five days off work, stood four days in lines, but I was not able to get any pants.' Another voice: 'I come from Dmitrov. There's absolutely nothing to buy there. Here, even though you have to stand in lines, you have a chance to get something.' Or again, 'I am standing in line for the fourth night, but I can't get a good overcoat for 800–1000 rubles.' There were constant quarrels with people who tried to push to the front and jump the queue. Other ways of gaining access to the objects desired included cunning, a personal connection to the department store staff or bribery. You could even buy places farther forward in the queue or 'give orders'. Osokina describes the queue as 'an encyclopaedia of the ways to survive'. 'Standing in lines became an art. It required being able to see and to take into account many things ahead of time. Any little thing could cause the loss of a place in the line. Where to stand? When to stand? And even, What to wear while standing? Clothes and appearance became very important after the shops in Moscow were limited to residents.'[14]

The authorities declared war on the queues by issuing a series of regulations for Moscow and Leningrad in 1939 and 1940. Later, measures were introduced against people coming from outside: they were expelled from the towns. Queues were patrolled, handbags searched; whoever had more than the permitted quantities had to give them back. 'Starting from seven o'clock in the morning, some people ... waiting for the opening of the stores pretended that they are shopping for meat, milk, and other groceries. They even have with them little milk containers, but when their turn comes they don't buy any milk; they go back to standing in line again ... people are standing in line for meat in order to hide from the police.'[15] In this way the customers outwitted the police; they even bought tickets for the elektrichka, the suburban railway, so as to evade the inspectors on the main-line platforms while distributing among fellow travellers the goods they had bought so as to get through the barriers unscathed.

Requiem: Waiting in the Face of Death

The epigraph to Anna Akhmatova's cycle of poems 'Requiem' (1935–1940), written at the peak of the Stalinist Terror, leads us to a very different dimension of the life consumed by the time spent queuing. We are speaking here of waiting in the corridors of power, where life and death decisions were made, of waiting for a sign of life from loved ones who had vanished into the expanses of the Gulags, and of the time of which Akhmatova wrote—in 1961:

> No, not far beneath some foreign sky then,
> Not with foreign wings to shelter me,
> I was with my people then, close by them
> Where my luckless people chanced to be.

And she wrote, instead of a foreword:

> In the fearful year of the Yezhov terror I spent seventeen months in prison queues in Leningrad. One day, somebody 'identified' me.

Beside me, in the queue there was a woman with blue lips. She had, of course, never heard of me; but she suddenly came out of that trance so common to us all and whispered in my ear (everybody spoke in whispers there): 'Can you describe this?' And I said: 'Yes, I can.' And then something like the shadow of a smile crossed what had once been her face.[16]

For all the efficiency with which the autocratic state expedited the oppression of its citizens and the annihilation of its real or imagined opponents, it was inevitable that the 'processing' of hundreds of thousands and even millions of people would result in disruption and blockages. Even in retrospect it is difficult to grasp how 'the organs' of the state—normally the apparatus of the NKVD—could have carried out the mass arrests, mass shootings and mass deportations, the deportations of hundreds of thousands of so-called kulaks during the period 1929–1932, the deportations from the eastern Polish territories and the Baltic occupied in 1939, the collective deportations of the Volga Germans, the Chechens, Ingush and Crimean Tatars—all in the shortest possible time and under wartime conditions. It was necessary to organise the arrests, move to the assembly points and railway stations, and transport to the transit camps and final destinations, which were frequently thousands of miles apart. This process on its own—transportation, travel in freight cars and arrival in regions without any shelter—led to hundreds of thousands of deaths. As we know from the memoirs of the survivors, every stop on this journey was a station on the road through Hell. From the outset there were delays and queues, though in these queues the problem was not the shortage of supplies but survival itself. Following the arrest of his mother in 1937, Stepan Podlubny, the son of a kulak who had gone to ground in Moscow, made his way through the Moscow police stations and prisons—Petrovka, Taganka, Butyrka and Sretenka—in search of her. He describes the process of queuing—how the queues formed and reformed and gradually worked their way to the counter at the front, which was likely to have closed down when one reached it.[17] He encountered the same situation everywhere:

A small, narrow, grimy room, full of the terrible smell of sweat. Because women with children are allowed in, a number of women have brought their squalling brats with them, who of course understand nothing of what is going on. . . . In front of the windows of the building a long queue has formed and next to them groups of people who have left the queue to stretch their legs. Every day over 1,000 people come to take part in the laborious business of standing in a queue. Half of them leave it in the evening without having achieved anything because they did not even reach the information counter. The other half will have learned of the whereabouts of the person they are looking for but will not be able to provide him with any help. All they are achieving is ruining their own health and wasting time. . . . Needless to say, there is much talk about the reasons for their imprisonment. There is a variety of offenses: theft, drunkenness, fighting while drunk, older crimes, words spoken at the wrong time and in the wrong place . . . but in many cases, the reasons for an arrest are not known.[18]

He wanted to send something to his mother and went to the prison. In the entry of 25 December 1937, he writes:

I hoped I was early enough to be at the front of the queue but I was in fact the 11th. Those before me had arrived around midnight. Moreover, there was a further queue with a list of its own for handing parcels over the following day. At 11 am I was told by the official that Yefrosinia was there. I cheered up somewhat. On my way home, I thought about what I would send her. I bought 40 rubles worth of goods and packed everything up, full of love. By evening the parcel was ready.

Towards morning, 5 o'clock. The same wintry cold as the previous day, but instead of a dozen people in the queue there were over 400. With their bundles and bags full of foodstuffs they had settled down half a kilometre away in the entrance hall of a vast building . . . other people kept coming in, who all had their names added to the list.[19]

Under the extreme conditions of the Leningrad siege, the queue become the basic site of the struggle for survival and of the discipline that thwarted the murderous plans of the Germans to starve the city to death. In her *Notes from the Blockade*, Lydia Ginzburg identified the queue, along with the trams and other modes of travel, as the locus of human self-assertion in a situation in which every civilised routine had broken down and all that was left was humankind's bare creaturely existence. 'It is just that what was concealed became obvious and the approximate literal; everything became condensed, manifest. This is what the conversation of blockade persons in queues, air-raid shelters, in canteens, in editorial offices, eventually became.'[20] Ginzburg recognises 'the essence of the queue' when she writes, 'A queue is a compulsory agglomeration of people, irritated with one another, yet at the same time concentrating on a single common circle of interests and aims. Hence the mixture of rivalry, hostility and collective feeling, the instant readiness to close ranks against the common enemy—the queue-jumper. The conversations here are stimulated by the enforced idleness and at the same time held together by the fixed nature of their content, concerned as it is with the object for which they are queuing.'

With a woman's eyes she highlights other aspects of the queue:

A queue is an assembly of people, doomed to a compulsory idle and internally isolated communality. Idleness, unless it be given point by way of recreation or diversion, is just suffering, a punishment (whether it be a prison, queue, or a waiting-room). A queue is utter idleness coupled with a grievous expenditure of physical energy. Men cope particularly badly with queues, since they are used to the idea that their time is valuable. The point is not even in the objective situation, it's simply a matter of inherited habits. Working women have inherited from their grandmothers and mothers time which is not taken into account. Their everyday lives do not allow that atavism to lapse. A man considers that after work he is entitled to rest or amuse himself; when a working woman comes home, she works at home. The siege queues were inscribed into an age-old background of things being issued or available, into the normal female irritation and the normal female patience.[21]

Men believed that standing in queues was a woman's business and that they should receive preferential treatment because they went out to work. Men believed that they were entitled to bread without having to queue.

> The shop was dark and full of vast impassable crowds, a hubbub of voices, threatening and imploring. The assistants struggled with the crowd across the counter. In the winter there were days when the pipes in the city froze up completely and people got water through holes in the river ice. The bakeries began to issue less than the ration. From four or five in the morning, hundreds of people queued for bread in the freezing darkness. A person suddenly remembers how he stood in line for the first time. He stood there thinking that he wouldn't get what he wanted in any case (he hadn't eaten anything since the soup of the day before). But all at once he thought that even if this lasted another five hours, or six, or seven—time would still be passing and would certainly pass over these five or six hours—however full those hours might be with agonies of immobility—therefore time itself would bear him on towards his goal. . . . In the queue the vast idea of a piece of bread was taking shape, whereas the sign embodied the infernal torpor of the queue. . . . On the day announced for the issue of fats and 'confectionery' there was a crowd outside the shop by five in the morning. People withstood all the agonies of an hours-long queue, knowing that by ten or eleven in the morning the shop would be empty. From the moment they became a possibility, it was psychologically impossible to sleep or busy yourself with anything else or simply exist, without joining in the process of approaching the fats and confectionery.

On the psychology of the queue we learn:

> Very few people read a book in a queue, or even a newspaper. This will surprise only those who have never stood for hours every day in queues. The psychology of the queue is based on a tense, wearing anxiety to reach the end; this weariness excludes anything else that might relieve it. The mental state of a person standing in a long queue is usually not fitted for any other occupation. The intellectual may naively take a book along, but he prefers to keep track of

what's going on. Having elbowed his way to the counter he watches the girl giving bread to those in front. . . . A person will go into genuine hysterics over anyone who tries to jump the queue—and then after getting his ration, the same person will stand for half an hour chatting to a friend, talking freely now, like someone here of his own free will. While he was in the queue, he was caught up, like all the rest, in the physical craving for movement, however illusory. Those at the back shout to those in front: 'Come on, get a move on, what's the hold up?' And there'd be some wise guy, ignorant of the mechanics of mental states, who will be sure to respond: 'Why push? It'll be no quicker for that'.[22]

The queue became the 'deadly crush' but also the 'human telegraph' in the Kyiv occupied by the Germans. As twelve-year-old Anatoly Kuznetsov observed:

At seven o'clock in the morning the doors of the shop opened. It was impossible to make out exactly what was going on: a terrible crush, groans and screams. The ones who got their flour first emerged from the shop with clothes all awry, battered and sweating, but with happy faces and clutching tightly their little bags bearing traces of white flour: it wasn't a dream and it wasn't a fairytale; it was real white flour. I went back to my place in the queue, but it still hadn't moved, although there was by this time as long a line behind me as in front. The women were saying that several men had been executed in Dymer after being caught listening to a crystal radio set; that *Swan Lake* was being performed at the ballet but that there was a notice up saying NO UKRAINIANS OR DOGS ADMITTED. Dropping their voices, they said the Germans had been brought to a complete halt, that they were lying around dead in their thousands around Moscow, that they had not even managed to take Tula, and that a second front was going soon to be opened in Europe. I listened eagerly, so that I could report it all back home. The bush telegraph worked marvellously! What is the use of forbidding people to listen to the radio? You have only to listen to the stories going around among the people; they nearly always turn out to be true.[23]

The queue became the barometer of social moods, the place of rumours and information in German-occupied Kyiv.

Destruction of the Market:
A Central Plan instead of the 'Invisible Hand'

In his exploration of the process of purchasing and consumption, the Hungarian economist János Kornai has analysed the significance of queuing for the act of buying something. He emphasises that this should be regarded not as a 'single moment' but as a 'dynamic process, taking time'. The formation of a queue is a form of waiting while making up one's mind on something, a search for a substitute for the object originally envisaged.[24] But what happens if there is no possibility of decision-making or choice because the potential customers are facing a systematically created situation of shortages?

According to Yelena Osokina: 'In the conditions created by an economy based on shortages, standing in queues becomes a way of life, but equally it was a way of surviving. Soviet queues only came to an end with the end of the planned economy that had brought them into being in the first place.' What was accepted and indeed had to be accepted as a blind natural process was the inexorable result of a historical development and of political decisions. In fact there was never a time when queues disappeared, only periods in which they became longer or shorter. They were an integral part of the centrally directed planned economy which had been depicted as superior to the anarchic practices of capitalism. In reality, it was a system for the central acquisition and redistribution of social surplus value. Its ambition was nothing less than the decision to supersede the 'invisible hand' of the market and replace it with a planning authority that regarded itself as a form of collective rationality. In theoretical or ideological terms, what held sway were the imperatives of the industrial means of production, of 'primitive accumulation', which would make it possible to finance the industrialisation of the country. This implied that from the very outset Soviet economic planning was one of systemic shortages, the redistribution of resources in favour of great state projects. It was based on doing away with private ownership of the means of production;

it envisaged the destruction of the market and the centralisation of social wealth in the hands of 'the state', which exploited and reconstructed the entire country in a kind of domestic colonial venture. Its crucial stages were war communism during the Civil War, the forced collectivisation and industrialisation of the first Five-Year Plan, the transformation of the entire economy of the Soviet Union imposed by the German invasion according to the motto 'Everything for the Front', and the attempts at the end of the Soviet Union to assert the authority of the regime over spontaneous market forces—an attempt that ultimately failed. These thrusts towards nationalisation, centralisation and state rationing—1918–1921, 1929–1932 and 1940–1945—contrast with phases in which more leeway was granted to the development of free initiatives and spontaneous market forces. Such were the years of the New Economic Policy (NEP), 1921–1928, and the brief period in 1935–1936 during which rationing was done away with for most foodstuffs. These phases of economic 'liberalisation' should be thought of as attempts to harmonise the market and the plan. But it was really always about oscillations within the fixed framework of an economic plan that not only tolerated scarcity but was predicated on it. Rising and falling curves are accurately reflected in the debates that formed the theoretical superstructure that presided over the economics of shortage and formed the intellectual framework underpinning the queues.[25]

However, the spontaneous energies of the 'free market' were never completely eliminated because without them the social crisis would never have been overcome. The chaotic hustle and bustle of the bazaar continued to function in the shadow of the state-planning authorities. In the shadow of the collectivised farms and nationalised agriculture, the kitchen gardens and tiny allotments of the peasants continued to thrive and the fruits of their toil provided food for the nation. The shadow economy never ceased to exist in the shadow of the official economy. And without the initiatives and the genius for improvisation of factory managers who knew how barter works, the planned economy could not have survived.

The paradoxes that manifested themselves in the Soviet economy can all be explained by reference to this basic policy decision and to the structures established in the course of modernisation: the fact that there could be famines in an agrarian country, that the rural population could only feed itself by migrating to the towns and cities since they had priority in the hierarchy of a centrally organised distribution system—Moscow primarily, but also Leningrad. Only 2 percent of the population lived in Moscow in 1939–1940, but it received 40 percent of the eggs and meat, over 25 percent of the fats, cheese and woollen textiles, 15 percent of sugar, fish, macaroni and kerosene (for Primus stoves), silk and footwear, and underwear. Over 50 percent of all available consumer goods went to Moscow and Leningrad.[26] The paradoxes include the fact that in order to survive, a large proportion of the population of working age had to be permanently on the move. The village travelled to the town to buy industrial goods but also food that had previously been taken from the village. A further absurdity was that the working lives and the actual lives of entire generations were blighted by the senseless processes of expropriation and redistribution. In short, the economy stood everything on its head and extracted everything possible from the countryside so as to redistribute it according to decisions taken at the centre.

The centralised command economy was the product of the war. It emerged in embryonic form during the First World War, was further developed in the emergency regime of the Civil War and then reached its apogee in the planned economy of the Great Patriotic War. It was shaped by military structures, as were the 'commanding heights' of the state and the Party. In this process consumption was treated as an appendage of production and the consumer was regarded as an irksome addition. People were even proud of the priority given to the production of the means of production. In 1940 around 30 percent of the national budget went towards armaments, 60 percent of capital investments into production of capital goods. The social rationality embodied in the institutions of the centralised command economy turned out to be too feeble to free the nation from the burden of production for its own sake. This remained the case even with the reforms of the 1950s and 1960s attempted or tolerated by Khrushchev. The command economy was never in a position to replace the intelligence of market forces—the 'invisible hand' of Adam Smith, Kant, Ricardo and Marx. The price exacted for this arrogant attempt to substitute for market forces can be seen in the chronically excessive demands the personnel on the commanding heights of the Soviet Union imposed on themselves, together with the stagnation, the wasted lives of generations—and ultimately, the demise of the Soviet system itself.

Post-Soviet Bazaar:
Collapse of the Order Represented by the Queue

The Russian Revolution of 1917 began with the disturbances triggered by the queues in the food shops in Petrograd. The end of the Soviet Empire that resulted from that revolution saw the disappearance of the queues. But the disappearance was not succeeded—for the moment at least—by a well-ordered and well-behaved marketplace as more than a few textbooks had envisaged, but by chaos and tumult. Overnight, town squares, stadiums, parks, metro-line terminuses and station forecourts turned into gigantic bazaars, black with people in every season and in all weather, in the dust-filled heat of summer or the autumn slush. The population of entire towns and cities seemed to have been transformed into traders. They spread out their wares or held them out in their hands on the pavements, street crossings, or park walkways in the middle of Moscow or Leningrad. There was nothing that was not on offer: self-knitted jackets, Chinese vases, newborn poodles, family albums, irons made in Belarus, mushrooms from the local forests. The collapse of the currency had brought with it a collapse in the pricing system. People who had practised their profession their entire lives—teachers, engineers, workers—found themselves part of the indistinguishable mass of buyers and sellers between Dzerzhinsky Square and Gorky Street, young people as well as babushkas offering for sale such things as a blouse or a kitchen knife made in Solingen.

Soviet towns and cities briefly transformed themselves into a great bazaar in which the order established by queues that until then had accompanied all transactions in an empire ruled by state planning had finally collapsed. You could see from the sudden, instinctual activity of the bazaar that this frenzied release of energy had been precipitated by the dissolution of the entire economy. Plans were swept

FIGURE 45.2. Alexander Ovchinnikov (1882–1941), *At the Lenin Mausoleum, 1939.* © Deineka Gallery, Kursk/akg-images.

aside; they had lost their meaning and their power to direct activity; relations between the productive sectors in the central ministries and industrial combines had been disrupted by the new frontiers in the newly created sovereign states. The division of labour consolidated over decades had ceased to function and from the very first moment the quickest and smartest fixers and operators had ruthlessly set about converting the property of the people into private property and launching their existence as oligarchs. The furious activity seen everywhere in the bazaars and the black markets was anything but an orderly transition to the marketplace, something for which there were no traditions, no experienced participants and no accepted rules. There was in fact nothing but a different kind of struggle for survival in anarchic conditions, in a space without leadership and in which right was on the side of the strongest. It would take years before the forces that had turned the public sphere into an unruly bazaar would sort themselves out and succeed in establishing a new order. This new order can be seen today in the great emporiums of the past whose monumental façades date from the 1930s and are illuminated nowadays like the department stores in Hamburg or Shanghai, or in the glass and crystal palaces and malls resembling extraterrestrial spaceships. No queues are to be found here; only artificial paradises for visitors to lose themselves in and make discoveries as long as they have the money those forced to remain outside do not. The queue has dissolved into polarised sectors of rich and poor with relatively few people in between. Queues now form elsewhere, such as at the visa departments of foreign embassies, at the customs and security checks in airports, at the entrances to concerts by Elton John or The Scorpions, or at the portals of churches and monasteries when pilgrims assemble for the Easter Vigil. These queues continue to grow while the queues that used to stretch for miles in front of the Lenin Mausoleum now melt and fade away altogether.

CHAPTER 46

'Think of the Parties We Had . . .'

Photos in family albums do not preserve the long trend in our lives but the outstanding moments. This holds true of Soviet family albums as well. Leafing our way through them resembles a staccato journey through someone's life. What is captured in these photos is a newborn child blinking, the first day at school, the group photo of the graduation class, pictures with which everyone can identify long afterwards. These photos are followed by those showing a person's entry into the adult world, a time when his or her own life has begun: first adventures, careers, the unexpected, premature deaths of people one has grown up with. Photograph albums are the summation of people's lives, pictures fixed reference points that dissolve the lengthy periods of grey everyday life and give life a retrospective order. Pictures of celebrations, social and private, play a key role in this process.

Alongside public holidays and parades—International Labour Day on 1 May, Victory Day on 9 May, the anniversary of the October Revolution on 7 November—we find recollections of private Soviet life stories. Plotting the annual public events is anything but difficult. The portraits of the General Secretaries and the associated slogans tell us in which 'era' and which part of the Five-Year Plan we find ourselves, how the Soviet leadership saw the world and who was Enemy No. 1 of the moment. The sight of people in their best attire enables us to identify the current fashions. The photographs reveal something of the mood in cities where hundreds of thousands of people from different neighbourhoods, institutes and workplaces have come together in a uniform procession, file past the prominent leaders of the Party and the state on the tribune and then proceed to the second, nonofficial part of the celebrations. Here they experience the pleasure of a day off work with somewhat restrained attractions and entertainments, dance floors, brass bands, fairgrounds, ubiquitous kiosks with food and drink, even varieties otherwise hard to obtain. The discipline of the demonstrators passing in rows of five or six people, the sea of banners and flags, the artificial flowers and balloons that have been distributed in the thousands, the voiceovers from the loudspeakers proclaiming the slogans of the day and the cheers erupting at regular intervals all reveal the hand of an organiser. And yet there is something else that can't quite be produced to order, a tension arising from the mass presence of expectant people—from million-strong capital cities, from provincial towns with several hundred thousands. It is a sort of nervous energy that arises when crowds encounter a police cordon, the mood of elation in a festive crowd in which children seated on their father's shoulders catch a glimpse of a leadership which is normally remote and now is close by. On these occasions, however, the partly voluntary, partly obligatory encounter with fellow workers and colleagues occurs not at their workplace, factory or institute but in the open air on what in spring is mostly a sunny day. All this shows that the public holiday, however smoothly orchestrated, still contains other elements: a basic need of sociability and community, of spontaneous self-expression. This human faculty exists a priori and the powerful know how to activate it, mobilise it and instrumentalise it.

Few groups in recent history have understood the development of media-staged public festivities as thoroughly as the Bolsheviks after 1917. If we can seriously speak of a specifically Soviet civilisation at all, this is at least in part due to the emergence of a genuine festival culture. We could illustrate the rise and fall of the Soviet Union by following the history of the Soviet mass festival, as Malte Rolf has done in detail.[1]

Birth of the Soviet Festival in the Carnival of History

'The history of official Bolshevik mass celebrations begins on 1 May 1918.'[2] The First of May—the traditional holiday of the international workers' movement, which in Tsarist Russia had been proscribed as an illegal May Day holiday and secretly observed in parks—was now openly celebrated in the central town squares. Boris Kustodiev's painting captured a moment when the entire city was bathed in a sea of red flags, when the five-pointed star gradually established itself as an emblem and the hammer and sickle became the signature of the new republic. Petrograd was redecorated: the palaces on Palace Square, the library on Nevsky Prospekt, the former Mariinsky Palace were all clad in metre-high Cubist paintings, while the Admiralty was decorated by Dobuzhinsky in the classical manner. The festivities for the first anniversary of the October Revolution were planned and organised by a commission of artists, directors and writers. Over sixty theatre groups were involved throughout the city. The costumes for the pageants and theatre performances were taken from the costume and prop stores of the theatres. Large red and orange rhombus-shaped canvas screens designed by Natan Altman were stretched over the baroque façades of Palace Square. In the House of Soviets, Mayakovsky's *Mystery Bouffe: The Heroic, Epic and Satirical Image of Our World Theatre* was performed, directed by Meyerhold. The Petrocommune distributed 350,000 free meals.

What began during that first year after the Revolution could be described as the invention of tradition; it was gradually expanded into full-fledged choreographies involving the entire city—and this at a time when the Civil War was still unresolved. This remained the case on 1 May and in October 1919, when Yudenich stood before the gates of Petrograd. In the spring of 1920, 'Theatrical Petrograd' emerged in all its glory: on 1 May the *Mystery of Liberated Labour* was produced; on 20 June *The Blockade of Russia* was staged; on 19 July there was a performance of the *World Commune* for the delegates to the Third Congress of the Comintern; and on 7 November, for the third anniversary of the October Revolution, *The Storming of the Winter Palace* was performed. In each case, the whole city was turned into a stage, with thousands of participants and a huge number of theatre professionals and media people. Behind this theatricalisation of life, this reinserting of theatre into life, stood elaborate theories that had circulated among Symbolist poets, artists and philosophers in the decades before the Revolution and become commonplaces of the period. Scholars such as Vyacheslav Ivanov had been influenced by Nietzsche and brought his cult of Dionysus into the contemporary world. Theatre people such as Meyerhold and Nikolay Yevreinov were concerned to eliminate the separation of audience and stage and took up Richard

Wagner's revolutionary project of a Gesamtkunstwerk that would overcome the gulf between life and art and between the action on the stage and its passive reception by the audience. In peacetime, such ideas might well have remained topics of debate among metropolitan intellectuals—for example, in the séances in Vyacheslav Ivanov's 'Tower' overlooking the gardens of the Tauride Palace—but during the collapse of the ancien régime, the streets became the property of whoever had occupied them and a kind of chaotic free space, a field for experimentation in which everything was possible. The activity on the streets encountered the ambitious projects of an intellectual Bohème, which at its best became synthesised into something later known as the 'Soviet avant-garde'. Vyacheslav Ivanov, Nikolay Yevreinov, Natan Altman, Vsevolod Meyerhold and many others, up until then socially marginalised figures who had often spent many years travelling abroad, were suddenly catapulted into a vacant space in which forms, sequences and scenes from festivals and theatre could be conceived—which then became the launch pad of an enduring tradition. All of this would surely have remained no more than abstract discourse about the Dionysus cult but for the fact that the collapse of the traditional social structures had made room for new, productive combinations.

Even earlier, the fall of the Tsar in the February Revolution with all its patriotic and republican pathos had produced a novel kind of public sphere with rallies and demonstrations, changes of flags and symbolic occupations of public space. The legacy of the French Revolution and its festivities had been adopted above all by the bourgeois classes and intellectuals and was generally debated and propagated by classical presentations of revolution.[3] But a far more powerful impulse came from the soldiers and their revolution in October. They were quite ignorant of the orgiastic cults of antiquity and had no need to be taught lessons about the festivals of the French Revolution. They had experience of their own festive tradition—the Russia of countless church festivals and holy days, of entertainments at carnivals and fairs, the holy days of local saints. These festivities often went on for days during which all work stopped, and were accompanied by clowns, jesters, satirical songs, hymns and entertainments. They attracted all sorts of itinerant folk from every corner of the Empire, and included

FIGURE 46.1. Audience in front of the Winter Palace, Leningrad 1933. http://humus.livejournal
.com/.

dancing bears together with drinking orgies and massive streetfights. Festivals are never more important than in times of crisis and deprivation; during the years 1917–1920 the 'carnival of history' became the moment of the Soviet festival's birth.[4]

The definitive elaboration of the festival calendar, the standardisation of procedures and the spread of a universal ritual throughout the entire Soviet realm was completed towards the end of the 1930s but before the beginning of the Soviet-German War. At the same time, a kind of ambivalence emerged, an ambiguity in the meaning of the festival as, on the one hand, a well-orchestrated and controlled ritual that served the purposes of mobilisation and indoctrination and, on the other hand, an act of spontaneous pleasure and self-expression with all the risks this entailed for the regime.

The evolution of the annual festivities enables us to trace the changing priorities and moods of the masses. The observer stands amazed at the imaginative richness of the pageants—the slogans, the masks and the interaction of music, political demonstration, farce and caricature. The years between the end of the Civil War and the onset of

Stalin's industrialisation witnessed a new onslaught on the 'burzhuys' of the NEP period who had regained some of their former prestige and prosperity, on the diplomats of the old capitalist world, on the 'White' émigrés and even the Pope.[5] With the Five-Year Plans, the enemy from the village moved to the centre of the campaign of defamation: a caricatured version of the kulak, the reactionary peasant—bearded, uncouth, given to alcohol and with the features of the bloodsucker and exploiter—who blocks the path to socialist construction. Pageants became the very opposite of those that had paraded through the streets before the Revolution. The priest—the kulak's ally, fat, unkempt and a threat to young girls—appeared as the very antithesis of everything progressive, enlightened, lucid and, well, Soviet. *Kulturnost* as opposed to illiteracy, electrification as opposed to the backwardness of the village, tractor as opposed to plough. *Lishentsy*, people who had been deprived of their right to vote on the grounds of their class membership, were not even permitted to be present at these public festivities.[6] Following a temporary relaxation in the mid-1930s, the years of the Great Terror were marked by mass pageants, processions and demonstrations that were nothing more than an initiation into a community of hate, which, once out of control, could even overturn the ritual of the festivities—portraits and names had to be removed because the people they referred to had become 'nonpersons' overnight and fallen victim to the purges.[7]

Here we find a different meaning of the pageant. The hate-filled choruses of thousands called for the annihilation of the enemies of the people, the spies, queues, traitors and double-dealers. They echoed the slogans that came from above but gave free rein to their own resentments and destructive impulses towards those whom they experienced as oppressors and held responsible for their past sufferings. Orgies of hatred and a furore of destructiveness—ordinary people settling accounts with the fat cats at the top. The people down below changed positions for a moment with those at the top, the classical conception of a carnival; everyone could be called out, no denunciation could be too extreme. But it all also had the effect of self-condemnation, self-purification, catharsis.[8]

The consummate organisation and standardisation of the pageants were not discontinued with the onset of the Second World

War, but merely interrupted. 'The rigidity of the widely standard-
ized culture of celebration continued after World War II and shaped
Soviet festivities until 1991. It was a process of standardization in
which the regions followed the instructions from Moscow ever more
carefully.'[9] The form taken by the processions increasingly mirrored
the Moscow 'paradigm'—flags, erecting the festival grandstand, decisions about portraits and slogans, the town illuminations, the sequence of marching columns right on down to the 'unpolitical' part
of the programme with theatrical performances, concerts and other
offerings in the cultural and recreational parks, and ending with a
firework display.[10]

By the end of the 1930s the new Bolshevik calendar was fully developed. The holidays established by law were 1 May (International
Labour Day), 7 and 8 November (the anniversary of the October Revolution), 5 December (Constitution Day). From 1935, 1 January was
reinstated as New Year's Day, and after the war, the most important
holiday to be introduced was 9 May (Victory Day), which only became
an official holiday after 1965.

The Red Calendar: New World, New Conception of Time

Temporal coordinates are as important as spatial ones. Human beings live in time and organise their lives in temporal intervals. They
find support in time just as they orientate themselves in space.[11] This
is why the transition to Soviet time, the entry into a new temporal
order, a new calendar, is of such importance. It is not just a matter
of 'historical time', of slowing down or speeding up, of stagnation or
energising; its importance is that it marks the introduction of a new
temporal framework with new significant dates for people to relate to
and record their life experiences and their memories. In this respect,
the Soviet and Russian experience is no exception.

All great social and political upheavals are linked to the introduction of new conceptions of time and new temporal regimes—or at
least with attempts to introduce them, as can be seen from the French
Revolution's proclamation of a new calendar. But there was even a
precedent in the case of Russia, when Peter the Great introduced the

Julian calendar in 1700 and ruled that the year should begin on 1 January. The Bolshevik government issued a decree on 24 January 1918, introducing the Gregorian calendar, thanks to which 1 February 1918 became 14 February 1918. This represented a symbolic rupture with the Tsarist regime at least on a chronological level, but at the same time, this was just the beginning of work on a new calendar, one which aimed to replace the holidays recognised by the Russian Orthodox Church.

In prerevolutionary Russia the course of the year was dictated by church holy days and popular festivals at all levels and in every region of the multinational empire until well into the twentieth century. In addition there were days of remembrance, anniversaries and jubilees that were celebrated in lavish festivals embracing the entire Empire. In 1911, for example, Russians commemorated fifty years since the emancipation of the serfs; in 1912, it was a century after the defeat of Napoleon; in 1913, three hundred years of the Romanov dynasty.[12] The Law of 1897 governing the working week fixed public holidays. They included 1 January, the Circumcision of Christ (Obrezanie Gospodne as well as the New Year); 6 January, the Baptism of Christ (Kreshchenie Gospodne); 25 March, the Annunciation (Blagoveshchenie Presvyatoy Bogoroditsy); 6 August, the Transfiguration of Jesus (Preobrazhenie Gospodne); 15 August, the Dormition of the Mother of God (Uspenie Bogoroditsy); 8 September, the Nativity of Mary (Rozhdestvo Presvyatoy Bogoroditsy); 14 September, the Feast of the Cross (Vozdvizhenie Kresta Gospodnya); 25–26 December, the Birth of Jesus; as well as Good Friday and Holy Saturday; Easter Day as well as Easter Monday and Tuesday; Ascension Day (Vosnesenie Gospodne) and Whitsun (Den Svyatoy Troitsy).[13] Taken together, these amounted to 140 festivals and holidays annually at the start of the twentieth century—not unusual for a society that still followed the natural rhythms of village life and was just starting to be drawn into those of industrial labour.

The Soviet government began, on the one hand, by legalising the holidays of the proletariat that had been banned by the old regime—such as 1 May (International Labour Day) and 8 March (International Women's Day)—and lending them new prestige. It also added holidays, such as 7 November (October Revolution), 18 March (Day of the Paris Commune) and the Harvest Festival in mid-October. All

religious public holidays were gradually removed from the calendar—
Vozdvizhenie in 1924, Kreshchenie and Blagoveshchenie in 1925. By
1930 all the church festivals had been eliminated. Processions during
the Easter Vigil and at Christmas were only permitted on church
premises. But the revolutionary powers-that-be could not simply
attack directly the calendar of the Russian Orthodox Church and
abolish it. Instead, when the Red calendar was introduced, a lengthy
transition period was built into it, creating a kind of dual time regime
with two overlapping chronologies: the Julian-Orthodox chronology
on the one hand, and the Bolshevik-Gregorian calendar on the other.
These overlapping chronologies were a form of coexistence between
two spiritual and social rivals. It had concrete implications since conflicts emerged between the religious and secular timetables in the
routines of daily life. These had started out as being halfway 'compatible', but they ended up in militant clashes, especially at the time
of the Great Change of 1929.

Thus alongside transitional social and economic regimes there
were comparable transitions in the realm of timetables. Societies
live concretely, but primarily 'in the mind'; they live simultaneously
in different chronological regimes, the old and the new, the religious
and the secular. This sometimes found expression when religious
processions still permitted in the early 1920s coincided with Soviet
demonstrations, which tacitly acknowledged their interaction. The
church banners, flags and icons held aloft by the faithful were in many
respects the forerunners of the banners and portraits carried by the
revolutionary workers in their rallies. The obvious superficial similarity between Easter processions and revolutionary demonstrations
makes it clear that ultimately the most promising way to destroy the
cultural hegemony of Russian Orthodoxy was not through direct,
frontal suppression but by taking over and adapting religious rites
and customs. After all, even in the 1937 Census well over half of the
population claimed to be religious. This meant that the Orthodox
faith still lingered in people's minds, even after the banning of religious processions and pilgrimages and even after the onslaught of the
League of Militant Atheists in the Cultural Revolution of 1929–1932,
when thousands of churches were closed down or destroyed and

bells were hurled down from the belfry. That faith stoutly resisted the competition of 'Red baptisms', 'Red Easter', 'Red weddings' and 'Red funerals'—so much so that at the moment of existential threat from the German invasion, it was revived and mobilised for the Great Patriotic War and in effect reinstated in its traditional role as a pillar of the state.

'Soviet Fordism': The New Time Pattern

The crudest expression of the new time pattern was doubtless the proclamation of the Red calendar in 1929. This abolished the seven-day week and introduced the five-day week.[14] This remained in force with slight variations until 1940. The month was subdivided into six weeks. To maintain the existing number of days in the year, five extra holidays were introduced. Dispensing with the seven-day week and replacing it with the five-day week was justified by the demands of accelerated industrialisation and the fuller, uninterrupted exploitation of industrial plants. The universal day of rest at the weekend had become superfluous, especially Sunday. This relentless rhythm could not be sustained, however, and was adjusted in 1931 when a universal day of rest was reintroduced every six days. Neither the five-day week nor the six-day week led to a general increase in industrial productivity which is probably why this experiment was discontinued in 1940.

The side effect or perhaps even the principal effect of this brutal manipulation of the working week was different, however. It destroyed the general relationship to the Christian Sundays and holy days; the weekend that had always functioned as the communicative heart of relationships with family and friends had been undermined. We might speak of the paralysis of the established rhythms of life and time, which contributed to the growth of restlessness and anxiety in Soviet society. Church festivals take a long time to prepare and set the mood; their cyclical nature, their alternation of work and rest, their fasts and celebrations were points of calm during the year. These had disappeared and been gradually replaced by the new Soviet holidays that in many ways were simply mutant versions of the religious festivals and indeed of even older, more archaic celebrations of the onset of spring or harvest time. They occurred, moreover, at similar intervals to church festivities—and neither was this by mere chance.

Secularisation: How Christmas Changed into New Year

An example of the restaging of traditional rites and customs was the introduction of a Harvest Festival on 14 October, a kind of Soviet Thanksgiving Day. 'Rural traditions were adopted deliberately and sovietised within the new system by adding the Soviet symbols of the hammer and sickle and the major rituals of the regime, such as singing the "Internationale". By usurping familiar symbols and practices for their own purposes, the Bolsheviks tried to link traditional customs to Soviet symbols and celebrations in an effort to introduce the notion of a Soviet harvest festival to the farmers.'[15]

Another representative example was the replacement of Christmas by New Year's Day, the festival of the New Year *yolka* tree—this was significant because it spoke to an increasingly urbanised population. The birth of Jesus is celebrated on 7 January in the Russian Orthodox Church calendar with a Christmas tree and all sorts of toys and sweets. After the Revolution, this custom was viewed as a 'vestige of the past'. In January 1929 the Central Committee of the Communist Party sent a statement to all Party members on 'measures to strengthen anti-religious work'. This was the basis for the struggle against the church holy days and associated traditions, such as Christmas and the Christmas tree. In 1931 the children's magazine *Chizh* (Siskin) published a poem with the words 'Only the friend of the priest / will enjoy the Christmas feast' ('Tolko tot, kto drug popov, / Yolku prazdnovat gotov'). Komsomol teams even tried to enter people's homes to see what was going on. As a result, Christmas was celebrated in secret, behind drawn curtains, with little trees that could easily be hidden.

Following a temporary relaxation and rethinking about certain traditions, Christmas customs were reevaluated. In December 1935 the chairman of the Ukrainian Communist Party, Pavel Postyshev, wrote an article in *Pravda* which went some way towards rehabilitating Christmas (Yolka), while at the same time moving it to New Year. From then on New Year became the quasi-legitimate heir of the traditional Christmas, which could now be celebrated openly and lavishly. Giant Christmas trees were set up in public squares and illuminated. Workingmen's clubs, schools and kindergartens celebrated New Year with dance music, tombolas, recorded speeches and bell-tolling from the Spassky Tower in the Kremlin. The top of the Christmas tree featured the five-pointed Red star, which had replaced the Star of Bethlehem. Glass ornaments and chains of electric lights appeared later. A special atmosphere was created when the tree was decorated and festooned with all sorts of garlands, little houses made of matchboxes, confectionary, chocolate bars and—more in the Soviet manner—miniature flags, airships made of cardboard and foil, and strings of coloured pearls. Such imagination and time were invested only in great festivals. Yolka now became mainly what it had been traditionally, before the Revolution, namely a festival for children and families who gathered around a richly laid table to welcome in the New Year.[16]

If there was any festival that preserved its religious character over the decades, however, it was Easter, with its painted eggs and spherical cakes (kulichi)—even at a time when the churches were shut and there was no community.

These may have been the most obvious examples of the secularisation of a formerly religiously defined calendar, but we can also point to the general practice of declaring holidays dedicated to specific professional groups or the memory of historical events, rather than particular saints. In this context we mention Engineers' Day (21 January), Geologists' Day (first Sunday in April), Radio Day (7 May), Border Guards' Day (28 May), Metalworkers' Day (third Sunday in July), Teachers' Day (5 October) and NKVD Day (20 December). Holidays commemorating historical events include the Battle of Stalingrad (2 February), the Battle of Kursk (23 August) and the Day of Commemoration and Mourning (22 June). Days of culture include Pushkin Day (6 June). These anniversaries and festivals have a kind of atmospheric importance for workplace relations and the work climate generally since their annual recurrence means that they form part of everyone's mental calendar and so belong to an internalised time pattern.

The Erosion of Soviet Festival Culture

The successful introduction of a standardised festival ritual based on the pattern of events in celebrations in the Soviet capital also signalled its downfall. Standardisation, planning and a schematic approach meant a growing distancing from the original (powerful) inspiration and the spontaneous impulse that had genuinely supported these festivals for a while. Festivals degenerated into mere ritual and ceremony and the original political or social motive fell increasingly into the background, while the 'second part' of the festivities—the entertainment, pleasure and relaxation—became the chief priority. The festival had become a cover for apolitical sociability, an experience of togetherness in which pleasure and the attractions on offer transcended the political statement. Established festivals could only rekindle enthusiasm and renew themselves by linking up with local and regional events, commemorations and traditions. But regionalisation spelled the fragmentation of the Soviet festival landscape. The familiar, the known and trusted reality to which the ordinary citizen could relate, became the focus of attention: city foundation dates, regional festivities—of the Volga region, the Urals—factory anniversaries, town festivals. These were the manifestations of a reawakened local patriotism and regional consciousness, all of which appeared brighter and more colourful when compared to the grey reality of the political celebrations. These countertrends spurred initiatives to make use of the festivities for people's own agendas. In 1965, for example, on 5 December, Constitution Day, the anniversary of the launching of Stalin's constitution in 1936, was taken over by the emerging dissident citizens' rights movement to put forward demands for bourgeois freedoms. This was followed by annual demonstrations on Pushkin Square, drawing attention to the victims of persecution and repression. The 'collapse of the ceremonial regime' that preceded the political collapse of the USSR could be seen even at the very heart of power. On 1 May 1990, when lines of demonstrators marched past the Lenin Mausoleum, their ranks included Baltic delegates armed with slogans demanding independence.[17]

The erosion of the Soviet festival calendar went chiefly in two directions and moved on two planes. The cycle of religious holy days regained more ground as against the secular holiday calendar—starting from the great festivals such as Easter, Christmas and Whitsun and moving on down to local events—baptisms, weddings and funerals. As in the incubation phase of the Red calendar in the 1920s, the end of the Soviet Union witnessed a rebirth of the 'dual time regime'—the emergence of different calendars and orders of time acting simultaneously, the juxtaposition of secular and religious holidays. The multiplication of religious festivals to include Islam, Judaism and other faiths led to a significant expansion of the number of holidays both secular and religious so that the days between them often acted as a work-free bridge joining them together. This led to a paradox: a society that achieved industrialisation and the radical reduction of work-free holidays ended up with an expanded period of work-free time and a revision of the very work and life rhythm imposed by industrialisation.

Globalisation has triggered an increase in events that is no less significant than the reactivation of religious festivities. It has helped to overturn the rigid sequence of secular and religious holidays. Great *events*, it would seem, have become more important than Christmas or Easter or the First of May. Megaevents from the world of culture and sports cast a long shadow before they actually happen and then leave traces in the minds of entire generations long after they have taken place. This includes the Olympic Games, football and other European championships, international film and music festivals—which all carve notches in the timeline. Annual and generational events have radically altered people's awareness of time since they brought the nation into temporal unity with the rest of the world. In this respect, the Soviet Union was no different from other countries where local and national cultures have been pulled into the slipstream of a global culture—though the process may have been more brutal in a country less well prepared for it. The easily understandable, precisely defined and circumscribed Soviet festival is disappearing in the welter of competing celebrations that are moving into vacated spaces. There was one occasion in the 1990s when, beneath the tent tops of the international circus festival, the great bands of the world—from Mick Jagger to Elton John—towered over Red Square and the 'best tenors in the world' drove a paying public of hundreds of thousands into a state of ecstasy—this where a quasi-sacral atmosphere had once prevailed. These celebrities brought more people to their feet than the late Soviet masters of ceremony. We shall no doubt see what will emerge from the disintegration of Soviet festival culture and the breakup of old and new traditions—perhaps a new hybrid, synthetic form. In the meantime, the professional archivists have incorporated the term *prazdnik* (holiday) in their indexes; this suggests that they have begun to take this element of the Soviet lifeworld seriously.

PART X

Bodies

CHAPTER 47

Fizkultura: Soviets as Athletes

THE ALTERNATIVE ROUTE TO STRENGTH AND BEAUTY

The annual *fizkultura* parades with thousands of athletes marching on Moscow's Red Square and in other Soviet towns and cities have always fascinated a wide range of observers. Had the population succumbed to an aesthetic of physical beauty or was something more mysterious at work? In 1936 André Gide watched the procession together with Maxim Gorky, standing on the podium of the Mausoleum. He, the great sceptic, made no secret of his admiration for the seventy-five thousand sportsmen and -women on parade: 'I was present in Moscow at the Festival of Youth in the Red Square. The ugliness of the buildings opposite the Kremlin was concealed by a mask of streamers and greenery. The whole thing was splendid and—I make haste to say it here, for I shan't always be able to—in perfect taste. The admirable youth of the Soviet Union, gathered together from the north and the south, east and west, was on parade. The march past lasted for hours. I had never imagined so magnificent a sight. These perfect forms had evidently been trained, prepared, selected; but how can one fail to admire a country and a regime capable of producing them?'[1] Yelena Bulgakova, who was out and about in the town centre, devoted a few lines of her diary to the parade of 12 July 1937 in which a portrait of Nikolay Yezhov was conveyed across the Square: 'Day of sport. Went to the dentist whom I had discovered by chance and she cheated us brazenly once she had elicited our names. Stopped on Arbat Square and gazed at the sportsmen marching past. A glorious sight from a distance—brown bodies, gaily coloured shorts. But looked at up close, there was scarcely an attractive face or a beautiful body.'[2]

As US ambassador, Joseph Davies enjoyed a privileged view from one of the seats on the tribune assigned to diplomats and was enraptured by the sight of the *fizkulturniki* on 14 July 1937:

It was quite wonderful and impressive in its way.

It was a bright sunny day. Both ends and the opposite façade were decorated profusely with flags and red bunting and various large emblems emblazoned with athletic medal designs, tributes to Stalin, etc.

Massed around three sides of the Square were companies of three or four hundred each of men and women, leaving the Square about half-filled for the marching and the various athletic tableaux and performances.

There were almost as many women as men in the parade and in the exhibitions. It was 'flaming youth'. And a very beautiful youth it was—all bareheaded and tanned to a deep brown, for the most part wearing only white shorts and coloured jerseys. Each company had a different uniform. Some were in Jansen suits and others were in regular gymnasium attire. The combinations of blues and whites, reds and whites, oranges and whites, crimsons and yellows, ma-roons and tans—all conceivable combinations—with white sneaker shoes, with colours in the hair of the women or carried in the hands of the marchers. It made a beautiful display. Added to this were thousands of tanned soldiers with shaved heads, in blue shorts and white 'sneakers'. Again there were two or three thousand athletes from various sections of the Soviet Union who were particularly colourful, especially those from the Ukraine, the Caucasus, and the Oriental section of the country. The latter brought reed, horn and drum bands, which made weird music for their sword dances and marches. The coloured gowns and robes of the performers as well as the beauty of the dances were unique and strange.

The parade lasted about four hours. It was estimated that there were forty or fifty thousand young people participating. There were all kinds of floral displays, extraordinarily well done; with bluebells and poppies and all manner of flowers in profusion. You know how beautifully they make pictures out of the massing of growing flow-ers over here.

The floats were designed for the most part to display various types of club activities. There were skiers actually skiing in com-panies of 1,500 young men. They apparently had ball bearings on their skis to enable them to get over the asphalt.

On some floats were the horizontal bars with the gymnasts actually performing; and springboards with acrobats doing double
high somersaults on the float. Others were skating or tobogganing
on the floats as the floats moved along in the parade. One athletic
exhibition consisted of forty or fifty young men and women, all
performing on the floats as they went moving by.

All in all, it was one of the most beautiful and extraordinary
exhibitions I have ever seen. Of course, the day was beautiful; and
the wonderfully fine-looking youth and perfect physiques and
healthful appearance all contributed to make the whole spectacle
most unusual.[3]

General Eisenhower, too, invited as a member of the anti-Hitler
coalition to watch the fizkulturniki parade following the end of the
Second World War, was overwhelmed by what he saw. At the parade of
12 August 1945, dedicated to the final victory and documented by cin-
ematographer and film director Vasily Belyaev, Eisenhower expressed
surprise that a dictator such as Stalin should show an interest in a
sports parade, but went on to explain:

We stood on the Mausoleum tribune for five hours, as long as the
parade lasted. None of us had ever seen anything remotely like a
show of this kind before. The sportspeople who appeared all wore
gaily coloured suits, thousands performed movements in a unified
rhythm. Folk dances, acrobatic numbers, gymnastic exercises, all
with spotless precision and visibly with great enthusiasm. It was
said that the orchestra consisted of a thousand musicians and
it played without interruption during the entire five-hour-long
performance. The Generalissimo showed not the slightest sign of
fatigue. On the contrary, he relished every moment. He stood next
to me and we talked with the help of an interpreter throughout the
entire proceedings.[4]

This was the first parade after the end of a war that had left millions
dead and many more wounded and disabled. It was almost as if the
festivities were being used to oppose those million-fold deaths with
the very force of life itself.

FIGURE 47.1. Parade of the fizkulturniki on the former Palace Square in Leningrad, renamed Uritsky Square, 1933, in front of the General Staff Building. http://humus.livejournal.com/.

These parades were not simply outstanding sporting occasions. In their presentation of immaculate, steely, seemingly invulnerable bodies, they were above all aesthetic events. We can see this for ourselves even today since the great fizkulturniki parades were recorded with impressive care. The parade of May 1935 was captured by ten directors and forty cameramen, that of 30 June 1935 in record time by thirty-five cameramen under the direction of V. Yosilevich. The resulting film, *Happy Youth* (*Shchastlivaya yunost*), was shown not just to the general public outside the capital, but also to the delegates of the Seventh World Congress of the Comintern, whose members met in Moscow in July and August of the same year. As critics wrote, 'One felt that a huge human brain, a great human heart, was directing and uniting the hundreds of thousands of people in the square and our whole country into the new invincible force of the Communist future of the world.'[5] The tableaux vivants of the parade of 24 June 1938 were captured in the cinematic masterpieces *Fizkulturny parad* (Sportsmen's parade), by Grigory Alexandrov, and *Tsvetushchaya yunost* (Blossoming youth), the technicolour film of 18 July 1939 by Alexander Medvedkin.[6]

The fizkulturniki parades provide the clearest proof that the Soviet Union had its own conception of the human body and that its notions of beauty circled around a physical ideal that derived in some respects from antiquity and the Renaissance, but added something new that had to do with the proletarian state and the altered status of human labour in modern society—with a different 'modernity', in fact. The ideal Soviet physique had its own moment of blossoming, but also its own decline.

It may be that the Soviet Union was nowhere as preeminent as on the field of sport and its demise can be seen quite drastically in the decline of its athletic prowess. To dismiss the history of Soviet physical culture as purely a matter of discipline or mere dressage would be a gross underestimation. The magic of sport and physical culture is to be found in play, in the free activation of human energies, in open-ended competitions in which the better and more agile athlete wins. In such activities there should be a referee or an umpire but no director or dictator. This was all well-known to such scholars as Johan Huizinga, the author of *Homo Ludens*, and the great anthropologist Helmut Plessner.[7] But it can be fatal if human behaviour that is supposed to be free and spontaneous should be forced into a plan, into what Mike O'Mahony calls an 'orchestrated spontaneity' in which external levers of play are controlled by others and the rules of dominion and power hold sway.[8]

The Russian 'Storm of Steel': The Birth of Physical Culture out of War and Revolution

Sport and physical training existed in Russia before the Revolution.[9] Trials of strength have formed an integral part of peasant Russia since time immemorial and boxing matches that degenerated into free-for-alls could still be found in villages in the early twentieth century. Prerevolutionary Russia also had its aristocratic sports, often imported from abroad—especially riding, rowing and sailing— and Russia had joined in modern international sports which were practised above all by the emerging middle class. Urban life featured gym and sports clubs; physical exercise was believed to be a tried-and-tested remedy for alcoholism and asocial behaviour. The workers' movement also provided its own angle: physical exercise as a counter to exploitation and the discipline of factory labour. Thus we find well-developed sporting activities in the towns even before the Revolution: regattas, horse shows, gymnastic competitions, bicycle racing, weight training and football. Women struggling for emancipation were part of these, and stars such as the Zaporozhian Cossack wrestler Ivan Poddubny, celebrated as the strongest man in the world, made appearances in fairgrounds, circuses and competitions. When the Olympic Games were reintroduced, Russia took part and sent small delegations in 1908 and 1912.

The outbreak of war and the Revolution took Russian sport in a different direction altogether. Horses were being superseded by the automobile, airships and planes. Physical training and control of the new technologies had become of critical importance for fighting wars, and so it is no surprise that the beginnings of Soviet sport should be linked to the need to increase combat fitness. These practical beginnings were preceded by elaborate theoretical and ideological reflections on the utterly different, nonbourgeois nature of working-class sport.

The date marking the first fizkulturniki parade is said to be 25 May 1919, with a march-past of young sportspeople in Red Square in the presence of Lenin and Trotsky. Significantly this had been organised by Vsevobuch (Vseobshchee voennoe obuchenie), the Universal Military Training Organisation, an outfit that trained raw recruits for the Red Army. The parade on Red Square was at the same time preparation for the Civil War front, which was in full swing at the time—a coincidence that would guarantee the close link between sport and defence for the decades to come.

Spartacus versus Olympia

With the end of military operations in Russia, other tasks and other traditions returned to the foreground of attention. Fizkultura was built up into a regular ideological and pedagogical complex. We should remind ourselves that Nikolay Chernyshevsky's novel *What Is to*

Be Done? of 1863—the cult work of entire generations of rebellious students—assigned a major role to asceticism, self-improvement and physical training in the development of the new people.[10] Gymnastics is a constant thread in the writings of the revolutionary democrats as well as those of the educationalist Pyotr Frantsevich Lesgaft. Physical fitness and strength are the marks of the new human being. At the same time, the one-sided developments arising from the division of labour, industrial machinery and unhygienic conditions are all to be overcome. The 'universal man' whom Marx had already presented to his readers in *The German Ideology* and which had been projected back into the Renaissance was now to be made a reality in the newly prevailing social conditions. For this reason, fizkultura and sport were discussed at the meetings of the Central Committee; this led to directives on sports education, town planning and sporting competition. Sport was in the first instance a matter of the proletariat, the modern class par excellence. The largest and most important clubs therefore had names such as Dynamo, Spartak, Locomotive, Torpedo and Soviet Wings. The sports movement of the 1920s renewed its links with international workers' sport. Emphasis was placed on its class character. It rejected the Olympic Games as middle-class in favour of games in the name of Spartacus, the rebel slave, as a challenge to elite bourgeois sports. In the summer of 1928, when over three thousand athletes from forty-six nations convened for the Olympic Games in Amsterdam, working-class sports delegations from around a dozen nations assembled in Moscow and thirty thousand athletes marched from Red Square to the newly built Dynamo Stadium. On 12 August 1928, more than two hundred thousand people came together for the inauguration of the culture park and to take part in the Spartakiad games.

In this way, sport became part of the international clash of class against class, socialism against capitalism. Between 1926 and 1937 Soviet teams travelled to Austria, Czechoslovakia, Sweden and Germany. Soviet athletes, boxers, gymnasts, footballers and weightlifters took part in the International Workers' Olympiads in Antwerp in 1937. Working people's sports were encouraged; they were held to be a form of education and cultivation. Cultural 'techniques' and forms of physical development were transmitted; peasant immigrants were to be transformed into urban proletarians. The emphasis was to be placed not on records and winning or losing but on strengthening class solidarity and toughening up the human body in and through everyday productivity.

The fizkultura parade became an annual fixture in July 1931 when some forty thousand men and women followed the slogan of the All-Union Council of the GTO (*Gotov k trudu i oborone SSSR*; Ready for Labour and Defence) and marched across Red Square. A year later, there were already seventy thousand marching past the Lenin Mausoleum. Yevgeny Kriger wrote at that time for *Izvestia*: 'For two hours and twenty-five minutes the *fizkultura* columns marched past. Finally the orchestras marched off towards GUM. The Conductor of Free Movement silently waves the flags. The Square instantly fills, like a flutter of wings, with gymnasts from the Institute of *Fizkultura*. This is a symphony of synchronicity, unity and precision. The Square, more accustomed to military marches, is now filled with the light sounds of a waltz. The flags wave. The whole atmosphere shimmers with lightning movements, and the words ring out from the people "Greetings Comrade Stalin".[11]

By this time everything was worked out in detailed choreographies, tableaux vivants, living sculptures, plane formations that spelled out slogans in the sky, staged boxing matches and three-story human pyramids driven through the parade on floats. 'From this moment on, the *fizkultura* parade truly entered into the spirit of the Hollywood musical', declared sports historian Mike O'Mahony.[12] A further twist was given in the parade of 1937 when the whole of Red Square was covered with a green carpet, goalposts set up and a game played between Dynamo Moscow (the team of the Commissariat for Internal Affairs, i.e., the NKVD) and Spartak Moscow. Red Square had been transformed into a stadium; the dictator and his team were the fans on the grandstand. What greater proof could there be of the power of sport and the importance of sport for power! How secure power must have seemed in a game where the better team determined the outcome, rather than the plan (Dynamo won 5–4). This was a memorable game with memorable photographs and memorable actors. Spartak's trainer, Nikolay Starostin, was later condemned and continued his career as team trainer in a camp in the Russian Far East. The initia-

tor of the game, Alexander Kosarev, the head of the All-Union Young
Communist League, was caught up in the purges and shot.[13]

From Modern Studies of Movement to Classical Sculpture: The Creation of Icons

The fizkultura parades acquired their definitive shape in 1935–1939.
They have been well recorded in film so even today we can form a clear
impression of what they were like. This enables us to demonstrate
the changes in physical education and the cult of the body in the
transition from the 1920s to the 1930s.

During this period sport became a preferred subject for the plastic
arts, especially photography, cinema and sculpture. The Soviet cult
of the body appears to be a variant of the new growth in interest in
the human body that began in Europe with the life-reform movement
of the late nineteenth and early twentieth centuries. It circled round
the bodies of workers modelled on the heroes of labour handed down
from antiquity—Vulcan, Hephaestus, Prometheus and Hercules—who
were supposed to reshape the world and clear out the modern 'Augean
stables of capitalism'. The human body fitted into the new world of
technology and itself acquired quasi-technical qualities. This too was
a characteristic feature of a euphoria that refused to recognise such
a thing as fate and insisted on placing the shaping of the planet in
human hands. In many respects, the machine became the model of
a rationalised body (see, for example, the drawings of Vladimir Krinsky).[14] The scientific organisation of work, the cinematic documentation of labour processes and Soviet Fordism all came together here
and pointed in a direction different from that of Leni Riefenstahl, who
in 1925 had titled her first film 'Ways to Strength and Beauty'. Just as
clothing and fashion had to be rational and functional—*profodezhda*,
workaday attire—so too did they have to be ergonomically designed
for sport.

Artists were fascinated. In 1922 Gustav Klutsis produced breath-
taking photomontages on sporting themes, geometric shapes of
gymnasts on the bars. In the same year El Lissitzky created illustrations of footballers for an Ilya Ehrenburg book. The black and white

striped sports' shirt—*futbolka*—became the outfit of the young man
who wanted to prove that he was au courant. Alexander Samokhvalov's paintings *Girl Wearing a Football Jersey* (1932) and *Girl with
a Shot Put* (1933) not only electrified the broad public in the Soviet
Union, but caused a furore at the 1934 Venice Biennale and the 1937
World Exhibition in Paris. Reproduced as postcards by the thousand,
they became the icons of the new human being. The fact was that the
masters of the Soviet sports picture had learned their trade from the
icon painters—Samokhvalov had studied them in the Russian Museum where he had been a regular visitor. 'These modern icons celebrated the *fizkulturnitsa* as the archetypal Soviet New Woman, whose
very image, replacing the saints of yesteryear, was designed to inspire devotion and veneration.'[15] With these images of sportswomen,
Samokhvalov and other painters displayed the transformation of the
baba, the peasant woman of Old Russia or the Muslim woman with
a black veil, into the modern emancipated woman. From the middle
of the 1930s, this woman was endowed with more evidently feminine
features. She appeared not just as a vigorous, child-bearing mother
capable of hard work but as a beautiful, desirable ideal partner for an
equally attractive, athletic man. Modern human beings discard their
clothes, they enjoy the sun, the air and movement; they display their
bodies without embarrassment. Swimming costumes are not a sign of
prudishness but of culture: they distinguish people from the customs
of the Russian village where nakedness was taken for granted.[16]

It is astonishing to see the many forms in which the sportsperson's
body appeared in the public space and how widely it was reproduced—
in the parades and sporting events, in stadiums and competitions.
Photographers such as Alexander Rodchenko, Boris Ignatovich and
Ivan Shagin produced iconic images of the beautiful athletic body in
motion. Naked sportsmen appear on the beach in Odesa in Dziga Vertov's *Man with a Movie Camera*. Alexander Deineka not only painted
sportsmen and -women but portrayed himself with a bare torso and
in boxer shorts. Vera Mukhina's *Worker and Kolkhoz Woman*, two ideal
figures, crowned the USSR Pavilion at the Paris World Fair in 1937.
Preliminary studies show that it had been inspired by the soaring
figure of the Nike of Samothrace. Three pictures stood at the centre of
the World Fair exhibition: Samokhvalov's *Soviet*, Deineka's *Respected*

Figures of the Soviet Union and Alexey Pakhomov's *Children of the Soviet Union.* Sportsmen and -women of almost every discipline are to be found in the stations of the Moscow Metro built between 1932 and 1958, especially in Ploshchad Revolyutsii, Mayakovskaya, Dynamo and Ploshchad Sverdlova. The seventy thousand workers who built the metro had their own sporting and cultural organisations. In the metro stations you come across sculptures by Matvey Manizer (Ploshchad Revolyutsii), mosaics by Deineka (Mayakovskaya), bas reliefs and sculptures of footballers, boxers and tennis players by Yelena Yanson-Manizer (Dynamo). In the Central Park of Culture and Recreation, Ivan Shadr's *Girl with an Oar* soars up into the sky; Joseph Chaykov, who had been associated with Osip Zadkin and Jacques Lipchitz in emigration in Paris before he returned to the Soviet Union, created a highly dynamic group of footballers that became an object of wonder in the Soviet Pavilion at the New York World Fair.[17]

It would be strange if the erotic and even homoerotic dimension had not asserted itself in this image world, if not always as explicitly as in Yury Olesha's novel *Envy* (1927):

> Kavalerov sees Valya standing on the lawn, her legs firmly spread apart. She is in black, cut-away shorts, her legs are terribly bare, and can be seen all the way up. She is wearing white sports shoes without socks; and these flat shoes make her posture firmer still, more like a man's or a child's than a woman's. Her legs are dirty, tanned and shiny: a little girl's legs which have been exposed so often to the sun and air, to tumbles onto grass and bangs, that they are coarse and covered with light brown cuts from prematurely torn-off scabs, and her knees are rough like oranges. Youth and an inner awareness of her physical beauty entitle her to treat her legs with such neglect. But higher up, under the black shorts, her skin is smooth and delicate, showing how lovely she will be when she becomes a mature woman, when she starts to take an interest in herself and wants to be attractive, and when the cuts heal, all the scabs fall off and her tan becomes even all over.[18]

The parallel between the body cults of national socialism and Stalinism is seductive, and there are undoubtedly visual affinities between such films as Leni Riefenstahl's *Triumph of the Will* (1935) and V. Yosilevich's *Happy Youth* (1935). However, their differences are equally obvious, despite the superficial similarity of the rhythms of the marching columns. Soviet youth and its cult were born out of the spirit of labour, the transformation of the world, of *perekovka*, 'reforging', and were never concerned with race or biological breeding, even though sociobiological ideas were not alien to the Soviet world in the 1920s and 1930s. Soviet icons of physical culture have other origins, as can be observed from the phenotype which is not too distant from the idea of the superman—the Russian intelligentsia was more than susceptible to Nietzsche's gospel of the Superman[19]—but this was the self-creating, self-perfecting Superman, not the Darwinian Superman of zoological selection. It was Gorky who, carried away by the sight of the beautiful bodies at the fizkulturniki parades, became convinced that 'the crippled Russian intellectual', with his overlarge head, spectacles (for the most part), frail physique and excess cerebral reflection as opposed to healthy pragmatism, would finally be superseded by an individual with an all-round personality of the kind envisaged by Michelangelo or Karl Marx.[20] The fact that the beauty of the Soviet body is not without a certain compensatory element is another matter altogether. It conceals the dark side of the history of the Soviet physique: the traces of violence, hunger, death from cold and exhaustion, physical liquidation on a massive scale.

War: A Meditation on the Living and the Dead

Alexander Deineka, the painter and choreographer of strong, muscular bodies in sun-drenched landscapes, also created images of vulnerable human bodies. In his painting *The Defence of Sevastopol*, sailors in white uniforms are threatened by German bayonets.[21] The bodies that had appeared invulnerable—the age group that had undergone parachute jumps and training in the stadiums and parks of culture and recreation, the DOSAAF and OSOAVIAKhIM,[22] people for whom physical training always implied military training as well—had been abandoned to starvation by the Germans; they were shredded and crushed by the hundreds of thousands. But the storm of steel and the armour of the tanks of the Soviet-German War were something very different. It is only against the background of twenty-seven million dead—flayed, tortured, shredded and crushed bodies that only a short time previously had been full of life and soul—that the entire horror of the war is revealed to us: a war of bodies, hand-to-hand fighting, injuries, crippling, and endless scars. The images of towns and villages destroyed are all that has been transmitted to us—softened pictures of a physical demographic catastrophe, a bodily rift that can only be healed after a recovery lasting generations. After the war, the Soviet Union was a nation of 'the living and the dead'—to cite Konstantin Simonov's great novel—a nation of millions of destroyed and wounded, many of whom suffered from the effects of their injuries to the end of their lives. Their history has not been told or even been made visible. Emblematic of their suffering is doubtless that Dantesque inferno far away in the north on the Island of Valaam in Lake Ladoga, the colony of mutilated and crippled victims, a place beyond the horizon of the visible world.[23] All the more impressive was the return of the survivors, the strong and unimpaired who made their appearance in the fizkulturni parade on Red Square on 12 August 1945 to the amazement of General Eisenhower. This was the reappearance of the living, the resurrection of the dead.[24]

The USSR/CCCP as a Global Sports Power

After the Second World War the Soviet Union did not return to the world of the worker Spartakiads of the 1920s but entered the international arena of the Olympic Games instead. The fizkulturni parades were moved from Red Square to the stadiums and competition took place in the framework of global sport. The key stages were those of Helsinki 1952, Melbourne 1956 and Rome 1960. The Soviet Union had become a world power in sport and its record-holders bore names familiar to an international public. Examples are the long-distance runner Vladimir Kuts, football legend Lev Lashin and high jumper Valery Brumel. Especially prominent, however, were particular sports where the Soviets had their own traditional strengths—their origins in workingmen's sports: weightlifting, boxing, wrestling, gymnastics (so close to ballet!), and shooting, where Soviet sportsmen and -women won medals and topped the international rankings. The Soviet Union often produced 'the strongest man in the world', with such athletes as Vasily Alexeev, Yury Vlasov and Leonid Zhabotinsky. For the acronym USSR to stand at the top of the medal boards was a point of patriotic duty which took precedence over personal aspiration and ambition. The team spirit of the collective was more highly regarded than individual prowess or individual style. Soviet sport valued its systematic and scientific approach—there was no university without its own chair of physical education and sport. Many athletes were more than sportspeople and had degrees in literature or the sciences, in line with the belief in 'all-round education'. The rise of the trainer was linked to this process of scientific selection and training. Trainers became models nationwide for young people and acquired great authority and even power. Poems and songs of the 1960s are full of tributes to these sporting icons as we can see from the writings of Yevgeny Yevtushenko, Robert Rozhdestvensky and Vladimir Vysotsky.

Stadiums became arenas of the Cold War and systemic competition. The medal tally now became the index of the superiority of one or the other system. But by the time the Olympic Games were held on Soviet soil for the first time, the nation was mired in the war in Afghanistan and the resulting boycott. On the eve of the opening-up of the nation, the high-achieving sporting culture promoted by the state over many decades could not have suspected that physical education would be one of the sectors hardest hit by globalisation and the collapse of the state, together with the fall of sporting idols, the training methods tried and tested over so many years and the shift in the prestige attached to sport in society in general. It turned out that physical training in line with a centrally dictated plan was now an outmoded approach. In the long run, the beauty of sport rooted in the free play of human energies was unsurpassed and irreplaceable—even in a world of increasing professionalisation and commercialisation.

After Yury Vlasov, Arnold Schwarzenegger

With the end of empire, national teams from the newly independent states emerged. The unitary league with such teams as Dynamo Kyiv, Zenit Leningrad and Dynamo Tbilisi ceased to exist. The shadow of the sporting empire remained visible for a long time in the biographies of the trainers, the (Russian-language) textbooks, the architecture of the stadiums and sports centres, the echo of the legendary clubs— Dynamo, Spartak and Zenit—the names of the athletes who came from all corners of the multinational empire and not least of all in the scandals that shook society when the doping empire collapsed along with the political one. Soviet sport was then sucked into the slip-stream of globalisation. The stadiums now displayed advertisements; clubs had to exploit their brands. Russian stars suddenly turned up in sports where previously Russia had been unrepresented—tennis, for example—while dropping down in the rankings in sports they had dominated for decades. Player transfers became all the rage and the internationalisation of the teams and their salaries changed the clubs' appearance. Brand names such as Locomotive and Dynamo suddenly seemed to hail from a distant Iron Age. The large towns witnessed the sudden emergence of fitness centres and gyms with the high-tech training gadgets that are now ubiquitous internationally and that have made the old gyms with their barbells and old-fashioned iron equipment look as if they came from nineteenth-century smithies. The international sports industry brands, outfits and bright uni-forms of leisure activities turned up in towns where previously men had exercised in worn-out training gear. The Spartakiads or fizkul-turniki parades were now something to be viewed from a distance, not without irony or even mockery, as if they had somehow come from an age irretrievably past. Personalities who had once served as role models for an entire generation, both for their character and for their sporting prowess, could now only keep up if they appeared on the title pages of glossy magazines and had revealing stories to tell about their families and their private yachts. Physical education was sidelined in favour of bodybuilding and the image of Yury Vlasov, who had once been the role model for the young Arnold Schwarzenegger, was displaced in favour of the armoured body of the terminator, the last representative of the power of good in the world.

The transition from the physical culture of one era to that of an-other was reflected in the thousands of posters to be found in the kiosks and gyms of even the remotest provincial villages. The military dimension that was always present in the fizkulturniki movement

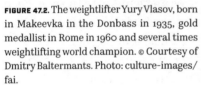

FIGURE 47.2. The weightlifter Yury Vlasov, born in Makeevka in the Donbass in 1935, gold medallist in Rome in 1960 and several times weightlifting world champion. © Courtesy of Dmitry Baltermants. Photo: culture-images/ fai.

FIGURE 47.3. Arnold Schwarzenegger, born in Styria in 1947. Bodybuilder, actor and governor of California, here with a dedication to Vlasov, whom he greatly admired. http:// citycelebrity.ru/citycelebrity/Post.aspx ?PostId=59062.

has disappeared or been repressed and relegated to the communities of fans always ready for a punch-up or to the booming industry of bodyguards and security men, if not to that of the paramilitary guerrillas on the margins of the former empire. It was self-evident that the nostalgia for strong human beings would inevitably grow in this confusion of competition, commerce and anxieties about the loss of control. If such figures were able to present themselves self-confidently on horseback, in the water, rising into the air or on the ice-hockey field, they would provide authority for a time at least, with that additional glamour without which even ruthless powers cannot succeed.

CHAPTER 48

Clothes for the New Human Being, or Christian Dior's Return to Red Square

Moscow 1959—what a year! It was exactly two years since Moscow had had an utterly new experience: the 1957 World Festival of Youth and Students with more than thirty thousand participants, especially young people, from 131 nations, a truly international and 'multicultural event'. If this latter concept was ever relevant, it was surely in those two weeks of August 1957. You could suddenly see faces, skin colours and clothes never seen before in Moscow, where previously every contact with a foreigner raised suspicions of spying. This was an event that allowed people to imagine what it might be like in a world that had left the war behind. In 1958 a young American—the pianist Van Cliburn—won the inaugural International Tchaikovsky Competition. In July/August 1959, parallel to the USSR exhibition in New York, the great US exhibition was held in Sokolniki Park in Moscow and visited by hundreds of thousands of astonished viewers. What amazed them was the standard of living of a wealthy country not simply as part of a propaganda campaign or a utopian dream, but actually featuring fridges, TVs, vacuum cleaners and cars—the American Way of Life at its most attractive, flanked by the visit of Richard Nixon and his wife, and framed by a cultural programme that three years later brought Benny Goodman to towns that themselves had once been centres of jazz, *Soviet jazz*, and had continued to thrive underground. The Moscow Film Festival of August 1959, the first after the war, belongs to this series of events occurring in rapid succession. Crowning it all was Khrushchev's trip to the United States in September 1959. It represented the emergence of a general secretary who impressed the world with his striking frankness. He appeared as a man who had partly liberated himself from his own inferiority complexes and this enabled him to express his admiration for American achievements—whether for growing corn or manufacturing automobiles—not to mention the spell cast by his unassuming and sympathetic wife, Nina Khrushcheva, who played the part of the Soviet First Lady. But a very different event showed most clearly that atmospherically and visually an era had come to an end: the brilliantly orchestrated appearance of the Christian Dior fashion house in Moscow on 10 June 1959. Following the death of Dior himself in 1957, leadership of the fashion house had been taken over by Yves Saint Laurent.

Like Butterflies from Another Planet

Even today it is possible to glean some sense of the impact of Dior's arrival in Moscow in 1959 from the photographs in *Life* magazine taken by Howard Sochurek. It meant the return of French fashion, a world that refused to be diverted or impressed by borders, however implacable, or by ruthlessly implemented Five-Year Plans.[1] Just to see the models descending the gangway, the graceful and dignified way they accepted bouquets. And to see their hats, with broad brims, or their short capes! Everything about them seemed simple and effortless, complete with movements that revealed nothing of the time and discipline that had been invested in creating their posture and gestures. The locations for the Dior models' appearances were chosen with care: in high heels on the cobblestones, with St. Basil's Cathedral in the background; in a marketplace in front of a flower stand; on Gorky Street, the Moscow Broadway. Their coquetry had nothing condescending about it, nothing offensive. These beautiful women appeared like butterflies in the harsh, rather grey city. They were quite simply a sensation. People stopped and stared in amazement. Like the three Graces, the models merged with a group of sailors, echoing the old motif from the days of the Revolution: they were like the aristocratic ladies who took up with men in working-class clothes or uniforms. What a contrast between these women in their expensive robes and the Russian women with their white, peasant headscarves, or the models leaning on the GUM balcony, stared at by young women with blond plaits. You could see the entire range of reactions, from wide-eyed surprise, incredulous amazement, curiosity to a slightly intimidated hesitation—and at the same time, a warm, enthusiastic welcome. These were images of changing times in which what had stood for enmity, decadence and foreignness was suddenly welcomed, without a trace of resentment or malice.

Needless to say, nothing had been left to chance in staging this event. In the days between 7 and 16 June, everything had been completely planned in advance. There were 129 suitcases full of clothes and accessories and 500 litres of perfume. There were two or three shows every day, with 120 presentations altogether. Palaces of culture and sports halls were not large enough to hold the public. The Krylia Sovetov stadium was lined with silk in the aristocratic grey of the House of Dior and the Dior logo was scattered in profusion throughout. Eleven thousand visitors, for the most part from the worlds of fashion, textile and art, followed the parade of models. There was a reception at the French embassy in Bolshaya Yakimanka 45 (Ulitsa Dimitrova, as it was then) for the crème de la crème of Moscow society. In addition to luxury gowns, the twelve models displayed everyday clothes that were made to be worn, not just for the show. This was in GUM, the very incarnation of Soviet consumption, a place where ordinary good-quality clothing was not always readily available. Wherever the Dior models appeared, everyone else turned instantly into Cinderella in comparison.[2]

It was the end of an era whose beginnings Christian Dior had experienced as a young man in 1931, when he journeyed to Moscow and saw the Soviet Union with his own eyes—like many before and after him, from Romain Rolland to André Gide, from Louis-Ferdinand Céline to Jean-Paul Sartre. Dior and many people of the same background—painters, actors and writers—were fascinated by the boldness of Soviet visions, the pictures of Kazimir Malevich or Pavel Tchelitchew, not to mention the best that the Russian culture of the early twentieth century had to offer: the Ballets Russes of Serge Diaghilev. As part of an organised travel group of architects, Dior wanted to witness this country with its explosive productivity. As the fashion revolutionary, the inventor of the 'New Look' after the war, what had struck him in 1931 was not a blaze of colour, untrammelled experimentation or unprecedented synthesis of art and everyday experience. Instead he found 'drab colours, a lack of vitality and the absence of freedom'. He was shocked by the 'peeling façades of the palaces, empty shop windows, the terrible poverty', greyness, squalor, unsmiling faces, and the feeling of emptiness. Conversely, he was fascinated by the nation's past culture. Dior had no political views; he reacted spontaneously and judged essentially according to aesthetic criteria.[3] He had arrived in the Soviet Union at a time when together with the cultural revolution, industrialisation and collectivisation, the Age of the Plan had begun—the conscious effort to control and manage people's time, a process to which all spontaneous utterances were to submit. And nothing was more alien to the idea and practice of the plan and of being planned than the most spontaneous form of expression: fashion.

What happened between Christian Dior's visit in the early 1930s and the visit of the House of Dior at the end of the 1950s has been described by historians of Soviet fashion as a process of rise and fall.[4] It was another visitor to Moscow, Walter Benjamin, who in his notes on the *Arcades Project* had asked, 'Does fashion die (as in Russia, for example) because it can no longer keep up the tempo—at least in certain fields?'[5] In this case, would fashion be destroyed by this acceleration—a Five-Year Plan in four years—by the subordination of the present to the future and of the spontaneous expression of life to conscious planning? Benjamin offered a key to the interpretation even of Soviet planning. The relevant extract in the *Arcades Project* runs as follows:

> For the philosopher, the most interesting thing about fashion is its extraordinary anticipations. It is well known that art will often—for example, in pictures—precede the perceptible reality by years. It was possible to see streets or rooms that shone in all sorts of fiery colours long before technology, by means of illuminated signs and other arrangements, actually set them under such a light. Moreover, the sensitivity of the individual artist to what is coming certainly far exceeds that of the *grande dame*. Yet fashion is in much steadier, much more precise contact with the coming thing, thanks to the incomparable nose which the feminine collective has for what lies waiting in the future. Each season brings, in its newest

FIGURE 48.1. Dior models parading through the GUM Moscow department store, photographed by *Life* journalist Howard Sochurek. © Getty Images/The LIFE Picture Collection/Howard Sochurek.

creations, various secret signals of things to come. Whoever un-
derstands how to read these semaphores would know in advance
not only about new currents in the arts but also about new legal
codes, wars and revolutions.—Here, surely lies the greatest charm
of fashion, but also the difficulty of making the charming fruitful.[6]

The Russian Revolution and the Casting-Out of Traditional Clothing

The dress code characteristic of the Tsarist Empire class system had
gradually begun to erode long before the Revolution. The members
of the estates and professional groups wore clothing appropriate to
their standing. By watching passersby on any street—as Gogol has
shown in the case of Nevsky Prospekt—you could read off the structure of society: peasants in their beards and smocks, students in their
uniforms, priests in their robes and hoods, professionals—engineers,
railway personnel—in their work clothes, merchants in Old Russian
attire or European dress.[7] Industrialisation and urbanisation altered
people's social physiognomy. Immigrant peasants were transformed
into workers wearing factory clothing. Anyone who could afford it
donned European garb, the emerging middle class in particular. The
future revolutionaries put on lounge suits, hats and ties, as if they
were in Geneva or London. At the meetings of the Bolshevik Council
of People's Commissars you could see distinguished-looking gentlemen who would have done credit to the boardroom of a bank or
an industrial company in an age when you could have encountered
a very different type in the streets of the town centres: the man in
a leather jacket or sailor's shirt with a bolt-action Mauser rifle, the
revolutionary leader in middle-class clothes, framed by the faces of
the masses in grey military coats and gazing intently at the camera.
This was more or less the ideal type of the members of Red Guard
battalions in 1918: 'One man in his uniform coat, an Astrakhan cap
on his head, a staved-in cartridge pouch on his belt, a revolver hanging from his belt, a rifle with fixed bayonet in his hand. The other
man had on a well-worn leather jacket. It was only half-buttoned and

under it you could see a striped sailor's shirt. The sailor's cap jauntily pushed down on the back of his head looked as if it might fall off at any moment. His bell-bottomed trousers were carefully ironed and his shoes were highly polished. He too was equipped with a revolver, while grenades peeked out of his pockets. Two cartridge belts crossed his chest. A Maxim machine gun stood at his feet.'[8]

Before the beginning of the Great War St. Petersburg and Moscow had become cities of haute couture with hundreds of studios and dressmakers that followed the fashions in Paris, London and Vienna. Paul Poiret, the pioneer of French fashion, came to St. Petersburg in 1911. Nadezhda Lamanova, Moscow's best-known fashion designer before the war and purveyor to the court of all things relating to fashion, travelled regularly to Paris. The wealthy and the beautiful in the Russian capitals spent months abroad every year and so were familiar with the Paris scene. You need only look at the photos taken in Nevsky Prospekt and Kuznetsky Most studios. In matters of fashion, Russia was up to the minute; indeed for the first time in the history of modern style, Russia was even in the lead throughout Europe. Diaghilev's Ballets Russes had achieved world fame with its sophisticated sets and costumes which combined Western fashions with elements of Russian folklore and Orientalising motifs. The designs of Léon Bakst, Alexandra Exter, Varvara Stepanova and Nadezhda Lamanova had not simply made Russian costumes stageworthy; they had created the foundation for the reputation of Russian designers and couturiers in Europe—which had major consequences, as we shall see in due course.[9]

St. Petersburg ceased to exist as a centre of fashion and luxury during the war years and the ensuing Revolution and Civil War. Hunger and rationing dominated and there were more important things to worry about than the latest evening-dress designs. To be well dressed in times of social unrest might easily have led to threats to life and limb. A smart suit, a white shirt and a top hat could be stigmatised just as much as epaulettes on an officer's uniform or the spectacles of a middle-class intellectual. On the black market, diamonds and expensive jewellery could save one's life—or, sewed into one's clothing, help aristocrats or relatives of the old rulers to survive in exile.[10]

FIGURE 48.2. 'The union member goes firstly to the Workers' Faculty and then to the universities.' His clothes, which are both practical and sporty—boots, leather jacket and a tunic with a belt—are the mark of his social advancement. From Tatiana Strizhenova, *Soviet Costume and Textiles 1917–1945*, Flammarion, Moscow, Paris and Verona 1991, 162.

Luxury shops were abandoned or plundered. Tailors had lost their clientele for the time being; the clothing and hosiery factories were nationalised and their first orders forthcoming only when the need for uniforms arose. These were now produced not for the Imperial Army but for the Red Army, albeit making use of a design that had been created before October 1917 and would serve as the outfit of the Red Army right up to the Second World War—with the long army tunic, the *valenki* (felt boots), and above all, the cap, the so-called *budyonovka*.[11]

Another item of clothing to gain celebrity after emerging from the tumult of modern motorised war was the car driver's black leather jacket. The leather jacket was in the vanguard of technological warfare, which had long since switched from horses and the cavalry to the vehicles of the modern age. Not only was it made from expensive and hard-wearing material but it would soon become the insignia of power itself. The leather jacket was worn by the commanders of the Red Guard, elite sniper regiments, bodyguards and, above all, members of the Cheka, the All-Russian Extraordinary Commission for Combating Counter-Revolution, Profiteering and Corruption, an organisation in charge of everything from ordinary policing activities right up to the practice of mass terror with all that signifies: arrests, torture and mass shootings. To the very end of Soviet communism, the semiotic and semantic links between leather jackets, Mauser pistols and Cheka-Bolshevism—with the frequent addition of 'Jewish Bolshevism'—became inseparable. It was the dire necessity of the Civil War, the flight into exile and the establishment of an imposed elite that destroyed the space in which fashion trends might have been able to flourish. Whatever valuables people still had, including fashionable possessions, were brought out and exchanged for food on the black market. Respected scholars were ashamed to be seen on the streets, according to H. G. Wells, because rags and slippers were all they had left. The best pieces of fashionable clothing were to be found in the theatre props departments. The places to profit most from the exodus of the nobility and the middle class were those where the émigrés settled—Berlin, Paris or Shanghai—thanks to the improvement in their aesthetic culture and fashion know-how.[12]

Fashion as Class Struggle

Only when the Civil War was over and everyday routines had resumed could the clothing and textile industry start to recover and with it the fashion industry—the Kersten knitwear factory was transformed into the Red Banner Textile Factory (Krasnoe znamya).[13] The 1930s became a struggle for the appropriate clothing for the new human being; its outcome was by no means a foregone conclusion. Thanks to the chaos of the New Economic Policy, the world has insight into one of the most fascinating chapters of the history of style in the twentieth century. A decade of confusion thanks to the war, the Revolution and the Civil War was followed by an explosion of creativity in which everything that had survived of prerevolutionary fashions awoke to a new life. Utilitarian notions of fashion flourished; clothes and fashions were embraced only as long as they were practical and without regard to aesthetic pretentions. The battle between different fashions was consciously fought out as class struggle, a war between old and new, the past and the future. Overnight the old establishments filled up again—with 'former people' and new 'NEP bourgeoisie'. In the same way, the insignia of the prewar fashions returned, but this time to the tune of the latest dances—the tango, foxtrot and two-step.[14] The views recalled Otto Dix's stylised scenes in the Berlin of the Golden Twenties: glittering costumes, deep décolletages, feather boas, evening dresses with smooth silhouettes and no waistlines, long cigarette holders, stoles, a form of dress that, following the appearance of the muscular proletarian figures of war communism, emphasised androgynous and metrosexual elements. The fashion scene of the NEP period had access to the Paris and Berlin fashion worlds via such magazines as *Vogue* and *Harper's Bazaar*—and not least through the resumption of travel from which people brought back samples of the latest creations.[15]

In sharp contrast to the return of the fashions of yesteryear or from the capitalist West, the revolutionary left saw itself obliged to work on an outfit for the new human being. The leading fashion designer in prerevolutionary Russia, Nadezhda Lamanova, had argued early on, in 1919, soon after the establishment of the first Soviet sewing laboratory, 'Art must penetrate every aspect of life. In the process it must develop the artistic taste and sensibility of the masses. . . . In the realm of apparel, artists must take the initiative and work on creating the simplest but also the most beautiful clothes, making use of simple materials that suit the new way of life of the workers.'[16]

Revolutionary clothing was not to be sumptuous and luxurious, but useful. It was to be free of superfluous decoration—jewellery, ornament and costly materials—and should enhance everyday culture. It was to serve not a particular, prosperous stratum of society, but the population as a whole. A woman was to abandon her role as the appendage or ornament of a man; she was predominantly proletarian or of peasant stock and strongly built, or at any rate, scarcely imaginable in an evening dress. The testing ground for the new attire was the theatre, a place where prototypes could be tried out. The path led from the Ballets Russes to the extravagant stage sets and costumes of such members of the Soviet avant-garde as Nikolay Yevreinov, Vsevolod Meyerhold and Alexander Tairov. Similarly, the abstract, geometrical costumes of the science fiction film *Aelita* (1924), which was based on Alexey Tolstoy's novel of the same name, could also be seen as a demonstration of avant-gardist fashion. Painters such as Kazimir Malevich, Varvara Stepanova and Lyubov Popova, who sought a radical simplification of forms, now appeared as designers of fabrics and clothes. They made use of colours and lines taken from Russian folk art and folklore. These were the designs and models that initially made their appearance at the first All-Russian Agricultural and Handicraft Industrial Exhibition held in Moscow in 1923 and which then caused a sensation at the Exposition Internationale des Arts Décoratifs in Paris in 1925. The fabrics, clothes, toys and jewellery made from the simplest of materials were rewarded with a Grand Prix. And all this took place in a climate not simply of openness towards Soviet Russia, but full of the most exalted expectations. These expectations had been nurtured not just by the contemporary fascination with the foreign and exotic, the lure of the rich colouring of 'folklore' and the 'primitive', but more especially by the very boldness of the functional approach to fashion that was subordinated to the work process and undeterred by any resulting harshness. Taken together, these ensured that Soviet design and fashion in the 1920s would have lasting recognition. Perhaps no one subjected fashion to the dictates of utility more rigorously than Nadezhda Lamanova, although it was not she who favoured the more ruthless versions of functionalism and Constructivism but designers such as Varvara Stepanova and her husband Alexander Rodchenko who designed stage costumes, 'agitprop'-style clothes with hammer and sickle emblems or working clothes (*profodezhda*) for specific activities or professions, including clothes that hardly anyone wore except the artists themselves.[17] Nadezhda Lamanova once defined this in terms reminiscent of a manifesto: 'The basic forms of folk costume are always wise. . . . By accepting the wonderful colour of traditional costumes and distributing it rhythmically on a rationally made costume, we create the kind of clothes that are in harmony with our contemporary life.'[18] A costume must not impose anything on the body, but should adjust to it, harmonise with it and be purposeful and useful. The new costume will be in line with the new life: working, dynamic and aware.[19]

Lamanova goes on to provide a quasi-programmatic account 'On the Rationality of Costume':

Costume is one of the most sensitive manifestations of social life and psychology. The unprecedented categorical restructuring of the entire social organism and the birth of the new mass consumer in Soviet Russia inevitably bring in their wake an equally sharp change of costume. Hence the necessity of creating a new costume that combines the artistic sense of form peculiar to our epoch with the purely practical requirements of our time. In contrast to West European fashion, whose changes depend on commercial considerations, we must assume as a basis of our costume considerations of social hygiene, the requirements of work, etc. It is not enough merely to create a comfortable costume; we need to ensure a proper correlation between the artistic elements of costume and the new forms and aspirations of the emerging new life. All these conditions require methods of artistic construction and practical realization of contemporary costume in the interests of mass production. Costume is in a sense a continuation of the body. It has functions to perform, like our bodies, in life and in work, and this is why clothes must be rational—they must not hinder the wearer, but in fact help him. Hence the most important factors dictating clothes design are the following:

1) The wearer's personal mood and taste in one form or another (the wearer's style).
2) The style of the epoch; its cultural physiognomy.
3) The form of the individual expressed in a definite silhouette.
4) The fabric, which being in itself a given form, predetermines some of the elements of the shape we are creating.
5) The utilitarian purpose of the costume.

Thus the task of creating an artistic costume involves the integration of the figure, the fabric and the purpose into a common form as appealing as possible in the eyes of the epoch and the wearer. The above can be expressed in the practical formula:

> For whom
> From what
> For what purpose
> And all this is synthesized in *how* (the form).

In creating the form according to these principles, it is necessary to observe its strict subordination to the plastic laws of proportions and relationships which govern any art. Such an interpretation of costume not only reflects the purely external life of society but also impels one to scrutinize the domestic, psychological, historical and national features of the Russian people; this, naturally, will lead to research into folk art, as manifested in the handicraft industry. Here will be found ample opportunity to use the splendour of folk art motifs and their profound rationality so in keeping with the Soviet way of life. Traditional embroidery, laces and linen fabrics are combined with the contemporary sense of form brought into existence by the renewed social and psychological life of society.[20]

Lamanova's relatively restrained functionalism and her concern for the undeniably aesthetic dimension of clothes presumably helps to explain her rise to become the haute couturière of the Soviet Union, the leading fashion designer of the Stalin era.[21] She survived the settling of accounts with the Formalists and Constructivists and with the establishment of the 'House of Models' in 1935, she founded the institutional framework for Soviet fashion design.

The 'House of Models' in 1935: Fashion and the Plan

Diplomats' wives and foreign visitors were surprised by the dramatic changes in the Moscow fashion scene in the mid-1930s. They found fashions in window displays and ateliers on a par with those to be seen in the West, albeit only in shop windows, not in the street. The French designer Elsa Schiaparelli was astonished by the orgy of chiffon and fur-lined garments, but her advice that clothing should be simple and practical fell on deaf ears. The fact that something fundamental had changed could be seen from the numerous fashion shows, posters and advertisements, especially from the 'House of Models' established on the Moscow Sretenka in 1935. It was decorated with frescoes by Vladimir Favorsky, expensive fixtures and fittings, and superior lighting. It was regarded as the place of choice in which to create a specific Soviet fashion. The aim was to make use of advanced Western manufacturing methods to mass produce high-value textiles with which to express the multiplicity of styles of the Soviet national cultures. It was later followed by decentralised fashion houses set up in the individual republics. Nadezhda Makarova, a pupil of Lamanova, had overall responsibility for this creation of Soviet or socialist fashion. The question was, how to create high-quality, individually handcrafted goods while using the methods of mass production—simplification, standardisation and reduction. This required solving a basic contradiction. Fashion springs from spontaneous expressions of taste; it matures in a subconscious mix of mood and feeling, which means it cannot really be planned. Yet, this was the period of the Five-Year Plans and fashion had to fit in with a production plan laid down in advance and ignore and even suppress the uncertainties and changes in the mood of the moment. Fashion ceased to be the spontaneous and unpredictable 'anticipation of the coming trend' but the translation into practice of a design that was scientifically grounded and not the product of 'the anarchy of the market'. It was a fashion that from its inception was and had to remain a 'prisoner of time'.[22] The prevailing system was in conflict with the ways of fashion design. Which models were produced and in what quantities was decreed from the top. The planners' interests and taste mattered more than customers' preferences. 'The powerful bureaucracy established under Stalinism that governed the industry through a rigid, hierarchically structured and overcentralized system determined the functioning of the field of fashion up to the end of socialism. With their activities informed by the hierarchical principle, socialist state textile factories did not respond to the desires of their customers but to the desires of their superiors from whom they received both supplies and orders to fulfil their plan.'[23]

Other factors also made it difficult to build up the Soviet fashion industry. These included shortages of materials, the low level from which Soviet industry was starting, poor manufacturing quality and the high rate of rejects. Despite all of Mikoyan's attempts at modernisation, textile production became a particularly tricky sector within a systematically backward and chronically underdeveloped consumer-goods industry. Queues in textile and clothes shops were part of the lifelong experience of Soviet citizens, as was the regular encounter with the irrationality of an inflexible system that had eliminated the interplay of supply and demand and, to put it crudely, produced summer clothes in winter and winter clothes in summer—all in conformity with the plan.

Demand was overwhelming, especially in the strata that had risen socially in the 1930s: top workers, technical personnel, Red directors, reputable scholars and artists. The transition from an egalitarian wages policy to one with material incentives had led to a situation in which many individuals had accumulated considerable amounts of money, money that now needed to be spent. The abolition of rationing and ration cards in 1935 had led to a growth in consumption in certain sectors. Furthermore, the image of women had undergone a change since the mid-1930s. Once again a woman was supposed to appear primarily as a wife and mother, as mistress of house and home. She was to be able to enjoy all the luxuries at her command without feeling guilty—including the jewellery, accessories and clothes displayed in the Soviet fashion magazines of the day: *Iskusstvo odevatsya* (The art of dressing) or *Atelie* (Atelier). What was sought was not simplicity or modesty, but 'grandness, classicism, uniqueness and preciousness.'[24] Clothes played an important role in the households of the worker aristocracy and the middle classes of the Stalin era. Foreign observers were struck by the crass contrast between ordinary workers and champion workers: the Stakhanovite workers who used their visits to Moscow for extensive shopping trips—perfumes, silk lingerie or furs—before returning to the pits of the Donbass or the Kuzbass. Stakhanovites often received ten times the average wages and this money was spent on ivory-coloured shoes costing 180 rubles or crêpe de chine dresses for 200 rubles each. Foreign visitors were astonished to discover that champion workers and academics could afford bespoke tailors.

Alexander Deineka and Alexander Samokhvalov immortalised these people in their paintings wearing their new clothes, often all in white and in a monumental format. The American journalist Hubert Knickerbocker described the ambitions of the new rising class: 'Stakhanoff bought a suit, hat and gloves for himself, a silk dress, coat sweater, perfume and silk lingerie for his wife. Alexander Busygin, an expert smith from Gorky, bought two dresses, shoes and gloves for his wife. Women Stakhanovites, Marusia and Dusia Vinogradova from the textile mills at Ivanovo-Voznesensk were "tough customers". "We showed them crêpe de chine dresses and they said 'We've already bought that kind'", a clerk in Moscow's biggest department store said. "We showed them other kinds of silk dresses with no better luck. 'We've bought that kind too', they declared." The Vinogradova sisters wanted wool dresses but could not find their sizes.'[25] The upshot was the development of two quite different market segments: an *haute couture soviétique* and mass production. There was little overlap between the two, something that would scarcely be worthy of mention if the separation into a luxury sector and the unchanging poor-quality provision of everyday clothing had not been so crass and enduring.

The Second World War only exacerbated the situation with the textile industry's shift to the needs of the front and the extreme destructiveness from which the country was just starting to emerge. This had also intensified hopes of a more general shift of direction—away from heavy industry towards light industry and a greater emphasis on consumer goods. But this did not really happen until the mid-1950s, following Stalin's death. An unexpected boost for the fashion industry came from the occupations and conquests of 1939–1941, the lend-lease deliveries of the Americans and the advance of the Red Army to the West. With the occupation of eastern Poland and the Baltic states in 1939/40 there was an influx into the Soviet Union of otherwise unobtainable consumer goods, including clothing and textiles of every kind; this trend was reinforced by the advance towards the West. With the seizure of UFA films featuring Marika Rökk and Lale Andersen, people could take a view of the state of fashion, and in the bazaars of the postwar period 'trophy fashions' not only became the most desirable objects but established something of a sense of style more broadly.

Nadezhda Lamanova, Couturière to the Soviet Union

If there ever was such a thing as an autonomous Soviet fashion—in the sense we have referred to—this was the achievement of one woman above all, Nadezhda Petrovna Lamanova, whom the historian Alexander Vasiliev named the 'couturière of the Soviet Union'.[26] She was born in 1861 into an impoverished aristocratic family close to Moscow and experienced the not atypical career of an emancipated woman of her generation: a girl's high school in Nizhny Novgorod, early independence and training in a Moscow embroidery workshop, followed by her own dressmaking business in the centre of Moscow (Bolshaya Petrovka 25, dom Adelgeima). By the beginning of the twentieth century she was already a much sought-after dressmaker and became 'Dress Designer to Her Imperial Majesty' and also costumière. She supplied the court from her new atelier on Tverskoy Bulvar and maintained contact with the European fashion scene with the aid of regular trips to Paris. From 1901 on, she worked as a costume designer for the Moscow Art Theatre under Konstantin Stanislavsky. After the Revolution, she was arrested for a short time with her husband in 1919 but freed again following the intervention of Maxim Gorky—she designed clothes for his always extravagantly dressed wife, the actress Maria Fyodorovna Andreeva—and went on to fill a leading position in the People's Commissariat for Enlightenment—like so many other artists and intellectuals dependent on rations for their survival.[27]

Instead of creating clothes for court society, she now designed simple clothes for ordinary people, inspired by Russian folklore. Together with other prominent artists—among them Vera Ignatievna Mukhina and Nadezhda Sergeevna Makarova—she created a sensation at the Paris Exhibition of 1925 and the Leipzig Fur Fair and turned fashion à la russe into a brand. Her work was crowned by the founding of the 'House of Models' with her pupil Nadezhda Makarova as director and herself as consultant. In the 1930s she worked as a costume designer for Soviet film—in such notable productions as Grigory Alexandrov's *Circus* and Sergey Eisenstein's *Alexander Nevsky*—and for such stars of the Soviet screen as Lyubov Orlova. She died dramatically from a heart attack on the square in front of the Bolshoi Theatre on 14 October 1941, having arrived too late to

FIGURE 48.3. Nadezhda Lamanova (1861–1941), haute couturière in the Tsarist Empire and the Soviet Union. © culture-images/fai.

be evacuated from Moscow, which was under attack from the Germans. She was buried in Vagankovo Cemetery and then forgotten for decades—the outstanding Russian and Soviet fashion designer of the day.[28]

At a time when agitprop textiles, the patterns and the clothes produced for theatrical productions by the Suprematists and Constructivists, were the talk of the day and travelled all over the world from one exhibition to the next, the work of Nadezhda Lamanova remained largely unknown—except to a few connoisseurs. And yet it was chiefly Lamanova, rather than such figures as Alexander Rodchenko, Varvara Stepanova or Lyubov Popova, who had set the tone in the incubation period of Soviet fashion. Her work contains all the riches of prerevolutionary fashion in Russia and Europe, the experience of a rupture with a world of luxury that had become problematic in times of war and revolution, the development of new elements in the repertoire of folk art and the debate with a sociologically inclined study of fashion and style. She found something of a middle way, a Soviet Art Deco, but it was not in her power to liberate fashion from the grip of bureaucratic and hierarchical planning institutes. She, too, like the fashion she wished to promote, was a 'prisoner of her time'. Fashion as the beating pulse of the age did not have the opportunity to reassert itself until the planning institutions had once again become enfeebled and outlived their usefulness. And this time began long before the agony of Soviet socialism had become public knowledge.

The Pulse of the Age: Stilyagi and Other Subcultures

There could be no return to prewar times after the horrendous war that turned the country upside down. However, by attempting to do just that, the Stalin regime tackled the issue head-on by plunging into a new campaign against terror which, even more bizarrely than in the 1930s, invented even more alarming enemies, fifth columns and so on, ultimately steering the country into the Cold War—the continuation of the war by peaceful means. But show trials, a propaganda war against America, an anti-Semitism disguised as anticosmopolitanism and anti-Zionism could ultimately not sustain the nation on its path to an overdue peaceful reconstruction. The housing shortage and dearth of consumer goods had worsened, if anything. Millions of people had not only experienced the horrors of the Nazis; they had been to Europe and brought back goods that provided proof of the unheard-of standard of living in the so-called decadent West. They had seen films that made quite clear that a world existed beyond the Soviet universe and that it was utterly different. The demobilised troops were the heroes of the time and those among them who had not been branded traitors because they were POWs or workers in the Eastern territories hoped finally to enjoy the fruits of victory. These factors had changed the nation and did not fit in with the plans of the paranoid dictator.

Ilya Ehrenburg used the metaphor of the 'Thaw' to refer to the political decisions and resolutions of the Twentieth Party Congress but also to the more molecular movements that were symptomatic of the coming changes. Representative was the emergence of the *stilyagi*— the term coined by a Soviet journalist to describe the young people who were fed up to the back teeth with the boredom, monotony and graveyard stillness in the land of the workers. This movement was essentially one of apolitical and antipolitical people who wanted to be left in peace by the propagandists, rather than members of a political opposition. The movement included the children of privileged public officials, the sons of diplomats who had had some experience of life abroad and could afford to copy jazz records (on X-ray film) or seek out private tailors because they had wealthy fathers or semilegal contacts. They indulged in cat-and-mouse games, but quite openly— sporting slicked-down hair, canary-yellow jackets, drainpipe trousers or 'Oxfords', bellbottoms, multicoloured socks and patent-leather shoes or crêpe soles with provocatively high heels. They had their own channels, accessed Western magazines, discovered Western dances and made sure that the sound of Eddie Rosner's jazz band or the 'Chattanooga Choo Choo' went beyond the bounds of a small circle of people and became all the rage. They had their own slang and revered everything that came from the West, particularly the USA. Nor did they let themselves be intimidated by the cartoonists of *Krokodil* who took pot shots at them as 'unsoviet', 'unpatriotic' and 'decadent', as 'Western bootlickers'. More than a few of them paid for their yearning for freedom and their insistence on expressing themselves with harsh punishments, loss of their jobs and even imprisonment. Once again fashion had become both a stigma and a sign of what was to come. It gained momentum over the following years and culminated in a political counterculture—the dissident and citizens' rights movement of the 1960s.

At the very moment Soviet fashion matured, it became apparent that it had in fact come to its end. Fashion was a matter not just of clothing but of behaviour and style; the dress code was also a guide, a manual on etiquette and 'proper living'. This becomes very clear from a typical statement in the magazine *Zhurnal mod* of 1958:

We have repeatedly written that the choice of clothes should follow the basic rule: time of day and particular circumstances. During the day, for example, it is not appropriate to pay visits or receive guests in a smart evening dress. In such situations a strictly elegant day dress is appropriate: of short length, high or just slightly open neckline, with short or long sleeves. . . . Such a dress is not served by loads of jewellery, it is better to restrict oneself to one piece: a brooch, a hairpin or a bracelet. Shoes, hats and gloves should be matched with such a day dress. Of course, everything should be co-ordinated according to the colour. Let us repeat: the dress that you wear during the working day should be modest and restrained in appearance. Matinées, parties at 1pm, cocktails and 'à la furshet' parties from 5 till 8pm, require a smarter day dress and a little elegant hat, which you are not supposed to take off. Evening dress, made from an expressive and decorative fabric that is not worn during the day, is necessary for grand receptions, theatre premieres and gala concerts especially if they happen after 8pm. Although not necessary, the evening dress is characterized by a lower neckline, short sleeves and a long skirt. Silk or lacy gloves can be added to such a dress, their length depends on the length of the sleeves: the shorter the sleeve, the longer the gloves, and the other way round. A small elegant handbag accompanies evening wear. Light, open shoes with high heels or medium heels for older women serve those occasions; shoes can be made from silk, brocade, or from golden or silver leather. Day shoes are not appropriate for evening wear. Evening wear may be embellished with jewellery. Here a sense of measure is welcome, as always.[29]

This style guide was quickly superseded by fashion, which prevails without any such guidance. At the very moment that fashion had finished defending itself, its definitive decline began.[30] The (chaotic and contradictory) phase of opening-up that had started under Khrushchev came to an end with his fall in 1964 and was followed by an even sharper phase of repression under Leonid Brezhnev. After a wave of persecution, the crushing of the Prague Spring in 1968 and a period of intensified rearmament, the nation entered into a phase of stagnation and even agony, which didn't come to an end until perestroika and the resulting dissolution of the Soviet Union in the early 1990s. It was not just a matter of individual campaigns and a youthful subculture. There was a growing economic interchange, tourism, a revolution in communication and information, the increasing seductions of the Western way of life; taken together, these posed a significant threat to 'the system', to the Soviet lifeworld as such. Towards the end of the 1980s there were no longer any fashion or lifestyle magazines with a mass distribution printed in the Soviet Union, let alone a censorship authority. Instead, such magazines as *Burda Moden*, *Vogue* and *Cosmopolitan* did a runaway trade. Even the dress patterns in *Burda Moden* or *Otto* catalogues had ceased to play a significant role here. Now there was a flood of goods into the country through tourist routes and drug dealers, the movements of millions shuttling between Istanbul and Moscow, between Sverdlovsk and the Chinese Ürümqi, between Khabarovsk and Harbin. They brought everything that people dreamt of onto the black markets and bazaars, albeit as fake copies of Gucci, Adidas, Reebok, Prada, Cartier and Givenchy. To run around in Western gear, with the brand names on one's forehead, was no longer the right of a privileged few or of smugglers. The time when only a star such as Lyubov Orlova could go to Paris to buy herself suitable gloves or when a prima ballerina such as Maya Plisetskaya had to apply to third parties to help her obtain the appropriate elegant outfit was long since over. The Soviet world that had long fought to produce a style of its own and striven to assert itself against 'seduction' by the soft power of lines and curves, the delicacy or tinting of exquisite materials, had not been strong enough. The return of Dior and Chanel to Red Square and the GUM department store signalled a retreat long before a political withdrawal had even been mooted.[31]

A Museum of Soviet Fashion:
A Retrospective of People's Anticipations

Alexander Vasiliev, a historian specialising in Soviet-Russian fashion, has proposed that a museum of Russian fashion be established. He has himself taken a step in this direction by mounting an exhibition in honour of Nadezhda Lamanova. For the location of such a museum, he nominates one of the pavilions on the site of the Exhibition of the Achievements of the National Economy (VDNKh) in Moscow, itself already a museum for the trade fair architecture of the Stalin era. Pavilions previously devoted to the conquest of the cosmos, the cotton production of the Republic of Uzbekistan or the exhibition *Leningrad: City of Culture and Science* could now serve as museums. They could provide the appropriate ambience for a fashion tradition that lived through every conceivable disaster, change of style, stigmatisation and symbolisation of the Russian twentieth century yet did not shrink from the hardest thing of all: the blunt severing of the link between fashion and the spirit of the times. Benjamin's talk of fashion as 'the anticipation of what is to come' might now be fully realised in a fashion museum, namely as a retrospective of those anticipations, while out in the city the search for the dernier cri would be underway with a renewed impetus.

CHAPTER 49

Manly Grace: Nureyev's Gesture

Notwithstanding all the vicissitudes of history, the great tradition of Russian ballet was never disrupted. Russian ballet took the lead in Europe in the nineteenth and early twentieth centuries. The original and enduring pieces of ballet music came from Russia—think of Tchaikovsky's *Nutcracker, Swan Lake* and *Sleeping Beauty* or Glazunov's *Raymonda*. It was to Russia that we owe such great choreographers as Marius Petipa and prima ballerinas such as Anna Pavlova, Tamara Karsavina, Mathilda-Marie Kshesinskaya, who became European and even international stars.[1] In a costume designed by Léon Bakst, Vaslav Nijinsky became a legend in the world of ballet with his incomparable interpretation of his role in *L'Après-midi d'un faune*. If proof were needed that Russia had become a global power at the beginning of the twentieth century as far as culture was concerned, it would be enough to look at Serge Diaghilev's Ballets Russes and their unique interaction with all the great representatives of modernity from every branch of music: Stravinsky, Prokofiev and Shostakovich; painting: Picasso, Matisse, Léger and Bakst; and dance: Vaslav Nijinsky, Serge Lifar, Michel Fokine, Anna Pavlova and Lydia Lopokova.

The Russian ballet had stepped onto the world stage—partly because there was no room on the stages of the Imperial Theatre and so the artistic sensations and scandals took place elsewhere: in Paris with the *Sacre du printemps* in 1913, and later in London, Monte Carlo, Buenos Aires and elsewhere.[2] These and other achievements of the Silver Age soon merged with the world of exiles since they had an impact on the artistic life of the different countries in which they were active: the foundation of ballet companies and schools in Constantinople, Paris, Copenhagen, and continuing work on choreography and artistic innovation.

Dance shifted its focus after the First World War and the Revolution and moved to the ballet of the Royal Opera in Copenhagen, London's Covent Garden and the New York City Ballet. In leading positions almost everywhere were dancers and choreographers with a Russian background: Serge Lifar, George Balanchine, Léonide Massine and Tatjana Gsovsky.

The Bolshevik Revolution and the succeeding 'Age of Steel' represented a profound caesura. Nevertheless, the ballet belonged to one of those traditions that outlived the revolutionary turmoil. In this respect it resembled elite organisations such as those involved in training engineers and technologists, the Academy of Sciences, the railways and other longstanding institutions essential to the support of the state that successfully survived systemic changes at least in part. Thus from time to time there were experiments with a new revolutionary ballet, such as *The Red Poppy*, but the restoration of the classical repertoire from the 1930s on was decisive.

On 17 April 1962, after a guest performance in Paris, a dancer from the Leningrad Kirov ensemble refused to board the plane for return to Moscow, while the rest of the ensemble flew on to London—clear evidence that a punishment was awaiting him. The dancer was Rudolf Khametovich Nureyev, born in 1938, who, together with his partner, had been a sensation in his appearances in Paris. The critics raved about his extravagant leaps and wildness but also his discipline, as well as the openness and evident curiosity he showed about Paris and the world of artists—all of whom wished to escape from the Cold War.[3] The East-West conflict had reached its climax; there had been defectors in both directions—Kim Philby and Oleg Penkovsky in 1963—and after Nureyev failed to return, others followed, including the dancer Mikhail Baryshnikov.

Following his defection, which had consequences for his relatives, colleagues and friends, Nureyev's stellar rise began into the world of celebrities, stars, the arty jet set and the international scene where artists, painters and politicians commingled. There was hardly anyone of note Nureyev did not have contact with in the thirty years up to his death, hardly any place of significance he failed to visit. The ballet world was in raptures. He was regarded as the reincarnation of Vaslav Nijinsky, the dancer of the century, and perhaps even as the greatest dancer of the twentieth century. His omnipresence in the newspapers and on TV is evidence of his unstoppable activity; he lived in a constant state of hypermobility. If we were to produce a catalogue of all his engagements—easily done since Nureyev's life was constantly monitored and observed, not to mention the many excellent biographies—we would still be left wondering just how he managed to fulfil his programme even given his extreme self-discipline. There were sometimes as many as three hundred appearances a year in locations around the globe: Paris, London, Copenhagen, New York, Toronto, Sydney, Atlanta, Buenos Aires, San Francisco, Berlin, Athens, Cairo, Beirut. Not until much later, not until the onset of perestroika, did he return to Leningrad and his hometown of Ufa in the Urals. Nureyev himself contributed to the publicity that surrounded him—with his bad manners, extravagances and loutish behaviour, his openly displayed homosexuality, his brazen show of opulence in The Dakota in Central Park. But it was his dancing that lay at the heart of the public's fascination. It thrilled thousands of people and if it did not actually trigger the rehabilitation of classical dance outside the Soviet Union, it undoubtedly provided a massive impetus. It was not so much the political scandal that surrounded him as his magical agility that made him appear like a shining comet whose lustre has not faded, even decades after his death.

Nureyev's dancing has been studied and analysed by professional observers, theatre and ballet critics and even nonexperts like me were spellbound by his appearances. I saw him in the Vienna State Opera and can no longer remember whether they were playing *Swan Lake*, *La Bayadère* or something altogether different.[4] What stayed in my memory was his gesture at the end of the performance, as he stepped in front of the curtain and bowed slightly to the audience, hand outstretched and right leg extended. He passed to his partner a rose that someone in the audience had thrown to him. His posture was sensational, what one might have referred to as 'natural grace' were it not for the fact that it was the result of years of training and the most stringent discipline conceivable. Analysing this graceful movement is far from easy. Describing its origins would involve accounting for its survival in conditions that—to put it mildly—were not always favourable.

To reconstruct Nureyev's movements and postures—or indeed those of anyone in his profession—we ought to take a look at the book that describes the theory and method that underpinned his

FIGURE 49.1. Rudolf Nureyev in Madrid in 1975. 'Since I had been forbidden to dance at home—and of course I couldn't stop dancing—I was forced to live a life full of lies. I had constantly to invent pretexts to leave the house and go to the exercises' (Elena Oboimina, *Rudol'f Nureev: Ia umru polubogom*, Algoritm, Moscow 2016, 27). © culture-images/GP.

training: Vera S. Kostrovitskaya's *School of Classical Dance: Textbook of the Vaganova Choreographic School*. This is where you can find the attempt to articulate the language of dance, as Ursula Kirsten-Collein, the German translator and editor of Kostrovitskaya's work, notes in the professional jargon of the ballet instructor.[5] In Kirsten-Collein's words, 'Dance is something indescribable. Dance lives because—like music—it can open up worlds in us that have no need of words.'[6] Despite her statement, it is possible to develop a language for movements, postures, positions and steps: 'Every emotional, spatial, musical and sculptural emanation of movements, postures and combinations can only be hinted at in words. After all, what is meant by "Effacé Devant; à la Seconde" when compared to the thrilling moment on the stage, and from the stage into the auditorium—a wave, a hand gesture, the line of a leg, the magic of the arms. All of this takes hold of our soul and stirs something indescribable in us.'

However serious the difficulties may be in 'notating' the language of movement and thus obtaining an idea of what is being described, the attempt has evidently been made—and not unsuccessfully, notwithstanding the limitations of the notation process. 'If, however, an aesthetic principle can be read between the lines, it is the law inherent in classical dance that beauty stems from the rightness, the logic and hence the harmonious coordination of movement. In other words, what proves to be most effective is whatever happens in an organic and functional manner and with the greatest economy.'

Kostrovitskaya's book, which reads like a dry, practical introduction to bodily movement, reproduces not the magic of dance—something that critics and observers strive to capture—but the almost mathematical dissection of the movements flowing through the body or articulated by it. The coordination of the arms, individual poses of a dancer's head and body, the relation to space as determined by the dancer's gaze, the relation to the body's core, that is, the body as key to the distribution of weight and hence to control of the body—all of these help to achieve a convincing technical and artistic effect. But what is required in addition is the development of an all-round personality, as can be seen from the subjects taught at ballet school: the classical languages, literature and history. Kostrovitskaya's pupil even arrives at the conclusion that 'Sense of responsibility, depend-

ability, readiness to help, conscious discipline (not to mention orderliness, cleanliness and punctuality) and right on to a sensitisation to
the other arts, but also the cultivation of a cultured lifestyle and a
sincere tact in human relations—all were crucial concerns in dealing
with the younger generation.[7]

The school of classical dance according to Vaganova sets out the
individual steps:

> Stability is one of the basic elements of classical dance. The stance
> of the body in the pose and in exercises on the whole foot, on demi-
> pointe and on pointe, on both legs and on one, must be assured
> and steady, without movement of the supporting leg and without
> hopping on it. Stability only acquires its aesthetic meaning (*aplomb*
> in its double meaning of stability and presence).
>
> To maintain prolonged stability on demi-pointe and on pointe
> on one leg in a fixed pose is difficult. And it is still more difficult
> not to lose the stability of a pose after landing on one foot from
> a big jump with a turn in the air, or in tours and pirouettes. The
> development of stability is begun in the first year with the train-
> ing of the legs and the body in the barre exercise through which
> the student acquires the ability to distribute the centre of the
> body's weight evenly on one or both legs. Generally speaking, for
> stability, the posture of the body must be vertical, without an
> inclination forward or back or a sagging in the waist; the back is
> erect and the buttocks muscles are tensed. The waist is strength-
> ened by the tension of the lower back muscles. However, in no
> case should the student attempt to hold the back by joining the
> shoulder blades, for this inevitably weakens the pulled up char-
> acter of the lower torso.
>
> The basis of stability lies in the preservation of the vertical axis,
> which passes through the middle of the head and body to the ball
> of the supporting foot, when one is standing on demi-pointe and
> in front of the heels when one is standing on the whole foot. To
> obtain stability in those cases where a bend of the body to the side
> or back or an inclination forward is required, the centre weight
> must be over the supporting leg, through which passes the vertical
> axis of the body.[8]

What is described here in relation to the *aplomb* is set out in detail for every other position and exercise—the *demi plié*, the *grand plié*, *relevé*, *battements*, and so forth. It is difficult for the lay observer to reconcile the elegant and apparently effortless flowing movements of the dancers with the mechanical descriptions of the positions and moves more reminiscent of the precise workings of a clock. But the detailed, moment-by-moment, 'calculated' reconstruction of the dancers' movements underpins what spectators see on the stage, without their having to be informed about how these were assembled. The magic of a single minute movement contains the anatomical knowledge and physical training of several generations of ballet teachers; each gesture contains a 'school', in this instance, the school of the Mariinsky Ballet, which in Soviet times had borne the name of Sergey Kirov, the Leningrad Party chief assassinated in 1934, but which had its old name restored to it in 1991.

Knowledge of dance is transmitted not primarily through books, but by working on movement, the ballet teacher together with pupils. This knowledge is then handed on from one teacher to the next, one ballet school to the next. The creation of the tradition is contingent on this living connection and transferred through lectures, demonstrations, imitations in the dance hall, rehearsals and actual performance. There is less emphasis on referring to passages in textbooks than on pointing to particular people, influential figures. Dancers, especially those who have achieved stardom, possess not only a particular talent but the accumulated labour of all those who set them on their path and onto the stages of the world.

No one had predicted that Rudolf Khametovich Nureyev would have a star-studded career. He was born into a Tatar-Bashkir family in 1938. His birth took place on the Trans-Siberian Express during his mother's journey to join his father, who was stationed in the Far East. His father, who later took part in the war, would go on to live modestly in Ufa. Nureyev's life was so full of events that it is difficult to give a coherent account of the extraordinary career that came to an end with his death in France in 1993. Growing up in humble circumstances in Ufa, he went to a kindergarten where singing and dancing were encouraged. He attended an ordinary school in the provinces, but one of his teachers taught English and, more especially, there was a dance teacher who had received her own training in prerevolutionary St. Petersburg and who noticed the talent of the young Rudolf (who was named after Rudolph Valentino, whose films his mother had admired in her youth).

The teacher's sharp eye for Rudolf's gifts as a dancer coincided with a selection system that sought out and assisted talented youngsters to send to Moscow or other cities. Rudolf attracted attention. Although he had no regular training in dance, he arrived at the dance school of the Leningrad Kirov Ballet in 1955—the school founded as far back as 1738 and located in Ulitsa Zodchego Rossi, St. Petersburg, since 1836. The elite training school of the Russian and later the Soviet ballet was situated in a street bordered by three theatres. There were rehearsal halls with bars, beams, classrooms and dormitories where the boys and girls were quartered—a kind of civilian barracks where early intimate friendships and rivalries were formed. The daily routine was strictly regimented. The structure of the programme can be followed in *School of Classical Dance*. But life did not consist solely of school and exercises. The city of Leningrad itself was a great educator. With its museums, palaces, monuments and façades, it was a highly concentrated cultural space. The Kirov Theatre was not just any old theatre; it was where Tamara Karsavina and Anna Pavlova had danced. Vaslav Nijinsky had appeared there. It was the theatre that had produced the talents who had written the history of ballet, men and women who were subsequently exported to the Bolshoi Theatre in the new capital city.

The teachers who taught Rudolf Nureyev had been instructed by people who received their own training before the Revolution. Their cultural style is easily recognisable in the photographs handed down. We can see how Alexander Ivanovich Pushkin, who taught Nureyev and Baryshnikov, conducted the exercises—in jacket and tie. We can see from the portrait of Natalia Dudinskaya, Nureyev's partner in his first solo performance, that she was herself very much the grande dame. And we can see the other friends and acquaintances he came to know or who took an interest in the young man from the provinces. They all belonged to the cultural milieu that was so concentrated and rich that it was able to survive the Revolution, the Civil War, the emigration of the elite and then the terrible period of the German siege—a milieu whose members could be recognised by their manners, their clothes, the books they admired and their habit of meeting up in the salon of the music shop director for readings, concerts and discussions. Even the leading teachers of the Kirov ensemble lived in shared apartments, like most of the members of the St. Petersburg intelligentsia. Rudolf Nureyev knew all about this world. It is the world that Brodsky described in *Less Than One*.[9] And it seems as if it was the respect for traditional cultural norms in the erstwhile capital of the Russian Empire that underpinned its own unconditional defence of formality.

Once he had come to the West, Nureyev regarded the rigour and the harsh discipline of his training as indispensable. That was the irreplaceable advantage of the school he had gone through in the Kirov. He had acquired his stature, his power and his self-confidence there—this too was the source of his boasting and arrogance towards the 'officials' in the corps de ballet whom he came to know later on, especially in Vienna. To his mind the school meant not only his teachers, Alexander Pushkin and Natalia Dudinskaya. It also included their predecessors, Agrippina Vaganova and the extraordinary Vakhtang Chabukiani.

Agrippina Yakovlevna Vaganova was born in 1879 not very far from the Mariinsky Theatre. She was accepted into the Imperial Ballet School when she was only ten; in 1897 she became a member of the corps de ballet. She made her appearance in the choreographies created by Marius Petipa and worked with stars of the St. Petersburg ballet scene such as Michel Fokine and Nikolay Legat.[10] Ballet suffered a setback during the Russian Revolution but was able to survive all its vicissitudes. The 1918/19 season contained productions of *Sleeping Beauty*, *Swan Lake*, *Raymonda*, *Giselle*, *Esmeralda* and *Chopiniana* among others.[11] It was fortunate that right up to the end of the 1920s, Fyodor Lopukhov, who strongly supported classical ballet but was also a champion of avant-gardist innovation, was the artistic director of the Mariinsky Theatre—he produced Beethoven's Fourth Symphony as a plotless 'symphonic ballet', almost anticipating the later Maurice Béjart (Lopukhov's sister, the dancer Lydia Lopokova, was a member of Diaghilev's ensemble and married to John Maynard Keynes).

In 1920 Vaganova took up teaching at a time when many of the best-known ballet teachers and dancers had gone into exile. She was a passionate instructor and produced the first Soviet ballerinas, including such outstanding dancers as Galina Ulanova. She showed no interest in avant-garde experiments in theatre, literature, art and ballet. She dismissed the modern movement as a destructive aberration. 'She believed in solid and lasting workmanship.' When the avant-gardist phase had passed and Lopukhov and 'Formalism' came under attack, she turned away from them. Shostakovich's *Golden Age* and *The Bolt* meant nothing to her—they were thought to be Western, un-Russian and bourgeois. In 1931 Vaganova was appointed artistic director of the Leningrad Ballet and stated that her primary duty was 'to preserve and revive ballets of Classical heritage'. Her second aim was to train new choreographers, and her third, to bring on a new generation of dancers. This tendency to restore classicism could be observed in every other branch of cultural life. This is where her *Basic Principles of Classical Ballet* came in, a textbook that became the authoritative work for the entire Soviet Union. Here she insisted on the autonomy of the Russian or Soviet ballet as distinct from the French or Italian varieties.[12] Following Kirov's assassination in 1934, the world of theatre and ballet had its victims too. One was the director Sergey Radlov. Maya Plisetskaya, who would become famous as prima ballerina of the Bolshoi Ballet, recalled that like her, many contemporaries in Moscow in 1937 had lost their parents 'in the same sweet Stalinist manner'—through imprisonment and the camps.[13] Shostakovich's ballet music *The Bright Stream* (1935) was sharply criticised; many ballet productions were cancelled because of the pervasive insecurity and climate of fear. Vaganova had to surrender her post as artistic director of the Kirov Ballet in December 1937, but she continued to teach and concentrated her energies on passing on the techniques of classical dance. Serge Lifar wrote to Vaganova from Paris in 1935, calling her 'the People's Artist, loved by Terpsichore in the Soviet country, loved by all of us in the whole world on whom today depends the Motherhood of dance and tradition.' Agrippina Vaganova died in Leningrad in 1951.[14]

There was a complete breakdown in the relationship between Nureyev and the Kirov ensemble, which had become the bastion of an increasingly conservative dance culture. The highly promising solo dancer of the world-famous Kirov ensemble developed into an international ballet star, gripping the imagination of a public that went well beyond the fans of classical dance. The breach came about because the Vaganova system had become too restrictive for him. It was glorious and far superior to other schools of dance as far as technique and training were concerned. But more recent developments had passed it by, much as the society to which the Kirov Ballet belonged seemed to have passed away.

With the end of the Stalin era and the arrival of the Thaw, the first signs of something new began to trickle through to the world behind the Iron Curtain. Guest performances by ballet companies and music ensembles made it possible to make comparisons. Above all, the skill and fame of artists, writers and scholars began to appear incompatible with constraints on their personal freedom of movement. Nureyev had become fed up with being shackled. It was not enough to take part in visits to Ryazan or the GDR. He wanted the freedom to travel more widely, to places where there were still pupils and heirs of Diaghilev, memories of Nijinsky and such creative minds as George Balanchine, people who continued to develop the older traditions. If classical ballet wished to retain its vitality, it would have to cast off the fetters of the excessively narrow Soviet canon.

PART XI

Kolyma: The Pole of Cold

Everything we know about suffering and death, about life and survival in the camps of the Far North is meaningless as long as we know nothing of the cold that pervades everything there nine months of the year. The cold is not an event or an episode but a condition that can lead to death unless precautions are taken or luck supervenes. The thermometer shows –50°C but only those who have been exposed to such a temperature can have any idea what it means. For everyone else 'the Siberian cold' is something they know only from hearsay; it is a literary cliché, perhaps a mere cultural construct.[1] The cold has killed off untold thousands of people. But the absence of those who can no longer speak is not the only explanation for the strange absence of the cold dimension from discussions of 'Stalinism'. It must have something to do with the limited imaginations of people who have been spared this experience. It leads us to the limits—or rather the heart—not of a climatic region but of a political order that was prepared to sacrifice everything for what it regarded as progress, including the human beings robbed of all protection. Kolyma, the name of the river in the extreme north of the Siberian Far East that flows into the Arctic Ocean, is associated in our minds with cold, slave labour and gold. Cold leads us to the capital of the Dalstroy empire. The Russian abbreviation stands for the 'Far North Construction Trust', which was established in 1931, a territory larger than the whole of Western Europe. Its unique wealth of mineral resources had been known since Tsarist times but exploiting them meant introducing a new regime of unprecedented brutality. The kingdom of Dalstroy swallowed up the life energies of the country for an ambitious project during which tens of thousands lost their lives. Its traces are still visible today.

Although Dalstroy was formally dissolved in 1957, it created a structure and a dependency from which the nation has been unable to free itself. The empire that reintroduced slave labour on such a massive scale itself came to an end because the work performed in it had proved to be not merely murderous but unproductive and the labourers had had enough of being enslaved. Traces of the abandoned camps still survive: the watchtowers and rolls of barbed wire.[2] What remains is the infrastructure: the capital, Magadan, port facilities, the highway, bridges and conveyor systems. People, young people especially, have been drifting away to the 'mainland', to warmer climes and to European Russia. Those who remain in the country of Eduard Berzin have to come to terms with this.

The territory of Kolyma at the northeastern end of the Eurasian Continent once lay beyond the bounds of the world. This almost inaccessible place could be reached only by boat from Vladivostok by landing in Nagaev Bay and going north from there. It is closer to Alaska, with which it has much in common, than to the Russian 'mainland'. The banks of the Kolyma River are inhabited by the indigenous Yakut and Evenk peoples but were settled during the twentieth century by colonists from all over the Soviet Empire. The area is now a multinational region of colonists, the vast majority of whom were brought there against their will: forced labourers serving out their sentences, deported peasants, criminals and people labelled as such, 'politicals' and people who were banished to the region or chose to settle there at the end of their sentences. After Dalstroy and the Gulag shut down, attempts were made to bolster the population of the region by a variety of material inducements—higher wages, longer leave. The terrain along the Kolyma is rocky with sparse vegetation; the river flows towards the northern ice seas, as do the Lena, the Ob and the Yenisei. Temperatures are extreme in winter—from 40° to 60° below zero. Photos from the pioneering days of the early 1930s and today's researchers on the lookout for traces of the olden days show an inhospitable, rocky landscape with stunted trees, reindeer herds and scattered settlements, all of which were established to wrest mineral riches from the stony soil: gold, tungsten, tin, diamonds, uranium and cobalt—resources that were supposed to make the country wealthy, while in the event they exacted a massive human toll.[3]

Yevgeniya Ginzburg: 'Minus 49 Degrees Celsius'

As a young woman and a passionate communist, Yevgeniya Ginzburg (1904–1977) was arrested in 1937 and then spent fifteen years in prisons and camps, with the longest single period in Kolyma. Her

memoirs *Into the Whirlwind* and *Within the Whirlwind* are among the
most shattering accounts of the Soviet Gulag world.[4] One chapter in
Within the Whirlwind—'Minus 49 Degrees Celsius'—is devoted to the
cold, which was a matter of life and death for the inmates. Minus
49° or 50° was the crucial question, one that might decide a human
being's fate: did you have to go out into the cold or could you stay in
the barracks? 'November, December, January, February. . . . For me,
life each day began with precisely this argument: minus 49 or minus
50 degrees?'[5] Hence the significance of the thermometer: 'The thermometer hung on the black log wall of the guard hut. It seemed an
anachronism; it was as if the universe had already succumbed to
some general cataclysm, while here on earth—otherwise restored to
the very first, primordial days of creation—this memento of a lost
civilisation had happened to survive. . . . Minus 49 degrees Celsius
was the worst possible reading of all, because the official humanity of the medical regulations could come into operation only when
the thermometer read minus 50 degrees. Minus 50 degrees meant
that the administration could cancel work in the forest that day.' The
beauty of the subpolar winter was lethal. 'There were low, sugar-loaf
hills, faultless in their symmetry. At night the sky blazed with galax-
ies that were somehow oppressively ancient, taking the imagination
back to the first beginnings.' But the ground was frozen solid, too
hard to bury the dead, who for that reason were piled up in heaps
in the snow until they were washed away by the melting snow in the
spring. Because of the cold it was too risky to go outside where there
was any amount of firewood to heat the room and where there were
ptarmigans and woodcock which would provide food aplenty. Even
the barrack walls were iced up. 'Incidentally, the reference to huts . . .
is not meant to be taken at face value. Only the one set aside for the
guards bore any resemblance to a proper hut. Our quarters were two
sagging shacks, barnacled with ice, overlaid with snow, and with holes
in the roofs. Every day, we had to plug these holes anew with lengths
torn from old, cast-off duffle coats.'[6] During the day Ginzburg was
outdoors sawing wood with the temperature at –49°, but at least she
was working close to the barracks, unlike others who were out in the
taiga felling trees. Ginzburg was saved by the fact that she was able to
work at the infirmary, thanks to her friendship with a fellow inmate

who was a doctor and her own experience as a medical orderly—this made her a 'privileged worker'. The post of doctor's assistant was in a sense one affording the privilege of survival, but it was equally one from which suffering and death could be witnessed in all their gradations and grim detail. The doctors, nurses and orderlies employed in the hospital barracks became some of the most important witnesses and analysts of doom and rescue.

The evidence that could provide a foundation for research into the complex 'Cold and the Camps' remains unexplored, buried in the archives of the departments in charge of ensuring that the inmates were still able to work and hence of the sanitary and hygienic regulations. These departments were also required to maintain sickness statistics and mortality charts. The 'archive revolution' since perestroika has shed light on internal life in Dalstroy, although up to now analysis of the physical and mental well-being of the forced labourers does not appear to have been the principal focus of attention.[7] Research into all the problems associated with people's adaptation to extreme climatic and environmental conditions is still only in its infancy. This is all the more remarkable since Russia has always possessed a culture of adjusting to and dealing with the extremes of climate and nature, a culture that has left its traces in the most subtle ramifications of everyday life right down to the present. It has developed a series of routines and practices in its efforts to come to terms with the cold. These vary from adapting one's clothing to different conditions, through constructing buildings resistant to the cold and technologies appropriate to living in the permafrost—the 'eternal ice'—right down to cold-resistant methods of transportation. Since a significant part of Russian/Soviet territory is in the polar and subpolar regions, there have always been good geographical reasons for taking a great interest in researching different ways of adapting to Arctic and sub-Arctic conditions—in this respect Russia is just like Canada, Finland or Alaska.[8]

This interest was concentrated on geological, geodetic, cartographical, economic and ethnological questions and was part of a particular desire to unlock the unexplored worlds of the Far North: Siberia as a frontier.[9] The battle in and against the cold became a public topic in the rescue action to save the crew of the *Chelyuskin*, which had

FIGURE XI.1. Masks to protect the face against the wind and cold, made between 1948 and 1953. 'Working was hard at minus 40–50°. Icicles froze on your nose and had to be removed somehow or other. Breathing was difficult, your lungs felt as if they were burning. Your eyelashes also froze. It was hard to keep your eyes open; you had to warm up the eyelids with your hands and remove the ice. . . . No sooner had we left the slopes and got back onto the path than the wind blasted you head-on and if there was even the smallest hole or tear in your clothing, the wind cut you to the bone. But you just had to protect your face somehow. The workers building the roads went to work with homemade masks they had patched together out of old vests. The masks had three holes—for the eyes and mouth—and greatly resembled the Ku Klux Klan hoods, except they were more unsightly. You wore a cap with earmuffs. We didn't have such masks and tried to walk sideways, using our shovels to shield us from the wind' (V. M. Lazarev, 'Das Jahr 1937 mit den Augen eines Augenzeugen', in *Pozhivshi v GULAGe: Sbornik vospominanii*, Moscow 2001, 7, 69). © Gulagmuseum Moscow. Photo: culture-images/fai.

been trapped in the Arctic ice in 1934, in the rescue of the Papanin expedition to the North Pole in 1936 and also in the flight across the North Pole. As a result, research into human behaviour under the extreme climatic conditions of the Far North has a long history. In the same way, during the phase of East-West rivalry the race to open up the polar regions, the last 'undiscovered continent', was of high importance.

But even when the polar theme was taken up again in the 1950s, the experience of the hundreds of thousands of forced labourers in the polar regions was not addressed. In December 1957, Vostok, the Soviet research station, was established in the Antarctic–1,300 kilometres from the coast and at a height of 3,500 metres–the aim was to demonstrate Soviet superiority over America and the limitless possibilities of opening up the South Pole. Inevitably, questions about how human beings could adapt to extreme conditions became the focus of extensive research projects. Natural resources were to be sought and towns would be built in the icy Antarctic wastes to provide a base not just for well-trained young men and expedition members, but for entire families. Accordingly, it was essential to discover how and whether the human organism could adapt to the conditions of extreme cold–down to–70°C–to the lack of oxygen, the four-month-long polar night and other exigencies. The *polyarniki*–the crew of the Vostok polar station–were subjected to extensive and regular medical checks for changes in their blood count, hormone balance, peripheral nervous system and mental state. This process was supposed to lead to practical recommendations for building stations–the right food, work rhythms and, above all, appropriate clothing. The heyday of 'polar medicine' fell in the 1960s and 1970s, and brought important insights into the health implications of extreme conditions: dizziness and flickering in the eyes, earpain and nosebleeds, sharp rise in blood pressure, choking, muscle and joint pains, sleeplessness, loss of appetite, and so on to rapid weight loss–all symptoms of polar stress. Abnormal lighting conditions and life in closed male communities brought on conflicts and gave rise to depression. Where men were healthy, well trained and warmly clad, the process of adaptation lasted up to three months. Work in the open air in these conditions was possible only to a limited degree. 'In the Vostok station,' admitted Sergey Bushmanov, a thirty-four-year-old physicist, after his expedition in 2009–2011, 'man does not live, he slowly dies.'[10]

It is all the more surprising that (to my knowledge) no Soviet studies on survival in extreme conditions refer to experiences in Kolyma, the Pole of Cold. There is an entire branch of research and numerous studies on the 'subjective feelings and physical state of overwintering (*zimovniki*)', on the susceptibility to particular illnesses and psychological conditions.[11] There have been investigations into blood circulation and the respiratory system, metabolism, immunological and

dermatological reactions; new methods of thermometry and ther-
mography have been tried out; comparisons have been made between
the behaviour of the indigenous population and new arrivals—but
this has all been achieved without reference to the experience of the
camps in Norilsk, Vorkuta or Kolyma.[12]

A further collection of essays—'Current Issues of Adaptation and
of the Life-Support Systems of Man in the Antarctic'—sets out to
explore the uses of polar medicine for improving health services for
the Soviet population. It asks how to improve the quality of cold-
resistant winter clothing, how to modernise temperature control and
hygiene facilities in buildings—but all this without any reference to
the massive experience of the world of the camps.[13] But there are
other witnesses and testimonies.

Varlam Shalamov's Kolyma Stories:
The Record of Death by Freezing

In a text of 1961, 'What I Saw and Understood in the Camps', Varlam
Shalamov, survivor of seventeen years on the Kolyma and together
with Alexander Solzhenitsyn author of the most devastating accounts
of the Gulag universe, wrote: 'The main means for depraving the soul
is the cold. Presumably in Central Asian camps people held out longer,
for it was warmer there.'[14] In 1954, after returning to Moscow from the
camp, he began to write his momentous *Kolyma Stories*.[15] It is perhaps
no mere coincidence that the German communist Trude Richter, in
her reflections on 'happiness' following her return to the GDR, should
put the 'cold' at the top of her list: 'I do not want to freeze! Forced for
years to spend the whole day in the open at minus 40–50°, badly fed
and inadequately clothed, I have learned how the frost can blot out all
your thoughts and feelings in a trice and reduce your entire being to
a miserable, shivering lump of flesh, which is then destroyed.'[16] Shalamov's stories go far beyond the problem of the cold and embrace the
entire universe of the camps: landscapes of death, biographies of the
people cast away and stranded there, lives of the so-called politicals
and the criminals or alleged criminals, the guards and those they were
guarding, the entire multinational cosmos, the camp as the represen-

tative centre of society, the camp capital as the capital of a society, a field for social experimentation, the centre of a universe.

Why the theme of the labor camps. The camp theme, broadly interpreted, in its fundamental sense, is the foundational and chief question of our day. Is the destruction of man with the help of the state not the main question for our time, for our ethics, that has entered into the psychology of every family? This question is much more important than the theme of war. War in some sense plays the role of psychological camouflage (history says that in times of war the tyrant draws closer to the people). They want to hide the 'camp theme' behind the statistics of war, statistics of any kind.[17]

Shalamov takes the cold seriously. He does not use it as a metaphor, an image, but as brute fact. The ability to reduce things is grounded in the futile, hopeless situation that allows for no relief, no alleviation. 'For prisoners, hope is a form of shackling. Hope is always an absence of freedom. A man who has hopes of something changes his behaviour, is more likely to go against his conscience than a man who has no hope.'[18] The only remaining option is to make a record of what he sees and witnesses. 'I trust the official record; I myself am a fact recorder, a fact hunter by profession, but what can one do if there are no such records? No personal files, no archives, no patient notes?' Shalamov's fear that one might forget one's own experience and that of one's contemporaries was and is all too justified. 'The documentation of our past has been destroyed, the guard towers have been sawn down, the barracks razed to the ground, the rusty barbed wire has been rolled up and taken away somewhere else. The rosebay willow herb—the flower of fires, of oblivion, the enemy of archives and human memory—has flowered over the ruins of the Serpantika [the place of mass executions in 1937]. "Did we exist?" I reply, "We did" with all the expressiveness of an official statement, with the responsibility, the precision of a document.'[19]

The ultimate guarantee of the document's validity is the body—one's own and that of one's fellow prisoners—and the alterations that can be observed in the process of exhaustion and emaciation. The body vouches for the authenticity of Shalamov's message to his contemporaries and posterity. 'One must and can write a story that is indistinguishable from a document. But the author must research his material with his own hide; not only with his heart but with every pore of his skin, his every nerve.'[20] As a writer, Shalamov was capable of expressing these experiences and as a medical orderly he became a specialist in case histories and camp pathologies. He could act as a companion to the dying—as well as a diagnostician such as can be produced only by extreme situations. He became an expert on 'alimentary dystrophy'—'starvation', in other words—with all of its symptoms: avitaminosis, polyavitaminosis, severe scurvy, pellagra, flu-like lung infections, heart failure and, again and again, frostbite. Shalamov was the expert forced to observe that 'No textbook of prisoners' diseases had yet been written. It never was.'[21] In a subsequent discussion of his story 'Cherry Brandy' [Sherri-brendi]—the story deals with Mandelstam's death in a transit camp near Vladivostok in 1938—he insists on fact-like precision and the nonmetaphorical nature of his account of his death. 'Here one finds an almost clinical description of death from nutritional edema, or simply speaking, from hunger, that same hunger of which Mandelstam died. . . . Here the death of a man is described. Is that really too little?'[22] This meticulous description, the product of precise observation, strikingly resembles that of Primo Levi—a chemist by profession—in his laconic scientific account of the physical deterioration of victims in Auschwitz.[23]

The *Kolyma Stories* deliver a phenomenology of cold not as a collection of isolated episodes but as an all-embracing condition that permeates everything, a condition in which people dressed in rags and cloth or rubber galoshes are utterly defenceless as they shuffle along. The clothing was never adequate—a padded-cotton winter jacket was supposed to last two years, padded winter trousers eighteen months; one pair of felt boots every two years, underwear every nine months—those were the allocations for 1943.[24] We might well read the *Stories* as an analysis of camp clothing. The textile engineer Garkunov dies because he refuses to hand over a woollen pullover; woollen pullovers were a matter of life and death for a man chopping down trees in the taiga ['On the Slate', 9]. Workers slept in their clothes—cap, tunic, pea jacket and padded trousers. How enviable were the foremen and brigade leaders who could afford reindeer-skin caps, Yakut boots or a short white fur jacket! Descriptions of nature are similarly grounded in the experience of the cold: 'In winter everything turned to ice. The mountains, the rivers, and the bogs seemed in winter to be one and the same being, ominous and hostile.' White mist, a small copse bowed down by the wind, a tunnel covered by metre-high snowdrifts—these always spell mortal danger. Earlier experiences of terror in prison seem less terrible: 'Now that they were here in the camp, the bright, clean, warm pre-trial prison, which they had so recently and so infinitely long ago left, seemed to absolutely everyone the best place on earth.'[25] Even the transition to brighter days in the summer months contains the risk of being blinded if eyes are not protected against the dazzling light reflected from the snow-covered ground.[26] As in Ginzburg, thermometers are often mentioned:

> The workmen were not allowed to see a thermometer, and they didn't need one. No matter what the temperature was, they had to go to work. In any case, the old hands could tell almost exactly how many degrees below zero it was. If there was a frosty mist, then it was minus forty centigrade outside; if there was a noise when you breathed out but you could still breathe normally, then it was minus forty-five; if your breath was noisy and you were out of breath, then it was minus fifty. Below fifty-five degrees a gob of spit freezes solid in mid-air. Spit had been freezing in mid-air for two weeks. Potashnikov woke up each morning hoping that the freezing temperatures had abated. After last winter, experience told him that, however cold it was, what you needed to feel warm was a sharp change in temperature, a contrast. Even if the weather got no warmer than minus forty or minus forty-five, you'd feel warm for a couple of days, and there was no point making any plans for longer than two days. But there was no let-up in the cold, and Potashnikov realized that he could not stand it anymore.

> Potashnikov 'had realized a long time ago what caused this dulling of the spirit, this cold lack of sympathy. The same cold that turned saliva to ice in mid-air had gotten to the human soul. If your bones

could freeze, then your brain could freeze into insensitivity and so could your soul. You couldn't think about anything in the freezing cold. Everything was simple. A cold hungry brain couldn't take in nutrition, the brain cells withered; this was clearly a physical process, and God knew if the pathosis could ever be reversed, as a medical man would put it, like frostbite, or if the destruction was permanent. That was what happened to the soul: it froze, it shrank, and, maybe, it would stay cold forever. All this had occurred to Potashnikov before, and now all that was left was a desire to endure, to outlive the spell of freezing cold.' Even the interior of the barracks where you 'could be warm for a day' offered no respite. 'The two of them barely had the strength to open the door, which had frozen shut. A red-hot iron stove was burning in the middle of the carpentry shop, and five carpenters, without jackets or hats, were bent over their workbenches. The two new arrivals kneeled in front of the stove's open door, worshiping the god of fire, one of humanity's first gods. They took off their gloves and held out their hands to the heat, almost shoving them into the fire. Their fingers, so often frostbitten, had lost their sensitivity and took time to feel the heat. After a minute, Grigoriev and Potashnikov took off their hats and undid their pea jackets but remained kneeling.'[27] Frostbite became a constant source of pain:

> If you remember the unheated damp barracks, with a thick layer of ice filling all the crevices inside, as if a tallow candle had melted in a corner of the barracks . . . the bad clothing and starvation rations, the frostbitten digits (frostbite meant everlasting agony, even if amputation was not resorted to); if you imagine how frequent were the inevitable appearances of flu, pneumonia, all sorts of chills and of tuberculosis in these marshy mountains, so fatal for anyone with heart trouble; if you recall the epidemics of self-harming by chopping off a limb or a digit; if you also consider the appalling moral dejection and the hopelessness, then you can easily see how much more dangerous clean air was to human health than prison. . . . It is difficult to form a true idea of this in advance, for everything there is too unusual, too improbable, and a poor human brain is simply incapable of conceiving concrete images of life there.[28]

The precision with which Shalamov registers the symptoms of the typical diseases of the camp population is astonishing. His descriptions are almost literal copies of the camp doctors' reports that Golfo Alexopoulos was able to evaluate: pellagra, dystrophy, physical and psychic exhaustion, which were chiefly the result of systematic undernourishment and lack of vitamins. In many respects they remind us of the accounts of German concentration camps and Robert Jay Lifton's analysis of the role of medicine in the German camp system.[29]

Even when the weather was milder, the dampness, the constant cold was still there. 'The bosses were relying on the rain, the cold streams of water lashing our backs. We had long been wet through—not to our underwear, though, because we didn't have any underwear. The bosses' crude secret calculation was that rain and wind would make us work. . . . The nights were too short to dry out our pea jackets; at night we nearly managed to get the tunics and trousers dry on our bodies.' But where horses could not stand a month of life here in the winter, in cold stables with hours and hours of heavy labor in subzero temperatures, human beings held out.[30]

For the systematic demolition of a human being—you might almost call it destruction 'by scientific design'—camp jargon coined the term *dokhodyaga*, a goner, a man reduced by his suffering to the point where he hovers between life and death, but is closer to death. Such people were known as 'Muselmänner' (Muslims) in the German concentration camps. Shalamov evokes this process in a few sentences in his story 'The Tatar Mullah and Clean Air':

In the camps, however, to turn a healthy young man, who had begun his career in the clean winter air of the gold mines, into a goner, all that was needed, at a conservative estimate, was a term of twenty to thirty days of sixteen hours of work per day, with no rest days, with systematic starvation, torn clothes, and nights spent in temperatures of minus sixty degrees in a canvas tent with holes in it, and being beaten by the foremen, the criminal gang masters, and the guards. The length of time required has been proven many times. Brigades that start the gold-mining season (the brigades are named after their foremen) have, by the end of the season, not a single man left alive from the start of the season, except for the

foreman and one or two of the foreman's personal friends. The rest
of the brigade is replaced several times over the summer. A gold
mine constantly discards its production refuse into the hospitals,
the so-called convalescent teams, invalid settlements, and mass
graves.[31]

The cold of the snowy wastes was also the greatest obstacle to
any attempts to escape. 'It's understandable why no escapes took
place in winter. . . . It's impossible to run away from Kolyma.'[32] There
was no point in even trying since nature herself had created a lethal
frontier. Notwithstanding this, there were repeated attempts, despite
the cold, thousands of German shepherd dogs and a huge supply of
guard posts, as well as the threat of a death sentence.

To cap it all, not even the earth could receive the dead. In the world
of permafrost there were no graves and when the ice thawed in the
spring and the snow retreated from the mountains, this became the
stage for a macabre 'camp mystery':

> In Kolyma bodies are consigned not to the earth but to the stones.
> Stone preserves and reveals secrets. Stones are more reliable than
> earth. Permafrost preserves and reveals secrets. Every one of those
> close to us who perished in Kolyma, everyone who was shot, beaten
> to death, exsanguinated by starvation, can still be identified, even
> after decades. There were no gas ovens in Kolyma. The corpses
> wait in the stones, in the permafrost. . . . The harsh winters and hot
> summers, the winds and rain had in six years taken the corpses
> away from the stone. The earth had opened and shown its under-
> ground stores, for the Kolyma's underground stores contain not
> just gold, not just lead, not just wolfram, not just uranium but un-
> decomposed human bodies. These human bodies were crawling
> down the slope, perhaps about to be resurrected.[33]

Shalamov speaks here explicitly of the mass shootings under Colonel S. N. Garanin, the so-called Garaninshchina in the Serpantika
camp in which 5,866 prisoners, mainly politicals, were murdered in
1938, almost half of the 12,566 condemned in Dalstroy in the same
year.[34] The mass operations of the 'Great Terror', that 'excess of

excess' as Alec Nove termed it, to which almost one million people fell victim in the course of a single year, exacted a specially high tribute in the camps. 'For many months the morning and evening roll calls involved the reading out of countless death sentences. In temperatures of minus 50, musicians who were non-political prisoners [from the group of *bytoviki*, the prisoners who had been sentenced for minor offences—K.S.] would play a flourish before and after the announcement of each death order. The smoking gas lanterns failed to disperse the darkness; they merely drew hundreds of eyes to the frosted sheets of thin paper on which those terrible words were typed.'[35]

The overwhelming number of people who met their deaths in the camps died of hunger, so-called alimentary dystrophy, cold, beatings, diseases, sheer exhaustion and wasting away. The camps were unable to cope with the hundreds of thousands of prisoners who had been 'delivered'; the infrastructure was inadequate, as were the accommodations and provisions. There were epidemics of typhus and dysentery. The deportation trains were unheated; there was not enough clothing, least of all for winter conditions. People often lay together—men and women, the sick and the healthy, patients with consumption or postoperative conditions; prisoners too weak for the long marches died where they stood. The total numbers of people forced through the camps and labour colonies between 1929 and 1953 has been estimated—with variations up and down—at around 18 million Soviet citizens. Adding the camp inmates together with those forcibly settled outside the camps totals 28.7 million forced labourers in the Soviet Union.[36] In the Dalstroy region there were around 170,000 forced labourers in place at the end of the 1930s.[37] The question of how many of these lost their lives through acts of violence—executions, beatings, murders at the hands of camp criminals—and how many through hunger and bad treatment, in other words, the question of how to explain the extraordinarily high mortality rates, will remain unanswered as long as the records remain unexamined. Of the 16,000 prisoners transported to Kolyma in the first year only 9,928 were still alive on arrival in Magadan.[38] There can be no doubt that forced labour and the camps affected millions of Soviet families.

Eduard Berzin's Villa and Gold

Shalamov arrived in Kolyma in 1937 at a time when Eduard Berzin was at the very zenith of his powers as the master of Kolyma. In the space of a few years he had built settlements, the highway and the camps. But in December 1937 Berzin was summoned to Moscow and shortly before arriving there on 19 December, he was taken off the train and arrested. The accusation against him and his entire team, which had built Dalstroy, was of spying on behalf of Japan and Britain, attempted coup and Trotskyism. Like thousands of other prisoners transported to Vladivostok via the Trans-Siberian route and from there by boat to Nagaev Bay, Shalamov had presumably passed the Rose Villa, the house previously lived in by the lord and master of the entire Far East and his family.[39] Shortly before his arrest, Berzin had journeyed to Italy with his wife, his first holiday after years of strenuous labour building the camp. The couple visited Venice, Florence, Rome and Sorrento, and made detours to Berlin and Paris. Eduard Berzin had earned this holiday, much as he had previously earned the highest distinctions. These included the Order of the OGPU in 1934 and the Order of Lenin in 1936. The Politburo and Stalin personally were impressed and even excited about his energy, his genius for organisation and the results of his efforts. Dalstroy delivered gold. The gold of Kolyma furnished the financial reserves required for Stalin's industrialisation programme.[40]

Photos of Berzin from the 1930s reveal an impressive figure standing beside a Rolls Royce and dressed in a gently flowing bearskin coat. He had himself photographed with his privately educated son, Petya, an image of the kind that might be found in the family album of an American millionaire. This is even truer of portraits of his wife Elza Yanovna Mittenberg. These reveal a lady with a fashionable hairdo, clothed in the 1930s style based on Parisian haute couture, with furniture undoubtedly taken from affluent middle-class or aristocratic homes in St. Petersburg or Moscow, along with a grand piano. Even if there is as yet no biography of the remarkable Berzin, some pieces of the puzzle can be put together. Some come from Shalamov himself, who came to know Berzin personally in the first place he was banished.

Eduard Petrovich Berzin was born on 7 February 1894 in Livonia, into a Latvian peasant family, and then moved with his family to the outskirts of Riga. There he attended a town school, followed by studies to be a painter. Since he wanted to be an artist, he moved to Berlin in 1913 and studied at the Academy of Fine Arts, where he met his wife, Elza Yanovna Mittenberg, who had studied at the Institute for Fine Arts in Riga. She hoped to continue her studies in St. Petersburg, but in the First World War Berzin was conscripted into the Tsarist army, where he distinguished himself by his bravery and was awarded a number of medals, among them the Cross of St. George. In 1917 he became an officer. In the October Revolution he took the side of the Bolsheviks and was made commander of the First Artillery Division of the Red Latvian Riflemen, which became a sort of praetorian guard to the Bolshevik leaders. The division was entrusted with protecting Lenin himself in his move to the new capital of Moscow and played a key role in suppressing the uprising of the left Socialist Revolutionaries in Moscow in 1918. Berzin played an outstanding part in exposing the Lockhart affair, an intrigue of the British secret services that was supposed to lead to the fall of the Bolsheviks. He was present on every front fighting the Whites—much like almost everyone called Berzin, even though the name was the only thing they had in common. He was involved in the All-Russian Cheka and also on the Executive Committee of the Comintern. Both soon brought him into contact with Felix Dzerzhinsky. In 1927 he proposed building a paper and cellulose combine in Vishera in the northern Urals. For this he travelled with a group of engineers to Germany and the United States in search of modern technology and equipment. With the aid of the machinery brought in from abroad, the cellulose combine was ready in the shortest possible time—eighteen months, in fact—thanks to the use of seventy thousand condemned prisoners. Shalamov wrote up his Vishera experiences in an antinovel.[41] This experience was one of the most important steps towards establishing the Gulag as a reservoir of labour in the so-called corrective labour camps. Together with the White Sea–Baltic Canal, Vishera set a precedent. Stalin personally charged Berzin with opening up the Kolyma territory and appointed him director of the Dalstroy project on 14 November 1931. 'As head of Dalstroy, the enterprise established to manage the Soviet

Far East, he had unlimited power over vast tracts of north-eastern Siberia. He single-handedly represented virtually all the branches of Soviet power: the party, the executive, the prosecution, the judiciary and the army. In exchange, the Kremlin expected just one thing—as much gold as possible.'[42]

On 4 February 1932, after a sea journey across the Sea of Okhotsk accompanied by an icebreaker, Berzin reached Nagaev Bay, which would eventually become the principal harbour of the new region. He was joined by a team he had chosen himself, consisting of mining engineers, guards—including many of his colleagues and comrades from Vishera—and a group of prisoners. A little later, he sent for his wife and children. Berzin spent all his time on the building sites and in the key points of the camps, not arriving home until late in the evenings.

> 'The children,' Elza explains, 'wanted to spend more time with him, but they only saw one another at breakfast and dinner. He only went hunting with Petia once; they shot three ducks and a wild goose. What a joy that was!' ... Berzin liked music and the couple used to listen to Tchaikovsky, Schubert and Grieg. 'We had a lot of good records by the Philadelphia Orchestra that Eddie had brought back from America on an official trip in 1930.' Their twelve-year-old [son] Petia was learning to play the piano. Their fifteen-year-old daughter Mirza grew flowers in the garden next to their house, including roses, which gave her father great joy. The children performed in the school theatre group run by actor-prisoners.

There were ambitious performances with directors likewise from among the prisoners, but also with stars from Moscow on a guest tour through the forced-labour colonies in the Far East. Chez Berzin there were productions of scenes from *Boris Godunov*, *Rusalka* and *Eugene Onegin*. '"It is better for the children in Magadan than in Moscow," wrote Elza Yanovna in her memoirs, "because they [have] lots of fresh air and space. On the whole, one can live quite well in the north."'[43]

In Moscow, in the circles of the Five-Year planners 'dazzled by their successes', Berzin must have appeared as a kind of star who could solve all financial problems by delivering gold and ever more gold. It amounted to half a tonne the first year; three years later, there were 14 tonnes; by 1936, 30 tonnes. But this comet-like rise was not enough to save him and in fact may have contributed to his downfall. He was accused of having organised a 'Kolyma anti-Soviet spy ring, an organisation of rebels, terrorists and saboteurs'. On 18 April 1938 he was expelled from the Communist Party together with twenty-one of his Kolyma colleagues and on 1 August 1938 he was condemned to death and executed by the Military Commission of the Supreme Court of the USSR for 'high treason', 'undermining state industry', 'carrying out terrorist acts', and 'organised activities aimed at destroying the existing order'. The ruler of the empire of Dalstroy, of the tens-of-thousands-strong army of forced labourers, and the provider of gold treasure was accused of being an enemy of the people and a spy who was supposed to have delivered the Kolyma gold to the Japanese! His family shared the fate of all families of prominent 'enemies of the people'. His wife Elza spent nine years in the camps; his son, Petya, went from an orphanage straight to the front and fell at Stalingrad. His daughter, Mirza, was taken in by her grandmother. Today a bust on the main square in Magadan commemorates Berzin. It was built in 1989 to commemorate the fiftieth anniversary of the awarding of a city charter to the Far Eastern port. Berzin's granddaughter was present at the ceremony and a street was named after him.

Berzin's career was breath-taking but not entirely untypical of the generation of young men who had grown up in the boom times and the turmoil of the later Tsarist Empire and been given the opportunity to rise in the Empire's educational corridors; whose principal experience had been surviving the Great War and the conquest of power after the fall of the ancien régime. As a twenty-year-old, Berzin—like many of his contemporaries—had already led several lives: the Latvian village; Riga, the booming Baltic metropolis; the Bohemian life of Wilhelminian Berlin; entry into the Tsarist army; and the rise of a member of a national minority from the western periphery of the Empire to the commanding heights of power and indeed the very heart of the state apparatus at the moment it destroyed the anti-Bolshevik forces in the Civil War. With the downfall of the Empire, the path was open for plans and projects that had long since been designed but could not

be implemented. Now the ruthless authority and expert personnel
needed to make them a reality were available. The members of discriminated minorities have always been especially energetic, eager to
achieve and better themselves socially. Berzin and many like him had
seen the world and felt something of the power of globalisation processes; they were just as fascinated by the achievements of the Silver
Age as by those of America and the New World, which had opened
up beyond the frontiers of 'Old Europe'—they were the modernists
who could get to work now that all obstacles had been thrust aside
by revolution. The conquest of the extreme North and the Far East
represented something like a frontier to a generation that now saw its
opportunity to rescue an entire continent from historical irrelevance
and carry out its *mission civilisatrice,* just as the most energetic and
ruthless pioneers of the European colonial powers had done in Africa
and Asia. It was an age of fantasy projects without precise calculation, carried out by adventurers and managerial figures in midcareer,
working in a society that had lost all possibilities of self-defence and
provided unlimited human resources. They had the necessary abilities and were on their way to becoming the pioneers of construction,
transcontinental and global actors.

Myths such as those concerning the savage north existed to be
refuted or to be made reality. Where icy wastes were to be found,
greenhouses and artificial paradises were introduced. There was
nothing that could not become reality. Even Bukharin on the eve of
his execution could dream of working as a museum director or gar-
dener in the icy wastes of northeast Siberia. The artificial biotope on
the Arctic Circle was not just an idiosyncratic idea: the monks in the
monastery on the Solovetsky Islands had built greenhouses there
as early as the sixteenth century and one of Berzin's colleagues in
building the Vishera cellulose combine, Tamarin, likewise a former
Tsarist officer, turned out to be a marvellous rose breeder. He had
gone to Kolyma with Berzin in order to build sovkhozy for producing
food, especially cabbage, for the prison population.[44] Looked at from
this angle, Kolyma is no remote province, nor the end of the world,
but a place of decision, a frontier in the wild east. One can even detect
this in Shalamov's description of the Kolyma highway, which had been
built on blood and bones:

The highway is Kolyma's artery and main nerve. . . . The refectories are places where you see geologists and prospectors for mining parties going on leave with their ruble bonuses, black-market tobacco and tea sellers, northern heroes and northern swine. Pure alcohol is always on sale in the refectories. People meet, argue, fight, exchange news, and are always in a hurry. . . . This is where you see nice tidy groups of prisoners being taken up-country to the taiga, and filthy heaps of human slag being brought down from up-country, back from the taiga. Here you see the special-operations search parties, hunting for escaped prisoners. And you see the escaped prisoners, too, often wearing military uniform. Here the chiefs, the lords of everyone's life and death, ride in ZIS limousines. A playwright ought to see this—it is in a roadside that you get the best scenes of the north.[45]

For Shalamov it was not Berzin who was the puzzle but the entourage who supported him: the artists and sculptors who portrayed him, the salon he hosted with his wife.

Something else is harder to understand. Why does talent not find enough inner strength, enough moral fiber to treat itself with respect and not to revere uniform and rank?

Why does an able sculptor make a statue of some Gulag boss with enthusiasm and self-abandon and reverence? Where is the compelling attraction for an artist in a Gulag boss? . . .

Well, let's say that an artist, a sculptor, a poet, or a composer may be inspired by an illusion, that he may be caught up in and carried away by a burst of emotion and then create some symphony, interested as he is only by the current of colors, the current of sounds. But why, all the same, should this current be generated by the figure of a Gulag boss?

Why does a scientist draw formulas on a blackboard for the same Gulag boss and feel inspired by this figure in his engineering searches for materials? Why does a scientist feel such reverence for some boss of a sub-camp? Only because he is the boss.

Scientists, engineers and writers, intellectuals who have ended up in chains, are ready to be sycophants for any semiliterate fool.

Shalamov never ceased to condemn people with a subaltern spirit, especially if they were members of the intelligentsia: 'All my life I have been observing the slavish self-abasement and self-degradation of the intellectuals, not to mention the other strata of society.'[46]

The frontier turns into a site for the creation of society. The same may be said of Yevgeniya Ginzburg, who also found herself in Magadan, admittedly some years after Berzin, and had imported a piano made by Red October. She began to feel that she too was part of a civilising mission. 'I nearly swooned with surprise and admiration. After seven years in the backwoods I was entering what was almost a real, genuine city. Multi-story buildings, limousines, bustling streets—at least that was how it appeared to me. It was only some weeks later that I noticed you could count the big buildings on your fingers. But at the time it really was a great metropolis for me.'[47] 'We spent the whole evening strolling up and down the main thoroughfare of Magadan, our golden city. . . . The whole of the Magadan beau monde was parading up and down Stalin Street that summer evening. The big bosses, for some reason, confined their perambulations to the right side of the street, from the House of Culture up to Kolyma Avenue.'[48] The documentation of the buildings listed in the 1930s and 1940s displays impressive images: the house of the Dalstroy management, including the Berzin villa; the administrative buildings, initially in wood and later in reinforced concrete; the culture and recreation park named after Yagoda, the head of the NKVD; the school buildings; the buildings on Ulitsa Stalina in 1952; and the telegraph station.[49] These are the impressions as reported by visitors from other 'advanced posts of civilisation'.

Dalstroy: Empire, Internal Colonisation

Established in 1931, Dalstroy—the abbreviation for the Construction Trust of the Far East, or alternatively, of the Far East and North (Glavnoe Upravlenie stroitelstva Dalnego Vostoka/Severa)—was transformed by the special powers conferred on it into a state within the state or an internal colony inside the Soviet Union. Far from the 'mainland'—*materik*—it was mainly criminals and other special groups who were imported to build the necessary infrastructure as quickly as possible—harbours, settlements, the highway, power lines and power stations. Procuring the labour force needed for Dalstroy was the job of Sevvostlag—Severo-Vostochny ispravitelno-trudovoy lager, the North-Eastern Corrective Labour Camps—a subsection of the OGPU (which became the NKVD from 1934) set up on the territory of Dalstroy with its headquarters in Magadan. Situated between the Pacific and the Norwegian Sea, Dalstroy encompassed the basins of the Lena, Indigirka and Kolyma Rivers, as well as the Chukchi Peninsula and the northern part of Kamchatka. With a territory of three million square kilometres, it was larger than Western Europe and included over 130 labour camps.[50] Dalstroy is the classic instance of what Alexander Etkind calls the colonisation of the Russian Empire and its Soviet successor.[51]

The expectations of gold extraction that led Moscow to embark on the building of Dalstroy were more than surpassed. The Old Bolshevik and finance expert A. P. Serebrovsky, who was executed in 1937, wrote: "Never, in the most feverish years of the capitalist gold rush that included all the metal taken out of Alaska, did a territory give as much gold as that produced this year by the new Kolyma region."[52] The 'Russian Klondike' was what Michael Solomon, a Romanian Jewish inmate, called Kolyma. From 1932 to 1934 output rose ten times—from 511 to 5,515 kilograms of pure gold. And that was just the beginning. In 1936 it was 30 tonnes; by 1937 it was already 51.5 tonnes. On its own, Dalstroy yielded one-third of all the gold of the Soviet Union.[53] Without the gold of Kolyma it would have been impossible to realise the ambitions of the Five-Year Plans; there would have been no build-up of the arms industries before and during the Soviet-German War.

The settling and colonisation were driven forward at a similar pace—the term 'colonisation' appears in all the documents of the time. As early as the end of the first year following the foundation of Dalstroy, 9,928 prisoners arrived in Nagaev Bay. The majority were 'de-kulakised' peasants and so-called criminals, for the most part people who had committed petty crimes—the 'theft of social property'. Up to the unleashing of the Great Purges, 'political prisoners' formed only a small proportion of the total. The overwhelming majority—85 percent—of the people working in the pits, shafts and factories were camp inmates; no more than 15 percent had been recruited as 'free workers' from the 'mainland'. By 1936 the number of inmates in Dalstroy had grown to 62,703 and they produced as much gold as the entire Tsarist Empire up to the outbreak of the First World War.[54] By the end of the 1930s there were around 163,000 inmates. However, these greater numbers were unable to sustain the rates of gold production of the preceding years—a consequence of the murderous 'mass operations' of 1937/38 and the inhuman living conditions, which undermined what was in any case the poor productivity and low efficiency of unfree labour. The goal of Gulag labour—gold extraction at any price—had increasingly been subordinated to political intrigues and grandstanding. 'The impressive mining output achieved by Dalstroy under Berzin evaporated in 1938 and 1939.'[55]

The changes at the top following Berzin's liquidation and subsequent attempts to introduce economic rationality did nothing to alter the fact that force alone was not enough to achieve greater efficiencies. Material inducements promised greater success as did amnesties and better treatment of more highly qualified inmates—one of them was Sergey Korolyov, the outstanding rocket scientist who was forced, as a prisoner, to struggle with menial physical tasks.[56] The predominance of inefficiency, irrationality and chaotic organisation, competing, incompetent and corrupt administrations proved that in the long run slave labour was unsustainable and would come to grief on obstacles it had itself created. The camp system was somewhat reduced during the war by the mobilisation of inmates. It did not grow again until after the war, when its population swelled with the arrival of German and Japanese POWs, Red Army soldiers suspected of collaborating and 'nationalists' deported from territories in the West—but it never regained the 'form' it had achieved through non-economic force, terror and ideological mobilisation. It was gradually dissolved owing to pressure from the inmates and the need for long overdue external reforms following Stalin's death. Dalstroy, established on 13 November 1931, ceased to exist on 29 May 1957, leaving behind a legacy shaped by forced labour, inhabited by thousands who for the most part had been taken there by force and no longer had the resources needed to return to the mainland and resume the life they had once led or else had decided that they would rather remain in Kolyma because it had become the centre of their universe and even their home.[57]

But what happens to an institution that owes its existence to the compulsion exercised by a despotic, colonial regime once that compulsion has vanished or been eliminated and the people involved are free to decide to go where they wish? The industrial centres and towns in the extreme conditions of the Far North could only exist because the human labour power that extracted the mineral resources cost nothing—was, in short, slave labour. As soon as such human labour became a cost factor, human life and work in the polar and subpolar regions acquired a 'value'—in other words, once it was no longer possible to induce the inmates to work by noneconomic methods, economic progress ceased to be sustainable.

The former infrastructure, the large towns made possible by forced labour or enhanced material rewards, were threatened with decline or forced to cut back. The settlers who had previously colonised and appropriated the land now wanted to retreat to regions where they could find work and a better life. The acquisition of the Far North through the creation of large settlements was a form of overstretch—Norilsk is a large town with a population of around 170,000, while there are around 70,000 in Vorkuta. Ultimately, this expansion proved a step too far for the resources of the Soviet Union. At the same time, it made the creation of self-supporting centres of civilisation by normal methods difficult or even impossible. Slave labour may be 'cheap' but not only is it murderous, it is also ineffective; and it does away with the pressure to innovate. The ultimate failure that led to dismantling was due not to the cold but rather to a regime that did not value human lives. In the same way, it is not the cold that now makes demolition the optimal solution but the fact that human lives do have value and that people can go where they want and where they can make the most of themselves and their country. What Fiona Hill and Clifford G. Gaddy call 'The Siberian Curse' could be remedied only by decommissioning the great settlements, pursuing a targeted policy of emigration and building transitional stations in which specialised workers could conduct the mining of resources in regularly changing shifts. A new economy would take account of the extremely cold conditions. Reversing the overstretched internal colonisation in the

Far North would liberate new energies in a post-Soviet Russia that a ruthless regime previously squandered over an extended period. And that would mean a real end to the Kolyma project rather than just letting it fade away.[58]

Preserving the Remains: Larches, Wheelbarrows, Gloves

Like other places, Kolyma has witnessed attempts to preserve the traces of that era. The archive revolution made available the Gulag administration documents that Shalamov had imagined lost. A private museum has been opened in Yagodnoe. Tomasz Kizny scanned the topography of the camp with his camera and captured the results in his photos. On the hill above Magadan looms the *Mask of Sorrow* monument. Designed by the dissident sculptor Ernst Neizvestny, it is made of concrete and as unyielding as the grey skies above Nagaev Bay. Events that took place on the Kolyma River were replicated in many other places. The camp universe has penetrated the local urban and regional museums, at times minimally and shame-faced, at other times candidly and confidently. The exhibits are almost always identical, as befits representation of the Gulag archipelago itself. Arrest warrants; court judgements; letters to the families, which read 'sentenced to 10 years without the right to letter contact'—which amounted to much the same thing as 'executed by shooting'; rusting barbed wire; tin cans; chess pieces made of dough; toys; pieces of embroidery; letters on birch bark; models of watchtowers; a heavy, rusty cell door, much recoated, from a remand gaol; a reconstructed, double-decker bunkbed; and occasionally, a railway wagon or so-called 'raven', which was used to transport prisoners; photos both full-face and in profile of people just before their execution; iron bars from isolation cells; a reconstructed detention room—all proof of what human beings can inflict on others when they have complete power over them. Nowadays social media make it possible to access almost all the regional museums online and to make one's way virtually through the exhibits. Nowhere can the world of the camps be studied as intensively, nowhere has it been documented in such detail as in the archives and data banks of Memorial, which from the moment of its foundation in 1988 sought to collect all the known facts, all the available documents and all the personal memorabilia before they vanished forever into the Hades of indifference and suffered, so to speak, a second death.[59]

Shalamov had objects, images and exhibits in mind with which to document, implausibly but irrefutably, all that had happened— perhaps with the premonition that with the passing of time later generations would have no idea that such things had ever been possible. Shalamov presented his evidence: himself, his body, his hands, his tools, so as to answer the question 'Did we exist? I reply, "We did" with all the expressiveness of an official statement, with the responsibility, the precision of a document.'[60]

Shalamov writes about a man who sends a larch twig from Kolyma to Moscow, where it is placed in a preserving jar and restored to life. 'The larch is alive, the larch is immortal, this miracle of resurrection is inevitable, after all, the larch has been put into a jar of water on the anniversary of the death in Kolyma of the husband of the lady of the house: he was a poet.' The larch has been witness to everything that has happened in the last two hundred years. 'The larch is the tree of Kolyma, the tree of concentration camps. No birds sing in Kolyma. Kolyma's flowers are garish, hasty, coarse, and they have no scent. The short summer—in the cold, lifeless air—is one of dry heat and chilling night cold. . . . Only the larch fills the forests with its vague smell of turpentine. . . . But on closer inspection when you take a really deep breath of this smell, you will understand that it is the smell of life. The smell of resistance to the north, the smell of victory.'[61]

Shalamov assigns a central role in any camp museum to the wheelbarrow: 'the wheelbarrow is a symbol of the era, its emblem is the prisoner's wheelbarrow.' Shalamov is the wheelbarrow expert, the wheelbarrow professor; he knows everything there is to know about this vehicle that was produced in its thousands and formed into a great collective to dispose of rubble from mines and opencast pits and carry off entire mountains.[62] 'How can you colonize the region? In 1936 a solution was found. Removal and preparation of the subsoil by explosive and pickaxe and loading that subsoil were inseparably linked. The engineers worked out the optimal movement of the wheelbarrow, the time it took to bring it back, the time it took to fill it using spades and pickaxes and sometimes crowbars to take apart a gold-bearing rock.'[63] The organisation of a total, integrated mechanism of wheelbarrow operators was a significant rationalisation and increase in efficiency. The wheelbarrow pushers created the Kolyma highway. 'In 1938 there were no mechanical excavators. The construction of the 600 kilometres of the highway had been constructed beyond Yagodny, and the roads to the Southern and Northern Administrations had already been built. Kolyma was now producing gold, and the bosses were getting medals. All those billions of cubic meters of dynamited rocks, all those roads, approaches, paths, the gold-panning equipment, the building of settlements and cemeteries was done by hand, with wheelbarrows and pickaxes.'[64]

The most important exhibit that Shalamov wished to bequeath to a future museum, however, was his Kolyma glove, the second skin covering his hand. Its fingerprints proclaimed his identity and had remained unaltered even many decades after his return from the camp. 'We believe in dactyloscopy.' 'These prints are kept forever in the case file.

The tag with the number of my case file preserves not only the place of death but its secret too. That tag number is written in graphite.' We have to be aware that the hands of fugitives from Kolyma were hacked off 'to obviate the need to transport the body for identification: two human hands in a soldier's knapsack were far more convenient to carry than bodies or corpses'.[65] Shalamov left his first 'skin', his glove, back in Kolyma, but the hand he writes with now is its twin. The first glove is marked by experiences of freezing, a worker's glove, a horny hand, rubbed by the crowbar until it bled, with fingers permanently bent to fit a spade handle. 'Those fingers couldn't unbend in order to pick up a pen and write about themselves.' This first glove was left in the Magadan Museum, the Museum of the Health Administration, bearing the stamp of the improvement works between the Belicha Hospital and the highway, tested in the 'ice centrifuges of the Kolyma', marked by the fight against scurvy and pellagra, when the skin peels off and disintegrates into scales and entire layers. 'For the time being the skin was falling off me in sheets. As well as having scurvy ulcers, my fingers and toes were rotting because of osteomyelitis following frostbite. I had loose scurvy teeth and pyodermic ulcers, which have left traces that are still visible on my legs. I remember the passionate, constant desire to eat and the crowning symptom: my skin coming off in layers.'[66] This discarded skin, together with the entire medical history, became 'a living exhibit for the museum of local history or at least of local medical history.'[67]

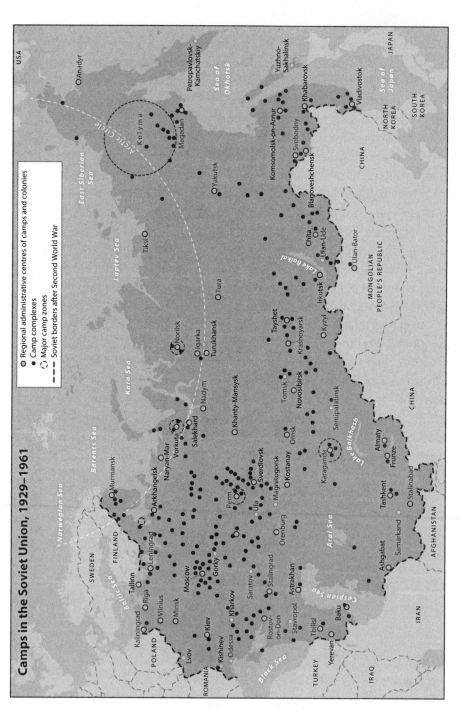

Camps in the Soviet Union, 1929–1961

Legend:
- ● Regional administrative centres of camps and colonies
- • Camp complexes
- ⌀ Major camp zones
- – – – Soviet borders after Second World War

FIGURE XII.1. Camps in the Soviet Union, 1929–1961. © Peter Palm, Berlin.

PART XII

The Solovetsky Special Camp—
Laboratory of Extremes:
Monastery Island
as Concentration Camp

Within sight of the Lubyanka, for decades the headquarters of the Cheka, the GPU, the OGPU, the NKVD, the MVD, the KGB and today the FSB, the Monument to the Victims of the Totalitarian Regime stands on the northern side of the Polytechnic Museum. It was built in 1990 at a time when Lubyanka Square still bore the name Dzerzhinsky Square and at its centre stood the monument to the founder of the Cheka, which was taken down in August 1991 and removed to the sculpture graveyard behind the Tretyakov Gallery on Krymsky Val. The new monument consists of an extremely heavy granite boulder brought to Moscow from the Solovetsky Islands by members of Memorial. Moscow citizens assemble there annually on 30 October to read out the names of victims murdered during the Great Terror and to honour their memory. The Solovetsky Stone refers to a place that is a household name to Soviet citizens. It evokes memories of the monastery island in the White Sea close to the Arctic Circle, an alluring destination for tourists and pilgrims and familiar to many, at least since Solzhenitsyn's book, as the birthplace of the Gulag system. There are even associations with pictures from a film, since in 1929 Maxim Gorky paid a visit to the island that was intended to show Soviet citizens and especially the foreign press that there was no truth in the rumours of inhuman conditions alleged to prevail there. In the memories of Soviet citizens Solovki evoked two images: one was the silhouette of the mighty, seemingly unreal monastery buildings rising out of the sea in the light of the White Nights; the other was the documentary featuring Gorky surrounded by OGPU personnel and prisoners, on the arrival of the boat from the mainland.

The Miracle in the White Sea

Hardly anyone outside Russia has heard of Solovki. No wonder. It refers to a group of islands in the Far North, no more than 160 kilometres from the Arctic Circle, in a dead corner of Europe. A signpost to Solovki from Tsarist times gives the distances in kilometres to the centres of the old Empire: Novgorod 755; Vilnius 1,530; Riga 1,359; Tallinn 1,080; Leningrad 625; Minsk 1,530; Kyiv 1,890; Moscow 1,200; Yerevan 3,150; Tbilisi 2,970; Vladivostok 7,950; Baku 3,240; Murmansk 455. According to an old photo, the distance to 'Berlin in Prussia' is 3,261 versts.

For most of the year the archipelago lies in a twilight zone; during autumn and winter there are no more than two hours of daylight at midday. In contrast, there is uninterrupted daylight in the summer months—for twenty-four hours straight. The island group in the White Sea rises radiantly out of the darkness. The brief summer months enable them to catch up with more moderate latitudes at two or three times the speed. The Arctic meadows burst into blossom; people and animals follow the lead of the sun. They no longer seem to need sleep and are still on the move at 4 a.m. The heavens shine brightly for a few weeks, nature is full of scent, beluga whales leap up out of the water like dolphins, seals lie around and bask in the sun. For a brief period, the Arctic Circle enjoys a Mediterranean climate. And that is not all. Anyone who approaches the island, which lies around 40 kilometres from the mainland, imagines they see a Fata Morgana, a grandiose fortress made of round boulders and monumental towers surmounted by gleaming white churches, bell towers and shimmering silver domes. Solovki is the name of a horrendous miracle, an outpost of European civilisation—its glory and its degradation.[1]

As far as ease of access is concerned, this island at the end of the world is not all that hard to find. You simply take the night train bound for Murmansk from St. Petersburg. At Kem, approximately halfway, where the rail line reaches the coast, you exit the train and continue to the pier in Belomorsk. This godforsaken spot is itself a place with a past: in the 1920s and 1930s this was known as Kemperpunkt, the notorious transit camp for prisoners being removed to Solovki. In the 1990s Kem had sixty thousand inhabitants; it was a settlement consisting of wooden huts, barracks and prefabricated apartment blocks—neither a town nor a village, with badly constructed streets leading nowhere. It was in short a temporary expedient that ended up being permanent. At its heart, there was an industrial plant processing timber, 'Karelia's Gold'. Today it lies abandoned.

FIGURE XII.2. Solovki as seen from the mainland. © akg-images/Sputnik.

In the ice-free navigation season between May and September, fishing boats cast off from here—not regularly, but from time to time—for the archipelago, which can be reached in a couple of hours. In the past this route was used by the steamer *Gleb Boky*, named after one of the camp commandants. Its hold was crammed full of prisoners, many of whom died before reaching their destination.

The Monks' Labour

Solovki, where the fishing boat lands after a journey lasting two hours, is a symbol of Russian culture. Its history falls into two parts: the era of a centuries-long monastic colonisation during which the monks and hermits of the Solovetsky Monastery played an outstanding role, and the era of the Gulag, the desecration of the monastery and the destruction of what had been built by generations in pious zeal and self-denying toil. In many respects the monastery's fate reflects that of the entire Russian church. Many thousands of priests and monks fell victim to persecution by the revolutionary regime. Hundreds of monasteries were expropriated and nationalised, their imposing buildings used as quarries but mainly adapted for other purposes—prisons, schools or colleges, camps or workshops.[2] The Russian Orthodox Church was the great rival in the struggle for cultural and intellectual hegemony over the old 'Holy Russia'. The history of the interaction between the Soviet state and the Orthodox Church, between communist dogma and popular beliefs, as well as between the church hierarchy and ordinary churchgoing people is marked by the use of force and submission, notwithstanding many intervening periods of milder, more relaxed treatment.[3] This was despite the fact that the Russian Revolution had created the opportunity to emancipate the church from its vassalage to the state, as was shown by the convening of the Council and the reestablishment of the patriarchate in 1917. However, what the Bolsheviks did was not just to enact the strict separation of church and state, but also to launch a general attack on the admittedly overpowerful position of the Orthodox Church. This involved the expropriation of church property, the confiscation of church wealth—which was justified as part of a campaign against famine—the desecration of sacred sites and relics, and the massive persecution and physical suppression of the clergy and the faithful. The attempt to undermine the position of the church by setting up the 'Living Church' loyal to the Soviets enjoyed little success. The militant Godless movement during the period of the culture revolution at the end of the 1920s and the brutal persecution in the wake of the Great Terror did severe damage to the church even though—as the 1937 Census reveals—most citizens clung to their faith either openly or in secret.

The rehabilitation of the church alongside the state came with the Second World War when the church proved to be the most ardent exponent of Soviet patriotism in the 'Great Patriotic War' and reverted to its traditional posture of harmony with the state that both empowered it and ensured its compliance. The Russian Orthodox Church was again marginalised in the decades after the war, more because of the general trend to modernisation and urbanisation than of the resumption of repressive policies towards the church, especially under Khrushchev during the years 1958–1972. It is undoubtedly true that for Russia, as elsewhere, the twentieth century can be regarded as a time of de-Christianisation, often carried out with utter ruthlessness. This process of secularisation did immense physical, cultural and spiritual damage, destroyed thousands of churches and monasteries, demolished church property and led to the destruction of traditions whose loss cannot be calculated in purely material terms. To be sure, the millennial celebrations in honour of the Christianisation of Rus in 1988, which included the reactivation of monastic life on Solovki, point to the reemergence of the Orthodox Church from the shadow of the Soviet period. But even in 1988 there were few signs that a time would come when the church would call for, and obtain, the restitution of its property and monasteries, and recover its treasures from the museums. It was scarcely conceivable at that time that the state would deck itself out with the glories of the liturgy of the Eastern Church or commemorate the martyrs of faith in public ceremonies. By the end of the 1980s some twenty monasteries had been reopened; this rose to five hundred by the end of the century.[4]

In 1429 the monks Savvaty, Herman and Zosima, later revered as saints, moved from the mainland and settled in the north of Solovetsky Island.[5] They themselves came from the important Kirillo-Belozersky Monastery and in their escape from the world into a solitary life, they founded their first settlement on Maura Mountain, the axe mountain (Sekirnaya Gora). Later on, they built the first monastery in the 'Bay of Well-Being'. Like the entire archipelago—apart from Bolshoi Solovetsky Island, this included Anzer, Bolshaya and Malaya Maksalma, Bolshoi Zayatsky and Maly Zayatsky—this belonged to the Novgorod Republic, which owned immeasurable territories in the North. It gradually developed over centuries into a giant complex whose history could be traced in 1989 in the new museum established in the monastery. The heyday of the monastery began when the monk Fyodor Kolychyov was made abbot there in 1558—later, he was appointed metropolitan of Moscow under the name Philip II and strangled following his opposition to the Terror instigated by Ivan the Terrible. Large stone buildings were constructed and equipped with amenities surprising for the age and their latitude: water supplies, sophisticated heating systems, a network of canals joining up the numerous lakes on the islands and opening them up to traffic. To take advantage of the milder microclimate of the archipelago, there were even greenhouses for the cultivation of fruit and vegetables. The monastery achieved great wealth through its own efforts, supplemented by endowments. The monks practised fishing and seal-hunting, extracting salt from the sea, trading throughout the entire White Sea basin, and processing skins in their tanneries. The monastery was regarded as a model economy until late into the nineteenth century when a power station was installed to produce electricity. The diligence of the monks and the economic miracle of Solovki were legendary in a Russia that was not exactly short of impressive monasteries. Thanks to the many pilgrims and schools for manual skills, the monastery could set up a large number of workshops and craft schools to which the children of peasants were sent from all over the North.

The monastery as a whole was a unique institution. Today it is a UNESCO World Heritage Site. At the close of the sixteenth century, the entire complex was surrounded with walls six metres thick, ten metres high and one kilometre long. These were built of boulders and basalt granite blocks following designs by the monk and master builder Trifon. Protected against 'fashionable' influences and conscious of its own traditions, the monastery saw itself as the guardian of the true faith, which it was unwilling to renounce even during the great church schism in the seventeenth century. From 1669 to 1676, the militant Old Believers fought to defend the monastery against the Tsar. For seven years it was besieged by troops from Moscow, who with the aid of treachery finally succeeded in overcoming the resistance of the monks, ending in a huge massacre. During the Crimean War, three British frigates approached the island and bombarded the monastery but without inflicting much damage. According to legend, the seagulls that were beloved and spoilt by the monks 'shot back' with such force that the English withdrew empty-handed. The monastery complex was surrounded by a settlement that provided for the monastery's needs as well as the growing number of pilgrims with brickworks, sawmills, fulling mills and vodka distilleries. The monks supported schools and training centres for icon painters. Documents from the great era of the monastery island are on show in the museum that was newly opened after 1990. They include postcards of the *Solovetsky*, the ship that brought pilgrims (and later, the future camp inmates) to the island, copies of the newspaper *The Pilgrim*, benches from the monastery school and all sorts of devotional paraphernalia. The botanical garden contains apple trees, Siberian cedars, lilac bushes and even roses. Until the 1920s the monastery was host to a large library with valuable manuscripts and one of the richest collections of icons in the Russian North. Large parts of these collections were plundered during the Soviet era or destroyed; little was salvaged and imported into the central museums of Moscow, Leningrad and Arkhangelsk. The most terrible blow of all was the fire of 25 May 1923, which destroyed the library together with its complete inventory and was probably intentional.

The First Concentration Camp

It was not for its beauty but for its isolation and harsh climate that the Bolsheviks chose the monastery as the site of a punishment camp. Nevertheless, its spiritual authority and educational tradition played a certain subliminal role in the decision to build a new type of camp at that location. The builders of communism wished to replace the old education with 'progressive' proletarian methods. In 1922, when the Soviet government handed the archipelago to the GPU to use as an internment camp for prisoners from the north Russian camps of Kholmogory and Pertaminsk, the monks were expelled from the island. Many were executed by shooting; some remained until the mid-1920s to supply the camp administration with food they produced themselves. On 1 July 1923 the first 150 political prisoners were brought to Solovki. The camp was then known by the abbreviation SLON, which means roughly 'Solovetsky camp for special purposes' but is also a pun on the Russian word for elephant. The harmless giant which was also depicted in the flower borders became the emblem of terror. It was the first concentration camp in the grand style, a place where the new methods to 'reeducate people and make new men of them' were tried out—a regular laboratory. During the 1920s, Solovki became the concentration camp for the old, prerevolutionary generation. This was where the 'former people' were 'concentrated'. They had belonged to all parties, from anarchists to monarchists, officers of the White Armies, former members of the Duma, businessmen and aristocrats, scholars from the St. Petersburg Religious-Philosophical Society, well-known actors and journalists, clerics of every confession and émigrés who had succumbed to their homesickness. But there were also others who had been unruly: survivors of the sailors' mutiny in Kronstadt and the peasants' rebellions in Tambov, as well as former commanders of the Red Army. What the political prisoners who had already experienced conditions in Tsarist prisons learned here was that their privileges—exemption from physical labour, access to newspapers—no longer counted for much and that tactics such as hunger strikes made no impression on their new masters. Numerous group photos show members of the prerevolutionary intelligentsia posing for their pictures.[6] This was where Chekists such as Nogtev, Boky or Eikhmans could demonstrate how in the shortest possible time self-confident citizens and revolutionaries tried and tested in underground activities could be turned into human wrecks. To achieve this, they used special torture methods that will forever be associated with the Solovki name—the 'stone sack', where prisoners were confined in recesses, forced to sit on poles for eighteen hours at a time and risked being killed if they fell off, being exposed to mosquitoes in summer or left in the snow in winter. Prisoners were handcuffed to tree trunks and pushed down the long stairway from Sekirnaya Gora, the axe mountain. Many of their tormentors themselves became the victims of senseless accusations, torture and death in 1937/38.

The museum conceived by the activists of Memorial at the end of the 1980s and opened in 1990 documents the development of Solovki as the first Soviet camp complex. Yury Brodsky and Alexander Bazhenov collected documents, photographs and objects found on the islands and brought them together in the first Gulag museum at the end of the Soviet Union and in the new Russia. In the succeeding years, it was dragged into the controversies about the dominant interpretation of events and the generally changing politics of history, which ended (for the time being at least) with handing over the island and the monastery complex, along with the authority to interpret its historical significance, to the Russian Orthodox Church.

In the 1990s the exhibition explored the radical opening-up of the Soviet past of the Solovetsky Islands. It worked out the key stages: during the first phase, 1923–1929, SLON was established. During the second, 1929–1937, a forced-labour and reforming camp was founded. In the third phase, 1937–1939, the island group became the Solovetsky prison—abbreviated to STON, which in Russian has the connotation of groaning or sighing. This was dissolved in 1939 when the island became a base and training centre for naval cadets and the vestiges of the camp were largely eradicated. The museum contains a copy of the decree of the Central Executive Committee of 17 May 1919, authorising the establishment of the forced-labour camp and signed by Avel Yenukidze, who subsequently fell victim to Stalin's purges. There is also a copy of Protocol No. 13 of the session of the Council of Commissars of 13 October 1923 concerning the establishment of SLON. On view is a door with baroque mountings, peephole and food hatch—it is the door to a monk's cell transformed into a prison cell. Also to be seen is Rykov's order to establish the camp with the stipulation that 70 of the 250 monks should be taken on as instructors and maintain the operation of the monastery—brickworks, dairy, leather and fur operations. Life followed a strict rhythm. The everyday activities of such a large number of people in such a confined space called for an efficient administrative structure and hierarchy. The 'new life' was enacted against the backdrop of the old monastic life. A wall with pious frescoes towers above the sickbeds in the quarantine lazaret. Monks operated the postal department for the inmates. Tracks were laid down for wagons to transport peat. Solovki became a production centre for valuable medicines.

In 1930 the concentration camp was transformed into a 'corrective labour camp', which was regarded at the time as a great reform, but merely meant that what had simply been prisons had to become self-financing. Above all, however, the camps were now required to supply millions of workmen for the 'great buildings of the first Five-Year Plan'. Most of the prisoners were peasants deported in the course of collectivisation together with their families. Work which had previously served to supply the camp itself—peat-cutting, logging, fishing, brick-making and various other enterprises—now became an economic factor included in Gosplan. The change of function became evident in the dramatic increase in the SLON prisoner population. In 1923 there were 3,049 prisoners. In 1924 this had risen to 4,100. By 1925 there were 6,800; in 1927, 12,700; in 1928, 13,366; in 1929, 21,900;

in 1930, 65,000; in 1931, 71,800; while in 1939, the numbers were back down to 4,500.[7] The monastery became a kremlin or citadel, the administrative centre of the archipelago. No more than a handful of Chekists lived there, while the chief labour of guarding, punishing and executing was assumed by privileged inmates, criminals for the most part. In the Solovetsky literature this became known as 'model self-administration'.

Dmitry Likhachyov, himself an inmate of the camp, described its topography in his memoirs. The population density on Solovki was greater than that of Belgium; it was a 'vast ant-heap'.[8] Based on the military model, the administration divided the inmates into hundreds. The commandant had his headquarters in Preobrazhensky Cathedral; the Guards Hundred was in the main building. The hundred was responsible for culture and education and brought actors, musicians and educators together. The prison was in the Arkhangelsk Gate. In addition, there was a giant lazaret that was always full to overflowing. Apart from living quarters, there were also service buildings in the kremlin: steam baths, the administration, the information and interrogation section where the informal collaborators and informers were interrogated, the tailoring shop, a theatre with a foyer that also doubled as a lecture hall, and the museum. Obtaining a ticket for the theatre was, according to the prisoners' memoirs, harder than getting a ticket to the Bolshoi Theatre nowadays. The monastery continued to function intermittently; monks lived there with the abbot and divine services were held. The clerics were also expert fishermen skilled in catching the famous Solovetsky herring that ended up on the tables of the Moscow Kremlin, which is why these fish were in fact called 'Kremlin herring'. Guards stood at the Nikolsky Gate. Executions by shooting took place in the monastery graveyard. Outside the kremlin was the old monastery hostel, which had become the home of the administration. In addition, the free workers on the island had a sports centre and a cafeteria at their disposal.

Solovki, where a person's life counted for little, was also a place of creative intellectual activities. These included publishing the camp newspaper, *The New Solovetsky*, which could even be subscribed to from abroad, establishment of the Solovetsky Society for Local History, a language laboratory for research into camp jargon, and a camp theatre that put on Mikhail Lermontov's *Masquerade* with stars such as Boris Glubovsky from the Moscow Tairov Theatre—with a Constructivist stage set, as befitted the period. In the cabinet of a well-known forensic expert, research was undertaken into criminality and statistics were evaluated. Dmitry Likhachyov, the later father of the Leningrad school of cultural history, wrote a study 'The Card Games of Criminals'. His friend I. M. Andrezhevsky published an essay in the *Solovetsky Islands* magazine on psychological and nervous illnesses on the archipelago. There were few places where so much learning and culture came together as with such prominent prisoners as the philosopher Alexander Meyer, the historian Nikolay Antsiferov, the young literary historian Dmitry Likhachyov and the great scholar Pavel Florensky. It was a concentration camp of the mind at whose entrance stood the motto not 'Work sets you free' but 'With an iron fist, we will lead humanity to happiness'.

News about what went on in Solovki spread to the outside world from early on. Sergey Malsagoff, a prisoner who managed to escape, published his book *An Island Hell* in London in 1925. Trade unionists and political parties issued protests and various 'investigating commissions' were sent out from Moscow to follow up accusations of cruelty and 'excesses' in the treatment of prisoners. In 1929 Maxim Gorky, the highly regarded writer who had returned to Russia after years of emigration, was sent to Solovki in a bid to rebut this 'anti-Soviet' propaganda. He had every opportunity to see what went on but either he did not see or he did not want to see. The young prisoner able to speak with him disappeared the day after Gorky left the island. The great writer who in his youth had come to know life in its 'Lower Depths' could only tell what he and his colleagues told the world years later as well—namely that he had been impressed by the enthusiasm of the new men and the successes achieved by the 'reforging' process. For people tortured on Solovki it was no consolation to learn that many of their tormentors suffered a cruel fate. A. P. Nogtev (1892–1946) spent years in the notorious camp in Norilsk and died shortly after his release; M. S. Kedrov (1878–1941) was shot; F. I. Eikhmans was arrested and executed in 1938. The 1990s museum exhibition displayed many documents from that time: ration cards, drawings, secret messages

FIGURE XII.3. Prisoners in the Kemperpunkt transit camp on their way to Solovki. Photograph from a propaganda film from the early 1930s dealing with the 'reforging' of the inmates. © culture-images/fai.

on birch rind discovered in the attic of the church on the axe mountain, letters from Pavel Florensky to his wife in Zagorsk (which was previously known as Sergiev Posad and once again bears that name today), messages carved in the beams of the building in the botanical garden, self-made cigarette packets, tobacco pouches, copies of *Solovetsky Islands*, the camp newspaper, homemade playing cards, Swiss banknotes, material singed in the monastery fire, spoons and cutlery from the SLON workshops, desk accessories made of clay, a photo of Gorky with OGPU personnel on the steamboat *Gleb Boky* on 20 June 1929. There is a quote from Gorky, saying, 'I am not able to convey my impressions in a few words. . . . I am happy and moved. Ever since 1929, I have been watching the OGPU re-educate people— it is fascinating. They are achieving something great, something phenomenal.'

In the 1930s the SLON became the Solovetsky prison, STON. The inmates were gradually transferred from the island to the mainland. In 1937, close to Sandarmokh on the White Sea–Baltic Canal, there was a mass execution of 1,111 Solovetsky prisoners, among them presumably Pavel Florensky and Les Kurbas, the Ukrainian theatre director.[9]

In 1939 the camp was closed down, not from humanitarian considerations but because it was not far from the Finnish border—in other words, it was too close to the front of the Finnish-Soviet 'Winter War'. Throughout the following decades naval cadets were stationed there and the islands remained a restricted zone in which attempts were made to remove traces of the camp. The mass graves scattered over the island were dug up and the remains thrown into the sea. The crown witness—the monastery—was turned into a regional museum during the Khrushchev Thaw so as to remove all reminders of this place of terror. But the clean-up job was slapdash. Up to the start of the 1990s and the initial stages of restoration of the monastery, rusting Soviet stars still crowned the domes of the Solovetsky cathedral. You could still see windows with bars and the camp barracks still housed people who had not managed to leave the island during the crisis. A cross has been placed in one of the former camp cemeteries.

Rebirth and Restoration

A journey to Solovki after the end of the Soviet Union was a journey into the confusions of the post-Soviet era as well as into the beginnings of the Gulag. Solovki in the 1990s was, like every island society, a miniature version of the great post-Soviet Russia. The archipelago in the White Sea, like the whole of the North, was hit by the disappearance of polar subsidies from central government. People there had to learn to survive through their own efforts. Half of the original population of two thousand had already left. 'Graveyard of hopes' was the name given to Solovki by Sergey Rubtsov, from the island's administration. The *Solovetsky Messenger* was discontinued. During the 1990s Russian tourists did not visit the Russian North in large numbers. Nevertheless, the archipelago did attract visitors from all over the nation: adventurers and deadbeats, romantics and critics of civilisation, a fluctuating elite that kept forming and reforming. We encountered a group of Moscow photographers who had set out to document the topography of terror; a music teacher who had contrived to bring thirteen pianos to the island and was determined to help one of her protégées study at the Moscow Conservatory; the Polish journalist Mariusz Wilk, a Solidarity activist who had settled there to explore the mysteries of Russia; an entrepreneur and all-round genius who refused to be defeated by the monstrous tax burden; students from Moscow and St. Petersburg who were helping to renovate the cathedral during their university vacations; and two young people who had opened a private hotel in the hope of attracting tourists and pilgrims. In a kind of hangar built for hydroplanes in 1925 that was still in use in the 1970s, some young people from Moscow and Arkhangelsk who already had some experience in New York were displaying their project of an underwater lighthouse. The programme included lectures on the mating habits of beluga whales and the fauna native to the Solovetsky archipelago. The industrial landscape of cranes, scrap metal and oil tanks was to be transformed back into a natural seashore and ancient pilgrims' hostels into comfortable hotels. Everywhere you could sense the atmosphere of a new beginning amid decline and dereliction.

In 1988 the millennial celebrations of the introduction of Christianity to Russia witnessed the rebirth of the monastery with the raising of the cross on the Filippovskaya Church. On 25 October 1990, the monastery reopened, initially with twelve monks under the direction of an abbot from Moldova. At Easter 1991 the bells were rung again for the first time. In August 1992 the relics of Zosima, Herman and Savvaty, the monastery's founders, which had been desecrated and put on display by the Bolsheviks, were returned to the island. An exhibition documented the activities of the monastery before its closure. The display included pictures of Sunday school classes, the arrival of pilgrims in the port, monks at work, a glorious liturgy and the visits of high dignitaries from the capital.

However, the wild 1990s when everything seemed possible are long since gone. The battle for the island and for the right interpretation of its past seems to be over. With state assistance, the Russian Orthodox Church appears to have regained the upper hand: it has the power to decide who can visit the archipelago. The church has called for the return of the territory and its art treasures and this has been granted. Throughout the nation a controversy has broken out about ownership of the icons that have ended up in the museums. The icon collections in the nation's exhibition halls—modest ones in the provinces, major ones in the big cities—are threatened by the demands for restitution. In many places, restorers' calls for the professional treatment of works of art are being rejected by fanatical clerics. The rival claims to ownership extend to the tragic chapters in Solovki's history. The Russian Orthodox Church has called for the closure or at any rate radical changes in the museums that were established during perestroika at the end of the 1980s. From now on, museums should cease to concentrate on the history of the Gulag archipelago; emphasis should be put on the history of the monastic archipelago, while the experiences of camps covering the whole of the Union are to be reduced to the status of a passing episode. Instead, the true focus of attention should be on the sufferings of the Christian martyrs. Were this programme to be implemented, it would present a place from which the twentieth century as we know it is wholly absent, a history cleansed of the cruelties of total power, a return that amounts to a restoration.

Much evidence points to such attempts to dispose of the Soviet phase of the monastery's history. Enjoying the magic of the Solovetsky Islands has become the privilege of the rich and beautiful. The runway of the former provincial airport whose radar system surpasses the monastery in size has been expanded because on high days and holy days the Patriarch, the President, oligarchs and other celebrities from the capital fly directly from Moscow to join the celebrations. The Moscow journalist Alexander Soldatov has described the combination of VIP tourism and history purified in the name of the church as a 'glamour Gulag'.[10] But the islands of the archipelago and the traces left behind by the Gulag will tell future tourists a different story. The day will come when Russia's tourists who have recently spent time in the Balearics and on Cyprus will find their way back to Solovki. Once there, they can gaze in wonder at things that can be seen only on Solovki, namely the peaks and troughs of the Russian spirit.

PART XIII

Corridors of Power

CHAPTER 50

K. in the Labyrinth of Everyday Soviet Reality

Until well into the 1960s Kafka was unknown to Soviet readers. This was the consequence of a censorship that had endured for four decades—if we set aside a few early mentions in the 1920s—on the grounds that Kafka was a decadent writer. The first Russian edition of Kafka appeared in 1965.[1] It was obvious that Kafka would fall foul of the Eastern bloc's censors—this was discussed openly in Lidice in 1964 at the Kafka Conference of the Czech Writers' Union, a landmark in the run-up to the Prague Spring. Kafka's novel *The Trial* seemed to anticipate the lurid events of the later show trials in Moscow and Prague. *The Castle* could be read as the key to the impenetrable, ubiquitous and anonymous power of a totalitarian state.[2] Kafka managed to describe in literary terms all the phenomena that historians, sociologists and the analysts of totalitarian power had struggled to understand: the enigmas of bureaucracies, alienation and the fragmentation of society. But Russia and the Soviet Union had writers of their own—Mikhail Saltykov-Shchedrin and Nikolay Gogol in the nineteenth century and Ilf and Petrov in the twentieth—whose writings throve on their depictions of absurd, surreal and even 'Kafkaesque' situations, which were doubtless literary inventions but derived from their authors' experience of the Tsarist bureaucracy that was subsequently 'embalmed in Soviet oil', as Lenin phrased it.

'Closed for Repairs'

Foreign visitors to the Soviet Union found it impossible to avoid Kafkaesque experiences even if they could attain only limited insight into living conditions there. It may be that their status as outsiders placed them in a privileged position, one that predisposed them to focus their attention on the paradoxes of everyday life in Soviet Russia to which they found themselves exposed. Of course, they often felt reluctant to explore too deeply the irritations and anxieties they felt, dismissing them as 'purely subjective' and not open to scientific analysis, perhaps because they wished to avoid giving the impression that they looked down on a country and a nation with which they wanted to empathise. Even Richard Stites, the great American historian and expert on Russia, admitted in his essay 'Crowded on the Edge of Vastness', 'My essay is a strictly subjective work based on personal observations over the past thirty years rather than a rigorous scholarly treatise based on a large database.'[3] But in reality, this led him to conceive a research project that would seek answers to the riddles that confronted everyone who had even a passing acquaintance with the country but that had never been researched. This included the fact that everyday work and going about one's business were organised in a manner that went against all common sense. The excessive complexity and bureaucratic nature of the simplest processes made a mockery of any idea of efficiency. In short, his project focuses on the irrational nature of specific, 'senseless' social practices concerning in particular the treatment and use of space public or private. The 'irrational use of space' diagnosed by Stites is striking because Soviet propaganda always emphasised the superiority of a model of society based on 'conscious planning', in stark contrast to the anarchy and chaos of capitalism. The issue was not so much the dramatic experiences of the prisons and camps as described by Yevgeniya Ginzburg and many others in their topographical prison narratives: 'People were walking busily about the corridors and from behind a glass door came the rattle of typewriters. A young man I had seen somewhere before actually nodded with a casual "Good morning!" An office just like any other.'[4] The puzzle lay rather in the long corridors and closed doors that characterised everyday life in the Soviet Union.

The phenomena are familiar. You approached magnificent entrances, which in fact were no entrances at all. With their ascending staircases, the monumental, even ostentatious buildings of ministries, authorities, institutes, libraries and museums often had grand entrances. And yet visitors were frequently not allowed to enter through the main entrance but only through a side or back door. They

FIGURE 50.1. 'Dear fellow citizens and guests of the city of Oryol, The Museum exhibition is closed for repairs.'

approached only to find a notice which always bore the same message: Closed for repairs/Closed for renovation/Closed for technical reasons/Closed for lunch/*Na obed.* Lunchtime seemed in general to be the untouchable, sacrosanct time. Or sometimes the notice just said, 'Closed', without further explanation.

In restaurants you regularly discovered a notice on the door, saying, 'No tables available', when it was crystal clear that the establishment was completely empty. Since this widespread practice was not a matter of singling anyone out for special treatment, we need to ask what lay behind it.

These experiences were more than once the butt of satirical pieces by Ilf and Petrov in their essays 'Bureaucrats Indifferent to the Whole World'. 'Locking doors has become a mania. It now happens even in theatres, department stores, public offices visited daily by thousands of people, everywhere, in short, where doors are most needed and ingenious architects have designed them in great numbers. People like this building superintendent have another hobby—building fences. No sooner has a house been built and richly festooned with pillars and reliefs than the management's first act is to nail up the glass front door with dirty boards and to glue a note on top with the words "Entrance closed. Access only from the rear."'[5] Such were the perceptions of the sharp-eyed observers of everyday Soviet life in the 1930s.

Sociology of the Threshold

There is an entire philosophy of doorways. We could develop a regular phenomenology of the significance of different thresholds: the imposing door as the embodiment of power and intimidation; the inviting doorway where the guest is received and helped over the threshold; the creaking door that hasn't been repaired for ages and tells us something about people's relation to their property; the heavy oak swing door at the entrance to the metro, which has to be pushed hard to gain entry and hits you in the chest when the person in front of you lets go; the pristine door with Art Nouveau ornamentation that has served for a century and is held together by numerous layers of paint; the clattering metal or aluminium door in the department store; the factory gate with the time clock or the porter's lodge; the padded door to the outer office through which no sound penetrates and which imposes a respectful air on people entering; the cell doors with a peephole, massive locks and a food flap on show in the Gulag Museum; the automatic doors on the metro trains and their loudspeaker announcements: 'The doors are about to close', followed by their warning signal—almost a universal sound, a tune now familiar to many generations. Portals, like entrance situations in general, are significant; they can be as two-faced as Janus, the Roman god of doorways.[6] They let you in or keep you out; they convey the first impression. The doors to public office buildings often have something forbidding about them, a fortress aspect, a proof that offices and authorities are not there for clients and citizens but the other way round.

The closed gateway has often been explained as a response to climatic conditions, with entrances that have a porch regarded as a lock linking the temperatures inside and out, especially in the winter season. Attempts have been made to explain the contrast between pompous and frequently monumental main entrances and more modest rear and side entrances as a feature of a prerevolutionary aristocratic and class-based society, particularly since the separate entrance for servants was a longstanding tradition in the middle-class world as well. This may be contrasted with the entrances to high-rise concrete apartment blocks with their always open and constantly slamming doors, flanked by benches occupied mostly by older women with a keen eye for comings and goings. These entrances were anonymous spaces, conveying impressions that ranged from a sense of indifference to downright neglect and vandalism. Thus we have two threshold situations: one leads to the well-guarded and protected official world of those at the pinnacle of society, while the other leads to a sort of no man's land, for 'common space is a no man's land'.

Richard Stites has pointed to the discrepancy between 'agoraphilia' and 'claustrophilia', the squandering of space on the one hand and cramped and crowded spaces on the other. This can be seen in the contrast between cavernous railway station concourses and the tiny ticket counters in front of which lengthy queues stand—not linear queues, but more amoeba-like lines—where the customer who has reached the counter is forced to bend down and even then is not able properly to see the person behind the pane of glass. Stites describes the apparently endless corridors with their long, narrow carpet runners and the tiny cabinets and offices leading off from them. And again, he describes the magnificent staircases in public buildings such as libraries and contrasts them with the crush in the catalogue halls or reading rooms.

The Meaning of Meaningless Motion

Offices, cabinets and secretariats were all valuable contact points in a centralised world of offices that required forms, approvals, signatures and countersignatures, all frequently associated with lengthy procedures. The approval of work-related trips (*komandirovka*), the issuing of special travel permits (*propusk*), approval for convalescent breaks in the sanatorium belonging to the works or the union (*putyovka*)— these were all channelled via the service provider: the secretariat or outer office. But here too we find what we have already reported in connection with the 'Closed' signs. The person responsible was often absent from his desk and so the applicant, whom one would like to get rid of, was simply told, 'He is not here today', 'I am very sorry', 'This is not my field of expertise', 'Come back next week, perhaps he will have returned by then'. Everyone seemed to be responsible solely for their own desk and even then only in emergencies since people only appeared to be working. It was as if someone had contrived to devise an even greater form of alienation than is represented by the principle of 'working to rule'. 'O indifference! It always strikes us unprepared since for the most part it is drowning in the great ocean wave of socialist creativity that has engulfed the entire Soviet nation. Indifference is a significant but iniquitous phenomenon. And it hurts.'[7] The 'thick-skinned boor' in the office treats citizens as 'suspect persons', unnerves them with endless formalities and shifts the responsibility for his own sloppy work onto their shoulders. 'In his opinion, the client lacks discipline, fails to abide by the rules and interrupts him in his work.'[8]

The space of alienated work was made bearable only by the personal touch: the plant, the kettle and the tea things behind the cupboard, the collection of private photos and some postcards. The lunch break was sacrosanct, if only because the food had to be prepared. What was actually a public space, 'the office', assumed the features of a private one, a home away from home, something true enough in many cases since unlike the shared apartment where one was surrounded by unloved fellow humans, the office housed one's colleagues, people of the same sort as oneself. This was a situation you could come to terms with. The office became a substitute home. We could describe this as the privatisation of a public space since the difference between workplace and private sphere blurred—at the expense of both. The work suffered since it called for efficiency, objectivity and alacrity, and an individual's privacy suffered likewise since it was unable to develop fully in the context of the workplace. This fusion of private and public could be pleasant, such as when you happened to come in on a good day or meet a fellow worker you liked, especially one of the opposite sex. As a rule, however, what predominated was the grumpy response to someone's concerns or at best indifference. The client was more likely to encounter rejection or actual warmth than commitment and politeness. Where you would have liked to be treated in a professional and experienced manner, you were more likely to find yourself dependent on an official's mood of the moment or a vast indifference that paralysed one's expectations of rational calculation, which oddly enough was something the Soviet way of life was especially proud of. If the daily routine cannot be planned in advance, it will become

FIGURE 50.2. A Soviet office in the House of Industry and Trade in Sverdlovsk/Yekaterinburg. Architects: Daniil Fridman, Gleb Glushtchenko, Pyotr Pasternak. From L. Tokmenikova, *Dom promyshlennosti i torgovli*, Tatlin, Yekaterinburg 2013.

dependent on chance. Calculations about the use of time collapse; muddling through and improvisation become the norm. Everything becomes unpredictable; you have to be ready for anything—a great virtue in itself but also a constant strain and waste of energy. All the intelligence that is 'actually' required for productive work flows into overcoming what are 'actually' unnecessary, superfluous obstacles that just make life more difficult.

Richard Stites gives a kind of 'thick description' of the daily Soviet routine familiar to most people who had anything to do with it.

Spatial irrationality is closely linked to other aspects of the culture of work and service. All of the Russian practices mentioned above sharply diminish the level of efficiency at work. The total effect is multiplied by the impact that each act or practice has upon everyone else. In the course of a day, one potentially productive worker at any task will lose about a third or even half a day's work due to the cumulative power of other citizens' work habits. Here I offer a fictional but plausible scenario. 10.00–5.00, a good enough workday in winter time. Citizen X plans to spend two hours in the library, have a business lunch with Y at 12.00, go for rail tickets at 1.00, meet another colleague, Z, for half an hour at 2.00, and then ride for half an hour to the university for teaching and consulting from 3.00 to 5.00. Call it a day and go home at five.

The reality we all know. The reading room without prior announcement (nobody's business but theirs) has been taken over for a special staff meeting—even though there are seven equally large rooms available for it. So X crosses town to another library and thus has only about 45 minutes of actual work that morning. Back to the meeting point for lunch. Y arrives forty minutes late because his plumber did not show up on time to do essential repairs. All nearby eating places are either 'full' (though nearly empty) or have long lines, so they go to a fast-food place and make it a short and not very productive stand-up business lunch. Then X gets to the railway ticket office at 2.00 instead of 1.00 and finds it closed for lunch until 3.00. Since the ticket is essential, he waits. The ticket-seller returns from lunch at 3.15, but her computer is down and the repairman has not yet come to fix it. After waiting in line at another window, X has his tickets by 4.00. He has of course missed his 2.00 appointment with Z thus throwing off Z's schedule as well. He calls the university but no one answers the phone because the receptionist has left early for the day to do the shopping and no one else in the office cares to answer (it's not their job). X rushes to his class and finds that all the students have left because he is more than one hour late.

The total professional productive work for X on that day: 45 minutes and about 15 minutes of business talk with Y. But note that Y and Z will face similar if not worse inefficiencies during the day as will perhaps every citizen of a major Russian city. And if X, Y and Z are relatively efficient people who want to do productive work, think of all those who are indifferent or even hostile to their jobs. This is all too obvious and familiar to those who have lived in Russia, even for a short time. What is striking and revealing is that no Russian I have ever met (inside the country) would venture to make an analysis of the real causes of an unproductive day, or week, or year. In the old Soviet days, the typical reaction of a critic—a dissident or someone indifferent to the Soviet system—would be 'it's the fault of our system', meaning socialism. A more honest and cogent reply that I have often heard—though no more trenchant analytically—is: 'it's Russia'.[9]

Private Property and the Economics of the Age

There is much to be said for holding old traditions responsible for inefficiency and chaos. Take the little peasant hut in the vast countryside—*izbushka*—where everything was packed together in the minutest space: the different generations, the extended family, in the winter the animals too. Contrast this with an ostentatiously monumental architecture even in prerevolutionary times, its showiness outweighing its practicality. Rather than looking for explanations in a centuries-old peasant tradition or the clash between an agrarian and an industrial culture, it would be more apposite to seek them in their destruction, dissolution and atomisation. The destruction of private property, people's loss of their own home, and the secular process of uprooting them played a far greater role in fundamentally upsetting the balance between public and private and so preventing the consolidation of the burgeoning culture of industry and efficiency. As a result, shock workers, the campaigns, the subjective and heroic commitment of individuals remained the standard by which to gauge all progress. To make this visible was the challenge for a post-Soviet social analysis that brought together Georg Simmel's sociology and the satirical insights of Ilf and Petrov.[10]

In the post-Soviet space both trends are present: the old indifference and the determination to break out of what Kant called 'self-incurred immaturity'; to continue the apathetic status quo or to take a leap into a new mode of effective work; indifference towards the general public or a new concern about what one has just acquired for oneself—as, for instance, in the private living space acquired at long last. Ever since people began to possess something of their

FIGURE 50.3. Office with padded doors in the House of Industry and Trade, built in Sverdlovsk/ Yekaterinburg in the 1930s. Architects: Daniil Fridman, Gleb Glushtchenko, Pyotr Pasternak. From L. Tokmenikova, *Dom promyshlennosti i torgovli*, Tatlin, Yekaterinburg 2013.

'own', they became more concerned about the security of their own apartment block or their own front door.[11] The more safety-conscious and prosperous have steel doors installed together with new locks, cameras or alarm systems so as to arm themselves against break-ins and attacks in these 'troubled times'. Many blocks have a sort of concierge or *dezhurnye*. Public buildings are guarded by Cerberuses in (mainly black) uniforms; the security and personal bodyguard business is flourishing. They are highly visible and have an intimidating effect. The naïvely youthful militiaman from the sticks who stands around with a bored expression is a thing of the past, succeeded by the battle-hardened and fighting-fit generation of the trained close-combat fighter, who may well have been in Afghanistan or Chechnya. The vehicles you see drawing up in front of banks or hotels nowadays are heavy, black limousines with darkened windows.

In the chaotic times following the abdication of the state, the palaces of culture of the past with their huge foyers, vestibules and theatre auditoriums could only stay afloat by adapting their facilities for commercial use. These were rented out for events, exhibitions and fairs. The extravagantly vast spaces were taken over by small businessmen for small exhibitions, start-ups, festivities, trade fairs, kiosks, stalls and shops. The new society created its own meeting places, offices and 'corridors of power', provisionally at first, but later they were made permanent. In the 1990s the dimly lit foyers were filled with *biznesmeny* in tracksuits; later on, men in violet jackets, all doing deals. Initially, they could be recognised by their preferred status symbols: cans of Coca-Cola and packs of Marlboro cigarettes. A decade later they were sitting in offices with windows to the ceiling and a view of the whole of Moscow. These offices had been designed by Italian or British architects or were full of gilt furniture in Empire style. But old or new, the ambience does not reveal whether a new workplace culture truly developed. The office personnel—mockingly referred to in the Russian press as 'plankton'—multiplied many times over. Whatever is really new is to be found among the young who sit with their laptops on their knees wherever they happen to be going between St. Petersburg and Silicon Valley. They are creating their own new spaces.

CHAPTER 51

The 'House on the Moskva': Machine for Living, Trap for People, Gated Community

The new Moscow is outgrowing the old Moscow. No city in Europe has changed as much since the collapse of the Soviet Union as the Russian capital. The 'change of decor', the phrase often used to refer to the Revolution in the so-called Aesopian language of the age of the censor, is complete. The capital of the USSR has become a Eurasian metropolis; what had been the centre of 'actually existing socialism' has become a genuine Babylon. In what was a world of grey, there has been an explosion of colour reminiscent of the Moscow paintings of Kandinsky or Lentulov. Newly built residential and office blocks spring up at annual intervals. All movement has accelerated—rising to a frenetic gridlock. Traffic flows over avenues and ring roads that are too narrow and crowded to cope with the stream of traffic despite their eight or ten lanes. The slogan 'Learning from Las Vegas' is one that Moscow has taken to heart. The posters on the traffic arteries and the ring roads around the city centre tower into the sky. Skyscrapers serve as billboards. The drab city of yesteryear now resembles a festival of light. Façade succeeds façade and then whole streets emerge from the gloom. The street lighting is so lavish, it's as if there were a competition to create the most dazzling effect with a new prize every day for the most extravagant idea. The Stalinist high-rise blocks gleam in the searchlights. The white, pink, violet and green lighting cascades down the façades and turns them into something different: American Art Deco towers, ziggurats or mountainous piles rising up on gigantic plinths. Gold—everywhere you glimpse the gold of the church domes: it dominates the horizon on the rebuilt Christ the Saviour Cathedral. Elsewhere, it blazes forth unexpectedly, shining out of the darkness of backyards. The colours are always strong, unmixed and garish. The ox-blood red of old factory buildings sits next to the turquoise or blue of a palace, the green roofs alongside the cream-coloured façades of buildings in the style of Moscow classicism. No colour respects other colours; each is sufficient unto itself. The colour palette produces a strong effect. No one abides by any rule or plan but somehow everything harmonises. None wants any truck with the others and each strives to surpass the others as best they can. But this creates the overpowering, dynamic effect with which the entire city vibrates. Something has come to an end, but something else has sprung into being.

This holds true even where Soviet Moscow was at its most massive: in the 'House on the Moskva' complex on the Bersenevskaya Embankment.[1] It's as if the sprawling, grey complex wished to offer resolute resistance to the dawning new age. The first to approach was the Kempinsky Hotels chain. Imagine the grandiose building from the early phase of Stalinism as a post-Soviet luxury hotel! Nothing came of this, but for an entire decade a Mercedes star was seen on the roof.

The 'House on the Moskva'

The House on the Moskva is really a city within a city, central and highly conspicuous. The terrain is around eight hectares and backed on two sides by the Kremlin and a canal. Formed as a series of massive rectangular prisms, the building rises eleven storeys and is arranged around three inner courtyards open to the city proper through large gateways yet also secluded. Anyone who goes from the Kremlin over the Great Stone Bridge and towards the old quarter of Zamoskvorechie passes by the house. Whoever goes to see a musical in the Variety Theatre [Teatr Estrady] has in fact entered the House club. The Udarnik cinema with a roof in the shape of a tortoise shell, the first sound-film theatre and at the time the largest cinema in Moscow, is also part of the House on the Moskva.[2] At the rear of the building, the four chimney stacks of an old electricity plant rise up, giving it the appearance of a steamer. There too you find the vestiges of church buildings and the old bakery and confectioner established by Theodor Einem and renamed Red October after the Revolution. Clouds of chocolate rise from the building at all hours. The drab complex belongs to the old Moscow; thanks to the addition of galleries, museums and cafés it is now completely integrated into the new Moscow, of which it is one of the most important locations.

The House on the Moskva, or House on the Embankment, is also known as 'Yofan's house', after its designer Boris Mikhailovich Yofan. Born in Odesa in 1891, Yofan studied in Italy before the Revolution, married an Italian countess and remained in love with Rome and the country of Palladio all his life. His name became familiar beyond the borders of the Soviet Union as the author of the fantastic Palace of the Soviets. Work had begun on this project in 1932 on the site of the recently demolished Cathedral of Christ the Saviour. The proposed tower was more like a sculpture; over four hundred metres tall, it was to feature a statue of Lenin more than seventy metres in height. Yofan was also the architect of the legendary USSR pavilion at the Paris International Exhibition of 1937—where he was the rival of Albert Speer—as well as at the New York World Fair of 1939. From 1931 until his death in 1976 he lived in the House on the Moskva and from his studio on the eleventh floor he had an overview of the Palace of the Soviets building site.[3]

In its day, the House on the Moskva was the largest 'machine for living' in Europe. Its style and volume supplied the benchmark for the new Moscow. Everything about this building was remarkable and scrupulously thought out. Exemplary solutions had been devised, so it was believed, for many of the new capital's problems. The aim was to bring together between five thousand and seven thousand employees of the people's commissariats and the government and Party apparatuses and 'concentrate' them at one location close to the Kremlin. Up to the time of the building's completion in 1929–1931, these officials had lived in 'Houses of the Soviets', scattered all over the city, for preference in the old luxury hotels such as the Metropol or National. Gosdom, or Government House, as the building was officially named, was designed to gather together everything needed to enable around five thousand people to live autonomously in five hundred apartments: kindergartens, theatres and cinemas, club rooms, sports halls, a roof tennis court, libraries and bookshops, an infirmary, laundries, a hairdresser, a shoemaker, chauffeurs, a variety of food shops and a department store for more upmarket goods. The apartments were allocated by the various people's commissariats and ministries, who also had the power to revoke them.[4]

The furnishings and decorations were of a high standard and considerable effort was made to satisfy contemporary ideas of a rationally organised new life. The apartments didn't just have waste-disposal chutes, central heating, refrigerators and lifts for people and goods, lots of light and sun and excellent ventilation in the courtyards. The building also featured all sorts of high tech—the snow-melting machine in the courtyards and the document shredders imported from the US. Life itself was to be reorganised. Yofan never went as far as some of his colleagues in eliminating individual kitchens in favour of canteens—impressive examples can be seen in the 'communal houses' in Moscow. But the idea of equality, of 'socialising' housework and redefining 'private life' is in evidence here.[5]

The Ambience of the Rising Class

Government House was a place of privilege even though its inhabitants were not really able to enjoy it free from anxiety. Something of this can be seen in one of the apartments, which, thanks to a private initiative by its owners, was established as a museum in 1989 and has been maintained by the city since 1997. It gives us a picture of what might be seen as prosperity in those heroic times of the first and second Five-Year Plans, the years of industrialisation and collectivisation, marred as they were by poverty and scarcity. We might regard this museum as the lifeworld of the 1930s, frozen in time.[6]

Everything is massive and heavy: the wardrobe in which uniform coats, caps and jackets resplendent with medals hang, the rectangular wooden folding table, the chairs that have taken on the elegant sweep of Thonet chairs, the sideboard, the bookcase and the divan covers. It was all meant to last for generations and perhaps even forever, like the oak floor planks. Smaller items from the old interiors have also been brought together: the samovar; the felt-covered desk; the Torpedo typewriter; the table lamp, which, unusually, has a green shade instead of a red one; the divan that can be converted into a bed. This is where you find the insignia of the new affluence, which was fully accessible to top employees and shock workers alike: the camera, the Pathephone and the bicycle. You can see the cultural icons that continued to hold their value beyond the Revolution: a Pushkin portrait and a landscape in the style of Isaac Levitan. A breath of cosiness in the hardest and cruellest of times: lace-edged tablecloths and china elephants on the shelf. Portraits as well as photos of families or groups testify to an almost comfortable prosperity, which must have existed in certain circles at least: ladies in furs, carefully kept clothes that were by no means proletarian in nature, and elegant hats; men for the most part with chests covered in medals and sometimes in white suits.

There are always surprises when discovering traces of the past: the postcard from a holiday in the Crimea, the grandfather clock that may have been brought back from a vanquished Germany, a variety of radios (including a Blaupunkt receiver of German provenance) or, as the unmistakable sign of a privileged position, the black ATC telephone of 1929. The bookcase contains the literature of the age: the so-called Short Course, that is, 'The History of the Communist Party of the Soviet Union (Bolsheviks)', the works of Lenin and Stalin, the Akademie Verlag's editions of the classics, brochures for the new Moscow of the General Plan of 1935 and photos of the *Chelyuskin* crew imprisoned in the ice. Everywhere you find vestiges of an ambience to which more than one generation had been forced to accommodate itself: photos of what Yury Trifonov called the 'sandbanks of the 1930s', happy holidays, ashtrays, presents from business trips abroad, violin cases and pianinos—which demonstrate the survival of chamber music even in times of Terror—wall hangings that lend a homely feeling to the apartments of the day, Party membership books and decorations. Four-room apartments, even if they at times served as home to several families, were a breath-taking, unheard-of luxury in the Moscow of the 1930s and 1940s, a city of mass immigration from the countryside. To come as far as this, a person must have reached the 'commanding heights' of Stalinist high society. Yofan's house provided a home for huge numbers of the powerful and even the most powerful. They included six members and candidate-members of the Politburo, sixty-three people's commissars or ministers, ninety-four deputy people's commissars, nineteen marshals and admirals, members of the Academy of Sciences, as well as writers and artists. The list of inhabitants reads like a Who's Who of Stalin's Soviet Union and anyone who reconstructs the layout of the apartments can follow the whereabouts of the Soviet elite entrance by entrance, door by door.[7] Many veterans of the revolutionary movement lived here—Yelena Stasova, Lenin's secretary (Apartment 231); Valentin Trifonov, the author's father and Civil War hero (Apartment 137); leaders of international communism; refugees; political émigrés such as Georgy Dimitrov (Apartment 235) and the Polish writer Bruno Jasieński (Apartment 176); and leading Party and state officials: Stalin's close friend Alexander Poskryobyshev (Apartment 231), the powerful head of the planning authorities Valerian Kuybyshev (Apartment 281), the 'conscience of the Revolution' Aaron Soltz (Apartment 193) and other prominent figures such as Ivar Smilga (Apartment 393) and Valerian Osinsky-Obolensky (Apartment 18). The secret police, the NKVD, the Gulag administration and the intelligence agencies were strongly represented, as were Red Army leaders—Marshals Mikhail Tukhachevsky (Apartment 221) and Georgy Zhukov (Apartment 219)— and a large number of plane builders and pilots, the true heroes of the 1930s. Others who frequented the house included the prosecutor in the Moscow show trials, Andrey Vyshinsky, and the procurator general Roman Rudenko (Apartment 2), both of whom may well have sat down opposite their victims here. Stalin was a frequent guest of his staff here. There were prominent diplomats too—People's Commissar for Foreign Affairs Maxim Litvinov (Apartment 14), as well as the leading shock workers to have achieved fame, such as Alexey Stakhanov (Apartment 55) and the geneticist Trofim Lysenko (Apartment 391), who developed pseudo-scientific theories and practices. Rising stars and younger officials, such as Nikita Khrushchev, the Moscow Party boss who came from Ukraine (Apartment 206), and Alexander Kosarev, the head of the Young Communists (Apartment 289), lived there. There were apartments where the so-called Swiss—those who had been in exile with Lenin and Plekhanov—would gather; others to meet there included 'Far Easterners' or Latvians. Richard Sorge came here on a visit to Yan Berzin (Apartment 153).

Like every little world that lives for itself, it was not without its bizarre features. Madam Tukhachevsky could be seen in her leather

FIGURE 51.1. The House on the Moskva at night. The illuminations are post-Soviet. © culture-images/fai.

jacket practising on the shooting range located in the cellar. Khrush-chev's mother-in-law, a village babushka, spent hours just sitting on a bench in the courtyard in front of the entrance to her son's apart-ment. Nikolay Yezhov was seen drunk and dancing the lezginka in Entrance 8. In 1937 waves of arrests by the NKVD took place while jazz played on the ground floor of the Udarnik cinema. The only people who seemed able to lead an untroubled life in the giant complex were the children and youngsters, who used the massive building as an adventure playground. In their eyes the House on the Embankment was the centre of the world, a place with clubs and circles, where they built model planes, collected stamps and were taught by the very best teachers. It remained like this right up to when the Revolution began to devour its own children and made many of them orphans and 'children of the enemies of the people'.

Yofan's machine for living was modelled on apartment complexes of the kind developed in the United States and was a symptom of the 'Soviet Americanism' (to use Hans Rogger's phrase) of those years.[8] The simple, laconic forms, the solid materials and the impeccable workmanship are all equally distant from both the Stalinist ostentation of the postwar period and the exaggerated simplicity of the mass-housing developments of the Khrushchev era. Yofan's building tells us something about the austere, even ascetic nature of an age that thought in terms not of fashion or economic trends but of historical epochs. It was a sort of Gesamtkunstwerk in which Yofan was in charge of the cherry-coloured lifts and the design of every detail—the porcelain door handles and the light fittings in the stairwells. This was a place where you became attuned to a 'cultured' life and learned not to throw cigarette butts down the washbasin. The Government House was the anticipation of life in the Moscow of the future.

The Trap: Purges and Moving House

To Muscovites the House on the Embankment is grey and gloomy, not so much because of its actual colour—chosen deliberately by the architect and doggedly defended today by the guardians of historical monuments—but because it was the setting for a grim history. It was literally a crime scene, a microcosm of Stalin's Soviet Union. The history of the building is the history of Russia in the twentieth century. Almost every one of the roughly five hundred apartments holds the story of the rise and fall of a generation. Almost all had a tragic tale to tell. The marble plaques on the façades in memory of distinguished residents are really epitaphs for people whose lives came to a premature end here—for the most part in 1937 and 1938, the years of the Great Terror. Stories and legends have built up around these walls. The spot where the structure was built had once been the court of Malyuta Skuratov, Ivan the Terrible's butcher. Lenya Chinchuk, the daughter of the former Soviet ambassador in Berlin, opened the gas taps when her father was taken away. Others threw themselves out of windows. Avgust Kork, a Red Army commander, burned all incriminating papers in his bath before his arrest. For Yury Trifonov, who spent a happy childhood there before his father was carried off and shot in 1938, the house and interest in time and place became a lifelong preoccupation.[9] Other longstanding residents such as Mikhail Korshunov and Viktoriya Terekhova have begun to write

up what they knew and what they could find out.[10] Their discoveries
have been brought together in the little museum set up on the ground
floor in 1989 and in their book *Mysterious Moscow*. Resident turnover
was high. Over time, each of the apartments was home to at least ten
families. The comings and goings were a precise reflection of social
advancement, the formation of a postrevolutionary elite and its self-
destruction in the 1930s.[11]

Based on the lists of residents, Wladislaw Hedeler has carried out
a meticulous reconstruction and produced an almost diagrammatic
picture of the 'movement of disappearance'.

The first wave of arrests merely brushed the House on the Embankment in July 1936. Six residents had vanished by the end of the
year. This was followed by 16 arrests in May 1937, while the number
leapt to 32 in June. In July the number fell to 25 and it fell further,
to 9, in August, only to climb again towards the end of the year:
11 in September, 16 in October and 22 in November. It fell again to
13 in December. In January 1938, it fell back again to 7 arrests, 5 in
February and 1 in March. In April it rose again to 14; in May it was
only 6, in June 7, in July 6 and in August only 2. This was followed
by a new increase: 4 in September, 5 in October, 9 in November and
4 in December. There were 8 further arrests up to April 1939. After
these ups and downs, Entrances 10 and 12 were almost completely
empty. New residents moved in.[12]

Within a brief period 'residents from 345 of the 505 apartments disappeared. Two residents were shot and buried in Butovo and 123 in
Kommunarka, while the ashes of 114 were scattered across the Donskoy
Cemetery close to the crematorium. Where the remains of a further 106
victims of shooting lie is uncertain. Ten men took their own lives so as
to escape arrest. After the men, it was the turn of the wives. They were
given a room in one of the three apartments assigned to the relatives
of arrested men. . . . The ordeals of 168 marriage partners living in the
Government House are more or less available to researchers. Seventeen were shot or died of the privations of camp life; the punishments
imposed on them lay between three and eight years. Forty-nine survived the camps from which they were released in 1946'.[13]

Every movement sent a message. Entry amounted to social advancement and a career. Exiting meant mainly transfer, arrest or death. Many of the apartments were staging posts on the way to the camps or firing squads. Many a kitchen and shared apartment were deemed by a paranoid power to be places where 'conspiracies' were hatched. Parents were arrested and only the children and the babushka were left behind—until they too were judged the children of enemies of the people and forced to leave. We can observe here codes of conduct dictated by fear. As long as people greeted one another in the hallways, the world was still in order. A person who was no longer greeted had become suspect, was excluded and as good as lost. People did not talk about this for no one could imagine that this might happen to them. But it happened to everyone. No one was immune and no one could explain why. It happened to members of the military, including Mikhail Tukhachevsky and Yakov Alksnis, who were shot in 1937. It happened to Comintern bigwigs, such as Karl Radek, Vilhelm Knorin and Solomon Lozovsky. Being a veteran of the Russian workers' movement no longer provided protection and so they lost their lives: Valerian Osinsky-Obolensky, the aristocrat among the Bolsheviks; Osip Pyatnitsky, who smuggled *Iskra* into Russia. The painter Heinrich Vogeler from Worpswede died during the evacuation from Kazakhstan. The House Club, today's Estrada Variety Theatre, was originally named after Alexey Rykov, the chairman of the Council of People's Commissars: he was condemned in a show trial and shot. Anna Larina, the wife of Nikolay Bukharin, who was also executed in 1938, lived in the house. There was only one other time when the residents were forced to pay such an exorbitant tribute: the Great Patriotic War. The list of victims can be inspected in the museum; it is horrifyingly long. The chaos wrought by the Great Terror in the House on the Embankment was so extensive that no proper inventory could be completed for 1937 and 1938. The confusion created by the wave of arrests ran out of control and many apartments had to be shut down. Looking down from the roof into the depth of the courtyards, you would be forgiven for thinking you were in a prison. The residence of the privileged stood exposed as a human trap—much like the Hotel Lux for members of the Comintern.

At some point after the death of the dictator, the situation calmed down. The nomenklatura admired the solid building close to the Kremlin. They included such dignitaries as Alexey Kosygin (Apartment 494), Nikolay Shvernik (Apartment 210) and Pyotr Abrassimov (Apartment 335). Jan Vogeler, the artist's son, lived in the house. George Blake, the British agent, found shelter there. There was a general refurbishment in the 1970s. The sense of solidarity among the 'old lags' gradually dissipated. By that time more comfortable and more modern apartments had become available farther out in the newly developed districts. The residents acquired a certain affluence. When Yury Trifonov tried to locate his father's library, which had been scattered throughout the building, the grandchildren and great-grandchildren of the founder generation could hardly wait to get rid of the old, worn-out furniture and throw it on the 'rubbish-heap of history'. The design and furnishings of the heroic phase of Soviet communism gradually disappeared. It took another while, down to the beginnings of perestroika in the 1980s, for the residents to start looking into the building's history and exploring its 'blank spaces'. We are indebted to their curiosity for the creation of the little museum, documentary films and informative guided tours.

Changing Times: From Gosdom to the Gated Community

The small exhibition at Entrance 1 presents the House on the Embankment as the museum of a vanished life form, a kind of *Titanic* of Soviet communism. There are still residents who can report on 'earlier times', before the great change. There are the children and grandchildren of the 'enemies of the people' who were gradually rehabilitated—after 1956 and again after 1985. There are people who collect vestiges of those times: Kuybyshev's phone, class photos, a sideboard and other relics. But only a small circle of people are interested in the museum. They meet once a year, hold minor conferences and keep the flame of memory alive. Today, the process of privatisation has turned the relic into a piece of real estate and the museum into a highly sought-after 'central location': opposite the Kremlin and the Cathedral of Christ the Saviour and all that goes with them—theatre, sport and culture. It has become a machine for living amid the turbulence of Russian capitalism. From the vantage point of the balconies from which sixty years ago you might have watched the demolition of Christ the Saviour, you can now see workers labouring night and day restoring the cathedral. The inner courtyards are full of parked cars, mostly foreign makes. The former 'Gastronom' for the elite has become a supermarket where you can buy anything you want and where people who can afford it do their shopping. There is no longer an Old Bolshevik such as Yelena Stasova to see to it that the salesgirls arrive for work on time. Instead, there are large numbers of security personnel who have to dress in black and ride around in black jeeps, as is the case everywhere else. The massive grey building has become a reef in whose gaps and pores the life of capitalist Moscow became lodged in the 1990s: kiosks, snack bars, small restaurants, shops and fitness studios. The battle for ownership of the prestigious piece of real estate has been going on for some time and has probably been resolved by now. Where Stalin's personal aide, Alexander Poskryobyshev, once lived is now the home of the Moscow representative of an international company. The internationalism of the business community has triumphed over the spirit of the Comintern. While age-old Bolsheviks, some of whom are still alive, are given regular meals in the refectory of a nearby monastery, American historians have rented accommodation in the house in order to research into the 'Stalin phenomenon'. With its eleven floors and massive volume, Gosdom had once anticipated the Moscow of the future. It is now fading into relative insignificance in the shadow of the dome of the Cathedral of Christ the Saviour, that remake of the nineteenth-century building designed by Konstantin Thon. The scent of chocolate no longer wafts over from the Red October factory. The Udarnik cinema presents Hollywood films and is illuminated in blue lights at night, like some phosphorescent deep-sea animal.

The heyday of the House on the Embankment now lies in the past. The privileged inhabitants of the new Moscow have a different lifestyle. Unlike their predecessors who lived modest, abstemious lives, they are not ashamed of their wealth and have learned how to put it on show. It does not occur to them to make do with the typical four-room apartments. They set about tearing down walls to create rooms that are vast for a town where people pay fairy-tale sums per square metre of space. They pay their architects and designers to create penthouse landscapes for them from the costliest materials. What they like best, however, is to build residences on forest land on Rublevskoe Chaussee: in Palladian, Georgian, Tudor, neo-Russian or some other style. They have now seen something of the world and wish to re-create that world for themselves.[14]

Even so, it is as if the House on the Embankment were experiencing something of a revival but in other locations. Everywhere in the city great compounds and new residential blocks are being built. They have names like 'Triumph Palace' or 'Purple Sail'. They are incomparably more luxurious and extravagant with their marble lobbies and foyers, their fountains, supermarkets, restaurants, banks, fitness and wellness centres, tennis courts and underground garages. It is no longer necessary to leave the city to be in contact with the outside world, for people have broadband, satellite dishes and internet connectivity. The House on the Embankment had been barred to outsiders, and so too are the new residential complexes, only for the latter the identity card and security system is incomparably more sophisticated. The city within the city has returned as a gated community and where once the House on the Embankment was the precursor of the Moscow of the future, today's gated communities anticipate the Moscow of tomorrow. An old story enters upon a new phase.

CHAPTER 52

The Aura of the Telephone and the Absence of the Phone Book

In the municipal or factory museums that could be found in every larger Soviet town, the age of industrialisation was represented for the most part by the office of a 'Red Factory Director' or the chairman of a town executive committee. The model inventory of such an office contained such items as a massive desk with a felt or leather blotting pad, an imposing set of matching bronze or porphyry writing utensils, a number of notebooks and files, a leather Art Deco–style armchair, a bookcase, perhaps a radio, a portrait of Stalin or the relevant people's commissar on the wall, a flower stand with an embroidered cloth and—an obligatory feature—a large telephone on the desk. It was as if this telephone represented a hot line to power, as if the directives issued from this office acquired their importance from the sheer size of the telephone itself. The room may also have had a carpet but apart from that the furnishings were minimal, Spartan even. The telephone was the emblem of the 'commanding heights of power'. Considered purely as an object, there was probably little to distinguish it from the phones in the headquarters of Western capitalist companies.

Now that the era of satellite phones, smartphones and tablets has arrived, traditional telephones of this kind look like fossils of an age long since vanished in both Russia and the West. And yet the Soviet phone also tells a different story about the connections between technical innovation, infrastructure development, social communication and the exercise of power. The telephone we remember from the late phase of the Soviet Union has left its traces in literature and especially the cinema. Boris Pilnyak's 1926 'Tale of the Unextinguished Moon' reads like fiction but contains a number of thinly veiled references to the story of the death of Mikhail Frunze, a high-ranking Red Army leader and Civil War hero, on the operating table of a Moscow hospital. The order to carry out this operation comes on the telephone of the 'unbending First Man', that is, Stalin. Pilnyak gives us a glimpse of his office:

> In this house unbroken silence settled, telephone bells were muf-
> fled, abacuses were quiet, people walked about noiselessly, people
> were not agitated, people did not stoop; the walls, covered with
> posters that had replaced paintings, stood erect; red carpets lay
> on the floor; at the doors stood men with red stripes on their uni-
> forms. In the study at the far end of the house, the heavy curtains
> were half-drawn, and beyond the windows the street hurried by; a
> fire was burning in the grate; on the red felt of the desk stood three
> telephones as if to affirm, in company with the crackling logs in the
> fireplace, the quietness of the room; the three telephones brought
> three of the city's arteries into the study, so that from its silence
> commands could be issued and so that everything going on in the
> city's arteries could be known. On the desk stood a writing set,
> bronze and massive, and in the penholder were stuck a dozen red
> and blue pencils. To the wall behind the desk was attached a radio
> receiver with two pairs of earphones and rows of electric buttons
> were lined up like a company of soldiers at attention—from one
> connecting with the reception room to one marked 'War Alarm'.
> Opposite the desk stood a leather armchair. Behind the desk the
> unbending man sat on a wooden chair. The heavy curtains were
> half-drawn, and on the desk an electric light burned under a green
> shade; the face of the unbending man was lost in the shadows.[1]

The telephone conveyed inquiries, reports and news items from the whole nation, indeed the whole world, from countless organisa-tions such as the Narkomvnudel [the NKVD], the Political and Eco-nomic Divisions of the OGPU, the Narkomfin [People's Commissariat for Finance], Narkomvneshtorg [People's Commissariat for Foreign Trade] and Narkomtrud [People's Commissariat for Labour].[2] It is by telephone that the consultant to carry out the operation receives his instructions; it is by means of the telephone that he himself became one of the privileged when 'he made a telephone call with a solemn face and a sort of nervous respectfulness': 'by means of all sorts of telephonic roundabout ways, the professor penetrated the network of about thirty or forty lines in all, calling the study of House Number

One [i.e., the Kremlin]' in order to ask 'respectfully if there would be any new instructions.' Professor Lozovsky 'went over to the window in the office where the telephone was, stood looking out at the first snow for a while, chewed his fingers, and then returned to the telephone; he penetrated the network that had thirty or forty lines, bowed to the receiver, and said that the operation had been successful, but the patient was very weak, and they, the doctors, had judged his condition to be grave—he begged to be excused from reporting in person immediately'.[3] Stalin's telephone calls were no literary invention; they have frequently been confirmed as fact. Notable examples were his nocturnal calls to Mikhail Bulgakov and Boris Pasternak, which might well have cost the lives of these writers and their friends.[4]

The phone plays a similar part in Mikhail Bulgakov's *The Master and Margarita*, when Woland's retinue activates anonymous phone calls from Apartment 50 or when all the phones in the Variety Theatre suddenly fail to work. Protagonists are also summoned by phone for interrogation.[5]

The role of the telephone as an instrument of power became completely clear in Solzhenitsyn's semifictional novel *In the First Circle*, set in a camp for scientists, a *sharashka*, at the end of the 1940s. The scientists are working to develop technology that would make it possible to identify the voices of suspect telephone users.[6] The telephone as an instrument of control, of state-organised spying, is not just a literary topos, but a reality right down to the end of the Soviet Union where dissidents avoided the phone on principle when they were arranging meetings or had important matters to discuss.

In other societies, too, the telephone was an emblem of progress, an index of the advances made in the creation of a modern infrastructure. This was especially the case in Russia, as can readily be seen from a comparison between telephone use and coverage in the USA, Britain and Germany in the early twentieth century. But the primary issue here is not the disparity in the sheer number of telephones but a specific connection between infrastructure and power.[7] Yevgeniya Ginzburg's arrest in 1937 begins with a telephone call:

Suddenly the telephone rang. It sounded as shrill as on that night in December 'thirtyfour. For a few moments none of us moved. We hated telephone calls in those days. Then my husband said in that same unnaturally calm voice he so often used now: 'It must be Lukovnikov. I asked him to ring up.' He took the receiver, listened, went white as a sheet and spoke even more quietly: 'It's for you, Jenny. Vevers of the NKVD'. Vevers, the Head of the NKVD department for special political affairs, could not have been more amiable and charming. His voice gushed like a brook in spring.[8]

At the end of Ginzburg's time in the camp on the Kolyma and her transfer to Magadan, the telephone becomes the medium signalling the end of an era: 'The final improbable miracle of miracles was the appearance of a telephone on our table ... I still remember to this day the number of that telephone, the first in the life that had begun for me on March 5, 1953: 22–71. There was no automatic exchange in Magadan in those days, and instead of a soulless buzz you heard a melodious little voice, saying conspiratorially, "I am putting you through..."'[9]

To own a telephone was a privilege until very late in the life of the Soviet Union—not very different, admittedly, from the situation in other European countries. The difference lay in the existence of a separate, self-contained phone system available only to a select circle of participants largely identical with the nomenklatura.

The self-contained phone network began in September 1918 with the establishment of a special telephone room in the Kremlin and soon became known as *vertushka*, a name that refers to a direct link to the Kremlin and was confined to a strictly limited circle of people. In 1922 an automatic exchange linked up the homes of around three hundred leading officials—Felix Dzerzhinsky's phone number was 007. This system was gradually extended, so that by the end of the 1940s the Kremlin network had 1,000 numbers; this had risen to a good 3,500 by the early 1950s. In the 1960s the governments of the socialist states adopted the same system together with its data encryption techniques. Likewise in the 1960s, radio networks were added that enabled the central system of governmental communications, which had existed hitherto only in Moscow, to expand to include other towns. By the mid-1980s around 7,000 telephones could be reached via ATC-2 and a further 10,000 phones in the entire country. By the mid-1990s the communications network of governmental agencies reached around 300 towns and special sites, totalling around 20,000 phone connections. Vertushka refers to the telephone network of the elite nomenklatura, a one-sided communication from above to below; the phones in this category really are emblems of access to power or membership of the ruling elite, much like the privilege of shopping in the special stores.[10] As for the 'normal' phone network, the horizontal communication of people among themselves, what stands out is the lack of provision and underdevelopment of the communications sector in the USSR.[11] From the 1960s on, the larger towns all had public phones—labelled TAKSOFON—known for their simple, robust construction, which enabled them to resist the weather and attacks by vandals until the very end. They were located in groups of two to six in the entrance halls of metro stations, the foyers of theatres and cinemas, institutes, and heavily frequented underpasses and intersections. Until 1992 there was no time limit on phone conversations, and since a call cost only two kopeks however long it might last, the telephone was the place for never-ending chats regardless of the length of the queue of people waiting. The indifference towards the lengthening queues was something of a demonstration of power. The endless palaver on the phone that did not let itself be disconcerted by anything or anyone was also the expression of a different sense of time and economy—as were the queues themselves. In the shared apartments too, where there was only one telephone for the numerous residents and lengthy waits and queues were a fact of life, the phone was a special focus of attention because all private conversations inevitably had other people listening in.

Special bureaucratic rules applied, leading to increased difficulties if you wanted to make a long-distance call or call someone abroad, since these often meant waiting for hours. But the feature that really distinguishes the Soviet telephone culture was the absence of the phone book. Books with telephone numbers and addresses in alphabetical order have a 'democratic' structure. In that sense they are abbreviated versions of society, an image of society reduced to its bare bones. They allow users to enter into direct, horizontal communication. They are navigation instruments with which to find one's way around the urban 'jungle'.[12] Russia, like all other modern states, had a long tradition of address books and telephone books before 1917. 'Ves Peterburg' or

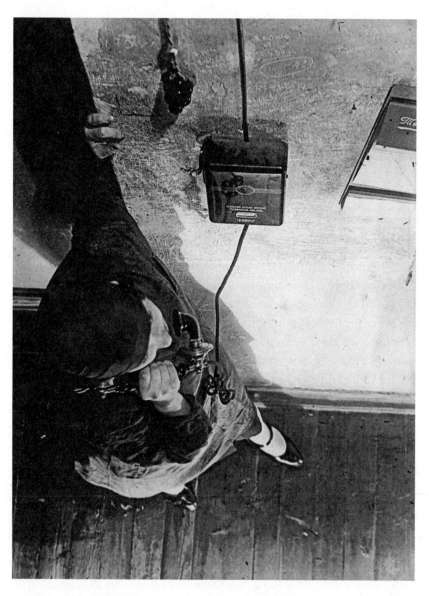

FIGURE 52.1. Alexander Rodchenko, *On the Telephone*, 1928. © VG Bild-Kunst, Bonn 2018, House of Photography, Moscow. Photo: akg-images/Archive Photos.

'Vsya Moskva' both date from before the Revolution. Today some annual editions from the 1920s are considered antiquarian rarities and key texts for the exploration of social and cultural topographies. The disappearance of general address books and phone books in 1937—and their reappearance during the 1980s—points to the lack of transparency in social relationships and its eventual return.

The Soviet-type address and phone books were distinguished by another kind of hierarchical arrangement as well. At the top of the 'power tree' were the supreme government offices, followed by central party echelons and authorities, social organisations, scientific institutions, health organisations, and public transport, and on to the local economy and services. The best comparison is with what is known in Western societies as the Yellow Pages, but reduced to a skeletal institutional framework. Because they were published in small editions, these phone books were limited to a relatively small number of users. The last of these books, 'Moscow: Telephones and Addresses of Organisations, Institutes and Enterprises', appeared in 1989, in an edition brought out by the Ministry of Communications. The private phone book, which remained unchanged over decades, greasy and the worse for wear from overuse, was a necessary expedient in the absence of a generally accessible and available phone book, which had once been an integral part of civilisation in Russia, as it was elsewhere.

With the advent of perestroika the phone book became generally available once again, but has itself been superseded by a far more fundamental change. The communication revolution has established itself in post-Soviet Russia with great speed and completely altered everyday life in ways that amount to a new understanding of time and space.[13] As a result the generation that has had no direct experience of the Soviet Union finds it difficult even to imagine what it was like in an age before mobile phones existed. The vast distances are still there but thanks to the satellite phones even the most remote part of Siberia can now be reached. Nobody has to stand in line any more in the Central Telegraph Office. That building, itself an architectural masterpiece of the late nineteenth century, lies abandoned and almost useless, waiting to be given a new function. Wherever people happen to be—in the metro, in midjourney, in the dacha—they create their own communication space directly, autonomously, horizontally, without requiring the mediation of a central authority. The phone, the vertushka, the all-seeing authority where the arteries of power all converge—the very essence of hierarchy and centralisation—has lost its dominant position. Even the classic telephone book that had a brief revival at the end of the 1980s has become superfluous in the age of the internet.

PART XIV

The Noise of Time

'The Noise of Time' is the title of a brilliant collection of essays by Osip Mandelstam in which he recalls the atmosphere of his childhood and youth in St. Petersburg at the beginning of the twentieth century, the high spirits in Pavlovsk Station, famous for one of the 'pleasure gardens' of the capital. Everything was peaceful and festive; he heard the rustle of clothing, orchestral music and the guest performances of famous conductors from everywhere in Europe.[1] Mandelstam had an ear for the noise of time. Epochs have their own background sounds. The absence of machines did not mean that all was silent, but everything was much fainter when compared to what followed. Coaches, horses' hooves, the bustle of the markets, the processions accompanied by pious hymns all produced a noise different from rotors, pumps, wheels, turbines and factory sirens. Eras were reorchestrated. Composers and music scores succeeded one another. A space that had been organised by church clocks and bell towers gave way to one regulated by the rhythm of railway timetables. Time now followed the progress of a wristwatch, which no one could afford to be without.

We have many pictures from the early years of the twentieth century, but few recordings. We watch on screen as the demonstrators on Nevsky Prospekt fall over, but we do not hear the shots that brought them down. We know all about the cannon shot fired by the cruiser *Aurora* and can see the traces of the (slight) damage caused by the explosion, but the noise created by this world-shaking bombardment has been lost to posterity forever. Pictures, when they exist (and have not been staged subsequently, as they were by Eisenstein), are silent and we have to imagine the sounds of the era prior to the emergence of recording technology, the documentary and the sound film.[2]

There are sharp caesuras in the noise of time but also transitions, overlapping sounds, and sometimes it is not quite clear whether the dominant sound is that of the past era or the new one. The march of the military band blends in with the solemn funeral march used by workers to accompany their fallen comrades to the grave.[3]

In contrast, the disappearance of many thousands of people without a trace occurred soundlessly. Quite early on there were soundtracks for the rituals of power—for appearances at Party congresses or for Dunaevsky's triumphal chorus, *Shiroka strana moya rodnaya* . . . , 'Wide is my motherland . . .', and for parades on Red Square. But there is no soundtrack leading to the trainloads of deportees, the camps on the Arctic Circle or the shooting ranges. But just think of all the sounds stored in the inner ear and the memory that ought to be recalled: the early morning ring at the door that announced that your house was about to be searched or that you would be arrested by NKVD personnel; the slamming of the car door when the Black Maria drove off; the noise made by the key turning in the cell door lock, the blow delivered to the cast-iron block that served as a gong, summoning the prisoners to the morning roll call; the metallic crackling of the loudspeakers announcing the latest achievements of top workers or celebrating the day with a rendition of the 'Internationale'. An entire continent has disappeared without a sound and can never be recovered. However, even the faintest whisper or the vaguest rumour is preserved in the informer reports that bear the label 'To be stored for all eternity'.[4]

CHAPTER 53

The Bells Fall Silent

Walter Benjamin, who was in Moscow in the winter of 1926/27, could not have known what he had missed when he noted approvingly in his diary that everything was peaceful in Moscow. 'Moscow has been virtually rid of the sound of bells that tends to spread such an irresistible sadness over large cities. This too is something one only realises and appreciates on one's return.'[1] For the visitor from the Berlin of the 1920s, a city that never slept but still had the chimes of bells, the absence of bells appeared to be the mark of a Russia in the process of opening itself up to a modern, secularised world. Benjamin had no idea of the phenomenon that had so fascinated Rainer Maria Rilke and his fellow travellers two decades earlier: the sound world of 'Holy Russia'. Moreover, he could not have imagined the change that would take place shortly after his return in 1929–1932, namely the systematic destruction of churches and bell towers and the unique sound world that had developed over centuries. It is difficult to describe in words sound worlds whose instruments and musical scores were largely destroyed during the twentieth century.[2]

Sound Clouds: The Acoustic Texture of Old Russia

A student of the world of Russian bells, N. I. Olovyanishnikov attempted in his standard work *History of Bells and the Bell Founder's Art*, published in Moscow in 1912, to convey something of the magic of the sound, in particular of the Ivan Veliky Bell Tower in the Moscow Kremlin.

> The sound—zvon—of the Ivan Bell Tower is extraordinarily festive, especially when all the bells are involved, which is what happens on the great holidays and other solemn occasions. This is called 'the beautiful sound'—*krasny zvon*—and it has its own particular melody.
> On the Easter Vigil the bells are rung in accordance with an ancient tradition. The morning peals sounding the call to divine

service begin from the Ivan Veliky Tower in the Kremlin. In order to develop the greatest possible solemnity and magnificence all the Moscow churches have to wait until the mighty Uspensky Bell in Ivan Veliky has chimed.

At its first stroke, an answer echoes back from the distant bell of the Strastnoy Monastery, and then, as if in response to a conductor's baton, the bells of all forty-times-forty Moscow churches ring out.

The clock on the Spassky Tower has not yet struck midnight when . . . the alarm bells from the Cathedral of the Dormition start to sound shrilly and urgently and the thousand-headed crowd on Kremlin Square falls silent. . . . Then the air begins to vibrate, interrupted by the sonorous but soft peal of the Uspensky Bell! Solemnly, a broad wave of sound arises, spreads out and rolls down from the Kremlin Hill over the Moskva River and far out into the surrounding countryside.

How wonderfully, how solemnly this compact, 'velvety' B Minor causes the cold night air to vibrate. The second stroke is already somewhat stronger, more powerful, and by way of reply it merges with the thunderous peal of a thousand bells of all the churches to form a sustained, booming roar.

More and more joyous tones resound, merge with one another and fade away in the solemn stillness of the night! You sometimes feel as if these sounds were not of earthly origin but as if this powerful peal of bells poured out from the dark heavens above onto a silent world frozen in hushed reverence.

This sublime, 'beautiful sound'—*krasny zvon*—of Moscow's, this celestial language, can best be heard from high up on the Sparrow Hills when the wind is blowing towards the city. The mass of sounds then becomes embroiled with the current of air and instead of reaching our ears all at once, arrives bit by bit and fills the mighty space that stretches out between the Sparrow Hills and the city.[3]

A. N. Muravyov was captivated by the same magic. He too toured the holy places:

In the midst of the mysterious stillness of this polyphonic night— *mnogoglagolivoy*—I suddenly heard from the top of Ivan Veliky, as if welling up from the depths of the heavens, the first note of the bell—*blagovest*—proclaiming the good news prophetically, like the archangel's clarion call announcing the universal resurrection. And there, at a signal from the Kremlin, thousands of bells obedient to the call from Ivan Veliky filled the air with their chimes, and their thunderous metallic roar passed over the entire venerable capital of the old Tsars; that capital was utterly transfixed by this solemn sound as if by a certain atmosphere peculiar to itself, permeated through and through by the sacred shudder of vibrating copper and by the joy of festive church music. The ear heard and could not hear enough of a wonderful harmony that seemed to waft over from another, heavenly world.[4]

Bells were a fixed component of everyday life in Russia, as in the rest of Europe. They told the hour and conveyed the rhythm of work and leisure time. Bells and the carpet of sound they produced created the 'musical framework of the day'.[5] They were rung when fires broke out, when there was a great disaster or when a hostile country launched an invasion. They rang out when people came together or had been summoned to battle against autocrats, as Alexander Herzen had attempted with his exile journal *The Bell (Kolokol)*. Birth, baptism and death were announced in the 'language of bells', as were everyday occurrences and events that affected the entire nation—a nuanced and irreplaceable communication system.

Bells and their peals fascinated foreign visitors to the Empire of the Tsars, from Adam Olearius to Rainer Maria Rilke, and down to this day the Tsar Bell, Tsar Kolokol, which was cast in 1735, can still be seen in the Kremlin. Weighing more than 200 tons, it remains a visitor attraction even though the bell has never been rung. The sound of Russian bells was different, as the philosopher and writer Vasily Rozanov once remarked:

Have you ever noticed that the Catholic Church and our church have bells that sound differently? In the Catholic Church the ringing of the bells sounds like the meowing of a cat. There is no accounting for taste. There is something of a cat's prowling and stretching itself about it. With us it is more like a heifer prancing about. Bass, tenor and descant—everything is harmonious. The 'choral element' of the Slavophiles? I don't know. At any rate, the choice of the specific sound of our bells is of far greater importance for Russian towns and villages than the 'filioque' that remains incomprehensible to everyone. How many sceptics and satirists have been dissuaded from protest, criticism and satire by the sad, melodious sound of the Russian bells at vespers and it may be because of that gentle ringing that no Voltaire or Renan ever saw the light of the world here.[6]

The bells hang in various storeys of the bell towers or separately in special structures. They don't swing but the clappers of different sizes and pitches are made to strike the bell walls by bell ringers—zvonari—using ropes and cords, which produce a multifaceted, almost filigree web of delicate, polyphonic sound reminiscent more of a silvery, shimmering tinkling than the steadily oscillating drone of the bells in Western European cathedrals; a sort of carillon with infinite variants and nuances, a specific grammar accessible only to initiates, and very different bell types—hourly chimes, Sunday chimes, Lenten bells, and so on—brought forth by ringers who have not learned their art by studying scores—there were none—but took over what they learned from their predecessors and teachers. The way the bell ringer manipulates the numerous ropes, threads and cords brings to mind work on a loom or the actions of a carpet weaver, in this instance creating a carpet of sound. There are different schools of bell ringing—such as those of Pskov and Novgorod. The first recordings of these polyphonic, symphonic 'performances' were produced in 1914.[7]

Dual Form of Rule: Bells versus Factory Sirens

Since bell towers and bell ringing stood wholly and completely for the power of the Orthodox Church, for the traditions of Old Russia, but also for a deeply embedded popular piety, conflict with Soviet power was unavoidable. Bells 'disturbed'; they demonstrated the presence of a spiritual and cultural hegemony that had to be broken. Bells should not be allowed to mobilise the faithful against the Soviet power. The bells aroused the appetite of the new rulers much as the other possessions of the churches and monasteries did. Iconostases, chandeliers, gold and silver chalices, wrought-iron rails and other 'cultural objects' could all be confiscated, melted down or sold off abroad and so too could bells if the authorities decided that they had an economic value. The 'bell war' was launched from the highest places while 'lower down', local authorities could not take possession of church property fast enough. Their wish was to put it to good use and turn 'useless' bell towers into 'useful' water towers or fire stations for the proletariat.

The 'War of the Bells', the conflict between two different sound worlds, surfaced in the experiments of the Soviet musical avant-garde and the theatre.[8] The bell towers were to be replaced by radio stations, the bell ringers by technicians and the bells by factory sirens; and the figure of the 'conductor', posted at a visible vantage point over the industrial terrain, was supposed to use flags and light signals to coordinate the orchestra composed of machines, steam boilers, the chugging of locomotives, honking and whistling. Alexander Mosolov's 'Iron Foundry' music still stands as an exemplary illustration of this trend.[9]

The early aesthetic concept of musical modernity that mobilised the noise of industry and the sounds of everyday life against the sacred aura of church music and liturgical song was rediscovered decades later, just like other pioneering achievements of Soviet modernity, such as street theatre. In the Soviet Union itself these remained isolated experiments—in Moscow, Ivanovo-Voznesensk or Baku—which never succeeded in competing with the daily sound routine of the Russian Orthodox world that had been practised and refined for centuries. The militant aggression of the Soviet atheist movement was the expression of an almost hopeless social isolation. To break out of that would have required a special degree of self-confidence, arrogance and sheer muscular violence—as well as the support of state power.

The attack on the sound world of the bell towers began with the industrialisation and collectivisation campaign and the accompanying culture revolution of 1928–1929. At that time, the activists of the atheist movement, for the most part young, militant communists, launched a campaign aimed at destroying churches, bell towers and the bells themselves. The 'resolute struggle against the sound of bells'—*zvon*—was a component of the programme of the League of Militant Atheists, which was determined to enforce its claims on the spot, always justifying its actions by arguing that it was essential to obey the imperatives of industrialisation: churches and bell towers were to be torn down or blown up to provide the construction materials for the buildings of communism, workingmen's clubs and palaces of culture, stadiums and Soviet municipalities. The sounds of bells were even said to be harmful to people's health.

In the preface to a book titled 'Church Bells in the Service of the Magic of Tsarism', by P. V. Gidulyanov, previously a professor of canon law, we read: 'With every year that passed, this violent noise became quieter and quieter. The time has come when church bells should finally fall silent throughout the entire territory of the USSR and make way for factories' and works' sirens. Today, in our opinion, it is the duty of active atheists to take possession of the vast quantity of valuable metal in the church bells, which still continue to ring out on the side of the exploiting classes, and hand it over to the smiths of our Five-Year Plan so as to further the progress of our Soviet industry.' Gidulyanov also recommended selling the bells to collectors of antiquities abroad instead of melting them down—a proposal that was in fact implemented.[10]

In the overheated, hysterical climate of collectivisation and the industrialisation campaign, this led to a hurricane of destruction, the upshot of which was that the rich culture and sound of bells were entirely lost to Russia. The famous bells of the cathedral of Kostroma were melted down in the foundry in Tula; the bells of the Suzdal monasteries were turned over to the State Commission of the Industrial Estate in Ivanovo. Frequently, the demolition and melting down of the bells went along with tearing down the bell towers as well. This was the case with the Zaikonospassky, Nikitsky and Sretensky Monasteries in Moscow. The bell towers of the Simonov and Andronikov Monasteries were also torn down. The resulting supply of bricks was used for new buildings such as the palace of culture designed by the Vesnin brothers for the ZIL car plant, a masterpiece of Constructivism. All these bells were not simply made of nonferrous metal whose values could be measured in tonnes and

FIGURE 53.1. Fallen bells, the early 1930s. Privately owned.

hundredweights; they had their own history and were closely bound up with the development of the Muscovite and Russian Empire. Now, they were torn down from their towers, smashed and transported to foundries.

The losses in the Holy Trinity Lavra Monastery of Sergiev Posad, at the heart of Russian Orthodoxy, must have been especially tragic. The writer Mikhail Prishvin, an eyewitness, noted in his diary:

> On 11 January 1930, they brought the Kornuchy Bell crashing down. How different the bells were in the manner of their death. The Great Tsar Bell, like the Great Bell, trusted humans to do it no harm and so surrendered quietly, settled down on the tracks and was swiftly removed. Masses of children went up to it and all this week they made the bell ring and even turned the interior of the bell into a regular children's nursery. The Kornuchy Bell somehow knew that something was amiss and resisted from the outset. It swayed around until it broke the lifting frame, splintered the wooden beam beneath it and then tore the rope. It strained against being lowered onto the track and had to be dragged with hawsers. . . . When it crashed down, it was smashed to pieces.

At the end of 1930 Prishvin observed in his diary: 'The anniversary of the destruction of the bells of Sergiev Posad is approaching. It is highly reminiscent of the theatre of a public execution.' And elsewhere he commented: 'Last month I witnessed the destruction of the Rastrelli bell tower, one of the rarest musical instruments in the world, it was indeed unique: the greatest bells of the world of the age of Boris Godunov were brought crashing down. This campaign was utterly senseless as far as its material benefits were concerned: it would have been easy to obtain 8,000 *pud* of bronze from ordinary bells. From the point of view of the League of Militant Atheists this action cannot be justified since from the very beginning of human culture bells have been at the service of human society as a whole, and not of the Church.'[11] There were attempts at resistance—by the composer and campanologist Konstantin Saradzhev, for example—as well as by restorers and museum professionals.[12] Moscow suffered disproportionately because of the profusion of churches and monasteries and also because of the ruthless implementation of the demolition and rebuilding programme in the first two Five-Year Plans. Some bells were saved by being handed over to the opera theatres whenever they didn't lose out to the offers for nonferrous metals from the powerful industrial combines. Many bells that had been melted down reappeared in new buildings as part of Stalin's General Plan for Moscow. The bronze reliefs on the façade of the Lenin Library are one example.

The commission set up to realise the value of cultural objects appears to have been less interested in preventing this chaotic, disorganised process of destruction than in regaining control of it and integrating it into the 'Plan'. This was achieved by passing the decision-making authority to regional and municipal councils, which in practice amounted to a 'death sentence' for the bells (V. F. Kozlov). The inestimable cultural value of the bells and the bell ringer's art was transposed into the language of bureaucratic planners; henceforth bells were appraised according to their weight, in hundredweights and tonnes. 'In the course of a few years almost all the bells that had been cast by a deeply pious Russian orthodoxy over the centuries were systematically destroyed. Early in the 1930s more than 100 bells were removed from the bell towers of old Novgorod and thrown into

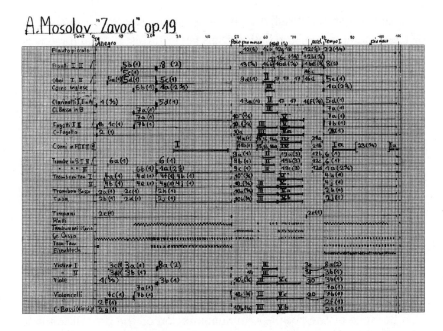

FIGURE 53.2. The tone and rhythm of the new age are supposed to resonate in Alexander Mosolov's machine music 'Iron Foundry', op. 19, 1928. From Detlef Gojowy, *Neue sowjetische Musik der 20er Jahre*, Laaber Verlag, Regensburg 1980.

the foundry furnaces. The same fate befell almost half the bells of the Moscow Kremlin. In the surrounding districts of Moscow and in other provinces special brigades were sent out with maps to register the bells with a view to "purging" the different regions.[13]

The position of the Orthodox Church improved for a while during the mobilisation of the Great Patriotic War. But there was a new setback with the militant persecution at the start of the 1960s even though the expropriations and demolition of buildings were—inevitably—not on the same scale as in the 1920s and 1930s. Moreover, the church remained in the background and under the control of the Communist Party, the secret services and the state up to the very end of the Soviet Union.

The sound of bells was banished from the public space. But anyone with ears could still hear them. The sound of the Russian world of bells survived in a sublimated form, in the operas of the Russian composers—Borodin's *Prince Igor*, Tchaikovsky's *Oprichnik* [*The*

Guardsman], Rimsky-Korsakov's *The Maid of Pskov* and *The Legend of the Invisible City of Kitezh*, as well as in Rachmaninov's cantata *The Bells* or Mussorgsky's *Boris Godunov*—and accessible to foreigners in Maurice Ravel's orchestration of *Pictures at an Exhibition*. In the West, Serge Jaroff's Don Cossack Choir moved audiences deeply and provoked thunderous applause for their performances of *Vecherny zvon* (Evening bells) in their tours through the centres of the Russian diaspora. Until recently, visitors to Lowell House on the Harvard University campus in Cambridge, Massachusetts, could hear the sound of bells that had been sold to American buyers to finance Stalin's Five-Year Plan. These bells had been set up in their new home by Konstantin Konstantinovich Saradzhev, the leading expert on Russian bell music. They have since returned to their original home, the Danilov Monastery in Moscow.[14] This was not the first time that bells that had fallen silent were brought back to life. Alexander Herzen's periodical *The Bell* was still available in Tsarist Russia long after he died in exile in France in 1870.[15]

Post-Soviet Soundtrack

The end of the Soviet Union has brought the bells back into the public sphere with everything that implies: the Russian Orthodox Church has resumed the position of power that it held at the time of the *symphonia*, the symbiosis of church and state in the Tsarist Empire. From a position of utter invisibility, it has returned to one of almost monumental visibility. Church property that had been confiscated was restored to it; icons and iconostases were taken from museums and given back to churches and monasteries. Thousands of churches and hundreds of monasteries have been expensively renovated. The church's new role as spiritual pillar of the state is expressed in such symbolically crucial buildings as the Cathedral of Christ the Saviour in the centre of Moscow, whose predecessor had been demolished in 1931 in favour of the Palace of the Soviets that was never completed. It is expressed in the liturgical ceremonies performed jointly by the patriarchate and the state, which led to what Richard Wortman calls the 'scenarios of power' that have become established in post-Soviet Russia.

Over the flat countryside the gleaming, golden domes of renovated churches are the emblems of a spiritual *reconquista* in jaded Russian villages. The church has a kind of foreign-policy function in creating a global protected 'Russian world' with grandiose new buildings, such as St. Vladimir's Cathedral in Paris. But even in the microdistricts of the large towns and cities the golden domes of new churches can be glimpsed between the massive high-rise apartment blocks. The bell foundries that had completely disappeared are enjoying a revival. The Moscow ZIL car plant and the St. Petersburg Baltic factory have taken to casting bells. In the markets you can find stalls for bells of every size and tuning, just like before the Revolution. The art of the carillon is again being learned and taught; its typical notes can again be heard. On holidays clouds of sound rise up to heaven—just as if they had never been silenced during the twentieth century.

CHAPTER 54

Levitan's Voice

'Citizens of the Soviet Union! Today at 4 o'clock a.m., without any claims having been presented to the Soviet Union, without a declaration of war, German troops attacked our country.' With these words Vyacheslav Molotov, People's Commissar for Foreign Affairs, addressed the Soviet population directly at noon on 22 June 1941 and informed them of Hitler Germany's attack on the Soviet Union. Photos of this moment show an entire nation rigid with shock, as in a torn film strip. A summer's day. People stopped just where they happened to be—on pavements, squares or in stations—and stared in silence at the loudspeakers mounted on house façades and lampposts. From that point on, the text of Molotov's speech was repeated every hour, nine times daily by Radio Moscow. But instead of Molotov's voice what people heard was the voice of Yury Borisovich Levitan. Few Soviet citizens of that time had not heard his voice; most recognised it instantly. The reporting of the course of the Soviet-German War has become so identified with the sound of Levitan's voice that Soviet citizens who lived through the Great Patriotic War tend to remember his voice rather than Molotov's. They may even remember Levitan's voice better than Stalin's for it was not until 3 July—eleven days after the outbreak of war—that Stalin recovered from his depression, pulled himself together and delivered his memorable address to his subjects, whom he, somewhat surprisingly, called his 'brothers and sisters'.

From 22 June 1941 until 9 May 1945 every day began and ended for millions of listeners with the news broadcasts of the Sovinformbyuro (Soviet Information Bureau) that had been founded two days after the outbreak of war. In the 1,418 days of the war, Levitan read the news from the front over two thousand times.[1] *Voix de mémoire*—not *lieu de mémoire*: we are concerned here with a voice rather than a place as the fixed point of the memory of an entire generation. Wherever he appeared in public after the war, Levitan would be perceived as the persona and the voice that everybody recognised. That voice was

FIGURE 54.1. 22 June 1941, the moment when everything changed. A sunny summer's day and the start of the German attack on the Soviet Union. The photo captures the moment when passersby on the Ilyinka in Moscow learned of the attack, which had been launched in the early hours of that morning. © akg-images/Voller Ernst/Chaldej.

present every day during times of mortal danger, when minute details take on a graver role: it was present in the trenches, in homes and factories, in Leningrad under siege as well as in the hinterland where everyone worked for the front.

Wherever he went after the war, Levitan found himself surrounded by veterans who had come out of the war alive. Right up to his death in a village in the Belgorod region on 4 August 1983—this last journey too had been undertaken for a reunion with veterans of the tank battle in Kursk—he received mail from people who had been in the war. If Levitan's voice was so completely identified with the experience of the war generation, this suggests that he was the personification of an age that was both catastrophic and heroic. Levitan was more *primus* than *primus inter pares* and this raises the question of why his voice mattered more than all others in a long list of spokespeople—where his voice came from and what it stood for. We must also ask what happened to it at the moment when the radio—the key medium of the age, a medium that had made him a figure of central importance—lost its status and was forced to give way to the primacy of television. For from that point on, voices counted for less than images.[2]

Technology and the Voice

We can experience Levitan's voice today without difficulty even though it has been pointed out in his biography that most broadcasts available today are re-recordings from the postwar period and don't convey the sound of the original live recordings.[3] Readers can obtain an impression of his voice by accessing online his news broadcasts on the German invasion (22 June 1941), the halting of the German offensive against Moscow (13 December 1941), breaking the siege of Leningrad (18 January 1943), the Soviet victory in Stalingrad (3 February 1943), and Germany's surrender (8 May 1945). It is worth listening to other recordings from the postwar and post-Stalin period by way of comparison: the announcement of Stalin's death on 5 March 1953, the success of the Soviet Sputnik on 4 October 1957, Yury Gagarin's space flight on 12 April 1961. The voice of the young Yury Borisovich Levitan, who was born on 2 October 1914 into a Jewish tailor's family

in the town of Vladimir to the northeast of Moscow, was widely felt
to be something special. His school fellows nicknamed him 'Trom-
bone' because of his resonant baritone voice; a friend in later years
advised him to donate his vocal cords to a museum of medicine after
his death. As an announcer his voice had a distinctive timbre, a deep,
sonorous sound. It had a medium volume and a characteristic melody;
his speech was even but not uniform. Every word, every syllable was
articulated clearly, almost overclearly. His speech flowed quietly but
not boringly. It quickened or slowed from time to time but not in an
overdramatised way; it was like listening to a musician moving between accelerando and ritardando. When he was reporting facts—the
number of tanks, divisions or casualties—he sounded as if reading
out statistics, one figure after the next, almost as if you were expected
to write them down, or like an inscription in which every letter has
been etched on a bronze plaque—not a steel plate. The even pace had
something of a litany, a liturgical hymn, an Our Father, and expressed
great calm and assurance, but sometimes it rose, hinting at the drama
and pathos of a given situation, such as the breaking of the blockade
of Leningrad. The animation and acceleration of his speech never
came close to hysteria or panic in either tone or tempo.

Levitan always gave voice to texts written by others but he did
not act as a mere loudspeaker; his speech was always shaped and
modulated—in other words, he put a lot of himself into it and even
into the way he articulated the sounds. He spoke in the name of an
institution or authority, but never adopted an officious or menacing
tone; instead his speech was simply weighty, as weighty as the facts
being reported. However 'subjective' and problematic it may be to
analyse his speech in this way, something in it evidently enabled
him to become the authoritative public voice of his day. Its sonorous
timbre avoided ecstatic tones of the kind found in agitators; it had
something thoughtful and perhaps even paternal about it, a certain
formality and rigour, but without menacing overtones. A calm voice
like this could be relied on; his listeners hung on his every word since
what he had to say could affect life-and-death decisions and the fate
of prisoners of war or family members at moments when it was vitally
important to obtain timely information about the war situation and
hence about personal and national tragedies. Anyone who wished to

keep up with events had to listen to the oral news bulletins—and the final news programme at night—since everything further depended on that. In an age when there was a lack of pictorial information—despite the ubiquity of propaganda billboards—the spoken word left an even deeper mark in the memory.[4]

That voice, which became embedded in the memory of his generation, was not simply the product of natural talent. It was the result of schooling, self-discipline and a learning process in the techniques of a profession, that of radio announcer, which had not existed previously any more than had the medium that now made use of it. The young Levitan had wanted to become an actor and at the age of fourteen he had applied in Moscow, where he failed to gain a place but attracted the attention of Vasily Kachalov, a then-famous actor and major figure of the Russian stage. At a second attempt, an audition for would-be radio announcers, he was given his chance, thanks to Kachalov, and began an unpaid internship with Radio Moscow. Levitan worked on his voice and diction, following Kachalov's advice on strengthening his voice. He studied breathing techniques, improved his articulation, sloughed off his provincial accent in favour of a metropolitan way of speaking and became something of a practised old hand by spending his nights in front of the microphone in the studio, reading out the leading Moscow press articles that had to be transmitted to the provincial offices. This very conscientious preparation in reading texts aloud bore fruit to the point where the interloper from the provinces soon developed into a professional speaker who then made a breathtaking career leap during the 1930s.[5] Stalin chanced to discover and identify him as the voice to which he most wanted to confide his own texts in the future: Levitan as Stalin's voice.

His rise would have been inconceivable without the rise of the medium whose history has been researched in recent years especially by Tatiana Goryaeva and Stephen Lovell.[6] Levitan owed his career to the radio and the population of the Soviet Union internalised the sound of his voice. The Soviet Union had recognised the radio and cinema as the most important media; the future would belong to them as means of communication, as the transmitters of political messages, as the instruments with which to produce an acoustic space that would encompass the entire nation, and as a collective organiser that surpassed all the media that had existed hitherto. The task of radio would be nothing less than to help create a single, indivisible Soviet country out of one that had been deeply divided and torn apart by revolution, civil war and radical change and to bring together into one Soviet people the many disparate ethnic groups that had existed up to then. Connecting the entire world with the aid of radio, broadcasting and wireless was of course part of a global process, but precisely because Russia was a 'backward' nation, this process acquired a sharper, more profound significance. The image encapsulating the leap from the 'dark Middle Ages' to the twentieth century was once again the bearded peasant, but he no longer held 'Lenin's lamp'—the symbol of electrification; instead he wore earphones—the symbol of the unification of the entire Soviet nation or even an international community of workers.

The data of the history of radio are impressive. Russia had its own pioneers of telephony and radio—Alexander Stepanovich Popov and Mikhail Alexandrovich Bonch-Bruevich. In 1921 loudspeakers were installed in Moscow for the first time. In 1924 the first radio transmission took place from the spectacular Comintern Radio Broadcasting Tower built by Vladimir Shukhov. In establishing a radio network, the Soviet government could rely above all on the passion for technology of young radio enthusiasts and radio hams. The radio was, like flying, parachuting and broadcasting in general, the very essence of the new mass movement of amateur enthusiasts that had sprung up, especially in North America. The range of the transmission masts was very limited to begin with; so too was the number of loudspeakers positioned in public places. Transmission quality was improved once cable was introduced. People listened in groups—in clubs, reading rooms and factory canteens. What they listened to was broadcast centrally and reception took place via the loudspeaker points. By the start of the Second World War over 80 percent of radio receivers (5.5 million) acted as such loudspeaker points.[7] Gradually a programme was built up, beginning with the transmission of speeches by the Party leadership, events on Red Square with bell ringing, demonstrations, bands, followed by entertainments with opera and other classical music, as well as educational programmes, talks and lectures. A new world of sound was in the making and loudspeakers, positioned on boulevards, marketplaces and parks, were its principal pillars. Loudspeakers would henceforth be an integral component of an omnipresent background sound that could not be switched off—whether in the factory or in the shared apartment block, as well as in the camp huts. The distribution of loudspeakers was very unequal—the overwhelming majority were to be found in the towns with only a few in rural districts. The soundscape of the Soviet Union, then, was marked by stark contrasts.

The uneven density of the sound and communication space produced by radio had significant consequences in the first weeks following the German invasion of the Soviet Union, when speedy and detailed information was at a premium. In the capital, people were informed about progress at the front, while on the periphery people were often left in the dark.[8] Our knowledge of the history of sound in the Soviet Union is indebted above all to what has been handed down from the centre and the towns and cities, although the majority of the population still lived on the land. The villages where many human tragedies were played out remain silent about the sounds and noises of their past, probably forever.

His Master's Voice

When Levitan stepped up to the microphone on 22 June 1941 he already had a career behind him as Radio Moscow's most prominent announcer. Notwithstanding his trademark introduction 'This is Moscow speaking', for most of the time during the war he spoke from a secret location in Sverdlovsk. Levitan was included high up in the Nazis' list of people to be arrested after the conquest of Moscow.[9]

To be a radio announcer in the 1930s meant describing day by day what was happening in the Union—and holding one's tongue about what was forbidden to report. There were news items about new production methods, reports on the largest dam in the world on the Dnieper, the socialist competition among Stakhanovite workers, the construction of new train lines, the opening of the Moscow-Volga Canal, and the fact that life as promulgated by Stalin had become better and more joyful. The radio transmitted broadcasts about major political developments,

FIGURE 54.2. Yury Borisovich Levitan (1914–1983), Radio Moscow's legendary announcer in the studio. © culture-images/fai.

Party congresses, Politburo decisions during 'a further escalation of the international class struggle' and 'the subversive activities of enemy agents, saboteurs, spies and terrorists'.

The new radio technology made it possible to report on events on the spot, to spread the news through the ether to the remotest regions of this giant country and so to make Soviet citizens direct witnesses of overwhelming innovations and triumphs. For example, they could follow the rescue of the crew of the Soviet steamer, the *Chelyuskin,* which had been trapped in polar ice in the Arctic in 1934, or the records of all-Union motor rallies or polar expeditions. Parades and festivals on Red Square, demonstrations and processions in Moscow could now be experienced throughout the country—with all the original band accompaniments, speeches and speaking choruses.

The public that had assembled in front of the loudspeakers became part of the great, Union-wide audio community, an unprecedented form of *communion,* of technical *sobornost.* The show trials no longer took place simply on the stage of the October Hall in the House of the Unions in Moscow, but in the space created by the radio transmissions before a nationwide public. Wolfgang Koeppen has written about the 'ethereal group-feeling' generated in this way and its relevance in the case of Nazi Germany: 'This creates a direct link between man and man at the intellectual level of speech, exclamation, understanding and listening. It embraces the entire nation in the concrete experience of the national community [*Volksgemeinschaft*], including those sections of the people who have been forced to live scattered throughout the world.'[10] The sensationalist accusations against 'spies', 'saboteurs' and 'fascist dogs', the confessions of the accused, the vitriolic tirades of the prosecutor and the enraged public penetrated to the furthest corners of the nation. The vitriolic chants of the Moscow workers marching through Red Square encouraged listeners as far away as Samara and Novosibirsk to follow their example and settle accounts with the 'enemies of the people'. Radio now proved its worth as an organiser of collective hysteria; it provided the cues for hate speech and even more for mistrust, vigilance and denunciation. It became the crucial medium for spreading fear and for uniting the country against enemies who were said to be everywhere, in every factory, in every family and in every circle of friends. The loudspeaker morphed into an instrument for forging a national community in whose midst even the most insignificant and seemingly uncontentious utterance could trigger a denunciation and a catastrophe.[11]

Even the radio itself was not spared by the waves of hysteria and denunciation. Slips of the tongue in reporting the news, playing questionable choices of music—a waltz or a funeral march at the wrong time and place—could have fatal consequences. Sabotage on air was discussed at the very highest levels, as in the plenum of February–March 1937.[12] It was also the radio that informed Soviet citizens (sometimes in live broadcasts) about the national socialist takeover in Germany, fighting on the fronts in the Spanish Civil War and Manchuria, the successes of Russian pianists and violinists in international competitions. All these things came together in the editorial offices of the mass media, so that during the 1930s a news broadcaster from Radio Moscow became the point at which news was concentrated and focused before going out into the world via microphone. Levitan was that focal point—or at least one of them— during the most tragic period of Soviet history, namely the years of the Great Terror that preceded the war. Levitan reported on the Party Congress of the victors in 1934 and was charged by Stalin to deliver his personal address at the congress. It was Levitan who broke the news on air of Kirov's assassination in December 1934. Levitan reported on the negotiations at the March 1937 plenum that signalled the start of the Great Terror, and he brought the news of the death sentences handed down during the Moscow show trials. He knew personally some of the accused and the condemned—in particular, Marshal Tukhachevsky, who was sentenced to death for treason in a trial that was held in camera. Having been compelled to read out the announcement describing Tukhachevsky's crimes and sentencing with his customary professionalism, Levitan suffered a heart attack.[13] He also had to witness the disappearance of his immediate superior Konstantin Alexandrovich Maltsev and a number of his Radio Moscow colleagues. None of these experiences left visible marks on Levitan. He retained his position, speaking neutrally as ever, with an unchanged intonation and no hint of irritation in his voice. He thus became the spokesman of the history of the 1930s, a sort of Hegelian World Spirit with a sonorous voice that allowed no doubts or hesitations. His biographer Ella Taranova offers this analysis:

> As with all Soviet people, Levitan believed in Stalin. And also in the leading, organising and mobilising role of the Party. As well as in the ideals of the Soviet social order as delineated by a powerful, Stalinist propaganda machine in which he felt himself to be a minor component. And sitting behind his microphone every day, he watched this machine crushing the enemies of the people. He enjoyed the closest possible relationship to this grandiose Moloch. He was not simply the voice of the Party and of Stalin personally; he also had a function and it was he who communicated the justice of the judgements passed on the enemies of the people and the workings of the court. The Party and the people condemned their enemies to death. The sentence had to be carried out! And he, Levitan, who read out the sentences handed down on the enemies of the Party and the people, added a steeliness of his own. An additional pinch of impatience. An extra portion of leaden gravity. Every word had something of the whiplash crack of a bullet in the

basement where the executions took place. It was as if Levitan
had personally carried out the execution himself. And had done
his duty in the process. His awareness of this must have been
the cause of his feeling of disquiet. With increasing frequency, in
the quiet stillness of the dawn, he caught himself thinking that
he was a murderer. That he who sat in front of the microphone
conscientiously reading out the sentences of the court thereby
released the safety catch on the Cheka agent's pistol. That it was he
who went along the row of men who had confessed to the craziest
crimes, shooting them in the back of the head. He was literally of
two minds. There was the Levitan who enthusiastically devoured
texts full of the achievements of the Soviet way of life. And the
other Levitan, the darker mirror-image, who read out the sentences
of the 'Troika' of judges.[14]

According to his biographer, it was the schizoid reactions of this Dr
Jekyll and Mr Hyde, rather than his fear for himself, that led him to
withdraw increasingly from his friends and colleagues.

Levitan was spared the fate of many others who unwittingly and
innocently fell into the meat grinders of the Stalinist purges in the
1930s and the period of his universal prominence during the Great
Patriotic War. He even escaped persecution in the very last years of
the Stalin regime, when the hunt was on for a new group of enemies,
namely the Jews, who were labelled agents of US imperialism and
its satellite 'Zionism'. In Moscow radio in 1952 he even met Lidiya
Timashuk, the doctor in the Kremlin hospital who played a fateful
part in unleashing the anti-Semitic campaign against the 'Doctors'
plot'.[15] And again, it was Levitan who with typical self-discipline read
out the medical bulletins on Stalin and then finally gave the citizens
of the Soviet Union the news of his death on 5 March 1953.

TV: The Veterans Take Their Leave

Everything that happened subsequently was a lengthy leave-taking
by an announcer whose voice will forever be linked to the war years.
That voice was embedded in a medium that was forced to make way

for another—the television—and hence for a world in which the image replaced the word as the deciding factor. Levitan's counterpart in Germany was Hans Fritzsche, the best-known announcer on German radio during the Nazi period. Fritzsche was put on trial at Nuremberg and acquitted but sentenced shortly afterwards to a lengthy period in prison. Despite being amnestied, he never found his way back into the media world in which he was so at home. In contrast, Levitan's voice is associated with some of the happiest moments of the postwar period of Soviet life. It was he who was able to report the successful launch of the first Sputnik in 1957, as well as Yury Gagarin's mission as the first man in space in 1961. The encounter of the two Yurys—Levitan and Gagarin—symbolises the continuity between the war generation and a society which, despite the Cold War, was preparing for peace and wished to enjoy the fruits of its own labour. Just as radio was representative of the construction phase of the 1920s and 1930s, of the Sturm und Drang period and the creation of the Soviet nation, so the new development stood for a departure from the mobilisation society and for its transition to a Soviet-type consumer society. The radio revolution had brought short-wave transmissions to the people, whereas from now on people could make their own programming and ceased to depend on a central radio team that could feed the public whatever it thought was right. The persistent bombardment by loudspeakers in public spaces gradually waned. Television became the natural medium for families who had moved out of the communal apartments into apartments of their own. It was the hearth around which family, friends and acquaintances could gather, a place to be private and left to oneself. It signified the development of an everyday life that had started to become 'normal'.

In the late phase of the Soviet Union, television began to exercise its greatest fascination just when debates about reforming the Soviet Union emerged from the apartments and kitchens and became a theme discussed in the newspapers, in public 'round tables' and even in the congress hall where the Supreme Soviet convened. From there these debates were reflected back into the private world of Soviet citizens. TV became the focal point of a disturbing process of self-discovery and a search for the path to a better life. The television set became something taken for granted, the natural centrepiece of a new consumerism, somewhat like a campfire around which the entire nation could warm itself.

The trajectory at the end of the Soviet Union led from the erosion of the state monopoly of news and communication systems to the unleashing of an often chaotic melee of voices. This was followed by a renewed clampdown under the extraordinarily media-savvy Putin regime. These changes led to a further radical transformation of the public sphere. Beneath the centrally manipulated media, networks running into the millions have been created that are busy speaking their own language and shaping their own ideas about the world.[16] In their eyes Levitan's voice is no more than an *objet trouvé* from a remote, alien past.

CHAPTER 55

Back in the USSR: Sound Traces

Since the war's end, it is probably true that no voice has been identified so completely with a particular period as was Levitan's during the war years. This is not to say that there haven't been other striking acoustic transitions, which lasted a long time and have become an integral part of the cultural memory of Soviet and even post-Soviet society. Admittedly, not all historical caesuras took on acoustic form. There was, for example, Khrushchev's 'secret speech' that proclaimed the end of the 'cult of personality', in other words, of Stalinism in its crudest form. This speech was given on 25 February 1956, the last day of the Twentieth Party Congress, and since it was intended for internal Party use only, it existed solely in copies and specific extracts, not in a sound recording. It remained a document that circulated underground, where it was quoted, but it was never actually heard outside the closed session of the Party Congress.[1] This does not mean that there was a lack of sound material for the aural memory. For the population of Leningrad under siege by the Germans, the radio and the loudspeakers scattered through the city were a veritable means of survival. It was through them that the population learned of developments at the front and received advice on how to defend themselves. The radio also enabled people to grasp the fact that they were still alive, despite everything. The sound of the metronome that in peacetime served to signal a broadcasting intermission became the vehicle of lifesaving information: when German planes approached the city, the beat quickened; when the all clear was sounded, the tempo sank to its accustomed frequency. In September 1941 Dmitry Shostakovich discussed on the radio the progress he was making with his Seventh Symphony and explained that the composition, which subsequently achieved fame as the 'Leningrad Symphony', proved merely that the city continued to live its life and that for everyone it was business as usual, composers included—a greater manifestation of self-confidence was inconceivable. The symphony's premiere was given in Kuybyshev, to which the orchestra and composer had been evacuated, but thereafter the 'Leningrad Symphony' was always on the air and became irrevocably associated with the city that had withstood the siege.[2]

Music almost seems to have developed into a distinctive marker. The 'Internationale', the national anthem that was broadcast at the end of the day from 1 January 1944 on, stood for the postrevolutionary Soviet Union that developed into a great power given the part it played in the coalition against Hitler. It could be heard by an international public at the Olympic Games award ceremonies right down to the end of the Soviet Union, when it was replaced by Mikhail Glinka's Tsarist anthem, which was replaced in turn a decade later by the reintroduction of the Soviet anthem with an adapted text by Sergey Mikhalkov, who had cowritten the original version. The sound of this anthem is associated in the general consciousness with the raising of the flag at award ceremonies, triumphal music in the sporting arenas of the world.

Music accompanied the political birthday of the head of state, reinforced his legitimacy and emphasised the unity of the multinational empire. Yevgeniya Ginzburg, in exile in Magadan in the Far East, recalled Stalin's seventieth birthday:

Julia insisted that the radio be kept permanently on. Her theory was: 'We must listen to everything.' And our loudspeaker blared away from morning to night, pouring out obsequious dithyrambs of hero-worship in honour of the Leader. The seventieth birthday celebrations lasted almost an entire week. The orgies of ecstatic raving and declarations of love and devotion went on for hours at a time. Each national minority performed a witch dance of its own. The Siberian bellowed heartrendingly about the wide-open spaces of their wonderful homeland, where they had supposedly devised their joyful song of praise to the Great Friend and Leader. The people of Ryazan and Voronezh put in some fast heel-and-toe work in honour of the Generalissimo, punctuating the strains of the accordion with wild cries. Then the radio transmitted the festivities on Red Square, with thunderous bands and choirs. This, too, was staged crescendo, and it looked as if the crescendo would never reach its peak.

It all seems hardly believable now. Did we not in fact dream up those dervish-like dances that accompanied the departure from the historic scene of that year of evil memory? Alas, no. Until quite recently the accuracy of our recollection was regularly confirmed every time we twiddled the knob and came across the sound of those piercing high soprano voices screeching out their superlatives in paroxysms of love for the Great Helmsman.[3]

Old times take their leave and new times announce their arrival to the accompaniment of music. The death of leaders is always framed by classical music. And so even Stalin's death could not be allowed to pass without the sound of classical music. Here is Ginzburg in Magadan in 1953:

> Suddenly, through all the crackling, I heard . . . Dear Lord, what was I hearing?
> 'There has been a deterioration . . . Intermittent heartbeat . . . pulse barely detectable.'
> The announcer's voice, tense as a violin string, throbbed with suppressed grief. A wild, improbable surmise flashed through my mind like a bolt of forked lightning, but I could not bring myself to trust in it. . . . 'I tell you as a doctor: recovery is impossible. Do you hear? Cheyne-Stokes respiration—that means he's in his death throes.'

And a little later music once again proclaimed what had happened. 'Both up to and after 5 March, in the harrowing days of the funeral rites of the Great and Wise One, Bach ruled supreme on the airways. Music occupied an unprecedented, colossal place in the radio broadcasts of that brief period. Majestic, musical phrases, slow and luminous, rolled forth from all the loudspeakers in our building, drowning out the clatter of children's feet in the corridor and the hysterical sobbing of the women.'[4] Ginzburg learns of the death of Beria, 'as an agent of the Okhrana and of the English secret service', in the same way:

> There was an unusual silence in the corridor. But you could hear music coming from the loudspeakers from behind the thirty closed doors (fifteen on either side).

'It's Bach again, I think,' said Anton, listening intently.

'That's good. It's a good omen. They always play Bach when they're at a loss for what to say next. . . .'

That was how Johann Sebastian Bach came to be drawn into the secular affairs of us poor sinners.[5]

Slow, solemn music broadcast through the loudspeakers was always a sign until late in the history of the Soviet Union that something of grave importance had occurred. The deaths in quick succession of Leonid Brezhnev (1982), Yury Andropov (1984) and Konstantin Chernenko (1985), along with their funerals, which included the journey from the House of the Unions to the Kremlin Wall to the accompaniment of the 'Warszawianka', came to represent something like the acoustic demise of the Soviet era. The rhythm and melody of the 'Warszawianka' take us back to the origins of the wars of liberation in the Russian Empire, the skirmishes on the barricades of the Revolution of 1905 and the emergence of working-class solidarity. It is a solemn funeral march.

Dignified funeral music rang out once again—this time it was excerpts from *Swan Lake*—when the putschists declared an emergency situation on 19–21 August 1991 but contrived only to accelerate the disintegration of the Empire. Anyone who spent the night of 21 August 1991 travelling in a sleeper (as I had) knew by dawn that something had happened because funeral music could be heard over the loudspeakers in the compartments (in my case it was the *Krasnaya Strela* night train from Moscow to Leningrad).

Although television had begun its triumphal march from the 1950s on in the USSR, as elsewhere, the Cold War was essentially a matter of the acoustic sphere, of sound waves, thanks to the rise of transistor radios. Powerful transmitters had been put in place on both sides. There was Radio Moscow but there were also broadcasting stations in a variety of languages in the so-called satellite states that attracted a broad public although the actual number of listeners in the West remained modest.[6] On the Western side there were such radio stations as Voice of America, Radio Liberty, Radio Free Europe, Deutsche Welle and the BBC, which offered a wide range of programmes in almost all the languages of the Soviet Union, entering a highly contested terrain in the process. Jamming stations attempted from time to time to interfere with or block Western transmitters. The reception of Western stations varied from region to region, with some areas favoured and others disadvantaged so that people who couldn't wait to hear the news often jumped aboard a train to reach the higher ground around Moscow from which they would be able to hear the latest developments about such matters as the Solidarity movement and the imposition of martial law in Poland.

The typical noise made by jamming, a crackling and hissing sound, could be heard everywhere in the 1980s, especially in households or courtyards inhabited by the urban intelligentsia. The ether became a battlefield and more than a few dissidents turned to it to amplify their voices and relay their concerns back to their own immediate vicinity via the Western media, or else, more importantly, to project them outwards into the Soviet 'provinces' by using the Western media as a springboard from which to reach a worldwide public. Whatever propagandistic aims may have been in play in these battles, there can be no doubt about the impact of the information broadcast by these stations. However, this impact was often counterproductive since it confirmed many people's belief that whatever was broadcast by their own media was a priori untrue and part of a campaign of disinformation. Even so, it was not so much the political news that broke through the blockade on information surrounding the Soviet Union and ultimately destroyed it but the knowledge that seeped in from every conceivable direction about what life was really like 'on the outside', beyond the confines of the Soviet world.

PART XV

Alien Territory, Contact Zones, In-Between Worlds

★

The division of the world was evident not just in external frontiers but also inside the country itself, above all in the capital, Moscow. Foreigners were more visible and even more exposed than elsewhere, especially if they came from the West. They were regarded as representatives of a different, alien and, often enough, hostile world. They lived apart in a special location where they had been forced together, were protected or isolated and to which as a rule ordinary Soviet citizens had no straightforward access. In describing the closed society of the Soviet Union we cannot ignore the enclaves inhabited by foreigners or people treated as the representatives of Western states regarded as enemies. The lives of people in these enclaves in the capital have been largely neglected by students of the Soviet way of life, yet they were never absent from the memoirs or reports of diplomats, journalists, businesspeople, students and expats who had dealings with them.

In the Soviet Union, foreigners were easily recognisable by their appearance, if by nothing else. They had not yet discovered how to dress for the Russian winter, as natives could easily tell from bare-headed passersby, or their woollen caps, or else their footwear. Where Soviet citizens favoured leather jackets, foreigners preferred coats and trench coats. The design of their spectacles was not just different: it was subject to regular changes according to fashion, whereas Soviet citizens had to put up with the same eyeglass frames more or less their entire lives. Foreigners even walked differently—as if accustomed to assuming that their path was smooth and that they wouldn't step into a hole or have to jump over a puddle. Most importantly, however, was that they all lived in the same area. For the most part they could be found only in the capital, apart from a few who had been deposited in a specialist organisation somewhere 'in the provinces'. During the first Five-Year Plans the settlements designed for foreign specialists and technical experts—with central heating, tennis courts and garages—were also known as 'Amerikanka'.[1]

In what follows we are not concerned with the visitors who featured prominently in the press, 'fellow travellers' or tourists of the Revolution,[2] nor with the delegations dedicated to a mission of some sort—trade unionists, writers and the World Council of Churches, which became increasingly infrequent with the passage of time—or with visitors from the Third World or students of the Patrice Lumumba University who stood out from the dominant grey because of their skin tone or colourful turbans and burnouses. We are concerned rather with 'Westerners' who had settled in Moscow for longer, mainly for professional reasons. Moscow was multiethnic and very colourful, as was only fitting for the capital of an empire, but in this respect it was strictly divided into 'us' and 'them'. Spatial segregation can be found everywhere in the world, sometimes strictly and at others more porously, and in ways that have changed over time: trendy neighbourhoods, red-light districts, exclusive residential areas, workers' districts, Chinatown, Little Italy, the London East End, Brooklyn with its ever-shifting ethnic and religious blocks, financial quarters, and so forth. Moscow is different. Here we find the world divided into two halves and this is reflected in territorial, civic terms. There is no division along ethnic, religious, social or cultural lines but along a systemic frontier. Even students were affected by it if they hailed from Germany: in Lomonosov Moscow State University, students from the Federal Republic of Germany lived in the wing for people coming from capitalist countries, while students from the German Democratic Republic lived in the wing for people arriving from the 'socialist countries'. There are areas even at the very heart of the city and the Soviet environment that have something of the reservation or the ghetto about them with all their attendant disadvantages or privileges. I am speaking of the world of diplomatic agencies, journalists and correspondents, specialised currency dealers and those hybrid spaces that belong to one or more of these spheres. This intermediate world is also home to cross-border commuters and adventurers. Isolated enclaves thriving in a grey zone of suspicion, rumour, semilegality, illegality—of people hovering between the shady and the criminal or the criminalised; this is the usual setting for thrillers and spy films.

The end of the Soviet Union seemed to signal the end of the foreigner as a specific cultural type. Now, with the whole world in thrall to international fashions, brands and logos, the figure of the foreigner as someone who stands out has also perished. For some this involves the loss of status; for others it spells the creation of a normality which they can at long last start to enjoy.

CHAPTER 56

'The Little Oasis of the Diplomatic Colony'

The history of embassies and embassy buildings can be told alongside that of international relations. In the case of German-Russian or German-Soviet relations this history might begin with the imposing embassy building of the German Empire on Isaakievskaya Ploshchad in St. Petersburg, an architectural masterwork by Peter Behrens built shortly before the outbreak of the First World War, topped by a quadriga, which was toppled into the Moyka River by an anti-German mob in August 1914 (the interior rooms have been preserved to this day, mostly in their original condition). It might continue via the Villa Berg in Denezhny Pereulok 5 in Moscow, which was occupied following the peace negotiations in Brest-Litovsk by the German ambassador Graf Wilhelm von Mirbach-Harff, who was then murdered by Socialist Revolutionary terrorists on 6 July 1918. After 1924 it became the home of the Italian embassy and remains so to the present day. This history would then proceed to the houses in Leontievsky Pereulok 10 and Chisty Pereulok 5, which are associated with the names of Graf Brockdorff-Rantzau, Herbert von Dirksen, Richard Nadolny and Graf von der Schulenberg. They continued to exist until the start of the German invasion of the Soviet Union. After the Second World War there were two German embassies—the GDR moved onto Leontievsky Pereulok, the Federal Republic of Germany into Bolshaya Gruzinskaya 17—with each embassy hosting its own diplomatic community.

We can learn about diplomatic relations not just from the study of treaties and personalities but also from the history of the embassies themselves. Whether they are open or inaccessible, launch pads for the development of relations or barriers, the stage for social and sociable living in capital cities or places of alienation and keeping people out can be discovered from the history of embassies in each of their phases.[1]

But anyone living in Moscow during the 1970s and early 1980s did not need to have heard of these historical figures to discern that embassies have their own specific territory. Scattered over the city and housed for the most part in palaces of the nobility or wealthy businessmen's villas, which frequently were among the most beautiful buildings of prerevolutionary Moscow, their entrances were flanked by porters' lodges—as was the case in other capital cities. However, in the period before the new terrorism, these lodges served not so much to protect the embassy personnel as to deter ordinary citizens from attempting to visit the embassies. In 'peaceful' Soviet times, mere mortals had no cause to have dealings with foreign embassies; further, they wanted nothing to do with them. Visits to embassies roused suspicions and mistrust; indeed, the guards posted prevented entry. So people did not go in; they simply walked on past. As long as emigration affected only a small number of people—under the heading of reuniting families, for example—embassy premises were frequented only by the various department employees, ex-pats, businesspeople, exchange academics or correspondents. You could collect your post there or read the current foreign newspapers not available in the Soyuzpechat kiosks. Thus embassies were primarily docking places, contact zones for the foreign communities, especially on national holidays.

This situation persisted until the 1970s and 1980s when it changed overnight with the onset of waves of émigrés, led by the Soviet Germans, Soviet Greeks and Soviet Jews. Lengthy queues formed in the boulevards and parks, as hundreds and even thousands of applicants from all quarters of the nation sought exit visas. Even so, the embassies were primarily places where consular and diplomatic duties were carried out as smoothly as possible. Only rarely did they also host social activities such as receptions, concerts, teas and readings. Earlier on, figures such as Graf Brockdorff-Rantzau, the passionate advocate of Rapallo diplomacy, and Georgy Chicherin, likewise a scion of the aristocracy but also People's Commissar for Foreign Affairs, would hold meetings that would last until long after midnight, in which people would converse and indulge their love of Mozart. But those times were over by the end of the 1920s.[2] Diplomatic missions were suspected from the outset of being the advance posts of hostile foreign countries, springboards for spying and sabotage. This remained true, as George F. Kennan has shown, even at the time of the very closest relations between the USSR and the USA—during the common struggle against Nazi Germany. They constantly kept an eye on one another.[3] Embassies became particular objects of surveillance during the long, drawn-out Cold War. Conversely, embassy staff sought to protect themselves with the aid of highly developed codes and ciphers, a high-security courier system and rooms specially protected against wiretapping and eavesdropping. During the late Soviet period many Western embassies withdrew their services and personnel into closed-off compounds where one's duties could be performed without ever having to leave the embassy grounds: they became cities within cities. With the aid of special permits, which could be obtained through special applications and approvals, it was possible to leave these enclaves and undertake journeys beyond the forty-kilometre zone around the city. At the city limits, posted guards were informed in advance which vehicle with which number plates would be passing through and knew the identity of its passengers. The situation with trains was similar and passengers arriving in Leningrad found that they were expected. Diplomatic cars with special plates were easily identified—as they are all over the world. Whereas travel was relatively free during the 1920s and 1930s—consulates were still fairly numerous outside the capital—restrictions and the entire machinery of rules and permits grew gradually over time. Progressive isolation and ghettoisation did not end until the years of Gorbachev's glasnost and perestroika, when the system of closed cities and regions—among them such important Russian towns as Nizhny Novgorod/Gorky—was abolished (at least temporarily); it was partially reintroduced in the early 2000s.

The 'little oasis of the diplomatic colony', to cite George Kennan's words from his time in Moscow in the 1930s, developed its own forms of life and survival. People met at official receptions, in collectively rented dacha colonies and holiday homes in the summer, and at tennis courts, and they kept meeting one another, like collectors *à la recherche du temps perdu*, in second-hand bookshops and antique shops whose preferred customers were the owners of foreign currency. One must doubtless think of the inhabitants of this oasis as a transnational, cosmopolitan community determined to maintain the mode of life it was accustomed to in the conditions imposed by the 'closed society'. At any rate, this is what we may conclude from the memoirs of such different diplomats as Herwarth von Bittenfeld and Gustav Hilger, and Americans such as George F. Kennan, Charles E. Bohlen and Averill Harriman.[4] Ambassadors' wives played a key role as society ladies who presided over salons and musical evenings. The colony lived its own life while the world around it changed at a breath-taking pace. One might converse with someone from Narkomindel—the Soviet Commissariat for Foreign Affairs—who the very next day would stand accused of being a 'spy' or an 'agent' and be relieved of his post. Neither was it unknown for diplomats to be delegated observers of the Moscow trials and to see at first hand yesterday's interlocutors, such as Karl Radek or Nikolay Krestinsky, sitting in the dock and facing accusations of having collaborated with German fascists. Meeting prosecutors and judges from the show trials at embassy receptions was by no means uncommon. Thus we learn from Ernst Köstring, the military attaché of the German embassy:

> So as to describe a comedy in between these tragedies, I should like to report on the party at the American embassy. Despite the entire diplomatic corps having been given an urgent warning about the food coming directly from the fridge (Madame controls all the refrigerator companies in America, providing her with an income of $5 million), absolutely everyone turned up. In addition, 50 Russians of the worst sort made their appearance. To improve the tone, judges with blood on their hands such as Vyshinsky and Ulrich had also been invited and they arrived with us of all people, whom they had reviled in the most appalling fashion only the week before. The highlight of the Russian group was our Orlov, who has been promoted to divisional commander and head of the Information Section—our Canaris, in short—whom our host even accompanied to the door as he took his leave! Budyonny, the traditional guest at diplomatic receptions, was absent, though whether he has been ditched has yet to be established.[5]

The embassy was a privileged location, an observation post. During parades military attachés stood on a raised tribune so as to assess

the new weapons filing past or the discipline of the new parachutists and report back home on their findings. Economic departments
carried out their analyses, assembled statistics and more than a few
used the knowledge they had gleaned in this way in quite different
contexts—as experts on the kolkhoz system during the German occupation, according to Otto Schiller—or later still, as 'experts on the
Soviet Union' on behalf of the Americans, according to Gustav Hilger.[6]
By visiting the Bolshoi Theatre, you could study the leaders of both
the Party and the state from close up and gauge shifts in hierarchy
ranking from their place in the seating arrangements. The diplomatic
procedures given shape in the nineteenth century had no chance of
surviving the contest with what Hannah Arendt called the 'paradiplo-
macy' of the movements of the age of totalitarianism. What Harold
Nicolson referred to as the 'freemasonry of professional diplomacy'
would be doomed in the altered circumstances.[7] Meetings that had
previously been held to exchange views and reach an understanding
away from the eyes of the public would henceforth be deemed conspiratorial and the active search for contacts regarded as high treason
and treated accordingly.[8] This is what happened in 1937 with a general
such as Tukhachevsky and with Karl Radek, the interlocutor universally esteemed. Gone were the days when it was generally believed
that more could be achieved in frank conversations like those held
by Brockdorff-Rantzau and Chicherin than in elaborate conferences
taking place in the public eye (of the world) and under the pressure
of international expectations. The ambassadors who had been rooted
to the spot for years found themselves elbowed out by leaders determined to take matters into their own hands—we need think only of
Hitler and Stalin, Molotov and Ribbentrop. In the twentieth century
old-style diplomacy came under pressure from two directions. On
the one hand, there was mass democracy, which called for transparency and categorically demanded the abolition of secret diplomacy,
as exemplified by President Wilson. On the other hand, there was
the totalitarian state, which undermined the formal approach and
ended up dispensing with it altogether. Diplomacy became no more
than a tool of implementation and was reduced to the status of an
appendage to the 'movement', a subsection of the Central Committee. And this amounted to the de facto abolition of diplomacy itself,

which henceforth was to be subordinated to the world-revolutionary movement. In this spirit Trotsky had declared that diplomacy was superfluous, while somewhat later Stalin used the reinstatement of secret diplomacy for his new imperial geopolitics.[9]

The long-lasting Cold War was marked by a series of diplomatic incidents, spying and bugging scandals. The end of the Cold War and the closed society gradually created new opportunities for diplomatic missions. One could look around the country and enter into contact with the public. Embassies could become social meeting points, a theatre in the capital. These were happy days in diplomats' lives. Whoever wished to recover from the stress and narrowness of life in the Soviet Union could now find refuge in the countryside or else take regular trips to the near abroad: Helsinki, Stockholm, Cologne/Bonn or Prague. Stockmann, Helsinki's department store, had adjusted to the Russian customers who flew in regularly, as had doctors' practices and the nightclubs where the guests could join in, secure in the knowledge that they wouldn't be exposed to the same temptations and risks that they might encounter in the Moscow scene.

What we read in so many memoirs by diplomatic personnel can probably be safely asserted of most cases: some simply accepted the restrictions involved in a Moscow posting. We could put it more strongly: they even 'fell for' the country and after they returned home or were transferred elsewhere, they were unable to shed their obsession with Russia. Others regarded a Moscow posting as a kind of banishment or a mere interlude.

CHAPTER 57

The Journalists' Ghetto: The View from Outside, Fixation with the Centre

The picture the West had of the Soviet Union was generated essentially by the reports, accounts and films produced by Moscow correspondents, day in, day out, year in, year out for an entire century. Agency news flashes, the reports of correspondents and the accounts of the journalists who travelled throughout the nation formed the basis of our knowledge and our attitudes. They were the recorders of current events and also long-term observers. They set the tone that created the mood music. The image we have of Russia and the Soviet Union is inconceivable without John Reed's *Ten Days That Shook the World*. There were the reports by William Henry Chamberlain, Pierre Pascal and Alfons Paquet from the Civil War period when Russia disappeared behind a wall created by a blockade; these later became the foundation of historical accounts. What would Paul Scheffer report in the *Berliner Tageblatt*? How large was the circle of readers of Joseph Roth's articles in the literary supplements? To what extent were people's attitudes influenced by the anti-Semitic reports of the Nazi journalist Theodor Seibert? And how significant were the journeys undertaken by the American journalist Hubert Renfro ('Red') Knickerbocker, who travelled all over the Soviet Union at the time of the first Five-Year Plan? The Third Reich and the Stalin period made journalism in its most basic sense impossible and replaced it with propaganda, disinformation and rabble-rousing that subsequently passed over into the actual conduct of war. But we can also learn something about the dangerous aspects of reportage when we read Walter Duranty's flattering and euphemistic accounts of the 1930s in which there was no starvation or mass terror.[1] And how much less would readers in the anti-Hitler coalition have found out about the war in the east were it not for the reports of Alexander Werth?[2]

From the outset there was the seductiveness of a great utopia but there was also the need to break through the propaganda of the new state and shed light on 'Russia in the Shadows', to quote the title of a book by H. G. Wells that appeared in 1921. The labours of whole generations of reporters would be needed to bring about a recovery from the devastation wrought in people's minds by the German war against the Soviet Union. We need think only of Klaus Mehnert's knowledgeable and insightful pieces, culminating in *The Anatomy of Soviet Man* at the end of the 1950s.[3] Or we should be aware of the pioneering writing of the young Gerd Ruge, working from his improvised office, as well as all the others who gradually became active as reporters, interpreters and bridge builders to a world divided by the Cold War and the Wall: Fritz Pleitgen, Klaus Bednarz, Thomas Roth, Dirk Sager and Kerstin Holm.[4] All have laboured to bring us closer to an alien country and helped to produce the images we hold of Russia.

Even though conditions have changed greatly, reporters in the closed society were always liable to be suspected of spying, of producing hostile pictures and ideological sabotage, unless they were outright supporters of the regime. This began at the chaotic start, when individual journalists were still battling on their own; it persisted during a period of increasing isolation and the censorship regime of the 1930s and 1940s, right on through the predictable process of 'normalisation' in the declining phase of the Cold War. Given the Soviets' destruction of an open public sphere, professional reporting inevitably became the biggest loser. Truthful reports were quickly denigrated as 'anti-Soviet propaganda' and often resulted in journalists' loss of accreditation and even expulsion. To be linked with the vestiges of the anti-Stalin opposition not only placed journalists in jeopardy— witness the fate of Paul Scheffer of the *Berliner Tageblatt*—it could even pose a threat to the internal Soviet opposition itself. Information was to be the exclusive province of the official agencies: the Russian Telegraph Agency (ROSTA), the later Russian News Agency (TASS) and the press sections of the relevant people's commissariats. Freedom of movement was restricted. Countrywide journeys required official approval and elaborate bureaucratic preparations, quite apart from the numerous restricted zones. Interpreters were often also informers and controllers. Telephone calls were eavesdropped on as a matter of course and meetings with dissidents were a risk for both parties. Moreover, journalists and correspondents lived in segregated compounds that might well have felt like ghettos. Threats and intimidation belonged to the everyday reality of the Moscow journalist, as did temptations to self-censor or directly collaborate with official 'organs'. The more difficult it was to form an accurate picture of the situation in the country and the more palpable the obfuscation by the Party and state media—*Pravda, Izvestia* and others—the more challenged the professional observer would feel in getting beyond the ordinary daily news or the usual round of high days and holidays.

This was the position with journalists and correspondents, who were committed to their profession, and, like nonconformist writers and poets, were concerned to convey an authentic picture of reality. This applied to both day-to-day reportage and the attempt to take a longer view. Many of them had fallen in love with the country and, in contrast to the facile and mystificatory but all too frequently quoted dictum of the poet Fyodor Tyutchev ['Who would grasp Russia with the mind?'], felt challenged to see Russia with their own eyes, to understand and 'comprehend it with their own reason'. They wished to explore the vast land and transcend its own propagandistic view of itself. What held them spellbound was an exciting country with harrowing destinies, inexhaustible creative energies and an incomparable talent for improvisation. This talent enabled people to face up to and overcome apparently insuperable predicaments—and all of this was in striking contrast to the rituals of power, the pompous and mendacious scenarios of the propaganda machinery. Moscow-based journalists grappled with topics that had been dismissed as insufficiently 'relevant' or sensational by the think tanks and established disciplines such as sociology. They described the overwhelming difficulties of everyday life, the microcosm of epiphanies and individual destinies— scenes which ordinary newspaper professionals failed to broach right to the very end. Many of the key books about the Soviet lifeworld represent the sum of many years of professional observation and analysis: Hedrick Smith's *The Russians*, Andrew Nagorski's reportages, Kerstin Holm's *Das korrupte Imperium* and a number of others.[5] We frequently learn more about the reality of Soviet life from such books than from studies by sociologists, political scientists or historians.

But we can also see the limitations of this journalistic reportage: its fixation on political decision-making processes about whose inner workings we know little and which (inevitably) resulted in the creation of the genre of Kremlin astrology. Alongside this focus on central committees, general secretaries, Party congresses, politburos and more generally 'the Kremlin', there was also a spatial concentration on Moscow that undeniably resulted in a Russocentric perception of the Empire, which was infinitely heterogeneous, fragmented, polyglot, multiethnic and multireligious, and had been thus even in times when the overarching Soviet domination was not in question. You needed a specific and for the most part urgent reason or a happy coincidence to justify travelling to the depths of the provinces, the non-Russian republics and the periphery. This generated a focus on the centre that produced its own blind spots, which only became visible when cracks began to appear in the Empire itself.

The appearance of the new media—first the radio, then TV and lastly the internet—radically changed the situation. During the Cold War the ether became the space for propaganda and information, for the battleground of competing worlds and ideologies. 'Secret speeches', such as Khrushchev's of 1956, could no longer remain secret. Protests, such as those of Sakharov and Solzhenitsyn, were no longer confined to a small circle of dissidents in the capital cities but were disseminated throughout the Soviet Union by Western broadcasters. The news of the explosion of the nuclear reactor in Chernobyl on 26 April 1986 did not just contain information about a deadly threat; it signalled the collapse of a news policy that put the denial of reality above the health and safety of Soviet citizens.

With the collapse of the monopoly of information held by the one-party state, journalism found itself confronted by entirely new tasks. Not a day passed without the discussion of events—past or present—that had previously been inconceivable.[6] Both the Moscow of the perestroika period, caught up in the daily storm of new events, and the Soviet Union, which could no longer be comprehended from its centre, had slipped from the grasp of journalists. Reportage now had to adapt itself to a new world and adjust its gaze to the postimperial situation.

CHAPTER 58

Beryozka Shops: 'Oases of Affluence'

Even people who had never entered a Beryozka shop knew that there were Soviet stores where in exchange for foreign currency—dollars, pounds sterling, German marks, Swiss francs or special cheques—you could obtain goods otherwise unavailable nationally or else in extremely short supply.[1] The ordinary Soviet shopper normally had no access to these shops. Outwardly, only the letters Берёзка (Beryozka) pointed to the shops; the word means 'little birch tree', a name that evokes or reinforces Russian associations for foreigners. In the republics of the Union the shops bear such names as Kashtan (chestnut) in Ukraine or Dzintars (amber) in Latvia. Other Eastern bloc countries followed the Beryozka model, so that there were Pewex shops in Poland, Tuzex shops in Czechoslovakia and Intershops in the GDR. Natalia Lebina quotes Marina Vlady, the French actress who lived for many years in the USSR: 'I can buy what I need in the Beryozka shops. You can buy everything there that you can't otherwise find: American cigarettes, instant coffee, toilet paper and even eggs, potatoes and lettuce that sometimes don't come into the ordinary shops for weeks on end.'[2]

Outside, the shops looked as if their operators knew about their morally debatable nature as capitalist islands in a socialist environment. They looked as if they suspected how provocative and humiliating they must have seemed in the eyes of ordinary citizens. The façades were kept very low key, with no publicity or glamorous window displays—it was almost as if they were ashamed of the official hypocrisy.[3] The shops had originally been designed to attract foreigners and other currency owners with first-class products 'Made in the USSR', but increasingly sold imported goods from the West. This was the source of their poor reputation in the Soviet population.

Entering them was not easy. The people who did go in were diplomats, businesspeople, journalists, tourists—and the doormen at
the entrances allowed them to pass with no questions asked. Other
people who went in innocently in search of goods in short supply
and had no hard currency or special vouchers were soon put right.
They would have to explain where they had obtained their dollars or
were simply shown the door. The goods on offer were not especially
extravagant; every Western supermarket had a greater choice. Even
so, the display was very telling.[4] This was where foreigners shopped
who could not be bothered to go to the local farmers' market and were
willing to pay higher prices to stock up on food ranging from potatoes
to pomegranates, Georgian spices and Moldovan wines. The Beryozka
shop in Moscow's Ulitsa Kropotkinskaya stocked all the things the ex-
pat did not wish to forgo: deep-frozen bilberries, Stolichnaya vodka,
Martell cognac and caviar. The product range reflected the goods that
were thought of as 'special' in Soviet Moscow and were for the most
part in short supply. It consisted of the goods that foreigners sought
or rather the taste ascribed to them. These included foodstuffs and
above all spirits: vodka, Armenian cognac, Riga Black Balsam and
Georgian wines. In the book section you could find works for which
you normally had to stand in line in regular bookshops or which were
otherwise unobtainable: Bulgakov's *The Master and Margarita*, Pasternak's *Aerial Ways*, the memoirs of Anastasia Tsvetaeva, as well as
the picture books assumed to be of particular interest to foreigners—
whether permanent residents or tourists in search of memorabilia:
costly, illustrated editions of Ilya Repin; the landscapes and forests of
Ivan Shishkin; the catalogues, mainly produced in Finland, of the great
collections of the Hermitage, the Pushkin Museum and the Tretyakov
Gallery. How pleased would friends and acquaintances be if you could
bring back one of the few obtainable volumes from the 'Lives of Important People' series or a monograph by historian and architect Selim O.
Khan-Magomedov?[5] In addition, catalogues from *Quelle* and *Otto* were
on display—the encyclopedias of Western consumer goods in fashion
at the time. Foreign newspapers such as *Der Spiegel* or the *New York
Times* were not available.

With the goods on offer, sales managers created the image that
tourists were supposed to take home with them: the Moscow of Red

Square and the GUM department store, the Leningrad of palaces and parks, the Kremlin with its armouries and palaces, the glories of the Bolshoi Theatre and the Russian ballet. For decades there was scarcely any change in this selection of images of Russia. The Moscow of businesspeople, Art Nouveau, Constructivism, the Soviet avant-garde, the municipal planning of the age of Stalin—none of these appeared. The choice of books in the Beryozka stores acted as a machine for the production of sympathetic stereotypes along the Intourist routes. The vinyl record departments were exceptionally stocked with famous names: David Oistrakh, Emil Gilels and Svyatoslav Richter, recordings with Heinrich Neuhaus, the choir of the Black Sea Fleet and the ensemble of the Red Army.

Another important section was designed to respond to the interest in folklore and crafts. There you could find the wonderful lacquer work of the Palekh masters, the red and gold lacquered bowls, spoons and plates from the Khokhloma workshops, the shawls and head-scarves of red-black and green cloth, and sometimes also the *valenki* (felt boots)—the Russian riposte to the Siberian cold. Particularly attractive were the dinner sets from the Leningrad Porcelain Factory—cobalt, gold, blue and white patterns—clay and porcelain vessels from Gzhel, carved toys and fairy-tale figurines, as well as Czechoslovak crystal, samovars, amber jewellery, precious and semiprecious gemstones from the Urals, fur caps and boxes of chocolates from 'Red Front' and 'Bolshevik', which people bought simply because of the exquisite wrapping paper. A further department offered household goods made in the West—tape recorders, cassette players and Philips televisions. Again and again, there was a profusion of cigarettes and jeans, which had become regular status symbols and even acted as a second currency outside the stores.

The history of the Beryozka shops began in the 1960s. They were established by a decree of the Council of Ministers of the USSR of 25 March 1961 at a time when more and more Soviet citizens were able to travel abroad, work there and earn money that they wanted to spend after returning home. These included members of the nomenklatura and the diplomatic corps (not just diplomats but other staff because Soviet embassies did not employ foreigners), specialists, engineers, university teachers, artists and others who were paid in hard currency.

Moreover, there were families with relatives living abroad who were able to give them financial support.[6] Soviet citizens were not permitted to hold hard currency and were forced to exchange through the state bank money they had earned for 'cheques' or 'certificates' at a predetermined rate that varied according to the particular currency. These sums could then be used in the Beryozka shops. Furthermore, it was possible to obtain goods and services that went far beyond those available in the shops themselves. For example, one could obtain a car (for which there were normally years-long waiting lists), a holiday or break in a sanatorium, a shared apartment or household goods in short supply such as fridges, vacuum cleaners and the like. Foreigners were amazed by the high prices the Beryozka shops could charge, thanks to their monopoly—a bar of chocolate would sometimes cost ten times more than in a Western supermarket.

Despite all this, the Beryozka system did not exist purely to satisfy the consumer wishes of privileged Soviet citizens or foreign visitors. Its principal aim was to sweep up the hard currency floating around in the economy and make use of it for the state budget and import of urgently needed industrial goods. In the 1960s, when profits from the export of agricultural goods had sharply declined, it was essential to mop up all the remaining valuables floating around in the economy. The Beryozka shops revived a practice that had existed earlier. Between 1932 and 1936 the Torgsin shops were established to raise revenue to finance the ambitious industrialisation programme of the Five-Year Plans. The figures gathered by Yelena Osokina are striking.[7] In the early 1930s, despite confiscations by the OGPU and NKVD, there were allegedly around 200 million gold rubles in the hands of ordinary Russians. When they handed in gold, jewels, works of art, medals or coins, they received 'Torgsin money' in return, albeit at a poor exchange rate. There were about 1,500 shops nationwide and in branches abroad. All sorts of things were sold there, from gold coins saved up over the years to a masterpiece of Dutch painting. People were driven to the Torgsin shops by necessity and Torgsin did not lose its raison d'être until hunger gradually abated, thus reducing the pressure to sell.

Some 287.2 million rubles were accumulated through the Torgsin shops, an essential contribution to the import of industrial materials

FIGURE 58.1. Torgsin antique shop in 1932, the favourite shopping destination of diplomats and other owners of valuables. Photo by Branson DeCou. © akg-images/Archive Photos.

required for the factories just being established: 42.3 million rubles for the Gorky automobile works, 35 million for the Stalingrad tractor works, 27.9 million for the Stalin automobile works, 31 million for the Dniprostroy power station, 22.5 million for the Chelyabinsk tractor factory, 15.3 million for the Kharkiv tractor plant, 44 million for Magnitogorsk, 25.9 million for Kuznetsk and 15 million for Uralmash in Sverdlovsk.[8] One-third of the takings from Torgsin was obtained from foreign currency, 70 percent from such valuables as coins, precious stones, artwork, wedding rings, jewellery and grandparents' gold medals—everything was transformed into turbines, machinery and the engines of industrialisation. In Torgsin's golden years one-third of Soviet imports were financed by the shops' transactions.[9] We can see from the reports of Western correspondents and diplomats such as Joseph E. Davies, the US ambassador to Moscow in the 1930s, just how this situation functioned:

> One of the most interesting of institutions here are the Commission Shops. These resemble our antique shops and are run by the state and sell all manner of things brought in by their owners, from pictures to bedroom sets and from jewels to china. Every now and then you can pick up something unusually good, but in general the supply has been well picked over. Up to a year and a half ago they had so-called 'Torgsin' shops which sold things for dollars (gold shops). Now all these things are being turned over to the Commission Shops. Dollars can't be used now; everything must be paid for in rubles. We have all had a lot of fun doing a little shopping in these places.

The American ambassador had lots of fun building up a significant collection of paintings and icons which he subsequently donated to his alma mater, the University of Wisconsin.[10]

And 'In its stores diplomats, foreigners, and Soviet elites bought delicacies while ordinary people went to Torgsin for their basic necessities. . . . Torgsin could not feed everyone, however. Its abundance was relative, and there were not enough goods. Chronic interruptions in supply were exacerbated by careless distribution of goods; for example, umbrellas and galoshes went to the northern regions and felt boots (*valenki*) went to Transcaucasia. Having Torgsin money did not guarantee the receipt of desired goods. Flour, groats, sugar, and other food in high demand during the famine were especially difficult to get. People stood in line for days and nights in order to buy them.'[11]

These shops left their mark in literature too. In Mikhail Bulgakov's *The Master and Margarita*, for example, we are presented with the 'foreigners' shop on the Smolensk Market' with its confectionery, sumptuous fish counter and impressive fashion department.[12]

It was inevitable that grey zones of the black market would develop around the 'oases of affluence'. The certificates that would entitle you to shop in a Beryozka store were sold and then sold on again at a considerable profit. Jeans, packs of Marlboro cigarettes, Coca-Cola,

French cosmetics and even plastic bags were bought and sold across the Union, between Leningrad and Alma-Ata. It was near obligatory for visitors to Moscow between the 1960s and the 1980s to make the acquaintance of the so-called *fartsovshchiki* (traffickers) who were prepared to pay up to 200–250 rubles for jeans—Levi's, Rifle, Wrangler or Lee—even though on average they did not earn more than 150 rubles.[13] Such currency deals not infrequently became a trap for foreigners willing to enter into them—and they could become even more of a trap for Soviet citizens. It was a grey zone between a closed society, with a fictitious ruble exchange rate, and a free market, with a genuine dollar exchange rate. This so-called second economy and the black market more generally launched more than a few people on their later careers as oligarchs, multimillionaires and billionaires amid the dissolving economy of the Soviet Union in the late 1980s. The initial stages of an entrepreneurial culture were formed in this world of semilegality that was always at risk and used and exploited by the power structures of the time. This period would shape the DNA of the economy following the demise of the Soviet Union.[14] To the people of the post-Soviet period who were born into the world of free currency exchanges, supermarkets and supermalls, the shops of the Beryozka chain must seem like relics of a Soviet Atlantis that has long since vanished.[15]

CHAPTER 59

Genius of the Collector: George Costakis and the Rediscovery of Soviet Avant-Garde Art

The Costakis collection has long been world-famous. Pictures from its stocks have been exhibited in the Düsseldorf Kunstmuseum, the Guggenheim in New York, the Moderna Museet in Stockholm and the Gropius Bau in Berlin. None of the great exhibitions of modern art in the second half of the twentieth century, whether 'Paris-Moscou' in the Centre Pompidou in 1979 or 'The Great Utopia' in the Museum of Modern Art in New York in 1992, would have been what they were without loans from this collection.[1] But the place they were all united under a single roof was a whole-floor apartment in the southwest of Moscow, more precisely, George Costakis's last apartment on the fifteenth floor of Vernadsky Prospekt 58. From its balcony there was a view of the mountain range of high-rise concrete apartment blocks built in the 1960s and 1970s. The drab appearance of this quarter gave no clue to the treasure it concealed: an explosion of colours and forms in pictures that no one had seen for decades, created by artists whose names were unknown or forgotten and finally salvaged by a man who originally had little experience of art but whose insatiable curiosity and enthusiasm led him to follow up every trace he uncovered and ultimately to assemble one of the greatest twentieth-century collections.

George Costakis, or, to give his Russian name, Georgy Dionisovich Kostaki, was born on 3 July 1913 in Moscow as the son of a Greek businessman. He died on 9 March 1990 in Athens, where he is buried.[2] From the 1970s on, a visit to the Costakis apartment became obligatory for artists and art enthusiasts from all over the world. The five volumes of visitors' books bear testimony to this and include such names as Igor Stravinsky, Marc Chagall, Andrzej Wajda, Michelangelo Antonioni, David Rockefeller, Pierre Trudeau and Edward Kennedy. There are a great many photographs of the apartment, showing the walls covered in pictures, individual masterpieces recognisable among them: Ivan Klyun's *Red Light Spherical Composition* (1923), glowing to the point of bursting the bounds of the frame, Lyubov Popova's *Spatial Force Construction* (1921), Alexander Drevin's *Woman with Long Hair* (1930). Alexander Rodchenko's mobile *Hanging Construction*, one of the icons of the Soviet avant-garde, appears suspended from the ceiling. Today it hangs in the MoMA in New York. This treasure house of long-forgotten art, rediscovered and rescued by Costakis, was also the setting for the breakup of the Costakis collection in Moscow in August 1977, scenes of which were captured by camera. Representatives of the Tretyakov Gallery can be seen in the apartment taking control of four-fifths of the collection, while Costakis, whose life had been made increasingly impossible in the Soviet Union, was allowed to take only the remaining one-fifth with him to Greece. The members of the Tretyakov Gallery Commission are seen sorting and taking notes, while Costakis and his wife Sina stay behind in the flat that has been stripped of its contents.

Vernadsky Prospekt is one of those depressing boulevards lined with gray apartment buildings of pre-stressed concrete that epitomize the 'new Moscow' as it was conceived in the 1960s. . . . In the living room of a fifteenth-floor apartment in building no. 58 a most curious event took place over several afternoons in August 1977. The entire floor of the twenty-by-twenty-six-foot room was strewn with drawings and watercolors, singly and in piles of several hundred each. Stacked against three walls were row after row of paintings. Amid this chaos sat three people, two of them curators from Moscow's Tretiakov Gallery, a third the host and owner, Georgii Dionisevich Kostaki, or as he is known in the West, George Costakis. From time to time tea would be served by Zinaida Panfilova, Mrs Costakis, a handsome and serene native of Moscow. Two of Costakis's Mediterranean-looking daughters were also present, watching intently as their heavy-set, sixty-four-year-old father chainsmoked and presided over the strange process.

Over a two-day period the Tretiakov was receiving one of the largest and most important gifts of art that any museum has received in the twentieth century. Since no record was kept of the transaction, it is impossible to determine the exact size of Costakis's gift to the Soviet Museum. Nor did Costakis ever bother to catalogue his collection during the three decades he devoted to assembling it. But the sheer quantity of works involved was staggering by any measure. Several years before these 1977 sessions, some 1500 works on paper were stolen from the apartment, but their loss did not significantly weaken the collection as a whole. Many times that number had to be dealt with now, not to mention some four hundred canvases, several score icons of the highest quality, and many manuscripts and catalogues, some of which included original prints, sketches and paintings.[3]

Whoever wishes to see the Costakis collection today has to visit two museums: the Tretyakov Gallery in its new building on the banks of the Moskva, opposite Gorky Park, and the former Lazarist Monastery in Thessaloniki, where the Greek portion of the collection has been held ever since it was acquired by the Greek government in 1995.[4] The great collector thought of all his pictures as his beloved 'children' so it is not difficult to imagine his feelings when the collection was broken up and he had to abandon it. He himself recalled the moment: 'It was like torture . . . every piece I gave up was a part of myself and left a bloody wound behind.'[5] And all the more so as his acquiescence in the breakup was accompanied by threats and humiliations: 'They treated me like a nigger who has found a jewel but had no idea of its value.'[6]

In 1977 he donated 839 artworks to the Soviet state, over 50 icons including his collection of folk art and applied art (*dekorativnoe iskusstvo*). In 2000 the Greek government purchased 1,277 works from his collection.

As if Struck by Lightning: How It All Began

Costakis did not come from the art scene; he was an autodidact, employed by the Canadian embassy as a chauffeur and general handyman and hence privileged in a sense but with no particular expertise. In his memoirs he describes a kind of moment of insight, an epiphany or turning point which transformed him into one of the most extraordinary collectors of the twentieth century. He had become familiar with the second-hand bookshops and with acting as a middleman, buying and selling art objects in the Soviet capital during the 1930s. He had acquired some experience as a collector of Chinese and Meissen porcelain, Dutch paintings and Afghan rugs. He was evidently thunderstruck when he first caught a glimpse of Olga Rozanova's *Green Stripe* on a visit to another experienced collector, Igor Vasilievich Kachurin, who actually gave him the painting as a present. Costakis described this momentous encounter as follows: 'I took a look and nearly had a heart attack. It was the *Green Stripe* of Olga Rozanova, and he somehow, somewhere, by chance, looking at some collection, saw it, and remembered that his friend Georgii Dionisovich loved cubes, squares and other such rubbish, and he (Kachurin) took this work and brought it to me and gave it to me. Today in my collection it is one of the crown jewels. It is a kind of miracle, from 1917.'[7] In 1946 he gave this account of the event: '"Somehow, completely by chance, I happened to be in somebody's apartment in Moscow. I don't remember at all where it was or whose it was. And there I saw two or three canvases, two or three works by the avant-garde artists. At the time I had no idea who these artists were. I remember one work . . . and later I understood that this one work was by Olga Rozanova. And it made a very strong impression on me." Thus "the ordinary Russian" ceased to be ordinary and the Costakis collection of the Russian avant-garde was born.'[8] From that point on, everything he had collected previously seemed boring and out-of-date.

At the time, no one was interested in the avant-garde. They all thought 'that the avant-garde was a thing of the past, buried for ever and ever amen, sprinkled with soil, blood and ice, and from this grave it would never rise. The works would never fetch a price. . . . Everyone

FIGURE 59.1. George Costakis's apartment, Vernadsky Prospekt 58, on the fifteenth floor. From *Russian Avant-Garde Art: The George Costakis Collection*, edited by Angelica Zander Rudenstine, Thames and Hudson, London 1981, 58; © George Costakis Collection; State Tretyakov Gallery, Moscow; Museum of Modern Art, New York; Thyssen-Bornemisza Foundation, Madrid.

brought things to this fool of a Greek. He buys this junk, let's take it to him. Even people with a good eye, who knew art, brought me things. They didn't believe in the avant-garde.'

Costakis remembers how the 'encounter' with Rozanova's painting changed his view of what he had collected hitherto. 'I started to think that if I went on with this collection, I would bring nothing new to art. Because what I collected was in every museum—in the Louvre, in the Hermitage, in every museum in every capital of the world. And in private collections. So that if I went on this way, I might get richer and—that's all.' He suddenly found his Dutch Masters dull; they were sombre and the original gilt frames often more interesting than the paintings. '[Collecting] was no longer giving me delight. It was as though I had spent all my life in a dark room with the windows closed—maybe a little lamp somewhere. But when I brought these (avant-garde) things home and put them down, the windows opened, the sunlight burst into the room and . . . my heart . . . and from that moment I decided to get rid of everything I had and start collecting the avant-garde.'[9]

We can see from this confession what Costakis, who tended 'to buy with his eyes', thought about collecting. 'At times, we collectors are like madmen who have forgotten everything else in the world.' Later, he formulated five rules that a collector had to obey:

1. A real collector must feel like a millionaire even when he is penniless; he must act as though he has money coming out of his ears. . . .
2. Rationalization is the collector's greatest enemy.
3. The real collector is ready to give up everything he has for a work he covets. It is easier for him to endure material hardship than to lose his new find. . . .
4. A collector must not haggle. It is more advantageous for him to pay too much than not to pay enough. . . .
5. One of the most important precepts for the collector is that he must precisely, even ruthlessly define the limits of his collection.[10]

Little by little, Costakis appears to have discovered the names of the artists and the works that he thought significant. He did not follow any well-worn path but opened up new territory. He added forty-five names to the twelve he already knew and redrew the map of modern Russian art by describing the competing aesthetic tendencies—Futurists, Rayonists, Suprematists, Constructivists, Productivists, etc.—and providing each group with its own profile. What looks to us in retrospect like a clearly defined field—the Soviet avant-garde—was a largely unknown, confused tangle when he began to collect. With his picture *The Funeral of the Avant-Garde* in the 1980s, he himself provided an image of its death from neglect, marginalisation and repression.[11] He relied on his own curiosity and his newly aroused interest in this forgotten trend of European art. He followed his own taste, the persistence of ever-new forays into unknown territory and his now sharpened judgement in aesthetic matters. And he repeatedly found himself the beneficiary of collector's luck. He gradually made the acquaintance of other Soviet collectors, each of them highly specialised—a tightly knit group of connoisseurs on the one hand, but keenly competitive on the other. There was a specialist for almost every artistic genre—whether seventeenth-century snuff boxes, Venetian glassware or old Russian silver. There were collectors in the grand style, such as Felix Yevgenievich Vishnevsky; Yevgeny Pavlovich Ivanov, whose apartment on Gorky Street was one great antiquarian bookshop; and Igor Lavrov, who possessed a collection of ethnic Chukchi art. However, Costakis did not buy just avant-garde art. He compiled an impressive collection of icons and another of toys.

When he started collecting, relatives of the avant-garde artists or the artists themselves withheld their works from sale because they thought them insignificant or unworthy. They feared that such works failed to meet the requirements of the socialist realism doctrine proclaimed in 1924 that had gradually come to dominate the art world, and would therefore be regarded as reactionary or decadent. Costakis's flair and persistence led him to the discovery of paintings by Lyubov Popova that had been used to cover broken windowpanes in a dacha. He was unable to buy them until he had acquired two plywood panels as a replacement. He found some of the most valuable pictures in his collection—those of Chagall, for instance—by tracking down the widow of Solomon Mikhoels, the Yiddish actor who, before his murder by Stalin in 1948, had spent time abroad as a member of the Jewish Anti-Fascist Committee. Kandinsky's painting *Red Square* came into his possession because he refused to exploit the previous owner's ignorance of prices on the Western art market and offered her an unimaginably elevated price by Soviet standards. He was permitted to bring Alexander Rodchenko's *Hanging Construction* down from the attic by the artist himself. He discovered the last surviving wing strut from Tatlin's final major work, *Letatlin*; this helped make possible a subsequent reconstruction of the model.

The search for further paintings brought him gradually into contact with circles who themselves either belonged to the avant-garde generation—like Rodchenko or Nikritin—or else were collectors conversant with the Soviet art world of the 1920s or 1930s.[12] He built the bridge between the 'first' and the 'second' avant-garde by making the art he had collected available to the 'nonconformist' artists of the 1960s and 1970s, such as Vasily Sitnikov, Anatoly Zverev, Dmitry

Krasnopevtsev, Vladimir Weisberg, Oskar Rabin, Ilya Kabakov and Oleg Tselkov.[13] He served as the 'contact man' between the generations. In the same way, he formed the link between Russian artists in exile and the native Soviet art scene—artists such as Natalia Goncharova and Mikhail Larionov, who had left Russia before the First World War and whom Costakis visited in France in 1955. Or again with Marc Chagall, who visited him in Moscow in 1973. With the aid of his collection he brought to light the work of the pioneers of Soviet modernity who had remained in obscurity until then: Lyubov Popova, Ivan Klyun, Gustav Klutsis, Kliment Redko, the entire Ender family, Solomon Nikritin, Drevin, Labas, Filonov, Matyushin—and so revised the genealogy and historiography of the avant-garde dominated by the great artists, Kandinsky, Chagall and Malevich, as has been attested to by no less an authority than John Bowlt.[14] Costakis not only expanded our knowledge but contributed decisively to a revision of the avant-garde canon. But behind his extraordinary collection lay an extraordinary life.

The Russian Greek: The Outsider between Two Worlds

Costakis was a Muscovite by birth—his father's address was Tverskaya 75, the house of the merchant Isaev; by nationality and more importantly by citizenship, he was a Greek. His father came from the Greek island Zakynthos and had arrived in Russia via Egypt as a representative of Bostancioglu, a tobacco company; he made his fortune in Russia, as had other Greeks. The different phases of young George's life coincided with those of the development of Soviet society. In the wake of the Revolution, the family lost its twelve-room apartment in Gnezdnikovsky Pereulok and moved houses several times—Malaya Bronnaya, Leningradskoe Chaussee, and finally Vernadsky Prospekt. Costakis could remember the shooting and unrest of the World War and the Civil War. He attended a Soviet school and experienced the turbulent period of the NEP like other young people. His father, expropriated, déclassé and stigmatised as a 'former person', made his peace with the new masters. George lived a niche existence and yet had access to an international public. He later learned how the art trade functioned outside the Soviet Union and this gave him an advantage over the traders limited to the Moscow markets that were cut off from all information about current market prices. The youthful Costakis knew about cars and motorbikes, especially Harley-Davidson—his brother was a celebrated motorbike racer. That was the basis for his later position as chauffeur and majordomo at the Greek embassy. In 1939, after Greece had broken off diplomatic relations in reaction to the Stalin-Hitler Pact, he continued to work as a jack-of-all-trades for Sweden by looking after the Finnish embassy, which had been abandoned after the 'Winter War' between the USSR and Finland. The German ambassador von der Schulenburg, whom Costakis had known from chance meetings in Moscow antique shops, offered him a job as chauffeur in the German embassy. Costakis turned the offer down, probably surmising that the Soviet/German rapprochement would be of short duration. Instead in 1943 he accepted a job offer from the Canadian embassy, remaining there until his departure from the Soviet Union in 1978.

Everything points to a kind of double existence. On the one hand, Costakis was wholly committed to the Soviet Union—school, training, and adjustment to everyday life. On the other hand, he was both protected and marginalised by his Greek citizenship and his employment in extraterritorial organisations such as embassies and consulates. Thus, while he experienced the consequences of social downgrading and marginalisation, he could enjoy the privileges connected with working in diplomatic organisations. Similarly, although subject to the limitations of Soviet society as far as information and consumption were concerned, he enjoyed the access to the outside world that comes with going in and out of embassies. His wages were paid in Canadian dollars and subject to a special exchange rate (250 percent higher than the usual rate for the ruble); this elevated his status even though he was only a chauffeur. Costakis thus occupied a privileged position that almost amounted to immunity, but equally, with a vulnerability in an environment plagued by distrust and spy mania. His life was full of tensions and divisions from the outset, inwardly and outwardly.

The blows of fate were not long in coming. In 1930 his brother Spiridon lost his life in a motorbike race. Some claim that since he

FIGURE 59.2. George Costakis (1913–1990). © UPI/Süddeutsche Zeitung Photo.

belonged to a sports club competing against the NKVD, he was the victim of an arranged accident. Shortly afterward, his father died of grief over his son's death. During the Great Terror of 1937/38 his mother, an aunt and his younger brother were condemned to imprisonment in the camps in accordance with Paragraph 58—'anti-Soviet

agitation and propaganda'. His brother was sent to Kotlas in the north
of Russia from where he sent George letters about the horrific living
conditions there. George Costakis reported subsequently about his
efforts to save his brother. He described how he took the train to Kotlas, rented a place to stay close to the camp, and gained the trust of
one of the guards who arranged a meeting with his brother. Costakis
later preserved a picture of the camp complex.[15] If there is any rationality to be discerned in the blind rule of Terror that also had its
impact on the Costakis family, it lies in the fact that the members of
non-Russian ethnic groups with cross-frontier links could be singled
out as belonging to a fifth column, as potential enemies, by the NKVD
and subjected to state repression. Greeks, especially the by no means
insignificant group around the Black Sea, were just as much in danger
as, say, the Polish, Lithuanian and German populations.

In the years before the outbreak of the Second World War, Costakis
had succeeded in making the acquaintance of people in the world
of antiques and art in Moscow. As chauffeur to the ambassador, he
knew the addresses of the antique shops on Stoleshnikov Pereulok,
Kuznetsky Most and on the Arbat. Middlemen bought goods on commission from natives and sold them at great profit. The Soviet state
was interested in foreign currency, and foreigners—diplomats, journalists and businessmen for the most part—represented 99.9 percent
of the customers of these shops. Native Russians were the principal
salespeople, driven by poverty to part with their last treasures. Or else
they did not know what to do with the 'old valuables' that had fallen
into their hands after the expropriation of the old, propertied classes.
In the words of Costakis, who knew what he was talking about, 'In
those years a lot went out of Russia. An awful lot. It was a kind of tor-
rent in jewels that changed hands every day, that piled up again, were
sold again, and still they brought in more.'[16] Other visitors to Moscow
and Leningrad described the antique shops there as gold mines, a
paradise, the new Klondike. Here, for example, is the American art
historian German Seligman: 'One room presented an extraordinary
sight: a giant hall which looked like a great cave of bronze gold with
stalactites and stalagmites made of gold and crystal. Hanging down
from the ceiling and on the floor or on tables there was an incredible
number of chandeliers—small ones, large or even giant ones. All of

them glittered and sparkled, since they were evidently well looked after, with gilt ornamentation and glass or crystal decorations. The tables they stood on likewise sparkled with their gold bronze ornaments and marble, onyx or agate surfaces or that extraordinarily vivid green malachite that the Russians love so dearly.' S. Frederick Starr, probably one of the best connoisseurs of the scene summed it up as follows: 'Nowhere in recent times had there been an art and antique market more opulent than that of Stalin's Moscow.'[17] But at some point Costakis ceased to be on the lookout for the collections of the old aristocracy that had now been scattered to the winds. He stopped looking for Fabergé eggs, Chinese porcelain, Roentgen furniture, Swiss clocks and Dutch *objets*. He was after something not yet in demand: the paintings of an art that was generally despised as decadent.

In the Cross-Hairs of Power

It never occurred to Costakis that he could leave the Soviet Union. He was married to a Russian, he attended the services of the Russian Orthodox Church, his children went to Russian schools. As he admitted later, he had never seen his 'historical homeland'. Through visits he had come to know the West, as early as 1956 with a trip to Sweden for a kidney operation, and subsequently with exhibition openings and lectures.

> But somehow the West never attracted me. From the first day I started going out of my mind. Of course there's lots of everything, the stores are full. Compared with Moscow, with the Soviet Union, it's some kind of paradise. But after a couple of weeks you start seeing there isn't much to it. . . . A sort of tedium sets in. I recall that after a month, or however long I was in a particular place, I felt a strong pull to go home. I wouldn't call it nostalgia. . . . But there was this pull. So I had no idea in my head of emigrating. I thought that at my age to start life in a new place, a new country was crazy. And at the time I was no longer so young. And I always had this thought that . . . I had done all this collecting, and, in the

end, probably I would give the collection to the Tretyakov Gallery, or maybe the Russian Museum in Leningrad, and keep the icons. I had maybe 140 icons, and very good ones. If I needed money, bit by bit, I could sell the icons. So I didn't want to live abroad. And my children weren't drawn by the West. So we lived quietly on in Moscow. But one fine day—one awful day, I should say—this quiet life was shattered. I was robbed for the first time, and right out of my apartment, out of the room where I stored my collection. They took seven or eight aquarelles of Kandinsky. It's true, at the bottom of the package they left two pieces, the sons of bitches, I suppose so I wouldn't die of a heart attack.[18]

In the course of these robberies, 'several hundred' works by Nikritin and Popova were taken.[19] And even worse, Costakis's dacha in Bakovka close to Moscow was also broken into and robbed and then burnt to the ground. However, these thefts and break-ins were just the start of a campaign against Costakis, which ended with his enforced emigration in January 1978.

There were several reasons Costakis was a thorn in the side of the Soviet authorities in general and the secret service in particular. People had started to talk about his collection. Prominent visitors from the West began to arrive at the Vernadsky Prospekt apartment. Artists who did not follow the official doctrine went in and out; Costakis became something of a patron and mediator. Paintings from his collection were put on show in exhibitions organised by scholars in institutes in Dubno and Novosibirsk and even in the Ministry for Nuclear Energy. He was personally present at the first exhibition of alternative art of 1974 that was disbanded by force by the authorities— the so-called Bulldozer Exhibition. His collection was written about in the *New York Times*. Many journalists classified him as a political dissident, something he never wanted to be and in fact never was. Rumours circulated to raise and even reinforce suspicion that with his salary as a chauffeur in the Canadian embassy, he could never have built up a collection like this one. There must have been something illegal or underhand about it and surely he had to be a speculator and art smuggler. Such rumours made their way to the West and Costakis developed a poor opinion of a number of museum directors and exhibition organisers there who looked down on him. The sharpest criticism and one that wounded him most deeply was the assertion that he wished to rob the Russian people of their art and culture and enrich himself at their expense. Peter Roberts, his biographer, summed up the barrage of criticism: 'Costakis was a victim of his growing fame in the world of art. That a foreigner, a hold-over from the old regime, the employee of a foreign embassy, should become one of the best-known and most admired collectors in the world, and should do it in Russia on the basis of a forbidden school of Russian art, was simply unacceptable in those days. He had to go, somewhere. And his collection had to stay, even if it did consist of depraved rubbish.'[20] The more he defended himself and the more Voice of America, the BBC and the Deutsche Welle reported on his activities, the more frenzied were the attempts to blacken his name and the more zealously he was pursued by official harassment. Since Costakis was familiar with KGB methods—observation, break-ins and nuisance phone calls—he never went in for dubious deals or transactions; he punctiliously abided by the current regulations and took the greatest care to avoid even the most trivial mistake. But even in the West rumours and doubts about him were rife among journalists, art dealers and exhibition organisers. How was it possible to assemble a collection of this quality without the assistance or at the very least the tacit approval of the Soviet secret services (i.e., the KGB)?

Costakis resented nothing more bitterly than the malicious insinuation that he was robbing the Russian nation of its art, that he was profiting from his privileged position and enriching himself at Russia's expense. As a man who had grown up in Moscow, knew every corner of the city and was one of the faithful members of the Orthodox Church, it was clear to him from the very beginning that his collection had to remain in the Soviet Union/Russia. In this respect he stands in a long line of Russian collectors that includes Shchukin and Morosov, who acquired the paintings of Matisse and Picasso not for themselves but for Russia. Speaking of himself, he said: 'God sent me into the world to save this art for the Russian people.'[21] He even insisted that the best works in his collection, some by Rodchenko, for example, should remain in the Tretyakov Gallery, even though the gallery did not wish to hold them because in their view Rodchenko was not a painter at all but a significant photographer. Costakis insisted that '[these works of art] belong to Russia. They must belong to the Russian people. The Russian people must not suffer as a result of the stupidity of the Soviet government. So in that kind of mood it was very easy for me to hand over most of the collection, and I tried to give them the best things, and I gave them the best things. If you look in the book, you'll see.' He wanted the entire collection to go to the Tretyakov Gallery. Admittedly, he insisted that certain conditions be satisfied, but these conditions were taken for granted elsewhere: the exhibition should be open to the public, the pictures should not be allowed to disappear into the vaults, the donor should be named and his daughter Aliki should become the curator of the collection.[22]

When it became clear to Costakis that he would not be able to hold out against all the harassment in the long run, and that his life's work might be destroyed, he sought help in the upper reaches of power. From early in the 1960s he had contacts with Minister of Culture Yekaterina Furtseva, who was favourably inclined towards people with a more liberal view of art. He eventually turned to a long-serving diplomat who was himself a notable collector, Vladimir S. Semyonov. It was Semyonov who put Costakis's request to the leadership of the Communist Party and in particular to the then-head of the KGB, Yury Andropov. The deal that finally emerged involved handing over the bulk of the collection to the Tretyakov Gallery and the export of the still significant remnant, which was transported by the Interdean Co. to the Düsseldorf Kunstmuseum. From there it went on through the great museums of the USA until it reached its final destination in Thessaloniki.

Between Sotheby's Triumph and the New Politics

When Costakis died in Athens on 9 March 1990, his history appeared to have come to an end. With the munificence of his donation, he had put to shame the apparatchiks who had made his life difficult, taken his brother from him and treated members of his family as enemies of the people. He had finally triumphed over the mean, shabby behaviour of the Soviet state. He did not live to see the formal end of the Soviet Union on 26 December 1991, but he did witness the dissolution of the Soviet world in the period of perestroika during which the artists he had discovered and who had long been ostracised were shown to the public for the first time. His own efforts had begun to be acknowledged in newspapers and the writings of art specialists. But he did not live to see the Sotheby's auction of 4 April 1990 at which only three-quarters of the works entered for sale found a buyer. The two events—the end of the Soviet Union and the Sotheby's auction—belong together. The return of the avant-garde restored one of the most productive and creative eras of Russo-Soviet culture to public awareness. This was a kind of reparation to Costakis for his achievement.[23] Russia was brought back into the global art market with exhibitions of Soviet artists abroad and the opening in Moscow of subsidiaries of the great international art dealers and auction houses. The frontiers had finally fallen; artists who had longed to travel at last went abroad, sometimes forever. In the 1990s Muscovite art—'unofficial', 'nonconformist' 'soc[ialist] art'—was given a boost on the international market, albeit briefly. Anyone who had made money in post-Soviet Russia took a greater interest in 'classical art', that is, nineteenth-century painting, Fabergé eggs and Empire furniture. Orthodox oligarchs of a patriotic bent began to collect icons. A quarter of a century after the end of the Soviet Union, the myth-making, apocalyptic and nationalist image world of the painter Ilya Glazunov with his portraits of Red commissars and White generals, the Golgotha of collectivisation and victory in the Great Patriotic War, is in greater demand than the experiments with light and colour with which the avant-garde aimed to illuminate the future.[24]

Russia's reintegration into the global art scene and the art market rekindled interest in the avant-garde and brought recognition for Russian art. At the same time, the transformation wrought by the perestroika phase destroyed the canonical certainties of the prevailing aesthetics and led to a 'revaluation' of numerous careers, with more than a few reputations ruined. It would be premature, even a quarter of a century after the end of the Soviet aesthetic world, to speak of 'normalisation' as long as exhibitions are vandalised and artists physically threatened, as was the case with the exhibition *Watch Out! Religion!* in 2003.[25]

PART XVI

The Railroads of Empire: Time Travel Back into the Russian Twentieth Century

The Russian Empire made its great, much-admired appearance on the global stage at the World Exhibition in Paris in 1900. The country regarded as the very incarnation of backwardness stood revealed as being at the cutting edge of the era, as the epitome of progressive modernisation. Frithjof Benjamin Schenk gave his major study the title 'Russia's Journey into Modernity: Mobility and Social Space in the Railway Age'.[1] One of the projects that had fired people's imagination worldwide from its inception was the building of the Trans-Siberian Railway and the carriage from this line on display at the exhibition proved to be a major attraction for an international public of millions. Visitors could enter the carriage and sit down while a scroll over one hundred metres long was drawn past the window, giving them a virtual journey through the Eurasian continent. Landscapes, towns and rivers flew past; endless plains were crossed, as were bridges over the great Siberian rivers. It was truly a journey into the twentieth century, for building had actually begun at five separate points and was well advanced. The first locomotives reached Vladivostok by 1916 and it was evident that travellers would soon be able to ride from the Atlantic to the Pacific, if not from Lisbon to Tokyo.[2]

Never had the power of the modern railway to cross frontiers and bring nations together seemed more palpable than with the building of the Trans-Siberian Railway and its 9,288 kilometres. No further proof was needed to show that modern methods of transport and communication—trains, shipping, the telegraph and the telephone—would overcome vast spaces and bring the world closer together.[3] Of all the grand imperialist, space-conquering projects—the Baghdad railway or the Union Pacific, for example—the Trans-Siberian Railway has best retained its mythic power down to the present day.[4] Russia became the railroad nation par excellence and its history could be narrated along its tracks, in a carriage like the one on show in Paris. The story would tell of a journey through time, through the twentieth century, at the end of which it would become very clear that like other countries Russia was preparing to leave both the Age of the Train and the Iron Age.[5]

Taking Leave of the Age of the Train

Russia is practising the transition to a new age on the line between St. Petersburg and Moscow. On 11 June 2001 the first Russian high-speed train was launched—an event that passed without much notice. The Nevsky Express of the class RE200 built by the Tver Carriage Works belongs to a new generation of trains that can travel up to two hundred kilometres per hour. The St. Petersburg–Moscow route currently takes four and a half hours in the Nova Express, as distinct from the at least six hours needed hitherto on the Aurora Express or by the fin-de-siècle-sounding Nikolaev Night Express. Anyone who boards the train at 7 a.m. at the Moscow Station in St. Petersburg will be in Moscow by lunchtime; anyone who leaves at 7 p.m. will arrive shortly after 11 the same evening. In the meantime, the Nevsky Express has been superseded by the Sapsan, the 'Peregrine Falcon' class (Velaro RUS) built by Siemens that went into service on 17 December 2009. It can travel the 635-kilometre route between the two metropolises in under four hours, to be reduced to two and a half hours in the future. This will still take a while as the infrastructure has to be updated and bridges, track and stations have to be modernised. Nevertheless, we are not just talking about a new train model, or a long since overdue timetable change or even a new aerodynamic design. Here is a more general step change: the rhythm, the perceived distance between the two cities, the changed sense of space and the perception of time. St. Petersburg and Moscow have effectively been transformed into a unified twin city. It is almost as if New York and Chicago had moved closer together. In Russia, too, high-speed trains have spelled the end of a chapter of railway history and with it a chapter of the history of movement. The St. Petersburg to Moscow route has been a trailblazer ever since it opened on 1 November 1851. Since 1999 other routes have opened up: between Moscow and Ryazan, Moscow and Tula, Moscow and Vladimir—complete with on-board bistro, air conditioning, WLAN [wireless local area network] and staff in uniforms reminiscent of those of flight attendants. The Iron Age, an epithet introduced into Russian literature by Alexander Pushkin, is drawing to an end; another age has begun.

The Boiling Samovar, Sandwiches Wrapped in Cellophane

Everything about the modern high-speed trains is new: the design, the speed and the rhythm. People who have taken the train to St. Petersburg from Murmansk or Arkhangelsk and then transferred to the Moscow Express have entered a new age. They will have spent an entire day and then an entire night on the train; changing trains for the Express, they will then travel the 635 kilometres to Moscow in a few hours. All Russian trains were previously designed with long distances in mind, and with journeys lasting days and nights. The Sapsan, in contrast, is a sprinter. If you want to, you can travel from St. Petersburg to Moscow and back in a single day. The Sapsan has something of a plane about it. With its streamlined shape and the way it lies deep in the track, it feels rather like a jet taking off. Painted in the national colours, white-blue-red, it reminds us also of the Aeroflot machines and contrasts with the pine green that has been the standard colour of Russian trains for generations. But even this does not convey the full extent of the culture change that has transformed the railway.

You no longer live in the train; you no longer settle down for the duration. You no longer get to know your fellow passengers. New-style passengers travel alone and have no interest in meeting fellow travellers or being entertained. They sit in one of the reserved, adjustable seats of the spacious carriage, which itself resembles a seat in a plane. They have a bundle of newspapers, reading matter for the brief trip or an iPad or laptop. Passengers sit behind one another. There is no longer anyone opposite to talk to. Instead you talk on your mobile phone to your partner, who is elsewhere. In the first-class section passengers can watch news and films on large screens, seek out conference and work compartments with fax and email connections and obtain something to eat. The journey which previously represented time away from work has become part of worktime in accordance with the new business model. You don't have to go beyond the platforms to realise that this mode of travel is that of a new class of people. They are not encumbered with large or heavy luggage such that you can't imagine where it can be stowed. No one has brought trunks or boxes. The train has ceased to be a vehicle for transporting goods in short supply that have to be taken home or to distant provinces. And since everything can now be procured everywhere there is no need for iron reserves or for stocking up. People simply bring the things they need for business trips or brief visits: an executive briefcase or a shoulder bag and a notebook. At most, there will be a few tourists dragging suitcases. Travelling is no longer an immersive activity but simply an interlude to be reduced as far as possible to the bare essentials. In such trains as these you no longer see passengers making themselves at home in pyjamas or tracksuits. You don't see them unpacking chickens or vobla [cured roach from the Caspian Sea], no tomatoes or pickled cucumbers—that would just be embarrassing. But the principal reason is that there is no longer enough time to enjoy a full meal of this kind. Instead, there are sandwiches wrapped in cellophane from the trolley. Tea comes in a plastic mug and the water for the tea from a thermos flask. There are no longer any samovars, which used to be boiling away in the conductor's compartment. The other thing that has disappeared is the faint, aromatic smell of cabbage that would envelop you everywhere on platforms in the Soviet Union even before you had entered the train.

The Sapsan Express is well staffed. There is no problem with buying a ticket. Nor do you have to buy it well in advance, as used to be the case, even if you want to be sure of getting one. The ticket offices are computerised and here too you can book online. The days when you had to stand in a queue with all the nerve-wracking waiting and people losing their tempers are long past. The downside is that travelling now costs more and for many people it has become a luxury.

One of the pair of high-speed trains no longer stops between St. Petersburg and Moscow. It can simply afford to bypass even such important stations as Tver and Klin, while also travelling nonstop through old junctions such as Bologoe. Travelling at a maximum speed of 200–250 km/h, passengers in the Moscow–St. Petersburg Express scarcely notice the landscape they are passing through. The contours become blurred and passengers are more preoccupied with their own affairs anyway. The world looks different from high-speed trains than from carriages moving along at 50–100 km/h.[6] If there have been problems, friction and disruptions this is because the supermodern trains of Western origin are not equipped for the winter temperatures and because the trains have been subjected to attacks. The corollary of greater speed is the reduction of local and regional traffic and the once-unified terrain where one could simply cross the rails on foot is now split up by the high-speed track.

Russian or Soviet History Is the History of the Railway

Despite the Sapsan Russia has remained a railway nation to this day and Russian history of the nineteenth and twentieth centuries played out along its railway lines. This can be seen in every railway museum—which Russia possesses in greater number than anywhere else on Earth, chiefly in the towns where the central stations are located together with the associated train depots, that is to say, in St. Petersburg, Moscow, Novosibirsk, Vladivostok, Vladikavkaz or in Ukrainian Kharkiv, which used to be the chief junction for the South Russian railway network. What we can learn from all of these railway museums—nowadays online as well—is about the power of rail to conquer space and help to build a state.[7] The railway stands for our ability to overcome our excessive dependence on nature, to develop mobility without regard to seasonal differences and to put an end to the centuries-old drama of the absence of tracks and pathways. It was not until the arrival of the train that Russia ceased to be a country in which accessibility was tied to rivers and the entire network of waterways. Only when the Russian Empire no longer had to be contemplated from the vantage point of ships' docking facilities on the great rivers and the veins and arteries of their tributaries and was instead organised by the 'geometry of train lines' did it become possible to escape from the fatalistic straitjacket of the natural order.[8] It amounted to the creation of a new Russia, with new distances, a new tempo, a hitherto unknown independence of natural conditions, the creation of a new space, inclusive of its associated risks: mobility, social convulsions and cultural fault lines—in short, railway lines are corridors and networks through which revolution spread in the vast empire.[9] The curse of Russia—being lost in the vast space of the realm, as Pyotr Chaadaev put it—appeared to have been broken with the construction of the railway.

If there was a Russian Empire, it was because there was a railway; if there was a Soviet Union, this was possible not least because a rail network already existed. An empire without the railway, without the great control of space, was as inconceivable as opening up North America without the great transcontinental railway corridors.[10] The fact that the railway functioned guaranteed the stability of the Empire. Expansions could only survive in the long run if new lines were laid and stations built. The Empire stretched as far as the broad-gauge tracks went. These tracks with their 1,520 mm width contrasted with the 'rest of the world', which had agreed on a standard width of 1,435 mm. They held together a space that would otherwise have fallen apart. Every train timetable on display in the concourse—now mostly on view electronically—brought the ends of the Empire together, day by day, month by month, year by year, down through the generations. The railway may be thought of as the Empire's DNA—like the highway system in the USA. As everywhere else, but to an even greater extent, the railway was the province of the state. In importance and status, and probably in the number of employees, it was, as Tsar Alexander III once said, the third most important pillar of the Empire after the army and the navy. It was the school of administrative and industrial discipline in a nation that still operated according to the agrarian cycle. Anyone who was employed by the railway—whether as official, station master or workshop hand—could think of themself as belonging to a kind of elite, almost as the member of a state within the state, a sort of 'school of the nation', with its carefully graded uniforms, solid system of rewards, lofty prestige and own ethos. The authority of this state within the state even extended to the train personnel, such as the ticket collectors, inspectors and the guards who waved the train through with outstretched arm, as if taking a march-past. Comfort on lengthy journeys such as from Moscow to Beijing depended very much on the solicitude of the women conductors.

The institutes where civil engineers received their training were elite schools, and railway engineers, land surveyors and tunnel and bridge builders were among the true pioneers of Russia's moderni-sation. Names such as Pavel Petrovich Melnikov (1804–1880) have not been forgotten in Russia. Masterpieces of engineering, such as the railway bridge over the Volga at Syzran, have remained icons of modern

РАСПИСАНИЕ ДВИЖЕНИЯ ПАССАЖИРСКИХ ПОЕЗДОВ (ВОКЗАЛЫ г. МОСКВЫ)

1. МОСКВА. Казанский вокзал Московской ж. д.

Куда отправляется и откуда прибывает	Род вагонов в поезде	Отпр. из Москвы			Приб. в Москву			№ маршрутных таблиц. начальных и конечных
		№ поезда	Время отпр.	Периодичность курсирования	№ поезда	Время приб.	Периодичность курсирования	
Абакан	ВР КПЖ	68	23.43	Ежедн.	67	13.45	Ежедн.	14, 14′, 388
Алма-Ата II	ВРСВКП	8	22.25	Ежедн.	7	15.38	Ежедн.	8, 8′, 125, 125′
Алма-Ата II	ВР КПЖ	84	4.20	Ежедн.¹)	83	22.26	Ежедн.¹)	12, 12′, 125, 125
Андижан	ВР СВКП	34	13.56	Ежедн.	33	5.36	Ежедн.	8, 8′, 126, 126′
Андижан	ВР КПЖ	320	0.15	Чет.¹)	319	18.14	Чет.¹)	10, 10′, 126, 126′
Андижан	ВР КПЖ	324	0.15	Неч.¹)	323	18.14	Неч.¹)	10, 10′, 126, 126′
Ашхабад	ВРСВМКП	12	17.15	Ежедн.	11	6.04	Ежедн.	8, 8′, 11
Барнаул	ВР КП	36	16.30	Чет.	35	11.20	Чет.	14, 14′, 132
Барнаул	ВР КПЖ	196	20.50	Неч.	195	15.05	Чет.	14, 14′, 132
Бийск	ВР КПЖ	548	20.50	пн., ср. сб.³	547	15.05	вт. пт., вс.³	14, 14′, 133
Вернадовка	КПЖ	602	21.30	Ежедн.	601	4.35	Ежедн.	12, 12′, 293
Волгоград	ВРСВК	2	14.28	Ежедн.	1	10.04	Ежедн.	8, 8′, 93
Волгоград	ВРСВКП	4	14.41	Ежедн.	3	11.12	Ежедн.	8, 8′, 93
Волгоград	ВР КПЖ	202	0.34	Ежедн.	201	21.18	Ежедн.	8, 8′, 93
Волгоград	ВР КПЖ	350	21.20	Ежедн.	349	16.10	Ежедн.	8, 8′, 93
Волгоград	ВР КПЖ	556	7.35	Чет.²)	555	23.33	Ежедн.³)	8, 8′, 93
Земетчино	КПЖ	606	19.44	Ежедн.	605	5.50	Чет.²)	12, 12′, 293
Душанбе	ВРСВКП	24	15.34	Ежедн.	23	5.15	Ежедн.	8, 8′, 354
Ейск	ВР КПЖ	598	8.50	Ежедн.¹)	597	23.20	Ежедн.²)	8, 8′, 317
Ижевск	ВРСВКП	50	18.15	Ежедн.	49	10.16	Ежедн.	14, 14′, 372
Ижевск	КПЖ	382	22.00	Ежедн.¹)	381	15.30	Ежедн.²)	14, 14′, 372
Жигулевское Море	ВРСВКП	66	16.40	Ежедн.	65	14.09	Ежедн.	12, 12′
Йошкар-Ола	СВКПЖ	58	14.52	Ежедн.	57	9.01	Ежедн.	14, 14′, 374
Казань	ВРСВМКП	28	20.20	Ежедн.	27	10.45	Ежедн.	14, 14′
Казань	ВР КПЖ	382	22.00	Чет.	381	15.30	Неч.	14, 14′
Караганда	ВР КПЖ	112	23.32	Ежедн.	111	22.17	Ежедн.	14, 14′, 130
Караганда	ВР КПЖ	220	13.22	Ежедн.	219	13.08	Ежедн.	10, 10′, 130
Караганда	ВР МКПЖ	372	9.45	сб., вс., чт.²)	371	21.59	пт., сб., ср.²)	14, 14′, 130
Краснодар	КП	348	6.53	Ежедн.³)	347	23.56	Ежедн.¹)	8, 8′, 403
Красноярск	ВРСВКП	56	13.12	Ежедн.¹)	55	5.45	Ежедн.¹)	14, 14′, 5, 5′
Красноярск	ВР КПЖ	176	9.20	Ежедн.	175	20.58	Ежедн.	14, 14′, 5, 5′
Куйбышев	ВР СВКП	10	19.28	Ежедн.	9	6.35	Ежедн.	12, 12′
Куйбышев	ВР КПЖ	46	20.35	Ежедн.¹)	45	10.57	Ежедн.¹)	10, 10′
Курган	ВР КПЖ	558	10.00	Неч.³)	557	23.30	Неч.³)	14, 14′
Кустанай	ВР КПЖ	214	0.44	Ежедн.²)	213	19.10	Ежедн.²)	12, 12′, 401
Лениногорск	ВР КПЖ	174	14.10	Ежедн.	173	23.00	Ежедн.	14, 14′, 353
Магнитогорск	ВР КПЖ	194	13.32	Ежедн.	193	5.08	Ежедн.	12, 12′, 437
Набережные Челны	ВР КП	234	9.30	Ежедн.¹)	233	4.05	Ежедн.¹)	12, 12′, 417
Новокузнецк	ВР КП	546	4.30	вт., чт., вс.³)	545	20.05	пн., ср., сб.³)	14, 14′, 62
Новокузнецк	ВР КП	32	12.17	Ежедн.	31	4.40	Ежедн.	14, 14′, 62, 62′
Нижний Тагил	ВР КП	70	12.57	Ежедн.	69	5.26	Ежедн.	60, 60′, 16
Омск	ВР КП	48	21.40	Ежедн.	47	13.55	Ежедн.	14, 14′, 12, 12′
Оренбург	ВРСВКП	44	0.04	Ежедн.	43	18.23	Ежедн.	12, 12′, 10, 10′
Орск	ВР КПЖ	192	13.44	Ежедн.	191	9.09	Ежедн.	10, 10′, 146
Павлодар	ВРСВКП	74	20.10	Чет.	73	14.22	Ежедн.	10, 10′, 132
Пенза	СВКП	52	21.50	Ежедн.	51	9.30	Ежедн.	10, 10′
Пенза	КПЖ	172	23.53	Ежедн.¹)	171	13.30	Ежедн.	10, 10′
Пермь	ВРСВКП	62	17.30	Ежедн.	61	9.50	Ежедн.	60, 60′ 5, 5′
Первомайск	КПЖ	624	21.00	Ежедн.	623	6.17	Ежедн.	14, 14′
Ряжск	КПЖ	608	22.46	Ежедн.	607	4.55	Ежедн.	10, 10′
Ростов	ВРСВКП	20	19.05	Ежедн.	19	14.38	Ежедн.	8, 8′
Ростов	ВРСВМКП	336	12.30	Ежедн.¹)	335	21.37	Ежедн.¹)	8, 8′
Рязань	КЖ	604	18.45	Ежедн.	603	10.20	Ежедн.	12, 12′
Самарканд	ВР КПЖ	98	0.24	Ежедн.	97	16.22	Ежедн.	10, 10′, 11
Саранск	СВКП	42	21.10	Ежедн.	41	5.54	Ежедн.	12, 12′, 32
Саранск	КПЖ	306	12.45	Ежедн.⁷	305	3.40	Ежедн.¹)	12, 12′, 32
Свердловск	ВР СВ КП	16	16.53	Ежедн.	15	10.37	Ежедн.	60, 60′, 5, 5′
Сергач	КПЖ	662	18.30	Ежедн.	661	4.25	Ежедн.	14, 14′
Ташкент	ВРСВКП	6	22.15	Ежедн.	5	14.30	Ежедн.	12, 12′, 10, 10′
Ташкент	ВРМ КПЖ	86	12.03	Ежедн.	85	4.45	Ежедн.	12, 12′, 10, 10′
Томск I	ВРСВКП	38	23.04	Неч.	37	16.02	Неч.	14, 14′, 63

FIGURE XVI.1. Departure times for passenger trains leaving Kazan Station, one of the seven Moscow stations (1988–1989). From *Raspisanie dvizheniia passazhirskih poezdov (kratkoe) na 1988–1989 gg.*, edited by V. F. Seliakova, Transport, Moscow 1988, 5.

technology down to the present day.[11] On its journey to modernity Russia owes as much to its engineers as to the far better-known financiers or ministers.[12] As to the enthusiasm for railways, there was scarcely any distinction to be drawn between the revolutionaries and the existing state. The elites of both the old and the new Empire had their own technological fantasies and technocratic dreams. Whoever had a name and a rank—from Sergey Witte to Konstantin Pobedonostsev, from Alexander Herzen to Leon Trotsky—revelled in philosophising about the railway, both as the instrument of expansion of imperial power and as a form of locomotion.

Without the railway the giant empire appeared to be no more than the lumbering, impotent 'colossus with feet of clay' that would collapse no sooner than it was attacked. With the railway, however, it would be able to hurl its vast resources at whatever front was at risk and so was virtually invincible. Train lines were like 'arteries' or 'sinews' that strengthened the body and the terminuses were treated often enough as signals pointing to the progress achieved by internal and external colonisation: Vladivostok ('Conquer the East') or Vladikavkaz ('Conquer the Caucasus'). Whoever controlled them controlled the Empire and could decide on victory or defeat. Connections with the rest of the world were established by the railway. It was through the railway that grain and timber could pass onto the world market via Odesa, Riga and St. Petersburg and it was through the railway that these towns became indissolubly tied to market cycles from that time on. Europe arrived in Russia via the railroad: Welsh coal, turbines made by AEG, soap from England, flowers from Nice, Gustav Mahler on a tour. Another person to travel from Switzerland in a 'sealed train' during the First World War was Lenin, the Revolution hard core, who arrived at the Finland Station in Petrograd in April 1917.[13] The railway, which held the Empire together in times of peace, became the engine of destabilisation in times of war and revolution. A new class had formed in the railway workshops and Gorky found the hero of his novel *Mother* there, in a Sormovo factory. It was by train that the exhausted, grey mass of soldiers was carried back to the homeland from the front so as to be present at the distribution of the land. Whoever had control of the railway junctions, signal boxes, stations and telegraphs had control of the entire country.

The railway lines became the tracks of the Revolution. The paths opened up to facilitate mobilisation for the Great War became the conduit for the masses on the move. Railway junctions, ships' landing stages and telegraph stations were the Archimedean points from which to turn the entire Empire upside down. Starting out from train tracks, Russia shifted from the steam engine to the armoured train. Locomotives and railway carriages formed a more crucial part of the inventory of the Russian Revolution than of any preceding revolution: armoured trains occupied and defended the strategic line; agitators travelled through the land in a futuristically painted agitprop train equipped with radios, studios for making posters and film cameras to spread the revolutionary message far and wide; the Trans-Siberian Railway became the via dolorosa of the Russian Civil War, alternately under the control of the Whites or the Reds—or indeed of third powers on Russian soil; trains filled with thousands and thousands of towns-folk foraging in the countryside.[14] One of the most perfect pictures illustrating the collapse of the old order depicts the railway graveyards filled with hundreds of broken-down locomotives that were shunted together to create veritable mountains. The characters in Pasternak's *Doctor Zhivago* move along the track of the Russian railways ruined by the Civil War; the first *subbotnik* was invented in the train depots of Moscow and Nikolay Ostrovsky found the hero of his novel *How the Steel Was Tempered* in the world along the railway lines.[15] Paralysed by a Time of Troubles lasting almost a decade, Russia had then fallen apart into mutually inaccessible territories.

However, the country made a speedy recovery in the 1920s and was forcibly propelled onto a second wave of modernisation. Examples are the completion of new routes already planned under the old regime, such as the Turksib or the Baikal-Amur Mainline (BAM).[16] A further example is the construction of routes already specified in the electrification plan of 1920 and that would lead to the creation of a new, autarchic USSR economy. The metaphors of 'catching up' and 'overtaking' were of central importance to the Stalinist industrialisation plan. Fellow travellers from the West who had seen little of the country enthused about the comfort they experienced in the new Night Express, the Red Arrow, which ran between Leningrad and Moscow. Something of its power and speed was mirrored in the newly

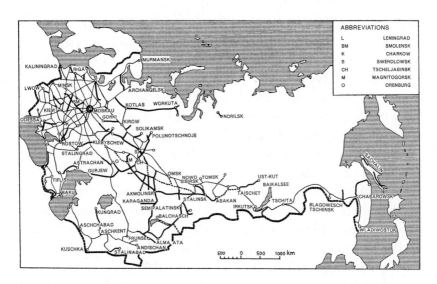

FIGURE XVI.2. The axes of empire in 1859. The thicker lines show railways completed since 1918 and the broken lines show railways under construction. From J. N. Westwood, *A History of Russian Railways*, Allen & Unwin, London 1964, 283.

developed class FD and JS locomotives in the 1930s—named after Felix Dzerzhinsky, founder of the Cheka and People's Commissar for Transport, and Joseph Stalin himself.[17] Today these may be thought of as the forerunners of the TGV. Even the darker side of modernisation has been immortalised in the photographs connected with the railway. We see it in the insanity of the extension to Salekhard just north of the Arctic Circle built by slave labour. We see it also in the cattle trucks used to deport hundreds of thousands of peasants and subsequently entire ethnic communities, such as the Chechens, Ingush, Volga Germans and Crimean Tatars, to Siberia or Central Asia. A railway network like the Soviet system in the phase of industrialisation was in a state of permanent stress and so ripe for accidents of every kind—derailments, explosions, collapsed bridges. This explains why it became a veritable battlefield for the 'disorganisation of the transport system' at the hands of 'parasites, saboteurs and agents' in the years of the Great Terror.[18]

But what is probably the most magnificent chapter in the history of the Soviet railways was written in the Second World War, which became the Great Patriotic War, when whole towns, factories and populations were evacuated to the east despite furious attacks by the German Wehrmacht and the Stuka dive-bombers, and the entire Soviet Union started to work in obedience to the motto 'Everything for the Front!' Initially, when the great train junctions were hit in Orsha, Veliky Luki and Bologoe, it looked as if the country would be bombed back into an archaic trackless waste and fall apart.[19] But the Soviet railway retaliated and became the logistical backbone of the great counterattacks. By the end of the war their restored broad-gauge tracks led all the way to the Schlesischer Bahnhof in Berlin.

The railway must inevitably be a concern of the state—one might almost say, a state within a state—for such a large country, which depends upon the strength of its transport system to encompass vast spaces and where every political authority owes its legitimacy in no small measure to its ability to maintain that system. This could be seen when the ruling dynasty resolved to create the first train connection between St. Petersburg and the royal residences in Tsarskoe Selo and Pavlovsk in 1837 and after that with the construction of the link between St. Petersburg and Moscow in 1851. The same applied to the secular project of the Trans-Siberian Railway in the 1890s and most especially in the case of the production of Soviet space. To be the minister or people's commissar for transport and communication was always to hold a very special office. This remained the case following the end of the Soviet Union since the Empire disintegrated into the national republics and the formerly transnational rail network with it. The disentangling and privatisation of the State Russian Railways was perhaps the hardest task to be accomplished en route to the denationalisation of the economy and the renewal of the nation's infrastructure. Once again, the railway has become the mirror or gauge of historical processes. There is a profound gulf between modernisation and increased speed on a few routes as against decline and reduced speed on many others. A centuries-old gulf.

Lifeworld of the Railway

And yet, we might almost say that in Russia the railway is less a concern of the state than a mode of transport, a concern of the lifeworld.[20] That is how it always was and how it still is today. And this explains why shifting over to the Sapsan Express is no mere trifle but a rupture within that *longue durée* with which we measure eras. Nowhere is the railway such a permanent fixture, such a well-established topos as in Russian literature. It moves from Tolstoy's Anna Karenina, who hurls herself in front of the train at Obiralovka Station in the winter of 1873, via Vsevolod Ivanov's *Armoured Train 14–69* and on to Solzhenitsyn's journey to the Gulag archipelago in the so-called Stolypin wagon. From the carriage window your gaze passes over the whole twentieth-century countryside. Russian literature is full of what Fyodor Stepun calls the 'musical melancholy of the train'.[21] In the cataclysms of the twentieth century it becomes the vehicle of mass movement, for the most part under coercion. The British historian Peter Gatrell in his study of the First World War has described this process with his title 'A Whole Empire Walking'. The railways were simply the chief means of transport in the age of general mobilisations, mass evacuations, deportations and mass emigration; they were vehicles of acceleration and the symbol of collapse. They were the means of transporting the millions of peasants uprooted from the doomed villages by collectivisation; they were the great conveyor belt—in Russian *Konveer*—in which prisoners were forced to stand in line for hours awaiting interrogation. It was on the trains that what was known as 'agrarian overpopulation' was shifted into the towns and the construction sites of socialism, a rupture of unprecedented brutality.

> We are made of rye and oatmeal
> We wear gaily coloured clothes as we sit in our farmstead
> You are made of cast iron and concrete,
> of electricity and milk. We are fire, water and fields,
> Winter corn and battered suns,
> You will be unable to tell the stories of the perfumed gardens.
>   Your songs are the hammer groans.
> Its chords are cinders and tin;
> The tree of life has been split,
> Instead of fruits heads hang from it.

These are the words of the peasant poet Nikolay Klyuev.[22]

What the highway and the automobile were for America—even during the Depression, when John Steinbeck's heroes in *The Grapes of Wrath* were making their way west—the trains, the stations, the spectacular landscapes through which the rail tracks ran and the rail junctions were for Russia and the Soviet Union. It was through these that millions sought their fortune in the freedom promised in the vast spaces of Siberia—or where they were sent to their deaths. 'On the road' in Russian was presumably acted out in the years of the post-Stalinist Thaw. It took place on the building sites of the Baikal-Amur railway or in the tent cities and container towns that brought hundreds of thousands of young people to the virgin territories of Kazakhstan. The stations were the great assembly points of Eurasia. As with their counterparts everywhere in Europe, they were also the relay stations of progress, and even a little more: they were 'the cathedrals of progress', centres of culture as can be seen today in the surviving station palaces along the Europe route (wherever they have not been modernised to death or even torn down).[23] But this is also exactly where the tracks with the 'Stolypin wagons' ran with their hundreds of thousands, and indeed millions, who were riding to their doom in camps and exile, if they did not collapse and die en route, whereupon they would simply be thrown off the train.[24] The stations were in a quite basic sense the places where the multinational Empire encountered itself and practised the modes of conduct without which empires of this kind and magnitude cannot function.

The train compartment was and still is a social venue par excellence: a place of experience, of meditation and reflection, of the enforced cohabitation of strangers meeting by chance, of erotic adventures and fateful encounters. It was a space in which even in the darkest times when you could trust no one, news circulated about the true state of the country. It was one of the few places where people spoke freely because everyone could reasonably assume that they would never meet again. Freedom and candidness *en passant*, between departure and arrival, we might call it. As Leonid Andreev, among many others, put it: 'I don't know why it is, but everyone becomes a philosopher while on a journey. Separated from everyday events, they seem to wake up and to look around them in surprise. They remember events of the distant past and dream of the no less distant future. If human ideas could assume a shape, every fast train would be enveloped by the multitude of their shadows and their thousand muffled and drawn-out voices would drown out its roar. For people in a train carriage there is no present, no damned present, that holds human thoughts and hand movements in an iron grip—perhaps this explains why people become philosophers on a train.'[25]

The train compartment as the place of truth is not exactly the typical bourgeois ideal of Western textbooks, but it is in a sense a kind of equivalent, a free space of great intensity and seriousness. Anyone who travelled through the land by train could count on the weirdest surprises and might encounter people they would never meet in 'normal' life: officials on work trips, businessmen, criminals or young people returning from camping in the wild in the Altai Mountains, veterans who had been present at the storming of the Seelow Heights on the threshold of Berlin, intellectuals who didn't know whether they would be able to endure living in the provinces any longer, jacks-of-all-trades, engineers conversant with the world of international congresses, journalists who knew all about mining in the Donbass, kolkhozniks, Siberian oil workers on leave in Ukraine, perhaps even an American from the Peace Corps. In the compartments of Russian and Soviet trains, you could learn more about the country and what was going on than from the newspapers or statistical analyses and all this remains true—or is true once again—even today, in the age of telecommunication and the internet. And almost every time you would discover a piece of 'society' of a complexity that had little to do with 'totalitarian society'—or what theoreticians schooled in social models understood by the term.

There are many reasons we should emphasise the importance of travelling by train in Russia or the Soviet Union and the human experiences to be encountered in the process. You meet strangers and yet spend so much time together—a day or, on occasion, many days—that you come to know one another and gradually understand who you are dealing with. There is also what might be called the almost domestic ambience associated with the Russian train compartment: from the embroidered curtains and blinds down to the real geraniums in the corridor, from the soothing rituals of bed-making down to the wake-up call. Then there is the discretion shown to many generations

of passengers that has become second nature; it is the discretion
characteristic of strangers who are forced to spend a certain period
of time together in the confined space of a coupé. This discretion is
shared by people from all walks of life and seems like the response to
that unavoidable 'tyranny of intimacy' that comes with living together
in tight quarters; it is a repeat of the kommunalka experience in a
moving train. We might almost call it the common cultural inheritance
of a nation of train travellers. In a certain sense, then, the Russian
train compartment is the space for the 'ideal conversation'; effortless, free and tactful. The rule of the conductor is based on natural
authority. The landscapes the train passes through and the stations
where it stops provide variety and endless fodder for conversation.
Such journeys offer the opportunity to learn about living conditions,
price differentials, merits or faults of particular governors or mayors,
the situation in local schools, and the quality of mushrooms or jams
on sale at the various stops along the line.

The railway as a part of Russian culture found an echo in the very
place it no longer exists: beyond its frontiers. For Fyodor Stepun,
living in exile, the railway carriage is a microcosm of Russia itself.

When I think back to my journeys through Russia, what I remember most vividly is the Russian railway carriage. The rhythm of its
wheels and the prevailing atmosphere were utterly different from
the rhythm and atmosphere of the trains in Western Europe. A
contemporary Russian philosopher has expressed the thought that
the Russian soul has little time for a solidly established household
since it regards every shelter in this life as no more than a staging
post on the path to the next world. . . . As is well known, the soul
of railway domesticity was tea. . . . In those days no one expressed
surprise at the presence of the samovar. But I was very moved—if
the reader will forgive my émigré sentimentality—when in 1928, on
my way to Dvinsk, which strictly speaking was in Latvia, I found
myself in what felt like a typical Russian railway carriage and saw
once again the native samovar! And in truth, it looked to me less
like a samovar than like the good spirit of my native hearth. No
less homely was the boiler man who brought me and my wife a
glass of hot, strong and aromatic tea of a kind rarely seen in West-

ern Europe. The nickel tray he held in a black hand that resembled a coal shovel, the slice of lemon on a saucer—all these things had been introduced in long-distance trains long before and had not been abolished by the Latvian government. They moved both of us almost to tears. Drinking tea on the train with a generous snack and endless talk went on for hours. The snack and the conversation were both very varied. They differed greatly in First Class and Second Class, in the express train and the local train. It was one thing when the train went to Warsaw and from there to the West and quite another when it headed for the Caucasus spas or the Volga territories.[26]

Of course, there have been times of greater insecurity and deprivation and hence of greater risk to travellers. Even in 1990 when the Soviet Union was falling apart, new borders were being created, prices had spiralled out of control and the state of the toilets pointed to the dissolution of order. Trains were transformed into bazaars on wheels, goods from China on their way to Europe piled up in the compartments and corridors.[27] Stations as junctions for the circulation of people have been superseded nowadays by airports, which have created new patterns of movement.

Journey into Noncontemporaneity

The track of the Sapsan Express is more or less identical with the route taken by Alexander N. Radishchev, one of the fathers of the Russian Enlightenment who embarked on his 'Journey from St. Petersburg to Moscow' in 1790. In his novel with the same title he spoke of the 'depravity of unfreedom' and dreamed of the miracles that would be achieved by the abolition of serfdom. As is well known, Radishchev paid for his candid description of conditions with censorship, banishment and suicide.[28]

The metropolitan corridor of today may perhaps show us, over two hundred years since Radishchev, where things are heading in Russia. Taking the Express at the end of the Second Millennium, one sees scarcely anything at all of the country being passed through. The traveller just changes trains—from the Metro to the Express—while remaining in the same time zone: capital city time, CNN time or global time. Clocks in Moscow have a different tick from those elsewhere in the country. Seventy percent of the capital of the Russian Federation flows together in Moscow. Ninety percent of the newspapers, journals and books published in the Russian Federation appear in Moscow. Year after year, Moscow propels new banking and residential towers into the sky at breath-taking speed. The Stalinist skyscrapers are illuminated like gigantic theatre sets and so the night sky over Moscow never becomes dark. On the banks of the Neva, St. Petersburg is all lit up.

Russia itself is somewhere outside all this, beyond the corridor that connects the two cities. Between the two cities there is an intelligentsia that knows little about what goes on outside that corridor and has little to do with it. Its members remain among themselves in the metropolitan corridor. This means that the illuminated vistas of Moscow and St. Petersburg with their private viewings and film locations are closer to Berlin, Stockholm or Istanbul than to medium-sized or small towns in the Russian provinces. Moscow is on another planet. It is almost a state within a state. You can see the metropolitan corridor from a plane, especially at night when it is all lit up and surrounded by the dark plain.

You have to be blind not to notice the gulf that opens up between the twin capitals and the countryside between them. The corridor between Moscow and St. Petersburg contains everything—the vast malls, bazaars, do-it-yourself shops, a branch of Ikea, drive-ins, outsize billboards, the beginnings of Las Vegas in Russia. The metropolitan corridor boasts ATMs, shops that never shut, internet cafés, a metro where the trains arrive every one-and-a-half minutes, and eight-lane streets where the traffic is stationary at peak times. Its edges are flanked by the towers of the mobile-phone companies and the posters showing the sun rising on the beaches of Cyprus and Miami. The limits of the new age are marked by the range of the mobile phones and the relative concentration of petrol stations. The zone around the fast lane is governed by other laws, other dynamics, a time scale of its own. Beyond the great cities in the corridor extends a different sort of zone, one that is little known but forms part of the Russia you fly over. It has no voice of its own; it is hidden in obscurity. It has no strength of its own; it is exhausted, worn out. Everything happens with great effort; it is all sluggish and lethargic. The corridor where everything moves faster collides with the zone where all movement has slowed down and may even have come to a halt. Were it not for the occasional church dome, newly decorated in gold, or the mobile-phone mast that you can glimpse through the trees, there would be nothing to suggest that anything at all is happening there.

It is as if there were two separate worlds, two different epochs. It is as if an entire country was left behind. Wherever the two worlds collide, you find resignation and hatred, resentment and envy. Russia has plenty of experience of the contemporary survival of the noncontemporaneous. The philosopher Nikolay Berdyaev once described the Russian Revolution as the clash between the sixteenth and twentieth centuries on Russian soil. 'Every nation lives in different times and centuries at every moment of its existence. But no nation except for the Russian has ever known such very different ages to be so closely intertwined as the sixteenth and the twentieth. And the union of these radically different ages is the source of the unhealthy situation of our national life and an obstacle to its integrity.'[29] In fact, the nation was almost destroyed by this collision of the ages in the Time of Troubles. Now, at the start of a new century we are again witnessing a new round in this clash of civilisations. No country can survive these noncontemporaneous events in the long run. Not even a country such as Russia, which has experienced so many crises and been tested by so many catastrophes.

What might a panoramic journey put on show today to compare with the one experienced by visitors to the 1900 Paris World Exhibition in a compartment of the Trans-Siberian Railway? Naturally, it would be able to take advantage of the advances in the media available in the early twenty-first century. It would probably be a journey through the twentieth century; it would show the Eurasian railway as a red thread running through a catastrophic age unforeseen in the forward projections of its creators.[30] The rail line that was supposed to link up the Atlantic with the Pacific was violently interrupted—by wars, the First and then the Second World War. A route that had been inaugurated as the axis of transcontinental change and trade became

FIGURE XVI.3. One of the many locomotive graveyards of the Civil War. From J. N. Westwood, *A History of Russian Railways*, Allen & Unwin, London 1964, 193. Photo from the Imperial War Museum.

the strategic axis for the movement of troops and weapons. It was the militarisation of a genuinely civil project.

The locomotives of progress turned into the armoured trains of internal Russian strife, the line forming a front between Red and White. Following the Eurasian axis, the centres of industrialisation pushed on from west to east, as early as the first Five-Year Plans of the 1930s, but chiefly in the course of the evacuations after the invasion of the Soviet Union, of European Russia, by Nazi Germany. The railway was the vehicle of transformation, industrialisation and urbanisation of the nation with new, aspiring settlements and the Trans-Siberian line, a truly Eurasian enterprise. It was the corridor through which the immeasurably vast river of deportees, the *katorzhniki* of the twentieth century, passed. But even the Siberians who were hurled into the front against Hitler's troops as the last reserves made use of this line. It was the new artery passing through the Empire; through this artery flowed the energy, the 'human material' for the internal colonisation.[31] The First and Second World Wars were followed by the Third War: the Cold War with frontiers that extended from the Elbe to the

Ussuri River and the Pacific. The Iron Curtain prevented any further attempt at pursuing the civilising mission of the Trans-Siberian Railway—to join up the world between Vladivostok and Lisbon. The track, which had been completed in 1916, never got going again. The end of the Soviet Union and the fall of the Iron Curtain allowed optimists, people of good will and project managers, to take another look at the Eurasian rail track—some even contemplated the idea of a bridge over the Bering Strait and a train travelling from Paris to New York. Post-Soviet Russia has up to now failed to deliver on the modernisation of the Eurasian rail track—despite all the announcements. It has few prospects when compared to the melting of the polar ice and the possible development of a northeast passage; no more indeed than the idea of a new Silk Road with containers rolling from Shanghai via Sinkiang through Central Asia to Istanbul and Central Europe, and all that without changing track and without the loss of time that is unaffordable in the world of globalisation. In all probability the Russian broad gauge—1,520 mm, with its 85 mm difference from standard gauge—is the most enduring trace to remind us of the Empire, long after it ceased to exist as a political reality.

PART XVII

Red Cube: The Lenin Mausoleum as Keystone

The image of the Lenin Mausoleum has become anchored in the memories of millions of people—in the Soviet Union and beyond. The cube on Red Square made of red granite, black labradorite and porphyry was the centre around which the great demonstrations and rituals of Soviet power unfolded every year over generations. It was from there that the Soviet state and Party leadership gazed at the troops parading past them on the square as well as at the crowds carrying paper flowers and balloons, children on their father's shoulders. From there speeches were made or orders given which were then carried out on the broad square below. This was the best place from which to appreciate the choreography of the tableaux vivants which folk-dance troupes or sports clubs had rehearsed with faultless precision. On 1 May, Victory Day on 9 May, or the anniversary of the October Revolution on 7 November, the platform became the strategic perch in front of which the latest launch vehicles passed by on their mountings and were displayed to the world. The state leaders who normally were hardly ever seen in public stood on the tribune. Foreign observers noted the presence of particular figures and the absence of others and drew their own conclusions about the political course to come. The details counted here. Once the holidays and victory parades were over and Red Square stood empty, the Red Cube came into its own once more.[1] This was where the never-ending queue of visitors slowly advanced to see the embalmed body of Lenin or to watch the changing of the guard that emerged from the Spassky Gate. In winter the Mausoleum rose up like a black cube against the snow-covered square. At night, when the square was only dimly lit, the Mausoleum itself appeared to be keeping watch.

An accelerated sequence of photos taken from the tribune would produce a history of the Soviet Union from its beginnings to its end, from the improvised and still somewhat uncertain movements of 1924, when what should be done with Lenin's body had not yet been decided, down to the moment in August 1991 when tens of thousands of people filed past the Mausoleum. Many of these had long since lost all respect for the 'leader of the proletariat' and not a few feared that there might be acts of violence. But all that happened was that someone left a crushed empty Coca-Cola can up against the Mausoleum wall as an almost casual act of desecration. The sequence would reflect rise and fall, a world-historical portrait gallery with such dramatis personae as Trotsky, Bukharin, Yezhov, Stalin, Beria and Khrushchev, along with record-breaking pilots and polar explorers, writers and generals. It would show crowds filled with enthusiasm or whipped up by hate-filled speeches filing past the tribune, but also moments of triumph and quiet reflection. In these pictures the Mausoleum would occupy a focal point, bringing together a variety of possible meanings. At its centre, holding the huge square together, is the chief monument in the row of graves along the Kremlin Wall; there is the block in front of the red-brick tower with the ruby-red Soviet star at its peak and behind it the yellow-and-white painted façade of Matvey Kazakov's Senate Building rising up beyond the Kremlin Wall; a tiered backdrop in different colours and an architectural triad of Soviet avant-garde, Italian Renaissance and Russian Classicism. It is a place of pilgrimage and a tourist destination. This is in fact one of the twentieth century's key pilgrimage sites, more significant perhaps than Mecca and Jerusalem, as Leonid Krasin, one of the progenitors of the Mausoleum, proclaimed as early as 1924, the year of Lenin's death.[2] Notwithstanding this, the Mausoleum was erected in a place where previously tramlines had run alongside the Kremlin walls.

The queues to enter the Mausoleum have long since petered out. Visitors are still allowed to enter at specified opening times; occasionally the music from a rock festival or open-air concert with opera stars from all over the world echoes around the square. On certain occasions the Mausoleum is clad in colour, as if it did not fit with modern times, as if people alive today should be spared the sight of a necropolis. The power of the tomb is welcomed when what is required—yet again—is the sight of military glory and tanks roll over a square that in its position and function was once the centre of empire and the most important marketplace in Moscow. No one knows what to do with this symbol of power, this necropolis at the heart of the capital of the former Empire; no one has an answer to the question of what should replace it. Many think the time has not yet come to free Lenin from his mummified existence and transfer his mortal remains to the family grave in St. Petersburg as family members and the Orthodox Church propose. It seems barely conceivable that he should be left just where he is, in the Kremlin Wall—along with Stalin. And to put Lenin's corpse on show, to turn it into an object in a museum of Soviet communism would mean relapsing into the practice of the Bolsheviks, who in their early years excavated relics from the graves and vaults of the churches and monasteries and then put them on public display. It would mean making use of Lenin's corpse as material proof of what was once known as 'Leninism'. The Red Cube stands in readiness, awaiting the time following the end of Soviet communism.

The Cube: The Search for Perfect Form

In its current state, the Mausoleum is the end result of a multistage development. The first version was a provisional building constructed for the funeral solemnities on 27 January 1924. The second resembled the present-day structure but was made of wood and built in the spring and summer of 1924. This was finally replaced in 1929–1930 by the still-standing Mausoleum in marble designed by Alexey Shchusev.[3]

> Shchusev's first design for a temporary wooden mausoleum provided a cubic base on which it was proposed to erect a monument consisting of four columns carrying an entablature. Tight construction schedules and building difficulties prevented the project from being fully carried out and the first mausoleum remained unfinished with only the base completed.
>
> In the course of designing the second wooden mausoleum, Shchusev attempted to return to his initial idea by crowning a stepped base with an extended colonnade, either circular or rectangular in plan. But the spare forms of the unfinished first mausoleum fitted well into the surroundings of Red Square and the very fact of their presence influenced all further design. As sketch followed sketch, the colonnade gradually shrank until it ultimately became the uppermost tier of the stepped design. Stylistically, the second wooden mausoleum was treated in the Classical manner

for compositional and formal purposes, with columns, pilasters, consoles, and so on.

Between 1924, when one wooden mausoleum followed the other, and 1929, when the stone one was designed, Shchusev's artistic outlook completely altered. . . . He was set the task of perpetuating the composition of the wooden one, which had become a familiar feature of Red Square, and of translating it into stone. Nevertheless, he completely discarded the traditional architectural elements incorporated in the previous monument and concentrated on spatial composition, so as to stress the simplicity of the geometric forms employed, the proportions of the composition and the relationship between the colours involved.[4]

Shchusev's first, persistent idea was this: 'Vladimir Ilyich is immortal. His name has entered the history of Russia and the history of mankind forever, for eternity. How shall we honour his memory and ennoble his grave? In our architecture the cube is immortal. Everything derives from the cube, the entire panoply of architectural creations. Let us then also derive the Mausoleum that we shall erect in memory of Vladimir Ilyich from the cube.'[5]

Shchusev had made his name as a cautious restorer and admirer of Russian church buildings even before the Revolution and had taken over the directorship of the All-Russian Agricultural and Handicraft Industrial Exhibition in 1923. The night after Lenin's death, he was summoned by the commission organising the funeral to the House of the Unions where Lenin's body lay in state and asked to produce a design for a mausoleum on Red Square. Shchusev remembered the occasion as follows:

Despite the lateness of the hour the agitated and shaken masses poured in to see the grave of the great man, the greatest friend of the workers. In the artists' room of the Hall of Columns to which I had been summoned, members of the government and the Commission for Lenin's Funeral were already present. I was commissioned by the Government to begin work on designing and building the provisional mausoleum for Lenin's tomb on Red Square. . . . I only had time to collect the necessary instruments from my studio and then to make my way to the building that had been assigned to me to carry out the work. The building of the tribune, the plan for the foundations and the scaffolding of the Mausoleum had to be arranged for the following day. Before making a start on the Mausoleum design I consulted L. A. Vesnin and Antipov, the architect, on the architectural principles involved. I explained to them that the Mausoleum should not be tall but should be stepped. For the inscription I proposed simply that we use the single word that contains the meaning that inspires the entire working population of the world. That word was 'Lenin'. . . . By four o'clock in the morning the design of the Mausoleum was already sketched out; I quickly put in the dimensions of depth, height and breadth and called the builders in to calculate the wooden construction. Early in the morning I went to Red Square, marked out the position of the building—you could already hear the first detonations of the frozen earth. At–25° the earth was too hard for shovels and crowbars to make an impression; explosives experts were needed. The detonations took up almost the entire day; only after that could workmen make a start on excavating the site. At the same time, a detachment from the Moscow municipal workforce brought wooden planks and boards to Red Square and carpenters began to build the scaffolding. The construction workers were able to keep warm by sleeping in special military tents outfitted with stoves. . . . The entire labour of building the Mausoleum lasted another three days. The workmen only left Red Square at the moment when the military arrived to take part in the solemnities in honour of the great leader.[6]

Once the initial solemnities were over on 27 February, it became evident that the population's interest and wish to visit the site was not fading; a discussion broke out within the Bolshevik leadership about whether there should be an at least temporary conservation of Lenin's body. This led to a decision in favour of a new, more stable Mausoleum that would contain Lenin's corpse, which had been transferred to a sarcophagus, and be more publicly accessible. Once again, Shchusev was commissioned to undertake the work. He retained the principal idea but proposed various modifications. The interior of the funeral chapel was designed by leading avant-garde artists—I. I. Nivinsky and

A. A. Exter. They maintained the lack of ornamentation and simple geometric shape, and added a tribune at the height of the first tier. But even this further wooden Mausoleum was only provisional and didn't fit the plan that had taken shape in the meantime: to preserve Lenin's body permanently and keep it on view for visitors.

As important as the final result were the various competitions and accompanying public debates. Dozens of proposals came in—some directly from the public. Everyone with a name in the architectural profession took part. The commission was represented by architects and intellectuals of the first rank: Leonty N. Benois, Anatoly Lunacharsky, Ivan Zholtovsky, Ivan A. Fomin and others.[7] Major architects of every persuasion were involved: Vladimir Gelfreikh, Vladimir Shchuko, Vladimir Krinsky. The battlefront in the struggle for an appropriate design for the tomb hinged on whether what was wanted was a monumental, concrete, figurative sculpture—in other words, a mausoleum dedicated specifically to Lenin—or whether Lenin's spiritual legacy would be best served by abandoning all thoughts of monumentality and instead honouring him by visibly improving the everyday life of the people. The camps were divided into supporters of a conventional monument and adherents of a functional building dispensing with merely symbolic gestures.

Both parties found prominent spokesmen. Vladimir Tatlin thought of the memorial as a kind of information bureau, which would be a 'triumph of engineering technology' in which visitors would make use of the 200–300 telephones installed to inform the world of events in the Soviet Union. The painter Alexander N. Samokhvalov advanced the idea of a building complex in Leningrad Harbour, resting on columns and reachable by bridges. The building would have an assembly hall, a library and a museum that would be illuminated at night by searchlight and also have a radio station.[8]

There was a similar project for the harbour in Odesa. Conversely, representatives of the classical, academic school, such as Fyodor Shechtel, Boris Yofan, Shchuko and Zholtovsky, called for monumental memorials whose aesthetic would express something of the revolutionary and subversive character of Lenin's own personality. Shechtel, the leading Art Nouveau architect in Moscow, cited the Mausoleum of Halicarnassus; Shchuko, subsequently the author of

FIGURE XVII.1. Alexey Shchusev (1873–1949); preliminary sketch for Lenin's Mausoleum 1924.
© culture-images/fai.

the design for the Palace of the Soviets, wanted an allusion to the
Tomb of Cyrus the Great. It goes without saying that they were all
steeped in the classics of sepulchral architecture, with the tombs on
the Appian Way, the Pyramid of Cestius and, above all, the Babylo-
nian/Assyrian and Egyptian monuments and pyramids, which were
thought of as symbols of eternity. But there was even a proposal
for a statue of Lenin in Leningrad Harbour as a counterpart to New
York's Statue of Liberty.

It was Shchusev who won the day and produced the final design,
which was then constructed in eighteen months between 1929 and
1930. The solemn inauguration—with Stalin on the tribune—took
place on 7 November 1930, the anniversary of the October Revolution. The final version of the Mausoleum was one of the key buildings of Russian Constructivism in form, functionality and material:
built of concrete and steel and faced with granite, bare of decoration
apart from a relief and the inscription, with functional lighting and
arrangements for shepherding visitors in and out. It was finished at a
time when Stalin was launching his 'revolution from above' and firmly
installed Leninism as the 'Marxism of our age'. The road to what was
later known as Stalinism had now been inaugurated.

Leninism and Lenin in His Sarcophagus:
'The King's Two Bodies'

People started to speak of 'Leninism' while Lenin was still alive. No one around him contested his position as *primus inter pares*. But condensing Lenin's thought and approach into a formula and a doctrine was Stalin's achievement. As early as spring 1924, Stalin defined Leninism as the 'Marxism of the age of imperialism and the proletarian revolution. . . . To be more exact, Leninism is the theory and tactics of the proletarian revolution in general, the theory and tactics of the dictatorship of the proletariat in particular.'[9] Lenin is presented as someone who rejected the orthodox beliefs of European socialism and left them behind because they failed to reflect the new realities of imperialism and war and stood in the way of revolutionary action. In this sense, he was above all the independent theoretician of practice, whatever predispositions and qualities he may have possessed— his uncompromising nature, his tendency towards factional conflict and his lack of scruple towards real or potential rivals, steeled by his experience of conspiracies. We can perhaps best understand the type of person he was by recalling Napoleon's saying 'On s'engage et puis . . . on voit'. He was less concerned with purity of doctrine than with his grasp of a reality on whose behalf he was acting—regardless of what Marxist theory said about bourgeois revolution and Russian backwardness. What he had was a boundless will to power at any price. His impassioned populism did not shy away from any change of course as long as it served the radicalisation of the movement and the defeat of the enemy. From a well-to-do background, he hated the regime not just out of ideological conviction but from the experience of a profound personal trauma—in 1887 he had lost his older brother Alexander, who was executed as a terrorist revolutionary.

Lenin was presumably better acquainted with the world of Europe between Munich, Zurich, Geneva and London, where he had spent most of his life, than with his native land. Even so, as with many other revolutionaries, his knowledge of his country's backwardness came from his exile to Shushenskoe on the Yenisei rather than from reading Marx in the British Museum and studying statistics in the Royal Library in Berlin. But he was unprepared for the outbreak of the First World War, which he explained as the product of the iron logic of imperialism. Even though he had longed for the revolution for years, that too took him by surprise, as it did almost everybody else. But once it had broken out, he plunged into the fray—he refused to be deterred despite his opponents' having accused him of being an agent financed by the German General Staff.[10] In April 1917, when he arrived in Petrograd with his theses about proletarian revolution and the tasks facing soviet state power, he appeared to most revolutionaries to be a fanatical scatterbrain out of touch with reality. And yet when the time for action came, he was the only one who felt confident enough to pick up 'the power lying in the streets'. His intuitive grasp of the weakness of the Provisional Government never left him and he was ready to deliver the fatal blow. It is surely true that without Lenin there would have been no October Revolution and no Bolshevik seizure of power. The formation of a Lenin cult was more or less inevitable, but not simply on account of his special abilities. It provided a solution to the overwhelming yearning for peace and stability in a world that was out of joint and full of despair and brutality. With Russian, German, Jewish and Kalmyk ancestors, he was a figure that could be produced only by a multiethnic country, a representative of empire. He was thought capable of extreme ruthlessness in his desire to destroy the republic, but also of the unscrupulous use of Red Terror to put a stop to a revolution that was getting out of hand. He was the only man whose single-minded desire to salvage the dictatorship of his party led him to accept the humiliations of the dictated Peace of Brest-Litovsk in March 1918, even though it earned him the accusation of 'high treason'. He was 'flesh of the flesh of the Russian intelligentsia', of the 'order' and intellectual community that took up the bitter struggle against the state on whose bayonets they nevertheless depended to protect them from the people in the 'Time of Troubles', as Mikhail Gershenzon, one of their acutest self-critics, observed.[11] And he was the only man capable of achieving the ultimate breach with Marxist orthodoxy. It was he who discovered a way to escape from the blind alley of 'war communism' by imposing the 'New Economic Policy'. Badly injured in an assassination attempt, paralysed by multiple strokes and kept away from political decisions, he left a number of texts all of which hinge on the limits of the Bolshevik revolution.

However, it was not these late self-critical reflections that came to form the kernel of Stalin's 'Leninism' and be given canonical shape in his *History of the All-Union Communist Party (Bolsheviks): A Short Course*. Stalin was the heir not of Lenin as a political mind open to rethinking his ideas, but of the unscrupulous power politician and pragmatist and followed in his footsteps in accordance with the ancient dictum: 'Le roi est mort, vive le roi'. Stalin's 'Lenin cult' soon developed into his 'cult of personality', Stalinism as the Leninism of the new age.[12] It would not be long before the main square of every town between Brest and Vladivostok would be called Lenin Square and no locality or railway station forecourt would be without its statue of Lenin. Statues of Lenin were placed on the plinths erected in the provincial capitals in 1913 to celebrate the three hundredth anniversary of the Romanov dynasty. Lenin existed as death mask, portrait, poster, statue, as the name of streets and institutes and as the script trailed by planes in the skies or as capital letters on the paving of Red Square to be danced on by athletes—all strictly regulated by the commission in charge of the cult. Above all, however, it was the *Selected Works* or *Complete Works* that were destined to carry Lenin's spirit and ensure it continued to thrive throughout eternity—in editions that ran into the millions, generation on generation beyond the frontiers of the 'proletarian fatherland'. In a country where all authority had been discredited and overthrown and in which there neither were nor should be any intellectual principles to act as a guide, it was now the unassailable leader who filled the place previously occupied by the trinity of autocracy, the church and national traditions. Members of his age group who, like his wife, Nadezhda Krupskaya, had been brought up in a secular and intellectual spirit now found themselves in a hopeless situation. They turned against the quasi-sacralisation, the quasi-heathen cult of Lenin, in whose creation they had participated. In consequence, they found themselves abandoned. Given this background, the erection of the Mausoleum and the embalming of Lenin were scarcely astonishing, but they were not the realisation of a long-cherished plan. Instead they were the product of circumstances. Just what circumstances were these?

There was a preexisting burial place in the Kremlin walls. This was where the revolutionaries killed in the street fighting and during the

Civil War years had been buried, as was the first head of state, Yakov
Sverdlov. But neither the construction of the Mausoleum for Lenin
nor his embalming was settled from the outset. Only the pressure of
hundreds of thousands of people who thronged to the Hall of Columns
persuaded the commission entrusted with the funeral solemnities to
prolong the time to enable 'the people to bid farewell to Lenin' and
to put the sarcophagus on display in a provisional wooden mausoleum. The extremely low temperatures made it possible to preserve
the body, at least for a while. This success inspired the leadership to
turn the provisional arrangement into something more permanent.
Hence the idea of an 'eternal' mausoleum and further work on the
preservation of Lenin's immortal remains.

Here, too, a variety of factors took hold. In the last years of his life,
Lenin had been surrounded by a number of eminent doctors who
attended to the diagnosis and treatment of his illnesses (arterioscle-
rosis among them). They included specialists from Germany such as
Otto Förster and Georg Klemperer who had access to the most modern refrigeration systems and medical technologies. International
research was then focused on the brain as the seat of genius and
criminality (Lenin's brain was not the only object of such research—
scientists examined that of Anatole France as well). Moreover, it was
a time when Soviet scientists, following the teachings of Nikolay Fyodorov, sought to conquer death, as well as disease. Alexander Bogdanov, 'Lenin's rival', died experimenting with a blood transfusion
carried out on himself.[13] Lenin's brain was dissected into many thousands of samples and preserved—down to the present day.[14] When,
to the surprise of the leadership, the population's interest in the
dead Lenin did not abate and when it became clear that his corpse
remained in good condition under the subzero temperatures, further
steps were taken. Scientists entrusted with the funeral preparations
were commissioned to look into permanent embalming. The chief
protagonists in these experiments were Vladimir Petrovich Vorobyov,
who held the chair in anatomy in Kharkiv University, had fought on
the White side in the Civil War and lived in Bulgarian exile after that;
and the St. Petersburg biochemist Boris Ilyich Zbarsky, who had received his education in Geneva. The two had come to know each other
on board ship for Riga. Both had successful careers and achieved fame

(something that did not give Zbarsky immunity from the persecution of 'cosmopolitans' at the end of the 1940s). It is their scientific expertise that the Soviet Union has to thank for the preparation of Lenin's body, which was laid out in state in a crystal sarcophagus designed by Konstantin Melnikov and Zbarsky and opened to the public on 1 August 1924 after a dress rehearsal in the presence of Dzerzhinsky, Molotov and others.[15] Over the following seventy years, more than seventy million people filed past Lenin's coffin.

With the enduring physical presence of the dead Lenin, the location itself underwent a change. It became a place of pilgrimage, a 'mecca', a spiritual and cultural focal point where what Ernst Kantorowicz defined as the 'king's two bodies' in his account of the ritual and continuity of sovereignty in the Middle Ages came together.[16] Embalming saints—something the Bolsheviks had once castigated as ecclesiastical obscurantism—now appeared as proof of the superiority of Soviet science and philosophy. Lenin's embalming was not the continuation of the ancient orthodox tradition of worshipping relics, but something new, a sign of scientific and technical progress, an index of the 'modernity' of the Soviet cult of the dead. It was the world-famous neurologist Vladimir Bekhterev who in 1927, the tenth anniversary of the October Revolution, called for the construction of a pantheon. This would be a place where the brains of famous Soviet geniuses should be preserved and made available for further scientific research.[17] The preservation of the body led to the establishment of distinguished chemical and medical institutes, which together with the storerooms, cooling systems and laboratories beneath the Mausoleum were responsible for the conservation of Lenin's body. The Pedagogic Centre for biomedical technologies founded in 1939 that is now part of the All-Russian Scientific Research Institute of Medicinal and Spice Plants (NPO VILAR) is to this day responsible for Lenin's preservation. At its zenith it had some two hundred employees,[18] and still has around forty today. Experiments were carried out on anonymous corpses to discover the best methods of conservation. Presumably the institute's most difficult operation was the evacuation of the sarcophagus from Moscow at the beginning of hostilities with Germany. It was taken to Tyumen in Western Siberia, where it survived the war in the building belonging to the

Agricultural Academy (although a piece of skin from the sole of Lenin's foot was lost during an experiment). From there, it returned to the capital in April 1945. On 16 September 1945, the Mausoleum on Red Square was reopened.

The next significant change involved rebuilding the Mausoleum to make room for Stalin's body after his death in 1953. The inscription over the entrance now reads: LENIN STALIN. But as early as the end of the Twenty-Second Congress of the CPSU in 1961 Stalin's sarcophagus was silently removed from the Mausoleum by night and the body reinterred in a grave in the Kremlin Wall necropolis. This moved Yevgeny Yevtushenko to write his poem 'The Heirs of Stalin', in which he calls for 'the doubling and trebling of the sentries guarding Stalin's grave'. Since that time, the communist death cult became a precedent which others followed with their own mausoleums. The experts of the Moscow institute have been consulted for advice on embalming Georgy Dimitrov in Sofia (in 1949; he has since been buried); Klement Gottwald in Prague (in 1953; the grave has since been removed); Ho Chi Minh (in 1969); as well as Kim Il-Sung and his son. Others—such as Fidel Castro—have refused this treatment—or else, like Mao Zedong, have achieved the same result without the assistance of Soviet experts.

The Pantheon That Was Never Built

Stalin's removal did not signal the end of the Mausoleum's history. Precisely one day after Stalin's death the Central Committee of the Communist Party and the USSR Council of Ministers resolved to erect a pantheon for the great men and women of the Soviet nation: 'A monumental building—a pantheon—shall be erected as a memorial to the eternal fame of the great men and women of the Soviet nation with the goal of immortalising the memory of the great leaders Vladimir Ilyich Lenin and Joseph Vissarionovich Stalin as well as outstanding politicians of the Communist Party and the Soviet State who are buried in the Kremlin Wall on Red Square.' It was to this pantheon that Lenin's and Stalin's sarcophaguses, along with the graves of over one hundred dead buried in the Kremlin Wall, were to be moved.[19]

The pantheon was to be erected in Moscow but, significantly, no particular location was specified. There were numerous proposals and design projects, frequently reminiscent of the competition designs for the construction of the Palace of the Soviets twenty years previously, a project never brought to fruition. The participants for the open competition included leading architects such as Vladimir Gelfreikh, and Mikhail A. Minkus, who had been responsible for the construction of some of the 'wedding-cake' skyscrapers in Moscow. Others involved included Arkady Mordvinov, Mikhail Posokhin, Leonid Polyakov, Dmitry Chechulin—in other words, the architects who played a major part in shaping the face of the new Moscow—as well as such established and independent architects as Konstantin Melnikov and Ivan Zholtovsky. Almost all the designs harked back to the mighty circular building in Rome or the Panthéon in Paris—with a circular colonnade in the case of Alexander Vlasov and Zholtovsky. Mordvinov envisaged a domed structure. Polyakov had evidently chosen the Lincoln Memorial in Washington as a model. Some designs remind us of Greek temples, of the Valhalla on the Danube, of the Vittorio-Emanuele II Memorial in Rome, or even of the great nineteenth-century opera houses.[20] But the entire building policy soon shifted away from monumental public buildings to mass housing and interest in the project gradually faded. Moreover, following the Twentieth Congress in 1956 with its criticism of Stalin's crimes and the removal of his sarcophagus in 1961, there ceased to be any question of monumental buildings such as a pantheon. Even so, the failure of the pantheon project meant only deferring the problem rather than eliminating it.[21]

Sixty years after the initial Soviet decision—never to be fulfilled—to build the pantheon, the Federal Memorial Military Cemetery was inaugurated on 22 June 2013 in Mytishchi in the northeast of Moscow. The pantheon planned there would have forty thousand graves and be Russia's principal military cemetery for the subsequent decades. It was dedicated with the burial of an Unknown Soldier who had lost his life on the Smolensk front in the Second World War. The most prominent person buried there is Mikhail T. Kalashnikov, the inventor of the eponymous submachine gun. The site was designed by the architect Sergey Goryaev 'in the style of the Putin era', with a sort of

Victory Avenue and a monumental, neoclassical columbarium. Since the opening of the pantheon, numerous prominent scientists and artists, but, above all, 'Heroes of the Soviet Union'—who have fallen in Chechnya and outside the Russian Federation—have been buried in the cemetery, which is under the control of the Ministry of Defence. Whether the 'Federal Military Cemetery' will become the pantheon intended for the known and unknown heroes of the Soviet century remains to be seen.[22] Moscow is a city with important necropolises. One is the cemetery of the New Maidens' Monastery (Novodevichie Cemetery); another, the memorial complex of Poklonnaya Gora, is dedicated to the fallen of the Second World War.[23] The creation of a new pantheon is hardly necessary.

When Lenin's corpse will finally be buried and the urns from the Kremlin Wall at long last find their final resting place in one of the Moscow cemeteries, the Mausoleum on Red Square will stand as a place of eternal remembrance of the victims of violence. It will be abstract and hard enough to absorb the immeasurable sufferings of the nameless and forgotten of the Soviet century.

PART XVIII

The Lubyanka Project:
Design for a *Musée Imaginaire*
of Soviet Civilisation

Everything that has been brought together and set out on the preceding pages amounts to an exhibition or museum of Soviet civilisation. The objects and shards appear to fit together into a *musée imaginaire* almost of their own accord. The idea of such a museum has been in the air for a long time and rehearsed in a variety of settings: as an exhibition in the Moscow Manege, as a theme in the Biennale in Venice, and elsewhere as local and provincial museums have been reconceptualised. There has even been talk about creating a museum of the 1990s.[1] We may have our doubts about whether it still makes sense to pursue such a project in an age when museums and galleries, even those in the deepest provinces, are available virtually, on the internet, to everyone at any time. What is primarily at issue are not the technical difficulties of navigating a boundless space but the far more puzzling question of being able to imagine 'the whole', to bring together once again in time and space the totality of a lifeworld even before the experts have successfully dissected it into its components and individual disciplines. What we find in that lifeworld is largely the overview and clarity that were denied to contemporaries, who moved around 'in the darkness of the lived moment' (as Ernst Bloch put it), but are available to subsequent generations who know how history actually played out.

To set up such a museum, there is hardly a better place than the Lubyanka in Moscow: the home of the secret services, which would be transformed into a forum of the open society. The giant complex, a 'city within a city', would be reabsorbed into the city. What was formerly a labyrinth of terror would be opened up and accessible. The site of interrogation would become a place for conversations. A place in which people fell silent would become one where names and voices are returned to the dead. The archive with the personal data of millions of people would become the material for an epic of life and afterlife in a state of emergency. The arcanum of world communism would be a place of enlightenment for visitors from all over the world. If this transformation were to succeed, the term 'Lubyanka' would cease to be solely the genius loci of evil.

FIGURE XVIII.1. The Lubyanka in its present state, not reached until the 1980s. http://www.system aspetsnaz.com/lubyanka -the-kgb-headquarter.

The process of transformation has already begun. In 1990 a granite boulder from the Solovetsky Islands was set up in memory of the victims of Stalinist terror within sight of the secret service headquarters. Since then, the names of the victims of violence have been read out from there annually on 30 October. In August 1991 the statue of Felix Dzerzhinsky, the founder of the Cheka, was removed, to the acclaim of thousands of Moscow citizens. The square itself, which had been known as Dzerzhinsky Square between 1926 and 1991, was changed back to Lubyanka Square. The museum in the Lubyanka, which the KGB had opened in the 1980s for training its own personnel, was opened for a time to the general public.[2] In 2016 the Russian action artist Pyotr Pavlensky staged a fire at the main gates of the Lubyanka in a dramatic protest against the continued existence of the 'organs' of power.[3]

On Lubyanka Square, which today is a large traffic roundabout, much of Moscow's history comes together: the remains of the walls of Kitay-gorod; the business district of prerevolutionary Moscow with offices and shops characteristic of the turn of the century; the neo-Russian-style Polytechnic Museum, a traditional meeting point of Moscow society; and the laconic façade of the Detsky Mir ('Children's world') department store from the 1950s. From Lubyanka Square streets and views radiate out both to Red Square via Ulitsa Nikolskaya (today a pedestrian zone) and to the Theatre and Manege Squares via Teatralny Proezd, which then merges into Ulitsa Okhotny Ryad,

formerly Karl-Marx Prospekt, passing the luxury Metropol and National Hotels as well as the monumental Gosplan building (nowadays
the home of the Duma). Lubyanka is also the name of the station on
the first Moscow Metro line, opened in 1935. The whole square forms
an ensemble composed of medieval city wall, turn-of-the-century
architecture, Constructivism, the Stalin era and the already superseded postmodern creations.[4] Following the Russian Revolution, the
Lubyanka building itself was, in Mikhail Ossorgin's words, the place
'where "goats had their horns set straight", where "the tongue was
sewn lower than the sole of the foot", where "people were weighed up
on a bone steelyard" . . . , and "had the gag put in firmly".' 'This is the
home of the fifth Moscow truth—the Lubyanka Truth.'[5]

The square is dominated by the famous or infamous 'Lubyanka',
a seven-storey box-shaped building, ochre-coloured with reddish
window frames and bronze portals that are always shut and have no
name or inscription over them. 'The Lubyanka! This is where all the
live nerves of pitiless despotism come together,' wrote Yury Tregubov, a member of the Russian émigré organisation NTS [National
Alliance of Russian Solidarists].[6] But that had not always been the
case. In 1894, the All-Russian Insurance Company based in St. Petersburg bought the land on which it stands with the prospects of
large profits from the booming real-estate market in Moscow and
built the block consisting of a hotel, offices and apartments to the
design of a Franco-Russian team of architects. Following the nationalisation of all insurance companies in 1918, the Cheka—more exactly,
the All-Russian Extraordinary Commission for Combating Counter-
Revolution, Profiteering and Corruption—under the leadership of
Felix Dzerzhinsky took over the complex, which kept on expanding
in the following years to the point where almost a quarter of the entire
neighbourhood had been overrun by its various organs, including the
famous Café Selekt and the garage in Varsonofievsky Pereulok 7–9,
which served as a place of execution.[7] Following the General Plan of
1935, the prerevolutionary building was to be added to and upgraded
in line with the dimensions and proportions of the new Moscow, a
task entrusted to Alexey Shchusev, architect of the Lenin Mausoleum.
However, after the embargo on construction work during the war, it
could not be completed until later on—not until 1984, in fact! Hence

the image that has remained fixed in the minds of observers down to this day—the symmetrical seven-floor building that monumentalises and integrates the original structure—is the product of a relatively late phase, a symbol of Brezhnevian stagnation, when political persecution was still an issue. But while the state pursued black-market smugglers (*fartsovshchiki*) and distributors of samizdat literature or continued to enrol students as spies, there was no longer any question of mass executions.

Ever since 1918 this building and its various annexes in the neighbourhood served the same 'organs' of state, even though the abbreviations they operated under constantly changed: Cheka, GPU, OGPU, NKVD, MVD, NKGB, KGB and, finally, the present-day FSB. The bosses' portraits hanging on the office walls change—Felix Dzerzhinsky, Vyacheslav Menzhinsky, Genrikh Yagoda, Nikolay Yezhov, Lavrenty Beria, Viktor Abakumov, Ivan Serov and Vladimir Semichastny, right down to Yury Andropov and Vladimir Putin—but the institution has survived.[8]

This building occupies an entire block from which thousands of people pour out at the end of a shift and automatic gates open to let out black automobiles. The changes that have taken place in the external appearance of the building reflect alterations introduced in the course of numerous renovations—prisoners' pencil drawings and scribblings on the cell walls have been scrubbed off. And yet, knowledge about the building is so extensive and precise that it would be a simple matter to identify the Lubyanka's growth rings. People who came here had to have their wits about them since a human life could hang on every gesture, every interrogation. Every detail has become ingrained in memory and if you were to collect up even the particles of memory, however fragmentary, you would still obtain the densest description of a place known to history, a true *lieu de mémoire*. 'Throughout the grinding of our souls in the gears of the great Night-time Institution, when our souls are pulverized and our flesh hangs down in tatters like a beggar's rags',[9] every little detail was noted—the lift, the corridor with the parquet floor, the smell of the floor polish, the desk with the lamp with the green shade, the armchair with the oilcloth cover, the plush leather sofa. Every staircase, the electric signals in the corridor, the temperature in the bathroom, the isolation cell—all left their marks in the memory. The prisoners could tell by the portraits hanging in the offices just what changes had been taking place in the leadership and during political crises. They learned to distinguish between the 'aristocratic' parts of the Lubyanka—the philosopher Nikolay Berdyaev saw polar bear skins on the floor—and the stairwell with steel netting: in 1925 Boris Savinkov, the famous or infamous terrorist, hurled himself out of a Lubyanka window and fell to his death. The prisoners gained knowledge of the layout of the Lubyanka, whether they wanted to or not. This explains why Alexander Solzhenitsyn could write: 'In the first place, it was very interesting to try to figure out the layout of the entire prison while they were taking you there and back, and to calculate where those tiny hanging courtyards were, so that at some later date, out in freedom one could spot their location. We made many turns on the way there, and I invented the following system: Starting from the cell itself, I would count every turn to the right as plus one, and every turn to the left as minus one . . . then back in the cell you could orient yourself and figure out what your own window looked out on.'[10]

The prisoners came to know the size of a cell in square metres even though it was stiflingly overfull; they knew that it was boiling hot under the roof in the summer and that you could die of cold in the isolation cell. Their internal clock could measure the time difference between getting up early in the morning and the arrival of night with an electric bulb that never switched off. The Lubyanka, according to Aleksander Wat, the Polish intellectual imprisoned there, 'was a laboratory for a total change in the way time is experienced.'[11] Walking around the courtyard on the seventh floor, the inmates heard the sounds of the city, the gun salutes on 1 May or 7 November festivities. Everyone who ever passed through the Lubyanka—or the other large Moscow prisons: Butyrka, Taganka, Lefortovo—and came out alive helped to complete the design of the ground plan of power. That goes for Margarete Buber-Neumann, whose husband Heinz Neumann, a leading member of the German Communist Party, was shot in 1937; Eddie Rosner, the jazz trumpeter, who also passed through the Lubyanka on his journey through the Gulag in 1946; Leopold Trepper, the leading member of the Rote Kapelle resistance group, at the end of the war; and Alexander Solzhenitsyn, who was brought to the Lubyanka straight from the East Prussian front. As a young dissident, Vladimir Bukovsky made the acquaintance of the Lubyanka several times and, like most other prisoners, could remember the number of his cell—102, right under the roof with a view of the 'exercise yards, tiny squares, like deep wells'.[12] One inmate reconstructed his routes through the Lubyanka from memory after his release and left a drawing. We have descriptions like this from him:

> We arrive at the lift. The cabin is small and divided into two by a door with two flaps. The man accompanying me pointed me to the rear half and remained in the front half himself. We moved upwards and soon left the lift. . . . A staircase, worn down by countless feet. . . . We went through a corridor, past crates. Finally, a door above which was an electric set of signals, as there was everywhere in the Lubyanka, a little red light and a green one. . . . One floor higher is a spacious, attractive lift fitted with polished redwood. . . . I enter and stand facing the wall. I count the floors, the lift stops on the sixth floor. Its door is of walnut. I am led out onto the corridor and am at once enveloped in a strange sweet smell. . . . My guard walks on and on; the corridor gets longer and longer, like a telescope; the room numbers light up. At last we stop at Number 693A. The room I am led into is lit by a harsh frosted glass light. A picture of Molotov hangs on the wall. We enter the room next to it. To the left of the window is a desk in front of which are some rather worn-out armchairs with oilcloth covers; a plush sofa and a leather sofa catch my eye. To the right on the wall, a portrait of Beria, to the left, one of Karl Marx.[13]

The details that Nikolay Berdyaev reported about his interrogation in the Lubyanka in 1920 seem somewhat macabre in comparison. Berdyaev remembered 'the endless corridors and up and down winding-staircases', a large brightly lit room with a white bearskin on the floor; he found himself sitting opposite a man 'with dull, grey and somewhat melancholic eyes' and good manners, who asked him to sit down and said, 'My name is Dzerzhinsky' and took him home after the interrogation. Lev Kamenev, one of the chiefs accused in the show trials of 1936 and an inmate in one of the Lubyanka cells

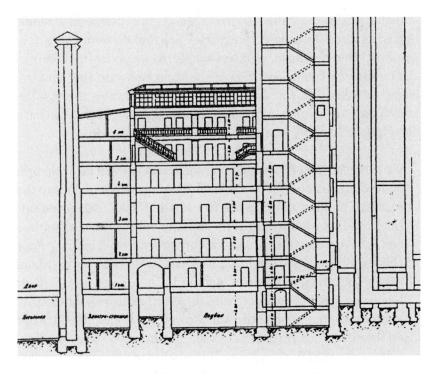

FIGURE XVIII.2. Cross-section of the Lubyanka. Memorial Society Archive.

before his execution, was also present at the discussion on 'idealism and materialism'.[14]

   We shall learn at some point what took place in the innermost circle of the Lubyanka, in the internal prison where many inmates spent their last days before sentencing and execution, or in the commandant's headquarters where experts in physical liquidation such as Vasily Blokhin had their offices. Inmates such as Nikolay Krestinsky, Karl Radek, Nikolay Bukharin, Lev Kamenev, Grigory Zinoviev and Alexey Rykov were worked on for the show trials that took place in the House of the Unions only a few minutes' walk away and for which the sentences were fixed in advance.[15] People to pass through the internal prison included antifascists who had sought refuge in the Soviet Union—Margarete Buber-Neumann; Zenzl Mühsam, the widow of Erich Mühsam who had been murdered in Oranienburg concentration camp; and many others—but also army generals such as Field Marshal Friedrich Paulus, the C-in-C of the

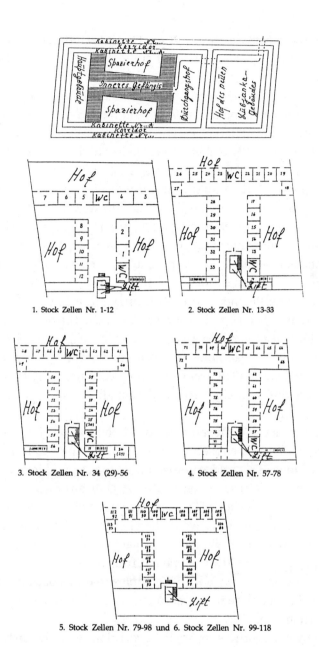

1. Stock Zellen Nr. 1-12

2. Stock Zellen Nr. 13-33

3. Stock Zellen Nr. 34 (29)-56

4. Stock Zellen Nr. 57-78

5. Stock Zellen Nr. 79-98 und 6. Stock Zellen Nr. 99-118

FIGURE XVIII.3. Ground plan of five storeys of the Lubyanka, drawn by Yury A. Tregubov, who was kidnapped from West Berlin in 1947 and spent two and a half years in the Lubyanka. He drew the plan following his release in 1955. From Jurij A. Treguboff, *Acht Jahre in der Gewalt der Lubjanka: Erlebnisbericht* [1st ed. in Russian 1957], Feuervogel-Verlag, Frankfurt am Main, 1999 © 1999 Feuervogel-Verlag, Frankfurt am Main (with the kind permission of Anita Treguboff).

German Sixth Army at Stalingrad. The internal prison was also the last staging post for Russian collaborators such as General Krasnov.

Before they were murdered, the victims of the anti-Semitic campaign against 'cosmopolitans' were held here. They included Solomon Lozovsky, David Bergelson and Itzik Feffer. This too is where the last traces of Raoul Wallenberg, the Swedish diplomat who saved the lives of thousands of Hungarian Jews, are lost. Few people could say what happened to the inmates at a time when 'the use of physical methods' was part of everyday life in the Lubyanka and NKVD bosses personally took part in torturing prisoners. The innermost core also contained the remnants of the former prison library whose riches had astonished Solzhenitsyn. There, probably for reasons of bureaucratic routine and indifference, you could always find the works of Yevgeny Zamyatin, Boris Pilnyak and even Dmitry Merezhkovsky, writings that would have been weeded out long before in the outside world.[16] Aleksander Wat remembers reading the copy of Proust's *Du côté de chez Swann* that he had borrowed from the library.[17] The vast building also houses the KGB archives, which contain many millions of files despite the campaigns to burn them all during the evacuation of Moscow in 1941.

The Lubyanka as a museum of Soviet civilisation—just as André Malraux spread out chosen images on his living room floor and formed the idea of a world art museum, so too can we picture to ourselves a museum of the Soviet century.[18] Only a very large building would suffice for such a project. Only a major centre where the fates of millions of people merge would be appropriate. Architects would have to consider how to handle the legacy of an entire century and create a place that would attract people from the whole nation and the world to come and grapple with a complex that has both fascinated and perturbed many generations, a place where they can learn what has held them together.

The Lubyanka, with its courtyards, corridors, galleries, driveways, staircases, cellars, lift shafts, endless array of offices and entire labyrinthine structure, may well be the best place from which to review a calamitous century. Visitors need not follow a linear, logical or even teleological route but may start their tour from the end or even from

FIGURE XVIII.4. André Malraux 1954, photographed by Maurice Jarnoux. From the *musée imaginaire* to the museum in the Lubyanka. © Getty Images/Paris Match Archive/Maurice Jarnoux.

the middle. On each floor you would move from one decade to the next. In one gallery you would go past photos of stars and heroes of the era, film stars such as Lyubov Orlova and the woman from the kolkhoz on the title page of *Pravda*. Here you could cast a glance at myriad portraits *en face* and *en profil*, portraits taken at the moment of arrest or after major torture or even in the face of death. Here you might gaze at a gallery of the truly great—from Tupolev to Shostakovich, from Malevich to Sakharov, from Anna Akhmatova to Sergey Korolyov—and pause in front of frames that are empty because

no camera could capture what had taken place in the camps of the
north or on 'Cannibal Island' on the Ob in 1933.[19] We would see the
smile of Yury Gagarin, in whom an entire generation saw their hopes
reflected, but also the images that display the destruction of those
hopes: the tanks in Prague in 1968 or Solzhenitsyn on the gangway
of the Aeroflot machine in Frankfurt in 1974. The façades of the Lubyanka would at long last be covered with memorial plaques for all
the people who suffered here. Loudspeakers in the inner courtyards
would reproduce the sounds of the age. Feature films, newsreels, doc-
umentaries would supply the images and original soundtracks for
the montage of a great film still being worked on. The immeasurable
numbers of rooms in the former secret service headquarters contain
enough space for everything: for a research centre, for the archive,
for the obligatory café and the bookshop with by far the world's best
selection of books in the section on 'communism'. Museums are places
in which to reflect, where visitors who are exhausted, overinformed
and frequently perplexed by all they have seen are able to gather their
wits again. They can take notes and go over everything in their minds
once more; they can try to get a handle on whatever they missed or
did not quite grasp. One of the inner courtyards could be turned into
an atrium in which the conversation about what the world will be like
after the end of Soviet civilisation can be continued; it would be a
conversation about the nature of Russia in the twenty-first century.
The roof on which the inmates used to do their regular circuit would
become a sky desk from which one's gaze would take in Moscow, the
capital city of a country that knows all about the abysses of history
and is able to draw strength from it for the future.

Aleksander Wat recollects one such circuit on the roof of the
Lubyanka.

Sometime before Easter we were taken up to the roof—I don't know
why—it was the first time in daylight as well. Darkness was falling,
dusk. But the sky and the air—the early spring easily overtook its
victims there, for we were its victims. My feelings grew keener. I
felt the early spring around me, and I could also hear music. They
were playing Bach's St. Matthew Passion on the radio for Easter—

can you imagine? It was just coming to an end, but it reached my section of the roof. . . . If the human voice, manmade instruments, and the human soul can create, even once in all of history, such harmony, beauty, truth, and power in such unity of inspiration—if this exists, then how ephemeral, what a nonentity all the might of empire must be.[20]

ACKNOWLEDGEMENTS

Everyone completing a book is aware that many people have gone into its making. This has given rise to a genre of its own, whose primary form takes the shape of a list naming those to whom the author is indebted. For the most part, these are the leading experts in the field, authoritative scholars who represent new approaches, paradigm changes and exemplary studies. There are such people in my case too, for example, Sheila Fitzpatrick, Richard Stites, Svetlana Boym and Natalia Lebina. It also often happens that quite crucial ideas behind a book may come from people who remain unmentioned because their influence is indirect, diffuse and not exactly measurable.

I would have to speak of all the people who aroused my curiosity in this great country and its inhabitants: the Soviet war veterans who decided to find out whether the young German was up to the challenge of drinking Riga Balsam; the tractor driver who raved on about 'Kant's city'—Kaliningrad, where he was stationed; the conductress on the train who knew about everything that had happened on the line for the previous twenty years; the helicopter pilot shot down over Afghanistan who showed me Magnitogorsk; the refugee from Dagestan who had to start all over again building up a farm in Central Russia. It was almost always meetings with people outside the 'corridors of power' that sparked my interest.

I cannot imagine this book without my encounters with Soviet dissidents and exiles of the 1960s and 1970s: Vladimir Bukovsky, Natalia Gorbanevskaya, Larisa Bogoraz, Leonid Plyushch, Alexander Zinoviev, Petro Grigorenko and, above all, Lev Kopelev and Raisa Orlova. It was an extraordinary privilege to be able to take part in seminars with Yury Levada and Grigory Pomerants in the 1980s, on evenings in Moscow kitchens or outside in dachas. Over the years I have profited from sober views and conversations with Lev Gudkov and Natalia Sorkaya. I owe thanks to the indomitable members of Memorial, principally Arseny Roginsky, the late Veniamin Iofe, Irina Flige and Yury Brodsky in St. Petersburg. My image of Leningrad/St. Petersburg would be the poorer without my meetings with Daniil Granin, Lev Lurie and Boris Kirikov. And how should I show my gratitude to Gabriel Superfin, coeditor of the 'Chronicle of Current Affairs', the most passionate archivist I have ever encountered, a 'German Boris Nicolaevsky' whose head is full of stories that would provide work for entire institutes and who makes me dizzy every time I meet him!

The first people to have heard about this book were my students at the University of Konstanz—a quarter of a century ago—and then in the Viadrina in Frankfurt an der Oder. They had no memory of the Soviet Union but were interested in what I had to tell them even though I was born in 1948 and a man of the twentieth century. They listened as if I were a kind of Homer talking about times long ago. The newly established Viadrina University was, notwithstanding all the obstacles mounted by the so-called Bologna process, a place where one could try things out—such as the German-Polish-Russian excursion to the Solovetsky Islands in 2001—and where thanks to my colleagues—Gangolf Hübinger and the prematurely deceased Heinz Dieter Kittsteiner—we could work on fascinating theoretical questions of cultural analysis. This period in Frankfurt an der Oder coincides with my collaboration with Michael Hagemeister, whom I always found stimulating. During those years I was always able to discuss complex questions of historical narrative with Hans Magnus Enzensberger, whose curiosity is as inexhaustible as the generosity with which he shared his own Soviet experiences with me. Jens and Eva Reich, as GDR citizens with long experience of Russia and the Soviet Union, drew my attention to one-sided perceptions in my account which could scarcely be avoided in someone who had grown up in the West. I should also like to express my warmest thanks to Stefan Bollmann and Angelika von der Lahr of the publishing house C. H. Beck for their inspired and always effective assistance in transforming my manuscript into the book that the reader is holding. Last but not least, I owe a great debt of gratitude to Karl-Konrad Tschäpe, my former colleague with a profound knowledge of cultural history, for his meticulous reading of the manuscript and detailed commentaries and insights which would not have occurred to me. Any remaining defects and errors are my own.

NOTES

Introduction: Archaeology of a Vanished World

1 I am basing my thoughts here above all on Juri Lewada, *Die Sowjetmenschen 1989–1991: Soziogramm eines Zerfalls*, Berlin 1992; Lev Gudkov and Boris Dubin, *Intelligentsiya: Zametki o literaturno-politicheskikh illyuziyakh*, Moscow 1995; Lev Gudkov, *Negativnaya identichnost: Stati 1997–2002*, Moscow 2004; Michel de Certeau, *The Practice of Everyday Life*, Berkeley, Los Angeles and London 1984.

2 In the sense of 'Soviet civilization' in Fernand Braudel, *A History of Civilizations*, New York 1987, 556–568.

3 On the crucial importance of different 'criteria' in historiography, see Jürgen Osterhammel, *Die Flughöhe des Adlers: Historische Essays zur globalen Gegenwart*, Munich 2016.

4 Walter Benjamin, *The Arcades Project*, translated by Howard Eiland and Kevin McLaughlin, Cambridge, MA and London 1999, 860.

5 Karl Schlögel, *In Space We Read Time: On the History of Civilization and Geopolitics*, translated by Gerrit Jackson, New York 2016.

6 Mikhail Bakhtin, 'Forms of Time and of the Chronotope in the Novel', in *The Dialogic Imagination*, edited by Michael Holquist, translated by Caryl Emerson and Michael Holquist, Austin and London 1981. On the problem of simultaneity, see Karl Schlögel, 'Chronotyp: Überlegungen zur Räumlichkeit von Geschichte nach dem "spatial turn"', in F. W. Graf, E. Hanke and B. Picht (eds.), *Geschichte intellektuell: Theoriegeschichtliche Perspektiven*, Tübingen 2015.

7 Stephen Kotkin, *Armageddon Averted: The Soviet Collapse, 1970–2000*, New York 2003.

8 Pioneering work on this subject has been carried out by Svetlana Boym, *Common Places: Mythologies of Everyday Life in Russia*, Cambridge, MA 1994; and especially impressively by the entire oeuvre of Natalia Lebina. Here I need mention only Lebina, *Entsiklopediya banalnostey: Sovetskaya povsednevnost—kontury, simvoly, znaki*, St. Petersburg 2006, and *Sovetskaya povsednevnost: Normy i anomalii. Ot voennogo kommunizma k bolshomu stilyu*, Moscow 2015.

9 As an instance of the variety of paradigms and paradigm shifts, see Hannah Arendt, *The Origins of Totalitarianism*, San Diego, New York and London 1973; and above all, the complete oeuvre of Sheila Fitzpatrick. Here I refer only to *Stalinism: New Directions*, edited by Sheila Fitzpatrick, London and New York 2000. On discourses, see Abbott Gleason, *Totalitarianism: The Inner History of the Cold War*, Oxford 1995.

10 Ernst Cassirer, *The Logic of the Cultural Sciences* (1942), translated by Steve G. Lofts, New Haven and London 2000 (previously translated in 1961 as *The Logic of the Humanities*); Heinz Dieter Kittsteiner (ed.), *Was sind Kulturwissenschaften? 13 Antworten*, Munich 2004; Peter N. Miller, *History and Its Objects: Antiquarianism and Material Culture since 1500*, Ithaca and London 2017.

11 On imperial history, see Andreas Kappeler, *Russland als Vielvölkerreich: Entstehung—Geschichte—Zerfall*, Munich 1992; Alexander Etkind, *Internal Colonization: Russia's Imperial Experience*, Cambridge 2011. On the postcolonial situation, see Frantz Fanon, *Peau noire, masques blancs*, Paris 1952 (*Black Skin, White Masks*, translation by Charles Lam Markmann,

New York 1967); Gayatri Chakravorty Spivak, *Can the Subaltern Speak?*, Basingstoke 1988, and *Selected Subaltern Studies*, edited with Ranajit Guha, Oxford 1988.

12 Walter Grasskamp, *André Malraux und das imaginäre Museum: Die Weltkunst im Salon*, Munich 2014; André Malraux, *Le Musée Imaginaire de la sculpture mondiale: La Statuaire—Des Bas-reliefs aux grottes sacrées*, Paris 1952–1954; Jonathan Spence, *The Memory Palace of Matteo Ricci*, London 1986.

Chapter 1. *Barakholka* in Izmailovsky Park, Bazaar in Petrograd

1 'Barakholka' and 'Tolkuchka' in Natalia Lebina, *Entsiklopediya banalnostey: Sovetskaya povsednevnost—kontury, simvoly, znaki*, St. Petersburg 2006, 55 and 347–349; 'Barakholka' in L. V. Belovinsky, *Entsiklopedichesky slovar istorii sovetskoy povsednevnoy zhizni*, Moscow 2015, 40–49.

2 On the role of the bazaars during the transitional phase, see Karl Schlögel, 'Basar Europa und die Arbeit der Weberschiffchen; Kiosk Eurasia, Berlin', in Schlögel, *Promenade in Jalta und andere Städtebilder*, Munich 2001, 9–21 and 199–207.

3 Svetlana Alexievich, *Second-Hand Time: The Last of the Soviets*, translated by Bela Shayevich, London 2016, 149–150.

4 A. Iu. Davydov, *Meshochniki i diktatura v Rossii 1917–1921*, St. Petersburg 2007.

5 *Oblomok imperii*, Sovkino 1929, and also *Gospodin fabkom*, starring Fyodor Nikitin and Lyudmila Semyonova.

6 Davydov, *Meshochniki i diktatura*, 295; N. D. Kondratiev, *Rynok khlebov i regulirovanie vo vremya voyny i revolyutsii*, Moscow 1922.

7 Mikhail [Michael] Ossorgin, *Quiet Street*, New York 1930, 173.

8 Waltraud Bayer, *Gerettete Kultur: Private Kunstsammler in der Sowjetunion 1917–1991*, Vienna 2006; *Antikvarno-khudozhestvenny rynok Peterburga*, St. Petersburg 2008.

9 Lebina, *Entsiklopediya banalnostey*, 55–57.

10 Boris Pilnyak, *The Volga Flows to the Caspian Sea*, London 1932.

11 Ibid., 13.

12 Ibid., 51.

13 Ibid., 54–55.

14 Quoted by Davydov, *Meshochniki i diktatura*, 344.

15 Yelena Osokina, *Za fasadom 'Stalinskogo izobiliya': Raspredelenie i rynok v snabzhenii naseleniya v gody industrializatsii, 1927–1941*, Moscow 1998, 141ff. (For a description of the Smolensky street market in the late 1920s/early 1930s, see E. Ashmead-Bartlett, 'The Riddle of Russia', in *The Daily Telegraph*, 22 January–20 February 1929). See also online at https://wdc.contentdm.oclc.org/digital/collection/russian/id/3454/rec/1 (accessed 29 May 2020).

16 Aleksander Wat, *My Century: The Odyssey of a Polish Intellectual*, edited and translated by Richard Lourie, with a foreword by Czeslaw Milosz, New York and London 1990, 323–324.

17 Lebina, *Entsiklopediya banalnostey*, 56f.

18 Anatoly Sorochan, 'Fartsa—kak mnogo v etom slove', in *Yuzhnaya pravda*,17 September 2015.

Chapter 2. The Soviet World as Museum

1 An excellent overview can be found in *Istoricheskie i kraevedcheskie muzei SSSR*, catalogue, Moscow 1988; *Vse muzei Rossii*, vol. 1, *Moscow, Moskovskaya oblast, Tsentr*, Moscow 2005; *Vse muzei Rossii*, vol. 2, *St. Petersburg, Severo-zapad, Privolzhie*, Moscow 2005; *Vse muzei*

Rossii, vol. 3, *Yug, Ural, Sibir, Dalny vostok*, Moscow 2006. For all museum and gallery addresses and opening times, see www.museum.ru (accessed 29 May 2017).

2 See Kerstin Holm's reports of her visits to provincial Russian museums in the *Frankfurter Allgemeine Zeitung* or her book *Rubens in Sibirien*, Berlin 2008.

3 On the history of museums as an institution, see Krzysztof Pomian, *Der Ursprung des Museums: Vom Sammeln*, Berlin 1988; more generally on memory and the culture of memory, see Aleida Assmann, *Erinnerungsräume: Formen und Wandlungen des kulturellen Gedächtnisses*, Munich 1999; more specifically on museums and the culture of objects, see Peter N. Miller, *History and Its Objects: Antiquarianism and Material Culture since 1500*, Ithaca and London 2017.

4 On the nature of exhibitions, see Marie-Louise von Plessen (with Daniel Spoerri), *Le musée sentimental de Prusse*, Berlin 1981.

5 See the comprehensive and controversial report *Muzei ili khram: Pochemu iz-za peredachi Isaakievskogo sobora RPTs vozniklo stolko sporov*, online at http://tass.ru/obschestvo /3932398 (accessed 29 May 2017).

6 Karl Schlögel, *In Space We Read Time: On the History of Civilization and Geopolitics*, translated by Gerrit Jackson, New York 2016, 42.

7 In my view, no work on the museum landscape begun in Soviet times can compete with the monumental guide to the archives by Patricia K. Grimsted. See her *Archives of Russia: Moscow and St. Petersburg; A Directory and Bibliographic Guide*, Russian edition, edited by Vladimir P. Kozlov and Patricia K. Grimsted, Moscow 1997; brief descriptions can be found in *Istoricheskie i kraevedcheskie muzei SSSR; Vse muzei Rossii*, vols. 1–3. In practice, all museums can now be accessed via the internet portal www.museum.ru (accessed 29 May 2017).

8 As for example in *Altaysky gosudarstvenny kraevedchesky muzey* with the supplement 'Soldaty Rossii XX vek' in Barnaul; see also http://www.agkm.ru/vistavka.html (accessed 29 May 2017).

9 N. K. Krupskaya, 'Otnoshenie Lenina k muzeyam', in A. A. Zhilyaev (ed.), *Avangardnaya muzeologiya 'Otnoshenie Lenina k muzeyam'*, Moscow 2015, 268.

10 We owe the reconstruction of these debates to A. A. Zhilyaev, 'Avangardnaya muzeologiya: K istorii odnogo pilotazhnogo eksperimenta', in Zhilyaev (ed.), *Avangardnaya muzeologiya 'Otnoshenie Lenina k muzeyam'*, Moscow 2015, 15–44; among others, see especially the contributions of N. F. Fedorov, 'Muzey, yego smysl i naznachenie', 45–112; I. K. Luppol, 'Dialektichesky materializm i muzeynoe stroitelstvo', 270–287.

11 Michael Hagemeister, *Nikolaj Fedorov: Studien zu Leben, Werk und Wirkung*, Munich 1989, 114f.

12 V. Kholtsov, 'Vystavka "Byt rabochego klassa 1900–1930 godov"', in Zhilyaev, *Avangardnaya muzeologiya*, 319–328.

13 In my descriptions of towns and cities, I have almost always tried to include accounts of the local museums. The last instance was of the Donbass Museum destroyed by shells in summer 2014. See Karl Schlögel, *Ukraine: A Nation on the Borderland*, translated by Gerrit Jackson, London 2018, 186–219.

14 Karl Schlögel, *Archäologie des Kommunismus oder Russland im 20. Jahrhundert: Ein Bild neu zusammensetzen*, Munich 2014.

15 Yury A. Brodsky, *Solovki: Dvadtsat let osobogo naznacheniya*, Moscow 2002.

16 A magnificent subject for a Leningrad exhibition might be provided by Daniil Granin, *Kerogaz i vse drugie: Leningradsky katalog*, Moscow 2003; the catalogue for the underwear exhibition in the Russian Museum: Olga Gurova, *Sovetskoe nizhnee belie: Mezhdu ideologiey i povsednevnostyu*, Moscow 2008.

17 Karl Schlögel, 'The Cube on Red Square: A Memorial for the Victims of Twentieth-Century Russia', in Marc Silberman and Florence Vatan (eds.), *Memory and Postwar Memorials: Confronting the Violence of the Past*, New York 2013, 31–50.

18 The impressive and extensive work of Memorial can be best accessed through the organisation's home page with its pointers to the topography of the camps, sites of executions, monuments, memorials, museums, and archives together with bibliographies at https://www.memo.ru/en-us (accessed 29 May 2017). *GULAG—das Lagersystem in der UdSSR: Eine CD-ROM-Dokumentation*, edited by Memorial Deutschland/Memorial Moskau, Berlin and Moscow 2006 (CD-ROM; with booklet). A bibliography on the subject can be found online at www.ausstellung-gulag.org/en/education/bibliography/current-research-literature .html (accessed 26 October 2021). A collection of model guides to the topography of terror for Syktyvkar, Komsomolsk-na-Amure, Voronezh, Krasnoyarsk, Penza and Ryazan is available in book/cassette form, *Topografia terrora*, Krasnoyarsk 2011.

19 The Museum of Ivan Panikarov in Yagodnoe, Magadan, is exemplary; see the exhibitions and photo documentations of the Polish historian Tomasz Kizny, *Gulag*, with prefaces by Norman Davies, Jorge Semprun and Sergey Kovalev, translated by Antonia Lloyd-Jones, Buffalo, NY and Richmond Hill, Ontario 2004; Kizny, *La Grande Terreur en URSS 1937–1945*, Lausanne 2013.

20 Uwe Neumärker and Andreas Nachama (eds.), *Massenerschießungen: Der Holocaust zwischen Ostsee und Schwarzem Meer 1941–1944*, Berlin 2016. Catalogue for the exhibition with the same title.

21 *Nizhegorodskaya fotografiya: Gorod. Lyudi. Sobytiya 1917–1970*, Nizhny Novgorod 2009, 86–163. On the history of the motor car in the Soviet Union, see Lewis H. Siegelbaum, *Cars for Comrades: The Life of the Soviet Automobile*, Ithaca 2008.

22 See Nikolai Anziferow, *Die Seele Petersburgs*, Munich 2003; further writings by Antsiferov are *Puti izucheniya goroda, kak sotsialnogo organizma: Opyt kompleksnogo podkhoda*, Leningrad 1925; *Teoriya i praktika ekskursy po obshchestvovedeniyu*, Leningrad 1926; *Gorod, kak vyrazitel smenyayushchikhsya kultur: Kartiny i kharakteristiki*, Leningrad 1926.

23 See the contributions of Osip Brik, Nikolay Punin, Alexander Rodchenko and others to the Museum Conference in Zhilyaev, *Avangardnaya muzeologiya*, 246–267.

24 I have written about chorology, flânerie, as a methodologically rigorous attitude towards knowledge in *In Space We Read Time*; for 'material culture' in the history of knowledge, see Miller, *History and Its Objects*.

25 This matter is also touched upon by Emily D. Johnson, *How St. Petersburg Learned to Study Itself: The Russian Idea of Kraevedenie*, University Park 2006.

26 Guido Hausmann, 'Die "kleinen" Themen und die "große" Geschichte: Neuere regionalgeschichtliche Arbeiten aus Russland', in *Jahrbücher für Geschichte Osteuropas* 50, 4/2002, 597–604.

27 Ronald G. Suny, 'Constructing Primordialism: Old Histories for New Nations; Contemporary Issues in Historical Perspective', in *Journal of Modern History* 73, 4/2001, 862–896.

28 K. Belenkina, I. Venyavkin, A. Nemzer and T. Trofimova (eds.), *Muzei 90-kh: Territoriya svobody*, Moscow 2016.

Chapter 3. Return to the Scene: Petrograd 1917

1 For literature on the Revolution, see W. H. Chamberlin, *The Russian Revolution, 1917–1921*, 2 vols., New York 1987 (1935); E. H. Carr, *The Bolshevik Revolution, 1917–1923*, 3 vols., New York 1953–1955; Alexander Rabinowitch, *Prelude to Revolution: The Petrograd Bolsheviks*

and the July 1917 Uprising, Bloomington 1968; Rabinowitch, *The Bolsheviks Come to Power: The Revolution of 1917 in Petrograd*, New York 1976; Rabinowitch, *The Bolsheviks in Power: The First Year of Soviet Rule in Petrograd*, Bloomington 2007; Michael S. Melancon and Donald J. Raleigh (eds.), *Russia's Century of Revolutions: Parties, People, Places—Studies Presented in Honor of Alexander Rabinowitch*, Bloomington 2012; Manfred Hildermeier, *Die Russische Revolution 1905-1921*, Frankfurt am Main 1989; Richard Pipes, *Russia under the Old Regime*, London 1974; Pipes, *The Russian Revolution*, New York 1990; Pipes, *Russia under the Bolshevik Regime, 1919-1924*, London 1994; Orlando Figes, *A People's Tragedy: The Russian Revolution, 1891-1924*, London 1996; B. I. Kolonitsky, 'Antiburzhuaznaya propaganda i "antiburzhuyskoe" soznanie', in *Anatomiya revolyutsii: 1917 god v Rossii—massy, partii, vlast*, St. Petersburg 1994.

2 Tamara Hovey, *John Reed: Witness to Revolution*, Los Angeles 1976; Robert A. Rosenstone, *Romantic Revolutionary: A Biography of John Reed*, New York 1975.

3 A. A. Kornikov, *Sudba rossiyskogo revolyutsionera: N. N. Sukhanov—chelovek, politik, memuarist*, Ivanovo 1995; J. Getzler, *Nikolai Sukhanov: Chronicler of the Russian Revolution*, New York 2002.

4 Nikolai Nikolaevich Sukhanov, *The Russian Revolution 1917: A Personal Record*, edited, abridged and translated by Joel Carmichael, Oxford 1955; the complete Russian edition in 3 vols., *Zapiski o revoliutsii*, St. Petersburg 1919-1923. Quoted here and subsequently from the English edition, 556.

5 Leon Trotsky, *History of the Russian Revolution*, translated by Max Eastman, London 1965, 1171f.

6 On social topography, see James H. Bater, *St. Petersburg: Industrialization and Change*, London 1976; B. M. Kotsakov (ed.), *Ocherki istorii Leningrada*, vol. 3 (1895-1917), vol. 4 (1917-1941), Moscow and Leningrad 1956, 1964; Karl Schlögel, *Petersburg: Das Laboratorium der Moderne 1909-1921*, Munich 2002; Karl Schlögel, Frithjof Benjamin Schenk and Markus Ackeret (eds.), *Sankt Petersburg: Schauplätze einer Stadtgeschichte*, Frankfurt am Main 2007.

7 Sukhanov, *Russian Revolution*, 547.

8 Ibid., 46, 59.

9 John Reed, *Ten Days That Shook the World*, London 2006, 86.

10 Ibid., 83.

11 Ibid., 105.

12 Sukhanov, *Russian Revolution*, 369.

13 Reed, *Ten Days*, 27f.

14 Sukhanov, *Russian Revolution*, 269.

15 Ibid., 277f.

16 Ibid., 280f.

17 Reed, *Ten Days*, 143.

18 Nikolaj Nikolajewitsch Suchanow, *1917: Tagebuch der russischen Revolution*, selected, translated and edited by Nikolaus Ehlert, preface by Iring Fetscher, Munich 1967, 339.

19 Reed, *Ten Days*, 80f.

20 Ibid., 92.

21 Ibid., 199.

22 On the Tauride Palace, see Ya. L. Sukhotin, *Tavrichesky dvorets*, Leningrad 1963.

23 V. I. Pilyavsky, *Lenin v Smolnom: 124 dnya*, Leningrad 1974.

24 On the Mariinsky Palace, see A. M. Kruglova, 'Mariinsky dvorets', in *Zdes svershalsya Veliky Oktiabr: Po mestam vooruzhennogo vosstaniya v Petrograde*, Leningrad 1967, 200-204; on the Winter Palace, V. I. Pilyavsky, *Zimny dvorets*, Leningrad 1967.

25 V. M. Kruchkovskaya, *Tsentralnaya gorodskaya duma Petrograda v 1917 g.*, Leningrad 1986.

26 On the soldiers' movement and the barracks complex, see Allan K. Wildman, *The End of the Russian Imperial Army*, vol. 1, *The Old Army and the Soldiers' Revolt (March–April 1917)*, and vol. 2, *The Road to Soviet Power and Peace*, Princeton 1980, 1988.

27 Astonishingly, there is very little literature on the Petrograd bridges. See A. L. Punin, 'Mosty Petrograda v dni Oktiabrskogo vooruzhennogo vosstaniya', in *Trudy instituta zhivopisi, skulptury i arkhitektury im. I. E. Repina*, Iskusstvovedenie series 2, Leningrad 1971; M. S. Bunin, *Mosty Leningrada*, Leningrad 1986.

28 On the role of the railway stations, see Frithjof Benjamin Schenk, *Russlands Fahrt in die Moderne: Mobilität und sozialer Raum im Wandel*, Stuttgart 2014; Roger Pethybridge, *The Spread of the Russian Revolution: Essays on 1917*, London and Basingstoke 1972.

29 See *Leningrad: Istoriko-geograficheskyy atlas*, revised and expanded ed., Moscow 1981, 26–28.

30 Trotsky, *History of the Russian Revolution*, 1071.

31 V. I. Lenin, *Collected Works*, vol. 33, Moscow 1965, 476. See https://www.marxists.org /archive/lenin/works/1923/jan/16.htm [Translation slightly modified].

Chapter 4. The Philosophy Steamer and the Splitting of Russian Culture

1 I am speaking here by and large of the 'Russian' emigration, even though following the collapse of the Russian Empire and the creation of the Soviet Union we are clearly looking at a multiethnic emigration (Georgians, Ukrainians, Armenians, Jews, Germans, etc., and later émigrés from the occupied Baltic states). The altered meaning—'Russian emigration' or 'emigration from Russia'—is reflected in various encyclopedias: *Russkoe zarubezhie: Zolotaya kniga emigratsii. Pervaya tret XX veka. Entsiklopedichesky biografichesky slo-var*, Moscow 1997; *Literaturnaya entsiklopediya Russkogo zarubezhia 1918–1940: Pisateli russkogo zarubezhia*, Moscow 1997; *Rossiya i rossiyskaya emigratsiya v vospominaniyakh i dnevnikakh: Annotirovany ukazatel knig, zhurnalnykh i gazetnykh publikatsy, izdannykh za rubezhom v 1917–1991 gg.*, 4 vols., Moscow 2003–2005.

2 Marc Raeff, *Russia Abroad: A Cultural History of the Russian Emigration 1919–1939*, New York and Oxford 1990 (Russian edition: *Rossiya za rubezhom: Istoriya kultury russkoy emigratsii 1919–1939*, Moscow 1994); Karl Schlögel (ed.), *Der Große Exodus: Die russische Emigration und ihre Zentren 1917 bis 1941*, Munich 1994.

3 The first analysis, whose logic was later confirmed by documents subsequently declassified, was by Michel Heller, 'Premier avertissement: Un coup de fouet; L'histoire de l'expulsion des personnalités culturelles hors de l'Union Soviétique en 1922', in *Cahiers du Monde russe et soviétique* 20, 2/1979, 131–172; this was also the foundation of Karl Schlögel, *Jenseits des Großen Oktober, Petersburg 1909–1921: Das Laboratorium der Moderne*, Berlin 1988, particularly the section 'Proskription, Ausweisung, das Schiff nach Stettin', 479–486.

4 The documents have been published in M. Ye. Glavatsky, *"Filosofsky parakhod": God 1922-y. Istoriograficheskie etyudy*, Yekaterinburg 2002; V. G. Makarov and V. S. Khristoforov (eds.), *Vysylka vmesto rasstrela: Deportatsiya intelligentsii v dokumentakh VChK-GPU 1921–1923*, Moscow 2005; V. G. Makarov, *Istoriko-filosofsky analiz vnutripoliticheskoy borby nachala 1920-kh godov i deportatsiya inakomyslyashchikh iz Sovetskoy Rossii*, Moscow 2010; Lesley Chamberlain, *Lenin's Private War: The Voyage of the Philosophy Steamer and the Exile of the Intelligentsia*, New York 2008.

5 Makarov and Khristoforov, *Vysylka vmesto rasstrela*, 87.

6 Chamberlain, *Lenin's Private War*, 121; see also Glavatsky, *"Filosofsky parokhod"*, 215.

7 Chamberlain, *Lenin's Private War*, 122.

8 Ibid., 130.

9 These questions were repeated at every interrogation, according to the memories of those affected; see Chamberlain's summary in *Lenin's Private War*, 116.

10 The record of the interrogation of 18 August 1922 can be found in Makarov and Khristoforov, *Vysylka vmesto rasstrela*, 214–216; the recollection of the conversation with Dzerzhinsky in 1920 can be found in Nicolas Berdyaev, *Dream and Reality*, translated by Katharine Lampert, London 1950, 237–238.

11 Despite the publication of the relevant documents, there are still (small) discrepancies on the question of numbers and classification both organisational and ideological. The list of deportees can be found in Chamberlain, *Lenin's Private War*, 305–312; Makarov and Khristoforov, *Vysylka vmesto rasstrela*, 38–48; Glavatsky, "Filosofsky parohhod", 182–197.

12 The lists have been compiled in Makarov and Khristoforov, *Vysylka vmesto rasstrela*, 41–43.

13 The topography of the diaspora is the entry point of analysis in Schlögel, *Der Große Exodus*, and Raeff, *Russia Abroad*; in the meantime, individual accounts covering all the diasporic centres have appeared, e.g., Van Chzhichen, *Istoriya russkoy emigratsii v Shankhae*, Moscow 2008.

14 Hannah Arendt is one of very few to have recognised and reflected on the significance of the Russian refugee movement, in particular in *The Origins of Totalitarianism*, San Diego, New York and London 1973, 267–302.

15 Robert C. Williams, *Culture in Exile: Russian Emigres in Germany 1881–1941*, Ithaca and London 1972.

16 Fritz Mierau (ed.), *Russen in Berlin 1918–1933: Eine kulturelle Begegnung*, Leipzig 1978; Karl Schlögel (ed.), *Russische Emigration in Deutschland 1918 bis 1941*, Berlin 1995, bibliography, 485–504; Schlögel, *Das russische Berlin: Ostbahnhof Europas*, Munich 2007; Karl Schlögel, Katharina Kucher, Bernhard Suchy and Gregor Thum (eds.), *Chronik russischen Lebens in Deutschland 1918–1941*, Berlin 1999.

17 ChSSR *dokumenty k istorii russkoy i ukrainskoy emigratsii v Chekhoslovatskoy respublike (1919–1939)*, Prague 1998; Miroslav Yovanovich, *Russkaya emigratsiya na Balkanakh 1920–1940*, Moscow 2005.

18 A. A. Romanov, *Na chuzhikh pogostakh: Nekropol russkogo zarubezhia*, Moscow 2000, 2003; Catherine Gousseff, *L'exil russe: La fabrique du réfugié apatride (1920–1939)*, Paris 2008.

19 Alexander Vasiliev, *Krasota v izgnanii: Tvorchestvo russkikh emigrantov pervoi volny—iskusstvo i moda*, Moscow 1998.

20 On the Russian emigration and anti-Semitism, see Michael Hagemeister, *Die 'Protokolle der Weisen von Zion' vor Gericht: Der Berner Prozess 1933–1937 und die 'antisemitische Internationale'*, Zurich 2017 (Publications of the Archiv für Zeitgeschichte der ETH Zürich, vol. 10); Hagemeister, 'Protokolle der Weisen von Zion', in Wolfgang Benz (ed.), *Handbuch des Antisemitismus: Judenfeindschaft in Geschichte und Gegenwart*, vol. 4, *Ereignisse, Dekrete, Kontroversen*, Berlin and Boston 2011, 321–325; Michael Kellogg, *The Russian Roots of Nazism: White Émigrés and the Making of National Socialism 1917–1945*, Cambridge 2009; Karl Schlögel and Karl-Konrad Tschäpe (eds.), *Die Russische Revolution und das Schicksal der russischen Juden: Eine Debatte in Berlin 1922/23*, Berlin 2014.

21 See the biographies in Schlögel and Tschäpe, *Die Russische Revolution*, 629–725.

22 V. G. Makarov, A. V. Repnikov and V. S. Khristoforov (eds.), *Tyuremnaya odisseya Vasiliya Shulgina: Materialy sledstvennogo dela i dela zaklyuchennogo*, Moscow 2010.

Chapter 5. *USSR in Construction*: The Power of Images

1 Cited in Helmut Lethen, *Der Schatten des Fotografen, Bilder und ihre Wirklichkeit*, Berlin 2014, 98.

2 A selection has been reprinted in *SSSR na stroyke: Illyustrirovanny zhurnal novogo tipa*, Moscow 2006.

3 On the origin and significance of the magazine, see Erika Volf, '"SSSR na stroyke": Zhurnal i ego chitatel, in *SSSR na stroyke*, 11–23.

4 Marc Jansen and Nikita Petrov, *Stalin's Loyal Executioner: People's Commissar Nikolai Ezhov*, Stanford 2000; J. Arch Getty and Oleg V. Naumov, with the assistance of Nadezhda V. Muraveva, *Yezhov: The Rise of Stalin's "Iron Fist"*, New Haven and London 2008.

5 Volf, '"SSSR na stroyke"', 11.

6 Ibid., 15–18.

7 Ibid., 17.

8 This question is explored by Leah Dickerman in 'The Propagandizing of Things', her contribution to the Museum of Modern Art exhibition catalogue: Magdalena Dabrowski, Leah Dickerman and Peter Galassi, *Aleksandr Rodchenko*, edited by David Frankel, with essays by Aleksandr Lavrent'ev and Varvara Rodchenko, New York 1998, 62–99.

Chapter 6. DniproHES: America on the Dnieper

1 V. V. Mayakovsky, 'Dolg Ukraine', quoted from Anne D. Rassweiler, *The Generation of Power: The History of Dneprostroi*, New York and Oxford 1988, 182.

2 This text is based on the author's visit to the dam in the summer of 2006.

3 Petrusov's photo can be found in *SSSR na stroyke* 4/1930.

4 Paul Scheffer, *Seven Years in Soviet Russia*, translated by Arthur Livingston, London and New York 1931, 96–97.

5 Here especially, K. B. Vasilchenko, V. B. Repin and A. A. Konovalenko (eds.), *Ogni Dneprostroya: Fotokniga*, Kyiv 1980.

6 Quoted from A. G. Chinyakov, *Bratia Vesniny*, Moscow 1970, 124; V. R. Yakubov, *Arkhitektory gidroenergetiki*, Moscow 2013, 30–32; for criticism of Chinyakov's and Khan-Magomedov's interpretation, see D. S. Khmelnitsky, *Zagadki Dneprogesa* (www.archi.ru) (accessed 1 April 2016), and Selim Khan-Magomedov, *Alexander Vesnin and Russian Constructivism*, New York 1986.

7 Quoted from Chinyakov, *Bratia Vesniny*, 124.

8 Ibid., 122.

9 Rassweiler, *The Generation of Power*, 11.

10 Scheffer, *Seven Years in Soviet Russia*, 103.

11 For I. G. Alexandrov, see S. I. Vavilov (ed.), *Lyudi russkoy nauki: Ocherki o vydayushchikhsya deyatelyakh estestvoznaniya i tekhniki*, Moscow 1948; one of the most accurate reports on the construction of DniproHES comes from a prominent engineer, V. E. Sproge, *Zapiski inzhenera*, Moscow 1999, 133–515.

12 Heiko Haumann, *Beginn der Planwirtschaft: Elektrifizierung, Wirtschaftsplanung und gesellschaftliche Entwicklung Sowjetrusslands, 1917 bis 1921*, Düsseldorf 1974. Cf. also the chapter 'GOELRO: Eros der Technik, Eros der Macht', in Karl Schlögel, *Petersburg: Das Laboratorium der Moderne 1909–1921*, Munich 2002, 353–408.

13 Scheffer, *Seven Years in Soviet Russia*, 102.

14 Ibid., 101.

15 Ibid., 99.

16 See Zara Witkin, 'An American Engineer in Stalin's Russia', in *The Memoirs of Zara Witkin 1932–1934*, edited by Michael Gelb, Berkeley 1991.

17 Rassweiler, *Generation of Power*, 147.

18 On Gastev, see Richard Stites, *Revolutionary Dreams: Utopian Vision and Experimental Life in the Russian Revolution*, New York 1989.
19 Margaret Bourke-White, *Portrait of Myself*, London 1964, 95.
20 'Ukrainian Activists Draw Attention to Little-Known WWII Tragedy', online at http://www.rferl.org/a/european-remembrance-day-ukraine-Little-known-tragedy/25083847.html (accessed 18 March 2016).

Chapter 7. Magnitogorsk: The Pyramids of the Twentieth Century

1 Stephen Kotkin, *Magnetic Mountain: Stalinism as a Civilization*, Berkeley 1995; see also Kotkin, *Steeltown, USSR: Soviet Society in the Gorbachev Era*, Berkeley and Los Angeles 1991.
2 Special issue of *SSSR na stroyke*, 1/1932: 'Magnitogorsk: Gigant vtoroy metallurgicheskoy bazy'.
3 Thomas Flierl (ed.), *Standardstädte: Ernst May in der Sowjetunion 1930–1933*, Berlin 2012; *Ernst May 1886–1970*, exhibition catalogue, Munich 2011.
4 John Scott, *Behind the Urals: An American Worker in Russia's City of Steel*, Bloomington 1973.
5 Ernst Jünger, *Der Arbeiter: Herrschaft und Gestalt*, Hamburg 1932.
6 Dagmara Jajeśniak-Quast, *Stahlgiganten in der sozialistischen Transformation: Nowa Huta in Krakau, EKO in Eisenhüttenstadt und Kunčice in Ostrava*, Wiesbaden 2010.
7 *Magnitka—Stal i lyudi: Fotoalbom*, Moscow 1979.
8 More recently, a museum devoted to one of the victims of Stalinist repression has been established in the town: the poet Boris Ruchyov's Apartment Museum (Muzey-kvartira Borisa Ruchieva) is a branch of the Magnitogorsk Local History Museum.
9 Moshe Lewin, *The Soviet Century*, edited by Gregory Elliott, London 2005; David L. Hoffmann, *Peasant Metropolis: Social Identities in Moscow 1929–1941*, Ithaca and London 1994.
10 The 1/1932 issue of *USSR in Construction* contains the story of the 'transformation' of a simple peasant into a self-confident and outstanding worker.
11 Margaret Bourke-White, *Portrait of Myself*, London 1964, 94 and 96.
12 See Karl Schlögel, 'Utopie als Notstandsdenken—einige Überlegungen zur Diskussion über Utopie und Sowjetkommunismus', in Wolfgang Hardtwig (ed.), *Utopie und politische Herrschaft im Europa der Zwischenkriegszeit*, Munich 2003, 77–96.
13 Flierl, *Standardstädte*.
14 Murray Feshbach and Alfred Friendly Jr., *Ecocide in the USSR: Health and Nature under Siege*, New York 1992.

Chapter 8. Black and White: The Photographer's Eye

1 Alexander Rodtschenko, *Schwarz und Weiss: Schriften zur Photographie*, edited by Schamma Schahadat and Bernd Stiegler, Paderborn 2011, 13–18, here 18. Henceforth cited as *Schwarz und Weiss*. (This translation in Aleksandr Rodchenko, 'Black and White: Autobiography', in *Experiments for the Future*, edited and with a preface by Alexander N. Lavrentiev, translated and annotated by Jamey Gambrell, with an introduction by John E. Bowlt, New York 2005, 307.)
2 *Schwarz und Weiss*, 227–244, here 243. (This translation in Rodchenko, 'The Paths of Contemporary Photography', in *Experiments for the Future*, 211.)

3 Rodchenko in his polemic 'Die Wege der modernen Photographie' of September 1928 in *Schwarz und Weiss*, 244. (This translation in Rodchenko, 'The Paths of Contemporary Photography', 211–212.)

4 Rodtschenko, 'Eine Warnung' (November 1928), in *Schwarz und Weiss*, 245–246, here 246. (This translation in Rodchenko, 'Reconstructing the Artist' and 'Warning!', in *Experiments for the Future*, 297, 213. [LEF is short for Left Front. It refers to a group of artists and also the magazine with the same title.])

5 Rodtschenko, 'Eine Warnung', 246. (This translation, slightly altered, in Rodchenko, 'Warning!', 213.)

6 Rodtschenko, 'Über die Komposition: Anstelle eines Vorworts (1941–42)', in *Schwarz und Weiss*, 319–323, here 323.

7 Rodtschenko, 'Das grosse Analphabetentum oder eine kleine Gemeinheit', in *Schwarz und Weiss*, 209. (This translation in Rodchenko, 'The Paths of Contemporary Photography', 212.)

8 Rodtschenko, 'Die Wege der modernen Photographie', in *Schwarz und Weiss*, 245–246, here 246. (This translation in Rodchenko, 'The Paths of Contemporary Photography', 212.)

9 Rodchenko, 'Warning!', 213.

10 M. Gorky, L. Averbakh and S. G. Firin (eds.), *Belomorsko-Baltiysky Kanal imeni Stalina: Istoriya stroitelstva*, Moscow 1934.

11 Rodtschenko, 'Der Meister und die Kritik: Ein Vortrag, der nicht gehalten wurde (September 1935)', in *Schwarz und Weiss*, 285–298, here 293.

12 Rodtschenko, 'Über die Komposition', 323.

13 Leah Dickerman, 'The Propagandizing of Things', in Magdalena Dabrowski, Leah Dickerman and Peter Galassi, *Aleksandr Rodchenko*, edited by David Frankel, with essays by Aleksandr Lavrent'ev and Varvara Rodchenko, New York 1998, 89.

14 Anne Brunswic gave me access to the photo collection. My thanks to the director of the Petrozavodsk museum. Some of the illustrations can be found in Yury A. Dmitriev, *Belomorsko-Baltiysky vodny put: Ot zamyslov do voploshcheniya*, Petrozavodsk 2003.

15 Rodchenko, 'Reconstructing the Artist', 297–298.

16 Ibid., 297–299.

17 Rodchenko, 'Letters to Varvara Stepanova 1930–1934', in *Experiments for the Future*, 289.

18 Dickerman, 'The Propagandizing of Things', 96.

Chapter 9. Excursion to the White Sea Canal

1 Aleksandr Solzhenitsyn, *The Gulag Archipelago*, translated by Thomas P. Whitney, New York 1975, especially vol. 2, pt. 3, 'The Destructive Labour Camps'; on the Gulag system, see Anne Applebaum, *Gulag: A History*, New York 2003; Michael Jakobson, *Origins of the Gulag: The Soviet Prison Camp System, 1917–1934*, Lexington 1993.

2 Cynthia A. Ruder, *Making History for Stalin: The Story of the Belomor Canal*, Gainesville 1998; Yury A. Dmitriev, *Belomorsko-Baltiysky vodny put: Ot zamyslov do voploshcheniya*, Petrozavodsk 2003.

3 Photos from the Petrozavodsk Archive in Dmitriev, *Belomorsko-Baltiysky vodny put*; Anne Brunswic, *Les eaux glacées de Belomorkanal*, Arles 2009.

4 Tomasz Kizny, *Gulag*, with prefaces by Norman Davies, Jorge Semprun and Sergey Kovalev, translated by Antonia Lloyd-Jones, Buffalo, NY and Richmond Hill, Ontario 2004.

5 M. Gorky, L. L. Averbakh and S. G. Firin (eds.), *Belomorsko-Baltiyskii Kanal imeni Stalina: Istoriya stroitelstva*, Moscow 1934. [Maxim Gorky, Leopold Averbakh and Semen Georgievich Firin (eds.), *The White Sea Canal: Being an Account of the Construction of the New Canal*

between the White Sea and the Baltic Sea, translated by Amabel Williams-Ellis, London 1935.]

6 Ibid., endpaper, left-hand side [Translation modified].

7 For a description of the geological, hydrological and technical aspects of the canal construction, ibid., 68–128.

8 Paul R. Gregory, *The Political Economy of Stalinism: Evidence from the Soviet Secret Archives*, Cambridge 2004; Paul R. Gregory and Valery Lazarev (eds.), *The Economics of Forced Labor: The Soviet Gulag*, Stanford 2003, ch. 8.

9 Information according to the Wikipedia entries on Suez and Panama, accessed 15 March 2016.

10 Dmitriev, *Belomorsko-Baltiysky vodny put*.

11 I. I. Gnetnev, *Lestnitsa k Belomu*, Petrozavodsk 1983; Michael Prischwin, *Der versunkene Weg ('Osudareva doroga')*, Stuttgart 1961.

12 Reprint of M. Gorky, L. L. Averbakh and S. G. Firin (eds.), *Belomorsko-Baltiysky Kanal imeni Stalina: Istoriya stroitelstva* [Moscow 1934], 1998, 105.

13 Ibid., 245.

14 Gregory, *The Political Economy of Stalinism*; Solzhenitsyn, *The Gulag Archipelago*, vol. 2.

15 N. V. Petrov and K. V. Skorkin, *Kto rukovodil NKVD 1934–1941: Spravochnik*, edited by N. G. Okhotin and A. B. Roginsky, Moscow 1999. On the question of the visibility and the representation of Jews in the early phase of the organs of Soviet repression, see O. V. Budnitsky, *Rossiyskie evrei mezhdu krasnymi i belymi (1917–1920)*, Moscow 2006; L. Krichevsky, 'Evrei v apparate VChK-OGPU v 20-e gody', in O. V. Budnitsky (ed.), *Evrei i russkaya revolyutsiya: Materialy i issledovaniya*, Moscow and Jerusalem 1999, 320–350; Yuri Slezkine, *The Jewish Century*, Princeton 2004; Karl Schlögel and Karl-Konrad Tschäpe (eds), *Die Russische Revolution und das Schicksal der russischen Juden: Eine Debatte in Berlin 1922/23*, Berlin 2014.

16 See Susanne Schattenberg, *Stalins Ingenieure: Lebenswelten zwischen Technik und Terror in den 1930er Jahren*, Munich 2002; Loren Graham, *The Ghost of the Executed Engineer*, Cambridge 1993.

17 Reprint of Gorky, Averbakh and Firin, *Belomorsko-Baltiysky Kanal imeni Stalina*, 234.

18 Ibid., 428.

19 The theme of reforging was also the subject of a film, *Zaklyuchennye* (Prisoners), directed by Yevgeny Chervyakov, screenplay by Nikolay Pogodin, USSR 1936.

20 Memoir Databank in Memorial. See under 'Belomor'.

21 On *tufta*, see the reprint of Gorky, Averbakh and Firin, *Belomorsko-Baltiysky Kanal imeni Stalina*, 377, 385.

22 Igal Halfin, *Terror in My Soul: Autobiographies on Trial*, Cambridge 2003; Jochen Hellbeck, *Revolution on My Mind: Writing a Diary under Stalin*, Cambridge 2006.

23 N. P. Antsiferov, *Iz dum o bylom: Vospominaniya*, Moscow 1992; for Antsiferov's biography, see Karl Schlögel, '"Die Seele Petersburgs" von Nikolai P. Anziferow: Ein legendäres Buch und sein unbekannter Autor', in Nikolai Anziferow, *Die Seele Petersburgs*, Munich 2003, 7–46.

24 Ekaterina Makhotina, *Stolzes Gedenken und traumatisches Erinnern: Gedächtnisorte der Stalinzeit am Weißmeerkanal*, Frankfurt am Main 2013.

Chapter 10. Landscape after the Battle

1 Wolfgang Schivelbusch, *Entfernte Verwandtschaft: Faschismus, Nationalsozialismus, New Deal 1933–1939*, Munich 2005.

2 Klaus Gestwa, *Die 'Stalinschen Großbauten des Kommunismus': Sowjetische Technik- und Umweltgeschichte 1948–1964*, Munich 2010; Dirk van Laak, *Weiße Elefanten: Anspruch und Scheitern technischer Großprojekte im 20. Jahrhundert*, Stuttgart 1999.

3 Hans Rogger, 'Amerikanizm and the Economic Development of Russia', in *Comparative Studies in Society and History* 23, 3/1981, 382–420.

4 A. I. Kokurin and Yu. N. Morukov, *Stalinskie stroyki GULAGa 1930–1953*, Moscow 2005.

5 Svetlana Alexievich, *Chernobyl Prayer: A Chronicle of the Future*, translated by Anna Gunin and Arch Tait, London 2016. New translation of the revised edition published in 2013.

6 Rudolf Bahro, *The Alternative in Eastern Europe*, translated by David Fernbach, London 1978.

III. Soviet Sign-Worlds

1 Roland Barthes, *The Empire of Signs*, translated by Richard Howard, New York 1983; Umberto Eco, *A Theory of Semiotics*, Indiana 1976; Jurij Lotman, *Studien zur Semiotik: Die Innenwelt des Denkens—Eine semiotische Theorie der Kultur*, Berlin 2010; Karl Schlögel, *Moskau lesen*, Berlin 1984; Nancy Condee (ed.), *Soviet Hieroglyphics: Visual Culture in Late Twentieth-Century Russia*, Bloomington and London 1995.

Chapter 11. The Writing on the Wall

1 Eric A. Peschler, *Künstler in Moskau: Die neue Avantgarde*, Schaffhausen 1988.

2 Kerstin Holm, *Das korrupte Imperium—ein russisches Panorama*, Munich 2003; Karl Schlögel, *Moskau lesen*, Berlin 1984, especially the section 'Zeichen auf goldenem Grund'.

Chapter 12. Decorations and Medals: Chest Badges

1 This entire chapter is based largely on Dietrich Herfurth, *Militärische Auszeichnungen der UdSSR*, illustrations by Jean Molitor, Berlin 1987, here 15.

2 Ibid., 20.

3 Ibid., 12.

4 Ibid., 27.

5 Ibid., 33.

6 'Dannye o kolichestve nagrazhdeny ordenami i medalyami SSSR za period 1918–1964 gg.', in *Istochnik* 3/1998, 132–159, here 137, table 3.

7 Ibid., 134, table 1; Herfurth gives a total of 14.9 million, *Militärische Auszeichnungen der UdSSR*, 33.

8 *Sovetskie ordena i ordenskie dokumenty iz sobraniya tsentralnogo muzeya revolyutsii SSSR*, catalogue, Moscow 1983.

9 'Dannye', 143, table 8.

10 Listed in A. A. fon Lampe, *Puti vernykh: Sbornik statey*, Paris 1960, 129–159.

Chapter 13. Body Language: Tattoos

1 Danzig Baldaev, Sergei Vasiliev and Alexei Plutser-Sarno, *Russian Criminal Tattoo Encyclopaedia*, vol. 1, translated by Andrew Bromfield, London 2003, foreword, 17–25.

2 Ibid., 27.

3 Ibid., 30, 35.

4 Ibid., 37, 39.

5 Ibid., 39, with the corresponding illustrations in Danzig Baldaev, *Drawings from the Gulag*, translated by Polly Gannon and Ast A. Moore, London 2010.

6 Baldaev, Vasiliev and Plutser-Sarno, *Russian Criminal Tattoo Encyclopaedia*, 48.

7 Ibid., 52.

Chapter 14. Moscow Graffiti: In the Beginning Was Futurism

1 John Bushnell, *Moscow Graffiti: Language and Subculture*, Boston 1990.

2 *Russian Art of the Avant-Garde: Theory and Criticism 1902–1934*, edited and translated by John E. Bowlt, London 1988; Felix Philipp Ingold, *Der große Bruch: Russland im Epochenjahr 1913, Kultur, Gesellschaft, Politik*, Munich 2000.

3 Vladimir Mayakovsky, David Burlyuk and A. Kamensky, 'Dekret No. 1 o demokratizatsii iskusstv', in *Gazeta futuristov*, Moscow, 15 March 1918. Cited here in the translation by James A. Reeves, http://atlasminor.com/decree-1-on-the-democratization-of-art/ (accessed 2 January 2019).

Chapter 15. Names Are Not Just Hot Air

1 Richard Stites, *Revolutionary Dreams: Utopian Vision and Experimental Life in the Russian Revolution*, New York 1989, 111f.

2 Lev Uspensky, *Ty i tvoe imya*, Leningrad 1962, xxx.

3 Ilya Ilf and Evgeny Petrov in *Pravda*, 7 June 1935.

4 K. Chukovsky, *Zhivoy kak zhizn': Razgovor o russkom yazyke*, Moscow 1962 (ch. 4, 'Umlsopogasy').

5 S. Marshak, *Sobranie sochineny v 8 tomah*, vol. 5, Moscow 1970, 532–533; Yevgeny Dolma-tovsky, cited in *Imena sovetskogo proiskhozhdeniya*, wikipedia.ru.

Chapter 16. Wrapping Paper, Packaging

1 On Soviet advertising, see Randi Cox, 'All This Can Be Yours! Soviet Commercial Advertising and the Social Construction of Space 1928–1956', in Evgeny Dobrenko and Eric Naiman (eds.), *The Landscape of Stalinism: The Art and Ideology of Soviet Space*, Seattle and London 2003, 125–162.

Chapter 17. The Fate of the Great Soviet Encyclopedia: The Organisation of Knowledge amid the Tumult of History

1 Brian Kassof, 'A Book of Socialism: Stalinist Culture and the First Edition of the *Bolshaya sovetskaya entsiklopediya*', in *Kritika: Explorations in Russian and Eurasian History* 6, 1/2005, 55–95.

2 *Bolshaya sovetskaya entsiklopediya*, vol. 1, Moscow 1927, editors' note.

3 *Entsiklopedichesky slovar*, edited by I. E. Andreevsky, Verlag F. A. Brockhaus and I. A. Efron, 41 vols. (82 half vols., supplementary vols. 1–2, 2 half vols.), St. Petersburg 1890–1907.

4 For the history of Brockhaus and Brockhaus-Efron, see Ulrich Hohoff, '200 Jahre Brockhaus: Geschichte und Gegenwart eines großen Lexikons', in *Forschung und Lehre* 2/2009, 118–120; exhibition in the Russian State Library on the 125th anniversary of the publication of the Brockhaus-Efron Encyclopedia, 6 August–15 September 2005; for the period in exile, see Gottfried Kratz: 'Russische Verlage und Druckereien in Berlin 1918–1941', in Karl Schlögel, Katharina Kucher, Bernhard Suchy and Gregor Thum (eds.), *Chronik russischen Lebens in Deutschland 1918–1941*, Berlin 1999, 514–515.

5 *Entsiklopedichesky slovar russkogo bibliograficheskogo instituta br. A. i I. Granat i Ko*, 7th revised ed., vols. 1–55 and 57–58, Moscow 1910–1948. Vol. 56 never appeared.

6 I have written about the key importance of the final editing of address books and reference works in *Moscow, 1937*, translated by Rodney Livingstone, Malden, MA and Cambridge 2012, ch. 3, 54–67.

7 The development of the 2nd and 3rd editions of the *BSE* is briefly told in A. Rewin and Ju. Schmuskis, 'Die Entwicklung der Enzyklopädien in der UdSSR', in Hans-Joachim Diesner and Günter Gurst (eds.), *Lexika gestern und heute*, Leipzig 1976, 263–296; for Stalin's influence on the editorial board, see Leonid Maksimenkov, '"Nachinaem rabotat pri bolshom pokrovitelstve": Ob uchastii I. V. Stalina v podgotovke vtorogo izdaniya BSE', in *Istochnik* 4/2003, 40–44.

8 *Bolshaya sovetskaya entsiklopediya*, edited by S. I. Vavilov, 2nd ed., 50 vols., 1 supplementary vol., Moscow 1950–1958, with two index vols., Moscow 1960.

9 *Bolshaya sovetskaya entsiklopediya*, edited by A. M. Prokhorov, 3rd ed., 30 vols., Moscow 1969–1978.

10 *Bolshoy entsiklopedichesky slovar*, 2nd revised and supplemented ed., Moscow and St. Petersburg 1997.

11 Sinaida Hippius, *Petersburger Tagebücher*, Berlin 2014, 326f.

Chapter 18. Galleries of Private Possessions: The China Elephant on the Shelf

1 Vera Dunham, *In Stalin's Time: Middleclass Values in Soviet Fiction*, enlarged and updated ed., Durham and London 1990.

2 Elena Yachnenko, 'Sovetsky farfor', in A. Golosovskaya and V. Zuseva (eds.), *Sovetsky stil. Vremya i veshchi: Ukrasheniya, moda, prazdniki, bele, eda, upakovka, dengi, dacha, igrushki, parfyumeriya, mebel, farfor*, Moscow 2012, 164–181.

3 On the art of Palekh craftsmen, see Monika Kopplin, *European Lacquer: Selected Works from the Museum für Lackkunst Münster*, Munich 2010, section on Russia, 273–317.

4 Vladimir Tolstoj, *Kunst und Kunsthandwerk in der Sowjetunion 1917–1937*, Munich 1990.

Chapter 19. The Piano in the Palace of Culture

1 Walter Benjamin, *Moscow Diary*, edited by Gary Smith, translated by Richard Sieburth, with a preface by Gershom Scholem, Cambridge, MA and London 1986, 28.

2 Mikhail [Michael] Ossorgin, *Quiet Street*, New York 1930, 126.

3 Ibid., 131.

4 Dmitry Likhachev, *Izbrannoe: Vospominaniya*, St. Petersburg 1995, 139.

5 Ossorgin, *Quiet Street*, 143f.

6 Yuri Orlov, *Dangerous Thoughts: Memoirs of a Russian Life*, translated by Thomas P. Whitney, New York 1991, 169–170.

7 This account follows that of M. V. Sergeev, 'Fortepiannoe delo v Peterburge XIX veka: Po materialam russkoy periodicheskoy pechati', in *Rossiyskaya kultura glazami molodykh uchennykh*, vol. 3, St. Petersburg 1994, 74–92.

8 M. V. Sergeev, 'Ekspertiza fortepiano rossiyskogo i sovetskogo proizvodstva', in *Muzykalnaya kultura i obrazovanie*, St. Petersburg 2010, 241–263.

9 A. Anatoli (Kuznetsov), *Babi Yar*, translated by David Floyd, London 1970, 215–216.

10 Norman Davies and Roger Moorhouse, *Microcosm: Portrait of a Central European City*, London 2002, 409. The quotation comes from Irena Strauss, in 'To było piękne miastu' (It was a beautiful city), in *Res Publica* 6/1990, 8.

11 Joseph Brodsky, 'In a Room and a Half', in *Less Than One: Selected Essays*, Harmondsworth and New York 1986, 470.

12 Likhachev, *Izbrannoe*.

13 Katja Petrowskaja, 'Rückschau auf die sowjetische Didaktik für die Kleinsten', in *Neue Zürcher Zeitung*, 13–14 April 2002, 55.

14 Stefan Melle, 'Auch Viktor Pawlowitsch verkauft', in *Berliner Zeitung*, 16 June 1999.

15 Special issue of *Sobaka*, 12, 72/2008, 'Istoriya vtoraya: Pro fortepianostroenie', sobaka.ru.

16 Eginald Schlattner, *Das Klavier im Nebel*, Vienna 2005.

17 Mikhail Korshunov and Viktoriya Terekhova, *Tayna tayn moskovskikh*, Moscow 1995, 121–132.

Chapter 20. Rubbish: A Phenomenology of Cleanliness

1 Reiner Keller, *Müll: Die gesellschaftliche Konstruktion des Wertvollen; Die öffentliche Diskussion über Abfall in Deutschland und Frankreich*, Wiesbaden 2009; for a sketch on the topic, see Karl Schlögel, *Das Wunder von Nishnij oder die Rückkehr der Städte: Berichte und Essays*, Frankfurt am Main 1991, section on garbage and waste, 174.

2 Ilya Utehhin, *Ocherki kommunalnogo byta*, 2nd expanded ed., Moscow 2004, 105; Nadežda Grigor'eva, Schamma Schahadat and Igor' Smirnov (eds.), 'Nähe schaffen, Abstand halten: Zur Geschichte von Intimität und Nähe in der russischen Kultur', Munich 2005 (*Wiener Slawistischer Almanach*, vol. 62), 439–456; Steven E. Harris, 'In Search of "Ordinary" Russia: Everyday Life in the NEP, the Thaw, and the Communal Apartment', in *Kritika: Explorations in Russian and Eurasian History* 6, 3/2005, 583–614.

3 Utehin, *Ocherki kommunal'nogo byta*, 195.

Chapter 21. Krasnaya Moskva: Chanel in Soviet-Speak

1 Maria Bykova, 'Dukhi "Krasnaya Moskva"—simvol epokhi', http://www.stranamam.ru/post/9724318/ and http://www.womenclub.ru/perfumery/2463.htm (accessed 2 June 2017).

2 Jürgen Raab, *Soziologie des Geruchs: Über die soziale Konstruktion olfaktorischer Wahrnehmung*, Konstanz 2001, 301; Hans J. Rindisbacher, *The Smell of Books: A Cultural-Historical Study of Olfactory Perception in Literature*, Ann Arbor 1992; Alain Corbin, *The Foul and the Fragrant*, translated by Miriam L. Kochan, Roy Porter and Christopher Prendergast, London 1986; Patrick Süskind, *Perfume*, translated by John E. Woods, Harmondsworth 1987.

3 Odours with which to identify political opponents were preserved in sealed glass jars by the state security services of the GDR.

4 Maria Bykova, 'Luchshie aromaty parfyumerii, sdelannoy v SSSR', https://mylitta.ru/761
   -soviet-perfume.html (accessed 3 June 2017); Bykova, 'Dukhi "Krasnaya Moskva"'; Marina
   Koleva, 'Sovetskaya parfyumeria', in A. Golosovskaya and V. Zuseva (eds.), *Sovetsky stil.*
   Vremya i veshchi: Ukrasheniya, moda, prazdniki, belie, eda, upakovka, dengi, dacha, igrushki,
   parfyumeria, mebel, farfor, Moscow 2012, 74–85.

5 Ernest Beaux, https://en.wikipedia.org/wiki/Ernest_Beaux (accessed 30 December 2021);
   Sasha Raspopina, 'Smells Like Soviet Spirit: A Brief History of Perfume and Cosmetics', in
   The Guardian, 19 November 2014; Tilar J. Mazzeo, *Chanel No 5: Die Geschichte des berühm-*
   testen Parfums der Welt, Munich 2014.

6 Cited in Natalia Lebina, 'Lemma Krasnaya Moskva,' in *Entsiklopediya banalnostey, Sovetskaya*
   povsednevnost—kontury, simvoly, znaki, St. Petersburg 2006, 207–208; E. Zhiritskaya, 'Legkoe
   dykhanie: Zapakh kak kulturnaya repressiya v rossiyskom obshchestve 1917–1930-kh gg.',
   in *Aromaty i zapakhi v kulture*, Moscow 2002, vol. 2.

7 Koleva, 'Sovetskaya parfiumeriya', 77–78.

8 Ibid., 81.

9 Lebina, 'Lemma Krasnaya Moskva', 207–208.

10 Mihail Lokutov, 'Grazhdanin frantsuzskoy respubliki', in *Sovetsky zhurnal khudozhestven-*
   nogo ocherka 'Nashi dostizheniya' 2/1937.

11 For the various versions, see Yevgenii Zhirnov, 'Pervy sekret "Shanel N° 5"', in *Zhurnal*
   Kommersant.ru, 15 October 2007, online at https://www.kommersant.ru/doc/813950
   (accessed at the time of the exhibition '*Shanel: Po zakonam iskusstva*, 3 June 2017). For
   Michel's biography, see http://www.casual-info.ru/wiki/МишеЛь+Август+/ (accessed
   3 June 2017).

12 Mikhail Bulgakov, *The Master and Margarita*, translated by Michael Glenny, London 1996,
   149.

13 Michael David-Fox, *Showcasing the Great Experiment: Cultural Diplomacy and Western*
   Visitors to the Soviet Union, 1921–1941, New York 2012.

14 For the sometimes contested information on the dates and careers of Beaux and Michel,
   see https://en.wikipedia.org/wiki/Ernest_Beaux (accessed 30 December 2021) and http://
   www.casual-info.ru/wiki/МишеЛь+Август+/ (accessed 3 June 2017).

Chapter 22. Stalin's Cookbook: Images of the Good Life in the Soviet Age

1 *Kniga o vkusnoy i zdorovoy pishche: Odobrena Institutom pitaniya Akademii meditsinskikh*
   nauk SSSR, Moscow 1953. My own copy, which I bought in the book market in Rostov-on-
   Don, first appeared in 1953 in an edition of 500,000 and cost 15 rubles at the time.

2 Ibid., 83–122 [Ministry of the Food Industry, *Book of Tasty and Healthy Food*, translated
   by Boris Ushumirskiy, Snoqualmie Pass, WA 2012, 93–168].

3 Ibid., 125–150 [*Book*, 169–214].

4 Ibid., 153–184 [*Book*, 215–281].

5 Ibid., 80. On the problem of vodka, see Sonja Margolina, *Wodka: Trinken und Macht in*
   Russland, Berlin 2004; William Pokhlebkin, *A History of Vodka*, London 1992.

6 *Kubanskie kazaki*, directed by Ivan Pyriev, 1949.

7 On Mikoyan, see Sheila Fitzpatrick, *On Stalin's Team: The Years of Living Dangerously in*
   Soviet Politics, Princeton and Oxford 2015; Anastas Mikoyan, *Tak bylo: Razmyshleniya o*
   minuvshem, Moscow 1999.

8 Jukka Gronow, *Caviar with Champagne: Common Luxury and the Ideals of the Good Life in*
   Stalin's Russia, London 2003.

9 An overview can be found in Marina Koleva, 'Eda v SSSR', in A. Golosovskaya and V. Zuseva (eds.), *Sovetsky stil: Vremya i veschi: Ukrasheniya, moda, prazdniki, belie, eda, upakovka, dengi, dacha, igrushki, parfiumeriya, mebel, farfor*, Moscow 2012, 86–97; Elena Osokina, *Our Daily Bread: Socialist Distribution and the Art of Survival in Stalin's Russia, 1927–1941*, translated by Kate Transchel and Greta Bucher, Armonk and London 2001.

10 See Vadim Volkov, 'The Concept of "kul'turnost": Notes on the Stalinist Civilizing Process', in Sheila Fitzpatrick (ed.), *Stalinism: New Directions*, London and New York 2000, 210–230.

11 *Podarok molodym khozyaykam ili sredstvo k umensheniyu raskhodov v domashnem khozyaystve*, online at http://www.molohovetc.ru/ (accessed 3 June 2017).

12 Alexander Kravetsky, 'Taynaya kukhnya Yeleny Molokhovets', in *Kommersant Dengi*, 22 September 2014, 49, online at https://www.kommersant.ru/doc/2558138 (accessed 3 June 2017).

13 Echbert Khartman, 'Yelena Ivanovna Molokhovets', in *Portrety i sudba*, in *Zhurnalny zal: Zvezda* 3/2000, online at http://magazines.russ.ru/zvezda/2000/3/hartman.html (accessed 3 June 2017).

14 Kravetsky, 'Taynaya kukhnya Yeleny Molokhovets'.

15 Address and telephone number can be found in *Spisok abonentov* [the list of subscribers] of 1915, 321, as Ye. I. Molokhovets, Suvorovsky prospekt 54, tel. 136–43.

16 Alena Dvinina, 'Kulinarnaya kniga kak otrazhenie istorii', in *Karelia*, 21 October 2002.

17 The address of the Museum of Social Nutrition in Moscow is Bolshoi Rogozhsky Pereulok 17, dom 17, stroenie 1.

Chapter 23. Geologists' Field Work and Other Breathing Spaces

1 For the history of tourism in the Soviet Union, see Anne E. Gorsuch and Diane P. Koenker (eds.), *Turizm: The Russian and East European Tourist under Capitalism and Socialism*, Ithaca and London 2006; Bernd Knabe, *Urlaub des Sowjetbürgers, Berichte des Bundesinstituts für Ostwissenschaftliche und Internationale Studien*, vol. 64, Cologne 1977; on foreign tourists in the USSR, see B. E. Bagdasarian, I. B. Orlov, J. J. Shnaydgen et al., *Sovetskoe zazerkale: Inostranny turizm v SSSR v 1930–1980-e-gody*, Moscow 2011.

2 *Vechernyaya Moskva*, 24 April 1930, quoted in Diane P. Koenker, 'The Proletarian Tourist in the 1930s: Between Mass Excursion and Mass Escape', in Gorsuch and Koenker, *Turizm*, 119–140, here 119.

3 Louise McReynolds, 'The Prerevolutionary Russian Tourist: Commercialization in the Nineteenth Century', in Gorsuch and Koenker, *Turizm*, 17–42.

4 *Komsomolskaya pravda*, 16 December 1926, 3, quoted in Koenker, 'The Proletarian Tourist', 121.

5 'Turizm' in L. V. Belovinsky, *Entsiklopedichesky slovar istorii sovetskoy povsednevnoy zhizni*, Moscow 2015, 662–663.

6 Vassili Galaktionov and Anatoli Agranovski, *Ein Strom wird zum Meer: Ein dokumentarischer Roman*, Berlin 1952, 76.

7 Katja Lebedewa, *Komm Gitarre, mach mich frei! Russische Gitarrenlyrik in der Opposition*, Berlin 1992.

8 A wonderful homage has been paid to this experience in Petr Vayl and Alexander Genis, *60-e: Mir sovetskogo cheloveka*, Ann Arbor 1988, especially the section 'Geography Instead of History: Sibiria', 69–75.

9 Christian Noack, 'Coping with the Tourist: Planned and "Wild" Mass Tourism on the Soviet Black Sea Coast', in Gorsuch and Koenker, *Turizm*, 281–304, here 295; Noack, '"Andere

Räume"—sowjetische Kurorte als Heterotopien: Das Beispiel Sotschi', in Karl Schlögel (ed.), *Mastering Russian Spaces: Raum und Raumbewältigung als Probleme der russischen Geschichte*, Munich 2011, 187–198.

10 Anna Rotkirch, 'Travelling Maidens and Men with Parallel Lives—Journeys as Private Space during Late Socialism', in Jeremy Smith (ed.), *Beyond the Limits: The Concept of Space in Russian History and Culture*, Helsinki 1999, 131–165.

11 Viktor Erofeev, *Muzhchiny*, Moscow 1997, 51–52, quoted in Anna Rotkirh, *Muzhskoy vopros: Liubov i seks trekh pokoleny v avtrobiografiyakh peterburzhtsev*, Gender series 2, St. Petersburg 2011, 214.

12 Illustrated perfectly in Ilya Kabakov, *My Mother's Album*, London 2017; Vitaly Bakanov, *Detstvo 50kh–6okh: Vospominaniya kievlyanina*, Kyiv 2012.

Chapter 24. Dacha: Chekhov's *Cherry Orchard* in the Twentieth Century

1 For an alternative view of the origins of the dacha in the GDR, see Henriette Brendler, *Die Kleingartenkultur in der DDR und BRD—ein Spiegel der politischen und gesellschaftlichen Systeme*, cultural studies BA, European University Viadrina, Frankfurt an der Oder 2007.

2 See 'Dacha' in Natalia Lebina, *Entsiklopediya banalnostey: Sovetskaya povsednevnost—kontury, simvoly, znaki*, St. Petersburg 2006; the history of the dacha has been written by Stephen Lovell, *Summerfolk: A History of the Dacha, 1710–2000*, Ithaca and London 2003.

3 For dacha suburbs, see M. V. Nashchokina, 'Dachnye poselki', in E. I. Kirichenko, E. G. Shcheboleva and M. V. Nashchokina (eds.), *Gradostroitelstvo Rossii serediny XIX–nachala XX veka: Goroda i novye tipy poseleny*, vol. 2, Moscow 2003, 347–389. A study of another prominent dacha centre is by Adrian V. Rudomino, *Legendarnaya Barvikha: Zapiski starozhila ob istorii, prirode i chastnoy zhizni*, Moscow 2009.

4 Quoted in Lovell, *Summerfolk*, 60.

5 Ibid., 105.

6 For the discussion of garden cities in Russia, see E. I. Kirichenko, 'Goroda-sady', in Kirichenko, E. G. Shcheboleva and M. V. Nashchokina, *Gradostroitelstvo Rossii serediny XIX–nachala XX veka: Goroda i novye tipy poseleny*, vol. 2, Moscow 2003, 506–544.

7 Sinaida Hippius, *Petersburger Tagebücher*, Berlin 2014, 166f.

8 Ibid., 200.

9 Ibid., 370.

10 Aleksandr Rodchenko, 'Working with Mayakovsky', in *Experiments for the Future*, edited and with a preface by Alexander N. Lavrentiev, translated and annotated by Jamey Gambrell, with an introduction by John E. Bowlt, New York 2005, 251.

11 On the question of conspiracies in dachas, see J. Arch Getty and Oleg V. Naumov, *The Road to Terror: Stalin and the Self-Destruction of the Bolsheviks, 1932–1939*, New Haven and London 2010, 314, 319.

12 Lovell, *Summerfolk*, 137.

13 See https://ru.wikipedia.org/wiki/Дача (accessed 12 April 2017).

14 Denis Babichenko and Nikolay Galkin, 'Ja zhivu na dache v Peredelkine ... Stalinsky "vishnevy sad" popal pod katok privatizatsii' [I live in Peredelkino—Stalin's 'cherry orchard' has been squeezed in the mangle of privatisation], in *Itogi*, 29 May 2001, 22–29; Lev Lobov and Kira Vasilyeva, *Peredelkino: A Tale of the Writers' Village*, Moscow 2011.

15 The catalogue of poets and writers can be found at https://ru.wikipedia.org/wiki/Передел -кино (accessed 3 June 2017); the catalogue of graves in the Peredelkino cemetery at

http://tropki.ru/rossiya/moskovskaya-oblast/poselok-pisateley-peredelkino#lt=55
.6572&ln=37.3473&z=14 (accessed 3 June 2017).

16 Frank Westermann, *Ingenieure der Seele: Schriftsteller unter Stalin—Eine Erkundungsreise*,
Berlin 2003, 153–180.

17 Lovell, *Summerfolk*, 236.

18 Vladimir Pribylovsky, *Vokrug Putina: Biograficheskyy spravochnik*, Moscow 2016; Karen
Dawisha, *Putin's Kleptocracy: Who Owns Russia?*, New York 2014.

Chapter 25. Health Resorts for Workers:
The Sanatorium as a Historical Locus

1 M. Gerschenson and W. Iwanow, *Briefwechsel zwischen zwei Zimmerwinkeln*, translated
by Nicolai von Bubnoff, with an afterword by Karl Schlögel, Stuttgart 1990 [Vyacheslav
Ivanovich Ivanov and Mikhail Osipovich Gershenzon, *Correspondence across a Room*,
translated by Lisa Sergio, Marlboro 1984]; Rainer Grübel (ed.), *Michail Geršenzon: Seine
Korrespondenz und sein Spätwerk*, Oldenburg 2007.

2 For more on convalescent homes, see V. F. Khodasevich, 'Zdravnitsa', in *Vozrozhdenie*, 14
March 1929.

3 I. I. Kozlov (ed.), *Zdravnitsy profsoyuzov SSSR: Kurorty, sanatorii, pansionaty i doma otdykha
profsoyuzov*, 5th ed., revised and expanded, Moscow 1979.

4 Ibid., 15.

5 Ibid., 12.

6 Ibid., 11.

7 For example, *Russland: Handbuch für Reisende* by K. Baedeker, Leipzig 1897, 393–408.

8 E. I. Kirichenko's contributions on the spa towns in the Caucasus and the Crimea can be
found in 'Goroda-kurorty', in E. I. Kirichenko, E. G. Shcheboleva and M. V. Nashchokina
(eds.), *Gradostroitelstvo Rossii serediny XIX–nachala XX veka: Goroda i novye tipy poseleny*,
vol. 2, Moscow 2003, 254–346.

9 Kozlov, *Zdravnitsy profsoyuzov SSSR*, 4f.

10 Illustrations ibid.

11 Ibid., 5.

12 Ibid., 6.

13 Dmitry Khmelnitsky describes him as 'Stalin's favourite architect'. Merzhanov, incidentally, worked as an architect for the defence of Moscow; then, during the 1940s and
1950s, he was condemned to ten years in a camp. He continued to work from prison and
the *sharashka*. His wife and closest colleagues were also present in the camp, where his
wife died in 1948 or 1949. In 1948 or 1949 he evidently designed a sanatorium in Sochi.
Cf. Wikipedia, which contains literature on Merzhanov, and also http://www.geokorolev
.ru/biography/biography_person_merzhanov.html (accessed 3 June 2017).

14 Description of the Caucasian Riviera complex can be found in Natalia Zaharova, 'Istoriya
kurorta "Kavkazskaya Riviera"', 28 November 2009, online at http://arch-sochi.ru/2009
/11/istoriya-kav-riv/ (accessed 3 June 2017).

15 A. V. Shchusev, 'Proekt gostinitsy v Matseste', in *Sovremennaya arkhitektura* 3/1927, 98–99,
cited in Natalia Zakharova, *Arkhitektura Sochi*, https://arch-sochi.ru/2016/04/a-v-shhusev
-proekt-gostinitsyi-v-matseste-1927-god/ (accessed 17 May 2022).

16 Selim O. Khan-Magomedov, *Pioneers of Soviet Architecture*, edited by Catherine Cooke,
translated by Alexander Lieven, London 1987, 514–516.

17 M. K., *Sochinskaya pravda*, 14 March 1936; see also N. Z. Nesis: Vladimir Kostinov, 'Plan-irovka kurorta Sochi-Mazesta', in *Arkhitektura SSSR* 9, September 1935, published in *Sochinsky kraeved*.

18 On N. Sokolov's early designs, see Natalia Zakharova, 'Kursovoy proekt Nikolaya Sokolova "Kurortnye gostinitsy v Matseste" 1928/29 uchebnyi god', with drawings, online at https://arch-sochi.ru/2016/05/kursovoy-proekt-nikolaya-sokolova-kurortnoy-gostinitsyi-v-matseste-1929-god/ (accessed 3 June 2017).

19 See Natalia Zakharova, L. A. and A. A. Vesniny, 'Proekt gostinitsy v Novoy Matseste. 1927 god', in *Sovremennaya arkhitektura* 3/1927, 96–97, https://arch-sochi.ru/2016/04/vesninyi-proekt-gostinitsyi-v-novoy-matseste-1927-god/; Khan-Magomedov, *Pioneers of Soviet Architecture*, 532.

20 This overview is based largely on the account given by Anzhela Adshar, http://arch-sochi.ru/2013/08/pamyatniki-arhitekturyi-goroda-sochi/ (accessed 3 June 2017). Sochi Central Station, built in the 1930s, may well have been the work of M. Ginzburg. The station built after the war was the work of A. N. Dushkin and G. G. Akvilev. The passenger port was constructed by K. S. Alabyan and L. B. Karlik.

21 On Stalin's favourite architect, see Boris Merzhanov, 'Erinnerungen an Stalins Architek-ten Miron Meržanov', in Peter Noever (ed.), *Tyrannei des Schönen: Architektur der Stalin-Zeit*, Munich and New York 1994, 55–61.

22 On the daily communications between Sochi and Moscow in the summer months, the best source is O. V. Khlevnyuk, R. U. Devis, L. P. Kosheleva, E. A. Ris and L. A. Rogovaya (eds.), *Stalin i Kaganovich: Perepiska 1931–1936*, Moscow 2001; on Sochi and Stalin's other residences, see Simon Sebag Montefiore, *Stalin: The Court of the Red Tsar*, New York 2004.

23 Margarete Buber-Neumann, *Schauplätze der Weltrevolution*, Stuttgart 1967, 296 ff.

24 Denis Babichenko, 'Uchtites otdykhat'! Kurortny rezhim dlya sovetskoy vlasti', in *Itogi*, 26 June 2001, 39.

25 Kerstin Holm, 'Die Sphäre sozialistischer Muße: In Sotschi am Schwarzen Meer hat das Architekturtheater des Sowjetsystems überdauert, ist nun aber vom Zerfall bedroht', in *Frankfurter Allgemeine Zeitung*, 27 January 2001, no. 23; Marianne Mösle, 'Zar und Zim-mermann. Prächtig verrostet: Das georgische Heilbad Borschomi wird endlich renoviert', in *Frankfurter Allgemeine Sonntagszeitung*, 1 May 2005, Travel Section V5.

Chapter 26. Doorbells: Nameplates and Signals

1 Klaus Mehnert, *Der Sowjetmensch: Versuch eines Porträts nach zwölf Reisen in die Sowjet-union 1929–1957*, Stuttgart 1958, 60. The entrance situation also plays a part in Philipp Pott, *Moskauer Kommunalwohnungen 1917 bis 1997: Materielle Kultur, Erfahrung, Erin-nerung*, Zurich 2009, 166.

Chapter 27. *Kommunalka*, or Where the Soviet People Were Tempered

1 Nadezhda Mandelstam, *Hope against Hope*, translated by Max Hayward, London 1971, 137; ZhAKT: *Zhilishchno-arendnye kooperativnye tovarishchestva*, i.e., shared rental apartments that existed in the period from the NEP up to 1937.

2 On the evolution of Soviet-Russian living conditions, see Irina Kulakova, *Istoriya moskovskogo zhilya*, Moscow 2006.

3 Yekaterina Yu. Gerasimova, *Sovetskaya kommunalnaya kvartira kak sotsialny institut: Istoriko-sotsiologichesky analiz (na materialakh Leningrada, 1917–1991)*, dissertation, St. Petersburg 2000, 10.

4 Hedrick Smith, *The Russians*, London 1976; Christian Schmidt-Häuer, *Das sind die Russen: Wie sie wurden, wie sie leben*, Hamburg 1980.

5 M. V. Vorobieva, 'Kommunalnaya kvartira v sovetskikh kinofilmakh i anekdotakh: Popytka obemnogo portreta', in *Labirint: Zhurnal sotsialno-gumanitarnykh issledovany* 2/2015, 19–31.

6 Sandra Evans, *Sowjetisch wohnen: Literatur-Kulturgeschichte der Kommunalka*, Bielefeld 2011; for novels, see 'Kommunalnye kvartiry v iskusstve', https://ru.wikipedia.org/wiki/Коммунальная_квартира (accessed 15 March 2017).

7 Svetlana Boym, *Common Places: Mythologies of Everyday Life in Russia*, Cambridge, MA 1994.

8 The outstanding studies here are Natalia Lebina, *Entsiklopediya banalnostey: Sovetskaya povsednevnost—kontury, simvoly, znaki*, St. Petersburg 2006; and Ilya Utekhin, *Ocherki kommunalnogo byta*, 2nd expanded ed., Moscow 2004. Also of importance are Gerasimova, *Sovetskaya kommunalnaya kvartira kak sotsialny institut*; Mark Meerovich, *Nakazanie zhilishchem: Zhilishchnaya politika v SSSR kak sredstvo upravleniya lyudmi 1917–1937*, Moscow 2008.

9 Julia Obertreis, *Tränen des Sozialismus: Wohnen in Petrograd/Leningrad zwischen revolutionären Entwürfen, sowjetischer Wohnpolitik und der Beständigkeit häuslicher Lebenswelten 1917–1937*, Cologne 2004; Paola Messana, *Soviet Communal Living: An Oral History of the Kommunalka*, London 2011; Evans, *Sowjetisch wohnen*.

10 Joseph Brodsky, *Less Than One: Selected Essays*, Harmondsworth and New York 1986, 448.

11 Ibid., 450.

12 Ibid., 452.

13 Ibid., 454.

14 Ibid., 454–455.

15 Ibid., 455.

16 Ilya Kabakov, *1964–1983: Stimmen hinter der Tür*, Leipzig 1998; Kabakov, *Die Kommunalwohnung*, Zurich 1989; Kabakov, *SHEK Nr. 8, Bauman-Bezirk, Stadt Moskau*, Leipzig 1994.

17 Kabakov, *1964–1983*, 22.

18 Ibid., 24. [See also Ilya Kabakov, *Ten Characters*, London and New York 1989, 50.]

19 Ibid., 34. [See Kabakov, *Ten Characters*, 50–51. The present translation is based on the English text where available, but otherwise follows the German version.]

20 Kabakov, *Ten Characters*, 52.

21 Kabakov, *1964–1983*, 39.

22 Ibid., 41.

23 For the debate about modern living, see William Craft Brumfield and Blair A. Ruble (eds.), *Russian Housing in the Modern Age: Design and Social History*, Cambridge 1993.

24 Peter Gatrell, *A Whole Empire Walking: Refugees in Russia during World War I*, Bloomington 2005.

25 Lebina, *Entsiklopediya banalnostey*, 201.

26 Golfo Alexopoulos, *Aliens, Citizens, and the Soviet State, 1926–1936*, Ithaca and London 2003.

27 Victor Buchli, *An Archeology of Socialism*, London 2000, 119.

28 https://ru.wikipedia.org/wiki/Коммунальная_квартира (accessed 15 March 2017). See the comprehensive account of housebuilding, Philipp Meuser, *Die Ästhetik der Platte: Wohnungsbau in der Sowjetunion zwischen Stalin und Glasnost*, Berlin 2015.

29 Utekhin, *Ocherki kommunalnogo byta*, 109.

30 Yuri Orlov, *Dangerous Thoughts: Memoirs of a Russian Life*, translated by Thomas P. Whitney, New York 1991, 96.

31 All this according to Utekhin, *Ocherki kommunalnogo byta*, 5–7. On new ways of living and privacy, see also Christina Kiaer and Eric Naiman (eds.), *Everyday Life in Early Soviet Russia: Taking the Revolution Inside*, Bloomington 2006; Catriona Kelly and David Shepherd (eds.), *Constructing Russian Culture in the Age of Revolution: 1881–1940*, Oxford 1998.

32 Yuri Slezkine, 'The USSR as a Communal Apartment, or How a Socialist State Promoted Ethnic Particularism', in Geoff Eley and Ronald Grigor Suny (eds.), *Becoming National: A Reader*, New York 1996, 203–238.

33 Cordula Gdaniec, *Kommunalka und Penthouse: Stadt und Stadtgesellschaft im postsowjetischen Moskau*, Münster 2005.

Chapter 28. The Interior as a Battlefield

1 See Walter Benjamin, *Moscow Diary*, edited by Gary Smith, translated by Richard Sieburth, with a preface by Gershom Scholem, Cambridge, MA and London 1986, 48.

2 See *Proekt Rossiya* 68, 2/2013, the issue of the architecture magazine dedicated to the interior, especially Artem Dezhurko, 'On the "Morphology of the Soviet Apartment"' (exhibition, 2011), 162–172; the analysis of the Kirov Museum in Leningrad is by N. Lebina. Almost all museums can be visited virtually online.

3 Ilya Utekhin, *Ocherki kommunalnogo byta*, 2nd expanded ed., Moscow 2004, 191 n. 5.

4 Walter Benjamin, 'The Return of the Flâneur', in *Selected Writings*, vol. 2, *1927–1934*, edited by Michael W. Jennings et al. and translated by Rodney Livingstone, Cambridge, MA and London 1999, 264.

5 Olga Strugova, 'Mebel i interier,' in A. Golosovskaya and V. Zuseva (eds.), *Sovetsky stil. Vremya i veshchi: Ukrasheniya, moda, prazdniki, bele, eda, upakovka, dengi, dacha, igrushki, parfiumeriya, mebel, farfor*, Moscow 2012, 148–163, here 152.

6 Quoted from Victor Buchli, *An Archaeology of Socialism*, London 2000, 44.

7 On the tyranny of the 'hearth', ibid., 46.

8 Ibid., 51.

9 Ibid., 53.

10 Strugova, 'Mebel i interier', 152.

11 Ibid., 148.

12 A. Vladimirsky and C. Sheftel, *Kulturno-Bytovaya Rabota v Domakh*, edited by N. Semashko, Moscow 1931, 14, quoted by Buchli, *An Archaeology of Socialism*, 53.

13 Ibid., 54.

14 Strugova, 'Mebel i interier', 151.

15 Buchli, *An Archaeology of Socialism*, 87–93.

16 Quoted in Strugova, 'Mebel i interier', 158.

17 Ibid., 158.

18 Ibid., 155.

19 B. Alekseev, 'O sovetskom interiere', in *Tvorchestvo* 4/1941, quoted in Strugova, 'Mebel i interier', 159.

20 Strugova, 'Mebel i interier', 160.

21 *Sovetsky Soyuz* 12/1954.

22 Buchli, *An Archaeology of Socialism*, 174.

Chapter 29. Hostel/*Obshchezhitie*: Soviet Melting Pot

1 'Obshchezhitie', in L. V. Belovinsky, *Entsiklopedichesky slovar istorii sovetskoy povsednev-noy zhizni*, Moscow 2015, 412–413; Natalia Lebina, *Entsiklopediya banalnostey: Sovetskaya povsednevnost—kontury, simvoly, znaki*, St. Petersburg 2006, 262.

2 Andrei Sakharov, *Memoirs*, translated by Richard Lourie, London, Sydney, Auckland and Johannesburg 1990, 43–54. See also Andrej Sacharov, *Mein Leben*, translated by Annelore Nitschke, Anton Manzella and Willhelm von Timroth, Munich and Zurich 1991, ch. 4, especially 83–88.

3 All this can be found in Andrei Grachev, *Gorbachev's Gamble: Soviet Foreign Policy and the End of the Cold War*, Cambridge 2008, and in Michail Gorbatschow, *Erinnerungen*, Berlin 1995, ch. 3, "Die Moskauer Universität," 67–80.

4 A. V. Zhidchenko, 'Povsednevnaya zhizn studencheskikh obshchezhity novykh rayonov krupnykh gorodov Sibiri v 1950–1960-e gg. (lokalny aspekt)', in *Labirint: Zhurnal sotsialno-gumanitarnykh issledovany* 2/2015, 52–62; see also G. Iu. Miagchenko, *Fenomen kultury povsednevnosti studencheskogo obshchezhitiya*, dissertation, Tambov 2006.

Chapter 30. Tent Cities, World of Barracks:
Finding One's Way in 'Russia in Flux'

1 On the significance of the barracks, see the entry in Natalia Lebina, *Entsiklopediya ba-nalnostey: Sovetskaya povsednevnost—kontury, simvoly, znaki*, St. Petersburg 2006, 54–55; as well as L. V. Belovinsky, *Entsiklopedichesky slovar istorii sovetskoy povsednevnoy zhizni*, Moscow 2015, 47–48.

2 On the life and work of Boris Ruchyov, the Magnitogorsk poet who suffered perse-cution during the Stalin period, see https://ru.wikipedia.org/wiki/Ручьёв,_Борис _Александрович (accessed 21 February 2016).

3 A. I. Mikoyan Meat Processing Plant: http://www.mikoyan.ru/ (accessed 3 June 2017).

4 Yuri Orlov, *Dangerous Thoughts: Memoirs of a Russian Life*, translated by Thomas P. Whit-ney, New York 1991, 72.

5 Alexander Kosarev, Chairman of the Komsomol 1932, cited in Lebina, *Entsiklopediya banalnostey*, 55.

6 On the transition from the barracks settlements to individual homes, see the interview with Yury Bubnov, the architect-in-chief of Nizhny Novgorod, in *Project Russia* 4/2010, 21ff.

7 Lebina, *Entsiklopediya banalnostey*, 55.

Chapter 31. Palm Trees in the Civil War

1 See Walter Benjamin, *Moscow Diary*, edited by Gary Smith, translated by Richard Sieburth, with a preface by Gershom Scholem, Cambridge, MA and London 1986, 83 and 29.

2 Walter Benjamin, *Berlin Childhood around 1900*, translated by Howard Eiland, in *Selected Writings*, vol. 3, Cambridge, MA and London 2002, 346.

3 Siegfried Kracauer, 'Unter Palmen', *Frankfurter Zeitung*, 19 October 1930, in Kracauer, *Werke*, vol. 5.3, *Essays. Feuilletons. Rezensionen*, edited by Inka Mülder-Bach and Ingrid Belke, Berlin 2011, 350–352.

4 Ibid.

5 On the general history of botanical gardens in the USSR, see P. I. Lapin, *Botanicheskie sady SSSR*, Moscow 1984; Peter Hayden and Frances Lincoln, *Russian Parks and Gardens*, London 2005, 65 and 220–223. On the history of the Moscow Botanical Garden, see https://ru .wikipedia.org/wiki/Аптекарский_огород (accessed 3 June 2017); on the history of the Botanical Garden in St. Petersburg, see http://walkspb.ru/sad/botanicheskiy_sad.html (accessed 3 June 2017).

6 Vsevolod Garshin, 'Attalea Princeps', in Garshin, *Short Stories*, translated by Rowland Smith, 2019, 117–124, online at https://www.globalgreyebooks.com/short-stories-vsevolod -garshin-ebook.html (accessed 5 February 2022).

7 Ibid.

8 Ibid.

9 Nikolai Anziferow, *Die Seele Petersburgs*, Munich 2003, 65. This is a clear reference to Heinrich Heine's poem No. 23 from the *Buch der Lieder* of 1822–1823:

> A pine is standing lonely
> In the North on a bare plateau.
> He sleeps; a bright white blanket
> Enshrouds him in ice and snow.
> He's dreaming of a palm tree
> Far away in the Eastern land
> Lonely and silently mourning
> On a sunburnt rocky strand.

Translation by Hal Draper published by Oxford University Press and Suhrkamp/Insel Verlag (1984). I am indebted to Karl-Konrad Tschäpe for pointing this out.

10 Quoted in Richard Buckle, *Diaghilev*, London 1984, 31.

11 Vladimir Nabokov, *Speak, Memory*, London 1969, 196.

12 Catherine Merridale, *Red Fortress*, London 2014, 273.

13 Mikhail Korshunov and Viktoriya Terekhova, *Tayna tayn moskovskikh*, Moscow 1995.

14 Cf. *Spravochnik-Putevoditel*, Moscow 1932, 219.

15 Norman Davies, *Heart of Europe: A Short History of Poland*, Oxford 1984, 389.

16 Svetlana Krymova, 'Zelenaya zhemchuzhina: Kupiv tri veka nazad "Aptekarsky ogorod" za 11 tysach rubley, Moskovsky universitet sdelal ego bestsennym', in *Poisk*, 10 September 2015.

Chapter 33. Ilya Kabakov's Installation: The Toilet as a Civilising Space

1 The Water Museum in St. Petersburg, http://www.vodokanal-museum.ru/ (accessed 3 June 2017); Water Museum in Moscow, http://www.mosvodokanal.ru/about/museum.php (accessed 3 June 2017).

2 Igor Bogdanov, *Unitaz: Ili Kratkaya istoriya tualeta*, Moscow 2007, 5 (see bibliography, 172–176). The following account is based chiefly on this historical sketch. For a review of the Vinzavod exhibition, see Ekaterina Degot, 'O chem grustit v "Tualete" Kabakova', http://os.colta.ru/art/events/details/2785/ (accessed 3 June 2017); A. S. Konchalovsky, *Nizkie istiny*, Moscow 2001.

3 Quoted in Bogdanov, *Unitaz*, 130.

4 Ilya Utekhin, *Ocherki kommunalnogo byta*, 2nd expanded ed., Moscow 2004, 94.

5 Vasile Ernu, 'Oda Sovetskomu tualetu', in Ernu, *Rozhdenny v SSSR*, Moscow 2007, 3.

6 V. I. Lenin, 'The Importance of Gold Now and after the Complete Victory of Socialism', in *Collected Works*, vol. 33, Moscow 1965, 109–116. https://www.marxists.org/archive/lenin/works/1921/nov/05.htm.

7 Quoted by Bogdanov, *Unitaz*, 86.

8 Ibid., 87.

9 Ilya Ilf and Evgeny Petrov, *The Little Golden Calf*, translated by Anne O. Fisher, Moscow 2009, ch. 13.

10 Mihail Zoshchenko, *Izbrannoe v dvukh tomakh*, vol. 1, Leningrad 1982, 170–172.

11 Mikhail Bulgakov, *The Heart of a Dog*, translated by Avril Pyman, Moscow 1990, 20, http://www.arvindguptatoys.com/arvindgupta/29r.pdf (accessed 3 February 2022).

12 Quoted in Bogdanov, *Unitaz*, 100.

13 Ibid., 116.

14 Ibid., 114; see also Ales Adamovich and Daniil Granin, *Blokadnaya kniga*, Leningrad 1989; Lydia Ginzburg, *Notes from the Blockade*, translated by Alan Myers and Angela Livingstone, London 1995 and 2016.

15 Catherine Merridale, *Red Fortress*, London 2014, 336.

16 Ibid., 348.

17 See Oleg Belov in the St. Petersburg *Izvestia* of 24 March 2004.

Chapter 34. The 'Moscow Kitchen', or the Rebirth of Civil Society

1 Andrei Amalrik, *Will the Soviet Union Survive until 1984?*, New York 1970.

2 Dietrich Beyrau, *Intelligenz und Dissens: Die russischen Bildungsschichten in der Sowjetunion 1917 bis 1985*, Göttingen 1993; Wolfgang Eichwede, *Samizdat: Alternative Kultur in Zentral- und Osteuropa. Die 60er bis 80er Jahre*, Bremen 2000.

3 Günter Hirt and Sascha Wonders (eds.), *Kulturpalast: Neue Moskauer Poesie und Aktionskunst*, with audio cassette and collection of index cards, Wuppertal 1984; Hirt and Wonders, *Moskau: Moskau*, videos, Wuppertal 1987; Yuly Kim on Vladimir Vysotsky and Alexander Galich, online at http://www.bards.ru/press/press_show.php?id=1598 (accessed 3 June 2017).

4 Yuly Kim's poem: http://www.bards.ru/archives/part.php?id=19148 (accessed 3 June 2017); the first eight lines were translated by Angela Livingstone.

5 One of the most comprehensive collections of documents on the history of dissident culture is the Archive of the Research Centre for East European Studies of the University of Bremen at https://www.forschungsstelle.uni-bremen.de/ (accessed 3 June 2017).

6 See the interview with Dmitry Prigov et al. on Radio Svoboda at http://www.svoboda.org/a/24200667.html (accessed 3 June 2017).

7 Tikhon Dzyadko and Kuhnya Ginzburga, in *Bolshoy gorod*, online at http://bg.ru/society/kuhnya_ginzburga-9471/ (accessed 3 June 2017).

8 See the series in *Bolshoy gorod*, online at http://bg.ru/series/9379/ (accessed 3 June 2017).

9 Karl Schlögel, 'Moskau: Die Rückkehr des Cafés', in Walter Prigge (ed.), *Städtische Intellektuelle: Urbane Milieus im 20. Jahrhundert*, Frankfurt am Main 1992, 162–181.

10 See, for example, Ludmila Ulitskaya, *The Big Green Tent*, translated by Polly Gannon, New York 2015 [2010], a novel with strong autobiographical overtones.

11 Marusya Ishchenko, 'Kukhnya Mitty', in *Bolshoy gorod*, online at http://bg.ru/society/kuhnya_mitty-9421/ (accessed 3 June 2017).

12 Ulitskaya, *The Big Green Tent*; Hans Magnus Enzensberger's reminiscences of his trips to Russia and the Soviet Union in Enzensberger, *Tumult*, Berlin 2014. There are also memories of visits to Moscow in Wolf Biermann, *Warte nicht auf bessre Zeiten! Die Autobiographie*, Berlin 2016; illuminating are Heinrich Böll and Lew Kopelew, *Briefwechsel*, Göttingen 2011; Raissa Orlowa and Lew Kopelew, *Wir lebten in Moskau*, Munich and Hamburg 1987.

13 Solomon Reyser and M. Aronson, *Literaturnye kruzhki i salony*, Moscow 2001 (1929).

14 Ludmilla Alexeyeva, *The Thaw Generation: Coming of Age in the Post-Stalin Era*, Pittsburgh 1990.

15 Alexander Solzhenitsyn et al., *From Under the Rubble*, translated under the direction of Michael Scammell, London 1975; Karl Schlögel, *Überdetermination und Selbstbestimmung: Die Intelligencija-Diskussion sowjetischer Dissidenten in den 70er Jahren = Berichte des BIOst*, 1982/83.

16 For the literature on dissidents and the civil rights movement, see Beyrau, *Intelligenz und Dissens*.

17 Alexander Nekritsch, *Entsage der Angst: Erinnerungen eines Historikers*, Frankfurt 1983; Roy A. Medvedev, *Let History Judge: The Origin and Consequences of Stalinism*, translated by Colleen Taylor, New York 1971.

18 Nikita Chruschtschow, *Chruschtschow erinnert sich*, Reinbek bei Hamburg 1971; William Taubman, *Khrushchev: The Man and His Era*, London 2005.

19 Petr Vail and Alexander Genis, *60-e: Mir sovetskogo cheloveka*, Ann Arbor 1988.

20 Borys Lewytzkyj, *Politische Opposition in der Sowjetunion 1960–1972: Analyse und Dokumentation*, Munich 1972.

21 See Franco Venturi, *The Roots of Revolution: A History of the Populist and Socialist Movements in 19th Century Russia*, Chicago 2001; Peter Scheibert, *Von Bakunin zu Lenin: Geschichte der russischen revolutionären Ideologien, 1840–1895*, Leiden 1956.

22 An overview of the development of the opposition and the civil rights movement can be found in *Kultura pamyati: Publikatsii na sayte Sakharovskogo tsentra—Soprotivlenie nesvobode v SSSR*: https://www.sakharov-center.ru/node/11682 (accessed 17 May 2022).

23 Petro Grigorenko, *Erinnerungen*, Munich 1981; Grigorenko, *Memoirs*, translated by Thomas P. Whitney, London 1983.

24 Donald M. Thomas, *Alexander Solzhenitsyn: A Century in His Life*, London 1998.

25 Alla Rosenfeld and Norton T. Dodge (eds.), *Nonconformist Art: The Soviet Experience 1956–1986*, New York 1995.

26 Leonid Pljuschtsch, *Im Karneval der Geschichte: Ein Leben als Dissident in der sowjetischen Realität*, Munich 1983; Leonid Plyushch, *History's Carnival: A Dissident's Autobiography*, edited and translated by Marco Carynnyk, London 1979.

27 Karl Schlögel, *Der renitente Held: Arbeiterprotest in der Sowjetunion (1953–1983)*, Hamburg 1984.

28 Andrei Sakharov, *Memoirs*, translated by Richard Lourie, London, Sydney, Auckland and Johannesburg 1990; Elena Bonner, *Alone Together*, translated by Alexander Cook, London 1986; Andrei Sacharow, *Stellungnahme*, Vienna 1974.

29 Lev Gudkov and Boris Dubin, *Intelligentsiya: Zametki o literaturno-politicheskikh illyuziyakh*, Moscow 1995.

30 Contributed by Alessandro Achilli, 4 January 2016, 13:31, https://www.antiwarsongs.org/canzone.php?lang=en&id=5159 (accessed 14 April 2019). The 'Moldau' is the Vltava River in the Czech Republic.

Chapter 35. Gorky Park: A Garden for the New Human Being

1 See the compelling account by Katharina Kucher, *Der Gorki-Park: Freizeitkultur im Stalin-ismus 1928–1941*, Cologne, Weimar and Vienna 2007. Moscow's Gorky Park is the prototype of parks in other towns and cities. See Ye. S. Kochukhova and Ye. I. Rabinovich, 'Kulturno-politichesky kombinat "pod otkrytym nebom": Tsentraly park 1930kh vs klubnye sady 1920kh: sluchay Sverdlovska', in *Labirint: Zhurnal sotsialno-gumanitarnykh issledovany* 2/2015, 6–18.

2 Karl Schlögel, 'Der Zentrale Gor'kij-Kultur- und Erholungspark (CPKiO) in Moskau: Zur Frage des öffentlichen Raums im Stalinismus', in Manfred Hildermeier (ed.), *Stalinismus vor dem Zweiten Weltkrieg: Neue Wege der Forschung*, Munich 1998, 255–274.

3 *Generalny plan rekonstruktsii goroda Moskvy*, Moscow 1936.

4 On exhibition culture, see M. I. Astafieva-Dlugach and Iu. P. Volchok, *Moskva stroitsya*, Moscow 1983, 106–124.

5 Today the park's history can be viewed in the museum of the reconstructed park.

6 L. B. Lunc and S. N. Palentreer, 'Zelenye nasazhdeniya Nyu-yorka', in *Stroitelstvo Moskvy* 10/1937, 17–19.

7 S. Frederick Starr, *Melnikov: Solo Architect in a Mass Society*, Princeton 1978.

8 M. P. Korzhev and M. I. Prokhorova (eds.), *Arkhitektura parkov SSSR*, Moscow 1940; Selim O. Khan-Magomedov, *Pioneers of Soviet Architecture*, edited by Catherine Cooke, translated by Alexander Lieven, London 1987, 514.

9 On the Palace of the Soviets, see Karl Schlögel, 'Im Schatten eines imaginären Turms', in *Moskau lesen*, Berlin 1984, 56–65.

10 Mikhail Zolotonosov, 'Gluptokratoz: Sovetskaya sadovo-parkovaya skulptura 1930-kh godov', in Zolotonosov, *Slovo i Telo: Seksualnye aspekty, universalii, interpretatsii russkogo kulturnogo teksta XIX–XX vekov*, Moscow 1999, 570–765.

11 For a detailed account, see Kucher, *Der Gorki-Park*. The reconstructed park subtly repro-duces this topography.

12 Klaus Mehnert, *Das zweite Volk meines Lebens: Berichte aus der Sowjetunion 1925–1983*, Stuttgart 1986, 89–90.

13 Yuri Orlov, *Dangerous Thoughts: Memoirs of a Russian Life*, translated by Thomas P. Whit-ney, New York 1991, 48.

14 Sheila Fitzpatrick, 'How the Mice Buried the Cat: Scenes from the Great Purges of 1937 in the Russian Provinces', in *Russian Review* 52, 3/1993, 299–320; Michail Bachtin, *Literatur und Karneval: Zur Romantheorie und Lachkultur*, Munich 1969.

15 On festival culture, see Malte Rolf, *Soviet Mass Festivals, 1917–1991*, translated by Cynthia Klahr, Pittsburgh 2013.

16 Wolfgang Leonhard, *Child of the Revolution*, translated by C. M. Woodhouse, London 1979; Markus Wolf, *Die Troika: Geschichte eines nichtgedrehten Films*, Berlin and Weimar 1989.

17 General Ernst Köstring, *Der militärische Mittler zwischen dem Deutschen Reich und der Sowjetunion 1921–1941*, edited by Hermann Teske, Frankfurt am Main 1965, 124–125.

18 Osip Mandelstam, 'After Having Dipped One's Little Finger . . .', from *The Moscow Notebooks*, translated by Richard and Elizabeth McKane, Newcastle upon Tyne 1991, 52.

19 For his photos of Gorky Park, see Henri Cartier-Bresson, *People of Moscow*, London 1955.

20 Filmed in 1983 from the novel *Gorky Park* by Martin Cruz Smith and starring Lee Marvin, William Hurt and Joanna Pacula.

Chapter 36. Diorama: View of a Landscape with Heroes

1 Marie-Louise von Plessen, *Sehnsucht: Das Panorama als Massenunterhaltung des 19. Jahrhunderts*, Frankfurt am Main 1993. Catalogue of the exhibition with the same name in the Kunsthalle Bonn, 28 May to 10 October 1993.

2 Walter Benjamin, 'Panorama', in *The Arcades Project*, translated by Howard Eiland and Kevin McClaughlin, Cambridge, MA and London 1999, 527–536; Stephan Oettermann, *Das Panorama: Die Geschichte eines Massenmediums*, Frankfurt am Main 1980.

3 See 'Diorama' in *Bolshaya sovetskaya entsiklopediya*, vol. 22, Moscow 1935, 487; V. P. Petropavlovsky, *Iskusstvo panoram i dioram*, Kyiv 1965; catalogue of dioramas in the territory of the USSR at https://ru.wikipedia.org/wiki/Диорама (accessed 3 June 2017).

4 Karl D. Qualls, '"Where Each Stone Is History": Travel Guides in Sevastopol after World War II', in Anne E. Gorsuch and Diane P. Koenker (eds.), *Turizm: The Russian and East European Tourist under Capitalism and Socialism*, Ithaca and London 2006, 163–185.

5 *Sovetskaya panoramnaya zhivopis, Sbornik statey*, Leningrad 1965.

6 Ivo Peterson, *Tsentralny muzey Velikoy Otechestvennoy voiny: Karta-putevoditel*, n.p. 2010.

Chapter 37. 'Zhilmassiv', or the Sublime Vistas of the Prefab Mountains

1 Walter Benjamin, *Moscow Diary*, edited by Gary Smith, translated by Richard Sieburth, with a preface by Gershom Scholem, Cambridge, MA and London 1986, 104.

2 Lewis H. Siegelbaum, 'Modernity Unbound: The New Soviet City of the Sixties', in Anne E. Gorsuch and Diane P. Koenker (eds.), *The Socialist Sixties: Crossing Borders in the Second World*, Bloomington 2013, 66–83.

3 Owen Hatherley, *Landscapes of Communism: A History through Buildings*, London 2015.

4 Philipp Meuser, *Die Ästhetik der Platte: Wohnungsbau in der Sowjetunion zwischen Stalin und Glasnost*, Berlin 2015, 707. [A partial translation can be found in Philipp Meuser and Dimitrij Zadorin, *Towards a Typology of Soviet Mass Housing: Prefabrication in the USSR 1955–1991*, Berlin 2015.]

5 Recording of the operetta conducted by Gennadi Rozhdestvensky, Russian State Symphonic Cappella, Residenz-Orchester Den Haag, 1997; film version directed by Gerbert Rappaport, Lenfilm 1962.

6 On Pimenov, see *Yury Ivanovich Pimenov*, Moscow 1986; Leonid Shishkin, *Yury Pimenov: K 11-letiyu so dnya rozhdenia*, Moscow 2013.

7 Quoted by Frank Nienhuysen, 'Wo bin ich?', in *Süddeutsche Zeitung*, 29–30 December 2012, V2/3; Meuser, *Die Ästhetik der Platte*, 33; prefab estates also provide the setting for Krzysztof Kieślowski's film cycle *Dekalog* of 1988/89.

8 M. V. Nashchokina, 'Cheremushki', in S. O. Shmidt, *Moskva entsiklopediya*, Moscow 1997, 894f.

9 Meuser, *Die Ästhetik der Platte*, 217f.

10 Ibid., 281.

11 Ibid., 229.

12 Monica Rüthers, *Moskau bauen von Lenin bis Chruščev: Öffentliche Räume zwischen Utopie, Terror und Alltag*, Vienna, Cologne and Weimar 2007, 236.

13 Meuser, *Die Ästhetik der Platte*, 708.

14 Ibid., 153f.

15 To borrow the title of Sir John Maynard, *Russia in Flux*, New York 1948.

16 Moshe Lewin, *The Soviet Century*, edited by Gregory Elliott, London 2005, 61f., 202.

17 Ibid., 63.

18 Ibid., 69.

19 Ibid., 72.

20 David L. Hoffmann, *Peasant Metropolis: Social Identities in Moscow 1929–1941*, Ithaca and London 1994.

21 Lewin, *The Soviet Century*, 203.

22 Helmut Altrichter, *Russland 1989: Der Untergang des sowjetischen Imperiums*, Munich 2009.

23 Dieter Hoffmann-Axthelm, *Die dritte Stadt: Bausteine eines neuen Gründungsvertrags*, Frankfurt am Main 1993.

Chapter 38. Russkaya Glubinka—the Country beyond the Big Cities

1 Christian Schmidt-Häuer, *Das sind die Russen—Wie sie wurden, wie sie leben*, Hamburg 1980, 44.

2 Tatiana Nefedova, 'Selskaya Rossiya: Prostranstvennoe szhatie i sotsialnaya polyarizatsiya', lecture on 13 May 2010 followed by discussion, online at https://polit.ru/article/2010/08/05/countryside/ (accessed 26 March 2017).

3 Carsten Goehrke, *Russischer Alltag: Eine Geschichte in neun Zeitbildern vom Frühmittelalter bis zur Gegenwart*, vol. 3, *Sowjetische Moderne und Umbruch*, Zurich 2005, 316; Goehrke, *Die Wüstungen in der Moskauer Rus': Studien zur Siedlungs-, Bevölkerungs- und Sozialgeschichte*, Wiesbaden 1968.

4 Tatiana Nefedova, 'Uvidet Rossiyu', reprinted in *Otechestvennye zapiski* 5/2006; Nefedova, *Selskaya Rossiya na pereputie: Geograficheskie ocherki*, Moscow 2003.

5 Vladimir Kagansky, 'Preodolenie sovetskogo prostranstva', lecture on 4 November 2004, in a series of 'Publichnye lektsii', online at https://polit.ru/article/2004/11/11/kagan/ (accessed 26 March 2017).

6 Vladimir Kagansky, 'Neizvestnaia Rossiya', lecture in the Bilingua Club on 19 April 2007, online at http://polit.ru/article/2007/05/04/kaganskiy/ (accessed 17 April 2017); Nefedova, 'Uvidet Rossiyu'; Vyacheslav Glazychev, 'Glubinnaya Rossiya nashikh dney', lecture in the Bilingua Club on 16 September 2004, online at http://polit.ru/article/2004/09/21/glaz/ (accessed 26 March 2017).

7 Tatiana Nefedova, 'Gorodskaya selskaya Rossiya', online at http://www.polit.ru/article/2004/01/13/demoscope141/ (accessed 26 March 2017).

8 Fiona Hill and Clifford G. Gaddy, *The Siberian Curse: How Communist Planners Left Russia Out in the Cold*, Washington, DC 2003.

9 On the problem of impassable roads in spring and autumn, see Nikolai Borisov, *Povsednevnaya zhizn russkogo puteshestvennika v epokhu bezdorozhia*, Moscow 2010.

10 Numerous Russian documentary and feature films about 'Russia off the beaten track' are available on YouTube.

11 Boris Rodoman, 'Rossiya—administrativno-territorialny monstr', lecture on 28 October 2004, online at http://polit.ru/article/2004/11/04/rodoman/ (accessed 3 June 2017).

12 Ye. I. Kirichenko, *Gradostroitelstvo Rossii serediny XIX–nachala XX veka: Stolitsy i provintsiia*, vol. 3, Moscow 2010.

13 Glazychev, 'Glubinnaya Rossiya nashikh dney'; Leonid Smirnyagin, 'Transformatsiya obshchestvennogo prostranstva Rossii', online at http://polit.ru/article/2007/01/08/smirnyagin/ (accessed 26 March 2017), reprinted in *Otechestvennye zapiski* 5/2006.

14 According to the analysis of Eugene M. Kulischer in *Europe on the Move: War and Popu-lation Changes, 1917–1947*, New York 1948.

15 Helmut Altrichter, *Die Bauern von Twer: Vom Leben auf dem russischen Dorf zwischen Revolution und Kollektivierung*, Munich 1984.

16 Stefan Merl, *Bauern unter Stalin: Die Formierung des sowjetischen Kolchossystems 1930–1941*, Berlin 1990.

17 Sheila Fitzpatrick, *Stalin's Peasants: Resistance and Survival in the Russian Village after Collectivization*, New York 1994.

18 J. Arch Getty and Oleg V. Naumov, *The Road to Terror: Stalin and the Self-Destruction of the Bolsheviks, 1932–1939*, New Haven and London 2010.

19 Nefedova, 'Gorodskaya selskaya Rossiya'.

20 Quoted in Glazychev, 'Glubinnaya Rossiya nashikh dney'.

Chapter 39. *Spetskhran*: Catalogue of Forbidden Books

1 Norbert Kunz, 'Die Nationalbibliotheken im ostslawischen Raum und die Entwicklung ihrer Funktion und Aufgaben in der postsowjetischen Ära', in *Berliner Handreichungen zur Bibliotheks- und Informationswissenschaft* 170/2005.

2 Peter Bruhn, 'Glasnost im sowjetischen Bibliothekswesen', in *Zeitschrift für Bibliotheks-wesen und Bibliographie* 36, 4/1989, 360–366; on the experience of foreign researchers in the 1960s, see Sheila Fitzpatrick, *A Spy in the Archives: A Memoir of Cold War Russia*, London 2013.

3 A. P. Shikman, 'Sovershenno nesekretno', in *Sovetskaya bibliografiya* 6/1988, 3–12.

4 S. Dzhimbinov, 'Epitafiya spetskhranu?', in *Novy mir* 5/1990 of 13 March 2002, 243–252, online at http://lib.ru/POLITOLOG/s_specchran.txt_with-big-pictu-res.html (accessed 2 April 2017).

5 N. V. Makhotina, 'Bibliotechnaya tsenzura v Rossii: K istoriografii voprosa', in *Bibliosfera* 1/2010, 61–64; S. F. Varlamova, 'Spetskhran bez tayn', in *Bibliotekar* 12/1988, 24–25.

6 Shikman, 'Sovershenno nesekretno'.

7 M. V. Zelenov, 'Spetskhran i istoricheskaya nauka v sovetskoy Rossii v 1920–1930-e gody', in *Otechestvennaya istoriya*, here 130, online at http://www.opentextnn.ru/censorship/russia/sov/libraries/books/zelenov?id=627 (accessed 3 June 2017).

8 Dzhimbinov, 'Epitafiya spetskhranu?'.

9 Zelenov, 'Spetskhran i istoricheskaya nauka'.

10 Ibid.; M. V. Zelenov, *Bibliotechnye chistki v 1932–1937 gg. v Sovetskoy Rossii*, online at http://www.opentextnn.ru/censorship/russia/sov/libraries/books/zelenov/?id=1218 (accessed 3 July 2017).

11 Zelenov, *Bibliotechnye chistki*.

12 Wolfgang Eichwede, *Samizdat: Alternative Kultur in Zentral- und Osteuropa. Die 60er bis 80er Jahre*, Bremen 2000.

13 Samizdat Archive, collected samizdat documents, Research Department, Radio Liberty, Munich 1973; Samizdat database, Open Society Institut, Budapest, Memorial Moscow, online at http://samizdat.memo.ru/samizdat/introen (accessed 3 July 2017). Samisdat-Katalog der Forschungsstelle Osteuropa der Universität Bremen, archive catalogue at https://www.forschungsstelle.uni-bremen.de (accessed 3 July 2017).

14 For the history of the censorship, see *Istoriya sovetskoy politicheskoy tsenzury: Dokumenty i kommentarii I*, Moscow 1997.

Chapter 40. Diagrams of Progress, Diagrams of Catastrophes

1 E. H. Carr and R. W. Davies, *Foundations of a Planned Economy*, 2 vols., New York 1969; R. W. Davies, *The Socialist Offensive: The Collectivization of Soviet Agriculture 1929–1930*, Cambridge, MA 1980; R. W. Davies, *The Soviet Collective Farm 1929–1930*, Cambridge, MA 1980.

2 Emma Minns, 'Picturing Soviet Progress: Izostat, 1931–4', in Christopher Burke, Eric Kindel and Sue Walker (eds.), *Design and Contexts 1925–1971*, London 2013, 257–281.

3 'Dognat i peregnat v tekhniko-ekonomicheskom otnoshenii peredovye kapitalisticheskie strany v 10 let', Moscow and Leningrad 1931.

4 'The Struggle for Five Years in Four/Profsoyuzy SSSR v borbe za pyatiletku v chetyre goda', Moscow 1932.

5 '15 let Oktyabrya', Moscow 1932.

6 'The Second Five-Year Plan in Construction', Moscow and Leningrad 1934.

7 Otto Neurath, *Gesellschaft und Wirtschaft: Bildstatistisches Elementarwerk*, Vienna 1930.

8 Quoted in Frank Hartmann and Erwin K. Bauer, *Bildersprache: Otto Neurath-Visualisierungen*, Vienna 2002, 43.

9 Neurath, *Gesellschaft und Wirtschaft*, 101.

10 Ibid.

11 Quoted in Hartmann and Bauer, *Bildersprache*, 66.

12 Otto Neurath, *Bildliche Darstellung sozialer Tatbestände*, Vienna 1926, quoted in *Gesammelte bildpädagogische Schriften*, edited by Rudolf Haller and Robin Kinross, Vienna 1991, 6.

13 Ibid.

14 Quoted in Hartmann and Bauer, *Bildersprache*, 79, 14, 26.

15 Ibid., 41.

16 Friedrich Stadler, *Vom Positivismus zur 'Wissenschaftlichen Weltauffassung': Am Beispiel der Wirkungsgeschichte von Ernst Mach in Österreich von 1895–1934*, Vienna and Munich 1982; Stadler, *Studien zum Wiener Kreis: Ursprung, Entwicklung und Wirkung des Logischen Empirismus im Kontext*, Frankfurt am Main 1997; Karl Sigmund, *Sie nannten sich Der Wiener Kreis: Exaktes Denken am Rand des Untergangs*, Wiesbaden 2015.

17 Julia Köstenberger, 'Otto Neurath und die Sowjetunion', in Linda Erker et al. (eds.), *Update! Perspektiven der Zeitgeschichte*, Innsbruck 2012, 101–107.

18 Walter Benjamin, *Moscow Diary*, edited by Gary Smith, translated by Richard Sieburth, with a preface by Gershom Scholem, Cambridge, MA and London 1986, 49–50.

19 Sophie Lissitzky-Küppers, *El Lissitzky: Maler, Architekt, Typograf. Fotograf. Erinnerungen, Briefe, Schriften*, Dresden 1992.

20 Minns, 'Picturing Soviet Progress'.

21 As reported in Gerd Arntz, *Zeit unterm Messer: Holz- & Linolschnitte 1920–1970*, Cologne 1988.

22 Astolphe de Custine, *Russische Schatten: Prophetische Briefe aus dem Jahr 1839*, Nördlingen 1985, 139.

23 Alen Blyum and Martina Mespule, *Byurokraticheskaya anarkhiya: Statistika i vlast pri Staline*, Moscow 2006.

24 Alain Blum, *Naître, vivre et mourir en URSS*, Paris 2004.

25 See Karl Schlögel, 'Blindness and Terror: The Suppressed Census of 1937', in *Moscow, 1937*, translated by Rodney Livingstone, Malden, MA and Cambridge 2012, 109–124.

26 Blum, *Naître, vivre et mourir en URSS*, 89.

854

NOTES TO CHAPTER 41

27 Peter Holquist, *Making War, Forging Revolution: Russia's Continuum of Crisis, 1914–1921*, Cambridge, MA 2002.
28 Manfred Hildermeier, *Geschichte der Sowjetunion 1917–1991: Entstehung und Niedergang des ersten sozialistischen Staates*, Munich 1998.
29 Ibid., 155.
30 Ibid., 389, 498.
31 Ibid., 400.
32 Ibid., 416.
33 E.g., Anton Antonov-Ovseenko, Roy Medvedev, Olga Shchatunovskaya, Dmitry Volkogonov and Robert Conquest. See the survey in Hildermeier, *Geschichte der Sowjetunion 1917–1991*, 454. Significant positions: J. A. Getty, G. T. Rittersporn and V. N. Zemskov, 'Victims of the Soviet Penal System in the Pre-War Years: A First Approach on the Basis of Archival Evidence', in *American Historical Review* 98/1993, 1017–1049, here 1021; S. Rosefield, 'Stalinism in Post-Communist Perspective: New Evidence on Killings, Forced Labour and Economic Growth in the 1930s', in *Europe-Asia Studies* 48/1996, 959–987; Robert Conquest, *The Great Terror*, Oxford 1968; Anne Applebaum, *Gulag: A History*, New York 2003; Stephen G. Wheatcroft, 'On Assessing the Size of Forced Concentration Labour in the Soviet Union, 1992–1956', in *Soviet Studies* 33, 2 /1981, 265–295; Stéphane Courtois (ed.), *The Black Book of Communism: Crimes, Terror, Repression*, translated by Jonathan Murphy and Mark Kramer, Cambridge, MA and London 2000; Nicolas Werth, *L'Ivrogne et la marchande de fleurs: Autopsie d'un meurtre de masse 1937–1938*, Paris 2009.
34 Hildermeier, *Geschichte der Sowjetunion 1917–1991*, 616. The statistics and visual representations in Volkhard Knigge and Irina Scherbakowa (eds.), *GULAG: Spuren und Zeugnisse 1929–1956*, commissioned by Memorial Moscow and the Buchenwald and Mittelbau Dora Memorials Foundation, Weimar 2012, 137–141.

Chapter 41. The Border at Brest—Rites of Passage

1 Quoted by Matthias Heeke, *Reisen zu den Sowjets: Der ausländische Tourismus in Russland 1921–1941—Mit einem bio-bibliographischen Anhang zu 96 deutschen Reiseautoren*, Münster 1999, 153; see also Bernhard Furler, *Augen-Schein: Deutschsprachige Reportagen über Sowjetrussland 1917–1939*, Frankfurt am Main 1987.
2 On the experience of crossing the Soviet-Chinese border, see Sören Urbansky, 'A Very Orderly Friendship: The Sino-Soviet Border under the Alliance Regime, 1950–1960', in *Eurasia Border Review* 3/2012, special issue, 'China's Post-Revolutionary Borders, 1940s–1960s' (ed. David Wolff), 33–52.
3 Eleonory Gilburd, 'Books and Borders: Sergei Obraztsov and Soviet Travels to London in the 1950s', in Anne E. Gorsuch and Diane P. Koenker (eds.), *Turizm: The Russian and East European Tourist under Capitalism and Socialism*, Ithaca and London 2006, 227–247.
4 See *Führer durch die Sowjetunion*, complete edition, revised by A. Radò, edited by Gesellschaft für Kulturverbindung der Sowjetunion mit dem Auslande, Berlin 1928.
5 For the period up to the First World War, see Jan Musekamp, 'From Paris to St. Petersburg and from Kovno to New York: A Cultural History of Transnational Mobility in East Central Europe', PhD dissertation, European University Viadrina, Frankfurt an der Oder 2016.
6 All quoted in Heeke, *Reisen zu den Sowjets*, 150f., 159.
7 Margarete Buber-Neumann, *Under Two Dictators: Prisoner of Stalin and Hitler*, translated by Edward Fitzgerald, London 1949; Alexander Cybulski Weissberg, *Conspiracy of Silence*, translated by Edward Fitzgerald, London 1952.

8 Steven Seegel, *Mapping Europe's Borderlands: Russian Cartography in the Age of Empire*, Chicago 2012; Mark Bassin, *Imperial Visions: Nationalist Imagination and Geographical Expansion in the Russian Far East 1840–1865*, Cambridge 1999.

9 Terry Martin, *The Affirmative Action Empire: Nations and Nationalism in the Soviet Union 1923–1939*, Ithaca 2001; Francine Hirsch, *Empire of Nations: Ethnographic Knowledge and the Making of the Soviet Union*, Ithaca 2005.

10 Aleksandr M. Nekrich, *Punished Peoples: The Deportation and Fate of Soviet Minorities at the End of the Second World War*, New York 1981; Nikolay Bugay, *Deportatsiya narodov v Sovetskom Soyuze*, New York 1996.

11 Emma Widdis, 'Borders: The Aesthetic of Conquest in Soviet Cinema of the 1930s', in *Journal of European Studies* 2000, 401–411.

12 On the philosophy steamer, see V. G. Makarov and V. S. Khristoforov (eds.), *Vysylka vmesto rasstrela: Deportatsiya intelligentsii v dokumentakh VChK-GPU 1921–1923*, Moscow 2005, and the relevant chapter in this volume.

Chapter 42. Choreographies of Power: Parades on Red Square and Elsewhere

1 The following account is based chiefly on *Voennye parady na krasnoy ploshchadi*, 3rd expanded ed., Moscow 1987, as well as Alexey Tarkhanov, 'Parady kak printsip', in Grigory Revzin et al., *Glavny Universalny Magazin: Entsiklopediya*, Moscow 2014, 100–101.

2 See Karl Schlögel, 'Rotes Forum', in *Moskau lesen*, Berlin 1984, 113–122.

3 Paul Scheffer, *Seven Years in Soviet Russia*, translated by Arthur Livingston, London and New York 1931, 179–180.

4 General Ernst Köstring, *Der militärische Mittler zwischen dem Deutschen Reich und der Sowjetunion 1921–1941*, edited by Hermann Teske, Frankfurt am Main 1965, 157.

5 *Voennye parady na krasnoy ploshchadi*, 79.

6 Köstring, *Der militärische Mittler*, 175.

7 These details can be found in Alexey Tarkhanov, 'Parad 7 noyabrya 1941 goda', in Grigory Revzin et al., *Glavny Universalny Magazin: Entsiklopediya*, Moscow 2014, 98–99.

8 Ibid., 99.

9 *Voennye parady na krasnoy ploshchadi*, 113.

10 Grigory Revzin et al., *Glavny Universalny Magazin: Entsiklopediya*, Moscow 2014, 104–105.

Chapter 43. A 'Temple of Modernity': The Crematorium

1 A new periodical has been dedicated to this topic: *Smert v SSSR: Pervy rossiysky nauchny zhurnal o death studies* 2/2016.

2 Philipp Kratz, 'Ernst-Wolfgang Topf, die Firma J. A. Topf & Söhne und die Verdrängung der Schuld in der Nachkriegszeit', in *Zeitschrift für Geschichtswissenschaft* 56/2008, 249–266.

3 D. Mallori, 'Ognennye pochorony', in *Ogonek*, 11 December 1927.

4 Natalia Lebina, '"Obryadnost krasnogo ognennogo pogrebenya" (O sotsiokulturnom kontekste pervogo sovetskogo krematoriya)', in *Teoriya mody* 20/2011, online at https://www.nlobooks.ru/magazines/teoriya_mody/20_tm_2_2011/article/19012/ (accessed 17 May 2022).

5 Ilja Ilf and Jewgeni Petrov, *Das Goldene Kalb oder Die Jagd nach der Million*, Berlin 2013, 60–61.

6 Natalia B. Lebina, *Peterburg sovetsky: 'Novy chelovek' v starom prostranstve*, St. Petersburg 2010, 50.

7 Ibid., 52; M. Shkarovsky, 'Stroitelstvo Petrogradskogo (Leningradskogo) krematoriya kak sredstva borby s religiey', in *Klio* 3/2006, online at http://www.krotov.info/history/20/1920/1920krematory.htm (accessed 4 June 2017).

8 Korney Chukovsky, *Dnevnik (1901–1929)*, Moscow 1991, 153.

9 Lebina, *Peterburg sovetsky*, 96.

10 Yuri Orlov, *Dangerous Thoughts: Memoirs of a Russian Life*, translated by Thomas P. Whitney, New York 1991, 38 and 135.

11 On the crematorium and cemetery, see http://www.pravmir.ru/istoriya-hrama-istoriyaveka (accessed 5 June 2017).

12 On the Donskoy Cemetery and the topography of terror: http://topos.memo.ru/donskoe-kladbishche-novoe (accessed 4 June 2017). Documents on the history of the cemetery/crematorium can be found at the same website. Yevgeniya Albats, 'Palachi i zhertvy', in *Novoe vremya*, 30 October 2014, no. 29 (340) of 14 September 2014, and https://newtimes.ru/stati/temyi/palachi-i-zhertvyi.html (accessed 5 June 2017).

13 On Blokhin, see https://ru.wikipedia.org/wiki/Блохин,_Василий_Михайлович_(чекист) (accessed 5 June 2017).

14 Arseny Roginsky and Yevgeniya Albats on the topography of terror and Donskoy Cemetery online at http://topos.memo.ru/donskoe-kladbishche-novoe (accessed 4 June 2017); Albats, 'Palachi i zhertvy', online at https://newtimes.ru/stati/others/archive-63663-palachi-u-hertvi.html (accessed 20 April 2017). Raoul Wallenberg's ashes too are said to lie in one of the mass graves; see Pawel Anatoljewitsch Sudoplatow and Anatolij Sudoplatow, *Der Handlanger der Macht: Enthüllungen eines KGB-Generals*, Düsseldorf 1994, 303.

Chapter 44. ZAGS, or the Rituals of Everyday Life

1 Barbara Stollberg-Rilinger, *Rituale*, Frankfurt and New York, 2013, 9.

2 Vladimir V. Mayakovsky, 'Stikhi o sovetskom pasporte', in *Sochineniya v odnom tome*, Moscow 1940, 261f.

3 Fannina W. Halle, *Die Frau in Sowjet-Russland*, Berlin, Vienna and Leipzig 1932. [*Woman in Soviet Russia*, translated by Margaret M. Green, New York 1933.]

4 As a response to the problem of millions of orphan children, see Anton S. Makarenko, *Der Weg ins Leben: Ein pädagogisches Poem*, Berlin 1971.

5 Barbara Evans Clements, 'The Birth of the New Soviet Woman', in Abbott Gleason, Peter Kenez and Richard Stites (eds.), *Bolshevik Culture*, Bloomington 1989, 220–237; Richard Stites, *The Women's Liberation Movement in Russia: Feminisms, Nihilism and Bolshevism, 1860–1930*, Princeton 1991; Catriona Kelly and David Shepherd (eds.), *Constructing Russian Culture in the Age of Revolution: 1881–1940*, Oxford 1998. ['The satisfaction of one's sexual desires should be as simple as getting a glass of water', often attributed to Alexandra Kollontay.]

6 Christel Lane, *The Rites of Rulers: Ritual in Industrial Society—The Soviet Case*, Cambridge 1981, 25.

7 Ibid., 71.

8 Alla Salnikova, *Istoriya yelochnoy igrushki, ili kak naryazhali sovetskuyu elku*, Moscow 2012.

Chapter 45. Queues as a Soviet Chronotope

1 Yelena Alexandrovna Osokina, *Proshchalnaya oda sovetskoy ocheredi*, online at https://magazines.gorky.media/nz/2005/5/proshhalnaya-oda-sovetskoj-ocheredi.html (accessed 17 May 2022); Osokina, *Our Daily Bread: Socialist Distribution and the Art of Survival in Stalin's Russia, 1927–1941*, translated by Kate Transchel and Greta Bucher, Armonk and London 2001.

2 Osokina, *Proshchalnaya oda sovetskoy ocheredi*.

3 See the article 'Ochered' in Andrey Lebedev (ed.), *Vita Sovietica: Neakademichesky slovar-inventar sovetskoy tsivilizatsii*, Ulyanovsk 2012, 160.

4 Ibid., 161f.

5 Ilya Utekhin, *Ocherki kommunalnogo byta*, 2nd expanded ed., Moscow 2004, 65.

6 Ibid., 200, 203.

7 Ibid., 204.

8 Vladimir Sorokin, *The Queue*, translated by Sally Laird, New York 2008.

9 Ibid., 3f.

10 The following account is taken from Osokina, *Our Daily Bread*.

11 Ibid., 187.

12 Ibid., 188.

13 Ibid., 187.

14 Ibid., 190.

15 Ibid., 193.

16 Anna Akhmatova, *Requiem and Poem without a Hero*, translated by D. M. Thomas, London 1976, 23. [Quatrain translated by Robin Kemball.]

17 *Tagebuch aus Moskau*, edited by Jochen Hellbeck, Munich 1996, 251.

18 Ibid., 242.

19 Ibid., 249.

20 Lydia Ginzburg, *Notes from the Blockade*, translated by Alan Myers and Angela Livingstone, London 1995 and 2016, 42f.

21 Ibid., 43, 39f.

22 Ibid., 38f, 40f.

23 A. Anatoli (Kuznetsov), *Babi Yar*, translated by David Floyd, London 1970, 252–253.

24 János Kornai, *Economics of Shortage*, vol. A., Amsterdam, New York and Oxford 1980, ch. 4, 'The Buyer: Shopping Process', 65–81, here 65.

25 Alexander Erlich, *Die Industrialisierungsdebatte in der Sowjetunion 1924–1928*, Frankfurt am Main 1991; Leo N. Kritzmann, *Die heroische Periode der großen russischen Revolution*, Frankfurt am Main 1971; Jewgenij A. Preobraženskij, *Die neue Ökonomik*, Berlin 1971 (1926); Jewsej G. Liberman, *Methoden der Wirtschaftslenkung im Sozialismus: Ein Versuch über die Stimulierung der gesellschaftlichen Produktion*, Frankfurt am Main 1974; Joseph Stalin, *The Economic Problems of Socialism in the USSR*, Peking 1972 (1951).

26 Osokina, *Proshchalnaya oda sovetskoy ocheredi*.

Chapter 46. 'Think of the Parties We Had . . .'

1 Malte Rolf, *Soviet Mass Festivals, 1917–1991*, translated by Cynthia Klahr, Pittsburgh 2013; Irina Sapozhnikova, 'Prazdniki i parady', in A. Golosovskaya and V. Zuseva (eds.), *Sovetsky stil. Vremya i veshchi: Ukrasheniya, moda, prazdniki, belye, eda, upakovka, dengi, dacha, igrushki, parfyumeriya, mebel, farfor*, Moscow 2012, 120–135; A. I. Mazaev, *Prazdnik kak*

sotsialno-khudozhestvennoe yavlenie, Moscow 1978; V. P. Tolstoy (ed.), *Agitatsionno-massovoe iskusstvo: Oformlenie prazdnestv*, Moscow 1984.

2 Rolf, *Soviet Mass Festivals*, 31.

3 Karl Schlögel, *Petersburg: Das Laboratorium der Moderne 1909–1921*, Munich 2002, 453–504.

4 Orlando Figes and Boris Kolonitskii, *Interpreting the Russian Revolution: The Language and Symbols of 1917*, New Haven 1999.

5 See the illustrations in the two-volume edition of Tolstoy, *Agitatsionno-massovoe iskussvto*.

6 Rolf, *Soviet Mass Festivals*, 90.

7 Ibid., 56.

8 Nathan Leites and Elsa Bernaut, *Ritual of Liquidation: The Case of the Moscow Trials*, Glencoe 1954.

9 Rolf, *Soviet Mass Festivals*, 58.

10 Ibid., 44–58.

11 Thomas Schmidt, *Kalender und Gedächtnis: Erinnern im Rhythmus der Zeit*, Göttingen 2000.

12 Richard S. Wortman, *Scenarios of Power, Myth and Ceremony in Russian Monarchy: From Peter the Great to the Abdication of Nicholas II*, Princeton 2006.

13 See 'Prazdniki', in *Entsiklopedichesky slovar Brokgauz-Efron*, vol. 24, St. Petersburg 1898, 940–942; 'Kalendar', in *Bolshaya sovetskaya entsiklopediya*, vol. 30, Moscow 1937, 691–693; N. Idelson, *Istoriya kalendarya*, Leningrad 1925.

14 Richard Stites, *Revolutionary Dreams: Utopian Vision and Experimental Life in the Russian Revolution*, New York 1989; Melanie Tatur, '"Wissenschaftliche Arbeitsorganisation": Zur Rezeption des Taylorismus in der Sowjetunion', in *Jahrbücher für Geschichte Osteuropas, Neue Folge*, 25, 1/1977, 34–51.

15 Rolf, *Soviet Mass Festivals*, 75.

16 Alla Salnikova, *Istoriya elochnoy igrushki, ili kak naryazhali sovetskuyu elku*, Moscow 2012, 201.

17 Rolf, *Soviet Mass Festivals*, 193.

Chapter 47. *Fizkultura*: Soviets as Athletes

1 André Gide, *Back from the USSR*, translated by Dorothy Bussy, London 1937, 25.

2 Jelena Bulgakowa, *Margarita und der Meister: Tagebücher, Erinnerungen*, Berlin 1993, 203.

3 Joseph E. Davies, *Mission to Moscow*, London 1942, 119–120.

4 Grigory Revzin, 'Parady fizkulturnikov', in Revzin et al., *Glavny Universalny Magazin: Entsiklopediya*, Moscow 2014, 87.

5 Valeriya Selunskaya and Maria Zezina, 'Documentary Film—a Soviet Source for Soviet Historians', in Richard Taylor and Derek Spring (eds.), *Stalinism and Soviet Cinema*, London and New York 1993, 171–185, here 180. *Happy Youth* can be viewed at https://www.youtube.com/watch?v=5bpN1pRA2Fw (accessed 6 June 2017).

6 Medvedkin's film can be seen at https://www.youtube.com/watch?v=xtMSvRuSkTE (accessed 6 June 2017).

7 Johan Huizinga, *Homo Ludens: A Study of the Play Element in Culture*, London 1970; Helmuth Plessner, 'Die Funktion des Sports in der industriellen Gesellschaft', in Plessner et al. (eds), *Schriften zur Soziologie und Sozialphilosophie*, Frankfurt am Main 1985, 147–166; Hans-Ulrich Gumbrecht, *Lob des Sports*, Frankfurt am Main 2005.

8 Mike O'Mahony, *Sport in the USSR: Physical Culture—Visual Culture*, London 2006.

9 On the history of sport in the Russian Empire and the Soviet Union, see Henry Morton, *Soviet Sport: Mirror of Soviet Society*, New York 1963; James Riordan, *Sport in Soviet Society*,

Cambridge 1977; Robert Edelman, *Serious Fun: A History of Spectator Sports in the USSR*, Oxford 1993.

10 Nikolay Gavrilovich Chernyshevsky, *What Is to Be Done? Tales about New People*, original translation by Benjamin R. Tucker, expanded by Cathy Porter, London 1982.

11 Quoted by O'Mahony, *Sport in the USSR*, 83.

12 Ibid., 84.

13 Ibid., 85; Nikolay Starostin, 'Futbol na Krasnoy ploshchadi', in Grigory Revzin et al., *Glavny Universalny Magazin: Entsiklopediya*, Moscow 2014, 94–95.

14 David L. Hoffmann, 'Bodies of Knowledge: Physical Culture and the New Soviet Man', in Igal Halfin (ed.), *Language and Revolution: Making Modern Political Identities*, London and Portland 2002, 269–286.

15 O'Mahony, *Sport in the USSR*, 48.

16 I. Barshova and K. Sazonova, *Alexander Nikolaevich Samokhvalov*, Leningrad 1963; Matthew Cullerne Bown and Brandon Taylor (eds.), *Art of the Soviets: Painting, Sculpture and Architecture in a One-Party State, 1917–1992*, Manchester 1993; Alessandro De Magistris, *Aleksandr Deineka (1899–1969): An Avant-Garde for the Proletariat*, Madrid 2011.

17 O'Mahony, *Sport in the USSR*, 145; Kerstin Holm, 'Die Superproletarier aus Stahl und Beton', in *Frankfurter Allgemeine Zeitung*, 3 November 2007, no. 256, 46.

18 Quoted by O'Mahony, *Sport in the USSR*, 70.

19 Bernice Glatzer Rosenthal, *Nietzsche and Soviet Culture: Ally and Adversary*, Cambridge 1994.

20 Hans Günther, *Der sozialistische Übermensch: Maksim Gor'kij und der sowjetische Heldenmythos*, Stuttgart and Weimar 1993; see also Alexander Izgojew's contribution to a volume that appeared originally in 1909, *Wegzeichen: Zur Krise der russischen Intelligenz*, Frankfurt am Main 1990, 176–211, in which 'mens sana in corpore sano' of the kind found in American colleges is presented as an educational ideal.

21 Deyneka, 'Oborona Sevastopolya', http://img-fotki.yandex.ru/get/4402/mazanov2005.13/0_48aa2_e6310598_XL (accessed 4 June 2017).

22 DOSAAF: Dobrovolnoe obshchestvo sodeystviya armii, aviatsii i flotu (Volunteer Organisation for the Advancement of Army, Airforce and Navy). OSOAVIAKhIM: Obshchestvo sodeystviya oborone aviatsionnomu i khimicheskomu stroitelstvu (Association for the Advancement of Defence, Aviation and Chemistry).

23 For the fate of invalids and the seriously injured on the Isle of Valaam, see the collection of materials *Istorii invalidov VOV, kotorykh soslali na Valaam za 'ubogy vid'*, online at https://newtambov.ru/best/dedy-voevali-govorite-smotrite-chto-oni-poluchili-ot-vlasti/ (accessed 4 June 2017).

24 On the body awareness of Soviet men after the war—analysed with reference to the works of Alexander Tvardovsky, Eldar Ryazanov, Vladimir Vysotsky and Vasily Shukshin—see Ethan Pollock, 'Real Men Go to the Bania', in *Kritika: Explorations in Russian and Eurasian History* 11, 1/2010 (new series), 46–76.

Chapter 48. Clothes for the New Human Being, or Christian Dior's Return to Red Square

1 For photos of Dior in Moscow, see 'Dior Models in Moscow, 1959: Photos by Howard Sochurek', https://www.youtube.com/watch?v=8ShdjjAYlJI (accessed 17 May 2022); http://fishki.net/40155-christian-dior-v-moskve-1959-god-30-foto.html (accessed 6 June 2017).

2 See the pictures in *Life* and reports from contemporary eyewitnesses such as Alexander Vasiliev, 'Vechno v mode', online at http://www.istpravda.ru/digest/1633/ (accessed 6 June 2017).

3 Quoted from Daria Yermilova, 'Sovetskaya moda', in A. Golosovskaya and V. Zuseva (eds.), *Sovetsky stil. Vremya i veshchi: Ukrasheniya, moda, prazdniki, belie, eda, upakovka, dengi, dacha, igrushki, parfiumeriya, mebel, farfor*, Moscow 2012, 10–37. On the Moscow visit, see F. M. Pochna, *Kristian Dior*, Moscow 1998, 23.

4 The most important studies of Soviet fashion are Tatiana Strizhenova, *Soviet Costume and Textiles 1917–1945*, Moscow, Paris and Verona 1991; Elena Huber, *Mode in der Sowjetunion 1917–1953*, Wien 2011; Djurdja Bartlett, *Fashion East: The Spectre That Haunted Socialism*, Cambridge, MA 2010; Sergey Zhuravlev and Iukka Gronov, *Moda po planu: Istoriya mody i modelirovaniya odezhdy v SSSR 1917–1991*, Moscow 2013 (bibliography 486–494).

5 Walter Benjamin, *The Arcades Project*, translated by Howard Eiland and Kevin McLaughlin, Cambridge, MA and London 1999, Convolute B, Fashion, 62–81, here 71.

6 Ibid., 63–64.

7 Alexander Vasiliev, *Russkaya moda*, Moscow 2004.

8 Cited in Huber, *Mode in der Sowjetunion*, 66.

9 Jane Pritchard (ed.), *Diaghilev and the Golden Age of the Ballets Russes 1909–1929*, London 2010.

10 Karl Schlögel, *Das russische Berlin: Ostbahnhof Europas*, Munich 2007, 128.

11 Yermilova, 'Sovetskaya moda', 13.

12 Alexander Vasiliev, *Krasota v izgnanii: Tvorchestvo russkikh emigrantov pervoy volny—iskusstvo i moda*, Moscow 1998.

13 Viktoriya Sevryukova, 'Sovetskoe belie', in A. Golosovskaya and V. Zuseva (eds.), *Sovetsky stil. Vremya i veshchi: Ukrasheniya, moda, prazdniki, belie, eda, upakovka, dengi, dacha, igrushki, parfiumeriya, mebel, farfor*, Moscow 2012, 38–51, here 42.

14 Irina Sirotkina, 'Fokstrot i moda v Sovetskom Soyuze', in *Intelros* 29/2013.

15 On fashion relations between East and West, see Strizhenova, *Soviet Costume*; Bartlett, *Fashion East*.

16 Quoted by Huber, *Mode in der Sowjetunion*, 31.

17 Yermilova, 'Sovetskaya moda', 17.

18 Strizhenova, *Soviet Costume*, documents on 309–311, here 309; originally in *Krasnaya niva* 30/1923, 32.

19 *Krasnaya niva* 27/1924, 662–663, quoted by Strizhenova, *Soviet Costume*, 310.

20 Quoted by Strizhenova, *Soviet Costume*, 310f.

21 Ada Raev, 'Zwischen konstruktivistischer "Prozodezhda" und extravaganter Robe—russische Avantgardistinnen als Modegestalterinnen', in *Frauen Kunst Wissenschaft*, 17 May 1994, 41–52; on Schiaparelli's visit, see Dilys E. Blum, *Shocking! The Art and Fashion of Elsa Schiaparelli*, catalogue of the exhibition with the same title, New Haven and London 2003.

22 Bartlett, *Fashion East*, 172.

23 Ibid., 84.

24 Ibid., 87.

25 Cited in Bartlett, *Fashion East*, 70.

26 Vasiliev, 'Vechno v mode'; especially T. Strizhenova, 'Nadezhda Petrovna Lamanova', in *Dekorativnoe iskusstvo* 6/1966, 16–20.

27 For information about her life, see Strizhenova, *Soviet Costume*; Raev, 'Zwischen konstruktivistischer "Prozodezda" und extravaganter Robe'.

28 Strizhenova, *Soviet Costume*, 95.

29 Quoted by Bartlett, *Fashion East*, 187.

30 Zhuravlev and Gronov, *Moda po planu*, 409–460.

31 Masha Lipman, 'Fade to Red? Style in the Land of Anti-Style', in *The New Yorker*, 21 September 1998, 106–113.

Chapter 49. Manly Grace: Nureyev's Gesture

1 See entries on ballet in *Entsiklopedichesky slovar Brokgauz-Efron*, vol. 4, St. Petersburg 1891, 797–800; and in *Bolshaya sovetskaya entsiklopediya*, vol. 4, Moscow 1926, 492–496.

2 From the rich literature on this subject, we mention only Richard Buckle, *Nijinsky*, London 1971; Buckle, *Diaghilev*, London 1984; Jane Pritchard (ed.), *Diaghilev and the Golden Age of the Ballets Russes 1909–1929*, London 2010; Lynn Garafola, *Diaghilev's Ballets Russes*, Oxford 1989. For an always perceptive observer and analyst of the Ballets Russes, see Count Harry Kessler, *The Diaries of a Cosmopolitan 1918–1937*, translated by Charles Kessler, London 2000; Harry Graf Kessler, *Das Tagebuch 1880–1937*, Stuttgart 2004; *Dyagilev i ego epoha*, St. Petersburg 2001.

3 The following account is based on Peter Watson, *Nureyev: A Biography*, London, Sydney and Auckland 1994; Julie Kavanagh, *Rudolf Nureyev: The Life*, London 2007; Elena Oboimina, *Rudolf Nureev: Ia umru polubogom*, Moscow 2016.

4 Andrea Amort (ed.), *Nurejew und Wien: Ein leidenschaftliches Verhältnis*, exhibition catalogue, Vienna 2003.

5 Vera S. Kostrowitzkaja, *Schule des Klassischen Tanzes: Die Waganowa-Methode in der Praxis*, translated by Ursula Kirsten-Collein, Berlin 2003. [New English edition: V. S. Kostrovitskaya and Alexei Pisarev, *School of Classical Dance: Textbook of the Vaganova Choreographic School*, translated by John Barker, London 1995.]

6 Ursula Kirsten-Collein, afterword to Kostrowitzkaja, *Schule des Klassischen Tanzes*, 312–318, here 312.

7 Ibid.

8 Kostrovitskaya and Pisarev, *School of Classical Dance*, 62f.

9 See the chapter on shared apartments, the kommunalka, in this volume.

10 This account follows that of Lynn Garafola, 'Introduction: Agrippina Vaganova and Her Times', in Vera Krasovskaya, *Vaganova: A Dance Journey from Petersburg to Leningrad*, translated by Vera Siegel, Gainesville 2005, xi–xxxvi.

11 See the diaries of the faithful chronicler of this transitional phase, Alexander N. Benua (Benois), *Moi vospominaniya (v dvukh tomakh)*, Moscow 2005; Benua (Benois), *Dnevnik 1916–1918 godov, Dnevnik 1918–1924 godov*, Moscow 2010.

12 Garafola, 'Introduction', xxi–xxviii and xxx.

13 Ibid., xxxi.

14 Krasovskaya, *Vaganova*, 255.

XI. Kolyma: The Pole of Cold

1 See the report by the Conference at the German Historical Institute in February 2012: Natalia Gadalova, 'Moroz, led i sneg: Kholodny klimat i russkaya istoriya', online at http://magazines.russ.ru/nlo/2013/119/g44.html (accessed 4 June 2017).

2 Photo documentations by Sergey Khalansky, *Kreshchennye adom*, Magadan 2003; Tomasz Kizny, *Gulag*, with prefaces by Norman Davies, Jorge Semprun and Sergey Kovalev, translated by Antonia Lloyd-Jones, Buffalo, NY and Richmond Hill, Ontario 2004.

3 For the literature on Kolyma and Dalstroy, see especially A. G. Kozlov (ed.), *Magadan: Konspekt proshlogo. Gody. Lyudi. Problemy*, Magadan 1989; I. D. Batsaev and A. G. Kozlov, *Dalstroy i Sevvostlag OGPU-NKVD SSSR v tsifrakh i dokumentakh*, vol. 2 (1941–1945), Magadan 2002; Jacques Rossi, *The Gulag Handbook: A Historical Dictionary of Soviet Penitentiary Institutions and Terms Related to the Forced Labour Camps*, with a preface by Alain Besançon, London 1987 (Rossi, *Spravochnik po GULAGu*, 2 vols., London 1987); Ivan Panikarov, 'Kolyma: Daten und Fakten', in *Osteuropa* 6/2007, 267–283; Mirjam Sprau, 'Gold und Zwangsarbeit: Der Lagerkomplex Dal'stroj', in *Osteuropa* 2/2008, 65–79; David Nordlander, 'Magadan and Economic History of Dalstroi in the 1930s', in Paul R. Gregory and Valery Lazarev (eds.), *The Economics of Forced Labor: The Soviet Gulag*, Stanford 2003, 105–125.

4 Eugenia Ginzburg, *Into the Whirlwind*, translated by Paul Stevenson and Manya Harari, London 1967; Ginzburg, *Within the Whirlwind*, translated by Ian Boland, introduction by Heinrich Böll, New York and London 1981. Other, highly informative reports have been written by Michael Solomon, *Magadan*, Princeton 1971; Elinor Lipper, *Eleven Years in Soviet Prison Camps*, translated by Richard and Clara Winston, London 1951; Trude Richter, *Totgesagt: Erinnerungen mit Nachbemerkungen von Elisabeth Schulz-Semrau und Helmut Richter*, Halle and Leipzig 1990, especially the section 'Death and Resurrection', 290–456.

5 Ginzburg, *Within the Whirlwind*, 35.

6 Ibid., 35–37.

7 The research embarking on this hitherto uncharted territory focuses on the problem not of cold but of hunger. See Golfo Alexopoulos, *Illness and Inhumanity in Stalin's Gulag*, New Haven 2017; Alexopoulos, 'Medical Research in Stalin's Gulag', in *Bulletin of the History of Medicine* 90, 3/2016; and Alexopoulos, 'Medicine and Mortality in the Gulag', https://www.youtube.com/watch?v=TwUgqHthjTs (accessed 17 May 2022).

8 Michael Balter, 'How to Survive a Siberian Winter', *Science*, 28 January 2013, online at https://www.science.org/content/article/how-survive-siberian-winter (accessed 10 March 2020); Mark Lawrence, 'How to Survive in Extreme Conditions—Siberia', online at https://secretsofsurvival.com/true-story-of-survival-the-way-back-siberia/#Upvrve%20eMFhTm3Lhc.99 (accessed 21 April 2017).

9 Galya Diment and Yuri Slezkine (eds.), *Between Heaven and Hell: The Myth of Siberia in Russian Culture*, New York 1993; Yuri Slezkine, *Arctic Mirrors: Russia and the Small Peoples of the North*, Ithaca 1994; Iwan Papanin, *Eis und Flamme: Erinnerungen*, Berlin 1981; John McCannon, *Red Arctic: Polar Exploration and the Myth of the North in the Soviet Union, 1932–1939*, New York and Oxford 1998; Karl Schlögel, 'Year of Adventures, 1937: A Soviet Icarus', in Schlögel, *Moscow, 1937*, translated by Rodney Livingstone, Malden, MA and Cambridge 2012, 294–313.

10 Sergei Bushmanov, Сергей Бушман, https://www.fresher.ru/2012/10/16/kakovo-eto-provesti-zimu-na-polyarnoi-stantsii-vostok/ (accessed 17 May 2022).

11 See, for example, the study by Nikolay Romanovich Deryapa, *Priroda antarktiki i akklimatizatsiya cheloveka*, Leningrad 1965.

12 See the summaries in N. R. Deryapa and I. F. Ryabinin, *Adaptatsiya cheloveka v polyarnykh rayonakh zemli*, Moscow 1977, 4; V. I. Korolev, *Klimaticheskaya adaptatsiya*, St. Petersburg 1998; A. V. Agafonov, *Temperatura okruzhayushchey sredy i zdorovie*, Alma-Ata 1983; *Diagnostika adaptatsionnykh i patologicheskikh reaktsiy cheloveka v usloviyakh severa (metodicheskie rekomendatsii)*, Moscow 1987.

13 V. P. Kaznacheev and N. R. Deryapa, 'Aktualnye voprosy adaptatsii i sistemy zhizneobespecheniya cheloveka v Antarktide', in *Adaptatsiya cheloveka v osobykh usloviyakh obitaniya: Trudy ordena Lenina arkticheskogo i antarkticheskogo nauchno-issledovatelskogo instituta*, vol. 356, Leningrad 1978, 5–10, here 9.

14 Varlam Shalamov, *Kolyma Stories*, translated by Donald Rayfield, New York 2018, xv.

15 Warlam Schalamow, *Wischera: Antiroman*, translated from Russian into German by Gabriele Leupold, Berlin 2016; Wilfried F. Schoeller, *Leben oder Schreiben: Der Erzähler Warlam Schalamow* (companion volume to the Literaturhaus exhibition), Berlin 2013; Manfred Sapper and Volker Weichsel (eds.), *Das Lager schreiben: Varlam Šalamov und die Aufarbeitung des Gulag*, Berlin 2007.

16 Richter, *Totgesagt*, 419.

17 Varlam Shalamov, 'On Prose', in *Late and Post Soviet Russian Literature: A Reader*, vol. 2, edited by Mark Lipovetsky and Lisa Wakamiya, translated by Brian R. Johnson, Brookline 2015, 125–126.

18 Varlam Shalamov, 'The Life of Engineer Kipreyev', in *Sketches of the Criminal World*, translated by Donald Rayfield, New York 2020, 184.

19 Shalamov, 'The Glove', in *Sketches of the Criminal World*, 331.

20 Shalamov, 'On Prose', 116.

21 Shalamov, 'The Geneticist', in *Kolyma Stories*, 599.

22 Shalamov, 'On Prose', 118.

23 Primo Levi with Leonardo de Benedetti, *Auschwitz Report*, edited by Robert S. C. Gordon, translated by Judith Woolf, London 2006, especially 29–78.

24 Anne Applebaum, *Gulag: A History*, New York 2003, 214.

25 Shalamov, 'The Tatar Mullah and Clean Air', in *Kolyma Stories*, 104.

26 'The most dangerous period in the north was between March and June, when the glare from the melting snow was blinding'; Solomon, *Magadan*, 116.

27 Shalamov, 'Carpenters', in *Kolyma Stories*, 14–18.

28 Shalamov, 'The Tatar Mullah and Clean Air', 105.

29 Alexopoulos, *Illness and Inhumanity in Stalin's Gulag*; Alexopoulos, 'Medical Research in Stalin's Gulag'; Robert Jay Lifton, *The Nazi Doctors: Medical Killing and the Psychology of Genocide*, London 1986; Primo Levi, *If This Is a Man* and *The Truce*, with an afterword by the author, translated by Stuart Woolf, London 1979.

30 Shalamov, 'Rain' and 'The Snake Charmer', in *Kolyma Stories*, 28–29, 94.

31 Shalamov, 'The Tatar Mullah and Clean Air', 100.

32 Shalamov, 'The Green Prosecutor', in *Kolyma Stories*, 643–644.

33 Shalamov, 'On Lend-Lease', in *Kolyma Stories*, 433.

34 Oleg V. Khlevniuk, *The History of the Gulag: From Collectivization to the Great Terror*, New Haven 2004, 171.

35 Shalamov, 'How It Began', in *Kolyma Stories*, 467.

36 Applebaum, *Gulag*, 518.

37 A. I. Kokurin and Yu. N. Morukov, *Stalinskie stroiki GULAGa 1930–1953*, Moscow 2005, 369–520 (ch. 3: 'Gold Extraction on the Kolyma'); Nordlander, 'Magadan and Economic History of Dalstroi in the 1930s', 114; for the most precise overview, see M. B. Smirnov (ed.), *Sistema ispravnitelno-trudovykh lagerey v SSSR, 1923–1960: Spravochnik*, Moscow 1998; Batsaev and Kozlov, *Dalstroy i Sevvostlag OGPU-NKVD SSSR*, vols. 1 (1931–1941) and 2 (1941–1945); Kozlov, *Magadan*.

38 Applebaum, *Gulag*, 99. See also the section on big data in the present volume.

39 A photograph of the spacious wood building can be seen in the illustration section of Kozlov, *Magadan*.

40 This account is based on Batsaev and Kozlov, *Dalstroy i Sevvostlag OGPU-NKVD SSSR*; Kizny, *Gulag*; and Schalamow, *Wischera*; a positive assessment of Berzin can be found in Kozlov, *Magadan*, 32ff.

41 Schalamow, *Wischera*.

42 Kizny, *Gulag*, 300–301.

43 Quoted by Kizny, *Gulag*, 301; see also Trude Richter's memoirs on the thinking in the Gorky House of Culture in Magadan; M. M. Korallov (ed.), *'Teatr GULAGa', Sbornik vospominany*, Moscow 1995.

44 For Tamarin, see Schalamow, *Wischera*, and the biographies of the Kolyma personnel in Batsaev and Kozlov, *Dalstroi i Sevvostlag OGPU-NKVD SSSR*, vols. 1 and 2.

45 Shalamov, 'The Lawyers' Conspiracy', in *Kolyma Stories*, 188–189.

46 Shalamov, 'By the Stirrup', in *Sketches of the Criminal World*, 275f.

47 Ginzburg, *Within the Whirlwind*, 201. Playing the piano as the saving grace for the shipwrecked is also found in Richter, *Totgesagt*, 366ff.

48 Ginzburg, *Within the Whirlwind*, 205.

49 All included among the illustration section in Kozlov, *Magadan*.

50 Batsaev and Kozlov, *Dalstroi i Sevvostlag OGPU-NKVD SSSR*, vols. 1 and 2.

51 Alexander Etkind, *Internal Colonization: Russia's Imperial Experience*, Cambridge 2011.

52 Quoted by Nordlander, 'Magadan and Economic History of Dalstroi in the 1930s', 107.

53 Khlevniuk, *The History of the Gulag*, 107; Alexei Yarotsky, *Zolotaya Kolyma*, 2003, online at https://shalamov.ru/authors/89.html (accessed 4 June 2017); M. V. Kurman, 'Vospominanya', in *Cahiers du Monde russe et soviétique* 34, 4/1993, 589–630.

54 Nordlander, 'Magadan and Economic History of Dalstroi in the 1930s', 109f.

55 Ibid., 117.

56 Ibid., 120.

57 A sense of the process of the gradual disintegration of Dalstroy together with an appreciation of the uprising in remote Norilsk can be found in Solomon, *Magadan*, chs. 14–18.

58 Fiona Hill and Clifford G. Gaddy, *The Siberian Curse: How Communist Planners Left Russia Out in the Cold*, Washington, DC 2003; for a critical view of this, see Leonid A. Bezrukov, 'Sibirsky kholod i ekonomika Rossii', in *Journal of Institutional Studies/Zhurnal institutsional'nykh issledovany* 3, 1/2011, 104–115.

59 See the Memorial home page: https://www.memo.ru/en-us/ (accessed 4 June 2017).

60 Shalamov, 'The Glove', 331.

61 Shalamov, 'The Resurrection of the Larch', in *Sketches of the Criminal World*, 325–327.

62 Shalamov, 'Wheelbarrow I' and 'Wheelbarrow II', in *Sketches of the Criminal World*, 396–398, 399–414.

63 Shalamov, 'Wheelbarrow I', 396–397.

64 Shalamov, 'Wheelbarrow II', 414.

65 Shalamov, 'Graphite', in *Sketches of the Criminal World*, 119–120.

66 Shalamov, 'The Glove', 360.

67 Ibid., 360–361. Objects for the world of the camps have been documented in the Gulag Museum in Moscow, Magadan and elsewhere. See *GULAG: Spuren und Zeugnisse 1929–1956*, edited by Volkhard Knigge and Irina Scherbakowa on behalf of Memorial Moscow and the Buchenwald and Mittelbau-Dora Memorials Foundation, Weimar 2012.

XII. The Solovetsky Special Camp—Laboratory of Extremes: Monastery Island as Concentration Camp

1 Both are marvellously captured by the photographer Yury A. Brodsky, *Solovki: Dvadtsat let osobogo naznacheniya*, Moscow 2002; Brodsky, *Solovki: Labirint preobrazheny*, Moscow 2017.

2 See the numerous examples of monasteries as camps in the Memorial cassette with guides: *Topografiya terrora*, Krasnoyarsk 2011; *Monastyri: Entsiklopedichesky spravochnik*, Moscow 2001.

3 Thomas Bremer, *Kreuz und Kreml: Kleine Geschichte der orthodoxen Kirche in Russland*, Freiburg im Breisgau 2007; Gregory L. Freeze, 'Von Entkirchlichung zu Laisierung: Staat, Kirche, und Gläubige in Rußland', in *Politik und Religion*, edited by Heinrich Meier, Munich 2013, 79–120.

4 *Monastyri*, 420f. On the history of the church, see Bremer, *Kreuz und Kreml;* Manfred Hildermeier, *Geschichte der Sowjetunion 1917–1991: Entstehung und Niedergang des ersten sozialistischen Staates*, Munich 1998; Carsten Goehrke, *Russland: Eine Strukturgeschichte*, Paderborn, Munich and Zurich 2010; Igor Smolitsch, *Geschichte der russischen Kirche 1700–1917*, Leiden 1964.

5 'Solovetsky stavropigialny monastyr' in *Entsiklopedichesky slovar Brokgauz-Efron*, vol. 60, St. Petersburg 1900, 782–784; 'Solovetsky monastyr' in *Bolshaya sovetskaya entsiklopediya*, vol. 52, Moscow 1947, 56–58.

6 Reports and memoirs from the Solovetsky camp are relatively common. Bibliographical references can be found in the excursus at www.Solovetsky.org/de/html/Literaturindex _de.html (accessed 20 April 2017); S. A. Malsagoff, *An Island Hell: A Soviet Prison in the Far North*, London 1926; N. P. Antsiferov, *Iz dum o bylom: Vospominaniya*, Moscow 1992 (ch. 3, 'SLON'); Dmitrij S. Lichatschow, *Hunger und Terror: Mein Leben zwischen Oktoberrevolution und Perestroika*, Ostfildern 1997; Michael Jakobson, *Origins of the Gulag: The Soviet Prison Camp System, 1917–1934*, Lexington 1993.

7 Tomasz Kizny, *Gulag*, with prefaces by Norman Davies, Jorge Semprun and Sergey Kovalev, translated by Antonia Lloyd-Jones, Buffalo, NY and Richmond Hill, Ontario 2004, 78–80.

8 Dmitry Likhachev, *Izbrannoe: Vospominaniya*, St. Petersburg 1995, 156.

9 Ekaterina Makhotina, *Stolzes Gedenken und traumatisches Erinnern: Gedächtnisorte der Stalinzeit am Weißmeerkanal*, Frankfurt am Main 2013.

10 Aleksandr Soldatov, 'Glamurny GULAG', in *Novaya gazeta*, 15 July 2016.

Chapter 50. K. in the Labyrinth of Everyday Soviet Reality

1 F. Kafka, *Roman. Novelly. Pritchi*, Moscow 1965; Anzhelika Sineok, 'Tsenzurnaya sudba Kafki v Rossii', online at http://www.kafka.ru/kritika/read/tsenzurnaya-sudba (accessed 4 June 2017); 'Roman, chelovek, obshchestvo: Na vstreche pisateley Evropy v Leningrade', in *Innostrannaya literatura* 11/1963, 204–246; *Sovremennye problemy realizma i modernizm*, Moscow 1965.

2 Eduard Goldstücker, *Franz Kafka: Aus Prager Sicht*, Prague 1965.

3 Richard Stites, 'Crowded on the Edge of Vastness: Observations on Russian Space and Place', in David Goldfrank (ed.), *Passion and Perception: Essays on Russian Culture by Richard Stites*, Washington, DC 2010, 47–57, here 47.

4 Eugenia Ginzburg, *Into the Whirlwind*, translated by Paul Stevenson and Manya Harari, London 1967, 44.

5 Ilja Ilf and Jewgeni Petrow, *Beziehungen sind alles: Erzählungen und Feuilletons*, Berlin 1981, 224, 223.

6 I am indebted to Karl-Konrad Tschäpe for pointing this out.

7 Ilf and Petrow, 'Gleichgültigkeit', in *Beziehungen sind alles*, 172–181, here 178.

8 Ilf and Petrow, *Beziehungen sind alles*, 225.

9 Stites, 'Crowded on the Edge of Vastness', 54f.
10 Georg Simmel, 'Brücke und Tür', in *Der Tag: Moderne illustrierte Zeitung*, no. 683, morning edition of 15 September 1909, illustrated section no. 216, 1–3 (Berlin).
11 Maksim Trudolyubov, *Lyudi za zaborom: Vlast, sobstvennost i chastnoe prostranstvo v Rossii*, Moscow 2015.

Chapter 51. The 'House on the Moskva': Machine for Living, Trap for People, Gated Community

1 Yuri Trifonov, *The House on the Embankment*, translated by Michael Glenny, London 1985.
2 The complex is described in Ye. I. Kirichenko, M. M. Posokhin and D. O. Shvidkovsky (eds.), *Pamyatniki arkhitektury Moskvy: Arkhitektura Moskvy 1910–1935 gg.*, Moscow 2012, 225–233.
3 For Yofan's life and work, see I. Yu. Eygel, *Boris Yofan*, Moscow 1978.
4 See the museum's home page: http://museumdom.narod.ru/index.html (accessed 4 June 2017).
5 The most compelling account of the architectural landscape of Moscow is still that of Selim O. Khan-Magomedov, *Pioneers of Soviet Architecture*, edited by Catherine Cooke, translated by Alexander Lieven, London 1987.
6 Olga Strugova, 'Mebel i interier', in A. Golosovskaya and V. Zuseva (eds.), *Sovetsky stil. Vremya i veshchi: Ukrasheniya, moda, prazdniki, belie, eda, upakovka, dengi, dacha, igrushki, parfiumeriia, mebel', farfor*, Moscow 2012, 148–163.
7 The alphabetic list of the residents can be found at http://museumdom.narod.ru/bio10 /kulman.html (accessed 26 April 2017).
8 For a typical product of the fascination with America, see Ilja Ilf and Jewgeni Petrow, *Das eingeschossige Amerika: Eine Reiseerzählung*, Frankfurt am Main 2013 (Russian 1st edition 1937). For an English-language edition, see *Ilf and Petrov's American Road Trip: The 1935 Travelogue of Two Soviet Writers/Ilya Ilf and Evgeny Petrov*, edited by Erika Wolf; with texts by Aleksandr Rodchenko and Aleksandra Ilf; translated by Anne O. Fisher, New York 2007.
9 Trifonov, *The House on the Embankment*; Juri Trifonow, *Widerschein des Feuers: Ein Bericht*, Neuwied 1979; Trifonow, *Zeit und Ort: Roman*, Munich 1982.
10 Mikhail Korshunov and Viktoriya Terekhova, *Tayna tayn moskovskikh*, Moscow 1995; T. I. Shmidt, *Dom na naberezhnoy: Lyudi i sudby*, Moscow 2009.
11 Catalogue of the repressed: http://museumdom.narod.ru/repres.html (accessed 26 April 2017).
12 Wladislaw Hedeler, 'Die Präsenz staatlicher Gewalt inmitten einer urbanen Umwelt: Das Beispiel Moskau', in Karl Schlögel (ed.), *Mastering Russian Spaces: Raum und Raumbewältigung als Probleme der russischen Geschichte*, Munich 2011, 199–252, here 210.
13 Ibid., 208f.
14 Bart Goldhoorn and Philipp Meuser, *Capitalist Realism: New Architecture in Russia*, Berlin 2007; Goldhoorn and Meuser, *Lust auf Raum: Neue Innenarchitektur in Russland*, Berlin 2007.

Chapter 52. The Aura of the Telephone and the Absence of the Phone Book

1 Boris Pilnyak, 'The Tale of the Unextinguished Moon', in *Mahogany & Other Stories*, translated by Vera T. Reck and Michael Green, New York and London 2013 [1988], 179.
2 Ibid., 181.

3 Ibid., 205f.

4 For Stalin's phone calls to writers, see Nadezhda Mandelstam, *Hope against Hope*, translated by Max Hayward, London 1971, 145–149; Lazar Fleishman, *Boris Pasternak: The Poet and His Politics*, Cambridge, MA 1990, 178–184; Simon Sebag Montefiore, *Stalin: The Court of the Red Tsar*, New York 2004, 136; Ralph Dutli, *Mandelstam: Meine Zeit, mein Tier*, Zurich 2003, 432; Dietrich Beyrau, *Intelligenz und Dissens: Die russischen Bildungsschichten in der Sowjetunion 1917 bis 1985*, Göttingen 1993, 164.

5 Lars Kleberg, 'K semiotike telefona', in Ben Hellman, Tomi Huttunen and Gennady Obatnin (eds.), *Varietas et Concordia: Essays in Honor of Professor Pekka Pesonen on the Occasion of His 60th Birthday*, Helsinki 2007, 362–378, here 373; R. D. Timentsik, 'K simvolike telefona v russkoy poezii', in *Zerkalo semiotika zerkalnosti: Trudy po znakovym sistemam 22/1988*, 155–163.

6 Aleksandr Solzhenitsyn, *In the First Circle: A Novel*, the restored text, translated by Harry T. Willetts, New York 2009, 243ff.; Lev Kopelev, *Ease My Sorrows: A Memoir*, translated from the Russian by Antonina W. Bouis, New York 1983 (ch. 9).

7 For the comparative figures, see Kleberg, 'K semiotike telefona', 363 n.

8 Eugenia Ginzburg, *Into the Whirlwind*, translated by Paul Stevenson and Manya Harari, London 1967, 41.

9 Eugenia Ginzburg, *Within the Whirlwind*, translated by Ian Boland, introduction by Heinrich Böll, New York and London 1981, 393.

10 The vertushka plays a major role in the analysis of Michail Woslensky, *Nomenklatura: Die herrschende Klasse der Sowjetunion*, Vienna 1980.

11 In the USA in 1982 there was 1 phone for every 1.3 inhabitants. In Italy it was 1 for every 2.7 and in the USSR, 1 for every 11.3. See Kleberg, 'K semiotike telefona', 363 n. 1.

12 Karl Schlögel, *In Space We Read Time: On the History of Civilization and Geopolitics*, translated by Gerrit Jackson, New York 2016, 275–291 (chapter on Berlin address books); Schlögel, *Moskau lesen*, Berlin 1984, 101–113 (chapter on All Moscow).

13 A. A. Petrenko-Lysak, 'Lichnoe v obshchih prostranstvakh: Mobilnye kommunikatsii v publichnykh mestakh', in *Labirint: Zhurnal sotsialno-gumanitarnykh issledovany 2/2015*, 32–40.

XIV. The Noise of Time

1 Osip Mandelstam, *The Noise of Time*, translated with critical essays by Clarence Brown, San Francisco 1986 (Music in Pavlovsk, 69–71).

2 Of key importance for the opening of aural space for historians is Alain Corbin, *Village Bells: Sound and Meaning in the Nineteenth-Century French Countryside*, New York 1998. For the transition from the silent film to the sound film in Soviet Russia, see Oksana Bulgakova, *Sovetsky slukhoglaz: Kino i ego organy*, Moscow 2010.

3 For my attempt to discuss the 'sound of the age', see Karl Schlögel, *Petersburg: Das Laboratorium der Moderne 1909–1921*, Munich 2002, 409–452 (The age discovers its sound; The conductor Serge Koussevitzky).

4 Orlando Figes, *The Whisperers: Private Life in Stalin's Russia*, London 2007.

Chapter 53. The Bells Fall Silent

1 Walter Benjamin, *Moscow Diary*, edited by Gary Smith and translated by Richard Sieburth, with a preface by Gershom Scholem, Cambridge, MA and London 1986, 114.

2 See the collection of essays on the culture of bells *Muzyka kolokolov: Sbornik issledovany i materialov, Traditsionnaya instrumentalnaya muzyka Evropy i Azii* series, issue 2, St. Petersburg 1999.

3 N. I. Olovyanishnikov, *Istoriya kolokolov i kolokoliteynoe iskusstvo*, Moscow 1912, 21.

4 Quoted in F. I. Rychin, *Putevoditel po moskovskoy svyatyne*, Moscow 1890, 144–145.

5 Michael Jeismann, 'Der hundertjährige Glockenkrieg', in *Frankfurter Allgemeine Zeitung*, 10 October 1995, no. 235, L43.

6 Wassilij Rosanow, 'Der russische Nil', in *Abschied von der Wolga*, edited and with a preface by Sonja Margolina, Berlin 1992, 23–114, here 65.

7 See 'Kolokola', in *Entsiklopedichesky slovar Brokgauz-Efron*, vol. 30, St. Petersburg 1895, 722–724; L. D. Blagoveshchenskaya, 'Zvonnitsa—muzykalny instrument', in *Kolokola: Istoriya i sovremennost*, Moscow 1985, 28–38; *Rossiysky gumanitarny entsiklopedichesky slovar'*, 2002, online at http://humanities_dictionary.academic.ru/7221/Колокол (accessed 4 June 2017).

8 As always, the magnificent and indispensable text is that of René Fülöp-Miller, *The Mind and Face of Bolshevism: An Examination of Cultural Life in Soviet Russia*, translated from the German by F. S. Flint and D. F. Tait, Texas 2007 [London 1927].

9 Alexander V. Mosolov, *Steel*, Ballet Suite, op. 19a (1926–28), including 'Iron Foundry'; Larry Sitsky, 'Aleksandr V. Mosolov: The Man of Steel', in Sitsky, *Music of the Repressed Russian Avant-Garde, 1900–1929*, Westport 1994, 60–86.

10 P. V. Gidulyanov, *Tserkovnye kolokola na sluzhbe magii i tsarizma*, Moscow 1929.

11 Quoted from V. F. Kozlov, *Gibel tserkovnykh kolokolov v 1920–1930-e gody*, Moscow 1994, 29f.; Mikhail Prishvin, 'Lesa k "Osudarevoy doroge": Iz dnevnikov 1909–1930', in *Nashe nasledie* 9/1990, 82–85.

12 A. I. Tsvetaeva, *Saradzhev K. K. Master volshebnogo zvona A. I. Tsvetaeva*, Moscow 1988.

13 Kozlov, *Gibel tserkovnykh kolokolov v 1920–1930-e gody*, 34.

14 Elif Batuman, 'The Bells', in *The New Yorker*, 27 April 2009, 28–29; 'Rescued Russian Bells Leave Harvard for Home', in *Harvard Gazette*, 10 July 2008, online at http://news.harvard .edu/gazette/story/2008/07/rescued-russian-bells-leave-harvard-for-home (accessed 4 June 2017).

15 See the charming study by Raissa Orlowa, *Als die Glocke verstummte: Alexander Herzens letztes Lebensjahr*, Berlin 1988.

Chapter 54. Levitan's Voice

1 The following account is based largely on the biography by Ella Taranova, *Levitan: Golos Stalina*, St. Petersburg 2010, 11; Wolf Oschlies, 'Levitan, Jurij Borisowitsch (1914–1943)', online at http://www.zukunft-braucht-erinnerung.de/jurij-borisowitsch-levitan/ (accessed 26 April 2017).

2 For fundamental reflections on the significance of the voice and radio for historical analysis, see Claudia Schmölders, 'Die Stimme des Bösen: Zur Klanggestalt des Dritten Reiches', in *Merkur: Zeitschrift für europäisches Denken* 581/1997, 681–693; I am also grateful to Claudia Schmölders for telling me about the important book on the subject by Marcel Beyer, *Flughunde*, Frankfurt am Main 1995.

3 For internet audio versions of Levitan's news broadcasts on the beginning of the war and the German surrender, see, e.g., https://commons.wikimedia.org/wiki/File:Levitan _USSR_attacked.ogg.

4 On media history, see the contributions in Jurij Murasov and Georg Witte (eds.), *Die Musen der Macht: Medien in der sowjetischen Kultur der 20er und 30er Jahre*, Munich 2003.

5 Taranova, *Levitan*, 47–51.

6 T. Goryaeva (ed.), *Istoriya sovetskoy radio-zhurnalistiki: Dokumenty. Teksty. Vospominaniya 1917–1945*, Moscow 1991; Goryaeva, *Radio Rossii: Politichesky kontrol sovetskogo radio*, Moscow 2000; Goryaeva, '"Velikaya kniga dnya": Radio i sotsiokulturnaya sreda v SSSR v 1920–30-e gody', in H. Giunter and S. Hensgen (eds.), *Sovetskaya vlast i mediya*, St. Petersburg 2006, 66–69; Stephen Lovell, 'How Russia Learned to Listen: Radio and the Making of Soviet Culture', in *Kritika: Explorations in Russian and Eurasian History* 12, 3/2011 (new series), 591–615; Lovell, *Russia in the Microphone Age: A History of Soviet Radio, 1919–1970*, Oxford 2015.

7 Lovell, 'How Russia Learned to Listen', 602 n. 43; James von Geldern, 'The Voice from the Center', in Richard Stites (ed.), *Culture and Entertainment in Wartime Russia*, Bloomington 1995, 45–61, here 45.

8 On the preeminent role of radio in the defence of Leningrad, see Alexander Rubashkin, *Golos Leningrada: Leningradskoe radio v dni blokady*, St. Petersburg 2005.

9 Werner Roeder, *Faksimile der 'Sonderfahndungsliste UdSSR' des Chefs der Sicherheitspolizei und des SD, das Fahndungsbuch der deutschen Einsatzgruppen im Russlandfeldzug 1941*, Erlangen 1977; for the Nazis' Wanted List, see Karl Schlögel, *Moscow, 1937*, translated by Rodney Livingstone, Malden, MA and Cambridge 2012, 538–543 (ch. 37, '"For Official Use Only": Moscow as a City on the Enemy Map').

10 Cited in Schmölders, 'Die Stimme des Bösen', 684.

11 Wendy Z. Goldman, *Inventing the Enemy: Denunciation and Terror in Stalin's Russia*, Cambridge 2011; Goldman, *Terror and Democracy in the Age of Stalin: The Social Dynamics of Repression*, Cambridge 2007; Jörg Baberowski, *Der Feind ist überall: Stalinismus im Kaukasus*, Munich 2003.

12 Schlögel, *Moscow, 1937*, 227f. ('Wreckers at Work in the Ether'); Taranova, *Levitan*, 72–78.

13 Taranova, *Levitan*, 84.

14 Ibid., 82.

15 On Lidiya Timashuk, see Taranova, *Levitan*, 139–141 and 146–152; Louis Rapoport, *Stalin's War against the Jews*, New York 1990 (ch. 10); Arno Lustiger, *Stalin and the Jews: The Red Book*, New York 2004.

16 Peter Pomerantsev, *Nothing Is True and Everything Is Possible: Adventures in Modern Russia*, London 2017.

Chapter 55. Back in the USSR: Sound Traces

1 *Die Geheimrede Chruschtschows: Über den Personenkult und seine Folgen*, Berlin 1990. [*The "Secret" Speech: Delivered to the Closed Session of the Twentieth Congress of the Communist Party of the Soviet Union*, by Nikita Sergeyevich Khrushchev, translated from the Russian by Tamara Deutscher; with an introduction by Zhores A. Medvedev and Roy A. Medvedev, Nottingham 1976.]

2 Aleksandr Rubashkin, *Golos Leningrada: Leningradskoe radio v dni blokady*, St. Petersburg 2005; Harlow Robinson, 'Composing for Victory: Classical Music', in Richard Stites (ed.), *Culture and Entertainment in Wartime Russia*, Bloomington 1995, 62–76.

3 Eugenia Ginzburg, *Within the Whirlwind*, translated by Ian Boland, introduction by Heinrich Böll, New York and London 1981, 305f.

4 Ibid., 356f.

5 Ibid., 370.

6 Alex Inkeles, *Social Change in Soviet Russia*, Cambridge, MA 1968 (section 5, 'Mass Communication and Public Opinion').

XV. Alien Territory, Contact Zones, In-Between Worlds

1 John Scott, *Behind the Urals: An American Worker in Russia's City of Steel*, Bloomington 1973.

2 Michael David-Fox, *Showcasing the Great Experiment: Cultural Diplomacy and Western Visitors to the Soviet Union, 1921–1941*, New York 2012.

Chapter 56. 'The Little Oasis of the Diplomatic Colony'

1 For a detailed recent account of the embassy as a social locality—from the Soviet standpoint—see Gabriel Gorodetsky (ed.), *Die Maiski-Tagebücher: Ein Diplomat im Kampf gegen Hitler 1932–1943*, Munich 2016.

2 For brilliant examples of parallel diplomatic lives, see Gordon A. Craig and Felix Gilbert (eds.), *The Diplomats 1919–1939*, 2 vols., Princeton 1953, in particular, Theodore H. von Laue, 'Soviet Diplomacy: G. V. Chicherin, People's Commissar for Foreign Affairs, 1918–1930', 234–281, and Carl E. Schorske, 'Two German Ambassadors: Dirksen and Schulenburg', 477–511.

3 George F. Kennan, *Memoirs 1925–1950*, New York 1967.

4 Hans von Herwarth, *Zwischen Hitler und Stalin: Erlebte Zeitgeschichte 1931–1945*, Frankfurt and Berlin 1982; Gustav Hilger, *Wir und der Kreml: Deutsch-sowjetische Beziehungen 1918–1941*, Frankfurt am Main 1956; Paul-Otto Schmidt, *Statist auf diplomatischer Bühne 1923–1945: Erlebnisse des Chefdolmetschers im Auswärtigen Amt mit den Staatsmännern Europas. Von Stresemann und Briand bis Hitler, Chamberlain und Molotow*, Bonn 1949; Erich Franz Sommer, *Geboren in Moskau: Erinnerungen eines baltendeutschen Diplomaten 1912–1955*, Munich 1997; Charles E. Bohlen, *Witness to History 1929–1969*, New York 1973.

5 General Ernst Köstring, *Der militärische Mittler zwischen dem Deutschen Reich und der Sowjetunion 1921–1941*, edited by Hermann Teske, Frankfurt am Main 1965, 198.

6 Jörn Happel, *Die Sowjetunion erklären: Gustav Hilger im deutsch-sowjetischen Jahrhundert*, thesis for the Department of History at the University of Basel 2015.

7 Harold G. Nicolson, *Diplomacy*, London 1963, 56.

8 Karl Schlögel, *Das russische Berlin: Ostbahnhof Europas*, Munich 2007, 233–262 ('Nikolai Krestinski und Graf von der Schulenburg: Diplomatie als Verrat').

9 The history of 'diplomacy as culture' has still to be written in the spirit of Jules Cambon, *Le Diplomate*, Paris 1926; Nicolson, *Diplomacy*.

Chapter 57. The Journalists' Ghetto: The View from Outside, Fixation with the Centre

1 For Duranty, a Pulitzer Prize writer, see S. J. Taylor, *Stalin's Apologist: Walter Duranty, the New York Times's Man in Moscow*, Oxford 1990; Richard Pipes, *Russia under the Bolshevik Regime, 1919–1924*, London 1994, 234–236.

2 Alexander Werth, *Russia at War 1941 to 1945*, London 1964.

3 Klaus Mehnert, *The Anatomy of Soviet Man*, translated by Maurice Rosenbaum, London 1961.

4 From the profusion of writers, we mention here only Gerd Ruge, *Weites Land: Russische Erfahrungen. Russische Perspektiven. Erfahrungsberichte*, Berlin 1996; Fritz Pleitgen, *Väterchen Don: Der Fluss der Kosaken*, Cologne 2008; Klaus Bednarz, *Mein Russland—Literarische Streifzüge durch ein weites Land*, Reinbek bei Hamburg 2006; Thomas Roth, *Russisches Tagebuch: Eine Reise von den Tschuktschen bis zum Roten Platz*, Munich 1995; Dirk Sager, *Russlands hoher Norden*, Berlin 2005; Kerstin Holm, *Das korrupte Imperium—ein russisches Panorama*, Munich 2003.

5 Hedrick Smith, *The Russians*, London 1976; Andrew Nagorski, *Reluctant Farewell: An American Reporter's Candid Look inside the Soviet Union*, New York 1985; David Satter, *Age of Delirium: The Decline and Fall of the Soviet Union*, New Haven 1996; Holm, *Das korrupte Imperium*.

6 Helmut Altrichter, *Russland 1989: Der Untergang des sowjetischen Imperiums*, Munich 2009.

Chapter 58. Beryozka Shops: 'Oases of Affluence'

1 The monograph on this subject—Anna Ivanova, *Magaziny 'Berezka': Paradoksy potrebleniya v pozdnem SSSR*, Moscow 2017—was not yet available at the time of writing.

2 Natalia Lebina, *Entsiklopediya banalnostey. Sovetskaya povsednevnost—kontury, simvoly, znaki*, St. Petersburg 2006, 59f.; M. Vladi (Vlady), *Vladimir, ili prervanny polet*, Moscow 1989.

3 A. Ivanova, 'Moralnaia otsenka privilegy i ekonomicheskikh prestupleny v sovetskom obshchestve: Diskussiya o magazinakh "Berezka" v kontse 1980-kh gg.', in *Die Konstruktion des Sowjetischen* (materials for the international conference in St. Petersburg 14–15 April 2011), *Bulletin. DHIM*, Moscow 2011; Ivanova, 'Magaziny Vneshposyltorga: Valyutnaya torgovlya v (1960–1980-e gody)', in *Vestnik Permskogo Universiteta, Istoriya vypusk* 3, 17/2011.

4 'Magaziny "Berezka": Opyt voploshcheniya mechty o kommunisticheskom izobilii', Vladimir Tolts and Anna Ivanova interview, Radio Svoboda, 13 March 2010.

5 'Chernaya "Berezka": Kak valyutnye magaziny dlya inostrantsev stali chast'yu sovetskoy kultury', online at https://theoryandpractice.ru/posts/15931-chernaya-berezka-kak-valyutnye-magaziny-dlya-inostrantsev-stali-chast-yu-sovetskoy-kultury (accessed 4 June 2017).

6 On the world of privileges and special deals, see Mervyn Mathews, *Privilege in the Soviet Union: A Study of Elite Life-Styles under Communism*, London 1978; Michail S. Voslensky, *Nomenklatura: Die herrschende Klasse der Sowjetunion*, Vienna and Munich 2005.

7 Elena Osokina, *Our Daily Bread: Socialist Distribution and the Art of Survival in Stalin's Russia, 1927–1941*, translated by Kate Transchel and Greta Bucher, Armonk and London 2001.

8 Ibid., 126–127.

9 Ibid., 127.

10 See Joseph E. Davies, *Mission to Moscow*, London 1942, entries of 22 March 1937 and 28 January 1937, pp. 94 and 38.

11 Osokina, *Our Daily Bread*, 124, 125.

12 Mikhail Bulgakov, *The Master and Margarita*, translated by Michael Glenny, London 1996, 391–403 (ch. 28, 'The Final Adventure of Koroviev and Behemoth').

13 Anatoly Sorochan, 'Fartsa—kak mnogo v etom slove', in *Yuzhnaya pravda*, 17 September 2015.

14 Karen Dawisha, *Putin's Kleptocracy: Who Owns Russia?*, New York 2014.
15 More recently, following the embargo on the import of various foodstuffs from the West, Foreign Minister Sergey Lavrov suggested that it would be a good idea to reintroduce the special shops: Karl Shrek and Alexander Gostev, 'Magazin edy, zapreshchennoy Putinym', online at http://www.svoboda.org/a/26842905.html (accessed 4 June 2017).

Chapter 59. Genius of the Collector: George Costakis and the Rediscovery of Soviet Avant-Garde Art

1 Catalogues from some of the great exhibitions include *Werke aus der Sammlung Costakis: Russische Avantgarde 1910–1930*, Kunstmuseum Düsseldorf and Kunstverein für die Rheinlande und Westfalen, Düsseldorf 1977; Margit Rowell, George Costakis and Angelica Zander Rudenstine (eds.), *Art of the Avant-Garde in Russia: Selections from the George Costakis Collection*, New York 1981; Angelica Zander Rudenstine (ed.), *Russian Avant-Garde Art: The George Costakis Collection*, introduction by S. Frederick Starr; 'Collecting Art of the Avant-Garde' by George Costakis, London 1981; Anna Kafestsi (ed.), *Russian Avant-Garde 1910–1930: The G. Costakis Collection*, under the auspices of the Ministry of Culture, Athens and Delphi 1996; *Licht und Farbe in der Russischen Avantgarde: Die Sammlung Costakis aus dem Staatlichen Museum für Zeitgenössische Kunst Thessaloniki*, Martin-Gropius-Bau Berlin, Berlin 2005.
2 This account follows that of the Russian-language autobiography *Moy avangard: Vospominaniya kollektsionera*, Moscow 1993—and the biography by Peter Roberts, *George Costakis: A Russian Life in Art*, New York 1994. Roberts was the Canadian ambassador and had known Costakis since 1957.
3 S. Frederick Starr, introduction to *Russian Avant-Garde Art: The George Costakis Collection*, edited by Angelica Zander Rudenstine, London 1981, 12; a photograph of the memorable meeting can be seen on p. 13.
4 I was fortunate enough to see the Costakis collection on a number of visits to the New Tretyakov Gallery, the Gropius Bau in Berlin and most vividly of all in Thessaloniki; my thanks to the curator, Angeliki Charistou, for the guided tour on 17 and 18 November 2016.
5 Quoted in Kafestsi, *Russian Avant-Garde 1910–1930*, 54.
6 Roberts, *George Costakis*, 201.
7 Ibid., 63.
8 Ibid., 34.
9 Ibid., 65, 61.
10 George Costakis, 'Collecting Art of the Avant-Garde', in *Russian Avant-Garde Art: The George Costakis Collection*, edited by Angelica Zander Rudenstine, London 1981, 65–67.
11 The reproduction appears as no. 312 in the Tretyakov Gallery exhibition catalogue *Georgy Kostaki: K 100-letiyu kollektsionera*, Moscow 2014, 373.
12 Since then, there has been a major Nikritin exhibition in Thessaloniki and Moscow: *Spheres of Light—Stations of Darkness: The Art of Solomon Nikritin (1898–1965)*, Thessaloniki and Moscow 2004.
13 Most of these artists were represented in the exhibition *Soviet Alternative Art (1956–1988) from the Costakis Collections* curated by Maria Tsantsanoglou, Athens 2006.
14 A detailed overview on the state of research can be found in John E. Bowlt, 'Towards a Historiography of the Russian Avant-Garde', in Anna Kafestsi (ed.), *Russian Avant-Garde 1910–1930: The G. Costakis Collection*, under the auspices of the Ministry of Culture, Athens and Delphi 1996, 591–611; Bowlt believes that no other collection was comparable to that

of Costakis in the 1950s; see also *Russian Art of the Avant-Garde: Theory and Criticism 1902–1934*, edited and translated by John E. Bowlt, London 1988.

15 The picture 'GULAG Kotlas' of 1989, no. 319 in *Georgy Kostaki: K 100-letiyu kollektsionera*, 372.

16 Roberts, *George Costakis*, 52.

17 Starr, introduction to *Russian Avant-Garde Art*, 29.

18 Cited in Roberts, *George Costakis*, 129f.; Kostaki, *Moi avangard*, 113–115.

19 Roberts, *George Costakis*, 132.

20 Ibid., 130.

21 Ibid., 148.

22 Ibid., 147, 175.

23 *Georgy Kostaki: K 100-letiyu kollektsionera* contains a reconstruction of the harassment that led to his emigration; see Irina Lebedeva, 'Georgy Kostaki: "Vyezd iz SSSR razreshit. . ."', 8–11; Irina Pronina and Lyubov Pchelkina, 'Zhivopis iz kollektsii Georgiya Kostaki v Tretiakovskoy galeree', 12–21; 'Letopis' zhizni Georgiya Kostaki', 334–338; Irina Pronina, 'Dar Georgiya Kostaki', 384–391.

24 For Glazunov's view of the world, see Michael Hagemeister, *In weiter Ferne so nah—vom Verstehen, Übersetzen und Vermitteln russischer Kultur*, inaugural lecture Mainz/Germersheim 27 June 2002 (unpublished manuscript).

25 On the storming of the exhibition in the Sakharov Centre in Moscow, the campaign and the court case, see the treatment of the topic in 'Religion and the State in Russia', in *Osteuropa* 4/2004.

XVI. The Railroads of Empire: Time Travel Back into the Russian Twentieth Century

1 The authoritative account of the history of the train in the Russian Empire, one that does justice to the complexity of the subject, is Frithjof Benjamin Schenk, *Russlands Fahrt in die Moderne: Mobilität und sozialer Raum im Wandel*, Stuttgart 2014, with a comprehensive bibliography, 387–430.

2 Eugen Zabel, *Transsibirien: Mit der Bahn durch Russland und China 1903*, edited by Bodo Thöns, Stuttgart and Vienna 2003 [originally 1904]; this also contains the report about the 1900 Paris Exhibition, 49f.

3 This has been systematically explored in Jürgen Osterhammel, *Die Verwandlung der Welt: Eine Geschichte des 19. Jahrhunderts*, Munich 2009; Wolfgang Zorn, 'Verdichtung und Beschleunigung des Verkehrs als Beitrag zur Entwicklung der "modernen Welt"', in Reinhart Koselleck (ed.), *Studien zum Beginn der modernen Welt*, Stuttgart 1977, 115–134.

4 Of fundamental importance for an understanding is Steven G. Marks, *Road to Power: The Trans-Siberian Railroad and the Colonization of Asian Russia 1850–1917*, Ithaca 1991.

5 Wolfgang Plat, 'Die Transsib', in *Die Zeit*, 15 May 1992, 102. Literature on the Trans-Siberian Railway is extraordinary in quantity. See John Poulsen and W. Kuranow, *Die Transsibirische Eisenbahn: Die längste Eisenbahn der Welt*, Malmö 1984; on the Trans-Siberian Railway today, see the various editions of the Lonely Planet guides.

6 The exemplary study here is still Wolfgang Schivelbusch, *Geschichte der Eisenbahnreise: Zur Industrialisierung von Raum und Zeit im 19. Jahrhundert*, Frankfurt am Main, Berlin and Vienna 1979.

7 Karl Schlögel (ed.), *Mastering Russian Spaces: Raum und Raumbewältigung als Probleme der russischen Geschichte*, Munich 2011; Friedrich Ratzel, 'Der Verkehr als Raumbewältiger', in

Ratzel, *Politische Geographie oder die Geographie der Staaten, des Verkehrs und des Krieges*, 2nd revised ed., Munich and Berlin 1903, 447–534.

8 On the absence of pathways, see Felix Philipp Ingold, *Russische Wege: Geschichte, Kultur, Weltbild*, Munich 2007; Roland Cvetkovski, *Modernisierung durch Beschleunigung: Raum und Mobilität im Zarenreich*, Frankfurt am Main 2006.

9 Roger Pethybridge, *The Spread of the Russian Revolution: Essays on 1917*, London and Basingstoke 1972.

10 On creating an empire and building a railway, see Ulrike von Hirschhausen and Jörn Leonhard (eds.), *Comparing Empires: Encounters and Transfers in the Long Nineteenth Century*, Göttingen 2011.

11 On bridge and tunnel building, see Evgeny Kraskovsky (ed.), *Istoriya zheleznodorozhnogo transporta Rossii i Sovestskogo Soyuza*, vol. 1, *1836–1917*, St. Petersburg and Moscow 1994, 225–241; *Zheleznye dorogi Rossii: Istoriya i sovremennost v fotodokumentakh*, St. Petersburg 1996.

12 Theodore H. von Laue, *Sergei Witte and the Industrialization of Russia*, New York 1969; *Putevoditel po Velikoy Sibirskoy zheleznoy doroge: Izdanie ministerstva putey soobshcheniya*, edited by A. I. Dmitrieva-Mamonova and A. F. Zdzharsky, St. Petersburg 1900; Kraskovsky, *Istoriya zheleznodorozhnogo transporta Rossii*, vol. 1, *1836–1917*; Kraskovsky (ed.), *Istoriya zheleznodorozhnogo transporta Rossii i Sovestskogo Soyuza*, vol. 2, *1917–1945*, St. Petersburg and Moscow 1997.

13 Catherine Merridale, *Lenin on the Train*, New York 2016.

14 Wsewolod Iwanow, *Panzerzug 14–69*, Frankfurt am Main 1970.

15 Lioubov Zoreva, *Die Eisenbahn im russischen kulturellen Raum*, PhD dissertation, Ludwig-Maximilians-University, Munich 2012, 259.

16 John Payne Matthew, *Stalin's Railroad: Turksib and the Building of Socialism*, Pittsburgh 2001; Johannes Grützmacher, *Die Baikal-Amur-Magistrale: Vom stalinistischen Lager zum Mobilisierungsprojekt unter Brežnev*, Munich 2012.

17 Pictures of these locomotives can be found in Kraskovsky, *Istoriya zheleznodorozhnogo transporta Rossii i Sovestskogo Soyuza*, vol. 2, *1917–1945*, 137, 140.

18 Edward Rees, *Stalinism and Soviet Rail Transport*, New York 1995.

19 Kraskovsky, *Istoriya zheleznodorozhnogo transporta Rossii i Sovestskogo Soyuza*, vol. 2, *1917–1945* (ch. 8); G. A. Kumanev, *Voyna i zheleznodorozhny transport SSSR 1941–1945*, Moscow 1988.

20 Schenk, *Russlands Fahrt in die Moderne*, especially chs. 3 and 4.

21 Fedor Stepun, *Das Antlitz Rußlands und das Gesicht der Revolution: Aus meinem Leben 1884–1922*, Munich 1961, 150–166 (Russian railways).

22 Cited in Zoreva, *Die Eisenbahn im russischen kulturellen Raum*, 228 n. 470.

23 The degree to which station buildings put their stamp on the spaces alongside the route and homogenised them can be seen from the relevant sections on railway building and urban development in Ye. I. Kirichenko and M. V. Nashchokina (eds.), *Gradostroitelstvo Rossii serediny XIX–nachala XX veka: Goroda i novye tipy poseleny*, vol. 1, Moscow 2001, 30–37; Ye. I. Kirichenko, Ye. G. Shcheboleva and M. V. Nashchokina (eds.), *Gradostroitelstvo Rossii serediny XIX–nachala XX veka: Goroda i novye tipy poseleny*, vol. 2, Moscow 2003, 470–506; Ye. I. Kirichenko and M. V. Nashchokina (eds.), *Gradostroitelstvo Rossii serediny XIX–nachala XX veka: Stolitsy i provintsiya*, vol. 3, Moscow 2010, 486–532.

24 The experience of transportation is to be found in all memoirs. See, for example, Aleksander Wat, *My Century: The Odyssey of a Polish Intellectual*, edited and translated by Richard Lourie, with a foreword by Czeslaw Milosz, New York and London 1990, 357ff.

25 Cited in Zoreva, *Die Eisenbahn im russischen kulturellen Raum*, 87.

26 Stepun, *Das Antlitz Rußlands und das Gesicht der Revolution*, 150ff.

27 One of the few studies of smugglers' networks in the 1990s is V. I. Dyatlov and K. V. Grigorichev (eds.), *Ethnic Markets in Russia: Space of Bargaining and Place of Meeting*, Irkutsk 2015; see also Karl Schlögel, 'Basar Europa und die Arbeit der Weberschiffchen', in Schlögel, *Promenade in Jalta und andere Städtebilder*, Munich 2001, 199–207.

28 Aleksandr N. Radishchev, *A Journey from St. Petersburg to Moscow*, edited by Roderick Page Thaler, translated by Leo Wiener, Cambridge, MA 2014 [1958].

29 N. A. Berdyaev, 'Dukhi russkoy revolyutsii', in *Iz glubiny*, Paris 1967, 72.

30 Francis W. Wcislo, *Tales of Imperial Russia: The Life and Times of Sergei Witte, 1849–1915*, Oxford 2011.

31 Alexander Etkind, *Internal Colonization: Russia's Imperial Experience*, Cambridge 2011.

XVII. Red Cube: The Lenin Mausoleum as Keystone

1 On the square and its history, see Ye. I. Kirichenko, M. M. Posokhin and D. O. Shvidkovsky (eds.), *Pamyatniki arkhitektury Moskvy: Arkhitektura Moskvy 1910–1935 gg.*, Moscow 2012.

2 For the history of the Lenin cult, see Benno Ennker, *Die Anfänge des Leninkults in der Sowjetunion*, Cologne and Weimar 1997, here 234; Nina Tumarkin, *Lenin Lives! The Lenin Cult in Soviet Russia*, Cambridge 1997.

3 Ennker, *Die Anfänge des Leninkults in der Sowjetunion*, 228; on the architectural history of the Mausoleum, see S. O. Khan-Magomedov, *Mavzoley Lenina: Shedevry avangarda*, Moscow 2013; Selim O. Khan-Magomedov, *Pioneers of Soviet Architecture*, translated by Alexander Lieven, London 1987; Kyrill N. Afanasiev, *A. V. Shchusev*, Moscow 1978.

4 Khan-Magomedov, *Pioneers of Soviet Architecture*, 236.

5 Cited by Ennker, *Die Anfänge des Leninkults in der Sowjetunion*, 229.

6 Afanasiev, *A. V. Shchusev*, 91–106, here 99–101.

7 Khan-Magomedov, *Mavzoley Lenina*, 43.

8 Ibid., 40.

9 J. V. Stalin, 'Concerning Questions of Leninism', in *Problems of Leninism*, 149, online at http://ciml.250x.com/archive/stalin/english/stalin_problems%20of_leninism_1954 _english.pdf.

10 The numerous Lenin biographies include Georg Lukács, *Lenin: A Study on the Unity of His Thought*, translated by Nicholas Jacobs, London 1970; Dmitri Wolkogonow, *Lenin: Utopie und Terror*, Düsseldorf 1994; Richard Pipes, *The Unknown Lenin: From the Secret Archive*, New Haven and London 1996; Robert Service, *Lenin: A Biography*, London 2000.

11 'As we are, we cannot even dream of merging with the people—we must fear them more than any state power, and we must praise that power, which alone can protect us from the rage of the people, thanks to its bayonets and prisons.' Michail Geršenzon, 'Schöpferische Selbsterkenntnis', in *Wegzeichen: Zur Krise der russischen Intelligenz*, Frankfurt am Main 1990, 140–175, here 165.

12 For the Stalin cult, see Jan Plamper, *The Stalin Cult: A Study in the Alchemy of Power*, New Haven 2012.

13 Dietrich Grille, *Lenins Rivale: Bogdanov und seine Philosophie*, Cologne 1966.

14 Tilman Spengler, *Lenins Hirn*, Berlin 2003.

15 For the biographies of Vorobyov and Zbarsky, see Yu. M. Lopukhin, *Bolezn, Smert i balz-amirovanie V. I. Lenina*, Moscow 1997, 104–107.

16 Ernst Kantorowicz, *The King's Two Bodies: A Study in Medieval Political Theology*, Princeton 1957.

17 V. M. Bekhterev, 'O sozdanii panteona v SSSR', in A. A. Zhilyaev (ed.), *Avangardnaya muzeologiya 'Otnoshenie Lenina k muzeyam'*, Moscow 2015, 166–171.

18 Yelena Kostyleva, 'Lenin mertv: Antropolog Alexey Yurchak sumel uznat mnogoe o sostoyanii tela Lenina v mavzolee. Yelena Kostyleva rassprosila o tom, kak i pochemu ego khranyat i pochemu ne pokhoronyat', online at http://www.colta.ru/articles/society/7482 (accessed 5 June 2017).

19 Quoted from Nikolay Petrov, 'Gudbay, Lenin', in *Novaya gazeta*, 12 July 2013.

20 Published in *Arkhitektura SSSR* 9/1954, 23–34. Illustrations and quotations in 'Proekt Panteona—Pamyatnika vechnoy slavy velikikh lyudey Sovetskoy strany na Leninskikh gorah', in *Livejournal*, 4 November 2010, online at http://cocomera.livejournal.com/310979 .html (accessed 5 June 2017).

21 Register of people buried in the Kremlin Wall in Alexej Abramow, *An der Kremlmauer: Gedenkstätten und Biographien revolutionärer Kämpfer*, Berlin 1984.

22 Irina Rezni, 'Panteon "epohi Putina": V Podmoskovie v subbotu otkroetsya pervoe v strane memorialnoe voennoe kladbishche', in *Gazeta.ru*, 21 June 2013, online at https://www .gazeta.ru/social/2013/06/21/5388897.shtml (accessed 5 June 2017); 'Proekt Panteona'.

23 For the most important Moscow cemeteries, see M. Artamonov, *Moskovsky nekropol*, Moscow 1995; for the home page of the Memorial complex, see http://mil.ru/memorial _cemetery.htm (accessed 5 June 2017).

XVIII. The Lubyanka Project: Design for a *Musée Imaginaire* of Soviet Civilisation

1 Museums of the Soviet Union already exist or are being planned in Simbirsk/Ulyanovsk, Novosibirsk and on the site of the VDNKh metro station in Moscow. See K. Belenkina, I. Venyavkin, A. Nemzer and T. Trofimova (eds.), *Muzey 90-kh: Territoriya svobody*, Moscow 2016.

2 By autumn 2016 it had once again ceased to be accessible. The museum's home page was archived at https://web.archive.org/web/20010204213700/; http://www.fsb.ru /eng/history/museum.html (accessed 5 June 2017); the phone number at the time was 007-095-224-19-82.

3 On Pavlensky, see the cover story by Noah Sneider, 'Body Politics', in *The Economist*, June/ July 2016.

4 For the history of the district and its building developments, see A. G. Mitrofanov, *Progulki po staroy Moskve*, Moscow 2009.

5 Mikhail [Michael] Ossorgin, *Quiet Street*, New York 1930, 244, 248.

6 Jurij A. Treguboff, *Acht Jahre in der Gewalt der Lubjanka: Erlebnisbericht*, Frankfurt am Main 1999, 39. [The NTS was a Russian anticommunist organization founded in 1930. It ran the Posev publishing house which published samizdat writings, including those of Alexander Solzhenitsyn.]

7 *Butovsky Poligon: V rodnom krayu. Dokumenty, svidetelstva, sudby . . .* , Moscow 2004; map with explanations: *Topografiya terrora. Lubyanka i okrestnosti*: www.memo.ru (accessed 2 May 2017).

8 On the structure and history of these organs, see A. I. Kokurin and N. V. Petrov (eds.), *Lubyanka: VChK-OGPU-NKVD-NKGB-MGB-MVD-KGB 1917–1960*, Moscow 1997; Kokurin and Petrov, *Lubyanka: Organy VChK-OGPU-NKVD-NKGB-MGB-MVD-KGB 1917–1991. Spravochnik*, Moscow 2003.

9 Aleksandr Solzhenitsyn, *The Gulag Archipelago*, translated by Thomas P. Whitney, vol. 1, London 1974, 144.

10 Ibid., 212.

11 Aleksander Wat, *My Century: The Odyssey of a Polish Intellectual*, edited and translated by Richard Lourie, with a foreword by Czeslaw Milosz, London and New York 1990, 220.

12 Vladimir Bukovsky, *To Build a Castle*, translated by Michael Scammell, London 1978, 136–137.

13 Treguboff, *Acht Jahre in der Gewalt der Lubjanka*, 39–51.

14 Nicolas Berdyaev, *Dream and Reality*, translated by Katharine Lampert, London 1950, 237–238.

15 See Wladislaw Hedeler, *Chronik der Moskauer Schauprozesse 1936, 1937 und 1938: Planung, Inszenierung und Wirkung*, Berlin 2003; Karl Schlögel, *Moscow, 1937*, translated by Rodney Livingstone, Malden, MA and Cambridge 2012, 68, 123–143, 544–557.

16 Solzhenitsyn, *The Gulag Archipelago*, vol. 1, 214–216.

17 Wat, *My Century*, 203ff.

18 For Malraux's idea of a *musée imaginaire*, see Walter Grasskamp, *André Malraux und das imaginäre Museum: Die Weltkunst im Salon*, Munich 2014.

19 Nicolas Werth, *Cannibal Island: Death in a Siberian Gulag*, translated by Stephen Rendall, Princeton 2007.

20 Wat, *My Century*, 238, 241.

SELECTED READING

Svetlana Alexievich, *Second-Hand Time: The Last of the Soviets*, translated by Bela Shayevich, London 2016.

Helmut Altrichter, *Russland 1989: Der Untergang des sowjetischen Imperiums*, Munich 2009.

Anne Applebaum, *Gulag: A History*, New York 2003.

Jörg Baberowski, *Scorched Earth: Stalin's Reign of Terror*, translated by Steven Gilbert, Ivo Komljen, and Samantha Jeanne Taber, New Haven 2017.

Svetlana Boym, *Common Places: Mythologies of Everyday Life in Russia*, Cambridge, MA 1994.

Stéphane Courtois (ed.), *The Black Book of Communism: Crimes, Terror, Repression*, translated by Jonathan Murphy and Mark Kramer, Cambridge, MA and London 2000.

Alexander Etkind, *Internal Colonization: Russia's Imperial Experience*, Cambridge 2011.

Orlando Figes, *Revolutionary Russia, 1891–1991*, London and New York 2014.

Sheila Fitzpatrick, *Everyday Stalinism: Ordinary Life in Extraordinary Times—Soviet Russia in the 1930s*, New York and Oxford 1999.

Sheila Fitzpatrick, *A Spy in the Archives: A Memoir of Cold War Russia*, London 2013.

Sheila Fitzpatrick and Michael Geyer (eds.), *Beyond Totalitarianism: Stalinism and Nazism Compared*, New York 2009.

J. Arch Getty and Oleg V. Naumov, *The Road to Terror: Stalin and the Self-Destruction of the Bolsheviks, 1932–1939*, New Haven and London 2010.

Carsten Goehrke, *Russischer Alltag: Eine Geschichte in neun Zeitbildern vom Frühmittelalter bis zur Gegenwart*, vol. 3, *Sowjetische Moderne und Umbruch*, Zurich 2005.

Carsten Goehrke, *Russland: Eine Strukturgeschichte*, Paderborn, Munich and Zurich 2010.

Handbuch der Geschichte Russlands, vol. 3, *Von den autokratischen Reformen zum Sowjetstaat*, edited by Gottfried Schramm with the assistance of Dietrich Beyrau, Gernot Erler, Helmut Gross, Heiko Haumann, Manfred Hildermeier, Heinz-Dietrich Löwe and Thomas Steffens, Stuttgart 1983.

Handbuch der Geschichte Russlands, vol. 5, *Vom Ende des Zweiten Weltkriegs bis zum Zusammenbruch der Sowjetunion 1945–1991*, edited by Stefan Plaggenborg with the assistance of Helmut Altrichter, Beate Fieseler, Donald Filtzer, Corinna Kuhr-Korolev, Stephan Merl and Donald O'Sullivan, Stuttgart 2002.

Heiko Haumann, *Geschichte Russlands*, Munich 1996.

Mikhail Heller and Aleksandr M. Nekrich, *Utopia in Power: The History of the Soviet Union from 1917 to the Present*, translated by Phyllis B. Carlos, New York 1986.

Manfred Hildermeier, *Geschichte Russlands: Vom Mittelalter bis zur Oktoberrevolution*, Munich 2013.

Manfred Hildermeier, *Geschichte der Sowjetunion 1917–1991: Entstehung und Niedergang des ersten sozialistischen Staates*, Munich 1998.

Geoffrey Hosking, *Rulers and Victims: The Russians in the Soviet Union*, Cambridge, MA 2006.

Felix Philipp Ingold, *Russische Wege: Geschichte, Kultur, Weltbild*, Munich 2007.

Andreas Kappeler, *Russland als Vielvölkerreich: Entstehung—Geschichte—Zerfall*, Munich 1992.

Oleg V. Khlevniuk, *Stalin: New Biography of a Dictator*, translated by Nora Seligman Favorov, London 2015.

Tomasz Kizny, *Gulag*, with prefaces by Norman Davies, Jorge Semprun and Sergey Kovalev, translated by Antonia Lloyd-Jones, Buffalo, NY and Richmond Hill, Ontario 2004.

Wasili Kljutschewskij, *Geschichte Russlands*, 4 vols., Berlin 1925–1926.

Gerd Koenen, *Utopie der Säuberung: Was war der Kommunismus?*, Berlin 1998.

Stephen Kotkin, *Magnetic Mountain: Stalinism as a Civilization*, Berkeley 1995.

Denis Kozlov and Eleonory Gilburd (eds.), *The Thaw: Soviet Society and Culture during the 1950s and 1960s*, Toronto, Buffalo and London 2013.

Natalia Lebina, *Povsednevnost epohi kosmosa i kukuruzy: Destruktsiya bolshogo stilya–Leningrad 1950–1960-e gody*, St. Petersburg 2015.

Natalia Lebina, *Sovetskaya povsednevnost: Normy i anomalii. Ot voennogo kommunizma k bolshomu stilyu*, Moscow 2015.

Moshe Lewin, *The Soviet Century*, edited by Gregory Elliott, London 2005.

Roy A. Medvedev, *Let History Judge: The Origin and Consequences of Stalinism*, translated by Colleen Taylor, New York 1971.

Dietmar Neutatz, *Träume und Alpträume: Eine Geschichte Russlands im 20. Jahrhundert*, Munich 2013.

Heinrich Nolte, *Russland, UdSSR: Geschichte, Politik, Wirtschaft*, Hannover 1991.

Richard Pipes, *The Russian Revolution*, New York 1990.

Stefan Plaggenborg, *Experiment Moderne: Der sowjetische Weg*, Frankfurt am Main and New York 2006.

Karl Schlögel, *In Space We Read Time: On the History of Civilization and Geopolitics*, translated by Gerrit Jackson, New York 2016.

Karl Schlögel, *Moscow, 1937*, translated by Rodney Livingstone, Malden, MA and Cambridge 2012.

Karl Schlögel, *Petersburg: Das Laboratorium der Moderne 1909–1921*, Munich 2002 (1988).

Lewis Siegelbaum and Andrei Sokolov, *Stalinism as a Way of Life: A Narrative in Documents*, New Haven and London 2000.

Andrei Sinyavsky, *Soviet Civilization: A Cultural History*, translated by Joanne Turnbull, New York 1990.

Timothy Snyder, *Bloodlands: Europe between Hitler and Stalin*, London 2010.

Richard Stites, *Revolutionary Dreams: Utopian Vision and Experimental Life in the Russian Revolution*, New York 1989.

Hans-Joachim Torke, *Historisches Lexikon der Sowjetunion 1917/22–1991*, Munich 1993.

Petr Vail and Alexander Genis, *60-e: Mir sovetskogo cheloveka*, Ann Arbor 1988.

Nicolas Werth and Mark Grosset, *Die Ära Stalin: Leben in einer totalitären Gesellschaft*, Stuttgart 2008. [*Les Années Staline*, Paris 2007.]

INDEX

abbreviations, 162–63, 193, 234, 289–90, 420, 523. *See also* language; names
Abramov, Fyodor, 446
Abrassimov, Pyotr, 688
Abrikosov, Vladimir, 64
Abukekirov, Alexander, 504
Adshar, Anzhela, 842n20
Aelita, 595
aesthetic asceticism, 215
aestheticization of violence, 121, 131
aesthetics: critiques of, 116, 428–29; and functionality, 87, 94–95, 275, 332, 586–87, 604–5, 798; perceptions of, 199, 569, 757. *See also* architecture styles; *specific styles*
Afghanistan, 184–85, 582
Agranov, Yakov, 63, 70
agriculture: infrastructure of, 446–47; low productivity of, 445, 452; organisation of, 440; prioritisation of, 177, 477. *See also* collectivisation; industrialisation
air-conditioning, 374
air travel, 81, 168, 263, 420, 503
Aisenberg, Mikhail, 381
Aitmatov, Chingiz, 280
Akhmatova, Anna, 381, 540, 817
Akhumadulina, Bella, 280
Alexadrov, Grigory, 572
Alexander III, 775
Alexander Nevsky (Eisenstein), 601
Alexandrov, Grigory, 601
Alexandrov, Ivan Gavrilovich, 86–91
Alexeev, Vasily, 582
Alexivech, Svetlana, 9–10
Alexopoulos, Golfo, 631
Alife as Life Itself (Chukovsky), 193
Aliger, Margarita, 280, 383
Alksnis, Yakov, 687
Alpert, Max, 78, 80
Althusser, Louis, 38
Altman, Natan I., 187, 216, 554–55
Alymov, Sergey, 125
Amalrik, Andrey, 376, 383

Amalrik, Gyuzel, 385
American Relief Administration (ARA), 62
Amerikana, 343–44, 732–33. *See also* Soviet Americanism
Anatomy of Soviet Man, The (Mehnert), 742
Andersen, Lale, 600
Andreev, Leonid, 782
Andrezhevsky, I. M., 660
Andropov, Yury, 393, 729
Annadov, Sariy, 504
Annenkov, Yury, 518
Anonov, Sasha, 385
anonymity, 209, 361–62, 364–65. *See also* privacy
anti-Semitism, 67, 71–72, 133, 593, 603, 723, 741, 816
Antonioni, Michelangelo, 753
Antsiferov, Nikolay, 35, 138–39, 355–56, 660
apartment museums, 24, 325, 831n8
April Theses, 51
Aragon, Louis, 242
Arbeiter-Illustrierte Zeitung, 78
Arcades (Benjamin), 3, 413, 588
archaeology, 1–2, 227, 366. *See also* history
architecture styles, 52, 87, 100–101, 110–11, 275, 286–88, 293, 326–28, 334, 401, 428–29, 675, 793–94, 797, 805, 810. *See also* aesthetics
Archive of Russia Abroad, 68, 72
archives: access to, xvii, 59, 462, 465, 829n11; analyses of, 808–9, 825n7; and gulags, 623, 631, 644–47, 658; and memory, 40; purposes of, 119; restrictions of, 78, 455–57, 464; of the Russian diaspora, 68–69. *See also* history; knowledge; libraries; museums
Ardis, 464
Arendt, Hannah, 67, 739, 823n9, 829n14
Arkhangelsky, Alexander A., 503
Armageddon Averted (Kotkin), 4
Armoured Train 14–69 (Ivanov), 781
Arntz, Gerd, 471–72
Around the Leader's Coffin (Brodsky), 350

art collecting, 754–57
Art Deco, 145, 334, 678, 691
Art Nouveau, 27, 161, 168, 237, 275, 288, 364, 524, 670, 747
Ashkenazy, Vladimir, 223
Asisi, Yadegar, 418
Astafiev, Viktor, 446
Atelie, 599
atheism, 23–24, 192, 514, 560–61, 706–7, 709. *See also* religion; secularisation
Atlas Shrugged (Rand), 71
Auschwitz, 514, 628
Austro-Marxism, 471
authenticity, 17
authoritarianism, 230, 332. *See also* totalitarianism
automobiles, 34, 50, 80–81, 299, 388, 479, 501, 531–32, 782
avant-garde aesthetics, 25, 87, 316, 388, 405, 617, 747, 793
avant-garde art, 752–67
Averbakh, L. L., 124–25
Avtorkhanov, Abdurakhman, 383
Axthelm-Hoffman, Dieter, 437
Aykhenvald, Alexandra, 384
Aykhenvald, Yuly I., 64, 68, 384

Babel, Isaac, 78, 280
Babitsky, Konstantin, 392, 511
Bakhtin, Mikhail, 3
Bakkal, Ilya Yurievich, 64
Bakst, Léon, 68, 591, 608
Balanchine, George, 618
Baldaev, Danzig, 179–81
Ballets Russes, 68, 587, 591, 595, 608
Baltermants, Dmitry, 251, 350
barakholka. *See* bazaars
Bardygin, Vasily, 64
barracks, 52–53, 345–47, 845n1, 845n6
Barthes, Roland, 160
Baryshnikov, Mikhail, 609
Basic Principles of Classical Ballet (Shostakovich), 617
Bauermeister, Friedrich, 471–72
Bauhaus, 110, 316, 430
bazaars, 9–11, 13–15, 17–18, 108, 547, 549, 785, 824n2
Bazhenov, Alexander, 657
Beaux, Ernest, 237, 242

Bedeneev, Boris Yevgenievich, 90
Behrens, Peter, 519
Béjart, Maurice, 616
Bekhterev, Vladimir, 803
Bell, The (Herzen), 704
bells, 702–5, 707–8, 710–11
Bells, The (Rachmaninov), 711
Belov, Vasily, 446
Belsky, Yakov, 78
Bely, Andrey, 138
Belyaev, Vasily, 571
Benjamin, Walter, 3, 121, 207, 219, 224, 326, 328, 349, 383, 413, 472, 494, 588, 607, 702
Benois, Alexandre, 356, 519
Benois, Leonty N., 797
Berberova, Nina, 64
Berdyaev, Nikolay, 59, 63–64, 69, 71, 73, 464, 787, 813
Bergelson, David, 816
Beria, Lavrenty, 793, 811
Berliner Tageblatt, 93, 741–42
Berman, Matvey, 132
Berman, Yakov, 129
Beryozka shops, 745–51. *See also* Torgsin shops
Berzin, A., 125
Berzin, Eduard Petrovich, 634–40, 642
Berzin, Petya, 634
Berzin, Yan, 505, 683
Biermann, Wolf, 383
Birulya-Byalynitsky, 334
Birzhevye novosti, 255–56
Bisti, Dmitry, 381
Bittenfeld, Herwarth von, 738
Black Sea, 90, 267–68, 287, 292
Blake, George, 688
Bloch, Ernst, 808
Blockade of Russia, The, 554
Blok, Alexander, 98, 406–7
Blokhin, Vasily, 521, 814
Blubovsky, Boris, 660
Blum, Alain, 474, 477
Bodanov, Alexander, 521
bodies, 30, 81–82, 150–55, 183, 246, 571–73, 577, 579–80, 609–13, 623–24, 627–30. See also *fizkultura*; New Human Being; sport
bodybuilding, 583
Bogdanov, Alexander, 802
Bogdanov, Igor, 367

Bogdanov, Ivan, 373
Bogoraz, Larisa, 392, 512
Bohlen, Charles E., 738
Bohm, Hark, 383
Böhme, Jakob, 138
Boky, 657
Böll, Heinrich, 383, 389
Bolshaya sovetskaya entsiklopediya. See
   Great Soviet Encyclopedia
Bolshevik, 463
Bolsheviks: opposition to, 52, 60, 63, 66;
   strategies of, 42–44, 552; violence by,
   44, 59, 517. *See also* Civil War; Russian
   Revolution
Bolshevism, 60, 71, 82, 206
Bolt, The (Shostakovich), 617
Bonch-Bruevich, Mikhail Alexandrovich, 718
Bonner, Yelena, 393
Book of Tasty and Healthy Food, 250–55,
   259–60; imagery of, 250–51, 253; legacy
   of, 245–46; and the nomenklatura,
   254–55; scope of, 248–49
books: as bourgois symbol, 212; culture
   of, 205; demand for, 197–98, 532, 746.
   See also consumer goods; literacy; Russian
   literature; Soviet literature
Boquet de Catherine II, 235, 242
Boris Godunov (Mussorgsky), 711
Borisov, Nikolai, 443
Borisov, Vadim, 381
Borodin, 710–11
botany, 351–57, 360, 654–55, 846n5
Botkin, Sergey P., 287
Bouquet de Catherine II, 237
Bourke-White, Margaret, 78, 84, 86, 96, 108
Bowlt, John, 759
Boym, Svetlana, 5, 307, 823n8
Boy with Fish (Makhtin), 402
brain drain, 64, 68, 70, 73, 395
brands, 197, 221–22, 226, 234, 583, 606, 677.
   See also capitalism; consumerism
Braudo, Yevgeny, 206
Brecht, Bertolt, 396
Brezhnev, Leonid, 150, 386, 393, 418, 510,
   605, 729
Bright Stream, The (Shostakovich), 617
Brik, Liliya, 242, 383
Brik, Osip, 25
Brocard, Henri Afanasievich, 236

Brocard & Co., 235, 237
Brockdorff-Rantzau, Graf, 735–36
Brockhaus, F. A., 203
Brockhaus-Efron Encyclopedic Dictionary,
   203, 212, 836n4
Brodsky, Isaak, 350
Brodsky, Joseph, 73, 224, 308–10, 325, 377,
   383, 392, 616
Brodsky, Yury, 29, 657, 864n1
Bruhn, Peter, 456–57
Brumel, Valery, 387, 581
Brutskus, Boris Davidovich, 64
Bryant, Louise, 41, 60–61
Buber-Neumann, Margarete, 297, 489,
   812, 814
Budantsev, S., 125
Budyonny, Marshal Semyon, 505–7
Bukharin, Nikolay, 94, 206–8, 242, 461, 522,
   638, 687, 793, 814
Bukovsky, Vladimir, 392, 492, 813
Bukshpan, Yakov Markovich, 64
Bulatov, Erik, 162
Bulgakov, Mikhail, 185–86, 191, 241, 372, 693, 750
Bulgakov, Sergey N., 64
Bulgakova, Yelena, 569
Bulla, Karl, 119
Bulla, Viktor Karlovich, 119
Bulldozer Exhibition, 764
Bunin, Ivan, 59, 69–70
Burda Moden, 606
bureaucracy: depictions of, 162, 667; ineffi-
   ciencies of, 152, 485–86, 668–69, 674;
   language of, 466; and oppression, 541;
   rituals of, 523, 528
Burlyuk, David, 187
Burov, Andrey, 292
Bushmanov, Sergey, 625
Bushnell, John, 185
Busygin, Alexander, 600
Bykova, Maria, 231, 233

Calvino, Italo, 21
capitalism: and globalisation, 73; inefficiencies of, 129, 152, 246–47, 689; perceptions
   of, 254, 531, 546, 668, 745; regulated forms
   of, 94; spread of, 17, 94, 276; symbols of,
   159, 169, 197; and unemployment, 101.
   See also brands; communism; consumerism; socialism

Carnap, Rudolf, 417

Carnegie, Andrew, 144

Carpine, Giovanni da Pian del, 102

Cartier-Bresson, Henri, 408–10

cartography, 54–55, 81. *See also* spatiality

Castle, The (Kafka), 667

Castro, Fidel, 387–88, 510, 804

Catherine II, 90, 352, 360, 447

censorship, 35, 42, 62, 124, 209, 394, 457, 459–63, 606, 667, 719, 743, 785, 816. *See also* knowledge; *spetskhran*

censuses, 431–32, 473–76, 560

Chaadaev, Pyotr, 490, 774–75

Chabukiani, Vakhtang, 616

Chabunya, Josef, 504

Chagall, Marc, 753, 758–59

Chamberlain, William Henry, 501–2, 741

Chanel No. 5, 235, 237, 242

Chantsev, Alyosha, 384

Chaplin, Charlie, 94, 107

Chayanov, Alexander, 474

Chaykov, Joseph, 579

Chechulin, Dmitry, 805

Chekhonin, Sergey Vasilievich, 216

Chekhov, Anton, 276–77, 289

Chelyuskin, 174, 623–24, 682, 720

Chernenko, Konstantin, 393, 729

Chernobyl nuclear disaster, 151, 155, 744

Chernyshevsky, Nikolay, 315, 574–75

Cherry Orchard, The (Chekov), 276–77

Cheryomushki (Shostakovich), 421

Chicherin, Georgy, 736

childhood, 3, 18, 248, 322, 332, 504, 526, 528–29, 541–42, 580, 684, 688

Children of the Soviet Union (Pakhomov), 579

China, 490

Chizh, 562

Chkalov, Valery, 405, 521

Christmas, 530, 560, 562–65. *See also* holidays

"Chronicle of Current Events," 391–92

chronotope, 3

Chubar, Vlas, 90

Chukovsky, Korney, 18, 193, 280–81, 356, 518

Church and Revolution, 518

CIAM Congresses, 316

cinema, 80, 94, 105–7, 414, 577, 585, 601, 700, 717

Circus (Alexandrov), 601

citational politics, 208

civil rights movement, 391–92. *See also* human rights

Civil War: continuation of, 44; death toll, 477, 801–2; disruption of, 13, 234, 327, 591, 593, 759; economy during, 219, 258, 547–48; end of, 800; everyday life during, 219–20, 283–84; and exile, 60–61; and *kommunalkas*, 317; normality after, 239, 252, 371; slogans of, 214; uncertainty after, 103, 554; US intervention in, 94; violence of, 26, 32, 44. *See also* Bolsheviks; Russian Revolution; Soviet Union

class distinctions, 14, 94, 205, 224, 238–39, 254–55, 257–58, 435, 551, 599–600, 681–82, 689–90, 697. *See also* luxury goods; middle class; petit-bourgeois

Class Struggles in France, The (Marx), 463

Cliburn, Harvey 'Van,' 388, 585

clothing, 593, 681–84, 732. *See also* fashion

Coco Chanel, 242

Cold War: acoustic sphere of, 729–30; arenas of, 582, 625, 788–89; and diplomacy, 740; dsiplays of military force, 496–97; embassies during, 736–39; emergence of, 603; end of, 386; holidays during, 496; and media during, 744; strategies of, 391. *See also* espionage

cold weather, 127, 198, 360, 620–22, 628, 651, 654–55

collectivisation: effectiveness of, 547; end of, 445; and labour supply, 92; legacy of, 475, 681–82; and religion, 706–7; representations of, 28; strategies of, 103, 219, 291, 444; victims of, 32, 93, 146, 477; violence of, 296, 449, 474, 707. *See also* agriculture; industrialisation

colonisation, 641, 652

Commission for the Study of Natural Productive Forces (KEPS), 91–92

Common Cause, The (Fyodorov), 25

Common Places (Boym), 823n8

communal apartments. See *kommunalkas*

communication technologies, 49, 725, 744, 770

communism, 3–4, 532. *See also* capitalism; socialism

Communist International, 68, 463

commuting, 276, 278, 317, 319, 338, 548, 771

company towns, 33

conceptualism, 162

Congress of Vienna of 1815, 491

Conquest, Robert, 146

Constructivism, 86–89, 100, 110, 214, 294–95, 329, 359, 400–401, 430, 487, 506, 514–15, 595, 597, 602, 660, 707, 747, 757, 798

consumer goods, 17–18, 164–68, 224, 230, 246, 252, 548, 600, 603, 682, 746–48, 772–73. *See also* books

consumerism, 18, 34, 150, 164, 217–18, 254, 388, 411, 476, 748. *See also* brands; capitalism; mass culture

contemporaneity of the noncontemporaneous, 239–40

Cooper, Hugh Lincoln, 90–91, 95

Corbin, Alain, 231

Correspondence across a Room (Gershenzon and Ivanov), 283

Corvalán, Luis, 392

cosmopolitanism, 207, 565, 737–38, 816. *See also* globalisation

Cossacks of the Kuban (Pyriev), 252

Costakis, George, 752–67

Coty, François, 237

crematoriums, 513–22. *See also* death

Crimea, xix, 74, 289–92, 299, 348

Crimean War, 655

Cuba, 387–88, 510

Cubism, 554

Curtius, Ernst Robert, 284

Czech-Jochberg, Erich, 487

Czechoslovakia, 68, 164–65, 379, 392

dachas: construction of, 274–75, 441; culture of, 279–81, 383, 840n1; locations of, 272–73; perceptions of, 275–76; security at, 764; and temporality, 279. *See also* nomenklatura

Dachniki (Gorky), 275–76

Daguerre, Jacques, 413–14

Dalstroy, 379, 620–23, 632–36, 640–44, 862n3, 864n57. *See also* Kolyma

dance, 609–18

Daniel, Yuly, 383, 386

Danilevsky, Nikolay, 491

Danko, Natalia Y., 217

Das Korrupte Imperium (Holm), 743

data encryption, 694

Davies, Joseph E., 569–70, 750

death, 513, 516, 518–21, 628, 632, 728, 802–4. *See also* crematoriums

Debabov, Dmitry, 78

Deborin, Abram, 207

Decline of the West (Spengler), 60

Defence of Sevastopol, The, 580

deindustrialisation, 144. *See also* industrialisation

Deineka, 578–79

Deineka, Alexander, 125, 578, 580, 600

Dekorativnoe iskusstvo, 337

Delaunay, Vadim, 379, 392, 511

Demag, 105

Der Spiegel, 461, 746

de-Stalinisation, 150, 162, 210, 318, 385–87, 417–18. *See also* Stalin, Josef

deurbanisation, 325. *See also* urbanisation

Diaghilev, Serge, 68, 73, 587, 591, 608, 618

dialectical materialism, 388

diaspora, xix, 58–59, 66–72, 461, 609, 759. *See also* exile

Dickerman, Leah, 121, 830n8

Didok, Pyotr, 504

Dimitrov, Georgy, 683

Dionisovich, Georgii, 755

Dior, Christian, 29, 388, 586–87

dioramas, 413–19

diplomatic procedures, 739–40, 747. *See also* embassies

Dirksen, Herbert von, 735

diseases, 55, 330, 373, 515, 633, 802

Dmitrov, Georgy, 804

DniproHES (Dniprovskaya Hidroelektrostantsiya): aesthetics of, 90–91, 94–95; construction of, 86–89, 92–96, 130; depictions of, 830n11; destruction of, 96; legacy of, 83–84, 97, 144–45, 148; scale of, 84–86

Dobrovolsky, Alexey, 391

Dobuzhinsky, 554

Doctor Zhivago (Pasternak), 280, 778

Dolgorukov, Nikolay, 500

Dolmatovsky, Yevgeny, 193

Donskoy, Dmitry, 507–8

doorbells, 303–4, 361

doorways, 670–71

Dostoevsky, Fyodor, 70, 275

Dreiser, Theodore, 109

Dremlyuga, Vladimir, 392, 511

Drevin, Alexander, 753, 759
drinking, 249–50, 322, 342, 409
Dubnow, Simon, 72
Dudinskaya, Natalia, 615–16
Dunham, Vera, 213
Duranty, Walter, 741
Duzhba narodov, 393
Dvinina, Alyona, 259
Dzerzhinsky, Felix E., 39, 63, 215–16, 291, 635, 694, 809
Dzhimbinov, S., 458

Eastman, Max, 41
Ebermann, V., 138
Eco, Umberto, 160
education, 19, 21, 27, 105, 107–8, 165, 202–3, 223–24, 388, 529, 656. *See also* knowledge; literacy
Efron, I. A., 203
egalitarianism, 446, 517
Ehrenburg, Ilya, 95, 242, 280, 386, 577, 604
Eikhmans, F. I., 657, 660
Eisenhower, Dwight D., 571
Eisenstein, Sergey, 48, 370, 601
Ekonomist, 60
electrification, 53, 84–85, 88–89, 91–92, 96, 147, 330, 457, 557, 655, 718. *See also* GOELRO (State Commission for the Electrification of Russia); modernisation
Elias, Norbert, 232, 369
Ellington, Duke, 389
embassies, 735–40, 760, 764. *See also* diplomatic procedures
Empire of Signs (Barthes), 160
Enlightenment spirit, 26, 205
Envy (Olesha), 579
Enzensberger, Hans Magnus, 383, 389
Erlikh, A., 125
Ermler, Fridrikh, 13
Eshliman, Karl I., 287
espionage, 736–37, 740, 742–43. *See also* Cold War
Etkind, Alexander, 641
European Functionalism, 214
EuroRemont, 337
everyday life: acceptance of, 311; crises of, 315–16; depictions of, 164, 225, 245, 251; harshness of, 339–40; household rituals, 324; and hygiene, 247–48; organisation
of, 216, 681; paradoxes of, 667–68; places of, 35, 167, 307, 382, 823n8; and queuing, 532–33, 538–39; and radio, 726; routines of, 29, 46, 164–69, 224, 267, 269, 510, 523–24, 529, 615, 672–73; sounds of, 303–4. *See also* standards of living; survival
excursionism, 24–25, 36, 138
exile, 58–63, 65–66, 68, 70–72, 94, 380, 392, 432, 476, 492, 511–12, 593, 608, 683, 759, 774. *See also* diaspora
Exter, Alexandra, 591, 797
eyewitness accounts, xviii, 4–5, 21, 40–42, 55, 59, 284, 622–23, 626–28, 685–86, 709, 719–20. *See also* history

factory environment, 33
Fadeev, Alexander, 280
Fairbanks, Douglas, 94
family: replacement of, 526; traditions of, 527–28
famine, 62, 93–94, 296, 432, 472, 475, 477, 548. *See also* hunger; scarcity
fashion, 30, 236, 552, 586–87, 593, 595–96, 604–7, 683–84, 732. *See also* clothing
Fast, Howard, 463
Favorsky, Vladimir, 598
Faynberg, Viktor, 392, 512
Feffer, Itzeik, 816
Ferrari, Giacomo, 52
Ferrein, Vladimir Karlovich, 236
Feuchtwanger, Lion, 358, 403, 463
Field of Mars, 519
Filonov, 759
Finish-Soviet Winter War, 662, 760
Firin, Semyon, 124, 126, 132, 137, 139
Fischer, Friedrich Ernst Ludwig, 352
Fitzpatrick, Sheila, 296–97
Five-Year Plans: costs of, 292, 641, 711, 748; and cultural revolution, 91, 255, 401, 557; forced labour in, 122; and foreigners, 732–33; goals of, 103, 105, 146, 466–67; and infrastructure construction, 92, 127, 341, 709; legacy of, 80, 201, 343, 681–82; and nationwide mobilisation, 126, 149, 586, 588; prioritisation of industry, 254, 598; promotion of, 100, 116–17, 146, 162, 502–3, 532, 707
fizkultura, 569–84. *See also* bodies; parades
Fizkulturny parad (Alexandrov), 572

Florensky, Florensky, 662
Florensky, Pavel, 25, 660–61
Florovsky, Georges, 70
Fokine, Michel, 616
Fomin, Ivan A., 518, 797
Fonda, Jane, 383
food, 163, 166, 246–48, 382, 530
forced labour, 121, 128, 131–32, 621; and
    railways, 778; scale of, 620; scale of
    workforce, 134; unsustainability of,
    642; valorisation of, 82. *See also* labour;
    prisons; re-education
Ford, Henry, 98, 145, 253
Fordism, 577
foreigners: access to the Soviet Union,
    98–99, 485; distrust of, 91, 667–68;
    encounters with, 113, 382, 585; tourists,
    163; visibility of, 732–33
Formalism, 120, 381, 597, 617
Förster, Otto, 802
Fortune, 78
Foul and the Fragrant, The (Corbin), 232
'Fragment of an Empire' (Ermler), 13
France, 67–69, 71, 236, 238, 240–42, 586, 591,
    594, 609
France, Anatole, 802
Frank, Josef, 472
Frankfurter Zeitung, 349
free speech, 4, 387, 395
French Revolution, 236, 527, 555
Frenkel, Naftaly, 132, 138–39
Frick, Henry Clay, 144
Fridman, Rudolf, 233
Fritzsche, Hans, 724
From Double Eagle to the Red Flag (Krasnov),
    72
From Under the Rubble (Solzhenitsyn), 386
Frunze, Mikhail, 691–92
Funeral of the Avant-Garde, The (Costakis),
    757
furniture: demand for, 532; high quality of,
    681; new styles of, 226, 329, 331, 334, 691;
    prerevolutionary styles, 27, 329; simple
    styles of, 335–36; symbolism of, 12–14,
    165, 219–20, 290, 327–28, 688
Furtseva, Yekaterina, 766
Futurism, 68, 109, 187–88, 757
Fyodorov, Nikolay, 25, 802
Fyodorov-Davidov, Alexey, 25

Fyodorovna, Alexandra, 460
Fyodorovna, Maria, 237, 601

Gabay, Ilya, 379
Gaddy, Clifford G., 643
Gagarin, Yury, 3, 176, 388, 510, 724, 818
Gaidar, Arkady, 18
Galanskov, Yury, 380, 391
Galich, Sasha, 380
Garanin, S. N., 632
Gardner, Francis, 216
Garshin, Vsevolod Mikhailovich, 353–56
Gary, Elbert H., 143
Gary, Indiana, 143–45
Gastev, Alexey, 96, 145
Gatrell, Peter, 781
Gausner, G., 125
Gegello, Alexander, 372
Gekht, S., 125
Gelfreikh, Vladimir, 292, 294, 455, 797, 805
gender roles, 256, 332, 526, 599
Genis, Alexander, 389
Georgia, 26, 165, 296
Gerlina-Aykhenvald, Valeriya, 384
German Democratic Republic, 164
German Ideology, The (Marx), 575
German Romantic architecture, 111
Germany: relation with Soviet Union, xix,
    93–94, 489, 503, 735; Russian disapora
    in, 66, 68
Gershenzon, Mikhail, 283–84, 800
Gesellschaft und Wirtschaft (Neurath), 469
Gessen, Yosif, 207
Geyer, Dietrich, 163, 275
Gide, André, 569
Gidulyanov, P. V., 707
Giedieon, 328
Gift, The (Nabokov), 71
Gift to Young Housewives, A (Molokhovets),
    255–60
Ginsberg, Allen, 383
Ginzburg, Alexander, 377, 381, 385
Ginzburg, Arina, 385
Ginzburg, Lydia, 543
Ginzburg, Moisey Y., 292, 326
Ginzburg, Yevgeniya, 383, 621–26, 640, 668,
    693–94, 727–28
Gippius, Zinaida, 212, 276–77
Girl with an Oar (Shadr), 402, 579

Glan, Betti, 404
glasnost, 4, 211, 386, 737. *See also* perestroika
Glazunov, Ilya, 767
Glinka, Mikhail, 727
globalisation: and culture, 29, 225, 259, 565; early phases of, 161, 299; and economics, 243, 360, 689; effects of, 638; of information, 390–91, 770; and sport, 581, 583; symbols of, 159, 260; and temporality, 413, 565; and travel, 263, 270, 406, 493. *See also* cosmopolitanism
Gnedin, Yevgeny, 383
Godless movement, 23–24
Godunov, Boris, 709
Goehrke, Carsten, 439
GOELRO (State Commission for the Electrification of Russia), 89–91, 95–96, 103, 147, 466, 474. *See also* electrification
Gogol, 590
Golden Age (Shostakovich), 617
Goldschmidt, Alfons, 488
Golosov, Ilya, 329
Golyzheva, Yelena, 384
Goncharova, Natalia, 759
Gontmakher, Yevgeny, 452
Goodman, Benny, 585
Gorbachev, Mikhail, 298, 339, 737
Gorbanevskaya, Natalia, 385, 391–92, 511
Gorky, Maxim, 34, 42, 78–80, 124, 174, 240, 275–76, 280, 284, 370, 401, 521, 569, 580, 601, 650, 660–61, 777
Gorky Park, 399–412, 849n20
Goryaev, Sergey, 805
Goryaeva, Tatiana, 717
Gosplan, 466, 658
Gottwald, Klement, 804
GPU. *See* OGPU
Graf, Oskar Maria, 403
graffiti, 184–88
Graftio, Genrikh Osipovich, 91
Grapes of Wrath, The (Steinbeck), 782
Great Depression, 94, 101, 145–46, 468, 782
Great Patriotic War. *See* World War II
Great Soviet Encyclopedia, 200–202, 205–12
Great Terror: arrests during, 55; awareness of, 472; depictions of, 13, 28, 163, 201–2, 540–41, 721–22; legacy of, 22–23, 34, 39, 150; memory of, 162, 277–78, 304, 809;

orchestration of, 296; and religious persecution, 653; survival strategies of, 108, 319; victims of, 55–56, 78, 106, 113–25, 140, 179, 241, 379, 388, 474, 491–92, 505, 521, 577, 632–33, 650, 658, 685–87, 723, 761–62. *See also* Stalin, Josef
Greaves, Ivan Mikhailovich, 25
Green Stripe (Rozanova), 755–56
Gregorian calendar, 558–60, 565
Grekov, Mitrofan, 415
Grigorenko, Petro, 392
Grimsted, Patricia K., 825n7
Gromov, Mikhail, 505
Gropius, Walter, 144
Grshebin Verlag, 42
Gründerzeit, 328
Guevara, Che, 387–88
Gulag system: administration of, 133; awareness of, 472; causes of death in, 633; closing of, 621; cold conditions of, 621–22, 626–27, 629–30, 632–33, 656, 862n7; depictions of, 134, 211, 540–41, 626–27, 631, 650, 660–61; establishment of, 122–23, 662; intellectual activities in, 659–60; as labour supply, 101, 635, 642, 658; memorialisation of, 644–47, 652, 826n18; populations of, 181, 478–80, 633, 641, 656–59; as reeducation project, 119–20; survivors of, 29, 387, 458, 626; traces of, 644–47, 658, 662, 701. *See also* prisons; re-education; violence
Gumilyov, Lev, 394
Gumilyov, Nikolay, 518
Gutsait, V. L., 243

Habermas, Jürgen, 51, 383
Hagemeister, Michael, 25
Halle, Fannina, 526
Hanging Construction (Rodchenko), 753, 758
Happy Youth (Yosilevich), 572, 580
Harper's Bazaar, 594
Harriman, Averill, 738
Hartman, Egbert, 256
Håstad, Disa, 384
Haxthausen, Baron von, 231
Heartfield, John, 78–79
Heart of a Dog, The (Bulgakov), 372
Hedeler, Wladislaw, 686
Heine, Heinrich, 846n9

Heller, Michel, 828n3
Hemingway, Ernest, 463
Herzen, Alexander, 704, 711
Hesse, Hermann, 207
Hildermeier, Manfred, 477
Hilger, Gustav, 738–39
Hill, Fiona, 643
history: artifacts of, 688, 816–17; control of, 29, 35, 463–64; end points of, 69, 360; of local areas, 22; material traces of, 214, 794; methods of, 1–5, 21, 34–36, 260, 307, 366; narratives of, 2–3, 24–26, 162; and national identity, 38; perceptions of, 30, 57, 208; purposes of, 20; reinterpretation of, 1, 28, 40, 206; and renaming, 158–59; representations of, 413–19; and spatiality, 30; and unified narratives, 19–20, 24–25, 36–37, 39, 80. See also archaeology; archives; eyewitness accounts; memory; museums
History of Bells and the Bell Founder's Art (Olovyanishnikov), 702
History of the Soviet Union (Hildermeier), 477
Hitler, Adolf, 59, 67, 96, 210, 490–91, 739
Hitler-Stalin Pact, 71–72
Ho Chi Minh, 804
Hoffman, David, 407
holidays, 137, 176, 257, 265–68, 291–92, 489, 496–97, 510, 530, 552–60, 562–65, 818–19. *See also* Christmas; religion; secularisation
Holm, Kerstin, 743
Holodomor famine, 26, 93
homoeroticism, 579
Homo Ludens (Huizinga), 573
homosexuality, 610
Honecker, Erich, 102
honours system, 95, 112, 133, 137, 170–73, 176–77, 508. *See also specific awards*
Hoover Dam, 94–95, 144–45, 345
Hornbostel, Henry, 144
Horowitz, Vladimir, 223
House of Models, 597–601
House on the Moskva, 679–90
How the Steel Was Tempered (Ostrovsky), 778
Hristoforov, V. S., 65
Huizinga, Johan, 573
human rights, 364–65, 386–87, 391–92, 564, 643. *See also* civil rights movement
Humboldt, Alexander von, 103

Hungary, 174, 510
hunger, 283–84, 339, 449. *See also* famine
Hunger Relief Committee (Pomgol), 62
hunger strikes, 60
hygiene, 247, 321, 329–30, 346, 357, 369, 372–73, 515

Ignatovich, Boris, 78, 578
Ilf, Ilya, 192, 358, 372, 669, 675
Ilyin, Ivan Alexandrovich, 64, 464
Ilyin, M., 145
imperialism, 799–800
Imperial Porcelain Factory (LFZ), 216
"In a Room and a Half" (Brodsky), 308–10
Inber, Vera, 125, 280
India, 405
indigenous peoples, 621
individualism, 108, 317, 331, 369
industrialisation: and automation, 253; costs of, 634, 636–37, 748–49; and cultural revolution, 219; destruction of, 707, 779; documentation of, 201, 479; economic effects of, 547; landscapes of, 144, 417; and mass housing, 421–22; memories of, 681; and national identity, 33–34; pace of, 274, 332, 344, 557, 561; paradoxes of, 565; phases of, 18, 93, 144, 477, 788; prioritisation of, 103, 428, 467, 546; and religion, 706–7; and specialisation, 253–54; symbols of, 77, 407, 503, 691; and urbanisation, 319. *See also* agriculture; collectivisation; deindustrialisation; Sturm und Drang phase
input-output matricies, 474
Insurrection (Redko), 56
intelligentsia: concentration of, 446; critics of, 276, 394–95, 580, 657; expulsion of, 58, 64, 66; living space of, 382, 384, 616, 730; perceptions of, 124, 386; re-education of, 133–34; replacement of, 61–62; symbolism of, 27; travel patterns of, 269–71, 275, 494
International Women's Day, 43, 231, 559
internet, 29, 270, 395, 645, 690, 698, 744, 808
In the First Circle (Solzhenitsy), 693
Into the Whirlwind (Ginzburg), 622
Iran, 492
"Iron Foundy" (Mosolov), 710
Irony of Fate (Ryazanov), 422–23
Iskra, 687

Iskusstvo odevatsya, 599
Islam, 527–28, 530, 565
Island Hell, An (Malsagoff), 660
ISOTYPE, 470
Ivan III, 489
Ivan IV, 489–90
Ivanov, P. V., 240
Ivanov, Vs., 125
Ivanov, Vsevolod, 781
Ivanov, Vyacheslav, 283–84, 554–55
Ivanov, Yevgeny Pavlovich, 758
Ivan the Terrible, 654, 685
Ivens, Joris, 102
Izgoev-Lande, Alexander Solomonovich,
    64–65
Izmailovsky Park, 9, 11
Izostat, 468–73
Izvestia, 121, 198, 451, 576, 743

Jähn, Sigmund, 176
Jakobson, Roman, 70–71
Japan, 490
Jarnoux, Maurice, 817
Jaroff, Serge, 711
Jasieński, Bruno, 125, 683
jazz, 389, 585, 604. *See also* music
Jones, David, 276
journalism, 41–46, 55–56, 741–44. *See also*
    propaganda
Judaism, 527–28, 530, 565
Jugendstil, 237
Julian calendar, 558–60, 565
Jünger, Ernst, 101, 145–46, 149

Kabakov, Emiliya, 525
Kabakov, Ilya, 311–13, 323, 363, 367, 370, 375,
    525, 759
Kachalov, Vasily, 716–17
Kachurin, Igor Vasilievich, 755
Kafka, Franz, 667
Kaganovich, Lazar, 411
Kahn, Albert, 144
Kalashnikov, Mikhail T., 805
Kalita, Ivan, 411
Kalmykov, Viktor, 107
Kamenev, Lev, 209, 280, 461, 813–14
Kandinsky, 678, 758–59
Kant, Immanuel, 548, 675
Kantorowicz, Ernst, 803

Kaplun, Boris G., 518
Kaplun, Ira, 380
Karmen, Roman, 78
Karsavin, Lev Platonovich, 63–65
Karsavina, Tamara, 63, 608, 615
Kassil, Lev, 280
Kataev, Valentin, 78, 82, 125, 280
Katkov, George, 70
Kedrov, M. S., 660
Kenna, George F., 737
Kennan, George F., 738
Kennedy, Edward, 753
Kennedy, John F., 389
Kersten, Kurt, 487–88
Keynes, John Maynard, 616
KGB, 394, 765, 809, 816. *See also* NKVD;
    OGPU
Khabibulla, Galiullin, 107
Khaldey, Yevgeny, 78
Khan, Batu, 102
Khan-Magomedov, Selim O., 866n5
Khariton, B. I., 65
Khasrevin, S., 125
Khayutina, Yevgeniya, 78
Khmelnitsky, Dmitry, 841n13
Khodasevich, Vladislav, 64
Khrushchev, Nikita: death of, 298; early life
    of, 683; and economic theory, 548; family
    of, 683–84; housing policy, 110, 150, 318,
    320, 336, 347, 411, 685; legacy of, 793;
    openness under, 183, 605, 653, 662; re-
    pression under, 389; resignation of, 386;
    and Stalin's cult of personality, 385–86;
    and the United States, 388, 585–86
Khrushchev's secret speech, 417–18, 726,
    744
Khrustalyov, N. I., 133, 139
Kibirov, Timur, 267
Kim, Yuly, 377–85
Kim Il-Sung, 804
Kirov, Sergey, 319, 326–27, 348, 358, 521,
    617, 722
Kirov ensemble, 617–18
Kirsten-Collein, Ursula, 612
Kisch, Egon Erwin, 328
Kissin, Yevgeny, 223
Kistyakovsky, Bogdan, 527
kitchens, 248, 250, 314, 321, 323, 325, 330, 339,
    376–86, 394–95

Kizevetter, Alexander Alexandrovich, 64
Kizny, Tomasz, 644
Klebanov, Vladimir, 392
Klemperer, Georg, 802
Klutsis, Gustav, 577, 759
Klyuchevsky, Vasily, 205–6
Klyuev, Nikolay, 781
Klyun, Ivan, 753, 759
Knickerbocker, Hubert Renfro, 600, 741
Knorin, Vilhelm, 687
knowledge: accessibility of, 21, 465; con-
    sistency of, 205; control of, 200–203,
    473, 741, 744, 785; dissemination of,
    713–14; marketplace of, 536; normal-
    isation of, 211; organisation of, 205–6,
    208–10. *See also* archives; censorship;
    education; memory; propaganda;
    spetskhran
Kochubey, Viktor, 352
Koeppen, Wolfgang, 721
Kogan, Lazar, 132, 138–39
Kogan, Moisey Lvovich, 124
Kohout, Pavel, 367
Kojève, Alexandre, 59, 71
Kolasin, Alexey, 504
Koleva, Marina, 239
kolkhozy, 447, 452. *See also* sovkhozy
Kollontai, Alexandra, 527
Koltsov, Mikhail, 78
Kolychyov, Fyodor, 654
Kolyma, 644. *See also* Dalstroy
Kolyma Stories (Solzhenitsyn), 626, 628
kommunalkas: community of, 230, 318–20,
    534; construction of, 317, 332–33; as
    contested spaces, 314–15, 3680; depic-
    tions of, 303–4, 372; dissolution of,
    325, 373, 380–81, 435; floor plans of,
    312–14, 320–25; legacy of, 305–7, 861n9;
    perceptions of, 307, 311; population
    density, 306, 309–10, 312, 372; tele-
    phones in, 695. *See also* mass-housing
    programme
kompromat, 462
Komsomolskaya pravda, 121
Konchalovsky, Andrey, 367
Kondratiev, Nikolay Dmitrievich, 64,
    474–75
Konstantinovich, Dmitry, 290–91
Kontinent, 464

Kopelev, Lev, 383
Korabelnikov, G., 125
Kork, Avgust, 502, 685
Kornai, János, 546
Kornfeld, J., 329
Korolyov, Sergey, 389, 642, 817
Korshunov, Mikhail, 685
Kosakov, M., 125
Kosarev, Alexander, 78, 577, 683
Kostaki, Georgy Dionisovich, 752–67
Köstring, Ernst, 407, 503–4, 738
Kostrovitskaya, Vera S., 612–13
Kosygin, Alexey, 688
Kotkin, Stephen, 4, 99, 112
Koussevitzky, Serge, 59, 70
Kovalyov, Ivan Sergeevich, 392
Kovan, Abram Saulovich, 64
Kozlov, V. F., 709
Kracauer, Siegfried, 349, 351
Kramer, F. A., 488
Krasin, Leonid, 793
Krasnaya Moskva, 231–44
Krasnopevtsev, Dmitry, 758–59
Krasnov, Nikolay P., 287, 290–91, 816
Krasnov, Pyotr, 72
Kraval, Ivan, 475
Krestinsky, Nikolay, 738, 814
Kriger, Yevgeny, 576
Krinsky, Vladimir, 577, 797
Kritsman, Lev, 206–8
Krokodil, 604
Krug, Karl, 206
Krupskaya, Nadezhda, 25, 460, 462, 801
Krzhizhanovsky, Gleb, 95–96
Kshesinskaya, Mathilda-Marie, 608
Kucher, Katharina, 849n1
Kulischer, Alexander, 72
kulturnost, 255, 557
Küppers, Sophie, 472
Kurbas, Les, 662
Kursky, Dmitry, 60
Kuskova, Yekaterina D., 60, 64
Kustodiev, Boris, 19, 553–54
Kutepov, Alexander, 71
Kuts, Vladimir, 581
Kutuzov, Mikhail, 414, 508
Kuybyshev, Valerian, 521, 683
Kuznets, Simon, 59
Kuznetsov, Anatoly, 222, 545

labour: artifacts of, 104–5; factory conditions, 574; and leisure time, 400; objectification of, 344; organisation of, 344, 550, 563, 577; potentials of, 100, 144; rationalisation of, 258, 426; rhythms of, 444, 559, 565, 673–74, 704, 772; sources of, 105; and specialisation, 105; and sport, 580; supply of, 92–93, 101, 635; valorisation of, 112, 145, 155. See also forced labour; leisure time

Lacis, Asja, 219

Lagutenko, Vitaly, 425

Lamanova, Nadezhda Petrovna, 591, 594–96, 601–3, 606–7

Lamprecht, Karl, 5

Landau, Grigory, 72

language, xviii–xix, 22, 78, 159, 179, 185, 191, 211, 382, 461, 469–70, 487, 614–15, 717. See also abbreviations; names

Lapin, B., 125

Lapshin, Ivan Ivanovich, 64

Larin, Yury, 206

Larina, Anna, 687

Larionov, Mikhail, 759

Lashin, Lev, 581

Lashko, N., 333

Lashkova, Vera, 391

Laurent, Yves Saint, 585

Lavrov, Igor, 758

Lavut, Alexander, 392

League of Militant Atheists, 707, 709

League of Nations, 67, 501–2

leather jackets, 593, 683–84

Lebedev, Andrey, 532

Lebedev-Kumach, Vasily, 403

Lebedev-Polyansky, Pavel Ivanovich, 460

Lebina, Natalia, 168, 347, 745

Le Figaro, 461

Legat, Nikolay, 616

Legend of the Invisible City of Kitezh, The (Rimsky-Korsakov), 711

leisure time, 264, 274, 288, 293, 399–400, 704. See also labour

Lemberg, Alexander, 125

Lenin, Vladimir: cult of personality, 330, 800; death of, 802; enemies of, 64; and ideological hegemony, 62–63; leadership of, 58–60, 316, 369, 667; legacy of, 55–56, 501, 507–8, 718, 795–800, 802–6, 875n10;

memorialisation of, 174, 258, 348, 358, 410, 792–94; modernisation strategies, 89, 457; monuments to, 89, 97, 111, 215, 402, 499–500, 510, 680, 801; and the Russian Revolution, 42–43, 48–49, 56–57, 777; and sanatoriums, 289; and sports, 574; writings by, 682

Leningrad: bazaars in, 549; central role of, 123, 130, 615; controlling queues in, 540; housing in, 308, 320, 326–27; parades in, 571–72; population of, 319, 548; siege of, 542–43, 715. See also Petrograd; St. Petersburg

Leninism, 386, 794, 798–99, 801. See also Stalinism

Lenin Library, 368, 455–56, 459, 465

Lenin's Mausoleum, 358, 387, 496, 499, 501–2, 520, 550, 564, 570–71, 792–98, 802–4, 806. See also Red Square

Leonidov, Ivan, 100–101

Leonov, Leonid, 282

Leontiev, Vasily, 474

Lesgaft, Pyotr Frantsevich, 575

Less Than One (Brodsky), 616

Letatlin (Tatlin), 758

Levi, Primo, 628

Levina, Natalia, 336, 516

Levitan, Yury Borisovich, 507, 713–30, 868n3

Lewin, Moshe, 430–31

Libikh-Lipold, 138

libraries, 455, 460, 463–64, 816. See also archives

Lifar, Serge, 617

Life, 78, 586, 588, 860n2

lifeworlds, 1–2, 21–24, 743, 780–82

Lifton, Robert Jay, 631

Likhachyov, Dmitry, 224, 659–60

Lilina, Z. I., 517

Lipchitz, Jacques, 579

Lippman, Walter, 41

Lissitzky, El, 78, 199, 472, 577

literacy, 48, 107–8, 136–37, 167, 409, 557. See also books; education

Little Golden Calf, The (Ilf and Petrov), 372

Litvinov, Maxim, 683

Litvinov, Pavel, 385, 392, 512

Litvinova, Renata, 233

Lockhart Affair, 635

Lokutov, Mikhail, 240–41

Lopokova, Lydia, 616
Lopukhov, Fyodor, 616–17
Lossky, Nikolay Onufrievich, 64, 71, 464
Louis Seize, 288
Lovell, Stephen, 717
Lozovsky, Solomon, 687, 816
lubok, 80
Lubyanka, 3, 39, 158, 521, 650, 808–19
Lunacharsky, Anatoly, 87, 206, 520, 797
Luppol, Ivan, 25
luxury goods, 108, 160, 166, 236, 238–39, 241, 252, 254, 287, 348, 592–94, 605, 682, 685, 689–90. *See also* class distinctions
Luzhkov, Yury, 159, 168, 230, 436
Lvov, Prince, 43
Lysenko, Trofim, 683
Lyubimov, Nikolay Ivanovich, 64

Mach, Ernst, 471
Machine in the Garden, The (Marx), 100
Magic Mountain, The (Mann), 283–84
Magnetic Mountain (Kotkin), 99
Magnitogorsk: construction of, 104–10; legacy of, 98, 100–102, 144–46, 148, 343; and pollution, 112, 142–44; scale of, 99, 104, 110
Magnitostroy (Polonsky), 105
Maid of Pskov, The (Rimsky-Korsakov), 711
Makarov, V. G., 65
Makarova, Nadezhda Sergeevna, 598, 601
Makhtin, Samuil, 402
Malevich, Kazimir, 19, 25, 187, 217, 327, 587, 595, 759, 817
Mallori, D., 515
Malraux, André, 6, 463, 816–17
Malsagoff, Sergey, 660
Manchuria, 721
Mandelstam, Nadezhada, 305, 383
Mandelstam, Osip, 383, 407, 700–701
Manizer, Matvey, 579
Mann, Henrich, 3
Mann, Thomas, 283–84
Man with a Movie Camera (Vertov), 578
Mao Zedong, 231, 804
Marchenko, Anatoly, 380
Margolina, Sonja, 384
Markov-Grinberg, Mark, 78
marriage, 340–41, 523–27, 530
Marshak, Samuil, 193

Marx, Karl, 211, 332, 344, 463, 500, 548, 575, 580, 799–800
Marx, Leo, 100
Marxism, 24, 98, 205, 207, 330, 386–87, 471, 799–800. *See also* neo-Marxism
Marxism-Leninism, 18, 209, 306
Masaryk, T. G., 68
Mask of Sorrow (Neizvestny), 644
Maslov, V. N., 131, 133, 139
mass culture, 406–8, 411, 413, 418–19. *See also* consumerism
mass-housing programme, 110, 420–24, 805. See also *kommunalkas*
Master and Margarita, The (Bulgakov), 185–86, 241, 693, 750
Matsesta, 292–96
Matyushin, 759
May, Ernst, 100–101, 111, 142–43
Mayakovsky, 88, 110, 199, 330, 358, 554
Mayakovsky, Vladimir, 68, 83–84, 101, 521, 524
McKee, Arthur, 143
McKee Company, 105, 142
Medvedkin, Alexander, 572
Mehnert, Klaus, 303, 307, 403, 742
Melgunov, Sergey M., 64
Melnikov, Konstantin, 80, 400–401, 514, 803, 805
Melnikov, Pavel Petrovich, 775
memorialisation, 23, 30–32, 123, 140, 809, 826n18
memory: and forgetting, 31, 202, 410, 662; locations of, 280, 792; and naming, 158; objects of, 6, 9–12; and photography, 77, 552–53, 700; and scents, 243–44; and sound, 700–701, 713–14, 716, 727–30. *See also* history; knowledge; monumentality; nostalgia
Mendeleev, Dmitry, 205
Mendelsohn, 328
Mensheviks, 42, 44, 55, 60, 66, 68
Mercader, Ramón, 211
Merezhkovsky, Dmitry, 816
meritocracy, 173–74
Merzhanov, Miron Ivanovich, 292, 295–97, 841n13
Meshlauk, Valery, 78
'Metaphysical sphinx' (Shemyakin), 38
Meuser, Philipp, 424
Meyer, Alexander A., 138, 660

Meyerhold, 554
Meyerhold, Vsevolod, 554–55, 595
Michel, Auguste, 240–43
Michel, Auguste Ippolitovich, 237
Michurin, Ivan, 174
middle class, 257–60, 274, 277–78, 281–83, 333, 590. *See also* class distinctions; petit-bourgeois
Mikhalkov, Nikita, 277
Mikhalkov, Sergey, 727
Mikhoels, Solomon, 758
Mikoyan, 599
Mikoyan, Anastas, 246, 249, 252
Miletich, Kolya, 384
Militant Godless movement, 653
military: authority of, 44; celebration of, 173, 508; disintegration of, 43; displays of power, 345, 499, 503–4, 512, 738–39; structure of, 175; training, 529, 574, 580, 583–84; valorisation of, 171–72
Military Revolutionary Committee of the Petrograd Soviet, 44
Miller, Yevgeny, 71
Milyukov, Pavel, 461
Milyutin, Nikolay, 142–43, 329
Milyutin, Vladimir, 474
Minin, Kuzma, 507–8
Minkus, Mikhail A., 805
Mirbach-Harff, Graf Wilhelm von, 735
Mirsky, Dmitry, 125
Mitin, Mark, 207
Mitta, Alexander, 383
Mittenberg, Elza Yanovna, 634–36
Mittenberg, Mirza, 637
Mittenberg, Petya, 637
modernisation: costs of, 82, 112; depictions of, 80, 467–68, 471; and fashion, 598–99; phases of, 203–6, 337, 778; prioritisation of, xviii, 441; strategies of, 36, 89, 98, 147, 328, 330; symbols of, 100–101, 190, 333–34, 501, 693, 724, 770–71, 777, 789; and technology, 96, 775; unequal experiences of, 448–49. *See also* electrification; progress
modernity, 77, 80–81, 88–89, 150, 217, 336–37, 608, 706, 803
Moldova, 165
Molokhovets, Franz, 256
Molokhovets, Yelena Ivanovna, 255–60
Molotov, Vyacheslav, 208, 240, 713, 739

money: collapse of currency, 549; control of, 53, 745, 748–49; foreign currency, 747, 760
Monighetti, I. A., 287
Montferrand, Auguste de, 287
monumentality, 38–39, 171, 176, 335, 644, 650, 668, 670–71, 675, 797, 805–6, 826n18. *See also* memory
Mordvinov, Arkady, 805
Moscow: bazaars in, 9, 549; building styles in, 294, 328, 678–79, 689, 747, 805, 866n5; centrality of, 28, 130, 242, 405, 484, 498, 744; compared to the countryside, 786–87; consumerism in, 586–87; and control of public space, 230, 275, 540; Dior models in, 587–88; divisions within, 732–33; embassies in, 735–36; and fashion, 591; festivals in, 564; and globalisation, 410; graffiti in, 185–86; parks in, 400; perceptions of, 81, 335, 472, 809–10; and perfume industry, 236, 240; population of, 401, 407, 548, 678–79; production in, 253; siege of, 506–8; suburbs of, 423–24; traffic in, 273, 277–78, 435–36, 678; urbanisation of, 436–37; visitors to, 403, 585. *See also* Red Square
Moscow Conceptualists, 392
Moscow Helsinki Group, 392
Moscow kitchens, 248, 250, 314, 321, 323, 325, 330, 339, 376–86, 394–95
Mosolov, Alexander, 706, 710
Mother (Gorky), 777
movement: and daily routine, 169; freedom of, 4, 73, 263, 387, 484, 493, 618, 671, 747; of refugees, 67; restrictions on, 484, 737, 742
Mühsam, Erich, 814
Mühsam, Zenzl, 814
Mukhina, Ignatievna, 601
Mukhina, Vera, 578
Muravyov, A. N, 703–4
musée imaginaire, 3, 6, 808–19
Museum of Canal Construction in Medvezhyegorsk, 139
Museum of the Metallurgical Complex, 104, 113
museums: and art, 754; and artifacts, 104–5, 108, 139, 644–47, 664, 688, 709; as contested space, 26; and cuisine, 260; culture of, 21, 26, 825n7; expertise of, 172; graffiti in, 186; and the Gulag system, 658,

660–61; and ideology, 387–88; and local history, 21–24, 28, 825n13; as memory, 687–88; organisation of, 19–21, 825n3; perceptions of, 19, 414, 818; purposes of, 25–27, 281, 664. *See also* archives; history; *specific museums*

music, 225, 403, 682, 706, 710, 747. *See also* jazz

Mussolini, Benito, 405

Mussorgsky, 711

Myakotin, Venedikt Alexandrovich, 64

Mysterious Moscow (Korshunov and Terekhova), 686

Mystery of Liberated Labour, 554

Nabokov, Vladimir, 59, 67, 70–71, 73, 356

Nadolny, Richard, 735

Nagibin, Yury, 17

Nagorski, Andrew, 743

Naître, vivre et mourir en URSS (Blum), 477

Nakhimov, 415

names: and collective memory, 158; renaming, 169, 189, 226, 234, 289–90, 372; sources of, 190–93. *See also* abbreviations; language

Nansen passport, 67

Napoleon, 414, 490, 799

Nashi dostizheniya, 80, 121, 240

natural resources, 90–92, 99, 102–3, 117–18, 141, 154, 440, 442, 621, 625, 634, 636–37, 641–42, 777

nature: access to, 90, 275, 402; appreciation of, 352–53; conditions of, 623; depictions of, 420, 628–29; destruction of, 141; in parks, 399; perceptions as limitless, 152, 154, 228; reclaiming space by, 356, 443, 452; superiority over, 86, 97, 120, 147–48, 774, 802–3; transformation of, 81–82, 117

Nazis, 71–72, 185

Nefedova, Tatiana, 439

Neizvstny, Ernst, 644

Nekrasov, Vika, 380

neoclassicism, 88, 187, 286, 294, 806

neo-Impressionism, 422

neo-Marxism, 4. *See also* Marxism

neomodernity, 217–18

neo-Renaissance, 415

Neuhaus, Heinrich, 223

Neumann, Heinz, 812

Neurath, Marie, 471–72

Neurath, Otto, 469, 471–72, 476

Nevsky, Alexander, 507–8

New Deal, 94–95, 101, 145–46

New Economic Policy (NEP): and abundance, 252; goals of, 400, 800; and housing policy, 317, 319; outcomes of, 466, 477, 502, 547, 557, 594; perceptions of, 759; and public conveniences, 369; symbols of, 162

New Human Being, 106–9, 120, 292–95, 329–31, 399–412, 575, 578, 580, 584, 593–94, 596. *See also* bodies

New Solovetsky, The, 659–60

newspapers, 166, 198, 464

Newsweek, 461

New York Times, 746, 764

Nicholas II, 237, 290, 460

Nicolson, Harold, 739

Nietzsche, 141–42, 554, 580

Nijinsky, Vaslav, 68, 608–9, 615, 618

Nikitsky Gardens, 291

Nikolaevich, Pyotr, 291

Nikritin, Solonon, 758–59

Nikulin, L., 125

Nivinsky, I. I., 796–97

Nixon, Richard, 585

NKVD: archives of, 119, 463, 537–38; arrests by, 72, 406, 684, 701; confiscation by, 748; and forced labour, 142, 641; logistics of, 541; power of, 692; victims of, 179, 211; violence of, 31, 450, 816. *See also* KGB; OGPU

Nogtev, A. P., 657, 660

nomenklatura, 216, 252, 254–55, 275, 277, 688, 694, 747. *See also* dachas

nonpersons, 461, 557

"Nosie of Time, The" (Mandelstam), 700–701

nostalgia, 37, 584, 763–64. *See also* memory

Noted on the Revolution (Gorky), 42

Notes from the Blockade (Ginzburg), 543

Novaya gazeta, 365

Novaya zhizn, 42, 53

Nove, Alec, 478–80, 633

Novikov, Mikhail Mikhailovich, 64

Novy mir, 387, 393

Novy zhurnal, 464

nuclear waste, 228. *See also* pollution

nuclear weapons, 148, 154, 496–97

Nureyev, Baryshnikov, 615

Nureyev, Rudolf, 615–16
Nureyev, Rudolf Khametovich, 609–10, 614, 617

Objectivism, 71
objects: collections of, 752–67; expertise of, 172; materiality of, 26–29, 150; ornmental and superfluous, 213–14, 330–31; returning artifacts, 664; significance of, 6; as traces of history, 9–13, 139, 214, 709
October, 121
October (Eisenstein), 370
Ogonyok, 80, 121, 393, 516
OGPU, 59, 63, 65–66, 105, 179, 291, 829n9; authority of, 132–33, 135; confiscation by, 748; and forced labour, 116–17, 122, 641; and the inner enemy, 135; and re-education, 126, 129; violence of, 137. See also KGB; NKVD
Okudzhava, Bulat, 280–81, 377
Olearius, Adam, 704
Olesha, Yury, 579
oligarchs, 550
Olivier, Lucien, 254
Olmsted, Frederick, 401
Olovyanishnikov, N. I., 702
Olšany Cemetery, 68
Olympics, 387, 565, 574–75, 581–82, 727. See also Spartakiad games
O'Mahony, Mike, 573, 575
One Day in the Life of Ivan Denisovich (Solzhenitsyn), 387
Oprichnik (Tcaikovsky), 710
Optimistic Tragedy, The (Vishnevsky), 503
Order of Lenin, 173–74, 176
Order of the Red Banner, 133
Order of the Red Banner of Labour, 95
Order of the Red Star, 173
Ordzhonikidze, 358
Ordzhonikidze, Sergo, 103, 521
Origins of Totalitarianism, The (Arendt), 823n9
Orlov, Yury, 220, 322, 346, 404, 520
Orlova, Lyubov, 240, 601, 606, 817
Orlova, Raisa, 383
Osinsky, Valerian, 206–8, 474
Osinsky-Obolensky, Valerian, 683, 687
Osipov, Dmitry, 514–15
Osokina, Yelena, 537, 539, 546, 748
Osokina, Yelena Alexandrovna, 531

Ossorgin, Mikhail [Michael], 14, 64, 69, 219, 810
Ostrovsky, Nikolay, 778
Otten, Nikolay, 384
Otto, 606
Our Daily Bread (Osokina), 531
Ovchinnikov, Alexander, 550
Overseas Press International, 464
Owen, Robert, 315

Pakhomov, Alexey, 579
Palace of the Soviets, 294, 402, 455, 680, 849n9
Palchinsky, Pyotr Ioakimovich, 64
Pallas, Peter Simon, 291
palm trees, 348–49, 351–55, 358–59
Panama Canal, 127–28
Panfyorov, Fyodor, 280
Panin, Count, 291
Paquet, Alfons, 741
parades: as displays of power, 496–98, 501, 505, 508, 583–84; for Five-Year Plans, 502–3; traditions of, 499–500, 512, 569–70. See also fizkultura
Parfyumeriya (Fridman), 233
Paris Exhibition of 1925, 326, 1925
Paris International Exhibition of 1937, 680
Pascal, Pierre, 741
Pashukanis, Yevgeny, 206–7
Pasternak, Boris, 242, 280–81, 381, 693, 778
Paul I, 499
Paulus, Friedrich, 814
Paustovsky, Konstantin, 280
Pavlensky, Pyotr, 809
Pavlov, Ivan P., 210, 247
Pavlova, Anna, 608, 615
Peace of Brest-Litovsky, 800
Penkovsky, Oleg, 609
People of Moscow (Cartier-Bresson), 408–9
Peredelkino, 280
Peredelkino Museum, 280–81
perestroika: economic stagnation, 606; and expansion of the public sphere, 184–85; fashion trends during, 178; formation of elites during, 385; introduction of, 158, 386, 393; and openness, 737; perceptions of, 259–60, 367, 393–94; re-organisation of knowledge, 29, 32, 211, 623, 697, 744, 767; uncertainty during, 376. See also glasnost
Pereulok, Bolshoi Kazyonny, 381
Perfume (Süskind), 232

perfume industry, 231–32, 234, 242–43
Pertsov, P., 125
Peter the Great, 16, 129, 174, 351–52, 360, 499, 558–59
petit-bourgeois, 213, 219, 290, 326, 331–33, 357–58. *See also* class distinctions; middle class
Petrishchev, A. B., 65
Petrograd, 15, 45–47, 51–54, 554. *See also* Leningrad; St. Petersburg
Petrov, Yevgeny, 192, 358, 372, 669, 675
Petrov-Vodkin, Kuzma, 252
Petrusov, Georgy, 78, 84–86
phenomenology, 26, 71, 227, 628, 670–71
Philby, Kim, 609
Philip II, 654
philosophy steamer, 58–74, 136, 492, 855n12
phone books, 695–97
photography: and authenticity, 77–78; censorship of, 124; as documentary evidence, 131–32, 134, 634; emotional influence of, 82, 96; and experiencing history, 413–14; influence of, 85–86, 498, 506, 508; and memory, 552–53, 700; and propaganda, 115, 117–18, 120; techniques of, 80, 115–16; traditions of, 80
photomontage, 80, 100, 115, 577
Piano in the Mist (Schlattner), 226
pianos, 219–26, 318, 663
Pickford, Mary, 94
pictograms, 479–80
Pictures at an Exhibition (Ravel), 711
Pilgrim, The, 656
Pilnyak, Boris, 15, 691–92, 816
Pimenov, Yury, 431, 527
Pittsburgh, 143–44
plastics, 150, 197, 199, 228
Platonov, Andrey, 25
Platonov, Sergey, 462
Plessner, Helmut, 573
Plisetskaya, Maya, 606, 617
Plutser-Sarno, Alexey, 179–80
Pobedonostsev, Konstantin, 258
Poddubny, Ivan, 574
Podiapolsky, Grisha, 380
Podlubny, Stephan, 541
Pogodin, Nikolay, 280
Pogudkin, A. V., 240
Pokrovsky, Mikhail, 26, 207

Poland, 174, 358, 510
political dissidents, 382, 384–87, 389–90, 393, 764. *See also* samizdat literature
political prisoners, 55, 182, 657. *See also* prisons
politics: centers of, 50; and communication media, 717; partisanship, 91, 162, 383; and religion, 710; and slogans, 163, 184, 198, 214; symbols of, 182. *See also* protests
Politkovskaya, Anna, 365
pollution, 112, 142, 151–52, 154, 338. *See also* nuclear waste
Polonsky, Vyacheslav, 105
Polyakov, Leonid, 805
Pomerants, Grigory, 385
Poniatowski, Stanisław August, 174
Popov, Alexander Stepanovich, 718
Popov, Pavel, 474
Popova, Lyubov, 595, 602, 753, 758–59
porcelain, 213–15
Portugalov, P. A., 404
Posev, 464
Poskryobyshev, Alexander, 683, 689
Posokhin, Mikhail, 805
postindustrial world, 154
Postyshev, Pavel, 562–63
Potashnikov, 629–30
Potemkin, Prince Grigory, 51, 352
poverty, 164, 309, 349
power: access to, 691–93, 698; displays of, 131, 510, 695; perceptions of, 667, 687; rituals of, 701; and spatiality, 54–55, 677, 744; symbols of, 163, 294, 497, 593, 792–93
Pozharsky, Dmitry, 507–8
Prague Spring, 386, 510–11, 605, 667, 818
Pravda, 53, 57, 61–62, 121, 198, 451, 562–63, 743, 817
Preobrazhensky, Yevgeny, 207
Princec Igor (Borodin), 710–11
Prishvin, Mikhail, 333, 708–9
prisons: conditions in, 53, 621–22, 633; cultural activities in, 137–39, 659–60, 816; executions in, 140; forced labour in, 621; frequent experience of, 183; populations of, 182, 478–80; records from, 817–18; return from, 387, 458; as subculture, 178–79; symbolism of, 182; traces of, 620–21. *See also* forced labour; Gulag system; political prisoners

privacy, 219, 306, 310, 314–15, 320–25, 332, 361–62, 364, 368, 373–74, 381, 784. *See also* anonymity
private property, 317, 427, 675–76, 688
private spaces, 325, 337, 373–74, 676–77, 724. *See also* public space
privatisation, 298, 317, 337, 365, 434–35, 447, 550, 688, 690, 780, 845n6
Productivists, 757
progress: celebrations of, 510; depictions of, 467–70, 501; symbols of, 592, 693. *See also* modernisation
Prokopovich, Feofan, 342
Prokopovich, Sergey, 64
propaganda, 26, 80, 115, 123, 147, 225–26, 336, 451, 461, 473, 500–502, 603, 660, 668, 716–17, 722, 730, 741–42, 830n8. *See also* journalism; knowledge
prostitution, 322
protests, 184–85, 379, 391, 436, 511, 564, 744. *See also* politics
Provisional Government, 43–44, 49, 51
Prozhektor, 121
Pshekhonov, Alexey Vasilievich, 64
public-private distinctions, 30, 219, 306, 310, 320–25, 364
public space: art in, 187–88; cleanliness of, 228–29; control of, 184, 187, 230, 327, 365, 374, 407, 672–73, 676; and mass movements, 45; perceptions of, 53, 326; privatisation of, 672, 676–77; responsibility for, 368, 373, 427; sound in, 710–11
public sphere, xvii, 4, 51, 62, 376, 383, 385, 394–95, 555, 742
Pugachev, Yemelian, 102
Puni, Ivan, 187, 327
Pushkin, Alexander Ivanovich, 70, 103, 215, 252, 406, 615–16, 770–71
Pushkin, Merkulov, 106
Pushkin Square, 564
Putin, 74, 299, 512
Putin, Vladimir, xix, 367, 395
Pyatakov, Georgy, 78, 206–7
Pyatnitsky, Osip, 687
Pyriev, Ivan, 252

Queue, The (Sorokin), 534–37
queues: depictions of, 534–37, 540–41, 543; prevalence of, 531–34, 544, 598–99;

psychology of, 544–45; as source of public opinion, 537–39, 545–46; and temporality, 532–33
Quiet Street (Ossorgin), 219

Rabin, Oskar, 759
Rabotnitsa, 239
Rachmaninov, Sergey, 226, 711
Radek, Karl, 206–7, 687, 738–39, 814
radiation, 151–52, 154–55
radio, 330, 391, 465, 498, 507, 706, 713–21, 724, 729–30, 744, 716o
Radio Moscow, 713, 717, 729
Radishchev, Alexander N., 785
Radlov, Ernest, 205
Radlov, Sergey, 405, 617
railways: competing with waterways, 129; and cultural changes, 772–73; depictions of, 777–78, 780–81; expansion of, 81, 274–75, 286–87, 344, 774–75, 778–79, 788–89; and limited access, 103; privatisation of, 780; reach of, 263, 651; social spaces of, 263, 278–79, 782–84; standards and guages, 485, 775, 789; strategic importance of, 53, 873n1; as symbol of modernisation, 770
Rallet, Alphonse, 236–37
Ramzin, Leonid, 207
Rand, Ayn, 71
Rappoport, Yakov, 132
Rasputin, Valentin, 446
rationing, 251, 538, 547, 591, 599. *See also* scarcity
Ratzel, Friedrich, 483
Ravel, Maurice, 711
Rayonists, 757
recycling, 198, 227, 707–10
Red calendar, 43, 527–28, 561, 565. *See also* temporality
Redchenko, 115–16
Redko, Kliment, 56, 759
Red Light Spherical Composition (Klyun), 753
Red Moscow, 231–44
Red Square, 496–99, 501–2, 510–11; and *fizkultura*, 576. *See also* Lenin's Mausoleum; Moscow
Red Square (Kandinsky), 758
Reed, John, 41–43, 46, 50, 53, 55, 60–61, 741

re-education, 119–20, 123, 125–26, 133–35, 137, 148, 224, 631, 656–57, 659–60, 833n19. *See also* forced labour; Gulag system
refrigerators, 150, 248, 253, 314, 681
Reich, Bernhard, 219
Reichstag, 184, 186
religion: festivals of, 555, 559–62; and holidays, 559–60, 562; influence of, 529–30, 557; suppression of, 527, 652, 707–10; and temporality, 561; traditions of, 515. *See also* atheism; holidays; Russian Orthodox Church
Renaissance style, 288, 401
"Requiem" (Akhmatova), 540
Respected Figures of the Soviet Union (Deineka), 578–79
Ribbentrop, 739
Ricardo, 548
Ricci, Matteo, 6
Richter, Svyatoslav, 223, 381
Richter, Trude, 626
Riefenstahl, Leni, 577, 580
Riesenkampf, Georgy K., 133
Riesman, David, 437
Rilke, Rainer Maria, 702, 704
Rimsky-Korsakov, 711
Roberts, Peter, 765
Robochy i soldat, 53
Rockefeller, David, 753
Rodchenko, Alexander, 25, 78, 82, 115–21, 125, 132, 140, 277, 326, 329, 407, 578, 595, 602, 696, 753, 758, 765–66
Rogger, Hans, 94, 149, 684
Rohe, Ludwig Mies van, 144
Rökk, Marika, 600
Rolland, Romain, 242, 358, 403
Rosenberg, Alfred, 72
Rosner, Eddie, 604, 812
Rostovtzeff, Michael, 70
Roth, Joseph, 483, 741
Rottert, Pavel Pavlovich, 86–91
Roubaud, Franz Alexeevich, 415
Rozanov, Vasily, 258–59, 484, 704
Rozanova, Olga, 755–56
Rozhdestvensky, Robert, 582
Rublyovka, 281
Rubo, Frants Alekseevich, 415
Rubtsov, Sergey, 662
Ruchyov, Boris, 344, 831n8, 845n2

Rudenko, Roman, 683
Rudnev, Lev, 519
Rudov, Vladimir, 384
Rudzutaks, Jānis, 502
Ruge, Gerd, 742
Russia and Europe (Danilevsky), 491
Russia in the Shadows (Wells), 742
Russian Classicism, 793
Russian Crimial Tattoo Encyclopaedia (Baldaev and Plutser-Sarno), 179, 182
Russian diaspora, xix, 58–59, 66–72, 461, 609, 759
Russian Empire, Russian Federation; art scene, 757, 765–66; backwardness of, xviii, 77, 82, 88, 95, 101, 149, 433, 518, 718, 770, 778, 799–800; borders of, 489–91; class hierarchy in, 67, 94, 282–83, 287, 689; cultural influence of, 68, 587–88; growth of, 174, 316, 477; and migration, 59, 430, 828n1; modernisation of, 22, 91, 328; Napoleon's campaign in, 414; national identity, 37, 215, 255–56; peasant values, 158, 528; perceptions of, 37, 39, 141–42, 747; reading culture in, 167, 242; relationship with France, 68; religion in, 555, 653, 663, 711; resilience of, 281, 623; soundscapes of, 702–7, 710–11; spa culture of, 286–87, 293; symbols of, 15, 27, 161, 163, 215, 274, 328, 331, 370, 407, 615–16, 652; traditions of, 16, 174, 221–23, 234, 255, 259, 351–52, 591, 595, 601, 747; and Western culture, 236, 281; as a world power, 608, 770. *See also* Soviet Union
Russian Federation, Russian Empire; bureaucracy of, 529; economy of, 751; and global markets, 442; national identity, 20; population growth, 273; religion in, 529; uncertain future of, 512; as a world power, xviii, 74, 360. *See also* Soviet Union
Russian language, xviii–xix, 6
Russian literature, 18, 34, 70–71, 149, 242, 275, 316, 381, 389, 448. *See also* books
Russian Orthodox Church: critics of, 388, 517, 652–53, 710; holidays of, 257, 529–30, 559; influence of, 191, 763; and land ownership, 281; reemergence of, 654, 663–64, 711; returning property to, 21, 521; symbols of, 330, 705–6. *See also* religion

Russian Revolution: abolishing rituals and traditions, 70, 518–19, 525; depictions of, 48–49, 52, 741; direct experiences of, 40–41; disruption of, 13, 25, 264, 327, 356, 591, 608–9, 615–16; and inventing tradition, 189–90, 193, 554; legacy of, 18, 311, 499, 803; perceptions of, xvii–xviii, 39–40, 55–56, 787; stages of, 43, 549; topography of, 44–51, 53–54; victims of, 477, 519–20. See also Bolsheviks; Civil War; Soviet Union

Russian Revolution, The (Sukhanov), 461

Russian Revolution of 1905, 42

Russians, The (Smith), 743

Russkaya mysl, 464

Russkaya volya, 53

Russo-Turkish War of 1877, 353

Rüthers, Monica, 426

Ryazanov, Eldar, 422–23

Rykov, Alexey, 461, 687, 814

Ryleev, Kondraty, 138

Saarinen, Eliel, 519

Sakharov, Andrey, 211, 338, 389, 393, 744, 817

Saltykov-Shchedrin, Mikhail, 667

samizdat literature, 342, 376, 382. See also political dissidents; *spetskhran*

Samokhvalov, Alexander, 348, 578–79, 600

sanatoriums, 283–85, 289–90, 293, 298, 748

Saradzhev, Konstantin, 709

Saturday Evening Post, 103

Savvaty, 663

scarcity, 17, 43, 219, 228–30, 245–51, 338, 364, 449, 532–33, 538, 540, 546, 591, 600–603, 745–46, 750, 785. See also famine; rationing; survival

Schchyuko, Yury, 410

Scheffer, Paul, 86, 93, 501–2, 741–42

Schenk, Frithjof Benjamin, 770, 873n1

Schiaparelli, Elsa, 598

Schiller, Otto, 739

Schlattner, Eginald, 226

Schmidt-Häuer, Christian, 307, 438

School of Classical Dance (Kostrovitskaya), 612, 615

Schuhuko, Vladimir, 88

Schwarzenegger, Arnold, 583–84

Scott, John, 101, 142–43

second modernity, 388, 430

secularisation, 527, 529, 653–54, 702. See also atheism; holidays

Sedyakin, Ivan, 518

Seibert, Theodor, 741

Seligman, German, 762

Selinsky, K., 125

semiotics, 179

Semyonov, Vladimir S., 766

Senkin, Sergey Yakovlevich, 348

Sennett, Richard, 310

Sensinov, M. A., 296

Serafimov, Sergey S., 518

Serebrovsky, A. P., 641

serfdom, 440

Serova, Valentina, 240

Seutin, Mikolay, 217

sex, 267–68, 321

sexuality, 527, 610

Shadr, Ivan, 402, 579

Shagin, Ivan, 578

Shaginian, Marietta, 280

Shaikhet, Arkady, 78

Shakhty trial of 1929, 91

Shalamov, Varlam, 626–28, 631, 634, 639–40, 644–45

Sharansky, Natan, 392

Shaw, George Bernard, 358, 403

Shcharansky, Anatoly, 392

Shchekochikhin-Pototskaya, V., 217

Shchukin, 765

Shchuko, Vladimir, 292, 294, 455, 797

Shchusev, Alexey V., 292, 294, 436, 794–98

Shechtel, Fyodor, 797

Shemyakin, Mikhail, 38

Sher, V. V., 17

Shestov, Lev, 69, 71, 464

Shikhanovich, Yury, 392

Shklovsky, Viktor, 125, 370

Shostakovich, Dmitry, 422, 617, 726, 817

show trials, 55, 207, 383, 391, 667, 683, 687, 722, 738, 813–14

Shpet, Gustav, 64

Shragin, Boris, 385

Shterenberg, David, 187–88

Shukhov, Vladimir, 514, 718

Shulgin, Vasily, 72

Shvernik, Nikolay, 688

Sidur, Vadim, 381

Siemens-Bau-Union, 93
Silver Age, 68
Silyagi, 603–6
Simmel, Georg, 5, 232, 324, 421, 675
Simonov, Konstantin, 580–81
Sinclair, Upton, 463
Sinoviev, Alexander, 73
Sintaksis, 464
Sinyavsky, Andrey, 383, 386
Sinyavsky, Vadim, 506
Siou, Adolphe, 236
Sitnikov, Vasily, 758–59
Skuratov, Malyuta, 685
Skurikhin, Anatoly, 118
slavery. *See* forced labour
Slezkine, Yuri, 325
slogans, 214, 254
Slovetsky Islands, 661
Smaokhvalov, Alexander N., 797
smells, 645–46, 837n3
Smena, 121
Smert v SSSR, 855n1
Smilga, Ivar, 683
Smith, Adam, 548
Smith, Hedrick, 307, 743
Smolyan, Alexander, 80
smugglers, 875n27
soap-making, 236
Sochi, 292, 299, 348
Sochinskaya pravda, 293
Sochurek, Howard, 598
socialism, 57, 557. *See also* capitalism;
    communism
socialist realism, 388, 758
Socialist Revolutionaries, 44, 61–63, 66
social localities, 306
social order, 160, 163, 215, 228, 230, 281, 526,
    549–50, 555, 564, 785, 827n6
Sofronitsky, Vladimir, 223
Soldatov, Alexander, 664
Solomon, Michael, 641
Solovetsky Islands, 660
Solovetsky Messenger, 662
Solovetsky Monastery, 652, 654–56, 659
Solovetsky Special Camp, 650–64
Solovki, 650–64
Solovyov, F. K., 513
Solovyov, Vladimir, 205
Solts, Aaron, 683

Solzhenitsyn, Alexander, 58, 73, 123, 154, 182,
    211, 386–87, 392, 464, 492, 626, 693, 744,
    781, 812, 816, 818
Sorge, Richard, 683
Sorokin, Pitirim, 59, 62, 64, 71, 464
Sorokin, Vladimir, 534–37
Sotsgorod, 142, 343–44
Soul of St. Petersburg, The (Antisferov), 35,
    138, 355–56
sound, 320–21, 700–704, 706–7, 710, 713–14,
    716, 727–30
Sovetskoe foto, 120
Soviet (Samokhvalov), 578
Soviet Americanism, 94–96, 109, 149, 684.
    See also Amerikana
Soviet Art Deco, 603
Soviet Century, The (Lewin), 431
Soviet civilisation, xviii, 1–2, 408, 808, 816,
    823n2. *See also* Soviet Union
Soviet Costume and Textiles (Strizhenova), 592
Soviet Fordism, 96, 577
Soviet literature, 280, 307–8, 389, 446,
    534–35. *See also* books
Soviet Modernism, 19
Soviet Photo, 80
Soviet sign-world, 158–60, 162–64, 170, 172
Soviet studies, 5–6, 306
Soviet Union: art scene, 757, 765–66; borders
    of, 270–71, 285, 483–84, 486–90, 492–93;
    changing moods in, 537–38; and citizen-
    ship, 759–60, 763; communication
    technologies in, 693–95, 725; countryside
    of, 438–43, 447–48; dacha culture in,
    277–78; decline of, 148, 151, 211, 218, 376,
    410–11, 548–49, 729, 734, 744, 785; diplo-
    matic relations, 231, 735–39; dissolution
    of, xvii, 6, 20, 111–12, 298, 549, 606, 751;
    diversity of, 22, 134, 341, 390; economy of,
    151–52, 386, 546–47, 605–6; elite classes
    in, 326, 517, 871n6; eras of, 110, 150, 817;
    exile from, 58–61, 64–66, 72; fashion
    industry in, 593–94, 597–98, 600–603,
    606; foreign relations, 163, 238; foreign
    visitors to, 29, 98–99, 163, 342, 382, 403,
    485, 585, 667–68, 732–33; free markets
    in, 243, 254, 538, 547, 745–51; growth of,
    149, 490; health resort system, 284–86,
    288–89, 291–93, 298; and high cultrure,
    30; housing shortages, 311, 316, 318, 320,

Soviet Union (*continued*)
337, 421–22, 425, 427–28, 430, 432, 434, 603; industrialisation of, 222, 234, 503; infrastructure in, 23, 91–92, 127, 147, 272, 298–99, 442, 693–95, 771; loyalty to, 63, 492, 760, 764; and migration, 394–95, 430, 736, 763, 828n1; modernisation of, 21, 26, 88–89, 91, 95, 98, 101, 133, 467–68, 501, 778; moral decline of, 124, 154; national identity, 33, 36, 81, 159–62, 200–201, 215, 336, 508–9, 524–25, 582, 653, 718–21; natural resources in, 90, 99, 102–3; perceptions of, 78–80, 93, 101, 163, 390–91, 484, 488, 496, 569–70, 588, 668, 689, 697, 739, 741, 743, 748, 792; population of, 106–7, 279, 306, 319–20, 372, 401, 425–26, 431–32, 441–42, 446, 475, 478–79; reading culture in, 167; relations with France, 238, 242; relations with Germany, xix, 93–94, 489, 503–4, 735; relations with the United States, 93, 388, 737; religion in, 526–27, 529–30, 560; social topography of, 827n6; soundscape of, 718–20, 724, 726–29, 818–19; and sports, 387, 573, 581–82; subcultures in, 178, 180, 185, 603–6; topography of, 31, 81, 168, 263, 266, 269–70, 440, 492–93, 533, 623, 638, 650–51, 774–75, 782–83; tourism in, 263, 839n1; urbanisation of, 105–7, 434; as world power, 145, 510. *See also* Civil War; Russian Empire; Russian Federation; Russian Revolution; Soviet civilisation; Sturm und Drang phase
sovkhozy, 447, 452. *See also* kolkhozy
Spanish Civil War, 342, 505, 721
Spartakiad games, 575–76, 581, 583. *See also* Olympics
Spartan style, 326
Spatial Force Construction (Popova), 753
spatiality, 24, 30, 44–50, 320–25, 483, 670–71, 673–74, 676–77, 732, 744, 771–72. *See also* cartography; temporality
Speak, Memory (Nabokov), 356
Speer, Speer, 680
spetskhran, 457–61, 463–64. *See also* censorship; knowledge; samizdat literature
sport, 575, 577–78, 582–83. *See also* bodies
Sputnik, 176, 388, 724
SSSR na stroike. See *USSR in Construction*

Stackenschneider, Andrey, 287
staircases, 361–63
Stakhanov, Alexey, 174, 683
Stalin, Josef: control of historical narrative, 25–26; critics of, 210, 805; cult of personality, 81, 147, 162, 202, 249–50, 254, 726, 801, 875n12; and the Dalstroy project, 635–36; death of, 29, 183, 298, 320, 386, 600, 642, 688, 723, 728, 804; depictions of, 211, 409, 691–92; desire for monumental style, 335; and diplomacy, 739–40; disconnect from reality, 252; doctrine of, 798–99; housing policy, 428–30, 436–37; industrialisation programmes, 634, 778; interest in sports, 571; legacy of, xix, 13, 217, 246, 332, 618, 685, 747, 793–94, 804–5; loyalty to, 126, 683, 689; and mass culture, 406–7; memorialisation of, 9, 111, 351, 358, 387, 691; and modernisation, 100, 133; perceptions of, 296–98, 388, 427–28, 501–2, 504–5, 722, 727; public speeches of, 506–8; repression under, 389, 474, 505; and sports, 575; summer home, 296–98; and the telephone, 693, 867n4; use of *kompromat*, 462; violence of, 58, 70, 491, 685, 798; voice of, 713, 717, 722; writings by, 682. *See also* de-Stalinisation; Great Terror
Stalin and the Politburo among Children in Gorky Park (Svarog), 409
Stalinism, 162, 387, 521, 579–80, 620, 726, 798, 801. *See also* Leninism
Stalin's Cookbook. See *Book of Tasty and Healthy Food*
Stalin's Dacha, 296–98
Stalin's Funeral (Baltermants), 350
Stalin's General Plan of 1935, 436–37
Stalin's Great Plan for the Transformation of Nature, 147
Stalinsky Park, 9
Stalin's Short Course, 26, 210, 463, 682, 801
standardisation, 336, 345–46, 420–21, 424–25, 523–24, 564
standards of living, 211, 247, 497, 585, 603, 843n2. *See also* everyday life
Stanislavsky, Konstantin, 174, 601
Starostin, Nikolay, 576–77
Starov, Ivan, 51
Starovoytova, Galina, 364–65
Starr, Frederick, 763

Stasova, Yelena, 683
statistics, 469–76, 532
Steffens, Lincoln, 41
Stein, Peter, 276
Steinbeck, John, 782
Steiner, Rudolf, 138
Stenberg, Georgy, 506
Stenberg, Vladimir, 506
Stepanov, Faddey, 504
Stepanova, Varvara, 78, 121, 591, 595, 602
Stepun, Fyodor, 62, 64, 73, 781, 784
Stern, 461
Stites, Richard, 190, 668, 670–73
Storming of the Winter Palace, The, 554
"Story of the Great Plan" (Ilyin), 145
St. Petersburg: dachas near, 274–76, 282;
    embassies in, 735–36; and fashion, 591;
    population of, 316; and the Romanov
    dynasty, 73. *See also* Leningrad; Petrograd
Stratonov, Vsevolod Viktorovich, 64
Stravinsky, Igor, 59, 68, 73, 512, 753
Strizhenova, Tatiana, 591
structuralism, 70–71
Struve, Pyotr, 69, 205, 464
Sturm und Drang phase, 141–45, 150, 210,
    240, 401, 724. *See also* industrialisation;
    Soviet Union
suburbs, 423–24, 840n3. *See also*
    urbanisation
Suez Canal, 127–28, 510
Sukhanov, Nikolay, 41–43, 46, 50, 53, 55–57, 461
Sukhoy, Mikhail, 504
Superfin, Gabriel, 392
Suprematism, 187, 214, 217, 602, 757
survival: and acts of resistance, 450; essen-
    tials of life, 310; and individuality, 108;
    and powerlessness, 308–9; and self-
    sufficiency, 278; strategies for, 13–14, 17,
    136, 170–71, 198; symbols of, 176, 645–46,
    726. *See also* everyday life; scarcity
Süskind, Patrick, 232
Suvorov, Alexander, 507–8
Svarog, Vasily, 409
Sverdlov, Yakov, 802
Swan Lake, 399, 729
Symbolism, 554

Tagore, Rabindranath, 515
Tairov, Alexander, 595

"Tale of the Unextinguished Moon" (Pilnyak),
    691–92
Tamarin, 638
Tarle, Yevgeny, 462
"Tatar Mullah and Clean Air, The" (Shalamov),
    631
Tatlin, Vladimir, 758, 797
tattoos, 178–81, 183
Tauride Palace, 51
Tchaikovsky, 710–11
Tchelitchew, Pavel, 587
technological solutionism, 95–96, 109, 149,
    151, 681, 694
Technology of Power, The (Avtorkhanov), 383
Teffi, 73
telegraph, 53, 130, 139
telephone, 49, 53, 139, 166–67, 321, 334,
    691–95, 698, 742–43
television, 341, 496–98, 724, 744
Telyatnikov, Abram, 402
temporality: and bureaucracy, 673–74; cal-
    endars, 530, 558–60; clashes of, 239–40,
    279, 443; and fashion, 598; and future-
    orientations, 532, 588; and globalisation,
    565; and industrialisation, 107–9, 565;
    and leisure time, 263–64, 400; and muse-
    ums, 19–20, 30; and nonsimultaneity,
    209; and queueing, 544–45; and railways,
    771–72, 776, 783, 785–86; regulation of,
    43, 700, 703–7, 709–10; and religious
    festivals, 527–28; re-organisation of,
    328, 485, 558, 560–61; rhythms of work,
    444; and simultaneity, 823n6; and
    stagnation, 532–33; symbols of, 3, 363;
    and urbanisation, 107. *See also* Red
    calendar; spatiality
Ten Years Khrushchev exhibition, 29
Terekhova, Viktoriya, 685
Terpsichore, 617
theater, 23, 110–11, 206, 405–6, 501, 553–55,
    595, 605, 615–17, 659–60, 706
The Stalin Canal (Gorky, Aveerbakh, and
    Firin), 124–25, 132–33
Thon, Konstantin, 689
Timashuk, Lidiya, 723
Time, 461
time zones, 485
Timoshenko, Semyon, 505
Tisse, Eduard, 78

toilets, 314, 321, 366–70, 372–75

Tolstoy, Alexey, 70, 125, 356, 595

Torgsin shops, 748–49. *See also* Beryozka
shops

Torleben, General von, 415

torture, 657, 816. *See also* violence

totalitarianism, 4, 201–2, 306, 473, 667,
823n9. *See also* authoritarianism

tourism, 263–64, 266, 270–71, 285, 298,
493–94, 839n1

Towards a Typology of Soviet Mass Housing
(Meuser), 424

trade unions, 285, 290, 294, 298

traditions: invention of, 105–6, 527–28, 554,
563, 614; sovietisation of, 562

Transylvania, 174

trash, 199, 227–30, 273–74, 361–62, 364, 374,
400, 688

Treaty of Rapallo, 62

Tregubov, Yury A., 810, 815

Trepper, Leopold, 812

Tretyakov, Sergey, 78

Trial, The (Kafka), 667

Trifonov, Valentin, 683

Trifonov, Yury, 682, 685, 688

Triolet, Elsa, 242

Triumph of the Will (Riefenstahl), 580

Troshin, Nikolay, 80

Trotsky, Leon, 43, 54, 58, 60–61, 94, 206, 211,
227, 405, 461, 463, 501, 518, 574, 740, 793

Trotsky, Noi A., 518

Trotskyism, 207–8, 634

Trubetskoy, Nikolay, 491

Trubetskoy, Sergey Yevgenievich, 64

Trudeau, Pierre, 753

TseKUBU (Central Commission for the
Improvement of the Everyday Lives of
Scientists), 284, 291

Tselkov, Oleg, 759

Tsereteli, Zurab, 281

Tsvetaeva, Marina, 70

Tsvetkov, Sergey Nikolaevich, 64

Tsvetushchaya yunost (Medvedkin), 572

tuberculosis, 291, 330

Tukhachevsky, Mikhail, 206–8, 683, 687,
722, 739

Tupolev, Andrey N., 503, 817

Twilight of Europe, The (Landau), 72

Ty i tyoye imya (Uspensky), 191

typhus, 55, 633

tyranny of intimacy, 784

Tyutchev, Fyodor, 743

Ukraine: 2022 war in, xix, 74; border with,
490; famine in, 26, 93; independence of,
90; relationship to Russia, 88

Ulanova, Galina, 617

Union of Soviet Writers, 280

United States: construction projects in,
94–95; cultural influence of, 94, 103, 107,
113, 530, 565, 604, 693; foreign aid, 62;
industrialisation of, 41–42, 100, 143; as
a model, 95, 252–53, 388, 468, 585–86,
684; and national identity, 69; relations
with, 388, 723, 737; Russian diaspora in,
69, 94; technical expertise from, 90–91,
93–96, 103, 142–43, 635, 681, 732–33;
vastness of, 782; as world power, 145

Unshlikht, 63, 70

Unter dem Banner des Marxismus, 463

urbanisation, 274, 319, 344, 421, 431–32, 441,
518, 562. *See also* deurbanisation; suburbs

Uspensky, Lev, 191

USSR in Construction, 78–82, 85, 100, 121, 132

Ustinov, Dmitry, 521

Utekhin, Ilya, 229, 321, 368–69, 534

Utomlyonnye solnstem (Mikhalkov), 277

Vaganova, Agrippina, 613, 616–18

Vail, Pyotr, 389

Valentino, Rudolph, 615

Vasiliev, Alexander, 601, 606

Vasiliev, Sergey, 179

Vavilov, Nikolay, 208

Vecherny zvon, 711

Vedeneev, Boris Yevgenievich, 86–89

Velikanova, Tatiana, 392

Vermenichev, Ivan D., 475

Vernadsky, Georges, 70

Vershbitsky, Konstantin, 132

Vertinsky, Alexander, 381

Vertov, Dziga, 578

Vesnin, Leonid A., 292, 294, 796

Vesnin, Viktor Alexandrovich, 86–89, 292

Vienna Circle, 469–73

Ville Radieuse, 316

Vinogradova, Dusia, 600

Vinogradova, Maurisa, 600

Vinter, Alexander Vasilievich, 86–91
violence: aestheticizing of, 121, 131; documentation of, 31–32, 201; topography of, 31–33. *See also* Gulag system; torture
Vishnevsky, Felix Yevgenievich, 758
Vishnevsky, Vsevolod, 503
Vkhutemas, 316
Vlady, Marina, 745
Vlasov, Alexander, 401
Vlasov, Yury, 387, 582–84
Vogeler, Heinrich, 687
Vogeler, Jan, 688
Vogue, 594, 606
Volfson, I. G., 243
Volga Flows to the Caspian Sea, The (Pilnyak), 15
Volkhov Hyroelectric Station, 90–91
von der Schulenburg, Graf, 735, 760
Vorobyov, Vladimir Petrovich, 802
Voroshilov, Kliment, 174, 208, 502, 504
Vostok polar station, 625
Voynovich, Vladimir Nikolaevich, 73
Voznesensky, Andrey, 280, 387
Vsevobuch (Vseobshchee voennoe obuchenie), 574
Vyazemsky, Orest V., 133, 139
vydvizhentsy, 255, 326
Vysheslavtsev, Boris, 6464
Vyshinsky, Andrey, 208, 683
Vysotsky, Vladimir, 377, 389, 582

Wagner, Richard, 555
Wajda, Andrzej, 753
Wallenberg, Raoul, 816
Warbug, Aby, 5
Wat, Aleksander, 17, 816, 818
"Ways to Strength and Beauty" (Riefenstahl), 577
Wedding in Tomorrow Street, 431
Weis, Igor, 138
Weisberg, Vladimir, 758–59
Weissberg, Alexander Cybulski, 489
Weissenhof Estate, 316
Wells, H. G., 593, 742
Werner, Ruth, 176
Werth, Alexander, 741
What Is to Be Done? (Chernyshevsky), 315, 574–75
White, Richard, 97

White Sea Canal, 116–25, 127–31, 134–36, 138–40, 833n7
Wilk, Mariusz, 663
Williams, R. C., 67
Will the Soviet Union Survive until 1984? (Amalrik), 376
Wilson, Woodrow, 739
Within the Whirlwind (Ginzburg), 622
Witte, Sergey, 460
Wolf, Friedrich, 176, 280
Wolf, Konrad, 176
Woman Pioneer with Gas Mask (Telyatnikov), 402
Woman with Long Hair (Drevin), 753
women: and fashion, 586–87; independence of, 247, 268, 526, 578, 595; perceptions of, 231, 238–39, 450, 542–44; in sport, 574; traditional gender roles, 256, 332, 526, 599
"Worker, The," 145
Worker and Kolkhoz Woman (Mukhina), 578
World Commune, 554
World Exhibition of 1900, 770, 787
World Exhibition of 1937, 578
World Exhibition of 1958, 223, 233
World Festival of Youth and Students of 1957, 3, 162, 387, 585
World War I: aftermath of, 284, 336, 490–91; allies of, 68–69; causes of, 799–800; death toll, 477; depictions of, 42, 283; disruption of, 316, 548, 608–9, 759; logistics of mobilisation, 778, 781; military awards during, 174–75; responses to, 91–92
World War II, xviii; aftermath of, 71–72, 111, 183, 341, 490, 526–27; beginning of, 713, 735; death toll, 26, 478, 521, 570–71, 580–81; depictions of, 23, 215, 217, 223, 414–15, 418, 507–8; destruction of, 373, 433, 450–51; disruption of, 208, 292, 335, 346, 357, 558, 600; and economics, 176, 254, 547–48; legacy of, 171, 222, 308, 510–11, 805; military awards during, 175; and military industries, 641; normality after, 150, 242, 251–52, 336; refugees of, 59, 67, 69; and religion, 653; Soviet victory in, 184, 506–9, 571; strategies of, 129, 476, 718, 779–80
World Youth Festival of 1957, 29

Wortman, Richard, 711–12
Wright, Frank Lloyd, 144, 297

Yagoda, Genrikh, 63, 70, 126, 132, 137
Yakhnenko, Yelena, 215–16
Yakobson, Anatoly, 392
Yakobson, Tosha, 380
Yanson-Manizer, Yelena, 579
Yashin, Lev, 387
Yeltsin, 112–13
Yenukidze, Avel, 70, 658
Yesenin-Volpin, Alexander, 385
Yevreinov, Nikolay, 554–55, 595
Yevtushenko, Yevgeny, 271, 280, 387, 582, 804
Yezhov, Nikolay, 78, 522, 569, 684, 793
YMCA Press, 464
Yofan, Boris Mikhailovich, 293, 334–36, 680, 685, 797
Yoffe, Abram, 206
Yon, V. A., 293
Yosilevich, V., 572, 580
Young Communists, 504
Young Pioneers, 528–29
Yudenich, 554
Yudina, Maria, 223

Yugoslavia, 68
Yusupov, Prince, 291

Zadkin, Osip, 579
ZAGS (Zapis aktov grazhdanskogo sostoyaniya), 523–24, 526, 529
Zamyatin, Yevgeny I., 64, 816
Zbarsky, Boris Ilyich, 802–3
Zemlya i Fabrika, 34
Zhabotinsky, Leonid, 582
ZhAKT (Zhilishchno-arendnye kooperativnye tovarishchestva), 317
Zhemchuzhina, Polina, 240
Zhilyaev, A. A., 825n10
zhilmassiv, 420–24
Zholtovsky, Ivan, 88, 292, 294, 797, 805
Zhuk, Sergey, 132–33, 139
Zhukov, Georgy, 508, 683
Zhumilova, Lena, 384
Zhuravlyov, Dmitry Nikolaevich, 381
Zhurnal mod, 604
Zimmerwald antiwar movement, 42
Zinoviev, Grigory, 206, 461, 517, 814
Zoshchenko, Mikhail, 125, 358, 372
Zverev, Anatoly, 758–59